Dictionary of Literary Biography

1 *The American Renaissance in New England,* edited by Joel Myerson (1978)

2 *American Novelists Since World War II,* edited by Jeffrey Helterman and Richard Layman (1978)

3 *Antebellum Writers in New York and the South,* edited by Joel Myerson (1979)

4 *American Writers in Paris, 1920-1939,* edited by Karen Lane Rood (1980)

5 *American Poets Since World War II,* 2 parts, edited by Donald J. Greiner (1980)

6 *American Novelists Since World War II, Second Series,* edited by James E. Kibler Jr. (1980)

7 *Twentieth-Century American Dramatists,* 2 parts, edited by John MacNicholas (1981)

8 *Twentieth-Century American Science-Fiction Writers,* 2 parts, edited by David Cowart and Thomas L. Wymer (1981)

9 *American Novelists, 1910-1945,* 3 parts, edited by James J. Martine (1981)

10 *Modern British Dramatists, 1900-1945,* 2 parts, edited by Stanley Weintraub (1982)

11 *American Humorists, 1800-1950,* 2 parts, edited by Stanley Trachtenberg (1982)

12 *American Realists and Naturalists,* edited by Donald Pizer and Earl N. Harbert (1982)

13 *British Dramatists Since World War II,* 2 parts, edited by Stanley Weintraub (1982)

14 *British Novelists Since 1960,* 2 parts, edited by Jay L. Halio (1983)

15 *British Novelists, 1930-1959,* 2 parts, edited by Bernard Oldsey (1983)

16 *The Beats: Literary Bohemians in Postwar America,* 2 parts, edited by Ann Charters (1983)

17 *Twentieth-Century American Historians,* edited by Clyde N. Wilson (1983)

18 *Victorian Novelists After 1885,* edited by Ira B. Nadel and William E. Fredeman (1983)

19 *British Poets, 1880-1914,* edited by Donald E. Stanford (1983)

20 *British Poets, 1914-1945,* edited by Donald E. Stanford (1983)

21 *Victorian Novelists Before 1885,* edited by Ira B. Nadel and William E. Fredeman (1983)

22 *American Writers for Children, 1900-1960,* edited by John Cech (1983)

23 *American Newspaper Journalists, 1873-1900,* edited by Perry J. Ashley (1983)

24 *American Colonial Writers, 1606-1734,* edited by Emory Elliott (1984)

25 *American Newspaper Journalists, 1901-1925,* edited by Perry J. Ashley (1984)

26 *American Screenwriters,* edited by Robert E. Morsberger, Stephen O. Lesser, and Randall Clark (1984)

27 *Poets of Great Britain and Ireland, 1945-1960,* edited by Vincent B. Sherry Jr. (1984)

28 *Twentieth-Century American-Jewish Fiction Writers,* edited by Daniel Walden (1984)

29 *American Newspaper Journalists, 1926-1950,* edited by Perry J. Ashley (1984)

30 *American Historians, 1607-1865,* edited by Clyde N. Wilson (1984)

31 *American Colonial Writers, 1735-1781,* edited by Emory Elliott (1984)

32 *Victorian Poets Before 1850,* edited by William E. Fredeman and Ira B. Nadel (1984)

33 *Afro-American Fiction Writers After 1955,* edited by Thadious M. Davis and Trudier Harris (1984)

34 *British Novelists, 1890-1929: Traditionalists,* edited by Thomas F. Staley (1985)

35 *Victorian Poets After 1850,* edited by William E. Fredeman and Ira B. Nadel (1985)

36 *British Novelists, 1890-1929: Modernists,* edited by Thomas F. Staley (1985)

37 *American Writers of the Early Republic,* edited by Emory Elliott (1985)

38 *Afro-American Writers After 1955: Dramatists and Prose Writers,* edited by Thadious M. Davis and Trudier Harris (1985)

39 *British Novelists, 1660-1800,* 2 parts, edited by Martin C. Battestin (1985)

40 *Poets of Great Britain and Ireland Since 1960,* 2 parts, edited by Vincent B. Sherry Jr. (1985)

41 *Afro-American Poets Since 1955,* edited by Trudier Harris and Thadious M. Davis (1985)

42 *American Writers for Children Before 1900,* edited by Glenn E. Estes (1985)

43 *American Newspaper Journalists, 1690-1872,* edited by Perry J. Ashley (1986)

44 *American Screenwriters, Second Series,* edited by Randall Clark, Robert E. Morsberger, and Stephen O. Lesser (1986)

45 *American Poets, 1880-1945, First Series,* edited by Peter Quartermain (1986)

46 *American Literary Publishing Houses, 1900-1980: Trade and Paperback,* edited by Peter Dzwonkoski (1986)

47 *American Historians, 1866-1912,* edited by Clyde N. Wilson (1986)

48 *American Poets, 1880-1945, Second Series,* edited by Peter Quartermain (1986)

49 *American Literary Publishing Houses, 1638-1899,* 2 parts, edited by Peter Dzwonkoski (1986)

50 *Afro-American Writers Before the Harlem Renaissance,* edited by Trudier Harris (1986)

51 *Afro-American Writers from the Harlem Renaissance to 1940,* edited by Trudier Harris (1987)

52 *American Writers for Children Since 1960: Fiction,* edited by Glenn E. Estes (1986)

53 *Canadian Writers Since 1960, First Series,* edited by W. H. New (1986)

54 *American Poets, 1880-1945, Third Series,* 2 parts, edited by Peter Quartermain (1987)

55 *Victorian Prose Writers Before 1867,* edited by William B. Thesing (1987)

56 *German Fiction Writers, 1914-1945,* edited by James Hardin (1987)

57 *Victorian Prose Writers After 1867,* edited by William B. Thesing (1987)

58 *Jacobean and Caroline Dramatists,* edited by Fredson Bowers (1987)

59 *American Literary Critics and Scholars, 1800-1850,* edited by John W. Rathbun and Monica M. Grecu (1987)

60 *Canadian Writers Since 1960, Second Series,* edited by W. H. New (1987)

61 *American Writers for Children Since 1960: Poets, Illustrators, and Nonfiction Authors,* edited by Glenn E. Estes (1987)

62 *Elizabethan Dramatists,* edited by Fredson Bowers (1987)

63 *Modern American Critics, 1920-1955,* edited by Gregory S. Jay (1988)

64 *American Literary Critics and Scholars, 1850-1880,* edited by John W. Rathbun and Monica M. Grecu (1988)

65 *French Novelists, 1900-1930,* edited by Catharine Savage Brosman (1988)

66 *German Fiction Writers, 1885-1913,* 2 parts, edited by James Hardin (1988)

67 *Modern American Critics Since 1955,* edited by Gregory S. Jay (1988)

68 *Canadian Writers, 1920-1959, First Series,* edited by W. H. New (1988)

69 *Contemporary German Fiction Writers, First Series,* edited by Wolfgang D. Elfe and James Hardin (1988)

70 *British Mystery Writers, 1860-1919,* edited by Bernard Benstock and Thomas F. Staley (1988)

71 *American Literary Critics and Scholars, 1880-1900,* edited by John W. Rathbun and Monica M. Grecu (1988)

72 *French Novelists, 1930-1960,* edited by Catharine Savage Brosman (1988)

73 *American Magazine Journalists, 1741-1850,* edited by Sam G. Riley (1988)

74 *American Short-Story Writers Before 1880,* edited by Bobby Ellen Kimbel, with the assistance of William E. Grant (1988)

75 *Contemporary German Fiction Writers, Second Series,* edited by Wolfgang D. Elfe and James Hardin (1988)

76 *Afro-American Writers, 1940-1955,* edited by Trudier Harris (1988)

77 *British Mystery Writers, 1920-1939,* edited by Bernard Benstock and Thomas F. Staley (1988)

78 *American Short-Story Writers, 1880-1910,* edited by Bobby Ellen Kimbel, with the assistance of William E. Grant (1988)

79 *American Magazine Journalists, 1850-1900,* edited by Sam G. Riley (1988)

80 *Restoration and Eighteenth-Century Dramatists, First Series,* edited by Paula R. Backscheider (1989)

81 *Austrian Fiction Writers, 1875-1913,* edited by James Hardin and Donald G. Daviau (1989)

82 *Chicano Writers, First Series,* edited by Francisco A. Lomelí and Carl R. Shirley (1989)

83 *French Novelists Since 1960,* edited by Catharine Savage Brosman (1989)

84 *Restoration and Eighteenth-Century Dramatists, Second Series,* edited by Paula R. Backscheider (1989)

85 *Austrian Fiction Writers After 1914,* edited by James Hardin and Donald G. Daviau (1989)

86 *American Short-Story Writers, 1910-1945, First Series,* edited by Bobby Ellen Kimbel (1989)

87 *British Mystery and Thriller Writers Since 1940, First Series,* edited by Bernard Benstock and Thomas F. Staley (1989)

88 *Canadian Writers, 1920-1959, Second Series,* edited by W. H. New (1989)

89 *Restoration and Eighteenth-Century Dramatists, Third Series,* edited by Paula R. Backscheider (1989)

90 *German Writers in the Age of Goethe, 1789-1832,* edited by James Hardin and Christoph E. Schweitzer (1989)

91 *American Magazine Journalists, 1900-1960, First Series,* edited by Sam G. Riley (1990)

92 *Canadian Writers, 1890-1920,* edited by W. H. New (1990)

93 *British Romantic Poets, 1789-1832, First Series,* edited by John R. Greenfield (1990)

94 *German Writers in the Age of Goethe: Sturm und Drang to Classicism,* edited by James Hardin and Christoph E. Schweitzer (1990)

95 *Eighteenth-Century British Poets, First Series,* edited by John Sitter (1990)

96 *British Romantic Poets, 1789-1832, Second Series,* edited by John R. Greenfield (1990)

97 *German Writers from the Enlightenment to Sturm und Drang, 1720-1764,* edited by James Hardin and Christoph E. Schweitzer (1990)

98 *Modern British Essayists, First Series,* edited by Robert Beum (1990)

99 *Canadian Writers Before 1890,* edited by W. H. New (1990)

100 *Modern British Essayists, Second Series,* edited by Robert Beum (1990)

101 *British Prose Writers, 1660-1800, First Series,* edited by Donald T. Siebert (1991)

102 *American Short-Story Writers, 1910-1945, Second Series,* edited by Bobby Ellen Kimbel (1991)

103 *American Literary Biographers, First Series,* edited by Steven Serafin (1991)

104 *British Prose Writers, 1660-1800, Second Series,* edited by Donald T. Siebert (1991)

105 *American Poets Since World War II, Second Series,* edited by R. S. Gwynn (1991)

106 *British Literary Publishing Houses, 1820-1880,* edited by Patricia J. Anderson and Jonathan Rose (1991)

107 *British Romantic Prose Writers, 1789-1832, First Series,* edited by John R. Greenfield (1991)

108 *Twentieth-Century Spanish Poets, First Series,* edited by Michael L. Perna (1991)

109 *Eighteenth-Century British Poets, Second Series,* edited by John Sitter (1991)

110 *British Romantic Prose Writers, 1789-1832, Second Series,* edited by John R. Greenfield (1991)

111 *American Literary Biographers, Second Series,* edited by Steven Serafin (1991)

112 *British Literary Publishing Houses, 1881-1965,* edited by Jonathan Rose and Patricia J. Anderson (1991)

113 *Modern Latin-American Fiction Writers, First Series,* edited by William Luis (1992)

114 *Twentieth-Century Italian Poets, First Series,* edited by Giovanna Wedel De Stasio, Glauco Cambon, and Antonio Illiano (1992)

115 *Medieval Philosophers,* edited by Jeremiah Hackett (1992)

116 *British Romantic Novelists, 1789-1832,* edited by Bradford K. Mudge (1992)

117 *Twentieth-Century Caribbean and Black African Writers, First Series,* edited by Bernth Lindfors and Reinhard Sander (1992)

118 *Twentieth-Century German Dramatists, 1889-1918,* edited by Wolfgang D. Elfe and James Hardin (1992)

119 *Nineteenth-Century French Fiction Writers: Romanticism and Realism, 1800-1860,* edited by Catharine Savage Brosman (1992)

120 *American Poets Since World War II, Third Series,* edited by R. S. Gwynn (1992)

121 *Seventeenth-Century British Nondramatic Poets, First Series,* edited by M. Thomas Hester (1992)

122 *Chicano Writers, Second Series,* edited by Francisco A. Lomelí and Carl R. Shirley (1992)

123 *Nineteenth-Century French Fiction Writers: Naturalism and Beyond, 1860-1900,* edited by Catharine Savage Brosman (1992)

124 *Twentieth-Century German Dramatists, 1919-1992,* edited by Wolfgang D. Elfe and James Hardin (1992)

125 *Twentieth-Century Caribbean and Black African Writers, Second Series,* edited by Bernth Lindfors and Reinhard Sander (1993)

126 *Seventeenth-Century British Nondramatic Poets, Second Series,* edited by M. Thomas Hester (1993)

127 *American Newspaper Publishers, 1950-1990,* edited by Perry J. Ashley (1993)

128 *Twentieth-Century Italian Poets, Second Series,* edited by Giovanna Wedel De Stasio, Glauco Cambon, and Antonio Illiano (1993)

129 *Nineteenth-Century German Writers, 1841-1900,* edited by James Hardin and Siegfried Mews (1993)

130 *American Short-Story Writers Since World War II,* edited by Patrick Meanor (1993)

131 *Seventeenth-Century British Nondramatic Poets, Third Series,* edited by M. Thomas Hester (1993)

132 *Sixteenth-Century British Nondramatic Writers, First Series,* edited by David A. Richardson (1993)

133 *Nineteenth-Century German Writers to 1840,* edited by James Hardin and Siegfried Mews (1993)

134 *Twentieth-Century Spanish Poets, Second Series,* edited by Jerry Phillips Winfield (1994)

135 *British Short-Fiction Writers, 1880-1914: The Realist Tradition,* edited by William B. Thesing (1994)

136 *Sixteenth-Century British Nondramatic Writers, Second Series,* edited by David A. Richardson (1994)

137 *American Magazine Journalists, 1900-1960, Second Series,* edited by Sam G. Riley (1994)

138 *German Writers and Works of the High Middle Ages: 1170-1280,* edited by James Hardin and Will Hasty (1994)

139 *British Short-Fiction Writers, 1945-1980,* edited by Dean Baldwin (1994)

140 *American Book-Collectors and Bibliographers, First Series,* edited by Joseph Rosenblum (1994)

141 *British Children's Writers, 1880-1914,* edited by Laura M. Zaidman (1994)

142 *Eighteenth-Century British Literary Biographers,* edited by Steven Serafin (1994)

143 *American Novelists Since World War II, Third Series,* edited by James R. Giles and Wanda H. Giles (1994)

144 *Nineteenth-Century British Literary Biographers,* edited by Steven Serafin (1994)

145 *Modern Latin-American Fiction Writers, Second Series,* edited by William Luis and Ann González (1994)

146 *Old and Middle English Literature,* edited by Jeffrey Helterman and Jerome Mitchell (1994)

147 *South Slavic Writers Before World War II,* edited by Vasa D. Mihailovich (1994)

148 *German Writers and Works of the Early Middle Ages: 800-1170,* edited by Will Hasty and James Hardin (1994)

149 *Late Nineteenth- and Early Twentieth-Century British Literary Biographers,* edited by Steven Serafin (1995)

150 *Early Modern Russian Writers, Late Seventeenth and Eighteenth Centuries,* edited by Marcus C. Levitt (1995)

151 *British Prose Writers of the Early Seventeenth Century,* edited by Clayton D. Lein (1995)

152 *American Novelists Since World War II, Fourth Series,* edited by James R. Giles and Wanda H. Giles (1995)

153 *Late-Victorian and Edwardian British Novelists, First Series,* edited by George M. Johnson (1995)

154 *The British Literary Book Trade, 1700-1820,* edited by James K. Bracken and Joel Silver (1995)

155 *Twentieth-Century British Literary Biographers,* edited by Steven Serafin (1995)

156 *British Short-Fiction Writers, 1880-1914: The Romantic Tradition,* edited by William F. Naufftus (1995)

157 *Twentieth-Century Caribbean and Black African Writers, Third Series,* edited by Bernth Lindfors and Reinhard Sander (1995)

158 *British Reform Writers, 1789-1832,* edited by Gary Kelly and Edd Applegate (1995)

159 *British Short-Fiction Writers, 1800-1880,* edited by John R. Greenfield (1996)

160 *British Children's Writers, 1914-1960,* edited by Donald R. Hettinga and Gary D. Schmidt (1996)

161 *British Children's Writers Since 1960, First Series,* edited by Caroline Hunt (1996)

162 *British Short-Fiction Writers, 1915-1945,* edited by John H. Rogers (1996)

163 *British Children's Writers, 1800-1880,* edited by Meena Khorana (1996)

164 *German Baroque Writers, 1580-1660,* edited by James Hardin (1996)

165 *American Poets Since World War II, Fourth Series,* edited by Joseph Conte (1996)

166 *British Travel Writers, 1837-1875,* edited by Barbara Brothers and Julia Gergits (1996)

167 *Sixteenth-Century British Nondramatic Writers, Third Series,* edited by David A. Richardson (1996)

168 *German Baroque Writers, 1661-1730,* edited by James Hardin (1996)

169 *American Poets Since World War II, Fifth Series,* edited by Joseph Conte (1996)

170 *The British Literary Book Trade, 1475-1700,* edited by James K. Bracken and Joel Silver (1996)

171 *Twentieth-Century American Sportswriters,* edited by Richard Orodenker (1996)

172 *Sixteenth-Century British Nondramatic Writers, Fourth Series,* edited by David A. Richardson (1996)

173 *American Novelists Since World War II, Fifth Series,* edited by James R. Giles and Wanda H. Giles (1996)

174 *British Travel Writers, 1876-1909,* edited by Barbara Brothers and Julia Gergits (1997)

175 *Native American Writers of the United States,* edited by Kenneth M. Roemer (1997)

176 *Ancient Greek Authors,* edited by Ward W. Briggs (1997)

177 *Italian Novelists Since World War II, 1945-1965,* edited by Augustus Pallotta (1997)

178 *British Fantasy and Science-Fiction Writers Before World War I,* edited by Darren Harris-Fain (1997)

179 *German Writers of the Renaissance and Reformation, 1280-1580,* edited by James Hardin and Max Reinhart (1997)

180 *Japanese Fiction Writers, 1868-1945,* edited by Van C. Gessel (1997)

181 *South Slavic Writers Since World War II,* edited by Vasa D. Mihailovich (1997)

182 *Japanese Fiction Writers Since World War II,* edited by Van C. Gessel (1997)

183 *American Travel Writers, 1776-1864,* edited by James J. Schramer and Donald Ross (1997)

184 *Nineteenth-Century British Book-Collectors and Bibliographers,* edited by William Baker and Kenneth Womack (1997)

185 *American Literary Journalists, 1945-1995, First Series,* edited by Arthur J. Kaul (1998)

186 *Nineteenth-Century American Western Writers,* edited by Robert L. Gale (1998)

187 *American Book Collectors and Bibliographers, Second Series,* edited by Joseph Rosenblum (1998)

188 *American Book and Magazine Illustrators to 1920,* edited by Steven E. Smith, Catherine A. Hastedt, and Donald H. Dyal (1998)

189 *American Travel Writers, 1850-1915,* edited by Donald Ross and James J. Schramer (1998)

190 *British Reform Writers, 1832-1914,* edited by Gary Kelly and Edd Applegate (1998)

191 *British Novelists Between the Wars,* edited by George M. Johnson (1998)

192 *French Dramatists, 1789-1914,* edited by Barbara T. Cooper (1998)

193 *American Poets Since World War II, Sixth Series,* edited by Joseph Conte (1998)

194 *British Novelists Since 1960, Second Series,* edited by Merritt Moseley (1998)

195 *British Travel Writers, 1910-1939,* edited by Barbara Brothers and Julia Gergits (1998)

196 *Italian Novelists Since World War II, 1965-1995,* edited by Augustus Pallotta (1999)

197 *Late-Victorian and Edwardian British Novelists, Second Series,* edited by George M. Johnson (1999)

198 *Russian Literature in the Age of Pushkin and Gogol: Prose,* edited by Christine A. Rydel (1999)

199 *Victorian Women Poets,* edited by William B. Thesing (1999)

200 *American Women Prose Writers to 1820,* edited by Carla J. Mulford, with Angela Vietto and Amy E. Winans (1999)

201 *Twentieth-Century British Book Collectors and Bibliographers,* edited by William Baker and Kenneth Womack (1999)

202 *Nineteenth-Century American Fiction Writers,* edited by Kent P. Ljungquist (1999)

203 *Medieval Japanese Writers,* edited by Steven D. Carter (1999)

204 *British Travel Writers, 1940-1997,* edited by Barbara Brothers and Julia M. Gergits (1999)

205 *Russian Literature in the Age of Pushkin and Gogol: Poetry and Drama,* edited by Christine A. Rydel (1999)

206 *Twentieth-Century American Western Writers, First Series,* edited by Richard H. Cracroft (1999)

207 *British Novelists Since 1960, Third Series,* edited by Merritt Moseley (1999)

208 *Literature of the French and Occitan Middle Ages: Eleventh to Fifteenth Centuries,* edited by Deborah Sinnreich-Levi and Ian S. Laurie (1999)

209 *Chicano Writers, Third Series,* edited by Francisco A. Lomelí and Carl R. Shirley (1999)

210 *Ernest Hemingway: A Documentary Volume,* edited by Robert W. Trogdon (1999)

211 *Ancient Roman Writers,* edited by Ward W. Briggs (1999)

212 *Twentieth-Century American Western Writers, Second Series,* edited by Richard H. Cracroft (1999)

213 *Pre-Nineteenth-Century British Book Collectors and Bibliographers,* edited by William Baker and Kenneth Womack (1999)

214 *Twentieth-Century Danish Writers,* edited by Marianne Stecher-Hansen (1999)

215 *Twentieth-Century Eastern European Writers, First Series,* edited by Steven Serafin (1999)

216 *British Poets of the Great War: Brooke, Rosenberg, Thomas. A Documentary Volume,* edited by Patrick Quinn (2000)

217 *Nineteenth-Century French Poets,* edited by Robert Beum (2000)

218 *American Short-Story Writers Since World War II, Second Series,* edited by Patrick Meanor and Gwen Crane (2000)

219 *F. Scott Fitzgerald's* The Great Gatsby: *A Documentary Volume,* edited by Matthew J. Bruccoli (2000)

220 *Twentieth-Century Eastern European Writers, Second Series,* edited by Steven Serafin (2000)

221 *American Women Prose Writers, 1870-1920,* edited by Sharon M. Harris, with the assistance of Heidi L. M. Jacobs and Jennifer Putzi (2000)

222 *H. L. Mencken: A Documentary Volume,* edited by Richard J. Schrader (2000)

223 *The American Renaissance in New England, Second Series,* edited by Wesley T. Mott (2000)

224 *Walt Whitman: A Documentary Volume,* edited by Joel Myerson (2000)

225 *South African Writers,* edited by Paul A. Scanlon (2000)

226 *American Hard-Boiled Crime Writers,* edited by George Parker Anderson and Julie B. Anderson (2000)

227 *American Novelists Since World War II, Sixth Series,* edited by James R. Giles and Wanda H. Giles (2000)

228 *Twentieth-Century American Dramatists, Second Series,* edited by Christopher J. Wheatley (2000)

229 *Thomas Wolfe: A Documentary Volume,* edited by Ted Mitchell (2001)

230 *Australian Writers, 1788–1914,* edited by Selina Samuels (2001)

231 *British Novelists Since 1960, Fourth Series,* edited by Merritt Moseley (2001)

232 *Twentieth-Century Eastern European Writers, Third Series,* edited by Steven Serafin (2001)

233 *British and Irish Dramatists Since World War II, Second Series,* edited by John Bull (2001)

234 *American Short-Story Writers Since World War II, Third Series,* edited by Patrick Meanor and Richard E. Lee (2001)

235 *The American Renaissance in New England, Third Series,* edited by Wesley T. Mott (2001)

Documentary Series

1 *Sherwood Anderson, Willa Cather, John Dos Passos, Theodore Dreiser, F. Scott Fitzgerald, Ernest Hemingway, Sinclair Lewis,* edited by Margaret A. Van Antwerp (1982)

2 *James Gould Cozzens, James T. Farrell, William Faulkner, John O'Hara, John Steinbeck, Thomas Wolfe, Richard Wright,* edited by Margaret A. Van Antwerp (1982)

3 *Saul Bellow, Jack Kerouac, Norman Mailer, Vladimir Nabokov, John Updike, Kurt Vonnegut,* edited by Mary Bruccoli (1983)

4 *Tennessee Williams,* edited by Margaret A. Van Antwerp and Sally Johns (1984)

5 *American Transcendentalists,* edited by Joel Myerson (1988)

6 *Hardboiled Mystery Writers: Raymond Chandler, Dashiell Hammett, Ross Macdonald,* edited by Matthew J. Bruccoli and Richard Layman (1989)

7 *Modern American Poets: James Dickey, Robert Frost, Marianne Moore,* edited by Karen L. Rood (1989)

8 *The Black Aesthetic Movement,* edited by Jeffrey Louis Decker (1991)

9 *American Writers of the Vietnam War: W. D. Ehrhart, Larry Heinemann, Tim O'Brien, Walter McDonald, John M. Del Vecchio,* edited by Ronald Baughman (1991)

10 *The Bloomsbury Group,* edited by Edward L. Bishop (1992)

11 *American Proletarian Culture: The Twenties and The Thirties,* edited by Jon Christian Suggs (1993)

12 *Southern Women Writers: Flannery O'Connor, Katherine Anne Porter, Eudora Welty,* edited by Mary Ann Wimsatt and Karen L. Rood (1994)

13 *The House of Scribner, 1846-1904,* edited by John Delaney (1996)

14 *Four Women Writers for Children, 1868-1918,* edited by Caroline C. Hunt (1996)

15 *American Expatriate Writers: Paris in the Twenties,* edited by Matthew J. Bruccoli and Robert W. Trogdon (1997)

16 *The House of Scribner, 1905-1930,* edited by John Delaney (1997)

17 *The House of Scribner, 1931-1984,* edited by John Delaney (1998)

18 *British Poets of The Great War: Sassoon, Graves, Owen,* edited by Patrick Quinn (1999)

19 *James Dickey,* edited by Judith S. Baughman (1999)

See also DLB 210, 216, 219, 222, 224, 229

Yearbooks

1980 edited by Karen L. Rood, Jean W. Ross, and Richard Ziegfeld (1981)

1981 edited by Karen L. Rood, Jean W. Ross, and Richard Ziegfeld (1982)

1982 edited by Richard Ziegfeld; associate editors: Jean W. Ross and Lynne C. Zeigler (1983)

1983 edited by Mary Bruccoli and Jean W. Ross; associate editor Richard Ziegfeld (1984)

1984 edited by Jean W. Ross (1985)

1985 edited by Jean W. Ross (1986)

1986 edited by J. M. Brook (1987)

1987 edited by J. M. Brook (1988)

1988 edited by J. M. Brook (1989)

1989 edited by J. M. Brook (1990)

1990 edited by James W. Hipp (1991)

1991 edited by James W. Hipp (1992)

1992 edited by James W. Hipp (1993)

1993 edited by James W. Hipp, contributing editor George Garrett (1994)

1994 edited by James W. Hipp, contributing editor George Garrett (1995)

1995 edited by James W. Hipp, contributing editor George Garrett (1996)

1996 edited by Samuel W. Bruce and L. Kay Webster, contributing editor George Garrett (1997)

1997 edited by Matthew J. Bruccoli and George Garrett, with the assistance of L. Kay Webster (1998)

1998 edited by Matthew J. Bruccoli, contributing editor George Garrett, with the assistance of D. W. Thomas (1999)

1999 edited by Matthew J. Bruccoli, contributing editor George Garrett, with the assistance of D. W. Thomas (2000)

Concise Series

Concise Dictionary of American Literary Biography, 7 volumes (1988-1999): *The New Consciousness, 1941-1968; Colonization to the American Renaissance, 1640-1865; Realism, Naturalism, and Local Color, 1865-1917; The Twenties, 1917-1929; The Age of Maturity, 1929-1941; Broadening Views, 1968-1988; Supplement: Modern Writers, 1900-1998.*

Concise Dictionary of British Literary Biography, 8 volumes (1991-1992): *Writers of the Middle Ages and Renaissance Before 1660; Writers of the Restoration and Eighteenth Century, 1660-1789; Writers of the Romantic Period, 1789-1832; Victorian Writers, 1832-1890; Late-Victorian and Edwardian Writers, 1890-1914; Modern Writers, 1914-1945; Writers After World War II, 1945-1960; Contemporary Writers, 1960 to Present.*

Concise Dictionary of World Literary Biography, 20 volumes projected (1999-): *Ancient Greek and Roman Writers; German Writers; African, Carribbean, and Latin American Writers; South Slavic and Eastern European Writers.*

Dictionary of Literary Biography® • Volume Two Hundred Thirty-Five

The American Renaissance in New England
Third Series

Dictionary of Literary Biography® • Volume Two Hundred Thirty-Five

The American Renaissance in New England
Third Series

Edited by
Wesley T. Mott
Worcester Polytechnic Institute

A Bruccoli Clark Layman Book
The Gale Group
Detroit • San Francisco • London • Boston • Woodbridge, Conn.

Matthew J. Bruccoli and Richard Layman, Editorial Directors
C. E. Frazer Clark Jr., Managing Editor
Karen L. Rood, Senior Editor

Printed in the United States of America

The paper used in this publication meets the minimum requirements of American National Standard for Information Sciences–Permanence Paper for Printed Library Materials, ANSI Z39.48-1984. ∞™

Library of Congress Cataloging-in-Publication Data

The American renaissance in New England. Third series / edited by Wesley T. Mott.
p. cm.–(Dictionary of literary biography: v. 235)
"A Bruccoli Clark Layman book."
Includes bibliographical references and index.
ISBN 0-7876-4652-0 (alk. paper)
1. American literature–New England–Dictionaries. 2. American literature–19th century–Dictionaries. 3. American literature–New England–Bio-bibliography–Dictionaries. 4. American literature–19th century–Bio-bibliography–Dictionaries. 5. Authors, American–New England–Biography–Dictionaries. 6. Authors, American–19th century–Biography–Dictionaries. 7. United States–Intellectual life–1783-1865–Dictionaries. 8. New England–Biography–Dictionaries. I. Mott, Wesley T. II. Series.

PS243.A543 2001
810.9'003–dc21 00-046628
[B] CIP

10 9 8 7 6 5 4 3 2 1

To Sandy

Contents

Plan of the Series

. . . Almost the most prodigious asset of a country, and perhaps its most precious possession, is its native literary product—when that product is fine and noble and enduring.

Mark Twain*

The advisory board, the editors, and the publisher of the *Dictionary of Literary Biography* are joined in endorsing Mark Twain's declaration. The literature of a nation provides an inexhaustible resource of permanent worth. We intend to make literature and its creators better understood and more accessible to students and the reading public, while satisfying the standards of teachers and scholars.

To meet these requirements, *literary biography* has been construed in terms of the author's achievement. The most important thing about a writer is his writing. Accordingly, the entries in *DLB* are career biographies, tracing the development of the author's canon and the evolution of his reputation.

The purpose of *DLB* is not only to provide reliable information in a convenient format but also to place the figures in the larger perspective of literary history and to offer appraisals of their accomplishments by qualified scholars.

The publication plan for *DLB* resulted from two years of preparation. The project was proposed to Bruccoli Clark by Frederick G. Ruffner, president of the Gale Research Company, in November 1975. After specimen entries were prepared and typeset, an advisory board was formed to refine the entry format and develop the series rationale. In meetings held during 1976, the publisher, series editors, and advisory board approved the scheme for a comprehensive biographical dictionary of persons who contributed to North American literature. Editorial work on the first volume began in January 1977, and it was published in 1978. In order to make *DLB* more than a reference tool and to compile volumes that individually have claim to status as literary history, it was decided to organize volumes by topic, period, or genre. Each of these freestanding volumes provides a biographical-bibliographical guide and overview for a particular area of literature. We are convinced that this organization—as opposed to a single alphabet method—constitutes a valuable innovation in the presentation of reference material. The volume plan necessarily requires many decisions for the placement and treatment of authors who might properly be included in two or three volumes. In some instances a major figure will be included in separate volumes, but with different entries emphasizing the aspect of his career appropriate to each volume. Ernest Hemingway, for example, is represented in *American Writers in Paris, 1920–1939* by an entry focusing on his expatriate apprenticeship; he is also in *American Novelists, 1910–1945* with an entry surveying his entire career, as well as in *American Short-Story Writers, 1910–1945, Second Series* with an entry concentrating on his short stories. Each volume includes a cumulative index of the subject authors and articles. Comprehensive indexes to the entire series are planned.

Since 1981 the series has been further augmented by the *DLB Yearbooks,* which update published entries and add new entries to keep the *DLB* current with contemporary activity. There have also been *DLB Documentary Series* volumes which provide biographical and critical source materials for figures whose work is judged to have particular interest for students. One of these companion volumes is devoted entirely to Tennessee Williams.

We define literature as the *intellectual commerce of a nation:* not merely as belles lettres but as that ample and complex process by which ideas are generated, shaped, and transmitted. *DLB* entries are not limited to "creative writers" but extend to other figures who in their time and in their way influenced the mind of a people. Thus the series encompasses historians, journalists, publishers, book collectors, and screenwriters. By this means readers of *DLB* may be aided to perceive literature not as cult scripture in the keeping of intellectual high priests but firmly positioned at the center of a nation's life.

DLB includes the major writers appropriate to each volume and those standing in the ranks behind

**From an unpublished section of Mark Twain's autobiography, copyright by the Mark Twain Company*

them. Scholarly and critical counsel has been sought in deciding which minor figures to include and how full their entries should be. Wherever possible, useful references are made to figures who do not warrant separate entries.

Each *DLB* volume has an expert volume editor responsible for planning the volume, selecting the figures for inclusion, and assigning the entries. Volume editors are also responsible for preparing, where appropriate, appendices surveying the major periodicals and literary and intellectual movements for their volumes, as well as lists of further readings. Work on the series as a whole is coordinated at the Bruccoli Clark Layman editorial center in Columbia, South Carolina, where the editorial staff is responsible for accuracy and utility of the published volumes.

One feature that distinguishes *DLB* is the illustration policy–its concern with the iconography of literature. Just as an author is influenced by his surroundings, so is the reader's understanding of the author enhanced by a knowledge of his environment. Therefore *DLB* volumes include not only drawings, paintings, and photographs of authors, often depicting them at various stages in their careers, but also illustrations of their families and places where they lived. Title pages are regularly reproduced in facsimile along with dust jackets for modern authors. The dust jackets are a special feature of *DLB* because they often document better than anything else the way in which an author's work was perceived in its own time. Specimens of the writers' manuscripts and letters are included when feasible.

Samuel Johnson rightly decreed that "The chief glory of every people arises from its authors." The purpose of the *Dictionary of Literary Biography* is to compile literary history in the surest way available to us–by accurate and comprehensive treatment of the lives and work of those who contributed to it.

The *DLB* Advisory Board

Introduction

Ralph Waldo Emerson issued a ringing challenge to the literary community of the young nation in his 1837 Harvard Phi Beta Kappa address, "The American Scholar": If American writers were "free and brave," with words "loaded with life," they would usher in a "new age." Emerson looms over that age, whether as an inspiration to reformers and artists of his generation and the next, or as a bugbear to those distrustful of social and institutional change or literary innovation. Never wishing to lead a "party" or to be imitated himself, he always thought it his role (and that of the "scholar") to "provoke" others to discover their own resources of genius and power. The rich literary production in New England during the next quarter century–in many senses a response to Emerson's provocation–constituted what has come to be known as the "American Renaissance."

This second of three *DLB* volumes dedicated to *The American Renaissance in New England* comprises forty-eight biographical/bibliographical essays on writers who flourished in Boston and Cambridge, Massachusetts, in the mid nineteenth century. The volume includes an appendix with an essay about the spirit and culture of Boston and Cambridge during that period, written by George Ripley and George P. Bradford, both of whom were reform-minded participants in the American Renaissance in New England.

To understand the lively and complex relationships among the writers of this important moment in literary history, readers should consult all three volumes of *The American Renaissance in New England:* Second Series (The Concord Writers), Third Series (Boston & Cambridge Writers), and Fourth Series (Regional Writers). William Dean Howells observed that many writers associated in the nation's mind with Boston actually lived throughout New England. "Yet Boston," he noted, "stood for the whole Massachusetts group, and Massachusetts, in the literary impulse, meant New England." Geographical categories for careers and residence are, of course, highly fluid. Several Concord and Regional writers, for example, were born or educated in Boston or Cambridge. Writers such as Nathaniel Hawthorne (associated with Salem, Massachusetts) chose to live in Concord because of its congenial setting and literary culture; others, such as Elizabeth Palmer Peabody (who had a long and diverse career in Boston), identified with the Emersonian or Transcendental climate of Concord. Many writers simply took up jobs and residence at several locations in New England and elsewhere, and are not easily classified by geography. (The major Transcendentalist reform communities and publications, moreover, though not physically based in Concord, are found in the Concord volume as a convenience and in recognition of their various indebtedness to the Concord writers.)

Together, the three *American Renaissance in New England* volumes supersede the 1978 *DLB 1* volume with the same title, edited by Joel Myerson. A pioneering work in its own right as well as the inaugural volume in the now-venerable *DLB* series, the 1978 version included ninety-eight biographical/bibliographical essays, some of which were comprehensive master essays but most of which were brief–several only a paragraph in length. The format of the *DLB* entries has evolved over the past twenty-two years. The new three-volume version provides significantly augmented essays, with full primary bibliographies, on most of the figures included in the original work. (George Henry Calvert is included in the new, augmented *Antebellum Writers of New York and the South,* edited by Kent P. Ljungquist; James Marsh and Edwin Percy Whipple, who have substantial essays in, respectively, *DLB 59* and *DLB 64,* do not appear in the new volumes, nor does Samuel Longfellow.) Ten new figures have been added in response to recent critical reevaluations of New England writers: the rediscovered women writers Lucy Larcom and Harriet Wilson; the Wampanoag William Apess; a neglected poet who bridges Romanticism and modernism, Frederick Goddard Tuckerman; and various orators and preachers whose published works were also important–Orville Dewey, Charles Follen, John Gough, Wendell Phillips, Charles Sumner, and Henry Ware Jr. Each volume concludes with a secondary bibliography encompassing standard modern studies as well as older titles that, although in many cases superseded by recent scholarship, retain historical value for their treatment of the literature of New England.

F. O. Matthiessen, in his *American Renaissance: Art and Expression in the Age of Emerson and Whitman* (1941), first termed the "half-decade of 1850–55" a national renaissance–not really a "*re-birth,*" he noted, but rather the flowering of "its first maturity . . . in the whole expanse of art and culture." This five-year period produced major works of Ralph Waldo Emerson, Nathaniel Hawthorne, Herman Melville, Henry David Thoreau, and Walt Whitman, which Matthiessen thought unsurpassed in "imaginative vitality" even as they were engaged with distinctly American issues. For all their differences, he maintained, the "one common denominator of my five writers . . . was their devotion to the possibilities of democracy."

Matthiessen's useful and compelling term for the era needs qualification in the context of the work at hand. First, the cast of characters does not neatly fit this regional focus. Emerson, Hawthorne, and Thoreau, of course, were New Englanders born and bred; but Melville (though he wrote *Moby-Dick, or, the Whale* [1851] at Pittsfield, Massachusetts) was first and last a New Yorker, and Whitman (though at crucial stages of his career he came under the influence of Emerson) is associated primarily with New York and New Jersey. Second, the period 1850–1855 is too restrictive to accommodate the many important New England writers, genres, and themes that flourished at midcentury. It has long been customary, in college courses and in monographs, to stretch Matthiessen's term back to 1836, the year Transcendentalism emerged, with books such as Emerson's *Nature* (1836), and ahead to the Civil War, during which event many of the reform issues that preoccupied the antebellum period culminated and by which time certain political, economic, and social developments that were transforming American life had accelerated and many of the leading literary figures of the period had become less productive or had died. Third, in an age of assaults on the traditional nineteenth-century literary canon, Matthiessen's heroes have come to many to seem decidedly too homogenous.

Matthiessen's scheme, however, has proved resilient, solidly endorsed, for example, by Robert E. Spiller's influential *Literary History of the United States* (revised third edition, 1963):

> In quality of style, and particularly in depth of philosophic insight, American literature has not yet surpassed the collective achievement of Emerson, Thoreau, Hawthorne, Melville, and Whitman. Having freed itself in these writers from its earlier tendencies either blindly to imitate or blindly to reject European models, American literature here for the first time sloughed off provincialism, and, by being itself–by saying only what it wanted to say and as it wanted to say it–attained, paradoxically, the rank and quality of world literature, a literature authentic not only in America but everywhere the English tongue is understood.

Matthiessen's monumental work has always invited interpretive refinement and theoretical challenges. But for all the specialized correctives and more broadly conceived cultural canvasses appearing in the past fifty-nine years, Matthiessen is still unsurpassed for the synthetic power of his grasp of the distinctive quality of an age, for the clarity of his expression, and for his own tenacious conviction that literary criticism in a democracy has moral implications.

Social observers of the young republic continually questioned whether these shores would be hospitable to the emergence of a homegrown literary culture. National anxiety marked the first two decades of the nineteenth century in the wake of the French Revolution, aggravated by ongoing tensions with Britain culminating in the War of 1812 and lingering fears about what President James Madison had called the greatest internal threat to democracy–"faction." Americans, moreover, prided themselves on dogged personal independence, preferring practicality to speculation and action to introspection. In "most mental operations each American relies on individual effort and judgment," noted the French social critic Alexis de Tocqueville in *Democracy in America* (volume 2, 1840); thus, he suggested wryly, "of all countries in the world, America is the one in which the precepts of Descartes are least studied and best followed." Yet, in Federalist Boston efforts to establish an original national culture had begun in earnest early in the new century. For example, *The Monthly Anthology* (1803–1811), forerunner of *The North American Review,* was founded by William Emerson and others to inculcate values of rationality, taste, and civic virtue–all deemed essential to order and stability in a republic–and to engender a sense of pride in New England culture. *The Christian Disciple* was established in 1813 to express and unify the growing spirit of liberal Christianity in Greater Boston; later called *The Christian Examiner,* this journal continued to play a crucial role as a more radical and innovative wing of Unitarianism–Transcendentalism–began to emerge in the 1830s.

In hindsight, these early efforts seem tame, parochial, even strangely in awe of and imitative of British culture. Ralph Waldo Emerson later mocked the labors of his father's generation as "that early ignorant & transitional *Month-of-March,* in our New England culture." By the 1820s the question "What is distinctive about American literature?"–a central question in literary study to this day–became a matter of some urgency as

American writers and critics sought their own identity and mission. The call for "literary nationalism" became a refrain as Americans insisted that the United States must cease imitating British and European literary models, that a great nation must have a great literature. As William Ellery Channing declared in his *Christian Examiner* review essay on a "National Literature" (January 1830), "A people, into whose minds the thoughts of foreigners are poured perpetually, needs an energy within itself to resist, to modify this mighty influence, and without it, will inevitably sink under the worst bondage, will become intellectually tame and enslaved." Channing was a nationalist, but he was no jingo. Great literature, he believed, consists of all original writings of "superior minds" that express a "nation's mind" and contribute "new truths to the stock of human knowledge." "We love our country much," he insisted, "but mankind more. As men and Christians, our first desire is to see the improvement of human nature." The special "genius" of the United States, as Channing saw it, was to bear witness to the potential of the unfettered human spirit. Prophetically he declared, "We want a reformation. We want a literature, in which genius will pay supreme, if not undivided homage, to truth and virtue." Emerson's more famous "The American Scholar" (1837) went on to outline the influence on, and duties of, "Man Thinking," leading Oliver Wendell Holmes years later to call this address "Our intellectual Declaration of Independence." Emerson's criticism of our dependence on the culture of other nations was secondary, however, to his radical celebration of the continually active, evolving power of mind, an *organic* process that could never stop to admire itself, to indulge in a sense of national superiority, or to congeal into institutional formalism. In this address, Emerson *was* renewing Channing's call for a national literature that, without being self-congratulatory, would express the potential of democratic culture as a contribution to the world.

The flowering of New England culture–in politics, education, religion, and literature–derives from the emergence of "liberal Christianity," or Unitarianism, in the early nineteenth century. Puritanism, the dominant religious and cultural force in the region since the 1630s, had held, in broadest terms, that man, being depraved, can be redeemed only by God's free grace. In fact, debates had simmered within Puritanism since the Reformation over the role man might play in *responding* to God's offer of grace. Eighteenth-century rationalism–manifest in the documents of the American Revolution–had only advanced the case for the ability of men and women to improve their own political as well as spiritual estates. The election of Henry Ware Sr. as Hollis Professor of Divinity at Harvard in 1805 signaled the arrival of the liberal theology in the halls of power in New England. The generation that came of college age in the 1820s, not satisfied with casting off the vestiges of Puritan theology, began to challenge the rationalist epistemology they associated with such philosophers as John Locke and William Paley, and they eagerly embraced theories maintaining that truth is perceived intuitively. William Ellery Channing's famous declaration in 1828 that self-knowledge is attained through "likeness to God" was the high point of this shift and prepared the way for the Transcendentalist movement that emerged in the mid 1830s. The Unitarians held that self-culture–a continual process of introspection, self-control, and moral growth–was the great project of life. Against this background, the Emersonian concept of *self-reliance*–often misinterpreted as a philosophy of self-absorption–was a profoundly moral stance.

The New England concern with self-culture, with its moral bent, manifested itself more naturally in forms outside merely belletristic kinds of fiction and verse. The archetypal regional genre since the founding of the Massachusetts Bay Colony in 1628 had been the sermon–always on these shores a means not simply to inculcate religious doctrine but also to exhort, to uplift, and to renew communal bonds. Despite the aridness implied by the misleading term "plain style," even Puritan sermons had been, of course, aesthetic performances. As Lawrence Buell and others have shown, the early-nineteenth-century Unitarians, largely freed from doctrinal burdens, exploited "literary" aspects of the genre to appeal to a new generation of parishioners–men and women who were bound less by appeals to authority and more by the power of pulpit eloquence to move intellect and emotion through narrative, dramatic, even "poetic" discourse. Many of the leading Transcendentalists had been trained for the ministry. Some (most dramatically, Emerson) left the pulpit for the lecture hall and the literary life; others continued to preach, some (most emphatically, Theodore Parker) to diverse audiences for whom denominational issues were subordinate to the power of sermons to affect feeling and to address the social concerns of a new age. Emerson's Harvard Divinity School Address (1838) struck many as a heretical challenge to religion; yet, it concludes by reaffirming "the institution of preaching,–the speech of man to men,–essentially the most flexible of all organs, of all forms."

Public eloquence, deriving from a two-hundred-year-old preaching tradition, an admiration for political oratory, and a new craving for information, education, and entertainment, now found an outlet in the lecture hall. Josiah Holbrook founded the first lyceum in Millbury, Massachusetts, in 1826 to satisfy the growing demand for more systematic instruction for working adults, and within a few years the lyceum movement had spread to the Ohio Valley. Figures as diverse as William Andrus Alcott, Frederick Douglass, Emerson, John Gough, Elizabeth Oakes Smith, and Thoreau were much anticipated on the lecture circuit. The ultimate extension of New England oral traditions, responding to the highly introspective demands of self-culture, was the Conversation. The most able practitioners of this most ephemeral genre, Bronson Alcott and Margaret Fuller, captivated the attention of select audiences by conducting seemingly spontaneous dialogues on topics ranging across the scholarly, the political, the aesthetic, and the speculative. The journal, a genre owing much to habits of New England spirituality, was practiced even by the nonliterary as a means of self-examination, of measuring growth in self-culture. In the hands of writers such as Emerson and Thoreau, the journal was also used pragmatically as a storehouse of quotations, anecdotes, and spontaneous thoughts, or artistically as a writing laboratory. Emerson called his extensive and carefully indexed journals his "savings bank," and he typically ransacked them for lecture material, and the lectures in turn often were polished into essays later collected in book form.

The deep-seated theological traditions of New England and attendant preoccupation with moral and spiritual development made the region somewhat biased against fiction as a frivolous diversion from the serious purpose of life. In the preface to his last novel, *The Marble Faun; or, The Romance of Monte Beni* (1860), Nathaniel Hawthorne named other cultural barriers to writing in a new land. America–with its materialism and self-confidence, its lack of history and tradition, and its insistence on practicality–failed to provide materials and context for works of the imagination. "No author, without a trial," Hawthorne declared, "can conceive of the difficulty of writing a Romance about a country where there is no shadow, no antiquity, no mystery, no picturesque and gloomy wrong, nor anything but a common-place prosperity, in broad and simple daylight, as is happily the case with my dear native land." Antebellum fiction, dominated by the didactic and the sentimental, was regarded as an appropriate vehicle for providing examples of virtue, heroism, and patriotism; for instructing youth; and for modeling domestic virtues for women. In the case of Louisa May Alcott, however, popular juvenile fiction became enduring art. *Little Women* (1868–1869), still a perennial favorite of young girls, resonates with themes that engage readers of all ages–home and family as the foundation of virtue, a sense of place, cultivation of personal and social reform, the difficulty of selecting a vocation–notably writing–and especially for a woman, the deepening of idealism that encounters reality, and reconciling the needs for self-reliance and community. Serious adult fiction began to explore such issues as regional history, the abilities of women, and racism. Hawthorne attained international status for tales and romances exploring psychological and tragic dimensions of human nature. New England poetry–seemingly taking its lead from Emerson's injunctions in "The Poet" that "it is not metres, but a metre-making argument, that makes a poem" and that poets are "liberating gods"–was as likely as fiction to aim at elevating language and thought. The best verse of the period, however, is moral in no narrow sense and achieves rich diversity of expression. Regional and national history, legends, and public issues mingled with deeply personal meditations and experiences to convey rich psychological and cultural landscapes. Emerson sought to show the miraculous in the common, speaking in the language of real people. Holmes and James Russell Lowell demonstrated that American poetry could be urbane and witty. John Greenleaf Whittier was the righteous poet as reformer who, in "Snow-Bound," could also win popular acclaim by capturing the post–Civil War elegiac mood, aching for loved ones and a past now lost. Henry Wadsworth Longfellow, steeped in the Romance languages, became the most revered American poet of his day by employing European models and verse patterns to elevate American events and legends to epic status. Emily Dickinson, little known in her own time, is perhaps the most radically innovative of all poets to emerge from this literary renaissance; though not as isolated from nature or society as stereotype has had it, her verse is the boldest exploration of the mind and the imagination.

The "American Renaissance" emerged, however, in a distinctly international context, warranting much of the recent scholarly criticism of the long celebration of American literary "exceptionalism." William Wordsworth, for example, appealed to New England writers with his call for poetry dealing with the commonplace, in language spoken by real people. Sir Walter Scott, for all his exotic and British settings, and Charles Dickens, with his rich evocation of English society and character, remained intimidating models of the great novelist. Samuel Taylor Coleridge and Thomas Carlyle were indispensable for introducing and interpreting Immanuel Kant and other German writers whose commentary on intuition and the workings of the mind fired the imaginations of young Transcendentalists eager to find an alternative to the pragmatic rationalism of Locke. The mystic Emanuel Swedenborg had a major influence not only on New England spirituality but also on theories of the origin and nature of language. Johann Wolfgang von Goethe and Alexander von Humboldt, moreover, were admired as examples of modern renaissance men, accomplished scientists as well as writers.

As Matthiessen knew, however–and depicted graphically in using as his frontispiece to *American Renaissance* a striking daguerreotype of David McKay, builder of the great clipper ship the *Flying Cloud*–the writers of this period shared in large degree the forward-looking spirit of their own nation. Emerson's statement that "Our American literature and spiritual history are, we confess, in the optative mood" (this last phrase provides the title for Matthiessen's first chapter) parallels the egalitarian optimism and the assertive "go ahead" attitude of the entrepreneurial class of the young nation that have come to seem so distinctively American. The Romantic individualism of young intellectuals in New England during the 1830s, however, was frequently at odds with the materialism of commercial and industrial expansion. New England, with its Federalist heritage, was naturally unfriendly turf for the presidency of Andrew Jackson (1829–1837). Although the Transcendentalists shared with Jacksonian democracy a belief in the common citizen and a distrust of big money, they abhorred its crude political leveling with its hypocritical callousness toward slavery, the plight of Native Americans, and principled political dissent. The antislavery activists of the region perceived the expansionist impulse of the nation in the 1840s and 1850s as entangled with imperialism and insidious strategies to expand the slave territory. Thus, they saw the originally idealistic concept of "Manifest Destiny" to be a cynical tool of jingoism, the Mexican War as an excuse for annexing Texas, and the Compromise of 1850–with its Fugitive Slave Law–as Daniel Webster's great moral sellout.

Consequently, even as major New England writers in various ways spoke for their age, an important strain of American literature began to stand in critical, often antagonistic, opposition to national habits and values. With such exuberant hope as that expressed by Channing and Emerson, with such expectations that a distinctive American literature would emerge to give voice to the distinctive genius of the young nation, disappointment and even alienation were perhaps inevitable. The discrepancies between the national "dream" and reality were felt keenly. The reading public has always sought entertainment and reassurance. The major writers of New England refused, however, to offer easy fare and smooth answers and in both openly defiant and subtle ways increasingly stood at odds with prevailing standards.

If, as Matthiessen thought, the most challenging writers of the age represented a high-water mark of democratic culture, they did so not only by celebrating what the United States had become but also by reminding the nation of what it had yet to become. Emerson's great project was to awaken the nation to its latent "power" and possibilities; yet, he saw that, in the present state of human nature, "A man is a god in ruins." For many writers of the period, the American Revolution was incomplete, its promises not yet realized. "Even if we grant that the American has freed himself from a political tyrant," declared Thoreau in "Life without Principle" (1863), "he is still the slave of an economical and moral tyrant. . . . What is the value of any political freedom, but as a means to moral freedom? . . . With respect to a true culture and manhood, we are essentially provincial still, not metropolitan,–mere Jonathans." Often heard during the literary renaissance of New England is the rhetoric of the jeremiad, a characteristic Puritan mode that in America, as Sacvan Bercovitch has shown, was a powerful means not simply of lamenting the national failings but of calling for renewal. The antebellum period was the Age of Reform in New England more than in any other region, as citizens sought to redeem the promises of the American Revolution in many crusades–for abolition, woman's rights, and temperance; for education reform, prison reform, and diet reform; for more humane treatment of convicts, the blind, and the insane; for free love and reform of marital laws; and in opposition to forced removal of Native Americans from their ancestral lands and to imperialist aggression toward Mexico. New England writers threw their support behind many such movements.

Racial hypocrisy in the United States was often exposed in terms that forced white Christians to redefine their own religious assumptions. The Wampanoag preacher William Apess in 1833 asked rhetorically, "What is all this ado about missionary societies, if it be not to Christianize those who are not Christians? And what is it for? To degrade them worse, to bring them into society where they must welter out their days in disgrace merely because their skin is of a different complexion." The escaped slave Frederick Douglass testified that Christianity could be a tool to enforce the "peculiar institution" by instilling passivity and acceptance in the slave, and that religious conversion could make the slaveholder more self-righteously vicious than he had been in a state of unbelief. Douglass's compelling autobiography is an extraordinary record of the unfolding of a mind gradually becoming aware–through experiences ranging from violent struggle to subterfuge to an awakening of the power of language–of its potential for integrity, independence, and growth. Even white New England abolitionists, however, were often reviled and abused on their own soil from 1831, when William Lloyd Garrison founded *The Liberator* in Boston, until the Civil War and its aftermath, when the self-aggrandizing myth of Northern moral righteousness became widespread and finally entrenched.

Women in disproportionate numbers were active in the antislavery movement. Many were struck by a stunning irony: they were permitted, even encouraged in certain circles, to agitate on behalf of chattel slaves hundreds of miles away; and yet, they themselves could not vote and did not enjoy legal protection even within matrimony. In *Woman in the Nineteenth Century* (1845) Margaret Fuller observed the dramatic change in women who were "champions of the enslaved African": "this band it is, which, partly in consequence of a natural following out of principles, partly because many women have been prominent in that cause, makes, just now, the warmest appeal in behalf of woman." Fuller had been fortunate in having a father "who cherished no sentimental reverence for woman, but a firm belief in the equality of the sexes." He demanded intellectual development and "addressed her not as a plaything, but as a living mind." What struck too many contemporaries as a threat to "family union" was to Fuller a natural extension of Transcendentalist "self-reliance": "This self-dependence, which was honored in me, is deprecated as a fault in most women. They are taught to learn their rule from without, not to unfold it from within."

Scholarship over the last several decades has stressed the deep cultural divide in the nineteenth century between the masculine world of industry, commerce, and politics, and "woman's sphere"–the home. Women, in this view, had the separate (but indispensable) role of nurturing. As mothers and as wives, their supposedly finer female susceptibility to sentiment, virtue, and piety rendered the domestic scene a realm of education in knowledge, feeling, and behavior–a veritable incubator of civic values crucial to a young republic. Many of the manuals, collections of verse, and novels of the period written by and for women were designed to enhance women's effectiveness in and satisfaction with their important but closely circumscribed "sphere" of activity. Some women writers, however, powerfully showed that domestic "female" virtues need not be cloistered. In that most influential of all American novels, *Uncle Tom's Cabin* (1852), Harriet Beecher Stowe employed "Christian" as well as maternal love in the service of moral suasion to move readers to a felt awareness of the horrors of slavery. The gender of Uncle Tom–and the recent discovery that "feeling" in oratory and literature was also directed at men–should be a reminder of the truth, even in the mid 1800s, of Fuller's claim that "Male and female represent the two sides of the great radical dualism. But, in fact, they are perpetually passing into one another." Indeed, several women writers began to challenge the validity of separate "spheres."

All of this scrutiny of social issues resulted not because New England writers were detached, privileged cultural observers but because they were enmeshed in economic forces transforming the region and the nation. The liberal Christian culture that had shaped nineteenth-century Boston was liberal theologically but conservative politically, and the connections between work, success, and civic virtue had become articles of faith. The population of Boston boomed by 40 percent in the 1820s, but there were causes for worry: economic panics in 1825 and 1837, and the proud shipping industry of Boston already being bested by that of New York City. The thirty years before the Civil War, moreover, ushered in an industrial revolution and market economy that was both exhilarating and threatening. Mills in Lowell and Lawrence, Massachusetts, reorganized patterns of work for thousands to manufacture efficiently raw materials supplied, in many cases, by the South (suggesting, to several writers, one form of Northern complicity in slavery). Symbolic of the new age for the Concord writers was construction of the Fitchburg Railroad by the shores of Walden Pond in 1844; Thoreau, who moved to Walden Woods the next year, announced ambivalently, "So is your pastoral life whirled past and away." In 1849 the California Gold Rush seemed to many writers a destabilizing form of gambling, as dangerous as Wall Street speculation. The emergence of money as the ultimate and pervasive measure of value, altering relationships and personal identity, was troubling. Emerson declared, "Society is a joint-stock company. . . . The virtue in most request is conformity. Self-reliance is its aversion." "This world," said Thoreau in disgust, "is a place of business. . . . It is nothing but work, work, work." Making a living as a writer was, then as now, difficult. Many writers–Emerson the most notable example–spent years traveling the arduous lecture circuit to supplement often meager income from book sales. Thoreau was bitterly disappointed by weak sales of his first book, *A Week on the Concord and Merrimack Rivers* (1849). Margaret Fuller turned to journalism in New York. Authorship in a competitive culture was an uneasy vocational choice for many men, and literary excellence too often was obscured by the marketplace success of hackwork, often sentimental tripe by and for women. Hawthorne had to rely on political patronage and resented the "d____d mob of scribbling women" that he blamed for his own predicament as a struggling author. American writers were as victimized as their English counterparts by the absence (until 1891) of international copyright protection.

If, as Emerson noted, it was "the age of the first person singular," it was also the age of association. Thus, two distinct means for reforming economic and social relationships are generally identified in antebellum New England: the individualistic and the communitarian. Adherents to each alternative agreed that if all people are endowed with intellectual and spiritual capacity for growth, then conditions that thwart such growth must be removed. Unitarian self-culture and Emersonian self-reliance embody the conviction that reform must start with the individual–a stance demanding imaginative if not literal solitude for reflection, balance, and moral integrity; Thoreau's two-year experiment in transcendental economy at Walden is in this sense the classic "community of one." Bronson Alcott's Fruitlands and George Ripley's Brook Farm are the most dramatic experiments in New England in group living. These polarities are useful, however, for describing not absolute alternatives but rather tendencies and tensions in reform thinking. Emerson and Thoreau were both interested in communal ventures but for various reasons declined to sign on to new social arrangements; but each demanded that personal character flower in action, and each looked hopefully for signs of social amelioration. Whatever personal and economic forces finally undid Fruitlands and Brook Farm, each in its own way sought (by rearranging and redefining economic relationships) to cultivate *individuals* in a group setting–thus, their wide appeal to writers and the various successes (at Brook Farm, at least) in education and the arts.

"Prophetic" writers of the American Renaissance–those lamenting national failures and disgraces–were often scorned in their own land. Serious writers who were not essentially reformers had other reasons, moreover, for being disaffected with American life. Their forms of literary "subversion" were aimed chiefly not at reforming society but at undermining deeper-seated complacencies about human nature, American self-images, and understandings of the function and purpose of literature itself. Hawthorne, for example, in "Earth's Holocaust" (1844) satirized the passion for reform sweeping his generation. Seeking to start the world anew, freed from all the corruptions and encumbrances of history and tradition, the idealist zealots in the tale toss into a huge bonfire the documents and symbols of virtually every contemporary institution. Watching the proceedings is a "dark-visaged stranger, with a portentous grin" who announces to the narrator the one fundamental thing not consigned to the "conflagration": "the human heart itself!" The stranger undercuts the myth of American exceptionalism by raising both the immediate specter of European corruptions that Americans prided themselves on having left behind, and the more ancient ghost of post-Edenic sin and evil, concluding, "Oh, take my word for it, it will be the old world yet!" Hawthorne had lived briefly at Brook Farm and initially found it physically and intellectually stimulating. He later satirized both the utopian impulse and his own ambivalent attitude toward reformers in *The Blithedale Romance* (1852), however, and was primarily concerned in his fiction to probe the complexities, contradictions, and hypocrisies of human psychology. Many of his tales and romances were popularly admired for their quaint depictions of colonial history, but his darker insights into human nature were often missed. Indeed, as Melville wrote in what may be the most famous review of one American author by another, "Hawthorne and His Mosses" (1850), "spite of all the Indian-summer sunlight on the hither side of Hawthorne's soul, the other side–like the dark half of the physical sphere–is shrouded in a blackness, ten times black." Like "Shakespeare and other masters of the great Art of Telling the Truth," Hawthorne told the truth, "even though it be covertly, and by snatches." Most readers, Melville held, would not even "discern" the truths of Hawthorne's works, for "some of them are directly calculated to deceive–egregiously deceive, the superficial skimmer of pages." Dickinson, too, knew, in her dazzling, tight, metaphysical verse, that true poetry is not smooth or easy: "Tell all the Truth but tell it slant– / . . . The Truth must dazzle gradually / Or every man be blind–." Even poets lionized in their own time–Longfellow and Whittier, for example–often subtly undercut the worship of progress during the age, with bittersweet verse evoking longing and memory or a cyclical, tragic sense of time and history.

An introduction to the themes and issues that occupied the great writers of New England would be incomplete and misleading if it failed to take note of the rich forms of collaboration and community that invigorated the region at midcentury. The strikingly original, even anticonventional, achievements of the American Renaissance in New England, combined with the tendency to think of writing as a solitary act of genius, obscures that much of the greatest literature of the age was fueled by apprenticeships, friendships, and mentoring–for example, Emerson and Thoreau; Hawthorne and Melville; Emerson and Fuller; Garrison and Douglass; Whittier and Larcom; and Higginson and Dickinson. Key collaborative literary ventures include such periodicals as *The Dial* and ambitious projects such as Ripley's *Specimens of Foreign Standard Literature* (1838–1842). The proliferation of clubs, beginning with the Transcendental Club (1836) and including the Town and Country Club and the Saturday Club, attest to the intellectual stimulation and fundamental sociability found in gatherings of the like-minded. Many of these groups were male-dominated, but the later growth of grassroots "women's clubs"–several formed by Julia Ward Howe–proved that the club impulse knew no gender.

Besides these smaller personal and social collaborations (and the reform communities of Fruitlands and Brook Farm), New England also produced literary communities within cities and towns. Boston and Cambridge, of course, dominated literary life in antebellum New England–its sheer size and wealth reflected by rich institutions of education, religion, and the arts. Regionally, Salem and New Bedford (Massachusetts), Hartford (Connecticut), Providence (Rhode Island), and Portland (Maine) sustained lively local cultures and produced important writers. Worcester, Massachusetts, a prosperous industrial city that was especially friendly to reform, was home to a particularly vibrant lyceum network that regularly brought leading authors to the platform. Thoreau, who professed disdain for the pretentious institutional and social world of Boston and Cambridge, found a congenial circle of friends in Worcester. The most striking literary community was the town of Concord, founded by Emerson's ancestor the Reverend Peter Bulkeley in 1635. Two hundred years later, Emerson, born and raised in Boston, returned to his ancestral ground, rendering Concord the American example of Romantic rural solitude and contemplation, and by the force of his reputation and personality making the town a mecca for Bronson Alcott, Fuller, Hawthorne, and many lesser figures. Of all the important writers who called Concord home, only Thoreau was a native son. By cultivating the Transcendentalist's heightened awareness of the epic and divine in the microcosmic, Thoreau did more than any other writer to celebrate–in Concord–a sense of place, asserting at once modestly and hyperbolically in *Walden,* "I have travelled a good deal in Concord." Its Revolutionary and literary history have combined to make Concord a living symbol of the American spirit.

A professional and commercial "community" was fostered by the publishing house Ticknor and Fields, which positioned itself as the publisher of leading New England writers, counting within its stable Emerson, Thoreau, Lowell, Longfellow, and Hawthorne. At midcentury, their offices at the corner of Washington and School streets–the fabled Old Corner Bookstore–became a gathering place for authors, and, in the popular mind as well, a virtual literary landmark. Through shrewd marketing, the firm that later evolved into Houghton, Mifflin–though not particularly sympathetic to Transcendentalism–helped create a myth of New England as the cradle of American literary culture.

Even as the literary myth of New England was being established, however, events were transpiring that changed the face of American literary culture. By 1850 New York City had a population of more than 500,000, and Boston, 136,881; the literary center of the nation inexorably shifted to New York as well. The Civil War was, in many ways, the culmination of the spirit of reform generated by the American Renaissance in New England. Julia Ward Howe's "Battle Hymn of the Republic" epitomized the self-image of the North as one of victorious moral righteousness. But the Civil War, with its bloodshed and with the accelerated urbanization, industrialization, political corruption, and national cynicism that followed in its wake, also overwhelmed the prewar moral idealism that had helped define the meaning of the war. The critical fortunes of the writers of the New England renaissance, too, have varied since the Civil War. With the exception of Dickinson, many of the poets of the period have come to be seen as the smug embodiment of Boston Brahmin privilege, exponents of refinement and safe middle-class values. Even Emerson, once deemed radical and dangerous, had become a national icon, his challenging concept of self-reliance safely denatured as an endorsement of industrial and economic growth and manifest destiny. The "Fireside poets" and other canonical figures came to be treasured not for their innovation but as reassuring voices from a seemingly simpler, more bucolic time. The popular image of New England authors gathered sociably at the Old Corner Bookstore evoked a still-palpable regional Golden Age. Forgotten in the haze of nostalgia was that the three decades before the Civil War had been a time in New England not of mere pastoral charm but of moral outrage and restless creative energy.

The influence of the American Renaissance in New England, however, has been profound. Antebellum idealism might have begun to seem quaint, but William Dean Howells, the great champion of literary realism, responded to the Transcendentalists' examination of the commonplace, and their moral vision and faith in democracy. Modernist poets have been attracted to the Transcendentalists' bold openness of form and embracing of the volatility of truth. Hawthorne was an essential example to later novelists as different as Henry James and William Faulkner. Today Thoreau exerts unprecedented appeal as a voice for social justice, the founder of American environmentalism, and a master of prose. Fuller is admired as the first and greatest literary feminist. Dickinson is regarded as the finest poetic experimenter. Emerson, for whatever purpose he is invoked, is widely considered the central figure in American culture. The literary canon continues to evolve. But the New England writers are as important as ever for the expression they gave to the possibilities of the American experience.

This volume is indebted not only to a fine group of contributors but also to several others who gave indispensable advice and help. Peggy Isaacson, of the WPI Publications Office, and Ray J. Emerson (WPI '01) offered expert computer assistance. Penny Rock and Margaret Brodmerkle, of the WPI Humanities & Arts Department, provided generous logistical support. For suggesting contributors, I am grateful to Steven C. Bullock, Phyllis Cole, Sterling F. Delano, Brenda Yates Habich, Len Gougeon, Kent P. Ljungquist, Beverly G. Merrick, Joel Myerson, Cameron C. Nickels, David Robinson, and Frank Shuffelton. Every editor should be as fortunate–in working with publishing-house editors–as I have been in working with Penelope M. Hope of Bruccoli Clark Layman, Inc.; she has been efficient, cooperative, scholarly, and professionally skillful at every stage of production. Besides the example of his own pioneering *DLB 1,* which the present volumes augment, Professor Joel Myerson, for two decades my professional colleague and friend, took time from his own daunting scholarly projects to offer guidance at every stage. For years of "provocation" and love, this work is dedicated to my wife, Sandy.

–Wesley T. Mott

Acknowledgments

This book was produced by Bruccoli Clark Layman, Inc. Karen L. Rood is senior editor. Penelope M. Hope was the in-house editor.

Production manager is Philip B. Dematteis.

Administrative support was provided by Ann M. Cheschi, Dawnca T. Williams, and Mary A. Womble.

Accounting supervisor is Ann-Marie Holland. Accounting assistant is Amber L. Coker.

Copyediting supervisor is Phyllis A. Avant. The copyediting staff includes Brenda Carol Blanton, Allen E. Friend Jr., Melissa D. Hinton, William Tobias Mathes, Nancy E. Smith, and Elizabeth Jo Ann Sumner. Freelance copyeditor is Rebecca Mayo.

Editorial associates are Andrew Choate and Michael S. Martin.

Layout and graphics supervisor is Janet E. Hill. The graphics staff includes Karla Corley Brown and Zoe R. Cook.

Office manager is Kathy Lawler Merlette.

Photography supervisor is Paul Talbot. Photography editors are Charles Mims and Scott Nemzek.

Permissions editor is Jeff Miller.

Digital photographic copy work was performed by Joseph M. Bruccoli.

SGML supervisor is Cory McNair. The SGML staff includes Frank Graham, Linda Dalton Mullinax, Jason Paddock, and Alex Snead.

Systems manager is Marie L. Parker.

Typesetting supervisor is Kathleen M. Flanagan. The typesetting staff includes Mark J. McEwan, Patricia Flanagan Salisbury, and Alison Smith. Freelance typesetters are Wanda Adams and Vicki Grivetti.

Walter W. Ross did library research. He was assisted by Steven Gross and the following librarians at the Thomas Cooper Library of the University of South Carolina: circulation department head Tucker Taylor; reference department head Virginia W. Weathers; Brette Barclay, Marilee Birchfield, Paul Cammarata, Gary Geer, Michael Macan, Tom Marcil, Rose Marshall, and Sharon Verba; interlibrary loan department head John Brunswick; and interlibrary loan staff Robert Arndt, Hayden Battle, Barry Bull, Jo Cottingham, Marna Hostetler, Marieum McClary, Erika Peake, and Nelson Rivera.

Dictionary of Literary Biography® • Volume Two Hundred Thirty-Five

The American Renaissance in New England

Third Series

Louis Agassiz

(28 May 1807 – 14 December 1873)

Laura Dassow Walls
Lafayette College

BOOKS: *Selecta genera et species Piscium, quos in itinere per Brasiliam* (Munich, 1829);

Recherches sur les poissons fossiles, 5 volumes (Neuchâtel, Switzerland: Petitpierre, 1833–1843);

Études sur les glaciers (Neuchâtel, Switzerland: Jent et Gassman, 1840);

Nomenclator zoologicus (Soloduri: Jent et Gassman, 1842–1846);

Monographie des poissons fossiles du vieux grès rouge ou système dévonien des Iles Britanniques et de Russie (Neuchâtel, Switzerland: Agassiz, 1844–1845);

Nouvelles études et experiences sur les glaciers actuels (Paris: Masson, 1847);

Catalogue raisonnè des familles, des genres et des espéces de la classe des èchinodermes (Paris: Martinet, 1847);

Bibliographia zoologiae et geologiae, 4 volumes (London: Ray Society, 1848–1854);

Principles of Zoölogy, with Augustus A. Gould (Boston: Gould, Kendall & Lincoln, 1848), revised and enlarged as *Outlines of Comparative Physiology* (London: Bohn, 1851);

Twelve Lectures on Comparative Embryology (Boston: Redding; New York: Dewitt & Davenport, 1849);

Lake Superior: Its Physical Character, Vegetation, and Animals, Compared with Those of Other and Similar Regions, with James Elliot Cabot, and others (Boston: Gould, Kendall & Lincoln, 1850);

Contributions to the Natural History of the United States of America, 4 volumes (Boston: Little, Brown; London: Trübner, 1857–1862);

Methods of Study in Natural History (Boston: Ticknor & Fields, 1863);

Geological Sketches (Boston: Ticknor & Fields, 1866);

A Journey in Brazil, with Elizabeth Cary Agassiz (Boston: Ticknor & Fields, 1868);

Address Delivered on the Centennial Anniversary of the Birth of Alexander von Humboldt (Boston: Boston Society of Natural History, 1869);

Geographical Sketches, Second Series (Boston: Houghton Mifflin, 1876).

OTHER: Josiah C. Nott and George R. Gliddon, *Types of Mankind,* with an introductory essay by Agassiz, "Sketch of the Natural Provinces of the Animal Worlds and Their Relation to the Different Types of Man" (Philadelphia: Lippincott, 1854);

Nott and Gliddon, *Indigeneous Races of the Earth,* with a preface by Agassiz (Philadelphia: Lippincott, 1857).

SELECTED PERIODICAL PUBLICATIONS–UNCOLLECTED: "Geographical Distribution of Animals," *Christian Examiner,* 48 (March 1850): 181–204;

"The Diversity of Origin of the Human Races," *Christian Examiner,* 49 (July 1850): 110–145;

"Contemplations of God in the Cosmos," *Christian Examiner,* 50 (January 1851): 1–17;

"Professor Agassiz on the Origin of Species," *American Journal of Science,* second series, 30 (July 1860): 142–154;

"Evolution and Permanence of Type," *Atlantic,* 33 (January 1874): 92–101.

The Swiss naturalist Louis Agassiz dominated American science and intellectual culture from his 1846 arrival in Boston until his death in 1873. From the first he generated a whirlwind of scientific activity. The nascent Lawrence Scientific School at Harvard quickly captured this European star for their new chair in zoology and geology, and from this platform, Agassiz organized the American Association for the Advancement of Science and the National Academy of Sciences; founded and ran the Museum of Comparative Zoology at Harvard; and professionalized the teaching of science in American colleges and universities. His students dominated the natural sciences in America for two generations. The Boston literati seated Agassiz at the head of their exclusive "Saturday Club" table; he counted Henry Wadsworth Longfellow, James Russell Lowell, Oliver Wendell Holmes, and Ralph Waldo Emerson among his closest friends. His lectures, campaigns, books, and articles spread his gospel of science into the far corners of America. At his death Agassiz was the last major scientist still to oppose Charles Darwin's theory of evolution, and the authority of Agassiz's name and the power of his popular appeals carried the argument for special creationism well into the twentieth century.

Jean Louis Rodolphe Agassiz was born on 28 May 1807 in Motier, Switzerland, to a solid and intellectual family. His father, Rodolphe Agassiz, was a pastor, and his mother, Rose Mayor Agassiz, was the daughter of a physician. Louis, their fifth child, was the first to survive infancy; he was followed by three more children–a brother, Auguste, and two sisters, Olympe and Cécile. Talented and charismatic, Louis rose rapidly through the Swiss educational system, at seventeen entering medical school at Zurich–a compromise that allowed him to continue study in natural science even as his parents urged him to a more practical career. He moved next to Heidelberg Germany, then concluded his formal training at the University of Munich, where he studied with the embryologist Ignatius Döllinger and the great *Naturphilosophen* (natural philosophers) Friedrich von Schelling and Lorenz Oken.

In 1829 the publication of Agassiz's first book, a taxonomy of Brazilian fishes (which he audaciously dedicated to Georges Cuvier, dean of European zoology), earned him his first doctorate and reconciled his parents to his chosen vocation; better still to them was the news in 1830 that he had finally earned his doctorate in medicine. Agassiz returned home briefly but soon persuaded his parents that he must go to Paris, the center of the scientific universe. This move was the turning point of his career: the renowned Cuvier received Agassiz kindly and was so impressed by his recent work on fossil fishes that he renounced his own work on the subject and passed on to Agassiz all his notes and illustrations. Cuvier's sudden death in May 1832 almost stranded the impoverished young naturalist, but Agassiz had made an even more powerful friend in Alexander von Humboldt, who rescued Agassiz with a grant of 1,000 francs and secured his appointment as Professor of Natural History at Neuchâtel, Switzerland.

Neuchâtel was the base for Agassiz's most productive period in science, from 1832 to 1846. In October 1833 he married Cécile Braun, a talented artist who drew many of his scientific illustrations. Cécile gave birth to their first child, Alexander, in 1835, then to Ida in 1837 and Pauline in 1841. Agassiz always had a dozen projects going at once, but two in particular made his reputation. The first was Cuvier's legacy, the great work on fossil fishes. Agassiz traveled all over Europe gathering information and at home set up, as his assistant Carl Vogt said, "a veritable scientific factory," employing as many as twelve people and running his own publishing house. Installments of *Recherches sur les poissons fossiles,* dedicated to Humboldt and detailing more than 1,700 species, were issued over the decade from 1833 to 1843; by the conclusion of the decade, Agassiz was recognized as one of the master naturalists of Europe, and in 1852 the work was awarded the highest possible honor, the Prix Cuvier. Agassiz's second

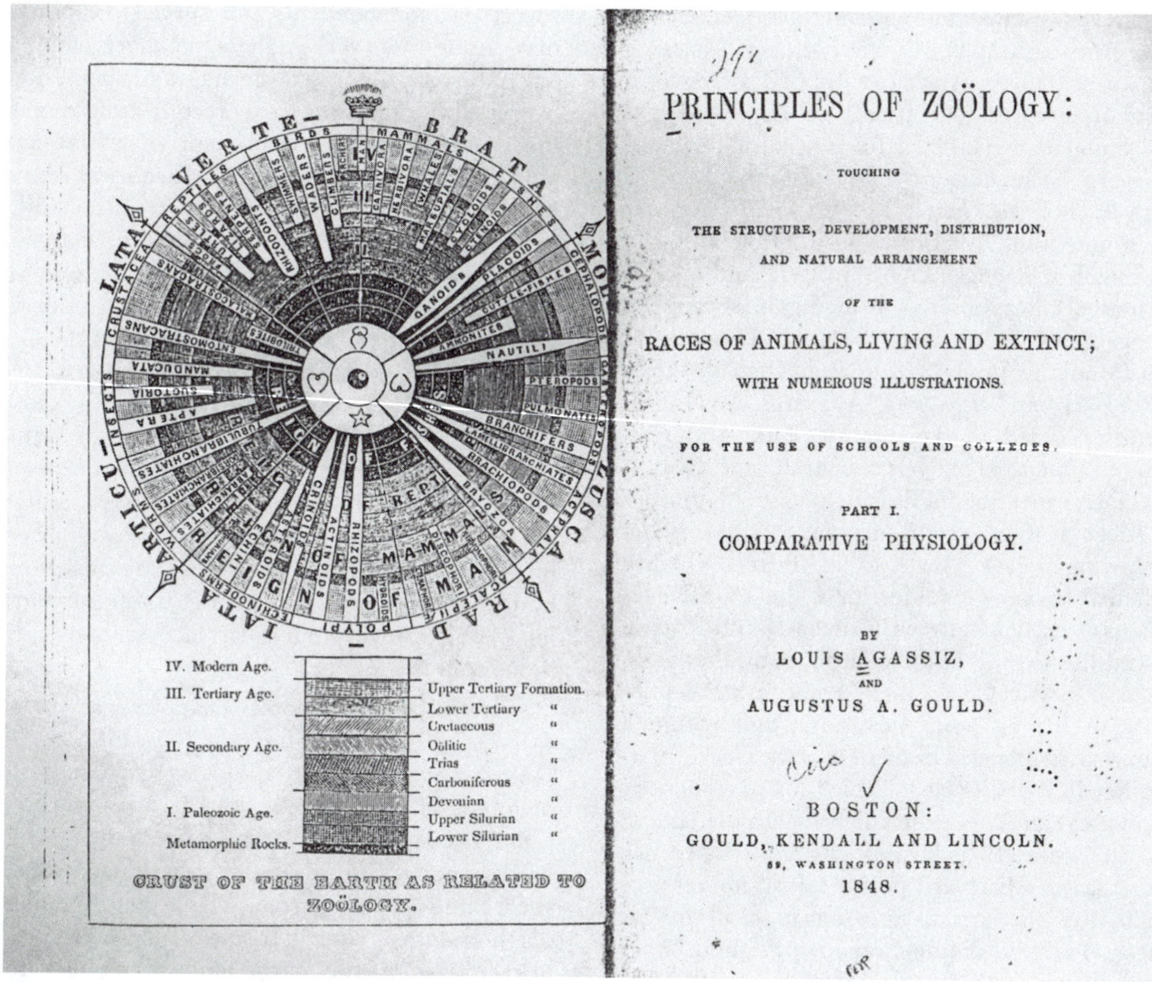

Frontispiece and title page for Agassiz's first book in English, a widely used textbook that went through sixteen editions during his lifetime

project was even more daring and earned him both fame and notoriety: an 1836 tour of alpine glaciers led Agassiz to propose that at one time a sheet of ice had covered all of Europe. His "Ice Age" theory aroused instant controversy and nearly universal opposition. Over the next several summers he and his scientific workers generated such an impressive body of evidence that ultimately he convinced virtually all the scientific community.

Agassiz was spending far beyond his modest salary, and by 1845 the reckoning was at hand: Cécile returned to her Carlsruhe home with the two girls (leaving Alexander at school), and mounting debts forced Agassiz to close his publishing house and disband his staff. Once again he was saved by powerful connections and fortunate timing: a long-deferred voyage to America suddenly materialized, as Humboldt engineered a supporting grant of 15,000 francs from the King of Prussia, Frederick Wilhelm IV. Meanwhile, in England, Charles Lyell put Agassiz in touch with John Armory Lowell of Boston, trustee of the Lowell Institute, who offered Agassiz $1,500 for a lecture series. Agassiz wrapped up his affairs in Europe and sailed out of Liverpool on 19 September 1846, bound for the United States.

After arriving in Boston on 3 October 1846, Agassiz's first act was to take a quick tour of the region, meeting scientists and dignitaries at every stop. While Agassiz was deeply impressed with what he saw, Americans in their turn found his massive knowledge and eternal good cheer equally impressive. Agassiz gave his Lowell lecture series, "The Plan of Creation in the Animal Kingdom," during the winter of 1846–1847 to an enthusiastic audience of up to five thousand; tickets were free (demand was so great they had to be distributed by lottery), and the lectures were repeated to a second audience. Soon Agassiz decided to make Boston his headquarters and began importing his old staff from Neuchâtel, meanwhile lecturing across New England. By

November 1847 Benjamin Silliman's *American Journal of Science* was triumphantly announcing Agassiz's decision to remain in America: Abbot Lawrence, a cotton manufacturer and friend of Lowell's, had donated $50,000 to Harvard for a scientific school, and Harvard hastened to create a professorship for Agassiz. Events continued to snowball: Agassiz helped found the American Association for the Advancement of Science (AAAS) in 1847, and his collecting network was already bringing in specimens (including many from Henry David Thoreau at Walden Pond); in June 1848 he published the textbook *Principles of Zoölogy* with Augustus A. Gould; that summer he led an expedition to Lake Superior, returning in time to give twelve separate addresses to the first AAAS meeting, in Philadelphia (and another twenty-seven at their second meeting, in Cambridge, the following year). Two other events further strengthened his new loyalties: first, the 1848 Revolution broke the ties between Neuchâtel and Prussia and forced the closing of the college; then, that summer Agassiz's wife Cécile died. Some months later Agassiz sent for his son, Alexander, and within a year he was courting Elizabeth Cabot Cary; marriage to her in April 1850 solidified his new identity as an American and his close alliance with the elite of Boston. In late 1849 a further gift from Lawrence secured Agassiz's Harvard position for another five years; finally, the arrival in August 1850 of his daughters, Ida and Pauline, made the household complete. None of the many extravagant offers he later received tempted Agassiz to return to Europe.

His first round of feverish activity had produced two books, which taken together give a fair overview of Agassiz's scientific ideas. Gould had already been planning a textbook of zoology, but his efforts were overtaken by Agassiz's energy and authority. *Principles of Zoölogy* became one of the most popular zoology textbooks of its time, going through sixteen editions during Agassiz's lifetime and a series of revisions after his death. In his first American book, Agassiz made his central ideas available to a popular audience. The frontispiece shows his version of Cuvier's original division of the animal kingdom into "four great departments," each based on a separate structural plan: vertebrates on top "with Man at their head"; mollusks and articulates at right and left; and at bottom, the lowest (that is, least complicated) class, the radiates. The time scale suggests two key elements of Agassiz's theory: first, all four branches were present from the earliest moment of creation; second, in successive ages all life forms were continually swept away and replaced according to a cosmic plan of creation. To the earlier and more primitive forms, each successive, independent, and special creation added new forms that were higher and more complicated. Scientific men identified the stages of succession both by reconstructing the fossil record and by studying the embryological development of living animals, which recapitulates the series of historical forms: fossil animals "bear a striking analogy to the embryonic forms of existing species." Although the diagram connected earlier forms to later ones, Agassiz insisted adamantly that the connection was not material but intellectual: it existed first in the mind of the Creator, then in the mind of the human observer. Indeed, the presence of such intelligible connections between the facts of nature proved "the existence of a thinking God" and the ability to apprehend them proved "our affinity with the Divine Mind." Agassiz found "indisputable" that the systems of classification were not human inventions but "in truth . . . translations into human language of the thoughts of the Creator." Each object, every physical fact in nature, was a thought in the mind of God.

Agassiz's next book, *Lake Superior: Its Physical Character, Vegetation, and Animals, Compared with Those of Other and Similar Regions* (1850), was written by several members of the expedition: Elizabeth's cousin James Elliot Cabot supplied the narrative of the journey and the taxonomy of birds; others discoursed on insects, shells, and Lepidoptera; Agassiz contributed essays on the physical characteristics of the lake, principles of classification, and glacial phenomena, plus one taxonomy of the fish of Lake Superior and another of its reptiles. The goal of the journey had been to gather evidence for Agassiz's conviction that every region of the globe formed a distinct zoological province with a unique array of animal life interconnected in a balanced harmony, the entire assemblage created on the spot by God's governing intelligence. Agassiz's glacial theory, for which he found evidence everywhere, was an integral part of his cosmic vision: he believed that the glaciers, "God's great plough," had swept down from the Arctic and wiped the slate clean for the current array of life. Agassiz laid down his scientific program: "There will be no *scientific* evidence of God's working in nature until naturalists have shown that the whole creation is the *expression of a thought,* and not the *product of physical agents.*" Thus, the great debate behind *Lake Superior* was over the unity or plurality of Creation: to Agassiz, creation had to be plural. To suggest otherwise attributed too much power to physical agents, such as the ability of creatures to migrate on their own, or of climate to modify an original form into variant species. Agassiz sent a gift copy to Charles Darwin, who responded warmly: "I have begun to read it with uncommon interest, which I see will increase as I go on."

Agassiz's next venture laid out the implications of his theory of the origin of species for human beings. In 1845, while still in Europe, he had affirmed that unlike animals, human beings had a single point of origin; but in 1846 his views received a shock when he visited Philadelphia and saw, for the first time, "negroes." A long-suppressed letter to his mother, of December 1846, registers his dismay:

> I can scarcely express to you the painful impression that I received, especially since the feeling that they inspired in me is contrary to all our ideas about the confraternity of the human type and the unique origin of our species. But truth before all . . . it is impossible for me to repress the feeling that they are not of the same blood as us. In seeing their black faces with their thick lips and grimacing teeth, the wool on their head, their bent knees, their elongated hands, their large curved nails, and especially the livid color of the palm of their hands, I could not take my eyes off their face in order to tell them to stay far away. . . . What unhappiness for the white race–to have tied their existence so closely with that of negroes in certain countries! God preserve us from such a contact!

This unreasoned revulsion was to have far-reaching consequences, as Agassiz adjusted his science to account for this grim "truth." He presented his ideas in 1850, first to the third AAAS meeting (held in Charleston, South Carolina), then in the Boston Unitarian journal *The Christian Examiner,* where in "The Diversity of Origin of the Human Races," Agassiz argues that man could be no exception to the laws of geography. Sensitive to at least some of the implications, Agassiz opens by recommending that "We recognize the fact of the Unity of Mankind" in a *spiritual* sense; but that the free domain of science had priority over the question of mankind's *physical* origin, and science showed that mankind had a diversity of origins, each race within its intended zoological province. These "natural groups" designed by God each had an individual character and rank: "The indomitable, courageous, proud Indian,–in how very different a light he stands by the side of the submissive, obsequious, imitative negro, or by the side of the tricky, cunning, and cowardly Mongolian! Are not these facts indications that the different races do not rank upon one level in nature . . . ?" His reluctance to apply the word "species" to these racial differences had been overcome by 1854. In his introduction to Josiah C. Nott's and George R. Gliddon's *Types of Mankind* (1854), the definitive statement of polygenesis, Agassiz put the entire volume on a scientific basis by developing his earlier ideas and adding the crucial

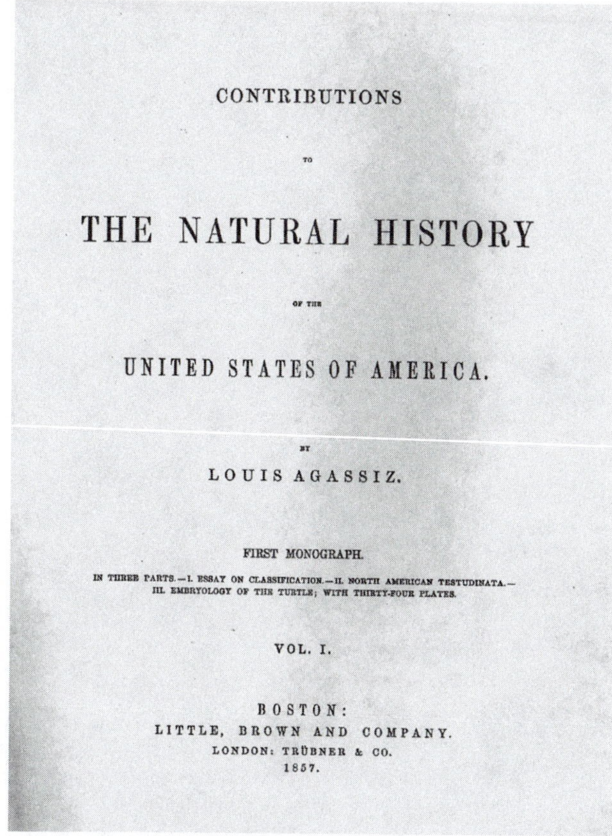

CONTRIBUTIONS

TO

THE NATURAL HISTORY

OF THE

UNITED STATES OF AMERICA.

BY

LOUIS AGASSIZ.

FIRST MONOGRAPH.

IN THREE PARTS.—I. ESSAY ON CLASSIFICATION.—II. NORTH AMERICAN TESTUDINATA.—III. EMBRYOLOGY OF THE TURTLE; WITH THIRTY-FOUR PLATES.

VOL. I.

BOSTON:
LITTLE, BROWN AND COMPANY.
LONDON: TRÜBNER & CO.
1857.

Title page for the book that prompted Oliver Wendell Holmes to rank Agassiz as one of the greatest natural scientists of all time

concept of "species" as "primordial organic forms," unchanging in time. To those who argued that races could not be separate species because they can interbreed, Agassiz countered that while species often interbreed, the resulting "half-breeds" or "mongrels" are weak and degenerate, eventually dying out to restore the original, pure type. Racial differences are dramatic enough to establish each race as a distinct species; in a remarkable foldout diagram, Agassiz presents eight separate species of humanity.

The burden of Agassiz's beliefs is clear, in this work and elsewhere: as he said in the *Christian Examiner* article, science must be free of both theological and political constraints to follow wherever the facts lead, no matter how morally uncomfortable or politically inexpedient; to "see what they can do with the results" is then up to the politicians. He advised that social policy must follow the lead of science: discourage miscegenation; encourage the maintenance of pure types; and make available to each human species the opportunities commensurate with their talents and limitations. His writings played directly into the hands of Southern slave owners, who were jubilant to have his authority on their side, and his dog-

Elizabeth Cabot Cary, whom Agassiz married in 1850

matic insistence on the "inferiority" of nonwhite races and his explicit and detailed descriptions of their racial characteristics contributed immeasurably to American racism and racist stereotypes.

In the 1850s Agassiz consolidated his rise to power: elected president of the AAAS for 1851–1852, he moved to establish a second, informal, and far more exclusive scientific society, whose membership would guide public policy. Calling themselves the "Scientific Lazzaroni," he and his associates–Benjamin Pierce, Augustus Gould, the classicist Cornelius Conway Felton (who soon became president of Harvard), James Dwight Dana, Joseph Henry, and Alexander Bache–formed a tight-knit group united to their mutual enhancement. Eventually, in 1863 the Lazzaroni established a formal American counterpart to the Royal Society of London and the French Academy of Sciences, calling it the National Academy of Sciences and limiting membership to fifty, chosen by election only. (The proposal found immediate favor with Congress, and President Abraham Lincoln signed it into law in March 1863.) Meanwhile, specimens were pouring into Cambridge from Agassiz's far-flung collecting network: he advertised in 1853 for a project on the fishes of the United States, then in 1855 advanced a still more ambitious plan for an all-inclusive zoological survey. His global subscription campaign netted more than 2,500 subscribers and $300,000 for the planned ten-volume work. To help finance the effort, Lizzie Agassiz established in their home a school for girls, which was a solid success, running from 1855 to 1863. The first families of Boston enrolled their daughters; Ralph Waldo and Lidian Emerson sent their daughter Ellen. Agassiz's social circle was further extended through his membership in the Saturday Club, which met monthly and included the leading intellectuals of Boston: in addition to his immediate neighbors–Felton, Longfellow, and James Russell Lowell–Agassiz developed warm and long-lasting friendships with Emerson, Holmes, Nathaniel Hawthorne, Charles Sumner, and many others. Agassiz's social connections opened the way to frequent publication in the *Atlantic* magazine, which from its first issue in 1857 became virtually a house organ for writings by and about Agassiz.

Agassiz pressed hard to complete the first two volumes of *Contributions to the Natural History of the United States of America* by his fiftieth birthday, and they were duly published in 1857. The first volume included a lengthy introduction, "Essay on Classification," Agassiz's most authoritative theoretical statement. It was followed by a demonstration of the resulting practice: one monograph classifying the North American Testudinata, or turtles, and, in the second volume, a monograph on turtle embryology. The set was beautifully produced and formidably technical, even though Agassiz declared in his preface that his book would be "read by operatives, by fishermen, by farmers, quite as extensively as by the students in our colleges or by the learned professions." The "Essay on Classification" reiterated ideas familiar from his previous books, with new stress on the parallels between the geological succession of animals, their embryology, their comparative anatomy, and their geographical distribution–all stacking into a single, fourfold sequence. The "imperial" grandeur of Agassiz's conception, together with the sheer mass of supporting details, caused Oliver Wendell Holmes to rank Agassiz with the greatest minds of natural science: Aristotle, Cuvier, Linnaeus, Humboldt–and Agassiz. No less a scientist than Richard Owen of England called it "the most important contribution to the right progress of zoölogical science in all parts of the world where progress permits its cultivation."

Agassiz's house on Quincey Street in Cambridge, Massachusetts

Agassiz's great vision was never completed; only two more volumes of *Contributions to the Natural History of the United States of America* were published before the project bogged down under the weight of newer labors. The most important of these fresh undertakings was the foundation of a great museum that would secure Agassiz's precious specimens from harm, embody in physical form his spiritual vision of nature, and rival any museum in Europe. Agassiz's angel this time was Francis Calley Gray, whose will deeded Agassiz enough money to found his museum. After Gray's death in 1856, Agassiz raised enough additional money from private donations, the Harvard Corporation, and the Massachusetts State Legislature to begin building. The museum went up in 1859 while Agassiz and his wife toured Europe, and it was opened to the public in November 1860. Successive additions over several decades enlarged it many times over; after Agassiz's death, his son, Alexander, dedicated himself to carrying on his father's mission.

The museum gave Agassiz the facilities to develop a new kind of education in America, postgraduate research training for scientists: he gathered a corps of bright and ambitious young men, fired them with the thrill of working on the frontiers of science, and trained them to think like true scientists. His innovative teaching methods–hands-on, interactive, and student-centered–remain famous to this day and in later years were warmly recalled by his former students. As the story goes, Agassiz abandoned the neophyte with a single specimen, asking him to prepare a report on all he could see. Agassiz then rejected report after report until, weeks later, the frustrated student learned to see not just details but the structural plan of the whole organism, whereupon Agassiz then set him to classifying entire families of bones or bottled specimens. William James, himself one of Agassiz's students, claimed that "there is hardly one now of the American naturalists of my generation whom Agassiz did not train." Agassiz's constant command was to learn from nature itself; as James added, "the hours I spent with Agassiz so taught me the difference between all possible abstractionists and all livers in the light of the world's concrete fulness, that I have never been able to forget it."

The first floor of Agassiz's museum, what he called "a temple of the revelations written in the material universe," was completed in November 1859, the month when he received Darwin's gift

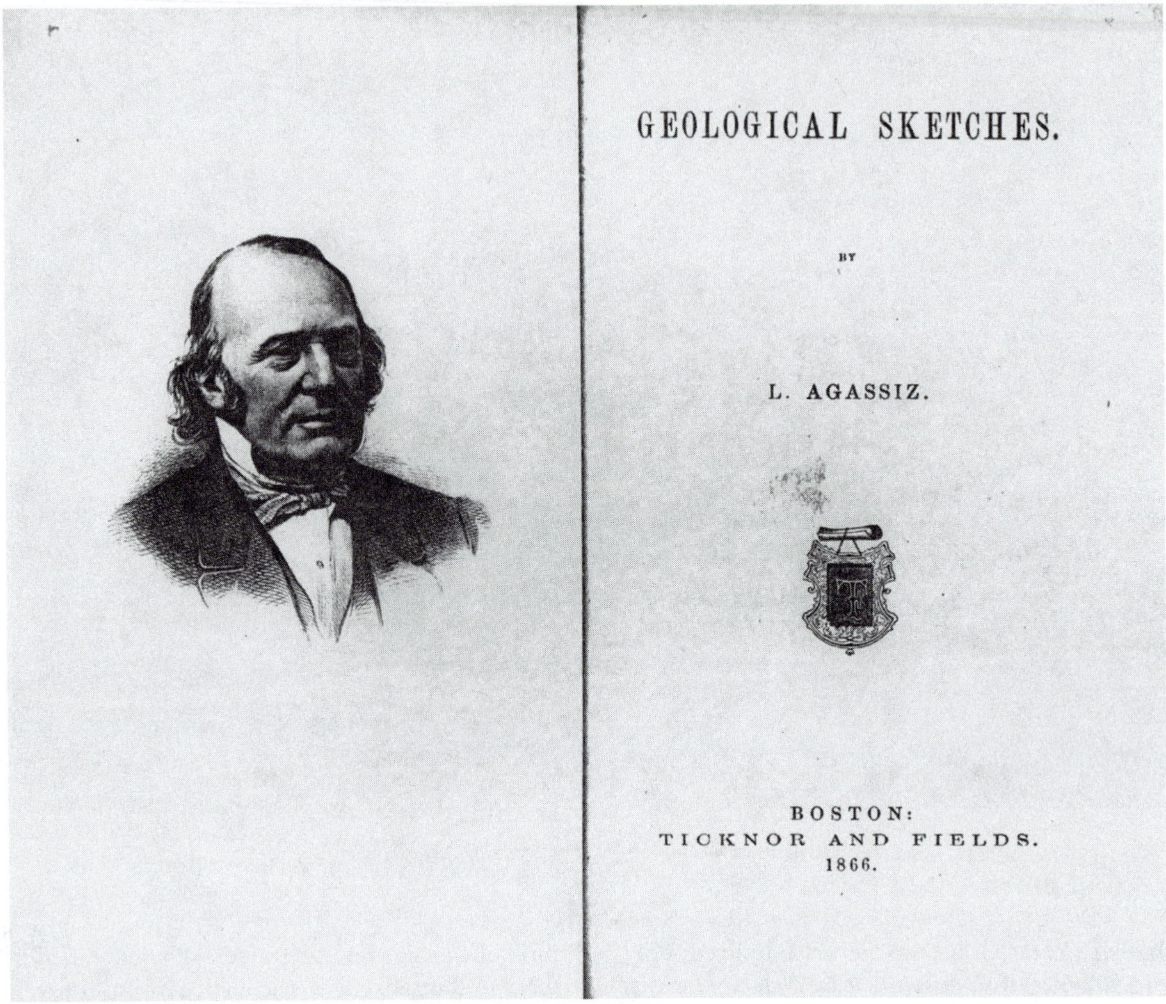
GEOLOGICAL SKETCHES.

BY

L. AGASSIZ.

BOSTON:
TICKNOR AND FIELDS.
1866.

Frontispiece and title page for one of the books in which Agassiz challenged the evolutionary theory of Charles Darwin

copy of *On the Origin of Species.* Agassiz had dedicated his life to the refutation of the "developmental hypothesis," whether Jean-Baptiste de Monet de Lamarck's, Étienne Geoffroy Saint-Hilaire's, Robert Chambers's, or Baden Powell's; and now here came still another version, by a naturalist he knew and respected. In the 1840s Agassiz's views had been entirely in the mainstream of modern science, and even by the early 1860s he was hardly alone; many scientists across the Atlantic–including Richard Owen, Karl Ernst von Baer, and Adam Sedgwick–stood with him. Yet, in the 1850s the winds were shifting, particularly in America. Darwin and the British botanist Joseph Hooker had been corresponding with the Harvard botanist Asa Gray, and through the 1850s Gray developed, in a series of thorough and thoughtful scientific papers, evidence for variation within species and the material connection of species across geographical distances. Gray was growing ever sharper in his criticism of his famous colleague's *a priori* and creationist views. Not surprisingly, *On the Origin of Species* positioned Gray and Agassiz in dramatic public opposition. The resulting debates, both oral and written, brought Darwin's ideas to the fore and made increasingly evident to the scientific community Agassiz's growing isolation. By the time of his death, his students, even his son, Alexander, had all declared their belief in evolution.

Agassiz's response was to renew his efforts to reach "operatives, fishermen, and farmers" and to educate the wider American public in the lessons of true science: he once again hit the lecture circuit. This time his lectures were printed as essays in the *Atlantic,* then gathered into popular books: the first of these books, *Methods of Study in Natural History* (1863), brought the concepts in the "Essay on Classification" to a lay audience. It proved to be Agassiz's most popular and successful volume, going through twenty-one editions by 1893. His preface registered his "earnest protest" against the "transmutation theory," which he called a "phantom" ever returning out of the desire for a simple solution to the puzzles of nature; but where others saw an answer, Agassiz saw rather "a repulsive poverty." The book offered a complete overview of the progress of zoology toward Agassiz's true method of natural history, which was to realize that in the classification of animal life "we are approaching the thoughts of the Creator, reading his conceptions, interpreting a system that is his and not ours." Science must be spread to all humanity, "woven into the common life of the world," for the results of science now "touch the very problem of existence," interpreting "the purposes of the Deity in creation, and the relation of man to all the past." Instead of being reserved for an "exclusive priesthood," science "should make a part of all our intellectual culture and of our common educational systems." The lesson taught by natural science was that the obvious and eloquent connection between animals could not be "material," caused by the "blind laws of matter," but only "intellectual": to study science was to realize the idea in the mind of God–to be, in the Platonic sense, an idealist.

These years were also the time of the Civil War, and Agassiz declared himself a fervent supporter of the North, even applying for American citizenship to prove his commitment. His wartime involvement in establishing the National Academy of Sciences was intended to demonstrate to Europe that the United States was a morally progressive and thoroughly modern and civilized state.

In the midst of war, Agassiz seized the chance to carry his message to another warring empire, Brazil. A modest idea for a vacation blossomed into a full-fledged scientific expedition under the sponsorship of Nathaniel Thayer and with the assistance of the American government and the Emperor of Brazil, Dom Pedro II. On 1 April 1865, Louis and Elizabeth Agassiz, together with their staff and volunteer assistants, set sail for Rio de Janeiro, returning in August 1866. Agassiz made the goals of his expedition clear in his shipboard lectures–not to discover new species, but to "look rather for the fundamental relations among animals," by confirming that each river basin of the Amazon had its peculiar species and by using embryology to confirm the relation of living animals to extinct types. Agassiz expected that his studies in Brazil would "give me the means of showing that the transmutation theory is wholly without foundation in facts." The only scientific publications that resulted from the trip were Louis's

Agassiz lecturing on the animals he classed as "radiates"

additions to Elizabeth's fine and thoughtful narrative from her "unprofessional" viewpoint, published as *A Journey in Brazil* (1868) by "Professor and Mrs. Louis Agassiz." The interplay of their two voices complicates the narrative: in particular, Louis's biological recounting of the inferior colored "species" of men jars against Elizabeth's sympathetic portraits of gentle and intelligent people leading decent lives in attractive thatched homes and riverfront villages. The book also announces Agassiz's discovery of abundant evidence of tropical glaciation, confirming the global grip of his ice age. Scientists greeted Agassiz's rampant geology with amazed disbelief, but the book was a great popular success, going through six editions in two years; people of note such as Holmes, George Bancroft, William James, Anna Eliot, and George Ticknor praised it, and Emerson wrote to Agassiz of his appreciation: "A very cheerful book to read: I am glad the expedition was sent, and in such dark times . . . glad that it attained such adequate results . . . glad that the social side should have been so honored . . . glad . . . that Mrs. Agassiz . . . was to be the angel of woman in Brazil."

In the years that followed, wealthy friends continued to sponsor Agassiz's adventures–in 1868, a trip to the American West, and in 1871–1872, a sea voyage around South America. Agassiz's health was strained: in 1869, following the exhaustive preparation for and delivery of a two-hour address honoring his great mentor Humboldt, he was paralyzed by a stroke and spent a year in recovery. The South American sea voyage again depleted his energies, but he rallied upon his return when given the chance to establish a summer school and marine research institute. With the donation of Penikese Island in Buzzard's Bay, Massachusetts and $50,000 by New York merchant John Anderson, and the near-miraculous efforts of construction crews, the Anderson School of Natural History opened its doors in July 1873 to a vibrant faculty and a student body composed of teachers, twenty men and ten women. After a glorious summer of teaching America's teachers, Agassiz returned to Cambridge ready to settle with Darwin for good; he began to draft what was to have been a series of popular articles. Only one was completed, "Evolution and Permanence of Type." In the midst of work, Agassiz collapsed in exhaustion and died a few days later, on 14 December 1873, of a cerebral hemorrhage.

Agassiz's sudden death shocked the literary world. The most memorable response was perhaps James Russell Lowell's long memorial ode "Agassiz," written in Florence, Italy, and published in *Atlantic* in May 1874. While scanning the newpaper with "vague, mechanic eyes," Lowell's reading is interrupted: "Three tiny words grew lurid as I read, / And reeled, commingling: *Agassiz is dead.*" Theodore Lyman, a close friend of Alexander Agassiz, ended his own long memorial in the February 1874 *Atlantic* by remembering Agassiz's burial: "The students laid a wreath of laurel on his bier, and their manly voices sang his requiem; for he had been a student all his life long, and, when he died, he was younger than any of them." Agassiz's essay on Darwin, published posthumously in the January 1874 *Atlantic,* stands as his own memorial to his work. In it, Agassiz reiterated all the reasons why a close examination of the facts confirmed that evolution existed only in the conjectures of Darwin's theory–and "I believe he has not even made the best conjecture possible in the present state of our knowledge." Himself honored as a great teacher, Agassiz concluded with the teacher's regret "that the young and ardent spirits of our day give themselves to speculation rather than to close and accurate investigation." For "Philosophers and theologians have yet to learn that a physical fact is as sacred as a moral principle. Our own nature demands from us this double allegiance."

To overestimate Agassiz's influence would be difficult. His implacable opposition earned Darwin's respect as his most "formidable" opponent, and his detailed and relentless arguments against all developmental theories forced Darwin's allies to build their case with similar care. The publicity Agassiz's powerful rhetoric and popular authority brought to evolution projected what might have been an arcane scientific discussion into the arena of popular American debate. With his passion for bringing science to ordinary people, Agassiz did more than any other single figure to construct science as a central part of the American imagination and to identify science with the search for spiritual, not merely physical, truth. His influence as a teacher marked American education indelibly, both for his insistence that Nature was the best classroom and that the classroom should be opened to women as well as men; Elizabeth Agassiz carried this idea much further, becoming a founder and the first president of Radcliffe College. At the same time, Agassiz's method was to interpret nature according to his one idea, and to insist in all confidence that the coherence of the resulting vision proved its absolute truth; that he was wrong only underscores the irony that Agassiz's aggressive idealism had for so long shaped the language of science in America.

Letters:

E. C. Herber, ed. *Correspondence between Spencer Fullerton Baird and Louis Agassiz–Two Pioneering Naturalists* (Washington, D.C.: Smithsonian, 1963).

Biographies:

Arnold Guyot, "Memoir of Louis Agassiz," *Biographical Memoirs* (Washington, D.C.: National Academy of Sciences, 1878, 1886), volume 2, pp. 39–73;

Elizabeth Cary Agassiz, *Louis Agassiz, His Life and Correspondence,* 2 volumes (Boston: Houghton, Mifflin, 1886);

Jules Marcou, *Life, Letters, and Works of Louis Agassiz,* 2 volumes (New York: Macmillan, 1896);

Alice Bache Gould, *Louis Agassiz* (Boston: Small, Maynard, 1901);

Edward Lurie, *Louis Agassiz: A Life in Science* (Chicago: University of Chicago Press, 1960).

References:

Ian F. A. Bell, "Divine Patterns: Louis Agassiz and American Men of Letters. Some Preliminary Explorations," *Journal of American Studies,* 10 (December 1976): 349–381;

Linda S. Bergmann, "A Troubled Marriage of Discourses: Science Writing and Travel Narrative in

Louis and Elizabeth Agassiz's *A Journey in Brazil,*" *Journal of American Culture,* 18, no. 2 (Summer 1995): 83–88;

Lane Cooper, *Louis Agassiz as a Teacher* (Ithaca, N.Y.: Comstock, 1917; revised edition, 1945);

Stephen Jay Gould, "Louis Agassiz–America's Theorist of Polygeny," in his *The Mismeasure of Man* (New York: Norton, 1981), pp. 42–50;

William James, "Louis Agassiz," in *The Works of William James,* edited by Frederick Burkhardt, volume 17 (Cambridge, Mass.: Harvard University Press, 1975), pp. 46–51;

Edward Lurie, "Louis Agassiz and the Races of Man," *Isis,* 45, no. 2 (July 1954): 227–242;

Lurie, *Nature and the American Mind: Louis Agassiz and the Culture of Science* (New York: Watson, 1974);

Ernst Mayr, "Agassiz, Darwin, and Evolution," *Harvard Library Bulletin,* 13 (Spring 1959): 165–194;

Brian Wallis, "Black Bodies, White Science: Louis Agassiz's Slave Daguerreotypes," *American Art,* 9 (Summer 1995): 38–61;

Laura Dassow Walls, "Textbooks and Texts from the Brooks: Inventing Scientific Authority in America," *American Quarterly,* 49 (March 1997): 1–25;

Mary P. Winsor, "Louis Agassiz and the Species Question," *Studies in History of Biology,* 3 (1979): 89–117;

Winsor, *Reading the Shape of Nature: Comparative Zoology at the Agassiz Museum* (Chicago: University of Chicago Press, 1991).

Papers:

The primary sources for Louis Agassiz materials are the Agassiz Papers at Houghton Library and at the Museum of Comparative Zoology, both at Harvard University. Additional materials, primarily letters, are on deposit at the Manuscript Division, Library of Congress (Alexander Dallas Bache Papers); Smithsonian Institution Archives (Spencer Fullerton Baird Papers); Rare Book Room, Yale University Library (James Dwight Dana Papers); the Academy of Natural Sciences of Philadelphia (Samuel S. Haldeman Papers); the New York State Museum (James Hall Papers); and the Manuscript Collections of the Library Company of Philadelphia and of the New York Public Library. Extensive information may be found in Edward Lurie's "Essay on Sources" in his biography, *Louis Agassiz* (1960).

Washington Allston

(5 November 1779 - 9 July 1843)

Kathleen Healey
Colby-Sawyer College

BOOKS: *The Sylphs of the Seasons, With Other Poems* (London: Pople, 1813; Boston: Cummings & Hilliard / Cambridge: Hilliard & Metcalf, 1813);

Monaldi: A Tale (Boston: Little, Brown, 1841; London: Moxon, 1841);

Lectures on Art, and Poems, edited by Richard Henry Dana Jr. (New York: Baker & Scribner, 1850);

Outlines and Sketches, engraved by J. and S. W. Cheney (Boston: Perkins, 1850).

Collection: *Autobiographical Works of Washington Allston,* introduction by Nathalia Wright (Delmar, N.Y.: Scholars' Facsimiles & Reprints, 1991)–comprises *Monaldi* and "The Angel and the Nightingale," from *Lectures on Art, and Poems.*

Washington Allston (portrait by George W. Flagg; from Jared B. Flagg, The Life and Letters of Washington Allston, *1892)*

Washington Allston is one of the most important artists to emerge in America after the American Revolution. A man of many talents, Allston was not only a visual artist but also a poet and novelist. Although his literary works have not been his legacy to American culture, they embody the Romantic ideals that fueled his artistic vision. Allston was a pioneer in his field, creating an art that pierced the exterior of existence to make the inner life visible and bringing the realm of the ideal into the real. While still adhering to the belief in the formal values of art and the moral ideals of his age, Allston chose to rely upon memory, imagination, and individual genius as the basis for his art. As a Romantic artist, his works bring a greater understanding to the literary and artistic endeavors of his contemporaries as well as the intellectual climate of his age.

Washington Allston was born on 5 November 1779 at Brook Green Domain on the Waccamaw River in All Saints Parish, District of Georgetown, South Carolina. He was the second of three surviving children born to Captain William and Rachel Moore Allston. Allston's father, a wealthy plantation owner who also fought in the American Revolution, died in 1781; four years later, Rachel Allston married Dr. Henry Collins Flagg of Newport, Rhode Island. About the time of his mother's marriage to Dr. Flagg, Allston went to Charleston, South Carolina, to study at Mrs. Colcott's school. There he began to draw and create landscapes out of sticks, pebbles, moss, and other natural items. In order to prepare for entering Harvard College, in the spring of 1787 Allston went to study in Newport, Rhode Island, at the school of Robert Rogers. In Newport, Allston befriended William Ellery Channing, who became an influential Transcendentalist, and Channing's sister, Ann, who later became Allston's first wife. The friendship between Allston and Channing lasted a lifetime. While he was in Newport, Allston also first

The Dead Man Revived by Touching the Bones of the Prophet Elisha *(1813), one of Allston's best-known paintings in the narrative style (Pennsylvania Academy of the Fine Arts, Philadelphia)*

met professional painters–including the miniature portrait painter Edward Greene Malbone–and began to work with oil paints. He entered Harvard in 1796, graduating in 1800.

After graduating from Harvard, Allston returned to Charleston in order to persuade his family to allow him to pursue painting as a career. Once he secured their consent, he sold his portion of the family land in order to finance his studies abroad. Though Allston was an artistic genius, he was not a skillful businessman, and he did not acquire the monetary worth of his property, nor did he use interest from his money for living expenses; instead, he drew freely upon the entire sum until it was gone. Allston's eventual financial problems had a significant impact on his painting.

America during Allston's lifetime was unfriendly soil for aspiring artists. The nation, newly born, was more concerned with expansion and with financial and material growth than with cultural development. There was little interest in the arts among the public and even less possibility for financial backing. Furthermore, the perceived lack of a past in America, especially in the arts, forced most aspiring artists to travel to Europe to train and become immersed in the great art of the "Old World." Following in the footsteps of many American artists before him, Allston traveled to Europe to study art. In May 1801 he sailed to England with the painter Malbone. Allston lived in London and petitioned for admission to the Royal Academy of Art; he was accepted as a student after he submitted his third drawing. There he studied art, visited art galleries, and met the famous American artist Benjamin West.

In 1803 Allston met New York painter John Vanderlyn, and together the two artists traveled through Holland and Belgium to Paris. While in Paris, Allston studied paintings at the Louvre, but not the works of contemporary French painters; rather, Allston was inspired by the works of the artists that his own age judged to be the greatest of the Western world, such as Nicolas Poussin, Peter Paul Rubens, and Salvator Rosa. Though his studies in London gave Allston the technical background he needed, his experiences in Paris and later Italy and the Swiss Alps helped him learn what he wanted to say through his art. Allston left Paris in the late spring of 1804, arriving in Rome in early 1805. His journey through the Alps on his way to Italy and Italy

Allston's 1814 portrait of Samuel Taylor Coleridge (National Portrait Gallery, London)

itself helped to form the tone of his love of nature and underlay his imagination the rest of his life. In Rome Allston continued to paint; he also became acquainted with American writer Washington Irving.

One of Allston's paintings executed in Rome, *Diana in the Chase,* attracted the attention of the English poet Samuel Taylor Coleridge, who was also traveling in Rome. Allston's friendship with Coleridge was one of the greatest experiences of his developing years, and the two men became lifelong friends. Writing to William Dunlap years later, Allston stated that "to no other man whom I have known, do I owe so much intellectually, as to Mr. Coleridge, with whom I became acquainted in Rome, and who has honored me with his friendship for more than five and twenty years." As a record of this association, Allston painted a portrait of Coleridge in Rome in 1806, which was left incomplete when the poet fled from Rome because of the Napoleonic Wars. The spiritual solitude and inner vitality evident in the portrait reflects Allston's Romantic vision, one that he brought to another portrait he painted of Coleridge ten years later.

Allston left Rome in 1808, returning to America to set himself up as a professional painter in a building on Court Street in Boston. He married Ann Channing on 19 June 1809. During this period Allston created many portraits of family and friends, but unlike many of his contemporaries, he did not support himself as a portraitist.

During the period in America following his marriage, Allston also wrote the majority of his poems appearing in the collection *The Sylphs of the Seasons, With Other Poems* (1813). Although Allston's poems were considered minor literary achievements in his day and are not read today, they are important for offering a glimpse of the complexity of Allston as an artistic personality; each of his poems can be considered a literary counterpart to his painting. They also embody the Romantic sensibility of the era. As a whole, his poems are concerned with the theme of the interior life, independent of nature and society, and the character of a dreamer or artist whose works include his own visions or memories. Like his paintings, his poems exude an aura of reverie and the mystical impressions of nature; they also include vivid pictorial descriptions, so that each brings to the mind's eye a carefully composed painting.

Of the longest poems in the collection, the title poem, "The Sylphs of the Seasons, A Poet's Dream," is the most notable. It begins with a poet who falls asleep and dreams of the spirits of the four seasons, each of whom tries to win his love. Each season appeals to his imagination and his memories, and reminds him of the ways in which she helped his creative growth. He wakens before making his choice, but winter is the most persuasive, in saying that her "purer" power ministered to him. The collection also includes some sonnets inspired by the great painters' works Allston viewed while in Europe. In the sonnet "On Rembrandt; occasioned by his Picture of Jacob's Dream," for example, Allston reflects upon the supernal quality of the painting, whose images and "random shadowings give birth / To thoughts and things from other worlds that come, / And fill the soul, and strike the reason dumb."

The Sylphs of the Seasons, With Other Poems received responses from a wide variety of readers. While acknowledging Allston's creative genius and the descriptive qualities of his poems, readers generally viewed Allston's poems as the product of a brief interlude from his true talent, painting. William Gilmore Simms wrote that Allston's talent as a painter naturally led him to the muse of poetry. While Simms found the poems "agreeable" and "gently contemplative," he called them "elegant trifles of a well drilled, well ordered mind. . . . His intercourse with the muse is not one of passions." Similarly, a reviewer from the August 1815 issue of the *Analectic Magazine* wrote that Allston was an amateur, not a professional, but praised his powers of description and ingenuity. Interest in Allston's literary endeavors was not confined to America. In a letter dated 4 November 1818 Allston's close friend William Collins, the English artist, described a discussion concerning Allston's volume of poems. Collins noted that the English writer Robert Southey said of the poems, "Whatever defects some of them might have . . . they could not have proceeded from any but a poetic mind; and Wordsworth who was present at the discussion, cordially agreed."

Before publishing *The Sylphs of the Seasons, With Other Poems,* Allston returned to England, accompanied by Ann Allston and the young painter and inventor Samuel F. B. Morse; a young art student from Philadelphia, Charles R. Leslie, joined them later. Allston resumed his friendship with Coleridge, who introduced him to William Wordsworth, Robert Southey, and Sir George Beaumont. Among the English painters, Allston's closest friend was the landscape painter William Collins, father of the novelist Wilkie Collins. Upon arriving in London, Allston took up the narrative type of painting, in which he depicted scenes from myth, history, literature, and the Bible. Allston's painting *The Dead Man Revived by Touching the Bones of the Prophet Elisha,* which won a prize of two hundred guineas at the British Institution in 1813, is one of many examples of the artist's work in this genre.

From his arrival in England, Allston worked diligently to establish his artistic reputation–so hard that his health ultimately suffered. Early in 1813 he took a trip to Hampton Court with his wife, Leslie, and Morse, and the group eventually traveled to Windsor, Oxford, and Blenheim. Yet, in the summer, near Windsor, Allston's health worsened. Coleridge came from London with a doctor, and although Allston's health improved so that he could resume his travels, this illness had a permanent effect; he was never again entirely well.

During 1814 Allston executed his last series of portraits, including the second picture of Coleridge. Upon returning from their travels, the Allstons took a house on Tinney Street in London. Soon after they moved into the new house, however, Allston experienced a tragedy. His wife became ill and died only two or three days after the onset of her illness, on 2 February 1815. Allston fell into a depression. He sought the support of Coleridge, and at this time he also joined the Episcopal Church. He returned to painting later in 1815. In 1817 he traveled to Paris with Leslie and Collins, but not before he began his first study of his famous incomplete picture *Belshazzar's Feast.*

Allston returned to the United States in 1818, a step that, in the opinion of many at the time, led to the end of his career. The atmosphere of London was conducive to the life of the artist. The city was filled with artists, exhibitions, collectors, dealers, and private collections–a great contrast to the lack of artistic activity in America. Allston's failure to complete *Belshazzar's Feast* has been blamed on his return to Boston and its lack of an atmosphere encouraging to the work of artistic genius. However, Allston's difficulty rendering this painting is much more complex than American indifference to the arts. Allston ran out of money upon his return to Boston and so had to paint pictures to earn a living; consequently, *Belshazzar's Feast* was pushed aside. A group of gentlemen in Boston collected money in order to help Allston finish the painting, but this financial backing only contributed to his inability to finish the picture. He worked on the painting until the end of his life, unable to complete it for a variety of reasons, including that he had lost the idea and interest in his subject. According to art historian Edgar Preston Richardson, Allston had "grown into another period of his life, in which the tranquil and meditative element of his art, reinforced by the introspective atmosphere of his new environment, displaced the grandiose and dramatic interests predominant in the preceding fifteen years."

Rosalie *(1835), a "dreamer" painting by Allston that is related to his 1850 poem with the same title (Society for the Preservation of New England Antiquities, Boston)*

Some of his energy in the last twenty-five years of his life went into literary endeavors. In 1818 Richard Henry Dana, the poet who later became Allston's clos-

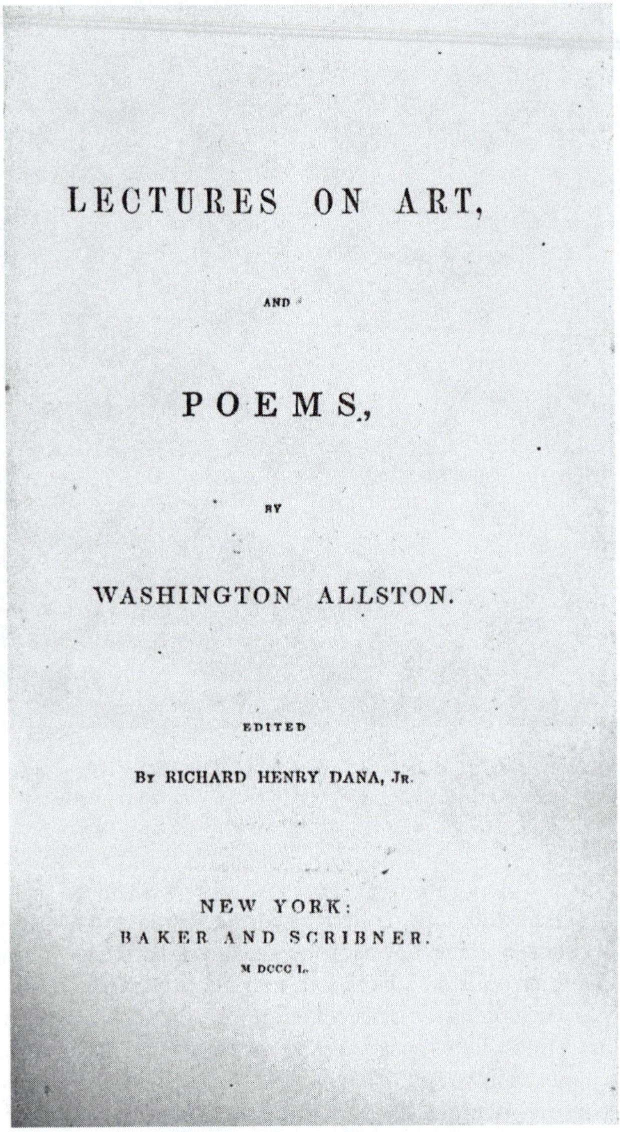
LECTURES ON ART,

AND

POEMS,

BY

WASHINGTON ALLSTON.

EDITED

BY RICHARD HENRY DANA, JR.

NEW YORK:
BAKER AND SCRIBNER.
M DCCC L.

Title page for the first American art treatise (courtesy of Special Collections, Thomas Cooper Library, University of South Carolina)

est friend, appealed to Allston for help with his new magazine, the *Idle Man.* By 1821 Allston had written "The Hypochondriac" and "Written in Spring," both of which appeared in the *Idle Man.* In 1822 he also started writing the gothic novel *Monaldi: A Tale,* but it was not published until 1841, long after the *Idle Man* folded.

Like the characters in Allston's poem, the title character of *Monaldi* is an artist who draws upon his inner life for inspiration. He withdraws from the external world in order to give life to images in his memory. To him "every object had a charm, and its harmony and beauty, its expression and character, all passed into his soul in all their varieties, while his quickening spirit brooded over them as over the elementary forms of a creation of his own." His paintings were infused with human emotion that would seem "unnatural . . . to him who *sees only with his eyes.*" Monaldi is described as the true successor to Raphael, who, in Monaldi's opinion, "speaks to the heart." Opposed to Monaldi is a friend from his childhood, an unsuccessful poet, Maldura, who is unable to see beyond the material world. While Monaldi is a great success, Maldura fails. He also is rejected by a woman who eventually marries Monaldi. Envious of Monaldi's professional and personal success, Maldura, with the help of a character named Count Fialto, destroys Monaldi. The schemers lead Monaldi to believe that Fialto is having an affair with Monaldi's wife, Rosalia, and Monaldi, in a jealous rage, attacks his wife. He believes he has killed her and becomes insane. However, she has not died, and the repentant Maldura seeks the insane Monaldi and confesses to the ruse. Despite Maldura's confession, Monaldi's mind is too fragile to recover, and he descends further into madness. Rosalia finds Monaldi and cares for him until his death. Moments before his death he recovers his sanity and reconciles with her. Maldura retires to a convent and dies feeling great remorse. While the theme of the novel is once again the examination of the interior world of the artist, it is also an indictment of a world hostile to the artist's pure inner nature. Maldura and Fialtro signify the influence of the world and evil, or sin, which threaten the artistic sensibility.

When Allston published *Monaldi* in 1841, the Gothic genre had fallen out of fashion. However, the novel did receive literary notice. Reviews of *Monaldi* were generally positive; the most uniform praise was for the pictorial quality of the work. A writer in the January 1842 edition of the *New York Review* wrote that "It paints to the 'minds eye' with the same exquisite coloring, and the same delicacy of taste, which are the peculiar charm of Mr. Allston's delineations upon canvas." Similarly, William Gilmore Simms praised the descriptions and the "delicate fancy" that he believed were "the distinct possessions of the genuine artist," although he found little in the material that was new. The novel was also praised for both its moral quality and Allston's ability to understand the nature of humankind. Like Allston's poetry, *Monaldi* is not currently a widely read or well-known work, but it offers a glimpse to the contemporary reader of the wide breadth of Allston's talents and his Romantic vision.

While Allston continued to paint during the years following his return to America in 1818, he also devoted his energy in the 1830s to recording his statement of his theory of art, which was published after his death. The five essays and "Preliminary Note" of his *Lectures on Art, and Poems* (1850) are his most important prose compositions, and the first American art treatise.

The essays combine actual creative experience and a clearly defined philosophical position. Allston defined a work of art as the "form" in which the artist's idea is manifested. The ultimate power in the universe, Allston contended, is spiritual and intellectual rather than physical, and the mind of the artist is the shaping force of creativity. The final work of art does not correspond to anything in nature, and its most distinctive character is "Human or Poetic Truth," or "the inward . . . outwardly manifested." This "intuitive power" is the means by which the artist creates and also the way by which man acquires knowledge of God and the divinely created world. Furthermore, the work of art is addressed to the inner life of the spectator, whose response is "the life or truth within, answering to the life, or rather its sign," before him. As in his literary endeavors, the recurring image by which Allston presents his concepts is that of the dreamer, or the mind in reverie.

Also published in *Lectures on Art, and Poems* are the contents of *The Sylphs of the Seasons, With Other Poems,* as well as poems never published before. In theme these poems are similar to the earlier poems. Of note in this volume are two poems, "The Tuscan Girl" and "Rosalie," which correspond to two Allston "dreamer" paintings of the same names. The poems delineate the birth of a new consciousness in which earthly scenes take on an otherworldly appearance. Several of the poems focus upon childhood memories and dreams. In "To My Sister," for example, Allston recalls carving a little bird out of a stalk of Indian corn, at the age of six, as a parting gift to his sister. The bird, a product of Allston's childhood and love for his sister, has true artistic power: "The life imparted by the loving Boy / Is truer life than now his Art can give." Like other Romantics, Allston celebrated childhood perceptions and experiences as closest to true creativity and the source of life. The feelings of childhood are also the strongest, as Allston notes in "To My Sister," for the bird, symbolic of his love for his sister, "Shall flit between us when we part again." Similarly, in "The Calycanthus," a poem to his mother, Allston writes of seeing, as an adult, a flower he loved in childhood, which transports him back to the land and dreams of childhood. His "teeming mind" of childhood "Had gifted with some wondrous story" all that he saw.

Lectures on Art, and Poems gained the notice of reviewers but was not a popular work. While a June 1850 review of the book in *Graham's American Monthly Magazine of Literature, Art and Fashion* found the poems disappointing, the reviewer praised highly the "Lectures." Encouraging the reader to look beyond the discussion of principles, the reviewer found the work to include "many specimens of that word-painting which gave such popularity to Ruskin's 'Modern Painters.'" He also praised Allston's criticisms of Michelangelo, Raphael, Titian, Poussin, and Claude Lorrain, noting the lectures were "unrivaled for discrimination as appreciation." Today, Allston's *Lectures on Art, and Poems* is deemed important in understanding Allston's approach to his art.

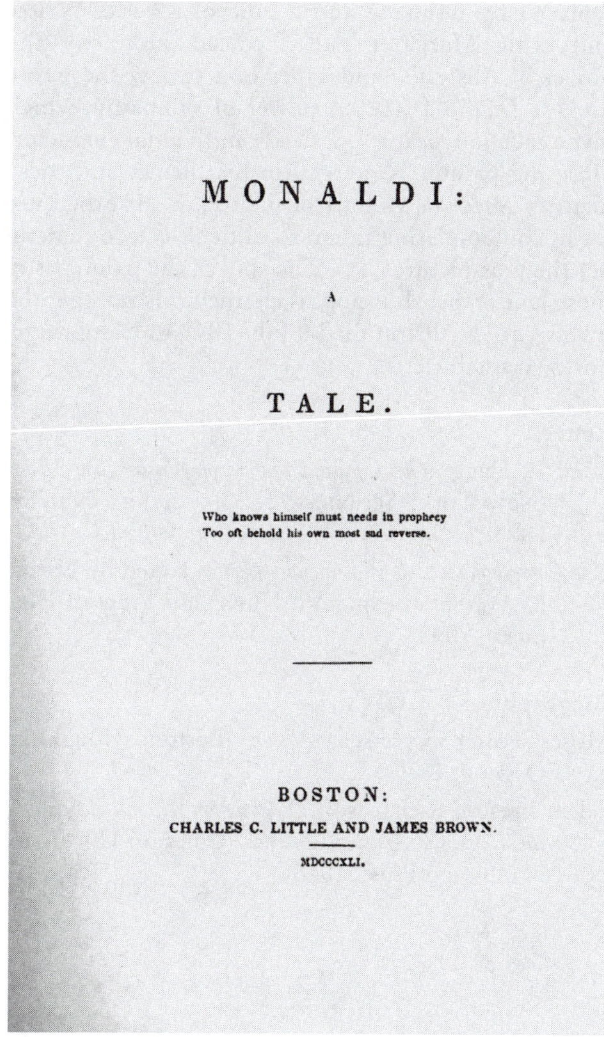
MONALDI:

A

TALE.

Who knows himself must needs in prophecy
Too oft behold his own most sad reverse.

BOSTON:
CHARLES C. LITTLE AND JAMES BROWN.
MDCCCXLI.

Title page for Allston's Gothic novel about an artist who draws on his inner life for inspiration

Allston spent the last years of his life in Boston and later Cambridgeport, Massachusetts, where, from 1831, he also kept his studio. He married Martha Remington Dana, the sister of the poet Richard Henry Dana, on 1 June 1830. He continued to be a productive painter, executing many landscapes, and worked intermittently and without success on *Belshazzar's Feast* until his death. The landscapes of his later years still reveal the wonder and solitude of his earlier works, but the heroic scale and excitement are replaced by intimacy and a tone of reverie. Writer and critic Margaret Fuller voiced succinctly the power of Allston's landscapes in a review she wrote for *The Dial* in 1840: "A power of sympathy, which gives each landscape a perfectly individual character. Here the painter is merged in his theme, and these pictures affect us as part of nature, so absorbed are we in contemplating them, so difficult is it to remember them as pictures. . . . The soul of the painter is in these landscapes, but not his character. Is not that the highest art?" Allston died 9 July 1843 in Cambridgeport, Massachusetts.

Letters:

Jared B. Flagg, *The Life and Letters of Washington Allston* (New York: Scribners, 1892; London: Bentley, 1893);

The Correspondence of Washington Allston, edited by Nathalia Wright (Lexington: University Press of Kentucky, 1993).

Biographies:

Moses Foster Sweetser, *Allston* (Boston: Houghton, Osgood, 1879);

Edgar Preston Richardson, *Washington Allston: A Study of the Romantic Artist in America* (Chicago: University of Chicago Press, 1948).

References:

David Bjelajac, *Millenial Desire and the Apocalyptic Vision of Washington Allston* (Washington, D.C.: Smithsonian Institution Press, 1988);

Bjelajac, *Washington Allston, Secret Societies, and the Alchemy of Anglo-American Painting* (Cambridge: Cambridge University Press, 1997);

Margaret Fuller, "A Record of Impressions Produced by the Exhibition of Mr. Allston's Pictures in the Summer of 1839," *Dial,* 1 (July 1840): 73–83;

William H. Gerdts and Theodore E. Stebbeins Jr., *"A Man of Genius": The Art of Washington Allston (1779–1843)* (Boston: Museum of Fine Arts, 1979);

C. P. Seabrook Wilkinson, "Emerson and the 'Eminent Painter,'" *The New England Quarterly,* 71 (March 1998): 120–126;

Nathalia Wright, "Introduction," in *Washington Allston, Lectures on Art and Poems and Monaldi* (Gainesville, Fla.: Scholars' Facsimiles & Reprints, 1967).

Papers:

The largest collections of Washington Allston's letters and papers are located at the Massachusetts Historical Society (including the Richard Henry Dana Collection), the Houghton Library at Harvard University, and the Historical Society of Pennsylvania. Miscellaneous letters can also be found in various public and private collections in the United States.

John Bartlett

(14 June 1820 – 3 December 1905)

Stephen N. Orton
University of North Carolina at Chapel Hill

BOOKS: *A Collection of Familiar Quotations* (Cambridge, Mass.: J. Bartlett, 1855; second edition, revised, 1856; third edition, revised, 1858); republished as *Familiar Quotations* (fourth edition, revised, Boston: Little, Brown, 1863; fifth edition, revised, 1868; sixth edition, revised, 1871; seventh edition, revised, 1875; eighth edition, revised, 1882; ninth edition, revised, 1891);

The Shakespeare Phrase Book (Boston: Little, Brown, 1881; London: Macmillan, 1881);

Catalogue of Books on Angling, including Icthyology, Pisciculture, Fisheries, and Fishing Laws (Boston: Little, Brown, 1882);

A New and Complete Concordance or Verbal Index to Words, Phrases & Passages in the Dramatic Works of Shakespeare, with a Supplementary Concordance to the Poems (London & New York: Macmillan, 1894).

John Bartlett

John Bartlett–publisher, editor, and lexicographer–remains famous for the volume of quotations that still bears his name. Bartlett's *Familiar Quotations,* a book he first published himself in 1855, went through nine editions in his lifetime. Bartlett also produced a concordance to William Shakespeare's works that was only supplanted by a computer-generated concordance of the 1974 Riverside edition.

John Bartlett was born on 14 June 1820 to William and Susan (Thatcher) Bartlett in Plymouth, Massachusetts; he counted among his ancestors two who came to Plymouth on the *Mayflower*. Educated in public schools in Plymouth, he started his career in Cambridge, where he found employment as a bookbinder in the Harvard College Bookstore at the age of sixteen. Soon he became a clerk, and by 1849, before he was thirty years old, he owned the store. He was young when he arrived in Cambridge. He lacked the education of his powerful, erudite customers. He compensated by reading widely and tirelessly, and by recording interesting ideas and turns of phrase in a commonplace book. Bartlett had always been a precocious reader, reportedly having read the entire Bible by age nine. He also had an impressive memory and a genius for detail.

In 1851 he married Hannah Staniford Willard, daughter of a Harvard professor of Hebrew and granddaughter of Joseph Willard, a past president of Harvard; they had no children. Bartlett loved Cambridge, cards, and fishing.

The bookstore provided a ready audience among students and faculty for his increasingly impressive knowledge of literature. He self-published the first edition of *A Collection of Familiar Quotations* in 1855, drawing on his own commonplace book and on a British model. He quickly published two more expanded editions out of the bookstore.

At the advent of the Civil War, Bartlett volunteered; at age forty-two he served as a Navy paymas-

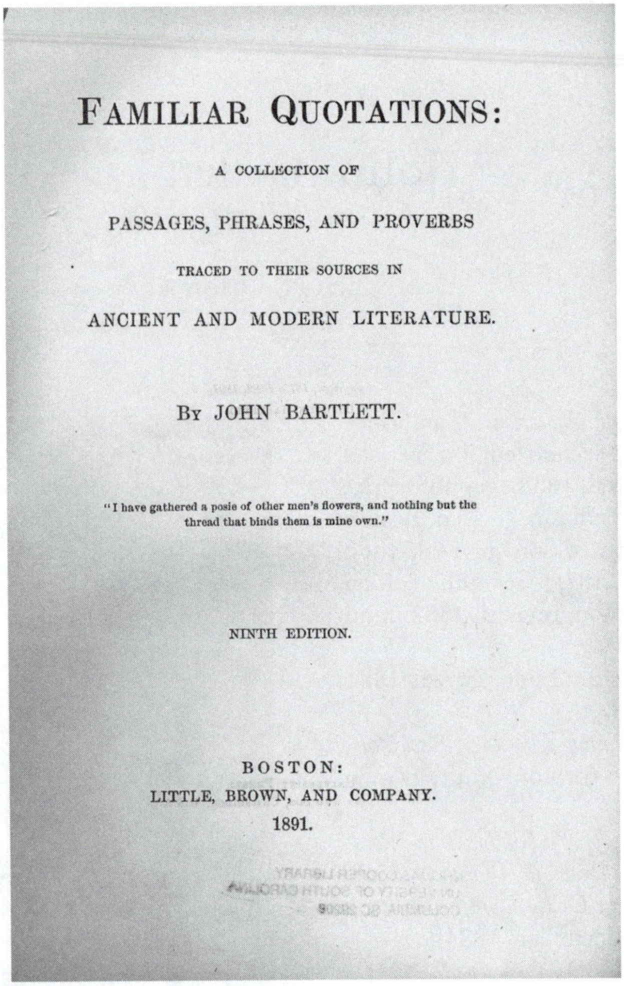

FAMILIAR QUOTATIONS:

A COLLECTION OF

PASSAGES, PHRASES, AND PROVERBS

TRACED TO THEIR SOURCES IN

ANCIENT AND MODERN LITERATURE.

BY JOHN BARTLETT.

"I have gathered a posie of other men's flowers, and nothing but the thread that binds them is mine own."

NINTH EDITION.

BOSTON:
LITTLE, BROWN, AND COMPANY.
1891.

Title page for the last edition of Bartlett's book that he revised himself. It had grown from 267 pages in 1855 to 1,158 in 1891

ter aboard a Union ship in the South. After this accounting stint, Bartlett returned to a position as an editor at Little, Brown and Company in Boston. In addition to his other editing duties at the company, Bartlett continued to expand and fine-tune the *Familiar Quotations*. Little, Brown published the fourth and all subsequent editions.

If his career as an editor and publisher and his marriage into the family of a Harvard president did not convey the Harvard imprimatur, Bartlett earned it in 1871 when the university conferred upon him an honorary Master of Arts degree. In fact, Bartlett was moving in rarefied literary circles by the mid 1860s. Among his friends he numbered James Russell Lowell, with whom he shared an interest in the works of Shakespeare and fishing. Lowell immortalized Bartlett in the poem "To J. B., who has sent me a seven-pound trout." Lowell also wrote a glowing review of the *Familiar Quotations* in the *North American Review* in July 1869.

John Holmes, the brother of Oliver Wendell Holmes, was a close mutual friend to both Bartlett and Lowell. Holmes frequently incorporated updates on "J. B." into his letters to Lowell. Lowell and Holmes played a regular game of whist with Estes Howe and Robert Carter, but Bartlett was a regular substitute when one member of the "Whist Club" was unable to play. Like Holmes, Bartlett had a ready wit, and friends such as Thomas Wentworth Higginson remembered him as an unparalleled storyteller with a vast store of tales, often involving books or fish. In 1873 Bartlett and his wife began building their dream house at 165 Brattle Street, in the middle of Cambridge. They lived out their lives together in the house. By 1878 Bartlett was a senior partner in charge of editing, marketing, and manufacturing at Little, Brown. In an 1878 letter to their mutual friend Lowell, Holmes said, "J. B. ambulates pleasantly along the asphalt sidewalk of life, going down to the Cape now and then, and returning to tell how narrowly he has escaped acute rheumatism from the truculent winds."

That same year Bartlett and his wife began working together on another daunting task–putting together a concordance to the works of Shakespeare. This book was the work of their "leisure time," according to Bartlett's self-effacing preface, but in fact the undertaking was a massive one. After publishing *The Shakespeare Phrase Book* in 1881–a precursor to the full concordance–Bartlett compiled another index, the *Catalogue of Books on Angling, including Icthyology, Pisciculture, Fisheries, and Fishing Laws* (1882). Bartlett developed this list while working on a deluxe edition of Izaak Walton's *Complete Angler* for Little, Brown in 1866.

In 1889 Bartlett retired from Little, Brown to finish work on *A New and Complete Concordance or Verbal Index to Words, Phrases & Passages in the Dramatic Works of Shakespeare, with a Supplementary Concordance to the Poems* (1894), but first he released his ninth and final edition of *Familiar Quotations* (1891). By that time, critics already regarded the book as an indispensable reference and a monument to Bartlett's unremitting labor and scholarship. The *Familiar Quotations* had grown from 267 duodecimo pages in 1855 to 778 pages by 1869, when Lowell reviewed the fifth edition. By 1891 Bartlett's commonplace book filled 1,158 octavo pages.

Besides impressive bulk, the ninth edition had a wide range. In addition to the Bible and Shakespeare, which dominated the first edition, the ninth edition included such widely diverse authors as the Sanskrit writer Pilpay, Hesiod, Geoffrey Chaucer, Omar Khayyám, Miguel de Cervantes, Charles Darwin, and Bret Harte. Bartlett included the ancient and the modern, the poet and the statesman: Lucretius, Martin Luther, Abraham Lincoln, James Russell Lowell, Charles Lamb (the English essayist), and Sir Edward Bulwer Lytton all had their own sections in his ninth edition.

Bartlett's final work had wide scope in time and topic, but it also demonstrated his careful, scholarly attention to detail. For example, Lytton's famous epigram "the pen is mightier than the sword" is cross-referenced with cognates by Robert Burton ("*Hinc quam sic calamus soevior ense, patet.* The pen worse than the sword") and a translation from Louis de Rouvroy, duc de Saint-Simon's memoirs ("So far had the pen under the king the superiority over the sword"). Almost every page includes a similar demonstration of Bartlett's ability to identify cognates and parallels to familiar quotations from a variety of fields and historical periods.

Despite its scholarly objectives, the book was something of an unexpected popular hit. The seventh and eighth editions reportedly sold more than forty thousand copies each in the United States. Indeed, especially as Bartlett came to include more contemporary authors, his book became a quick, quantitative measure of fame: critics could not withstand the temptation to count the number of entries for authors to determine whether their stars were waxing or waning. Lowell's July 1869 review mentioned this function of the book. It is still interesting today to compare the relative space Bartlett provided to different authors: the ninth edition devoted more space to Lowell than to Ralph Waldo Emerson, for instance, and included John Greenleaf Whittier, but not Walt Whitman.

The book also provided a ready shortcut to clever quoting, of course. Lowell's review warned that this was not the purpose of Bartlett's work: the "object has not been to supply us with ready-made learning and impromptu felicity of allusion, but to restore the estrays of literature to their rightful owners." Lowell, however, also readily admits the ability to measure fame with the book and appreciates its function as a "lesson in rhetoric," designed to highlight the "turn of phrase so perfect as to seem inevitable."

Bartlett's *Familiar Quotations* still bears his name in the twenty-first century. Much less familiar to modern readers is his concordance to the *Globe* edition of Shakespeare, a reference work even more massive than the one for which Bartlett is justly famous. The concordance includes 1,769 pages of words and phrases, in context, from the bard's plays, and 140 more pages indexing words and phrases in the sonnets. The work took close to twenty years to complete. The concordance was reissued regularly through 1953, and has only been superseded as the standard concordance by the publication of the Riverside edition of Shakespeare's works, the concordance, which was prepared with the help of a computer.

Bartlett's *Familiar Quotations* reinvented the commonplace book. At his death, a notice in *Scribner's* in March 1906 said that Bartlett's book had entered a crowded market of similar titles and "vanquished the many others." Predictably, the notice referred to Bartlett's "useful diligence"; *Outlook* similarly noted the man's "patient and industrious" nature. To his contemporaries, Bartlett's mind was secondary to his energy and industry. For the almost unimaginable scope of his work and reading, not for the power of his intellect, has Bartlett been reckoned an American Samuel Johnson.

The huge, scholarly *Familiar Quotations* is anything but pretentious: it humbly intended to "show . . . the obligations our language owes to various authors for numerous phrases and familiar quotations which have become 'household words,'" according to Bartlett's preface. Although a secondary intent was clearly to identify valuable and beautiful contributions to the language, Bartlett's work was primarily descriptive in nature; only more recent editors of the *Familiar Quotations* have voiced more proscriptive, taste-forming objectives for it.

Bartlett was a collector and an organizer, finding and sorting the threads of meaning running through literature. His skill was well appreciated by his contemporaries. The ninth edition of the *Familiar Quotations* includes this quotation from Lowell's "For an Autograph": "Though old the thought and oft exprest, / 'Tis his at last who says it best." Bartlett files this couplet in the index under the heading "Quotations," cross-referenced with an epigram from the work of Emerson: "Next to the originator of a good sentence is the first quoter of it." These two ideas, recognizing and quoting the best of literature, encompass Bartlett's lasting contribution.

By 1927 editors of his *Familiar Quotations* had begun removing old Bartlett quotations such as these–quotations that no longer seemed so familiar–but the book continues to be known as Bartlett's. The name endures because of the lasting quality of the scholarship and because of the fact that Bartlett, self-made man, bookbinder, publisher of his own books, so well embodies the up-by-the-bootstrap American ideals of hard work and self-reliance.

Biographies:

M. H. Morgan, "John Bartlett," *Proceedings of the American Academy of Arts and Sciences*, 41 (July 1906): 841–846;

"Reminiscences of John Bartlett," *Cambridge Historical Society Publications I* (Cambridge, 1906), pp. 67–87;

Thomas Wentworth Higginson, "John Bartlett," *Carlyle's Laugh and Other Surprises* (Boston: Houghton Mifflin, 1909), pp. 194–198.

Reference:

Letters of John Holmes to James Russell Lowell and Others, edited by William Roscoe Thayer (Boston: Houghton Mifflin, 1917)–includes several letters to and about John Bartlett.

Papers:

An autobiographical manuscript, including a list of books John Bartlett read, "A Record of Idle Hours," can be found at the Houghton Library of Harvard University.

Cyrus Augustus Bartol

(30 April 1813 – 16 December 1900)

William G. Heath
Lakehead University

BOOKS: *Influence of the Ministry at Large in the City of Boston, as a Spectator* (Boston: Munroe, 1836);

A Discourse Delivered in the West Church In Boston, March 3, 1839 (Boston: Freeman & Bolles, 1839);

An Address Delivered Before the First Congregational Society in Groton: At the Funeral of Their Late Pastor, Rev. George W. Wells, March 21, 1843 (Boston: Crosby, 1843);

Confession of Faith: A Sermon Delivered at the West Church, in Boston, January 28, 1844 (Boston: Greene, 1844);

Individual and Public Reform: A Discourse Delivered on Fast Day, April 2, 1846, at the West Church in Boston (Boston: Crosby & Nichols, 1846);

The New Planet; or, An Analogy between the Perturbations of Matter and Spirit (Boston: Bowles, 1847);

Christ the Way: A Sermon Preached at the Ordination of the Rev. George M. Bartol, as Minister of the First Church of Christ, in Lancaster, Mass., Wednesday, August 4, 1847 (Lancaster: Ballard & Messinger, 1847);

Public Causes for Gratitude: A Sermon Preached on Thanksgiving Day, November 25, 1847, in the West Church, Boston (Boston: West Parish Association, 1848);

Discourses on the Christian Spirit and Life (Boston: Crosby & Nichols, 1850; revised edition with an introduction, Boston: Crosby & Nichols, 1850);

The Cure: A Sermon Preached in the West Church, Boston, on Fast-Day, April 10 (Boston: Crosby & Nichols, 1851);

The Hand of God in the Great Man: A Sermon Delivered in the West Church, Occasioned by the Death of Daniel Webster (Boston: Crosby & Nichols, 1852);

Discourses on the Christian Body and Form (Boston: Crosby & Nichols, 1853);

A Discourse on the Life and Character of Samuel Putnam (Boston: Crosby & Nichols, 1853);

Motive-Powers: A Sermon Preached in the West Church, Boston (Boston: Bowles, 1853);

The Relation of the Medical Profession to the Ministry: A Discourse Preached in the West Church, on Occasion of the Death of Dr. George C. Shattuck (Boston: Wilson, 1854);

The Traveller's Report (Boston: Crosby & Nichols, 1854);

The Alarm: A Discourse on the Introduction of the New Fire Alarm, Preached in the West Church, Boston (Boston: Bowles, 1854);

Grains of Gold; or, Select Thoughts on Sacred Themes (Boston: American Unitarian Association, 1854);

Pictures of Europe, Framed in Ideas (Boston: Crosby & Nichols, 1855);

The West Church and Its Ministers (Boston: Crosby & Nichols, 1856);

"Snow and Vapor": A Sermon Preached in the West Church (Boston: Bowles, 1856);

Christ's Humanity and His Divinity the Same Thing: A Discourse Preached in the West Church, and before the Sunday School Teachers' Institute, in Boston (Boston: Office of the Quarterly Journal, 1856);

Dying with Our Friends: A Sermon on the Character of Rev. Ephraim Peabody, D.D. Delivered in the West Church, Boston, Sunday, December 7, 1856 (Boston: Office of the Quarterly Journal, 1857);

The Voice of Twenty Years: A Discourse Preached in the West Church on the First Day of March, Being the Twentieth Anniversary of His Ordination (Boston: Wilson, 1857);

Jesus and Jerusalem; or, Christ the Saviour and Civilizer of the World: A Discourse Preached before the Benevolent Fraternity of Churches, on Sunday Evening, April 12, 1857, in Behalf of the Ministry at Large (Cambridge: Metcalf, 1857);

An Address Delivered Before the Alumni of the Divinity School in Harvard University, Tuesday, July 20, 1858 (Boston: Office of the Quarterly Journal, 1858);

Church and Congregation: A Plea for their Unity (Boston: Ticknor & Fields, 1858);

The Key of the Kingdom: An Address before the Ministerial Conference in Bedford Street, Boston (Boston: Bowles, 1859);

Religion in Our Public Schools: A Discourse Preached in the West Church, Boston (Boston: Ticknor & Fields, 1859);

The Word of the Spirit to the Church (Boston: Walker, Wise, 1859);

Cornering Religion (Albany: Weed, Parson, 1860);

The Immediate Vision of God: A Sermon Preached in the West Church (Boston: Walker, Wise, 1860);

A Discourse, Preached in the West Church, on Theodore Parker (Boston: Crosby & Nichols, Lee, 1860);

The Duty of the Time. A Discourse Preached in the West Church Sunday Morning, April 28, 1861 (Boston: Walker, Wise, 1861);

Our Sacrifices. A Sermon Preached in the West Church, November 3, 1861, Being the Sunday after the Funeral of Lieut. William Lowell Putnam (Boston: Ticknor & Fields, 1861);

Proceedings in the West Church on the Occasion of the Decease of Charles Lowell, D.D.: Its Senior Pastor (Boston: Walker, Wise, 1861);

The Recompense. A Sermon for Country and Kindred (Boston: Ticknor & Fields, 1862);

The Remission by Blood: A Tribute to Our Soldiers and the Sword (Boston: Walker, Wise, 1862);

The Nation's Hour: A Tribute to Major Sidney Willard, Delivered in the West Church, December 21, Forefathers' Day (Boston: Walker, Wise, 1862);

Conditions of Peace: A Discourse Delivered in the West Church, in Memory of David Kimball Hobart (Boston: Walker, Wise, 1863);

The Unspotted Life: A Discourse in Memory of Rev. Thomas Starr King, Preached in the West Church, March 6, 1864 (Boston: Walker, Wise, 1864);

The Purchase by Blood: A Tribute to Brig.-Gen. Charles Russell Lowell, Jr. Spoken in the West Church, Oct. 30, 1864 (Boston: Wilson, 1864);

Extravagance: A Sermon for the Times (Boston: Walker, Wise, 1864);

The Fall: A Sermon Preached in the West Church, Nov. 27, 1864, the Sunday after the Decease of Mrs. Sarah Putnam (Boston: Wilson, 1865);

The Memorial of Virtue: A Sermon Preached in the West Church, Jan. 22, 1865, After the Death of Edward Everett (Boston: Walker, Wise, 1865);

The Significance of Abraham Lincoln as Man and President: A Sermon Preached in the West Church, on Fast Day, June 4 (Boston: Bowles, 1865);

Congregational Freedom: A Discourse after Thirty Years' Ministry, Preached in the West Church, March 3, 1867 (Boston: Printed for the Society, 1867);

Loving Words from Our Good Pastor (Boston: Privately printed, 1869);

Sensations in the Church and on the Exchange: A Sermon Preached in West Church, Boston, January 14, 1872 (Boston: Williams, 1872);

Sincerity: An Address Before the Essex Conference, Feb. 28, 1872 (Boston, 1872);

The Upper Standing: A Sermon Preached in the West Church, Boston, March 3, 1872 (Boston: Bowles, 1872);

True Childhood: A Sermon Delivered in West Church, June 2, 1872, after the Death of Mrs. Mary Avery Upham (Cambridge, Mass.: Wilson, 1872);

The Trial by Fire. A Sermon Preached in the West Church, Boston, Sunday, Nov. 17, 1872 (Boston: A. Mudge, 1872);

Radical Problems (Boston: Roberts, 1872);

The War Cloud: A Sermon Preached in the West Church, Boston, Sunday, Nov. 24, 1873 (Boston: Williams, 1873);

Senatorial Character: A Sermon in West Church, Boston, Sunday, 15th of March, after the Decease of Charles Sumner (Boston: Williams, 1874);

The Rising Faith (Boston: Roberts, 1874)–includes an enlarged version of *Sincerity;*

Christianity on Trial: A Sermon (1876);

The Five Ministers: A Sermon in West Church (Boston: Williams, 1877);

The Man and the Physician: A Sermon [upon Dr. Edward H. Clarke], Preached in the West Church, Boston, Sunday, Dec. 9, 1877 (Boston: Williams, 1878);

Reason and Rome in Education: A Sermon Preached at the West Church, Boston, Sunday, November 23, 1879 (Boston: Ellis, 1879);

Principles and Portraits (Boston: Roberts, 1880);

James T. Fields: A Discourse in West Church, Boston (Boston: Williams, 1881);

Music in Religion (Boston: Ellis, 1881);

The President's Death: A Discourse Delivered in the West Church, on Sunday, the 25th of September (Boston: Williams, 1881);

Ralph Waldo Emerson: A Discourse Preached in West Church (Boston: Williams, 1882);

Webster as Man and Statesman: A Sermon . . . in West Church, Boston, Sunday, January 29, 1882 (Boston: Ellis, 1882);

Henry Whitney Bellows (Boston, 1882);

The Andover Bottle's Burst: A Sermon in West Church, Sunday, April 30, 1882 (Boston, 1882);

The Preacher, the Singer, and the Doer: Dewey, Longfellow, and Bertram: A Sermon in West Church (Boston: Williams, 1882);

Otis Norcross, Civic and Patriotic Worth in Boston: Sermon Preached by Cyrus A. Bartol, in the West Church, Boston, Sunday, Sept. 17, 1882 (Boston: Marvin, 1883);

The Image Passing Before Us. A Sermon after the Decease of Elizabeth Howard Bartol . . . (Boston: Cupples, Upham, 1883);

Mind-Cure: A Sermon Preached in the West Church, Boston, Mass., May 4, 1884 (New York: Funk & Wagnalls, 1884);

The Beloved Physician: A Sermon in West Church, after the Decease of Dr. Calvin Ellis (Boston: Cupples, Upham, 1884);

Spiritual Specifics. Mind in Medicine; Embracing Two Sermons Preached in the West Church, Boston, Mass., October 5th and 12th (Boston: Carter & Karrick, 1884);

Charles Faulkner: A Sermon in West Church, Sunday, Oct. 18, 1885 (Boston: Mudge, 1885);

The West Church, Boston: Commemorative Services on the Fiftieth Anniversary of Its Present Ministry, and the One Hundred and Fiftieth of its Foundation, on Tuesday, March 1, 1887, with Three Sermons by Its Pastor (Boston: Damrell & Upham, 1887);

Amos Bronson Alcott: His Character (Boston: Roberts, 1888).

OTHER: *Hymns for the Sanctuary,* prepared by Bartol and others (Boston: Crosby & Nichols, 1849);

"Emerson's Religion," in *The Genius and Character of Emerson: Lectures at the Concord School of Philosophy,* edited by F. B. Sanborn (Boston: James R. Osgood, 1885), pp. 109–145;

Poems and Essays by Jones Very, edited by James Freeman Clarke, with a preface by Bartol (Boston: Houghton, Mifflin, 1886).

SELECTED PERIODICAL PUBLICATIONS–UNCOLLECTED: "Theodore: or, The Skeptic's Conversion," *Christian Examiner,* 31 (January 1842): 348–373;

"Poetry and Imagination," *Christian Examiner,* 42 (March 1847): 250–270;

"*Representative Men,*" *Christian Examiner,* 48 (March 1850): 314–318;

"The Theological Transition," *Radical,* 2 (January 1867): 287–296;

"The Church of the Spirit," *Radical,* 2 (March 1867): 385–397;

"The Clerical Business. An Address before the Senior Class in the Divinity School at Cambridge, 14 July 1867," *Radical,* 3 (October 1867): 65–77;

"Ralph Waldo Emerson, the Man," *Literary World,* 11 (22 May 1880): 174–175;

"The Nature of Knowledge: Emerson's Way," *Unitarian Review and Religious Magazine,* 17 (October 1882): 289–312.

Cyrus Augustus Bartol figured prominently in the religious, intellectual, and literary life of nineteenth-century Boston. As minister of the historic West Church for fifty-two years, he participated in the Unitarian, Transcendentalist, and free religious movements. However, just as the West Church was nominally Unitarian but remained staunchly independent of sectarian creed and label, so was Bartol in, but never totally of, these movements. His dissatisfaction with temporal forms and institutions inspired a lifelong search for what he called the Church of the Spirit. Bartol's core belief, from which flowed all his ideas concerning religion, nature, and man in society, was his abiding faith in a personal theism. His spiritual odyssey originated in his identity as a visionary and critic, a kind of religious Man Thinking. As he wrote to his friend, Reverend Henry W. Bellows, on 16 June 1849: "Your destiny in this world is cast as irrevocably as mine. It is to be an exponent and director of the wants & thinking of the times." A prolific author, Bartol fulfilled this destiny in ten books and in many sermons and addresses on the vital issues of the day.

The third of five children of George Bartol and Ann (Given) Bartol, Cyrus Augustus Bartol was born on 30 April 1813 and grew up in the coastal town of Freeport, Maine, a thriving agricultural and commercial center where his father was in business. Bartol descended from a long line of successful Yankee merchants from whom he inherited a keen business sense that complemented his spiritual calling and that served him well in later years. His maternal great-grandfather was a Catholic priest who left the Church to marry, a possible augury of Bartol's own eventual theological independence. A childhood spent amid rural surroundings, with the ocean sights and sounds for his playground, inspired in Bartol an ecstatic love of nature and provided a fertile source of metaphor for his writings.

Nature to him was never a static emblem of spiritual truth but a living force imbued with God's presence. As he confided to Bellows on 31 August 1879, "I . . . dissolve & mix with the universe, and find I come out of the spiritual ocean, as out of the actual sea, refreshed & feeling like an angel."

Spontaneously pious as a child, Bartol was reared a Calvinist and remembered his religious upbringing as a gloomy time. "When women fainted in church," he recalled in *The Rising Faith* (1874), "I thought they were called to the judgment. I walked about, hanging down my head, saying over and over again, hour after hour, *'God be merciful to me a sinner!'*" Bartol grew spiritually younger and more mystical with the years. His religious liberation began at age seven when, as he later recalled, he overheard his father and uncle discussing William Ellery Channing's preaching. As he wrote in *Principles and Portraits* (1880), "The joy of my relatives in their new-found teacher of liberty and love was for me . . . nothing less than the removal of a curse." Bartol's liberation continued when his father moved the family to Portland in 1825 to take advantage of greater business opportunities. There, Bartol came under the influence of the Unitarian minister of the First Parish Church, Ichabod Nichols, whom he called in a letter to John G. Palfrey on 7 February 1837 "the spiritual guide of my youth." Nichols, a trustee of Bowdoin College in nearby Brunswick, may also have influenced Bartol to enroll there in 1828 when he was just fifteen. At Bowdoin, Bartol took courses from Henry Wadsworth Longfellow and distinguished himself in religious and literary studies. He became a convert to Samuel Taylor Coleridge's *Aids to Reflection* (1825) and was elected president of the college literary society in his junior year on the basis of exceptional character and scholarship.

Bartol graduated from Bowdoin with honors in 1832, after which he entered the Harvard Divinity School in the same class as Charles Timothy Brooks, Christopher Pearse Cranch, and John Sullivan Dwight. These years also marked Bartol's first contact with the early stages of the Transcendental revolt against Unitarian orthodoxy. He wrote approvingly in his journal of hearing Ralph Waldo Emerson lecture at the Cambridge Lyceum on 10 March 1835 on the aim and uses of biography, describing Emerson's style as "concise, definite, naked." Even more important was Bartol's discovery of Elizabeth Peabody's *Record of a School* (1835), which introduced him to Amos Bronson Alcott's belief in the Spirit as "the only ground of true Religion," a doctrine that proved to be the main catalyst in the emergence of Bartol's latent personalism. The two men enjoyed a warm, reciprocal friendship that spanned half a century. Bartol acknowledged his indebtedness to Alcott's "vital conception of Personality" in his 1872 essay, "Transcendentalism," as well as in the memorial tribute he delivered at Alcott's funeral in 1888. Alcott was no less complimentary of Bartol, praising his address to the Harvard Divinity School seniors in a letter on 18 September 1867, "for the added *Personality,* without which the spirit were but symbolized not identified, nor known experimentally," and calling Bartol "Poet of the Pulpit" in "Sonnet XXI" of *Sonnets and Canzonets* (1882).

After graduating from divinity school in 1835, Bartol spent six months as an apprentice preacher at the First Congregational Church in Cincinnati. While there, he was in touch with William Henry Channing and James Freeman Clarke, editors of the Transcendentalist *Western Messenger,* and possibly attended meetings of the Semi-Colon Club, which they founded. In April 1836 Bartol returned to Boston for more apprentice preaching at Gray's Chapel and to do missionary work as minister at large for the city. On 1 March 1837 he was ordained and called to the West Church as junior pastor to Charles Lowell, father of James Russell Lowell. Henry Ware Jr., one of Bartol's Harvard professors, delivered the ordination sermon. One year later, on 7 February 1838, Bartol strengthened his ties to the West Church by marrying Elizabeth Howard, whose grandfather Simeon Howard had been minister of the church during the American Revolution. Their only child, Elizabeth, became a successful painter in Boston, a disciple of the portraitist William Morris Hunt. Among her paintings is a portrait of Frederic Hedge, one of the founders of the Transcendental Club.

Bartol joined the West Church in its centennial year and, upon Charles Lowell's death in 1861, became only its fifth and, as it turned out, last minister. Established in 1737 at the height of the Great Awakening as a refuge from Calvinistic theology, the West Church came to be considered one of the most liberal scions of the Unitarian stock. In the Unitarian *Year Book* the West Church was listed as an "independent Congregational Society," the only church in Boston so designated. This tradition of religious independence fit well with Bartol's nonsectarian instincts, allowing him room over the years for the unrestricted development of his increasingly radical beliefs. His reputation as a freelancer who used the pulpit to lead and shape public opinion on secular as well as religious issues and who was known for his incisive wit and oracular style as a preacher made him something of an attraction in Boston for many years. In 1868 the *New-York Tribune* called Bartol "probably the most successful minister in Boston." On 28 February 1887, amid much-publicized observances of the sesquicentennial of the West Church and the fiftieth anniversary of Bartol's ordination, the *Boston Daily Journal* wrote that "his sermons might be

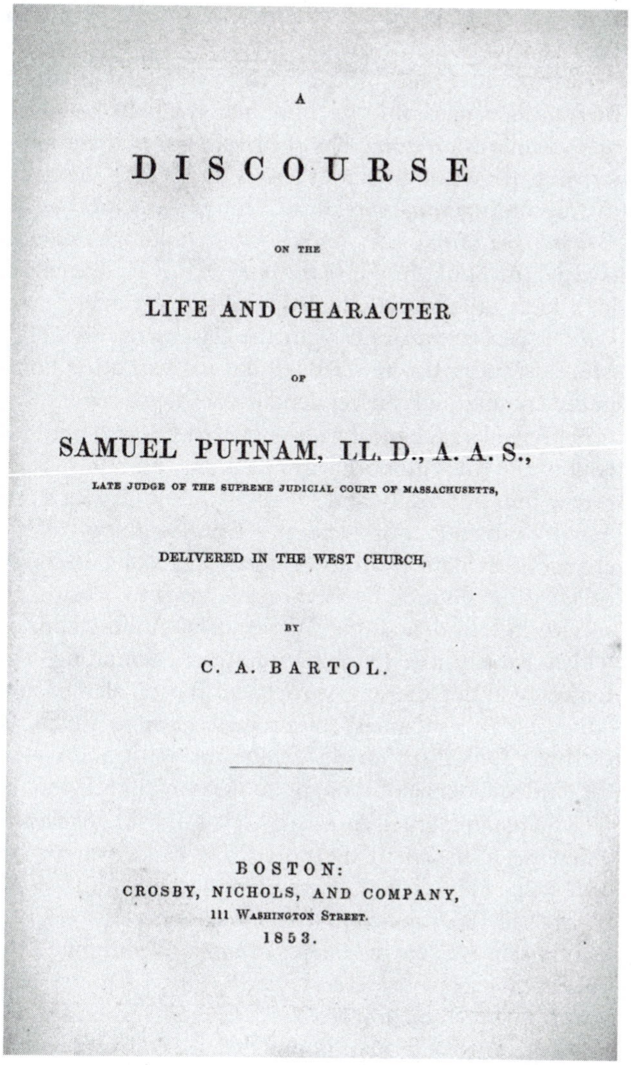
A

DISCOURSE

ON THE

LIFE AND CHARACTER

OF

SAMUEL PUTNAM, LL. D., A. A. S.,

LATE JUDGE OF THE SUPREME JUDICIAL COURT OF MASSACHUSETTS,

DELIVERED IN THE WEST CHURCH,

BY

C. A. BARTOL.

BOSTON:
CROSBY, NICHOLS, AND COMPANY,
111 WASHINGTON STREET.
1853.

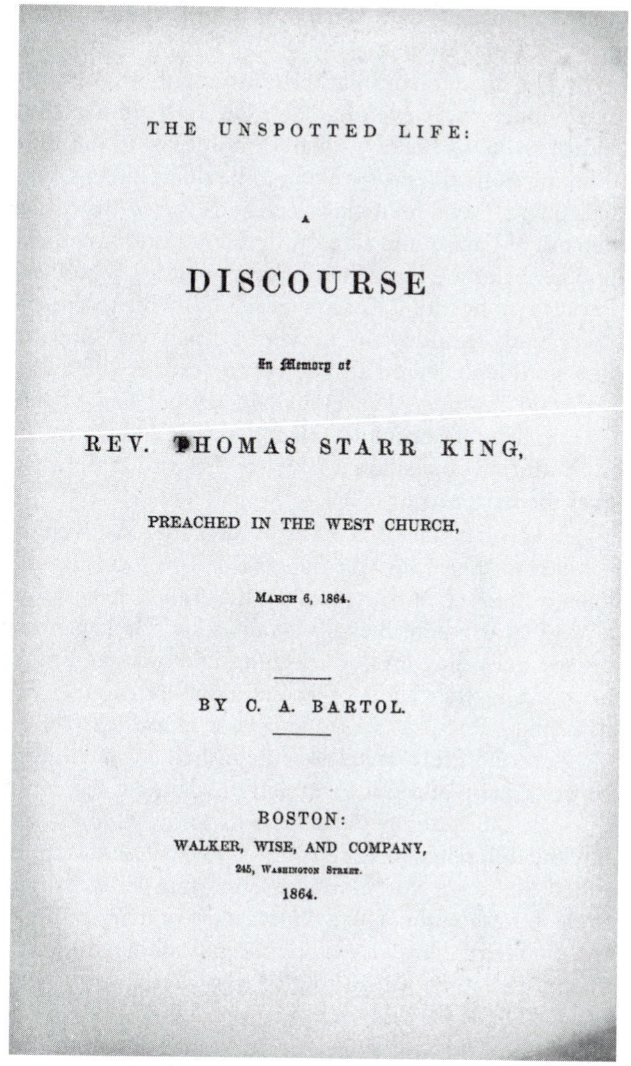
THE UNSPOTTED LIFE:

A

DISCOURSE

In Memory of

REV. THOMAS STARR KING,

PREACHED IN THE WEST CHURCH,

MARCH 6, 1864.

BY C. A. BARTOL.

BOSTON:
WALKER, WISE, AND COMPANY,
245, WASHINGTON STREET.
1864.

Title pages for two of Bartol's funeral sermons (Collection of Joel Myerson)

consulted as giving an index to the great social, scientific and religious phases of American life during the past half century." The *Catholic Review,* on the other hand, politely demurred, citing the fanfare as evidence of what it called "the Bartol cult" and suggesting that if Bartol were canonized, he should be called "St. Cyrus the Vague."

By the time of his ordination, Bartol was a regular member of the Transcendental Club, likely having joined at the second meeting on 19 September 1836. Over the next four years he attended at least fourteen of the thirty meetings held, hosting six of them in his home at 17 Chestnut Street, including the one on 18 September 1839 at which the idea for launching what became the *The Dial* was first openly discussed. Along with George Ripley and Convers Francis, Bartol was considered one of the more serious students of German literature within the club.

Initially, Bartol saw Transcendentalism as an antidote to a moribund orthodoxy. He stood by Emerson during the controversy surrounding his Divinity School Address, and twice he opposed moves to oust Theodore Parker from the Boston Association of Congregational Ministers following the latter's inflammatory 1841 discourse on "The Transient and Permanent in Christianity," telling his congregation some years later that if Parker had been forced out, he would have left as well. But his actions were more a sign of respect for these men as individuals than an endorsement of their spiritual positions. By the late 1840s Bartol was sounding like a Christian apologist as he openly criticized what he considered the excesses of Transcendentalism. Reviewing Emerson's *Poems* (1847) and *Representative Men* (1850) in the conservative *Christian Examiner,* he criticized his friend's doctrine of the Over-Soul as vague, cold, and above all impersonal, and he warned that Emersonian self-reliance could erode social cohesion.

His dissent from Parker's position, both privately and publicly, was even harsher. On 2 December 1852 Bartol wrote to Bellows, "I have no desire to put him, thinking as he does & speaking as he does, into a Christian pulpit." The following year he reversed his earlier defense of Parker and sided with the ministerial association in excluding him. The sticking point for Bartol was Parker's notion of "absolute religion," which, like the Over-Soul, excluded the notion of a personal Creator. In a sermon delivered after Parker's death in 1860, Bartol again defended Parker's character but faulted him for proclaiming absolute religion over Christianity. "I must affirm his position a false one," Bartol said, "however the man was true."

As Octavius Brooks Frothingham observed in *Transcendentalism in New England* (1876), during the debate over church reform in the 1850s it was not always clear where Bartol's loyalties lay. He began the decade defending traditional Unitarian forms and practices against the claims of an intuitional religion. In his first book, *Discourses on the Christian Spirit and Life* (1850), a collection of sermons, he distinguished between inner consciousness and outer revelation, claiming that only through the latter could a person know God. In an obvious reference to Emerson's *Representative Men,* published the same year, Bartol asserted that Jesus "is not, in the phrase of the day, a 'representative man,' but representative of deity. . . . He transcends all our transcendentalism." Not surprisingly, the book was well received in conservative circles. Andrew Peabody, writing in the *Christian Examiner,* praised the discourses for their eloquence and piety, and Horace Bushnell rated the book above the writings of Channing. In his next book, *Discourses on the Christian Body and Form* (1853), Bartol continued to rebuke what he considered the "extreme of free-thinking, endless speculation, and well-nigh savage independence and solitary vagrancy in religious matters."

In 1854 a yearlong leave of absence gave Bartol a much needed respite from his pastoral duties. "I am *tired* body & soul," he wrote to Bellows on 1 May 1854; "I want to get out of the ruts." He did so by traveling in Europe for six months, starting in England, where he called on James Martineau–"he knew of me," Bartol wrote Bellows on 29 May 1854–and continuing on to France, Belgium, Holland, Prussia, Austria, and Italy. He visited art galleries and cathedrals and reveled in the natural wonders of Europe, especially the Alps. When he returned home, at the urging of friends he published an account of his impressions, *Pictures of Europe, Framed in Ideas* (1855), his most Transcendentalist book to date and the most literary of all his books. Like Emerson's *Nature, Pictures of Europe* is a prose poem on the Swedenborgian theme of the correspondences between matter and spirit. The early chapters, in which he translates natural forms into their symbolic language and meaning, are unified by the metaphor of the double journey, prompting Charles Foster to describe the book as "an international version of Thoreau's *A Week on the Concord and Merrimack Rivers.*" Contemporary readers praised the book. In the *Christian Examiner,* Hedge called it "a kind of spiritual Childe-Harold's Pilgrimage" and said "it deserves to rank with the classics of the land." More recently, Lawrence Buell has discussed the book in the context of Transcendentalist aesthetics.

Bartol's sabbatical from the West Church got him "out of the ruts" in more ways than one. Not only did it renew him physically and mentally, but it also inspired him to adopt a more liberal religious outlook. This change is evident from the chapter in *Pictures of Europe* called "The Church," based on his visits to a Catholic service in Dresden and to Westminster Abbey, both of which experiences left him unmoved. Sounding like Parker without the angry rhetoric, Bartol blamed the "dividing . . . dogmas" of Protestantism as much as Catholic formalism for deadening the spirit and called for "independence of thought and action" in religion.

That quality is precisely what Bartol displayed when he returned to the pulpit. He caused a stir by establishing a policy of "open communion" at the West Church in 1857, an action that one member of the Association said was a worse heresy than any committed by Parker. Bartol considered resigning his pastorate and wrote to Emerson for advice. Emerson responded by sending Bartol the manuscript of his 1832 resignation sermon and urging him "to write a stinging pamphlet" but not to resign. The pamphlet became a book-length defense of the new policy, *Church and Congregation: A Plea for their Unity* (1858). When the American Unitarian Association refused to publish it, Bartol instead gave the book to Ticknor and Fields. As the decade wore on, he became disillusioned with the polarizing effect of denominational squabbles. Not even the honorary Doctor of Divinity degree he received from Harvard in 1859 could conceal his growing estrangement from the Unitarian establishment. In what he called "a little taste of excommunication," he was ostracized from Unitarian and Universalist pulpits and denied access to publish in certain religious journals because they considered his views too radical for publication in their pages.

While some Unitarian leaders, notably Bellows, were calling for denominational unity, Bartol began to preach what he called the Unity of the Spirit as a solution to factional strife. When Bellows urged him to embrace "the Church-Idea," Bartol reminded him in a letter on 13 October 1859 that "it is not the only or the chief Idea. The Spiritual idea . . . is higher. It is my nature and necessity to *emphasize that,* in the face of all discouragement and doubt." This concept became the constant refrain of Bartol's writing from this point on, beginning with his next book, *The Word of the Spirit to the Church* (1859). The Spiritual Idea was an adjunct of his personal theism. Upon it he based his ideal church, the "Church of the Spirit," a community of believers united by the indwelling "Person." An idealized Church of the Spirit offered Bartol an escape from the narrow, creed-bound theology of denominational Unitarianism.

During the 1860s Bartol pinned his hopes for a realization of this ideal on a small group of young, similarly disenchanted radicals who were seeking an alternative to Bellows's "Church Idea." The *New-York Tribune* commented that "The young radicals have found no better friend, no abler advocate of their faith than Dr. Bartol." Following their defection from the National Conference of Unitarian Churches in Syracuse on 10–11 October 1866, Bartol offered his home as a gathering place for the radicals, eight of whom–including John Weiss, Samuel Johnson, and Frederic Ellingwood Abbot–met there three times over the winter to plan a new religious society. Out of these discussions came the Free Religious Association, or FRA, which was officially launched at a public meeting in Horticultural Hall in Boston on 30 May 1867. The purpose of the association, as stated in its articles, was "to promote the interests of pure religion, to encourage the scientific study of theology, and to increase fellowship in the spirit." That same year, Bartol also organized the Radical Club as a forum for the expression of free thinking on radical ideas.

Characteristically, Bartol never joined the FRA, although he spoke briefly at four of its annual meetings. Before long, the growing domination of the association by policies that seemed to have no truly spiritual basis produced in him the same kind of disillusionment that had earlier marked his response to Transcendentalism and Unitarianism. He complained that free religion was too scientific and empirical, that it preached a hollow individualism, and that it advocated the secularization of society. For Bartol, free religion turned out to be not a religion at all but a dry, rationalistic philosophy.

He voiced his strongest critique of free religion in his next two books, *Radical Problems* (1872) and *The Rising Faith* (1874). These books mark Bartol's full, belated flowering as a Transcendentalist and are written in the terse, epigrammatic, and richly allusive style for which he is best known. In the essay "Transcendentalism" in *Radical Problems,* he argued that the Transcendentalist "made consciousness, not sense, the ground of truth; and, in the present devotion to physical science and turn of philosophy to build the universe on foundations of matter, we need to vindicate and reassert his premise." But Bartol did not reject science totally. He proposed a kind of transcendental empiricism, a harmonization of science and intuition based on his conviction that truth lies in "an atonement [literally, an at-one-ment] of opposites." He demonstrated this harmonization in his essay on "Personality" in *The Rising Faith* by emphasizing the empirical basis of his personal theism, noting that it seeks to explain the infinite reality in terms of finite persons. In short, conceiving of God as a Person is consistent with the scientific method employed in any intellectual undertaking–moving to the unknown by way of the known.

Bartol's last book, *Principles and Portraits* (1880), combined philosophical essays on such topics as art, business, law, and politics with biographical essays on William Shakespeare, Channing, Bushnell, Weiss, William Lloyd Garrison, and the painter Hunt, all linked by his favorite themes of spirit and personality. Two years later, Emerson died. In a sermon at the West Church that was personal and anecdotal, Bartol eulogized his friend while also noting that Emerson's primary defect as a thinker was his failure to take proper notice of evil. Alcott's death followed six years later. Bartol was now one of the elder statesmen of the religious and intellectual community in Boston. He divided his time between preaching, writing, and lecturing annually at the Concord School of Philosophy. His contribution to the school was literary rather than metaphysical; along with Ednah Dow Cheney, David Wasson, and Elizabeth Peabody, he helped provide the Transcendentalist element at the sessions. Twice he lectured on Emerson–"The Nature of Knowledge: Emerson's Way" (1882) and "Emerson's Religion" (1884). Other topics included "Goethe and Schiller" (1885), "Dante's Tropes" (1886), and "Shakespeare's Poetics" (1887).

In "The Tidings," a sermon preached on 6 March 1887, an aging Bartol offered his resignation from the West Church. Population shifts within the city had shrunk the congregation to a handful; the sanctuary, he said, resembled "a big withered pod, in which the grains or kernels rustle or rattle around." He stayed on for two more years, finally retiring with the title of Pastor Emeritus on 30 September 1889 because of failing health. The West Church was dissolved as a body; in 1892 it closed its doors for good. Andrew C. Wheelwright, a philanthropist, bought the historic building to save it from being turned into a factory, and in 1894 he sold it to the city for use as a branch of the public library.

Bartol spent his last years at his seaside home in Manchester-by-the-Sea, Massachusetts, an area he did much to develop and promote as a fashionable resort.

In 1871 he purchased sixty acres of seemingly useless property for $600 per acre, a price that many considered ludicrously high. But Bartol's critics did not have his visionary eye. Where they saw only barren rocks and sand, he pictured beautiful homes, spacious lawns, and people enjoying the benefits of nature. He gradually improved the property by dividing it into house lots and putting in streets and roads. Proof of his sagacity came when he sold the lots for between $10,000 and $12,000 per acre, or twenty times what he paid. Over the next quarter century, Bartol bought, improved, and sold additional properties in Manchester. In his *History of the Town of Manchester* (1895), Darius Francis Lamson wrote that "Rev. Dr. Bartol has done more than any other man to bring Manchester into notice. By his early, far-sighted and well-managed investments, he has proved himself more of a 'seer,' even from a financial and economic point of view, than many who have been bred in the art of money-making."

Bartol's contemporaries expressed surprise that such a mystical and unworldly clergyman was also a shrewd speculator in real estate, but there was nothing ironic or paradoxical to Bartol about his success. Whereas other Transcendentalists such as Alcott and Thoreau preached the virtues of simplicity, Bartol defended wealth as a means to a spiritual end. He used his activities in Manchester as an extension of his ministry. As he wrote in *Radical Problems,* "The toil of the man that makes my roads, lays out my grounds, turns my rock ravine into a stairway to the sea, and beneath boulders and rough fragments–the wreck of ages–discovers a beach, I rate as of more value than some sermons and prayers."

Bartol died of bronchitis at his home on 16 December 1900. A funeral service was conducted at the Church of the Disciples by Charles G. Ames and Horatio Stebbins, a longtime friend. Many friends and former parishioners attended, including Julia Ward Howe and Booker T. Washington. Bartol was buried at Forest Hills Cemetery. F. B. Sanborn aptly observed that "Old Boston–the Boston of the first half of our century–may be said to have died with [him]." Indeed, of all those associated with the movement, only Moncure Conway, Thomas Wentworth Higginson, Ellery Channing, and Sanborn outlived Bartol. But Bartol alone could claim to have been instrumental in both the early and later phases of the movement, could claim in a sense, in the words of the anonymous writer in *Time and the Hour,* to be "the last of the Transcendentalists."

Bibliographies:

William G. Heath, "A Bibliography of the Writings of Cyrus Bartol," in *Cyrus Bartol, On Spirit and Personality,* edited by Heath (St. Paul, Minn.: John Colet, 1977), pp. 185–203;

Literary Writings in America: A Bibliography (Millwood, N.Y.: KTO, 1977).

References:

Charles G. Ames, "Cyrus Augustus Bartol," *Heralds of a Liberal Faith,* 3 volumes, edited by Samuel A. Eliot (Boston: American Unitarian Association, 1910), III: 17–22;

Lawrence Buell, *Literary Transcendentalism: Style and Vision in the American Renaissance* (Ithaca, N.Y.: Cornell University Press, 1973);

George Willis Cooke, *An Historical and Biographical Introduction to Accompany The Dial,* 2 volumes (Cleveland, Ohio: Rowfant Club, 1902);

"Cyrus Augustus Bartol," *Time and the Hour* (13 May 1899): 7–8;

Octavius Brooks Frothingham, *Transcendentalism in New England: A History* (New York: Putnams, 1876), pp. 341–343;

William G. Heath, "Cyrus Augustus Bartol," *The Transcendentalists: A Review of Research and Criticism,* edited by Joel Myerson (New York: Modern Language Association of America, 1984), pp. 97–99;

Heath, "Cyrus Bartol's Transcendental Capitalism," *Studies in the American Renaissance, 1979,* edited by Myerson (Boston: Twayne, 1979), pp. 399–408;

Heath, Introduction to *Cyrus Bartol, On Spirit and Personality* (St. Paul, Minn.: John Colet, 1977), pp. ix–xliv;

William R. Hutchison, "To Heaven in a Swing: The Transcendentalism of Cyrus Bartol," *Harvard Theological Review,* 56 (October 1963): 275–295;

Hutchison, *The Transcendentalist Ministers: Church Reform in the New England Renaissance* (New Haven: Yale University Press, 1959);

Darius Francis Lamson, *History of the Town of Manchester, Essex County, Massachusetts, 1645–1895* (Manchester: Published by the Town, 1895), pp. 192–195;

Guy R. Woodall, "Cyrus Augustus Bartol," *Biographical Dictionary of Transcendentalism,* edited by Wesley T. Mott (Westport, Conn.: Greenwood Press, 1996), pp. 14–16.

Papers:

Cyrus Augustus Bartol's "Memorandum Books, 1834–1848," "Sermon Book," and thirty-seven-year correspondence with Henry W. Bellows are housed in the Massachusetts Historical Society. The Houghton Library of Harvard University and the Boston Public Library possess additional Bartol letters.

Francis Bowen

(8 September 1811 - 21 January 1890)

William Rossi
University of Oregon

See also the Bowen entry in *DLB 59: American Literary Critics and Scholars, 1800–1850.*

BOOKS: *Critical Essays on a Few Subjects Connected with the History and Present Condition of Speculative Philosophy* (Boston: Williams, 1842);

Lowell Lectures, on the Application of Metaphysical and Ethical Science to the Evidences of Religion, Delivered Before the Lowell Institution in Boston, in the Winters of 1848–1849 (Boston: Little, Brown, 1849); revised as *The Principles of Metaphysical and Ethical Science Applied to the Evidences of Religion* (Boston: Little, Brown, 1855); annotated for use of colleges as *The Principles of Metaphysical and Ethical Science to the Evidences of Religion* (Boston: Hickling, Swan, & Brown, 1855);

The Principles of Political Economy, Applied to the Condition, the Resources, and the Institutions of the American People (Boston: Little, Brown, 1856); revised as *American Political Economy* (New York: Scribner, 1870);

A Treatise on Logic; or the Laws of Pure Thought, Comprising both the Aristotelic and Hamiltonian Analyses of Logical Forms and Some Chapters on Applied Logic (Cambridge, Mass.: Sever & Francis, 1864);

Modern Philosophy, from Descartes to Schopenhauer and Hartmann (New York: Scribner, Armstrong; London: Sampson Low, Marston, Searle & Rivington, 1877);

Gleanings from a Literary Life, 1838–1880 (New York: Scribners, 1880);

A Layman's Study of the English Bible, Considered in Its Literary and Secular Aspect (New York: Scribners, 1885).

OTHER: "Life of Sir William Phips," in *The Library of American Biography,* volume 7, first series, edited by Jared Sparks (Boston: Hilliard, Gray; London: Richard James Kennett, 1837), pp. 1–102;

"Life of Baron Steuben," in *The Library of American Biography,* first series, volume 9, edited by Sparks (Boston: Hilliard, Gray; London: Richard James Kennett, 1838), pp. 1–88;

Publius Maro Vergilius, *Bucolica, Georgica et Aeneis,* edited by Bowen (Boston: Williams, 1842);

"Life of James Otis," *The Library of American Biography,* second series, volume 2, edited by Sparks (Boston: Little, Brown, 1844), pp. 1–199;

"Life of Benjamin Lincoln," in *The Library of American Biography,* second series, volume 13, edited by Sparks (Boston: Little, Brown, 1847), pp. 205–434;

Georg Weber, *Outlines of Universal History, from the Creation of the World to the Present Time,* translated by M. Behr; edited, revised, and supplemented with a history of the United States of America by Bowen (Boston: Jenks, Hickling & Swan, 1853);

Documents of the Constitution of England and America, from Magna Charta to the Federal Constitution of 1789, compiled and edited, with notes, by Bowen (Cambridge, Mass.: Bartlett, 1854);

Dugald Stewart, *Elements of the Philosophy of the Human Mind,* revised and abridged, with notes for use in schools and colleges by Bowen (Boston: Munroe, 1854);

William Hamilton, *The Metaphysics of Sir William Hamilton,* collected, arranged, and abridged by Bowen (Boston: Allyn, 1861);

Alexis de Tocqueville, *Democracy in America,* translated by Henry Reeve, edited, with translations revised and supplemented by Bowen (Boston: Allyn / Cambridge, Mass.: Sever & Francis, 1862).

SELECTED PERIODICAL PUBLICATIONS–UNCOLLECTED: "Transcendentalism," *Christian Examiner,* 21 (January 1837): 371–385;

"A Theory of Creation," *North American Review,* 60 (April 1845): 426–478;

"The War of the Races in Hungary," *North American Review,* 70 (January 1850): 78–136;

"The Action of Congress on the California and Territorial Question," *North American Review,* 71 (July 1850): 221–268;

"The Rebellion of the Slavonic, Wallachian, and German Hungarians against the Magyars," *North American Review,* 72 (January 1851): 209–249.

Best known for his attack on the speculative and stylistic excesses of Ralph Waldo Emerson's *Nature* (1836), Francis Bowen was an outspoken opponent of philosophical and literary Transcendentalism during the controversial defining years of the movement between 1836 and 1842. A Unitarian and younger admirer of Andrews Norton, Bowen worked hard to rise into the Harvard establishment and then to defend Unitarian social and intellectual values against forces that threatened them. He was a fixture in Harvard philosophy for thirty-six years, contributing to the University Lectures for graduate students in 1869–1870, along with such men as Emerson, John Fiske, and Frederic Henry Hedge, and serving as an important, if little acknowledged, influence on his more famous students and colleagues Chauncey Wright, Charles Peirce, and William James.

Francis Bowen was born on 8 September 1811 in Charlestown, Massachusetts, to Dijah and Elizabeth (Flint) Bowen. Educated at the Mayhew Grammar School in Boston, Francis clerked in a publishing office there for a few years before entering Phillips Exeter Academy in January 1829 and then the sophomore class at Harvard College in 1830. For four years, while attending Exeter and Harvard, Bowen taught school at Hampton Falls, New Hampshire, and Lexington, Northborough, and Concord, Massachusetts, before graduating with highest honors in 1833. After teaching mathematics for one year at Exeter, he returned to Harvard for four years as a tutor of Greek and then instructor of philosophy and political economy. In 1839 Bowen resigned his instructorship for a year of travel in Europe, returning to Cambridge to continue his chosen profession of letters. On 1 November 1848 he married Arabella Stuart; they had a son and two daughters.

In 1837, in his first year as instructor at Harvard and eager to begin a literary career, the twenty-five-year-old Bowen stepped forward as the Unitarian spokesman against "the new school of philosophy" with two articles in the *Christian Examiner:* a review essay attacking Emerson's *Nature* as symptomatic of the errors of the movement and an essay on "Locke and the Transcendentalists." Published in January and November, Bowen's assaults followed on the heels of key Transcendentalist publications the year before by Emerson, George Ripley, Orestes Brownson, Elizabeth Peabody, and Bronson Alcott. The combined effect of Bowen's essays was to declare publicly a philosophical and theological schism between conservative Unitarians and their liberal brethren, a split soon exacerbated by the Miracles Controversy.

Because of the resemblance of *Nature* to contemporary treatises of natural theology, which sought to identify the attributes and effects of God in nature, Bowen approved of the subject and organization of the book, particularly up through "Discipline," a chapter he singled out for the "great energy and directness" with which "the lessons of Nature are enforced." But he objected strenuously to Emerson's poetic language, his endorsement of idealism, and the "vein of mysticism that pervades . . . [his] whole course of thought." As but "the latest representative" of the movement whose "adherents" have "dignified it with the title of Transcendentalism," the defects of *Nature* equally infected the writings of other Transcendentalists, defects Bowen attributed to the "foreign influence" of German and Coleridgean metaphysics. In addition to Emerson's apparent denial of the independent existence of material nature, the primary error of these writers was to have rejected rigorous empirical observation and induction in favor of intuitive modes of apprehending truth. Emerson wants his readers to dispense with logic, Bowen wrote sarcastically, "for the truths which are *felt* are more satisfactory and certain than those which are *proved*." Bowen deplored as well the importation of new philosophical terms and the mixing of poetic and philosophical discourses, both of which generated merely "a mirage of meaning" and "encourage[d] tyros to prate foolishly and flippantly about matters, which they can neither master nor comprehend." This preference for rarefied speculation, arcane terminology, and poetic expression, he suggested, rendered Transcendentalism inaccessible to all but a few and thus fundamentally undemocratic.

Two months later, in the first issue of his *Boston Quarterly Review,* Brownson responded directly to Bowen, countering that since the intuitive truths of "spontaneous reason" are "the property alike of all men," the true elitist was the "disciple of Locke" who denied intuitive access to universal truth and "look[ed] upon the instinctive beliefs of the masses with contempt." How, Brownson asked pointedly, will "those who [thus] rail against Humanity . . . save us from universal Skepticism?" As a conservative Christian moral philosopher, this question was, in fact, Bowen's most fundamental concern–that what he saw as the skeptical influence of Transcendentalism and of "foreign" metaphysics generally would undermine the religious foundations and moral fabric of American society.

In a series of review essays published in the *Christian Examiner* and the *North American Review* over the next four years, Bowen undertook to stem this tide by examining the link between epistemological and religious skepticism in the continental sources of Transcendentalist thought. Collected in 1842 with "Locke and the Transcendentalists" and other pieces as *Critical Essays on a Few Subjects Connected with the History and Present Condition of Speculative Philosophy,* these essays constitute Bowen's most sustained effort to undermine "the growth of a native [that is, Transcendentalist] school of speculative philosophy." In contrast to his first polemical attacks, however, these essays aim to acquaint his educated audience with the chief arguments and technical terminology of European philosophy while at the same time identifying the practical and spiritual consequences of Immanuel Kant's strictures on knowing noumenal reality, Johann Gottlieb Fichte's deification of conscience, Victor Cousin's substitution of universal reason for the activity of an autonomous thinking self, and the anti-empiricism of Bishop George Berkeley. Because these philosophers relied on a priori reasoning, Bowen argued, they substituted an abstraction or a mere "universal idea" for the actual being and personality of God. Without naming names, he concluded that the like views held by his contemporaries must therefore be reckoned as "downright atheism." Besides countering this pernicious tendency, Bowen also wished, more positively, to showcase the superiority of British empiricism and to establish a native American school of philosophy along lines begun by Edinburgh philosophers Dugald Stewart and Sir William Hamilton. Toward this end he developed the Scottish Common Sense position that philosophy, or "mental science," should be grounded in the observed evidence of the senses, an inductive empirical method as trustworthy in metaphysics and theology as it had proved to be in physical science. For Bowen, as for other Harvard Unitarian moral philosophers, the exemplar of this method in theology, employing a mode of reasoning "substantially the same" as that "of Bacon and Locke," was Archbishop William Paley, whose popular natural theology Bowen defended and further elaborated in two long essays. Reasoning from experience rather than from intuition, Bowen sought to reestablish the independent existence of material nature, the personal being of God, and the reality of a unified moral self necessarily in touch with both. These essays proved to be the germ of two lecture courses Bowen delivered during the winters of 1848 and 1849 at the prestigious Lowell Institute on "The Application of Metaphysical and Ethical Science to the Evidences of Religion," a work he subsequently revised as both a popular and a college text.

In 1843 Bowen became chief owner and editor of the *North American Review*. Never friendly to Transcendentalist writers, during Bowen's ten-year term the journal developed a reputation for dull respectability, a quality that led Henry David Thoreau to boast in his journal that "it is one of my qualifications that I have not written an article for the N.A. Review" and to dismiss it as a "venerable cobweb . . . which has hither to [*sic*] escaped the broom." An active contributor, Bowen's writings exhibited his pugnacious spirit, penetrating intellect, and conservative politics. In the first extensive American review of the evolutionary tract *Vestiges of the Natural History of Creation,* published anonymously by Robert Chambers in 1844, Bowen provided a detailed summary and then dismissed Chambers's naturalistic account of the origin and development of organic life as newfangled atheistic materialism. As a Cotton Whig, Bowen's views on slavery continued the opposition of the *North American Review* to immediate emancipation, while supporting the 1850 Compromise and the Fugitive Slave Law. Against the tide of popular support for the Hungarian revolution and its leader, Lajos Kossuth, in 1850 Bowen condemned Kossuth's cause as a sham that would only extend Austrian despotism in another form. The furor in Boston over Bowen's essays so angered ex officio politicians on Harvard's Board of Overseers that his appointment as McLean Professor of History (made by Jared Sparks when he became president of Harvard in 1850) was rescinded.

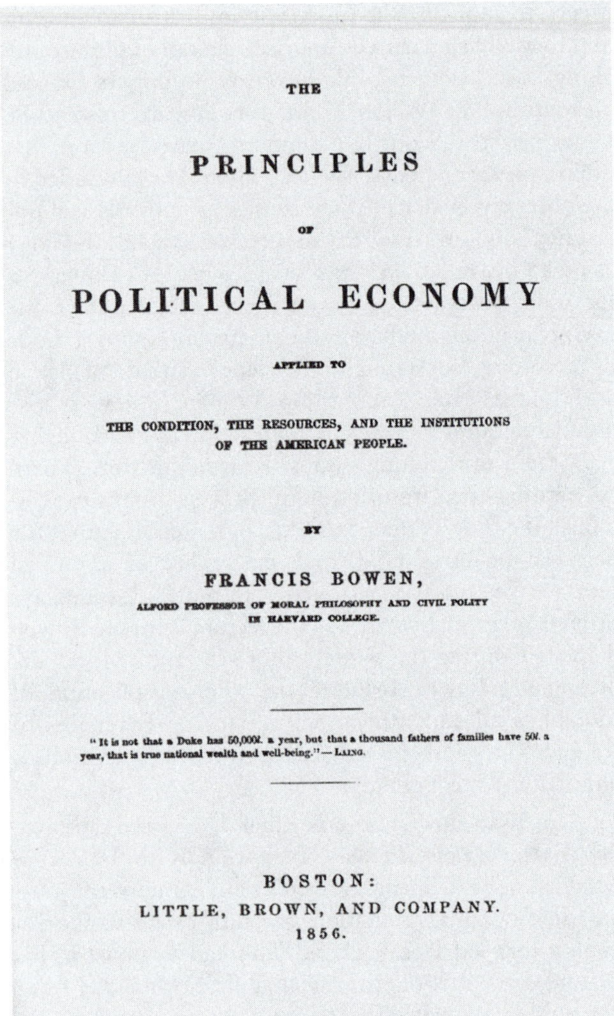
THE

PRINCIPLES

OF

POLITICAL ECONOMY

APPLIED TO

THE CONDITION, THE RESOURCES, AND THE INSTITUTIONS
OF THE AMERICAN PEOPLE.

BY

FRANCIS BOWEN,

ALFORD PROFESSOR OF MORAL PHILOSOPHY AND CIVIL POLITY
IN HARVARD COLLEGE.

"It is not that a Duke has 50,000*l.* a year, but that a thousand fathers of families have 50*l.* a year, that is true national wealth and well-being."—LAING.

BOSTON:
LITTLE, BROWN, AND COMPANY.
1856.

Title page for the book in which Bowen applied Adam Smith's economic theories to America

In 1853, however, Bowen was appointed Alford Professor of Natural Religion, Moral Philosophy, and Civil Polity (no doubt partly on the strength of his Lowell lectures), a position he held for thirty-six years. Although with academic specialization these areas soon became distinct domains, for Unitarian moral philosophers particularly, natural religion, moral philosophy, and civil polity (comprising what is now sociology and political science) were intimately linked. For them, the possibility of moral and spiritual achievement required a foundation of material prosperity, and the "harmony" established between material and moral elevation appeared to testify to the same benevolent Providence evident in the natural world. Bowen's belief in this harmonious order and his admiration for "the merchant princes of Boston" are evident in *The Principles of Political Economy,* a work published in 1856 that adapted the classical economics of Adam Smith to the American scene. In it Bowen defended the security of property as necessary for the growth of capital and argued that (with the exception of moderate, temporary protection for the developing industries of the United States) laissez-faire principles best facilitated the smooth operation of economic laws and the "beneficent designs of Providence in the constitution of society."

While he hoped this book would have an impact on statesmen and legislators, Bowen's immediate audience was his students. Responsible for instructing students in political economy as well as philosophy and believing that inculcating information through textbooks and manuals rather than lecturing better served the purposes of education, Bowen prepared several texts for college use, including editions of Dugald Stewart's *Elements of the Philosophy of the Human Mind* in 1854, Sir William Hamilton's metaphysics in 1861, and Alexis de Tocqueville's *Democracy in America* in 1862. In addition to *Principles of Political Economy* and a revision of the Lowell lectures, he wrote his own text on logic as well as *Modern Philosophy, from Descartes to Schopenhauer and Hartmann* (1877), according to Bruce Kuklick "the finest history of modern philosophy produced by a Harvard scholar."

Outside Harvard during these years, Bowen continued a strong conservative voice in public affairs, advocating traditional liberal arts education based in the study of classical literature over "utilitarian studies," opposing increases in the national debt, and staunchly defending orthodoxy and Christian theism. A tireless adversary of Charles Darwin's development theory and of the philosophical materialism he believed it encouraged, Bowen contributed many essays during the 1860s, 1870s, and 1880s against "the dirt philosophy," several of which he collected in *Gleanings from a Literary Life, 1838–1880* (1880). In his review of Darwin's *On the Origin of Species* (1859), he praised Darwin's ability and his candor at admitting the weaknesses of his theory. But Bowen saw clearly that the theory would destroy the basis for the traditional argument from design he had himself developed from Paley. Attacking the most empirically vulnerable of these points, the absence of "any direct proof" of transmutation "either from observation or testimony" and the vast time required by Darwin's hypothesis for evolution to work, Bowen recurred to an argument similar to that advanced in a different setting by Emerson and William Henry Furness twenty years earlier–that the continuous activity of God in creation, a process "constantly going on all around us," is a miracle "wholly inexplicable" by science.

Bowen came to fear that widespread acceptance of Darminian materialism, besides invalidating traditional natural theology, Bowen came to fear that widespread acceptance of Darwinian materialism would foster pessimism, leading to catastrophic moral and social consequences, particularly among the educated classes. Increasingly demoralized by "the Philosophy of Despair," less and less willing to reproduce and train their kind, these classes would eventually suffer extinction along with the refinement and values they represented. Bowen's stance against materialism also led him in later life to shift allegiance away from common sense realism toward Kantian constructivism, an interesting reversal, considering he had begun his career by attacking Transcendentalism. For whereas, in the prevailing philosophical climate, emphasizing the independent existence of material nature could be tantamount to granting that mind was only an epiphenomenal effect of matter, acknowledging the constructive power of mind now helped Bowen affirm the spiritual ontology of the self.

In 1889 Francis Bowen retired; he died six months later on 21 January 1890, the only Harvard Unitarian moral philosopher to remain active after the Civil War. As an ardent intellectual and social conservative, Bowen ultimately resisted more of the dramatic postwar transformations of American life than he either adapted to or affected. His greatest impact was as a philosophical writer and historian of philosophy. As his early opposition to Transcendentalism had served to define sharply the epistemological and metaphysical underpinnings of Boston Unitarianism, so his later teaching and philosophical work at Harvard, his interest in the extension of consciousness into bodily experience, and his concern for the pragmatic application of ideas left their marks on a new generation of American philosophers.

References:

Joseph Dorfman, *The Economic Mind in American Civilization: 1606–1865,* volume 2 (New York: Viking, 1946), pp. 835–844;

Waldo Higginson, ed., *Memorials of the Class of 1833 of Harvard College* (Cambridge, Mass.: Wilson, 1883), pp. 100–103;

Daniel Walker Howe, *The Unitarian Conscience: Harvard Moral Philosophy, 1805–1861,* revised edition (Middletown, Conn.: Wesleyan University Press, 1988);

Bruce Kuklick, *The Rise of American Philosophy: Cambridge, Massachusetts, 1860–1930* (New Haven: Yale University Press, 1977);

Perry Miller, ed., *The Transcendentalists: An Anthology* (Cambridge, Mass.: Harvard University Press, 1950);

Frank Luther Mott, *A History of American Magazines,* 5 volumes (Cambridge, Mass.: Harvard University Press, 1938–1968), II: 219–245;

David Robinson, *The Unitarians and the Universalists* (Westport, Conn.: Greenwood Press, 1985).

Papers:

A small collection of Francis Bowen's papers (1860–1882) is in the Harvard Archives; his correspondence and materials relevant to the *North American Review* are held in the Houghton Library, Harvard University.

Edward Tyrrel Channing

(12 December 1790 - 8 February 1856)

Alfred G. Litton
Texas Woman's University

See also the Channing entry in *DLB 59: American Literary Critics and Scholars, 1800–1850s.*

BOOKS: *An Oration Delivered July 4, 1817, at the Request of the Selectmen of the Town of Boston, in Commemoration of the Anniversary of American Independence* (Boston: Buckingham, 1817);

Inaugural Discourse Delivered in the Chapel of the University in Cambridge, December 8, 1819 (Cambridge, Mass.: Hilliard & Metcalf, 1819);

Lectures Read to the Seniors in Harvard University (Boston: Ticknor & Fields, 1856).

SELECTED PERIODICAL PUBLICATIONS–UNCOLLECTED: "On Models in Literature," *North American Review,* 3 (July 1816): 202–209;

"Philosophical Essays. By James Ogilvie," *North American Review,* 4 (March 1817): 378–408;

"A Review of *Two Years Before the Mast,*" *North American Review,* 52 (January 1841): 56–75.

Edward Tyrrel Channing, circa 1852 (portrait by G. P. A. Healy; Harvard University Portrait Collection)

Edward Tyrrel Channing was, arguably, the most influential American rhetorician of the nineteenth century. A roster of Channing's students reads like a "Who's Who" of nineteenth-century American letters. Ralph Waldo Emerson, Henry David Thoreau, Oliver Wendell Holmes, Richard Henry Dana Jr., Francis Parkman, Edward Everett Hale, and many others shared in common the tremendous influence of Channing's rhetorical instruction at Harvard College during the middle decades of the century. Though neither an educational innovator nor a revolutionary in the field of rhetorical theory, Channing's devotion to demanding standards of style and organization and his passionate views on the role of the orator and writer in a democratic society left indelible impressions upon an entire generation of American writers and statesmen.

Edward Tyrrel Channing was born on 12 December 1790 in Newport, Rhode Island, to William and Lucy (Ellery) Channing. The youngest of nine children, Edward (or "Ned" as he was later called by close friends) was a member of a highly successful New England family. His father, a distinguished lawyer, had been the district attorney of the United States, as well as the attorney general of the state of Massachusetts until his death in 1793. His mother, an educated and highly respected daughter of William Ellery, proved more than capable of raising her many children, even after being widowed at age forty-one. Edward's older brother, William Ellery Channing, became one of the most important religious figures of the century, leading the newly established Unitarian denomination in its earliest years; his other siblings distinguished themselves as physicians, lawyers, and university professors. Like his brothers, Edward was educated at Harvard College, which he entered in 1804 and where he would have graduated in 1808 had he not participated in the celebrated student rebellion of 1807. Though he eventually received the degree, Edward was far more interested in pursuing a legal career (under the tutelage of his older brother Francis Dana Channing) in his first years out of Harvard than in an academic career, but within a few years Channing's interests became primarily literary.

The change in Channing's career was brought about in no small part by his participation in a small club of young men who, in the winter of 1814–1815, began what became one of the most influential American magazines of the nineteenth century, the *North American Review*. Together with men such as John Kirkland, Dana, and Josiah Quincy, Channing saw an opportunity to create a literary review that would foster a distinctively American literary culture and would provide an outlet for the writers of the new nation. In time, the periodical grew to be one of the most respected literary reviews in the United States. Channing contributed to the growth of the magazine through his membership in the editorial club and later through his brief editorship of the publication with Dana. His essay "On Models in Literature" (1816) warned about the use of exemplary literary texts in helping students cultivate good writing style. The work went beyond the standard nationalistic condemnation of foreign works and argued that genius suffers from too much "reading and obeying." A year later, Channing expanded upon his thoughts regarding literary and rhetorical education by publishing his review of James Ogilvie's *Philosophical Essays* (1816), a work in which he praised the style of the British writer while maintaining his view that great literary stylists should not be memorized by students but should be placed on the shelves of libraries for students to consult in their leisure hours. These thoughtful pieces foreshadowed both his interest in rhetorical education and his vigorous defense of radical individualism in matters of literary style. Channing's considerable reviews for the *North American Review* enhanced his reputation as an astute literary critic and opened the path to the academic career for which he has been remembered.

The academic post to which Channing aspired was the Boylston Professorship of Rhetoric and Oratory at Harvard College. Established by Nicholas Boylston in 1771, the post remained unfilled for more than forty years. John Quincy Adams first held the position, serving from 1806 to 1809, and he was followed by Joseph McKean from 1809 until his death in 1818. Adams had been a classicist, and his *Lectures on Rhetoric and Oratory* (1810) demonstrated a complete commitment to the ancient Greek and Roman models of oratory. Since the statute of the endowment stipulated that the holder of the Boylston Chair teach rhetoric and oratory from the classical model, Adams was a perfect theoretical fit for the position. But as the unenthusiastic reception of his *Lectures on Rhetoric and Oratory* illustrates, the classical approach had largely fallen out of favor by his time. McKean, actually more a mathematician than a rhetorician, was appointed principally because he had had a successful ministerial career. In the decade in which he held the post, he made no substantive changes or innovations. Thus, for its first fifteen years, the Boylston professorship remained a rather undistinguished position. That changed when, in the fall of 1819, the corporation at Harvard elected Edward Channing to fill the post.

When Channing was appointed the Boylston Professor of Rhetoric and Oratory at Harvard in 1819, he ushered in a new era of rhetorical instruction at the school. Channing's election proved to be controversial. Some pointed to his participation in the 1807 student rebellions while others contended that his election owed much to the influence of his older brother William Ellery Channing. Those who were critical of the appointment made their sentiments clear in letters to the *Boston Daily Advertiser* and other papers. The controversy centered as much on Channing's views of literature and rhetoric as upon his preparation for the post, for his ascension signaled the death of the classical tradition and the triumph of the enlightenment rhetorical philosophies of George Campbell, Hugh Blair, and Richard Whately, which wedded literary criticism with rhetorical theory. These eighteenth-century British rhetoricians were just as concerned with the cultivation of literary style as they were with developing skill in public oratory. Additionally, for these neoclassical theorists, whose assumptions concerning just about every aspect of the discourse act were heavily influenced by the epistemology of Locke, the goal of rhetoric was for the speaker or writer to appeal to the "faculties" of the auditor, to reproduce the original experiences of the observer through the use of language. In such a system, the seat of reality is external, and the communication process is viewed as essentially a mimetic act. Channing's definition of rhetoric as "a body of rules derived from experience and observation, extending to all communication by language and designed to make it efficient" reflects the degree to which he concurred with the leading eighteenth-century British rhetoricians, and Channing's lectures, pedagogical approaches, and assignments were also consistent with their assumptions about the nature and function of rhetoric.

Before he had even been offered the Boylston position, Channing had made his thoughts on oratory and citizenship well known to the Boston elite. In fact, there is little doubt that his impressive *An Oration Deliv-*

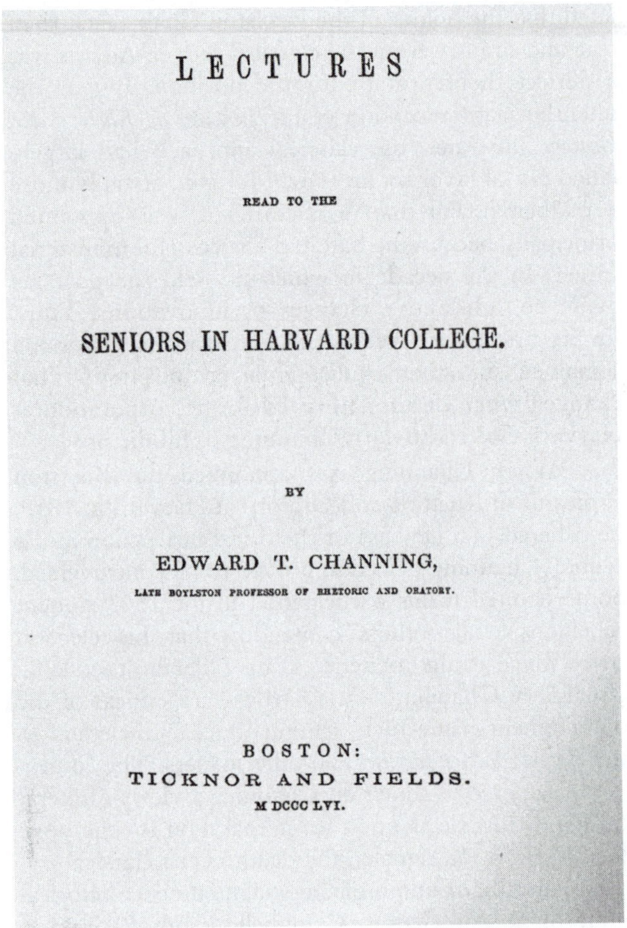
LECTURES

READ TO THE

SENIORS IN HARVARD COLLEGE.

BY

EDWARD T. CHANNING,

LATE BOYLSTON PROFESSOR OF RHETORIC AND ORATORY.

BOSTON:
TICKNOR AND FIELDS.
M DCCC LVI.

Title page for the posthumous collection of Channing's lectures, including one in which he describes the ideal democratic orator

ered July 4, 1817, at the Request of the Selectmen of the Town of Boston, in Commemoration of the Anniversary of American Independence (1817) contributed greatly to his reputation as an eloquent speaker and as a perceptive social and political thinker. In his praise of the "new order of things" and "new growth of society" Channing's staunch Federalism tempers his nationalistic views. The leaders of the American Revolution, he argues, "were not compelled to practice arts upon the multitude, to kindle them into rebellion . . . they were not a crowd of hot-headed boys . . . they were men of great soberness and forecast." In the aftermath of the French Revolution, Channing was concerned that the new American political leadership maintain "a sound judgment" and not use oratory for the purposes of demagoguery. His ideal orator-statesman was one who not only did not reject all things European but also acted as a restraining force on the "mob" of libertines who inevitably (in his mind) rise to positions of influence in the wake of a popular revolution. Thus, Channing's interest in rhetoric, though strongly influenced by his ideas on literary style, were partly political as well. For Channing, how rhetorical instruction was offered to the future leaders of the new nation would determine, in part, the success or failure of its newly established political institutions and also its ability to define its own cultural voice.

From his earliest months at Harvard, Channing strove to put these ideals into practice. His *Inaugural Discourse Delivered in the Chapel of the University in Cambridge, December 8, 1819* sets forth clearly his vision of rhetorical instruction, and that vision expanded and became more detailed as he delivered his lectures. Though not collected and published until shortly after his death, Channing's *Lectures Read to the Seniors in Harvard College* (1856) include his most powerful and thoughtful works delivered throughout the three decades of his tenure at the university and cover a broad range of subjects, from matters of elocution to literary composition to more-philosophical works touching on the subject of the orator himself. In what is perhaps his most famous lecture from the collection, "The Orator and His Times," Channing discusses in depth the characteristics of his ideal democratic orator. The portrait of such an individual is a study in contradictions. Such an orator must be democratic though ever distrustful of the mass of men, a populist in sentiment but an elitist in practice, one who knows (even better than the general public) what is in the best interest of society but who must, nevertheless, obtain consent from the populace using his own persuasive abilities. As a defender of the establishment, Channing's orator is no militant activist. For him, it is "one of the happiest and we trust most permanent distinctions between our state of society [that is, a constitutional republic] and the ancient . . . that the power of the individual is lessened; we do not encourage any man to aspire after an overwhelming greatness and sway." The diminished power of the modern orator means that "He can no longer be a despot, either to save freedom or destroy it. He is not the important personage he once was."

Unquestionably, Channing's ideal orator was something new in rhetorical history. Far, indeed, from the orator Cicero or even Quintillian had envisioned, the new American orator was one who was to help the mass of men avoid, at all cost, the anarchy and brutality that had followed the French Revolution. Naturally, Channing felt strongly that he must instill in his students an appreciation of their responsibilities as part of the intellectual elite of the new nation. These were to be the writers, orators, clergymen, and statesmen who, first and foremost, defended the established institutions against the ever-changing passions of the mob. Many of the essay topics that Channing assigned reflect this view as well. Topics ranging from "What is

Meant by Popular Feelings?" to "The Methods of Gaining or Exercising Public Influence" to "The Duties, Inconvenience, and Dangers of Conformity" all required students to consider carefully the roles of writers and public speakers in a democratic society and the relationships those writers and speakers have with the public. An examination of Thoreau's essays written for Channing's classes demonstrates just how influential the rhetoric professor's assignments were on the aspiring writer. Thoreau's earliest compositions for Channing's classes compelled him to explore and refine ideas that later recurred throughout his writings. Responding to Channing's topic on conformity, for example, Thoreau characteristically writes of the need to conform to the dictates of an inward arbiter. In the many essay assignments in which students were called on to discuss their ideas of literary accomplishment, Thoreau and other students were allowed to explore their own thoughts on such subjects, albeit with the sometimes imposing and always opinionated figure of the conservative Channing serving as critic. One can only speculate on the influence that Channing's own lectures on "Permanent Literary Fame," "A Writer's Preparation," and "A Writer's Habits" had upon students such as Thoreau, Holmes, and James Russell Lowell.

Students could rely on Channing to be open to new ideas, but they also were well aware that they had better be prepared to defend those ideas if they differed from Channing's. In the classroom, Channing could be quite a daunting figure. His practice of conferring individually with each student for each composition might have been laudable, but his audible critiques were dreaded by even the most accomplished student. As Hale recalled, no detail escaped Channing's eye: "you sat down in the recitation-room, and were called man by man, or boy by boy, in the order in which you came into the room; you therefore heard his criticism on each of your predecessors. 'Why do you write with blue ink on blue paper? When I was young, we wrote with black ink on white paper . . . Hale, you do not mean to say that you think a Grub Street hack is the superior of John Milton?'" Thomas Wentworth Higginson recalled that "never in my life have I had to meet such exacting criticism on anything written as came from Professor Channing, and never have I had any praise so encouraging as his." Later in his life, Hale contended that Channing's students absorbed their teacher's stylistic, mechanical, and organizational habits so completely that he could recognize whether a man graduated from Harvard before or after Channing retired in 1851.

Channing married Henrietta Abby Shaw Ellery in 1826, and though their union was a long and apparently happy one, they did not have children. The couple seems to have had close relationships, however, with many students over the years as Richard Henry Dana Jr.'s recollections of Channing's weekly Saturday dinners and the voluntary reading classes held in Channing's study attest. Many of his former students recalled his wit and eloquence in conversation, but nearly all acknowledged a sense of reserve and a constant concern with decorum and propriety. His sense of humor, though generally acknowledged, was used sparingly. Channing seems to have been as conservative in his private life as he was in his political views.

Earlier in his career, he had decided to retire at the age of sixty, and in 1851, he resigned his post after thirty-two years of service. In his later years, Channing continued to contribute literary reviews to the *North American Review,* most notably his favorable review in 1841 of Dana's *Two Years Before the Mast* (1840), but the strenuous workload of teaching and lecturing proved too great to allow for extensive writing. His writing and speaking style have been remembered for the biting satire (and occasional sarcasm) that he employed. Far more important than his own writing or lectures, however, was the important contribution Channing made to Harvard's growing reputation in the nineteenth century as the hub of literary achievement. In ways his predecessors could not, Channing was able to take instruction in composition and oratory to a new level, one appropriate to the changing era his students found themselves emerging into. Along the way, he trained an entire generation of writers and thinkers and compelled them to confront essentially American issues in the classrooms, halls, and meeting rooms. He did so from the perspective of one who maintained a new vision of the mission and style of American oratory. Perhaps more than any other figure, then, Channing deserves to be regarded as the first truly American rhetorician.

Channing died on 8 February 1856 while still preparing his lectures on literature and rhetoric for publication. His students published the works without alteration and saw the project through to completion in that year. He is buried beside his brother William in the famed Mount Auburn Cemetery of Cambridge, Massachusetts.

References:

Dorothy I. Anderson, "Edward T. Channing's Definition of Rhetoric," *Speech Monographs,* 14 (1947): 81–92;

Anderson, "Edward T. Channing's Teaching of Rhetoric," *Speech Monographs,* 16 (1949): 69–81;

Anderson and Waldo W. Braden, "Introduction" to Edward T. Channing, *Lectures Read to the Seniors in*

Harvard College (Carbondale: Southern Illinois University Press, 1968), pp. ix–lii;

Kenneth Walter Cameron, "Thoreau, Edward Tyrrel Channing and College Themes," *Emerson Society Quarterly,* no. 42 (First Quarter 1966): 15–34;

Richard Henry Dana Jr., "Biographical Notice," in Edward T. Channing, *Lectures Read to the Seniors in Harvard College* (Boston: Ticknor & Fields, 1856), pp. vii–xx;

Richard H. Dillman, "Thoreau's Harvard Education in Rhetoric and Composition: 1833–1837," *Thoreau Journal Quarterly,* 13 (July–October 1981): 49–62;

Nan Johnson, *Nineteenth-Century Rhetoric in North America* (Carbondale: Southern Illinois University Press, 1991);

Elizabeth Larsen, "The Progress of Literacy: Edward Tyrrel Channing and the Separation of the Student Writer from the World," *Rhetoric Review,* 11 (1992): 159–171;

Andrew W. Peabody, "Edward Tyrrel Channing," in *Harvard Reminiscences* (Boston: Ticknor, 1888), pp. 84–90;

Ronald F. Reid, "The Boylston Professorship of Rhetoric and Oratory, 1806–1904: A Case Study in Changing Concepts of Rhetoric and Pedagogy," *Quarterly Journal of Speech,* 45 (October 1959): 239–257.

Papers:

A single volume of manuscript material from Edward Tyrrel Channing himself can be found in the Papers of Edward Tyrrel Channing at the Harvard University Archives. This collection should be consulted for the nearly nine hundred "Subjects Which I Gave out for Themes" that Channing passed on to his successor. The William Ellery Channing Papers at the Houghton Library of Harvard University include family correspondence–in particular, some of Edward Channing's letters to his brother. Letters from Channing can also be found in the Claude Halstead Van Tyne Papers at the Bentley Historical Library of the University of Michigan, Ann Arbor.

William Ellery Channing

(7 April 1780 – 2 October 1842)

David M. Robinson
Oregon State University

See also the Channing entry in *DLB 59: American Literary Critics and Scholars, 1800–1850.*

William Ellery Channing (portrait attributed to Washington Allston; from Madeleine Hooke Rice, Federal Street Pastor: The Life of William Ellery Channing, *1961)*

BOOKS: *The Duties of Children. A Sermon Delivered on Lord's Day, April 12, 1807, to the Religious Society in Federal Street, Boston* (Boston: Manning & Loring, 1807; Liverpool: F. B. Wright, 1828);

A Sermon, Delivered at the Ordination of the Rev. John Codman, to the Pastoral Care of the Second Church of Christ in Dorchester, Dec. 7, 1808 (Boston: Joshua Belcher, 1808);

A Sermon Preached in Boston, April 5, 1810, the Day of the Public Fast (Boston: John Eliot, 1810; Boston: Samuel Avery, 1810);

A Sermon Preached in Boston, July 23, 1812, the Day of the Publick Fast, Appointed by the Executive of the Commonwealth Massachusetts, in Consequence of the Declaration of War Against Great Britain (Boston: Greenough & Stebbins, 1812; Boston: Greenough & Stebbins / Birmingham, U.K.: C. Wilks, 1812);

A Sermon Preached in Boston, August 20, 1812, the Day of Humiliation and Prayer, Appointed by the President of the United States, in Consequence of the Declaration of War Against Great Britain (Boston: C. Stebbins, 1812);

Elements of Religion and Morality in the Form of a Catechism (Boston: John Eliot, 1813);

Two Sermons on Infidelity, Delivered October 24, 1813 (Boston: Cummings & Hilliard / Cambridge, Mass.: Hilliard & Metcalf, 1813);

A Discourse, Delivered in Boston at the Solemn Festival in Commemoration of the Goodness of God in Delivering the Christian World from Military Despotism, June 15, 1814 (Boston: Henry Channing / Cambridge, Mass.: Hilliard & Metcalf, 1814; London: J & J Hardy, 1815?);

A Sermon, Delivered in Boston, September 18, 1814 (Boston: Henry Channing, 1814);

A Letter to the Rev. Samuel C. Thacher, on the Aspersions Contained in a Late Number of the Panoplist, on the Ministers of Boston and the Vicinity (Boston: Wells & Lilly, 1815);

Observations on the Proposition for Increasing the Means of Theological Education at the University in Cambridge (Cambridge, Mass.: Hilliard & Metcalf, 1815);

Remarks on the Rev. Dr. Worcester's Letter to Mr. Channing, on the "Review of American Unitarianism" in a Late Panoplist (Boston: Wells & Lilly, 1815);

Remarks on the Rev. Dr. Worcester's Second Letter to Mr. Channing, On American Unitarianism (Boston: Wells & Lilly, 1815);

A Sermon, Delivered at the Ordination of the Rev. John Emery Abbot to the Pastoral Care of the North Church of Christ in Salem, April 20, 1815 (Salem: Thomas C. Cushing, 1815);

A Sermon on War: Delivered before the Convention of Congregational Ministers of Massachusetts, May 30, 1816 (Boston: Wells & Lilly, 1816);

An Examination of Passages of Scripture Supposed to Prove the Deity of Jesus Christ (Boston: Bowles, 1819; Liverpool: F. B. Wright, 1828);

A Letter to Professor Stuart, in Answer to his Letters to Rev. William E. Channing, and in Vindication of a Large and Respectable Body of the New England and Other Clergy, From the Unfounded Aspersions Cast on Them, in Said Letters, anonymous (Boston: Sylvester T. Goss, 1819);

Objections to Unitarian Christianity Considered (Boston: Christian Register Office, 1819; London: R. Hunter, 1831?; London: Smallfield, 1831);

A Sermon Delivered at the Ordination of the Rev. Jared Sparks, to the Pastoral Care of the First Independent Church in Baltimore, May 5, 1819 (Baltimore: Benjamin Edes, 1819; Newcastle, U.K.: J. Marshall, 1820);

Note for the Second Baltimore Edition, of the Rev. Mr. Channing's Sermon, Delivered at the Ordination of the Rev. Jared Sparks. Together With a Table of Errata, in the Baltimore and Boston Editions of That Publication (Boston: Hews & Gross, 1819);

Religion a Social Principle. A Sermon, Delivered in the Church in Federal Street, Boston, December 10, 1820 (Boston: Russell & Gardner, 1820);

Memoir of John Gallison, Esq. (Boston: Wells & Lilly, 1821); republished as *Christian Biography. A Memoir of John Gallison, Esq. of Boston in New England, Counsellor at Law, Who Died Dec. 24, 1820, Aged 32 Years* (Bristol, U.K.: William Browne, 1828);

A Discourse on the Evidences of Revealed Religion, Delivered before the University in Cambridge, at the Dudleian Lecture, March 14, 1821 (Boston: Cummings & Hilliard, 1821; Bristol, U.K.: Parsons & Browne, 1822);

A Sermon, Delivered at the Ordination of the Rev. Ezra Stiles Gannett, as Colleague Pastor of the Church of Christ, in Federal Street, Boston, June 30, 1824 (Boston: Christian Register Office, 1824); republished as *Christianity Adapted to Every Age and Condition of Mankind* (Liverpool: F. B. Wright, 1824);

Discourse Delivered at the Dedication of Divinity Hall, Cambridge, 1826 (Boston: Carter & Hendee, 1826);

Remarks on the Character and Writings of John Milton; Occasioned by the Publication of His Lately Discovered "Treatise on Christian Doctrine" (Boston: Isaac R. Butts, 1826; London: Edward Rainford, 1826);

A Discourse, Preached at the Dedication of the Second Congregational Unitarian Church, New-York, December 7, 1826 (New York: Second Congregational Unitarian Church, 1826); republished as *The Superior Tendency of Unitarianism to Form an Elevated Religious Character* (Liverpool: F. B. Wright, 1827);

Remarks on the Character of Napoleon Bonaparte, Occasioned by the Publication of Scott's Life of Napoleon (Boston: Bowles & Dearborn, 1827; Boston: Bowles & Dearborn / Liverpool: W. Wales, 1828); republished as *Analysis of the Character of Napoleon Bonaparte, Suggested by the Publication of Scott's Life of Napoleon* (London: Edward Rainford, 1828);

A Continuation of Remarks on the Character of Napoleon Bonaparte, Occasioned by Publication of Scott's Life of Napoleon (Boston: Bowles & Dearborn, 1828); republished as *Thoughts on Power and Greatness, Political, Intellectual, and Moral; in Continuation of an Analysis of the Character of Napoleon Bonaparte* (London: Edward Rainford, 1828);

A Discourse Delivered at the Installation of the Rev. Mellish Irving Motte, as Pastor of the South Congregational Society, in Boston, May 21, 1828 (Boston: Bowles & Dearborn, 1828; London: R. Hunter, 1828); republished as *The Great Design of Christianity. A Discourse, Delivered at the Installation of the Rev. Mellish Irving Motte, as Pastor of the South Congregational Society, in Boston, May 21st, 1828* (Liverpool: F. B. Wright, 1828);

A Discourse Delivered at the Ordination of the Rev. Frederick A. Farley, as Pastor of the Westminster Congregational Society in Providence, Rhode Island, September 10, 1828 (Boston: Bowles & Dearborn, 1828; London: Edward Rainford, 1829); republished as *Man the Image of His Maker. A Discourse Delivered at the Ordination of the Rev. Frederick A. Farley, as Pastor of the Westminster Congregational Society, in Providence, Rhode Island, September 10, 1828* (Liverpool: F. B. Wright, 1829);

Sermons and Tracts, Including the Analysis of the Character of Napoleon Bonaparte and Remarks on the Writings of John Milton (London: R. Hunter, 1828);

Remarks on the Character and Writings of Fenelon (London: Edward Rainford, 1829); republished as *An Essay, on the Character and Writings of Fenelon* (Liverpool: F. B. Wright, 1829);

Discourses, Reviews and Miscellanies (Boston: Carter & Hendee, 1830); republished in 2 volumes (London: John Mardon, 1834; London: O. Rich, 1834);

The Importance and Means of a National Literature (London: Edward Rainford, 1830);

Remarks on the Disposition Which Now Prevails to Form Associations, and to Accomplish All Objects by Organized Masses (London: Edward Rainford, 1830);

A Sermon, Preached at the Annual Election, May 26, 1830, Before His Excellency Levi Lincoln, Governor, His Honor Thomas L. Winthrop, Lieutenant Governor, the Honorable Council, and the Legislature of Massachusetts (Boston: Carter & Hendee, 1830; London: British & Foreign Unitarian Association, 1830);

The System of Exclusion and Denunciation Considered (London: R. Hunter, 1831?);

Discourses (Boston: Charles Bowen, 1832; London: Richard James Kennett, 1833);

Remarks on the Associations Formed by the Working Classes of America, Designed to Relieve the Distresses of Mechanics and Their Families, to Promote Inventions and Improvements in the Mechanic Art, by Granting Premiums and Assisting Young Mechanics by Loans of Money (London: John Mardon, 1833);

Political Writings of W. E. Channing, D. D., of Boston (Edinburgh: W. Tait, 1835);

The Future Life. A Sermon Preached on Easter Sunday, 1834, in the Federal Street Church, Boston (Boston: James Munroe, 1835; London: John Mardon, 1836);

A Sermon on War, Delivered January 25, 1835 (Boston: Homer & Palmer, 1835); republished as *On War. A Discourse* (London: R. Hunter / John Mardon / Manchester: T. Forrest, 1835);

The Ministry for the Poor. A Discourse Delivered Before the Benevolent Fraternity of Churches in Boston, on Their First Anniversary, April 9, 1835 (Boston: Russell, Odiorne & Metcalf, 1835; London: Richard James Kennett, 1835);

Slavery (Boston: James Munroe, 1835; London: Rowland Hunter, 1836; Edinburgh: Thomas Clark, 1836);

Dr. Channing's Letter, on Catholicism, &c (Louisville: Morton & Smith, 1836; Liverpool: Willmer & Smith, 1837; Glasgow: J. Hedderwick, 1837);

Letter of William E. Channing to James G. Birney (Boston: James Munroe, 1836); republished as *Letter of Dr. William E. Channing to James G. Birney* (Cincinnati: A. Pugh, 1836);

A Discourse Delivered at the Dedication of the Unitarian Congregational Church in Newport, Rhode Island, July 27, 1836 (Boston: S. N. Dickinson, 1836; London: Richard Kinder, 1837);

An Address on Temperance (Boston: Weeks, Jordan, 1837; London: John Green, 1837; Glasgow: J. Hedderwick, 1837);

Character of Napoleon, and Other Essays, Literary and Philosophical, 2 volumes (London: Charles Tilt / Edinburgh: J. Menzies / Philadelphia: T. Wardle, 1837);

Essays, Literary & Political (Glasgow: James Hedderwick / London: Simpkin, Marshall / Edinburgh: Oliver & Boyd, 1837);

A Letter to the Abolitionists (Boston: Knapp, 1837);

A Letter to the Hon. Henry Clay, on the Annexation of Texas to the United States (Boston: James Munroe, 1837; Glasgow: James Hedderwick / London: Simpkin, Marshall / Edinburgh: Oliver & Boyd, 1837); republished as *Thoughts on the Evils of a Spirit of Conquest, and on Slavery. A Letter on the Annexation of Texas to the United States* (London: John Green, 1837);

Remarks on Creeds, Intolerance, and Exclusion (Boston: James Munroe, 1837); republished as *Letter on Creeds, & C* (Liverpool: Willmer & Smith, 1837);

The Sunday School. A Discourse Pronounced Before the Sunday School Society (Boston: James Munroe, 1837; London: R. J. Kennett, 1837);

A Tribute to the Memory of the Rev. Noah Worcester, D.D. (Boston: James Munroe, 1837; Boston: J. Dowe, 1837); republished as *A Discourse Delivered in Boston, November 12, 1837. Being a Tribute to the Memory of the Reverend Noah Worcester, D.D.* (London: John Green, 1838);

The Evidences of Christianity (Glasgow: J. Hedderwick, 1838);

Self-Culture. An Address Introductory to the Franklin Lectures, Delivered at Boston, September, 1838 (Boston: Dutton & Wentworth, 1838; London: William Strange / Joseph Noble, 1838?);

The Worship of the Father, a Service of Gratitude and Joy (Boston: James Munroe, 1838);

Lecture on War (Boston: Dutton & Wentworth, 1839; London: John Green, 1839);

Remarks on the Slavery Question, in a Letter to Jonathan Phillips, Esq. (Boston: James Munroe, 1839; London: John Green / Bristol: Philip & Evans, 1839; London: Wiley & Putnam / Charles Fox, 1839);

Treatises on Self-Culture, Immortality, and the Future Life (Edinburgh: Thomas Clark, 1839);

A Discourse Occasioned by the Death of the Rev. Dr. Follen (Boston: James Munroe, 1840); republished as *Christian Views of Human Suffering* (Boston: James Munroe, 1840);

Emancipation (Boston: E. P. Peabody, 1840; London: Charles Fox, 1841);

Lectures on the Elevation of the Labouring Portion of the Community (Boston: William D. Ticknor, 1840; Bristol: Philip & Evans / London: John Green, 1840; Manchester: Abel Heywood, 1840);

The Power of Unitarian Christianity to Produce an Enlightened and Fervent Piety (Boston: James Munroe, 1840);

Letter of the Rev. William E. Channing to the Standing Committee of the Proprietors of the Meeting-House in Federal

Street, in the Town of Boston, Read at the Annual Meeting, May 6, 1840; and the Reply of the Proprietors Thereto (Boston: Joseph Dowe, 1840);

The Church. A Discourse, Delivered in the First Congregational Unitarian Church of Philadelphia, Sunday, May 30th, 1841 (Philadelphia: J. Crissy, 1841; London: John Green, 1841; Glasgow: James Hedderwick / Edinburgh: Oliver & Boyd / London: Simpkin, Marshall, 1841);

A Discourse on the Life and Character of the Rev. Joseph Tuckerman, D.D. Delivered at the Warren Street Chapel, on Sunday Evening, Jan. 31, 1841 (Boston: William Crosby, 1841); republished as *The Obligation of a City to Care For and Watch Over the Moral Health of Its Members; With Remarks on the Life & Character of the Rev. Dr. Tuckerman, Founder of the Ministry at Large. A Discourse, Delivered at the Warren-Street Chapel, Boston, Jan. 31, 1841* (Glasgow: James Hedderwick / Edinburgh: Oliver & Boyd / London: Simpkin, Marshall, 1841);

An Address, Delivered Before the Mercantile Library Company, of Philadelphia, May 11, 1841 (Philadelphia: J. Crissy, 1841); republished as *The Present Age: An Address Delivered Before the Mercantile Library Company of Philadelphia, May 11, 1841* (Glasgow: James Hedderwick / Edinburgh: Oliver & Boyd / London: Simpkin, Marshall, 1841; Manchester: Abel Heywood, 1841);

An Address Delivered at Lenox, on the First of August, 1842, the Anniversary of Emancipation, in the British West Indies (Lenox, Mass.: J. G. Stanly, 1842); republished as *Dr. Channing's Last Address, Delivered at Lenox, on the First of August, 1842, the Anniversary of Emancipation in the British West Indies* (Boston: Oliver Johnson, 1842; London: John Green, 1842); republished as *Address on Occasion of the Anniversary of the Emancipation of the Slaves in the British West India Islands* (Glasgow: J. Hedderwick, 1842);

The Duty of the Free States, or Remarks Suggested by the Case of the Creole, 2 parts (Boston: William Crosby, 1842; Glasgow: James Hedderwick / Edinburgh: Oliver & Boyd / London: Simpkin, Marshall, 1842);

A Discourse on the Church (Boston: James Munroe, 1843);

Memoir of William Ellery Channing, with Extracts from His Correspondence and Manuscripts, 3 volumes, edited by William Henry Channing (Boston: Crosby & Nichols / London: J. Chapman, 1848);

The Perfect Life. In Twelve Discourses, edited by William Henry Channing (Boston: Roberts, 1873; London: Williams & Norgate, 1873);

Dr. Channing's Note-Book Passages from the Unpublished Manuscripts of William Ellery Channing, edited by Grace Ellery Channing (Boston & New York: Houghton, Mifflin, 1887);

Remarks on Some Texts of Scripture, Frequently Alleged in Defence of the Supreme Deity of our Lord Jesus Christ (Belfast: Unitarian Society for the Diffusion of Christian Knowledge, n.d.);

"A Study and Transcription of William Ellery Channing's Unfinished Treatise on Man," edited by Morton deCorcey Nachlas, dissertation, Meadville Theological School, Chicago, 1942;

"Two Unpublished Sermons," edited by Richard E. Myers, *Unitarian Universalist Christian,* 35 (Spring 1980): 40–47.

Collection: *The Works of William Ellery Channing, D.D.,* 6 volumes (Boston: James Munroe, 1841–1843);

The Works of William E. Channing, D.D. (Boston: American Unitarian Association, 1875);

William Ellery Channing: Selected Writings, edited by David Robinson (Mahwah, N.J.: Paulist Press, 1985).

William Ellery Channing was the most prominent preacher and theologian in the early Unitarian movement in New England. He was one of the founders of the Unitarian denomination and was a major intellectual influence on Ralph Waldo Emerson and the New England Transcendentalist movement. His theory of self-culture, the belief that the religious life was centered on the cultivation and growth of the individual's inherent spiritual potentiality, was a central premise of early Unitarian theology and had an important formative impact on the thinking of Transcendentalists such as Emerson, Orestes Brownson, Elizabeth Palmer Peabody, James Freeman Clarke, Margaret Fuller, Frederic Henry Hedge, and Theodore Parker. Without becoming a Transcendentalist himself, Channing nevertheless stood as one of the most potent influences on the movement, delineating many of Emerson's key ideas and setting an example in both pulpit eloquence and literary enterprise. Channing's sermons and essays–which combined logical trenchancy, oratorical eloquence, and emotional fervor–set an important literary standard for both Unitarians and Transcendentalists who followed him. He was thus an influential figure in the formation of American literary culture in the 1820s and 1830s.

William Ellery Channing was born in Newport, Rhode Island, on 7 April 1780, the son of William Channing, an attorney and member of the Rhode Island legislature, and Lucy (Ellery) Channing, the daughter of William Ellery, a member of the Continental Congress and signer of the Declaration of Independence. As one of Channing's biographers, Madeleine Hooke Rice, notes, "The marriage of William Channing and Lucy Ellery united two of Newport's substantial and useful families." Channing went to New London, Connecticut, in 1792 to study with his uncle Henry Channing, minister of the First Church of New London. In 1793 his father, William, died, an event that placed some financial strain on the family.

Channing entered Harvard College in 1794 and graduated in 1798, forming there his intention to enter the ministry. During his studies at Harvard he made one particularly important intellectual and spiritual discovery–the idea of "disinterested benevolence" in the works of the Scottish moral philosopher Frances Hutcheson. Hutcheson argued that humans were capable of acts of purely unselfish benevolence. Hutcheson's view of the basis of ethics in a benevolent concern for others impressed Channing by establishing a grounding for a positive view of human nature, one that would counter both theories that ethical acts were ultimately grounded in self-interest and Calvinist arguments that the human condition was one of original sin or innate depravity. Because of this human capacity for moral action based not on selfish interests but on an unselfish care for the condition of others, one could assume an innate capability for virtue within human nature. Channing was thus able to form a more positive view of the spiritual potential of the individual, and this concept became the cornerstone of an emerging liberal theology that challenged New England Calvinism.

Channing completed his undergraduate studies at Harvard, still intending to prepare for the ministry. Hoping to support himself financially while he continued his studies for the ministry, he accepted a position as a tutor for the Randolph family in Richmond, Virginia. During his two-year stay in Virginia, while he continued to extend his reading in theology, he underwent a significant period of spiritual trial and self-examination. His spiritual discipline included experimentation with some forms of ascetic self-denial. John White Chadwick's account of this period reveals the remarkable intensity of Channing's spiritual quest, even its self-destructive qualities:

> Not only did he remain at his books till two or three o'clock in the morning, and often till the daylight broke, but he made harsh experiments in living, went insufficiently clothed, without an overcoat in winter weather, sleeping upon the bare floor in a cold room, eating very little, and that what he did n't like. He fancied he was curbing his animal nature, when the temptations that assailed him were the spawn of his own ascetic glooms. He thought he was hardening himself when he was making himself frail and pervious to every wind that blew.

The effect of this period of experimentation, whatever spiritual results it produced, was to weaken his health permanently. "On Channing's return to Newport the family received him the more tenderly because his broken health seemed ominous of fatal ill." While he lived into his sixties, he lost any previous robustness and had to manage his energy with great care for the rest of his life.

The Old Federal Street Meetinghouse, where Channing was ordained

Channing returned to Cambridge in 1800 to serve as a regent, or residence-hall supervisor, at Harvard and to complete the theological studies that he had been pursuing independently. He was approbated to preach in 1802 and ordained as minister of Federal Street Church in Boston on 1 June 1803, a post he held until his death in 1842. Some two decades later Channing would emerge as the leader of the liberal wing of the New England Congregational churches, which split to form the Unitarian denomination in the 1820s and 1830s. Channing's ministerial and theological career is closely linked to the origins of New England Unitarianism, and his developing religious philosophy was profoundly affected by the religious controversies that caused the rise of that religious movement.

There has been much analysis of Channing's early theological development, and the general theological situation surrounding it deserves particular attention. New England congregationalism, which had its origins in the churches established by the Puritans after their migration from England, was in a state of profound transition in the late eighteenth century. Calvinism had been the theology of the Puritans, and though it was a complex and evolving system of belief, subject to several shades of emphasis and interpretation, two of its fundamental doctrines became increasingly controversial after 1750–the belief in innate depravity and in election to grace. Calvinists held that all humans were corrupt or sinful and therefore unworthy of salvation by a God of purity, but that Christ's death had atoned for the sin of some, whose fate had been predetermined and known by an omnipotent God from the beginning of the Creation.

While these doctrines were supported by a logical structure and generated a remarkably intense introspective piety, they could also seem arbitrary and harsh. Conrad Wright's account of the gradual unfolding of liberal dissent to Calvinist doctrines in the late eighteenth century (*The Beginnings of Unitarianism in America,* 1955) shows how a liberal party within congregationalism gradually coalesced in Boston and eastern Massachusetts, with its adherents becoming increasingly outspoken in calling for theological revision. They developed a greater emphasis on human moral capacity, countering the Calvinist doctrines of innate depravity and election to grace, and also stressed the benevolence of God. By the early nineteenth century, when Channing began his ministry, Massachusetts congregationalism was divided into two broad factions–the orthodox, who upheld Calvinism, and the liberals or Arminians, who had rejected or substantially modified the harsher elements of Calvinism. Though not yet divided institutionally, the pressure was building for the split of the churches that occurred in the 1820s and 1830s.

Channing's development suggests a variety of possible influences in his early theological outlook. His Newport minister, Samuel Hopkins, was an influential defender of Calvinism, attempting to renew it with his own rigorous reinterpretation, which stressed the necessity of an absolutely selfless devotion to God as the cornerstone of the Christian life. But Channing was also subject to other more liberal influences, both from his uncle Henry, whose theological tendencies were moderate or Arminian, and from the general atmosphere of Harvard, which was becoming the center of New England theological liberalism. Channing's early devotion to the philosophy of Hutcheson suggests that he was attracted toward a positive view of human nature, a position that eventually linked him with liberalism. Soon after Channing took the Federal Street pulpit, the rift between orthodox Calvinists and liberals erupted in controversy in 1805 over the appointment of a liberal, Henry Ware, to the Hollis Professorship of Divinity at Harvard. For the next thirty-five years New England theology was consumed by this division, resulting in a permanent split of the original churches in Massachusetts and the eventual formation of the Unitarian denomination.

Channing became the chief spokesman of the liberal movement in the second decade of the nineteenth century, entering the theological discourse as a strong advocate of reason as a principle of authority in religious belief and of the spiritual potential of the individual. In 1815 he defended the openness and sincerity of the Boston liberals against Calvinist attacks in his *A Letter to the Rev. Samuel C. Thacher, on the Aspersions Contained in a Late Number of the Panoplist, on the Ministers of Boston and the Vicinity,* arguing that despite their differences with orthodox Calvinists, the liberals did not seek to separate from the church to form their own denomination. But he made clear the liberals' discontent with the prevailing theology and their commitment to an ever-enlarging sense of religious discovery. "We profess to believe, that candid and impartial research will guide mankind to a purer system of christianity, than is now to be found in any church or country under Heaven."

Four years later he outlined the principal liberal doctrines and accepted the name "Unitarian" for the movement in his influential *A Sermon Delivered at the Ordination of the Rev. Jared Sparks, to the Pastoral Care of the First Independent Church in Baltimore, May 5, 1819* (1819), known as "Unitarian Christianity." Countering the Calvinist criticism of the liberals as overly committed to reason in the interpretation of the Bible, Channing declared, "We object strongly to the contemptuous manner in which human reason is often spoken of by our adversaries, because it leads, we believe, to universal skepticism." Of all books, he argued, the Bible most needs the exercise of reason for its interpretation. "Our leading principle in interpreting Scripture is this, that the Bible is a book written for men, in the language of men, and that its meaning is to be sought in the same manner as that of other books." This assertion left open to question, among many other points, the doctrine of the Trinity, which Channing believed was unfounded and dangerously confusing as the Calvinists presented it. Calling it a "corruption of Christianity," he termed the doctrine "alike repugnant to common sense and to the general strain of Scripture," making it "a remarkable proof of the power of a false philosophy in disfiguring the simple truth of Jesus."

Even more open to attack for Channing were the Calvinist doctrines of innate depravity and election to grace, as his vivid depiction of those doctrines suggests:

> This system [Calvinism] also teaches, that God selects from this corrupt mass a number to be saved, and plucks them, by a special influence, from the common ruin; that the rest of mankind, though left without that special grace which their conversion requires, are commanded to repent, under penalty of aggravated woe; and that forgiveness is promised them, on terms which their very constitution infallibly disposes them to reject, and in rejecting which they awfully enhance the punishments of hell. These proffers of forgiveness and exhortations of amendment, to beings born under a blighting curse, fill our minds with a horror which we want words to express.

Clearly Channing had become a powerful controversialist, stating the liberal critique of Calvinism with singular and memorable authority.

As the liberals coalesced into a new denomination in the 1820s and 1830s, Channing provided important intellectual leadership through a series of sermons and addresses that emphasized human reason and moral capacity, a more benevolent characterization of the nature of God, and the possibility of cultivating a likeness to God through a disciplined program of spiritual self-culture. In these years Channing also became one of the most influential ministers in Boston. He was an early leader in the development of religious education, taking important steps to establish a Sunday School at his Federal Street Church. He was also influential among his ministerial colleagues in the Boston area, playing an important part in the eventual formation of the Unitarian denomination as the Boston area churches split between liberals and orthodox. Channing accepted the inevitability of the split reluctantly and was distrustful of the sectarianism involved in the formation of a new denomination. While he was a powerful critic of Calvinism, his major effort in theology was to establish the positive principles of the new Unitarian movement.

In 1814 Channing was married to Ruth Gibbs, whose wealth transformed Channing's outward life and provided him with a certain measure of freedom in his relationship with his Federal Street congregation. The importance of this freedom increased when Channing became an outspoken antislavery advocate, in opposition to some of the more-conservative members of his congregation. Because of his continuing uncertain health and the freedom that his wife's wealth provided, he reduced his duties at the Federal Street Church after

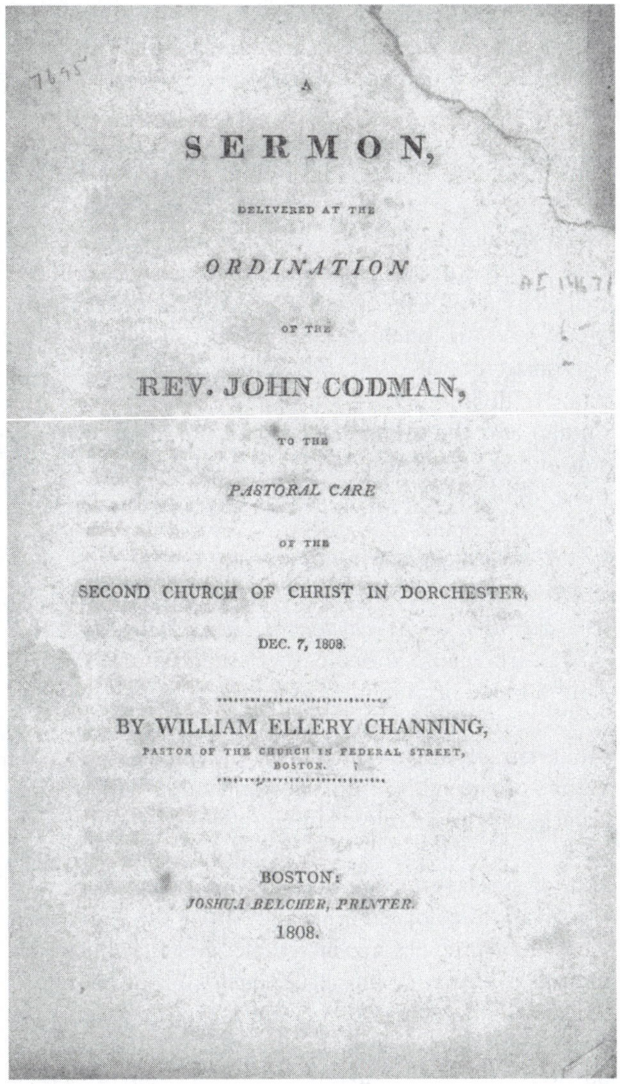
A

SERMON,

DELIVERED AT THE

ORDINATION

OF THE

REV. JOHN CODMAN,

TO THE

PASTORAL CARE

OF THE

SECOND CHURCH OF CHRIST IN DORCHESTER,

DEC. 7, 1808.

BY WILLIAM ELLERY CHANNING,

PASTOR OF THE CHURCH IN FEDERAL STREET, BOSTON.

BOSTON:

JOSHUA BELCHER, PRINTER.

1808.

Title page for one of Channing's sermons (Collection of Joel Myerson)

1830, becoming less a week-to-week pastor, passing those duties on to his associate minister, Ezra Stiles Gannett. Rice reports that after 1832, Channing preached only five to six times a year at Federal Street but maintained his position as minister of the church.

The construction of the liberal position in theology that Channing had begun in his *A Letter to the Rev. Samuel C. Thacher* and "Unitarian Christianity" was extended in "The Moral Argument against Calvinism" (1820), a critique of the deleterious effect of Calvinism on the conception of the moral character of God. Channing's characterization of the fatalistic quality of Calvinism was stinging. "Calvinism teaches, that, in consequence of Adam's sin in eating the forbidden fruit, God brings into life all his posterity with a nature wholly corrupt, so that they are utterly indisposed, disabled, and made opposite to all that is spiritually good, and wholly inclined to all evil, and that continually." Such a system, he argued, "which contradicts our best ideas of goodness and justice, cannot come from the just and good God, or be a true representation of his character." By showing that a doctrine of human corruption actually implicated God, making God as corrupt as his creatures, Channing forged a link between the nature of God and the nature of humans that became an important element of his religious outlook. An affirmative theology had to celebrate the nature of God and to demonstrate that men and women could also participate in divinity. This affirmative bond between the human and the divine had a great influence on Emerson and the Transcendentalists, and in this emphasis, more than any other, Channing helped to spark the Transcendentalist movement.

Channing's Dudleian lecture, *A Discourse on the Evidences of Revealed Religion, Delivered before the University in Cambridge, at the Dudleian Lecture, March 14, 1821* (1821) articulated a theology of "supernatural rationalism," a blend of Enlightenment rationalism and affirmation of the biblical miracles characteristic of early Unitarian thought. Channing accepted the factual nature of the biblical miracles and other supernatural aspects of Christianity, but he accepted them on the basis of rational assent, thus preserving both the supernatural aspects of Christian belief and the authority of reason as a theological principle. Noting the widely held view "that miracles are incredible, and that the supernatural character of an alleged fact is proof enough of its falsehood," Channing argued that "no adequate cause for [Christianity] can be found in the powers or passions of human nature, or in the circumstances under which it appeared." The absence of such possible explanations forces the conclusion that Christian belief "can only be accounted for by the interposition of that Being, to whom its first preachers universally ascribed it, and with whose nature it perfectly agrees."

Channing's Dudleian lecture made a strong impact on Emerson, who noted it in his journal as one of the influences that pulled him toward the vocation of the ministry. The significance of the address was less its defense of the miracles than its frank confrontation with modern rationalistic skepticism and its strategy of bringing the "natural" and "supernatural" into a more holistic synthesis that preserved the essence of both. Conrad Wright has traced the development of supernatural rationalism in eighteenth-century philosophy, noting that for advocates of this outlook, "Natural Religion and Revealed Religion were conceived of as sustaining and supporting each other." In his Dudleian lecture Channing sought to present a religion that was supported by the evidences of both nature and Scripture, working to resolve the perceived conflicts between them.

Channing's most significant statements of his mature religious outlook were *A Discourse Delivered at the Ordination of the Rev. Frederick A. Farley, as Pastor of the Westminster Congregational Society in Providence, Rhode Island, September 10, 1828* (1828), known as "Likeness to God," which describes the religious life as a progressive process of conformity to the divine principle, and *Self-Culture. An Address Introductory to the Franklin Lectures, Delivered at Boston, September, 1838* (1838), an address in which he envisioned a life of progressive "culture," a continual effort of self-improvement and spiritual growth. "Likeness to God" is in part an extension of Channing's belief that one's view of human nature is dependent on one's view of the nature of God. Channing argued that "high aspirations, hopes, and efforts" were vital aspects of religious experience and that such aspirations grew out of mankind's sense of relation to God. "To honor him, is not to tremble before him as an unapproachable sovereign, not to utter barren praise which leaves us as it found us. It is to become what we praise. It is to approach God as an inexhaustible Fountain of light, power, and purity. It is to feel the quickening and transforming energy of his perfections." In this description of the human relationship with God, Channing emphasized feeling and action, the internal or personal transformation of religious experience and its outward expression in ethical action. In becoming "what we praise" humans enact the principles associated with perfection, making the abstract real. Such action need not be heroic in any unusual or romantic sense. "Whenever we think, speak, or act, with moral energy, and resolute devotion to duty," he argued, "be the occasion ever so humble, obscure, familiar; then the divinity is growing within us, and we are ascending towards our Author." Every act, indeed every decision of life, has in this sense a moral and spiritual dimension, offering the ever-present possibility to nurture the likeness to God that is a human being's innate potential.

Channing termed this process of the constant development of the spiritual nature "self-culture," and his 1838 lecture by that title, addressed to a working-class audience, proposed it as a guide to both the practical and the spiritual aspects of life. Channing insisted that self-improvement was compatible with the life of labor, even given the constraints on time and resources that a laborer faced. "An earnest purpose finds time or makes time," he argued. "A man, who follows his calling with industry and spirit, and uses his earnings economically, will always have some portion of the day at command; and it is astonishing, how fruitful of improvement a short season becomes, when eagerly seized and faithfully used." The metaphor of a

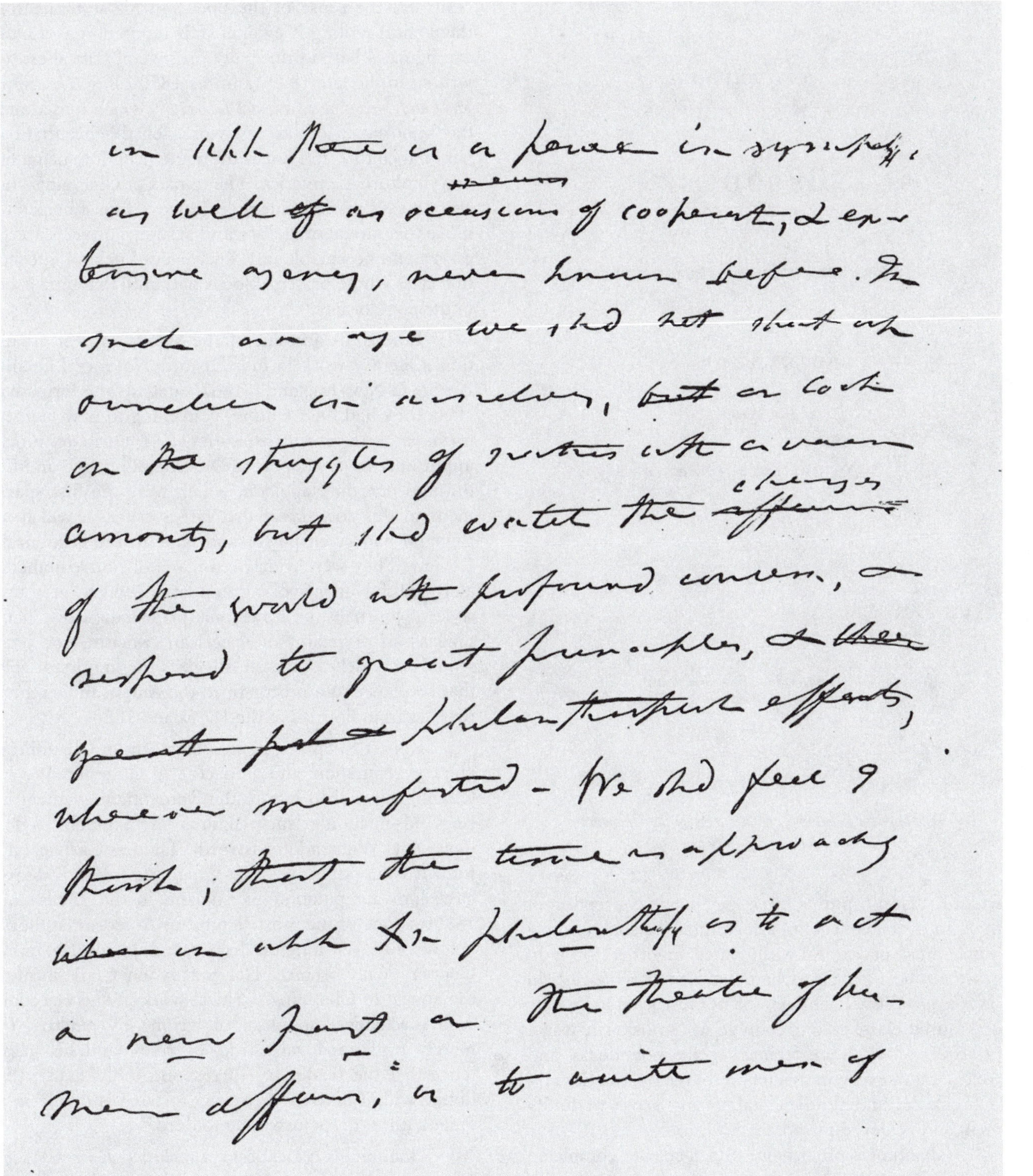
in which there is a power in sympathy, as well ~~of~~ as occasions of cooperation, & extensive agency, never known before. In such an age we shd not shut up ourselves in ourselves, ~~but~~ or look on the struggles of nations with a vain amusement, but shd watch the changes ~~affairs~~ of the world with profound concern, & respond to great principles, & ~~these~~ ~~greater prot~~ philanthropic efforts, wherever manifested. We shd feel that the time is approaching ~~when~~ in which Xn philanthropy is to act a new part on the theatre of human affairs, & to unite men of

Page from the manuscript for the discourse Channing delivered in Boston in June 1831, after his return from St. Croix and Havana (from Autograph Leaves of Our Country's Authors, *edited by John Pendleton Kennedy and Alexander Bliss, 1864)*

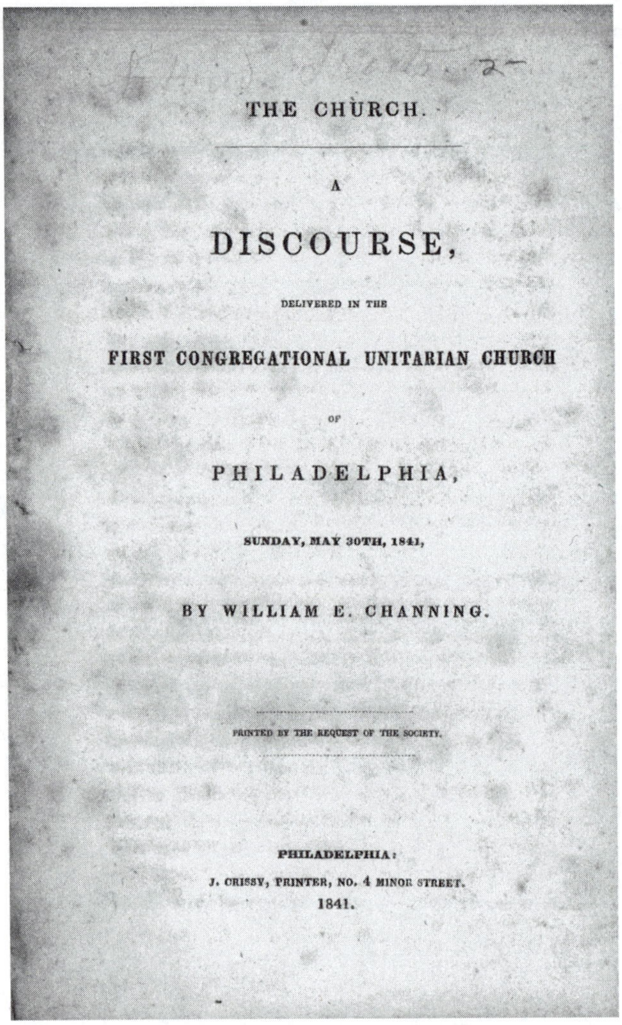
THE CHURCH.

A

DISCOURSE,

DELIVERED IN THE

FIRST CONGREGATIONAL UNITARIAN CHURCH

OF

PHILADELPHIA,

SUNDAY, MAY 30TH, 1841,

BY WILLIAM E. CHANNING.

PRINTED BY THE REQUEST OF THE SOCIETY.

PHILADELPHIA:
J. CRISSY, PRINTER, NO. 4 MINOR STREET.
1841.

Title page for Channing's observations on the Unitarian Church (Collection of Joel Myerson)

fruitful season captures the larger poetic conception at the root of the concept of self-culture: the soul, a living thing, must be carefully cultivated in order for it to grow and bear fruit. As Channing tried to make clear in *Self-Culture,* this view of life was not restricted to an elite or leisured class, able to indulge its curiosity. It was a principle of vital importance to the soundness and well-being of every individual, a source of integrity and self-reliance, and fundamental to any sense of fulfillment and achieved purpose.

Channing's philosophy of self-culture completed his reformation of New England theology, a singular intellectual achievement, and his fundamental claim to philosophical importance. He also made a significant cultural impact as a literary essayist and reviewer in the 1820s and as an antislavery advocate in the 1830s and 1840s. Channing wrote comparatively little that could be regarded as purely "literary," though the rhetorical craft and the sense of the poetic in his sermons and theological writing is evident. His reputation as a literary figure is based principally on several critical essays written in the late 1820s and his 1830 essay *The Importance and Means of a National Literature,* which underlined the importance of literary work for the health of a national culture and noted the acute need for such a literary culture in America. The impact of Channing's literary essays was considerable, however, for it helped to make the pursuit of literary and aesthetic projects a necessary and acceptable task for a New England intellectual class whose principal focus had until that time been in theology or law.

Emerson's account of the significance of Channing's literary work in his "Historic Notes of Life and Letters in New England" (1867) suggests the formative effect they had on a culture awakening to new literary forms and to poetic aspirations: "I attribute much importance to two papers of Dr. Channing, one on Milton and one on Napoleon, which were the first specimens in this country of that larger criticism which in England had given power and fame to the Edinburgh Review. They were widely read, and of course immediately fruitful in provoking emulation which lifted the style of Journalism." Emerson's presentation of Channing as an originator of American criticism, one who would be widely emulated, suggests the important role that he played as a precursor to the American literature that began to flourish in the 1840s and 1850s.

Robert E. Spiller, in an assessment of Channing's literary reputation and impact ("A Case for W. E. Channing"), linked him to the Romantic movement in England–including such figures as Samuel Taylor Coleridge, William Wordsworth, Thomas Carlyle, and John Ruskin–and notes that Channing's critical essays gave him a reputation in England in the 1820s and 1830s as one of the most significant American authors, below only Washington Irving and James Fenimore Cooper in importance. Harry Hayden Clark located the appeal of Channing's critical work in "his rejection of a mechanical appraisal of writing by external or merely traditional yard-sticks or rules, and his insistence that the reader try to respond individually, the divine within himself answering to what is divine in a great author, deep answering to deep."

Channing's critical essays included *Remarks on the Character and Writings of Milton: Occasioned by the Publication of His Lately Discovered "Treatise on Christian Doctrine"* and *Remarks on the Character of Napoleon Bonaparte, Occasioned by the Publication of Scott's Life of Napoleon,* both of which were reviews of recent books that expanded to become thorough reassessments of the figures under consideration. His essay *The Importance and Means of a National*

Literature focused on the paucity of American literary and intellectual culture:

> The truth ought to be known. There is among us much superficial knowledge, but little severe, persevering research; little of that consuming passion for new truth, which makes outward things worthless; little resolute devotion to a high intellectual culture. There is nowhere a literary atmosphere, or such an accumulation of literary influences, as determines the whole strength of the mind to its own enlargement, and to the manifestation of itself in enduring forms.

Channing's essay was a reminder to the young nation that it could not be complete without an independent and productive intellectual class, and a distinctive and compelling national literature. It was also a call for newness that had a ring of appeal to those such as Emerson, who held poetic and literary aspirations and were drawn to the idea of creating a new kind of literature:

> Still we feel, that all existing literature has been produced under influences, which have necessarily mixed with it much error and corruption; and that the whole of it ought to pass, and must pass, under rigorous review. . . . The most interesting questions to mankind are yet in debate. Great principles are yet to be settled in criticism, in morals, in politics; and, above all, the true character of religion is to be rescued from the disguises and corruptions of the ages. We want a reformation.

Channing's belief in the potentially progressive direction of his age and nation and his confidence in the contributions that a reformulated literature and religion could make to that progress were enormously helpful and inspiriting to the younger intellectuals such as Emerson, Margaret Fuller, and Theodore Parker, who took his call for a "reformation" of intellectual life to heart in propounding the "new views" of Transcendentalism.

While Channing's contributions to the formation of American literature in the 1820s were important, his career began to take a different direction and emphasis in the 1830s as he became a more committed social reformer and, in particular, a strong critic of slavery. The roots of his antipathy toward slavery were deep. His Newport minister, Samuel Hopkins, had been an early opponent of slavery, and Channing was able to witness slavery firsthand during his stay in Virginia. There he found that even the Randolphs and others of the Virginia planter class had deep reservations about slavery. New England was the center of the national opposition to slavery, and Channing was much impressed by Lydia Maria Child's 1833 volume, *An Appeal in Favor of That Class of Americans Called Africans*. In

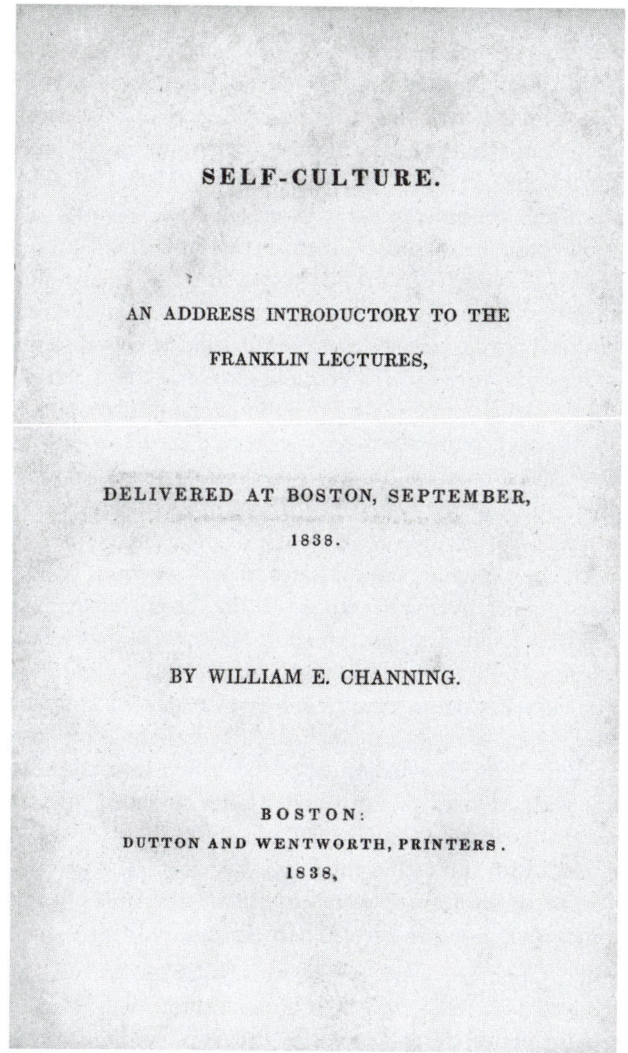
SELF-CULTURE.

AN ADDRESS INTRODUCTORY TO THE

FRANKLIN LECTURES,

DELIVERED AT BOSTON, SEPTEMBER,

1838.

BY WILLIAM E. CHANNING.

BOSTON:

DUTTON AND WENTWORTH, PRINTERS.

1838.

Title page for the lecture in which Channing explains his theory of the cultivation of spiritual growth (Collection of Joel Myerson)

Slavery (1835), Channing presented the moral case against slavery–a system that obviously violated the deepest principles of his theology, which stressed the spiritual dignity and potentiality of every individual. The enslavement of a man or woman was thus a violation of his or her spiritual nature, as well as a violation of natural rights. It denied dignity to an individual whose deepest characteristic was a "likeness to God." Channing thus argued that a philosophy of the dignity and potential Godlikeness of each individual was utterly incompatible with the dehumanizing institution of slavery. It was the forceful application of theological principle to a social and political problem, and it indicated the increasing intellectual momentum of the antislavery movement in New England.

Channing continued to speak out against slavery, even over the opposition of the controlling conservative faction of his parishioners at the Federal Street Church. He did not, however, align himself with the more-radical versions of abolitionism espoused by such men as William Lloyd Garrison and thus remained open to criticism from both conservative and abolitionist parties during the late 1830s and early 1840s. "Most Unitarian ministers, though antislavery, were not abolitionists and took pains to dissociate themselves from the Garrisonians," Conrad Wright has noted, in a description that includes Channing. "They were gradualists, who in due course became free-soilers, insisting on the containment of slavery within its traditional boundaries, and relying on the development of more enlightened public opinion to support public policy that would bring about its eventual extinction." Clearly Channing struggled with the nature of his commitment to the antislavery cause and was torn between the demands of abolitionism and a temperamental caution and deep aversion to the harsh and divisive rhetoric of the Garrisonians. As Andrew Delbanco has argued in *William Ellery Channing: An Essay on the Liberal Spirit in America* (1981), Channing was also insistent that evil not be externalized and that any form of political and moral condemnation also include an acknowledgment of the critic's own complicity with the existence of evil. "Channing said for his time," Delbanco explained, "what Reinhold Niebuhr has said for ours–that the forgetting of evil is the catastrophe of modern man, but that if we remember it, we must remember that we *all* participate in it."

Channing's last public address, at Lenox, Massachusetts, in 1842, was a commemoration of England's emancipation of the slaves in the West Indies, an act that he held up as an important example to America. He did not argue for the immediate abolition of slavery in America but rather for the North to free itself "from all constitutional or legal obligations to uphold slavery." Then, "we must give free and strong expression to our reprobation of slavery," trusting to the work of moral suasion bringing about the eventual end of slavery. "The North has but one weapon, moral force, the utterance of moral judgment, moral feeling and religious conviction. . . . Whoever spreads through his circle, be it wide or narrow, just opinions and feelings in regard to slavery, hastens its fall." Channing was already in failing health when he delivered this address. He died some two months later. In an elegy that stressed Channing's visionary commitment to the ideal in human nature, James Freeman Clarke said, "He did not respect man's character, but his nature–not his attainments, but his capacities–not man as he is, but man as he was made to be. He looked through the outward, and saw beneath his ignorance and sin the struggling form of an angel of God."

The evolution of Channing's thought from theological controversy to a focus on ethics and politics is an important indication of the broader course of American intellectual history in the nineteenth century. Channing's early polemics against Calvinism marked the end of the Puritan hold on the New England mind, and in the rejection of Calvinism, Channing also discovered a powerfully positive agenda that was the foundation of the liberal tradition in American intellectual and political culture. Grounded in a faith in the dignity and capacity of the individual but also concerned for the strengthening of American community and public culture, Channing's thought not only shaped the Transcendentalist movement but also helped alter the direction of American culture as a whole.

Letters:

The Correspondence of William Ellery Channing, D.D., and Lucy Aiken, edited by Anna Letitia Le Breton (Boston: Roberts, 1874).

Bibliographies:

Conrad Wright, "A Channing Bibliography: 1929–1959," *Proceedings of the Unitarian Historical Society,* 12, no. 2 (1959): 22–24;

Joel Myerson, "William Ellery Channing 1780–1842," in *First Printings of American Authors: Contributions toward a Descriptive Checklist,* volume 4, edited by Matthew J. Bruccoli and others (Detroit: Gale Research, 1979), pp. 77–90;

David Robinson, "William Ellery Channing," in *The Transcendentalists: A Review of Research and Criticism,* edited by Myerson (New York: Modern Language Association, 1984), pp. 310–316.

Biographies:

William Henry Channing, *Memoir of William Ellery Channing,* 3 volumes (Boston: Crosby & Nichols, 1848);

Elizabeth Palmer Peabody, *Reminiscences of Rev. Wm. Ellery Channing, D.D.* (Boston: Roberts, 1880);

John White Chadwick, *William Ellery Channing: Minister of Religion* (Boston: Houghton, Mifflin, 1903);

Madeleine Hooke Rice, *Federal Street Pastor: The Life of William Ellery Channing* (New York: Bookman, 1961);

Jack Mendelsohn, *Channing: The Reluctant Radical* (Boston: Little, Brown, 1971).

References:

Sydney Ahlstrom, "The Interpretation of Channing," *New England Quarterly,* 30 (March 1957): 99–105;

Lawrence Buell, "The Literary Significance of the Unitarian Movement," *American Unitarianism, 1805–1865,* edited by Conrad Edick Wright (Boston: Massachusetts Historical Society and Northeastern University Press, 1989), pp. 163–179;

Buell, *Literary Transcendentalism: Style and Vision in the American Renaissance* (Ithaca, N.Y.: Cornell University Press, 1973);

Harry Hayden Clark, "Changing Attitudes in Early American Literary Criticism: 1800–1840," in *The Development of American Literary Criticism,* edited by Floyd Stovall (Chapel Hill: University of North Carolina Press, 1955), pp. 15–73;

James Freeman Clarke, *A Sermon Preached in Amory Hall, October 9th, 1842, Being the Sunday Succeeding the Death of William Ellery Channing* (Boston: Greene, 1842);

Andrew Delbanco, *William Ellery Channing: An Essay on the Liberal Spirit in America* (Cambridge: Harvard University Press, 1981);

Ralph Waldo Emerson, "Historic Notes of Life and Letters in New England [1867]," in *The Complete Works of Ralph Waldo Emerson,* volume 10, Centenary Edition, edited by Edward Waldo Emerson (Boston: Houghton, Mifflin, 1903–1904), pp. 323–370;

Daniel Walker Howe, *Making the American Self: Jonathan Edwards to Abraham Lincoln* (Cambridge: Harvard University Press, 1997);

Howe, *The Unitarian Conscience: Harvard Moral Philosophy, 1805–1861* (New Haven: Yale University Press, 1970);

Robert Leet Patterson, *The Philosophy of William Ellery Channing* (New York: Bookman, 1952);

David Robinson, *Apostle of Culture: Emerson as Preacher and Lecturer* (Philadelphia: University of Pennsylvania Press, 1982);

Robinson, "The Legacy of Channing: Culture as a Religious Category in New England Thought," *Harvard Theological Review,* 74 (April 1981): 221–239;

Robinson, *The Unitarians and the Universalists* (Westport, Conn.: Greenwood Press, 1985);

Herbert Wallace Schneider, "The Intellectual Background of William Ellery Channing," *Church History,* 7 (March 1938): 3–23;

Robert E. Spiller, "A Case for W. E. Channing," *New England Quarterly,* 3 (January 1930): 55–81;

Conrad Edick Wright, *The Beginnings of Unitarianism in America* (Boston: Starr King Press, 1955);

Wright, "The Channing We Don't Know," *Unitarian Universalist Christian,* 35 (Winter 1980–1981): 39–47;

Wright, *The Liberal Christians: Essays on American Unitarian History* (Boston: Beacon Press, 1970).

Papers:

The major holdings of William Ellery Channing's papers are at the Andover-Harvard Theological Library of Harvard Divinity School; the Houghton Library, Harvard University; the Massachusetts Historical Society; and the Meadville-Lombard Theological School, Chicago.

Francis James Child

(1 February 1825 – 11 September 1896)

Janice L. Edens
Macon State College

See also the Child entry in *DLB 64: American Literary Critics and Scholars, 1850–1880.*

WORKS: *Four Old Plays: Three Interludes: Thersytes, Jack Jugler, and Heywood's Pardoner and Frere: and Jocaste, a Tragedy by Gascoigne and Kinwelmarsh,* edited, with introduction and notes, edited by Child (Cambridge, Mass.: G. Nichols, 1848);

The Poetical Works of Edmund Spenser, 5 volumes, edited, with biographical and philological notations, by Child (Boston: Little, Brown, 1855);

English and Scottish Ballads, 8 volumes, selected and edited by Child (Boston: Little, Brown, 1857–1859);

Il pesceballo, opera seria in un atto; musica del maestro Rossibelli-Donimozarti, Italian words by Child, English version by James Russell Lowell (Cambridge, Mass.: Riverside Press, 1862);

"Observations on the Language of Chaucer," *Memoirs of the American Academy of Arts and Sciences,* new series, 8 (1862): 445–502;

War-Songs for Freemen, compiled by Child (Boston: Ticknor & Fields, 1862);

Poems of Religious Sorrow, Comfort, Counsel and Aspiration, selected and edited by Child (New York: Sheldon, 1863; revised edition, New York: Hurd & Houghton, 1866);

Observations on the Language of Gower's Confessio Amantis (Boston: F. B. Dakin, 1868); originally submitted for publication in 1866, published in *Memoirs of the American Academy of Arts and Sciences,* new series, 9, part 2 (1873): 265–315;

The English and Scottish Popular Ballads, 5 volumes, collected and edited by Child (Boston: Houghton, Mifflin, 1882–1898; London: Henry Stevens & Stiles, 1882–1898);

The Childe of Bristowe, a Legend of the Fourteenth Century, edited by Child (Cambridge, Mass.: J. Wilson, 1886).

OTHER: "Ballad Poetry," in *Johnson's New Universal Cyclopedia,* edited by Frederick A. P. Barnard and Arnold Guyot (New York: A. J. Johnson, 1878), pp. 365–368;

"Introductory Note," in *The Epic Songs of Russia,* by Isabel Florence Hapgood (New York: Scribners, 1886).

SELECTED PERIODICAL PUBLICATIONS–UNCOLLECTED: "Bishop Percy's Folio Manuscript," anonymous, *Nation,* 5 (29 August 1867): 166–167;

"Ballad Books," anonymous, *Nation,* 7 (1868): 192–193;

"Old Ballads. Prof. Child's Appeal," *Notes and Queries,* Series 4, 11 (4 January 1873): 12.

Francis James Child is best remembered for *The English and Scottish Popular Ballads* (1882–1898), published first in ten parts, then in five quarto volumes. The set included 305 different ballads with their many variants and notes, and a glossary of terms. Child preceded each ballad with a preface explaining its history, sources, and foreign language parallels in as many as thirty different languages. The work is still considered one of the most important and painstaking collections of ballad literature, with its publication eventually paving the way for the study of folk literature in its own right. Thomas R. Lounsbury, Professor of English at Yale College, called *The English and Scottish Popular Ballads* "not merely one of a kind that has never before been done, in the English Language at least, but which will never have to be done a second time." Although this publication is Child's crowning achievement, he is also remembered for his illuminating study of Geoffrey Chaucer's language and his contribution to the development of comparative study in folklore research. His work in instigating the study of folklore and oral literature resulted in his becoming the first president of the American Folklore Society (1888), founded in Cambridge, Massachusetts. He also founded and became first president of the American Dialect Society.

Francis James Child was born in Boston on 1 February 1825, the third child of eight, to Joseph Child, a sailmaker, and Mary (James) Child. Such a modest background could have prevented Child from attaining a higher education. However, Epes Sargent Dixwell, headmaster of the Boston Latin School, noticed Child's intellectual gifts and encouraged him to prepare for Harvard College by attending his institution. Child graduated from Harvard in 1846, coincidentally the year the term "folklore" was coined.

Shortly after graduating from Harvard, Child was appointed as an instructor of math. He published his first book, a new edition of *Four Old Plays: Three Interludes: Thersytes, Jack Jugler, and Heywood's Pardoner and Frere: and Jocaste, a Tragedy by Gascoigne and Kinwelmarsh* (1848), when he was just twenty-three. His early editing of this volume foreshadows the kind of meticulous work he later did with *The English and Scottish Popular Ballads.* Like his later triumph, *Four Old Plays* includes an introduction, notes, and a glossary, all prepared by Child himself.

In 1849 Child became a tutor in history and political economy and an instructor of elocution. Shortly thereafter, in 1849, Jonathan I. Bowditch, to whom Child had dedicated *Four Old Plays,* loaned him the money to go to Germany. With a leave of absence provided by Harvard, Child left for Germany to do graduate work in philology at the universities of Berlin and Göttingen from 1849 to 1851. Although he began working on a doctoral thesis under Friedrich Wilhelm Schneidewinn and Karl Friedrich Hermann, well-respected philologists, Child returned to Harvard in 1851 without finishing his degree. However, in 1854 the University of Göttingen awarded him an honorary doctorate. Another important result of Child's brief stint in Germany was the influence of Jacob Grimm, a man who saw the literature of the world as interconnected, a view reflected in Child's later work with the ballads.

In August 1851, after returning from Germany, Child became Boylston Professor of Rhetoric and Oratory at Harvard. In 1860 he married Elizabeth Ellery Sedgewick of New York with whom he later had four children–Helen, Susan, Henrietta, and Francis. Because of the large number of student themes and recitations required by his position at Harvard, he was not able to pursue his great work until he changed his teaching assignment from Rhetoric and Oratory to English studies (eventually, in 1876, becoming the first Professor of English at Harvard). One of the problems of studying English literature during the 1850s and 1860s was the difficulty of obtaining authentic texts in America. To cope with this problem, scholars began issuing reprints of English texts, taking pains to verify their faithfulness to the original. In just such an attempt in 1852 Child became general editor of the reprints of the 130 volumes of *British Poets* (1853–1866), based on *The Aldine Edition of the British Poets* (1830–1853). Child also contributed *The Poetical Works of Edmund Spenser* (1855) to the effort. Though his work was based on another's edition, Child included some up-to-date material in his sketch of Spenser's life and additional philological apparatus. In the late 1850s Child published, as part of the *British Poets* series, *English and Scottish Ballads* in eight volumes (1857–1859), an important precursor to his life's work. This earlier work included the narrative poetry of anonymous British poets, which he collected and edited, the most comprehensive collection to date. However, it was not the product of the remarkable research efforts that Child later employed. It included all works considered ballads at that time and used printed sources. Child included some of the ballads from Thomas Percy's *Reliques of Ancient English Poetry* (1765) and was influenced by this work that helped shape his own. By the time of the second edition of *English and Scottish Ballads,* however, the influence had shifted from Percy to Svend Grundtvig and his ballad collection, *Danmarks gamle Folkeviser* (1853–). By comparing the prefaces of the 1857 and 1860 editions of Child's work, one can see his growing and changing concept of the ballad. By the second edition, Child had clarified his ballad theory, distinguishing

Drawing of Child while he was on leave from Harvard to do graduate work in philology at the University of Göttingen (Harvard University Archives)

between the true ballads of oral tradition, "spontaneous products of nature," and the more suspect "artificial literature." He began to see that to do a proper collection, he would have to abandon the printed texts and go back to the original manuscripts. He had been critical of Sir Walter Scott's *Minstrelsy of the Scottish Border* (1802–1803) because he doubted the authenticity of many of Scott's ballads and deplored changes Scott had made to the original manuscripts. He did not want to be responsible for making such changes.

His growing concern with authenticity can be seen when he was asked to do work with Chaucer similar to what he had done previously with Spenser. He declined because he did not think he could obtain an authentic version of Chaucer's text to work from. Because of Spenser's care with seeing his work published, one could have confidence in the published text of that poet's work, but the various manuscripts of Chaucer's work were all suspect.

Child did deliver "Observations on the Language of Chaucer" to the American Academy of Arts and Sciences on 3 June 1862. This lecture appeared as private preprints, available in September 1862, and then in the new series of the *Memoirs* of the Academy, volume eight (1862). This work is noteworthy because of Child's research that provided logical methods of determining when Chaucer's final *e* was and was not pronounced. His work influenced modern reading of Chaucer's language. On 9 January 1866 Child presented a similar paper on the language of John Gower's *Confessio Amantis* (1390), "Observations on the Language of Gower." This lecture was also distributed privately as a preprint during spring 1868. The *Memoirs* of the Academy did not appear until 1873. Both of these lectures were eventually condensed and rearranged in Alexander John Ellis's *On Early English Pronunciation* (1869–1889).

During the 1860s Child was heavily involved in supporting the Union cause. Unable to join the Union army because of bad eyesight, he aided the soldiers in several other ways. He compiled *War-Songs for Freemen* (1862), songs used by soldiers at the front. Some of these songs were written by Child, including the ballad "The Lass of Pamunky." Other contributors were James Russell Lowell, Oliver Wendell Holmes, John Greenleaf Whittier, and Julia Ward Howe. Child also wrote political tracts and broadsides and edited a collection, *Poems of Religious Sorrow, Comfort, Counsel and Aspiration* (1863), for those left behind. He prepared *Il pesceballo* (1862), a burlesque operetta, to raise money for war relief. This work was an eleven-scene parody of operatic conventions using well-known Italian and German texts and classical European music familiar to his literate audience, who would understand the humor. Its plot was probably based on an experience told to him by Harvard friend George Martin Lane, who had joined Child in his studies in Germany. Though Child began working on his parody in 1854, he did not finish it until 1862, spurred on by the war. The amateur production was first performed in Bessie Parson's home as a benefit for the Sanitary Commission, a charity for sick and injured soldiers. Further performances were held at Chickering Hall in Boston in 1864 to benefit Union soldiers in East Tennessee. The libretto was published in 1862, at the time of its first performance, with an English translation by James Russell Lowell.

Child's civic concerns were not limited to the Civil War, as evidenced by his canceling of classes one Tuesday in 1864 in order to distribute Republican ballots in front of Lyceum Hall. Even before the war he had taken his civic duties seriously. According to President Charles W. Eliot of Harvard, "Professor Child was, in the fifties, an ardent reformer in municipal politics. He was in the habit of attending the caucuses and other public meetings that were called in Cambridge to nominate candidates for municipal office, or to further measures of reform in the city."

In 1873 Child went abroad for his health, and in 1874 he wrote an article for *A. J. Johnson's New Universal*

Cyclopaedia (1877), the first to use American scholars for all its contributions. In this article he elaborated on the ballad theory he had suggested in the second edition of *English and Scottish Ballads*–that popular ballads are "spontaneous products of nature" whereas broadsides are "artificial literature." He saw the true ballad as international and universal, not individual, and he saw popular poetry as "before and beyond class." Popular ballads, according to Child, predated print, came from people of high and low classes, and reflected shared, public values. This concern with ancient, simple productions of the common people suggests Child's connection to the Romantic movement.

His evolving attitude toward the ballad was realized in his approach to his magnum opus, *The English and Scottish Popular Ballads,* in which he went back further than printed sources to manuscripts. Child wanted to gather all the genuine English ballads and to include only those taken down word for word from oral transmissions. He hoped to find old manuscripts that had transcribed the words of actual singers before cheap printing had allowed corruptions to creep into the texts. To retain the authenticity of the ballads, he planned to use only works orally transmitted by uneducated people. Part of his rationale was to preserve and document an early form of culture and literature to serve in comparison to later forms. To obtain these manuscripts he advertised for "Old Ballads" (in "Old Ballads. Prof. Child's Appeal") in *Notes and Queries* of 4 January 1873. Furthermore, he sent one thousand fliers to American college students, asking them to look for Irish-American ballads. For several years thereafter he continued to post notices in *Notes and Queries,* seeking additional manuscripts. During this time he was assisted by Frederick J. Furnivall, who served as an intermediary in receiving copies of manuscripts that Child's inquiries had elicited. Furnivall also helped Child by sending out queries to clergymen and schoolmasters who might have access to original manuscripts. Probably Furnivall's greatest benefit to Child had come previously, however, when he finally obtained permission to publish Percy's manuscript in 1867. Child had come to suspect that Percy's *Reliques of Ancient English Poetry* were less than authentic ballads and felt he could do no genuine work on these ballads until he saw the original manuscript that Percy had used. However, those in possession of the manuscript were refusing to release it. Furnivall eventually negotiated its publication, which enabled Child to begin his researches in earnest. Much had already been lost. When Percy had found the manuscript, pages of it were being used to light the fire in his friend's parlor; even more was lost when the bookbinder Percy sent it to have the edges trimmed. Finally, before publishing the ballads, Percy edited and polished the texts himself, ending up with corrupted versions. With the original manuscript Child could avoid duplicating these errors in his own work.

Other men also aided Child in his research. William Macmath of Edinburgh volunteered to help Child gather ballads, and Grundtvig, who had set the standard with his earlier work *Danmarks gamle Folkeviser* in regard to "scope and arrangement," gave Child advice and criticism during their correspondence from 1872 to 1882. Child's letters reveal his concern with the order as well as the content of his volumes, and he persisted in asking Grundtvig for help in these areas until Grundtvig provided him with concrete suggestions; Child followed the advice, organizing the ballads according to form (those of two-line stanzas first, four-line stanzas next, and so on). Another one of Child's major assistants was Mrs. Brown of Falkland, in Fife. She preserved almost thirty-six ballad texts, four of which are the only versions in existence. Child also obtained additional material through the agency of Child's longtime friend James Russell Lowell, who, as Minister to the Court of St. James in England, was able to put Child in touch with manuscript holders. Additional help with the ballads came from his many years of correspondence with William Walker of Aberdeen, Scotland. One of his last letters to Walker suggests Child intended to write a preface to the entire *English and Scottish Popular Ballads* series, but he died before he could produce more than a few lines.

Yet, for all this original work and as much as he decried the broadsides and garlands, he cites them for at least one version of a third of his ballads, and 20 percent of all the ballads come solely or primarily from them. Even though he had decided on a new method to apply in choosing ballads for his new volumes and dropped 115 of the ballads originally included in *English and Scottish Ballads,* only 90 of the 305 ballads in *The English and Scottish Popular Ballads* had not also been included in *English and Scottish Ballads.* One reason for this apparent discrepancy was that some of the oral ballads had a literary quality to them, and some of the broadsides came directly from the oral ballads. Furthermore, some broadsides had better and more extensive versions than the oral version. Child even admitted that Mrs. Brown could have been influenced by printed versions. In spite of his avowed purpose, he realized that the line between genuine and artificial was often hard to define. Another problem with authenticity was Child's own squeamishness about sexual matters, which he was reluctant to include in the texts of the ballads and often arbitrarily omitted.

Child continued to work on the ballads until his death, in spite of the gout and rheumatism that plagued him. The care with which he approached his work can be seen in this observation from a letter of 19 January

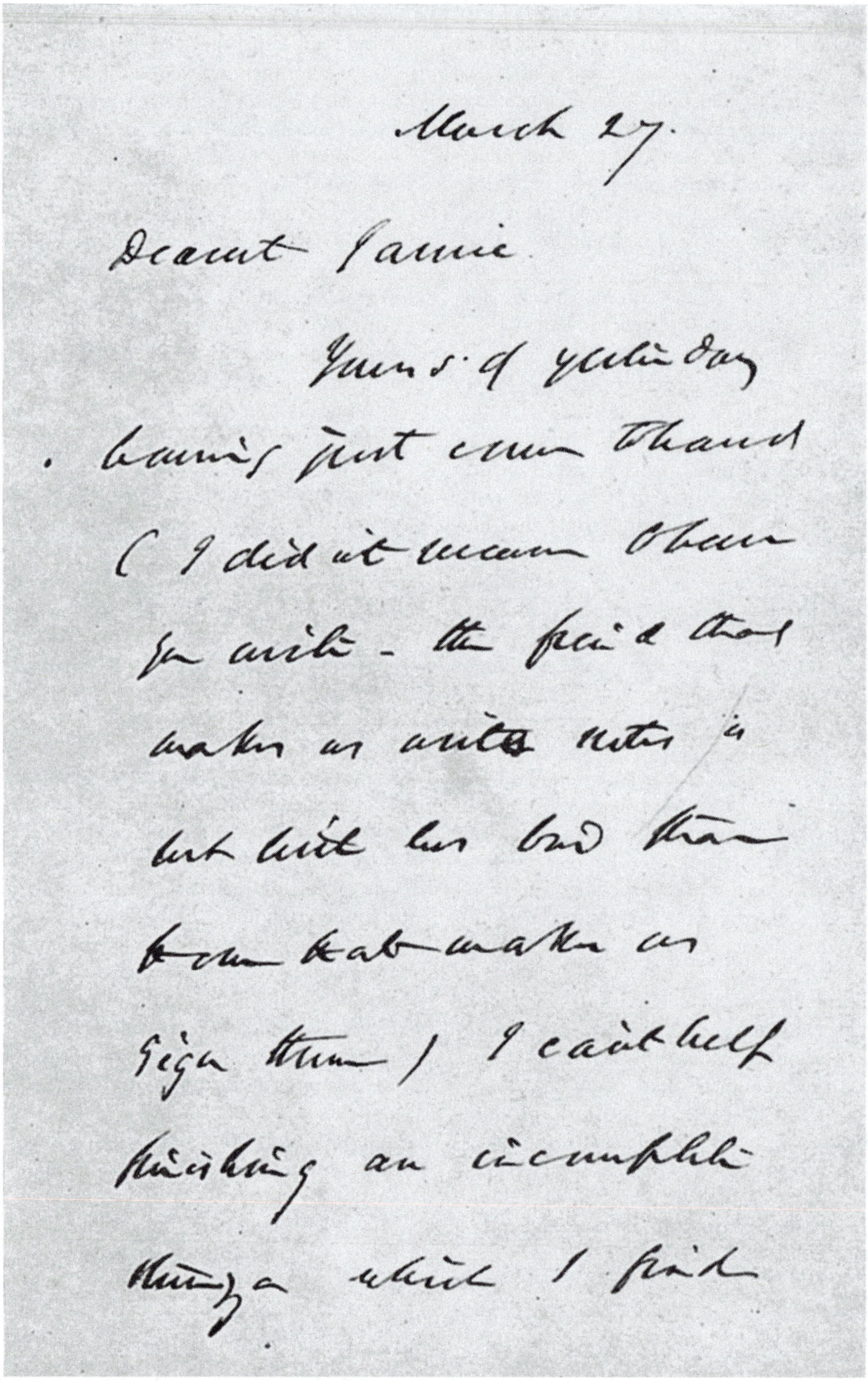

March 27.

Dearest Jamie

Page from Child's 27 March 1888 letter to James Russell Lowell (Harvard University Archives)

1895 to William Walker: "I have aimed to put into the Glossary every word and phrase likely to trouble any reader, and I have also registered almost every phenomenon in the language which might be of the least philological interest. No doubt I have done rather more than was strictly necessary."

Devoted to the ballads as he was, Child also had a thriving personal life during this time. For many years he corresponded with Emily Tuckerman of Stockbridge, Massachusetts, who later collected the letters and allowed them to be published as *A Scholar's Letters to a Young Lady* (1920), though at the time she wished to remain anonymous. Child had many friendships with women, and there is some evidence that his wife, Elizabeth, was annoyed by her husband's somewhat romantic correspondence with other women but learned to tolerate the situation. Child himself delighted in life and in what he called his "superstitions": "love of women, roses (including apple-blossoms), popular poetry, Shakespere [sic], my friends, wild flowers, trees, violin music, *voila*!" He cultivated more than three hundred rose bushes, of many varieties, in his front yard.

In the 1890s Child became chairman of the new Division of Modern Language at Harvard and as chairman was responsible for the English, German, French, Italian, Spanish, and Germanic and Romance Philology departments. He also continued to teach and, during the last two years of his life, conducted a graduate seminar on "The English and Scottish Popular Ballads." Though he could be impatient and sarcastic, Child was revered by students, who affectionately referred to him as Stubby because of his short, round, and stooped physique.

Child died on 11 September 1896 of kidney failure in Massachusetts General Hospital. Students and colleagues, who had been preparing a festschrift to honor his fifty years at Harvard, turned the book into the *Child Memorial Volume* (1896). He was eulogized by many of his famous contemporaries, who commented on Child's impact as a man, not just as a scholar. Charles Eliot Norton called him "original, quaint, humorous, sweet, sympathetic, tender-hearted, faithful." William James wrote about Child: "I *loved* Child more than any man I know"; he claimed Child "had a moral delicacy and a richness of heart that I never saw and never expect to see equalled [sic]." Henry James in *Notes of a Son and Brother* (1914) called Child a

> delightful man, rounded character, above all humanist and humorist. As he comes back to me with the quite circular countenance of the time before the personal cares and complications of life had quite gravely thickened for him, his aspect, all finely circular, with its golden rims of the largest glasses, its finished rotundity of figure and attitude, I see that there was the American spirit, since I was 'after it,' of a quality deeply inbred; beautifully adjusted to all extensions of knowledge and taste, and as seemed to me quite sublimely quickened by everything that was, at the time, so tremendously in question.

Child in his garden

The 1 November 1897 minutes of the Library Council of Harvard University, whose secretary Child was from 1867 until his death (he had also been elected secretary in 1865 of the Library Committee, the predecessor of the Council), paid tribute to him: "For all these the University is mainly indebted to Professor Child's loyal and indefatigable exertions. The frequenters of the Library will long miss him in his accustomed place before the little table at the East end of the old Stack, and the members of the council deeply mourn the loss of one who was wise, farseeing, and unselfish in his consideration of every department of learning with which the Library is concerned."

Letters:

A Scholar's Letters to a Young Lady: Passages from the Later Correspondence of Francis James Child, edited, with a biographical introduction by M. A. DeWolfe Howe (Boston: Atlantic Monthly Press, 1920 [limited edition]; Westport, Conn.: Greenwood Press, 1970);

"Appendix A, The Grundtvig-Child Correspondence," edited by Sigurd Bernhard Hustvedt, in *Ballad Books and Ballad Men* (Cambridge, Mass.: Harvard University Press, 1930), pp. 241–299;

Letters on Scottish Ballads, from Professor Francis J. Child to W. W., Aberdeen (Aberdeen, Scotland: Bon Accord Press, 1930;

The Scholar Friends: Letters of Francis James Child and James Russell Lowell, edited by Howe and G. W. Cottrell Jr. (Cambridge, Mass.: Harvard University Press, 1952).

References:

Michael J. Bell, "'No Borders to the Ballad Maker's Art': Francis James Child and the Politics of the People," *Western Folklore,* 47 (October 1988): 285–307;

Bertrand Harris Bronson, *The Ballad as Song* (Berkeley: University of California Press, 1969);

Bronson, *The Traditional Tunes of the Child Ballads: With their Texts, according to the Extant Records of Great Britain and America,* 4 volumes (Princeton: Princeton University Press, 1959–1972);

Tom Cheesman and Sigrid Rieuwerts, eds., *Ballads into Books: The Legacies of Francis James Child* (Berne, N.Y.: Peter Lang, 1997);

Francis Barton Grummere, "A Day with Professor Child," *Atlantic Monthly,* 103 (March 1909): 421–425;

Dave Harker, "Francis James Child and the 'Ballad Consensus,'" *Folk Music Journal,* 4, no. 2 (1981): 146–164;

Joseph Harris, ed., *The Ballad and Oral Literature* in *Harvard English Studies,* 17 (Cambridge, Mass.: Harvard University Press, 1991);

Walter Morris Hart, "Professor Child and the Ballad," *PMLA,* 21 (1906): 755–807;

Sigurd Bernhard Hustvedt, *Ballad Books and Ballad Men: Raids and Rescues in Britain, America, and the Scandinavian North Since 1800* (Cambridge, Mass.: Harvard University Press, 1930);

Hustvedt, *Ballad Criticism in Scandinavia and Great Britain during the Eighteenth Century* (New York: American-Scandinavian Foundation, 1916);

George Lyman Kittredge, "Francis James Child," *Atlantic Monthly,* 78 (December 1896): 737–742; slightly revised for *The English and Scottish Popular Ballads* (Boston: Houghton, Mifflin, 1883–1898), pp. xxiii–xxxi;

Jo McMurtry, "Francis James Child (1825–1896), Harvard, and *The English and Scottish Popular Ballads,*" in *English Language, English Literature: The Creation of an Academic Discipline* (Hamden, Conn.: Archon, 1985), pp. 65–110;

Charles Eliot Norton, "Francis James Child," *Harvard Graduate's Magazine,* 6 (December 1897): 161–169;

Roy Palmer, "'Veritable Dunghills': Professor Child and the Broadside," *Folk Music Journal,* 7, no. 2 (1996): 155–166;

James Reppert, "F. J. Child and the Ballad," *The Learned and the Lewd: Studies in Chaucer and Medieval Literature,*" edited by Larry D. Benson, *Harvard English Studies,* 5 (Cambridge, Mass.: Harvard University Press, 1974), pp. 197–212;

Sigrid Rieuwerts, "The Folk-Ballad: The Illegitimate Child of the Popular Ballad," *Journal of Folklore Research,* 33 (September–December 1996): 221–226;

Rieuwerts, "From Percy to Child: The 'Popular Ballad' as a Distinct and Very Important Species of Poetry," in *Ballads and Boundaries: Narrative Singing in an Intercultural Context,* edited by James Porter (Los Angeles: UCLA, 1995), pp. 13–20;

Rieuwerts, "'The Genuine Ballads of the People': F. J. Child and the Ballad Cause," *Journal of Folklore Research,* 31 (1994): 1–34;

Irwin Stambler and Grelun Landon, *Encyclopedia of Folk, Country and Western Music* (New York: St. Martin's Press, 1969);

Robin Varnum, "Harvard's Francis James Child: The Years of the Rose," *Harvard Library Bulletin,* 36, no. 6 (Summer 1998): 291–319.

Papers:

The papers of Francis James Child are in the *Child MSS,* 30 volumes, arranged and indexed by George Lyman Kittredge, the Houghton Library at Harvard University.

James Freeman Clarke

(4 April 1810 – 8 June 1888)

Alan D. Hodder
Hampshire College

See also the Clarke entry in *DLB 59: American Literary Critics and Scholars, 1800–1850.*

James Freeman Clarke

BOOKS: *False Witnesses Answered* (Boston: Leonard C. Bowles, 1835);

The Unitarian Reform (Boston: James Munroe, 1839);

Letter to the Unitarian Society in Louisville (Louisville, Ky.: Morton & Griswold, 1840);

The Well-Instructed Scribe; or, Reform and Conservatism. A Sermon Preached at the Installation of Rev. George F. Simmons, and Rev. Samuel Ripley, as Pastor and Associate Pastor over the Union Congregational Society in Waltham, Mass. October 27, 1841 (Boston: Benjamin H. Greene, 1841);

A Sermon Preached in Amory Hall, October 9th, 1842, Being the Sunday Succeeding the Death of William Ellery Channing (Boston: Benjamin H. Greene, 1842);

A Tract for the Times. No. 1. Repentance toward God (Boston: Office of the Christian World, 1843);

Slavery in the United States. A Sermon Delivered in Amory Hall, on Thanksgiving Day, November 24, 1842 (Boston: Benjamin H. Greene, 1843);

The Pilgrim Fathers: A Poem Recited in the Church of the Disciples, Boston, on the Festival of the Pilgrims, December 22d, 1842 (Boston: Thurston & Torry, 1843);

The Annexation of Texas. A Sermon, Delivered in the Masonic Temple, on Fast Day (Boston: Office of the Christian World, 1844);

The Peculiar Doctrine of Christianity; or Reconciliation of Jesus Christ (Boston: James Munroe, 1844);

A Protest Against American Slavery (Medford, Mass.: 1845);

A Sketch of the History of the Doctrine of the Atonement (Boston: James Munroe, 1845);

The Story of a Converted Sceptic (Boston: Crosby & Nichols, 1846);

The Church of the Disciples in Boston. A Sermon on the Principles and Methods of the Church of the Disciples, Delivered Sunday Morning and Evening, Dec. 7, 1845 (Boston: Benjamin H. Greene, 1846);

A Poem, Delivered before the Phi Beta Kappa Society, Alpha of Massachusetts, on its Anniversary, August 27, 1846 (Boston: Crosby & Nichols, 1846);

Charge at the Ordination of T. W. Higginson. (1847);

Dilemma of Orthodoxy (Boston: Office of the Christian World, 1847);

An Important Question. (Boston: Office of the Christian World, 1847);

The Church . . . As It Was, As It Is, As It Ought to Be. A Discourse Delivered at the Dedication of the Chapel, Built by the Church of the Disciples, Wednesday, March 15, 1848 (Boston: Benjamin H. Greene, 1848);

On the Spiritual Doctrine of Forgiveness (Manchester, U.K.: Johnson, Rawson, 1850?);

James Freeman. Discourse of Dedication of Freeman Place Chapel. [Boston?], 1850;

Slavery in its Relation to God. A Review of Rev. Dr. Lord's Thanksgiving Sermon, in Favor of Domestic Slavery, Entitled the Higher Law, in its Application to the Fugitive Slave Bill. By a Minister of the Gospel, in Massachusetts (Buffalo: A. M. Clapp, 1851);

The Christian Doctrine of Forgiveness of Sin: An Essay (Boston: Crosby & Nichols / New York: C. S. Francis, 1852);

Eleven Weeks in Europe; And What May Be Seen in That Time (Boston: Ticknor, Reed & Fields, 1852);

The Christian Doctrine of Prayer. An Essay (Boston: Crosby & Nichols, 1854);

The Rendition of Anthony Burns. Its Causes and Consequences. A Discourse on Christian Politics, Delivered in Williams Hall, Boston, on Whitsunday, June 4, 1854 (Boston: Crosby & Nichols, 1854);

Jesus Christ Himself the True Cornerstone: A Sermon Preached at the Montreal Convention, October, 1854 (Boston: Leonard C. Bowles, 1854);

Obituary of H. J. Huidekoper (Boston: Crosby & Nichols, 1854);

Polemics and Irenics. An Address on Theology, before the Ministerial Conference, at Bedford Street Chapel, Wednesday, May 31, 1854 (Boston: Crosby & Nichols, 1854);

A Church and Its Methods (Albany: Weed, Parsons, 1859);

Present Condition of the Free Colored People of the United States (Boston & New York: American Anti-Slavery Society, 1859);

Theodore Parker, and his Theology: A Discourse Delivered in the Music Hall, Boston, Sunday, Sept. 25, 1859 (Boston: Walker, Wise, 1859);

Causes and Consequences of the Affair at Harper's Ferry. A Sermon Preached in the Indiana Place Chapel, on Sunday Morning, Nov. 6, 1859 (Boston: Walker, Wise, 1859);

The Good Hospital (Boston, 1859);

A Look at the Life of Theodore Parker: A Discourse concerning Theodore Parker; Delivered in the Indiana-Place Chapel, June 3, 1860 (Boston: Walker, Wise, 1860);

Secession, Concession, or Self-Possession: Which? (Boston: Walker, Wise, 1861);

"Two Ways in Religion" Reviewed: A Letter to Rev. F. D. Huntington, D.D. (Boston: American Unitarian Association, 1862);

Discourse on the Aspects of the War, Delivered in the Indiana-Place Chapel, Boston, on Fast Day, April 2, 1863 (Boston: Walker, Wise, 1863);

The Word in the Beginning with God: A Sermon Preached at the Ordination of William Brown as Pastor of the First Church, Sherborn, Mass., November 5, 1863 (Boston: John Wilson, 1863);

Is Evil Eternal? A Reply to Dr. Mansel (1864);

The Hour Which Cometh, and Now Is: Sermons, Preached in Indiana-Place Chapel, Boston (Boston: Walker, Wise, 1864); revised, *The Hour Which Cometh and Now Is.* (Boston: William V. Spenser, 1868);

Natural and Artificial Methods in Education. Lectures Delivered before the American Institute of Instruction, at Concord, N.H., August 27, 1863 (Boston: Ticknor & Fields, 1864);

A Sermon Preached before the Delegates to the National Unitarian Convention, New York, Tuesday Evening, April 4, 1865 (Boston: Walker, Fuller, 1865);

Orthodoxy: Its Truths and Errors (Boston: American Unitarian Association; Boston: Walker, Fuller; New York: James Miller, 1866);

Inspiration of the New Testament (Boston: American Unitarian Association, 1867);

The Duties of Massachusetts. A Sermon Delivered before the Executive and Legislative Departments of the Government of Massachusetts, at the Annual Election, Wednesday, Jan. 1, 1868 (Boston: Wright & Potter, 1868);

Steps of Belief; or, Rational Christianity Maintained against Atheism, Free Religion, and Romanism (Boston: American Unitarian Association, 1870);

Ten Great Religions: An Essay in Comparative Theology (Boston: James R. Osgood, 1871);

The Atonement (New York: Office of the "Liberal Christian," 1872);

What Do Unitarians Believe? (New York: Office of the "Liberal Christian," 1872);

Common-Sense in Religion: A Series of Essays (Boston: James R. Osgood, 1874);

Peter at Antioch; or, The Vatican vs. Bismark and Gladstone. A Sermon Preached by James Freeman Clarke, to the Church of the Disciples, Boston, Dec. 20th, 1874 (Boston: Office of the Saturday Evening Gazette, 1875);

Oration Delivered before the City Government and Citizens of Boston, in Music Hall, July 5, 1875 (Boston: Rockwell & Churchill, 1875);

Essentials and Non-Essentials in Religion. Six Lectures Delivered in the Music Hall, Boston (Boston: American Unitarian Association, 1877);

Go Up Higher or Religion in Common Life (Boston: Lee & Shepard; New York: Charles T. Dillingham, 1877);

The Old South Speaks (Boston, 1877);

Clarke's 1835 watercolor of the First Unitarian Church of Louisville, his first ministerial assignment (The Filson Club and the First Unitarian Church of Louisville, Kentucky)

Why Am I a Unitarian? A Lecture Delivered in the Music Hall, Boston, Sunday Evening, June 10th, 1877 (Boston: George H. Ellis, 1877; London: British & Foreign Unitarian Association, 1894);

How to Find the Stars with Indications of the Most Interesting Objects in the Starry Heavens, and An Account of the Astronomical Lantern and Its Use (Boston: Lockwood, Brooks, 1878);

Memorial and Biographical Sketches (Boston: Houghton, Osgood, 1878);

The New Theology (N.p., 1878);

One God, The Father (1878);

The State of the Nation; or, What the Nation Asks of Congress and the President. Discourse Delivered by James Freeman Clarke, Fast Day, April 11, 1878 (Boston, 1878);

Orthodox Views of the Atonement Examined, with Especial Reference to Some Recent Statements of Joseph Cook (Boston: American Unitarian Association, 1879);

On Giving Names to Towns and Streets (Boston: Lockwood, Brooks, 1880);

Self-Culture: Physical, Intellectual, Moral, and Spiritual. A Course of Lectures (Boston: James R. Osgood, 1880);

Events and Epochs in Religious History: Being the Substance of a Course of Twelve Lectures Delivered in the Lowell Institute, Boston, in 1880 (Boston: James R. Osgood, 1881);

The Legend of Thomas Didymus the Jewish Sceptic (Boston: Lee & Shepard; New York: Charles T. Dillingham, 1881);

Rational Sunday Observance (London: W. Reeves, 1881);

Work of Unitarians in the Past and the Future, A Sermon Preached at the Annual Meeting of the Association, Unity Church, Islington, May 31st, 1882 (London: British & Foreign Unitarian Association, 1882);

Anti-Slavery Days, A Sketch of the Struggle Which Ended in the Abolition of Slavery in the United States (New York: J. W. Lovell, 1883);

Christ and Christianity (London: British & Foreign Unitarian Association, 1883; Boston: George H. Ellis, 1902);

Ten Great Religions. Part II. A Comparison of All Religions (Boston & New York: Houghton, Mifflin, 1883);

Sermon on Channing Preached at Newport, July 15, 1883, on the Dedication of the Memorial Window, Representing a Sower Going Forth to Sow (Boston: George H. Ellis, 1883);

A Collection of Twelve Sermons Preached at the Church of the Disciples (N.p., 1884);
The Ideas of the Apostle Paul Translated into Their Modern Equivalents (Boston: James R. Osgood, 1884);
Manual of Unitarian Belief (Boston: Unitarian Sunday-School Society, 1884);
Address of Rev. James Freeman Clarke, at Tremont Temple, October 1, 1884. And the Letter of Rev. Robert Collyer, D.D. (Chicago: Central Committee of Republicans & Independents, 1884);
Christ and His Antichrists. A Sermon Preached to the Church of the Disciples, Boston (Boston: George H. Ellis, 1885);
The Introduction to the Gospel of John. A Sermon Preached to the Church of the Disciples, Boston (Boston: George H. Ellis, 1885);
The Five Points of Calvinism and the Five Points of the New Theology. A Sermon Preached to the Church of the Disciples, Boston, May 10, 1885 (Boston: George H. Ellis, 1885);
Messages of Faith, Hope and Love (Boston: George H. Ellis, 1885);
The Sin Against the Holy Ghost. A Sermon Preached to the Church of the Disciples, Boston (Boston: George H. Ellis, 1885);
Agnosticism vs. Positivism. An Essay (Boston: George H. Ellis, 1886);
Every-Day Religion (Boston: William Ticknor, 1886);
Memoir of Ralph Waldo Emerson (Boston, 1886);
The Fourth Gospel: The Question of Its Origin Stated and Discussed (Boston: George H. Ellis, 1886);
The Hercules and Wagoner of To-Day or State Help vs. Self Help. An Essay (Boston: George H. Ellis, 1886);
Is Probation or Education the End of Life: A Sermon Preached to the Church of the Disciples, Boston (Boston: George H. Ellis, 1886);
Old and New Ideas Concerning the Divinity of Jesus (Boston: George H. Ellis, 1886);
The Scientific Basis of Prayer. An Essay (Boston: George H. Ellis, 1886);
The True Coming of Christ. A Sermon Preached to the Church of the Disciples, Boston (Boston: George H. Ellis, 1886);
Vexed Questions in Theology. A Series of Essays (Boston: George H. Ellis, 1886);
Anarchy and Law (Boston: George H. Ellis, 1887);
Dorothea L. Dix (Boston: George H. Ellis, 1887);
From Faith to Faith (Boston: George H. Ellis, 1887);
A Happy New Year (Boston: George H. Ellis, 1887);
Ministry of the Letter and the Ministry of the Spirit (Boston: George H. Ellis, 1887);
The Mutual Obligations of Science and Religion (Boston: George H. Ellis, 1887);
The Pew System and the Free-Seat System (Boston: George H. Ellis, 1887);
Rejoice Evermore (Boston: George H. Ellis, 1887);
A Sermon on Scolding (Boston: George H. Ellis, 1887);
Temperance Efforts and Temperance Methods (Boston: George H. Ellis, 1887);
The Wrath of the Lamb (Boston: George H. Ellis, 1887);
Be Not Weary in Well-Doing (Boston: George H. Ellis, 1888);
The Broad Church (Boston: George H. Ellis, 1888);
Christ and Other Masters (Boston: George H. Ellis, 1888);
Five Sources of Our Knowledge of Jesus Christ (London: Christian Life Publishing, 1888);
The Hereafter–23 Answers by as many Teachers (Boston: George H. Ellis, 1888);
Homes in Heaven and on Earth (Boston: George H. Ellis, 1888);
The Joys of Christmas (Boston: George H. Ellis, 1888);
The Lord's Prayer. Being the Last Eight Discourses of the Rev. James Freeman Clarke, D.D. (London: Christian Life Office, 1888; Boston: American Unitarian Association, 1891);
The Mind of Christ (Boston: George H. Ellis, 1888);
The Old and New View of the Hereafter (Boston: George H. Ellis, 1888);
The Theology of the Future (London: Christian Life Publishing, 1888);
The Transformation of Years into Life (Boston: George H. Ellis, 1888);
What God Gives He Gives Forever (Boston: George H. Ellis, 1888);
Woman Suffrage: Reasons For and Against (Boston: George H. Ellis, 1888);
Church-Going: Past, Present, and Future (Boston: George H. Ellis, [188?]);
Selections from Sermons Preached to the Church of the Disciples (Boston: Lowell & Co., [188?]);
Deacon Herbert's Bible-Class (Boston: George H. Ellis, 1890);
What Do Unitarians Believe About God? (Boston: George H. Ellis, 1890);
What Do Unitarians Believe About Jesus Christ? (Boston: George H. Ellis, 1890);
What Do Unitarians Believe About Sin and Salvation? (Boston: George H. Ellis, 1890);
James Freeman Clarke: Autobiography, Diary and Correspondence, edited by Edward Everett Hale (Boston & New York: Houghton, Mifflin, 1891);
What Do Unitarians Believe About the Holy Ghost? (Boston: George H. Ellis, 1892);
Nineteenth Century Questions (Boston & New York: Houghton, Mifflin, 1897; London: Gay & Bird, 1898);
The Resurrection of Jesus (Boston: George H. Ellis, 1900);
The Genuine Prayer (Boston: George H. Ellis, 1901);

Salvation by Character (Boston: George H. Ellis, 1905);
God Loves all Souls (Boston: American Unitarian Association, 1906);
Keep the Bible (Boston: American Unitarian Association, 1906);
The True Self Is the Best Self (Boston: American Unitarian Association, 1906);
What is Heaven? (Boston: American Unitarian Association, 1906);
Hymns and Poems (Boston: George H. Ellis, 1908);
Conference Sermon, Preached at the First Meeting of the National Conference of Unitarian and Other Christian Churches, April 4, 1863 (Boston: George H. Ellis, 1909);
The Transfiguration of Life (Boston: American Unitarian Association, 1909);
The Blessings of Our Knowledge and of Our Ignorance in Regard to a Future State (Boston: George H. Ellis, 1910);
Not Unclothed, but Clothed Upon (Boston: George H. Ellis, 1910);
Why Women Ought to Desire the Ballot (Boston: Lilian Freeman Clarke, 1913);
The Lessons of the American Civil War (Boston: George H. Ellis, 1916);
Many Mansions in God's House (Boston: American Unitarian Association, 1925);
What Good Has the Birth of Jesus Brought to the World (Boston: American Unitarian Association, 1926);
A Christmas Parable (Boston: General Alliance of Unitarian and Other Liberal Christian Women, 1926);
The True Doctrine of Liberal Christianity (Boston: American Unitarian Association, 1937);
Charles Sumner. His Character and Career (Boston: n.d.; republished by George H. Ellis, 1911);
Do not be Discouraged (Boston: American Unitarian Association, n.d.);
The Experiment of a Free Church; Its Difficulties and Advantages (Boston, n.d.);
The Fatherhood of God (Boston: George H. Ellis, n.d.);
From the Old Faith to the New (Boston: American Unitarian Association, n.d.);
Has Unitarianism Done Its Work? A Sermon Preached to the Church of the Disciples, Boston (Boston: American Unitarian Association, n.d.);
How to Get Eteranl Life (Boston: American Unitarian Association, n.d.);
How to Get the Most out of the Coming Year (Boston: George H. Ellis, n.d.);
The Leadership of Jesus (Boston: George H. Ellis, n.d.);
Man Doth not Live by Bread Alone (Boston: George H. Ellis, n.d.);
Old and New Views Concerning the Bible (Boston: George H. Ellis, n.d.);

Self-portrait in Clarke's "Journal for 1839-1840"
(Houghton Library, Harvard University)

Revivals, Natural and Artificial (Boston: American Unitarian Association, n.d.);
Some Reasons for Believing in a Future Life (Boston: George H. Ellis, n.d.);
Unitarian Belief in Regard to the Supernatural Element in Christianity (Boston: George H. Ellis, n.d.);
Unitarian Belief in Regard to Vicarious Sacrifice (Boston: George H. Ellis, n.d.);
We Need to Know God (Boston: American Unitarian Association, n.d.);
What do Unitarians Believe about Heaven and Hell? (Boston: George H. Ellis, n.d.).

OTHER: *The Disciples' Hymn Book: A Collection of Hymns and Chants for Public and Private Devotion, edited by Clarke* (Boston: Benjamin H. Greene, 1844);
Service Book: For the Use of the Church of the Disciples (Boston: Benjamin H. Greene, 1844);
Memoirs of Margaret Fuller Ossoli, 2 volumes, edited by Clarke with Ralph Waldo Emerson and William Henry Channing (Boston: Phillips, Sampson, 1852); republished in 3 volumes (London: Bentley, 1852);
William Hull and the Surrender of Detroit (Boston: George H. Ellis, 1912).

TRANSLATIONS: *Wilhelm Martin Leberecht de Wette, Theodore; or, The Skeptic's Conversion. History of the Culture of a Protestant Clergyman. Translated from the*

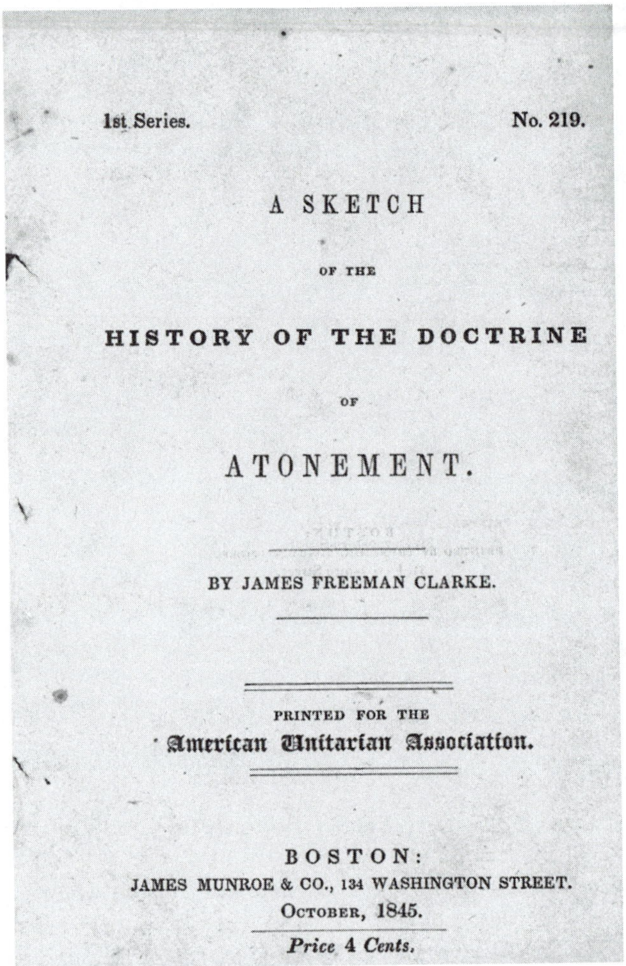
1st Series. No. 219.

A SKETCH

OF THE

HISTORY OF THE DOCTRINE

OF

ATONEMENT.

BY JAMES FREEMAN CLARKE.

PRINTED FOR THE

American Unitarian Association.

BOSTON:
JAMES MUNROE & CO., 134 WASHINGTON STREET.
October, 1845.

Price 4 Cents.

Title page for one of Clarke's religious pamphlets (Collection of Joel Myerson)

German of De Wette, 2 volumes, translated by Clarke (Boston: Hilliard, Gray, 1841);

Karl Hase, *Life of Jesus. A Manual for Academic Study,* translated by Clarke (Boston: Walker, Wise, 1860);

Exotics: Attempts to Domesticate Them, translated by Clarke with Lilian Rebecca Clarke (Boston: James R. Osgood, 1875).

In recent historiography, the name of James Freeman Clarke usually occurs in connection with the movement of religious reform and literary emergence known as American Transcendentalism. Among the young Unitarian ministers sympathetic to the new Romantic views of the 1830s, however, Clarke typified those who espoused a more conservative church-based brand of Transcendentalist vision. In marked contrast to Ralph Waldo Emerson, who resigned his pastorate in 1832 and subsequently moved beyond the pale of the Christian churches altogether, or Theodore Parker, who, while remaining active in the ecclesiastical life of Boston, embraced a form of radical post-Christian theology, Clarke quietly insisted on the privileged place of Jesus for the life of faith and remained active in his denomination until the end of his long career in the ministry. A close friend and contemporary of several leaders of the movement–including Margaret Fuller, William Henry Channing, and Frederic Henry Hedge–Clarke contributed crucially to the group's early sense of itself, both socially and intellectually, and despite his resistance to the more radical expressions of Transcendentalism, he stoutly defended the views of his friends from their more conservative detractors. Particularly significant to the movement was Clarke's informed sponsorship of German literary, theological, and philosophical writings. Together with Fuller and Hedge, Clarke played a key role in helping to translate and popularize representative texts of the German Romantic tradition generally recognized as sources for the new views but inaccessible to most of his contemporaries. Yet, despite his better-known role in the Transcendentalist movement, Clarke's contributions to the religious and literary culture of nineteenth-century Boston and, more widely, of the country at large, extended well beyond the confines of the movement itself. Clarke was a prolific and apparently indefatigable writer–author of more than a hundred books and pamphlets on subjects including theology, education, church practice and polity, comparative religion, and even astronomy. He was a leading shaper of nineteenth-century Unitarian thought and practice, serving throughout his career as a voice of reason and moderation in the sometimes heated exchanges between the radicals and the traditionalists of his denomination. He was an effective activist and often indispensable spokesman for a host of consequential reform movements of his time, in particular, abolitionism, and, toward the end of his life, female suffrage. Finally, in his lectures and scholarly writings on comparative religion, Clarke became a pioneer of the serious academic study of world religions in America.

James Freeman Clarke was born on 4 April 1810 in Hanover, New Hampshire, the third of five children of Samuel Clarke and Rebecca Hull Clarke. Clarke's father, a reserved and silent man, was full of enterprise but short on follow-through: over the course of his life, he worked variously as an inventor, sheepherder, architect, artist, mechanic, physician, lawyer, and druggist. Clarke's mother was a practical, sociable, and sometimes outspoken woman who resigned herself early in life to her husband's quixotic career and, after his death in 1830, took on boarders to support the family. Rebecca Clarke was the daughter of General William Hull, a flinty veteran of Valley Forge, who, after a humiliating surrender to British forces at Detroit in the War of 1812, returned home to an ignominious retirement in Newton, Massachusetts. In 1846 Clarke wrote an account of the campaign of 1812 to redeem his grandfather's blighted reputation. On the other side of the family was James Freeman, Clarke's stepgrandfather and namesake, who, in the years following the American Revolution, had turned old King's Chapel in Boston into a cornerstone of the Unitarian establishment. Though fond of all his grandchildren, Freeman felt a special attachment to the young James and petitioned successfully to raise and educate his grandson in his own household in Newton. Clarke later praised his grandfather Freeman as a "wonderful teacher" who anticipated by sixty years "the best methods of modern instruction."

Not until the age of ten, when Clarke enrolled in the Boston Latin School, did he experience firsthand the inside of a New England schoolroom. Though his grandfather had prepared him well in the classics, mathematics, and history, Clarke found the emphasis on drills and rote memorization discouraging. When he entered Harvard College in 1825, the situation hardly seemed any better. Every student was expected to pursue the same tedious curriculum in the classics, mathematics, philosophy, history, and rhetoric, together with a smattering of science. Spoiled at an early age by his grandfather's enlightened educational methods, he thought the Harvard curriculum stultifying, despite the presence there of several eminent scholars: "No attempt was made to interest us in our studies. We were expected to wade through Homer as though the Iliad were a bog, and it was our duty to get along at such a rate *per diem*. Nothing was said of the glory and grandeur, the tenderness and charm of this immortal epic." Yet, Harvard did have some distinct advantages. Among the members of the celebrated "Class of 1829" were several men who later led notable careers, including the mathematician Benjamin Pierce, the eminent jurist Benjamin Robbins Curtis, and the physician and author Oliver Wendell Holmes. William Henry Channing, Clarke's classmate from the Latin School and a lifelong friend, was also a member of the Class of 1829. On entering the Harvard Divinity School, Clarke became acquainted with an even wider circle of acquaintances whose lives intersected his for years to come. Besides Cambridge society, Clarke enjoyed Professor John Farrar's lectures on philosophy, physics, and astronomy, and under the supervision of pioneering Germanist Charles Follen, Clarke became an avid gymnast. To supplement his physical education programs, Follen had erected a seventy-foot mast, equipped with ropes for climbing, on the old delta north of Harvard Yard. Clarke gained a reputation for

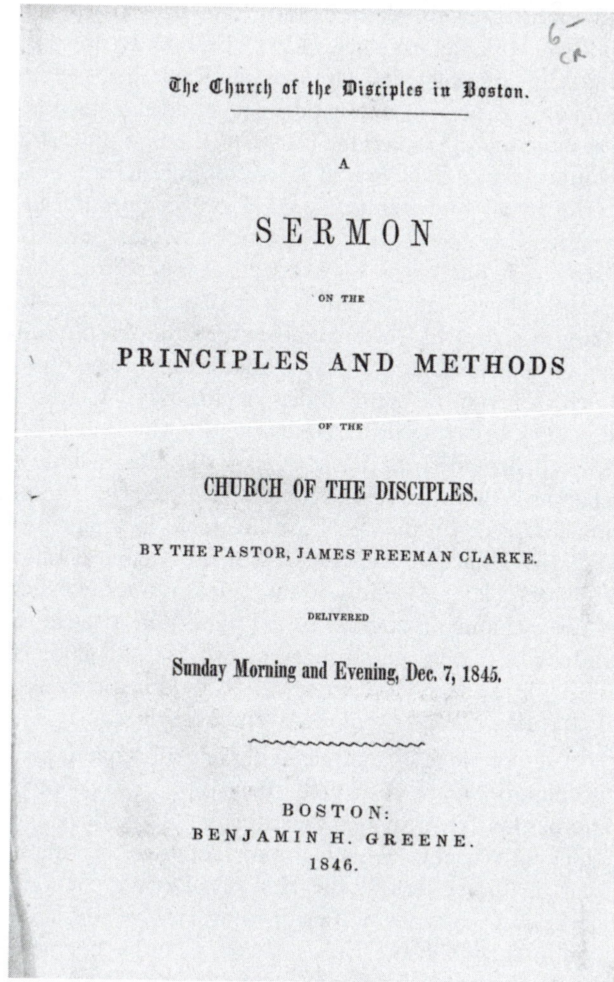
The Church of the Disciples in Boston.

A

SERMON

ON THE

PRINCIPLES AND METHODS

OF THE

CHURCH OF THE DISCIPLES.

BY THE PASTOR, JAMES FREEMAN CLARKE.

DELIVERED

Sunday Morning and Evening, Dec. 7, 1845.

BOSTON:
BENJAMIN H. GREENE.
1846.

Title page for one of Clarke's sermons (Collection of Joel Myerson)

fearlessness among his classmates for his famously vertiginous ascents to the top of Follen's mast.

For many students the other principal advantage of Harvard was the college library. Putting aside their assigned copies of Hugh Blair's *Rhetoric* (1784), Clarke and his classmates found themselves captivated instead by the works of Sir Thomas Browne, Ben Jonson, Charles Lamb, Sir Walter Scott, and William Wordsworth. These writers were "our real professors of rhetoric," Clarke later remarked. During his senior year, he also stumbled for the first time upon James Marsh's American editions of Samuel Taylor Coleridge's prose works. Coleridge precipitated a sea change in Clarke's developing philosophical outlook and opened the way to his subsequent embrace of German Romantic thought and Transcendentalism. Throughout the 1820s and 1830s, educated New Englanders were still held in thrall by the philosophy of John Locke. Clarke himself encountered Locke's works in his grandfather's library but found Locke's sensationalism and particularly his "polemic . . . against innate ideas" personally unpalatable. In arguing with Immanuel Kant that while "knowledge begins *with* experience it does not come *from* experience," Coleridge provided the first powerful rebuttal Clarke had seen of Lockean empiricism. This insight struck him with the force of a revelation. Recalling this discovery later in life, Clarke wrote: "Then I discovered that I was born a transcendentalist . . . I became a great reader of Coleridge, and was quite ready to accept his distinction between the reason and the understanding. . . . This distinction helped me much in my subsequent studies of theology." Clarke's discovery of Kant and Coleridge had lasting repercussions. It provided the basic rationale for his hallmark religious inclusivism and his rejection of creed as a criterion for sectarian divisions. As he wrote in a letter to Unitarian colleague and friend William Greenleaf Eliot a few years later, "Faith is, in my opinion, not the belief of propositions or dogmas of any kind, but a sense of truth, which may be stronger or weaker. All faith is essentially faith in God, inasmuch as God is the source of all truths, the centre of the spiritual world. . . ."

If Coleridge inaugurated Clarke's subsequent preoccupation with German Romantic philosophy, Thomas Carlyle provided the impetus for what became a lifelong romance with German literature. During a break in his studies at the Harvard Divinity School, Clarke ran across some unsigned articles by the flamboyant Carlyle in the *Edinburgh Review* and other periodicals. Through these provocative pieces, Clarke was first made aware of the rich German Romantic tradition, particularly the works of Johann Wolfgang von Goethe. Abetting these new literary interests was the brilliant young Margaret Fuller, a distant family relation, with whom Clarke had struck up an acquaintance during his senior year. The two young people shared much in the way of Cambridge society and were galvanized by many of the same intellectual enthusiasms. Clarke was at first "puzzled" and a bit overwhelmed by his precocious and dauntingly accomplished cousin but was quick to pronounce her "the most remarkable of women." Soon they saw or wrote to each other on almost a daily basis. In Fuller, Clarke found a much prized confidante and mentor; in Clarke, Fuller discovered a sensitive and appreciative friend. In an 1830 letter Clarke expresses gratitude for the "wonderful epoch" that had dawned in his life with her friendship and resolves, through her inspiration, "to live out of my own soul." After Fuller's tragic death by shipwreck off Fire Island in 1850, Clarke agreed to collaborate with Emerson and William Henry Channing in editing her scattered memoirs. The sections of the *Memoirs of Margaret Fuller Ossoli* (1852) attributed to him are animated by fervent admiration and unqualified gratitude for her contributions to his own personal growth. She possessed a genius, he wrote, for recognizing "the secret interior capability" in each of her friends and an uncanny skill for knowing how best to draw them out. The two had responded similarly, he recalled, to "the wild bugle-call of Thomas Carlyle" and had undertaken the demanding study of German together.

By the end of 1832 Clarke had also become acquainted with Emerson, describing in his journal a conversation they had had about their mutual interests in Goethe, German literature, and Carlyle. Having himself graduated from the Harvard Divinity School, Emerson had recently stepped down from his position as minister of the Second Church of Boston and was contemplating a new career as a lecturer and author. By the end of the decade, Emerson's writing and addresses became a lightning rod for attacks by the traditionalists of the Divinity School against the dangerous influence of German philosophy and the alleged infidelities of some of the younger ministers of the denomination. While Clarke himself felt that Emerson had gone too far in overthrowing the traditional role of Christ in the Christian faith, he admired Emerson personally and agreed with his basic philosophical premise. "As for Mr. Emerson," he wrote to his prospective wife in 1838, "When we are permitted to meet a man whose life is holiness, whose words are gems, whose character is of the purest type of heroism, yet of childlike simplicity,–shall we stop to find fault with the shape of his coat, or the coherence of his opinions, instead of gratefully receiving this Heaven's gift?"

Precisely these heterodox Transcendentalist influences, in particular the writings of Coleridge, spurred his call to the Christian ministry. Like most of his friends, Clarke had been raised under the liberal banner of the New England churches. His own grandfather had been among the first Boston ministers openly to avow himself a Unitarian, and Clarke looked with warm admiration on the example of William Ellery Channing, the spiritual leader of his generation. Since 1805 the Harvard Divinity School had itself functioned as a Unitarian seminary, and by the time Clarke graduated in 1833, he too had resolved to dedicate his life to the ministry. For his first sermon, he preached from Ecclesiastes: "Whatsoever thy hand findeth to do, do it with thy might"–a passage that reminded him of Goethe's maxim, "Do your present duty!" which in later years came to serve as the motto of his life. Yet, Clarke was not content to slip into the predictable, preassigned role of a local minister and chose instead to take on the exhausting work of a missionary preacher in what was then the Western hinterlands of Louisville, Kentucky. Nothing he had learned at the Harvard Divinity School prepared him for the frustrations of a frontier ministry. He went to Kentucky to plead the cause of liberal religion but realized when he arrived that his first order of business was simply to preach the gospel of Christ: "I believed that every church should have for its object the teaching of positive Christianity . . . and seldom went out of my way to engage in controversy." But Clarke's work in Louisville was frustrating: the pastoral work was tedious, and genuine converts were slow in coming. Furthermore, he missed the culture and lively intellectual exchange of Cambridge and Boston.

In part to compensate for the cultural aridity of his new environment, Clarke began to devote more attention to his writing. In 1836 he agreed to take over publication and chief editorial responsibilities of the *Western Messenger,* a monthly magazine of religion and literature that fellow Unitarian Ephraim Peabody had started in Cincinnati the previous year. Conceived as a vehicle for spreading liberal culture to the Ohio Valley, the *Western Messenger* had enjoyed modest success as a mouthpiece for the Western Unitarian mission. In his capacity as editor, Clarke sought to expand the focus of the magazine to include material on antislavery, labor relations, German literature, and contemporary poetry. Actively soliciting materials from his Transcendentalist friends, Clarke published many essays, poems, and translations reflecting their Romantic views and on occasion defended Emerson and "the new school of literature and religion." Under Clarke's stewardship the *Western Messenger* became in effect the first journal of the Transcendentalist Movement. But Clarke also found in its pages a convenient venue for his own literary and theological projects. One of these undertakings, appearing serially beginning in February of 1836, was his massive translation of a novel by the German theologian Wilhelm Martin Leberecht de Wette. Published in toto in 1841 as *Theodore; or, The Skeptic's Conversion. History of the Culture of a Protestant Clergyman, Translated from the German of De Wette,* the narrative takes the form of a theological bildungsroman in which the protagonist struggles to come to terms with a host of competing theological positions before arriving at a just and convincing theological vision of his own. Clarke presented de Wette's novel to his English-speaking readership as a convenient demonstration of the range and sophistication of German theological work.

Despite the consolations afforded by Clarke's literary activities during his Louisville period, he longed to return to the more cosmopolitan setting of eastern Massachusetts. In 1839 he married Anna Huidekoper, the daughter of Harm Jan Huidekoper, a wealthy Unitarian businessman from Meadville, Pennsylvania, who had supported and encouraged Clarke's work in the

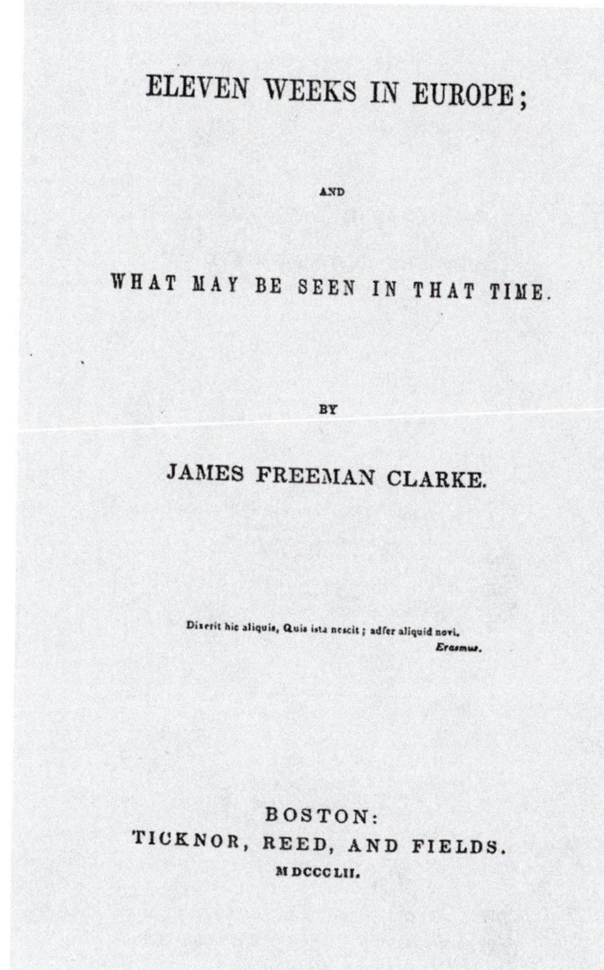

ELEVEN WEEKS IN EUROPE;

AND

WHAT MAY BE SEEN IN THAT TIME.

BY

JAMES FREEMAN CLARKE.

Dixerit hic aliquis, Quis ista nescit; adfer aliquid novi.
Erasmus.

BOSTON:
TICKNOR, REED, AND FIELDS.
MDCCCLII.

Title page for Clarke's book about his travels during the summer of 1849

Ohio River Valley. The next year Clarke brought his wife and their infant son, Herman, to Boston to resettle, and over the next decade, the Clarkes welcomed three more children–Lilian, Eliot, and Cora–into their growing household. In 1841 Clarke founded the Church of the Disciples in Boston with the aim of putting into practice his burgeoning ideas about church reform. He conceived his new congregation along the lines of what he called a "free church," open to all worshippers without regard to wealth or status. To finance the activities of the church, Clarke instituted a system of voluntary contributions in place of the traditional sale or rental of pews and encouraged his parishioners to participate actively in all aspects of its social, liturgical, and organizational functions. Apart from a loosely defined stipulation of faith in Jesus, Clarke's church was also committedly nondogmatic and strove to mediate between the opposing camps of radicals and conservatives to which the Unitarian churches in Boston had

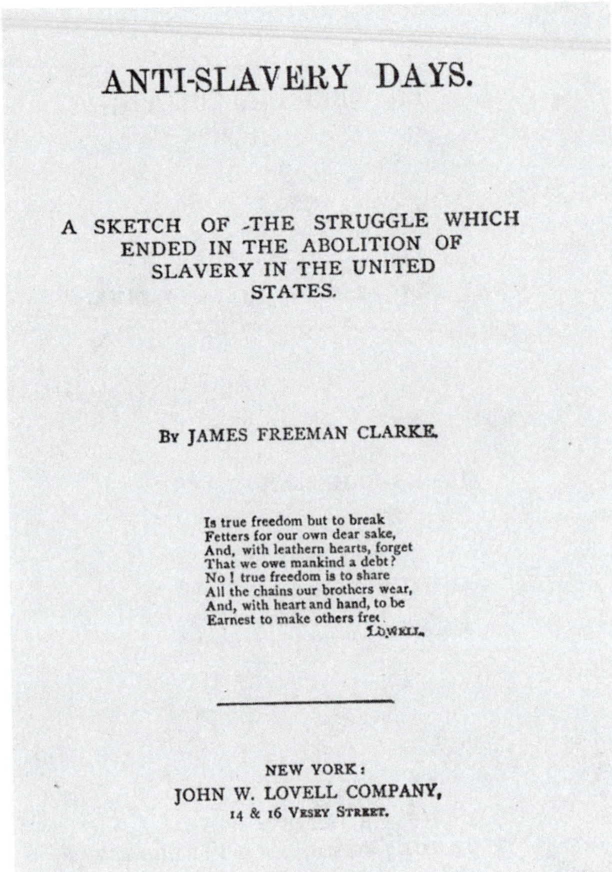
ANTI-SLAVERY DAYS.

A SKETCH OF THE STRUGGLE WHICH ENDED IN THE ABOLITION OF SLAVERY IN THE UNITED STATES.

By JAMES FREEMAN CLARKE.

Is true freedom but to break
Fetters for our own dear sake,
And, with leathern hearts, forget
That we owe mankind a debt?
No! true freedom is to share
All the chains our brothers wear,
And, with heart and hand, to be
Earnest to make others free.
LOWELL.

NEW YORK:
JOHN W. LOVELL COMPANY,
14 & 16 VESEY STREET.

Title page for Clarke's history of the slavery conflict, including some recollections of his own first encounters with slavery in Louisville

lately been reduced. From its inception, the congregation of the Church of the Disciples also conceived of itself as activist with a strong commitment to social justice. By this point in his career, Clarke had put himself clearly on record as resistant to the more extreme religious views expressed by such men as Emerson and Parker. Yet, his loyalties to his Transcendentalist friends remained strong, and when most of the Unitarian ministers of Boston voted to deny Parker access to their pulpits shortly after the delivery of his famously incendiary address of 1841, "The Transient and Permanent in Christianity," Clarke refused to do so. Though he felt little sympathy for Parker's radical overturning of Christian tradition, Clarke adamantly rejected the move to silence him. While the repercussions of Clarke's support for Parker were felt for several years, the respect generally accorded Clarke by his denomination, in spite of this conspicuous nonconformity, was attested by his election in 1845 to the Board of Directors of the American Unitarian Association.

For six years, Clarke's professional reputation in Boston grew, and the prosperity of his family increased. But the end of the decade brought a series of staggering blows that threatened to destroy everything for which Clarke had striven. In the spring of 1848 he came down with a virulent case of flu that left him incapacitated for weeks. The next winter eight-year-old Herman died abruptly from scarlet fever. The following summer Clarke found some solace traveling in Europe for eleven weeks. Visiting Salisbury, he felt vigorous enough to climb to the top of the four-hundred-foot cathedral and even, in a harrowing reprise of his Harvard College days, to clamber out onto the spire itself–to the horror and dismay of his companions. By the time he returned to Boston in October, his health problems seemed to have dissipated, but in January they flared up once again in a serious attack of typhoid fever. With his church in financial disarray and his family still reeling from the shock of Herman's death and his own unrelenting illnesses, Clarke gave up his pastorate to convalesce at the Huidekoper estate in Meadville. The family remained there from 1850 to 1853. But the forced exile from Boston proved enabling in other respects. As his health gradually improved, he began to involve himself in the life of the local church, as well as the nearby seminary–the Meadville Theological School. Freed from the daily pressures of the ministry, he also began to devote himself to reading and several writing projects published during the Meadville period or shortly thereafter, including *The Christian Doctrine of Forgiveness of Sin* (1852); *Eleven Weeks in Europe; And What May Be Seen in That Time* (1852), a travel account of his trip to Europe; *The Christian Doctrine of Prayer* (1854); and a translation in 1860 of Karl Hase's *Leben Jesus*.

With the loss of its minister in 1849, the tightly woven society of the Church of the Disciples began to unravel. Many early members left, and the church building was sold. Yet, in spite of these setbacks, a nucleus of the old membership survived Clarke's three-year absence. With his health finally restored in late 1852, he was eager to resuscitate his old church, and by the start of 1853 he was back ministering to his former congregation, the position he would retain for the next thirty-five years. This time fortune supported his efforts. His own health now continued strong, and his revived church gradually began to coalesce under his careful stewardship. In 1855 he bought a spacious house in Jamaica Plain in what was still a rural location on the outskirts of town. There he and Anna established the pattern of housekeeping that characterized their lives for the next three decades. Family life blossomed. Even as the three surviving children grew to adulthood, the house continued to be a center of the near and extended family. Clarke was a solicitous father and grandparent. When one of Eliot's children became ill, Clarke took the infant up in his arms and paced up and down the hall, reciting Horatian odes to soothe her. He spent his free time pruning his fruit trees or puttering in the garden. At night he could sometimes be heard making astronomical observations on the roof.

Ever mindful of Goethe's maxim "Do your present duty!" Clarke had dedicated himself from the beginning of his ministry to various causes of social reform. In Boston he became actively involved in temperance work and, during the war with Mexico, the peace movement; he lobbied hard for social and educational reform, supporting what he called "constructive socialism"; and in later years, he became an outspoken advocate for women's suffrage and access to higher education. But no social injustice fired his indignation as slavery did. Edward Everett Hale, in his memoir of Clarke, pointed out that his friend had never joined any of the antislavery parties, since he was opposed on principle to some of the abolitionists' more confrontational tactics. But few of the religious or secular leaders of the city spoke out against slavery as effectively as Clarke did. "I learned my anti-slavery lessons from slavery itself," he noted ruefully in *Anti-Slavery Days, A Sketch of the Struggle Which Ended in the Abolition of Slavery in the United States* (1883), a late-life history of the struggle to end slavery in the United States that includes some recollections of his first encounters with slavery in Louisville. No sooner had he taken charge of the *Western Messenger* than he began turning it into an organ of protest against slavery. In his first issue he published excerpts from a pamphlet by William Ellery Channing that, while it deplored slavery, nevertheless argued for a peaceful and conciliatory approach to its abolition. From the standpoint of the radical followers of abolitionist William Lloyd Garrison, Channing's cautious recommendations smacked of moral weakness, but this gradualist approach to abolition seemed judicious to Clarke at the time. With the passage of years, however, Clarke's resentment began to mount. When in May of 1854, to the shock and consternation of hundreds of Bostonians, the fugitive slave Anthony Burns was remanded to his Southern overseer by a federal magistrate in Boston, Clarke's outrage boiled over. For him and many with similar views, this action was the last straw. The effect of the Burns affair was to radicalize Clarke's subsequent agitation on behalf of the abolitionist movement. After the outbreak of hostilities, Clarke worked tirelessly to aid the Northern war effort, and even in the darkest early days, he dispensed from his pulpit a constant stream of hope and encouragement to his anxious congregation.

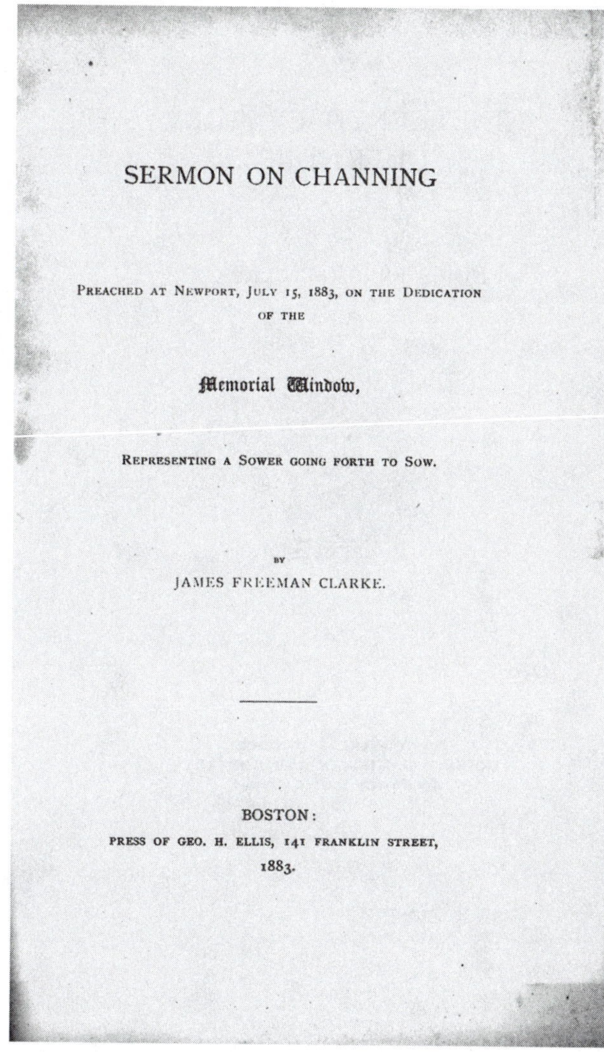
SERMON ON CHANNING

PREACHED AT NEWPORT, JULY 15, 1883, ON THE DEDICATION OF THE

Memorial Window,

REPRESENTING A SOWER GOING FORTH TO SOW.

BY

JAMES FREEMAN CLARKE.

BOSTON:
PRESS OF GEO. H. ELLIS, 141 FRANKLIN STREET,
1883.

Title page for Clarke's funeral oration on William Ellery Channing, a friend and fellow Transcendentalist (Collection of Joel Myerson)

Following the Civil War, Clarke's reputation grew. He was active in both state and national politics. Widely respected for his probity and moderation, he was frequently sought out to help mediate political and ecclesiastical disputes. When the National Conference of Unitarian Churches, which Henry Whitney Bellows organized in 1865, threatened to break down over disagreements between the creedal conservatives of the denomination and radical free religionists, Clarke emerged as a leader of the "broad church" coalition that sought to give wide latitude to differences of religious belief without altogether sacrificing the traditional Christian identity of the denomination. While the Unitarian community as a whole moved inexorably away from its Christian roots in the last few decades of the century, Clarke epitomized the principled but open-minded church leadership of his day. His *Manual of Unitarian Belief,* which he prepared in 1884 as a kind of liberal Sunday-School catechism, provided a teach-

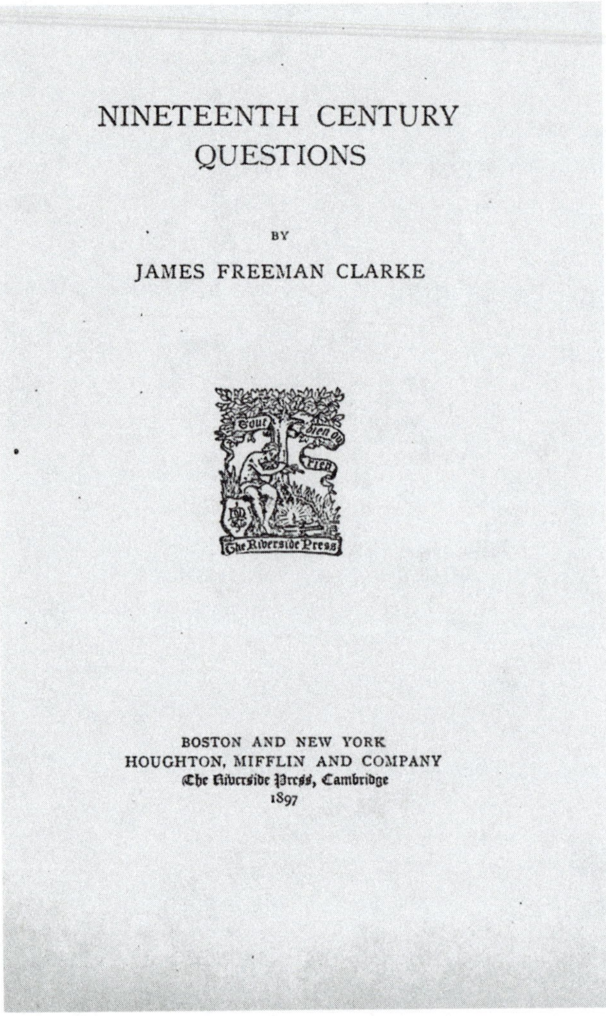

NINETEENTH CENTURY
QUESTIONS

BY

JAMES FREEMAN CLARKE

BOSTON AND NEW YORK
HOUGHTON, MIFFLIN AND COMPANY
The Riverside Press, Cambridge
1897

Title page for the posthumously published collection of Clarke's literary criticism

erly formulation of the main items of the Unitarian faith, and *Vexed Questions in Theology* (1886), a series of essays published two years before his death, offered the classic late-nineteenth-century summation of the liberal creed. In explicit contradistinction to the five planks of Calvinism, Clarke elaborated a set of five corresponding liberal doctrines, including "the fatherhood of God, . . . the brotherhood of man, . . . the leadership of Jesus, . . . salvation by character, . . . and the progress of mankind onward and upward forever."

The growth of Clarke's fame in this last period of his life was fueled in considerable part by the growing public estimation of his writings. Since his first return to Boston in 1841, Clarke's sermons and essays had appeared often in the religious and popular press. The period of his greatest literary and theological productivity, however, came after the Civil War. From 1866 to 1881, works by Clarke appeared on the average of one every year and a half, and for fifteen years beginning in 1873, the *Saturday Evening Gazette* reserved one of its columns for the regular publication of his sermons. *Orthodoxy: Its Truths and Errors,* published under the auspices of the American Unitarian Association in 1866, sets out to provide a fair-minded, even at times sympathetic, critique of the conventional doctrines of New England Orthodoxy. In a notable departure from the polemical writing of an earlier period, Clarke seeks not to disparage the theological contributions of Orthodoxy but "to find and state the truth contained in their doctrines" on the grounds that aspects of these doctrines have something to teach the liberals themselves. *Common-Sense in Religion,* a sermonlike series of essays published in 1874, considers the meaning of some twenty themes of traditional Christianity from the standpoint of "common-sense," which Clarke defines as "a method of judgment derived from experience."

The first volume of the work for which Clarke was best known, *Ten Great Religions: An Essay in Comparative Theology,* appeared in 1871. The publication of this work, followed in 1883 by its companion volume, *Ten Great Religions. Part II. A Comparison of All Religions,* represented the culmination of twenty-five years of scholarly study. Drawing liberally on almost a hundred years of European scholarship, Clarke provided a detailed historical examination of each of the major religious traditions of the world, with special attention to their respective contributions to what he conceived to be the evolution of "universal religion." Implicitly following the comparative method espoused by the Orientalist Max Müller, Clarke employed this new "science of religion" as a way both to understand and to legitimize religion generally. Though Clarke finds much to admire in the other religious traditions of the world, he sees Christianity as a "pleroma," a more catholic and "all embracing" faith and therefore the best candidate for the universal religion of the future. While *Ten Great Religions* is still a product of a Christian perspective and a nineteenth-century historical consciousness–evident especially in its unself-conscious evolutionism and its preoccupation with origins, essentialist typologies, and universals–it represents one of the first serious attempts by an American to survey historically the burgeoning field of the comparative study of religion. Another work of this period, *Events and Epochs in Religious History: Being the Substance of a Course of Twelve Lectures Delivered in the Lowell Institute, Boston, in 1880* (1881), exemplifies Clarke's ongoing interest in bringing the results of his research on religious history to the notice of a wider public. In *The Legend of Thomas Didymus the Jewish Skeptic,* his historical novel appearing the same year, Clarke recounts the story of Jesus from the standpoint of Thomas, the notoriously doubting disciple. Resorting for the first and only time in his career to a fictional mode, Clarke offers his own considered version of the life of Jesus, which characteristically stakes out a middle position between those advocates of the higher criticism, who debunk the supernatural claims of the New Testament narratives, and those orthodox Christians, who insist on taking them all at face value. In these later years, a substantial portion of Clarke's time was taken up with his educational priorities. Throughout his career Clarke had voiced strong support for educational reform. From 1863 until 1869 he served on the State Board of Education; in 1867, and again in 1876, he joined the faculty at the Harvard Divinity School to introduce its first courses in the comparative history of religion; and from 1866, he began what turned out to be a twenty-year tenure as an Overseer of Harvard College. The most important literary expression of Clarke's lifelong interest in education was his series of lectures published in 1880 as *Self-Culture: Physical, Intellectual, Moral, and Spiritual.* In it he sets out his mature philosophy of education and a blueprint for educational reform in the United States.

Taken as a whole, Clarke's vast literary corpus may be fairly characterized as more workmanlike than inspired. "People read my books," he readily acknowledged, "because they are *intelligible.* They are written for a useful purpose, not a literary." In this sense his literary contributions were much of a piece with his preaching and social activism and arose from the same ethical and pastoral concerns. Yet, despite the somewhat prosaic cast of his literary work, Clarke was also an avid poet. Speaking shortly after Clarke's death on 8 June 1888, Hedge remarked: "You do not get a true estimate of Clarke unless you see him as a poet. He approached all subjects from the poetical side." Indeed, as did his more famous literary contemporaries–Holmes, Emerson, and Fuller–Clarke loved poetry and wrote poetry his entire life, though his poems were never as well received as those of his more gifted friends. Nevertheless, some of his poems did appear in Transcendentalist and other magazines, and in 1875, in collaboration with his daughter Lilian, he also published a volume of translations, mostly of his beloved German poets, *Exotics: Attempts to Domesticate Them.* Highlights of Clarke's literary criticism–including essays on William Shakespeare, Thomas Gray, Emerson, Carlyle, and Voltaire–were collected and published posthumously as *Nineteenth Century Questions* (1897). Clarke's writings have not in general withstood the test of time, since they always responded overwhelmingly to the specific and more pressing requirements of his immediate social and historical circumstances. What obvious gifts he had–of imagination, intellect, and social conscience–he always willingly subordinated to the needs of his church and his century, consistent with the purpose of his life: "Whatsoever thy hand findeth to do, do it with thy might."

Letters:

The Letters of James Freeman Clarke to Margaret Fuller, edited by John Wesley Thomas (Hamburg: Cram, de Gruyter, 1957);

Robert D. Habich, "James Freeman Clarke's 1833 Letter-Journal for Margaret Fuller," *ESQ,* 27 (First quarter 1981): 47–56.

Bibliographies:

Edward Everett Hale, *James Freeman Clarke: Autobiography, Diary, and Correspondence* (Boston & New York: Houghton, Mifflin, 1891), pp. 416–419;

Theresa Layton Hall, "A Bibliography of the New England Transcendentalist Movement," M.A. thesis, Columbia University, 1929;

Arthur S. Bolster Jr., "The Life of James Freeman Clarke," dissertation, Harvard University, 1953;

Joel Myerson, "James Freeman Clarke 1810–1888," *First Printings of American Authors,* volume 4 (Detroit: Gale, 1979), pp. 93–107;

Leonard Neufeldt, "James Freeman Clarke: Notes toward a Comprehensive Bibliography," *Studies in the American Renaissance 1982,* edited by Joel Myerson (Boston: Twayne, 1982), pp. 209–226.

Biographies:

Lilian Freeman Clarke, "James Freeman Clarke 1810–1888," *Heralds of a Liberal Faith,* 3 volumes, edited by Samuel A. Eliot (Boston: American Unitarian Association, 1910), III: 67–75;

John Wesley Thomas, *James Freeman Clarke: Apostle of German Culture to America* (Boston: J. W. Luce, 1949);

Arthur S. Bolster Jr., *James Freeman Clarke: Disciple to Advancing Truth* (Boston: Beacon, 1954);

Derek K. Colville, "The Transcendental Friends: Clarke and Margaret Fuller," *New England Quarterly,* 30 (September 1957): 378–382;

Joel Myerson, "James Freeman Clarke," *The New England Transcendentalists and the Dial: A History of the Magazine and Its Contributors* (Rutherford, N.J.: Fairleigh Dickinson University Press, 1980), pp. 127–133.

References:

Catherine Albanese, *Corresponding Motion: Transcendental Religion and the New America* (Philadelphia: Temple University Press, 1977);

Robert C. Albrecht, "The Theological Response of the Transcendentalists to the Civil War," *New England Quarterly,* 38 (March 1965): 21–34;

Charles E. Blackburn, "James Freeman Clarke: An Interpretation of the Western Years (1833–1840)," dissertation, Yale University, 1952;

Paul F. Boller Jr., *American Transcendentalism, 1830–1860: An Intellectual Inquiry* (New York: Putnam, 1974);

Kenneth Walter Cameron, *Transcendental Reading Patterns* (Hartford: Transcendental Books, 1970);

George Willis Cooke, *Unitarianism in America: A History of its Origin and Development* (Boston: American Unitarian Association, 1902);

Octavius Brooks Frothingham, *Transcendentalism in New England: A History* (New York: Putnam, 1876);

Margaret Fuller, *Summer on the Lakes, in 1843* (Boston: Little & Brown, 1844);

Harold Clarke Goddard, *Studies in New England Transcendentalism* (New York: Columbia University Press, 1908);

Clarence L. F. Gohdes, *The Periodicals of American Transcendentalism* (Durham: Duke University Press, 1931);

Judith A. Green, "Religion, Life, and Literature in the *Western Messenger,*" dissertation, University of Wisconsin, 1981;

Robert D. Habich, *Transcendentalism and the Western Messenger: A History of the Magazine and Its Contributors, 1835–1841* (Rutherford, N.J.: Fairleigh Dickinson University Press, 1985);

Robert Hudspeth, ed., *The Letters of Margaret Fuller,* volume 6 (Ithaca & New York: Cornell University Press, 1994);

William R. Hutchison, *The Transcendentalist Ministers* (New Haven: Yale University Press, 1959);

Carl T. Jackson, *The Oriental Religions and American Thought: Nineteenth-Century Explorations* (Westport, Conn.: Greenwood Press, 1981);

Elizabeth McKinsey, *The Western Experiment: New England Transcendentalism in the Ohio Valley* (Cambridge, Mass.: Harvard University Press, 1973);

Leonard Neufeldt, "James Freeman Clarke," *The Transcendentalists: A Review of Research and Criticism,* edited by Joel Myerson (New York: Modern Language Association, 1984), pp. 112–116;

David Robinson, *The Unitarians and the Universalists* (Westport, Conn.: Greenwood Press, 1985);

Ralph L. Rusk, *The Literature of the Middle Western Frontier,* volume 1 (New York: Columbia University Press, 1925);

Douglas C. Stange, *Patterns of Anti-Slavery Among American Unitarians, 1831–1860* (Rutherford, N.J.: Fairleigh Dickinson University Press, 1977);

Arthur Versluis, *American Transcendentalism and Asian Religions* (New York: Oxford University Press, 1993);

Stanley M. Vogel, *German Literary Influences on the American Transcendentalists, 1810–1840* (New Haven: Yale University Press, 1955);

Conrad Wright, ed., *A Stream of Light: A Sesquicentennial History of American Unitarianism* (Boston: Unitarian Universalist Association, 1975).

Papers:

Most of James Freeman Clarke's papers and manuscripts are found in libraries and depositories in the greater Boston area. The largest concentration of them is located, however, in the Houghton Library of Harvard University, the Massachusetts Historical Society, and the Andover-Harvard Theological Library at Harvard Divinity School. In his bibliographic treatment of 1982, Leonard Neufeldt provides a helpful inventory of these and other collections.

Caroline Healey Dall

(22 June 1822 - 17 December 1912)

Helen R. Deese
Tennessee Technological University

Caroline Healey Dall, circa 1836 (portrait by Alvin Clark; from The College, the Market, and the Court, *Memorial Edition, 1914)*

BOOKS: *Essays and Sketches* (Boston: Samuel G. Simpkins, 1849);

"Woman's Right to Labor": or, Low Wages and Hard Work (Boston: Walker, Wise, 1860);

Historical Pictures Retouched: A Volume of Miscellanies (Boston: Walker, Wise, 1860; London: Edward S. Whitfield, 1860);

Woman's Rights under the Law (Boston: Walker, Wise, 1861);

Sunshine: A New Name for a Popular Lecture on Health (Boston: Walker, Wise, 1864);

Nazareth (Boston: American Unitarian Association, 1866);

The College, the Market, and the Court; or, Woman's Relation to Education, Labor, and Law (Boston: Lee & Shepard, 1867);

Egypt's Place in History: A Presentation (Boston: Lee & Shepard, 1868);

Patty Gray's Journey: From Boston to Baltimore (Boston: Lee & Shepard, 1869);

Patty Gray's Journey: From Baltimore to Washington (Boston: Lee & Shepard, 1870);

Patty Gray's Journey: On the Way, or, Patty at Mt. Vernon (Boston: Lee & Shepard, 1870);

The Romance of the Association: or, One Last Glimpse of Charlotte Temple and Eliza Wharton (Cambridge, Mass.: John Wilson, 1875);

My First Holiday: or, Letters Home from Colorado, Utah, and California (Boston: Roberts, 1881);

What We Really Know about Shakespeare (Boston: Roberts, 1885);

Sordello: A History and a Poem (Boston: Roberts, 1886);

Life of Dr. Anandabai Joshee: A Kinswoman of the Pundita Ramabai (Boston: Roberts, 1888);

Barbara Fritchie: A Study (Boston: Roberts, 1892);

Otis; the Story of an Old House (Washington, D.C., 1892);

Margaret and Her Friends: or Ten Conversations with Margaret Fuller (Boston: Roberts, 1895);

Transcendentalism in New England: A Lecture (Boston: Roberts, 1897);

"Alongside": Being Notes Suggested by "A New England Boyhood" of Doctor Edward Everett Hale (Boston: Thomas Todd, 1900);

The Story of a Boston Family (Boston: Thomas Todd, 1903);

Of "Lady Rose's Daughter": A Defense and an Analysis (Boston: Thomas Todd, 1903);

Fog Bells: A Sequel to Nazareth (Boston: Thomas Todd, 1904);

Reverend Charles Lowell, D.D.: Pastor from January 1, 1806, to January 20, 1881, of the West Church, Boston, Massachusetts (Boston: Thomas Todd, 1907).

OTHER: *A Practical Illustration of "Woman's Right to Labor"; or, A Letter from Marie E. Zakrzewska, M.D.,* edited by Dall (Boston: Walker, Wise, 1860);

Memorial to Charles Henry Appleton Dall, edited by Dall (Boston: Beacon Press, 1902).

SELECTED PERIODICAL PUBLICATION–UNCOLLECTED: "Pioneering," *Atlantic Monthly,* 19 (April 1867): 403–416.

Caroline Healey Dall, known as the most able writer in the women's movement in the 1850s and 1860s, was a second-generation Transcendentalist and a memorialist of the Transcendentalist movement and its major figures. Reformer, lecturer, and miscellaneous writer, she was shaped by her early associations with Elizabeth Palmer Peabody, a willing mentor who introduced her into the wider circle of the Boston-area intellectuals; Margaret Fuller, whose "Conversations" she attended when she was eighteen; and a host of male Transcendentalists, whose lectures and sermons she heard, whose books and articles she read, and with many of whom she was on close personal terms. She attended Ralph Waldo Emerson's lectures and took notes on them as early as the age of twelve, and she was profoundly influenced by the radical Transcendentalist preacher Theodore Parker. Dall became an early apologist for Margaret Fuller, her most significant role model. The Transcendentalist influence is most evident in Dall's commitment to reform causes, especially the cause of women's rights.

Caroline Wells Healey was born in Boston, the oldest child of wealthy Boston merchant Mark Healey and his wife, Caroline (Foster) Healey. Mark Healey provided an excellent education for his daughter through governesses, private schools, and tutors, but this education ended when she was fifteen. Her father discussed religious, philosophical, and political questions with his daughter as an equal from an early age; he expected great things of her, and she responded by writing novels as a child and publishing short pieces in religious periodicals by the time she was thirteen. Because her father was in financial difficulty, when Caroline Healey was twenty, she went to Georgetown, District of Columbia, to teach in an exclusive girls' school, sending her earnings home to help pay for the education of her siblings. In Washington she met and in 1844 married Charles Henry Appleton Dall, a Baltimore Unitarian minister to the poor. For eleven years Caroline Dall was an active minister's wife. The Dalls had a son (William H. Dall, destined for prominence as an early explorer of Alaska and a Smithsonian naturalist) and a daughter (Sarah K. Dall, later Munro).

Dall's commitment to writing for publication continued into her marriage and motherhood, and in 1849 she published (with her father's financial backing) *Essays and Sketches,* a collection of pieces on questions of religion and reform. It attracted little attention and is remarkable today chiefly to illustrate how far she later moved from the extremely cautious positions on abolitionism and the women's question that she expressed in it. In the early 1850s while living in Toronto, where her husband was preaching, she became significantly involved in both movements, writing pieces for the *Liberty Bell* and contributing prolifically to an early paper devoted to the women's question, *The Una,* edited by Paulina Wright Davis. Moving back to the Boston area in 1855, Dall became for a short time before its demise the co-editor of *The Una.*

After Charles Dall left his family in February 1855 to become a missionary to Calcutta (where, except for rare visits home, he remained until his death in 1886), Caroline Dall became more intensively involved in the women's movement. She organized conventions in Boston, addressed a committee of the legislature, circulated petitions, spoke at meetings in New York City, wrote reports, and delivered lectures. These activities were associated with four publications in 1860–1861. The first of these, *"Woman's Right to Labor": or, Low Wages and Hard Work* (1860), consisted of three lectures that she had delivered in the previous year, attempting to revolutionize the kinds of work that were open to women and the attitude of both women and the general public toward women working in nontraditional areas. This publication was followed, also in 1860, by an edited work, *A Practical Illustration of "Woman's Right to Labor"; or, A Letter from Marie E. Zakrzewska, M.D.* Zakrzewska was a German-born pioneering American female physician, recipient of an M.D. degree in 1856 from Western Reserve University in Cleveland, Ohio. Dall declared in her introduction: "The object of my whole life has been to inspire in women a desire for *thorough training* to some special end, and a willingness to share the training of men." When she first heard Zakrzewska speak in 1856, Dall recognized in her at once the perfect model that she had been seeking for young women–the example of an ordinary woman who had persisted in the face of all impediments and professional requirements to forge for herself meaningful work and who was committed to "the uplifting of the fallen, the employment of the idle, and the purification of society." The text proper of the book consists of Zakrzewska's lengthy letter to Mary L. Booth recounting the story of her struggles to realize her ambitions. Dall's third book publication of the year was *Historical Pictures Retouched: A Volume of Miscellanies,* largely a collection of articles that Dall had first published in *The Una,* many of which comprised an early version of women's studies. Dall scrutinized history for instances of overlooked, suppressed, or maligned women of intelligence, independence, and virtue. Not content with simply highlighting the work of such figures as Margaret Fuller and Mary Wollstonecraft, Dall reread in a favorable light some of the female pariahs of male-written history–Aspasia, for example, the reputed courtesan who caused Pericles to leave his wife and family. She "retouched" the portraits of these figures–that is, she took the known facts and showed how they could be reinterpreted in a way favorable to these women whom history had thus far read in the least sympathetic light or simply ignored. In 1861 Dall published another series of her lectures, *Woman's Rights under the Law,* the product of extensive research, in which she surveyed the legal status of woman, highlighting the inequities and disabilities. All four of these works attracted considerable, and for the most part favorable, attention in newspapers and periodicals, including even a few English periodicals.

In 1866 Dall, a great admirer of Abraham Lincoln, visited his law partner, William F. Herndon, in Springfield, Illinois. From her conversations with him and her perusal of the papers that he was collecting in preparation for writing a Lincoln biography, Dall found evidence that Lincoln was a much earthier man than she had imagined and that the true love of his life was Ann Rutledge. Her admiration for the man was undiminished, but she now saw him as a product of a rough Western culture, one that had, however, fortuitously fitted him for the role he played in history. She worked out these ideas in the article "Pioneering," published in the *Atlantic Monthly* (1867). The article attracted a great deal of attention, much of it negative, for it was seen as an attack on the martyred hero's greatness and a slur on Mary Todd Lincoln. Although Emerson was said to have admired the article, Dall noted that almost all reviewers had missed its point, the theme implied by its title of the peculiar quality of the Western pioneer culture that had produced such a man.

The Civil War had produced a self-imposed moratorium on the women's movement, but within two years of the close of the war Dall reentered the fray by publishing her most significant reform work, *The College, the Market, and the Court; or, Woman's Relation to Education, Labor, and Law* (1867). This volume included the three lectures already published in *"Woman's Right to Labor,"* the three published in *Woman's Rights under the Law,* three unpublished lectures on women and education, and an appendix that updated these lectures (at that time eight to ten years old) with new statistics and information on the education of women at Vassar, Oberlin, and Antioch colleges. The book received wide recognition in both the United States and England. By its nature controversial, it had many detractors but was repeatedly recognized as

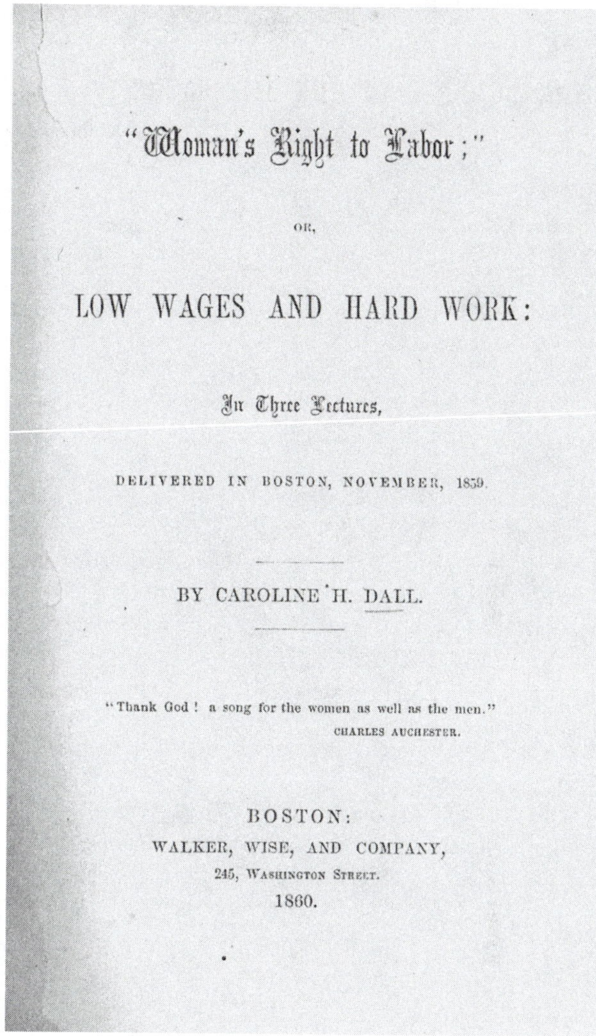

"Woman's Right to Labor;"

OR,

LOW WAGES AND HARD WORK:

In Three Lectures,

DELIVERED IN BOSTON, NOVEMBER, 1859.

BY CAROLINE H. DALL.

"Thank God! a song for the women as well as the men."
CHARLES AUCHESTER.

BOSTON:
WALKER, WISE, AND COMPANY,
245, WASHINGTON STREET.
1860.

Title page for Dall's book about the right of women to work at so-called men's jobs (Collection of Joel Myerson)

the fullest and most eloquent statement of the women's question to date, and it shortly went into a second edition. Dall observed that history, largely written by men who viewed women as inferior, simply reflected and validated their prejudices. She strongly urged the expansion of opportunities for higher education for women, including the admission of women to the Harvard Medical School. On the economic front, she argued that women's labor should be valued at the same rate as men's; sympathetically portrayed the lot of prostitutes, whose only choices often were "death or dishonor"; encouraged women of means to become entrepreneurs; suggested an early version of temporary employment agencies; and looked forward to a (somewhat romanticized) era of dual-career couples. She demonstrated the absurdities of English common law (upon which most state laws were based) with regard to women's issues such as divorce and property rights. Her plea for the franchise and full

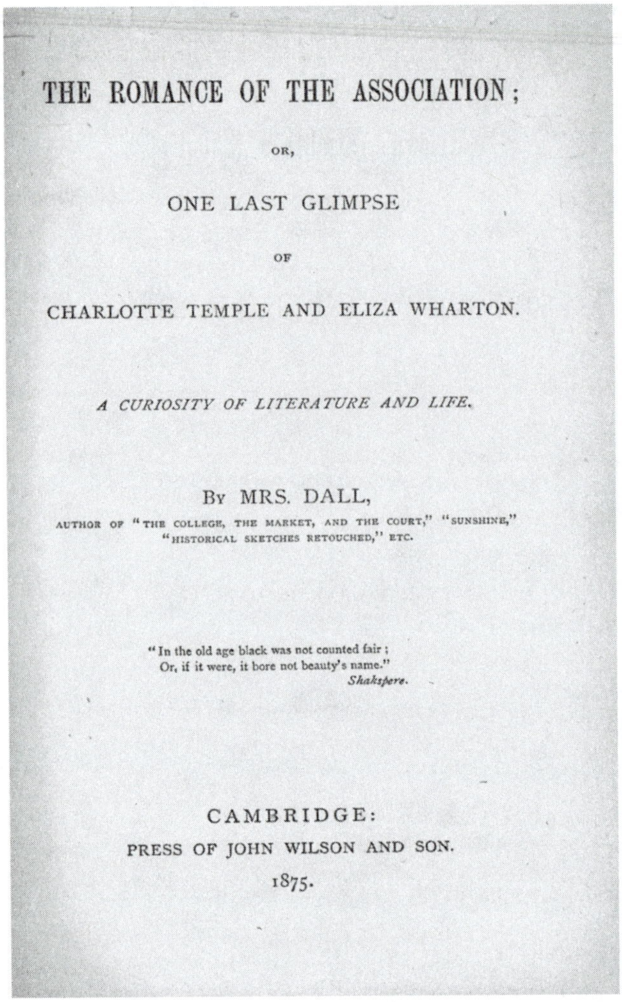
THE ROMANCE OF THE ASSOCIATION;

OR,

ONE LAST GLIMPSE

OF

CHARLOTTE TEMPLE AND ELIZA WHARTON.

A CURIOSITY OF LITERATURE AND LIFE.

BY MRS. DALL,

AUTHOR OF "THE COLLEGE, THE MARKET, AND THE COURT," "SUNSHINE," "HISTORICAL SKETCHES RETOUCHED," ETC.

"In the old age black was not counted fair;
Or, if it were, it bore not beauty's name."
Shakspere.

CAMBRIDGE:
PRESS OF JOHN WILSON AND SON.
1875.

Title page for Dall's book about the real-life models for two fictional women

equality for women in the educational, economic, and legal arenas was couched in terms of the Christian doctrines of the worth of all human souls and the duty to develop one's God-given faculties. The *National Anti-Slavery Standard* (3 August 1867) judged that Dall had "wielded, in the interest of woman, by far the most effective and vigorous pen." The *New York Tribune* (22 June 1867) carried a highly favorable review that spoke of Dall as "widely known as one of the ablest and most earnest advocates of a radical change in the social position of woman," praising both the "storehouse of evidence, argument, and illustration" presented in the book and its literary merits, its "glowing and vigorous eloquence." This publication marked the high point of Dall's involvement in the women's movement. Her personality did not fit well with that of other leaders of the movement, nor did she approve of the association of Elizabeth Cady Stanton and Susan B. Anthony with George Francis Train. She gradually withdrew from active participation but late in the century was remembered and celebrated as one of the pioneers of the movement. In the meantime she was a founder and longtime officer of a new and more generalized "scientific" reform group, the American Social Science Association, organized in 1865.

In the last half of her life Dall published works in a great variety of fields. Her *Egypt's Place in History: A Presentation* (1868), a work that Emerson at least is said to have found useful, is a redaction of the five-volume work by Baron Christian Bunsen, *Egypt's Place in Universal History* (1848–1867). Dall's contribution to the genre of children's literature was the three-volume series *Patty Gray's Journey* (1869–1870). These books trace the young heroine's travels, soon after the close of the Civil War, from Boston to Baltimore, then on to Washington, D.C., and finally to Mount Vernon. Mildly moralistic, the stories are calculated to impress upon young readers the evils of slavery, the righteousness of the Union cause and the heroism of its soldiers, the necessity of quality education for blacks, and the basic goodness of many Southerners, even former slaveholders. They further attempt to instill a sense of national pride and patriotism by introducing young readers to the Capitol, the Smithsonian, Mount Vernon, and other points of interest in the Washington area. In *The Romance of the Association: or, One Last Glimpse of Charlotte Temple and Eliza Wharton* (1875) Dall delved into the question of the real-life models for Hannah Foster's *The Coquette; or The History of Eliza Wharton* (1797) and Susanna Rowson's *Charlotte: A Tale of Truth* (1791). In 1877, in recognition of her "position . . . in the front ranks of those who labor for the elevation of woman," Dall received from Alfred University the LL.D. degree, surely one of the earliest such degrees granted to an American woman.

In 1878, largely retired from active reform work, Dall moved from Boston to Washington, D.C., where she was the friend of political and scientific luminaries, the intimate of first lady Frances Cleveland, and a well-known hostess and leader of a reading group for young women. She continued to write, as indeed she did throughout most of her life, for newspapers and periodicals. She published in such religious papers and periodicals as the *Christian Register, Christian Examiner, Radical,* and *Index* and in such reform and secular serials as the *Liberator, Boston Daily Advertiser, Springfield Republican, Cambridge* (Massachusetts) *Tribune,* and *The Nation.* Among her book publications of this period was her sole contribution to the genre of travel literature, *My First Holiday: or, Letters Home from Colorado, Utah, and California* (1881), recounting the railroad trip that she took unaccompanied to California, with stops in Colorado and Utah. Her revulsion at the degradation of mining camps was balanced by her appreciation of Yosemite Valley in east central California and other sites of natural beauty. Several of her late miscellaneous book publications were works of historical and literary scholarship: she undertook in *What We Really Know about Shakespeare* (1885) to review the known facts of William Shakespeare's life; in *Sordello: A History and a Poem* (1886) to explain the context of Robert Browning's poem of the same title; and in *Barbara Fritchie: A Study* (1892) to prove the truth of the legend celebrated in John Greenleaf Whittier's poem "Barbara Frietchie."

In Dall's late years she recognized that the period of her young womanhood in the Boston area had been no ordinary time; she saw it as a kind of New England Golden Age that she had been in a position to observe. Having read and reviewed in the last several decades many biographies of major figures of the American Renaissance, by the 1890s she began formulating her own reminiscences. Three works written in her seventies looked back to the events and personages of her youth and are important records and interpretations of that world. In 1895 she published her transcription of the Margaret Fuller Conversation series that she had attended in 1841, *Margaret and Her Friends: or Ten Conversations with Margaret Fuller.* The eighteen-year-old Dall had been a wide-eyed but unintimidated participant (along with Emerson, George Ripley, and Peabody, among others), and this contemporary record is one of the few of that elusive and quintessentially Transcendentalist form, the Conversation. In the same year Dall delivered in Washington, D.C., a lecture that she published two years later as the pamphlet *Transcendentalism in New England: A Lecture* (1897). Of her retrospective publications on the intellectual climate of her youth, this one is the most original and provocative. When she delivered this lecture, Dall was nearly seventy-three years old. Rather than simply drawing upon the stores of her memory and her journals to produce an entertaining talk consisting of personal anecdotes of the now-celebrated Transcendentalists, Dall, addressing the Society for Philosophical Enquiry, deliberately chose to challenge the standard history of Transcendentalism, O. B. Frothingham's *Transcendentalism in New England: A History* (1876). She undertook to construct a revisionist interpretation of the movement, one that is, among other things, unabashedly feminist. The Transcendentalist movement began and ended, Dall asserted, with a woman: Anne Hutchinson was a foremother of the central belief of the movement in "the immanence of the Divine in the Human," and Fuller's death essentially marked its end. Dall was a vigorous apologist for Fuller, objecting to the prevailing view of her as a detached intellectual and pointing particularly to her involvement in the practical business of improving women's lives. Dall attempted to restore Frederic Henry Hedge (overlooked entirely by Frothingham) to a central place in the movement and to diminish the importance of A. Bronson Alcott. In 1900 she published *"Alongside": Being Notes Suggested by "A New England Boyhood" of Doctor Edward Everett Hale,* a more general reminiscence of the Boston of her youth.

Dall's pamphlet publications in the last decade of her life represent her venture into theology. Though never ordained, she had occasionally filled Unitarian pulpits, claiming to be the first woman to do so. *Nazareth* (1866), presented first as a sermon, was a learned exploration of the environment–physical, intellectual, and spiritual–in which Jesus grew up, and a speculation on how this environment produced the great teacher. Dall considered it one of the great validating events of her old age that the American Unitarian Association chose to reprint this pamphlet in its "Memorable Sermons" series, a series that also included sermons by William Ellery Channing, Theodore Parker, and Emerson. *Fog Bells: A Sequel to Nazareth* (1904), first published as a series of articles in *The Friend* in 1867, addressed the question of biblical miracles. Its original publication was anonymous, for Dall feared that such radicalism expressed by a woman would shut her and other women out of the pulpit. She wrote in a journal entry for 4 January 1867 that through these articles she hoped "to turn men a little

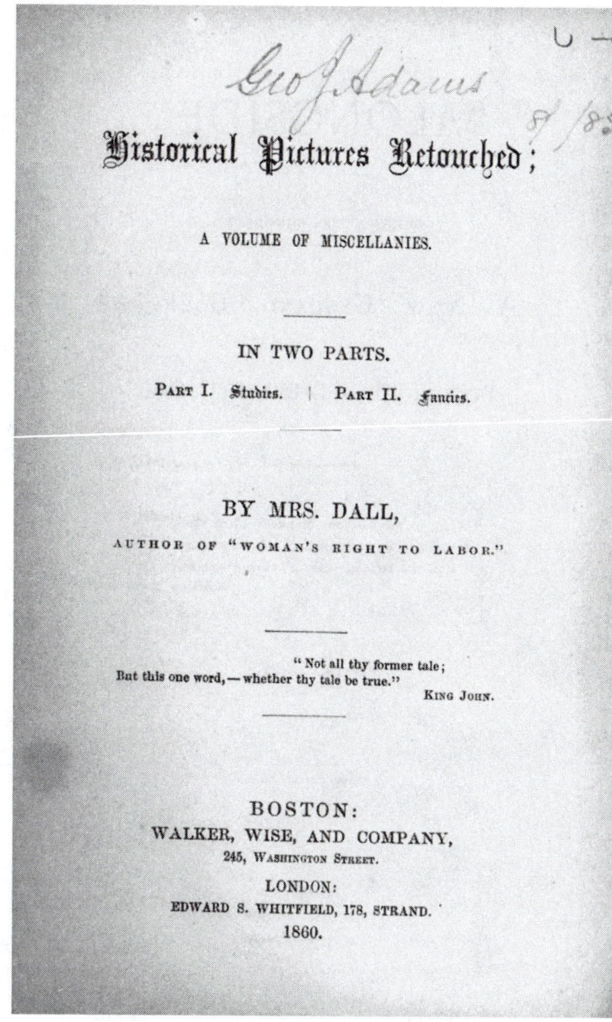
Historical Pictures Retouched;

A VOLUME OF MISCELLANIES.

IN TWO PARTS.

PART I. Studies. | PART II. Fancies.

BY MRS. DALL,

AUTHOR OF "WOMAN'S RIGHT TO LABOR."

"Not all thy former tale;
But this one word,—whether thy tale be true."
KING JOHN.

BOSTON:
WALKER, WISE, AND COMPANY,
245, WASHINGTON STREET.
LONDON:
EDWARD S. WHITFIELD, 178, STRAND.
1860.

Title page for essays, in which Dall reexamines the reputations of well-known women whose actions were misunderstood (Collection of Joel Myerson)

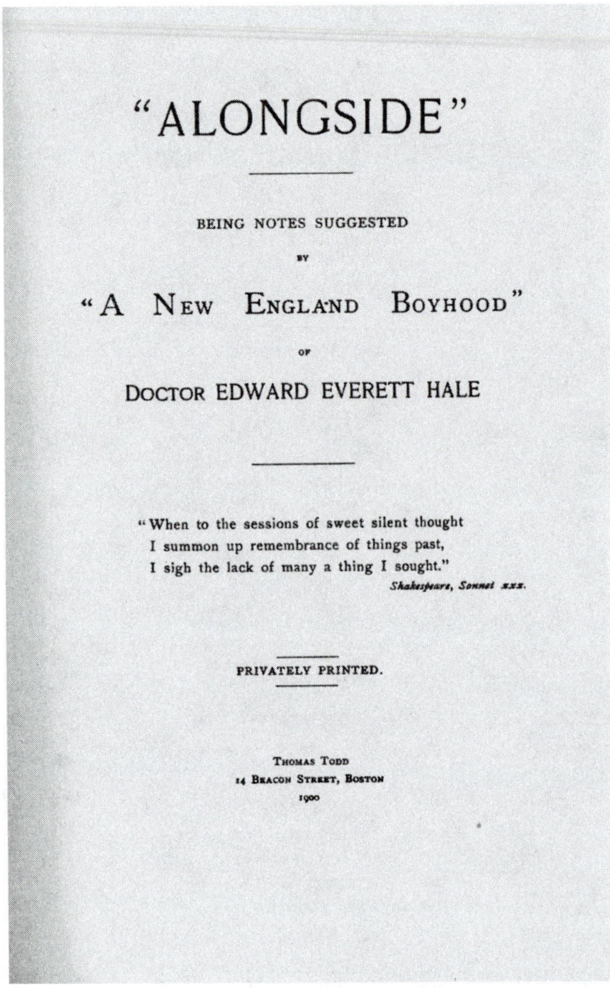
"ALONGSIDE"

BEING NOTES SUGGESTED

BY

"A NEW ENGLAND BOYHOOD"

OF

DOCTOR EDWARD EVERETT HALE

"When to the sessions of sweet silent thought
I summon up remembrance of things past,
I sigh the lack of many a thing I sought."
Shakespeare, Sonnet xxx.

PRIVATELY PRINTED.

THOMAS TODD
14 BEACON STREET, BOSTON
1900

Title page for Dall's reminiscence of her Boston childhood

toward what is at *once* independent and reverent before I die."

Dall continued to lead an active life until her last few years, when she suffered greatly from arthritis and other maladies of old age. She continued to keep a journal, sporadically at the last, until a year and a half before her death on 17 December 1912. As yet unpublished, Dall's manuscript journals–covering three-quarters of a century and many major literary, religious, and reform movements–may yet prove her most lasting contribution to American literature.

References:

Helen R. Deese, "'Alcott's Conversations on the Transcendentalists': The Record of Caroline Dall," *American Literature,* 60 (March 1988): 17–25;

Deese, "A Liberal Education: Caroline Healey Dall and Emerson," in *Emersonian Circles Essays in Honor of Joel Myerson,* edited by Wesley T. Mott and Robert E. Burkholder (Rochester, N.Y.: University of Rochester Press, 1996), pp. 237–260;

Deese, "A New England Women's Network: Elizabeth Palmer Peabody, Caroline Healey Dall, and Delia S. Bacon," *Legacy: A Journal of American Women Writers,* 8 (Fall 1991): 77–91;

Deese, "Transcendentalism from the Margins: The Experience of Caroline Healey Dall," in *Transient and Permanent: the Transcendentalist Movement and Its Contexts,* edited by Charles Capper and Conrad Edick Wright (Boston: Massachusetts Historical Society, 1999), pp. 527–547;

Gary Sue Goodman, "'All About Me Forgotten': The Education of Caroline Healey Dall 1822–1912," dissertation, Stanford University, 1987;

William Leach, "From Personal Disunion to Social Community: The Feminist Career of Caroline Dall," in his *True Love and Perfect Union: The Feminist Reform of Sex and Society* (New York: Basic Books, 1980), pp. 263–291;

Joel Myerson, "Caroline Dall's Reminiscences of Margaret Fuller," *Harvard Library Bulletin,* 22 (October 1974): 414–428;

Rose Norman, "'Sorella di Dante': Caroline Dall and the Paternal Discourse," *A/B: Auto/Biography Studies,* 5 (Fall 1990): 124–139;

Howard M. Wach, "A Boston Feminist in the Victorian Public Sphere: The Social Criticism of Caroline Healey Dall," *New England Quarterly,* 68 (September 1995): 429–450;

Barbara Welter, "The Merchant's Daughter: A Tale from Life," *New England Quarterly,* 42 (March 1969): 3–22.

Papers:

Caroline Healey Dall left her manuscript journals, incoming correspondence, scrapbooks, and other papers to the Massachusetts Historical Society. The collection has been microfilmed and comprises forty-five microfilm reels. Important collections of her papers also exist at the Arthur and Elizabeth Schlesinger Library on the History of Women in America, Radcliffe College, and at the Bryn Mawr College Library. Because of her extensive correspondence with hundreds of prominent contemporaries, Dall's letters are to be found in scores of libraries, notably the Houghton Library of Harvard University, the Boston Public Library, and the Andover-Harvard Theological Library.

Richard Henry Dana Jr.

(1 August 1815 - 6 January 1882)

Michael McLoughlin
University of South Carolina

BOOKS: *Two Years Before the Mast: A Personal Narrative of Life at Sea* (New York: Harper, 1840; London: Moxon, 1841);

The Seaman's Friend, Containing a Treatise on Practical Seamanship, with Plates; a Dictionary of Sea Terms; Customs and Usages on the Merchant Service; Laws Relating to the Practical Duties of Master and Mariners (Boston: Little, Brown & Loring, 1841); reprinted as *The Seaman's Manual* (London: Moxon, 1841);

Remarks of Richard Henry Dana, Jr., Esq. before the Committee on Federal Relations, on the Proposed Removal of Edward A. Loring, Esq., from the Office of Judge of Probate, March 5, 1855 (Boston: Alfred Mudge, 1855);

To Cuba and Back: A Vacation Voyage (Boston: Ticknor & Fields, 1859; London: Smith, Elder, 1859);

An Address upon the Life and Services of Edward Everett (Cambridge, Mass.: Sever & Francis, 1865);

Oration at Lexington, April 19, 1875 (Boston: Franklin, 1875; Boston: Lockwood, Brooks, 1875);

Speeches in Stirring Times and Letters to a Son, edited by Richard Henry Dana, III (Boston & New York: Houghton Mifflin, 1910);

An Autobiographical Sketch (1815–1842), edited by Robert F. Metzdorf (Hamden, Conn.: Shoe String, 1953);

The Journal of Richard Henry Dana, Jr., 3 volumes, edited by Robert F. Lucid (Cambridge, Mass.: Harvard University Press, 1968).

OTHER: Washington Allston, *Lectures on Art, and Poems,* edited, with a preface, by Dana (New York: Baker & Scribner, 1850);

"Biographical Notice," in Edward T. Channing, *Lectures Read to the Seniors in Harvard College* (Boston: Ticknor & Fields, 1856), pp. vii–xx;

Henry Wheaton, *Elements of International Law,* edited by Dana (Boston: Little, Brown, 1866); edited, with notes, by George Grafton Wilson (Oxford: Clarendon Press; London: H. Milford, 1936).

SELECTED PERIODICAL PUBLICATION–UNCOLLECTED: "Journal of a Voyage from Boston to the Coast of California, by Richard Henry Dana, Jr.," edited by James Allison, *American Neptune,* 12 (July 1952): 177–185.

The enduring critical reputation of Richard Henry Dana Jr. derives largely from his popular memoir *Two Years Before the Mast: A Personal Narrative of Life at Sea* (1840), a work addressing what Edgar Allan Poe referred to in an early review as "the exact *letter* of the sea." Dana's book went beyond strict autobiography, however, by participating in the literary promotion of social reform. With this work, Dana contributed to an ongoing tradition in American letters that formed a vital element in the works of Ralph Waldo Emerson, Henry David Thoreau, and Walt Whitman. In subject and theme, *Two Years Before the Mast* is an important influence on such authors as Herman Melville, who significantly remarked that he felt connected to Dana "by a sort of Siamese link of affectionate sympathy."

Dana came from a well-established, distinguished Massachusetts family. One of his great-grandfathers had signed the Declaration of Independence, and his grandfather Judge Francis Dana was a highly respected Revolutionary patriot. His father, Richard Henry Dana Sr., had a legal background but also enjoyed literary pursuits as the founder and editor of the *North American Review*.

Richard Henry Dana Jr. was born in Cambridge, Massachusetts, on 1 August 1815, the second of four children. His mother, Ruth Charlotte (Smith) Dana, died when Richard Jr. was only six years old. He entered Harvard at the age of sixteen, but his education was cut short by vision problems resulting from measles. Always eager for new experiences, nineteen-year-old Dana set sail from Boston in the middle of August 1834 on the brig *Pilgrim,* which was bound around Cape Horn to the coast of California. Dana returned to Boston on the ship *Alert* a little more than two years later, in September of 1836. With his eyesight significantly restored and his enthusiasm heightened, Dana returned to Harvard and graduated first in his class. After this achievement, he attended Harvard Law School and was licensed to practice law in Massachusetts in 1840.

Dana had assiduously recorded his experiences at sea in journals and spent much of his time during these busy years transforming these travelogues into a coherent dramatic narrative. Unfortunately, when Dana's work was completed, publishers expressed little interest. Dana finally sold his manuscript for *Two Years Before the Mast* to Harper and Brothers for $250. The book, which has since emerged as Dana's most critically acclaimed work, was published in 1840 as part of the "Harper's Family Library" Series.

Dana argued that *Two Years Before the Mast* was the first "authentic and accurate" depiction of a common sailor's life. In writing it, he was attempting to dispel romantic misconceptions about "life before the mast" popularized by the sea novels of James Fenimore Cooper and his imitators. Dana observed that these works were all written either from the point of view of officers or of passengers, who were unable to give accurate portrayals of the sailors' actual lives. He felt compelled to expose the true nature of the seaman's profession and to demonstrate "that the sailor has no romance in his every-day life to sustain him, but that it is very much the same plain, matter-of-fact drudgery and hardship, which would be experienced on shore." To this important end, Dana hoped that *Two Years Before the Mast* would help to "raise" sailors "in the rank of beings" and to promote "their religious and moral improvement, and diminish the hardships of their daily life."

Two Years Before the Mast provides an unvarnished account of the day-to-day hardships that comprised a sailor's life in mid-nineteenth-century America. For example, he describes his quarters in the forecastle as "a little, wet, leaky hole," where the air was always foul. One of the few comforts he came to experience derives from the companionship offered by his fellow crew members:

> No man can be a sailor, or know what sailors are, unless he has lived in the forecastle with them–turned in and out with them, eaten of their dish and drank of their cup. After I had been a week there, nothing would have tempted me to go back to my old berth, and never afterwards, even in the worst of weather, when in a close and leaking forecastle off Cape Horn, did I for a moment wish myself in the steerage.

Dana thus conveys his belief that the friendship of his fellow sailors more than compensated for his uncomfortable lodgings.

In his book Dana complains little about the unsavory fare in the sailors' mess–salt beef and stale biscuits–washed down with hot, weak tea twice a day. Dana quickly adapts to this less than ideal "grub," mentioning that it was occasionally supplemented by fresh fruit or vegetables to prevent scurvy. His only complaint is that sailors were not given hot tea or coffee at regular intervals during their work in the chilling passage around the cape.

Dana remarks that one of the ships on which he served, the *Alert,* was a temperance ship, but "the temperance was all in the forecastle." Though the sailors were categorically denied alcohol, the captain could always "have his brandy-and-water in the cabin, and his hot coffee at the galley."

In sum, although Dana recognizes that some measure of discomfort was unavoidable by the very nature of the profession, he nevertheless finds much of the sailors' suffering to be needless and cruel. He repeatedly offers valuable suggestions for ways in which the lot of seamen can be improved.

Dana had firsthand awareness of the rigor and the danger of a sailor's life. The routine tasks of a sailor were often monotonous and unpleasant. The harshness of this profession was augmented by the strict discipline observed aboard ship. Dana notes that "in no state prison are the convicts more regularly set to work and more closely watched." Dana served under a barbarous captain who tyrannized his mates and "hazed" the crew. On one occasion he flogged two sailors with minimal provocation, and

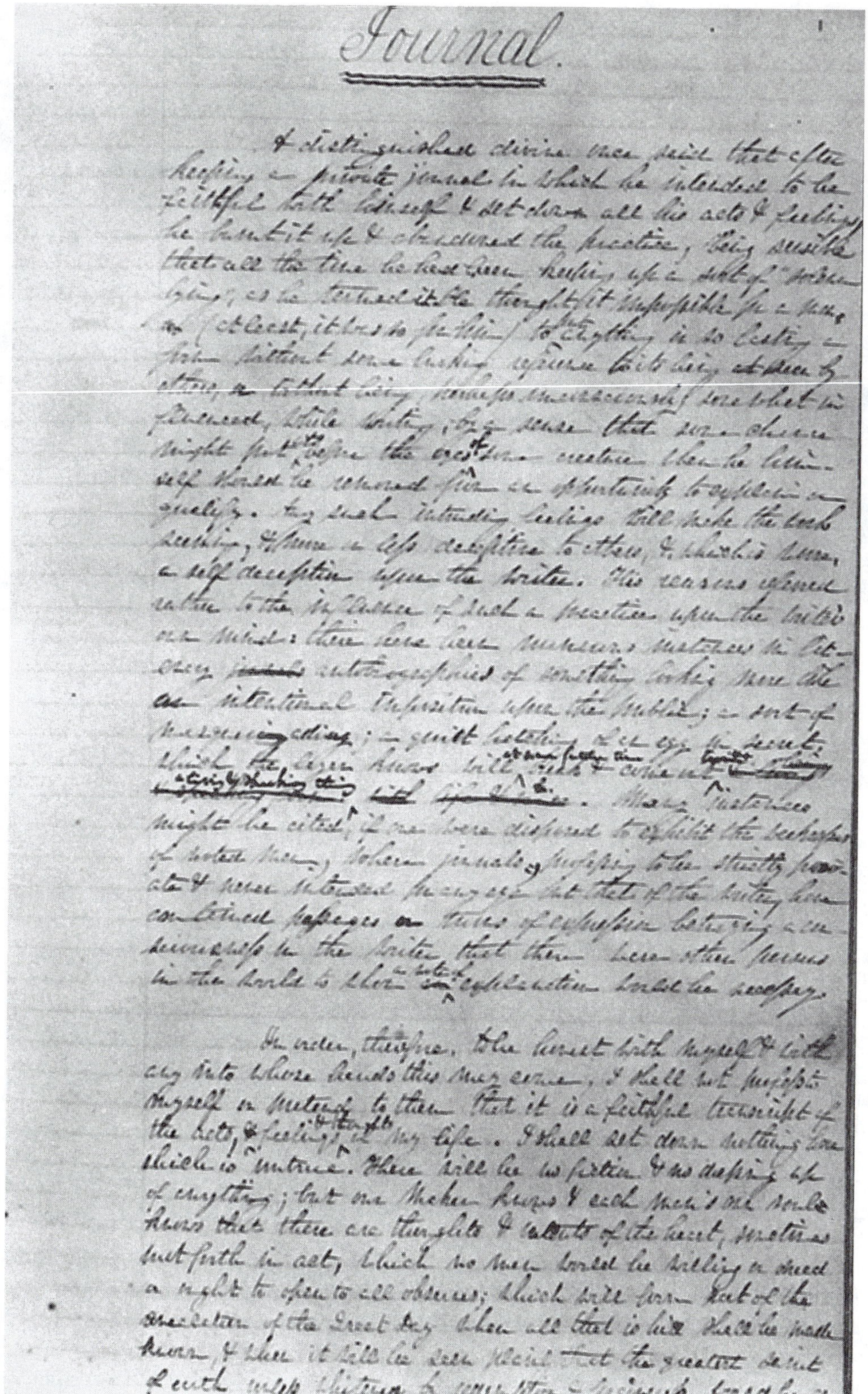
Journal.

First page of Dana's journal (Massachusetts Historical Society)

Dana's first house in Cambridge, Massachusetts, on the corner of Phillips and Berkeley Places

Dana reveals that he was repulsed by the brutal, undignified, and unjust punishment. While he recognized the necessity of the captain's absolute authority, Dana despised the arrogance and sadism of a tyrant who so abused his power. But even this objectionable act had some compensation: "The behavior of the two men who were flogged toward one another showed a delicacy and a sense of honor, which would have been worthy of admiration in the highest walks of life."

Equally interesting as Dana's description of life at sea is his unaffected chronicle of his own development from a privileged schoolboy into a strong, capable adult. He portrays himself as reveling in the self-confidence and sense of accomplishment that his competence in his work conferred upon him. After his "first act of what sailors will allow to be seamanship" (sending down a royal yard in the Bay of Monterey), "I heard the 'well done' of the mate, when the yard reached the deck, with as much satisfaction as I ever felt at Cambridge on seeing a 'bene' at the foot of a Latin exercise." Later, in describing the hard work of cutting and loading bull hides along the coast of California, he gives further testimony to his abilities as an adaptable, self-sufficient, and skilled worker, fully capable of fending for himself.

Coming at the time when he was growing into manhood, such experiences made Dana more sympathetic than others of his high social rank to the working class. He later wrote that he never in his life met men he more admired and respected than some of the sailors and other working-class persons with whom he associated during those two years. Among these men were Bill Jackson, "the best specimen of the thoroughbred English sailor that I ever saw," and Tom Harris, "the most remarkable man I have ever seen," who had a perfect memory, incomparable reasoning powers, and a more acute intelligence than any of "the young men of my acquaintance and standing at college." He continues, "I would not part with the hours I spent in the watch with that man for any given hours of my life passed in study and social intercourse." A special friend of Dana's was the Sandwich Islander (Hawaiian) "Hope," a representative specimen of a people whom Dana repeatedly called "the most interesting, intelligent, and kind-hearted people that I ever fell in with." He notes that he "felt an interest and affection for many of these simple, true-hearted men, such as I never felt before but for a near relation."

Dana was greatly moved by experiences such as witnessing the captain's barbarities to the crew and the loss of a shipmate overboard. Such incidents strengthened his commitment to his fellowman. At the same time, the various scenes of life he observed made him more aware of differences in individuals and cultures than he would have been if he had not viewed life from a humble station during two impressionable years of his youth. He was interested in the contrast between Yankees and the Spanish Americans he met in California, calling the latter "an idle, thriftless

Dana's wife, Sarah Watson Dana, with two of their daughters, Elizabeth Ellery Dana (left) and Angela Henrietta Channing Dana

people" but also the most dignified and well-bred persons he had ever seen: "Even a Spanish beggar wears his rags with an air." He met sailors of all nations in the ports of California and was fascinated with the distinctions of national character: the vivacity of Italians, who wore bright colors and spontaneously burst into song; the haughty pride of the English; and the "brutish" appearance and manners of Russians, "a stupid and greasy-looking set."

Dana spent roughly sixteen months in California–from January 1835 to May 1836. As a common sailor and hide curer he had little opportunity to study the social and geographical characteristics of the place, but his story nevertheless richly describes California life in vivid detail. This period was about a decade before the United States won California from Mexico. Dana saw the immense possibilities of the Pacific Coast and exclaimed, almost prophetically, "In the hands of an enterprising people, what a country this might be!" Although Dana noted that Americans and Englishmen "are fast filling up the principal towns, and getting the trade into their hands," he apparently did not foresee that his own country would soon make a conquest of this beautiful coastal region.

Dana's "two years before the mast" were really only about eight months, since he spent two-thirds of the time in California. The real core of his narrative, however, is the story of the voyage from Boston to Santa Barbara on the *Pilgrim* and of the return voyage from San Diego to Boston on the *Alert.* His youth and the fact that he viewed nautical scenes with naive eyes lend the work originality and freshness. Dana effectively expresses the heroism of the sailors in descriptions of gales and calms. The pleasant and beautiful scenes of sea life are gracefully rendered: albatross and dolphins, icebergs and corposants, and the beauty of a ship under full sail, "the most glorious moving object in the world."

Dana weaves all these experiences into a leisurely but never languid narrative, diversified with anecdotes and interspersed with humor. He tells of sailors' pranks and holidays as well as of their hardships and hazards. His rhetoric brims with nautical expressions, which lend it the right sea flavor but seldom seem obtrusive.

Dana's vivid story was an immediate critical and popular success. *Two Years Before the Mast* ran through many editions, was translated into many foreign languages, and

The three Richard Henry Danas (Longfellow House)

was praised by common readers, by nautical men, and by later writers of sea-related works. The British Admiralty Board paid Dana the compliment of distributing his book in the Royal Navy as an informative chronicle of sea life. Unfortunately, however, Dana never matched this work, published when he was twenty-five, with an equal achievement during the remaining half-century of his ambitious, purposeful, and busy life.

He channeled his energy and ambition instead into giving legal aid to sailors and to fugitive slaves. His experiences aboard the *Pilgrim* and in California had developed within him a compassionate understanding of the difficulties endured by such people, and he worked hard to redress the many injustices they suffered. He specialized in admiralty law in order to assist sailors, and *The Seaman's Friend, Containing a Treatise on Practical Seamanship, with Plates; a Dictionary of Sea Terms; Customs and Usages on the Merchant Service; Laws Relating to the Practical Duties of Master and Mariners,* published in 1841, became a standard manual. Shortly before its publication, Dana married Sarah Watson, with whom he had six children.

In the late 1840s Dana became interested in aiding fugitive slaves and in preventing the further spread of slavery into the southwestern region of what is now the United States. He opposed the Mexican War and was one of the founders of the Free-Soil Party. Though his wealthier clients began to take their business elsewhere, and his elitist friends balked at his espousal of such a cause, he doggedly followed his conscience despite the injury to his professional career and his social relationships. His self-righteousness expressed his pride: "I am a Free-Soiler, because I am (who should not say so) of the stock of the old Northern gentry, and have a particular dislike to any subserviency or even appearance of subserviency on the part of our people to the slave-holding oligarchy."

Dana believed that the opposition of respectable Boston to Abolitionists and Free-Soilers was based on their financial interest; his analysis thus coincided with that of Emerson, Thoreau, and James Russell Lowell. "The spindles and daybooks are against us," he wrote, despairing of the cause. In the 1850s Dana took a leading part in the defense of fugitive slaves and of those who aided their escape. He volunteered to defend Anthony Burns, the last fugitive slave captured in Massachusetts, without payment. Dana's defense of Burns in this famous trial was eloquent but unsuccessful. However, Burns was later freed by Northern sympathizers. In the excitement surrounding the trial, Dana was actually clubbed in the streets by a hired thug, but nothing deterred his legal championship of the degraded and outcast classes of humanity.

Although Dana's career was fueled by his strenuous and heroic humanitarianism, he never actually became a true "man of the people." He always retained his class-consciousness and class pride, and his tastes and values were conservative, even for his social rank. He was one of the founding members of the Saturday Club (1856), an elite intellectual group that met monthly to discuss such topics as literature, politics, and philosophy. Even his aristocratic associates in the club noted "a certain Episcopal flavor about his manners and speech." By "Episcopal flavor" such acquaintances referred not only to Dana's newly adopted religious denomination but also to the formality and haughtiness of manner that was thought to characterize it. Despite his progressive attitude regarding slavery and the working class, Dana was drawn to tradition in many ways and shunned certain "modern" and particularly American concepts. He preferred high European culture to American; his literary preferences were for English classics, particularly the works of William Shakespeare, John Milton, and Christopher Marlowe. He was repulsed by Charles Darwin's ideas about evolution and reveled in the company of his Saturday Club associates because of their "gentility" and their "true Christianity." In 1861 Abraham Lincoln appointed Dana United States district attorney for the district of Massachusetts.

In his later legal career Dana continued to advocate the causes he had espoused as a young lawyer. He specialized in maritime law and also lectured on international law at Harvard during the years 1866 to 1868. He served as counsel for the United States in the prosecution of Jefferson Davis from 1867 to 1868 for high treason. Though these activities added to his professional eminence, they probably prevented him from attaining his political goals. His hard legal fighting for humane causes had deprived him of the support of rich and influential people, and his aristocratic stiffness prevented his gaining a popular following. Thus, political enemies blocked his confirmation when, as a reward for services to the Republican Party, President Ulysses S. Grant nominated him for the post of ambassador to England. Dana later ran for Congress but was overwhelmingly defeated.

Though Dana wrote and traveled throughout his life, he never produced another work rivaling *Two Years Before the Mast.* He did write another travel book, *To Cuba and Back,* published in 1859, which was successful and ran through several editions, but it has since fallen into obscurity. Most of his other writing was on the subject of international law, which of course did not add to his literary reputation. He did much miscellaneous newspaper and magazine writing between 1840 and 1870 but on topics of momentary and therefore fleeting significance.

As an old man, Dana acknowledged bitterly that his only important success had been "a boy's work." However, to have written such a clean, fresh, and honest report of the life of common sailors as *Two Years Before the Mast* is hardly an inconsequential achievement.

Letters:

"Five Dana Letters," edited by James Allison, *American Neptune,* 13 (July 1953): 162–176.

Biographies:

Charles Francis Adams, *Richard Henry Dana: A Biography,* 2 volumes (Boston: Houghton, Mifflin, 1890);

Samuel Shapiro, *Richard Henry Dana, Jr.: 1815–1882* (East Lansing: Michigan State University Press, 1961).

References:

James M. Cox, "Richard Henry Dana's *Two Years Before the Mast:* Autobiography Completing Life," *The Dialectic of Discovery: Essays on the Teaching and Interpretation of Literature Presented to Lawrence E. Harvey,* edited by John D. Lyons and Nancy J. Vickers (Lexington, Ky.: French Forum, 1984), pp. 159–177;

Robert A. Ferguson, "The Richard Henry Danas: Father and Son," in *Law and Letters in American Culture* (Cambridge, Mass.: Harvard University Press, 1984), pp. 241–272;

Robert L. Gale, *Richard Henry Dana, Jr.* (New York: Twayne, 1969);

James D. Hart, "The Education of Richard Henry Dana, Jr.," *New England Quarterly,* 9 (March 1936): 3–25;

Douglas B. Hill Jr., "Richard Henry Dana, Jr., and *Two Years Before the Mast,*" *Criticism,* 9 (Fall 1967): 312–325;

Margaret S. Thompson, "Ben Butler Versus the Brahmins: Patronage and Politics in Early Gilded Age Massachusetts," *New England Quarterly,* 55 (June 1982): 163–186.

Papers:

The letters, private papers, and manuscripts of Richard Henry Dana Jr. are housed primarily at the Houghton Library of Harvard University and the Massachusetts Historical Society in Boston.

Dorothea Lynde Dix

(4 April 1802 - 18 July 1887)

Suzanne Disheroon Green
Northwestern State University

BOOKS: *Conversations on Common Things; or, Guide to Knowledge, With Questions* (Boston: Munroe & Francis, 1824; ninth edition, revised, 1842);

Evening Hours (Boston: Munroe & Francis; New York: Charles S. Francis, 1825);

The Prize; or, The Three Half Crowns, by the author of "Self Conquest" (Boston: Bowles & Dearborn, 1827);

Meditations for Private Hours, by the author of "Evening Hours" (Boston: Munroe & Francis, 1828);

The Pearl; or, Affection's Gift: A Christmas and New Year's Present (Philadelphia: Thomas T. Ash, 1829);

American Moral Tales for Young Persons (Boston: Leonard C. Bowles & B. H. Greene, 1832);

Memorial to the Legislature of Massachusetts, 1843. Protesting against the Confinement of Insane Persons and Idiots in Almshouses and Prisons (Boston: Munroe & Francis, 1843);

Address by a Recent Female Visiter [sic] to the Prisoners in the Eastern Penitentiary of Pennsylvania (Philadelphia: White, 1844);

Memorial. To the Honourable the Senate and General Assembly of the State of New Jersey (Trenton, N.J., 1845);

Memorial Soliciting a State Hospital for the Insane, second edition (Trenton, N.J., 1845);

Remarks on Prisons and Prison Discipline in the United States (Boston: Munroe & Francis, 1845);

A Review of the Present Condition of the State Penitentiary of Kentucky, with Brief Notices and Remarks Upon the Jails and Poor-houses in Some of the Most Populous Counties (Frankfort, Ky.: A. G. Hodges, 1845);

Memorial Soliciting a State Hospital for the Insane (Pennsylvania) (Philadelphia: I. Ashmead, 1845);

Memorial Soliciting a State Hospital for the Insane (Harrisburg, Pa.: J. M. G. Lescure, 1845);

Memorial Soliciting Enlarged and Improved Accommodations for the Insane of the State of Tennessee, by the Establishment of a New Hospital (Nashville: B. R. M'Kennie, 1847);

Memorial of D. L. Dix, Praying a Grant of Land for the Relief and Support of the Indigent Curable and Incurable Insane in the United States (Washington, D.C.: Tippin & Streeper, 1848);

Dorothea Lynde Dix, 1846 (Houghton Library, Harvard University)

Memorial Soliciting a State Hospital for the Insane (Montgomery, Ala.: Office of the Advertiser and Gazette, 1849);

Memorial Soliciting Adequate Appropriations for the Construction of a State Hospital for the Insane in the State of Mississippi, February 1850 (Jackson, Miss.: Fall & Marshall, 1850);

Memorial of Miss D. L. Dix, to the Honorable the General Assembly in Behalf of the Insane of Maryland (Annapolis, 1852);

"Memorial of Miss Dix, the Honorable the Senate and House of Representatives of the State of Illinois," in *Reports of the Illinois State Hospital for the Insane, 1847–1862* (Chicago: F. Fulton, 1863), pp. 9–31;

On Behalf of the Insane Poor; Selected Reports (New York: Arno Press, 1971);

Asylum, Prison, and Poorhouse: the Writings and Reform Work of Dorothea Dix in Illinois, edited by David L. Lightner (Carbondale, Ill.: Southern Illinois University Press, 1999).

OTHER: *Hymns for Children: Selected and Altered, With Appropriate Texts of Scripture* (Boston: Munroe & Francis, 1824);

The Garland of Flora, compiled and edited by Dix (Boston: S. G. Goodrich; Carter & Hendee, 1829).

Dorothea Lynde Dix is best remembered for her work on behalf of the indigent, the insane, and the mentally disabled. She tirelessly lobbied the U.S. Congress and individual state legislatures alike for the improvement of residential facilities for these populations as well as for the regulation and supervision of the treatments that took place in these facilities. However, Dix's biographer Thomas J. Brown has aptly pointed out that Dix's legacy extends beyond her important work on behalf of the downtrodden. Her life also exemplifies the evolving role of women in the nineteenth century. On one hand, existing social mores dictated that she exist in the traditionally female sphere, which consisted of very narrowly defined occupations and roles. Conversely, she successfully interacted with the male establishment that populated the government of her era. According to Brown, Dix, unlike many of her female compatriots, "lived at the center of both the so-called separate spheres of female virtue and public affairs." Dix's importance extends to her pioneering work as a woman in a man's era, well beyond the scope of lobbying for changes in the treatment of insanity.

Dorothy Lynde Dix, born on 4 April 1802 in Hampden, Maine, often remarked upon the unhappy nature of her childhood. Her father, Joseph Dix, was in many ways a disappointment to his family–in part because of his lack of ambition and squandering of opportunities while attending Harvard College and in part because of his choice of a wife. His domineering parents viewed his marriage to Mary Biglow as a poor choice because, according to Brown, Joseph Dix "cast aside [an] important chance to solidify a place in the Boston elite." The Biglows possessed a longstanding family name, but not a particularly prestigious one. The eldest child resulting from this union, Dorothea described herself as an "orphan prematurely deprived of parental attention and burdened with the grave responsibilities of adulthood" at the age of ten. She chafed under the consistent ridicule of her grandmother, who was especially disdainful of her needlework, and this blatant disregard by the person for whom Dix was named led the reformer to change her name to Dorothea during her teenage years, renouncing both her given name and her longstanding nickname, "Dolly," which was also borrowed from her grandmother.

Dix rarely spoke of her early family life, but her few comments are telling. She identified the age of ten as "the fundamental dividing line of her life" rather than following the traditional pattern of dating "her uniqueness from the day of her birth." During her tenth year, also, she embraced Unitarianism, finding the principles of salvation through "gradual, self-disciplined cultivation of piety and rectitude" ideals that she could espouse with the "fervor of an ardent evangelical." She also marked this year as significant because of the birth of her younger brother, the child who "orphaned" her by diverting her parents' attention. She emphasized the importance of her conversion to the Unitarian faith and the birth of the first of two younger brothers, saying, "I trace many of my governing principles to that one year"–principles that included a "resilient pride in the independence and tenacity that she would always consider to be her chief character traits."

Because of her tenuous familial relationships, Dix sought love and companionship in other homes. At the age of fourteen, she moved out of her parents' home and began to develop a friendship with Anne Heath, a woman five years her senior who served as something of a mentor. Dix engaged in a brief, subdued flirtation with a Unitarian minister, Ezra Stiles Gannett, but she rapidly lost interest in him when she heard, mistakenly, that he was courting another young lady. Gannett remained single for many years, but Dix's infatuation had waned. She decided instead to remain unmarried, despite what Brown has called "the daunting economic and social consequences of spinsterhood" in the early 1800s. Although her Lynde relatives tried several times to match her with an appropriate partner, Dix steadfastly refused to play courting games or to waste time attending balls and parties.

Dix began teaching at a young age and saw teaching as her true vocation. She was appointed in 1824 to the Female Monitorial School, which was one of the premier schools in Boston at the time. She

Dorothy Dix, the grandmother for whom Dix was originally named (Houghton Library, Harvard University)

developed the reputation of being one of the finest schoolmistresses in Boston and began writing in her spare time. Plagued by ill health throughout much of her life, however, Dix was forced to give up teaching for a time. She almost became a professional author "under the financial pressure of her respite from school-teaching." Her first book, *Conversations on Common Things; or, Guide to Knowledge, With Questions* (1824), was intended as a grammar-school text that answered common childhood inquiries in the form of a dialogue between a mother and daughter. The book was quite successful and remained in print for more than forty years. She followed this volume in 1825 with *Evening Hours,* which used a format similar to that of *Conversations on Common Things* to aid children in reading the Christian Scriptures, and in 1828 with *Meditations for Private Hours,* which "summarized some of the lessons she had drawn from her experiences." During her early adulthood, she also worked as a governess and tutor for the children of William Ellery Channing, whose religious views and sermons she greatly admired. This chapter of her life closed with the publication of *The Garland of Flora* (1829), an anthology geared to "those who love flowers and fine sentiments." Although commercially oriented, the book was less of a success than her earlier volumes. After the lukewarm reception of this volume, she concluded that "professional writing led away from her primary goals of moral instruction," and she resolved to return to teaching and leave literature behind her.

In March of 1841, Dix made two educational inspection visits that changed her life. Recently returned from Europe, where biographer David Gollaher has speculated that she suffered a mental breakdown, Dix discovered that the family estate had been sold upon the death of her grandmother. Rather than dividing her real estate equally among her grandchildren, as she had promised, she offered free use of her home to minister Thaddeus Harris and his family for the remainder of his life, and the executor of Dorothy Lynde's estate took this as a sign that the property should be sold to Harris. While Dix was prepared for such financial independence, she was not as well equipped emotionally. She described herself as being adrift the better part of a year, until she made an inspection at the Middlesex County House of Correction. Intrigued by the conditions and the state of the incarcerated individuals, she began teaching Sunday school classes at the prison and arranging for ministers to come and speak at the prison as well. Her repeated visits to the prison "spurred her interest in the moral education of prisons" and convinced her of the propriety of the "moral treatment" for mental and social illnesses that had "superseded the heroic treatment of insanity by bloodletting and other aggressive measures that were intended to exhaust or overpower mental patients . . . ; the moral treatment attempted to inculcate self-control in patients rather than impose violent coercion." This moral treatment, according to Sonya Michel, consisted of therapy whereby the inmates were "to be treated kindly but held to a clearly defined routine. This type of therapy began to gain acceptance among American physicians just after the turn of the eighteenth century. Previously, insanity treatment consisted mainly of confining and attempting to subdue the insane, who were regarded as subhuman because they were believed to have lost their reason."

Dix's conviction that this type of treatment was superior to the heroic measures widely used in her era reflected two aspects of her personality: an active belief, according to Brown, in the "superior piety and benevolence of women [which] endowed them with a distinctive moral authority" and her perception that in "teetering between sinful passions and redeeming affections, the insane brilliantly demonstrated the central tenet of Dix's strain of Unitarianism, the promise that religious piety could channel ardor into the achievement of self-control."

Dix's belief in the moral treatment led her to crusade tirelessly for the rights of the insane. Despite repeated remonstrances from friends that an overzealous travel schedule would damage her already frail health, Dix undertook a brutal visiting schedule, touring as many as thirty-five asylums and houses of correction in one week. These visits led to the composition of her first "memorial" in 1843. Initially, she intended to work in conjunction with Samuel Gridley Howe, who won a seat in the Massachusetts legislature around this time and shared her concern over the treatment of the insane. According to Michel, unlike her male counterparts, who could speak in legislative sessions because they were men who could address themselves to men, Dix's "chief avenue of access to legislative bodies was the memorial, which had to be read aloud by a willing male representative." These lengthy narrative essays–some ran to thirty pages or more–summarized the argument presented. Despite the potential difficulty of getting her arguments presented, Dix struck out on her own when Howe did not fully support the well-documented claims in her first memorial, despite his urging that she publish it and his assisting with its editing. She continued to write these memorials, which were generally presented with success to numerous state legislatures throughout the eastern and southern United States. Her later memorials became more scientifically oriented, generally offering an overview of the moral treatment and its development. Dix also presented her arguments to the U.S. Congress, the only governmental body that she lobbied without success. Although she succeeded in convincing Congress to pass a bill in 1854, President Franklin Pierce vetoed the measure.

Most of Dix's memorials were quickly issued as pamphlets as well, but they were not met with instant popularity. Legislators resisted her ideas because of the large appropriations of money that the suggested reforms involved. Wardens and keepers of almshouses were outraged at the way in which they were characterized: not as deliberately cruel, but as possessing a brutal indifference to the welfare of their charges." Despite the criticism she received, Dix was straightforward concerning the state of the asylums that she visited. She "emphasized repeatedly that she had accepted no secondhand accounts. '*I tell what I have seen!*' she promised." Accordingly, she described individuals held in "*cages, closets, cellars, stalls, pens! Chained, naked, beaten with rods,* and *lashed* into obedience!" She told of men confined in dead rooms, of men and women locked in the same cells with no heat, clothing, or sanitation. The public outcry raised at the publication of her *Memorial to the Legislature of Massachusetts, 1843. Protesting against the Confinement of Insane Persons and Idiots in Almshouses and Prisons* (1843) ultimately led to the passage of a bill to enlarge a Massachusetts asylum from 250 to 400 beds. Far from satisfied with her success, however, Dix took her crusade to other states and was the only New England reformer to spend a substantial amount of time in the Southern states attempting to improve the situation of the mentally ill.

Dix's friend and mentor Anne Heath in 1864 (Massachusetts Historical Society)

Brown has noted that many historians have misunderstood the nature of Dix's crusade, identifying her as a "humanitarian visionary" rather than a "participant in American politics." She campaigned for six years in Congress to establish a network of state hospitals, a plan that she argued should be funded by a revenue-sharing program similar to that adopted to establish land-grant colleges, a plan that according to Brown, was based not on the "nature of insanity but the nature of public lands." What came to be known as "Miss Dix's bill"

The New Jersey State Lunatic Asylum at Trenton, which Dix helped to establish

> intersected with related controversies about the federal domain that defined the major political parties, absorbed vast profit-seeking energies, framed sectional disputes over slavery, and convulsed the nation between the acquisition of the Mexican Cession and the passage of the Kansas-Nebraska Act. As a result, careful examination of Dix's measure not only exposes neglected dimensions of Victorian womanhood but also sheds new light on some of the most thoroughly reviewed questions of American political history.

Unfortunately, this political victory–the victory of being heard–for the female gender did not translate in this instance to a victory for Dix's cause.

Historians often find Dix interesting because of her connection to notable figures in the Transcendentalist movement. She served as the tutor/governess in William Ellery Channing's household for several years and is reputed to have been part of a group that serenaded Ralph Waldo Emerson with a requiem that he requested. This odd type of frivolity does not reflect Dix's general character, however, as she took her duty as a teacher and a woman seriously–roles that she believed required her to set a high moral example for others. She was acquainted with Bronson Alcott, and Margaret Fuller was well acquainted with Dix's personality and reputation as an uptight, prudish spinster. Fuller correctly predicted to Emerson that Dix would refuse to give her a copy of a new edition of *Private Hours* so that the volume might be reviewed in *The Dial,* in part because Dix had refused to participate in a Conversation class led by Fuller since Dix disagreed with the topics under discussion. Despite her extensive good works, many of Dix's compatriots found her difficult and unpleasant because of her narrow-minded attitudes and religious fanaticism. This inflexibility led to her failure as the Union Superintendent of Nurses during the Civil War.

Because of her "faith in the divine vocation of benevolent womanhood," Dix volunteered for active nursing duty at President Abraham Lincoln's first call. She came to view the Southern cause in much the same way as she viewed mental illness–as a sickness that could be cured with the moral treatment and the positive example of a morally upright person. Convinced that she could set this shining example and help speed the end of the conflict, she lobbied the President's private secretary and was appointed the Superintendent of Nursing for the Union Army, a position that was essentially created for her by the U.S. War Department. She attempted to instill rigorous standards of cleanliness and care and held her nurses to impossibly high criteria for personal and professional behavior. She found herself in direct conflict with both the Union doctors and the Sanitary Commission as the result of both procedural disagreements and her unwillingness to compromise. Many of her nurses found her difficult to work for as well. Louisa May Alcott, also a nurse to the Union troops, summed up the popular opinion of Dix, stating that she was "a kind old soul, but very queer, fussy and arbitrary. No one likes her and I don't wonder." In the end, Dix's ambitious nursing program was considered a failure, and the program was abolished by the War Department in 1863.

Dix continued to pursue the improvement of conditions for the insane for most of the remainder of her life. However, by the end of her life, she resided in a guest house in the Trenton hospital that she had helped to start, feeling alone and deserted. Her health continued to fail, and she lost most of her hearing and sight, losses that ironically caused her to open her room to more visitors than she had previously allowed despite her complaints of loneliness. Upon the death of William Greenleaf Eliot, a minister whom she considered "almost a brother," she became visibly more feeble and passed away shortly thereafter on 18 July 1887. She was buried in Mount Auburn Cemetery, not twenty paces from the grave of William Ellery Channing, one of the ministers she had most admired. She was "at home at last" in the Boston Unitarian cemetery.

Letters:

The Lady and the President: The Letters of Dorothea Dix & Millard Fillmore, edited by Charles M. Snyder (Lexington: University Press of Kentucky, 1975).

Biographies:

David Gollaher, *Voice for the Mad: The Life of Dorothea Dix* (New York: Free Press, 1995);

Thomas J. Brown, *Dorothea Dix: New England Reformer* (Cambridge: Harvard University Press, 1998).

References:

Seth Curtis Beach, *Daughters of the Puritans* (Freeport, N.Y.: Books for Libraries Press, 1905);

Sonya Michel, "Dorothea Dix; or, the Voice of the Maniac," *Discourse,* 17, no. 2 (1994–1995): 48–66;

Martha Saxton, *Louisa May* (Boston: Houghton Mifflin, 1977).

Papers:

A substantial collection of Dorothea Lynde Dix's papers is held by the Houghton Library, Harvard University.

John Sullivan Dwight

(13 May 1813 - 5 September 1893)

Ora Frishberg Saloman
Baruch College and The Graduate School, City University of New York

BOOKS: *Report Made at a Meeting of the Honorary and Immediate Members of the Pierian Sodality, in Harvard University, Cambridge, August 30th, 1837, with a Record of the Meeting* (Cambridge, Mass.: Folsom, Wells & Thurston, 1837);

Address, Delivered before the Harvard Musical Association, August 25th, 1841 (1841);

A Lecture on Association, in its Connection with Education, Delivered before the New England Fourier Society, in Boston, February 29th, 1844 (Boston: Benjamin H. Greene, 1844).

OTHER: *Select Minor Poems, Translated from the German of Goethe and Schiller,* translated and edited, with notes and a preface, by Dwight (Boston: Hilliard, Gray, 1839);

Dwight's Journal of Music, A Paper of Art and Literature, 41 volumes, edited by Dwight (Boston: Edward L. Balch, 1852–1881);

"The History of Music in Boston," in *The Memorial History of Boston, including Suffolk County, Massachusetts, 1630–1880,* 4 volumes, edited by Justin Winsor (Boston: James R. Osgood, 1881–1883), IV: 415–464;

Charles C. Perkins, Dwight, William F. Bradbury, and C. Guild, *History of the Handel and Haydn Society, of Boston, Massachusetts,* 2 volumes, chapters 4–15 of volume 1 written by Dwight (Boston: Alfred Mudge, 1883–1934).

SELECTED PERIODICAL PUBLICATIONS–UNCOLLECTED: "Music, as a Branch of Popular Education," *Boston Musical Gazette: A Semi-Monthly Journal Devoted to the Science of Music,* 1 (16 May 1838): 9–10;

"Review of Gardiner's *Music of Nature* By Rev. J. S. Dwight," *Boston Musical Gazette: A Semi-Monthly Journal Devoted to the Science of Music,* 1 (19 September 1838): 81–82; (3 October 1838): 89–90;

"The Concerts of the Past Winter," *Dial,* 1 (July 1840): 124–134;

"Address, Delivered Before the Harvard Musical Association, August 25th, 1841," *Musical Magazine,* 3 (28 August 1841): 257–272;

"Academy of Music–Beethoven's Symphonies," *Pioneer* (January 1843): 26–28; (February 1843): 56–60;

"Haydn," *United States Magazine, and Democratic Review,* 14 (January 1844): 17–25;

"*Musical Review*. Music in Boston During the Last Winter.–No. III: Concerts of the Boston Academy of Music," *Harbinger,* 1 (16 August 1845): 154–157;

"*Musical Review*. The Virtuoso Age in Music. The New School of Pianists and Violinists," *Harbinger,* 1 (15 November 1845): 362–364; (22 November 1845): 378–381;

"*Musical Review*. 'Father Heinrich' in Boston," *Harbinger,* 3 (4 July 1846): 58–59;

"How Stands the Cause?" *Harbinger,* 3 (7 November 1846): 348–351;

"Concerts of the Past Week," *Dwight's Journal of Music,* 2 (12 February 1853): 149–151;

"Richard Wagner: Third Article," *Dwight's Journal of Music,* 2 (26 February 1853): 165–166;

"Too Much Heavy Music," *Dwight's Journal of Music,* 6 (17 March 1855): 189–190;

"Concert Review," *Dwight's Journal of Music,* 22 (28 March 1863): 410–411;

"'Light' and 'Heavy,'" *Dwight's Journal of Music,* 24 (17 September 1864): 310;

"The Past Musical Year in Boston," *Dwight's Journal of Music,* 26 (9 June 1866): 254–255;

"Music in its larger Meanings," *Dwight's Journal of Music,* 26 (1 September 1866): 302–303.

John Sullivan Dwight, a Transcendentalist writer and critic on music, literature, and social reform, was founder and sole editor of the first long-lasting nineteenth-century periodical of art music in America, *Dwight's Journal of Music, A Paper of Art and Literature*. He was a respected translator of German and French literature, teacher of music and Latin at Brook Farm, and effective advocate for the establishment of music in the curriculum at Harvard University and for many cultural organizations in Boston, Massachusetts.

Oldest of the four children of Dr. John Dwight–a Calvinist-turned-freethinker who then became a physician–and Mary (Corey) Dwight, John Sullivan Dwight was born 13 May 1813 in Boston, Massachusetts. He was educated at the Boston Latin School and at Harvard College, from which he graduated in 1832. Supplied with fine faculty recommendations in the classics and in German, he expected to obtain a suitable position as a teacher of languages and literature. Without full commitment to a career in the ministry when he entered Harvard Divinity School in 1834, Dwight interrupted his work there briefly to become a tutor in Pennsylvania before returning to complete his studies in 1836.

During his graduate years Dwight was in the vanguard of those who studied Ludwig van Beethoven's sonatas for piano in an era when that composer's music was little known in America. Dwight's attention was a sign of his prescience and interest in furthering knowledge about Beethoven. The nature of Dwight's early musical education is not precisely known, but his sensitivity to the field had been recognized during early piano study with his father and perhaps a sister. He had been an enthusiastic flutist during his undergraduate years and played the clarinet in the Arionic Sodality at Harvard before joining the more advanced Pierian Sodality in his senior year. These informal groups were the only musical outlets then available on the campus; the discipline of music had not yet become part of the formal college curriculum.

For four years following graduation from the Harvard Divinity School, Dwight filled temporary pulpits while pursuing his interests in literature and music. As an early participant in the discussions of the group later known as the Transcendental Club, Dwight admired the leadership of Ralph Waldo Emerson. Dwight's outlook, however, was closer to that of his mentor and friend George S. Ripley, who founded the community Brook Farm in West Roxbury, Massachusetts, based on the view that individuality could be joined effectively to collective cooperation for the benefit of society. Following an unhappy year as an ordained minister in Northampton, Massachusetts (1840–1841), Dwight joined the Ripleys at Brook Farm and became an active member of that community.

During the late 1830s and the 1840s Dwight was increasingly productive as a writer and an editor. In his *Report Made at a Meeting of the Honorary and Immediate Members of the Pierian Sodality* (1837), he enunciated a concept of music as literature to form the basis for proposals intended initially to advance the cause of music as a field of learning at Harvard College. He was convinced that Beethoven must be honored as much as William Shakespeare. He expanded the notion of music as a written literature of the world to that of a "pure Literature of the affections" to be made accessible to all, in "Music, as a Branch of Popular Education," which appeared in the *Boston Musical Gazette* (1838). Expressing the hope that sensitivity to art music could eventually become as common as that to poetry or fine writing, he advocated attuning the "public ear" through public musical education and concerts made available to everyone.

Dwight's early advocacy of wide access to musical culture has been obscured by contemporary critics familiar only with his later nineteenth-century musical and social conservatism. His plea that musical compositions be regarded as literature may be elucidated in connection with his contemporaneous, intensive study of Friedrich Schiller's and Johann Wolfgang von Goethe's works during 1837 and 1838 in preparation for his critically admired translation, with notes, *Select Minor Poems, Translated from the German of Goethe and Schiller* (1839). Schiller had emphasized that literature, conceived broadly, was capable of leading humanity toward ennobling moral truth; Dwight proposed an approach to music as literature understood in the Schillerian sense of creative imaginative expression addressing the exalted in human character. Dwight's interpretation was based on Schiller's poetry and aesthetic treatise, as well as on material gleaned from Thomas Carlyle's *The Life of Friedrich Schiller* (1825). Dwight dedicated his poetry volume to Carlyle, who had referred to Schiller's view of genuine literature as including "the essence of philosophy, religion, art, whatever speaks to the immortal part of man." Dwight's initial perception and communication of a strong connection between aesthetic education and social progress may also be traced to Schiller's thought and Carlyle's discussion of Schiller's *Briefe über die aesthetische Erziehung des Menschen* (On the Aesthetic Education of Man, 1795).

For the volume he edited and for which he supplied eighty pages of notes as well as a preface, Dwight translated sixty-nine poems by Goethe and sixteen by Schiller. Describing the project to James Freeman Clarke, editor of *The Western Messenger* (10 March 1837), Dwight explained his organization of the lyrics to exhibit their spirit and mark "the different *phases* thro' wh. their minds passed." He specified his method of translation as the preservation of the author's idea through the form as part of the substance, and thus saw it as organic rather than literal; his intention was to retain the original rhythm and "grace of expression" to the greatest possible extent, an aim in which he appears to have been largely successful. In his informative notes, Dwight stressed the significance of the poetry in speaking to universal common interests, an important critical criterion he applied to musical compositions as well.

Dwight's work, the third volume of Ripley's series *Specimens of Foreign Standard Literature,* earned him esteem. Carlyle praised Dwight's perceptive comments and skill. Among modern critics, J. Wesley Thomas lauds Dwight's application of a connected poetic-musical approach to poetic translations and literary reviews, but he misjudges Dwight's critical criteria in music. Stanley M. Vogel regards Dwight's contributions in "belletristic forms of German culture" as important, yet asserts that his translations, although accurate, possess neither grace nor charm. Henry A. Pochmann, however, considers many of Dwight's translations to have been among the best translations made of the shorter poems of Goethe and Schiller.

Dwight contributed three articles to the Transcendentalist periodical *The Dial* during 1840–1841, of which one, "The Concerts of the Past Winter" (July 1840), was a substantial review essay. In it he broached many themes on which he elaborated with remarkable consistency throughout his career. One is his conviction that "genuine classic music," with a preference for instrumental music, represents the aspiration of the heart to the Infinite. Orchestral music should not seek to imitate physical nature, nor should listeners seek to identify specific images in it. His strong encouragement of regular orchestral rehearsals and concerts stems from his belief that with frequent public performances "orchestra and audience would improve together" in order to build toward the playing of more difficult music and the development of a large public capable of appreciating it. Another aspect of his definition of "true classic" works emerges in his recognition of recent compositions for the piano as performed by visiting European virtuosi. Although enthusiastic about hearing idiomatic pieces by Sigismund Thalberg, Frédéric François Chopin, and Franz Liszt, he acknowledges that he would have been more pleased to hear sonatas by Beethoven or other works written solely to communicate inspired artistic feeling, rather than for instrumental display.

Ripley, then managing editor of *The Dial,* praised the essay: "Your article on 'Concerts' is an atoning offering for the many sins of the 'Dial'" (7 July 1840). In the mid twentieth century, Irving Lowens surveyed writings about music in Transcendentalist periodicals and judged Dwight to have possessed the sharpest critical intelligence in the United States. Joel Myerson offers a general appreciation of the critic's contributions to the magazine.

By 1842 Dwight was residing and teaching at Brook Farm. He was active in the new Harvard Musical Association formed with other members of the Pierian Sodality and enjoyed a growing reputation as a writer on music when he accepted an invitation to contribute to James Russell Lowell's periodical, *The Pioneer.* In "Academy of Music–Beethoven's Symphonies" (January–February 1843), Dwight described the sound of the Second Symphony and originated a theory of criticism applied initially to the Fifth Symphony. As preparation, he attended rehearsals and performances by the orchestra of the Boston Academy of Music at the Odeon and played arrangements of the symphonies on the piano at Brook Farm. In defining how to write well about music, he cautioned that a story could never be an interpretation of instrumental music, which transports the listener beyond visual imagery, but "allegorical illustration" in the spirit of the music could create a correspondence between the two. Avoiding previously defined literary interpretations, Dwight suggested a generalized character for each movement, interspersed biographical references drawn from writings by such writers as Anton Schindler and Bettina Brentano von Arnim, and attempted basic musical description of the structure of the first movement.

Three essays by Dwight appeared in the *United States Magazine, and Democratic Review*–on George Frideric Handel, Wolfgang Amadeus Mozart, and Franz Joseph Haydn (March and November 1843, January 1844). Each composer is associated with a particular genre. Handel's treatment of the oratorio, and especially *Messiah,* is emphasized; Mozart is considered for his dramatic handling of music as the language of the passions through opera; Haydn, together with Beethoven, is proposed as having introduced the new "boundless world" of instrumental music in which Haydn had succeeded in bringing out the individual capacities of the instruments and combining them effectively. Revealing his knowledge of an important German essay, "Symphonie oder Sinfonie" by Gottfried Wilhelm Fink published in the *Encyclopädie der gesammten musikalischen Wissenschaften, oder Universal-Lexicon der Tonkunst* (1835–1838), Dwight stressed that the challenges of the symphonic genre are to achieve unity from the greatest variety and the characteristic activity of all instruments as one unit. Dwight's essays of 1843 and 1844, particularly those treating the symphony, are more extensive in detail and scope than others by American writers of that era. They reveal his efforts to explain fundamental structural and instrumental aspects of music along with emotive description, biographical references, and autobiographical comments.

In 1844 Brook Farm officially adopted principles based on the social theory known as Fourierism, after the social philosopher Charles Fourier. Dwight wrote about and translated from Fourier's books, lectured to the New England Fourier Society, on whose executive committee he served, and revised the constitution of the community. Believing in a movement that called for universal harmony through the reform of society, he also considered art music vital to knowledge of the self, of Nature, and of God, as well as a harbinger of a better future in America. In his *A Lecture on Association, in its Connection with Education, Delivered before the New England Fourier Society, in Boston, February 29th, 1844* (1844), he articulated a vision for the improvement of society based on the joining of individuality with universality as mutually reconcilable. He explained it through a musical metaphor: just as "each note in the great world-symphony is a whole, a unit in itself," and must insist on its own sound while dedicating itself to "the harmony of the whole," so in society each member must live "most effectually to himself" yet find himself "in true relations with the whole" of humanity. In universal unity, each would attain unity of relations in real, social, and ideal spheres through the appropriate use of human capabilities.

Fourier's doctrine provided the theoretical framework for Dwight's educational philosophy, which he applied the following year when he became director of education for the entire school program at Brook Farm. His plan affirmed the importance of self-culture in an associative setting that encouraged development in groups through a graduated program of exercises, tasks, lessons, and studies from infancy through high school. During these years Dwight led a busy and satisfying life. Another role in which he took pleasure was his organization of the music for many convivial events in the community. The kindly and patient Dwight enjoyed the companionship of people of all ages. Memoirs and letters suggest that the affection of the young people for him was genuine and reciprocated.

Dwight's most important musical accomplishment during the Brook Farm years was his establishment of an excellent music column in the official Associationist organ published by Ripley, with Dwight's editorial assistance, called *The Harbinger* (1845–1849). Founded at Brook Farm as an expansion of *The Phalanx,* a journal published by the American Fourierist disciple Albert Brisbane, *The Harbinger* provided a supportive intellectual environment within which Dwight formulated his musical ideas as he heard a varied repertory in performance and integrated aspects of Fourierist thinking as appropriate. In it Dwight wrote essays heralding the earliest regular series of public orchestral performances in the United States of Beethoven's symphonies held concurrently in Boston and New York. During this epoch, Dwight joined his societal hopes for the future to his intrinsic musical preferences, for he was convinced that particularly Beethoven's music, technically difficult and aesthetically challenging, was a "presentiment of coming social harmony." He encouraged the Boston Academy of Music to rehearse the symphonies carefully until the musicians had "really got to feel them, and cooperate as one in the production of them," a process that would enable them to work together harmoniously, in the Fourierist sense, to benefit both music and audience. In his 1845 essay on Beethoven's Fifth Symphony, Dwight asserted that Beethoven's music encompassed the "aspiration of this age" and was prophetic of the great world movement of social reform. Americans had a need, a capacity, and a "destiny in this age and in this land to love Beethoven."

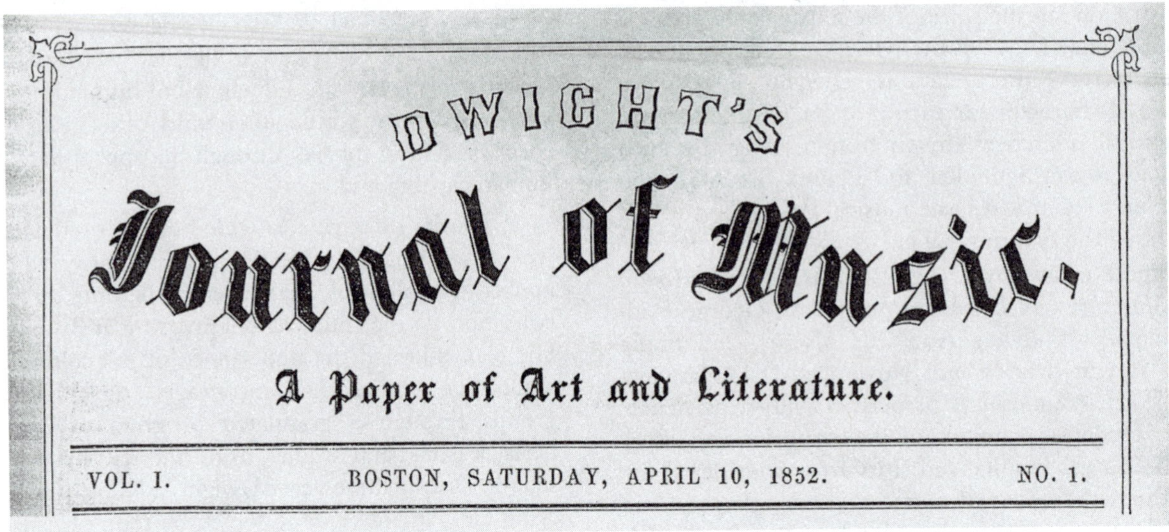
DWIGHT'S
Journal of Music,
A Paper of Art and Literature.
VOL. I. BOSTON, SATURDAY, APRIL 10, 1852. NO. 1.

Flag for the long-running periodical that Dwight founded

By 1846, as outlined in a lecture series in New York, Dwight had developed a general view of the history of music as divided into three phases: the "scientific," with Johann Sebastian Bach as its main representative; the "expressive," including music by Mozart and Beethoven; and the "modern music of effect," comprising compositions and performances by instrumental virtuosos. Significant articles written for *The Harbinger* in 1845 and 1846 enabled Dwight to admired brilliance in performance but considered certain pieces composed by virtuosi (such as Ole Bull) to lack unity and to be excessively individualistic. This mixed reception of virtuosos and their repertory continued throughout his career, a tendency misunderstood by modern critics unfamiliar with the full range of Dwight's writings, but acknowledging the legitimacy of virtuoso music in nineteenth-century concert life.

Sterling F. Delano has devoted one chapter to Dwight's music criticism, written between 1845 and 1849, in his broad study of the various departments of the Associationist journal. Ora Frishberg Saloman has analyzed Dwight's published and unpublished writings on music from 1835 to 1846, with emphasis on material in *The Harbinger,* in her book *Beethoven's Symphonies and J. S. Dwight: The Birth of American Music Criticism* (1995). In studying the European critical and intellectual foundations of Dwight's writings, she proposes that he pioneered in furthering public understanding of art music in America before the mid nineteenth century. Dwight described Beethoven's symphonies as the highest exemplars of expressive instrumental music, but this view impeded the critic's capacity, particularly in later decades, to evaluate divergent new instrumental approaches. For example, Dwight discerned a lack of "poetic or dramatic unity" in Anthony Philip Heinrich's narrative instrumental compositions because their vivid imagery did not accord with his essentially abstract Beethovenian symphonic model.

Dwight's activity on behalf of Associationism as a writer, translator, lecturer, and board member of The American Union of Associationists is well exemplified by his essay "How Stands the Cause?" published in *The Harbinger* (7 November 1846). His commitment to collective association as social ideal resulted in the plea that Brook Farm be sustained and recognized as its successful practical embodiment, despite the failure of the industrial sector. Moving through a summary of European associative organizations, Dwight clarified his abiding faith that the movement for social unity could best fulfill its high promise in the United States. Characteristically searching for connections between elements in society as in music and in education, he described three aspects: a "Synthetic mode," to nourish small groups as they coalesce; an opposite "Analytic mode," to enumerate the necessary attributes of a model Association; and an earnest conviction that Brook Farm could be the intellectual and moral nucleus of the movement. He imbued his prose with terminology and concepts proposed originally by Fourier and expounded by Brisbane in *Social Destiny of Man* (1840). Dwight expressed the conviction that despite its precarious existence, Brook Farm was central to the continued vitality of *The Harbinger,* the well-regarded school, the Associationist lectures and meetings, and the concept of honoring both manual labor and intellectual activity. If the essay testifies to the author's belief in social progress, it also serves as a poignant reminder that with the closing of Brook Farm in 1847, one of its strongest and last defenders would be left once again, as after his brief pastoral experience in Northampton, without prospects of a secure future.

Dwight continued to write from Boston for *The Harbinger* when it moved its central headquarters to New York. It ceased publication in 1849, and an uncertain period of three years followed during which Dwight contributed freelance essays and music reviews to several papers, including *Sartain's Magazine.* One positive event was his marriage on 12 February 1851 to Mary Bullard, an attractive singer who had participated with Dwight in musical events at Brook Farm. In 1852, with the sponsorship of the Harvard Musical Association, he founded *Dwight's Journal of Music,* which survived until 1881. Initially published weekly and then fortnightly from 1863, it is an invaluable chronicle of concert activities in America, as well as musical developments in Europe. Dwight was its editor and proprietor as well as its primary author and translator. He dedicated its pages to instruction, enlightenment, aesthetic guidance, improvement in public taste, and the broadening of appreciation for the role of music, arts, and literature in human life.

The forty-one volumes of *Dwight's Journal of Music* fulfill the aims set forth in the prospectus of the first volume (10 April 1852). Contents include critical reviews of all genres, with essays on the composers by various contributors; notices of new music published in America and abroad; summaries of musical news gathered from European and domestic papers; correspondence representing varied geographic locations and points of view; articles on musical styles, periods, compositions, theories, musical education at all levels, and music in diverse social settings; translations from significant German and French writers on music and art; occasional notices about artistic or literary matters; and original poetry or short fiction.

During the 1850s Dwight experienced a transitional era. He continued to be an effective guide to readers struggling to account for the indefiniteness of expression in abstract instrumental music by many composers, but he increasingly resisted new dramatic and programmatic genres. This conflict is observable in his response to the music and writings of Richard Wagner, whose work stimulated Dwight to publish a large number of commentaries in *Dwight's Journal of Music.* His capacity for tolerating dissimilar views was sufficient that in praising Beethoven's Ninth Symphony on its premiere in Boston as the culmination of that composer's achievements, he described Wagner's differing perspective about it as "a consistent and . . . intelligible whole" (12 February 1853). However, he also spiritedly refuted Wagner's thesis from *Opera and Drama* that instrumental music vainly struggles to attain definite expression through the human voice and the word. This belief was the basis for Wagner's then-radical interpretation of the Ninth Symphony as pivotal in the history of music in projecting toward new music of the future intrinsically allied to the word. Dwight asserted (26 February 1853), in contrast, that instrumental music transports the listener beyond specific thoughts and suggests more deeply "than words and voices can convey" through its powers as a subtle expressive medium. Characteristically, Dwight frequently took a strong position in controversies but maintained editorial integrity by publishing a wide range of ideas and sources of information.

The music publishing firm of Oliver Ditson and Company took over the business management of *Dwight's Journal of Music* for twenty years, beginning in April 1858. On 7 July 1860 Dwight undertook his only trip to Europe, returning in November 1861. During his absence of seventeen months, a period marred by the unexpected death of his wife on 6 September in Boston, the suddenly bereaved critic confirmed his earlier musical predilections. He visited London and Paris, then Leipzig, Dresden, Berlin, Hanover, and other German cities. Hearing a broad repertory performed well by larger forces than those in America and meeting major figures in music–including Joseph Joachim and Clara Wieck Schumann–enabled him to send admiring reports for publication in *Dwight's Journal of Music.* When he resumed its editorship on his return, he observed concert life in Boston from a more sophisticated musical perspective, and from then on he devoted increased attention to issues concerning performance.

To educate readers, Dwight frequently introduced technical terms into his own accounts or reprinted essays including analytical detail by Hector Berlioz, Robert Schumann, and other leading musical figures. One of the recurrent themes in Dwight's critical career was a defense of making art music accessible to a wide audience of listeners who might instinctively appreciate beauty without possessing detailed understanding of compositional techniques. Although he disseminated the idea that basic knowledge contributed to greater satisfaction in the arts, he disavowed artistic exclusivity: "Do painters paint only for painters, or doctors preach only to doctors, or musicians make music only for musicians?" He did not agree with those who suggested that light, entertaining items be placed on concert programs as a means of leading gradually to higher standards. He made an analogy to literature in asking, "How long a course of sentimental blood and thunder novels, of clap-trap melodramas, and of popular weeklies does it take to nurse up a true appetite for

Chaucer, Shakspeare, [*sic*] and Milton? No, this is not the way" (17 March 1855).

When writing about the building of balanced programs of quality in a young concert culture, Dwight favored emphasis on contrasts and connections: "We are no exclusive sticklers for one style of music. There is as wide room for difference of style within, as there is without, the so-called 'classical' boundaries." By setting these limits, Dwight tried to encourage stimulating the imagination of audiences through the playing of only certain kinds of "light" music, such as Felix Mendelssohn's incidental music to *A Midsummer Night's Dream* or the "Hunters' Chorus" from Carl Maria von Weber's *Der Freischütz* (17 September 1864).

During the long course of *Dwight's Journal of Music,* the critic enthusiastically guided American listeners to understand multiple genres and works not only by George Frideric Handel, Bach, Haydn, Christoph W. Gluck, Mozart, and Beethoven but also by Luigi Cherubini, Weber, Franz Schubert, Gioacchino Rossini (the comic operas and *Guillaume Tell*), Vincenzo Bellini, Adrien Boieldieu (*La Dame blanche*), Mendelssohn, Schumann, Chopin, Liszt, and Pyotr Ilich Tchaikovsky. Dwight responded favorably to Wagner's orchestral overtures but resisted his music dramas. Negative comments about operas by Giacomo Meyerbeer, Fromental Halévy, Giuseppe Verdi, and Charles Gounod stem from his view that they strove excessively for dramatic effect. Works by young Americans who had studied abroad, particularly in German cities, often received Dwight's encouraging support. Dwight also urged collection and preservation of the African American vocal heritage.

Dwight's own critical judgments, as well as his editorial choices of articles, were often astute. For example, he advised readers that a symphony by Carl Philipp Emanuel Bach should be heard for its "modern" tendencies similar to later architecturally supple and instrumentally varied symphonies by Haydn rather than in association with contrapuntal music composed by his father, Johann Sebastian Bach. According to Dwight, "in form, in style, in spirit, it bears far more resemblance to Haydn than to the old Bach" (28 March 1863).

When the Harvard Musical Association organized a new series of orchestral concerts in 1865, Dwight extended his strong influence on musical life and taste, especially in Boston, to assure that concerts might become "in the best sense more truly musical" than those offered previously (9 June 1866). Dwight's hope that many Americans would learn to respect art music preoccupied his increasingly subjective perspective. During this period he was a member of the informal Saturday Club, a group of eminent literary, scientific, and professional men who dined together on the last Saturday of each month (except July, August, and September), amidst literary and political figures of the establishment. His unusual musical authority and participation in prominent circles created an impression of the critic in later years that varied sharply with his earlier vital but obscured musical contributions and social aims; nevertheless, this conservative image dominated in secondary literature until near the end of the twentieth century.

Dwight's goals in music criticism remained consistent: "to guide public taste in its selection, to inspire artists in their performance, and above all to exhort the musician to a high sense of the dignity of his profession, and teach others to respect it, too" (1 September 1866). In the 1870s Dwight recognized that his journal no longer filled the same need in society that it had at its inception. When he finally announced that *Dwight's Journal of Music* would cease publication in its twenty-ninth year and his sixty-eighth, he experienced regret mixed with relief and a sense that he had contributed significantly to American cultural history. The latter assessment is widely shared even by contemporary critics who oppose Dwight's later positions.

George Willis Cooke wrote the earliest biography of Dwight in 1898; despite its lack of documentation and unpretentious goal to honor a friend through warm reminiscences, it continues to be a regularly cited source. The standard modern biography was written in 1952 by Walter L. Fertig as a doctoral dissertation in American Studies. It surveys Dwight's writings in literature, politics, and music. It offers a convenient overview but is deficient in its musical perspective. The author considers Dwight a "literary amateur of music," a misnomer borrowed inappropriately from H. Theodor Hach, a contemporaneous professional cellist from Germany residing briefly in Boston, who reprinted writings by Dwight–then still a young minister in Northampton–in his own short-lived music journal. The appellation and viewpoint have been reflected in many subsequent publications. Far more precise and sound in musical scholarship, is Marcia Wilson Lebow's doctoral dissertation systematically examining *Dwight's Journal of Music.*

The most extended essay of Dwight's last years is his "The History of Music in Boston," published in Justin Winsor's *Memorial History of Boston* in 1881–1883. Divided into four eras, its scant detail for the years 1810 to 1841 attests to Dwight's glaring lack of knowledge of that period. For the period spanning 1841 to 1852, Dwight refers to concert programs in describing highlights from series presented by the Boston Academy of Music, the Musical Fund Society, the Germania Musical Society, and other groups. Materials for the third era, between 1852 and 1866, are accessible from Dwight's own *Journal of Music.* As an officer and resident librarian of the Harvard Musical Association during the last twenty years of his life, Dwight recounts its sponsorship of the *Journal of Music,* the Boston Music Hall, and an early series of chamber-music concerts, along with its role in fostering the acceptance of music among humanistic disciplines. A champion of instrumental music, he describes efforts to establish a permanent symphony orchestra in Boston but also reflects a yearning for a resident opera company.

Chronicling events from 1865 to 1881, Dwight ultimately acknowledges the "conservative ground" maintained in the orchestral series sponsored by the Harvard Musical Association. He credits conductor Theodore Thomas with reorganizing his own competing orchestra, which presented better performances of classic as well as modern works. Nevertheless, Dwight justifies the Harvard Orchestra's "pure programmes" as having guarded against the encroachments of commercial concert organizers. In conceding that art music needed to be financially secured by a nucleus of the socially influential and aesthetically defended by enlightened audiences, the elderly critic reflects his ultimate disappointment that a broad public had not supported it.

Dwight took pleasure, nonetheless, in having played a major role in establishing the significance of art music in American educational institutions and cultural life. The Harvard Musical Association achieved one of its objectives when composer John Knowles Paine was appointed Harvard University's first professor of music, and Dwight expressed the hope that a full faculty of music would soon be organized to join those in medicine and theology. Reviewing eight culminating signs of musical health, he noted the growth of an independent musical culture in Boston for many genres and a marked improvement in the "tone of musical literature and criticism, particularly in the daily and weekly press," rendering "almost superfluous" a music journal such as his own. He died in Boston on 5 September 1893.

Biographies:

George Willis Cooke, *John Sullivan Dwight: Brook-Farmer, Editor, and Critic of Music; A Biography* (Boston: Small, Maynard, 1898; republished, New York: Da Capo Press, 1969);

Walter L. Fertig, "John Sullivan Dwight: Transcendentalist and Literary Amateur of Music," dissertation, University of Maryland, 1952.

References:

Sterling F. Delano, *"The Harbinger" and New England Transcendentalism: A Portrait of Associationism in America* (Rutherford, N. J.: Fairleigh Dickinson University Press; London: Associated University Presses, 1983);

Marcia Wilson Lebow, "A Systematic Examination of the *Journal of Music and Art* Edited by John Sullivan Dwight: 1852–1881, Boston, Massachusetts," dissertation, University of California, Los Angeles, 1969;

Irving Lowens, "Writings about Music in the Periodicals of American Transcendentalism (1835–1850)," *Journal of the American Musicological Society,* 10 (Summer 1957): 71–85;

Joel Myerson, *The New England Transcendentalists and the "Dial": A History of the Magazine and Its Contributors* (Rutherford, N.J.: Fairleigh Dickinson University Press; London: Associated University Presses, 1980);

Henry A. Pochmann, *German Culture in America: Philosophical and Literary Influences, 1600–1900* (Madison: University of Wisconsin Press, 1957);

Irving Sablosky, *What They Heard: Music in America, 1852–1881, from the Pages of "Dwight's Journal of Music"* (Baton Rouge & London: Louisiana State University Press, 1986);

Ora Frishberg Saloman, *Beethoven's Symphonies and J. S. Dwight: The Birth of American Music Criticism* (Boston: Northeastern University Press, 1995);

Saloman, "Continental and English Foundations of J. S. Dwight's Early American Criticism of Beethoven's Ninth Symphony," *Journal of the Royal Musical Association,* 119, part 2 (Autumn 1994): 251–267;

J. Wesley Thomas, "John Sullivan Dwight: A Translator of German Romanticism," *American Literature,* 21 (May 1950): 427–441;

Stanley M. Vogel, *German Literary Influences on the American Transcendentalists* (New Haven: Yale University Press, 1955).

Papers:

The John Sullivan Dwight Papers are in the Rare Book Room, Boston Public Library. Other materials are located at the Harvard Musical Association Library in Boston; the Houghton Library, Harvard University; the Rare Book and Special Collections Division as well as the Music Division of the Library of Congress; and the Massachusetts Historical Society.

Edward Everett

(11 April 1794 - 15 January 1865)

James W. Mathews
State University of West Georgia Emeritus

See also the Everett entry in *DLB 59: American Literary Critics and Scholars, 1800–1850.*

BOOKS: *American Poets* (Cambridge: Hilliard & Metcalf, 1812);

A Defence of Christianity Against the Works of George B. English, A.M., Entitled The Grounds of Christianity Examined, by Comparing the New Testament with the Old (Boston: Cummings & Hilliard, 1814);

An Address Pronounced October Twenty-first at the Funeral of Rev. John Lovejoy Abbot, Pastor of the First Church of Christ in Boston (Boston: Munroe, Francis & Parker, 1814);

A Sermon, Preached at the Dedication of the First Congregational Church in New York, January 20, 1821 (New York: Van Winkle, 1821);

Address of the Committee Appointed at the Meeting Held in Boston, December 19, 1823 for the Relief of the Greeks, to Their Fellow Citizens (Boston: Press of the North American Review, 1824);

A Memorial of the Professors and Tutors of Harvard University to the Corporation (N.p., 1824);

A Letter to John Lowell, Esq. In Reply to a Publication Entitled Remarks on a Pamphlet, Printed by the Professors and Tutors of Harvard University, Touching Their Right to the Exclusive Government of that Seminary (Boston: Oliver Everett, 1824);

An Oration Pronounced at Cambridge Before the Society of Phi Beta Kappa (Boston: Oliver Everett, 1824);

An Oration Delivered at Plymouth, December 22, 1824 (Boston: Cummings, Hilliard, 1825);

An Oration Delivered at Concord, April the Nineteenth, 1825 (Boston: Cummings, Hilliard, 1825);

The Claims of Citizens of the United States of America on the Governments of Naples, Holland, and France (Boston: Cummings, Hilliard, 1825);

Speech of Mr. Everett on the Proposition to Amend the Constitution of the United States. Delivered in the House of Representatives, March 9, 1826 (Washington, D.C.: Gales & Seaton, 1826);

Remarks of Mr. Everett on the Bill for the Relief of the Revolutionary Officers, in the House of Representatives, April 25, 1826 (Cambridge, Mass.: Hilliard & Metcalf, 1826);

An Oration Delivered at Cambridge, on the Fiftieth Anniversary of the Declaration of the Independence of the United States of America (Boston: Cummings, Hilliard, 1826);

An Address Delivered at Charlestown, August 1, 1826, in Commemoration of John Adams and Thomas Jefferson (Boston: W. L. Lewis, 1826);

Speech of Mr. Everett, of Mass. On the Subject of Retrenchment: Delivered in the House of Representatives of the United States, Feb. 1, 1828 (Washington, D.C.: Gales & Seaton, 1828);

An Oration Delivered Before the Citizens of Charlestown: On the Fifty-second Anniversary of the Declaration of the Independence of the United States of America (Charlestown, Mass.: Wheildon & Raymond; Boston: Hilliard, Gray, Little & Wilkins, 1828);

An Address Delivered at the Erection of a Monument to John Harvard, September 26, 1828 Erected in the Graveyard at Charlestown by the Graduates of the University (Boston: Nathan Hale, n.d.);

Speech of Mr. Everett, of Mass.: On the Proposal of Mr. McDuffie to Repeal the Laws of 1828 and 1824, Imposing Duties on Imports: Delivered in the House of Representatives, on the 7th and 8th May, 1828 (Washington, D.C.: Gales & Seaton, 1830);

Remarks on the Public Lands, and on the Right of a State to Nullify an Act of Congress (Boston: Gray & Bowen, 1830);

An Address Delivered on the 28th of June, 1830, the Anniversary of the Arrival of Governor Winthrop at Charlestown: Delivered and Published at the Request of the Charlestown Lyceum (Charlestown, Mass.: William W. Wheildon; Boston: Carter & Hendee, 1830);

Speech of Mr. Everett of Massachusetts, on the Bill for Removing the Indians from the East to the West Side of the Mississippi: Delivered in the House of Representatives, on the 19th of May, 1830 (Washington, D.C.: Gales & Seaton, 1830; Boston: Office of the Daily Advertiser, 1830);

A Lecture on the Working Men's Party: First Delivered October Sixth, Before the Charlestown Lyceum (Boston: Gray & Bowen, 1830);

Speech of Mr. Everett, of Massachusetts in the House of Representatives, on the 14th and 21st of February, 1831, on the Execution of the Laws and Treaties in Favor of the Indian Tribes (Washington, D.C., 1831);

Address Delivered Before the American Institute of the City of New York, at Their Fourth Annual Fair, October 14, 1831 (New York: Van Norden & Mason, 1831);

An Address Delivered as the Introduction to the Franklin Lectures, in Boston, November 14, 1831 (Boston: Gray & Bowen, 1832);

Speech of Mr. Edward Everett, on the Proposed Adjustment of the Tariff. Delivered in the House of Representatives of the United States, on the 25th June, 1832 (Washington, D.C.: Gales & Seaton, 1832);

The Progress of Reform in England, by the author of *The Prospect of Reform in Europe* (London: O. Rich, 1832);

Address of the Hon. Edward Everett, Before the Young Men's Temperance Society of Salem, Mass. June 14, 1833 (Boston: Dutton & Wentworth, 1833);

An Address Delivered Before the Citizens of Worcester on the Fourth of July, 1833 (Boston: J. T. Buckingham, 1833);

An Address Delivered Before the Phi Beta Kappa Society in Yale College, New Haven, August 20, 1833. By Edward Everett. Published by request of the Society (New Haven: Hezekiah Howe, 1833);

Eulogy on Lafayette, Delivered in Faneuil Hall, at the Request of the Young Men of Boston, September 6, 1834 (Boston: N. Hale/Allen & Ticknor, 1834);

Remarks of Mr. Edward Everett on the French Question, in the House of Representatives . . . on the 7th of February and 2d of March, 1835 (Boston: Nathan Hale, 1835);

An Address, Delivered at Lexington, on the 19th (20th) April, 1835 (Charlestown, Mass.: William W. Wheildon, 1835);

Oration Delivered on the Fourth Day of July, 1835, Before the Citizens of Beverly, Without Distinction of Party (Boston: Russell, Odiorne, 1835);

An Address Delivered Before the Literary Societies of Amherst College. August 25, 1835 (Boston: Russell, Shattuck & Williams, 1835);

An Address Delivered at Bloody Brook, in South Deerfield, September 30, 1835, in Commemoration of the Fall of the "Flower of Essex," at That Spot, in King Philip's War, September 18, (o.s.) 1675 (Boston: Russell, Shattuck & Williams, 1835);

Address of His Excellency Edward Everett, to the Two Branches of the Legislature, on the Organization of the Government, for the Political Year Commencing January 6, 1836 (Boston: Dutton & Wentworth, 1836);

Orations and Speeches on Various Occasions (Boston: American Stationers' Co., 1836); revised and expanded, 4 volumes (Boston: Little, Brown, 1850–1868);

Address of His Excellency Edward Everett to the Two Branches of the Legislature on the Organization of the Government for the Political Year Commencing January 4, 1837 (Boston: Dutton & Wentworth, 1837);

An Address Delivered Before the Adelphic Union Society of Williams College, on Commencement Day, August 16, 1837 (Boston: Dutton & Wentworth, 1837);

An Address Delivered Before the Massachusetts Charitable Mechanic Association, 20th September, 1837, on Occasion of Their First Exhibition and Fair (Boston: Dutton & Wentworth, 1837);

A Discourse on the Importance to Practical Men of Scientific Knowledge, and on the Encouragement to Its Pursuit (Edinburgh: T. Clark, 1837);

Address of His Excellency Edward Everett: To the Two Branches of the Legislature on the Organization of the Government for the Political Year Commencing January 3, 1838 (Boston: Dutton & Wentworth, 1838);

An Address Delivered Before the Mercantile Library Association at the Odeon in Boston, September 13, 1838 (Boston: William D. Ticknor, 1838);

Address of His Excellency Edward Everett to the Two Branches of the Legislature on the Organization of the Government

Brattle Street Church, of which Everett became minister at the age of nineteen

for the Political Year Commencing January 2, 1839 (Boston: Dutton & Wentworth, 1839);

Selections from the Works of Edward Everett, with a Sketch of His Life (Boston: James Burns, 1839);

Importance of Practical Education and Useful Knowledge, a Selection from His Orations and Other Discourses (Boston: Marsh, Capen, Lyon & Webb, 1840; New York: Harper, 1840);

A Memoir of Mr. John Lowell, Jun., Delivered as the Introduction to the Lectures on His Foundation, in the Odeon, 31st December, 1839; Repeated in the Marlborough Chapel, 2d January 1840 (Boston: Little, Brown, 1840);

Address at the Inauguration of the Hon. Edward Everett, L.L.D., as President of the University at Cambridge, Thursday, April 30, 1846 (Boston: Little, Brown, 1846);

Address Delivered at the Opening of the New Medical College in North Grove Street, Boston, November 6, 1846 (Boston: William D. Ticknor, 1846);

Twenty-first Annual Report of the President of the University at Cambridge to the Overseers: Exhibiting the State of the Institution for the Academical Year 1845–46 (Cambridge, Mass.: Metcalf, 1847);

A Eulogy on the Life and Character of John Quincy Adams, Delivered at the Request of the Legislature of Massachusetts, in Faneuil Hall, April 15, 1848 (Boston: Dutton & Wentworth, 1848);

Speech in Support of the Memorial of Harvard, Williams, and Amherst Colleges: Delivered Before the Joint Committee on Education, in the Hall of the House of Representatives, Boston, on the 7th of February, 1849 (Cambridge, Mass.: Metcalf, 1849);

An Oration Delivered at Charlestown, on the Seventy-Fifth Anniversary of the Battle of Bunker Hill, June 17, 1850 (Boston: Redding, 1850);

Address of the Hon. Edward Everett at the Anniversary of the American Colonization Society, Washington City, January 18, 1853 (Boston: Massachusetts Colonization Society, 1853; Boston: T. R. Marvin, 1853; Hartford, Mass.: Case, Tiffany, 1853);

Speech of Hon. Edward Everett, of Mass., on the Central American Treaty. Delivered in the Senate of the United States, March 21, 1853 (Washington, D.C.: Congressional Globe Office, 1853);

The Discovery and Colonization of America, and Immigration to the United States: A Lecture Delivered Before the New York Historical Society, in Metropolitan Hall, on the 1st of June, 1853 (Boston: Little, Brown, 1853; London: J. Miller, 1853);

Stability and Progress. Remarks Made on the 4th of July, 1853, in Faneuil Hall (Boston: Eastburn's Press, 1853);

Remarks at the Plymouth Festival, on the First of August, 1853, in Commemoration of the Embarkation of the Pilgrims (Boston: Crosby, Nichols, 1853);

Speech of Mr. Everett, of Massachusetts, Delivered in the Senate of the United States, Feb. 8, 1854, on the Nebraska and Kansas Territorial Bill (Washington, D.C.: Congressional Globe Office, 1854);

Dorchester in 1630, 1776, and 1855: An Oration Delivered on the Fourth of July by Edward Everett. . . . Also an Account of the Proceedings in Dorchester at the Celebration of the Day (Boston: David Clapp, 1855);

In Memory of Daniel Webster (Boston: Office of the Daily Courier, 1856);

The Uses of Astronomy: A Discourse Delivered at Albany on the 28th of August, 1856, on Occasion of the Inauguration of the Dudley Observatory (Boston: Little, Brown, 1856);

Speech: At the Dinner Given in Honor of George Peabody, Esq., of London, by the Citizens of the Old Town of Danvers, October 9, 1856 (Boston: H. W. Dutton, 1857);

Academical Education. An Address Delivered at St. Louis, 22d April, 1857, at the Inauguration of Washington University of the State of Missouri (St. Louis: Washington University/Boston: Little, Brown, 1857);

Address Delivered Before the N.Y. State Agricultural Society . . . at Buffalo, Friday, October 9, 1857 (Albany, N.Y.: Van Benthuysen, 1857);

Eulogy on Thomas Dowse, of Cambridgeport: Pronounced Before the Massachusetts Historical Society, 9th December, 1858 (Boston: J. Wilson, 1859);

A Defence of Powers' Statue of Webster: Being the Substance of Remarks Made on the 8th of June, 1859, at a Meeting of the General Committee of One Hundred on the Webster Memorial (Boston: W. White, 1859);

Daniel Webster, an Oration by the Hon. Edward Everett, on the Occasion of the Dedication of the Statue of Mr. Webster, in Boston, September 17, 1859 (New York: H. H. Lloyd, 1859);

The Death of Washington Irving. An Address before the Massachusetts Historical Society. Delivered at Boston, December 15, 1859 in *A Tribute to the Memory of Washington Irving* (New York: Putnam, 1860), pp. 233–240;

The Mount Vernon Papers (New York: New York Ledger, 1858–1859; New York & London: D. Appleton, 1860);

The Life of George Washington (New York: Sheldon; Boston: Gould & Lincoln, 1860);

Oration Delivered Before the City Authorities of Boston: On the Fourth of July 1860 (Boston: George C. Rand & Avery, 1860; Boston: Ticknor & Fields, 1860); republished as *Success of Our Republic: An Oration . . . , Delivered in Boston, Mass., July 4, 1860* (New York: H. H. Lloyd; London: Trübner, 1860);

The Great Issues Now Before the Country. An Oration by Edward Everett, Delivered in the New York Academy of Music on the Fourth of July, 1861 (New York: James G. Gregory, 1861; London: Trübner, 1861);

An Address: Delivered Before the Union Agricultural Society of Adams, Rodman, and Loraine, Jefferson County, New York, 12 September, 1861 (Cambridge, Mass.: H. O. Houghton, 1861);

An Address Delivered at the Inauguration of the Union Club, 9 April 1863 (Boston: Little, Brown, 1863); republished as *Address of the Hon. Edward Everett Delivered Before the Boston Union Club, Thursday, April 9, 1863* (Liverpool: Daily Post, 1863);

An Address Delivered at the Annual Examination of the United States Naval Academy, 28 May, 1863 (Boston: Ticknor & Fields, 1863);

Address Delivered at the Consecration of the National Cemetery at Gettysburg, 19th November, 1863 (New York: Baker & Godwin, 1863; Boston: Little, Brown, 1864; Glasgow: George Gallie, 1864);

Address by the Hon. Edward Everett, Delivered in Faneuil Hall, October 19, 1964. The Duty of Supporting the Government in the Present Crisis of Affairs (Boston, 1864);

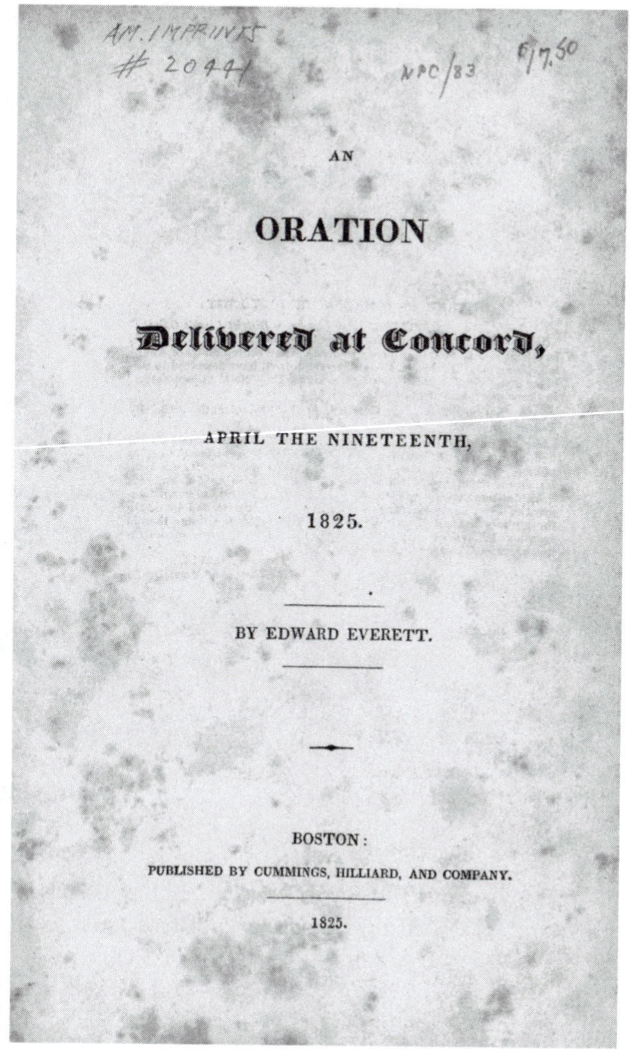

AN

ORATION

Delivered at Concord,

APRIL THE NINETEENTH,

1825.

BY EDWARD EVERETT.

BOSTON:

PUBLISHED BY CUMMINGS, HILLIARD, AND COMPANY.

1825.

Title page for the speech Everett delivered on the fiftieth anniversary of the Battle of Concord (Collection of Joel Myerson)

Account of the Fund for the Relief of East Tennessee: With a Complete List of the Contributors (Boston: Little, Brown, 1864);

First Battle of the Revolution: Lexington, Concord, Bunker Hill (New York: Maynard, c1890);

Cuba: The Everett Letters on Cuba (Boston: G. H. Ellis, 1897).

OTHER: *Greek Grammar, Translated from the German of Philip Buttmann* (Boston: O. Everett, 1822; Boston: Cummings, Hilliard, 1826; Boston: Hilliard, Gray, Little & Wilkins, 1831);

The Greek Reader, by Frederic Jacobs. From the 7th German Edition, Adapted to the Translation of Buttman's Greek Grammar (Boston: O. Everett, 1823; Boston: Hilliard, Gray, Little & Wilkins, 1827, 1829);

Harvard College about 1830

"Life of John Stark," in *Library of American Biography,* volume 1, edited by Jared Sparks (Boston: Hilliard, Gray, 1834; London: R. J. Kennett, 1834), pp. 3-116;

"Biographical Memoir of the Public Life of Daniel Webster," in volume 1, *The Works of Daniel Webster,* 6 volumes, edited by Edward Everett (Boston: Little, Brown, 1851); revised and expanded as *The Writings and Speeches of Daniel Webster,* National Edition, 18 volumes (Boston: Little, Brown, 1903);

"Peter Chardon Brooks," in *Lives of American Merchants,* 2 volumes, edited by Freeman Hunt (New York: Office of Hunt's Merchant Magazine, 1856-1858), I: 132-183;

"George Washington," in *Encyclopaedia Britannica,* eighth edition (Boston: Little, Brown, 1859), XXI: 740-766; with appendix, republished as *The Life of George Washington* (Boston: Gould & Lincoln, 1860);

"Alexander Baring (Lord Ashburton)," II: 634-636; "George William Frederick Villiers (Lord Clarendon)," V: 285-286; "Thomas Dowse," VI: 595-597; "Henry Hallam," VIII: 659-661; "George Washington," XVI: 238-257; "Daniel Webster," XVI: 311-323, in *The New American Cyclopaedia: A Popular Dictionary of General Knowledge,* 18 volumes, edited by George Ripley and Charles A. Dana (New York: D. Appleton, 1863).

SELECTED PERIODICAL PUBLICATIONS–UNCOLLECTED: Review of *Christian Gottlob Heyne–Biographisch dargestellt,* by Arn. Herm. Lud. Helren, *North American Review,* 2 (January 1816): 201-217;

Baron Munchhausen, extract of a letter to the editor from a friend in Germany, *North American Review,* 3 (July 1816): 214-215;

Review of *Aus meinem Leben–Dichtung und Wahrheit. Von Göethe. From My Life–Fiction and Fact,* by Johann Wolfgang von Göethe, *North American Review,* 4 (January 1817): 217-262;

Review of *An Appeal from the Judgments of Great Britain Respecting the United States of America. Part First, Containing an Historical Outline of Their Merits and Wrongs as Colonies; and Strictures upon the Calumnies of the British Writers,* second edition, by Robert Walsh Jr., *North American Review,* 10 (April 1820): 334-371;

Review of *A Grammar of the English Language,* by John Barrett, *North American Review,* 12 (April 1821): 310-317;

Review of *Poems,* by James G. Percival, *North American Review,* 14 (January 1822): 1-15;

Review of volume 1 of *The Comedies of Aristophanes,* by T. Mitchell, *North American Review,* 14 (April 1822): 273–296;

Review of *Bracebridge Hall, or the Humorists, a Medley, "by Geoffrey Crayon, Gent.," North American Review,* 15 (July 1822): 204–224;

Review of *A Report to the Secretary of War of the U. S. on Indian Affairs, comprising a narrative of a Tour performed, in the Summer of 1820, under a Commission from the President of the U. S., for the purpose of ascertaining, for the use of the government, the actual State of the Indian tribes, in our Country,* by Rev. Jedidiah Morse, *North American Review,* 16 (January 1823): 30–45;

Review of *The Life of Francis Bacon, Lord Chancellor of England,* by David Mallet, *North American Review,* 16 (April 1823): 300–337;

Review of *The Works of Maria Edgeworth, in six volumes, North American Review,* 17 (October 1823): 383–389;

Review of *The Ethics of Aristotle to Nicomachus,* revised and edited by A. Coray, *North American Review,* 17 (October 1823): 389–424;

Review of *Orpheus Poetarum Graecorum Antiquissimus,* by Georgio Henrico Bode, *North American Review,* 21 (October 1825): 383–385;

Review of *Russian Tales; from the French of Count Xavier de Maistre,* translated by M. de Wallenstein, *North American Review,* 24 (January 1827): 188–193;

Review of *The Speeches of Henry Clay, Delivered in the Congress of the United States; to which is Prefixed a Biographical Memoir . . . , North American Review,* 25 (October 1827): 425–451;

Review of *An Historical Sketch of the Greek Revolution,* by Samuel G. Howe, M. D., *North American Review,* 29 (July 1829): 138–199;

Review of *A History of the United States, from the Discovery of the American Continent to the Present Time,* volume 1, by George Bancroft, *North American Review,* 40 (January 1835): 99–122;

Review of *The Crayon Miscellany, by the Author of the Sketch Book. No 1.–A Tour of the Prairies, North American Review,* 41 (July 1835): 1–28;

Review of *Speeches and Forensic Arguments,* by Daniel Webster, *North American Review,* 41 (July 1835): 231–251;

Review of *On the Democracy of America,* by Alexis de Tocqueville, *North American Review,* 43 (July 1836): 178–206.

Edward Everett was one of the most accomplished Americans of the nineteenth century. He was a preacher and orator, a classical scholar, an editor and critic, and a politician and diplomat. Oliver Wendell Holmes commented only half facetiously, "We [in Boston] all carry the Common in our heads as the unit of space, the State House as the standard of architecture, and measure off men in Edward Everetts as with a yard-stick."

Born in Dorchester, Massachusetts, on 11 April 1794, Edward Everett was the son of the Reverend Oliver Everett, pastor of the New South Church in Boston from 1782 until 1792, and Lucy (Hill) Everett. Edward's younger brother, Alexander Hill Everett, became a writer and diplomat. In 1807, at age thirteen, Edward entered Harvard College, graduating in 1811 and delivering the valedictory English oration. A year after graduation, on 27 August 1812, he delivered the annual Phi Beta Kappa poem, "American Poets," which gave evidence of his youthful espousal of "literary nationalism."

Having remained at Harvard as a tutor and divinity student, Everett received his M.A. in 1814 and gave the English oration on "The Restoration of Greece." In February of the same year, at age nineteen, he was called as minister of the prestigious church in Brattle Square, the Everetts' home congregation; its former pastor was J. S. Buckminster. There Everett established his reputation for oratorical eloquence. During this period he published his first book, *A Defence of Christianity Against the Works of George B. English, A.M., Entitled The Grounds of Christianity Examined, by Comparing the New Testament with the Old* (1814), a precocious but ephemeral work of apologetics. After a little more than a year at Brattle Square, he accepted the Eliot Professorship of Greek Literature at Harvard, a newly endowed chair, and embarked for Europe, in the company of George Ticknor, to prepare himself for teaching. He received a Ph.D. at Göttingen University in 1817, the first American to receive that degree. After two additional years of assimilating European culture, Everett assumed his duties at Harvard. In 1822 he married Charlotte Gray Brooks, daughter of self-made millionaire Peter Chardon Brooks, one of whose daughters married Charles Francis Adams and another, Nathaniel L. Frothingham, minister of Boston's First Church. Another important alliance had been forged in 1816 when Everett's sister Sarah became the wife of Nathan Hale, editor of the *Boston Daily Advertiser.*

According to his students, one of whom was Ralph Waldo Emerson, Everett was an eloquent and inspiring professor, breathing new life into the Greek classics. To fill the vacuum in teaching resources, he translated from German both a Greek grammar and a reader. While at Harvard his most applauded public discourse was given before the Phi Beta Kappa Society on 24 August 1824. This address, which was delivered with the Marquis de Lafayette in the audi-

The Everett House on Sumter Street in Boston

ence, was called by Emerson "the high water mark which no after tide has reached" and was cited by Frederic Henry Hedge as "a performance which made an era in the literary history of the college, as it did in the intellectual history of many who heard it." Anticipating Emerson's "American Scholar" address thirteen years later, Everett announced as his theme "the peculiar motives to intellectual exertion in America." American thinkers must abandon the distant past, he said, for "an impending future, teeming with life and action." Native institutions are most "favorable to intellectual improvement, because their foundation is in dear nature." In a democratic environment, more minds can be brought into action "on equal terms" and more voices heard. Advocating practical endeavors as the best stimulation for intellectual processes, he declared that no great literary productions ever appear "but in the pressure, the din, and crowd of great interests, and dazzling rewards."

About the same time Everett began teaching at Harvard, he succeeded Edward Tyrrell Channing as editor of *The North American Review,* having written for the journal intermittently since 1816. Under Everett's editorship, *The North American Review* became more intellectual in tone and international in scope while still giving considerable attention to American culture. After two years under Everett the circulation of the journal increased from 600 to 2,500. He relinquished his editorial duties at the end of 1823 to enter politics but continued to write regularly into the 1830s, resuming the editorship briefly in 1828 during Jared Sparks's leave of absence. In a typical article Everett surrounded his subject with a scholarly framework constructed from his encyclopedic knowledge of literature, history, and politics. He marshaled extensive evidence, often including lengthy quotations, to support his opinions, which, like his basic nature, were moderate and diplomatic. In addition to literature, he reviewed histories, biographies, travel reports, and books on current national and international issues.

Everett's earliest significant periodical essay and a milestone in the history of American criticism was his review of Johann Wolfgang von Göethe's autobiography (1811, 1812, 1814) in *The North American Review* for January 1817. Other than introducing Göethe to American readers, Everett's review of the autobiography is an interesting example of primitive sociopsychological criticism. Perplexed at first by Göethe's use of *Dichtung und Wahrheit* (fiction or poetry and fact) as a subtitle to his *Leben,* Everett deduced that the poet was differentiating between immediate, verifiable events of one's life and indistinct events "of which memory makes uncertain reports." Although he made no specific reference to current Romantic epistemology, it is inherent in his conclusion: Our "indistinct and uncertain remembrance" is aided by "reason or fancy, to connect or adorn the actual; and hence the fiction and fact." While poetry does blend the real and the imaginary, it is basically the product of conflict between the individual and environment–"a struggle between unequal powers, between the man who is a conscious moral person, and nature, or events, or bodies of men. . . ." Although Everett seemed comfortable to a degree with environmental determinism, his Christian orthodoxy could not accommodate Göethe's theology. Everett said that Göethe's conception of "the person of God, which, though it may pass for tolerable Platonism of the heathen school, we confess is very little to our taste."

In another area of German letters, Everett hailed the philological approach in criticism, of which he had gained firsthand knowledge during his European sojourn. "While the foundation was laid [for the new criticism] in a most laborious grammatical study," he wrote in a review of Mitchell's *Comedies of Aristophanes* (1820), "the superstructure was carried up in the boldest, most elevated, and adventurous spirit of criticism." For taking the lead in reinterpreting the classics, in particular clarifying Aristophanes' satire, Everett praised brothers August Wilhelm and Friedrich von Schlegel, even though he did not agree with their whitewashing of Aristophanes' private character.

Everett was never a militant literary nationalist, but he did find merit in Robert Walsh's *An Appeal from the Judgments of Great Britain* (1819). While decrying the political partisanship behind the hostility toward Great Britain, he admitted that a certain anti-British sentiment was justifiable. In one of the areas of contention, the attack of the British reviews on the English language in America, Everett defended linguistic innovation and insisted that American English is no more corrupt than British English. Despite his strong advocacy of American literature, Everett refused to praise poetry simply because it emanated from these shores. In his review of James G. Percival's *Poems* (1821), he wrote that he could "see no consideration of duty or patriotism . . . in encouraging the multitude of indifferent poetical essays which are made among us." On another aspect of the subject of language, Everett was ahead of his contemporaries when he objected to the traditional method of teaching English. In reviewing John Barrett's *A Grammar of the English Language* (1819), he lamented the use of Latin to elucidate English grammar and maintained that imitation of correct practice is more efficacious than abstract rules.

In fiction Everett gave the highest praise to Washington Irving, calling him in an 1835 review of *A Tour of the Prairies* "the best living writer of English prose." Everett's review of *Bracebridge Hall* (1822) thirteen years earlier, however, had chided Irving for writing "as an Englishman would write." Although Everett considered *Bracebridge Hall* "quite equal to any thing, which the present age of English literature has produced in this department," he felt that Irving should have been "representing the literary interests of America abroad" and exploring American topics, emotions, and judgments. Among contemporary English novelists, Sir Walter Scott was Everett's favorite, but in his 1823 review of *The Works of Maria Edgeworth* he ranked Maria Edgeworth not far behind in "great qualities of invention, observation of manners, familiarity with life, both elegant and common, of wit and sense. . . ."

Everett's impressive Phi Beta Kappa speech in 1824 brought him to the attention of influential citizens, who engineered his election to the U.S. House of Representatives, where he served from 1825 through 1834. On 9 March 1826 Everett gave his first speech in the House–a three-hour argument against a constitutional amendment that would remove election of the President from the House. In his strong defense of the Constitution, he also tacitly defended slavery and immediately stirred the ire of early abolitionists. In 1835, with the backing of Senator Daniel Webster, Everett was elected governor of Massachusetts. In his inaugural address he again touched off controversy when he upheld the legality of slavery. During his four years as governor he helped create "normal schools" for prospective teachers, established the state board of education, and supported state aid for the expansion of railroads. Since Everett was preoccupied with civic responsibilities, his periodical articles slowed to a trickle after the mid 1830s. Even though in the 1820s he had set the tone for a new, progressive American thought, now he seemed uninterested in contemporary literary or intellectual movements. Despite his education in Germany, he remained distrustful of German idealistic philosophy and was privately antipathetic to Transcendentalism, which flourished in his own backyard.

While traveling in Europe in 1841, Everett was confirmed as minister plenipotentiary to the Court of St. James, having been recommended to President William Henry Harrison by Daniel Webster, at that time U.S. Secretary of State. Because of his savoir faire and linguistic expertise, Everett seemed quite at home in London society and was an effective emissary of the New World to the Old. Rejecting Webster's proposal to send him to China on a trade mission, Everett remained in London until relieved by President John Tyler in 1845. No sooner had Everett returned to Boston than he accepted the presidency of Harvard and entered the most difficult four years of his public life. He was appalled by the indifference of students in class and their general misbehavior, the tepid religious atmosphere on campus, and the inferiority of graduate education. His legacy as Harvard president includes restoring the original motto, *Christo et Ecclesiae,* to the seal, employing Louis Agassiz as a professor, and establishing the Lawrence Scientific School, although Harvard treasurer Samuel A. Eliot tried to take credit for the last.

After resigning the Harvard presidency, Everett planned to write a history of Greece, as well as the United States, but he held these projects in abeyance while he edited Webster's speeches and wrote a long biographical essay as an introduction. After Webster, who again became Secretary of State under President Millard Fillmore, died in October 1852, Everett filled that post until Fillmore left office. Everett's most notable act in the State Department was framing the historic letter to the emperor of Japan that resulted in Commodore Matthew Calbraith Perry's opening diplomatic and trade relations with

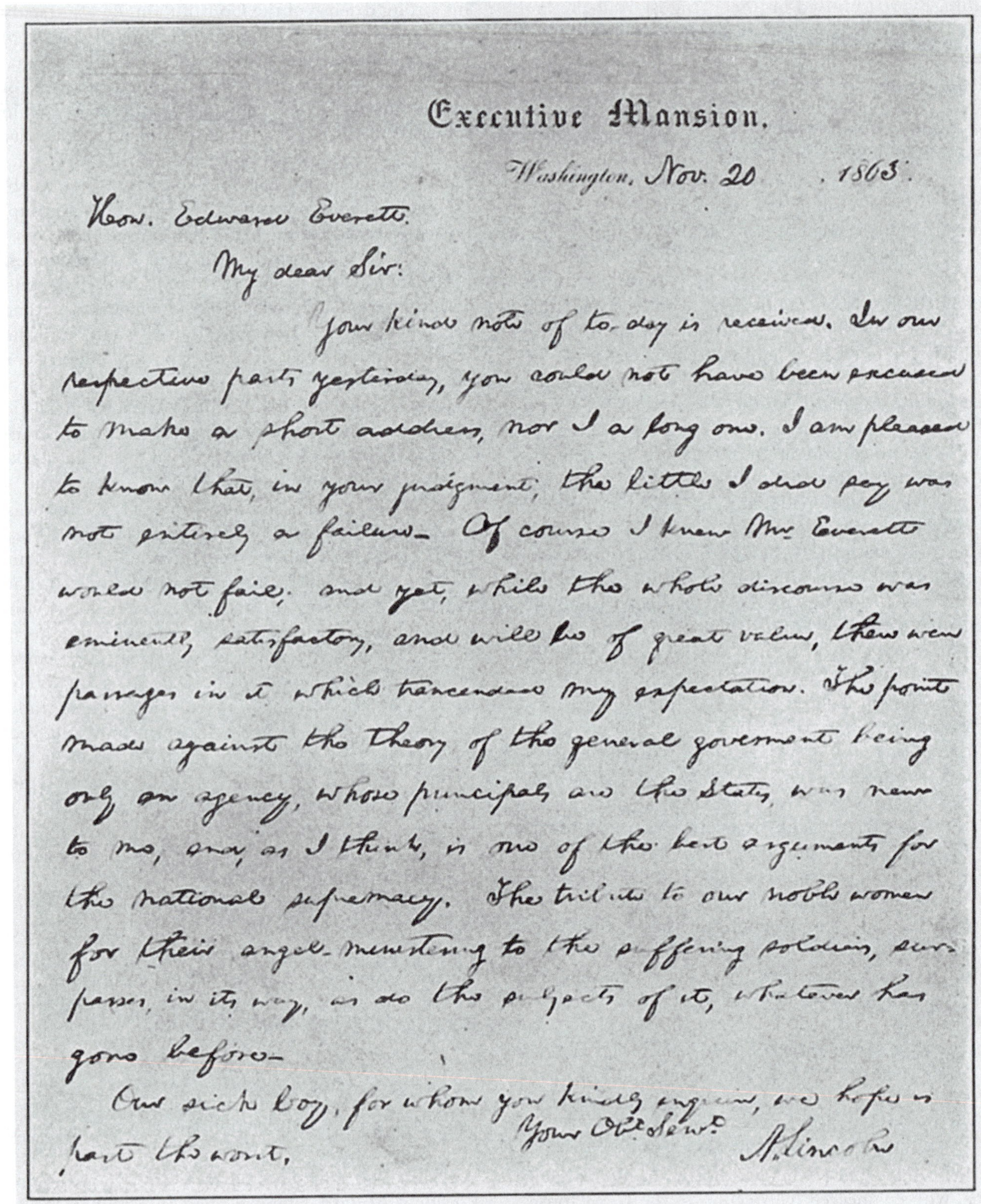

Executive Mansion,

Washington, Nov. 20, 1863.

Hon. Edward Everett.

My dear Sir:

Your kind note of to-day is received. In our respective parts yesterday, you could not have been excused to make a short address, nor I a long one. I am pleased to know that, in your judgment, the little I did say was not entirely a failure. Of course I knew Mr. Everett would not fail; and yet, while the whole discourse was eminently satisfactory, and will be of great value, there were passages in it which trancended my expectation. The point made against the theory of the general government being only an agency, whose principals are the States, was new to me, and, as I think, is one of the best arguments for the national supremacy. The tribute to our noble women for their angel-ministering to the suffering soldiers, surpasses, in its way, as do the subjects of it, whatever has gone before—

Our sick boy, for whom you kindly enquire, we hope is past the worst.

Your Obt. Servt.

A. Lincoln

Letter to Everett from President Abraham Lincoln, written the day after they both spoke at the dedication of the national cemetery on the Gettysburg battlefield (from Paul Revere Frothingham, Edward Everett: Orator and Statesman, *1925)* that nation. Everett also authored the controversial letter to England and France, insisting that the status of Cuba was exclusively an American concern. Despite Webster's long patronage (Emerson called him Everett's "evil genius" for spiriting him away from scholarship), Everett had not approved Webster's famous Seventh of March speech (1850) upholding the Fugitive Slave Law and refused to sign a public letter of approbation. In March 1853 the Massachusetts legislature elected Everett to the U.S. Senate, but he resigned fifteen months later, broken in spirit. He had been roundly criticized by liberals for missing a key vote on the Kansas-Nebraska Bill–ostensibly because of illness, although he had spoken against the bill in committee and on the Senate floor.

Having abandoned the turbulent political arena, for which he had never been temperamentally suited, Everett now deployed his oratorical powers in areas more compatible with his personality–lyceums, patriotic events, dedications, and memorials to prominent persons. From his early days as minister of the church in Brattle Square, he enjoyed renown as an orator and was in constant demand until his final illness. Although he was erudite, he was not pedantic and thus was appreciated by all classes of people. Over the years he tempered his excessive ornateness with a more direct, substantive style while retaining its richly allusive character. Most of the speeches were written beforehand and memorized, an amazing feat when one considers their great length and comprehensiveness. Among his late public services were joining George Ticknor in firmly establishing the Boston Public Library and repeating a speech on "The Character of George Washington" countless times across the country. While the immediate purpose of this speech was to raise money for the preservation of Mount Vernon, it was intrinsically a patriotic appeal for national unity.

In 1860 Everett reluctantly allowed his name to be placed on the Constitutional Union Party ballot for vice president of the United States. As a conservative and staunch unionist, he was disturbed by Abraham Lincoln's election but came to support the President's war policies, giving an oratorical endorsement, "The Causes and Conduct of the War," more than sixty times. Everett's oratorical tour de force was delivered at the dedication of the Gettysburg, Pennsylvania, cemetery on 19 November 1863, although President Lincoln gave the more celebrated "Gettysburg Address." Everett, who, as the most distinguished orator in the nation, was the principal drawing card, spoke for two hours, demonstrating his careful scholarship as well as his fervent patriotism. He opened by comparing the present occasion to burial rites in ancient Athens and then presented an analysis of the causes of the Civil War and a painstaking review of the three-day battle of Gettysburg, concluding with the prediction of a restored Union.

Everett (engraving by H. Wright Smith, after a portrait by M. Wight)

Everett was a man of enormous energy and intellect, one of the most versatile persons in a century of giants. He was known best in his own time as a spellbinding orator, but his accomplishments in several fields, including literature, were remarkable. In his alacrity to duty, conscientiousness, and industry, he epitomized the Puritan ethic–the proposition that from those to whom much is given much is expected. Privately Everett was staid and aloof, characteristics that probably precluded a rousing political success but that might have undone a person less gifted. Although he was not a "popular" personality, when he died on 15 January 1865 he was mourned by all of Boston and eulogized in many memorial services.

Biographies:

Paul Revere Frothingham, *Edward Everett: Orator and Statesman* (Boston: Houghton Mifflin, 1925);

Irving H. Bartlett, "Edward Everett Reconsidered," *New England Quarterly,* 69 (September 1996): 426–460.

References:

William Kenneth Christian, "The Mind of Edward Everett," dissertation, Michigan State College, 1952;

Harry Hayden Clark, "Literary Criticism in the *North American Review,* 1815–1835," *Transactions of the Wisconsin Academy of Sciences, Arts and Letters,* 34 (1940): 299–350;

John O. Geiger, "A Scholar Meets John Bull: Edward Everett as U.S. Minister to England, 1841–1845," *New England Quarterly,* 49 (December 1976): 577–595;

Frederic Henry Hedge, *Discourse on Edward Everett, Delivered in the Church of the First Parish, Brookline, on the Twenty-Second of January* (Boston: George C. Rand & Avery, 1865);

Orie William Long, *Literary Pioneers: Early American Explorers of European Culture* (Cambridge: Harvard University Press, 1935);

James W. Mathews, "Fallen Angel: Emerson and the Apostasy of Edward Everett," *Studies in the American Renaissance, 1990,* edited by Joel Myerson (Charlottesville: University of Virginia Press, 1990), pp. 23–32;

Allen Walker Read, "Edward Everett's Attitude toward American English," *New England Quarterly,* 12 (March 1939): 112–129;

Ronald Reid, *Edward Everett: Unionist Orator* (Westport, Conn.: Greenwood Press, 1990);

Robert Streeter, "Critical Thought in the *North American Review,* 1815–1865," dissertation, Northwestern University, 1943;

Paul A. Varg, *Edward Everett: The Intellectual in the Turmoil of Politics* (Selinsgrove, Pa.: Susquehanna University Press, 1992);

Gary Wills, *Lincoln at Gettysburg: The Words That Remade America* (New York: Simon & Schuster, 1992).

Papers:

Most of the papers of Edward Everett are held by the Massachusetts Historical Society. Other major holdings are in the Houghton Library, Harvard University, the Boston Public Library, and the Library of Congress; minor holdings are in various libraries around the country.

Cornelius Conway Felton

(6 November 1807 – 26 February 1862)

C. P. Seabrook Wilkinson
College of Charleston

BOOKS: *An Address Pronounced August 15, 1828, at the Close of the Second Term of the Livingston County High School on Temple Hill, Geneseo, N.Y.* . . . (Cambridge, Mass.: Hilliard, Metcalf, 1828);

An Address Pronounced on the Anniversary of the Concord Lyceum, November 4, 1829 . . . (Cambridge, Mass.: Hilliard & Brown, 1829);

A Lecture on the Classical Learning, Delivered before the Convention of Teachers, and Other Friends of Education, Assembled to Form the American Institute of Education (Boston: Hilliard, Gray, Little & Wilkins, 1831);

A Discourse Pronounced at the Inauguration of the Author: As Eliot Professor of Greek Literature in Harvard University, August 26, 1834 (Cambridge, Mass.: Munroe, 1834);

An Address Delivered at the Dedication of the New Building of Bristol Academy in Taunton, August 25, 1852 (Cambridge, Mass.: Metcalf, 1852);

An Address Delivered before the Association of the Alumni of Harvard College, July 20, 1854 (Cambridge, Mass.: J. Bartlett, 1854);

The Schools of Modern Greece (Boston, 1861);

Familiar Letters from Europe (Boston: Ticknor & Fields, 1865);

Greece, Ancient and Modern. Lectures Delivered Before the Lowell Institute, 2 volumes (Boston: Ticknor & Fields, 1867);

Athens (n.d.).

OTHER: Homer, *Homeroy Ilias = The Iliad of Homer. From the Text of Wolf, with English Notes and Flaxman's Illustrative Designs,* edited by Felton, 2 volumes (Boston: Hilliard, Gray, 1833; revised edition, Boston: Munroe, 1854);

"Life of William Eaton," in *Lives of Baron Steuben, Sebastian Cabot, and William Eaton,* volume 9 of *The Library of American Biography,* edited by Jared Sparks (Boston: Hilliard, Gray, 1838; London: R. J. Kennett, 1838);

Select Modern Greek Poems (Cambridge, Mass.: Owen, 1838);

A Greek Reader: For the Use of Schools: Containing Selections in Prose and Poetry, with English Notes and a Lexicon: Adapted Particularly to the Greek Grammar of E. A. Sophocles (Hartford, Conn.: Huntington, 1840);

Aristophanes, *The Clouds of Aristophanes,* with notes by Felton (Cambridge, Mass.: Owen, 1841);

Classical Studies: Essays on Ancient Literature and Art, with the Biography and Correspondence of Eminent Philologists, edited, with contributions, by Barnas Sears, B. B. Edwards, and Felton (Boston: Gould, Kendall & Lincoln, 1843);

Edward Augustus Brackett, *Works,* with notes by Felton (Boston, 1844);

Aeschylus, *The Agamemnon of Aeschylus,* with notes by Felton (Boston: Munroe, 1847);

Isocrates, *The Panegyricus of Isocrates,* from the text of Bremi, with notes by Felton (Cambridge, Mass.: G. Nichols, 1847);

Aristophanes, *The Birds of Aristophanes,* with notes and a metrical table by Felton (Cambridge, Mass.: J. Bartlett, 1849);

Selections from the Greek Historians; Arranged in the Order of Events, with notes by Felton (Cambridge, Mass.: J. Bartlett, 1852);

"Biographical Sketch of the Rev. John Snelling Popkin," in *A Memorial of the Rev. John Snelling Popkin,* edited by Felton (Cambridge, Mass.: J. Bartlett, 1852), pp. i–lxxxviii;

Diary in Turkish and Greek Waters. By the Earl of Carlisle, edited by Felton (Boston: Hickling, Swan & Brown, 1855);

Selections from Modern Greek Writers, in Prose and Poetry, notes by Felton (Cambridge, Mass.: J. Bartlett, 1855);

Sir William Smith, *A History of Greece from the Earliest Times to the Roman Conquest with Supplementary Chapters on the History of Literature and Art . . .,* with notes and a continuation to the present time by Felton (Boston: Hickling, Swan & Brown, 1857);

Washington Irving. Mr. Bryant's Address on His Life and Genius. Addresses by Everett, Bancroft, Longfellow, Felton, Aspinwall, King, Francis, Greene. Mr Allibone's Sketch of His Life and Works (New York: Putnam, 1860).

TRANSLATIONS: Aeschylus, *Prometheus Bound* (London: A. J. Valpy, 1833);

Wolfgang Menzel, *German Literature, Translated from the German of Wolfgang Menzel,* 3 volumes (Boston: Hilliard, Gray, 1840);

Arnold Guyot, *The Earth and Man: Lectures on Comparative Physical Geography in Its Relation to the History of Mankind* (Boston: Gould, Kendall & Lincoln, 1849).

SELECTED PERIODICAL PUBLICATIONS–UNCOLLECTED: Review of *A Year's Life,* by James Russell Lowell, *North American Review,* 52 (April 1841): 452–466;

Review of *Essays,* by Ralph Waldo Emerson, *Christian Examiner,* 30 (May 1841): 253–262;

"Charles Stearns Wheeler," *Christian Examiner,* 35 (November 1843): 232–244;

Review of *Poems,* by James Russell Lowell, *North American Review,* 58 (April 1844): 283–299.

A productive and versatile college administrator in his day, Cornelius Conway Felton is all but forgotten except, perhaps, in the footnotes and indices of books on the Transcendentalists, with whose views he had little sympathy but some of whom he influenced greatly, and nearly all of whom he knew personally. Classical scholar, translator, essayist, reviewer, bon viveur, clubman, professor, administrator, and nineteenth president of Harvard, Felton is remembered less for his own writings, which were copious and various, than for the influence he exerted on the course of classical studies in the United States, on educational reform, and on individual minds that he helped to mold during his thirty-five years of teaching at Harvard. His greatest legacy may indeed be his role in shaping the extraordinary and erratic genius of Henry David Thoreau. Felton earned the affection and respect of students as diverse as Jones Very and James Russell Lowell. In an age of great teachers, he stood out; in an age of prodigious linguists, he was equally outstanding. He had a talent for friendship scarcely excelled in the Boston and Cambridge of his day. In 1837–with George Stillman Hillard, Henry Russell Cleveland, Henry Wadsworth Longfellow, and Charles Sumner–he founded the "Five of Clubs" to promote literary conversation. The apogee of his career of conviviality came with his election to the Saturday Club twenty years later in 1857. This club, founded by Emerson,was the most exclusive intellectual establishment in Boston in the 1850s and 1860s; its members met at the Parker House on the last Saturday of the month for dinner and conversation. Felton was, for most of his life, absolutely at the center of the intellectual and social life of the 'Hub of the Universe,' as Boston with surprisingly little irony considered herself to be. He was also a man of titanic industry who yet was able to relax and display a lighter side in social intercourse, if less often in his writings. Even if none of his own writings remain current, he was responsible for commissioning one of the major landmarks of American literature, Emerson's 1837 Phi Beta Kappa address, *The American Scholar.*

Cornelius Conway Felton, a son of Cornelius Conway and Anna (Morse) Felton, was born in West Newbury, Massachusetts, on 6 November 1807. On both sides of his family he was descended from early settlers of Massachusetts Bay, but by his father's time the family was in straitened circumstances. A harness-maker, the elder Felton went bankrupt, and early poverty much affected his son's schooling, indeed largely shaped his life until he secured a teaching appointment at Harvard. Felton's intellectual powers manifested themselves at an early age. Ably prepared by Simeon Putnam of North Andover, Felton entered Harvard College in 1823, graduating with the class of 1827. While an undergraduate, and for a time after graduation, he was obliged to work as a tutor and schoolteacher to finance his education. As he continued his own reading of classical texts, Felton taught for two years at the Livingston High School in Geneseo, New York. His energy and appetite for learning were such that his intellectual development was stimulated by the economic restraints he experienced. By the time he was appointed Tutor in Latin at Harvard in 1829 he was one of the best classical linguists in the United States. At Harvard, he rose quickly, becoming Tutor in Greek in 1830, Professor of Greek in 1832, and Eliot Professor of Greek Literature in 1834. Felton held the latter distinguished chair until his elevation to the presidency of the University in 1860; as Eliot Professor he taught every Harvard undergraduate for nearly two generations, and he brought the classical curriculum at Harvard out of the eighteenth century.

Profoundly learned classicist though he was, Felton was a man of wide-ranging interests, with a particularly strong commitment to science and to the visual arts. Friend of Louis Agassiz and André-Marie Ampère, Felton served as a Regent of the Smithsonian Institution, where he often lectured. The Feltons of Essex County boasted a bold streak of Yankee pragmatism; Cornelius Felton's younger brother Samuel Morse Felton was a distinguished engineer and railway pioneer. One of Felton's first acts as president of Harvard was, appropriately in view of his strong commitment to science education, opening the Museum of Comparative Zoology. His translation of Arnold Guyot's pioneering work of comparative physical geography, *The Earth and Man: Lectures on Comparative Physical Geography in Its Relation to the History of Mankind* (1849), had gone through sixteen editions by 1874 and was still being reprinted in 1900.

An indefatigable committeeman, Felton served on both the local Cambridge school board and the Massachusetts Board of Education. His constant aim was to bring education within the reach of all. If he felt that everyone was entitled to some education, he was also a pragmatist interested in "securing the best possible education within the reach of all who are qualified to benefit by it." Felton was a friend of Emerson and a close friend of Washington Allston in the great poet-painter's final years. Felton's friendships with great scientists and painters reflect the breadth of his intellectual enthusiasms. In letters Longfellow playfully addressed his former colleague and close friend as "Feltonius"; less playfully, Poe in "The Rationale of Verse" dismissed Felton and Longfellow as "the Frogpondian Professors collectively." Charles Sumner was also an intimate, but Felton did not share Sumner's politics or his combativeness; he was miraculously untouched by the wrangling and rancor of the Abolitionist controversy, even though Samuel Gridley Howe was another close friend, at whose wedding to Julia Ward he was present. Felton finally went to see the Greece about which he had

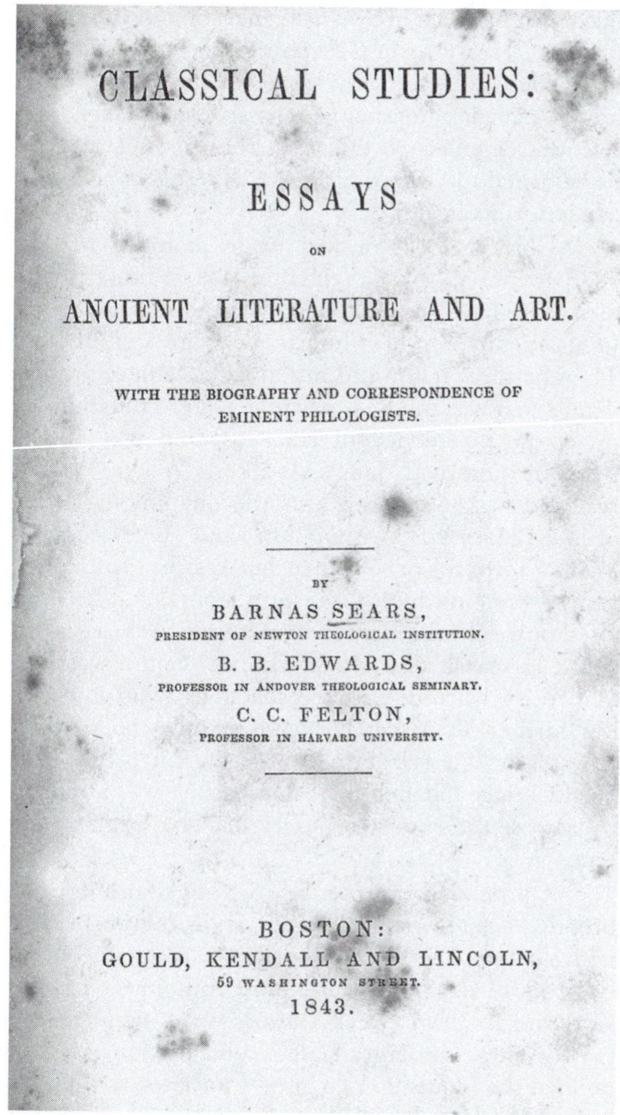
CLASSICAL STUDIES:

ESSAYS

ON

ANCIENT LITERATURE AND ART.

WITH THE BIOGRAPHY AND CORRESPONDENCE OF EMINENT PHILOLOGISTS.

BY

BARNAS SEARS,

PRESIDENT OF NEWTON THEOLOGICAL INSTITUTION.

B. B. EDWARDS,

PROFESSOR IN ANDOVER THEOLOGICAL SEMINARY.

C. C. FELTON,

PROFESSOR IN HARVARD UNIVERSITY.

BOSTON:

GOULD, KENDALL AND LINCOLN,

59 WASHINGTON STREET.

1843.

Title page for a book on which Felton collaborated with other eminent classicists been writing for more than a generation in the spring of 1853. This year in Greece, on the Continent, and in England was the only sustained interruption in a life of placid domesticity, intense conviviality, and relentless intellectual effort. In the summer of 1858 he returned to Greece, partly to investigate sites and partly for his health.

Cornelius Felton was twice married, first in 1838 to Mary, the daughter of Asa Whitney, who died in 1845. In the following year he married Mary Louisa, daughter of Thomas G. Carey of Boston. The one time Felton did not quickly achieve an academic goal was in 1853, when he sought the ultimate prize, the presidency of Harvard, and was passed over in favor of James Walker. When Walker resigned in 1860, Felton was the unanimous choice of the Harvard Corporation and Overseers as Walker's successor. By then he was, unfortunately, nearly worn out by his incessant labors, and he exercised power for little more than a year. Advised to go south in search of a kinder climate, Felton was prevented by wartime travel restrictions from journeying farther than Pennsylvania, where he died at Chester on 26 February 1862. His funeral in Harvard College Chapel on 4 March 1862 was attended by almost the entire hierarchy of New England letters.

Cornelius Felton's major writings fall into four broad categories: college texts, translations, addresses, and reviews. His editions of classical texts, histories of Greek literature, and anthologies of classical and modern Greek authors were intended primarily for undergraduate consumption. Felton defined the requisites of a good translator as "genius, learning, and industry"; he possessed the latter two in prodigious degree. His translations were wide-ranging, from Greek (both ancient and modern) to French and German. Felton was a pioneer in the study of modern Greek literature and one of the first to translate modern Greek texts into English. His public utterances were mostly on various aspects of education; in most of these speeches he addressed questions long since answered or discarded. Perhaps his liveliest writing is in his many reviews. Often Felton was assigned the most important books by the most prestigious journals, as when he reviewed Emerson's first series of *Essays* (1841) for the *North American Review*. He wrote more than seventy-five articles for the *North American Review* and for the *Christian Examiner,* together with enormous quantities of journalism for the daily papers and dozens of articles for reference works such as the *New American Encyclopedia*. As might be expected, so sociable a man was also a good collaborator, teaming up with fellow classicists such as Barnas Sears and with literary men such as his great friend Longfellow, for whom he supplied most of the biographical notices for *The Poets and Poetry of Europe* (1845). Felton nearly collaborated with Nathaniel Hawthorne as well: in 1848 he expressed an interest in turning over his materials for a history of the Acadians to Hawthorne, but the fabulist wrote to Longfellow, intimating his intention of leaving the project in the "abler hands of Professor Felton"–in whose hands it languished, for Felton never managed to complete his history.

As with so many nineteenth-century men of letters, much of Felton's most interesting thought is buried in the lengthy reviews of which the age was so fond and that he duly provided for decades. His 1841 review of James Russell Lowell's *A Year's Life* (1841) presented Felton with an excuse for an assessment of the major English Romantic poets. Like that other dedicated classicist Hugh Swinton Legaré, Felton is surprisingly enthusiastic about George Gordon, Lord Byron. Felton objects in Lowell's writing to what he also finds repellent in Emerson, "its very strong infusion of personality." He is not, however, an Augustan such as William John Grayson (a classicist who is not a late-blooming Augustan is something of a premium in antebellum America). A century before Robert Lowell's *Life Studies* (1959) appeared, Felton accused his kinsman James Russell Lowell of presenting the public with "versified confessions." Not surprisingly, as a language teacher Felton believed in the importance of mastering the technical aspects of prosody. He finds James Russell Lowell a true poet, but deficient in technique: "A poet has no right to deal with his words as a sailor with his ropes, splicing them where they are not long enough." Colloquial and witty turns enliven Felton's reviews, which, even when they are lengthy, do not seem so endless as those of Orestes Brownson. One of the defects to which Felton objects most strongly is a tendency to artificial prettiness; he locates true poetry beneath poeticism, observing that "good poetry is prose before it is poetry; it is reason, before it is rhyme." At the end of the review of *A Year's Life,* Felton gives some advice to his former student; Felton's criticism–even that of Emerson, his senior by four years–often sounds as though he is quietly reproving an impulsive undergraduate.

Perhaps the most noteworthy of Felton's reviews is that of the first series of Emerson's *Essays,* published a month after his critical assessment of Lowell's first book. In this review Felton expresses cogently a belief many readers of Emerson have shared: that much of what Emerson says is just filler holding together his main points. He disbelieves in

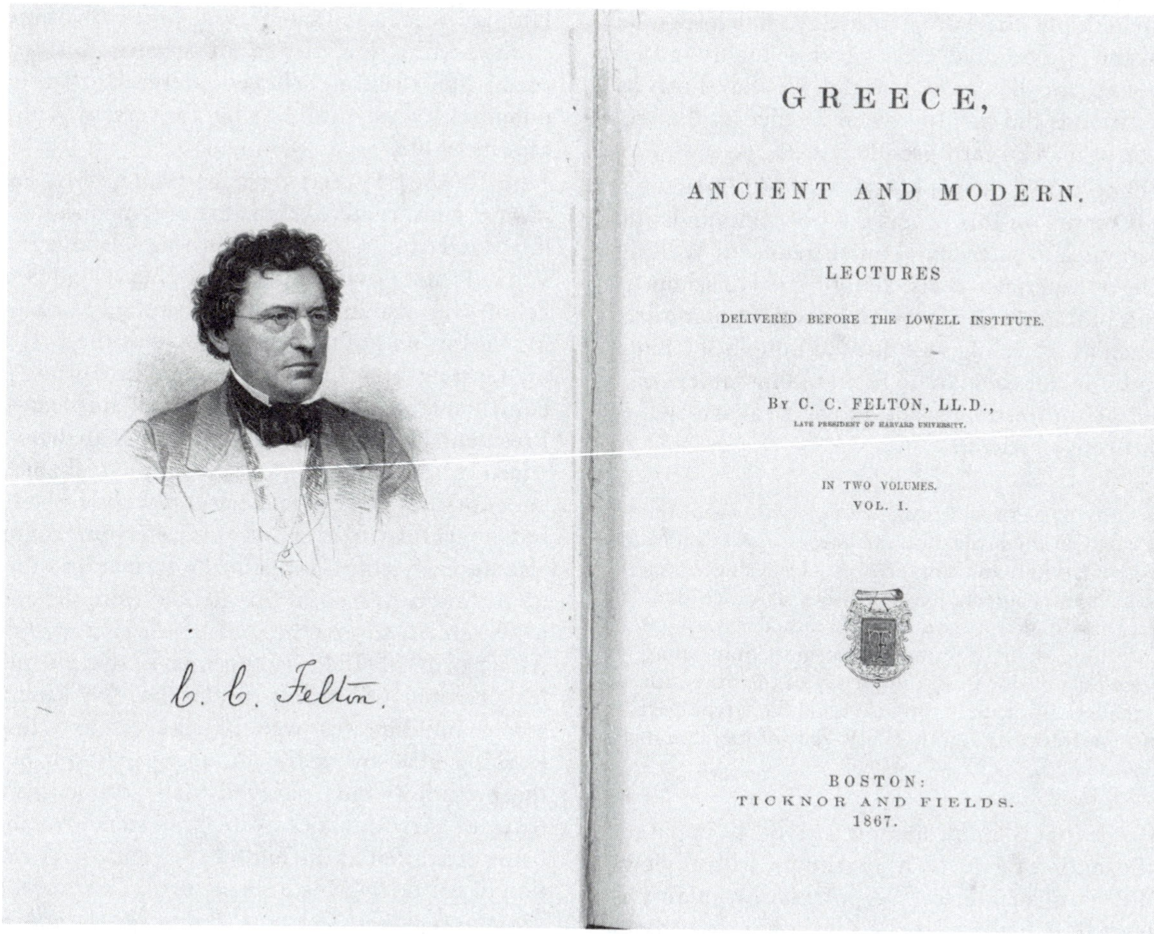
C. C. Felton.

GREECE,

ANCIENT AND MODERN.

LECTURES

DELIVERED BEFORE THE LOWELL INSTITUTE.

By C. C. FELTON, LL.D.,

LATE PRESIDENT OF HARVARD UNIVERSITY.

IN TWO VOLUMES.

VOL. I.

BOSTON:

TICKNOR AND FIELDS.

1867.

Frontispiece and title page for one of Felton's popular lecture series

Emerson's radical originality: "To a very great extent, the new opinions, if such they may be called, are ancient errors and sophistries, mistaken for new truths." He is not afraid to put Emerson in his place, finding him "full of significant hints" but unwilling to be tied down to any definite belief or position. Felton offers the damning opinion that much of Emerson's thought is not thought at all: "Mr. Emerson's whimsical associations often lead him out of the regions of thought, into the realm of vague, shadowy impressions."

Acknowledging Emerson's sincere love of nature, Felton finds beauty in Emerson's prose but too much gratuitous oddity, "a studied quaintness of language." Felton is aware that even in 1841 he is reviewing a school as well as a charismatic individual: "all the airs and affectations these fantastic euphuists put on only make them look like awkward children, dressed up in the brocade gowns and high-heeled shoes of their great grandmothers." This description shows Felton's healthy dislike of pomposity–and he finds a great deal of pomposity in the Transcendentalists. He expresses dismay at Emerson's tendency to train his sarcasm on religion. Felton finds his friend's writing amusing but unsound; Felton, in print, is often rather uneasy being amused. In his summing up his assessment of Emerson, he acknowledges beauty, independence, manliness, flashes of "dazzling brilliancy," but subtracts many marks from Emerson's genius "on the score of oddity, whim, and affectation." Felton had what, as a teacher, he needed: a sense of responsibility, together with a profound appreciation of literary decorum and moral seemliness.

In his 1843 biographical sketch of the deceased Charles Stearns Wheeler, Felton is again weighing a former student. As in the review of Emerson's *Essays,* he detects and deplores a tendency to whimsy, but he warms to the "beauty and simplicity" of Wheeler's prose. When he says admiringly of Wheeler, "He possessed the rare talent of using his time well," Felton is accurately describing himself, for he seemed able to multiply the hours in a day. In closing he praises the "honorable toil" of this highly gifted young man and bemoans a useful life cut short–as Felton's friends did in 1862 when he died in the second year of his Harvard presidency.

Felton's review of Lowell's 1844 *Poems* is a progress report on this promising poet. He finds the "affectations and puerilities" much reduced. Writing of younger American poets, Felton is as conscious as Emerson of the need to forge an American literature: poets such as Lowell have a duty to uphold the highest standards, for they are to be founding fathers of a national literature. He is not above a savage swipe, as with Bronson Alcott:

> The study of German became an epidemic about the time that Carlyle broke out; the two disorders aggravated each other, and ran through all the stages incident to literary affectation, until they assumed their worst form and common sense breathed its last, as the "Orphic Sayings" came,–those most unmeaning and witless effusions–we cannot say of the brain, for the smallest modicum of brains would have rendered their appearance an impossibility,–but of mere intellectual inanity.

Felton's devotion to "common sense" is apparent over the entire range of his writings. His reviews often advert to manliness. To possess this quality is to be worthy of high praise: he speaks approvingly of Lowell's "manly reach of mind." Again the pedagogue in Felton comes to the fore when he considers the question of proper models, of influences healthy and otherwise, and finds Tennyson a dangerous model for an impressionable young poet. Felton dislikes inversion and gratuitous ornament and stresses the need to condense. His preference is for an unaffected, unadorned style. "'A Glance behind the Curtain' is excellent in parts, but is a terribly protracted glance." Near the end of this review Felton enunciates a major principle of his criticism: "*Subjective* feelings, to use the jargon of philosophical criticism, should be but rarely and reservedly expressed in books." In this belief he is diametrically opposed to Emerson. For Felton, subjective feelings are appropriate in clubs, but not before the reading public. The final paragraph of the review expresses impatience with the posturings of the Transcendentalists, as Felton contemplates the mature Lowell he hopes will emerge. Felton is describing the sort of man he strove to be himself, the sort of Harvard man he tried to mold, hoping that Lowell "will soar above the spirit of *coteries;* that he will reject the bad taste of cultivating singularities in thought and expression, and descend from the clouds of vague philosophy and Utopian reforms; that he will brace his mind with strengthening knowledge in science, history, and social life." Felton believed literature that has the potential to last needs to be conversant with many aspects of life.

In 1861 Francis Barnard wrote, "Mr. Felton is always conservative," but this judgment is too absolute, for Felton's conservatism was selective. Conservative in many ways, notably in his religious beliefs, Felton was also an innovator, especially in his teaching and as an administrator. He was the first holder of the new post of regent at Harvard–roughly the equivalent of a modern undergraduate dean–under President Jared Sparks in 1849. A man who found "deep in the human heart an inextinguishable reverence for the past" would naturally have been galled by the jaunty irreverence of Emerson. Felton was also an early contributor to the formation of aesthetics in America; he and Longfellow were the audience to whom Allston read aloud his *Lectures on Art* in the winter of 1842–1843. Felton was, in sharp contrast to his personal friend but intellectual foe Emerson, a spider building his web of classical and linguistic learning year by year, edition by edition. Some of those editions long outlived their author: his edited texts of Aristophanes were still standard and still being reprinted at the end of the century. A compilation of his Lowell Institute lectures, *Greece, Ancient and Modern. Lectures Delivered Before the Lowell Institute* (1867), reached a tenth edition by 1896. Felton's influence on students of the classics and on the general reader extended far beyond Harvard.

Felton was much a part of his age. His own background naturally made him a willing participant in the age of self-improvement, and, indeed, he was a tireless lecturer at the Concord Lyceum. To call Felton a harbinger of inclusiveness, even an advocate of multiculturalism, is no exaggeration, for he argued that "the social body, in its collective capacity, may include all cultures." A true believer in a liberal education, Felton worked to make the curriculum of Harvard more liberal by adding courses in art and the sciences. He was also a pioneer in the education of women, for he taught at Agassiz's Cambridge female academy, the ancestress of Radcliffe, from 1856. Not notably active in reforms other than educational ones, Felton, who had many British friends, did work with such men as Emerson, Hawthorne, and Longfellow for reform of copyright to secure equity for British authors in America.

Henry Wadsworth Longfellow, who was devastated by his friend's premature death on 26 February 1862, adapted some Greek elegiacs by E. A. Sophocles for Felton's gravestone:

> Felton, dearest of friends, to the Land Unseen thou departest,
> Snatched away, thou hast left sorrow and sighing behind;
> On thy companions, the dear ones, alas! the affliction has fallen,
> Hellas, of thee belov'd, misses thy beautiful life.

Indeed, Cornelius Felton's life was in many respects an unfulfilled one. Assuredly, he was useful in his generation, but he spent most of his life preparing for the ultimate prize and challenge of the Harvard presidency and then was too ill to institute the reforms of which he had dreamed. As it is he has no memorial at Harvard, or anywhere else. His books lie in the Harvard Depository. His memorial is, however, what is for a dedicated teacher the most desirable sort–the influence on great minds that have gone on to inspire and influence all subsequent generations. Felton's edition of the *Iliad* was in Thoreau's cabin on Walden Pond, and Felton, as a teacher, made Thoreau the best classicist among the Transcendentalists. Modern in his insistence that one cannot really learn a foreign language without immersing oneself in the whole culture that produced and spoke the language, Felton was an early advocate of "Classical Studies." A great philologist, he helped to move the study of the classics in America away from narrow philological obsessions. If Felton moved easily in a great variety of circles, Harvard was ultimately, as with his friend Washington Allston, his world. His was the complete Harvard life–for all his cosmopolitan learning and travels at home and abroad, his absorption in so many modern European languages and his enthusiasm for scientific discoveries, Felton never really outgrew the university that educated his own mind and the young minds he helped to shape for so long in so many capacities.

References:

Henry Barnard, "Cornelius Conway Felton," *American Journal of Education,* 10 (March 1861): 265–296;

George S. Hillard, "Memoir of Cornelius Conway Felton," *Proceedings of the Massachusetts Historical Society,* 10 (1867–1869): 352–368.

Papers:

The papers of Cornelius Conway Felton are preserved in the Harvard University Archives.

James T. Fields

(31 December 1817 – 24 April 1881)

Ellery Sedgwick
Longwood College

BOOKS: *Anniversary Poem, Delivered Before the Mercantile Library Association of Boston, September 13, 1838* (Boston: William D. Ticknor, 1838);

Songs and Sketches (1849?);

Poems (Boston: William D. Ticknor, 1849);

Poems (Cambridge, Mass.: Metcalf, 1854);

A Few Verses for a Few Friends (Cambridge, Mass.: Privately printed, 1858);

Yesterdays with Authors (Boston: Osgood, 1872; London: Sampson Low, 1872; enlarged edition, 1876);

A Conversational Pitcher (Boston: Briggs, 1877);

Underbrush (Boston: Osgood, 1877; enlarged, Boston: Houghton, Mifflin, 1881);

Verses for a Few Friends (Cambridge, Mass.: University Press, 1879);

Ballads and Other Verses (Boston: Houghton, Mifflin, 1881);

Some Noted Princes, Authors, and Statesmen of Our Times, James T. Fields and others, edited by James Parton (New York: Crowell, 1885).

OTHER: *The Boston Book: Being Specimens of Metropolitan Literature,* edited by Fields (Boston: Ticknor & Reed, 1850);

Thomas De Quincey, *Thomas De Quincey's Writings,* 23 volumes, edited by Fields (Boston: Ticknor, Reed & Fields, 1850);

Favorite Authors: A Companion Book of Prose and Poetry, edited by Fields (Boston: Osgood, 1861);

Sir Thomas Browne, *Religio Medici: A Letter to a Friend, Christian Morals, Urn-Burial, and Other Papers,* edited, with a biographical note, by Fields (Boston: Ticknor & Fields, 1862);

William Makepeace Thackeray, *Early and Late Papers Hitherto Uncollected,* edited by Fields (Boston: Ticknor & Fields, 1867);

Family Library of British Poetry from Chaucer to the Present Time, edited by Fields and E. P. Whipple (Boston: Houghton, Osgood, 1878).

James T. Fields

James T. Fields was the preeminent publisher of American and British literature in the United States at a time when Boston proclaimed itself capital of literary culture in the nation, and American writing was beginning to achieve a wider readership both at home and abroad. He helped substantially to create the reputations of many New England writers, to develop a broader national market for their books, and to make authorship a paying profession. He accomplished these aims through personal charm, cultivating friendships with authors and publicists, a genuine love of literature, an instinct for public taste, astute entrepreneurship, and effective use of a variety of promotional strategies.

These strategies included producing attractive-looking books, geographically expanding distribution, increasing advertisement, cultivating close relationships with newspaper editors and journalists, eliciting sympathetic reviews, creating a reputation for generous treatment of authors, and promoting an aura of literary celebrity identified with his publishing house.

For the last decade of his career as a publisher (1861–1871), Fields was also an able editor in chief of the *Atlantic Monthly,* which was owned by his firm, Ticknor and Fields, and which he brought to the high point of its literary influence. He used the magazine effectively to disseminate New England culture to the nation and, not coincidentally, to give his authors an additional source of revenue and increased exposure to a broader public. Fields had literary aspirations himself, in his youth writing sentimental and occasional poetry and, after retirement, reminiscences of the authors he had published. But his major achievement remained his publication and promotion of the works of others and cultivation of a wider readership, particularly for American literature.

James Thomas Fields was born on 31 December 1817 in Portsmouth, New Hampshire, the first of two sons of Michael and Margaret (Beck) Fields. His father, captain of a ship, was seldom home and died of a fever in New Orleans when James was two. His widowed mother was apparently affectionate, pious, and supportive of his education. Fields finished the available high school curriculum before moving to Boston in 1831 at the age of thirteen to serve as a clerk in the bookstore of Timothy H. and Richard Carter and Charles Hendee (Carter and Hendee), soon to become the Old Corner Bookstore. Fields continued to educate himself in much the manner Benjamin Franklin educated himself during his early years in Philadelphia. Fields read widely in the books available in the shop, developed associations with other young men from the provinces similarly eager for self-education, and joined the Boston Mercantile Library Association. During his first decade or so in Boston, Fields not only developed literary ambitions but also gained some local success by being selected to read his poems on several public occasions (once sharing the platform with Governor Edward Everett) and having some of them published as far afield as New York.

Fields was by character an expansive extrovert with a talent for friendship that contributed much to his professional success. Handsome, hearty, good-natured, and enthusiastic, he was an attractive and lively companion. As a young man, he was something of the modish, cane-carrying, literary dandy. As he aged he became more corpulent and comfortable, though still a conspicuous personage with his large head accentuated by unruly hair and full beard. He was good-humored and fond of talking, talented at mimicry and anecdote. But he also had the capacity to make others feel noticed, heard, and appreciated. "His real interest is in what interests another," his wife said, and this capacity served him well as publisher, editor, and general intermediary between authors and the public. Both his early literary ambitions and a lifelong deference for writers, perhaps stemming from self-consciousness about his lack of formal education, made him popular with authors. While his personality seemed perfectly suited to advance his professional interests, and a few found him inclined to flattery, his sociability, good humor, and sympathy were usually genuine. Many of his friendships–such as those with E. P. Whipple, Mary Mitford, Henry Wadsworth Longfellow, and Charles Dickens–were deep, and he was unfailingly loyal.

Fields's attractive personality, his combination of enthusiasm and deference, his literary interests and connections, and his business sense gradually won recognition and reward from his employers during the 1830s and 1840s. A year after Fields arrived, Carter and Hendee sold the Old Corner Bookstore to a publishing partnership of Allen and Ticknor, and in 1834 William Davis Ticknor, who had come to Boston from a New Hampshire farm in 1817, became the sole owner. Under Ticknor's management, the shop was an eclectic affair, not untypical of the book trade at the time. It was partly a retail store from which Fields apparently developed a fine instinct for public taste in books. He later claimed to have learned as clerk to predict exactly what titles each customer entering the shop would buy. Like many retail booksellers, however, Ticknor was a publisher as well. In fact, Ticknor's publishing activities were ambitious for the time (seventy-seven new titles and eight attempted magazine start-ups in nine years). But they were also sporadic, eclectic in subject matter, and often unremunerative for publisher and author. The publishing side of the business was what drew Fields, however, particularly where it connected with his literary interests.

While working seventy-hour weeks for twelve dollars as a clerk during the 1830s, Fields experienced some modest success with his own poetry, publishing in such annuals or periodicals as John Greenleaf Whittier's *North Star, The Token, The Knickerbocker,* and Horace Greeley's *New-Yorker,* as well as giving occasional lectures on literary subjects. Through these activities, he established a web of connections with writers, editors, and publishers–mainly in Boston, but as far afield as New York and Philadelphia–that later proved useful.

By 1840 Fields began proposing to his employer the publication of works that would strengthen the liter-

The Old Corner Bookstore in Boston, where Fields started out as a clerk working for Carter and Hendee

ary side of the house. Initially he recommended British poetry and prose because he knew that they would sell and, in the absence of international copyright, would require no royalties, thus making a surer profit. But in 1842 he persuaded Ticknor that the long-term interest of the firm would best be served by voluntarily paying Alfred Tennyson the standard royalty of 10 percent of the retail price for an authorized American edition of his early poems, thus establishing a precedent, unusual for the time, that helped to make the house over the next twenty years a major American publisher of contemporary British poetry and fiction.

By 1843 Fields had proved his value sufficiently that when the firm was reorganized, Ticknor made him a junior partner purely on the strength of his professional experience and connections, a status that required no capital but entitled him to $800 of the annual profits. During the next decade, Fields vindicated Ticknor's judgment of his value to the firm by continuing to expand its list in British literature, including a multivolume collection of *Thomas De Quincey's Writings,* which he compiled and edited himself. More importantly, however, he established it as the sole publisher of several New England writers who were beginning to emerge as major American authors–including Longfellow, Whittier, Oliver Wendell Holmes, James Russell Lowell, and Nathaniel Hawthorne. Fields secured the loyalty of these writers not only through his personal attention to and confidence in them, but more importantly by convincing them that there was a significant market for their literature, that he would publish their works attractively and promote their reputations vigorously, and that he would make writing pay them more than it had in the past.

Fields's account in *Yesterdays with Authors* (1872) probably exaggerates his role in the genesis of *The Scarlet Letter* (1850), but many of the facts are true and characteristic. Fields had tried unsuccessfully in 1849 to help Hawthorne retain his custom house sinecure. Although Hawthorne's *Twice-Told Tales* (1837) had failed to sell, Fields visited the struggling author to solicit his current work, read the nucleus of *The Scarlet*

Letter, encouraged him to expand it, and offered to publish a first edition of 2,500, rather than the usual 1,000 copies, with a royalty of 15 percent rather than the standard 10 percent.

As Fields's professional career gathered momentum in the 1840s and early 1850s, he experienced a series of personal losses. In 1844 he became engaged to Mary Willard, the daughter of a Boston clockmaker, only to witness her painful decline and death from consumption over the following year. In 1847 he lost his mother, to whom he had always been close. During this period, he maintained close ties with Mary Willard's family and gradually fell in love with Mary's younger sister, Eliza, who had been only thirteen at Mary's death but now was emerging into womanhood. In March 1850 Fields, thirty-two, and Eliza, eighteen, were married. For a year they lived in what Fields called a state of "permanent happiness." But it was far from permanent. Eliza contracted the tuberculosis that had killed her sister, and Fields for a second time experienced the agony of seeing the slow, hopeless decline and death of the woman he loved.

Emotionally numbed and physically weakened, Fields had difficulty recovering from the desolation of his wife's death. Encouraged by Ticknor and friends, he embarked for Europe in an attempt to shake his melancholy. He visited Paris, Marseille, Naples, and Rome, but the focal point of his trip was a return to England, where during a visit in 1847 he had made many friends, transacted some business, and developed full-blown Anglophilia. In England he was warmly received and ceaselessly entertained by old friends such as Barry Cornwall, Francis Bennock, and Mary Mitford. He was also introduced to most of the established literary figures of the era, including Robert and Elizabeth Barrett Browning, whose work he had published; the curmudgeonly Thomas Carlyle; Walter Savage Landor; Thomas De Quincey; Dickens, briefly; and William Makepeace Thackeray, whom he convinced to undertake an American speaking tour.

Fields somewhat reluctantly returned to Boston in September 1852 after eleven months in Europe, his old exuberance, energy, and purpose restored. By 1854 he had fallen in love and determined to marry again. His choice was Annie Adams, daughter of a Boston doctor, a cousin of Eliza Willard, and, like her, much younger than Fields. Fields was thirty-seven, and Annie was twenty when they married. Pretty, gracious, and adoring as a young bride, she had the intellect and character to grow.

The marriage, like Fields's temperament, seemed a fortunate blend of genuine personal happiness and professional success. Annie Fields's literary interests evolved under his tutelage, and she herself began writing. Together they developed their house on Charles Street into what Henry James satirically referred to as a "waterside museum" of literary treasures and a salon for entertaining a constant stream of celebrities and those who hoped Fields would make them so. Annie not only became the consummate hostess and gave loyal emotional support but also formed strong personal ties, particularly among the women authors whom Fields sought to publish–most notably Harriet Beecher Stowe, Celia Thaxter, and Sarah Orne Jewett. Having developed during their long marriage into a personage of her own, she lived for thirty-four years after Fields's death, entering a long relationship with Jewett and memorializing the decades of the literary celebrity of Boston that she and her husband had done so much to promote.

Fields's publishing partner, William D. Ticknor, in 1862 (etching by S. A. Schoff)

In the year of Fields's marriage, 1854, Ticknor and Company was again reorganized, this time as Ticknor and Fields, with Fields contributing a fifth of the capital. Fields was now in a position to move more quickly toward his goals of concentrating on publishing rather than retailing and achieving a reputation as the premier publishing house in the United States for good literature by both American and British authors. Over the next decade Ticknor and Fields remained or became the publisher not only of most of the major writers in New England but also of many from New York and Philadelphia, though few yet from points south and west. The firm's American list expanded to include not only Longfellow, Lowell, Whittier, Holmes,

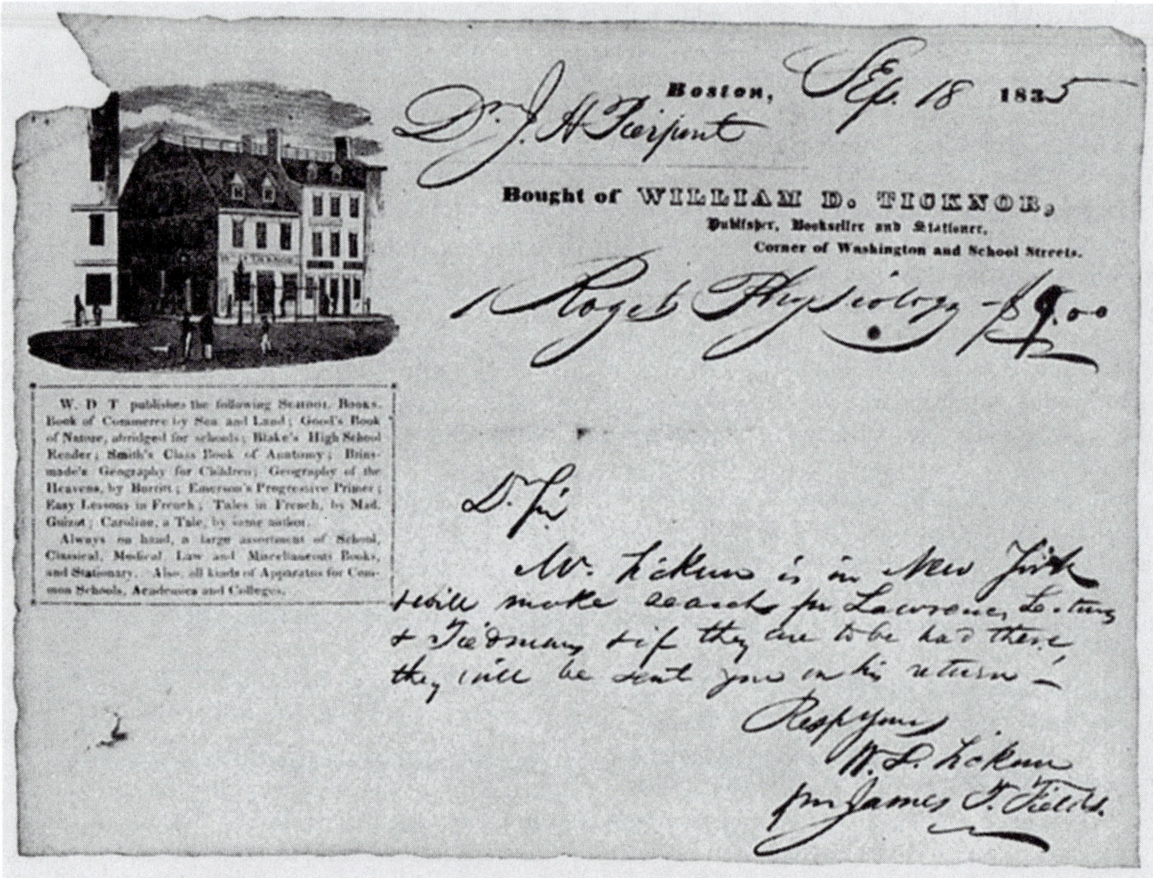
Boston, Sep. 18 1835

Dr. J. H. Pierpont

Bought of WILLIAM D. TICKNOR,
Publisher, Bookseller and Stationer,
Corner of Washington and School Streets.

1 Roget Physiology $5.00

W. D. T. publishes the following School Books. Book of Commerce by Sea and Land; Good's Book of Nature, abridged for schools; Blake's High School Reader; Smith's Class Book of Anatomy; Brinsmade's Geography for Children; Geography of the Heavens, by Burritt; Emerson's Progressive Primer; Easy Lessons in French; Tales in French, by Mad. Guizot; Caroline, a Tale, by same author.

Always on hand, a large assortment of School, Classical, Medical, Law and Miscellaneous Books, and Stationary. Also, all kinds of Apparatus for Common Schools, Academies and Colleges.

Dr. Sir

Mr. Ticknor is in New York & will make search for Lawrence, Lectures & Tiedeman & if they are to be had there they will be sent you on his return.

Resp yours
W. D. Ticknor
pr James T. Fields

A bill from the Old Corner Bookstore after it became the property of William D. Ticknor (Berg Collection, New York Public Library, Astor, Lenox, and Tilden Foundation)

and Hawthorne, but also Henry David Thoreau, Ralph Waldo Emerson, John Saxe, Grace Greenwood, Alice and Phoebe Cary, George Hillard, Harriet Beecher Stowe, Henry Giles, Julia Ward Howe, Charles Sumner, Paul Hayne, George Boker, Richard Stoddard, and Edmund C. Stedman. Among the British authors attached to the house by Fields's solicitations and relatively generous royalties were Tennyson, Robert Browning, De Quincey, Barry Cornwall, Leigh Hunt, Charles Kingsley, Thackeray, Charles Reade, Matthew Arnold, Coventry Patmore, Thomas Hughes, Owen Meredith, and later Dickens. Fields's effectiveness as a publisher, his reputation for fairness, and the prevailing "courtesy of the trade" (which encouraged authors to keep their books with a single publisher and discouraged publishers from bidding for authors identified with another house) insured that Ticknor and Fields remained the publisher for virtually all of the works by these authors until the sale of the firm on Fields's retirement in 1871.

Successful authors are likely to attribute sales of their books solely to the literary merits of the books, unsuccessful ones to the publisher's failure to promote them. But whether they chose to recognize the fact or not, Fields's authors benefited tangibly from his instinct for promotion. Fields was an early advocate of plentiful advertising in newspapers and magazines, much of the copy written by himself. Quick to understand that publishing and book distribution were evolving from local to national enterprises, he advertised not only locally but also in major cities across the country. He also initiated the practice of tipping lists of the books published by the firm into volumes before they were bound.

Under Fields's guidance, the advertising budget of the firm expanded exponentially. He got considerable mileage out of it, however, not only directly through ads but often indirectly through sympathetic reviews. If Ticknor and Fields patronized a newspaper by placing a large volume of advertisements in it, Fields reasoned that the firm could expect sympathetic treatment of its books. This form of reciprocity, common at the time, worked well until an independent-minded reviewer for the Boston *Traveller* panned Longfellow's "Hiawatha" as "a mass of the most childish nonsense that ever dropped from human pen." Fields, outraged, thoughtlessly fired off a letter saying that his firm would no longer "trouble you with our publications or the advertisements of them," to which the *Traveller* responded by prominently announcing an "Attempt to Coerce the Press." For once, Fields was left with an embarrassing public revelation of the underside of literary publishing.

Most reviewers, however, were more tractable than the one for the *Traveller,* often grateful merely for the free review copy of the book or anxious to promote the goodwill that would lead to reciprocal favors. As William Charvat describes in *Literary Publishing in America: 1790–1850,* Fields early established a network of personal and professional contacts among editors such as Rufus Griswold and reviewers such as his close friend E. P. Whipple, or later, Thomas Bailey Aldrich–influential people who, in the words of an early Fields poem, could be counted on to "puff the pills," and "pills thus puffed," he knew, "will sell."

Fields was also early to recognize the importance of magazines to book publication and promotion. Although Ticknor was the one who purchased the *Atlantic Monthly* when it was sold by Phillips and Sampson in 1859, while Fields was on another European sojourn, Fields was the one who assumed editorship of the *Atlantic* from James Russell Lowell in 1861 and added four periodicals to the firm in the mid 1860s: the *North American Review,* a resolutely scholarly quarterly edited by Lowell and Charles Eliot Norton; *Our Young Folks,* a "juvenile" edited by Lucy Larcom; *Every Saturday,* an eclectic weekly edited by T. B. Aldrich; and the *Atlantic Almanac,* a popular annual.

Fields did not acquire and maintain these magazines expecting to develop a mass circulation and large profits through either subscriptions or advertising. That was accomplished by the New York magazines that largely displaced Fields's publications over the remainder of the nineteenth century. Certainly Fields wanted profits and actively boosted both circulation and advertising where he could. But he was willing to subsidize even periodicals that perennially ran in the red, such as the *North American Review,* to augment the prestige of Ticknor and Fields and its reputation for literary quality. His purpose was to build the reputations of his firm and its authors by developing a wider exposure among the literate public. While the first edition of an average book was likely to run about one thousand to two thousand copies, regular circulation of most of these periodicals might range from ten thousand to fifty thousand. Magazines also served the firm by helping to solicit new authors, connecting them with the house, and providing them with an additional source of income beyond book publication, particularly important for younger

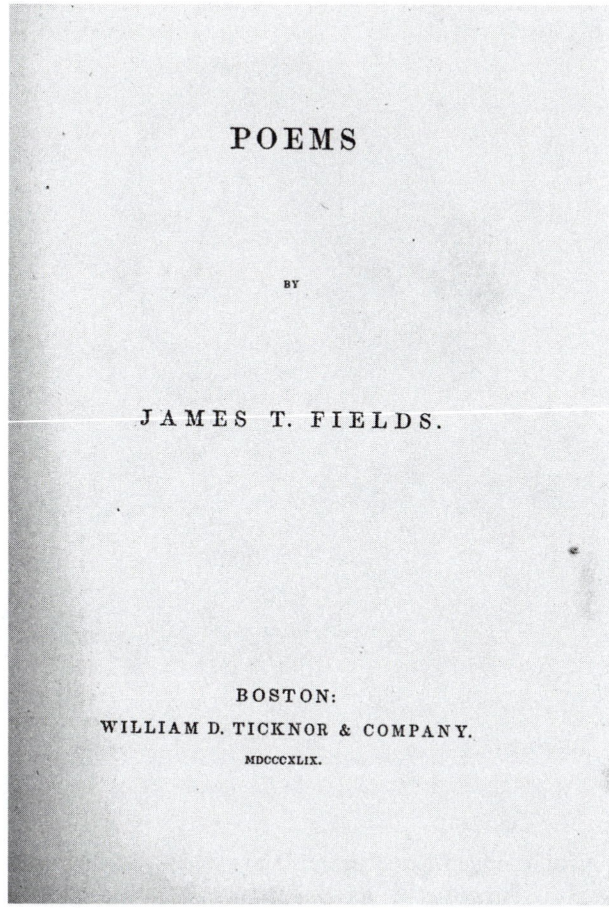
POEMS

BY

JAMES T. FIELDS.

BOSTON:
WILLIAM D. TICKNOR & COMPANY.
MDCCCXLIX.

Title page for the first collection of Fields's poems, many previously published in journals (Collection of Joel Myerson)

authors without a significant stream of royalty income. Finally, magazines served as vehicles for advertising the publications of the firm targeted at precisely the audiences most likely to buy them.

Fields's successful editorship of the *Atlantic Monthly* from 1861 to 1871 at the height of his career reflects many of his major accomplishments: his advocacy of good literature, his development of a market for it, his talents at promoting it, and his contributions to making authorship a paying profession. It reflects also his balance between literary culture and commerce. As might be expected, the change of editorship from the scholar Lowell to the publisher Fields brought a degree of popularization. Scholarly articles were sent to the *North American Review;* fiction and short pieces on the contemporary scene were increased. But these changes by no means made the magazine an intellectual lightweight. Circulation rose gradually from thirty-two thousand in 1861 to more than fifty thousand in 1866–the highest for the magazine during the nineteenth century. Fields added "The Atlantic Advertiser and Miscellany"–eight to fifteen pages of advertising for everything from

Annie Adams at about the time of her marriage to Fields (portrait by Rouse; Boston Athenaeum)

patent medicines to spiritualists to artificial limbs, as well as announcements of Ticknor and Fields books, reprints of favorable reviews, and literary chatter. He also used the magazine effectively to promote the idea of "the Atlantic circle," a coterie of admired New England writers who made Boston the center of national literary culture and Ticknor and Fields the hub of this universe. This promotion was epitomized in the offer to every new subscriber of a large print (suitable for framing) of the literary Olympian of their choice. These prints of Emerson, Hawthorne, Whittier, Lowell, and Longfellow adorned the walls not only of many New England homes but also of farmhouses across the midwest in which, as William Dean Howells and others testify, the *Atlantic Monthly* was literary culture.

As editor of the *Atlantic Monthly,* Fields was an early exponent of celebrity publishing; probably he overrelied on "the Atlantic circle," particularly for poetry. But he also published much of the best literature being written at the time, paid its authors relatively well for it, and frequently welcomed new talent. Fields solicited several essays by Emerson–including pieces calling for and celebrating emancipation–and he made a particular effort to bring Thoreau back to the magazine with a series of nature essays and "Life without Principle." He declined Harriet Beecher Stowe's proposal for a separate women's department but, fully aware that a majority of his readers were women, retained Stowe as a staff writer on yearly contract, publishing not only two-year-long series of her "domestic essays" but also much of her fiction, including her "Old Town" novel and stories, as well as controversial essays on emancipation, Sojourner Truth, and George Gordon, Lord Byron. This last one, exposing the poet's incest, lost the magazine many thousands of outraged readers. Hawthorne, whose letters to Fields suggest that he was on the edge of psychological collapse, indicated that probably he would not have written either "Our Old Home" or the unfinished "Dolliver Romance" without Fields's solicitations and constant mollification with "soft-soap." Fields published approximately thirty-five pieces by Holmes–as well as poetry by Longfellow, Lowell, and Whittier, as often as he could get it, including works that are still anthologized.

While Fields could rely on established writers and was not as aggressive as later editors in soliciting nationally, he published and encouraged many younger writers and clearly recognized the need to cultivate the next generation, including those beyond the New England pale. Early in his editorship, he appointed Thomas Wentworth Higginson to "cast about for good things" among young writers of promise. Too often remembered solely as Emily Dickinson's "Dear Mentor" who discouraged her from publishing, Higginson lent substantial support to the early careers of such writers as Rose Terry, Harriet Prescott, Charlotte Hawes, Thaxter, and Dickinson's friend Helen Hunt. In 1866 Fields hired as his assistant editor and talent scout a twenty-nine-year-old Ohioan named William Dean Howells, through his fifteen years at the *Atlantic Monthly* and his subsequent work at *Harpers' Monthly* the most effective advocate for the next two generations of American writers. But Fields himself published "Life in the Iron Mills," "The Story of To-Day," and other works by Rebecca Harding (later Davis) of West Virginia, found merit in an early western story by the unknown Bret Harte, and featured as the lead for March 1865 the first of many *Atlantic Monthly* publications by Henry James.

In 1864 Fields's partner, Ticknor, died suddenly on a trip undertaken to restore Hawthorne's declining health. The firm was again reorganized, with Fields as senior partner, clearly responsible for the policies and success of the house. By the mid 1860s, he had every evidence of his success. He had expanded Ticknor and Fields into a major publishing house, shed its eclectic retail operation, given it a distinctive literary focus, attracted the most admired American and British writers of the era, acquired five periodicals–the most distinguished of which he edited himself–and established a national and international reputation in literature for the *Atlantic Monthly* and the house. But success and the growth of the house seemed to multiply problems, and Fields was beginning to tire.

Fields hired Howells in 1866, in part to free himself of the daily operation of the *Atlantic Monthly,* but problems continued to develop. Some of these were caused by the recession in the book trade and the economy in general during the late 1860s, but others were caused by Fields himself. In 1867 Fields decided to cut the number of new books issued almost in half and to rely increasingly on cheap editions of his established authors. But he also supported a costly and abortive experiment proposed by his new junior partner, James Osgood–who was enterprising but often lacking in business judgment–to illustrate *Every Saturday* lavishly in the vain hope of competing with *Harpers' Weekly*. Also in 1867, Fields sponsored a lecture tour by Dickens (with whom he developed a genuine friendship) that was an immense, though exhausting, financial and personal success for both men. He stirred up a firestorm among publishers, however, for violating the courtesy of the trade on which he himself depended heavily by luring Dickens from the Harpers with an offer of 10 percent on all volumes sold rather than a flat rate on advance sheets.

In 1868 Fields initiated an acrimonious reorganization of the firm to force out Ticknor's son, Howard, ostensibly for being caught embracing a secretary, and give additional weight to James Osgood, whose name was added to the new combination: Fields, Osgood and Company. But far more painful were Gail Hamilton's accusations in 1868 that Fields had shortchanged authors with sharp business practices. In the inflationary period after the Civil War, Fields had contracted with many of his authors to pay a flat fee of 15 cents per book rather than the previous 10 percent of retail. As long as book prices remained at $1.50 or below, as they were when the contract was originally made, all was well, but when they escalated to $2 in the mid 1860s, authors lost royalties. A tribunal concluded that there was no fraud, only loosely made business arrangements leading to misunderstanding. But Fields was personally hurt by the defection of authors he considered friends and professionally hurt by Hamilton's savaging of his reputation for liberality.

Largely to escape troubles at home, the Fieldses made another European trip in 1869, but on resuming the burden of his business interests upon their return, Fields experienced a deterioration of his health. He was only fifty-three, but his former vigor and optimism had eroded under anxieties that manifested themselves in migraines, insomnia, and exhaustion. Fields decided to retire. He sold his holdings for more than $100,000, put a public announcement in the newspapers that he would read no more manuscripts, and was honored on his last day at the firm, 1 January 1871, by a gathering of many of the authors with whom he had developed both personal and business relationships–including Longfellow, Whittier, Emerson, Holmes, and Howells. In retirement, Fields kept his distance from James Osgood and Company, partly from disillusionment with Osgood himself. As a result of the Boston fire of 1872, the panic of 1873, and a series of poor business decisions, Osgood gradually failed. The firm was absorbed into Houghton, Mifflin and Company, which thus became the eventual successor to the house of Ticknor and Fields.

Fields in 1878 (Boston Athenaeum)

Fields had always seen himself as primarily a literary man rather than a businessman, and on retirement from business he immediately threw himself into an intensive schedule of writing and lecturing. In 1871 he began writing a series of recollections and appreciations of the writers who had been his friends, which was serialized in the *Atlantic Monthly* as "Our Whispering Gallery" and published with alterations as *Yesterdays with Authors*. During the 1870s he also wrote and published several books of poetry and occasional essays. His major occupation, though, was lecturing. Soon after retirement, he wrote out twenty-eight lectures, mainly

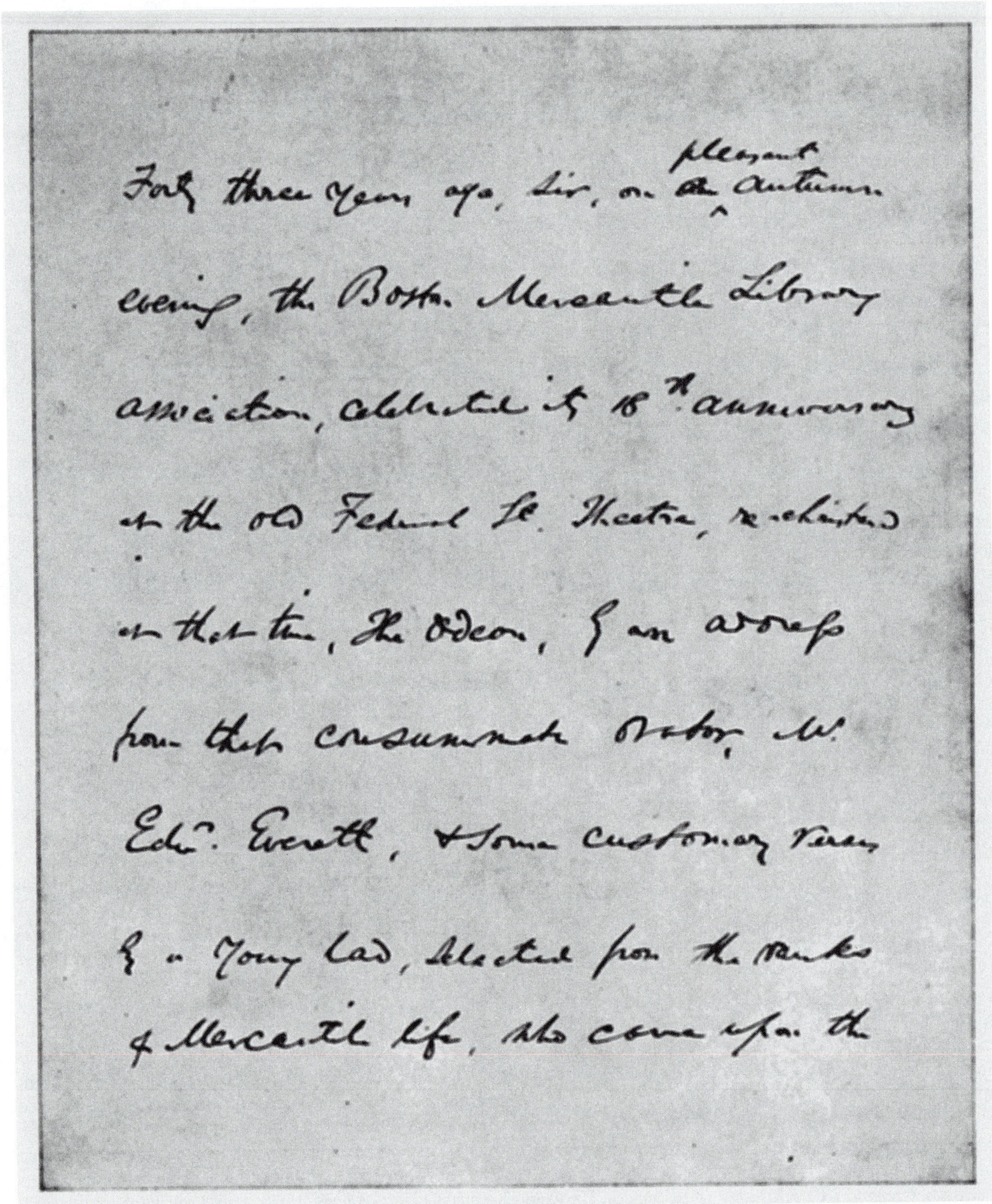

Forty three years ago, Sir, on a pleasant autumn evening, the Boston Mercantile Library association, celebrated its 18th anniversary in the old Federal St. theatre, re-christened at that time, the Odeon, by an address from that consummate orator, Mr. Edw. Everett, & some customary verses by a young lad, selected from the ranks of Mercantile life, who came upon the

First page of a lecture Fields wrote a few weeks before his death (from W. S. Tryon, Parnassus Corner: A Life of James T. Fields, *1963)*

on literary figures he had known but also some inspirational pieces such as "Cheerfulness." He then advertised nationally, hired a booking manager, and spent extended parts of the next five years spreading Yankee literary culture in person as far as Wisconsin, Iowa, and Nebraska. Exhausted, he canceled his schedule in 1876 but continued to lecture frequently around Boston, even after collapsing from a brain hemorrhage while delivering a talk at Wellesley College in 1879. In January 1881 he suffered a major heart attack and on 24 April 1881 died of a seizure at the age of sixty-three.

Fields had led a fortunate life. He had begun his career as the New England literary renaissance was flowering and ended it while the New England Indian summer was still fruitful. He had entered publishing at a time when it was evolving from a local enterprise to a national one, but before mass culture. He was blessed with good nature, sociability, and a happy marriage. But he had also accomplished a great deal with his good fortune. He had begun with little and achieved material prosperity by building a profitable business. He had been motivated, moreover, not only by profit but also by a genuine enthusiasm for literature and respect for those who wrote it. In the words of his biographer, he was "at once the patron of letters and the huckster of the product." By combining these roles, he built a publishing house and a magazine that contributed importantly not only to the New England literary movement in its golden age, but also to developing new readers for American literature and to establishing the profession of authorship in America.

Letters:

James C. Austin, *James T. Fields of the Atlantic Monthly* (San Marino, Cal.: Huntington Library, 1953).

Bibliography:

Jacob Blanck, *Bibliography of American Literature* (New Haven, Conn.: Yale University Press, 1959), III: 142–158.

Biographies:

Annie Fields, *James T. Fields. Biographical Notes and Personal Sketches* (Boston: Houghton, Mifflin, 1881; London: Sampson & Low, 1881);

W. S. Tryon, *Parnassus Corner: A Life of James T. Fields* (Boston: Houghton Mifflin, 1963).

References:

William Charvat, "James T. Fields and the Beginnings of Book Promotion, 1840–1855," in *Literary Publishing in America 1790–1850* (Philadelphia: University of Pennsylvania, 1959);

Ellery Sedgwick, *A History of the Atlantic Monthly: 1857–1909* (Amherst: University of Massachusetts Press, 1994);

Michael Winship, *American Literary Publishing in the Mid-Nineteenth Century: The Business of Ticknor and Fields* (Cambridge: Cambridge University Press, 1995).

Papers:

The major collection of James T. Fields's papers is at the Huntington Library, San Marino, California. The Houghton Library at Harvard also has a substantial collection of letters to and from Fields, as well as financial and other records of the publishing house of Ticknor and Fields and its successors. Other papers may be found at the American Antiquarian Society, Boston Public Library, Dartmouth College, Essex Institute, Exeter Academy, New York Public Library, Historical Society of Pennsylvania, Library of Congress, Longfellow House, Massachusetts Historical Society, and Portsmouth, New Hampshire, Public Library.

Charles Follen

(4 September 1796 – 13 January 1840)

Thomas S. Hansen
Wellesley College

BOOKS: *Beiträge zur Geschichte der teutschen Sammtschulen seit dem Freiheitskrieg 1813* (Germany, 1818);

Deutsches Lesebuch für Anfänger (Boston: S. G. Simpkins, 1826);

A Practical Grammar of the German Language (Boston: Phillips, Sampson, 1828);

Inaugural Discourse Delivered Before the University in Cambridge, Massachusetts, September 3, 1831 (Cambridge, Mass.: Hilliard & Brown, 1831);

Funeral Oration, Delivered Before the Citizens of Boston, Assembled at the Old South Church Nov. XVII at the Burial of Gaspar Spurzheim (Boston: Marsh, Capen & Lyon, 1832);

An Address, Introductory to the Fourth Course of the Franklin Lectures, Delivered at the Masonic Temple, Nov. 3, 1834 (Boston: Tuttle & Weeks, 1835);

Religion and the Church (Boston: James Munroe, 1836);

Blessed Are the Pure in Heart: A Sermon Preached at the First Congregational Church in Chambers Street, on Sunday, February 5th, 1837 (New York: Charles S. Francis, 1837);

The Works of Charles Follen, with a Memoir of his Life, 5 volumes, edited by Eliza Lee Cabot Follen (Boston: Hilliard, Gray, 1841, 1842)–comprises volume 1, *The Life of Charles Follen,* by Eliza Lee Cabot Follen; volume 2, *Sermons;* volume 3, *Lectures on Moral Philosophy; Fragment of a Work on Psychology;* volume 4, *On Schiller's Life and Dramas;* and volume 5, *Miscellaneous Writings;*

Christmas, and Poems on Slavery (Cambridge, Mass.: Privately published by the author for the Massachusetts Anti-Slavery Fair, 1843).

OTHER: Thomas Carlyle, *The Life of Friedrich Schiller: Comprehending an Examination of his Works,* edited by Follen (Boston: Carter & Hendee, 1833).

SELECTED PERIODICAL PUBLICATIONS–UNCOLLECTED: "On the Future State of Man," *Christian Examiner,* 7 (1829); 8 (1830);

Charles Follen

"Peace and War," *U.S. Magazine and Democratic Review,* 5 (1839).

Charles Follen's career as professor, preacher, and social reformer may be divided into two distinct periods. The first twenty-eight years of his life were spent in Europe, where he gained a reputation for political activism in the radical student movement at the German universities. He was trained in the field of law and he pressed for political reform and German unification. Because of his reputation for extremism, however, he was pursued by the police for his clandestine revolutionary activities and fled Germany for Switzerland in 1819 to live in exile before immigrating to America in 1824. He spent the second part of his life in the United

States, involved with the equally combative antislavery movement. He lived in Philadelphia for a year and then in western Massachusetts; soon he was made an instructor and, ultimately, a professor of German at Harvard University. He became a major force in the early dissemination of German language and culture in the United States. His interest in Unitarianism grew, and he became a minister in that denomination, finally leaving academic life for the pulpit. He was active in the antislavery movement and contributed to the theory and practice of abolitionism. His unswerving political convictions, as uncompromising and subjective in his American years as they had been during the German freedom movement, won him a reputation among his contemporaries for ideological rigidity. In Germany he is viewed as an antiauthoritarian, idealistic fighter for modern liberal reform. His role as teacher and activist in the United States, combined with his political profile as an abolitionist, have also earned him a place in American intellectual history.

Charles Theodore Christian Follen, who was born Karl Follenius, anglicized his Christian name and Germanized his surname (which his father, Christoph, had Latinized) when he immigrated to America. He was born in Romrod (Hesse-Darmstadt) near Giessen, where his father was a respected judge. A baptized Lutheran, Follen always showed keen interest in religion. His mother, Rosine, died when he was three years old. He proceeded from the grammar school to the classical "Gymnasium" (European secondary school), where he excelled in ancient and modern languages. Follen was born into, and grew up in, a generation at war with France–a conflict that produced clear political and emotional allegiances of a strongly nationalistic streak. He responded at an early age to the patriotic poetry of Friedrich Schiller and of contemporaries such as Friedrich ("Turnvater") Jahn or Ernst Moritz Arndt. He also liked Theodor Kõrner's poetry, which nurtured the national ideal of a united Germany liberated from foreign domination. After his schooling at a gymnasium, Follen studied law at the University of Giessen, where he and his two brothers answered the patriotic fervor of the day by joining a student corps of riflemen who pursued Napoleon's retreating armies to France (without, however, ever seeing actual combat). Follen, who contracted typhoid early in his short-lived military career, lacked the physical strength to participate in the greater part of the march. He returned to his studies in 1814 infused with a sense of national identity and the idealistic rhetoric of patriotic and religious pathos that helped him formulate notions of freedom and duty. The University of Giessen (like that of Jena) was a hotbed of liberal ideas in this movement, and Follen studied political issues and joined a *Burschenschaft,* or fraternity, dedicated to the nationalist ideal. He was obsessed with the concept of freedom and wrote of the subjugation of tyranny within oneself as a basis for combating unjust dominion in the world. The goal of reform, he believed, was to promote universal brotherhood as taught by Jesus Christ, who was ever Follen's model. Follen joined that group of educated elite–notably, professors and students–at the forefront of the nationalist movement interested not only in reforming university life but also the German political situation. As his biographers note, Follen developed his ideas into a systematic propaganda for the political, social, and religious reform of Germany, eventually leaving the political mainstream to become an extreme radical and advocate of political murder and revolutionary upheaval. Follen was a leading member of a student group called the "Giessen Blacks," who wore black clothing, wrote essays and poems about their experiences and political goals, and engaged in *Turnen* (gymnastics) as a regimen of physical discipline. The great master of the *Turnen* movement, Friedrich Ludwig Jahn, had opened the first athletics training ground in Berlin in 1811, from which the movement soon spread to German student societies. Gymnastics had an important influence upon Follen, who spent much time training in fencing, swimming, and other sports. All these secret, radical, nationalistic activities forged a strong sense of Christian Germanness and anti-French sentiment that brought the students under suspicion of sedition and lèse-majesté. In his pamphlet *Beiträge zur Geschichte der teutschen Sammtschulen seit dem Freiheitskrieg 1813* (Contributions to the History of German Universities since the War for Freedom 1813, 1818) Follen tried to portray the Giessen Blacks as inoffensive or harmless, whereas their goals were radical and fed by agitators outside the university. This political activity led Follen to a life that was increasingly secretive, so much so that he fled Giessen for the University of Jena, where his new group, "The Unconditionals," was dedicated to political revolution.

By 1818, at age twenty-two, Follen was well known to, and feared by, authorities for his successful agitation against a law that had sought to levy a tax upon peasant communities to finance the war debts of the state of Hesse-Darmstadt. All subsequent political work had to be clandestine. He maintained relations with student groups and worked for radical causes, often alienating allies by his insistence on violent measures. Historians have argued that Follen (whom the Prussian historian Heinrich von Treitschke called "the German Robespierre") could have deterred the student Carl Ludwig Sand from murdering the playwright and actor August von Kotzebue in March 1819, a move that sent shock waves not only through the public but also

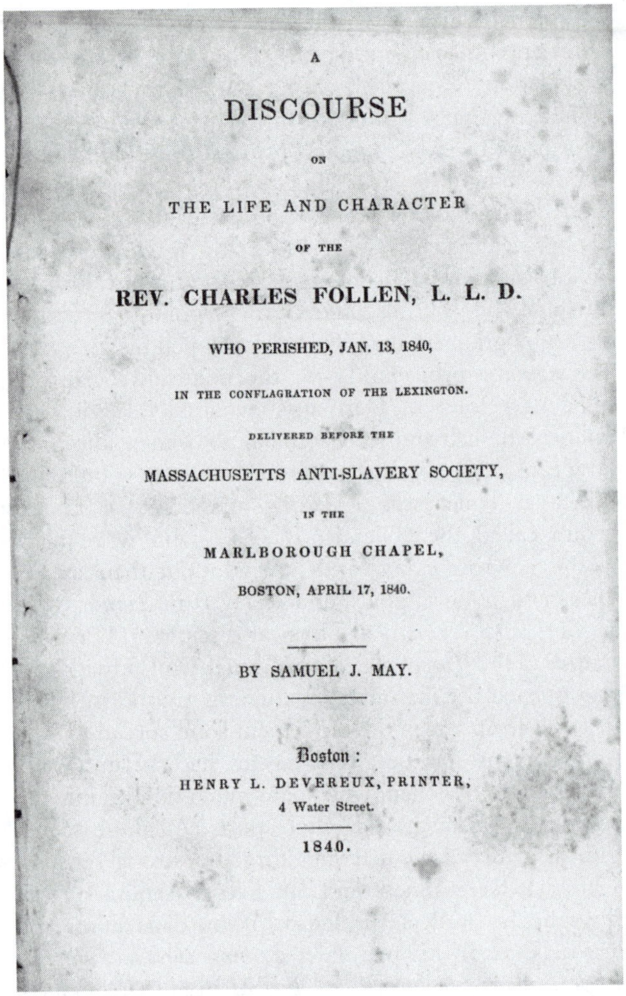
A

DISCOURSE

ON

THE LIFE AND CHARACTER

OF THE

REV. CHARLES FOLLEN, L. L. D.

WHO PERISHED, JAN. 13, 1840,

IN THE CONFLAGRATION OF THE LEXINGTON.

DELIVERED BEFORE THE

MASSACHUSETTS ANTI-SLAVERY SOCIETY,

IN THE

MARLBOROUGH CHAPEL,

BOSTON, APRIL 17, 1840.

BY SAMUEL J. MAY.

Boston:

HENRY L. DEVEREUX, PRINTER,

4 Water Street.

1840.

Title page for a pamphlet written after Follen died in the fire that sank the steamboat Lexington

through the moderate German student organizations and governments. Follen was close to Sand and, although courts could not link Follen directly to the murder plan, later evidence suggests undeniable complicity. Follen's sympathizers blamed his extremism for weakening the liberal cause and gradually abandoned him. By the fall of 1819 the severe Carlsbad Decrees ended radical political opposition in the German Confederation. In the wake of this crackdown, Follen and his brother August were arrested and interrogated about Charles Follen's connection with the Kotzebue murder. Because Follen was able to destroy some of his sensitive papers, the commission lacked enough evidence to connect him to the plot.

Follen had no chances for a university post and was in danger from the authorities. In the winter of 1819–1820 he fled to France. While in Paris for two weeks, he studied French radicalism and met intellectual and political figures, among them the Marquis de Lafayette, Benjamin Constant, and the Germanophile philosopher and political radical Victor Cousin. When foreigners were expelled from France for political reasons, Follen went to Switzerland, where he spent a productive time as lecturer at the University of Basel and as a teacher in a cantonal school. From Basel, which was a center of German political activity in exile and asylum to many of the original "Giessen Blacks," he tried to influence German politics by founding another secret revolutionary group. He also became engaged to the daughter of a professor at the university, but she refused to leave Switzerland with him. In Basel he made friends with a German scholar, Karl Beck, who accompanied Follen to America three years later (changing his name to Charles Beck) and even followed him to Harvard and influenced New England intellectual life. While the Prussian government was trying to effect his extradition, Follen fled to France on a false passport and eventually sailed to New York in November 1824.

He was twenty-eight years old when he arrived in the United States, and for the sixteen remaining years of his life Karl Follenius–calling himself Charles Follen–engaged in new social and political crusades but never changed his personality or ethical position. He always brought his own personal biases and agendas to an issue. He and his friends soon abandoned a plan he had concocted to form an autonomous German state in North America. Instead, reality dictated that Follen assimilate, perfect his English, acquire citizenship, and eventually marry an American woman. He turned from utopian political dreams to concrete issues of American reform movements while his personal style remained dominated by a rigorous and uncompromising sense of moral and political duty that cost him both jobs and friendships.

Follen's first letters home to his family in Hesse describe America as a place of democracy, freedom, and hope for oppressed German refugees. This positive view was soon amended by his realization of the existence of slavery in the U.S.; in fact, abolitionism was the reform movement with which he allied himself. Follen spent his first year in New York City, where he had arrived in December 1824 along with Beck. Lafayette eased their arrival by giving Follen advice and arranging contacts with prominent Americans. In January 1825 Follen moved to Philadelphia and sought employment with the established German community in the region. Realizing that a career in law was almost impossible, he settled upon teaching. His first position was in Northampton, Massachusetts, at the Round Hill School, which was founded in 1823 by Göttingen-trained graduates of Harvard George Bancroft and Joseph Cogswell with the help of Harvard president John Thornton Kirkland, and modeled on the German *Gym-*

nasium. All pupils there studied German and gymnastics, an emphasis that has made the school interesting to historians of American physical education. Follen taught there a year.

In January 1825 Follen met with the young Harvard professor of modern languages, George Ticknor, in Philadelphia. Ticknor, recently returned from his own German studies at Göttingen, had been asked by Lafayette to find employment for Follen, preferably at Harvard. As a result, Follen was hired by Harvard in November 1825 as instructor of the German language; prior to his appointment German had been offered only by private tutorial outside the normal curriculum.

There is vivid documentation of Follen at Harvard that preserves a picture of a man who was as enthusiastic and engaging a teacher as he had been a committed political agitator. While he taught both French and German, he also set up the first gymnastics program at Harvard. President Kirkland had offered the position first to Jahn, the "father of modern gymnastics," but Jahn's advanced age prevented him from entertaining such an offer. Follen, however, had the expertise to introduce physical education, which, at its inception, was closely associated in America with the study of German language and literature. James Freeman Clarke, Germanophile cousin of Margaret Fuller and later Unitarian minister, described gymnastics at Harvard in 1825:

> It so chanced that in our Freshman year, Dr. Follen, recently from Germany, was enabled, by some happy influence, to introduce gymnastic exercises into Harvard College. We began with a large room, fitted up with parallel and horizontal bars, ladders, climbing poles, wooden horses, dumb-bells and the like. Afterward the triangular piece of ground, called the Delta, where Memorial Hall now stands, was fitted up with a more elaborate apparatus.

Follen was appointed superintendent of the newly established Harvard gymnasium, where he supervised the exercise regimen. By the end of 1827, however, he had retired from this post to devote himself to other duties; furthermore, attendance had dwindled as the novelty of gymnastics wore off.

Not only did the students initially take to German gymnastics but also to Follen's German classes. Andrew Peabody left a famous description in his *Harvard Reminiscences* (1888) of the experience of Follen as a professor:

> German had never been taught in college before; and it was with no little difficulty that a volunteer class of eight was found, desirous, or at least willing, to avail themselves of his services. I was of that [first] class. We were looked upon with very much the amazement with which a class in some obscure tribal dialect of the remotest Orient would be now regarded. We knew of but two or three persons in New England who could read German; though there were probably many more, of whom we did not know. There were no German books in the bookstore. A friend gave me a copy of Schiller's "Wallenstein," which I read as soon as I was able to do so, and then passed it from hand to hand among those who could obtain nothing else to read. There was no attainable class-book that could be used as a "Reader." . . . The "German Reader for Beginners," compiled by our teacher, was furnished to the class in single sheets as it was needed, and was printed in Roman type, there being no German type in easy reach. There could not have been a happier introduction to German literature than this little volume. It contained choice extracts in prose, all from writers that still hold an unchallenged place in the hierarchy of genius, and poems from Schiller, Goethe, Herder, and several other poets of kindred, if inferior, fame. But in the entire volume, Dr. Follen rejoiced especially in several battle-pieces from Kõrner, the soldier and martyr of liberty, whom we then supposed to have been our teacher's fellow-soldier, though, in fact, he fell in battle when Dr. Follen was just entering the University. I never have heard recitations which impressed me so strongly as the reading of those pieces by Dr. Follen, who would put into them all of the heart and soul that had made him too much a lover of his country to be suffered to dwell in it. He appended to the other poems in the first edition of the Reader, anonymously, a death-song in the memory of Kõrner, which we all knew to be his own, and which we all read so often and so feelingly, that it sank indelibly into permanent memory; and I find that after an interval of sixty years it is as fresh in my recollection as the hymns I learned in my childhood. . . .
>
> Dr. Follen was the best of teachers. Under him we learned the grammar of the language, in great part, *in situ,*–forms and constructions, except the most elementary, being explained to us as we met them in our reading-lessons, and explained with a clearness and emphasis that made it hard to forget them. At the same time he pointed out all that was specially noteworthy in our lessons, and gave us, in English much better than ours, his own translations of passages of particular interest or beauty. He bestowed great pains in bringing our untried organs into use in the more difficult details of pronunciation, particularly in the ö, the ü, the r, and the ch, on which he took us each separately in hand.

As Peabody records, Follen had to write his own texts for the new project of the teaching of German in the United States. His *Deutsches Lesebuch für Anfänger* (German Reader for Beginners, 1826) and *A Practical Grammar of the German Language* (1828), which were the fruits of his classroom experience, went through many editions in the nineteenth century. The writers included in the reader represented Follen's own interest in social

Frontispiece for Thomas Carlyle's biography, The Life of Friedrich Schiller, *edited by Charles Follen*

and political reform. They included Gotthold Ephraim Lessing, Johann Gottfried von Herder, Heinrich Friedrich von Wieland, Friedrich Schiller, and Novalis (Friedrich Leopold von Hardenberg). The subjectivity of this selection is obvious when one encounters texts by the patriotic martyr Theodor Kõrner and even poems by the editor's brother, August Follen. The absence of Goethe is conspicuous, for Follen chose German writers who, in his opinion, best exemplified issues of German nationhood and political freedom. Goethe, whose classical mind sought to represent the universal condition of man, did not fit this contemporary agenda.

By 1830 Follen's reputation had spread to the point that he attracted sixty students, among whom were Ralph Waldo Emerson, Bronson Alcott, and Theodore Parker. Margaret Fuller encountered Follen informally in a private reading group in Cambridge. Not only must he have influenced the Transcendentalists, but he was also an important figure in Boston, where fascination with German language and culture was strong. He soon was accepted in social circles of the educated elite from which his wife, Eliza Lee Cabot, came. They married in 1828. The Cabots, an old family of Boston merchants, funded the professorship for Follen in 1830, which was to pay his salary of $500 per year for five years. The Follens had one son, Charles Christopher, born in 1830.

Once settled in Cambridge, Follen became an active scholar, promoting German thought and literature. His attitude toward the two great German writers of his generation is indicative of his approach. While he elevated Schiller as the people's hero, he also contributed to Goethe's negative reputation in New England. Schiller's social conscience and freedom-loving pathos he found superior to Goethe's highly personal aesthetics. Follen identified Goethe with the aristocratic state and Schiller with the ideals of republicanism. Furthermore, Follen's moral objections to Goethe's private life as licentious (an attitude shared by Emerson but not Margaret Fuller) slowed acceptance of Goethe in the United States in some circles.

Follen remained interested in scientific and intellectual developments in Germany. Therefore, because these develpments included phrenology, when the phrenologist Johann Christoph Kaspar Spurzheim died in America on a lecture tour, Follen presented the funeral oration. He also wrote about psychology, or mental philosophy, as the study was known in America. He believed that, like phrenology, psychology was a key to better self-knowledge and therefore an aid to man's self-improvement.

Not surprisingly, given Follen's record of public defiance of authority, his career at Harvard was precarious and short-lived. During the tense years of student rebellion between 1834 and 1838, President Josiah Quincy, a conservative man not skilled in handling his youthful charges, introduced strict disciplinary measures and expulsions. For these he was attacked by students and faculty alike. The leader of the dissident faction at the college was apparently none other than Charles Follen, who advocated less administrative interference and more autonomy in student life. By 1834 Follen, labeled a troublemaker, had fallen out of favor. He and his wife were seen to be too close to student life, hosting the undergraduates privately and fomenting criticism of President Quincy. Although Follen and his friends intimated that his abolitionist views were the source of his dismissal from the university in 1835, the real reason for his leaving Harvard was most likely his central role in the campus unrest.

From the time of his arrival in the Boston area, Follen was always present in Unitarian circles. In the winter of 1826–1827 he met William Ellery Channing, who became a significant influence upon him. Follen was accepted as a candidate for the Unitarian ministry in 1828 and was ordained eight years later upon leaving Harvard in 1836. He had been interested in religion even in his Giessen days when he had realized that it could be a powerful force for molding a political agenda. He found the example of Jesus particularly instructive for its uncompromising devotion to, and sacrifice for, a cause. The idea of martyrdom became central to Follen's understanding of religion. Both he and his wife spread the idea in their writings and sermons that religion should liberate the human mind from prejudices and doctrinaire assumptions. Follen's position was accepted in the intellectual climate of Boston as representative of German philosophical idealism and theological liberalism, which were both central to the spiritual systems of Unitarianism and Transcendentalism that placed so much emphasis on the freedom of individual conscience. Follen also used his ministry to promote his own belief in this idea of freedom, which most considered too radical. As a result, in 1830 he resigned a position of lecturer at the Harvard Divinity School, a position that he had held for just a short time. After his ordination in 1836 he took a pulpit in New York but was dropped by the congregation soon thereafter for the radical antislavery views that pervaded his sermons. He lectured and published on religion, but the social and financial prosperity he had attained were threatened by his insecure employment and his wife's health. The Follens sold their new house when Eliza's condition declined and she was advised to move to a healthier climate.

In 1838 the famous case of Abner Kneeland gave Follen an opportunity to put to the test the religious convictions about which he had lectured and preached. Kneeland, who was serving a prison term for blasphemy and atheism, based on statements he had published, had been found guilty when his appeal was heard for the fourth time. Follen was among the prominent Bostonians who co-authored a petition to the governor for Kneeland's pardon. They argued for freedoms of speech, press, and religious expression. By throwing his support behind Kneeland's cause, Follen was striking a blow for the practical, worldly expression of religion. Although the petition was unsuccessful, Follen gained a higher public profile as a result of the case.

In 1839 Follen's situation improved when he was hired as a minister in a Unitarian parish in East Lexington, Massachusetts. Plans for the new parish proceeded. Follen moved to Lexington and was prepared to help build the church that he had designed himself.

The issue of slavery–by far the most divisive topic of the day–continued to engage Follen profoundly. Following the lead of many in the Unitarian circle (particularly William Lloyd Garrison and William Ellery Channing), he satisfied his need for polemics in the cause of freedom by writing essays, giving speeches, and joining or founding antislavery societies. As he had sided with the cause of the Hessian peasants twelve years earlier, he now supported the emancipa-

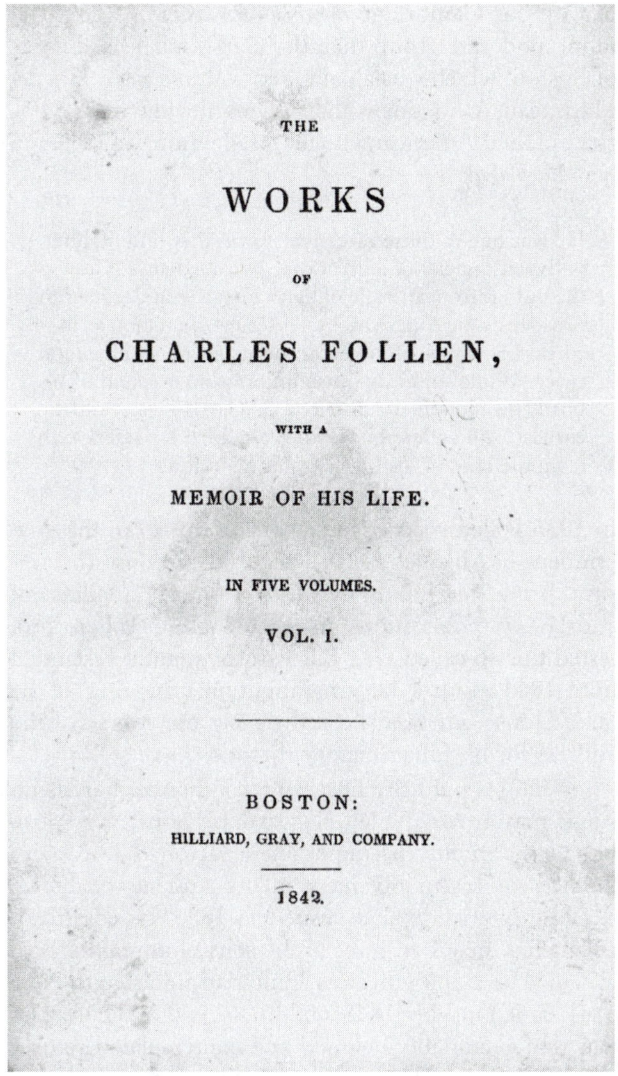
THE

WORKS

OF

CHARLES FOLLEN,

WITH A

MEMOIR OF HIS LIFE.

IN FIVE VOLUMES.

VOL. I.

BOSTON:

HILLIARD, GRAY, AND COMPANY.

1842.

Title page for the posthumously published collection of Follen's writings edited by his wife, Eliza Lee Cabot Follen

tion of American slaves. As usual, Follen's heated rhetoric and radical intensity cost him support of colleagues and parishioners. Still, as Edmund Spevack has said, Follen "wanted to work within the framework of the existing legal and political institutions and never publicly advocated an overthrow of the American government." He used legal methods to test public conscience, acquainting himself during the 1830s with the arguments and problems of the antislavery movement and rising in the organizational ranks of the American Antislavery Society. When this group held the first New England Antislavery Convention in Boston in 1834, Follen was chairman of the committee that drafted a public statement against slavery; in his "Address on Slavery" he advocated absolute and immediate elimination of the institution. Follen was also a founding member of the Cambridge Antislavery Society (1834), a more moderate group than the Garrisonian hard-liners of Boston, which was abandoned within a year. Harriet Martineau, who knew the Follens during the 1830s, championed American abolitionists, writing of Follen in her *Autobiography:*

> He was one of those rare great spirits that find no alternative at the call of a great case but obedience. He was the only European exile of that vintage who declined to prosper as an American by flattering the nation's sin,—so rare is the virtue that can pour out of its life-blood twice. While suffering proscription from the land of his birth, he identified himself with Garrison among the earliest, and suffered, with the rest, a fresh proscription from the land of his love and his adoption.

In 1835 Follen tried to force concessions from the government of Massachusetts, which (in response to pressure from the South) tried to stop the mailing of antislavery publications to Washington. Follen protested this so-called Gag Bill (which was not rescinded until 1844) with a fiery harangue in a hearing at the State House but was silenced during the course of the address for his inflammatory rhetoric.

All this publicity hurt Follen. Whereas there is no single reason why he left Harvard, his antislavery position was certainly as important a factor as university finances or his involvement in the student rebellions. Because of friction that ensued in 1835, he could not even keep the job of tutor to the sons of a wealthy Bostonian. His employment as Unitarian minister in New York ended in May 1838, and by the end of the year he was understandably dejected and contemplated returning to Germany. He canceled these travel plans, however, when he was offered the parish in East Lexington. In January 1840 Follen was earning money by lecturing in New York City. Leaving his wife and son, he traveled back to Massachusetts to dedicate the new church building with his congregation. When the steamboat *Lexington,* on which he was a passenger, caught fire and sank in a storm in Long Island Sound on 13 January 1840, Follen lost his life. William Ellery Channing, who was shaken by the senseless death of a man who had fought to better the world, wrote a moving tribute to Follen. The Unitarians and abolitionists all saw him as a martyr, while Eliza Follen's biography of her husband is a positive picture of an idealist staunchly devoted to his political causes.

Letters:

Follen-Briefe: Briefe Karl Follens und seiner Verwandten aus der Zeit seines Aufenthaltes in der Schweiz und in Nordamerika (Chicago, Ill.: Deutsch-amerikanische historische Gesellschaft, 1914), pp. 7–82.

Bibliography:

George Washington Spindler, *The Life of Karl Follen: A Study in German-American Cultural Relations* (Chicago: University of Chicago Press, 1917), pp. 229–234.

Biographies:

William Ellery Channing, *A Discourse Occasioned by the Death of the Rev. Dr. Follen* (Cambridge, Mass.: Metcalf, Torry & Ballou, 1840); republished as *Christian Views of Human Suffering* (Boston: J. Munroe, 1840);

Samuel Joseph May, *A Discourse on the Life and Character of the Rev. Charles Follen, LL.D.; who Perished, Jan. 13, 1840, in the Conflagration of the Lexington* (Boston: Henry L. Devereux, 1840);

George Washington Spindler, *The Life of Karl Follen: A Study in German-American Cultural Relations* (Chicago: University of Chicago Press, 1917);

Edmund Spevack, "Charles Follen's Search for Nationality and Freedom in Germany and America, 1795–1840," dissertation, Johns Hopkins University, 1992;

Spevack, *Charles Follen's Search for Nationality and Freedom; Germany and America 1795–1840* (Cambridge, Mass.: Harvard University Press, 1997).

References:

Douglas Percy Brayton, *The History of the Follen Church* (East Lexington, Mass., 1939);

Sigrid Bauschinger, *The Trumpet of Reform: German Literature in 19th Century New England,* translated by Thomas S. Hansen (Columbia, S.C.: Camden House, 1998);

James Freeman Clarke, *Autobiography, Diary, and Correspondence,* edited by Edward Everett Hale (Boston: Houghton, Mifflin, 1891);

Kuno Francke, "Karl Follen and the German Liberal Movement (1815 to 1819)," *American Historical Association. Papers of the American Historical Association* (New York, 1891), V, parts 1–2: 63–81;

Erich Geldbach, "Die Verpflanzung des deutschen Turnens nach Amerika," *Stadion,* 1 (1975): 331–376;

Herman Haupt, "Karl Follen und die Giessener Schwarzen," *Mitteilungen des Oberschlesischen Geschichtsvereins,* NF, 15 (1907);

Gustav Phillip Körner, *Das deutsche Element in den Vereinigten Staaten von Nordamerika 1818–1848* (Cincinnati: A. E. Wilde, 1880);

Fred Eugene Leonard, *Pioneers of Modern Physical Training,* revised and enlarged (New York: Association Press, 1919);

Harriet Martineau, *Harriet Martineau's Autobiography,* 2 volumes, edited by Maria Chapman (Boston: Houghton, Mifflin, 1877);

Friedrich Munch, *Erinnerungen aus Deutschlands trübster Zeit. Dargestellt in den Lebensbildern von Karl Follen, Paul Follen, Friedrich Munch* (St. Louis, Mo.: C. Witter, 1873);

Andrew P. Peabody, *Harvard Reminiscences* (Boston: Ticknor, 1888), pp. 116–123;

Henry A. Pochmann, *German Culture in America: Philosophical and Literary Influences 1600–1900* (Madison: University of Wisconsin Press, 1957);

Richard Pregizer, *Die politischen Ideen des Karl Follen: ein Beitrag zur Geschichte des Radikalismus in Deutschland* (Tübingen: C. Mohr, 1912);

Douglas Stange, "The Making of an Abolitionist Martyr: Harvard Professor Charles Theodor Christian Follen," *Harvard Library Bulletin,* 24 (1976): 17–24;

Helena Szépe, "Zur Problematik von Karl Follens 'Grossem Lied,'" *Monatshefte für den deutschen Unterricht,* 63 (1971): 335–340;

Heinrich von Treitschke, *Deutsche Geschichte im Neunzehnten Jahrhundert,* 5 volumes (Leipzig: S. Hirzel, 1879–1889), II: 437–443;

Louis Viereck, *Zwei Jahrhunderte deutschen Unterrichts in den Vereinigten Staaten* (Braunschweig: F. Vieweg, 1903);

Stanley Vogel *German Literary Influences on the American Transcendentalists* (New Haven: Yale University Press, 1955);

Robert Wesselhöft, *Teutsche Jugend in weiland Burschenschaften und Turngemeinden* (Magdeburg: W. Hinrichshofen, 1828);

J. Wuest, *Karl Follen; Festgabe der Deutschen und Giessener Burschenschaft zur Studentenhistoriker-Tagung 1935* (Giessen: O. Kindt, 1935), "Aus den Mitteilungen des Oberhessischen Geschichtsvereins," 33 (1935).

Papers:

Charles Follen's own collection of his papers disappeared in the nineteenth century and has not been rediscovered. See Spevack, 279 (note 1) and 282 (notes 33, 35), for discussion of archival sources at Harvard University, Boston Public Library, and others. The Massachusetts Historical Society has some miscellaneous letters and papers relating to Follen–Papers I: 1801–1840, Archive/Manuscript Control (1 folder), Miscellaneous Letters and Papers Relating to the Rev. Charles Follen, Unitarian Minister and Harvard Professor of German literature, and Papers II: 1815–1860, Archive/Manuscript Control (1 folder), Miscellaneous letters, chiefly to members of the family of the Rev. Charles Follen, Unitarian minister and Harvard professor of German literature.

Eliza Lee (Cabot) Follen

(15 August 1787 - 26 January 1860)

Mary Ann Wilson
University of Louisiana at Lafayette

BOOKS: *The Well-Spent Hour* (Boston: Wait, Greene, 1827, 1828; London: E. T. Whitfield, 1830);

Hymns, Songs and Fables for Children (Boston: Carter, Hendee & Babcock, 1831; revised and enlarged, Boston: Crosby & Nichols, 1847);

A Sequel to the Well-Spent Hour, or The Birthday (Boston: Carter & Hendee, 1832);

Words of Truth (Cambridge, Mass., 1832);

Little Songs for Little Boys and Girls (Boston: Leonard C. Bowles, 1833);

The Skeptic (Boston & Cambridge: J. Munroe, 1835; London, 1853);

Sketches of Married Life (Boston: Hilliard, Gray, 1838);

Hymns and Exercises for the Federal Street Sunday School (Boston: Green, 1839);

Nursery Songs (New York: S. Colman, 1839);

Poems (Boston: William Crosby, 1839; London: J. Chapman, 1840);

The Life of Charles Follen (Boston: T. H. Webb, 1840; London: J. Chapman, 1842);

The Liberty Cap (Boston: Leonard C. Bowles, 1840);

To Mothers in the Free States (New York: American Anti-Slavery Society, 1855);

Made-Up Stories (Boston: Whittemore, Niles & Hall, 1855);

The Old Garret, 3 volumes (Boston: Whittemore, Niles & Hall, 1855);

The Pedler of Dust Sticks (Boston: Whittemore, Niles & Hall, 1855);

True Stories about Dogs and Cats (Boston: Whittemore, Niles & Hall, 1855);

Travellers' Stories (Boston: Whittemore, Niles & Hall, 1858);

May Morning and New Year's Eve (Boston: Whittemore, Niles & Hall, 1858);

Conscience (Boston: Whittemore, Niles & Hall, 1858);

What the Animals Do and Say (Boston: Whittemore, Niles & Hall, 1858);

Our Home in the Marshland; or Days of Auld Lang Syne (London: Griffith & Farran, 1877).

Collections: *Twilight Stories,* 12 volumes (Boston: Whittemore, Niles & Hall, 1858).

OTHER: *The Christian Teachers' Manual,* edited by Follen (Boston: American Sunday School Union, 1828–1830);

François de Salignac de La Mothe-Fénelon, *Selections from the Writings of Fenelon: With a Memoir of His Life,* translated and edited by Follen (Boston: Hilliard, Gray, Little & Wilkins, 1829; enlarged, Boston & Cambridge: J. Munroe, 1859);

Sacred Songs for Sunday Schools, Original and Selected (Boston: Green, 1839);

Gammer Grethel, or German Fairy Tales and Popular Stories, translated and edited by Follen (Boston: J. Munroe, 1840);

The Works of Charles Follen, with a Memoir of His Life, 5 volumes, edited by Follen (Boston: Hilliard, Gray, 1841, 1842);

Anti-Slavery Hymns and Songs (New York: American Anti-Slavery Society, 1855);

Adélaïde de Montgolfier, *Piccolissima,* translated by Follen (Boston: Whittemore, Niles & Hall, 1858);

Home Dramas for Young People, compiled by Follen (Boston: J. Munroe, 1859).

The writings and causes of Eliza Lee (Cabot) Follen intersect several historical and intellectual currents in the nineteenth century. Her contributions to children's literature, her work with William Ellery Channing and the Sunday School Movement, and her tireless efforts in the abolitionist cause reveal a woman who took full advantage of her education to further humanitarian ends. She wrote sentimental domestic fiction, children's poetry, and antislavery tracts; she edited both *The Child's Friend* and the *Christian Teachers' Manual,* publications of the American Sunday School Union; and she wrote for the abolitionist periodical *The Liberty Bell.* Viewed as a whole, her life and work exhibit a remarkable coherence; from her early efforts in children's education at Channing's Federal Street Church in Boston to her passionate antislavery tracts of 1855 addressed to the mothers of the free states, Follen consistently ventured outside her domestic borders while simultaneously arguing for the family's crucial role in the cultural enterprise of nation building. Deeply religious and committed to a Christian ethos, Follen saw her literary activities as a means of promoting these beliefs. Her 1828 marriage at the age of forty-one to German political refugee Charles Follen, who later became a Unitarian minister and an ardent abolitionist, strengthened Eliza Follen's commitment to social activism. Charles Follen's appointment as the first German instructor at Harvard College plunged both husband and wife into a heady intellectual environment in Cambridge, where they were frequently visited by luminaries such as British activist Harriet Martineau. But Eliza Follen's importance lies in more than her role as a "Harvard wife," as she is called in a 1965 article by Elizabeth Bancroft Schlesinger. Follen's domestic fiction, her works in children's literature, and her antislavery writings reveal a woman bent on educating a growing U.S. populace at a pivotal time in its history. Follen's career illustrates in miniature the gradual broadening of nineteenth-century woman's sphere and embodies Follen's belief in what came to be called "republican motherhood"–creating citizens for the newly forming country and ultimately envisioning that country free from the taint of slavery.

Born on 15 August 1787 in Boston, Massachusetts, to Samuel and Sarah (Barrett) Cabot, Eliza Lee Cabot was the fifth of thirteen children in a prominent and visible Boston family. Her father was a descendant of John Cabot, who emigrated in 1700 from the British Channel island of Jersey to Salem, Massachusetts. In 1796 he became secretary of the United States commission appointed by President George Washington to negotiate claims against England from the American Revolution, a duty that kept him away from home for four years. His able and educated wife, Sarah (or Sally, as she was called), was the granddaughter of Richard Clarke, a wealthy loyalist tea merchant who had fled to England at the outbreak of the American Revolution. Samuel Cabot's poor health kept the family in unstable circumstances, calling upon the considerable managerial skills of Eliza's capable mother, Sally. Her parents' connections put Eliza in touch with other prominent Boston families, and she grew up in the company of many Perkins, Cary, and Higginson cousins, receiving an excellent education. She was cultivated, deeply interested in religious and social problems, and firm and outspoken in her convictions. After her mother's death in 1809 and her father's ten years later in 1819, Eliza and two of her sisters established a home together at 1 Mt. Vernon Street in Boston.

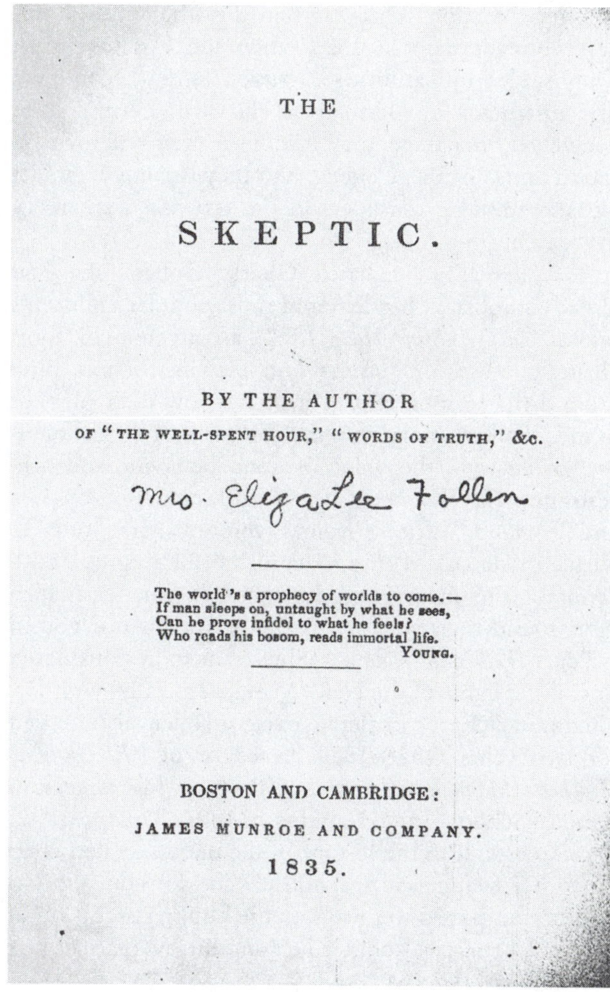
THE

SKEPTIC.

BY THE AUTHOR

OF "THE WELL-SPENT HOUR," "WORDS OF TRUTH," &c.

mrs. Eliza Lee Follen

The world's a prophecy of worlds to come.—
If man sleeps on, untaught by what he sees,
Can he prove infidel to what he feels?
Who reads his bosom, reads immortal life.
YOUNG.

BOSTON AND CAMBRIDGE:

JAMES MUNROE AND COMPANY.

1835.

Title page for Eliza Lee Follen's first novel, which expresses her belief in the power of Christian mothers to shape the American Republic

Eliza Cabot eventually focused her religious and educational fervor on the Unitarian Church, specifically William Ellery Channing's Federal Street Church in Boston, and on the then newly forming Sunday School Movement. During these years, she cultivated her interest in children's education and formed a close working relationship with the charismatic Channing, meeting often at his home and the home of her writer friend Catharine Sedgwick, along with other like-minded people. Through Sedgwick, Eliza met her future husband, Charles Theodore Christian Follen, a political refugee from Germany, nine years her junior. She encouraged Follen's interest in the ministry by bringing him to meetings of the Sunday school teachers at Channing's Unitarian church. Eliza and Charles had similar humanitarian interests and enthusiasms, and when Charles's German fiancée refused to join him in America, what had begun as friendship blossomed in another direction. Eliza married the brilliant and earnest younger man in 1828 when she was forty-one. They settled in Cambridge, where Charles became the first instructor of German at Harvard. During their twelve-year marriage, they combined their zeal for education and religious training, and they became formidable and untiring crusaders in the growing antislavery movement.

When Eliza married Charles Follen, she had already published her first and most popular children's book, *The Well-Spent Hour* (1827), a conventional, moralizing tale bent on spiritual and civic instruction. Built around the sermon text "Let them show their piety at home," Follen's story uses the contrast of two girl cousins to illustrate the value of good behavior and self-restraint. *The Well-Spent Hour* was popular in America and England. Writing from Liverpool, Mrs. John T. Kirkland remarked in a letter dated 23 August 1830: "Among the literary productions of America which have found their way across the Atlantic is our cousin Follen's *Well-Spent Hour*. . . . She seems to be considered one of the lights of the New World, associated with Dr. Channing." Early in her marriage, Follen also served for two years (1828–1830) as editor of *The Christian Teachers' Manual,* an organ of the growing American Sunday School Union founded in 1824. Thus, early in her career and in the history of the nation, Follen combined her evangelical zeal and passion for education in efforts that paved the way for the public schools amid national concerns about educating an ever-expanding population.

Eliza Follen's adult fiction, *The Skeptic* (1835) and *Sketches of Married Life* (1838), also show the powerful early influence of William Ellery Channing and Follen's own interest in educating not just children, but young women for their roles in marriage and motherhood. Both works share elements of the sentimental domestic fiction of the time written by Lydia Sigourney, Follen's friend Catharine Sedgwick, and Susan Warner. Indeed, the earlier work, *The Skeptic,* is suffused with a sententious, piously didactic tone; but *Sketches,* as Nina Baym has pointed out in *Woman's Fiction* (1993), portrays an independent heroine whose competence and resourcefulness anticipate future fictional heroines.

The Skeptic is the story of Alice Grey, her husband, James, and James's friendship with a "free-thinker," Ralph. Ralph's liberal religious views and his taste for whiskey punch make him a double threat to James. Alice's friend Jane is in love with Ralph, but she, too, fears his liberal ways. Told from a third-person omniscient point of view, which is conducive to frequent moral discourses on the events dramatized, Follen's work is permeated with images of woman as ennobler and spiritualizer (Ralph's father wants him to marry Jane and thus be converted) and framed with overtly biblical chapter headings, such as "The Things Unseen are Real." Tackling issues such as reason versus faith and the education of women, *The Skeptic* reveals Jane as bemoaning that she feels intellectually ill equipped to argue theological points with Ralph, and Alice as vowing never to let her children be caught in a similar situation. Follen thus easily conflates the issues of religious education and maternal influence, inviting the reader to share her vision of a Christian republic shaped and molded by its mothers. She even contrives her characters' regeneration through a sick child: James's ailing daughter Fanny becomes the means by which his weakened faith in God is renewed, and the good Christian doctor incidentally proposes that James read all of Dr. Channing's works. In a convergence of stock melodramatic situations, the child Fanny dies, Ralph commits suicide after being disinherited by his father, and Jane nurses Ralph's grieving father into his old age, as she vows celibacy and a life devoted to good works. Follen's story, beneath its pious veneer, demonstrates the necessity for educating women not only as mothers but also as equal intellectual opponents for the freethinkers who might assault their faith. Both Alice and Jane anticipate Amy in *Sketches of Married Life,* a character whose strong ego and independent mind make her a worthy and equal partner for her husband, Edward.

Dedicated to Charles Follen, *Sketches of Married Life* juxtaposes two marriages–one based on mutual respect and esteem and the other on rigidly prescribed and internalized gender roles of submissive wife and dominant husband. Unlike other sentimental domestic fiction of the period, which preached patience and submission as requisites for a happy marriage, Follen's novel presents an independent heroine who supports her family in its poverty and defies society by going to the hospital and nursing her desperately ill fiancé back to health. Both *The Skeptic* and *Sketches of Married Life* include the larger social and cultural issues that dominated popular discourse–education, women's rights, and the formation of a Christian republic–and both illustrate their author's engagement with the concerns that ultimately define woman's role and function outside the domestic sphere.

Eliza Cabot's marriage to Charles Follen and the birth of their only son, Charles Christopher, in 1830 gave her ample opportunity to combine her public and private spheres. During these years, while she wrote and edited educational treatises and children's moral tales, she and her husband opened their home to four Harvard students and began the work of preparing their son and other young boys for Harvard. The couple's religious and educational concerns inevitably led them to involvement in the growing antislavery movement, a venture that some sources believe eventually cost Charles Follen his job at Harvard. Schlesinger points out that only one or two Boston clergymen, notably Channing, would even read notices of antislavery meetings from the pulpit. Thus deprived of academic employment, Charles Follen turned to the ministry and with preaching, lecturing, and writing tried to support his family. Eliza now redoubled her efforts at writing.

Charles's untimely death in 1840, in a fire aboard the steamboat *Lexington* while traveling home from a lecture engagement in New York, ended a fruitful and productive personal and professional union. Eliza Follen subsequently traveled to Germany to collect materials for a biography of her husband and a compilation of his works. Shortly after her husband's death, *The Life of Charles Follen* (1840) appeared. Obviously a labor of love, the biography traces Charles Follen's early life in Germany and his journey to America as a political refugee under the sponsorship of George Ticknor, distinguished professor of Spanish at Harvard, who secured Follen a teaching post there. She chronicles her husband's attempts to start his own church in New York, his efforts on behalf of women's rights and abolition, and his gifts as a loving husband and father. In 1841 and 1842, *The Works of Charles Follen, with a Memoir of His Life* appeared. The works show Charles Follen as a man of courage and character, passionately devoted to freedom and equality, unafraid to stand before an often hostile crowd in public gatherings and proclaim his feelings about the abolitionist cause. His life stands as an obvious model for his wife's own later impassioned efforts for the same cause.

Eliza Follen's untiring antislavery work reflects the larger cultural shift at midcentury away from mere moral advocacy toward more politically focused action. She served on the executive committee of the American Anti-Slavery Society, was a counselor of the Massachusetts Society, and was a member of the Boston Female Anti-Slavery Society, working as chief organizer of the annual Anti-Slavery Society bazaars held in Fanueil Hall. Such public activities helped to compensate nonvoting women for their virtual powerlessness in the public domain and gave them an arena for their actions. As feminist historians have further pointed out, women devoted to antislavery ultimately served to redefine the notion of true womanhood, projecting, as Jean Fagan Yellin maintains in *Women and Sisters* (1989), an ideal alternative to the image of woman as angel in the house. Follen's writings during the late 1830s and 1840s both in children's and in antislavery literature reflect her increasing involvement in the abolitionist cause.

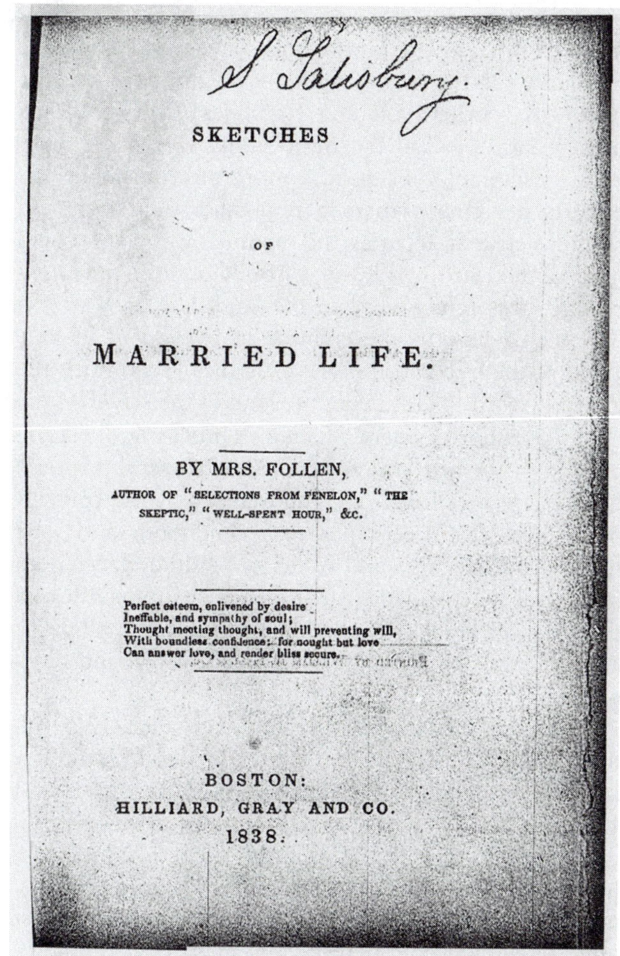
S Salisbury.

SKETCHES

OF

MARRIED LIFE.

BY MRS. FOLLEN,

AUTHOR OF "SELECTIONS FROM FENELON," "THE SKEPTIC," "WELL-SPENT HOUR," &c.

Perfect esteem, enlivened by desire
Ineffable, and sympathy of soul;
Thought meeting thought, and will preventing will,
With boundless confidence: for nought but love
Can answer love, and render bliss secure.

BOSTON:
HILLIARD, GRAY AND CO.
1838.

Title page for Follen's second novel, in which the strong heroine is her husband's equal

After her husband's death, Follen assumed a more public role in her writing endeavors, editing the Sunday school publication *The Child's Friend* from 1843 to 1850. This children's magazine was a compendium of stories from the Bible; tales from foreign lands; poems with moralizing tags; essays inculcating piety, obedience, and civic virtue; and an occasional brief geography lesson. Some issues ended with notes from the editor to the Sunday school teacher, giving a healthy dose of educational theory as framework for the contents of the issue. A publication espousing kindness to the poor and thoughtfulness of others' feelings easily found room for poems and stories that embodied a more concrete concern for the plight of the slave, sentimentalized though it was. Such poems are Follen's "For the Fourth of July" and "Children in Slavery," both recently collected in Janet Gray's 1997 *She Wields a Pen: American Women Poets of the Nineteenth Century*. The first poem uses the occasion of American Independence Day to illuminate the disparity between white freedom and black enslavement: "O, how the foul stain canst thou bear, / Of being the land of the slave?" Invoking the humanity of the slave, Follen's poem plays on the theme of brotherhood and combines the Old Testament notion of God the stern Father with the gentler New Testament concept of a more merciful God. She exhorts her countrymen to remember their civil and religious strife in forming the republic, and warns them not to expect further blessings from God until the blight of slavery is removed from the land. She ends with a moral challenge to the country to live up to its title "land of the free and the brave" and to "send forth the glorious word, / This is not the land of the slave!"

The shorter poem, "Children in Slavery," continues the theme of a country cursed by slavery, this time narrowing the focus to children and the contrast between a carefree, innocent childhood and one marked by the cares and wants of adulthood. Such an unnatural state, Follen writes, must be symptomatic of a deeper social ill: "When children pray with fear all day, / A blight must be at hand: / Then joys decay, and birds of prey / Are hovering o'er the land."

Eliza Follen's poems dealing with social and cultural issues such as slavery help readers understand her later, more public abolitionist efforts in the 1840s and 1850s. Perhaps her greatest interest to contemporary literary scholars lies in her antislavery work. Other contributing factors are recent trends in culture studies, women's studies, and African American studies–which have essentially rewritten the text of American literary history and reshaped the notion of what constitutes literature.

Follen's antislavery writings appeared during a time when the propriety and efficacy of women's entering public discourse were being debated–when activists such as Lydia Maria Child were editing newspapers of public policy (for example, *The National Anti-Slavery Standard*) and when the Grimké sisters were speaking out in public forums on the issues of women's rights and slavery. Two of Follen's early pieces appeared in *The Liberty Bell,* a publication of the Massachusetts Anti-Slavery Society, and the annual gift book that Maria Weston Chapman edited for the Boston Female Anti-Slavery Society. The first essay, "A Morning Walk," is framed around two incidents–one that Follen witnessed and another that she heard related. "Passing occurrences become histories," Follen begins as a way of putting her two stories in context; then she begins subtly to undercut her initial observations that "the poor have nothing to give." Observing a poor black man giving money to a poorer black woman, Follen reflects on the joy such benevolence obviously gave the man and reasons that if, despite the contempt in which they are held, blacks can still be capable of such generosity, then it must be "a strong original principle of their nature." She thus critiques and undercuts her initial rather facile assumptions about the poor by relating what she has witnessed. Such a scene occasions Follen's hopes for "the final elevation of this much injured race." She continues with a story about a black woman who, at a certain time every day, donned her best clothes and went up to a garret to pray, giving thanks to God for her comfortable home with a family who treated her well. Follen ends her piece with a heartfelt plea that the day will come when all this woman's brothers and sisters may be equally grateful–with cause–and may leave their labors and give thanks to God for deliverance. The Christian framework denotes a kind of evangelical abolitionist sentiment that allowed women such as Eliza Follen to use their religious beliefs in the service of such immediate humanitarian causes as the one against slavery.

A year later, in *The Liberty Bell,* Follen published a more polemical essay called "Women's Work," an overtly political statement framed in Christian rhetoric that takes as its thesis the belief that abolishing slavery is indeed women's work. Echoing earlier women writers such as Anne Bradstreet, Follen begins by rehearsing what she calls the whole "catechism" of reasons that many believe women should confine themselves to the domestic sphere. She challenges her audience to consider whether women are not called upon more than men to work at abolishing slavery, since she believes that women, by virtue of their physical vulnerability, sympathize more with the plight of the female slave. In targeting the bondage of the woman slave, Follen, like some of her female contemporaries, linked the fight for women's rights with the abolitionist crusade. Her essay obliquely refers to the difficulty she had in securing women's signatures on the petitions she circulated as part of her efforts in the movement. Follen uses rhetorical questions effectively, leading her readers subtly by cumulative emotional appeals–challenging women to send in their names, to do something for their suffering sisters. Midway through her essay, Follen shifts the appeal from women's innate sympathy for each other to their Christian duty and responsibility toward those less fortunate than they. In a stunning reversal of public sentiment, she affirms that women, precisely because they are not politicians, not "money-makers nor law-makers," are more likely to look clearly and judge the morality of the slavery question. In the absence of an opportunity to work actively for the cause, women can still pray for the sufferers, for the mothers who, unlike them, must face the inevitable separation from their children. Appealing to women's roles as mothers and wives, Follen thus sets the terms of the debate in the domestic sphere while arguing from a public pulpit.

She ends by reiterating her belief that abolishing slavery is women's work; but she broadens the scope of her argument by invoking a specific Christian context–inviting her readers to imitate those holy women who followed Christ despite the angry mobs who vilified them. Such women, Follen asserts, were faithful to the man they knew to be the Son of God. Finally, she denounces those fathers, brothers, or husbands who would hold women back and appeals to her readers' common humanity and shared Christian beliefs.

Eliza Follen's most famous antislavery tract is *To Mothers in the Free States* (1855), in which she continues the empathic stance of "Women's Work" and echoes the maternal discourses of the antislavery conventions by appealing to the sympathy of mothers with children. Her audience is her fellow countrywomen, whom she invites to think of themselves as slave mothers. Daughters of slave mothers, Follen argues, are prey for lascivious white men who exploit, abuse, and dehumanize them. Follen directs those listeners who think she exaggerates to Harriet Beecher Stowe's *Key to Uncle Tom's Cabin* (1853), the author's defense of the facts in her novel. Follen maintains that the owner regards the slave woman the same as he does his cattle: "the law of the land and the customs of society give her to him." Follen claims that the abuse of power resulting from this corrupt system ultimately usurps the prerogative of the Almighty.

After such inflammatory rhetoric, Follen counters probable protests by reiterating the mother's power to mold sons who will refuse to vote for the Fugitive Slave Law or the Nebraska Bill. Such an argument recalls earlier Sunday School publications promoting mothers as shapers of true Christian character; but mothers, Follen contends, must transmit more than generic Christian charity. They can and must teach principles of social justice, just as did the biblical mother in the story of the Maccabees or the early American mothers. Biblical and national history merge in Follen's tract as she leads her audience from these broad concerns to the immediate situation and the climax of her argument–that while Southerners may be the slave owners, the residents of the free states are the slaveholders. Follen maintains that the free states, by their complicity in the South's slaveholding system, remain morally responsible for slavery. She ends her appeal with a series of dramatic rhetorical questions exhorting mothers to heed the cries of the enslaved and realize that "the tender heart of the boy is in the hands of the mother." The mother in Follen's tract ultimately emerges as the angel in the house, called to a "Higher Law" that she must voice and pass on to the future sons of the republic.

During the last decade of her life, Follen became a powerful and persistent voice for the growing abolitionist cause, the concern she shared with her late husband. She wrote and spoke out in public forums, earning a reputation as a strong and respected member of her community. She inspired poet James Russell Lowell, who included her in his poem "Letter from Boston," which is about the antislavery women who conducted bazaars in Faneuil Hall. He writes, "And there, too, was Eliza Follen, / Who scatters fruit-creating pollen / Where'er a blossom she can find / Hardy enough for Truth's north-wind." Follen died in Brookline, Massachusetts, of typhus fever in 1860 at the age of seventy-three.

References:

Nina Baym, *Woman's Fiction: A Guide to Novels by and about Women in America 1820–1870* (Urbana: University of Illinois Press, 1993), pp. 73–75, 80;

Janet Gray, ed., *She Wields a Pen: American Women Poets of the Nineteenth Century* (Iowa City: University of Iowa Press, 1997), pp. 3–6;

Anne Scott MacLeod, *A Moral Tale: Children's Fiction and American Culture* (Hamden, Conn.: Archon Books, 1975), pp. 31–33, 111–113;

Cornelia Meigs, and others, *A Critical History of Children's Literature* (New York: Macmillan, 1953), p. 287;

Helen Waite Papashvily, *All the Happy Endings* (New York: Kennikat Press, 1956), pp. 44–45;

Elizabeth Bancroft Schlesinger, "Two Early Harvard Wives: Eliza Farrrar and Eliza Follen," *New England Quarterly,* 38 (June 1965): 141–167;

Jean Fagan Yellin, *Women and Sisters: The Antislavery Feminists in American Culture* (New Haven: Yale University Press, 1989), p. 60.

Papers:

Eliza Lee (Cabot) Follen's papers are located in the Massachusetts Historical Society, Boston.

Convers Francis

(9 November 1795 – 7 April 1863)

Guy R. Woodall
Tennessee Technological University

Convers Francis

BOOKS: *A Sermon, Delivered January 17, 1821, to the Pastoral Charge of the Third Church and Parish at the Ordination of Mr. Charles Brooks, in Hingham 1821* (Boston: Printed by E. Lincoln, 1821);

On Experimental Religion (Boston: Bowles & Dearborn, 1827);

A Discourse Delivered in Bedford April 30, 1828, before the Middlesex Bible Society (Boston: Bowles & Dearborn, 1828);

Errors in Education: A Discourse Delivered at the Anniversary of the Derby Academy, in Bingham, May 21, 1828 (Bingham, Mass.: Farmer & Brown, 1828);

An Address Delivered 4th of July 1828 at Watertown, in Commemoration of the Anniversary of National Independence (Cambridge, Mass.: Hilliard & Brown, 1828);

An Historical Sketch of Watertown, Massachusetts, from the First Settlement of the Town to the Close of its Second Century (Cambridge, Mass.: E. W. Metcalf, 1830);

The Value of Enlightened Views of Religion (Boston, 1831);

The Christian Change. Described by the Apostle Peter (Boston: Gray & Bowen, 1832);

A Discourse Delivered at Plymouth, Mass., Dec. 22, 1832, in Commemoration of the Landing of the Fathers (Plymouth: Printed by A. Danforth, 1832);

Popery & Its Kindred Principles Unfriendly to the Improvement of Man; A Lecture Delivered May 8th 1833. The Dudleian Lecture, Delivered before the University at Cambridge (Cambridge, Mass., 1833);

The Dust to Earth, the Spirit to God: A Discourse Delivered before the Congregational Society in Watertown, on Sunday, March 17, 1833 (Boston: I. R. Butts, 1833);

Christianity as a Purely Internal Principle (Boston: L. C. Bowles, 1836);

Life of John Eliot, the Apostle to the Indians, in *Library of American Biography,* edited by Jared Sparks (Boston: Hilliard, Gray, 1836), V: 1–357;

Three Discourses Delivered before the Congregational Society in Watertown; Two upon Leaving the Old Meeting-House; and One at the Dedication of the New (Cambridge, Mass.: Folsom, Wells & Thurston, 1836);

Memoir of Dr. Gamaliel Bradford, M.D. (Cambridge, Mass.: E. W. Metcalf, 1839);

The Death of the Aged: A Discourse Preached to the First Church and Society in Concord, Mass., on the Morning of Sunday, September 26, 1841, the Sabbath after the Funeral of Their Late Senior Pastor, Rev. Ezra Ripley, D.D. (Boston: Munroe, 1841);

Christ the Way to God (Boston: Munroe, 1842);

Memoir of Hon. Judge John Davis, LL.D. (Cambridge, Mass.: E. W. Metcalf, 1848).

OTHER: *Life of Sebastian Rale, Missionary to the Indians,* in *Library of American Biography,* edited by Sparks (Boston: Little & Brown, 1845), VII: 157–233;

"The Journals of Convers Francis," edited by Guy R. Woodall, part 1, in *Studies in the American Renaissance 1981,* edited by Joel Myerson (Boston: Twayne, 1981), pp. 265–343; part 2, in *Studies in the American Renaissance 1982,* edited by Myerson (Boston: Twayne, 1982), pp. 227–284;

"The Selected Sermons of Convers Francis," edited by Woodall, part 1, in *Studies in the American Renaissance 1987,* edited by Myerson (Charlottesville: University Press of Virginia, 1987), pp. 73–129; part 2, in *Studies in the American Renaissance 1988,* edited by Myerson (Charlottesville: University Press of Virginia, 1988), pp. 55–131.

SELECTED PERIODICAL PUBLICATIONS–UNCOLLECTED: "On the Use of the Word 'Mystery,'" *Christian Disciple,* 2, new series (November–December 1820): 429–436;

"Remarks on Matt. XXVIII: 19, translated from the German," *Christian Disciple,* new series, 3 (March–April 1821): 89–97;

"The Gospel, a New Creation," *Christian Disciple,* new series, 4 (July–August 1822): 225–235;

"Obituary Notice of the Late Rev. Dr. Osgood," *Christian Disciple,* new series, 4 (November–December 1822): 464;

"Reason and Faith," *Christian Examiner,* 3 (March 1826): 99–103;

"South's Sermons with a Sketch of his Life and Character," *Christian Examiner,* 4 (January 1827): 230–242;

"On Love to Christ," *Liberal Preacher,* 1 (November 1827): 73–82;

"Paley's *Life and Writings,*" *Christian Examiner,* 5 (March 1828): 113–134;

Johann Gottfried von Herder, "Aurora's Complaint to the Gods," "The Lily and the Rose," and "The Complaint of the Rose," translated by Francis, in *Juvenile Miscellany,* 4 (March, May, and July 1828): 90; 221–223; 269–270;

Herder, "The Dying Swan," "Echo," and "Night and Day," translated by Francis, in *Juvenile Miscellany,* 1, new series (September, November 1828; January 1829): 36–39; 133–135; 284–285;

"An Article in the *North American Review* on the Removal of the Indians," *American Monthly Magazine,* 1 (January 1830): 701–718;

"The Presence of God with the Good Man," *Liberal Preacher,* new series, 1 (July 1831): 100;

"Old English Writers. The Library of Old English Prose Writers," *Christian Examiner,* 11 (September 1831): 1–26;

"Natural Theology; or Essays on the Existence of Deity, and of Providence, on the Immateriality of the Soul, and a Future State," *Christian Examiner,* 12 (March 1832): 193–220;

"The Value of Enlightened Views of Religion," *Liberal Preacher,* new series, 2 (May 1832): 73–86;

"'The Friendship of the World,'" *Unitarian Advocate,* new series, 5 (May 1832): 204–212;

"Plan of the Founder of Christianity by Reinhart and Memoirs and Confessions of Reinhart," *Christian Examiner,* 13 (September 1832): 364–385;

"Popery and Its Kindred Principles Unfriendly to the Improvement of Man. A Dudleian Lecture on Popery, May 8, 1833," *Christian Examiner,* new series, 9 (July 1833): 371–395;

"Grace as Connected with Salvation," *Liberal Preacher,* new series, 3 (November 1833): 141–164;

"Anti-slavery Principles and Proceedings," *Christian Examiner,* third series, 25 (September 1838): 228–255.

The Reverend Convers Francis, D.D., was one of the most erudite Unitarian ministers and university professors of his time. His career was almost evenly divided by his tenure of twenty-three years as pastor of the First Parish Congregational Church in Watertown, Massachusetts, and his professorship of twenty-one years in the Divinity School at Harvard. After his death, memorialists remembered him as a pioneer in the German language and theology in America, an excellent biographer and historian, a collector of rare and esoteric books, a popular teacher, a supporter of public reforms, and a beloved pastor and pulpit minister. He was a member of the Massachusetts Historical Society and the New England Historic and Genealogical Society. Although he was a member of the Transcendental Club, he was never a major force in the New England Transcendentalist movement, though he was a strong influence in it. His name was often linked to that of his famous sister, the poet-novelist-reformer Lydia Maria Child. Because of his amiable nature and ability as a conversationalist, he was always a welcomed guest at Boston and Cambridge social gatherings, but his reserved manner precluded wide popularity. As an author, Francis wrote altogether in the interest of scholarship and the dissemination of knowledge, confining himself to histories, biographies, religious pamphlets, translations, and miscellaneous reviews. While not so copious as that

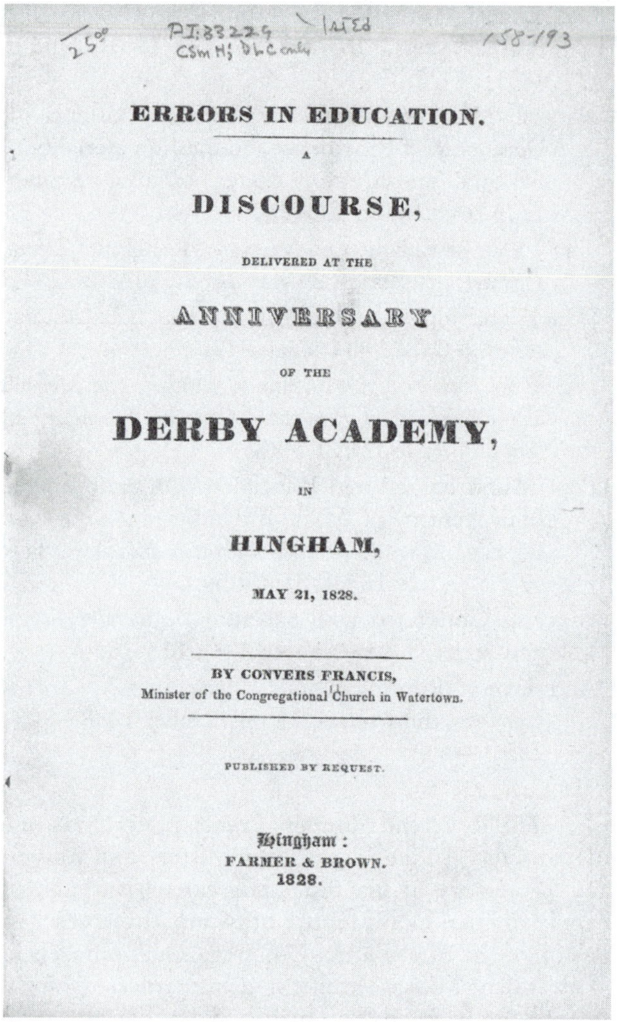
ERRORS IN EDUCATION.

A

DISCOURSE,

DELIVERED AT THE

ANNIVERSARY

OF THE

DERBY ACADEMY,

IN

HINGHAM,

MAY 21, 1828.

BY CONVERS FRANCIS,

Minister of the Congregational Church in Watertown.

PUBLISHED BY REQUEST.

Hingham:

FARMER & BROWN.

1828.

Title page for a discourse in which Francis called for educational reforms (Collection of Joel Myerson)

of many of his illustrious contemporaries, his literary output was quite substantial and respectable.

Convers Francis was born on 9 November 1795 in West Cambridge, Massachusetts, the fifth of six children of Convers Francis Sr. and Susanna (Rand) Francis. Convers Francis Sr., a baker first in West Cambridge and then in Medford, traced his ancestors to Richard Francis, an early colonist who settled in 1640 in Cambridge. Young Convers helped his father in the bakery and was first educated in the Medford town school. In his fifteenth year, in what he called "the great event of my boyhood," his father offered him the opportunity, which he accepted, to go to college. He entered Harvard College in August 1811 and was graduated with an A.B. degree with honors on 30 August 1815. Since at the time there was no organized school of divinity at Harvard (it was in its formative state), he remained in Cambridge for three years to study divinity under some of the most learned Congregational theologians of the time, among whom were Dr. Henry Ware and Andrews Norton. By the time Francis finished his studies at Harvard, he had mastered Latin, Greek, and Hebrew, and he soon afterward became proficient in French, Spanish, and German. At Francis's death, the Reverend Frederic Henry Hedge, himself a pioneer in the German language and theology in America, praised Francis's contributions as a scholar and innovator in German and as one of the best read scholars in German theology in America. From his youth a lover of books, he systematically collected from home and abroad an impressive library that eventually numbered about eight thousand volumes, many of which were esoteric and rare.

He was licensed to preach by the Boston Association of Congregational Ministers on 15 November 1818. The First Parish Congregational Society and the Selectmen of Watertown called him in the spring of 1819 to be their minister. On 23 June 1819 he was formally ordained. He preached at Watertown for twenty-three years; it was his first and only parish. On 15 May 1822 Francis married Abby Bradford Allyn, daughter of the Reverend John Allyn, D.D., of Duxbury, Massachusetts. To Convers and Abby were born four children, two of whom died in infancy and Abby Bradford and George Convers. Neither ever married.

At Watertown Francis quickly earned a reputation as an effective pulpit minister and untiring shepherd of his flock. His popularity extended beyond Watertown. In a time when pulpit exchanges were the ultimate test of fellowship, there was scarcely a Unitarian minister in the whole Boston area with whom he did not repeatedly exchange. His pulpit manner was simple and unaffected. He invariably read his carefully written sermons. He prepared his sermons to inspire his listeners to greater knowledge and spirituality, never to frighten or to intimidate them. The subject matter of his sermons fell generally into the categories of external nature, religious doctrine, reform, and civic responsibilities. Francis's natural affection for and responsiveness to nature were hardly surpassed by that of William Wordsworth, his favorite poet. Many of his sermons were larded with references to nature, but many more were written altogether on the subject of nature. To Francis there was never a conflict between natural religion and revealed religion, since they were both consonant to the soul's own law of belief. Another distinctive group of his sermons deals wholly with the subject of religion per se. In these sermons a recurring idea is that true religion addresses the mind and soul of man, not the body and physical senses. External forms–for example, the Lord's Supper–in religion, however, are not to be despised and discarded, for they are outward helps to man for effecting internal changes of the heart. Since they are only means to an end, however, they are not absolutely indispensable in religion. A second thread that runs through the sermons on religion is that intuition or a priori reasoning is extremely important, but religious truths cannot be apprehended exclusively by it; one must depend also upon the revealed scriptures. A third group of Francis's sermons deals with social reforms. At Watertown, Francis was slow to embrace the popular reforms, but after moving to the Divinity School, he began cautiously to accept some of them, though he never became as highly vocal or conspicuous a reformer as his friends Theodore Parker, Amos Bronson Alcott, James Freeman Clarke, or Francis's sister, Lydia Maria Child. At the end of Francis's life, though, Parker remembered with appreciation Francis's positive stance against slavery, and Franklin Benjamin Sanborn remembered Francis as "a friend of all practical reforms."

Francis was not long at Watertown before he began to establish a reputation as a writer–publishing articles, reviews, and translations; tracts and pamphlets on biographical, historical, and theological subjects; and books. His first four periodical articles were published in the *Christian Disciple* between 1820 and 1822. Three of these essays dealt with matters of hermeneutics; the fourth was an obituary notice of his former pastor, David Osgood of Medford. Between 1828 and 1832 Francis translated from German six fables and moral tales by Johann Gottfried von Herder and also supplied at least a dozen brief essays for a column titled *Scripture Illustrations* for the *Juvenile Miscellany,* a Boston journal published by Lydia Maria Child. He published eight articles between 1826 and 1838 in the *Christian Examiner;* most were reviews of the works of British and German clerics and theologians. Two of the *Examiner* articles are singular: "Popery and Its Kindred Principles Unfriendly to the Improvement of Man" (1833) is a printing of the Dudleian lecture that he had delivered at Harvard in May 1833, and "Anti-slavery Principles and Proceedings" (1838) is an essay that calls attention to the dangers of philanthropic associations in effecting public reforms, though he pleads for a respectful hearing of the abolitionists. In "An Article in the *North American Review* on the Removal of the Indians. The Letters of William Penn" in the *American Monthly Magazine* (1830), Francis expresses outrage at the perfidious treatment of the Indians by the U.S. government. Between 1832 and 1834 he contributed other pieces to the *American Monthly Review, Unitarian Advocate, Scriptural Interpreter,* and *Liberal Preacher.*

In 1821 Francis had printed as a pamphlet, or tract, the first of many sermons. Several of these pamphlets were a part of the American Unitarian Association Tract series, the first of which was *On Experimental Religion* (1827). In this tract he stressed that true "experimental religion" was experienced with the feelings. His first full-length book was *An Historical Sketch of Watertown, Massachusetts, from the First Settlement of the Town to the Close of its Second Century* (1830). This history grew out of an historical address that Francis gave upon the occasion of a celebration in Watertown marking the second centennial of the town. Reviewers praised the history for its completeness and its just balance between events related to the church and town.

The year 1836 was a memorable year in Francis's life because the publication of some works brought him recognition, which in turn brought about new group associations. In this year he published his *Life of John Eliot, the Apostle to the Indians,* in Jared Sparks's *Library of American Biography.* The Reverend George Putnam said in a review of the biography in the *Christian Examiner* (September 1836) that no one was so intimately acquainted with New England antiquity as Francis and that he had set a high standard for accuracy in treating colonial history. On the merits of his history and biography, Francis was elected a member of the Massachusetts Historical Society in 1837. He remained an active member of this society for the rest of his life and at his death was ninth member in seniority. Another signal event in 1836 was the publication of *Christianity as a Purely Internal Principle,* his second tract in the American Unitarian Tract Series. In it he held that true religion relies much upon intuition: "It dwells not," he said, "among the poor corruptible things of the sense." With this tract he clearly identified himself with the liberal branch of the Unitarian Church.

Many passages in Francis's journals and letters deal with the division of the orthodox Congregationalists and Unitarians, and then the Unitarians into liberal and conservative groups. His sympathies usually lay with the more liberal Unitarians. Noting accounts of recent publications in 1836 by such friends and acquaintances as the Reverend George Ripley, Orestes A. Brownson, William H. Furness, and Amos Bronson Alcott, Francis said he had long seen that the Unitarians were going to divide into two parties–the English (the materialists or empiricists) and the German (the spiritualists or idealists). He felt that the latter had more truth but would for a

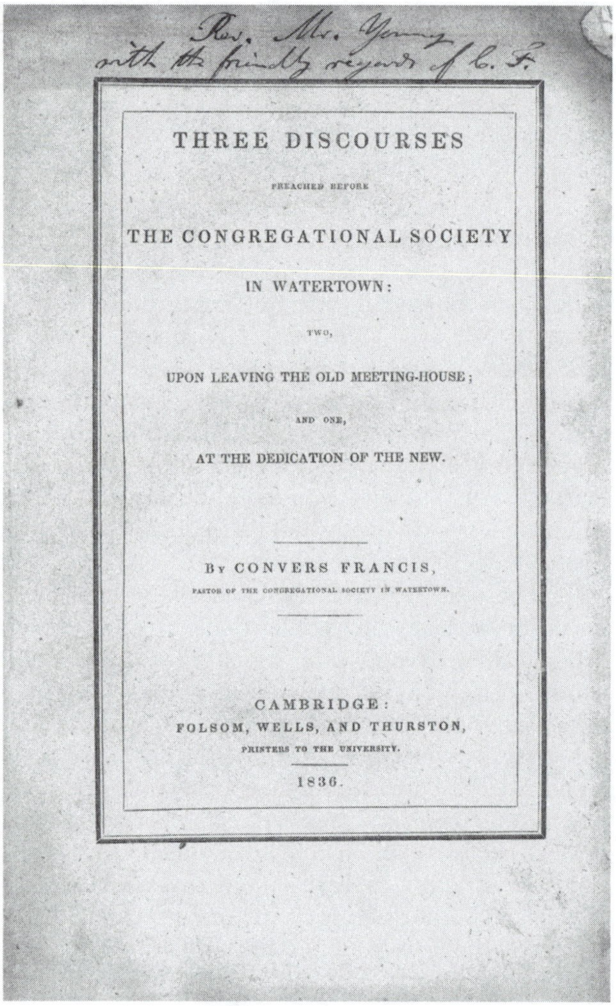
Rev. Mr. Young
with the friendly regards of C. F.

THREE DISCOURSES

PREACHED BEFORE

THE CONGREGATIONAL SOCIETY

IN WATERTOWN:

TWO,

UPON LEAVING THE OLD MEETING-HOUSE;

AND ONE,

AT THE DEDICATION OF THE NEW.

BY CONVERS FRANCIS,

PASTOR OF THE CONGREGATIONAL SOCIETY IN WATERTOWN.

CAMBRIDGE:
FOLSOM, WELLS, AND THURSTON,
PRINTERS TO THE UNIVERSITY.

1836.

Title page for a collection of Francis's sermons (Collection of Joel Myerson)

time be ridiculed. He wrote in his journal, though, that the cause of spiritual truth would gain far more by them than the others. About the time of this journal entry, Francis entered a new and stimulating phase of his life: on the evening of 19 September 1836, he met with the Transcendental Club in its first gathering in Boston at the home of Ripley. In no place was Francis more closely and more conspicuously linked with the liberal party of the Unitarian Church than in his association with the Transcendental Club, variously called Hedge's Club and the Symposium; it included, among others, such liberal young ministers as Ralph Waldo Emerson, Ripley, Brownson, Furness, Hedge, Clarke, Parker, Cyrus A. Bartol, and Caleb Stetson. Several women, including Margaret Fuller, often met with the group. Francis was the eldest member of this coterie and by reason of his age served as moderator at the meetings. His genial nature and freedom from dogmatism fitted him well for this role. Octavius Brooks Frothingham, in his *Boston Unitarianism: 1820–1850* (1890), characterized Francis as "absolutely free from dogmatism,–the dogmatism of the liberal as well as the dogmatism of the conservative." In a letter to Emerson on 9 May 1837, club member Alcott, the educator-philosopher, praised Francis as a moderator, saying, "In the spiritual Horolog he is an admiral balance wheel to keep all movements in fit order. Such Men are most useful." Francis's attraction to the club was always more literary and philosophical than theological. Unlike some of the others, especially Ripley and Parker, he was not an active church reformer. He was comfortable with the traditional Unitarian theism, forms, and dogma, and he allowed others wide latitude in interpreting such things as they wished. His tolerance for the views of others and disdain for exclusiveness endeared him to the liberal Unitarians.

After the Transcendental Club ceased to meet, Francis continued to maintain a close friendship with most members. He and Emerson, whom he had watched grow up, were frequent visitors in each other's homes. When Emerson was a divinity student at Cambridge, he preached in Francis's pulpit, and later when Emerson was pastor of the Second Church in Boston and then in East Lexington, the two exchanged pulpit favors. When Emerson turned to a career as lecturer, Francis often attended the lectures and recorded his reaction to them, nearly always favorably, in his journals. When Emerson's orthodoxy was questioned after the controversial Divinity School Address in 1838, Francis was a faithful apologist and defender. Francis did not always share Emerson's views on theological matters, but he was tolerant of them and praised Emerson's saintliness and eloquence. Francis thought that Emerson sometimes dwelled too much in the ideal rather than the actual but recorded in his journal that it was unfortunate that the Divinity School faculty and Boston clergy were unable to see Emerson as a "gifted seer" but instead branded him as a "visionary," "pretender," and "fanatic."

Among the heterodox Unitarians, Parker was the one whom Francis most admired and whose intellectual companionship he most valued. Francis was Parker's mentor. Their friendship was secured by Francis's vast classical and theological knowledge and great library, and by Parker's love of books and desire to learn. In 1832 and 1833 Francis prepared the young Parker to enter Harvard and eventually interceded successfully in 1840 for Harvard to grant Parker an honorary M.A. degree. Francis was Parker's principal source for books and help in theological matters. Francis greatly respected Parker's independent thinking and prodigious intellect but did not always agree with his radical theology. Francis quietly supported Parker when he incurred the wrath of the Boston Association of Congregational Ministers with his pamphlet *The Previous Questions between Mr. Andrews Norton and His Alumni . . .* (1840); his Charles C. Shackford ordination sermon, *The Transient and the Permanent* (1841); his article "The Hollis St. Council" in the *Dial* (1842); and his pamphlet *A Discourse of Matters Pertaining to Religion* (1842). When the Boston Association denounced *A Discourse of Matters Pertaining to Religion* as "vehemently deistical" and "subversive to Christianity as a particular religion," Francis wrote in his journal that he regretted the condemnation but felt, in fairness, that Parker had to bear some blame because his spirit was "bad, derisive, sarcastic, arrogant, contemptuous of what the wise and good hold sacred."

In Francis's Watertown years he maintained close connections with his alma mater. In the 1820s he was a frequent and popular speaker in college chapel–engagements that, as he confided in his private journals, were daunting. In 1829 he was invited to deliver the Phi Beta Kappa oration. He was chosen to deliver the annual Dudleian lecture on 8 May 1833, the subject of which was "Popery & Its Kindred Principles Unfriendly to the Improvement of Man." In 1836 he delivered the valedictory sermon before the senior class in the Divinity School. In 1837, in recognition of his attainments and services, Harvard awarded him the S.T.D. (Doctor of Sacred Theology) degree. On many later occasions he was elected to the Board of Overseers in the Divinity School.

But Francis's periodic connection with Harvard and his career changed completely when on 15 June 1842 he accepted an appointment succeeding the Reverend Henry Ware Jr. as the Parkman Professor of Pulpit Eloquence and Pastoral Care in the Divinity School at Harvard University. He moved to Cambridge to begin his teaching in September 1842. Because of the doctrinal differences between the conservative ministers in the Boston Association of Congregational Ministers and the liberal Unitarian ministers, the choice of a successor for Ware was not easy; but after a painstaking consideration, Francis was offered the position, mainly because of his superb theological credentials and his gentle spirit. He agonized over whether or not to accept the appointment but finally did so at the encouragement of the Reverend James Walker, Parker, and other liberal and moderate ministers. The compelling reason for his acceptance, as he suggested in his journal on 24 September 1842, was that he felt his appointment would be good for the denomination and for the Divinity School. The opportunity to exchange his pulpit in a rural parish for the classroom and a world of books at the Divinity School was surely a factor also in his decision to move, as perhaps was a substantial increase in salary. Probably the most painful aspect of his move to Cambridge came when he asked Parker to free him from a previous commitment to fill his pulpit. Francis felt that the cancellation would meliorate some of the animosity of the conservative ministers. Parker acceded to Francis's request for a cancellation but felt betrayed by Francis's lack of courage. Parker's disappointment was short lived, however, for within a brief time Francis was again preaching for him.

Before and even after Francis accepted the professorship at Cambridge, he was suspected by some of the conservative ministers of being a dangerous Transcendentalist. The Boston Association tested Francis's orthodoxy by asking him to speak at the Thursday Lecture on 23 July 1842. Of the unpleasant affair, he wrote somewhat sarcastically in his journal: "The sermon, I believe, gave some satisfaction to those who have been disposed to accuse me of the horrible crime of transcendentalism! Oh the folly, as well as wickedness, of the *odium theologicum!* It is just as bad in the nineteenth as in the fifteenth or sixteenth century,–just as bad among Unitarians as among straitest of the Orthodox." The sermon that he preached, "Afar Off–Made Nigh by the Blood of Christ," was doctrinally conservative and probably did satisfy some of his critics because it affirmed the value of historical Christianity. But the sermon was not a retreat from his liberal views or his tolerance for heterodoxy. Moreover, he continued to preach in the pulpits of known liberal ministers, including all those with whom he was associated in the Transcendental Club. When Parker went abroad for the sake of his health in 1843–1844, Francis regularly filled his pulpit at West Roxbury. He was quite aware that his friendship with Parker had incurred the displeasure of many in the Boston Association, but their reaction did not trouble him much. On 22 June 1844 he wrote with humor on this matter to Parker, then in Italy: "If the bigotry of Unitarian *liberality* should bind me up in the bundle of condemnation with you, why I would rather go to hell with you than to heaven with them, though I am inclined to think the direction of the two parties might be the reverse of this." Francis never directly confronted the conservative clergymen because they never made any definite charges against his teaching. By 1845 he found fewer occasions to express his disappointment with the exclusive spirit of the Boston ministers because the

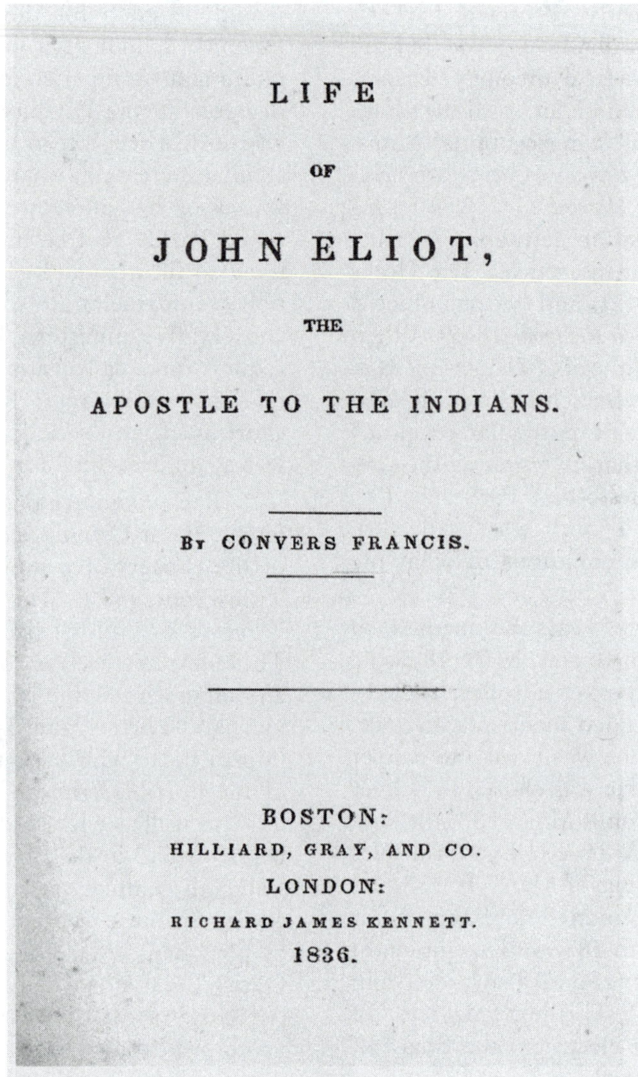
LIFE

OF

JOHN ELIOT,

THE

APOSTLE TO THE INDIANS.

BY CONVERS FRANCIS.

BOSTON:
HILLIARD, GRAY, AND CO.
LONDON:
RICHARD JAMES KENNETT.
1836.

Title page for Francis's biography of the revered Puritan clergyman who in 1663 translated the Bible into Algonquian for the use of Massachusetts Indians, one of his contributions to Jared Sparks's collection of American biographies

Transcendentalist ministers had so risen in popularity as not to be threatened by them.

When Francis began teaching at the Divinity School, he entered immediately upon courses titled Lectures on Ecclesiastical History, The Review of the Criticism of Sermons, Composition of Original Sermons (with the Senior Class), Style and Composition, Writing of Essays, the Doctrine and Office of Prayer (with the Middle Class), Cicero, and *De Natura Deorum* (with the Junior Class). For one-half of each year he preached to the college students on Sundays and until 1856 conducted a daily chapel program. Francis strove to inspire his students with a love of learning. His favorite method of teaching was to present all points of view on a subject and then have his students weigh and sift them to arrive at what they felt was the truth. Once, after reading in Cicero about the injurious effect of *auctoritas,* or a teacher's being dictatorial, Francis wrote in his journal, "I believe the way of *auctoritas* would have made me more popular, both among the students and in the Unitarian denomination, strange as it may seem. Most people like to be told what to accept, than to be put upon finding it out for themselves." Some did indeed accuse him of lacking commitment to any one point of view because of his refusal to dogmatize, but most who knew him seemed to understand and appreciate his teaching method. At times Francis was at a loss to understand the slothful and indifferent study practices of some students. In a letter to Parker, 14 April 1844, he attributed the lack of "manly" hard study among his students to their chasing after popular current philanthropies and relying too much upon intuition, a "one-sided" misconception they had gotten from Emerson, which made them think books were but "fetters and encumbrances."

Once established in the Divinity School, Francis did not write quite as often for publication as he had in his Watertown years. One work, however, that drew favorable notices was *Life of Sebastian Rale, Missionary to the Indians* in Sparks's *Library of American Biography* (1845). In 1846 he published the "Memoir of Dr. Gamaliel Bradford" in the *Collections of the Massachusetts Historical Society,* and in 1849 he published the "Memoir of Judge Davis" in the same journal. (Both had earlier been published separately.) Francis's historical and biographical scholarship earned him membership in the New England Historic and Genealogical Society in 1847.

Francis's salutary influence in the Divinity School began to be noticed soon after his arrival at Cambridge. Parker wrote to Francis on 26 September 1842 that he had heard of the good changes already evident in the school: "The school already wears a new aspect, as it has a new soul; that you stimulate the dull and correct the erratic, and set right such as have prejudices inclining to narrowness, if not bigotry." Samuel Johnson, a former student of Francis, wrote to Edward Everett Hale in August 1850, praising Francis for encouraging freedom of thought among the students. Johnson said that any trouble that the Divinity School had experienced lay not with Francis but rather with the "meddlesome Boston Association." The Reverend John Weiss, Francis's successor at Watertown, observed that Francis's generous spirit was responsible for the more generous attitude of the young ministers who were presently being graduated from the Divinity School. Frothingham, in his *Boston Unitarianism,* said Francis's influence in broadening the Unitarian pulpit was "second to none." In her *Transcendentalism in New England* (1897), Caroline Healey Dall recalled Francis's liberalizing influence on others as probably his most salient feature. One telling evidence that liberal changes took place in the Divinity School after Francis's arrival was that several ministers once associated with the Transcendentalist movement were invited from time to time to speak on commencement occasions. Among these ministers were Samuel J. May (1847), Frederic Henry Hedge (1849), and Thomas Treadwell Stone (1856). Theodore Parker was invited in 1857 by the divinity students themselves but was rejected by the college administration. When May was invited by the students to speak, he was informed that he been chosen specifically "to represent that movement called Transcendentalism."

Francis was devoted to his students and the classroom to the end of his life. In his last days he had become so weakened by a debilitating disease that he had his students carry him to his lecture room in a chair. Soon, when he was unable even to be carried to the classroom, he had them meet classes in his home study. He continued to give instruction until Friday, 27 March 1863, when his increasing weakness obliged him for the first time in his career to dismiss a class before the hour was over. He died on 7 April 1863 of a "scirrhous disease." His funeral was conducted on 10 April 1863 at his home in Cambridge, where George R. Noyes, a colleague, read the scriptures, and the Reverend John Weiss made some "most touching and appropriate" remarks. Francis was interred at the Watertown Cemetery in a grave beside that of his beloved wife, who had died in 1860. Francis bequeathed his massive library to the Divinity School, and on 3 September 1863 his old friend and colleague Hedge selected 2,300 books from the library to be placed in a special room and catalogued under the title "The Francis Library."

Francis's contributions to the American Renaissance were positive but modest when considered beside those of his many popular and illustrious friends and colleagues in the Brahmin and Transcendentalist circles. His early study of Plato, Henry More, Immanuel Kant, and Samuel Taylor Coleridge led him philosophically to esteem highly a priori reasoning and the organic principle and to value less John Locke's empiricism and Sir Isaac Newton's mechanism. Francis's faith in intuition and organicism helped establish a favorable climate in which new intellectual movements in New England, including Transcendentalism, could flourish. Without being aware of it, he became an apostle of change when he early became a devoted student of the German language and German theology. He, along with George Bancroft, Hedge, and Ripley, opened the door for the liberalizing influence of the New Criticism of the German theologians to enter more freely into the Unitarian denomination and into the Divinity School at Harvard. His literary remains are relatively small, but they are large and significant enough to help document the social and religious changes in the American Renaissance. Some writers–such as the historian John Gorham Palfrey, the poet Henry Wadsworth Longfellow, the poet-essayist Emerson, the theologian-reformer Parker, the educator-philosopher Alcott, and the poet-novelist-reformer Lydia Maria Child–sought his advice on literary and theological matters, but he seems to have exerted little or no direct influence upon the thinking of any of his contemporaries, with the exception of

Parker. He opened Parker's mind to liberal German theology and inspired him to humane preaching. As an apologist for a more liberal and inclusive Unitarianism, moreover, Francis helped to create a congenial atmosphere that allowed the ideas of diverse groups to be heard with less prejudice.

Letters:

Gary L. Collison, "A Critical Edition of the Correspondence of Theodore Parker and Convers Francis, 1836–1859," dissertation, Pennsylvania State University, 1979.

Biographies:

John Weiss, *Discourse Occasioned by the Death of Convers Francis, Delivered before the First Congregational Society, Watertown, April 19, 1863* (Cambridge, Mass.: Welch, Bigelow, 1863);

William Newell, "Memoir of the Rev. Convers Francis, D. D.," *Proceedings of the Massachusetts Historical Society,* 8 (1865): 233–253;

Mossetta Vaughan, *Sketch of the Life and Work of Convers Francis, D.D.* (Watertown, Mass.: Historical Society of Watertown, 1944).

References:

Octavius Brooks Frothingham, *Boston Unitarianism 1820–1850: A Study of the Life and Works of Nathaniel Langdon Frothingham* (New York: Putnam, 1890), pp. 170–174;

Frothingham, *Transcendentalism in New England: A History* (New York: Putnam, 1876), pp. 353–356;

Joel Myerson, "Convers Francis and Emerson," *American Literature,* 70 (1978): 17–36;

Guy R. Woodall, "Convers Francis," in *The Transcendentalists: A Review of Research and Criticism,* edited by Joel Myerson (New York: MLA, 1984), pp. 167–170;

Woodall, "Convers Francis and the Concordians: Emerson, Alcott, and Others," *Concord Saunterer,* 1 (Fall 1993): 23–58;

Woodall, "Convers Francis, the Transcendentalists, and the Boston Association of Ministers," *Proceedings of the Unitarian Universalist Historical Society,* 21, part 2 (1989): 41–48;

Woodall, "The Record of a Friendship: The Letters of Convers Francis to Frederic Henry Hedge in Bangor and Providence 1835–1850," in *Studies in the American Renaissance 1991,* edited by Myerson (Charlottesville: University Press of Virginia, 1991), pp. 1–57.

Papers:

About two thousand of Convers Francis's manuscript sermons, one section of his journals, and holographic records in Francis's hand of the First Parish Congregational Church of Watertown are in the Free Public Library at Watertown, Massachusetts. One large fragment of Francis's journals is in the Houghton Library of Harvard University. There are about two hundred and fifty manuscript letters by and to Francis in the holdings at the Boston Public Library; three Harvard University libraries–the Houghton Library, the Harvard University Archives at the Pusey Library, and the Andover-Harvard Theological Library; the Massachusetts Historical Society; and the Bangor Historical Society.

William Henry Furness

(20 April 1802 - 30 January 1896)

Esther Lopez
University of Rochester

BOOKS: *A Discourse Preached at the Dedication of the First Congregational Unitarian Church, Philadelphia, November 5, 1828* (Philadelphia: Printed for First Congregational Unitarian Church, 1828);

A Discourse, Preached in the First Congregational Unitarian Church (Philadelphia: Printed for R. H. Small, 1829);

A Discourse, Preached in the First Congregational Unitarian Church, on the Morning of the Lord's Day, May 24, 1829. Occasioned by the Recent Emancipation of the Roman Catholics Throughout the British Empire . . . (Philadelphia: Printed for R. H. Small, 1829; Liverpool & London: F. B. Wright, 1829);

The Genius of Christianity (Boston: Gray & Bowen, 1830; London, 1830);

An Address Delivered in the First Congregational Unitarian Church in Philadelphia, on the Morning of the Lord's Day, Sept. 4, 1831 (Philadelphia, 1831);

A Sermon Delivered in the First Congregational Unitarian Church on the Evening of the Lord's Day, January 1, 1832 (Philadelphia: Jesper Harding, 1832);

A Sermon, Delivered in the First Congregational Unitarian Church in Philadelphia, on the Morning of the Lord's Day, October 20, 1833 (Philadelphia: John C. Clark, 1833);

An Address, Delivered in the Room over the Northern Liberties Reading-Room: On the Afternoon of Sunday, Dec. 13, 1835 (Philadelphia: John C. Clark, 1836);

A Sermon, Preached at the First Church in Medford, Sunday, May 1, 1836 (Charlestown, Mass.: Office of the Aurora, 1836);

Remarks on the Four Gospels (Philadelphia: Carey, Lea & Blanchard, 1836; London: C. Fox, 1837); revised as *Jesus and His Biographers* (Philadelphia: Carey, Lea & Blanchard, 1838);

Our Benevolent Institutions: A Discourse Occasioned by the Death of Julius R. Friedlander, Principal of the Pennsylvania Institution for the Blind, and Delivered, Sunday, March 24, 1839 (Philadelphia: C. Sherman, 1839);

Domestic Worship (Pittsburgh: C. H. Kay, 1839);

William Henry Furness

A Discourse Delivered on the Morning of the Lord's Day, January 19, 1840, in the First Congregational Unitarian Church, Occasioned by the Loss of the Lexington (Philadelphia: C. A. Elliott, 1840);

A Discourse Delivered on the Occasion of the Death of John Vaughan, in the First Congregational Unitarian Church, Sunday, Jan. 16, 1842 . . . with the Services at the Funeral (Philadelphia: J. Crissy, 1842);

A Discourse, Delivered on the Occasion of the Erection in the Church of Tablets: In Memory of John Vaughan, Ralph Eddowes, and William Y. Birch, August 20th, 1842 (Philadelphia: J. Crissy, 1842);
Communion with the Unseen; Discourse, Oct. 1, 1843 (Philadelphia: J. Crissy, 1843);
The Ministry of Women. A Discourse, Delivered Nov. 20, 1842 (Philadelphia: J. Crissy, 1843);
Two Discourses Occasioned by the Approaching Anniversary of the Declaration of Independence. Delivered June 25, A.M., and July 2, A.M., 1843 (Philadelphia: J. Pennington, 1843);
Religion, a Principle, Not a Form. A Discourse, Delivered on the Lord's Day, March 17, 1844, in the First Congregational Unitarian Church, in Reference to the Question Concerning the Use of the Bible in the Public Schools . . . (Philadelphia: J. Crissy, 1844);
A Christmas Sermon, December 25, 1844 (Philadelphia? 1844);
A Brief Statement of the Christian View of the Atonement (Boston: J. Munroe, 1845);
A Funeral Discourse . . . May 4th, 1845 (Philadelphia? 1845);
The Exclusive Principle Considered: Two Sermons on Christian Union and the Truth of the Gospels (Boston: B. H. Greene, 1845);
A Word for Peace: A Christmas Discourse . . . December 25th, 1845 (Philadelphia: J. Crissy, 1845);
Two Discourses Delivered in the First Congregational Unitarian Church, on the Sundays, January 26, and February 2, 1845 (Philadelphia: J. Crissy, 1845);
A Thanksgiving Discourse . . . Nov. 27th, 1845 (Philadelphia, 1845);
The Kingdom of Heaven: A Sermon Preached at the Installation of Rev. John T. Sargent, as Pastor of the First Congregational Church in Somerville, Mass., Wednesday, February 18, 1846 (Somerville, Mass.: E. Tufts, 1846);
The Spirit of the Pilgrims: An Oration Delivered Before the Society of the Sons of New England of Philadelphia December 22d, 1846, in Commemoration of the Landing of the Pilgrims CCXXVI Years Ago (Philadelphia: J. C. Clark, 1846);
Nature and Christianity: A Dudleian Lecture: Delivered in the Chapel of the University of Cambridge, Wednesday, May 12, 1847 (Boston: Crosby & Nichols, 1847);
Doing Before Believing: A Discourse Delivered at the Anniversary of the Derby Academy in Hingham, May 19, 1847 (New York: W. S. Dorr, 1847);
The Son of Man Cometh: A Discourse Preached Before the Society of the Cambridgeport Parish, Sunday, May 30, 1847 (Boston: J. Munroe, 1847);
The Mediation of Christ: A Discourse Delivered . . . October 10th, 1847 (Philadelphia, Thomas H. Town, 1847);
The Memory of the Just: A Discourse Delivered in the First Congregational Unitarian Church, in Philadelphia, February 27, 1848 (Philadelphia: Crissy & Markley, 1848);
An Address Delivered before the Art Union of Philadelphia in the Academy of Fine Arts . . . October 12th, 1848 (Philadelphia: Griggs & Adams, 1848);
A Sermon on the True Nature of Worship, Preached Febr. 11, 1849 . . . (New York, 1849);
Sunday Travel: A Discourse Delivered Sunday Morning, April 28, 1850, in the First Congregational Unitarian Church in Philadelphia (Philadelphia: C. Sherman, 1850);
A History of Jesus (Boston: Crosby & Nichols, 1850);
An Address Delivered Before a Meeting of the Members and Friends of the Pennsylvania Anti-slavery Society During the Annual Fair December 19, 1849 (Philadelphia: Merrihew & Thompson, 1850);
Discourse, Delivered 5 Jan. 1851, in the First Congregational Unitarian Church in Philadelphia (Philadelphia, 1851);
The Moving Power. A Discourse Delivered in the First Congregational Unitarian Church in Philadelphia, Sunday Morning, Feb. 9, 1851, after the Occurrence of a Fugitive Slave Case (Philadelphia: Merrihew & Thompson, 1851);
A Discourse Occasioned by the Boston Fugitive Slave Case, Delivered in the First Congregational Unitarian Church, Philadelphia, April 13, 1851 (Philadelphia: Merrihew & Thompson, 1851);
Faith in Christ: A Discourse Delivered at Ordination of the Rev. Charles E. Hodges as Colleague Pastor of the First Parish in Barre, Mass., June 11, 1851 (Boston: Crosby & Nichols, 1851);
A Few Words to Children and Parents in Two Discourses Delivered in the First Congregational Unitarian Church in Philadelphia (Philadelphia: B. Mifflin, 1851);
A Discourse for the Time: Delivered January 4, 1852 in the First Congregational Unitarian Church (Philadelphia: C. Sherman, 1852);
Discourse in Memory of Thomas W. Morgan by W. H. F. (Philadelphia, 1854);
A Tribute to the Memory of Joseph Sill (Philadelphia? C. Sherman, 1854?);
Christian Duty (Philadelphia: Merrihew & Thompson, 1854);
Discourses (Crosby & Nichols, 1855);
Julius, and Other Tales from the German (Philadelphia: Parry & McMillan, 1856);
A Discourse Delivered on the Occasion of the Death of Edwin Cowperthwait, June 21st, 1857 (Philadelphia: Crissy & Markley, 1857);
The Revivals: A Discourse. Delivered in the First Congregational Unitarian Church in Philadelphia on Sunday April 11th 1858 (Philadelphia: Crissy & Markley, 1858);

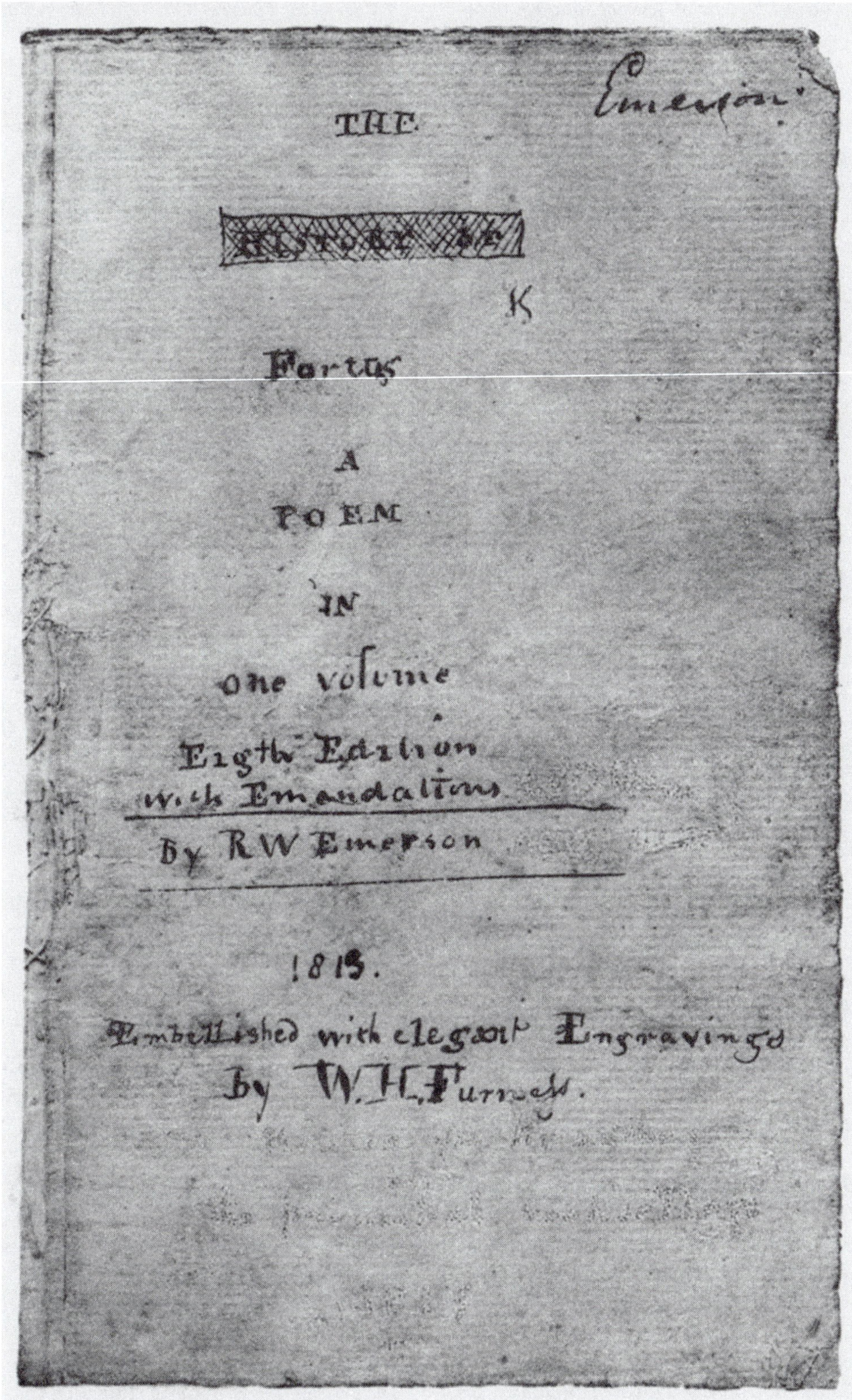

Cover for the manuscript of a poem written by Ralph Waldo Emerson and illustrated by Furness (from Horace Howard Furness, ed., Records of a Lifelong Friendship, 1807–1882, Ralph Waldo Emerson and William Henry Furness, *1910)*

Thoughts on the Life and Character of Jesus of Nazareth (Boston: Phillips, Sampson, 1859);

The Body of Christ: A Discourse Delivered in the First Congregational Unitarian Church Sunday April 17, 1859 (Philadelphia: C. Sherman, 1859);

The Right of Property in Man: A Discourse Delivered in the First Congregational Unitarian Church, Sunday July 3, 1859 (Philadelphia: C. Sherman, 1859);

A Word to Unitarians: A Discourse Delivered in the First Congregational Unitarian Church Sunday Sept. 4 1859: On the Occasion of First Assembling for Public Worship after the Summer Vacation (Philadelphia: C. Sherman, 1859);

Thy Holy Child Jesus (Albany, N.Y.: Ladies' Religious Publication Society, 1859);

Religion and Politics: A Discourse Delivered . . . Sunday March 20th, 1859 (Philadelphia: T. B. Pugh, 1859);

Put up Thy Sword: A Discourse Delivered Before Theodore Parker's Society, at the Music Hall, Boston, Sunday, March 11, 1860 (Boston: R. F. Wallcut, 1860);

The Blessings of Abolition, a Discourse Delivered . . . Sunday, July 1, 1860 (Philadelphia: C. Sherman, 1860);

Schiller. An Address Delivered Nov. 10, 1859, in the Academy of Music, Philadelphia, on the Occasion of the Celebration of Schiller's Birthday (Cincinnati, 1860);

Our Duty as Conservatives. A Discourse Delivered in the First Congregational Unitarian Church Sunday, November 25, 1860. Occasioned by the Threatened Secession of Some of the Southern States (Philadelphia: C. Sherman, 1860);

Christianity a Spirit: Discourse at the Ordination of William J. Potter to the First Congregational Church in New Bedford, Dec. 28, 1859 (New Bedford, Mass., 1860);

A Discourse Delivered on the Occasion of the National Fast, September 26th, 1861: In the First Congregational Unitarian Church in Philadelphia (Philadelphia: T. B. Pugh, 1861);

England and America: A Discourse Delivered . . . Sunday, December 22, 1861 (Philadelphia: C. Sherman, 1861?);

A Thanksgiving Discourse: Delivered in the First Congregational Unitarian Church . . . April 13th, 1862 (Philadelphia: T. B. Pugh, 1862);

The Declaration of Independence: A Discourse Delivered in the First Congregational Unitarian Church in Philadelphia, June 19, 1862 (Philadelphia, 1862);

A Word of Consolation for the Kindred of Those Who Have Fallen in Battle: A Discourse Delivered September 28 1862 (Philadelphia: Crissy & Markley, 1862);

Our American Institutions: A Thanksgiving Discourse Delivered in the First Congregational Unitarian Church in Philadelphia, August 6th, 1863 (Philadelphia: T. B. Pugh, 1863);

A Voice of the Hour: A Discourse Delivered in the First Congregational Unitarian Church (1864);

The Veil Partly Lifted and Jesus Becoming Visible (Boston: Ticknor & Fields, 1864);

The Fountain of Christian Truth: A Discourse Delivered . . . March 5th, 1865 (Philadelphia: C. Sherman, 1865);

Ecclesiastical Organizations: A Discourse Delivered in the First Congregational Unitarian Church in Philadelphia March 19, 1865 (Philadelphia: C. Sherman, 1865);

Remarks on Renan's Life of Jesus (Philadelphia, 1865);

The Authority of Jesus: A Discourse Delivered Before a Conference of Liberal Christians, Held in Northumberland, Pa., April 10th, 1867 (Philadelphia: King & Baird, 1867);

In Memoriam. Philadelphia, Sunday March 17, 1867. [Occasioned by the Death of His Son, W. H. Furness] (Philadelphia, 1867);

The Unconscious Truth of the Four Gospels (Philadelphia: J. B. Lippincott, 1868);

Robert Collyer and His Church: A Discourse Delivered in the First Congregational Church in Philadelphia, November 12, 1871 (King & Baird, 1871);

Jesus (Philadelphia: J. B. Lippincott, 1871);

Jesus and the Gospels (Philadelphia, 1872);

Faith in Christ: A Discourse Delivered at the Dedication of Unity Church under the Pastoral Care of Robert Collyer; Chicago, December 7, 1873 (Philadelphia: C. Sherman, 1873);

The Power of Spirit Manifest in Jesus of Nazareth (Philadelphia: J. B. Lippincott, 1877);

Jesus, the Heart of Christianity (Philadelphia: J. B. Lippincott, 1879);

God and Immortality: A Discourse in Memory of Lucretia Mott, Who Departed this Life November 11, 1880, in the 88th Year of Her Age (Philadelphia: Office of the Journal, 1881);

The Nativity: A Christmas Sermon (Philadelphia: J. B. Lippincott, 1883);

The "Power of His Resurrection" Easter 1884 (Philadelphia, 1884);

The Story of the Resurrection of Christ Told Once More, with Remarks upon the Character of Christ and the Historical Claim of the Four Gospels (Philadelphia: J. B. Lippincott, 1885; enlarged, 1886);

A Christmas Sermon, Sunday December 21, 1884 (Philadelphia: J. B. Lippincott, 1885);

The Faith of Jesus (Philadelphia: Privately printed, 1887);

The Personal Power of Christ (Philadelphia, 1887);

The Great Festival (Philadelphia, 1888);

Jesus and Christianity: A Discourse (Philadelphia: Privately printed, 1889);

Immortality. A Discourse by W. H. Furness, D.D. Read Sunday, May 5th, at "The Hayes Mechanics Home," after the

Death of Charles D. Reed, a Generous Benefactor of the Institution (Philadelphia, 1889);

Jesus, the Revelation of God in Man: A Discourse Delivered in Philadelphia, 28th Oct., 1889 (Philadelphia, 1889);

A Christmas Discourse Delivered in the First Congregational Unitarian Church of Philadelphia, December 21, 1890 (Philadelphia? 1890?);

An Easter Sermon Delivered in the First Congregational Unitarian Church of Philadelphia April 17th, 1892 by W. H. Furness, D.D. (Philadelphia? 1892?);

A Glad Religion: A Sermon Delivered in the First Unitarian Church in New York . . . Jan. 10th, 1892 (New York? 1892?);

Address Before the Middle States Unitarian Conference by W. H. Furness, D.D. November 16th, 1892 (Philadelphia? 1892?);

Pastoral Offices (Boston: Houghton, Mifflin, 1893);

"God Is Love": A Sermon Delivered in the First Congregational Unitarian Church of Philadelphia, November 12th, 1893 (Philadelphia? 1893?);

The Resurrection of Jesus: A Discourse, Easter, 1894 (Philadelphia, 1894);

Heart-Faith. A Sermon, Nov. 11, 1894 (Philadelphia, 1894);

The Historical Christ: A Discourse Delivered in the First Unitarian Church in Philadelphia, December 23, 1894 (Philadelphia? 1894?);

Recollections of Seventy Years: A Discourse Delivered in the First Unitarian Church in Philadelphia (Philadelphia? 1895);

The Gospels: A Historical Address Delivered at the Unitarian Conference in Washington, D.C., October, 1895, and Other Sermons (Philadelphia: Unitarian Book Room Association, 1896).

OTHER: *Prose Writers of Germany* (Philadelphia: Carey & Hart, 1848);

Johann Christoph Friedrich von Schiller, *Song of the Bell,* translated by Furness (Philadelphia: C. Sherman, 1849);

Gems of German Verse, edited by Furness (Philadelphia: W. P. Hazard, 1851; revised and enlarged, 1860);

Gotthif Heinrich von Schubert, *The Mirror of Nature,* translated by Furness (London: W. Tweedie, 1854);

David Schenkel, *Character of Jesus Portrayed,* translated by Furness (Boston: Little, Brown, 1866);

Emma Seiler, *The Voice in Singing,* translated by Furness (Philadelphia: J. B. Lippincott, 1868);

Seiler, *The Voice in Speaking,* translated by Furness (Philadelphia: J. B. Lippincott, 1875);

First Unitarian Church (Philadelphia, Pa.) Exercises at the Meeting of the First Congregational Unitarian Society, January 12, 1875: Together with the Discourse Delivered by Rev. W. H. Furness, Sunday, Jan. 10, 1875, on the Occasion of the Fiftieth Anniversary of his Ordination, January 12, 1825 (Philadelphia: C. Sherman, 1875);

Verses Translated from the German and Hymns (Boston: Houghton, Mifflin, 1886).

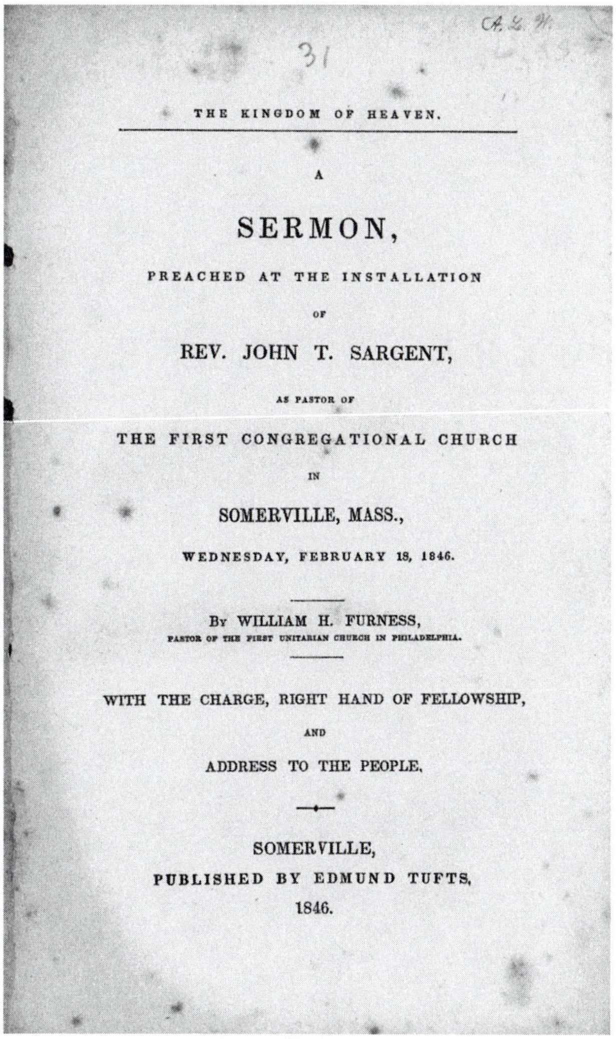
THE KINGDOM OF HEAVEN.

A

SERMON,

PREACHED AT THE INSTALLATION

OF

REV. JOHN T. SARGENT,

AS PASTOR OF

THE FIRST CONGREGATIONAL CHURCH

IN

SOMERVILLE, MASS.,

WEDNESDAY, FEBRUARY 18, 1846.

BY WILLIAM H. FURNESS,

PASTOR OF THE FIRST UNITARIAN CHURCH IN PHILADELPHIA.

WITH THE CHARGE, RIGHT HAND OF FELLOWSHIP,

AND

ADDRESS TO THE PEOPLE.

SOMERVILLE,

PUBLISHED BY EDMUND TUFTS,

1846.

Title page for a sermon Furness preached at the installation of a fellow minister (Collection of Joel Myerson)

In an undated letter written in the 1880s, William Henry Furness remarked, "My interest in the view of Jesus of the Gospels, which I have been taking more and more to heart for these fifty years past, is almost insane." A Unitarian clergyman, theologian, reformer, translator, and author, Furness was both an unyielding abolitionist and one of the first Americans to distinguish between the life of Jesus and the theology of Christ. Someone once remarked of Furness that his life and work were driven by "two themes,–the man of Naza-

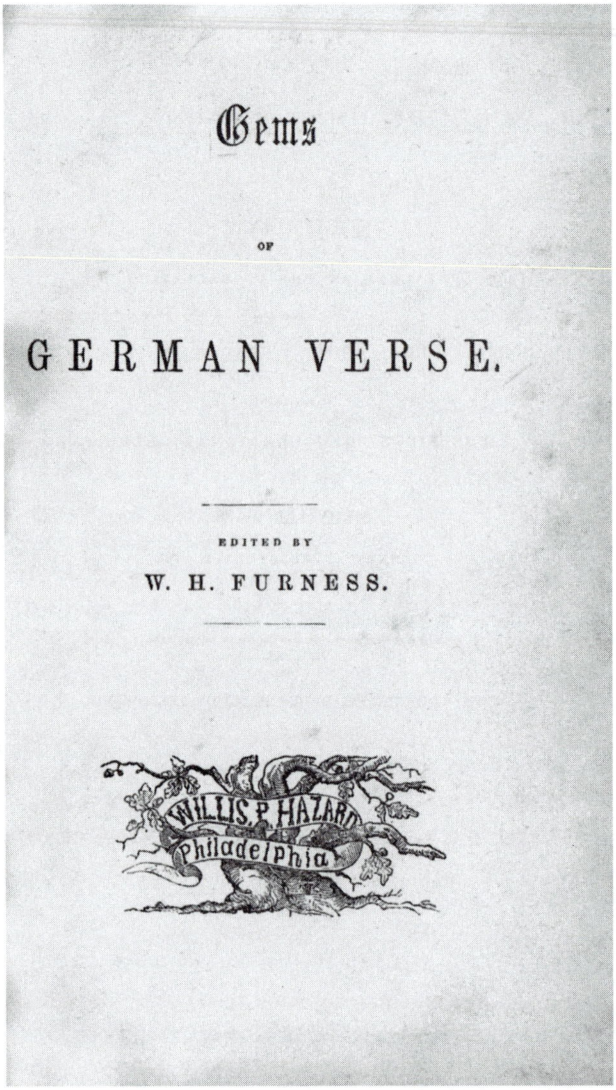

Gems

of

GERMAN VERSE.

EDITED BY

W. H. FURNESS.

WILLIS P. HAZARD

Philadelphia

Title page for a collection of poems translated by Furness

reth and the man of Africa." As a member of the Transcendental Club, despite his distance from the community, Furness corresponded regularly with Convers Francis, Frederic Henry Hedge, Theodore Parker, James Freeman Clarke, Moncure Daniel Conway, and Christopher Pearse Cranch. He maintained a lifelong friendship with Ralph Waldo Emerson and conducted his private funeral service. Emerson wrote of Furness to Margaret Fuller that he was his "dear gossip, almost a gossip for the gods, there is such a repose and honour in the man." Furness also enjoyed a lengthy intimate relationship with Amos Bronson Alcott, who included a verse portrait of him in his *Sonnets and Canzonets* (1882).

The son of William and Rebekah (Thwing) Furness, William Henry Furness was born on Federal Street in Boston, Massachusetts, on 20 April 1802. His ancestors on his mother's side included the noted Captain Clapp, who moved from England in 1629. Furness's father was a clerk in the Union Bank on State Street in Boston. Young William's education began at Mrs. Whitwell's school, where he met Emerson. The two also attended Boston Latin School together, where at nine and ten they collaborated on at least one poem. Emerson supplied the verse–Furness, the art.

Furness entered Harvard College in 1816, graduating from the college in 1820 and from the Divinity School in 1823. He preached his first sermon in Watertown, Massachusetts. Seeking a pastorship, he preached in the Boston area until May 1824. After working as an assistant in Baltimore for three months, he went to Philadelphia in the summer of 1824 to preach at the Unitarian society, founded by Dr. Joseph Priestley in 1796. The organization had been without a minister for twenty-nine years, and they immediately invited Furness to become their first pastor. His ordination, delayed because of the difficulty of obtaining ministers to take part in it, finally took place on 12 January 1825. Among those presiding was Dr. Aaron Bancroft, George Bancroft's father. The congregation prospered under Furness's guidance. In 1828, about three years after he became pastor, they built a large house of worship, where Furness preached throughout the remainder of his life.

In 1825 Furness married Annis Pulling Jenks of Salem, Massachusetts. Furness and his wife had four children, three of whom survived them. Their son Horace Howard Furness, a distinguished Shakespearean scholar, edited *Records of a Lifelong Friendship 1807–1882* (1910), a collection of letters exchanged between Emerson and Furness.

Throughout the 1830s, Furness, like Emerson, did not publicly address the slavery question. However, several events in 1834 foreshadowed his later activism. Lucretia Mott, a Quaker abolitionist, reported that Furness was "becoming increasingly interested in the Abolition cause, and we hope it will ere long be with him a pulpit theme." During this time also Harriet Martineau, an English Unitarian reformer, was his houseguest, and Fanny Kemble, later famous for her abolitionist writings, joined his church. By December 1834 Furness was already, according to Martineau's report, labeled a heretic by certain individuals in Boston, presumably because of his beliefs on miracles and other controversial subjects.

Furness preached his first antislavery sermon in July 1839. Afterward he wrote to Mary Jenks: "It is a great relief to have preached this sermon–not that I want to be an advocate of abolition, but I want to have my opinions fully known. . . ."

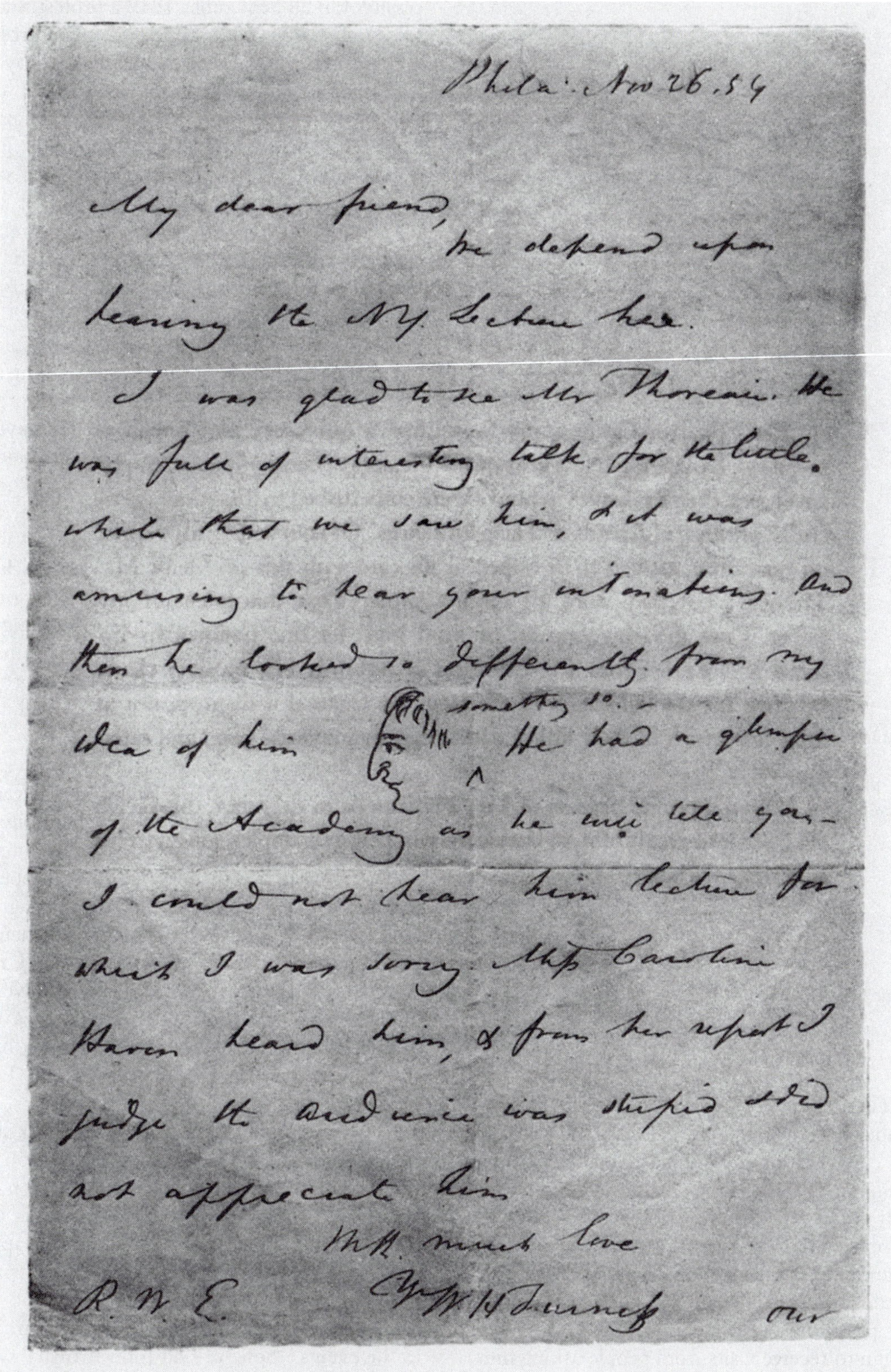

Phila: Nov 26. 54

My dear friend,
We depend upon hearing the N.Y. Lecture here.

I was glad to see Mr Thoreau. He was full of interesting talk for the little while that we saw him, & it was amusing to hear your intonations. And then he looked so differently from my idea of him something so. He had a glimpse of the Academy as he will tell you. I could not hear him lecture for which I was sorry. Miss Caroline Haven heard him, & from her report I judge the audience was stupid & did not appreciate him.

With much love

R.W.E. Yrs W.H. Furness our

Letter from Furness to Emerson (from Horace Howard Furness, ed., Records of a Lifelong Friendship, 1807–1882, Ralph Waldo Emerson and William Henry Furness, *1910)*

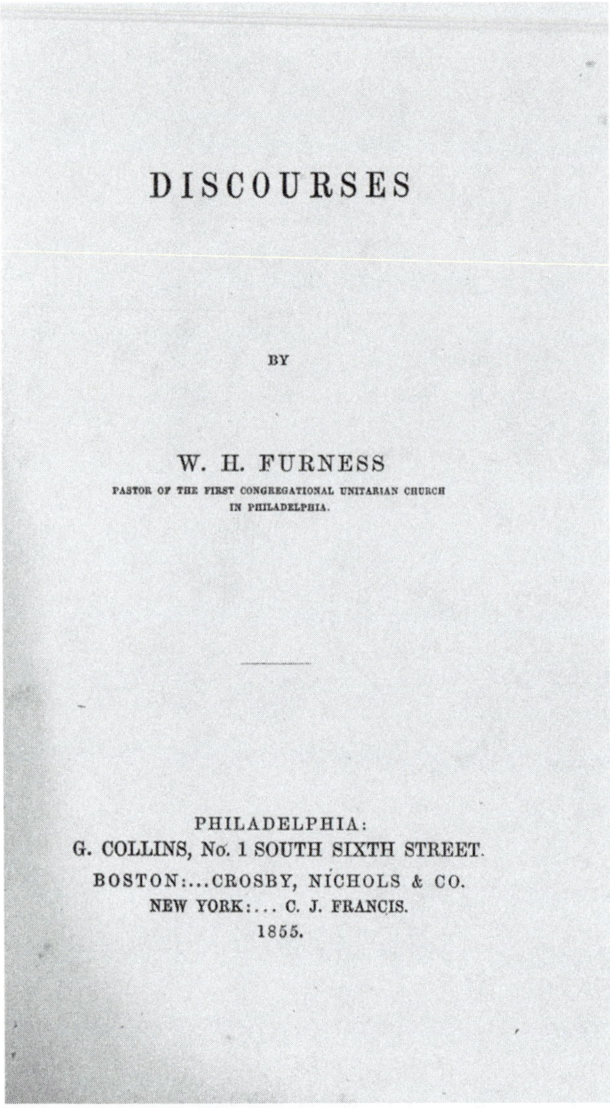
DISCOURSES

BY

W. H. FURNESS

PASTOR OF THE FIRST CONGREGATIONAL UNITARIAN CHURCH IN PHILADELPHIA.

PHILADELPHIA:
G. COLLINS, No. 1 SOUTH SIXTH STREET.
BOSTON:...CROSBY, NICHOLS & CO.
NEW YORK:... C. J. FRANCIS.
1855.

Title page for a collection of Furness's orations

Once Furness decided to speak out, he did not tire of the subject. Len Gougeon writes that "A member of Furness' congregation noted that 'for twenty-five years not a Sunday passed when Dr. Furness did not in sermon or in prayer make some reference to slavery.'" His dedication to the issue caused some dissent in his church. An anniversary sermon on 3 January 1841 provoked a letter on his "obnoxious doctrines." After preaching a particularly strident sermon on 14 May 1841, he began to receive visits from people asking him to stop preaching antislavery sermons. When he announced that he would preach on abolition on 3 July 1842 several church members rose and left. Although a member of the trustees, Joshua Tervis, resigned his position and tried to censure Furness, he was not successful. On 23 September 1842 a protest was submitted to the Trustees with thirty-nine signatures, but loyal members had learned of the protest and by November had seventy-eight signatures in support of Furness. When offered the opportunity to take the pastorship of a church in New Bedford, Massachusetts, Furness presented the offer to his congregation for a vote. On 28 September 1846 a meeting was held at which they voted three hundred to three in favor of retaining him. Some members of the congregation did not attend because Furness preached antislavery sermons while waiting for the decision.

A passionate believer in the abolitionist cause, Furness nevertheless refrained from joining any antislavery society because of his distrust of all organizations. He did, however, speak to several antislavery groups, including the Pennsylvania Anti-Slavery Society, on 19 December 1849. By far the greatest event for Furness in 1850 was his address to the American Anti-Slavery Society in New York, where he joined William Lloyd Garrison, Wendell Phillips, and Frederick Douglass. *The Nation* later reported that the occasion was "the proudest recollection of his life." Recalling the event, Furness wrote that "Depths were stirred in me never before reached." This event sparked more passionate efforts toward social reform and moved him farther away from traditional Unitarianism.

The passage of the Fugitive Slave Law was another defining moment in his antislavery activity. Furness and Emerson both became painfully aware that individual moral conscience was not strong enough to oppose legislated evils and that civil disobedience was necessary. Furness announced to his congregation his intention to oppose the law and urged them to do the same; he also became involved in the Underground Railroad. His defiance of the Fugitive Slave Law made him the object of federal scrutiny. James Buchanan's cabinet discussed whether or not to indict him for treason but, at the urging of John K. Kane, U.S. District Judge of Pennsylvania, decided against it.

Senator Charles Sumner, who was attacked by Congressman Preston Brooks in May 1856, was a personal friend of both Furness and Emerson and stayed with the Furness family in Philadelphia for several weeks during his recovery. Furness also appears to be the only clergyman involved in John Brown's case and was upset that Brown's body was not allowed to remain in Philadelphia. He wrote a hymn in response to the events, "Song of Old John Brown," which Emerson called "the most effective song that theme has found."

A tireless worker, Furness continued writing and translating in addition to his antislavery activities throughout the Civil War years. His translation of the

German theologian David Schenkel's *Character of Jesus Portrayed* (1866) is perhaps his most important because of the heavy influence of German scriptural criticism. Collaborating with Frederic Henry Hedge, he had helped translate a volume of *Prose Writers of Germany* (1848). The following year, in perhaps his best verse translation, he prepared Johann Christoph Friedrich von Schiller's *Song of the Bell* (1849).

Furness's pleasant, even temperament and good manners served him in good stead. In his obituary, *The Nation* recalled his "fine face and noble presence, [with] a voice remarkable for depth and melody." Similarly, *The Critic* noted that "Dr. Furness was averse to controversies, restricting himself to the criticism of ideas, never of persons." Without these qualities, one can only speculate on whether or not he would have remained sole minister of his church for fifty years. In 1875 he became Pastor Emeritus.

Remarks on the Four Gospels, a work that Furness revised as *Jesus and His Biographers* (1838), established his reputation. Heavily influenced by his readings of German scriptural text criticism, the work was something of an anomaly. Before its publication, Furness circulated the manuscript among members of his evening lecture series, which he had started in 1828. Fearing that it would not be acceptable to mainstream Boston Unitarians, they advised him to ask his former professor at the Harvard Divinity School, Andrews Norton, for advice. Furness took their concerns seriously, and on 2 July 1836 he wrote to Norton, outlining his project. Citing his disagreement with Furness's basic interpretation of the miracles and dismissal of the angels at Christ's tomb as Jewish superstitions, Norton responded by stating that if he were asked to review the manuscript, he would feel bound to express his disapproval. Furness wrote to Norton twice more before the publication and received another similar response. In his last letter, of 14 August 1836, he informed Norton that although he desired his opinion on the miracles, at this point the book must go to press without it.

On 12 November 1836 *Remarks on the Four Gospels* was on sale in Boston. It outlined Furness's philosophy of Jesus, and he returned to these ideas in one form or another in every subsequent book. Its publication marked Furness's alignment with the Transcendentalists; the publication of the book swept him into the Miracles Controversy of 1836. The Miracles Controversy exposed the theological conflicts between conservative Unitarians and the new Transcendentalists. Conservative Unitarians such as Andrews Norton generally subscribed to Lockean sensationalism, contending that empirical evidence was necessary to understand the true revelation of Christ. This position was symptomatic of their belief that common people could not understand religious truth directly and needed supernatural evidence to convince them. Transcendentalists such as Furness believed that truth could be perceived through intuition and that common people were capable of directly experiencing religious truth. Even a cursory examination of *Remarks on the Four Gospels* suggests, therefore, why Norton was reluctant to respond to Furness.

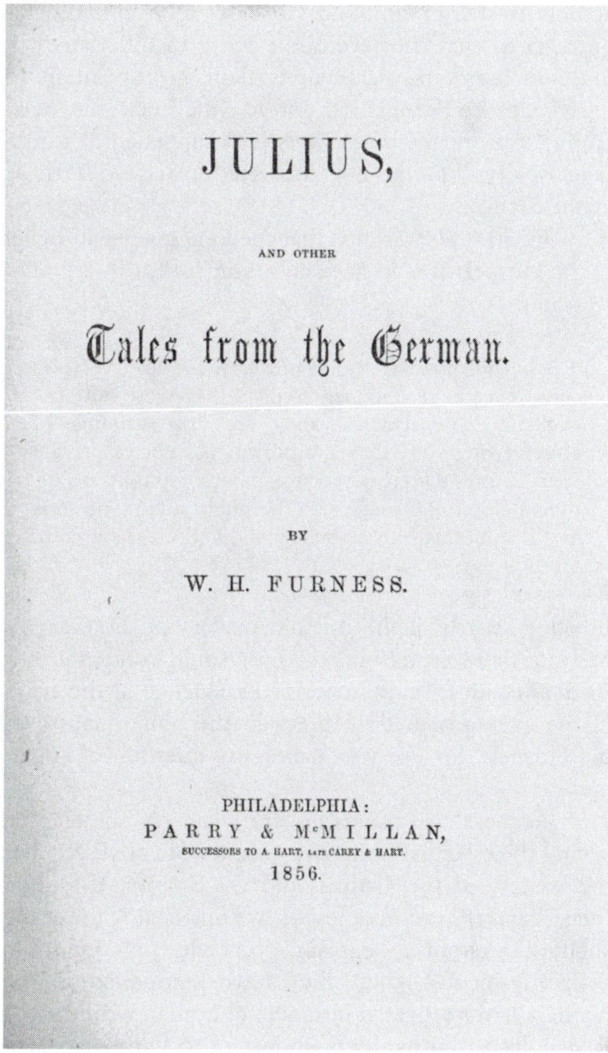
JULIUS,

AND OTHER

Tales from the German.

BY

W. H. FURNESS.

PHILADELPHIA:
PARRY & McMILLAN,
SUCCESSORS TO A. HART, LATE CAREY & HART.
1856.

Title page for a collection of tales translated by Furness

Furness begins by establishing the historical character of the four gospels. He argues that they must be historically accurate, for if they are not, "If they had designed to deceive–to relate what they knew was not true, they never would have been so prodigal of circumstances, so profuse in allusions to public persons, places, and events." Affirming the truth of the Gospels is important because it allows Furness to argue that all information necessary to believe his version of the miracles is present in the Bible. He allowed for inaccuracies but argued that they were due more to differences in individual writers' perceptions than to any intent to deceive. Since Furness did not, like the Lockeans, need empirical evidence that events had happened in a particular way, he did not concern himself with these inconsistencies.

Furness also argued that the long history of belief in the Gospels was in itself an argument for their validity and that

> it is hardly possible to imagine how the four Gospels could ever have obtained credit if they were not substantially true, because they are not accounts of abstract opinions, they are narrations, not of private visions and secret experiences, but of public occurrences closely affiliated with the public affairs, persons and institutions of a certain period and a certain community.

In other words, if the original readers of the Gospels had not detected falsehoods, how could contemporary readers claim to have superior knowledge of the truth of the events related? Moreover, the public nature of the Gospels, for Furness, belies any question of supernatural revelation.

Furness also builds his argument on miracles by noting the essential humanity of Jesus. He observes that the writers of the Gospels did not attempt to soften their characterization of Jesus: "we find that without the slightest attempt to explain, reconcile, or soften the apparent inconsistency, they have mentioned in the plainest terms repeated instances of human weakness in Jesus." Jesus' humanity is important to Furness's argument, because if one sees Jesus as a human being who is simply doing a better job of living up to his potential, then the idea that miracles represent nonhuman powers is called into question. Creation itself is miraculous, so God does not need to prove himself by supernatural means.

After carefully establishing the historical nature of the Gospels and the humanity and consistency of Jesus' character, Furness turns his attention to the miracles. The etymology of the word "miracle" provides the basis for his argument. Throughout the work, Furness is fond of invoking etymology to make a point. He notes that miracle "is derived from the Latin word '*miraculum*' which means simply a wonder." Therefore, everything is miraculous. According to traditional Unitarians, "Miracles are usually conceived of and represented as departures from the natural order of things,–interruptions, violations of the laws of Nature." Furness maintains that human beings cannot know whether or not something is miraculous because they cannot yet claim to understand what the natural order of the universe is: "With our very limited knowledge of Nature, how, I ask again, shall we pronounce an alleged fact a violation of its order?" Although this argument may sound perfectly logical, conservative Unitarians fervently rejected the idea that miracles are simply a part of the natural world. Unitarians such as Andrews Norton, as followers of the Lockean tradition, believed that miracles were necessary evidence of the superiority of Jesus. Furness claimed that if one accepted miracles as part of the natural order, then the truth about Jesus could be known only by intuition. This conclusion did not, however, mean that miracles were ordinary occurrences. Miracles were possible because of Jesus' extraordinary moral character.

Clarke reviewed *Remarks on the Four Gospels* in the December 1836 *Western Messenger*. He found much to admire and later spent three days in Philadelphia discussing the book with Furness. He agreed with Furness's idea that miracles were not interruptions of the natural order and that miracles were not devices to force people into believing in Christianity. Not surprisingly, the response from the conservative Unitarian community was much harsher.

In March 1837 Martin Luther Hurlbut's review of *Remarks on the Four Gospels* appeared in *The Christian Examiner*. Although the journal had abstained from commenting on the increasing divisions in the Unitarian community, Hurlbut's review changed its stand. He wrote that

> there is a class of writers among us, who are, consciously or unconsciously, *philosophizing* away the peculiarities of the Gospel, and reducing it to a level with mere naturalism. Such, we verily believe, to be the *tendency* of Mr. Furness' theory of the miracles. . . . We are persuaded that Mr. Furness would disavow any such purpose. . . . Still, it is not in his option to check, limit or qualify the tendency of his book.

Hurlbut's refusal to believe that Furness intends to discredit the Gospels is important because it reflects the level of esteem Furness was held in. Nevertheless, Hurlbut is scandalized, particularly by the suggestion that "all men are endued with miraculous powers; that the human mind, as such, possesses a 'supremacy over' material things." Addressing the heart of the differences between the conservatives and liberals, Hurlbut writes, "If the miracles of the Gospel are to be regarded as 'natural facts' capable of being reduced to natural laws, and explained by them, it does appear to us, that Christianity, as a system of revealed truth, ceases to be. We are thrown back upon *mere naturalism*." Clearly, Hurlbut found Furness's views heretical.

The Transcendentalists themselves were divided about Furness's position. William Ellery Channing, a

Samuel Bradford, Ralph Waldo Emerson, and William Henry Furness (a 1910 composite from photographs by F. Gutenkunst, Philadelphia)

friend whom Furness openly criticized in the book, valued its biblical criticism but found the arguments on miracles lacking. However, Cranch wrote to his brother enthusiastically about the book, and Francis incorporated Furness's discussion of the miracles into his sermons. After the publication of *Jesus and His Biographers* Furness wrote to Emerson on 27 April 1840: "You gratified me by the good opinion you expressed that of that humble labour of mine to elucidate the Gospels. But I do not know whether you accord with me in my love of those wondrous and enlightening facts of the life of Christ." Emerson actually did not completely agree with Furness's conclusions on the miracles, since he believed that they were ordinary natural phenomena.

Jesus and His Biographers omits two chapters from the original and adds eight, including new chapters such as "The Baptism" and "The Temptation." In his preface Furness acknowledges that his former discussion of the miracles has been misinterpreted and offers this book as an attempt to clarify his position. He chose to integrate new material on Jesus' life with the *Remarks on the Four Gospels* rather than publishing it separately because he wanted to stress the connection between the two books.

Furness was not alone in his belief that the miracles were not necessary evidences of Christianity. George Ripley, who agreed with Furness on many points, was engaged in a nasty public debate with Norton at the same time that Furness was writing. Norton by all accounts had both Ripley and Furness in mind when he published *A Discourse on the Latest Form of Infidelity* (1839), in which he railed against certain Transcendentalist understandings of miracles. Norton sent Furness a copy, and Furness graciously thanked him. He did, however, make clear that he sincerely believed he was not a heretic.

Although Furness constantly revised his work, lay readers may have difficulty seeing substantial theoretical differences between his earlier and later works. Nevertheless, there were subtle changes in his philosophy over the course of his career. For example, as R. Joseph Hoffman observes, Furness's position on scientific discovery, while fairly positive in the late 1840s, was by the time he published *Discourses* (1855) rather negative. Furness stated that "Science . . . is atheistic, not professedly, not consciously so perhaps, but still it is so." Rejecting science, he moved toward a stronger belief in intuition.

By the time Furness published *The Veil Partly Lifted and Jesus Becoming Invisible* (1864), German biblical scholarship, which he had been instrumental in bringing to critical notice, was changing. Although he had always found certain elements of German scholarship problematic, Ernst Renan's *Vie de Jesus* (1863) troubled him because it did not acknowledge the moral nature of Jesus' life. To Furness's taste, Renan also tried too hard to discover the truth about Jesus through learning rather than intuition.

Despite Furness's theological changes, *The Veil Partly Lifted* reiterates many of the ideas he developed in *Remarks on the Four Gospels*. He continues to stress the relationship between truth and nature, asserting that "if a thing is to be seen as true, it must be seen . . . to be consistent, not only with itself, but with everything that is known to be true." He posits that the reason some people do not believe in Christ is that his "harmonious" relationship with nature has become obscured, making it seem unnatural.

Although *The Nation* noted that "there was something pathetic" in Furness's persistence in rewriting his books long after others had moved on, Furness was well aware of this tendency. He remarked to a friend, "I suppose you write many sermons. . . . I write only one, but I keep writing it over and over." No doubt because of Furness's lifelong dedication to his one sermon, Octavius Brooks Frothingham called him "A Transcendentalist of the most impassioned school." In the 1870s Emerson wrote that he, Furness, and their childhood friend Samuel Bradford "had agreed not to grow old." Furness obliged, continuing to preach occasionally even into his nineties. Even after the death of his wife, Annis, in 1884, Furness published several books. On 30 January 1896, in Philadelphia, he finally broke his agreement with Emerson and died. At the time of his death, he was the oldest living graduate of Harvard College, outliving all the other Transcendentalists.

Letters:

Records of a Lifelong Friendship 1807–1882, edited by Horace Howard Furness (Boston: Houghton Mifflin, 1910).

References:

Christian Register, 6 February 1896, pp. 84–86;

Critic, 8 February 1896, p. 99;

Samuel A. Eliot, ed., *Heralds of a Liberal Faith* (Boston: American Unitarian Association, 1910);

Elizabeth Geffen, "William Henry Furness: Philadelphia Anti-Slavery Preacher," *Pennsylvania Magazine of History and Biography,* 82 (July 1958): 259–291;

Len Gougeon, "Emerson and Furness: Two Gentlemen of Abolition," *American Transcendental Quarterly,* 41 (Winter 1979): 17–31;

R. Joseph Hoffman, "William Henry Furness: The Transcendentalist Defense of the Gospels," *New England Quarterly,* 56 (June 1983): 238–260;

Elisabeth Hurth, "That 'Grand Model of Humanity': William Henry Furness and the Problem of the Historical Jesus," *Studies in the American Renaissance 1995,* edited by Joel Myerson (Charlottesville: University Press of Virginia, 1995), pp. 101–126;

William R. Hutchison, *The Transcendentalist Ministers: Church Reform in the New England Renaissance* (New Haven: Yale University Press, 1959);

Perry Miller, ed., *The Transcendentalists: An Anthology* (Cambridge, Mass.: Harvard University Press, 1950);

Nation, 6 February 1896, pp. 114–115;

Guy R. Woodall, "William Henry Furness' *Remarks on the Four Gospels* in the 'Annus Mirabilis' (1836)," *American Transcendental Quarterly,* new series, 3 (September 1989): 233–244.

Papers:

The H. H. Furness Memorial Library, located in the VanPelt library at the University of Pennsylvania, houses the largest collection of William Henry Furness's correspondence.

William Lloyd Garrison

(10 December 1805 - 24 May 1879)

Len Gougeon
University of Scranton

See also the Garrison entry in *DLB 43: American Newspaper Journalists, 1690–1872.*

William Lloyd Garrison, 1825 (portrait by William Swain; from Walter M. Merrill and Louis Ruchames, The Letters of William Lloyd Garrison, *volume 1, 1981)*

BOOKS: *An Address: Delivered Before the Free People of Color, in Philadelphia, New York, and Other Cities, During the Month of June, 1831* (Boston: Printed by Stephen Foster, 1831);

An Address on the Progress of the Abolition Cause: Delivered Before the African Abolition Freehold Society of Boston, July 16, 1832 (Boston: Garrison & Knapp, 1832);

Thoughts on African Colonization (Boston: Garrison & Knapp, 1832);

Address Delivered in Boston, New-York and Philadelphia: Before the Free People of Color, in April, 1833 (New York: Free People of Color, 1833);

The Maryland Scheme of Expatriation Examined. By a Friend of Liberty (Boston: Garrison & Knapp, 1834);

A Brief Sketch of the Trial of William Lloyd Garrison for an Alleged Libel on Francis Todd, of Newburyport, Massachusetts (Boston: Printed by Garrison & Knapp, 1834);

An Address Delivered in Marlboro Chapel, Boston, July 4, 1838 (Boston: Knapp, 1838);

An Address Delivered at the Broadway Tabernacle, N.Y., August 1, 1838. By Request of the People of Color of the City, in Commemoration of the Complete Emancipation of 600,000 Slaves on That Day, in the British West Indies . . . (Boston: Knapp, 1838);

An Address, Delivered Before the Old Colony Anti-Slavery Society, at South Scituate, Mass., July 4, 1839 (Boston: Dow & Jackson, 1839);

Sonnets and Other Poems (Boston: O. Johnson, 1843);

American Slavery. Address on the Subject of American Slavery, and the Progress of the Cause of Freedom throughout the World. Delivered in the National Hall, Holborn, on Wednesday Evening, September 2, 1846 (London: Printed by R. Kinder, 1846?);

Letter from William Lloyd Garrison. Read at the Annual Meeting of the Pennsylvania Anti-Slavery Society (Boston: J. M. M'Kim, 1851);

Principles and Mode of Action of the American Anti-slavery Society: A Speech (London: W. Tweedie, 1853);

West India Emancipation. A Speech by Wm. Lloyd Garrison, Delivered at Abington, Mass., on the First Day of August, 1854 (Boston: American Anti-Slavery Society, 1854);

No Compromise with Slavery: An Address Delivered to the Broadway Tabernacle, New York, February 14, 1854 (New York: American Anti-Slavery Society, 1854);

"No Fetters in the Bay State!" Speech of Wm. Lloyd Garrison, Before the Committee on Federal Relations, in Support of

the Petitions Asking for a Law to Prevent the Recapture of Fugitive Slave, Thursday, Feb. 24, 1859 . . . (Boston: R. F. Wallcut, 1859);

The New "Reign of Terror" in the Slaveholding States, for 1859–1860 (New York: American Anti-Slavery Society, 1860);

The "Infidelity" of Abolitionism (New York: American Anti-Slavery Society, 1860);

A Fresh Catalogue of Southern Outrages upon Northern Citizens (New York: American Anti-Slavery Society, 1860);

The Abolition of Slavery: The Right of the Government under the War Power (Boston: R. F. Wallcut, 1861);

The Spirit of the South Towards Northern Freemen and Soldiers Defending the American Flag Against Traitors of the Deepest Dye (Boston: R. F. Wallcut, 1861);

The Loyalty and Devotion of Colored Americans in the Revolution and War of 1812 (Boston: R. F. Wallcut, 1861);

The Abolitionists and Their Relations to the War: A Lecture by William Lloyd Garrison, Delivered at the Cooper Institute, New York, January 14, 1862 (New York: E. D. Barker, 1862);

Southern Hatred of the American Government, the People of the North, and Free Institutions (Boston: R. F. Wallcut, 1862);

Fillmore and Sumner. A Letter from William Lloyd Garrison (Boston, 1874);

Helen Eliza Garrison, A Memorial (Cambridge, Mass.: Printed at the Riverside Press, 1876);

The Philosophy of the Single Tax Movement (New York: Sterling, 1895);

The Nature of a Republican Form of Government (New York: National American Woman Suffrage Association, 1900);

Garrison's First Anti-Slavery Address in Boston. Address at Park Street Church, Boston, July 4, 1829 (Boston: Directors of the Old South Work, 1907).

Collections: *Selections from the Writings and Speeches of William Lloyd Garrison* (Boston: R. F. Walcutt, 1852);

The Words of Garrison, A Centennial Selection (1805–1905), edited by Wendell Phillips Garrison and Francis Jackson Garrison (Boston: Houghton, Mifflin, 1905);

William Lloyd Garrison on Non-resistance, together with a Personal Sketch by His Daughter, Fanny Garrison Villard, and a Tribute by Leo Tolstoi, edited by Fanny Garrison Villard (New York: Nation Press, 1924).

OTHER: *The Narrative of the Life of Frederick Douglass, An American Slave, Written by Himself,* preface by Garrison (Boston: Boston Anti-Slavery Society, 1845);

Documents of Upheaval, Selections from William Lloyd Garrison's the Liberator, 1831–1865, edited by Truman Nelson (New York: Hill & Wang, 1966)–includes articles by Garrison;

William Lloyd Garrison and the Fight Against Slavery: Selections from the Liberator, edited by William E. Cain (Boston: St. Martin's Press, 1995).

William Lloyd Garrison is generally considered to be, more than any other person of his time, the leading figure in the American antislavery movement. Because of his absolute dedication to his cause and his tendency to offer caustic, unsparing, and sometimes ferocious denunciations of both pro-slavery apologists and fellow reformers who disagreed with any of his positions, opinions of the man differed greatly among his contemporaries. Early biographers, however, were uniformly laudatory of his accomplishments. Thus, John Jay Chapman, in his early study *William Lloyd Garrison* (1913), refers to his subject as "the central figure in American life" during his time and insists that "the day Garrison established the *Liberator* he was the strongest man in America. . . . Tide and tempest served him." Modern biographers have been more critical and discriminating, but all agree that Garrison was without a doubt the most significant single force for reform in an age generally denominated the "Era of Reform" (1830–1860) in U.S. society. His impact derived largely from his effectiveness as an agitator, organizer, platform speaker, and, most tellingly, through his thirty-five years of service as founder, editor, and publisher of the most influential antislavery journal in the United States, the *Liberator* (1831–1865).

William Lloyd Garrison was born in Newburyport, Massachusetts, on 10 December 1805 to Abijah and Frances Maria (Lloyd) Garrison. His father had emigrated from Nova Scotia, seeking improved economic opportunities as a sailing master. Bad luck, poor work habits, and a propensity to drink, however, caused Abijah to fail in both his profession and his marriage. He deserted his wife and three children when William was less than three, leaving the family in dire poverty, a condition that persisted throughout William's youth. His strong-willed mother, whom he always admired, made a gallant effort to provide for her family, but life was a constant struggle for them. As a result, William was afforded little education in the local grammar school before being apprenticed as a printer at the *Newburyport Herald* at age fifteen. Young William took considerable pleasure in the role of compositor and printer and soon acquired the skill that eventually propelled him into national prominence. His name appeared in print for the first time three years later when he published an essay defending bachelorhood.

After completing his seven-year apprenticeship, Garrison became owner of the Newburyport *Free Press.* Around this time he began to develop an interest in the issue of slavery, which he considered a moral abomination. Other political interests, however, kept him from focusing exclusively on this issue. Through his role as editor and publisher of the *Free Press* he met John Greenleaf Whittier and published several of his early poems, which had been submitted anonymously by Whittier's sister. Garrison was taken with the young Quaker's work and sought him out; the two became lifelong friends. Eventually, Whittier followed Garrison into the antislavery camp in 1833 and soon emerged as its poet laureate.

After the *Free Press* failed, the youthful Garrison moved to Boston in late 1826. Two years later he joined Nathaniel H. White in editing the *National Philanthropist,* which was primarily a prohibition journal. In the interval, he made the acquaintance of the major moving spirit of Boston's evangelicals, Lyman Beecher, who stoked the fires of reforming zeal in young Garrison. Beecher's Hanover Street Church, in the words of one biographer, became "Garrison's spiritual home and Beecher his mentor." Some of that evangelical fervor began to manifest itself in Garrison's writings for the *Philanthropist.* In editorials he promoted a moral reform of politics that included a plea to elect only Christian candidates. The theory that Garrison articulated held that social reform begins with the moral reform of individuals. Once this change has been accomplished, society will purge itself of such abominations as slavery, intemperance, promiscuity, and Sabbath breaking. In his editorials Garrison also appealed to women to make their influence felt in promoting the cause of reform. This inclination to reach out to women and to enjoin them to take an active role in social reform characterized Garrison's reforming philosophy and was the source of both great strength and great controversy for his cause.

Around this time Garrison made the acquaintance of Benjamin Lundy, a Quaker reformer whose main interest was in attacking the institution of slavery. Lundy's Boston meetings found little enthusiasm for the antislavery cause among local clergy and others. Garrison, however, was impressed with Lundy's dedication and sincerity and was won over to his cause. Garrison's commitment bore little fruit at first. He was called away to Bennington, Vermont, to serve as publisher of the *Journal of the Times,* an anti-Andrew Jackson paper. The proprietors of the press were willing to allow Garrison to discuss slavery and other reforms within the pages of the political journal in return for his services. About this time Garrison began to articulate his theory of absolute human equality, which characterized his campaign against slavery for the next thirty-five years. During the debates in Congress concerning a proposal by Representative Charles Miner of Pennsylvania that slavery be abolished in the District of Columbia, a proposal that was introduced in January of 1829, Garrison ran editorials denouncing the New England representatives who opposed the measure. In his attack on the waywardness of this opposition, Garrison noted that some fifty-three years earlier the Declaration of Independence had declared that all men were born free and equal and that this principle should be duly recognized as applicable to all, regardless of race. Garrison insisted that God had created all men simultaneously and that all were, therefore, equally the children of God and entitled to the same rights and privileges. He maintained this position throughout his reforming career, despite the development of later "scientific" theories that maintained the inherent inferiority of Negroes and the notion of multiple creations bearing races with varying talents and abilities. For Garrison, skin color and physiology had nothing to do with a person's moral and intellectual capacities. The harshness of his attacks on the moral backsliding and wrongheadedness of his opponents brought censure from various quarters, a response that occurred frequently throughout his lengthy career, and Garrison left the

Garrison's birthplace, the Farnham House on School Street in Newburyport, Rhode Island

Journal of the Times and returned to Boston in April 1829. While there, he met with Benjamin Lundy, and the two decided to join forces. They agreed that Garrison would take over as the editor of the *Genius of Universal Emancipation,* and Lundy would be free to continue his lecturing on Haitian colonization. While in Boston, Garrison gave his first major antislavery address on Independence Day at the Park Street Church. In his address he spoke for abolition and offered the Declaration of Independence as an example of a document of righteousness that, along with the Bible, provided a body of spiritual law that superseded any contrived legal tradition that supported the abomination of human slavery. He also attacked the established churches for their failure to take the high moral ground by attacking the heinous institution. Moral suasion, he thought, through the raising of moral consciousness, would soon bring an end to American slavery. The speech was barely noticed in the Boston community.

Following this performance, Garrison departed for Baltimore, where he met Lundy, and together they worked on the *Genius of Universal Emancipation.* In his earliest writings for the *Genius of Universal Emancipation,* Garrison articulated his commitment to the "immediate emancipation" of all slaves–by far the most radical of the antislavery positions. While never defining the mechanism through which such a wholesale emancipation would occur or how the former slaves would be integrated into free society, Garrison saw this position as the only one that was morally satisfying. Colonization, which he had once supported, he now saw as a mere halfway measure that would not result in the abolition of slavery and that was also based on the racist assumptions of inferiority that he so thoroughly rejected. Although he was not the first to assert the "immediate emancipation" position, he was one of the more articulate spokespersons for this radical philosophy, and he was completely and rigidly dedicated to it.

Garrison's writings in the *Genius of Universal Emancipation* reflected his increasing dedication to this cause, a dedication that soon got him into trouble. Not long after his arrival in Baltimore, Garrison began running a "Black List" in the paper. In this column he printed examples of slavery's outrages, such as kidnappings, whippings, murders, and the like. On one occasion he noted that a ship called the *Francis* had recently sailed from Baltimore with a cargo that included seventy-five slaves. The ship, as it turned out, was owned by a New Englander from Garrison's own Newburyport–Francis Todd, a wealthy merchant. In the *Genius of Universal Emancipation,* Garrison castigated Todd for his immorality in dealing in the slave trade and for mistreating the slaves he transported. Garrison subsequently sent a copy of the article to Todd and also to the *Newburyport Herald.* The article could be seen as libelous in its accusations, and Todd responded by bringing suit against both Garrison and Lundy in Baltimore City Court. Garrison, as the author of the article, was found guilty of libel and fined $50, which he could not pay. As a result, he was sent to jail for a term of six months. Garrison accepted his jail term as the price he had to pay for conscience, and while incarcerated, he wrote an eight-page pamphlet, *A Brief Sketch of the Trial of William Lloyd Garrison for an Alleged Libel on Francis Todd, of Newburyport, Massachusetts* (1834). The sketch was eventually read by Arthur Tappan, a wealthy New York philanthropist, who subsequently came forward to pay Garrison's fine. As a result, forty-nine days after his initial incarceration, on 5 June 1830, Garrison walked forth a free man and a budding hero to the cause of antislavery.

Shortly after his release, Garrison returned to Boston and, after lecturing for a time, issued a prospectus for a new antislavery journal to be called the *Liberator.* Joining with a like-minded partner, Isaac Knapp, he launched the *Liberator* with the help of various supporters, including Ellis Gray Loring, a successful Boston business lawyer and antislavery advocate; David Lee Child, a liberal Unitarian reformer; Amos Phelps, a Congregational minister; and Oliver Johnson, a devout evangelical who later edited the *National Anti-Slavery Standard.* The first number, printed on a hand press and using borrowed type, was published on 1 January 1831. Four hundred copies were printed and carried Garrison's famous manifesto:

> I will be as harsh as truth, and as uncompromising as justice. On this subject, I do not wish to think, or speak, or write, with moderation. No! no! Tell a man whose house is on fire to give a moderate alarm; tell him to moderately rescue his wife from the hands of the ravisher; tell the mother to gradually extricate her babe from the fire into which it has fallen;–but urge me not to use moderation in a cause like the present. I am in earnest–I will not equivocate–I will not excuse–I will not retreat a single inch–AND I WILL BE HEARD.

And thus began what became a lifetime career in challenging the moral lethargy of the age regarding the greatest moral abomination of the age. The *Liberator,* the circulation of which never exceeded three thousand and the finances of which were frequently in perilous arrears, became the conscience of the nation. It was in continuous publication until the

THE LIBERATOR.

VOL. I.] WILLIAM LLOYD GARRISON AND ISAAC KNAPP, PUBLISHERS. [NO. 1.

BOSTON, MASSACHUSETTS.] OUR COUNTRY IS THE WORLD—OUR COUNTRYMEN ARE MANKIND. [SATURDAY, JANUARY 1, 1831.

THE LIBERATOR
IS PUBLISHED WEEKLY
AT NO. 6, MERCHANTS' HALL.

WM. L. GARRISON, EDITOR.

Stephen Foster, Printer.

TERMS.

☞ Two Dollars per annum, payable in advance.

☞ Agents allowed every sixth copy gratis.

☞ No subscription will be received for a shorter period than six months.

☞ All letters and communications must be POST PAID.

THE LIBERATOR.

THE SALUTATION.

To date my being from the opening year,
I come, a stranger in this busy sphere,
Where some I meet perchance may pause and ask,
What is my name, my purpose, or my task?

My name is 'LIBERATOR'! I propose
To hurl my shafts at freedom's deadliest foes!
My task is hard—for I am charged to save
Man from his brother!—to redeem the slave!

Ye who may hear, and yet condemn my cause,
Say, shall the best of Nature's holy laws
Be trodden down? and shall her open veins
Flow but for cement to her offspring's chains?

Art thou a parent? shall thy children be
Rent from thy breast, like branches from the tree,
And doom'd to servitude, in helplessness,
On other shores, and thou ask no redress?

Thou, in whose bosom glows the sacred flame
Of filial love, say, if the tyrant came,
To force thy parent shrieking from thy sight,
Would thy heart bleed—*because thy face is white?*

Art thou a brother? shall thy sister twine
Her feeble arm in agony on thine,
And thou not lift the heel, nor aim the blow
At him who bears her off to life-long wo?

Art thou a sister? [illegible]
Awake thy sleeping brother, while thine eye
Beholds the fetters locking on the limb
Stretched out in rest, which hence, must end, for him?

Art thou a lover?—no! naught e'er was found
In lover's breast, save cords of love, that bound
Man to his kind! then, thy professions save!
Forswear affection, or release thy slave!

Thou who art kneeling at thy Maker's shrine,
Ask if Heaven takes such offerings as thine!
If in thy bonds the son of Afric sighs,
Far higher than thy prayer his groan will rise!

God is a God of mercy, and would see
The prison-doors unbarr'd—the bondmen free!
He is a God of truth, with purer eyes
Than to behold the oppressor's sacrifice!

Avarice, thy cry and thine insatiate thirst
Make man consent to see his brother cursed!
Tears, sweat and blood thou drink'st, but in their turn,
They shall cry 'more!' while vengeance bids thee burn.

The Lord hath said it!—who shall him gainsay?
He says, 'the wicked, they shall go away'—
Who are the wicked?——Contradict who can,
They are the oppressors of their fellow man!

Aid me, NEW ENGLAND! 'tis my hope in you
Which gives me strength my purpose to pursue!
Do you not hear your sister States resound
With Afric's cries to have her sons unbound?

*. *. *.

TO THE PUBLIC.

In the month of August, I issued proposals for publishing 'THE LIBERATOR' in Washington city; but the enterprise, though hailed in different sections of the country, was palsied by public indifference. Since that time, the removal of the Genius of Universal Emancipation to the Seat of Government has rendered less imperious the establishment of a similar periodical in that quarter.

During my recent tour for the purpose of exciting the minds of the people by a series of discourses on the subject of slavery, every place that I visited gave fresh evidence of the fact, that a greater revolution in public sentiment was to be effected in the free states—*and particularly in New-England*—than at the south. I found contempt more bitter, opposition more active, detraction more relentless, prejudice more stubborn, and apathy more frozen, than among slave owners themselves. Of course, there were individual exceptions to the contrary. This state of things afflicted, but did not dishearten me. I determined, at every hazard, to lift up the standard of emancipation in the eyes of the nation, *within sight of Bunker Hill and in the birth place of liberty*. That standard is now unfurled; and long may it float, unhurt by the spoliations of time or the missiles of a desperate foe—yea, till every chain be broken, and every bondman set free! Let southern oppressors tremble—let their secret abettors tremble—let their northern apologists tremble—let all the enemies of the persecuted blacks tremble.

I deem the publication of my original Prospectus* unnecessary, as it has obtained a wide circulation. The principles therein inculcated will be steadily pursued in this paper, excepting that I shall not array myself as the political partisan of any man. In defending the great cause of human rights, I wish to derive the assistance of all religions and of all parties.

Assenting to the 'self-evident truth' maintained in the American Declaration of Independence, 'that all men are created equal, and endowed by their Creator with certain inalienable rights—among which are life, liberty and the pursuit of happiness,' I shall strenuously contend for the immediate enfranchisement of our slave population. In Park-street Church, on the Fourth of July, 1829, in an address on slavery, I unreflectingly assented to the popular but pernicious doctrine of *gradual* abolition. I seize this opportunity to make a full and unequivocal recantation, and thus publicly to ask pardon of my God, of my country, and of my brethren the poor slaves, for having uttered a sentiment so full of timidity, injustice and absurdity. A similar recantation, from my pen, was published in the [illegible] in September, 1829. My conscience is now satisfied.

I am aware, that many object to the severity of my language; but is there not cause for severity? I *will be* as harsh as truth, and as uncompromising as justice. On this subject, I do not wish to think, or speak, or write, with moderation. No! no! Tell a man whose house is on fire, to give a moderate alarm; tell him to moderately rescue his wife from the hands of the ravisher; tell the mother to gradually extricate her babe from the fire into which it has fallen;—but urge me not to use moderation in a cause like the present. I am in earnest—I will not equivocate—I will not excuse—I will not retreat a single inch—AND I WILL BE HEARD. The apathy of the people is enough to make every statue leap from its pedestal, and to hasten the resurrection of the dead.

It is pretended, that I am retarding the cause of emancipation by the coarseness of my invective, and the precipitancy of my measures. *The charge is not true.* On this question my influence,—humble as it is,—is felt at this moment to a considerable extent, and shall be felt in coming years—not perniciously, but beneficially—not as a curse, but as a blessing; and posterity will bear testimony that I was right. I desire to thank God, that he enables me to disregard 'the fear of man which bringeth a snare,' and to speak his truth in its simplicity and power. And here I close with this fresh dedication:

'Oppression! I have seen thee, face to face,
And met thy cruel eye and cloudy brow;
But thy soul withering glance I fear not now—
For dread to prouder feelings doth give place
Of deep abhorrence! Scorning the disgrace
Of slavish knees that at thy footstool bow,
I also kneel—but with far other vow
Do hail thee and thy herd of hirelings base:—
I swear, while life-blood warms my throbbing veins,
Still to oppose and thwart, with heart and hand,
Thy brutalising sway—till Afric's chains
Are burst, and Freedom rules the rescued land,—
Trampling Oppression and his iron rod:
Such is the vow I take—SO HELP ME GOD!'

WILLIAM LLOYD GARRISON.

BOSTON, January 1, 1831.

* I would here offer my grateful acknowledgments to those editors who so promptly and generously inserted my Proposals. They must give me an available opportunity to repay their liberality.

DISTRICT OF COLUMBIA.

'What do many of the professed enemies of slavery mean, by heaping all their reproaches upon the south, and asserting that the crime of oppression is not national? What power but Congress—and Congress by the authority of the American people—has jurisdiction over the District of Columbia? That District is rotten with the plague, and stinks in the nostrils of the world. Though it is the Seat of our National Government,—open to the daily inspection of foreign ambassadors,—and ostensibly opulent with the congregated wisdom, virtue and intelligence of the land,—yet a fouler spot scarcely exists on earth. In it the worst features of slavery are exhibited; and as a mart for slave traders, it is unequalled. These facts are well known to our two or three hundred representatives, but no remedy is proposed; they are known, if not minutely at least generally, to our whole population,—but who calls for redress?

Hitherto, a few straggling petitions, relative to this subject, have gone into Congress; but they have been too few to denote much public anxiety, or to command a deferential notice. It is certainly time that a vigorous and systematic effort should be made, from one end of the country to the other, to pull down that national monument of oppression which towers up in the District. We do hope that the 'earthquake voice' of the people will this session shake the black fabric to its foundation.

The following petition is now circulating in this city, and has obtained several valuable signatures. A copy may be found at the Bookstore of LINCOLN & EDMANDS, No. 59, Washington-street, for a few days longer, where all the friends of the cause are earnestly invited to go and subscribe.

Petition to Congress for the Abolition of Slavery in the District of Columbia.

To the Honorable Senate and House of Representatives of the United States of America in Congress assembled, the petition of the undersigned citizens of Boston in Massachusetts and its vicinity respectfully represents—

That your petitioners are deeply impressed with the evils arising from the existence of slavery in the District of Columbia. While our Declaration of Independence boldly proclaims as self-evident truths, 'that all men are created equal, that they are endowed by their Creator with certain inalienable rights, that among these are life, liberty, and the pursuit of happiness,'—at the very seat of government human beings are born, almost daily, whom the laws pronounce to be from their birth, not *equal* to other men, and who are, for life, deprived of *liberty* and the free *pursuit of happiness*. The inconsistency of the conduct of our nation with its political creed, has brought down upon it the just and severe reprehension of foreign nations.

In addition to the other evils flowing from slavery, both moral and political, which it is needless to specify, circumstances have rendered this District a common resort for traders in human flesh, who bring into it their captives in chains, and lodge them in places of confinement, previously to their being carried to the markets of the south and west.

From the small number of slaves in the District of Columbia, and the moderate proportion which they bear to the free population there, the difficulties, which in most of the slaveholding states oppose the restoration of this degraded class of men to their natural rights, do not exist.

Your petitioners therefore pray that Congress will, without delay, take such measures for the immediate or gradual abolition of Slavery in the District of Columbia, and for preventing the bringing of slaves into that District for purposes of traffic, in such mode, as may be thought advisable; and that suitable provision be made for the education of all free blacks and colored children in the District, thus to preserve them from continuing, even as free men, an unenlightened and degraded caste.

If any individual should be unmoved, either by the petition or the introductory remarks, the following article will startle his apathy, unless he be morally dead—dead—dead. Read it—read it! The language of the editor is remarkable for its energy, considering the quarter whence it emanates. After all, we are not the only fanatics in the land!

[From the Washington Spectator, of Dec. 4.]

THE SLAVE TRADE IN THE CAPITAL.

[illegible]

It is well, perhaps, the American people should know, that while we reiterate our boasts of liberty in the ears of the nations, and send back across the Atlantic our shouts of joy at the triumph of liberty in France, we ourselves are busily engaged in the work of oppression. Yes, let it be known to the citizens of America, that at the very time when the procession which contained the President of the United States and his Cabinet was marching in triumph to the Capitol, to celebrate the victory of the French people over their oppressors, another kind of procession was marching another way, and that consisted of colored human beings, handcuffed in pairs, and driven along by what had the appearance of a man on a horse! A similar scene was repeated on Saturday last; a *drove* consisting of males and females chained in couples, starting from Roby's tavern on foot, for Alexandria, where, with others, they are to embark on board a slave-ship in waiting to convey them to the South. While we are writing, a colored man enters our room, and begs us to inform him if we can point out any person who will redeem his friend now immured in Alexandria jail, in a state of distress amounting almost to distraction.* He has been a faithful servant of a revolutionary officer who recently died—has been sold at auction—parted from affectionate parents—and from decent and mourning friends. Our own servant, with others, of whom we can speak in commendatory terms, went down to Alexandria to bid him farewell, but they were refused admission to his cell, as was said, 'the sight of his friends made him feel so.' He bears the reputation of a pious man. It is but a few weeks since we saw a ship with her cargo of slaves in the port of Norfolk, Va.; on passing up the river, saw another ship off Alexandria, swarming with the victims of human cupidity. Such are the scenes enacting in the heart of the American nation. Oh patriotism! where is thy indignation? Oh philanthropy! where is thy grief? OH SHAME, WHERE IS THY BLUSH? Well may the generous and noble minded O'Connell say of the American citizen, '*I tell him he is a hypocrite. Look at the stain in your star-spangled standard that was never struck down in battle. I turn from the Declaration of American Independence, and I tell him that he has declared to God and man a lie, and before God and man I arraign him as a hypocrite.*' Yes, thou soul of fire, glorious O'Connell, if thou could but witness the spectacles in Washington that make the genius of liberty droop her head in shame, and weep her tears away in deep silence and undissembled sorrow, you would lift your voice even to tones of thunder, but you would make yourself heard. Where is the O'Connell of this republic that will plead for the EMANCIPATION OF THE DISTRICT OF COLUMBIA? These shocking scenes must cease from amongst us, or we must cease to call ourselves free; ay, and we must cease to expect the mercy of God—we must prepare for the coming judgment of Him who, as our charter acknowledges, made all men '*free and equal!*'

* At the same time this man was sold, another—a husband—was knocked off. The tears and agonies of his wife made such an impression on the mind of a generous spectator that he bought him back.

When a premium of Fifty Dollars is offered for the best theatrical poem, our newspapers advertise the fact with great unanimity. The following is incomparably more important.

PREMIUM.

A Premium of Fifty Dollars, the Donation of a benevolent individual in the State of Maine, and now deposited with the Treasurer of the Pennsylvania Society for promoting the Abolition of Slavery, &c. is offered to the author of the best Treatise on the following subject: 'The Duties of Ministers and Churches of all denominations to avoid the stain of Slavery, and to make the holding of Slaves a barrier to communion and church membership.'

The composition to be directed (post paid) to either of the subscribers—the name of the author in a separate sealed paper, which will be destroyed if his work shall be rejected.

Six months from this date are allowed for the purpose of receiving the Essays.

The publication and circulation of the preferred Tract will be regulated by the Pennsylvania Society above mentioned.

W. RAWLE,
J. PRESTON, } *Committee.*
THOMAS SHIPLEY,

Philadelphia, Oct. 11.

The first issue of the most influential American antislavery journal

The flag used on The Liberator *from 23 April 1831 until 23 March 1838*

passage in 1865 of the Thirteenth Amendment, which ended slavery.

The influence of the *Liberator* was far greater than its circulation numbers suggest. It was read by some of the most influential people of the age, including Ralph Waldo Emerson, and articles printed in the *Liberator* were often reprinted in other newspapers through the clever use of exchanges. Garrison sent the *Liberator* to Southern newspapers, which reprinted articles as examples of Yankee fanaticism on the subject of slavery and included their own commentary. These were then picked up by Northern papers, which reprinted both the original and the Southern commentary and added commentary of their own. Garrison then reprinted everything and added yet another commentary on the total; the chain reaction continued. In the early years especially, the paper struggled for existence. Its finances were always shaky. The majority of subscribers were poor blacks, who could contribute little to its maintenance. As a result, Garrison often solicited aid from benefactors. Eventually, in 1840, a "financial committee" was formed to help keep the paper afloat and its affairs in order. The members of this committee were Francis Jackson, Ellis Gray Loring, Edmund Quincy, Samuel Philbrick, and Wendell Phillips–all longtime Garrison supporters.

Southern irritation with the *Liberator* and its editor became intense following the Nat Turner rebellion in August 1831. In this famous uprising, a band of slaves, whose numbers have been estimated as between fifty and seventy, went on a rampage and killed sixty-one whites before being tracked down and executed. A nearly hysterical fear of similar uprisings spread through the South, and Yankee agitators such as Garrison were seen as incendiaries who sought to foment a dangerous unrest through the publication and distribution of their abolition propaganda. Garrison, who was a committed nonresistant at the time, did not approve of the bloody uprising but, at the same time, indicated that he could well understand how people held in abusive bondage might react in such a way and how this rebellion might be a sign of worse things yet to come. In an editorial in the 3 September 1831 issue of the *Liberator* he wrote:

> What we have long predicted,–at the peril of being stigmatized as an alarmist and declaimer,–has commenced its fulfillment. The first step of the earthquake, which is ultimately to shake down the fabric of oppression, leaving not one stone upon the other, has been made. The first drops of blood, which are but the prelude to a deluge from the gathering clouds, have fallen. The first flash of lightening, which is to ignite and consume, has been felt. The first wailings of a bereavement, which is to clothe the earth in sackcloth, have broken upon our ears.

Because of such writings, there were calls for the suppression of the *Liberator*. In November the Georgia

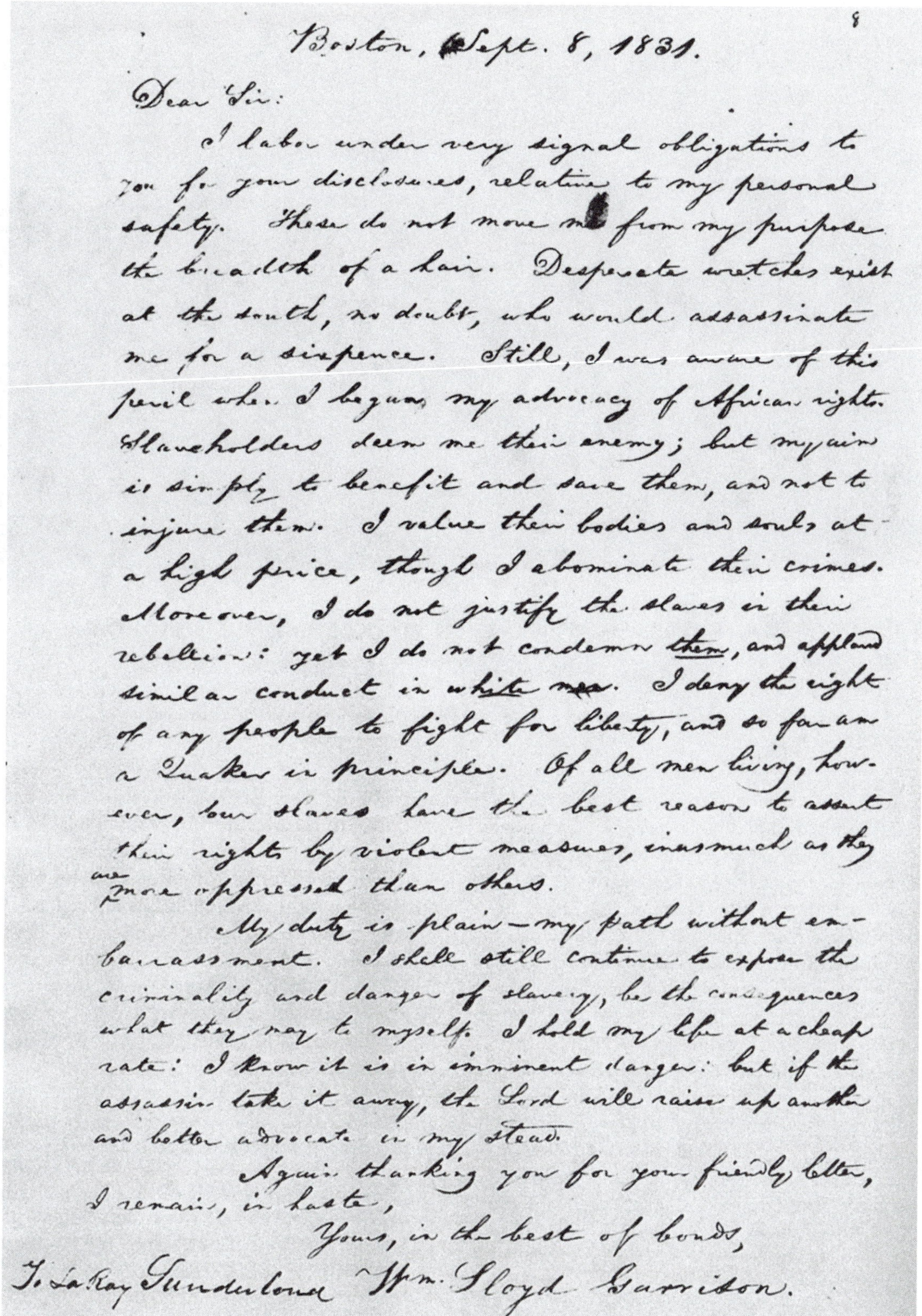

Boston, Sept. 8, 1831.

Dear Sir:

I labor under very signal obligations to you for your disclosures, relative to my personal safety. These do not move me from my purpose the breadth of a hair. Desperate wretches exist at the south, no doubt, who would assassinate me for a sixpence. Still, I was aware of this peril when I began my advocacy of African rights. Slaveholders deem me their enemy; but my aim is simply to benefit and save them, and not to injure them. I value their bodies and souls at a high price, though I abominate their crimes. Moreover, I do not justify the slaves in their rebellion: yet I do not condemn them, and applaud similar conduct in white men. I deny the right of any people to fight for liberty, and so far am a Quaker in principle. Of all men living, however, our slaves have the best reason to assert their rights by violent measures, inasmuch as they are more oppressed than others.

My duty is plain—my path without embarrassment. I shall still continue to expose the criminality and danger of slavery, be the consequences what they may to myself. I hold my life at a cheap rate: I know it is in imminent danger: but if the assassin take it away, the Lord will raise up another and better advocate in my stead.

Again thanking you for your friendly letter, I remain, in haste,

Yours, in the best of bonds,

To LaRoy Sunderland Wm. Lloyd Garrison.

Letter in which Garrison acknowledged a warning that his life was in danger (Boston Public Library)

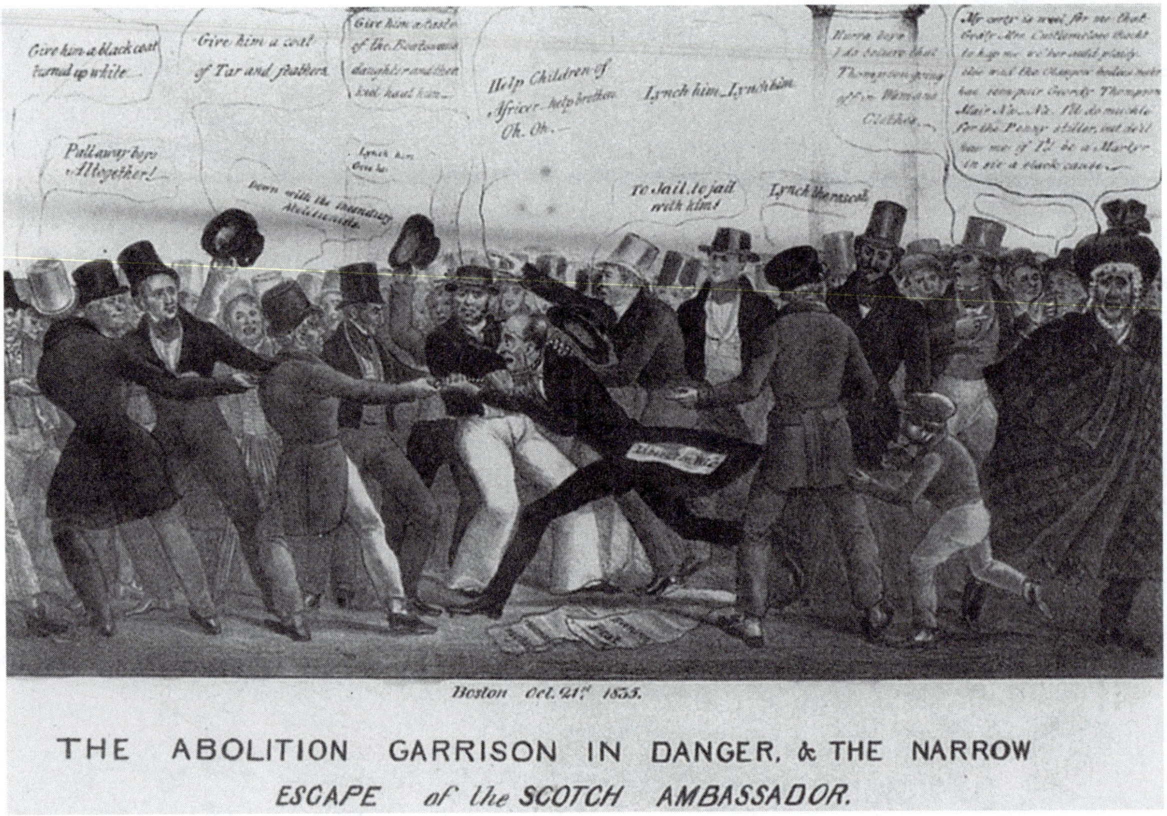

An 1835 editorial cartoon applauding the actions of a Boston mob that nearly lynched Garrison (Library Company of Philadelphia)

legislature took the extreme step of passing a resolution offering a reward of $5,000 to anyone who might kidnap the editor of the *Liberator* and bring him to justice in Georgia. Garrison was pleased with the attention and pointed out in the *Liberator* that such an outrageous attack on free speech only confirmed the moral bankruptcy of the Southern slave culture.

Garrison now set about establishing an organization to focus and direct the efforts of those who were coming forward in increasing numbers to express their opposition to slavery. In November and December of 1831 initial organizational meetings were held. In January of 1832 the New England Anti-Slavery Society was established and elected a Quaker, Arnold Buffum, as its first president. Garrison was named corresponding secretary and later became a salaried agent for the organization. All of these developments were duly reported in the *Liberator,* along with repeated calls for membership.

By this time Garrison had become a solid opponent of colonization and its goals, which he saw as subversive of true abolitionism. In 1832 he published his *Thoughts on African Colonization,* a lengthy pamphlet outlining his opposition to an organization he had once supported. In 1833 he sailed for England as an agent of the New England society. While in England, he hoped to raise money for a manual-labor school for Negroes. Also, as part of his personal agenda, he sought to undermine the efforts of the Colonization Society to continue raising funds in England. Garrison found some success in both endeavors. He managed to establish himself with British abolitionists, and he made many friends among them. In an address to "The Patrons of the Liberator and the Friends of Abolition," in the 12 October 1833 edition of the *Liberator* he announced,

> The great object of my mission,–namely, the exposure of the real character and object of the American Colonization Society,–has been accomplished, expeditiously, comprehensively, and effectually. The philanthropists of Great Britain now see clearly the deformity and foulness of that Society, and their detestation of it is equalled only by their indignation at having been so basely deceived, and so extensively defrauded, by its corrupt and pusillanimous "representative."

After returning from England, Garrison, who had once written on the advantages of bachelorhood, met and eventually married Helen Benson. Helen's father, who was eighty-two at the time of his daugh-

Abolitionists Wendell Phillips, William Lloyd Garrison, and George Thompson in 1851 (Boston Public Library)

ter's marriage on 4 September 1834, had been an abolitionist since 1792. In 1834 he was serving as president of the New England Anti-Slavery Society. Helen, who was twenty-three at the time of her marriage, was highly supportive of and dedicated to her husband. The marriage was a happy one. Seven children were born to the couple, two of whom died in infancy. By all reports Garrison was a loving and devoted father. Two of his children eventually honored him in their extensive biography, *William Lloyd Garrison, 1805–1879; The Story of His Life as Told by His Children* (1885–1889).

Around this time Garrison met with antislavery proponents in New York City and in December of 1833 joined with several others in forming the American Anti-Slavery Society. The movement continued to gain momentum throughout the later 1830s, a growth that did not please the more conservative elements in his immediate society. Their displeasure was vividly demonstrated when Garrison invited the British abolitionist George Thompson to Boston. On 21 October 1835 Thompson was scheduled to appear at a meeting of the Boston Female Anti-Slavery Society. The Boston press ran notices of the scheduled event and encouraged proper Bostonians, "gentlemen of property and standing," to turn out to protest the appearance. By noontime on the twenty-first a handbill was circulated advertising that "a purse of $100 has been raised by a number of patriotic citizens to reward the individual who shall first lay violent hands on Thompson, so that he may be brought to the tar-kettle before dark." Thompson was forewarned and stayed away from the meeting, but the angry mob that gathered found Garrison there instead. After a brief effort at flight, Garrison was seized by the mob and dragged though the streets with a rope about him. Before the crowd could drag him to his intended fate, perhaps the tar-kettle prepared for Thompson, Garrison was rescued by the intervention of the mayor of Boston and several deputies. After spending the night in protective custody, Garrison was released the following day and departed the city for a few weeks. Soon the *Liberator* published full accounts and comments on the event (7 November 1835), and Garrison's reputation rose substantially in the minds of his supporters and admirers. His conduct was seen as courageous and exemplary.

Admiration for Garrison, however, was by no means uniform. Some of his supporters saw him as too inflexible in his positions and too harsh both toward his opponents and toward his supporters with whom he disagreed. Some considered him autocratic, self-righteous, and irritating. Perhaps these traits were, in part, the products of his personality, but they were also made conspicuous through his commitment to Christian "Perfectionism." Perfectionist doctrine held that, by accepting Christ, men could achieve a state of

Detail from E. C. Del's "Practical Illustration of the Fugitive Slave Law" (1851), showing Garrison, a pacifist, employing force in defense of a runaway slave (Wichita State University)

sinlessness, if they so wished. The emulation of Christ's sinless example would allow Christ to act through them, to save their souls, and also to regenerate society. Perfectionists attempted to fulfill in their daily lives the simple but daunting command: "Be ye perfect even as your heavenly Father is perfect." Such a commitment to perfection, of course, tends to make one's personal piety the standard against which all others are measured, and while it might be a grand stimulant to the individual, it could often present a special challenge in those situations in which the organized cooperation of many is the goal. Perfectionism is a reflection of the religious origins of the antislavery movement. Garrison was in many ways a missionary of righteousness preaching to a corrupt society, and his editorials often were jeremiads.

Throughout his lengthy career, Garrison deliberately appealed to women, as the presumed guardians of morality and virtue in the world, to come forward in the service of the antislavery cause. This invitation was both a source of his strength and a source of controversy for the movement he promoted. The assumption of the time was that women were able to maintain virtue and morality to a higher degree than men–largely because they lived in the protective environment of the home and, thus, were not subject to the corrupting effects of society at large with its various commercial, political, and professional enterprises. This "cult of domesticity," as it is commonly known today, allowed for only an indirect influence on the part of women. They were intended to have a positive effect on society by encouraging virtuous behavior in their husbands and sons. By calling women out from the protection of hearth and home, Garrison not only challenged the dominance of men in all areas of social life but also, in the eyes of many, put women at risk by exposing them to the corruptions that he hoped to ameliorate. This danger, however, did not dissuade him. In the 14 July 1832 issue of the *Liberator* he ran the following editorial:

> Two capital errors have extensively prevailed, greatly to the detriment of the cause of abolition. The first is, a proneness on the part of the advocates of immediate and universal emancipation to overlook or depreciate the influence of women in the promotion of this cause; and the other is, a similar disposition on the part of the females in our land to undervalue their own power, or through a misconception of duty, to excuse themselves from engaging in the enterprise. These errors, we repeat, are capital, and should no longer be suffered to prevail. The cause of bleeding humanity is always, legitimately, the cause of WOMAN. Without her pow-

erful assistance, its progress must be slow, difficult, imperfect.

A million females in this country, are recognized and held as property–liable to be sold or used for the gratification of the lust or avarice or convenience of unprincipled speculators–without the least protection for their chastity–cruelly scourged for the most trifling offenses–and subjected to unseemly and merciless tasks, to severe privations, and to brutish ignorance! Have these not claims upon the sympathies–prayers–charities–exertions of our white countrywomen?

Among the most famous women who first made their presence felt in Garrison's camp were two Southern sisters, Angelina and Sarah Grimké. These two women shocked conservatives by appearing as speakers at abolition gatherings and thus taking on a public role heretofore reserved exclusively for men. Many women naturally gravitated toward the abolition movement because it provided them with an opportunity for self-expression and also because, as Margaret Fuller noted in *Woman in the Nineteenth Century* (1845), they recognized a compelling similarity between the subjugation of black slaves and the subjugation of women in American society. Eventually the woman's rights movement became a cause in itself, with strong support from Garrison, Frederick Douglass, Wendell Phillips, and other antislavery men.

In 1839, however, Garrison had to face a rebellion within the ranks of the abolitionists–those who wished to exclude women from active roles. He was able to fend off this initial assault, but the opponents soon withdrew to form their own organization, the Massachusetts Abolition Society, which was for men only. The rebels also sought to free antislavery from the deleterious distractions of perfectionism, nonresistance, and the pursuit of woman's rights–all of which Garrison favored. A similar defection occurred in New York in 1840 when the new American and Foreign Anti-Slavery Society was formed by Garrison's opponents. This defection left Garrison in command of the "old organization," the American Anti-Slavery Society, which immediately elected Lucretia Mott, Maria Weston Chapman, and Lydia Maria Child to the new Executive Committee. The latter was put in charge of editing a new journal, the *National Anti-Slavery Standard*. The schism came about not only because of the woman question but also because of opposition to Garrison's no-government principles whereby he refused to utilize political instruments, such as voting and party support, to achieve his reformist goals. The theory behind the no-government position held that human governments are by nature corrupt, like man himself, and therefore reliance upon them as instruments of reform is pointless. As he noted in the *Liberator* in December of 1838: "The present governments of the world are the consequence of disobedience to the commands of God. But Christ came to bring men back to obedience 'by a new and living way.' When the cause is taken away, must not the effect cease?" Garrison's conclusion is "We are for subverting the rotten, unequal, anti-Christian government of man, and establishing, as a substitute that which is divine."

Helen Eliza Benson Garrison, the abolitionist's wife, in 1853 (Sophia Smith Collection, Smith College)

The instrument of choice for this reform was moral suasion, which, in Garrison's view, was the mode appointed by God to conquer evil and destroy the works of darkness. No other could be effective. This opinion remained central to his philosophy of reform until the advent of the Civil War, which led to a substantial reconsideration of its efficacy.

In June 1840 Garrison traveled to London to attend the World's Anti-Slavery Convention. When he arrived, he was disappointed to discover that the women delegates–Lucretia Mott, Ann Phillips, and Elizabeth Cady Stanton–had been seated in the balcony and not allowed to participate except as observers. Wendell Phillips, a Garrison supporter and probably the most articulate orator in the movement,

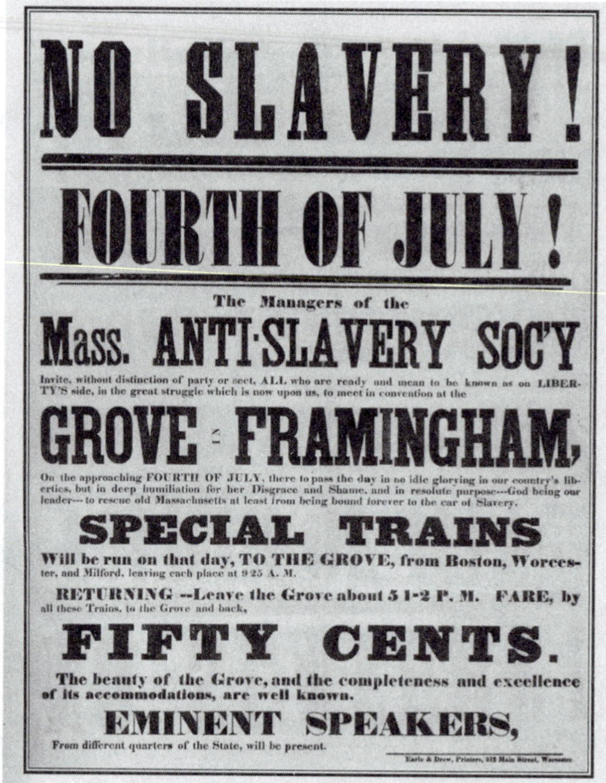

Poster for an 1854 rally at which Garrison burned a copy of the U.S. Constitution to protest the recent return of a fugitive slave to his owner (Massachusetts Historical Society)

proposed that all persons representing any antislavery organization be admitted to the convention, regardless of gender. He was voted down by a majority of conservative delegates. In protest of the exclusion of the women, Garrison took his place with them in the balcony, where he remained, in silence, for the duration of the convention.

Upon returning to the United States, Garrison attended, in November of 1840, the famous Chardon Street Convention of the friends of Universal Reform. Emerson, who was also in attendance, published an extended account of the affair in the July 1842 issue of *The Dial.* His essay, later republished as "The Chardon Street Convention," states that the "Madmen, madwomen, men with beards, Dunkers, Muggletonians, Come-outers, Groaners, Agrarians, Seventh-day Baptists, Quakers, Abolitionists, Calvinists, Unitarians and Philosophers,–all came successively to the top, and seized their moment, if not their hour, wherein to chide, or pray, or preach, or protest." Despite his mild amusement at such a miscellaneous gathering of reformers, Emerson also noted that "If there was not parliamentary order, there was life," and that "these men and women were in search of something better and more satisfying than a vote or a definition, and they found what they sought, or the pledge of it. . . ."

Emerson, who was at this time skeptical of one-issue, self-appointed reformers, nevertheless eventually warmed to the abolitionists, and Garrison in particular. In a journal entry in 1839 Emerson describes Garrison as "a man of great ability in conversation, of a certain longsightedness in debate which is a great excellence . . . and an eloquence of illustration which contents the ear & the mind." Later, in 1846, Emerson's estimation of the man had grown to the point at which he saw Garrison as one of "the five or six personalities that make up . . . our American existence." Bronson Alcott, Emerson's fellow Transcendentalist, was also impressed with Garrison upon hearing him lecture in 1830, and Alcott's brother-in-law, Samuel J. May, eventually became one of Garrison's strongest supporters.

Throughout the 1840s Garrison became increasingly prominent in the antislavery movement. While his preferred instrument of expression was the *Liberator* and the editorials and commentaries that he published there, he also possessed a poetic spirit, to which he sometimes gave expression. In 1843 he published his *Sonnets and Other Poems,* a collection with more fervor than grace. Emerson reviewed the volume in *The Dial* (4 [1843]) and noted the following:

> Mr. Garrison has won his palms in quite other fields than those of the lyric muse, and he is far more likely to be the subject than the author of good poems. He is rich enough in the earnestness and the success of his character to be patient with the very rapid withering of the poetic garlands he has snatched in passing. Yet though this volume contains little poetry, both the subjects and the sentiments will everywhere command respect. That piece in the volume, which pleased us most, was the address to his first-born child.

National events throughout the 1840s served to increase concerns about the deleterious influence of slavery on the entire society. In January of 1843 the American Anti-Slavery Society, with prompting from Garrison, passed a resolution condemning the U.S. Constitution as "a covenant with death and an agreement with hell." His disunion sentiments became even more pronounced with the annexation of Texas in 1845. Many saw the ensuing war with Mexico (1846–1848) as an effort to extend slaveholding territories and influence. The war elicited a variety of protests from many quarters in the Free States, including Henry David Thoreau's famous one-night stay in jail. The "no Union with slaveholders" crusade that Garrison promoted seemed to some to be increasingly plausible, while others felt that a more substantive political engagement would be more effective in containing slavery.

Garrison in Scotland, 31 July 1877 (from Walter M. Merrill and Louis Ruchames, The Letters of William Lloyd Garrison, *volume 6, 1981)*

In 1846 Garrison visited England once again, and in 1847 he set out on a lecture tour with Frederick Douglass, former slave and author of the classic *The Narrative of the Life of Frederick Douglass, An American Slave, Written by Himself* (1845) for which Garrison provided an introduction. Douglass had been associated with Garrison since his escape from slavery in 1838. Shortly after arriving in New Bedford, Massachusetts, Douglass discovered the *Liberator*. "The paper became my meat and my drink," he said. "My soul was set all on fire. Its sympathy for my brethern in bonds–its scathing denunciations of slaveholders–its faithful exposures of slavery–and its powerful attacks upon the upholders of the institution–sent a thrill of joy through my soul, such as I had never felt before!" Douglass's reaction is probably typical of many Negro subscribers at the time who felt that they had finally found a voice. Garrison soon discovered Douglass's intellectual and oratorical powers and hired him as an agent. In 1847 Douglass was elected president of the New England Anti-Slavery Society. Eventually, however, he split from Garrison because of philosophical differences regarding the best way to pursue the reform of American society. Douglass had a striking presence and was a powerful speaker. The speaking tour of 1847, which took Garrison and Douglass beyond the Alleghenies, was a rigorous experience for both, and Garrison's health began to suffer, but even greater challenges lay just ahead.

The Compromise of 1850, which included the infamous Fugitive Slave Law, came as a great shock to abolitionists and others throughout the North. The law provided for the forcible return from Free States of escaped slaves, who previously could live unmolested under the protection of various personal liberty laws that had been enacted in many free states. Massachusetts was one of them. Under the new law, fugitive slaves were denied trial by jury. They were not allowed to testify in their own behalf in hearings, which were conducted by appointed commissioners. Additionally, any citizen attempting to prevent the return of an escaped slave was subject to a fine of $5,000, six months imprisonment, and damages of up to another $1,000 dollars. Emerson, as well as many others, was enraged at this "filthy enactment," and he vowed never to obey it. Individuals who were largely indifferent to the slavery issue before, now became politicized by this

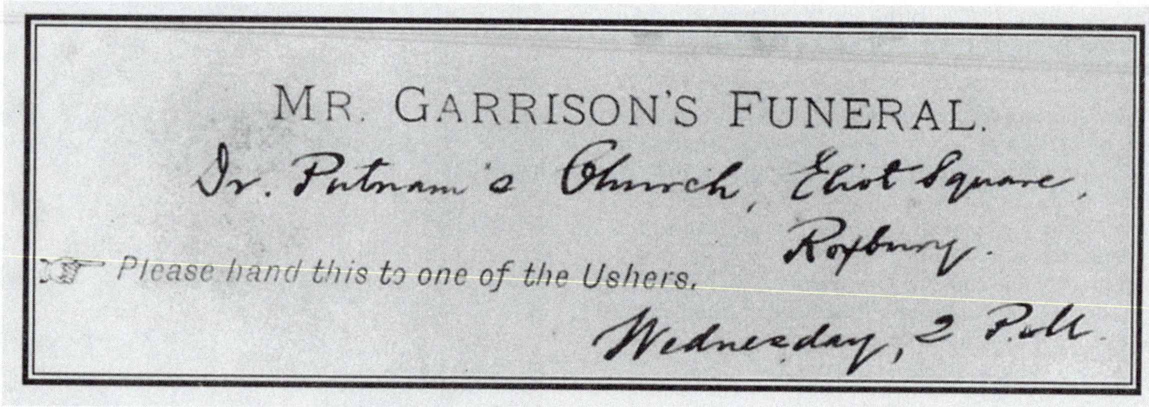
MR. GARRISON'S FUNERAL.
Dr. Putnam's Church, Eliot Square,
Roxbury.
Please hand this to one of the Ushers.
Wednesday, 2 P.M.

Admission card to Garrison's funeral, 28 May 1879 (Department of Special Collections, Ablah Library, Wichita State University)

intrusion of the slave power into their own states. Garrison condemned the compromise in no uncertain terms and also Daniel Webster's speech on 7 March, which supported and thereby made the compromise possible. Garrison referred to the oration as "indescribably base and wicked," as well as "dishonorable" and "infamous." Emerson used similarly harsh terms in his "Fugitive Slave Law Address" of 1851 and in another address on the same topic in 1854. Clearly, the national situation was deteriorating rapidly, and separation from the South seemed to many to be the only certain way to stop the contagion. Needless to say, Garrison's stock continued to rise as abolition became less of a moral abstraction and more of an immediate reality to many.

During the 1850s tensions between North and South over the slavery issue constantly escalated. Garrison was alternately praised and despised for his efforts in pressing for immediate and universal emancipation as the ultimate and only solution to the problem. In May of 1850 the annual meeting of the American Anti-Slavery Society was disrupted by an unruly mob led by the notorious Isaiah Rynders. Both Garrison and Douglass were subjected to Rynders's verbal abuse and threats, but they held their own, and bloodshed was avoided. The rendition of slaves under the Fugitive Slave Law became a constant source of agitation for abolitionists, especially in the Boston area. Vigilance groups were formed to protect possible victims of the law and initially proved effective. In October of 1850 William and Ellen Craft were protected from their pursuers by members of the Vigilance Committee, who frightened the Southerners off. In February 1851 the fugitive slave known as Shadrach was captured by Southern agents but was eventually freed from custody by a mob. He was then spirited off to Canada. Garrison, though still a nonresistant, celebrated Shadrach's rescue by force. Unfortunately, the forces of the slaveholders, reinforced by the power of the federal government, proved relentless. In April 1851 Thomas Sims, a seventeen-year-old fugitive, was arrested in Boston. This time a substantial contingent of armed guards was employed to ensure that an escape was impossible. Despite the angry protests of abolitionists and other outraged citizens of Boston, after a short hearing Sims was placed on a ship and returned to his master in Savannah, Georgia, where he was publicly whipped on 19 April. Under a headline that read "THE VICTIM HAS BEEN SACRIFICED," Garrison reported,

> Thomas Sims was taken from his prison room in the Court House a few minutes before five o'clock this morning, under the direction of Marshal Tukey, and marched through Court square, Court and State streets, to the head of Long Wharf, "in the center of a hollow square," and placed on board the Brig Acorn, . . . and is now on his way to Georgia and the auction-block of slavery! Mayor Bigelow composed a part of the escort! As early as 1/2 past 3 o'clock, Marshal Tukey began to muster the men who were to aid him in disgracing Massachusetts, and dooming a young man–a free citizen of Massachusetts–into slavery. (*Liberator,* 18 April 1851)

It was a sight that most abolitionists never thought they would see. The disgrace was followed by the return of another famous victim, Anthony Burns, in 1854. The return of fugitives was now such a bitterly controversial matter that an escort of two thousand Federal troops accompanied Burns through the streets of Boston on the day of his rendition. The same year marked the passage of the Kansas-Nebraska Act, which rescinded the Missouri Compromise and allowed slavery in the territories of Kansas and Nebraska on the basis of popular sovereignty, or the will of the people living there. By this time, Garrison was so outraged at the actions of the federal government, which was now seen as little more than a tool of the slave power, that at an antislavery gathering in Framingham, Massachusetts, on Independence Day 1854, he burned a copy of the Constitution of the United States and cried out, "So perish all compromises with tyranny!" At this same gathering Thoreau delivered his acerbic address "Slavery in Massachusetts," in which he described his thoughts as "murder to the State." Earlier in March, Emerson repeated his condemnation of Daniel Webster and the federal government in his famous address "The Fugitive Slave Law." Everywhere, positions were hardening.

During the remainder of the decade, partisan warfare increased in Kansas as New England immigrants were terrorized by "Border Ruffians," who wished to preserve the territory for slavery. In response, support groups were formed in Massachusetts to supply Sharp's rifles, or "Beecher's Bibles," as they were called by some, to the New England farmers. Garrison wrote in the *Liberator* that the Kansas-Nebraska Act was "against the laws of God and the rights of universal man–in subversion of plighted faith, in utter disregard of the scorn of the world, and for purposes as diabolical as can be conceived of or consummated here on earth." However, his nonresistance principles led him to condemn the use of violence. In a report of the annual meeting of the Massachusetts Anti-Slavery Society, which appeared in the *Liberator* (6 February 1857), Garrison is quoted as saying, "But our work is not carried on by Sharp's rifles. We wish to send the living speaker to carry truth to the hearts of men. Those who give here, give for this purpose, not for Sharp's rifles. It is our purpose to deal by moral instrumentalities."

The dire developments of the 1850s strained Garrison's previous commitment to nonresistance, perfectionism, and no-government policies. In the Presidential election of 1856 he endorsed a candidate for the first time. His support went to John C. Frémont because of his stand against the extension of slavery into the territories. This compromise with political reality became more pronounced as Garrison reacted to the various provocative events leading up to the Civil War.

One of the most significant of these events was John Brown's raid on the federal arsenal at Harpers Ferry, in October 1859. While condemning the raid as ill advised and rash, Garrison nevertheless saw Brown as a hero and a martyr to the cause. Following the execution of Brown, Garrison ran the following notice in the *Liberator* on 23 December 1859:

> It is utterly impossible for us to chronicle in our columns a hundredth part of what is transpiring in the country. To do this we would need to publish a daily *Liberator,* of twice its present size. We have on hand the proceedings of scores of commemorative meetings held in different parts of the country on the day of the execution of John Brown, all of which we should be glad to publish if it were practicable. No such popular demonstration of sympathy and exalted appreciation has been witnessed at the North since the death of George Washington. Well may the South tremble!

Shortly thereafter Garrison, for all practical purposes, abandoned his pacifist stand, as well as his opposition to organized political activity. He came to support the Republican Party. During the Civil War he at first felt some reservations about Abraham Lincoln as a champion of freedom for the slave, but after the Emancipation Proclamation became a reality in 1863, Garrison was a warm supporter of the President.

At the conclusion of the war, Garrison moved for the dissolution of the American Anti-Slavery Society in 1865. Other members of the society, especially Wendell Phillips, felt that there was still much work to be done to bring about equality in American society, and they successfully opposed dissolution. Garrison, however, declined a twenty-third term as president of the organization, sensing that his work was done. After the passage of the Thirteenth Amendment to the Constitution, which abolished slavery in the United States, Garrison wrote a farewell address for the *Liberator* and set and printed the final issue on 29 December 1865.

During his years of retirement Garrison was revered by those who saw him as the most notable reformer in the United States. In 1868 a testimonial fund of more than $30,000 was raised and presented to him in recognition of a lifetime of sacrifice. He continued his efforts at reform by supporting Prohibition, woman's rights, the protection of Native Americans, and other causes. He died of kidney disease on 24 May 1879.

Letters:

The Letters of William Lloyd Garrison, 6 volumes, edited by Walter M. Merrill and Louis Ruchames (Cambridge, Mass.: Belknap Press of Harvard University Press, 1971–1981).

Biographies:

Oliver Johnson, *William Lloyd Garrison and His Times* (Boston: B. B. Russell, 1880);

Wendell Phillips Garrison and Francis Jackson Garrison, *William Lloyd Garrison, 1805–1879; The Story of His Life as Told by His Children,* 4 volumes (New York: Century, 1885–1889);

Archibald Henry Grimké, *William Lloyd Garrison: The Abolitionist* (New York: Funk & Wagnalls, 1891);

Lindsay Swift, *William Lloyd Garrison* (Philadelphia: G. W. Jacobs, 1911);

Walter M. Merrill, *Against Wind and Tide: A Biography of William Lloyd Garrison* (Cambridge, Mass.: Harvard University Press, 1963);

John L. Thomas, *The Liberator: William Lloyd Garrison* (Boston: Little, Brown, 1963);

George Fredrickson, *William Lloyd Garrison* (Englewood Cliffs, N.J.: Prentice-Hall, 1968).

References:

James Brewer, *William Lloyd Garrison and the Challenge of Emancipation* (Arlington Heights, Ill.: Harlan Davidson, 1992);

James Duban, "Thoreau, Garrison, and Dymond: Unbending Firmness of the Mind," *American Literature,* 57 (May 1985): 273–286;

Thomas Wentworth Higginson, *Contemporaries* (Boston: Houghton, Mifflin, 1899);

Aileen Kraditor, *Means and Ends in American Abolitionism: Garrison and His Critics on Strategy and Tactics, 1834–1850* (New York: Pantheon, 1969);

William B. Rogers, *"We are all together now": Frederick Douglass, William Lloyd Garrison, and the Prophetic Tradition* (New York: Garland, 1995);

O. J. Villard, *Some Newspapers and Newspaper-Men* (New York: Knopf, 1923);

Henry Wilson, *History of the Rise and Fall of the Slave Power in America,* 3 volumes (Boston: J. R. Osgood, 1872–1877).

Papers:

Most of William Lloyd Garrison's letters, papers, and manuscripts can be found in the Boston Public Library. There are also collections of Garrison Family Papers at the Houghton Library, Harvard University, and in the Sophia Smith Collection at Smith College, Northampton, Massachusetts.

Asa Gray

(18 November 1810 - 30 January 1888)

E. Kate Stewart
University of Arkansas at Monticello

BOOKS: *Elements of Botany* (New York: G. & C. Carvill, 1836); revised as *The Botanical Text-Book for Colleges, Schools, and Private Students* (New York: Wiley & Putnam / Boston: Little, Brown, 1842); revised as *Introduction to Structural and Systematic Botany, and Vegetable Physiology* (New York: Ivison, Blakeman, Taylor, 1857); revised as *Structural Botany, or Organography on the Basis of Morphology* (New York & Chicago: Ivison, Blakeman, Taylor, 1879);

A Flora of North America, 2 volumes (New York & London: Wiley & Putnam, 1838, 1843);

A Manual of the Botany of the Northern United States (Boston: J. Munroe / London: Chapman, 1848; revised edition, New York: Putnam / Ivison & Phinney, 1856; revised again, New York: Putnam, 1859; revised again, 1863; revised again, New York: Ivison, Blakeman, 1867);

Genera floræ Americanæ boreali-orientalis illustrata, 2 volumes, illustrations by Isaac Sprague and descriptions by Gray (Boston: J. Monroe / New York & London: Wiley, 1848, 1849);

Plantæ Wrightianæ texano-neo-mexicanæ, 2 volumes (Washington, D.C.: Smithsonian Institution, 1852, 1853);

Botany. Phanerogamia, volume 15 of *United States Exploring Expedition, during the Years 1838, 1839, 1840, 1841, 1842* (Philadelphia: Printed by C. Sherman, 1854);

First Lessons in Botany and Vegetable Physiology (New York: Putnam / Ivison, Phinney, 1857); revised as *The Elements of Botany for Beginners and for Schools* (New York: American Book Company, 1887);

Botany for Young People and Common Schools. Part I: How Plants Grow: A Simple Introduction to Structural Botany (New York: Ivison, Blakeman, 1858);

Field, Forest, and Garden Botany (New York: Ivison, Blakeman, Taylor / Chicago: S. C. Griggs, 1868);

Sequoia and Its History: An Address (Salem, Mass.: Salem Press, 1872);

Asa Gray, 1865

Botany for Young People. Part II: How Plants Behave (New York & Chicago: Ivison, Blakeman, Taylor, 1872);

Darwiniana: Essays and Reviews Pertaining to Darwinism (New York: Appleton, 1876);

Synoptical Flora of North America, volume 2, part 1 (New York: Ivison, Blakeman, Taylor / London: Trübner, 1878); volume 1, part 2 (New York: Ivison, Blakeman, Taylor / London: Wesley & Trübner, 1884); second edition, revised, of both parts (New York: Ivison, Blakeman, Taylor / London: Wesley & Trübner, 1886); volume 1, part 1 (New York: American Book Company, 1895);

Jane Lathrop Loring, whom Gray married in 1848

Natural Science and Religion: Two Lectures Delivered to the Theological School of Yale College (New York: Scribners, 1880);

The Elements of Botany for Beginners and for Schools (New York: American Book Company, 1887; Chicago: Ivison, Blakeman, Taylor, 1887; revised, New York: American Book Company, 1887).

Collections: *Gray's School and Field-Book of Botany* (New York: Ivison, Phinney, Blakeman, 1869)–comprises *First Lessons in Botany and Vegetable Physiology* and *Field, Forest, and Garden Botany;*

Scientific Papers of Asa Gray, 2 volumes, compiled by Charles Sprague Sargent (Boston & New York: Houghton, Mifflin, 1889; London: Macmillan, 1889).

OTHER: *The Botanical Works of the Late George Engelmann,* edited by William Trelease and Gray (Cambridge, Mass.: John Wilson, 1887).

SELECTED PERIODICAL PUBLICATIONS–UNCOLLECTED: "A Sketch of the Mineralogy of a Portion of Jefferson and St. Lawrence Counties (N.Y.)," *American Journal of Science,* first series 25 (1834): 346–350;

"Notes of a Botanical Excursion to the Mountains of North Carolina," *American Journal of Science,* first series 42 (1842): 1–49;

"The Longevity of Trees," *North American Review,* 59, no. 124 (July 1844): 189–238;

"Account of Argyroxiphium, A Remarkable Genus of Compositae, Belonging to the Mountains of the Sandwich Islands," *Proceedings of the American Academy,* 2 (1852): 159–160;

"The Smithsonian Institute," *American Journal of Science,* second series 20 (1855): 1–21;

"Statistics of the Flora of the Northern United States," *American Journal of Science,* second series 22 (1856): 204–232;

"Statistics of the Flora of the Northern United States," *American Journal of Science,* second series 23 (1856): 62–84, 369–403;

"Wild Potatoes in New Mexico and Western Texas," *American Journal of Science,* second series 22 (1856): 284–285;

"Centrostegia," *Pacific Railroad Surveys,* 7 (1857): 19;

"Action of Foreign Pollen upon Fruit," *American Journal of Science,* second series 25 (1858): 122–123;

"Trichomanes Radicans, Swartz," *American Journal of Science,* second series 28 (1859): 440–441;

"Fertilization of Orchids through the Agency of Insects," *American Journal of Science,* second series 34 (1862): 420–429;

"Harvard University Herbarium," *American Journal of Science,* second series 39 (1865): 224–226;

"Story about a Cedar of Lebanon," *American Journal of Science,* second series 39 (1865): 226–228;

"Descriptions of Eleven New California Plants," *Proceedings of the California Academy,* 3 (1869): 101–103;

"Characters of New Genera and Species of Plants," *Proceedings of the American Academy,* 8 (1873): 620–631;

"The Botanic Garden," *The Harvard Book,* 1 (1875): 313-315;

"Roots and 'Yarbs'–in the Mountains of North Carolina," *American Agriculturist* (September 1879): 337–338;

"The Flora of Boston and its Vicinity, and the Changes It Has Undergone," in Justin Winsor, *Winsor's Memorial History of Boston,* 4 volumes (Boston: J. R. Osgood, 1880), I: 17–22;

"Note on the Musaratic Chapel of the Cathedral of Toledo, *Nation,* 884 (1882): 482;

"The Scientific Principles of Agriculture," *Science,* 5 (1885): 76;

"Botanical Nomenclature," *Britten's Journal of Botany,* 25 (1887): 255–355.

Asa Gray had a profound impact on the development of scientific study in nineteenth-century America.

He shaped the course of the study of botany into the twenty-first century, and his textbooks, especially the notable *A Manual of the Botany of the Northern United States* (1848), remain standards of the discipline. Beginning in 1834 Gray contributed copiously to such illustrious scientific journals as the *American Journal of Science* even as he wrote for such general readership magazines as the *Nation*. During his tenure at Harvard, Gray tended and nurtured the herbarium and expanded its holdings significantly by receiving and cataloguing untold numbers of plants that he collected personally or received from colleagues in the field. He is perhaps best remembered for his reviews of Charles Darwin's *Origin of Species* (1859), which styled Gray as the primary Darwin apologist in the United States. Through a life filled with laudable deeds, Asa Gray prepared the way for modern scientific study.

Born on 18 November 1810 in Sauquoit, New York, Asa Gray was the eldest child of Moses and Roxana (Howard) Gray. His Gray ancestors were of Scottish Presbyterian stock and had migrated from Ireland, settling in Worcester, Massachusetts. Eventually, his paternal grandparents settled in the Mohawk Valley in 1793. His Howard forebears also moved to Sauquoit, arriving around the same time as the Grays.

Beginning school at three, Asa demonstrated an early academic inclination. His formative training involved instruction in the basics. He especially relished reading, an occupation he held throughout his life. In 1823 the thirteen-year-old Gray began a two-year matriculation at Hamilton College in Clinton, New York. Had that institution been more stable at the time, Gray likely would have completed his education there. At Hamilton Gray received intensive training in Latin and Greek, languages that proved necessary to his career. The Gray family had hoped that Asa could go to Yale, but economic realities crushed that dream. Instead, Gray entered Fairfield (Connecticut) Medical School and received his M.D. degree in 1831. While at medical school, Gray began collecting and studying plants. In 1834 he accepted a position as an assistant to John Torrey, a chemistry professor at the College of Physicians and Surgeons in New York City. Their shared interest in botany resulted in a lifelong association that produced the celebrated *A Flora of North America* (1838, 1843).

Gray assumed the Fisher Professorship of Natural Science at Harvard College in 1842. Before his retirement in 1873, he had managed to establish in essence the botany department of that institution. His commitment to the discipline and his promotion of it brought botany from the shadows to the foreground of scientific research.

To be sure, Gray's endeavors at Harvard earned him a significant place in the annals of botanical study.

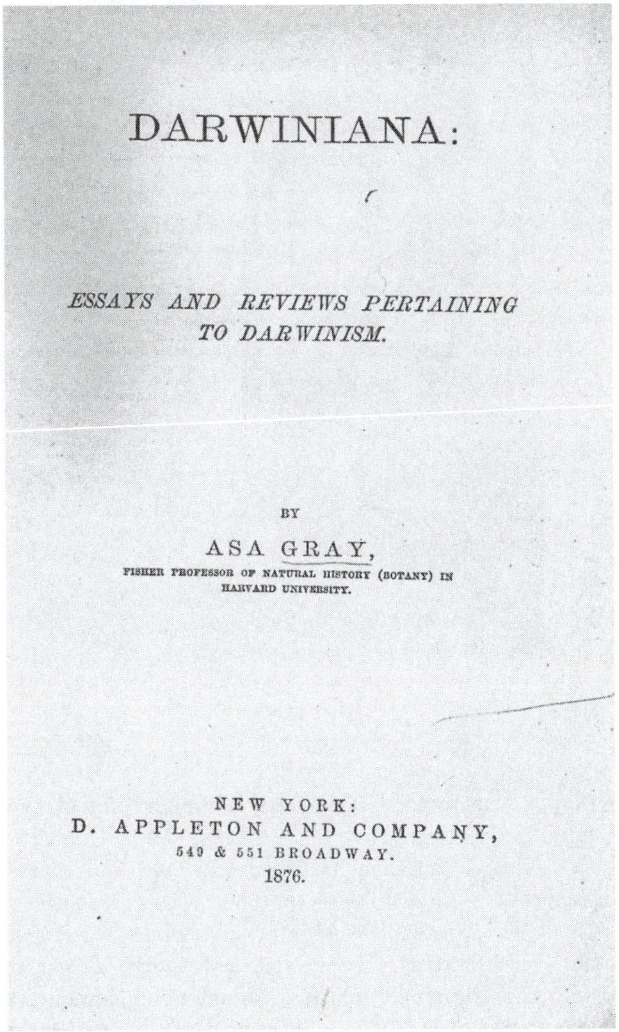

Title page for essays in which Gray introduced and defended Charles Darwin's theory of evolution to the American public

His publication record, though, defines him as a scholar who possessed remarkable attributes. Beginning in 1834 until his death in 1888, Gray hardly missed a year in making significant contributions to the study of botany. His array of writings includes textbooks, notes on discoveries of new plants, reviews of significant scientific scholarship, and sketches of celebrated scientists.

With the publication of his first textbook, *Elements of Botany* (1836), Gray notified the world that he approached the study of botany from a rather different perspective than did others. Gray was convinced that botany was far more than the mere study of taxonomy. Naming and classifying a plant was, he believed, necessary, but he posited further that a plant should be understood more fully so that one could determine the plants useful in, for instance, medicine. On that premise he built *Elements of Botany*. From the onset, the 420-page

Gray in his study

volume was praised widely, thus establishing Gray's reputation.

Elements of Botany has been reprinted and republished several times. It was combined with *First Lessons in Botany and Vegetable Physiology* (1857), which was originally published as *Field, Forest, and Garden Botany* in 1868. Gray designed the latter volume as an elementary introduction to both the wild and the cultivated common plants that grew east of the Mississippi River. Both of these texts demonstrate Gray's belief that botany could be studied by young students and lay people.

Gray's next significant publication was his collaborate effort with his friend and mentor John Torrey. Torrey had conceived of a work such as *A Flora of North America* some twenty years before he teamed with Gray to make the project a reality. The two sought in the work to describe native plants of North America according to the natural system. This system of classification was not new, but most botanists in the United States continued to rely on the Linnaean method, which grouped plants broadly by looking at only one aspect of the subject. The natural system, on the other hand, classified plants by examining many characteristics of the plant.

Torrey and Gray spent hours collecting plants themselves, but they also secured the help of a large cadre of field botanists from across the United States. The two men analyzed and wrote a description of each of the specimens collected. These descriptions comprised the content of *A Flora of North America.* The first volume opens with a brief description of "Cormophyta," which the writers describe as plants that consist of a root and stem. Gray and Torrey describe further the appearance of the root and the stem. Following the discussion of the general type, they move to the various members of the group. In every case the commentary is clear enough that even the lay reader can understand the material.

Because *A Flora of North America* relied on the natural system, it heralded a new day in botanical studies in the United States. With some opposition from more traditional naturalists, Torrey and Gray ushered the country into "modern" science.

Ten years after Torrey and Gray had published the first portions of *A Flora of North America,* Gray wrote a similar volume–*A Manual of the Botany of the Northern United States.* On 4 May of that same year, he married Jane Lathrop Loring, daughter of Charles Greeley Loring. She shared her husband's interest in his work and upon his death edited his autobiography and his letters.

Since he relied so heavily on the work of amateur botanists in the field, Gray saw a need for a more systematic and scientific approach to collecting specimens. *A Manual of the Botany of the Northern United States* answered that need by offering the classification of plants, descriptions of them, and illustrations.

Gray's work, though, extended beyond field study. He advocated a more sophisticated approach to teaching botany in the classroom. Gray believed that teaching botany should involve a truly scientific approach, but he also noted that the methodology should be accessible to the general audience.

Published in 1842, *The Botanical Text-Book for Colleges, Schools, and Private Students* filled the need as a source of instruction for burgeoning botanists. Heretofore, botany textbooks had been overly simplistic and bore only traces of truly scientific content. *The Botanical Text-Book for Colleges, Schools, and Private Students,* which underwent several title changes and revisions in its publication life, marked the first of a series of teaching aids. The 1842 volume was geared primarily toward a college audience and thus proved too advanced for younger students. Gray responded with such texts as *First Lessons in Botany and Vegetable Physiology* (1857), *How Plants Grow: A Simple Introduction to Structural Botany* (1858), and *The Elements of Botany for Beginners and for Schools* (1887). Each of these volumes retains Gray's scientific method though each is presented in a style more accessible than that of *The Botanical Text-Book for Colleges, Schools, and Private Students.*

As important as his manual and his textbooks are in shaping the course of current scientific study, Gray is perhaps best remembered for his response to the publication of *Origin of Species.* Because of the acquaintanceship Gray and Darwin had developed in the course of Gray's sojourns in England, which began in 1838, Darwin asked Gray to review *Origin of Species* before its publication. Gray recognized immediately that theories espoused in the work, especially the theory of natural selection, would be offensive to people of orthodox views. He recognized further that Darwin had produced a groundbreaking work that deserved attention.

Reared as an orthodox Christian himself, Gray questioned some of Darwin's notions. Unlike many of his religious counterparts, though, he believed that natural selection could coexist with the biblical account of creation. In a series of articles for the *Atlantic Monthly,* Gray essentially introduced Darwin and evolution to the American public. His analyses of *Origin of Species* are clear and well-written. He follows a consistent pattern of quoting at length passages from Darwin's work, then discussing them carefully. Because Gray's assessment is so balanced, many might charge him with waffling. His reviews and assessments, though, doubtless reflect his own struggle with reconciling his faith and scientific theory.

Besides notable textbooks and the articles on Darwin, Gray also published many articles in the leading scientific journals of the day. He contributed most frequently to the *American Journal of Science,* for which he also served as an editor. These essays consist of notations of discoveries of new plant species, reviews of current scientific works, and biographical sketches of leading scholars in science in the nineteenth century.

Asa Gray successfully introduced scientific botanical studies to the United States. He continued his contributions to scholarship up to his death on 30 January 1888 in Cambridge, Massachusetts. His texts and articles brought respectability to an important field of study.

Letters:

Letters of Asa Gray, 2 volumes, edited by Jane Loring Gray (Boston & New York: Houghton, Mifflin, 1893).

Bibliography:

J. Watson, "List of the Writings of Dr. Asa Gray," *American Journal of Science,* third series 36 (1888): 785–825.

Biography:

A. Hunter Dupree, *Asa Gray: American Botanist, Friend of Darwin* (Cambridge, Mass.: Belknap Press of Harvard University Press, 1959).

References:

Paul Jerome Croce, "Probabilistic Darwinism: Louis Agassiz and Asa Gray on Science, Religion, and Certainty," *The Journal of Religious History,* 22, no. 1 (1998): 35–58;

James Dwight Dana, "Asa Gray," *American Journal of Science,* third series 35 (1888): 23;

George C. Fry, *Congregationalists and Evolution: Asa Gray and Louis Agassiz* (Lanham, Md.: University Press of America, 1989);

Michael McGiffert, "Christian Darwinism: The Partnership of Asa Gray and George Frederick Wright, 1874–1881," M.A. thesis, Yale University, 1977.

Papers:

The majority of Asa Gray's manuscripts and letters are located at Harvard University.

Horatio Greenough

(6 September 1805 - 18 December 1852)

Sally C. Hoople

BOOKS: *Aesthetics at Washington,* no. 1 (Washington, D.C.: J. T. Towers, 1851);

The Travels, Observations, and Experience of a Yankee Stonecutter, as Horace Bender (New York: G. P. Putnam, 1852);

Form and Function: Remarks on Art by Horatio Greenough, edited by Harold A. Small, with an introduction by Erle Loran (Berkeley & Los Angeles: University of California Press, 1947);

An American Sculptor's Drawings, compiled by Richard H. Saunders (Middlebury, Vt.: Middlebury College Museum of Art, 1999)–exhibition catalogue.

Horatio Greenough, 1852 (daguerreotype attributed to John Adams Whipple)

Horatio Greenough was a sculptor by profession, but some critics have praised him more for his writings than for his artistic creations. He was an exponent of the organic theory in sculpture and architecture whose essays place him in the early school of rationalism in the United States as a predecessor to Louis Sullivan and his famous declaration that "Form follows function." Greenough's struggle to develop distinctly American artistic ideals and works persisted throughout his life, and he attacked revivalism, especially Gothic, as derivative and unoriginal. While he did not reject classical models, he believed that the artist should emulate their finest features, but with inventiveness.

Born in Boston, Massachusetts, on 6 September 1805 to a family with deep roots in that city, Horatio Greenough early adopted Yankee "notions" that remained, in his words, "intact," combined with "others acquired by a long sojourn on different points of the earth's surface." His father, David Greenough, was a successful realtor and builder whose contribution to outstanding architectural projects brought early prosperity to him and his family. His mother, Elizabeth (Bender) Greenough, was born in Marlborough, Massachusetts. A voracious reader, she also wrote poetry, but she had little interest in art. Greenough was one of eleven children; of the nine who survived to adulthood, seven were artists and/or writers. His interest in art flourished when he was still a boy. Inspired by a marble statue of Phocion in the family garden, visits to the Boston Athenaeum, which contained a sizable collection of statuary, tutelage from Solomon Willard–a carver, architect, and tombstone maker–and modeling lessons from John B. Binon, Greenough decided to become a sculptor.

In 1821 Greenough entered Harvard, the college of three of his brothers–John, Henry, and Alfred. There he read the classics, English literature, and art history, and also studied anatomy, as well as foreign languages, especially French and Italian. During his college years he met Washington Allston and Richard and Edmund Dana, whose friendships profoundly influenced his artistic and literary development. In 1825

Greenough submitted a design to the Bunker Hill Monument Association, proposing an obelisk instead of a column, to which he objected on the basis of its lack of completion. In a letter he stated that the column, intended to support an entablature as an appendage to a greater construction, "grand and beautiful as it is *in its place,*" loses its function when it is erected in isolation: "It steps forth from that *body* of which it has been made a harmonious *part* to take a situation which of all others requires *unity* of form." Although the final design was not Greenough's, it was an obelisk.

After his graduation from Harvard that same year, Greenough sailed to Europe, where he finally settled in Rome to study sculpture. There he shared rooms with New York painter Robert Weir, with whom he absorbed the artistic culture of the city. The Danish sculptor Bertel Thorvaldsen, whom he met in Rome, was probably the most significant force in the development of Greenough's aesthetic theories. In a May 1826 letter to Washington Allston, Greenough acknowledged that "the acquaintance of Thorvaldsen made the greatest change in my views." Thorvaldsen taught Greenough to think for himself and to progress from emphasis on the means of art to excellence in execution. Additionally, Greenough hoped "to pay much attention to *character,*" in his opinion a neglected beauty that "none but the very first minds have seized . . . or discovered its principles." In a letter Greenough said that he regarded the Italian view of art as "narrow" and sculptor Antonio Canova as "clever" but "superficial and sensual in his style–& a most barefaced misrepresenter of Nature–He I am convinced will fall *very low very shortly.*" During his brief stay in Rome, Greenough produced copious sketches and models, but during the latter half of 1826 he suffered a life-threatening illness, probably malaria. In January 1827 he went to Naples to try to recuperate from recurring symptoms. During this illness he showed some signs of depression and derangement. In March he and Weir, who had cared for him while he was ill, sailed for Boston.

Toward the end of 1827 Greenough modeled a bust of George Washington and other portraits, and completed a marble bust of Josiah Quincy, mayor of Boston. During that autumn he wrote a review of Richard Henry Dana Sr.'s *Poems* (1827). The review was published in *American Quarterly Review* in March 1828. The most significant aspect of his review, according to biographer Nathalia Wright, was that "he set forth at the beginning of his essay a theory of American culture." The late entrance of America into history, Greenough wrote, precluded "an intellectual infancy. . . . Discovered, America, like the statue of Prometheus touched by an enlivening fire, awoke, as far as poetry is concerned, in adult vigor." Early in 1828 Greenough met Samuel F. B. Morse, Thomas Cole, and William Cullen Bryant in New York. Later he went to Washington, D.C., where he began modeling a bust of President John Quincy Adams. In May Greenough once again sailed for Italy.

Back in Florence, which he referred to as "the most inspiring place in the world," Greenough criticized the art of Italy in an October 1828 letter to Washington Allston. Greenough believed that most of the young Italian artists, unlike their illustrious predecessors Michelangelo and Leonardo Da Vinci, were deficient in portraits and landscapes and distorted nature, which they found "so excessively true that they must dilute a little the *reality* of her character to bring it into the circle of the Bello" (Beauty). Claiming as an exception the sculptor Lorenzo Bartolini, he wrote in a letter that "Nature is his idol and to imitate her exactly his whole desire"; he asked Bartolini to serve as his teacher. Under Bartolini's tutelage and generous offer of facilities, Greenough worked on many commissions from the United States, including the *Medora* for Robert Gilmor and the *Chanting Cherubs* for James Fenimore Cooper, who helped him financially, intellectually, and emotionally. In a 17 November 1829 letter to Allston, Greenough described Cooper as "the noblest patron I have yet found–[he] has the broadest ideas on the subject of art and wishes me well personally." In that same letter he set forth his ideas about truth and beauty. While he acknowledged that "truth is not always beauty," he considered a work devoid of beauty "the lowest in the order of works of sculpture" and sought to convey "all that's dear in beauty all that's moving in passion all that's grand in thought."

In August 1831 Greenough went to Paris, where he visited the Louvre, met the Marquis de Lafayette and artist Jean-Auguste-Dominique Ingres, and participated in the cultural life of the city. He considered Paris splendid but rejected French art generally and dismissed "the french-greek physiog" of J. L. David's "ideal figures" as "nauseous." Writing to Allston from Paris, Greenough compared American architecture to European and concluded that imitations of classical and Gothic styles were unsuccessful. He dismissed the Second Bank of the United States in Philadelphia, designed to resemble the Greek Parthenon, as a "shorn" structure that "reminds us of a noble captive stripped alike of arms and ornaments." Calling Nature "the only true school of art," he planted the seeds of his architectural ideals of rationalism. Rather than sacrifice use to "an abstract idea of form–we would that the shell of each fabric be as it were, moulded on the wants and conveniences desired." He cited the functional nature of naval architecture as the ideal principle of construction: "Our fleets alone can shew that the world is not retrograde." Thus, the architect must consider, above all, the "requi-

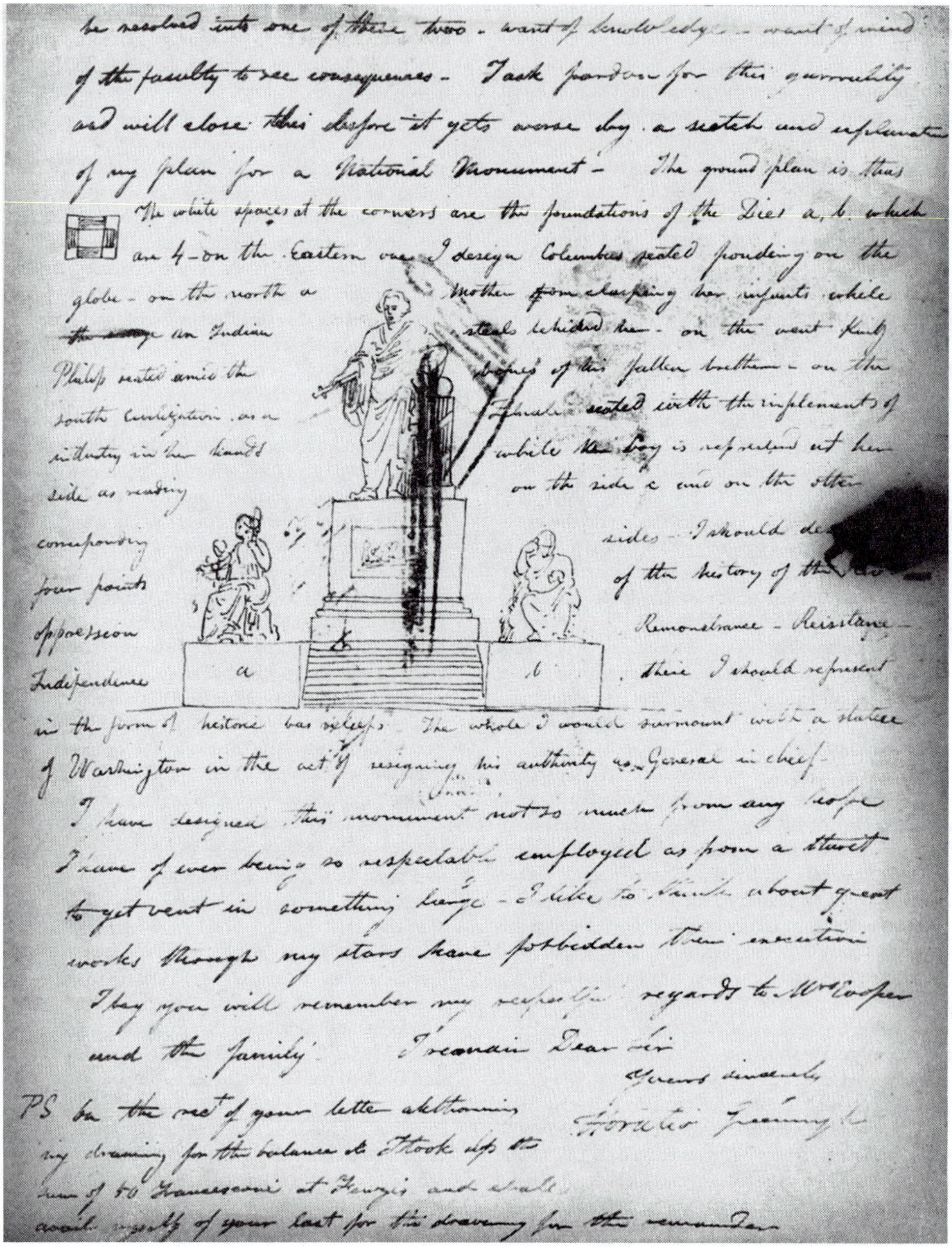

be resolved into one of these two - want of knowledge - want of mind of the faculty to see consequences - I ask pardon for this garrulity and will close this before it gets worse by a sketch and explanation of my plan for a National Monument - The ground plan is thus

The white spaces at the corners are the foundations of the Dies a, b. which are 4 - on the Eastern one I design Columbus seated pondering on the globe - on the north a ~~the savage~~ an Indian Mother clasping her infants while steals behind her - on the west King Philip seated amid the bones of his fallen brethren - on the south Civilization as a Female seated with the implements of industry in her hands while the boy is represented at her side as reading on the side c and on the other sides - I should de… corresponding of the history of the Rev… four points Remonstrance - Resistance - Oppression Independence these I should represent in the form of historic bas reliefs. The whole I would surmount with a statue of Washington in the act of resigning his authority as General in chief-

I have designed this monument not so much from any hope I have of ever being so respectably employed as from a thirst to get vent in something large - I like to think about great works though my stars have forbidden their execution

Pray you will remember my respectful regards to Mrs Cooper and the family. I remain Dear Sir

Yours sincerely

Horatio Greenough

PS On the rect of your letter authorizing my drawing for the balance I took up the sum of 80 Francesconi at Fenzi's and shall avail myself of your last for the drawing for the remainder

Page from Greenough's 7 March 1831 letter to James Fenimore Cooper, in which the artist describes his design for a national monument (Cooper Collection, Beinecke Rare Book and Manuscripts Library, Yale University)

The statue of George Washington (1843) that Greenough was commissioned to sculpt for the rotunda of the U.S. Capitol. It was later moved to the Smithsonian Institution.

sites of a building by those who are to occupy it." He concluded his letter with a call for originality in American architecture: "If we continue to stand tip-toe along the Atlantic shore endeavouring to catch the last word from Europe nothing great will surely be done." In an 8 November 1831 letter to Rembrandt Peale, Greenough asked him to convince fellow Americans "that one American Work is of more value to the U.S. than 3 foreign ones even of superiour merit . . . the scholars of America have looked so much abroad for salvation in letters arts and manners that they have not only overlooked home but have unfitted all under their influence for judging impartially of any thing American. They have carted sand in upon a fine soil." At the end of November, Greenough left Paris and returned to Florence.

Greenough wanted to create a massive work and thus "emulate others who have made statues for my country, while I'm young." In an 1832 letter to Cooper, Greenough explained that he "would fain do something in the large before *habit* shall have cramped my hand to the little." That year Congress granted Greenough a commission to sculpt a statue of George Washington for the United States Capitol. Ambivalent about where to execute his Washington statue, in 1833 Greenough wrote to Cooper, "Like the ass between 2 bundles of hay I cast my eye from continent to continent and sigh that I can't plant one foot in the states and the other on the boot [Italy]." From 1832 to 1844 Greenough worked on several private commissions and executed the group sculpture *Angel and Child,* which was exhibited in Boston. Greenough cultivated the friendship of several writers during those years, and Ralph Waldo Emerson's visit to Florence for a month in 1833 produced a bond between the two men. In 1836 Greenough returned to the United States.

On 27 July, three days after Greenough arrived in Boston, his ailing father died. In a letter to Cooper, Greenough described his father's last words to his gathered offspring: "My trust is in an unknown God!" Contrasting "the simplicity and kindness of his last words" to "the mannered jargon of the priest whose duty it was made to console this family," Greenough concluded that "Christianity is in the heart & in the heart only–any admixture of head-work spoils all–and in those of the trade all is spoiled." To Richard Henry Wilde he wrote, "I have lost the man on earth whom I esteemed and loved the most & who was rather a companion, than a governor of my youth." In September, Greenough sailed to England with his sister Louisa. In December he went to Paris and in January returned to Florence. On 14 October 1837 he married Louisa Ingersoll Gore of Boston. With her substantial inheritances, the Greenoughs lived comfortably. In September 1840 Greenough was granted the Diploma of the Royal Academy of the Fine Arts in Florence.

By the end of 1840 he had completed his statue of Washington, whom he described as "the *apotheosis of abnegation*–he is a conductor standing between God and man, the channel of blessings from heaven, and of prayer and praise from earth." After some delay, the statue was shipped in June 1841. In September 1842 Greenough sailed for America; after a stay of a few weeks in Boston, he went to Washington in November. Critical opinion about his statue was sharply divided. While the public praised his artistic skill, they sneered at the anachronistic drapery and deemed the nudity of the upper body barbaric and indecent. While the criticism offended Greenough, he did agree with their objections to the location of the statue in the Rotunda. Thus, he requested that it be moved outside to the Capitol grounds. Today the statue occupies a prominent position in the Smithsonian Institute. In April 1843 Horatio and Louisa Greenough moved to Wilmington, Delaware, and in July they sailed to Europe.

At this time Greenough turned his attention more to reading and writing and acquired a sizable library. In 1843 his essays "Remarks on American Art" and

"American Architecture" were published in the *United States Magazine and Democratic Review*. In "Remarks on American Art" he protested the European critics of New World culture who, he believed, viewed Americans as skillful and clever but artistically undeveloped: "Seeing us intently occupied during several generations in felling forests, building towns, and constructing roads," Europe "thence formed a theory that we are good for nothing except these pioneer efforts." Europe ridiculed American lack of "statues or frescoes in our log cabins; she pronounced us unmusical because we did not sit down in the swamp, with an Indian on one side and a rattlesnake on the other, to play the violin." Belying those judgments, Greenough pointed to the more recent spate of artists and concluded that "the same powers displayed in clearing the forest and tilling the farm will trim the garden." He argued that to educate those artists, imitation has value for learning rudiments, but insistence upon routine and drudgery will stifle the truly creative students.

In "American Architecture" Greenough observed that in America the subject of building had been subordinated to "matters of more pressing importance"; thus, the nation indiscriminately adopted building styles imported from Europe without attempting "to adapt, to distinguish,–nay, to understand." Modifying a Greek temple to "serve for a customhouse or bank, departs from its original beauty and propriety as widely as the crippled gelding of a hackney coach differs from the bounding and neighing wild horse of the desert." His concept of organic beauty, influenced in part by his studies in anatomy, demanded that a work be harmonious in itself and consistent with its environment. Marking the grace and functionalism of a ship at sea, he observed that if Americans carried "into our civil architecture the responsibilities that weigh upon our shipbuilding, we should ere long have edifices . . . superior to the Parthenon, for the purposes that we require" and proposed that "our blunders on terra firma be put to the same dread test that those of shipbuilders are." Rather than forcing the inhabitants and functions of a building to adhere to one outer form, artists should organically "begin from the heart as the nucleus, and work outward."

In 1843 Greenough and his wife turned to hydrotherapy to improve their health. Water was their only beverage, and they took cold baths every day. Louisa Greenough had suffered several miscarriages; thus, in 1844 they went to Gräfenberg, Austria, to seek *das Wasser kur* (the water cure) from Vincent Priessnitz. The vigorous daily exercise and cold baths seem to have proved efficacious. Not only did both of the Greenoughs enjoy excellent health, but on 11 May 1845, Henry Saltonstall, nearly eleven pounds, was

Greenough's studio on the Piazza Independenza in Florence

born and, in Greenough's words, "plunged at once into water so cold that I cannot drink a full glass of it without stopping." In a 26 May 1845 letter, presumably to John Louis Sullivan, Greenough defended "the system of Hydrotherapeutics." Claiming to have seen more than a thousand patients treated with the Priessnitz method, he said that only four had died, in spite of the range of illnesses from common colds to leprosy and syphilis, and he affirmed that he had "yet to see one who does not confess that he is better." He described bedridden patients with chronic illnesses who gradually improved and at last rose "with the lark and as merry as he." He declared that the system fostered cleanliness, simplicity, and decency, and required daily labor, "which makes it clear that idleness is decay." He concluded that not only did he respect the medical efficacy of hydrotherapy, but he also believed in it "as a system of living."

In the late summer of 1845 Greenough and his family returned to Florence, where he studied German, read extensively, and wrote critical essays that were published in the *United States Magazine and Democratic Review* in February 1846. These four "Etchings with a Chisel" included "The Miraculous Picture," a description of the Annunciation painting in the Florence church of SS. Annunziata; "Do Not be Afraid of Grace and Beauty," a portrayal of Fanny Elssler's dancing; "Prince Metternich," an account of Greenough's meet-

The Rescue *(1851), in which Greenough "endeavoured to convey the idea of the triumph of the whites over the savage tribes." The statue was commissioned for the U.S. Capitol, where it stands on a buttress of the east portico.*

ing with the Chancellor; and "By Their Fruits Ye Shall Know Them," a discussion of contrasting political systems. In the spring of 1846 Greenough and his family went to Freiwaldau, Silesia, and returned in the fall to Florence, where he built a studio on Piazza Maria Antonia. On 25 July 1847 Louisa Greenough gave birth to Mary Louise and on 16 September 1850 to Charlotte.

In July 1851 Greenough completed his group sculpture *The Rescue,* and in October he and his family sailed for America. In November he went to Washington, D.C., to await the arrival of *The Rescue,* only to learn that it had not yet been shipped. Distressed by the delay and what he considered the cavalier attitude of the Commissioner of Public Buildings, he wrote *Aesthetics at Washington* (1851), a pamphlet comprising five essays. Decrying the reliance of the United States upon imported civilization and its "stern disregard of everything not materially indispensable," Greenough called for "working normal schools of structure and ornament," where students might learn valuable basics by designing for mechanics and manufacturers. Disparaging many buildings in Washington, he found the stone used to build the Capitol defective and the cost of paint to cover that fragile material deplorable. He considered the vines on the Capitol grounds incongruous with "the character and functions of this edifice" and the statuary poorly situated. He objected to the iron railings, inadequate lighting, and the foliage that obscured the inscription on his statue of George Washington. He believed that a standard should be established to counteract "the heterogeneous and chaotic character of these buildings" lest the city soon become "but a patchwork of as many whims, fancies, and artistic dogmas as have found favor in the eyes of the temporary occupants." Rather than warp the Greek temple to their use, the men who "have reduced locomotion to its simplest elements, in the trotting wagon and the yacht *America*" more nearly approach the Greek ideal. "If a flat sail goes nearest wind, a bellying sail, though picturesque, must be given up." Turning to the Washington Monument, Greenough objected to the incongruous juxtaposition of an Egyptian obelisk with a Greek Doric colonnade. The "dark pile" that composed the Gothic Smithsonian made him shudder as he saw in front of the Capitol that threatening "tower and battlement, and all that medieval confusion, stamped . . . on the halls of Congress, as ink on paper! Dark on that whiteness–complication on that simplicity!"

Early in 1852 Greenough saw much of Emerson, Henry David Thoreau, and Henry Wadsworth Longfellow. On 18 and 19 August he stayed with Emerson, who described in his journal the brilliance and magnanimity of his visitor. That year G. P. Putnam's published, under the name Horace Bender, Greenough's volume of essays *The Travels, Observations, and Experience of a Yankee Stonecutter* (1852). It included his earlier essays "Aesthetics at Washington" and "American Architecture," as well as other commentaries on art and miscellaneous subjects. In "Fourier et Hoc Genus Omne" Greenough expressed mistrust of the theorist who has "no wholesome, working, organic relation with God's ground or with his fellow-men." He objected to "transcendental theories of life . . . because they threaten to pare down and clip the tendrils by which I cling to the concrete." Because he loved "the concrete my brother," he knelt "to Willy Shakespeare, who guessed to a drop how much oil goes to a Lombard's salad." In "The Stonecutter's Creed" he set forth three characteristics of man worthy of "love and thought," "Beauty–Action–Character":

> By beauty I mean the promise of function.
> By action I mean the presence of function.
> By character I mean the record of function.

"Relative and Independent Beauty" expands Greenough's insistence upon organicism and calls upon science "to arrest the tide of sensuous and arbitrary embellishment." He maintains "that the first downward step was *the introduction of the first inorganic, non-functional element, whether of shape or color.*" In "The Cooper Monument" Greenough again assailed embellishment, which tended to proliferate from acanthus leaves to a desire for "jasper, and porphyry, and serpentine, and giallo antico [an ornamental marble] at last" and the twist from straight to spiral columns. "By degrees you find yourself in the midst of barbaric pomp, whose means must be slavery, nothing less will supply its waste, whose enjoyment is satiety, whose result is corruption."

Greenough's *The Rescue* was placed on a buttress of the Capitol portico. Although the statue was not finished until 1851, Greenough had begun the work in 1837. In a 15 November 1837 letter to John Forsyth, Greenough enclosed a design for *The Rescue* and remarked that with it he "endeavoured to convey the idea of the triumph of the whites over the savage tribes." In his essay "Abolition" Greenough claimed that "the black perishes in the process of civilization." He believed that the lowliest slave in America enjoyed a condition superior to that of the African and attacked the antislavery agitation that ignored "the rights of property in the south . . . similar or analogous abuses at the north," and "the constitution itself" right up to the point of civil war. To a friend who defended the agitation he responded, "You say slavery is a curse! I say that black freedom is annihilation to the blacks here. . . . Why are you so intolerant of the sin of the south in holding slaves, so tolerant of the sin of the north in holding prostitutes." Greenough and Emerson vigorously disagreed upon this issue. In response to Emerson's primary objection to Greenough's essays, which otherwise he wholeheartedly endorsed, Greenough wrote in an 11 September 1852 letter to Emerson a defense of his "adhesion to the South." He blamed the North for purchasing products produced by slaves and concluded, "I am a staunch believer in free discussion & have no objection to hear any amount of abuse of slavery and slave holders–provided there be also a fair hearing for the defense–So far as the negro himself is concerned I fully believe & roundly declare that I believe he *can exist here* only as a bondsman."

In late November of 1852 Greenough delivered two lectures in the Lecture Room of the New Music Hall. On 4 December, showing symptoms of severe irrationality, he was hospitalized, and on 18 December he died. According to the Cambridge Death Records, the cause of death was "nervous derangement." He was buried in Mount Auburn Cemetery in Cambridge.

Letters:

Letters from Horatio Greenough to his Brother Henry, edited by Frances Boott Greenough (Boston: Ticknor, 1887);

Letters of Horatio Greenough, American Sculptor, edited by Nathalia Wright (Madison: University of Wisconsin Press, 1972).

Biography:

Nathalia Wright, *Horatio Greenough: The First American Sculptor* (Philadelphia: University of Pennsylvania Press, 1963).

References:

Alexander H. Everett, "Greenough's Statue of Washington," *United States Magazine and Democratic Review,* 14 (June 1844): 618–621;

F. O. Matthiessen, *American Renaissance: Art and Expression in the Age of Emerson and Whitman* (New York: Oxford University Press, 1941), pp. 140–152;

Charles R. Metzger, *Emerson and Greenough: Transcendental Pioneers of an American Esthetic* (Westport, Conn.: Greenwood Press, 1954);

Lorado Taft, *The History of American Sculpture* (New York: Macmillan, 1924), pp. 37–56;

Henry T. Tuckerman, *Book of the Artists* (New York: G. P. Putnam, 1867), pp. 10, 85–86, 188, 247–275;

Tuckerman, *A Memorial of Horatio Greenough* (New York: G. P. Putnam, 1853);

Nancy Wynne and Beaumont Newhall, "Horatio Greenough: Herald of Functionalism," *Magazine of Art,* 32 (January 1939): 12–15.

Papers:

Manuscripts of letters to Horatio Greenough's brother Henry and many other papers have apparently been destroyed. Other primary manuscripts are scattered. Four essays are in the posssession of Henry G. Nickerson, Dedham, Mass. A few drafts of letters and other items are in the collection of Nathalia Wright.

Edward Everett Hale

(3 April 1822 – 10 June 1909)

Peter Valenti
Fayetteville State University

See also the entries on Hale in *DLB 42: American Writers for Children Before 1900* and *DLB 74: American Short-Story Writers Before 1880.*

Edward Everett Hale, 1855

BOOKS: *Jenny's Journey* (Boston: Carter, Hendee, 1840?);

How to Conquer Texas, Before Texas Conquers Us (Boston: Redding, 1845);

The Rosary of Illustrations of the Bible (Boston: Phillips, Sampson, 1849);

"What Is the Worth of Doctrine?" A Sermon Preached at the Anniversary of the Charleston Unitarian Book and Tract Society (Charlestown, Mass.: Walker & Burke, 1848);

Margaret Percival in America: A Tale, by Hale and Lucretia P. Hale (Boston: Phillips, Sampson, 1850);

Christian Duty to Emigrants: A Sermon Delivered Before the Boston Society for the Prevention of Pauperism, at the Old South Church in Boston, May 9, 1852 (Boston: J. Wilson, 1852);

The Lord Visits and Redeems His People: A Sermon Preached at the Installation of E. B. Willson as Minister of the First Parish of West Roxbury, July 18, 1852 (Boston: J. Wilson, 1852);

Letters on Irish Emigration (Boston: Phillips, Sampson, 1852);

Sketches of Christian History (Boston, 1850); republished as *Scenes from Christian History* (Boston: Crosby & Nichols, 1852);

The Gospel of Freedom Extended by the Organization of Emigration: An Essay on the Scriptural and Political Remedy for the North in the Present Crisis on Slavery (Boston, 1853);

Kanzas and Nebraska (Boston: Phillips, Sampson, 1854);

The Immaculate Conception: A Sermon Preached in the Church of the Unity, Worcester, and in the Second Congregational Church, Worcester, on the 14th and 21st of January, 1855 (Boston: Phillips, Sampson, 1855);

The Last Voyage of the Resolute (Boston, 1856);

Address before the Worcester Children's Friends Society (Worcester, Mass., 1856);

Public Amusement for Poor and Rich. A Discourse Delivered Before the Church of the Unity, Worcester, December 16, 1855 (Boston: Phillips, Sampson, 1857);

The Relief of the Poor by Individuals, by the State, and by Benevolent Societies: A Discourse Delivered Before the Howard Benevolent Society, Sunday Evening, Dec. 14, 1856, at the South Congregational Church, Boston (Boston: J. Wilson, 1857);

How to Seek God. The Duties and the Dangers of a Revival: A Sermon Preached at the South Congregational Church, Boston, on the 14th of March, 1858 (Boston: Phillips, Sampson, 1858);

A Sermon Delivered Before His Excellency Nathaniel P. Banks, Governor, His Honor Eliphalet Trask, Lieutenant-governor, the Honorable Council, and the General Court of Massachusetts, at the Annual Election, Wednesday, Jan. 5, 1859 (Boston: W. White, 1859);

Elements of Christian Doctrine and Its Development (Boston: Walker, Wise, 1860);

Christian Ministry in Large Cities (Boston, 1860);

A Sermon Delivered at the Ordination of Mr. Chas. B. Ferry, in Peterborough, N. H., June 13, 1860 (Peterborough, N.H.: K. C. Scott, 1860);

Thirty Years of Boston: An Address Delivered at Hollis-Street Church, Jan. 27, 1861: On Occasion of the Celebration of "The Silver Birthday" of Warren-Street Chapel (Boston?, 1861);

Ninety Days' Worth of Europe (Boston: Walker, Wise, 1861);

The Future Civilization of the South: A Sermon Preached, on the 13th of April, 1862, at the South Congregational Church, Boston (Boston, 1862);

The Desert and the Promised Land. A Sermon (Boston: Moody, 1863);

The Emigration of Women to Oregon: A Report to the Directors of the New-England Emigrant Aid Co. (Boston, 1864);

Edward Everett in the Ministry of Reconciliation: A Sermon Preached in the South Congregational Church, Boston, Jan. 22, 1865 (Boston: A. Mudge, 1865);

The Public Duty of a Private Citizen: A Sermon Preached in the South Congregational Church, Boston, Sept. 3, 1865, the Sunday Following the Death of Mr. George Livermore (Cambridge, Mass.: J. Wilson, 1865);

The Man Without a Country (Boston: Ticknor & Fields, 1865);

The Christian Unity: A Sermon Preached at the South Congregational Church, Boston, November 11, 1866, with the Reports of the Christian Unity from its Beginning (Boston: A. Mudge, 1866);

Free Schools for the South (N.p., 1866);

Silver Wedding Memorial of Mr. and Mrs. Thos. C. Stearnes (Boston, 1866);

If, Yes, and Perhaps. Four Possibilities and Six Exaggerations, with Some Bits of Facts (Boston: Ticknor & Fields, 1868); republished as *The Man Without a Country and Other Tales* (Boston: Ticknor & Fields, 1868);

The Ingham Papers (Boston: Fields, Osgood, 1869);

How They Live in Boston and How They Die There (N.p., 1869);

Sybaris and Other Homes (Boston: Fields, Osgood, 1869);

Col. Ingham's Visit to Sybaris (Boston: Fields, Osgood, 1869);

People and Minister: An Anniversary Sermon, Preached at the South Congregational Church, Boston, January 9, 1870 (Boston: Rand, Avery & Frye, 1870);

Ten Times One Is Ten: The Possible Reformation. A Story in Nine Chapters, as Colonel Frederic Ingham (Boston: Roberts, 1871);

How To Do It (Boston: J. R. Osgood, 1871);

His Level Best and Other Stories (Boston: Roberts, 1872);

In His Name: A Christmas Story (Boston: Proprietors of Old and New, 1873);

Christmas Eve and Christmas Day: Ten Christmas Stories (Boston: Roberts, 1873);

Ups and Downs: An Every-day Novel (Boston: Roberts, 1873);

A Summer Vacation: Four Sermons (Boston: Roberts, 1874);

Workingmen's Homes (Boston: J. R. Osgood, 1874);

Early Maps of America; and a Note on Robert Dudley and the Arcano Del Mare. Read Before the American Antiquarian Society, October 21, 1873 (Worcester, Mass.: C. Hamilton, 1874);

Sketches of the Lives of the Brothers Everett (Boston: Little, Brown, 1875);

One Hundred Years Ago: How the War Began. A Series of Sketches from Original Authorities (Boston: Lockwood, Brooks, 1875);

Our New Crusade: A Temperance Story (Boston: Roberts, 1875); also published as *The Good Time Coming; or Our New Crusade* (Boston: Roberts, 1875);

Philip Nolan's Friends: A Story of the Change of Western Empire (New York: Scribner, Armstrong, 1876);

A Free-born Church: Sermon Preached Before the National Conference of Unitarian and Other Christian Churches, Sept. 12, 1876 (Boston, 1876);

Fall of the Stuarts (Boston: Estes & Lauriat, 1876);

Biographical Sketch of James Edward Root (Albany: J. Munsell, 1877);

G. T. T.; or, the Wonderful Adventures of a Pullman (Boston: Roberts, 1877);

The Wolf at the Door, anonymous (Boston: Roberts, 1877);

Salvation: A Sermon Preached in Music Hall, Sunday Evening, May 6th (Boston, 1877?);

Back to Back: A Story of To-day (New York: Harper, 1878);

Mrs. Merriam's Scholars (Boston: Roberts, 1878);

What Career? (Boston: Roberts, 1878);

The Duty of the Church in Cities: A Paper Read at the Philadelphia Conference, Oct. 31, 1878 (Boston: George H. Ellis, 1878);

Looking Back: A Sermon Preached at the South Congregational Church, Boston, Nov. 17, 1878 (Boston: A. Williams, 1878);

Yourselves. A Sermon Preached at the South Congregational Church, Boston, Jan. 12, 1879 (Boston: A. Williams, 1879);

Hale's birthplace (far left) at the corner of Tremont and School Streets in Boston

What It Is to Be a Catholic: Sermon Jan. 26, 1879 (Boston: A. Williams, 1879);

Stories of War Told by Soldiers (Boston: Roberts, 1879);

Blasphemy Against the Holy Ghost (Boston: A. Williams, 1879);

The Joy of Life: A Sermon Preached in the South Congregational Church, Boston, February 9, 1879 (Boston: A. Williams, 1879);

The Future of New England. A Sermon Preached in the South Congregational Church, Boston, Fast Day, April 3, 1879 (Boston: A. Williams, 1879);

Emigration to Kansas: An Address Delivered in Bismarck Grove, Lawrence, Kansas, on the 18th of September, 1879 (Boston: George H. Ellis, 1879);

The Associated Charities: A Sermon Preached in the South Congregational Church, Boston, February 16, 1879 (Boston: A. Williams, 1879);

Lent: A Sermon Preached in the South Congregational Church, Boston, March 9, 1879 (Boston: A. Williams, 1879);

Mental Discipline: A Sermon Preached at the South Congregational Church, Boston (Boston: George H. Ellis, 1879);

New Life: A Sermon Preached in the South Congregational Church, Boston, March 16, 1879 (Boston: A. Williams, 1879);

Body, Mind and Soul: A Sermon Preached at the South Congregational Church, May 25, 1879 (Boston: George H. Ellis, 1879);

Spiritual Exercises: A Sermon Preached at the South Congregational Church, Boston, June 22, 1879 (Boston: George H. Ellis, 1879);

Happy Homes: A Sermon Preached Before the First Religious Society, Roxbury, July 20, 1879, and at the Church of the Messiah, New York, August 24, 1879 (Boston: George H. Ellis, 1879);

Candor in the Pulpit: A Sermon Preached at Boston, Sept. 7, 1879 (Boston, 1879);

Daily Bread: A Sermon Preached at Sage Chapel, Cornell University, October 29, 1879 (Boston: George H. Ellis, 1879);

The Later Pharisees: A Sermon Preached at the South Congregational Church, Boston, Nov. 16, 1879 (Boston: George H. Ellis, 1879);

The Pattern in the Mount: A Sermon Preached at the South Congregational Church, Union Park Street, Dec. 21, 1879 (Boston: George H. Ellis, 1879);

The Bible and Its Revision: Three Addresses (Boston: Wilson, 1879);

The Life in Common: A Sermon Preached Before the Unitarian Conference at Weir's Landing, N. H. (Boston: George H. Ellis, 1879);

Bodily Training: A Sermon Preached at the South Congregational Church (Boston: George H. Ellis, 1879);

Prayer: A Sermon Preached at the South Congregational Church, Boston (Boston: A. Williams, 1879);

Ritual: A Sermon Preached at the South Congregational Church, Boston, January 4, 1879 (Boston: A. Williams, 1879);

Respectability: A Sermon Preached at the South Congregational Church, Boston, January 19, 1879 (Boston: A. Williams, 1879);

The Bible: A Sermon, Preached in the South Congregational Church, Boston (Boston: A. Williams, 1879);

The Revision of the Bible: A Sermon Preached in the South Congregational Church, Boston, Feb. 23, 1879 (Boston: A. Williams, 1879);

The Seventy Returned: A Sermon Preached at the South Congregational Church, Boston, Nov. 9, 1879 (Boston: George H. Ellis, 1879);

From Thanksgiving to Fast (Boston: George H. Ellis, 1879);

Time and Grief: A Sermon Preached at the South Congregational Church, Boston, Dec. 28, 1879 (Boston: George H. Ellis, 1880);

Aggressive Christianity: A Sermon (Boston: George H. Ellis, 1880);

Exaggeration: A Sermon Preached at the South Congregational Church (Boston: George H. Ellis, 1880);

The Centennial of the Constitution: A Sermon Preached at the South Congregational Church, Sunday, Jan. 11, 1880, by Edward E. Hale (Boston: George H. Ellis, 1880);

Public Worship: A Sermon Preached at the South Congregational Church, Boston, Jan. 18, 1880 (Boston: George H. Ellis, 1880);

God's Love: A Sermon Preached in the South Congregational Church on the 15th of February, 1880 (Boston: George H. Ellis, 1880);

Conscience and Will: A Sermon Preached at the South Congregational Church, Feb. 29, 1880, by Edward E. Hale (Boston: George H. Ellis, 1880);

Is Life Worth Living?: A Sermon Preached at the South Congregational Church, Boston, April 25, 1880 (Boston: George H. Ellis, 1880);

Where Will Sect Go?: A Sermon Preached at the South Congregational Church, Feb. 22, 1880 (Boston: George H. Ellis, 1880);

Palm Sunday: A Sermon Preached at the South Congregational Church, March 21, 1880 (Boston: George H. Ellis, 1880);

The Channing Centennial: A Sermon Preached at the South Congregational Church, Boston, April 11, 1880, by Edward E. Hale (Boston: George H. Ellis, 1880);

Life and its Enemies: An Easter Sermon Preached at the South Congregational Church, Boston, by Edward E. Hale (Boston: George H. Ellis, 1880);

The Sunday Laws: A Sermon Preached at the South Congregational Church, Boston, June 27, 1880 (Boston: George H. Ellis, 1880);

New Year to Midsummer: Twenty Sermons (Boston: George H. Ellis, 1880);

Mary Magdalene: A Sermon Preached in the South Congregational Church (Boston: George H. Ellis, 1880);

From Fast to Christmas: Sixteen Sermons (Boston: George H. Ellis, 1880);

Purity and Temperance: Two Sermons Preached at the South Congregational Church, Boston (Boston: George H. Ellis, 1880);

Subsoiling: A Sermon Preached at the South Congregational Church, Boston, October 31, 1880 (Boston: George H. Ellis, 1880);

Law and Gospel: A Sermon Preached at the South Congregational Church, Boston, Nov. 28, 1880 (Boston: George H. Ellis, 1880);

The Men of Gadara: A Sermon Preached at the South Congregational Church, Boston, Dec. 5, 1880 (Boston: George H. Ellis, 1880);

Crusoe in New York, and Other Tales (Boston: Roberts, 1880);

The Kingdom of God, and Twenty Other Sermons (Boston: Roberts, 1880);

The Shiftless: A Sermon Preached in the South Congregational Church, Feb. 8, 1880, by Edward E. Hale (Boston: George H. Ellis, 1880);

The Life in Common, and Twenty Other Sermons (Boston: Roberts, 1880);

Stories of the Sea, Told by Sailors (Boston: Roberts, 1880);

Christ the Giver, and, Christ the Friend. Two Sermons Preached at the South Congregational Church, Boston, Dec. 25 and Dec. 26, 1880 (Boston: George H. Ellis, 1881);

All Things New: A Sermon Preached at the South Congregational Church, Boston, Jan. 2, 1881, by Edward E. Hale (Boston: George H. Ellis, 1881);

The Abolition of Pauperism: A Sermon Preached at the South Congregational Church, Boston, Jan. 9, 1881 (Boston: George H. Ellis, 1881);

Things Above: A Sermon Preached at the South Congregational Church, Boston, Jan. 16, 1881, by Edward E. Hale (Boston: George H. Ellis, 1881);

Hale's parents, Nathan and Sara Hale

Not Less, but More: A Sermon Preached in the South Congregational Church, Boston, Jan. 30, 1881 (Boston: George H. Ellis, 1881);

Christian Realism: A Sermon Preached in the South Congregational Church, Boston, Feb. 6, 1881, by Edward E. Hale (Boston: George H. Ellis, 1881);

Thomas Carlyle: A Sermon Preached in the South Congregational Church, Boston, Feb. 13, 1881 (Boston: George H. Ellis, 1881);

God Is a Spirit: A Sermon Preached in the South Congregational Church, Boston, Feb. 20, 1881 (Boston: George H. Ellis, 1881);

Send Me: A Sermon Preached in the South Congregational Church, Boston, Feb. 27, 1881 (Boston: George H. Ellis, 1881);

The Religion of America: A Sermon Preached in the South Congregational Church, Boston, March 6, 1881 (Boston: George H. Ellis, 1881);

Parable and Bible: A Sermon Preached in the South Congregational Church, Boston, March 13, 1881 (Boston: George H. Ellis, 1881);

Indifference: A Sermon Preached in the South Congregational Church, Boston, March 20, 1881 (Boston: George H. Ellis, 1881);

The Possible Boston: A Sermon Preached in the South Congregational Church, Boston, March 27, 1881 (Boston: George H. Ellis, 1881);

The King's Work: A Sermon Preached in the South Congregational Church, Boston, on Palm Sunday. 1881 (Boston: George H. Ellis, 1881);

Increase of Life: A Sermon Preached in the South Congregational Church, Boston, April 3, 1881 (Boston: George H. Ellis, 1881);

Honor and Idolatry: A Sermon Preached at the South Congregational Church, Boston, May 1, 1881 (Boston: George H. Ellis, 1881);

The Victory of the Few: A Sermon Preached in the South Congregational Church, Boston, on Easter Sunday, 1881 (Boston: George H. Ellis, 1881);

I Must See Rome: A Sermon Preached at Brookline, Mass., April 24, 1881 (Boston: George H. Ellis, 1881);

The Oedipus Tyrannus and Christianity: A Sermon Preached in the South Congregational Church, Boston, May 29, 1881 (Boston: George H. Ellis, 1881);

What Will He Do with It? A Baccalaureate Address Delivered at the Commencement of Cornell University, June 12, 1881 (Boston: A. Williams, 1881);

A Family Flight through France, Germany, Norway, and Switzerland, by Hale and Susan Hale (Boston: Lothrop, 1881);

June to May: The Sermons of a Year (Boston: Roberts, 1881);

Capt. Nathan Hale. An Address Delivered at Groton, Connecticut, on the Hale Memorial Day, September 7, 1881, by Edward E. Hale (Boston: A. Williams, 1881);

Church of the Unity in Worcester, Massachusetts, where Hale was minister from 1846 until 1856

Stories of Adventure, Told by Adventurers (Boston: Roberts, 1881);

A Congregational Church: A Sermon Preached in the South Congregational Church, Boston, on the Twentieth Anniversary of its Dedication, January 8, 1882 (Boston: George H. Ellis, 1882);

Work and Labor: Sermon in South Congregational Church (Boston: George H. Ellis, 1882);

A Family Flight Over Egypt and Syria, by Hale and Susan Hale (Boston: Lothrop, 1882);

Stories of Discovery, as Told by Discoverers (Boston: Roberts, 1883);

Luther Memorial Addresses at the Meeting of the Suffolk Conferences of Unitarian and other Churches, Nov. 18, 1883 (Boston, 1883?);

Loneliness: A Sermon Preached at the South Congregational Church, Boston, Mass. (Boston: George H. Ellis, 1883);

Our Christmas in a Palace, a Traveller's Story (New York: Funk & Wagnalls, 1883);

Seven Spanish Cities, and the Way to Them (Boston: Roberts, 1883);

Christmas in Narragansett (New York: Funk & Wagnalls, 1884);

A Family Flight Around Home, by Hale and Susan Hale (Boston: Lothrop, 1884);

A Family Flight through Spain, by Hale and Susan Hale (Boston: Lothrop, 1884);

The Fortunes of Rachel (New York and London: Funk & Wagnalls, 1884);

Consider the Lilies: A Sermon Preached at the South Congregational Church, Boston (Boston: George H. Ellis, 1884);

The Stories of the Wadsworth Club (Boston: J. S. Smith, 1884);

The Joy of the Lord: A Sermon Preached at the South Congregational Church, Boston, June 21, 1885 (Boston: George H. Ellis, 1885);

The Nearer World (Boston: George H. Ellis, 1885);

My Father's Business: A Sermon Preached at the South Congregational Church, Boston (Boston: George H. Ellis, 1885);

What Is the American People?: An Address Delivered Before the Phi Beta Kappa of Brown University, and Repeated Before the Adelphic Union of Williams College (Boston: J. S. Smith, 1885);

Boys' Heroes (Boston: Lothrop, 1885);

Stories of Invention, Told by Inventors and Their Friends (Boston: Roberts, 1885);

The Chautauqua System: Two Addresses . . . One Delivered at the Dedication of the Hall of Philosophy, Framingham; and the Other at the Commencement at Chautauqua, Before Members of the Graduating Class of 1885 (Boston: Chautauqua Press, 1886);

The Holy Spirit (Brooklyn, N.Y.: Tremlett, 1886);

A Family Flight through Mexico, by Hale and Susan Hale (Boston: Lothrop, 1886);

Easter: A Collection for a Hundred Friends (Boston: J. S. Smith, 1886);

History of the United States (New York: Chautauqua Press, 1887);

The Story of Spain, by Hale and Susan Hale (New York and London: Putnam, 1886); republished as *Spain* (London: Putnam, 1898);

Red and White: A Christmas Story (Boston: J. S. Smith, 1887);

Franklin in France, 2 volumes, by Hale and Edward Everett Hale Jr. (Boston: Roberts, 1887, 1888);

Books That Have Helped Me (New York: Appleton, 1888);

Daily Bread: A Story of the Snow Blockade (Boston: J. S. Smith, 1888);

Tom Torrey's Tariff Talks (Boston: J. S. Smith, 1888);

The Law of Investment (Boston: George H. Ellis, 1888);

How They Lived in Hampton: A Study of Practical Christianity Applied in the Manufacture of Woollens (Boston: J. S. Smith, 1888); republished as *Practical Christianity, or How They Lived in Hampton* (London: Cassell, 1892);

Emily and Ellen Hale, the writer's wife and first child, in 1855

The Life of George Washington, Studied Anew (New York & London: Putnam, 1888);

Mr. Tangier's Vacations, a Novel (Boston: Roberts, 1888);

My Friend the Boss: A Story of To-day (Boston: J. S. Smith, 1888);

Sunday-School Stories; on the Golden Texts of the International Lessons of 1889, by Hale and others (Boston: Roberts, 1889);

The Twentieth Century: A Sermon Preached at Washington, D. C. on the 3rd of March (Boston: J. Stilman, 1889);

Beggary and Prayer: Sermon (Boston: George H. Ellis, 1889);

Neither Scrip Nor Money, a Christmas Story (Boston: J. S. Smith, 188?);

The Temperance Puritan . . . an Address Delivered at a Meeting of the Unitarian Church Temperance Society, Held at Tremont Temple, Boston, May 30, 1890 (Boston, 1890?);

Afloat and Ashore (Chicago: Searle & Gorton, 1891);

Idealists in the State of Rhode Island, Hazard Memorial Address, Oct. 9, 1891 (Narragansett?: J. A. & R. A. Reed, 1891);

James Russell Lowell (Boston, 1891);

Autobiography, Diary and Correspondence of James Freeman Clarke, edited and with substantial material supplied by Hale (Boston: Houghton, Mifflin, 1891);

Four and Five: A Story of a Lend-a-Hand Club (Boston: Roberts, 1891);

The Worth of Enthusiasm: A Sermon Preached at the South Congregational Church, Boston, Jan. 24, 1891 (Boston: J. S. Smith, 1891);

The Life of Christopher Columbus (Chicago: G. L. Howe, 1891); republished as *The Story of Columbus, as He Told It Himself* (Boston: J. S. Smith, 1893);

The Story of Massachusetts (Boston: Lothrop, 1891);

The Massachusetts Convention of Congregational Ministers (Boston, 1891);

East and West: A Story of New-Born Ohio (New York: Cassell, 1892); republished as *The New Ohio: A Story of East and West* (London: Cassell, 1892);

Every-Day Sermons (Boston: J. S. Smith, 1892);

Five Questions (Boston: J. S. Smith, 1892);

Installation of Mr. Cuckson by Edward E. Hale, Minister of South Congregational Church, Boston (Boston: J. S. Smith, 1892);

The New Harry and Lucy: A Story of Boston in the Summer of 1891, by Hale and Lucretia P. Hale (Boston: Roberts, 1892);

Sybil Knox; or, Home Again: A Story of To-day (New York & London: Cassell, 1892);

A New England Boyhood (New York & London: Cassell, 1893);

For Fifty Years: Verses Written on Occasion, in the Course of the Nineteenth Century (Boston: Roberts, 1893);

Ralph Waldo Emerson, by Edward E. Hale. An Address Delivered Before the Brooklyn Institute on the 24th of May, 1893, the Ninetieth Anniversary of Mr. Emerson's Birth (Boston: J. S. Smith, 1893);

One Good Turn, a Story (Boston: J. S. Smith, 1893);

Philips Brooks (Boston: J. S. Smith, 1893);

How to Use the Bible (Boston: J. S. Smith, 1893);
Sermons of the Winter (Boston: J. S. Smith, 1893);
Love of Country . . . at the South Congregational Church, Feb. 25, 1894 (Boston: Commonwealth Publishing, 1894);
40th Anniversary of the Ordination of Caleb David Bradlee, December 11, 1854–1894, poems by Hale and Alfred Manchester (N.p., 1894);
The Life of God. Edward E. Hale at the South Congregational Church, March 25, 1894 (Boston: Commonwealth Publishing, 1894?);
Lent: What It Is and What It Is Not. Edward E. Hale at the South Congregational Church, March 4, 1894 (Boston: Commonwealth Publishing, 1894?);
All Souls' (Boston: J. S. Smith, 1895);
American Town Government (New York: American Institute of Civics, 1895);
Aunt Caroline's Present (Boston: J. S. Smith, 1895);
A Safe Deposit (Boston: J. S. Smith, 1895);
If Jesus Came to Boston (Boston: Lamson, Wolffe, 1895);
Studies in American Colonial Life (Meadville, Pa.: Flood & Vincent, Chautauqua Century Press, 1895);
The Lord's Prayer (Boston: J. S. Smith, 1895);
My Double & How He Undid Me (Boston & New York: Lamson, Wolffe, 1895);
Susan's Escort (Boston: J. S. Smith, 1895);
Fellowship? By Edward E. Hale, June, 1895 (Boston: J. S. Smith, 1895);
Colonel Clipsham's Calendar (Boston: Lend a Hand Society, 1895);
The Foundation of the Nation (Boston: J. S. Smith, 1896);
'Tis Sixty Years Since a Harvard (N.p., 1896);
Man and Beast (Boston: J. S. Smith, 1896);
A Permanent Tribunal of International Arbitration (Boston: American Peace Society, 1896);
The Formation of Character . . . South Congregational Church, Boston (Boston: J. S. Smith, 1896);
God and Man [Preached Oct. 11, 1896] (Boston: J. S. Smith, 1896);
Emmanuel: God with Us: A Sermon Preached at the South Congregational Church, Boston (Boston: South Congregational Branch Alliance, 1896);
Independence Day: Address (Philadelphia: H. Altemus, 1896);
Yourselves: A Sermon Preached at the South Congregational Church, Boston, January 12 1879, Edward E. Hale (Boston: A. Williams, 1897);
The Contribution of Boston to American Independence: Oration Delivered Before the Mayor and Citizens of Boston at the One Hundred and Twenty-first Celebration of the Declaration of Independence, Monday, July 5, 1897 (Boston: Printed by order of the City Council, 1897);
Susan's Escort, and Others (New York: Harper, 1897);
The New Revival . . . a Sermon Preached at the South Congregational Church, Sunday, Jan. 10, 1897 (Boston? 1897?);
I Am: A Sermon Preached at the South Congregational Church, Boston, January 2, 1898 (Boston: Rockwell & Churchill Press, 1898);
Fervent in Spirit: A Sermon Preached in the South Congregational Church, Boston, Jan. 30, 1898 (Boston: Rockwell & Churchill Press, 1898);
Historic Boston and Its Neighborhood (New York: D. Appleton, 1898);
Personal Purity (Boston: Unitarian Temperance Society, 1898);
Memoir of Benjamin Marston Watson (Cambridge, Mass.: J. Wilson, 1898);
Young Americans Abroad, by Hale and Susan Hale (Boston: Lothrop, 1898);
Comfort and Comforters: A Sermon Preached at the South Congregational Church, Boston, Sunday, Jan. 8, 1899 (Boston: Rockwell & Churchill, 1899);
James Russell Lowell and His Friends (Boston: Houghton, Mifflin, 1899);
The Brick Moon, and Other Stories (Boston: Little, Brown, 1899);
In His Name; and Christmas Stories (Boston: Little, Brown, 1899);
Ralph Waldo Emerson . . . Together with Two Early Essays of Emerson (Boston: Brown, 1899);
The Old Diplomacy, Arbitration and the Permanent Tribunal (Boston: American Peace Society, 1899);
A Permanent Tribunal: The Emperor of Russia and His Circular Regarding Permanent Peace (Boston: George H. Ellis, 1899);
The Pilgrim Covenant of 1620: A Covenant for the Churches of To-day: A Sermon Preached Before the Massachusetts Convention of Congregational Ministers at the South Congregational Church, Boston, on the 31st Day of May, A.D. 1900 (Cambridge, Mass.: Co-operative Press, 1900);
How to Do It; to Which Is Added, How to Live (Boston: Little, Brown, 1900);
Addresses and Essays on Subjects of History, Education, and Government (Boston: Little, Brown, 1900);
American Unitarianism: Its History and Development (Boston: Christian Register Association, 1900?);
The Empty House: A Sermon Preached at the South Congregational Church (Boston: Lend a Hand Society, 1900?);
The New Century: Three Sermons Preached in the South Congregational Church, Boston, by Hale and Edward Cummings (Cambridge, Mass.: Co-operative Press, 1901);
About Books (Boston, 1901);

The Five Great Duties of the Twentieth Century. A Commencement Address Delivered Before the University of Ohio June the Nineteenth Nineteen Hundred and One (N.p., 1901);

The Real Philip Nolan (Oxford, Miss., 1901);

The President's Death. Address Delivered on the Day of the President's Funeral, in the South Congregational Church, Boston (Haverhill, Mass.: Ariel Press, 1901);

Commencement Day Address, Delivered to the Graduating Class of Smith College, Northampton, Mass., June 17, 1902 (N.p., 1902);

How to Live (Boston: Little, Brown, 1902);

Gosnold at Cuttyhunk (Worcester, Mass.: C. Hamilton, 1902);

Memories of a Hundred Years, 2 volumes (New York: Macmillan, 1902; revised, New York & London: Macmillan, 1904);

How Shall Unitarianism Reach the People? A Plea for a Central Unitarian Temple in Boston. An Address Delivered at the Hotel Vendome Nov. 12, 1902 (Boston: Unitarian Club, 1903);

"We, the People": A Series of Papers on Topics of To-day (New York: Dodd, Mead, 1903);

New England History in Ballads, by Hale and others, illustrated by Ellen D. Hale, Philip L. Hale, and Lilian Hale (Boston: Little, Brown, 1903);

The Gospel of Emerson, for His Time and Ours: The Last Address in the Emerson Celebration, Huntington Hall, July 31, 1903 (Boston: South End Industrial School Press, 1903);

Thomas Starr King: A Memorial Address Delivered in the South Congregational Church, Boston, Mass., March 1, 1903, for the Anniversary of His Death (Westwood, Mass.: Ariel Press, 1903?);

Prayers in the Senate (Boston: Little, Brown, 1904);

The Ideas of the Founders: An Address Delivered Before the Brooklyn Institute, November 4, 1903 (Boston: Lend a Hand Society, 1904);

Thanksgiving Day: A Sermon Preached at the South Congregational Church, Boston, Nov. 24, 1904: The Real Presence of the Living God (Boston: George H. Ellis, 1904);

The Great Treaty: A Sermon Preached at the Second Church, Boston, Massachusetts, Sept. 10, 1905 (Boston: Lend a Hand Society, 1905);

The Foundations of the Republic (New York: J. Pott, 1906);

Tarry at Home Travels (New York: Macmillan, 1906; London: Macmillan, 1906);

For Christmas and New Year; Dedicated to My Own Friends (Boston: Privately printed, 1906);

Whitsunday: A Sermon Preached at the South Congregational Church, Boston, Mass., May 19, 1907 (Boston: George H. Ellis, 1907);

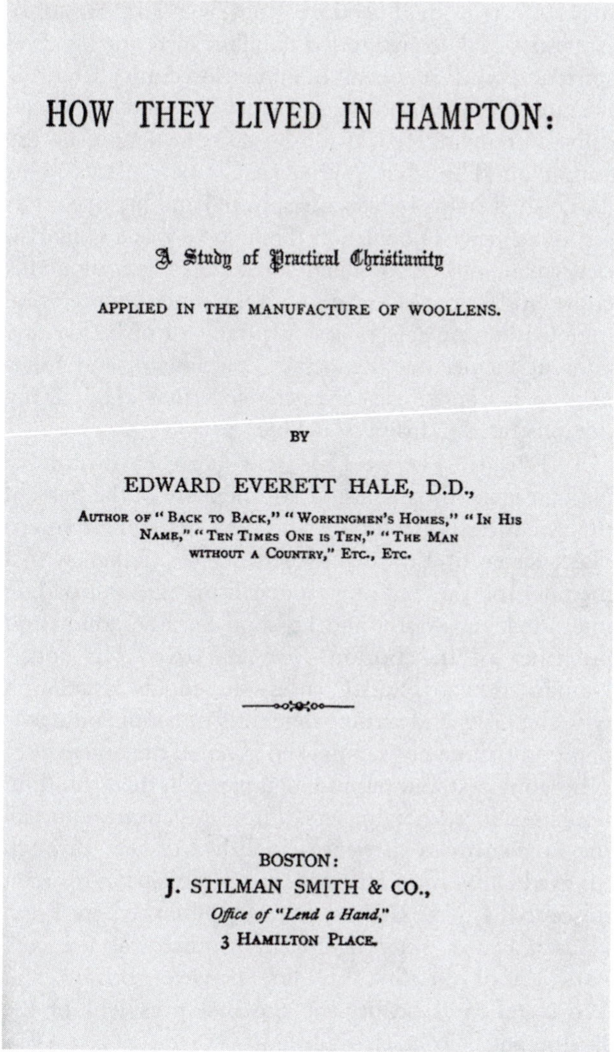

HOW THEY LIVED IN HAMPTON:

A Study of Practical Christianity

APPLIED IN THE MANUFACTURE OF WOOLLENS.

BY

EDWARD EVERETT HALE, D.D.,

AUTHOR OF "BACK TO BACK," "WORKINGMEN'S HOMES," "IN HIS NAME," "TEN TIMES ONE IS TEN," "THE MAN WITHOUT A COUNTRY," ETC., ETC.

BOSTON:
J. STILMAN SMITH & CO.,
Office of "Lend a Hand,"
3 HAMILTON PLACE.

Title page for the 1888 book in which Hale offered a plan for providing affordable housing to people of all social classes, focusing particularly on the needs of workers in Massachusetts woolen mills

Christianity Is a Life: A Sermon by E. E. Hale Preached at the South Congregational Church, Boston, April 28, 1907 (Boston: George H. Ellis, 1907);

The Old South Meeting House: A Sermon Delivered in the Old South Meeting House August 4, 1907 (Boston? 1907?);

Mohonk Addresses, by Hale and David J. Brewer (Boston: International School of Peace, 1910).

Collection: *The Works of Edward Everett Hale,* Library Edition, 10 volumes (Boston: Little, Brown, 1898–1900).

When Edward Everett Hale died in 1909 at the age of eighty-seven, he was one of the most revered Americans living in the first years of the twentieth century. Along with Theodore Roosevelt and Susan B. Anthony, Hale commanded public respect for his civic spirit and work on behalf of others. A century later, his position in American life and letters has altered drastically. If remembered at all, he is known only as the author of "The Man Without a Country" (1863); his diminished status reflects the spiritual and literary interests of a changed population. Though he was a Unitarian clergyman with responsibility for large congregations his entire professional life, he found the time to write voluminously on diverse topics. Virtually all of his writing aims at inculcating democracy, patriotism, and tolerance in his audiences–characteristics that Hale amply demonstrated in his personal life.

Edward Everett Hale was born in Boston to Nathan Hale, the namesake and nephew of the hero of the American Revolution, and Sara Preston (Everett) Hale, sister of Edward Everett. Hale's father was a member of the bar, but journalism and railroading interested him more, and he soon became editor and publisher of the Boston *Daily Advertiser*. His sons–Nathan, Edward, and Charles–shared his fascination with the tasks and writing demands of running a newspaper; the three boys mimicked in small the practices of generating text and publishing a paper in their youthful home-produced newspapers. These adventures, and all the noteworthy experiences in Edward's life through his graduation from Harvard, are chronicled in his reminiscence *A New England Boyhood,* published in 1893. Nathan Hale's other significant venture was the construction of the first rail line between Boston and Worcester, and he became the first president of the Boston and Worcester Railroad.

Edward regarded his father's achievements carefully, for these accomplishments showed the impressionable Edward how an individual's determination and commitment could triumph against a skeptical public and how in order to work for the general good of society, a person had to be willing to face a long labor and frequent disappointment. Many residents of Boston thought the railroad a ridiculous idea and the concept of a profitable line operating to the west of Boston even more ridiculous, but Nathan Hale calmly persevered. Edward's willingness throughout his life to work long hours at his craft and to champion one social cause after another, right up until the time of his death, reflects lessons learned in the household of his youth. Evenings in the family parlor often featured benevolent society meetings or prolonged discussions of current affairs (with Edward Everett and Daniel Webster frequently in attendance).

A precocious youth, Edward was enrolled in Miss Whitney's dame school at the age of two. He attended Mr. Dowes's school before enrolling at the Boston Latin School, where his brother Nathan preceded him. Edward spent approximately four years at each of these schools before enrolling in Harvard at age thirteen. Though other students of that period might have enrolled at an even younger age, Edward was allowed to register a year early because his beloved brother Nathan was a freshman during Edward's last year at Boston Latin School, and Edward spent much of his time visiting his brother's room at Harvard. The brothers roomed together when Edward enrolled in 1835. Edward continued his outstanding academic work at Harvard, where he was one of only six boys admitted that year without condition.

Graduating second in the Class of 1839, Edward was elected to Phi Beta Kappa and was named class poet. He was active in many student clubs and enthusiastic about various parts of the curriculum, following his own interests when the prescribed courses proved too dull. During his senior year he began reporting the activities of the state legislature for the Boston *Daily Advertiser,* a duty he continued after graduation. He returned to Boston Latin School as a teacher for two years, though he knew he wanted to prepare for the ministry. His distaste for regular classes precluded his enrolling in divinity school, so he studied theology independently. Moving along through his religious studies with the same vigor he demonstrated in all his endeavors, he was granted a license to preach at the end of his twentieth year.

During the decade following his graduation from college, in addition to his theological study, he continued to write prolifically and to give speeches frequently. Combining his journalistic work with more formal essays, he began to produce the prose of social concern that was to mark his entire career. In *A New England Boyhood* Hale provides clues to his success as a preacher and public speaker: as a result of his training and discipline at Boston Latin School, he always felt confident and poised when speaking, declaiming, or debating. Harvard provided additional experiences that confirmed his self-assurance on public stage or pulpit, a confidence that served him well as he began to preach in various churches.

On 29 April 1846 Hale was ordained as minister in the Church of the Unity in Worcester and began a highly successful ten-year tenure. Gratified by the growth of his congregation, he increasingly championed social causes as he wrote more and more frequently on various subjects. His early journalistic training in direct, unadorned prose prepared him to be an efficient writer who thought out a sermon or essay and then wrote it out, usually in a single draft with little need for revision. Later in his life, he commented that his sermons–which were held in high regard for their content and effectiveness–were often written in three hours.

In 1852 Hale married Emily Baldwin Perkins, niece of Harriet Beecher Stowe and Henry Ward Beecher, members of a Massachusetts family as illustrious as his own. The Hales had eight children–Ellen, Arthur, Charles, Philip, Herbert, Harry, Roberta, and Edward Everett Jr. Hale's domestic life paralleled the harmony he enjoyed when he was growing up. In 1854 he published *Kanzas and Nebraska,* his first important book, to sway the American public to look at the newly opened territory as a site for the fulfillment of American democratic ideals of tolerance and to turn away from the institution of slavery. Even the title of the book reflects this concern: he prefers "Kanzas" to "Kansas" because the *z* reflects more accurately the Indian name of the territory. He continued his antislavery, pro-peace, pro-tolerance teaching in his sermons when, two years later, he became pastor of the South Congregational Church of Boston, a position he held for forty-three years.

He widened his field of writing interests: travel writing jostled with collected sermons for his attention, and his output of fiction increased. In 1863 "The Man Without a Country" appeared in the *Atlantic Monthly* as a call to all Americans to hold fast to the Union. Perhaps the most widely reprinted and best-known American short story through its first century of existence, this tale of Philip Nolan's tragic rejection of his country touched mythic depths in the national psyche. When a young Nolan, seduced by the self-promoting Aaron Burr's dreams of a western empire, is found guilty by a jury while the clearly culpable Burr escapes punishment, the young officer cries, "Damn the United States! I wish I may never hear of the United States again!" He is granted his wish: he spends the rest of his life on board ships at sea, never returning to his country, never hearing another passenger speak of the United States. Ahasuerus, the Flying Dutchman, Samuel Taylor Coleridge's Ancient Mariner, and–closer to home in Boston–Peter Rugg are Nolan's fictional precursors as figures doomed to wander because of rash acts.

Nolan is devastated by the results of his rash remark and becomes a tragic figure who shows the effects of losing a national allegiance. Reading the story as an encouragement to patriotic spirit and as a warning of the dangers of overzealous individualism propelled its popularity beyond the printed story into other media, such as radio, television, and motion picture. Later audiences, however, often read the story as a warning against jingoism, xenophobia, and dangerous abridgments of free speech.

Hale wrote other stories popular during his lifetime. "My Double, and How He Undid Me," first published in the *Atlantic Monthly* in September 1859, tells of a busy farmer who finds a look-alike to take up some of his social obligations, only to find that his stand-in wants to take over other aspects of his personal life. "The Skeleton in the Closet," first published in *Galaxy* in 1866, explains how discarded hoops from hoop skirts ("skeletons") caused the downfall of the Confederacy. Collected with "The Man Without a Country" in *If, Yes, and Perhaps* (1868), these two stories demonstrate masterful management of first-person narration for humorous effect. Only rarely in the remainder of his career did Hale reach the level of craft shown in the 1868 collection of fiction, though *In His Name* (1873) displays careful plotting and attention to period details. The 1876 novel *Philip Nolan's Friends: A Story of the Change of Western Empire* presents a fictionalized account of the real Philip Nolan, whom Hale distinguished from his fictional creation to set the real Nolan's record straight. Hale's most successful fantasy, "The Brick Moon," first published in the *Atlantic Monthly* in 1869 (first collected in *His Level Best and Other Stories,* 1872) anticipates construction of twentieth-century satellites.

Hale at work in his study

Most of Hale's writing, however, was in support of his causes. *Workingmen's Homes* (1874) and *How They Lived in Hampton: A Study of Practical Christianity Applied in the Manufacture of Woollens* (1888) describe humane solutions to the problem of affordable housing for all social classes, with particular regard for the needs of the workers in woolen mills. His fictional utopia, Sybaris, enthrones the simple routines of community life of an earlier time. Hale's belief that writing and human endeavor should aim at collective good through individual commitment and effort probably grew out of his boyhood household. Hale's "Lend a Hand Society" aimed at increasing public awareness of how every citizen might help others; his story *Ten Times One Is Ten: The Possible Reformation. A Story in Nine Chapters* (1871) illustrates these principles by creating fictional situations for illustration. Likewise, Hale's fascination with Leo Tolstoy's civic projects indicates how deeply the Bostonian thought about how to make writing and speaking instruments of social change.

Resigning because of his age from the South Congregational Church in 1899, Hale accepted nomination as Chaplain of the U.S. Senate in 1903. Upon his death in 1909, publications universally mourned the loss of a great American figure. Across the country, front-page obituaries and features testified to a larger-than-life public figure; in his own way, Hale was a figure as memorable and inspiring as his fictional creation, Philip Nolan.

Letters:

The Life and Letters of Edward Everett Hale, 2 volumes, edited by Edward E. Hale Jr. (Boston: Little, Brown, 1917).

Biography:

Jean Holloway, *Edward Everett Hale: A Biography* (Austin: University of Texas Press, 1956).

References:

Lyman Abbott, "Edward Everett Hale, an American Abou Ben Adhem," in his *Silhouettes of My Contemporaries* (Garden City, N.Y.: Doubleday, Page, 1921), pp. 100–125;

John R. Adams, *Edward Everett Hale* (Boston: Twayne, 1977);

Jean Holloway, "A Checklist of the Writings of Edward Everett Hale," *Bulletin of Bibliography,* 21 (May–August, September–December, January–April 1954–1955): 89–92, 114–120, 140–143.

Papers:

Major holdings of Edward Everett Hale's correspondence and manuscripts are found in the New York State Library at Albany and the Massachusetts Historical Society. Collections of his letters are also held in the Houghton Library of Harvard University, the American Antiquarian Society, the New York Public Library, the Boston Public Library, and the University of Rochester.

Richard Hildreth

(28 June 1807 – 11 July 1865)

Christine Brooks Macdonald
University of Colorado, Boulder

See also the Hildreth entries in *DLB 30: American Historians, 1607–1865* and *DLB 59: American Literary Critics and Scholars, 1800–1850.*

BOOKS: *An Abridged History of the United States of America. For the Use of Schools. Intended as a Sequel to Hildreth's View of the United States,* as Hosea Hildreth (Boston: Carter, Hendee & Babcock, 1831);

The Slave: or Memoirs of Archy Moore, 2 volumes, anonymous (Boston: J. H. Eastburn, 1836); expanded as *The White Slave; or, Memoirs of a Fugitive* (Boston: Tappan & Whittemore / Milwaukee: Rood & Whittemore, 1852; London: Routledge, 1852);

The History of Banks: To Which is Added, A Demonstration of the Advantages and Necessity of Free Competition in the Business of Banking (Boston: Hilliard, Gray, 1837; London: J. S. Hodson, 1837); revised and enlarged as *Banks, Banking and Paper Currencies* (Boston: Whipple & Damrell, 1840);

Brief Remarks on Miss Catharine E. Beecher's Essay on Slavery and Abolitionism, by the author of *Archy Moore* (Boston: Isaac Knapp, 1837);

My Connection with The Atlas Newspaper (Boston: Whipple & Damrell, 1839);

The People's Presidential Candidate; or The Life of William Henry Harrison, of Ohio (Boston: Weeks, Jordan, 1839);

A Letter to His Excellency Marcus Morton, on Banking and the Currency (Boston: Kidder & Wright, 1840);

The Contrast; or William Henry Harrison versus Martin Van Buren (Boston: Weeks, Jordan, 1840);

Inducements to the Colored People of the United States to Emigrate to British Guiana (Boston: Kidder & Wright, 1840);

A Letter to Emory Washburn, Wm. M. Rogers, and Seventy-Eight Others, Dissentients from the Resolution Touching Political Action, Adopted at the State Temperance Convention (Boston: Kidder & Wright, 1840);

A Letter to Andrews Norton on Miracles as the Foundation of Religious Faith (Boston: Weeks, Jordan, 1840);

Richard Hildreth, 1858 (portrait by Robert M. Pratt; New-York Historical Society)

Despotism in America; or, An Inquiry into the Nature and Results of the Slave-Holding System in the United States (Boston: Whipple & Damrell, 1840); revised and enlarged as *Despotism in America: An Inquiry into the Nature, Results, and Legal Basis of the Slave-Holding System in the United States* (Boston: John P. Jewett / Cleveland: Jewett, Proctor & Worthington, 1854; Boston: John P. Jewett / New York: Sheldon, Lamport & Blakeman, 1854; London: Sampson Low, 1854);

What Can I Do for the Abolition of Slavery? (Boston: J. W. Alden for the New England Anti-Slavery Tract Association, 1844);

Theory of Morals: An Inquiry Concerning the Law of Moral Distinctions and the Variations and Contradictions of Ethical Codes (Boston: Little, Brown, 1844);

Native-Americanism Detected and Exposed. By a Native American (Boston: Privately printed, 1845);

A Joint Letter to Orestes A. Brownson and the Editor of the North American Review: In Which the Editor of the North American Review is Proved to Be No Christian, and Little Better than an Atheist (Boston, 1845);

The Truth Revealed. Statement and Review of the Whole Case of the Reverend Joy H. Fairchild, from its Commencement to its Termination, Compiled from Original Documents by a Member of the Suffolk Bar, anonymous (Boston: Wright, 1845);

"Our First Men:" A Calendar of Wealth, Fashion and Gentility, Containing a List of Those Persons Taxed in the City of Boston, Credibly Reported to Be Worth One Hundred Thousand Dollars, with Biographical Notices of the Principal Persons, anonymous (Boston: Published by all the Booksellers, 1846);

The History of the United States of America, from the Discovery of the Continent to the Organization of Government Under the Federal Constitution, 3 volumes (New York: Harper, 1849); revised as volumes 1–3 of *The History of the United States of America;*

The History of the United States of America, from the Adoption of the Federal Constitution to the End of the Sixteenth Congress, 1788–1821, 3 volumes (New York: Harper, 1851, 1852); revised as volumes 4–6 of *The History of the United States of America;*

Theory of Politics: An Inquiry into the Foundations of Governments, and the Causes and Progress of Political Revolutions (New York: Harper, 1853);

The "Ruin" of Jamaica (New York: American Anti-Slavery Society, 1855);

Japan as It Was and Is (Boston: Phillips, Sampson / New York: J. C. Derby, 1855); revised as *Japan and the Japanese* (Boston: Bradley, Dayton, 1860);

The History of the United States of America, 6 volumes (New York: Harper, 1856–1860).

OTHER: Jeremy Bentham, *Theory of Legislation,* translated from French by Hildreth (Boston: Weeks, Jordan, 1840).

SELECTED PERIODICAL PUBLICATIONS–UNCOLLECTED: "Novels and Novel Reading," *Ladies Magazine,* 1 (April 1828): 145–147;

"National Literature," *American Monthly Magazine,* 1 (September 1829): 379–385;

"A Plea for Sunday Freedom: In a Letter to John Quincy Adams, President of the late Baltimore Lord's-day Convention. By 'One of the New Generation,'" *Liberator,* 24 (January 1845): 16;

"The Legality of American Slavery," anonymous, *Massachusetts Quarterly Review,* 2 (December 1848): 32–39;

"Uncle Tom, The White Slave, Ida May and the N.Y. Evening Post," anonymous, Boston *Evening Telegraph,* 13 (November 1854).

Richard Hildreth is most often remembered as an historian who wrote the six-volume *History of the United States* (1849; 1851, 1852). But Hildreth also was a lawyer, a successful newspaper editor, an active pamphleteer, an ardent abolitionist, and the author of the first novel-length work of abolitionist fiction. His contribution to antislavery literature has begun to attract the interest of literary scholars.

Richard Hildreth was born on 28 June 1807 in Deerfield, Massachusetts, the son of Hosea and Sarah (McLeod) Hildreth. On his father's side Richard was descended from among the earliest English settlers in North America: his namesake, Richard Hildreth, arrived on the shores of Massachusetts sometime in 1635. In 1811 Hosea Hildreth obtained a teaching position as a professor of mathematics and natural philosophy at Phillips Exeter Academy in Exeter, New Hampshire, where Richard spent his early childhood and in 1816 became the youngest student at Phillips Exeter. In 1822 Richard entered Harvard, where he formed friendships with men with whom he later became active in the cause against slavery, such as antislavery lawyer Ellis G. Loring and Edmund Quincy.

In 1832 Hildreth helped found the Boston *Daily Atlas,* a political newspaper that came to be identified with Whig policies. Hildreth wrote many of the lead editorials, including a series that he later claimed helped William Henry Harrison gain the Whig presidential nomination for the 1840 election. In 1834 Hildreth left the paper for health reasons and temporarily moved to Florida, although he continued to contribute articles describing the territory and early developments in the Seminole War. After returning to Boston in April of 1836, Hildreth renewed his formal connection with the *Atlas;* after an unsuccessful effort to preserve the Massachusetts temperance laws, which resulted in much infighting in the Whig party, Hildreth's health again broke down, and he recuperated for some months in South America. On 7 June 1844 Hildreth married Caroline Gould Negus, an artist. The portraits she painted helped the couple survive financially in later years after Hildreth's literary endeavors proved less remunerative than he originally hoped.

During the eighteen months he spent on a Florida plantation Hildreth had developed what became a lifelong aversion to slavery and the attendant desire to help bring about its demise. After observing the interactions between masters and slaves, Hildreth wrote his first and only novel, *The Slave: or Memoirs of Archy Moore* (1836), which inaugurated the genre of antislavery fiction. As the first antislavery novel as well as the first fictional slave narrative written by a white person, it established many of the conventions of the genre, including the use of the theme of miscegenation as a means to undermine the logic of race-based slavery and the theme of racial "passing."

The plot of the novel centers on the slave Archy Moore, whose father, Colonel Moore, fought as a young man on the side of liberty in the American Revolution. Hildreth contrasts Colonel Moore's love of liberty with his status as a slave owner who keeps slave mistresses, including Archy's mother, and who sees nothing wrong in enslaving his own son. Through Archy's narration, readers are exposed to the anguish of a male slave who witnesses and experiences unjust cruelty by masters toward their slaves, who cannot legally protect the chastity of his wife, who becomes separated from his wife and child when they are sold to different owners, and who finally escapes, alone, to the North and from there to England. The 1836 edition ends with Archy declaring his determination to return to America to seek his wife and child.

Hildreth's project is to shock slave-owner tyrants into reforming their actions and to prevent a new generation from taking their place: "perhaps within some youthful breast, in which the evil spirits of avarice and tyranny have not yet gained unlimited control, I may be able to rekindle the smothered and expiring embers of humanity." Perhaps the most radical aspect of Hildreth's first edition is that it has an unhappy and unresolved ending. Archy escapes to England and becomes wealthy, but he remains separated from his wife and son.

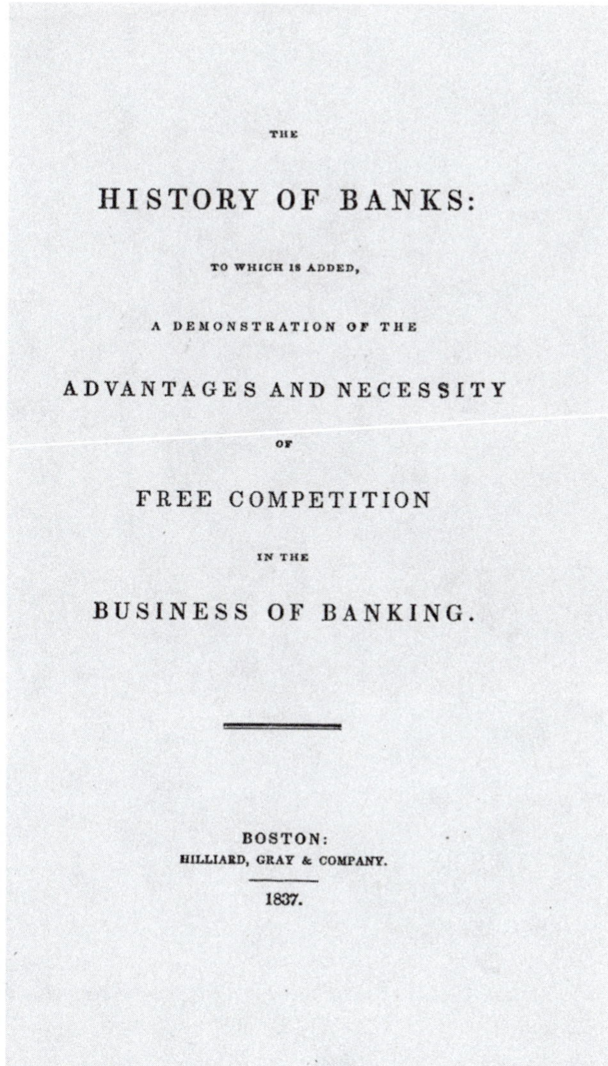
THE

HISTORY OF BANKS:

TO WHICH IS ADDED,

A DEMONSTRATION OF THE

ADVANTAGES AND NECESSITY

OF

FREE COMPETITION

IN THE

BUSINESS OF BANKING.

BOSTON:
HILLIARD, GRAY & COMPANY.

1837.

Title page for the book in which Hildreth advocated a uniform system of U.S. currency

As a literary effort, Hildreth's novel lacks the emotional power and Christian framework that drew so many readers to Harriet Beecher Stowe's *Uncle Tom's Cabin* (1852). Hildreth later claimed that his novel provided Stowe with some of her ideas; unlike Stowe, however, Hildreth depicts Christianity not as a sustaining force for individual slaves nor as a powerful means of retribution for evil, but as a belief system that helps slave owners maintain control of their slaves. Hildreth, however, put in place many of the arguments that later were used again and again in antislavery fiction. His fictional character challenges the rationale of race-based slavery because Archy looks white; since his body provides no visible rationale for his enslavement, his slave status reveals that slavery is based not upon a natural hierarchy but upon laws defining racial categories in an arbitrary way. Hildreth shows the pervasiveness of racism even within the slave community, as Archy has to learn that skin color has nothing to do with self-worth. Eventually he rejects the rationale behind the hierarchy of race, from which he benefited as a light-colored slave: "I no longer took sides with our oppressors by joining them in the false notion of their own natural superiority;–a notion founded only in the arrogant prejudice of conceited ignorance, and long since discarded by the liberal and enlightened."

In 1852 Hildreth revised and republished his novel under the title *The White Slave; or, Memoirs of a Fugitive*. In this expanded version, which almost doubles the length of the novel, Archy returns to the

A FREEHOLDERS' COURT. Page 157.

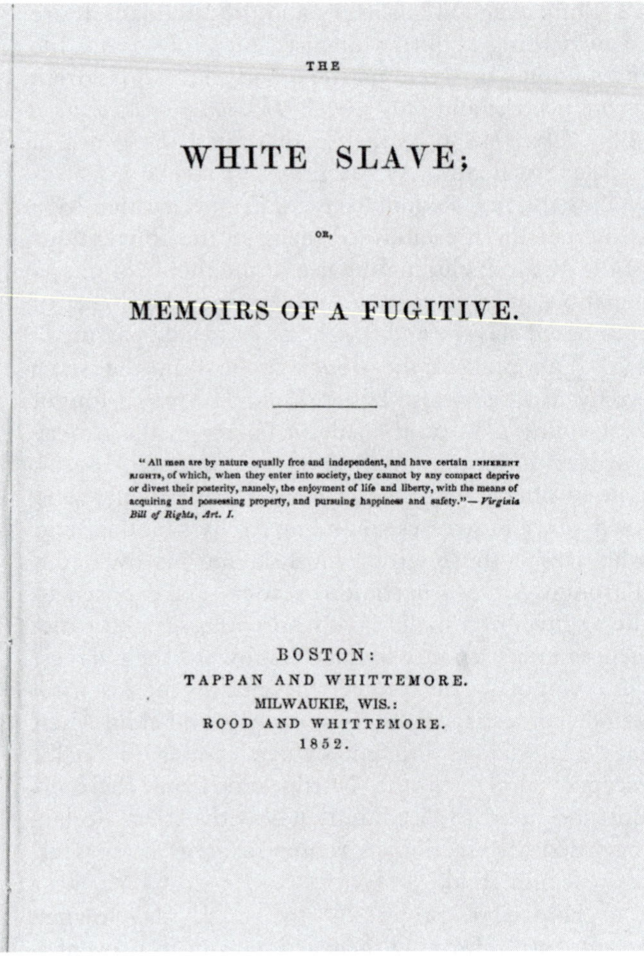

THE

WHITE SLAVE;

OR,

MEMOIRS OF A FUGITIVE.

"All men are by nature equally free and independent, and have certain INHERENT RIGHTS, of which, when they enter into society, they cannot by any compact deprive or divest their posterity, namely, the enjoyment of life and liberty, with the means of acquiring and possessing property, and pursuing happiness and safety."—*Virginia Bill of Rights, Art. I.*

BOSTON:
TAPPAN AND WHITTEMORE.
MILWAUKIE, WIS.:
ROOD AND WHITTEMORE.
1852.

Frontispiece and title page for the revised and expanded version of Hildreth's antislavery novel

United States and travels the South posing as a white English gentleman while he searches for his lost wife and son. He witnesses lynch mobs kill fugitive slaves and harass moderate citizens. The theme in this section of the book is that southern hysteria over imagined slave revolts is eroding both free speech and freedom from unreasonable search and seizure–rights that are essential to democracy. This version of the novel ends more happily than the first, with Archy successfully reunited with his wife and son; all three resettle in the free country of England.

Both *Archy Moore* and *The White Slave* went through several editions, although Hildreth relates in the introduction to *The White Slave* that he initially had difficulty finding a publisher for *Archy Moore:* "No bookseller dared to publish anything of the sort, and so complete was the reign of terror, that printers were almost afraid to set up the types. The author was obliged to have the book printed at his own expense." Hildreth's allusion is to a series of violent incidents against abolitionists in the early 1830s, a time in which public opinion against abolitionists in both the North and the South was high. Thus, initial sales of *Archy Moore* amounted to seven or eight thousand copies and were confined mostly to abolitionists. Before he made his authorship known, there was some speculation that the author of *Archy Moore* was either Lydia Maria Child or Harriet Martineau. Hildreth later took care to preserve his status as the progenitor of the genre of antislavery fiction, especially after the success of Stowe's *Uncle Tom's Cabin.* In the introduction to *The White Slave* Hildreth concludes, "Such is the history of this book, in virtue of which the author claims as his invention, (as applicants for a patent say in their specifications,) the first successful application of fictitious narrative to anti-slavery purposes. At the success of others, who have adopted this invention, no one rejoices more heartily than he does . . . but . . . he claims, at the same time, the respect and honor due to the father of all of them."

In many ways *Archy Moore* was ahead of its time; even some dedicated opponents of slavery did not support the novel when it first appeared. As the first fictional treatment of slavery from a slave's point of view, *Archy Moore* may have undermined the efforts of various antislavery societies that were insisting that the stories of the cruelties of slavery mentioned within their abolitionist pamphlets were true. Hildreth relates that the New York Anti-slavery Society refused to sell *Archy Moore* because it included details "too revolting to be made public," because some of the characters swore, and because it was fiction. Even though reviews of the novel indicate an understanding that the book was, in fact, fiction, the apprehensions of the New York Anti-slavery Society were not entirely unfounded; after the abolitionist cause had risen in popularity in the 1850s, several editions of a slave pamphlet republished episodes compiled from the novel and identified Archy and his friend Thomas, or "Wild Tom," as actual fugitive slaves.

William Dean Howells noted that the novel left "an indelible impression" upon him: "The impression is still so deep that after the lapse of nearly forty years since I saw the book, I have no misgiving in speaking of it as a powerful piece of realism." While the plot is contrived and the characters melodramatic and somewhat one-dimensional, literary scholars of today have begun to notice this novel and to consider its place within the larger context of abolitionist literature. If for no other reason, its status as the first work of fiction to make the critique of slavery its central theme should continue to attract scholars' attention.

A nonfiction counterpart to *Archy Moore* is Hildreth's *Despotism in America; or An Inquiry into the Nature and Results of the Slave-Holding System in the United States* (1840), which he also wrote during his stay in Florida. Juxtaposing his book title against Alexis de Tocqueville's *De la Démocratie en Amerique* (1835, 1840; Democracy in America), Hildreth sought to contrast the "experiment of Democracy" with "another experiment, less talked about, less celebrated, but not the less real or important, to wit, *the experiment of Despotism.*" The book's five sections focus on different aspects of the slaveholding system: the relation of master and slave; the political, economical, and personal results of the system of slavery; and, in the expanded version of 1854, the legal basis of the institution. The only solution to the system of slavery, argued Hildreth, was emancipation, and freedom for the slaves was not solely for their benefit but necessary for the continuation of democracy. Slavery was "a fatal obstacle to the progress of our free institutions, a consuming cancer eating into the heart of our liberties, and threatening the extinction of those principles upon which our constitutions are founded." As proof, Hildreth documented repeated attempts, some successful, of slavery's supporters to suppress freedom of speech and freedom of the press, and to thwart justice through lynching.

Hildreth reiterates the theme that he dramatized in *Archy Moore,* that there is no natural hierarchy of race, but that race-based slavery and the degradations that are an integral part of the slave system help perpetuate the false perceptions that feed racial prejudice: "That contempt, that antipathy, that disgust which the degraded condition of servitude naturally inspires . . . is artfully, though imperceptibly, transferred from condition to race. . . . In consequence, the . . . privileged cease to consider the servile class as belonging to the same scale of being with themselves."

Hildreth joined the New England Anti-Slavery Association, and his activism was often noticed in William Lloyd Garrison's antislavery newspaper, *The Liberator.* Hildreth wrote numerous articles against slavery and used his legal training to dispute its legitimacy. For example, in "The Legality of American Slavery" he endeavored to prove that slavery had had no legal standing in the British Colonies and was not legally sanctioned by the Constitution of the United States but instead functioned under the "*lynch* law of force and violence."

Hildreth's pamphlet writing kept him engaged in controversy. He defended the Transcendentalists in a forty-page *Letter to Andrews Norton on Miracles as the Foundation of Religious Faith* (1840). Andrews Norton was the chief spokesman for the Unitarians who were outraged by Ralph Waldo Emerson's explanation of the Transcendentalist position in his Harvard Divinity School Address. Hildreth's rebuttal to Norton was just one pamphlet in a larger controversy about the true nature and source of religious faith. Although Hildreth himself was not a Transcendentalist, he objected to Norton's assertion that "Religion is founded upon knowledge derived, and derived only, from the critical study and rational interpretation of the sacred books." The Transcendentalist position, observed Hildreth, posited the more "modest" assertion that "Religion, in its true and vital sense, is a matter of feeling, which feeling leads to knowledge. This is the reverse of your process." Hildreth argued that Norton's position made "impossible . . . that we should have any personal knowledge of the supernatural, the invisible." What particularly seemed to irk Hildreth was Norton's charge that those who disagreed with his position were infidels and atheists; it appeared that the only

Hildreth's grave in Florence

person whom Norton deemed to have interpreted the Scriptures accurately was Norton himself. Norton must indeed be "lucky," observed Hildreth, "to possess the gift of infallibility."

Hildreth's most ambitious project was *The History of the United States* (1849). The first three volumes began with the "Voyages of Discovery" and ended with the ratification of the Constitution. The next three volumes appeared in 1851 and 1852 and covered the period from the adoption of the Constitution in 1788 to the end of the Sixteenth Congress in 1821. The history met with mixed reviews. Some praised Hildreth's use of original sources and his objectivity; others compared it unfavorably to George Bancroft's popular history of the United States written and published at roughly the same time. Bancroft followed an approach to writing about history that Hildreth criticized as too nationalistic; Hildreth opened his first volume with the declaration: "Of centennial sermons and Fourth-of-July orations, whether professedly such or in the guise of history, there are more than enough."

One of the most enduring images of Hildreth was captured by Nathaniel Hawthorne, who observed him at work on his history of the United States in 1850 in the Boston Athenaeum:

> The library is in a noble hall, and looks splendidly with its vista of alcoves. The most remarkable sight, however, was Mr. Hildreth, writing his history of the United States; he sits at a table, at the entrance of one of the alcoves, with his books and papers before him, as quiet and absorbed as he could be in the loneliest study; now consulting an authority, now penning a sentence or a paragraph, without seeming conscious of anything but his subject. It is very curious, thus to have a glimpse of a book in the process of creation under one's eye. I know not how many hours he sits there; but while I saw him, he was a pattern of diligence and unwandering thought; he had taken himself out of this age, and put himself, I suppose, into that which he was writing about. Being deaf, he finds it much the easier thus to abstract himself. Nevertheless, it is a miracle. He is a thin, middle-aged man in black with an intelligent face, rather sensible than scholarlike.

Hildreth did not earn as much from his history of the United States as he had hoped and turned to other types of writing to make a living. In 1854 he began contributing to Horace Greeley's *New-York Tribune* and moved to New York in 1856 to take up the duties of "principle editor." The paper was committed to the antislavery cause, and Hildreth wrote many articles against the institution, contributing to the paper's efforts to form political opposition to slavery, which eventually resulted in the formation of the Republican Party. In the meantime, in 1855 he had published his *Japan as It Was and Is,* a compilation of early interactions other nations had had with Japan. Interest in that country was high after Commodore Matthew Calbraith Perry's expedition, and Hildreth's book went through several editions in his lifetime.

After the financial crisis of 1857 wiped out most of his savings, Hildreth's health again began to fail. His wife, Caroline, engaged the help of friends, who influenced Abraham Lincoln to appoint Hildreth consul to Trieste in 1861. The state of his health forced Hildreth to resign this post in 1864. William Dean Howells described a visit with Hildreth during this period:

> . . . I remember him always reading, reading, reading. He could with difficulty be roused from his book by some strenuous appeal from his family to his conscience as a host. The last night he sat with *Paradise Lost* in his hand, and nothing could win him from it till he had finished it. Then he rose to go to bed. Would not he bid his parting guest good-bye?

> The idea of farewell perhaps dimly penetrated to him. He responded without looking round,
>
> "They, hand in hand, with wandering steps and slow,
> Through Eden took their solitary way,"
>
> and so left the room.

Hildreth died on the night of 10–11 July 1865, and was buried in Florence, Italy.

References:

Donald E. Emerson, "Hildreth, Draper, and 'Scientific History,'" in *Historiography and Urbanization: Essays in American History in Honor of W. Stull Holt,* edited by Eric Goldman (Baltimore: Johns Hopkins Press, 1941), pp. 139–170;

Emerson, *Richard Hildreth, Johns Hopkins University Studies in Historical and Political Science,* series 64, no. 2 (Baltimore: Johns Hopkins Press, 1946);

Louis B. Friedland, "Richard Hildreth's Minor Works," *Papers of the Bibliographical Society of America,* 40 (Second Quarter 1946): 127–150;

Alfred H. Kelly, "Richard Hildreth," in the *Marcus W. Jernegan Essays in American Historiography,* edited by William T. Hutchinson (Chicago: University of Chicago Press, 1937), pp. 25–42;

Martha M. Pingel, *An American Utilitarian: Richard Hildreth as a Philosopher* (New York: Columbia University Press, 1948);

Arthur M. Schlesinger Jr., "The Problem of Richard Hildreth," *New England Quarterly,* 13 (June 1940): 223–245.

Papers:

There is no central collection of Richard Hildreth's papers. Harvard University Archives has some items. A few letters can be found in the Houghton Library at Harvard, the Boston Public Library, and the Massachusetts Historical Society.

Oliver Wendell Holmes

(29 August 1809 – 10 October 1894)

Scott Slawinski
University of South Carolina

See also the Holmes entry in *DLB 189: American Travel Writers, 1850–1915.*

BOOKS: *Poems* (Boston: Otis, Broaders, 1836; revised edition, London: O. Rich, 1846; Boston: William D. Ticknor, 1849);

Boylston Prize Dissertations for the Years 1836 and 1837 (Boston: Little, Brown, 1838);

Homeopathy, and Its Kindred Delusions (Boston: William D. Ticknor, 1842);

The Position and Prospects of the Medical Student (Boston: John Putnam, 1844);

Urania: A Rhymed Lesson (Boston: William D. Ticknor, 1846);

An Introductory Lecture, Delivered at the Massachusetts Medical College, November 3, 1847 (Boston: William D. Ticknor, 1847);

Astræa: The Balance of Illusions (Boston: Ticknor, Reed & Fields, 1850);

The Benefactors of the Medical School of Harvard University (Boston: Ticknor, Reed & Fields, 1850);

Puerperal Fever, as a Private Pestilence (Boston: Ticknor & Fields, 1855);

Semi-Centennial Celebration of the New England Society (New York: William C. Bryant, 1856);

The Autocrat of the Breakfast-Table (Boston: Phillips, Sampson, 1858; London: Hamilton, Adams, 1859);

Valedictory Address, Delivered to the Medical Graduates of Harvard University, at the Annual Commencement, Wednesday, March 10, 1858 (Boston: David Clapp, 1858);

The Professor at the Breakfast-Table (Boston: Ticknor & Fields, 1860; London: Sampson Low, 1860);

Currents and Counter-Currents in Medical Science (Boston: Ticknor & Fields, 1861);

Elsie Venner: A Romance of Destiny, 2 volumes (Boston: Ticknor & Fields, 1861; Cambridge, Mass.: Macmillan, 1861);

Songs in Many Keys (Boston: Ticknor & Fields, 1862);

Oration Delivered Before the City Authorities of Boston, on the Fourth of July, 1863 (Boston: J. E. Farwell, 1863);

Soundings from the Atlantic (Boston: Ticknor & Fields, 1864; London: Sampson Low, 1864);

Humorous Poems (Boston: Ticknor & Fields, 1865);

The Guardian Angel (Boston: Ticknor & Fields, 1867; London: Sampson Low, Son & Marston, 1867);

Teaching from the Chair and at the Bedside (Boston: David Clapp & Son, 1867);

The Medical Profession in Massachusetts (Boston: John Wilson, 1869);
Mechanism in Thought and Morals (Boston: James R. Osgood, 1871; London: Sampson Low, Son & Marston, 1871);
The Poet at the Breakfast-Table (Boston: James R. Osgood, 1872; abridged edition, London: J. Camden Hotten, 1872; complete edition, London: George Routledge, 1872);
Crime and Automatism (Cambridge, Mass.: Riverside Press, 1875);
Songs of Many Seasons (Boston: James R. Osgood, 1875);
Favorite Poems (Boston: James R. Osgood, 1877);
The Poetical Works of Oliver Wendell Holmes (Boston: James R. Osgood, 1877);
John Lothrop Motley: A Memoir (London: Trübner, 1878; Boston: Houghton, Osgood; Cambridge, Mass.: Riverside Press, 1879);
The School-Boy (Boston: Houghton, Osgood; Cambridge, Mass.: Riverside Press, 1879);
The Iron Gate, and Other Poems (Boston: Houghton, Mifflin; Cambridge, Mass.: Riverside Press, 1880; London: Sampson Low, Marston, Searle & Rivington, 1881);
Medical Highways and By-Ways. A Lecture Delivered Before the Students of the Medical Department of Harvard University, May 10, 1882 (Cambridge, Mass.: Riverside Press, 1882);
Farewell Address . . . to the Medical School of Harvard University, Tuesday, November 28, 1882 (Cambridge, Mass.: Riverside Press, 1882);
Grandmother's Story and Other Poems (Boston: Houghton, Mifflin; Cambridge, Mass.: Riverside Press, 1883);
Medical Essays (Boston & New York: Houghton, Mifflin; Cambridge, Mass.: Riverside Press, 1883);
Pages from an Old Volume of Life (Boston & New York: Houghton, Mifflin; Cambridge, Mass.: Riverside Press, 1883);
Illustrated Poems (Boston & New York: Houghton, Mifflin; Cambridge, Mass.: Riverside Press, 1885; London: Macmillan, 1885);
Ralph Waldo Emerson (Boston & New York: Houghton, Mifflin; Cambridge, Mass.: Riverside Press, 1885; London: Kegan Paul, 1885);
A Mortal Antipathy (Boston & New York: Houghton, Mifflin; Cambridge, Mass.: Riverside Press, 1885; Sampson Low, Marston, Searle & Rivington, 1885);
Selections from the Poetical Works of Dr. Oliver Wendell Holmes (Boston: Howe Memorial Press, 1885);
Our Hundred Days in Europe (Boston & New York: Houghton, Mifflin; Cambridge, Mass.: Riverside Press, 1887; London: Sampson Low, Marston, Searle & Rivington, 1887);
Before the Curfew and Other Poems (Boston & New York: Houghton, Mifflin; Cambridge, Mass.: Riverside Press, 1888; London: Sampson Low, Marston, Searle & Rivington, 1888);
My Hunt after the Captain and Other Papers (Boston & New York: Houghton, Mifflin; Cambridge, Mass.: Riverside Press, 1888);
The Holmes Birthday Book (Boston & New York: Houghton, Mifflin; Cambridge, Mass: Riverside Press, 1889);
Over the Teacups (Boston & New York: Houghton, Mifflin; Cambridge, Mass.: Riverside Press, 1891; London: Sampson Low, Marston, Searle & Rivington, 1891);
The Writings of Oliver Wendell Holmes, 13 volumes (Boston & New York: Houghton, Mifflin; Cambridge, Mass.: Riverside Press, 1891);
The One Hoss Shay With its Companion Poems How the Old Horse Won the Bet & The Broomstick Train (Boston & New York: Houghton, Mifflin; Cambridge, Mass.: Riverside Press, 1891);
Dorothy Q. together with A Ballad of the Boston Tea Party & Grandmother's Story of Bunker Hill Battle (Boston & New York: Houghton, Mifflin; Cambridge, Mass.: Riverside Press, 1893).

During his long career, Oliver Wendell Holmes wrote in a variety of genres and attained considerable popularity among his nineteenth-century contemporaries. Though interest in his work has declined, he is still remembered for four significant works, three of them literary, the fourth scientific. Even these four works reveal the range of Holmes's authorial abilities, for each is in a different genre. Two of them–his poem "Old Ironsides" (1830) and his medical investigation of puerperal fever (1843)–appeared early in his career. The other two–his collection of essays *The Autocrat of the Breakfast-Table* (1858) and his novel *Elsie Venner: A Romance of Destiny* (1861)–were published in mid career, just as Holmes entered his most productive period. Taken together, the four works represent Holmes's versatility and his dedication to writing.

The fourth of five children and a descendant of Anne Bradstreet, Oliver Wendell Holmes was born to Abiel Holmes and his second wife, Sarah, on 29 August 1809 in Cambridge, Massachusetts. His father was a graduate of Yale and a moderate Congregationalist minister, while his mother was part of what was eventually called the Unitarian Church. In matters of religion, Holmes came to favor his mother's beliefs after finding the stern Calvinist understanding of original sin and predestination wanting. Nevertheless, his father proba-

Holmes's birthplace in Cambridge, Massachusetts

bly is the parent who fostered Holmes's interest in books and authorship. Abiel Holmes possessed a good-sized library that included some British classics among its largely theological texts. Moreover, he was the author of *Annals of America* (1805), one of the first books to recount the history of the eastern seaboard as American rather than colonial. He also wrote some verse and helped compile *The Family Tablet* (1796), a collection of writings concerning friendship. He did not encourage an interest in fiction, however; for novels Holmes had to turn to his brother, who borrowed them from the library at Harvard.

Holmes began his education with Dame Prentiss at her Dame School, continued it at William Biglow's school, and then entered the private Port School, which his father had helped found. Here Holmes first met Richard Henry Dana Jr. and Margaret Fuller. To prepare him for college, Abiel then sent his son to the Phillips Academy in Andover, Massachusetts. Perhaps he felt his son needed stricter training in Calvinism, for the Andover academy was conservative in matters of Congregationalist doctrine. The school only served, however, to push Holmes further away from the faith of his father. A year later, in 1825, Holmes entered Harvard, and after his 1829 graduation, he began to study law, eventually abandoning it in favor of medicine.

In his four years of college he gained a reputation as a wit and a punster, and here his interest in writing blossomed for the first time. In Andover, when he was fifteen, Holmes had already begun to produce a little poetry, having translated a passage from Virgil's *Aeneid* into heroic couplets. He had received praise for his efforts, which no doubt encouraged him when the college government asked him to compose a poem for the 1829 commencement ceremonies. His poem met with approval from both its listeners and from the newspapers. Possibly Holmes published some of his work prior to his 1829 graduation, but his earliest known pieces appeared in *The Collegian,* a monthly magazine begun by his college friends. The first copy was published in February 1830 and featured three of Holmes's poems. Thereafter he contributed to every issue until the periodical ceased production later that year. Occasionally the newspapers picked up his poems and provided them with a wider circulation. Before the end of 1830 Holmes had already produced fifty poems, and in 1831 he wrote one of his most popular ones, "The Last Leaf." The poem depicts Major Thomas Melvill–Herman Melville's grandfather–as the last of his generation, an anachronism in contemporary Boston. The poem was one of his finest achievements and eventually gained approval from both Edgar Allan Poe and Abraham Lincoln.

None of Holmes's early poems, however, produced the sensation that "Old Ironsides" did in late 1830. On 14 September 1830 the *Boston Daily Advertiser* printed a brief notice stating that the *U.S.S. Constitution* was to be dismantled and used as scrap. Outraged that the United States would allow one of the most prized and famous vessels in the short history of the country to meet with such an end, Holmes wrote his poetic response and submitted it to the *Advertiser,* which printed it on 16 September. Soon, the poem appeared across the country in newspapers and on broadsides, stirring up enough public outcry to ensure the preservation of the ship for future generations. While Holmes had not used his full name (he was in the habit of publishing anonymously or with his initials), "Old Ironsides" significantly shaped his career. For the next sixty-four years Holmes continued to produce occasional poems, many of them linked to specific gatherings such as college commencements and professional meetings.

In the early 1830s Holmes became a regular contributor to Frederick Hill's *New England Galaxy* and to the newly founded *Amateur,* both literary newspapers. Hill also collected some poems written about a Boston art exhibit into a now rare pamphlet, *Illustrations of the Athenaeum Gallery of Paintings* (1830); nine of these poems were by Holmes. Though local audiences knew Holmes to be the author of "Old Ironsides" and his other poems, many readers outside of New England were familiar with his verses, but not with the name of their author. In fact, as late as 1848 a Kentuckian reported carrying some of Holmes's poems in his hat with the hope of someday identifying their author's name. Only in 1833, when "The Wasp and the Hornet" appeared in *The Token,* did Holmes begin to employ his full name when he published. In addition to poetry, this early part of Holmes's career was the beginning of another significant literary project, one that did not fully bloom until the 1850s. An essay by him appeared in the November 1831 issue of the *New England Magazine,* and a second appeared in February 1832. Both featured a small group of characters gathered around a boardinghouse table (Holmes was living in a boardinghouse at the time), talking among themselves. Though he wrote no more than two of these essays in the 1830s, twenty-five years later they evolved into his popular series, *The Autocrat of the Breakfast-Table.*

Holmes's father, the Reverend Abiel Holmes (portrait by an unknown artist; from Life and Letters of Oliver Wendell Holmes, *volume 1, part 1, 1896)*

By 1833 Holmes had advanced his medical education as far as he could in the United States. The really good American doctors of the period spent at least some time training in Europe, so on 10 March 1833 he sailed for England. Stopping there long enough to visit Stonehenge, Salisbury Cathedral, and the estate of the Earl of Pembroke, he then traveled on to Paris on 4 May. There he studied under the pathologist Charles Pierre Alexandre Louis. Parisian medical studies were highly respected in the 1830s, and Holmes learned the scientific method, worked with the newly invented microscope, and gained an appreciation for the value of observation and experience. While Holmes learned the latest developments in medicine at the medical school in Paris, he also attended several play performances; thus began his love of the stage. While such outings were occasionally possible, his medical studies took up most of his time, and his literary production dropped off sharply. In the two years preceding his departure for Europe, Holmes had produced twenty-five poems; while he was in Paris he wrote practically nothing, despite several solicitations from magazines in the United States. He turned down requests from John O.

Holmes and his wife, Amelia Jackson Holmes, whom he married in 1840

Sargent in 1834 and from Park Benjamin in late 1835. He stayed on in Europe for two years, studying and traveling, and in November 1835 he boarded the *Utica* for New York City, landing there 14 December 1835.

The first composition Holmes wrote upon his return was the medical thesis required for completion of his degree. He wrote furiously for three days in January on acute pericarditis, consulting both his notes and books from his private library. His thesis passed on 11 February 1836, and three months later he received his medical degree. Back in the United States and with his thesis completed, Holmes returned to writing poetry. The editors of the *American Monthly Magazine*–one of whom was Benjamin–succeeded in getting contributions from Holmes, but he refused to submit more poetry when one of the lines in "The Last Reader" was changed without his knowledge or permission. Phi Beta Kappa members convinced him to present a poem at one of their gatherings, and both Harvard and Brown successfully solicited poems from him for their commencements; he also wrote a poem for the anniversary of the founding of Harvard. By the end of the year Holmes was gathering these verses and those from the previous five years into one volume, fixing forever their authorship. *Poems* appeared in November 1836, and Holmes used its publication to attempt a graceful exit from literary authorship. He claimed to be too busy for poetry and intended to dedicate himself to his new profession, despite protests from the *North American Review* and other periodicals and despite Ralph Waldo Emerson's recommendation that he join the lyceum lecture circuit. The only requests for poems that Holmes granted in the next few years came from friends such as James Freeman Clarke, who was editing the *Western Literary Messenger* at the time, and Holmes only submitted a work if he already had one on hand when the request came.

Holmes did indeed focus on medicine for a time after he received his degree and won an unprecedented three consecutive Boylston prizes in 1836 and 1837 for medical essays dealing with neuralgia, intermittent fever (malaria) in New England, and the use of the stethoscope, a relatively unknown instrument in the United States. The three essays appeared in a single-volume edition in January 1838. Holmes also introduced medical students to the microscope, becoming one of

Holmes (seated second from left) with other members of the Boston Society for Medical Improvement, 1843 (Boston Medical Library)

the first instructors in America to employ the invention for teaching. In the summer of 1838 he joined the faculty at Dartmouth College, and members of a New Hampshire chapter of Phi Beta Kappa quickly requested he write a poem for the 1839 commencement, a work that received a positive review in the *Boston Daily Atlas*.

Despite his attempted retreat into medicine, people still demanded that Holmes make public appearances. In 1837 he presented a poem on the same occasion that Emerson declared literary and intellectual independence in front of Phi Beta Kappa members with his "American Scholar" address. Though Holmes made his debut on the lecture circuit in late 1837 at the Boston Lyceum, his appearances were irregular, and he did not lecture consistently until the 1850s. His early lectures do not survive, and notices in the newspapers are sparse, but the title of one, "English Versification," suggests his continued interest in poetry. These years were busy personally for Holmes as well. On 15 June 1840 he married Amelia Jackson, and a year later Oliver Wendell Holmes Jr., future Supreme Court justice, was born. This first son was followed by daughter Amelia in 1843 and a second son, Edward, in 1846. Also in 1840, Holmes began to use his lyceum lectures to expose medical quackeries publicly, attacking hydropaths and homeopaths with particular vehemence. Privately, he thought William Cullen Bryant and Henry Wadsworth Longfellow foolish for believing in homeopathy. Such public attacks naturally drew responses from supporters of homeopathy, and at least one was outraged enough to publish a pamphlet defending the practice and attacking Holmes.

In the meantime, Holmes regularly began to attend meetings of the Society for Medical Improvement. In 1842 the society asked the medical community whether puerperal fever, which infects women during and after childbirth, was contagious. Holmes began his research in December 1842. He did not conduct a laboratory investigation, choosing instead to examine all recorded incidents of the disease that came into his hands. On 13 February 1843 he presented his findings, concluding that puerperal fever was indeed contagious. While predecessors had only speculated that the disease could be transmitted from person to person, Holmes's investigation revealed that doctors themselves carried the disease from childbed to childbed, infecting the pregnant women under their care. Holmes's conviction and the persuasiveness of his essay led the society to request he publish the piece. It appeared in its entirety in the fourth number of the *New England Quarterly Journal of Medicine and Surgery* for 1843, and an editor's abstract later appeared in the *American Journal of the Medical Sciences.* While the abstract gained wider circulation throughout the nation, it lacked the persuasiveness of Holmes's writing abilities. Moreover, the *New England Quarterly Journal* ceased publication after 1843, an occurrence that made the original essay difficult for medical men to find. Thus, the contagiousness of puerperal fever remained in question until 1855, when Holmes republished his essay with a new and extensive introduction. Throughout Holmes's life, this essay provided its author with tremendous satisfaction because he was certain it had saved the lives of many pregnant women.

Holmes continued to speak out on public matters, and throughout the 1840s his public appearances as an occasional poet increased. His after-dinner poem for Phi Beta Kappa members in 1843 (which he later published in *Graham's Magazine* under the title "Terpsichore") criticized homeopathy and Transcendentalism. He also drew on contemporary manners and customs for the subject matter of other poems and satirized the follies of the day. Naturally, his views drew criticism, some of it from James Russell Lowell. After Holmes read his poem "Urania," Lowell criticized its political stance. Many of the popular reforms of the day, including temperance and antislavery, which Lowell vigorously supported, did not appeal to Holmes. He also found Transcendentalism wanting. Nevertheless, in the mid 1840s, with an open mind, he reevaluated Emerson's poetry. He still objected to its unnatural rhymes and rhythms, but he did grow to appreciate it. Despite his many public appearances throughout the 1840s, Holmes still turned down editors' requests for poetry–including those from Sarah Josepha Hale of *Godey's Lady's Book.* Holmes continued not to think of himself as a professional author, even while he negotiated for an expanded British edition of his 1836 *Poems* and produced a second American edition.

In 1847 Holmes accepted the position of Dean of the Medical School at Harvard, a position he held for six years, and delivered the opening address of the year for the Medical School. Delivering addresses and presenting poems came to characterize this portion of his life. Eventually, in January 1849, he notified his patients that he was giving up private practice, and in April he resigned from Massachusetts General Hospital, where he had worked since 1846. Holmes appeared frequently and regularly on the lyceum lecture circuit in the 1850s. He made daily presentations throughout New England and New York, and he occasionally traveled as far as Cincinnati, Ohio, and Louisville, Kentucky. Holmes's lectures were more entertaining than they were informative, a characteristic that reflected how the circuit had changed since the 1830s and 1840s. Then, lecturers on the circuit had sought to educate their audiences, but in the 1850s the invitations Holmes received frequently requested the lectures he had written for the amusement of his listeners. Generally, audiences and critics alike both in and outside of New England found his presentations on the love of nature and medicine pleasurable. Holmes's lectures on British poets forced him to become familiar with both older and contemporary poets from across the ocean, and through his research he gained a late appreciation for the British Romantics.

Holmes also continued to take criticism throughout the 1850s for his lectures and writings. Cornelius Matthews, reviewer for Evart Duyckinck's *The Literary World,* apparently took the satire of critics in the poem "Astræa" more personally than Holmes had meant it. When Holmes published the poem, which he had presented to the Yale Phi Beta Kappa members in August 1850, Matthews vehemently attacked both poem and author. While Holmes was not averse to receiving criticism for his writings, in a letter to James T. Fields he did object to the injustice of this particular review. Criticism of more import came after one of Holmes's lectures. He had dared to criticize extreme abolitionists, especially those whom he felt endangered the Union, and he drew a round of condemnation for it. His speech in New York City in front of the New England Society of New York was grossly misrepresented in the New York papers. It was not just misquoted; some reprints hardly corresponded to the original speech. Holmes censured the press in his lectures, and the press responded by mocking Holmes; some papers marked their protest by not reporting his lectures at all. By the late 1850s lecturing was losing its appeal for Holmes. The lecture was becoming a less popular form; lecturers were running out of new material; and the schedule was draining to the speakers. After 1856 Holmes dramatically decreased the number of appearances he made. Unfortunately, the loss of income forced him to sell his farm in Pittsfield, Massachusetts, which had been in the Holmes family for years. He had been in the habit of spending his summers in Pittsfield, and his time there had allowed him to be among those who witnessed the important first meeting between Nathaniel Hawthorne and Herman Melville on 5 August 1850.

Though the criticism he took for his lectures and the tapering off of his appearances might suggest that he was once again retreating from his public status, Holmes actually was on the verge of his most productive literary period. James Russell Lowell, who had become editor of a new periodical, *The Atlantic Monthly,* made sure Holmes became a contributor. Lowell

Massachusetts General Hospital (left), where Holmes practiced medicine until 1849, and Harvard Medical School (right), where he became dean in 1847

believed that to ensure the success of the magazine he must publish a variety of items by both conservative and liberal authors. The first issue of *The Atlantic Monthly* appeared in November 1857, and on page 47 of that issue appeared the first of Holmes's revamped *Autocrat of the Breakfast-Table* essays. The format had remained essentially the same as that in the two issues published in the early 1830s–a group of boarders having a conversation at their breakfast table. Holmes, however, was a better writer than he had been twenty-five years earlier, and the essays reflected his increased abilities. Integrating poetry with prose, the *Autocrat of the Breakfast-Table* papers are witty and philosophical. Moreover, Holmes wrote what he knew, many times drawing on his own varied experiences as source material. He was a member of the Saturday Club–which claimed among its members Emerson, Hawthorne, Lowell, and Longfellow–and wrote about one of its meetings. Themes from previous lectures and poems reappeared in the essays as well. Holmes spontaneously wrote each essay to meet a deadline, and he had no overall plan for them; yet, the *Autocrat of the Breakfast-Table* series was well received just about everywhere, and readers drew comparisons between Holmes and major essayists from Montaigne to Charles Lamb. Even the *Charlestown Courant* of South Carolina, which disliked *The Atlantic Monthly* as a whole, praised Holmes's essays. The series also provided him with a significant British audience in addition to his growing American audience. In fact, the series became central to the success of *The Atlantic Monthly,* significantly increasing orders for its second number, and Holmes incorporated mail from both detractors and fans into his essays. When the series was published in book form, Ticknor and Fields made sure it was well advertised, and it garnered several favorable reviews, including one in the *Boston Transcript.* As a result of the advertisements and the overall popularity of the essays, the book sold ten thousand copies in the first three days and more than double that in the next several weeks.

The Holmes family, circa 1859: Edward Jackson, Mrs. Holmes, Amelia, Oliver Wendell Jr., and Dr. Holmes

Though Holmes was no doubt pleased with the success of *The Autocrat of the Breakfast-Table,* he increased public interest by allowing another boarder, the Professor, to take over the conversation. *The Professor at the Breakfast-Table* began appearing in *The Atlantic Monthly* in January 1859. This new series was in some ways not new at all. Holmes used the same format and took up some of the same themes that he had explored in the *Autocrat of the Breakfast-Table* papers, but close inspection reveals that the Professor is not exactly the same character as his predecessor. He jokes less than the Autocrat does and pays more attention to his fellow boarders. The papers also have a pseudoplot and some action. A romance develops between the patriotic Little Boston and Iris, and Holmes actually allows one of the characters to die at the end of the book. He also deals with religion more openly and sternly in the *Professor at the Breakfast-Table* series. His essays and his lecture "The Chief End of Man" drew fire from furious orthodox Congregationalists. Church papers and ministers criticized the series for its religious views, and *The Atlantic Monthly* lost a few subscribers. The orthodox also felt that Holmes had committed heresy in his lecture by suggesting that the chief purpose of life might differ for each individual and by arguing that it might be sought and found during an earthly existence. For Congregationalists, Holmes was suddenly more of a threat to orthodoxy than Emerson. Despite the controversy surrounding Holmes, the *Professor at the Breakfast-Table* essays were popular; Holmes's literary reputation increased accordingly, and *The Professor at the Breakfast-Table* appeared in book form in 1860.

Though Holmes had been dedicating much of his time to producing literary pieces, he had not abandoned medicine altogether. Soon after *The Professor at the Breakfast-Table* he published *Currents and Counter-Currents in Medical Science* (1861), a collection of his best medical essays. In this volume appeared his now classic essay on puerperal fever and his attacks on the use of "cures" and "remedies" to treat illness. Quacks peddling cures that really only treated the symptoms of illness or had no effect at all disgusted Holmes. He believed that drugs were merely a medical aid to relieve the pain and suffering of patients, and he severely criticized those who claimed otherwise. In his view, too many doctors prescribed medicines when actually the body's immune system should be let alone to do its work without unnecessary intervention from physicians. By this time, Holmes's writings were frequently subjects of controversy, and *Currents and Counter-Currents in Medical Science* was no exception. Some practitioners in the medical community reacted heatedly to the book and disavowed its arguments concerning their "remedies."

Controversy surrounded Holmes's next book as well. The addition of a slight plot to *The Professor at the Breakfast-Table* and a degree of depth to some of the other boarders had already suggested that Holmes was moving in the direction of fiction. The result of the move toward fiction was his first novel, *Elsie Venner: A Romance of Destiny.* To an extent, Holmes's story employs the conventions of the day. It includes a mysterious heroine, a marriage plot, and a touch of the Gothic. Still, Holmes showed great creativity in developing his story by writing what he knew–medicine and Calvinist doctrine. Throughout the book, the narrator describes his heroine, Elsie, as wild and having an apparent kinship to snakes. Eventually, the plot reveals that a snake had bitten Elsie's mother while she was pregnant with Elsie, and the poison had infiltrated the girl and altered her development, thus providing her with snakelike qualities. By drawing on medical investigation and the developing science of genetics, Holmes shifted the focus of his novel away from psychological reasons for his heroine's behavior toward physiological reasons. In the process, he created a religious allegory involving original sin and parental inheritance. Although early-twentieth-century readers criticized Holmes for being too politely Victorian about matters of sex, the content shocked and outraged some of his conservative contemporaries. Religious conservatives in particular singled out *Elsie Venner,* and the *Northwest Christian Advocate* of Chicago chose to run an attack on the novel each time a new installment appeared in *The Atlantic Monthly.* The story apparently placed too much emphasis on Elsie's physicality for some people, while his religious remarks infuriated others. Nevertheless, the work was popular with many readers, and in 1861 Ticknor and Fields brought out *Elsie Venner* in book form. Several subsequent editions have appeared, including a centennial edition, and it has become the best known of Holmes's novels.

Meanwhile, on 3 January 1861, at his Harvard reunion, Holmes presented the patriotic poem "A Voice of the Loyal North," for which he once again received criticism from the press, this time for his partisanship. They urged him not to overreact to the secession of South Carolina on 20 December 1860. This poem nevertheless set the tone for Holmes's poetry during the war. When he wrote at all, his poems were largely patriotic, and the writings he produced in these years that were unconnected to the Civil War were strictly oriented toward medicine. Like so many of his contemporaries, Holmes also had a personal link to the conflict. In 1861 his oldest son and namesake had enlisted, and Holmes went about securing a commission for him. Young Lieutenant Holmes did see action, and on 21 October 1861 the Holmes family received a telegram notifying them that Oliver Jr. had been wounded at the Battle of Ball's Bluff and was recovering in Philadelphia. The anxious father immediately trekked to Pennsylvania, found his son, and brought him back to Boston for recuperation. After his full recovery, young Holmes went back into battle, and the Holmes family received a second telegram informing them that Oliver Jr., now a captain, had been wounded during the Battle of Antietam. Once again the father journeyed to Philadelphia, but this time Holmes searched Philadelphia in vain for nine days. Finally, he learned that his son's wound was not serious and that the young captain had not even left his unit. Holmes turned this adventure into "My Hunt After 'the Captain.'"

The business of supporting and promoting new authors also occasionally drew Holmes's attention. In 1860 he met William Dean Howells, a guest at a meeting of the Saturday Club, and declared the event a "laying on of hands," seeing Howells as the successor to his literary generation. In addition, the war had fostered in Holmes an interest in war poetry and poets. He promoted those authors he liked when opportunities presented themselves and made war poetry the subject of one of his public lectures.

Though an 1865 dramatization of *Elsie Venner* proved unsuccessful, by September 1866 Holmes had already planned out and written a portion of his next novel. That same year *The Guardian Angel* began its run in *The Atlantic Monthly.* Now owner of the magazine, James T. Fields was paying Holmes $250 per installment–an unheard-of price–and he was giving the piece considerable publicity by beginning each issue with the latest chapters. When *The Guardian Angel* eventually appeared in book form in 1867, its run in *The Atlantic Monthly* having come to an end earlier in the year, Holmes dedicated the novel to Fields. Once again

Holmes had to suffer through a round of condemnation. Holmes chose hysteria as the focus of *The Guardian Angel* and related the affliction to the sexual development of its heroine, Myrtle Hazard. Naturally, several critics disliked Holmes's investigation of such a topic, but the criticism printed in the *Nation* upset him more than past criticism had, because the magazine was financed by Charles Eliot Norton, a friend and remote relative of Holmes. He was surprised and disturbed by both the source of the criticism and its vehemence. Despite the objections to it, *The Guardian Angel* sold well enough to equal about half the sales of *Elsie Venner*.

After finishing *The Guardian Angel,* Holmes spent the latter part of the 1860s focusing on his other profession–medicine. Younger members of the Harvard faculty were urging reform in the medical school. They wanted to institute longer terms and favored research over clinical teaching; a few of the reformers even advocated admitting women. While Holmes was not opposed to teaching women, he did reject the other reforms, strongly believing that laboratory experimentation, though important, should not have priority over the practice of medicine. Nevertheless, reform did come in 1871, and medical students found their terms lengthened and a mixture of lectures, laboratory, and clinical work included in their curriculum. Holmes benefited from the changes, finding that his salary had stabilized once it no longer depended on enrollment numbers. In addition to involving himself in the debate over reform at Harvard, he also continued to publish articles about medicine, producing *Mechanism in Thought and Morals* (1871) and *Crime and Automatism* (1875), both of which articulated his views on determinism. Medicine and Harvard occupied much of his time in the latter half of the 1860s, and his literary pursuits amounted only to a trip to Montreal to negotiate a Canadian printing of *The Guardian Angel* and occasionally delivering lectures, as he did for the Lowell Institute on the subject of the medical profession in Massachusetts.

By 1870, though, Holmes was ready to dedicate more time to literature, and the result was *The Poet at the Breakfast-Table* (1872), the final book in the "trilogy." He had talked the project over with William Dean Howells, now editor of *The Atlantic Monthly,* and in January 1872 the series began its run. *The Poet at the Breakfast-Table* develops some of the same themes as *The Professor at the Breakfast-Table* and *The Autocrat of the Breakfast-Table.* The Poet differs, however, from both the Professor and the Autocrat, for he is less bold and confident, more reserved and modest than his predecessors. Holmes also continued to draw on episodes from his own life for subject matter; the reforms at Harvard and the sale of his Cambridge boyhood home both find their way into the essays. To link this book directly to

Holmes's eldest son, future Supreme Court justice Oliver Wendell Holmes Jr., during his service as a lieutenant in the Union Army

the other volumes, Holmes uses the opening essay to reintroduce the boarders gathered around the table, while the reappearance of the Landlady and her family adds continuity to the series. Unlike the earlier books, however, *The Poet at the Breakfast-Table* provides no pseudoplot, so there is little narration found in the essays. Perhaps Holmes knew that the series had peaked, for near the end of *The Poet at the Breakfast-Table,* he predicts diminished readership for his Breakfast-Table series in the coming years, a prediction that has proved prophetic. The trilogy comes to a close with *The Poet at the Breakfast-Table,* and with the publication of the essays in book form in 1872, Holmes capped his most productive literary period.

While Holmes published *The Poet at the Breakfast-Table* and essays on determinism during the 1870s, the number of pieces he produced generally decreased, and his other productions consist only of a few reviews and poems. He had grown weary of the occasional poem and even turned down an opportunity to present a poem at the Harvard commencement ceremonies. Howells, still editor of *The Atlantic Monthly,* continued to ask Holmes for a new piece of fiction, but Holmes pre-

Holmes at seventy (Harvard University Archives)

ferred to allow the stories of Howells and Henry James to command the pages of the magazine. The 1870s were a sad time for Holmes personally, because he suffered the loss of his sister and his son-in-law as well as several close friends and colleagues. Despite his personal difficulties and his hiatus from writing literature, major literary figures of both the pre- and post-war generations turned out on 3 December 1879 to celebrate his seventieth birthday. William Dean Howells organized the breakfast, and many of the guests delivered presentations. John Greenleaf Whittier, Annie Fields, Julia Ward Howe, and Julia Dorr all contributed poems. James T. Fields could not attend in person, but his piece for Holmes was read to the crowd, and Mark Twain found a more receptive audience than he had for his speech at Whittier's birthday party.

While Holmes may have retreated some from literary writing in the 1870s, by the next decade he was energetically back at work and about to enter another productive phase. He had resigned from the Harvard medical faculty in 1882, making his last appearance there on 28 November. Thomas Bailey Aldrich, now the editor of *The Atlantic Monthly,* begged Holmes for a contribution, and he complied, submitting a few poems and prose pieces. Popular demand for his writings also led Holmes in 1882 to begin re-editing his work. Though the process took him years to complete, the eventual result was the multivolume Riverside edition of his writings. Meanwhile, he continued to extend the range of his writing by agreeing to write a biography for the American Men of Letters Series. His subject was his old friend Ralph Waldo Emerson. Though Holmes had never fully subscribed to Emerson's ideas, and the biography occasionally shows the subject matter to be beyond his abilities, Holmes did write a well-balanced narrative that steers a middle course between the opinions of those who idolized Emerson and those who severely criticized him.

Writing the Emerson biography tired Holmes immensely, but by the time it appeared in print in December 1885, he was already working on his third novel, *A Mortal Antipathy* (1885). The novel includes several reminiscences about the early part of the nineteenth century, but the mystery surrounding the hero, Maurice Kirkland, moves the plot along. Kirkland is the victim of a phobia, a strong antipathy toward women. Holmes was apparently drawing on the "Woman Question" for his material, and the narrative appears to satirize both sides of the issue. The novel covers familiar ground by making medical conditions central to the plot (in addition to Kirkland's phobia, the feminist in the novel is a hysteric); yet, it differs from his other fiction through the absence of any significant criticism of Calvinism, and it reveals a tension between his desire for realism and the fantastic nature of his subject matter.

By the publication of *A Mortal Antipathy* in the mid 1880s, Holmes was well into his seventies; yet, he continued to live an active life. On 29 April 1886, after having received many invitations to visit, he and his daughter, Amelia, left on a trip to England. Though he meant the trip to be a restful vacation, his time there was taken up with social gatherings and dinner parties. Henry James, Robert Browning, Oscar Wilde, and Walter Pater all met with him, and Holmes visited Alfred, Lord Tennyson, at his private home on the Isle of Wight. Holmes also received British honorary degrees from Cambridge, Edinburgh, and Oxford. He then visited Paris and, while there, called on Louis Pasteur. Unfortunately, in Holmes's absence his wife had become seriously ill, and her deteriorating health demanded he cut his vacation short and return home. Nevertheless, the experience netted him enough material for *Our Hundred Days in Europe* (1887), a travel narrative that appeared first in *The Atlantic Monthly* and then in book form, with sales approaching those of *The Guardian Angel* twenty years earlier.

Also in 1886, Harvard was celebrating its 250th anniversary. Quite naturally, Holmes was there to present a poem, and equally unsurprising, he created a controversy by continuing to criticize Calvinism. His remarks were infuriating enough to force the president of Princeton to walk out during the presentation. The address by his friend James Russell Lowell was equally upsetting to the audience because he chose to criticize university policies. While the antebellum generation may have aged, it still possessed the ability to unsettle its listeners. Though *Our Hundred Days in Europe* was barely behind him and he was approaching eighty, in 1888 Holmes began a new series for *The Atlantic Monthly*. The first essay of *Over the Teacups* made its debut in March, but the series was barely under way before Holmes abandoned it when he lost his wife and his best friend, James Freeman Clarke, in quick succession. Then, a year later, on 4 April 1889, his daughter, Amelia, died. These losses devastated Holmes, but he could never permanently keep away from writing, and the autumn after Amelia's death he returned to his *Over the Teacups,* eventually completing the series and publishing it in *The Atlantic Monthly* in 1890 and in book form in 1891. Holmes continued to lose friends to death throughout these years. James Russell Lowell died in 1891, and in 1893, a year after producing his last poem (for Holmes's eighty-third birthday), John Greenleaf Whittier died. Perhaps the best moment of the decade for Holmes was the publication of *The Writings of Oliver Wendell Holmes* (1891). In November 1893 Holmes made his last public appearance. His literary career had slowed considerably; he produced only a few poems and introductions in the 1890s. A long illness plagued him in the spring of 1894. On 10 October 1894 he was sitting with his son talking when he simply stopped breathing, having become the last of his literary generation to die, "the last leaf" to fall.

Bibliographies:

Thomas Franklin Currier and Eleanor M. Tilton, *A Bibliography of Oliver Wendell Holmes* (New York: New York University Press, 1953);

Barry Menikoff, "Oliver Wendell Holmes," in *Fifteen American Authors Before 1900,* edited by Robert A. Rees and Earl N. Harbert (Madison: University of Wisconsin Press, 1971; revised edition, 1984).

Biographies:

William Sloane Kennedy, *Oliver Wendell Holmes: Poet, Litterateur, Scientist* (Boston: S. E. Cassino, 1883);

John T. Morse Jr., *Life and Letters of Oliver Wendell Holmes,* 2 volumes (Boston: Houghton, Mifflin, 1896);

E. E. Brown, *Life of Oliver Wendell Holmes* (Akron, Ohio: Saalfield, 1903);

M. A. DeWolfe Howe, *Holmes of the Breakfast-Table* (New York: Oxford University Press, 1939);

Eleanor M. Tilton, *Amiable Autocrat: A Biography of Oliver Wendell Holmes* (New York: Shuman, 1947);

Edwin P. Hoyt, *The Improper Bostonian: Dr. Oliver Wendell Holmes* (New York: William Morrow, 1979).

References:

Clarence P. Oberndorf, *The Psychiatric Novels of Oliver Wendell Holmes* (New York: Columbia University Press, 1943);

Miriam Rossiter Small, *Oliver Wendell Holmes* (New York: Twayne, 1962).

Papers:

Most of Oliver Wendell Holmes's papers are located in the Houghton Library at Harvard University, but other items can be found at the Library of Congress, the Frances A. Countway Library of Medicine in Boston, the Harvard University Archives, and the Henry E. Huntington Library.

Julia Ward Howe

(27 May 1819 - 17 October 1910)

Camille A. Langston
Texas Woman's University

See also the entry on Howe in *DLB 189: American Travel Writers, 1815–1850.*

BOOKS: *Passion-Flowers,* anonymous (Boston: Ticknor, Reed & Fields, 1854);

Words for the Hour, by the author of "Passion-Flowers" (Boston: Ticknor & Fields, 1856);

The World's Own (Boston: Ticknor & Fields, 1857); another version published as *Leonore; or, The World's Own, A Tragedy, in Five Acts,* Stuart's Repertory of Original American Plays, no. 1 (New York: Baker & Godwin, 1857);

A Trip to Cuba (Boston: Ticknor & Fields, 1860);

Later Lyrics (Boston: J. E. Tilton, 1866);

From the Oak to the Olive. A Plain Record of a Pleasant Journey (Boston: Lee & Shepard, 1868);

Sex and Education; A Reply to Dr. E. H. Clarke's "Sex in Education" (Boston: Roberts, 1874);

Memoir of Dr. Samuel Gridley Howe (Boston: Albert J. Wright, 1876);

Modern Society (Boston: Roberts, 1881);

Margaret Fuller (Marchesa Ossoli) (Boston: Roberts, 1883);

Is Polite Society Polite? and Other Essays (Boston & New York: Lamson, Wolffe, 1895);

From Sunset Ridge: Poems Old and New (Boston: Houghton, Mifflin, 1898);

Reminiscences 1819–1899 (Boston & New York: Houghton, Mifflin, 1899);

At Sunset (Boston & New York: Houghton, Mifflin, 1910);

Julia Ward Howe and the Woman Suffrage Movement; A Selection from Her Speeches and Essays, edited by Florence Howe Hall (Boston: Dana Estes, 1913);

The Walk with God . . . Extracts from Mrs. Howe's Private Journals, edited by Laura E. Richards (New York: Dutton, 1919).

OTHER: *Woman's Work in America,* introduction by Howe (New York: Holt, 1891);

The National Exposition Souvenir: What America Owes to Women, introduction by Howe (Chicago: Moulton, 1893);

Sketches of Representative Women of New England, edited by Howe and M. H. Graves (Boston: New England Historical Publishing Company, 1904).

SELECTED PERIODICAL PUBLICATION–UNCOLLECTED: "The Battle Hymn of the Republic," *Atlantic Monthly,* 9 (February 1862): 10.

Howe's parents, Samuel and Julia Ward (from Louise Hall Tharp, Three Saints and a Sinner, *1956)*

Julia Ward Howe was a writer, poet, reformer, lecturer, and author of "The Battle Hymn of the Republic"; she dedicated her life to a number of causes, but especially to restoring and maintaining peace after the Civil War. Most of her writings include the central theme of peace, accompanied by reform issues pertaining to women, slavery, and war.

Howe was born on 27 May 1819 in New York City to well-to-do parents, Samuel, a New York banker, and Julia (Cutler) Ward. Julia Ward died of tuberculosis when her daughter, Julia, was five, and an aunt, Eliza Cutler, reared young Julia and educated her privately. In her early twenties, Julia Ward met Bostonian Samuel Gridley Howe, a well-known hero of the Greek Revolution and head of the Perkins Institute for the Blind in Boston. According to Howe biographer Deborah Pickman Clifford, Samuel's maturity, good looks, and popularity as a philanthropist captivated Julia Ward's attention. In 1843, when she was twenty-three, Julia Ward married forty-two-year-old Samuel Howe. Soon after their marriage, the couple moved to Dorchester, just south of Boston. They had six children.

Although Howe wrote nonfiction essays and published letters and diaries, drama, and an autobiography, she was best known for her poetry. While still a teenager, Howe met the popular poet Henry Wadsworth Longfellow and asked him to critique her verses. Longfellow kindly reviewed her poetry and encouraged her to continue writing. During difficult times Howe often turned to poetry as an outlet for her emotions. When motherless Howe was a young adult, her father died; shortly after her father's death, her favorite brother, Henry, died; and within months of Henry's death, her sister-in-law and nephew died. Howe expressed her mourning in poems, especially in a poem about her brother Henry. Later, Howe shared these poems with Margaret Fuller, and Fuller encouraged Howe to continue writing.

Once Howe married, she subjugated her writing to her duties as a subservient housewife. Her husband, Samuel, discouraged her from writing since it distracted Howe from her responsibilities as a mother and wife. While still on her honeymoon, Howe realized that she had lost her freedom and that her husband was not interested in what she thought or did. During these first few months of marriage, Howe wrote,

> I feel my varied powers all depart
> With scarce a hope they may be born anew
> And nought is left, save one poor loving heart,
> Of what I was–and that may perish too.

Of course, she did not share her poetry with her new husband. Although her husband disapproved of her gregariousness, Howe continued to write poetry, organized a woman's club called the Crochet Party, and devoted

The Ward children, circa 1825: Henry, Samuel, and Julia (miniature by Anne Hall; from Laura E. Richards and Maud Howe Elliott, Julia Ward Howe, 1819–1910, *1916)*

her time to learning Latin, Hebrew, and philosophy. After three years of marriage, Howe published several of her pieces in Rufus Griswold's *Female Poets of America* (1849).

In 1850 Howe spent several months in Rome with her sisters, and during this time she briefly reexperienced the freedom she had known before her marriage. On her dreaded monthlong return to Boston, Howe wrote about her Roman vacation. In one poem, "Rome," she expresses her independence:

> I knew a day of glad surprise in Rome
> Free to the childish joy of wandering,
> Without a "wherefore" or "to what good end?"
> By querulous voice propounded, or a thought
> Of punctual duty, waiting at the door
> Of home, with weapon duly posed to slay
> Delight ere it across the threshold bound. . . .

In this same poem, she expresses her dreaded return to her husband:

> The gate is closed–the air without is drear.
> Look back! the dome! gorgeous in the sunset still–
> I see it–soul is concentrate in sight–
> The dome is gone–gone seems the heaven with it.
> Night hides my sorrow from me. Oh my Rome,
> As I have loved thee, rest God's love with thee!

Against her husband's desires, Howe anonymously published these poems in her first collection, *Passion-Flowers* (1854). The collection became hugely successful; however, its success was based more on the daring of the work–emotional outbursts by a genteel woman–than on its poetic genius. Because of the popularity of the collection, Howe's husband eventually discovered that his wife was the author of *Passion-Flowers.* He came to accept the work and Howe's ability to write poetry, but when he heard rumors about "Mind Verses Mill-Stream," a poem about a miller's unsuccessful attempts at damming a stream, Samuel became outraged. Most readers recognized Howe's poetry as autobiographical, and many readers interpreted this poem as a metaphor for Samuel and Julia's marital problems. When Samuel heard of the interpretation and of the rumors that he could not control his wife, he became so upset that he developed a physical illness, which lingered for months. Howe refrained from publishing poetry for a while after his illness.

Eventually, Howe published a second book of poetry, *Words for the Hour* (1856), and a travel journal, *A Trip to Cuba* (1860). After the Civil War she wrote poetry for the periodical press, including *The Galaxy* and *The Atlantic Monthly.* Her last new collection of poetry, *Later Lyrics,* was published in 1866.

Howe and her husband actively participated in the abolitionist movement. Samuel was one of the "Secret Six" who financed John Brown's expedition in Virginia. During the late 1850s Howe worked with her husband on antislavery issues and assisted him with the publication of the antislavery newspaper *The Commonwealth.*

Howe's husband, Samuel Gridley Howe, in the garb of a Greek soldier (portrait by John Elliott; from Laura E. Richards and Maud Howe Elliott, Julia Ward Howe, 1819–1910, *1916)*

Howe's most famous contribution to American literature, "The Battle Hymn of the Republic" (1862), derived from her work as an abolitionist. She wrote the song as an inspiration to Union soldiers. Various stories on the composition of "The Battle Hymn of the Republic" exist. One version claims that she wrote the song when she and her husband went to the White House to meet Abraham Lincoln in the fall of 1861. Evidently, the Howes joined a group that traveled a few miles outside Washington, D.C., to see the Army of the Potomac perform a military review. At the review, everyone sang patriotic songs, including "John Brown's Body," and some of Howe's friends, knowing her as a poetess, suggested that she write a similar song. According to this version, Howe wrote the lyrics to "The Battle Hymn of the Republic" that night at Willard's Hotel. Later, the lyrics were set to the tune of "John Brown's Body." A second version claims that after visiting a camp near the capital with the party of Governor John A. Andrew of Massachusetts, she scribbled the lines in a tent. A third story asserts that James Freeman Clarke urged her to write suitable words to the hymn. The hymn was first published in James T. Fields's *Atlantic Monthly* (February 1862). For publication of the work, Howe was paid five dollars.

Frequently, "The Battle Hymn of the Republic" is cited for its biblical references and direct appeals to Jesus Christ and God. These references are said to have stirred a nation at war. Jeffrey J. Polizzotto describes the hymn not only as "the most famous poem to emerge from the American Civil War" but also as part of "a religious crusade for freedom, of cosmic importance in history comparable to the death and resurrection of Jesus Christ." Howe wrote,

> In the beauty of the lilies Christ was born across the sea,
> With a glory in his bosom that transfigures you and me;
> As he died to make men holy, let us die to make men free,
> While God is marching on.

In the song, Howe describes a vengeful, judging, Old Testament God. Clifford asserts that the "religious nationalism of the 'Battle Hymn' asserts God's justice rather than his mercy." Howe's stern God sounds "out the trumpet that shall never call retreat," carries a sword, and marches with the Union soldiers as he crushes the South, symbolized by "the serpent," with "his heel."

After twenty years of marriage, Howe approached her husband about her future intentions of public speaking. Although Samuel Howe spent much of his energy supporting the abolitionist cause, he did not fully support the woman's movement. He disagreed with the concept of married women leading active public lives, and he objected to Julia's projecting her public image through speaking appearances. In opposition to her husband's desires, Howe found that she had much to say and that she could no longer express her views through poetry, so she planned to give a series of parlor readings on ethical subjects. Samuel finally accepted the parlor readings on the condition that Howe would not accept compensation for her speeches. Howe held her parlor readings and expanded her public speaking engagements. She preached her first sermon to the Parker Fraternity (1863), read an essay at the Church of the Disciples (1864), and shared her six parlor readings as a lecturer in Washington (1864).

The Howes' conflicting viewpoints on women's roles caused much stress within their marriage. The National Women's Hall of Fame refers to Howe's marriage as "stifling . . . where none of her ideas were valued or accepted" and claims that Samuel's prohibitive view of women may have inspired Howe to dedicate her life to fighting for woman's suffrage and individuality. Additionally, Howe spent much of the 1860s working with other women on reform issues, and she found herself persuaded by Immanuel Kant's claim that women were the moral and spiritual equals of men. The combination of her resentment toward her husband, her association with other women activists, and her Kantian philosophy led Howe to devote most of her later life to furthering women's rights. She allied herself with women's reforms, especially the women's club movement and woman's suffrage.

Women's clubs provided semipublic opportunities for women to share knowledge, gain an informal education, and build a community. In the early 1860s Howe formed one of her early clubs, the Ladies Social Club of Boston, familiarly known as the Brain Club. Artists and writers presented lectures, charades, music, and recitations to the meetings. Later, along with Lucy Stone and others, Howe founded and ran the New England Women's Club (1869); she served as president of the Association for the Advancement of Women (1873); she organized the Washington Ladies Literary and Social Club (1874); and she served as president of the South Boston Women's Club (1876).

As the first president of the New England Woman Suffrage Association and a leader of the American Woman Suffrage Association, Howe assumed an active role in fighting for woman's suffrage. She lectured twice at the first Convention for the American Woman Suffrage Association (1869), served as the foreign corresponding secretary of the association, and edited the journal of the association, the *Women's Journal* (1870). During the following year, Howe traveled throughout New England and lectured about woman's suffrage to various groups.

Once the optimism for the woman's suffrage movement abated, Howe directed her energies to the promotion of peace. She felt that women, as the mothers of mankind, had a duty to preserve peace and to halt war, so she initiated a woman's peace movement. She wrote treatises on peace, attempted to convene a world congress of women in behalf of international peace, became first president of the American Branch of the Women's International Peace Association, and held annual Mothers' Day for Peace festivals.

Howe pioneered the Mother's Day for Peace movement. She publicized her argument throughout the western world, arguing that Mother's Day should be to the women of the United States as Memorial Day was to veterans. Howe wanted to commemorate mothers who worked to fulfill the dream of peace. In her Mother's Day petition, "An Appeal to the Women of the World," Howe exclaims, "Arise, then, women of this day! As men have often forsaken the plough and the anvil at the summons of war, let women now leave all that may be left of home for a great and earnest day of counsel." Later, in her autobiography titled *Reminiscences 1819–1899* (1899), Howe states, "The little document which I drew up in the heat of my enthusiasms implored woman, all the world over, to awake to the knowledge of the sacred right vested in them as mothers to protect the human life which costs them so many pangs." Not only did Howe's movement for peace succeed in establishing Mother's Day, but it also provided her with the opportunity to assert publicly her position on the importance of mothers, their connection to the peace movement, and their responsibilities as protectors of human life.

After her husband's death in 1876, Howe found herself confronted with financial worries. Consequently, she embarked on a two-month lecture tour throughout the West. Her lectures were well attended and well received in cities such as Chicago and Topeka. Shortly after this tour, Howe took her daughter Maud to Europe for a two-year tour and found herself lecturing throughout the continent. She lectured in Geneva in protest of legalization of prostitution in England and in Paris on the woman question.

Within months of her return to Boston, Howe was called upon to give lectures on her travels. In October 1881 the *Woman's Journal* listed the lectures she was prepared to deliver: "Paris, Historical, Social and Political," "Greece Revisited," "Cairo and the Nile," and "Philosophy in Europe and America." She prepared one lecture especially for Bronson Alcott's Concord School of Philosophy. The lecture, titled "Modern Society" (1879), drew more than 1,500 people, a crowd larger than those gathered by Emerson.

In 1888 Howe embarked on what Clifford calls the "most extensive and triumphant lecture tour of her career." She lectured in cities such as Chicago, Walla Walla, and San Francisco on topics ranging from "Women in Greek Drama" to "Woman as Social Power." Throughout the 1890s Howe continued to lecture, although her physical strength was diminishing. As she neared her eightieth birthday, her doctor insisted that she no longer attempt long lecture tours.

Although Howe discontinued her lecture tours, she continued to work for world peace. She served as president of the United Friends of Armenia in 1896, and she helped found the American Friends of Russian Freedom in 1897.

Howe, described by George S. Hellman as "the most notable woman of letters born and bred in the metropolis of America," died on 17 October 1910 in Oak Glen, Rhode Island. "The Battle Hymn of the Republic" was sung at her memorial service in the Boston Symphony Hall.

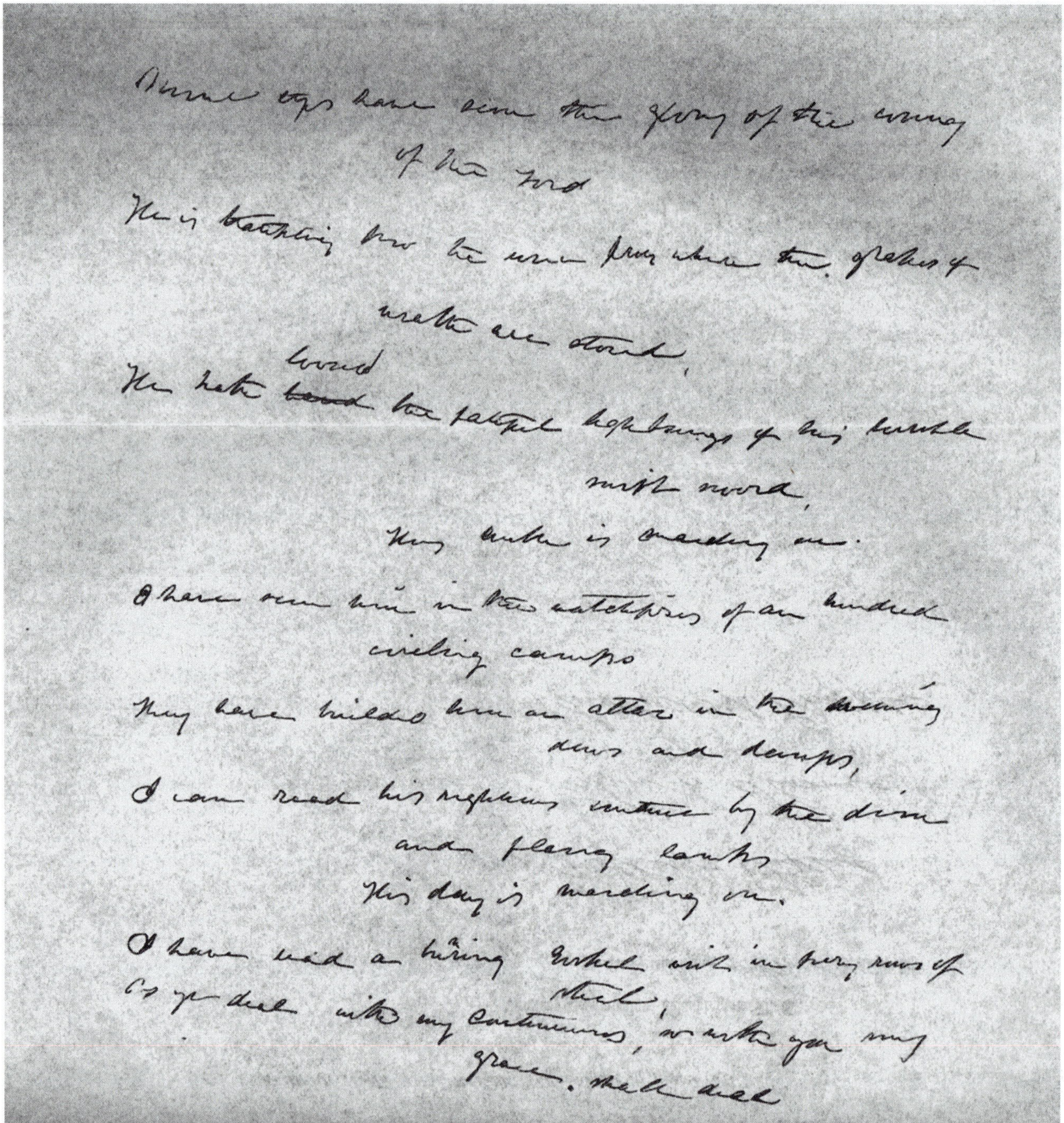

Mine eyes have seen the glory of the coming
of the Lord
He is trampling out the wine press where the grapes of
wrath are stored,
He hath ~~[illegible]~~ loosed the fateful lightnings of his terrible
swift sword,
His truth is marching on.
I have seen him in the watchfires of an hundred
circling camps
They have builded him an altar in the evening
dews and damps,
I can read his righteous sentence by the dim
and flaring lamps
His day is marching on.
I have read a burning Gospel writ in fiery rows of
steel,
As ye deal with my contemners, so with you my
grace shall deal

The first draft of "The Battle Hymn of the Republic" (from Laura E. Richards and Maud Howe Elliott, Julia Ward Howe, 1819–1910, *1916)*

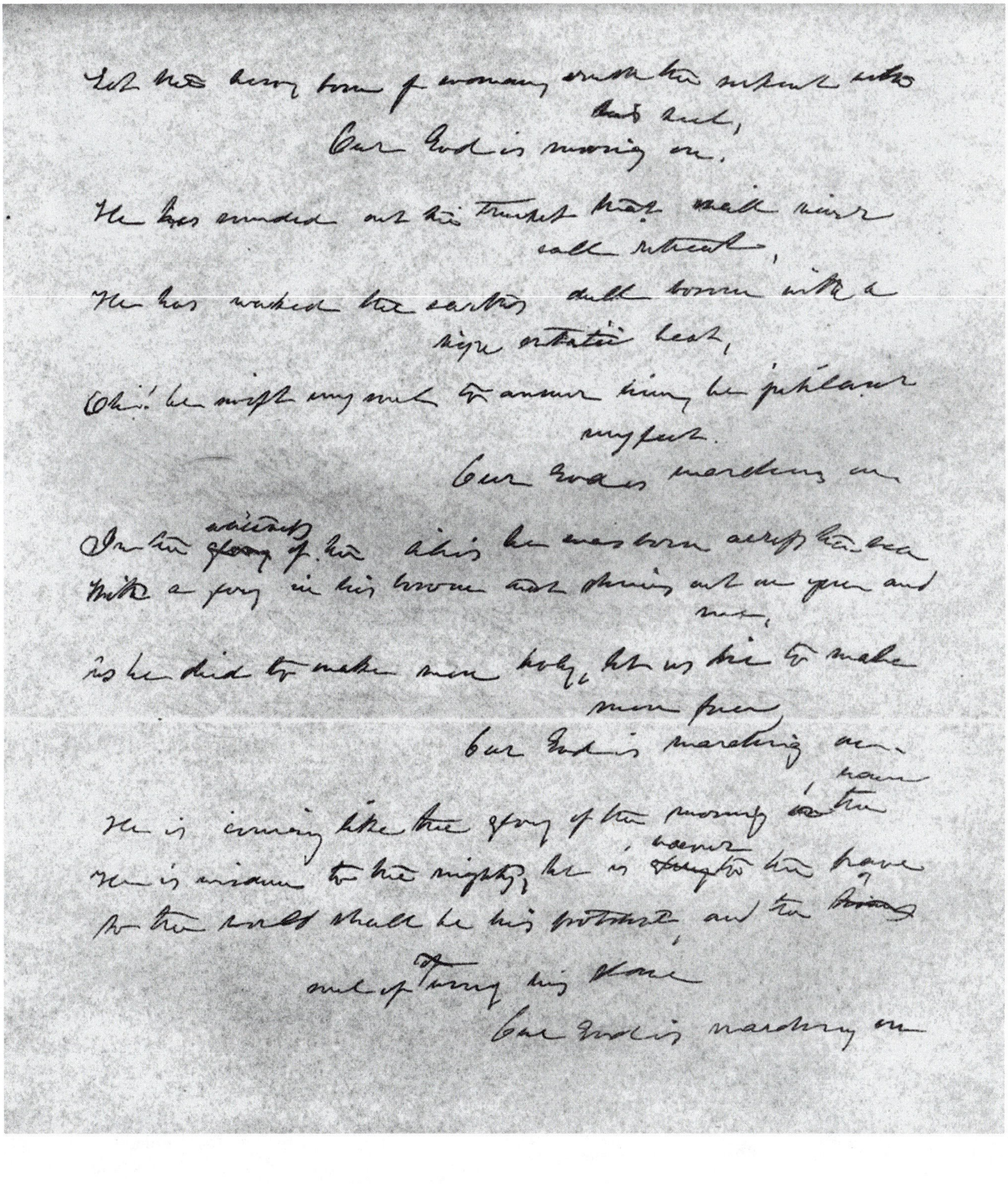
Let the hero born of woman crush the serpent with his heel,
Our God is moving on.

He has sounded out his trumpet that shall never call retreat,
He has waked the earth's dull bosom with a high ecstatic beat,
Oh! be swift my soul to answer him, be jubilant my feet.
Our God is marching on

In the ~~glory~~ whiteness of the lilies he was born across the sea
With a glory in his bosom that shines out on you and me,
As he died to make men holy, let us die to make men free,
Our God is marching on.

He is coming like the glory of the morning on the wave
He is wisdom to the mighty, he is honor to the brave
So the world shall be his footstool, and the soul of Time his slave
Our God is marching on

Howe in the parlor of her house in Oak Glen, Rhode Island (photograph by Major Dudley Mills)

Letters:

Letters, excerpted in *Julia Ward Howe 1819–1910,* 2 volumes, edited by Laura Elizabeth Howe Richards and Maud Howe Elliott (Boston: Houghton, Mifflin, 1915).

Biographies:

Laura Elizabeth Howe Richards, *Two Noble Lives: Samuel Gridley Howe, Julia Ward Howe* (Boston: Dana Estes, 1911);

Richards and Maud Howe Elliott, *Julia Ward Howe 1819–1910,* 2 volumes (Boston: Houghton Mifflin, 1915);

Deborah Pickman Clifford, *Mine Eyes Have Seen the Glory: A Biography of Julia Ward Howe* (Boston: Little, Brown, 1979);

Mary H. Grant, *Private Woman, Public Person, An Account of the Life of Julia Ward Howe from 1819 to 1868* (Brooklyn, N.Y.: Carlson, 1994).

References:

Florence Howe Hall, *The Story of the Battle Hymn of the Republic* (New York & London: Harper, 1916);

George S. Hellman, *Lanes of Memory* (New York: Knopf, 1927);

Jeffrey J. Polizzotto, "Julia Ward Howe, John Brown's Body, and the Coming of the Lord," in *Worldmaking,* edited by William Pencak (New York: Peter Lang, 1996), pp. 185–191;

Louis Hall Tharp, *Three Saints and a Sinner: Julia Ward Howe, Louisa, Annie and Sam Ward* (Boston: Little, Brown, 1956);

Gary Williams, *Hungry Heart: The Literary Emergence of Julia Ward Howe* (Amherst: University of Massachusetts Press, 1999).

Papers:

Julia Ward Howe's papers are held at the Library of Congress Manuscript Division, Washington, D.C. More than two hundred items in five containers are catalogued. Items include Howe's speeches and writings, together with correspondence, notes, and printed materials pertaining to education, immigration, prison reform, race relations, religion, and woman's rights. Correspondence relates to family and other matters and to Howe's work with the New Orleans Exposition. Correspondents include William Henry Channing and Francis Lieber.

Henry Wadsworth Longfellow

(27 February 1807 – 24 March 1882)

Jane Donahue Eberwein
Oakland University

See also the Longfellow entry in *DLB 59: American Literary Critics and Scholars, 1800–1850.*

BOOKS: *Outre-Mer; A Pilgrimage beyond the Sea,* 2 volumes (volume 1, Boston: Hilliard, Gray, 1833; volume 2, Boston: Lilly, Wait, 1834); enlarged edition (New York: Harper, 1835; London: Bentley, 1835);

Hyperion, A Romance (New York: Samuel Colman, 1839; revised edition, Boston: Fields, Osgood, 1869);

Voices of the Night (Cambridge, Mass.: John Owen, 1839);

Poems on Slavery (Cambridge, Mass.: John Owen, 1842);

Ballads and Other Poems (Cambridge, Mass.: John Owen, 1842);

The Spanish Student. A Play, in Three Acts (Cambridge, Mass.: John Owen, 1843);

The Belfry of Bruges and Other Poems (Cambridge, Mass.: John Owen, 1845);

Evangeline, A Tale of Acadie (Boston: William D. Ticknor, 1847; London: Kent & Richards, 1848);

Kavanagh, A Tale (Boston: Ticknor, Reed & Fields, 1849);

The Seaside and the Fireside (Liverpool: John Walker / London: David Bogue; Hamilton, Adams; John Johnstone / Edinburgh: Oliver & Boyd; John Johnstone / Dublin: J. M'Glashan, 1849; Boston: Ticknor, Reed & Fields, 1850);

The Golden Legend (Boston: Ticknor, Reed & Fields, 1851; London: David Bogue, 1851);

The Song of Hiawatha (London: David Bogue, 1855; Boston: Ticknor & Fields, 1855);

Poems by Henry Wadsworth Longfellow, 2 volumes (Boston: Ticknor & Fields, 1857);

Prose Works of Henry Wadsworth Longfellow, 2 volumes (Boston: Ticknor & Fields, 1857);

The Courtship of Miles Standish and Other Poems (London: Kent, 1858; Boston: Ticknor & Fields, 1858);

Tales of a Wayside Inn (London: Routledge, Warne & Routledge, 1863; Boston: Ticknor & Fields, 1863);

Henry Wadsworth Longfellow, 1840 (portrait by C. G. Thompson; Longfellow House, Cambridge)

Flower-de-Luce (London: Routledge & Sons, 1867; Boston: Ticknor & Fields, 1867);

The New England Tragedies . . . I. John Endicott. II. Giles Corey of the Salem Farms (Boston: Ticknor & Fields, 1868; London: Routledge, 1868);

The Divine Tragedy (Boston: Osgood, 1871);

Christus, A Mystery, 3 volumes (Boston: Osgood, 1872)–includes *The Divine Tragedy, The Golden Legend,* and *The New England Tragedies;*

Three Books of Song (Boston: Osgood, 1872; London: Routledge, 1872);

Aftermath (Boston: Osgood, 1873; London: Routledge, 1873);

The Hanging of the Crane (Boston: Osgood, 1874; London: Routledge, 1874);

The Masque of Pandora and Other Poems (Boston: Osgood, 1875; London: Routledge, 1875);

Kéramos and Other Poems (Boston: Houghton, Osgood, 1878; London: Routledge, 1878);

The Early Poems of Henry Wadsworth Longfellow, edited by Richard Herne Shepherd (London: Pickering, 1878);

Ultima Thule (London: Routledge, 1880; Boston: Houghton, Mifflin, 1880);

In the Harbor, Ultima Thule–Part II (Boston: Houghton, Mifflin, 1882; London: Routledge, 1882);

Michael Angelo (Boston: Houghton, Mifflin, 1883; London: Routledge, 1883).

Editions: *The Writings of Henry Wadsworth Longfellow,* Riverside Edition, edited by Horace E. Scudder, 11 volumes (Boston: Houghton, Mifflin, 1886); reprinted in Standard Library Edition with *Life,* by Samuel Longfellow, 14 volumes (Boston: Houghton, Mifflin, 1891);

The Complete Poetical Works of Henry W. Longfellow, Cambridge Edition, edited by Horace E. Scudder (Boston: Houghton, Mifflin, 1893); republished as *The Poetical Works of Longfellow,* introduction by George Monteiro (Boston: Houghton Mifflin, 1975).

OTHER: *Manuel de Proverbes Dramatiques,* edited by Longfellow (Portland, Me.: Samuel Colman / Brunswick, N.J.: Griffin's Press, 1830);

Charles Francois Lhomond, *Elements of French Grammar and French Exercises,* translated by Longfellow (Portland, Me.: Samuel Colman / Brunswick, N.J.: Griffin's Press, 1830);

Novelas Españolas: El Serrano de las Alpujarras; y el Cuadro Misterioso, edited by Longfellow (Portland, Me.: Samuel Colman / Brunswick, N.J.: Griffin's Press, 1830);

Oliver Goldsmith, *Le Ministre de Wakefield,* French translation by T. F. G. Hennequin, edited by Longfellow (Boston: Gray & Bowen, 1831);

Syllabus de la Grammaire Italienne, edited by Longfellow (Boston: Gray & Bowen, 1832);

Saggi de' Novellieri Italiani d'Ogni Secolo, edited by Longfellow (Boston: Gray & Bowen, 1832);

Coplas de Don Jorge Manrique, translated by Longfellow (Boston: Allen & Ticknor, 1833);

The Waif: A Collection of Poems, edited by Longfellow (Cambridge, Mass.: John Owen, 1845);

The Poets and Poetry of Europe, edited, with biographical notes, by Longfellow (Philadelphia: Carey & Hart, 1845; revised and enlarged, Philadelphia: Porter & Coates, 1871);

The Estray: A Collection of Poems, edited by Longfellow (Boston: Ticknor, 1846);

The Divine Comedy of Dante Alighieri, 3 volumes, translated by Longfellow (Boston: Ticknor & Fields, 1865–1867; revised, 1867; London: Routledge, 1867);

Poems of Places, edited by Longfellow (volumes 1–19, Boston: Osgood, 1876–1877; volumes 20–31, Boston: Houghton, Osgood, 1878–1879).

By far the most widely known and best-loved American poet of his time, Henry Wadsworth Longfellow achieved a level of national and international prominence possibly unequaled in the literary history of the United States. Poems such as "Paul Revere's Ride," *Evangeline, A Tale of Acadie* (1847), and "A Psalm of Life" became mainstays of national culture, long remembered by generations of readers who studied them in school. Longfellow's celebrity in his own time, however, has yielded to changing literary tastes and to reactions against the genteel tradition of authorship he represented. The only American writer honored in the Poets' Corner of Westminster Abbey (his bust was installed there with due ceremony in 1884) has suffered an eclipse of reputation nearly as unparalleled as his original success. Still, Longfellow's achievements in fictional and nonfictional prose, in a striking variety of poetic forms and modes, and in translation from many European languages resulted in a remarkably productive and influential literary career–one achieved despite pressures of college teaching and repeated personal tragedies. Even if time has proved him something less than the master poet he never claimed to be, Longfellow made pioneering contributions to American literary life by exemplifying the possibility of a successful authorial career, by linking American poetry to European traditions beyond England, and by developing a surprisingly wide readership for romantic poetry.

Born on 27 February 1807, in Portland while Maine was still a part of Massachusetts, Henry Wadsworth Longfellow grew up in the thriving coastal city he remembered in "My Lost Youth" (1856) for its wharves and woodlands, the ships and sailors from distant lands who sparked his boyish imagination, and the historical associations of its old fort and an 1813 offshore naval battle between American and British brigs. His father, Stephen Longfellow, was an attorney and a Harvard graduate active in public affairs. His mother, Zilpah (Wadsworth) Longfellow, was the daughter of General Peleg Wadsworth, who had served in the American Revolution. She named this second son among her eight children for her brother, Henry Wadsworth, who had died heroically in Tripoli harbor in 1804. The family occupied the first brick house in Port-

Longfellow's birthplace in Portland, Maine

land, built by the general and still maintained as a literary shrine to its most famous occupant. Henry began his schooling at age three, when he and his older brother, Stephen, enrolled in the first of several private schools in which they prepared for entrance to Bowdoin College. Aside from a leg injury that nearly resulted in amputation when he was eight, Henry apparently enjoyed his school friendships and outdoor recreation both in Portland and at his Grandfather Wadsworth's new home in the frontier village of Hiram, Maine. His father's book collection provided literary models of a neoclassical sort, and family storytelling acquainted him with New England lore dating to pilgrim days. The boy's first publication, appearing in the 17 November 1820 *Portland Gazette* and signed simply "Henry," drew on local history for a melancholy four-quatrain salute to warriors who fell at "The Battle of Lovell's Pond." A family friend's dismissal of the piece as both "stiff" and derivative may have discouraged Henry's ambition for the time. Also at age thirteen he passed the entrance examinations for Bowdoin College, although his parents chose to have both Henry and Stephen complete their freshman studies at Portland Academy and delay the twenty-mile move to Brunswick and the new college until their sophomore year.

Bowdoin College, when Henry and Stephen Longfellow arrived for the fall 1822 term, was a small and isolated school with a traditional curriculum and conservative Congregational leadership. The stimulus Henry Longfellow found there came less from classes or the library (open one hour a day and allowing students only limited borrowing privileges) than from literary societies. Elected to the Peucinian Society, he mixed with the academically ambitious students of the college (more serious than his brother or than classmates Nathaniel Hawthorne, Franklin Pierce, and Horatio Bridge–all belonging to the Athenean Society). The book holdings of the Peucinian Society, its formal debates, and its informal Conversations about contemporary writing and American authors encouraged Henry to direct his ambition toward literary eminence despite his practical father's preference for a career in law or one of the other established professions. Favorable responses to poems, reviews, sketches, and essays he contributed to the *Portland Advertiser, American Monthly Magazine,* and *United States Literary Gazette* sparked hopes for editing and writing opportunities that collided against the materialistic pragmatism of New England culture. Public speaking provided other outlets for Henry's artistic and rhetorical skills at Bowdoin: in his Junior Exhibition performance he anticipated *The Song of Hiawatha* (1855) by speaking as a "North American Savage" in a dialogue with an English settler, and his commencement address argued for redirection of national values in support of "Our American Authors."

Unenthusiastic about the legal career to which his father apparently destined him, Longfellow bargained for a year of postgraduate study in literature and modern languages while he explored possibilities of supporting himself by writing. Fate, however, intervened to protect him from the bar. Mrs. James Bowdoin, for whose late husband the college had been named, contributed $1,000 to endow a professorship in modern languages (only the fourth in the United States), and–on the strength of Longfellow's translation of a Horace ode that had impressed one of his father's colleagues among Bowdoin trustees–college authorities offered the position to the young graduate at his 1825 commencement on the condition that he prepare for the post by visiting Europe and becoming accomplished in Romance languages. On the advice of George Ticknor of Harvard, Longfellow decided to add German to French, Spanish, and Italian. He sailed from New York to Le Havre in May 1826 and spent the next three years rambling through cities and countryside, absorbing impressions of European cultures and places, living with families in Paris, Madrid, and Rome, and developing linguistic fluency. Before he settled down in the university town of Göttingen, to which Ticknor had directed him, Longfellow's approach to language acquisition was less systematic than impressionistic and even desultory. His model was Washington Irving, to whom he was introduced while in Spain, and Longfellow envisaged putting his experience to Irvingesque literary use. Homesickness, however, prompted him to develop a proposal for a never published new-world sketchbook featuring New England settings and stories, rather than any literary account of European materials; "The Wondrous Tale of a Little Man in Gosling Green," which appeared in the 1 November 1834 *New Yorker,* exemplifies his intent for that projected volume. In Germany, Longfellow settled down to relatively disciplined study in preparation for his Bowdoin professorship, though his readings there focused more on Spanish literature than German.

Returning to Maine in summer 1829, Longfellow as a young professor soon found himself immersed in the unpoetic routines of pedagogy. Later, he distilled memories of European wanderings (along with material from his college lectures) into *Outre-Mer; A Pilgrimage beyond the Sea* (1833, 1834) and the anticipatory "Schoolmaster" pieces he published between 1831 and 1833 in the *New-England Magazine,* but not before directing his talents to more practical kinds of writing.

Back at Bowdoin in his new role, Longfellow felt stultified in a college atmosphere so different from what he had experienced at Göttingen and stifled by the provincial atmosphere of Brunswick. He also found himself overburdened with instructional tasks–introducing students to the rudiments of various languages and developing teaching materials he could use in classes to replace rote recitation of grammar with literary conversation and translation. Most of his publications for the next few years involved textbooks for students of Spanish, French, and Italian. Aspiring to scholarly recognition beyond Brunswick, Longfellow also regularly wrote essays on French, Spanish, and Italian languages and literatures for the *North American Review* between 1831 and 1833. Aside from two Phi Beta Kappa poems–the first at Bowdoin in 1832 and the other the next year at Harvard–the poetry he was composing consisted chiefly of translations from Romance languages that he used in his classes and articles. His continuing concerns about the place of poetry in American culture emerged, however, in his 1832 review essay on a new edition of Sir Philip Sidney's "The Defence of Poetry," in which Longfellow argued that "the true glory of a nation consists not in the extent of its territory, the pomp of its forests, the majesty of its rivers, the height of its mountains, and the beauty of its sky; but in the extent of its mental power,–the majesty of its intellect,–the height and depth and purity of its moral nature."

Despite the frustrations Longfellow experienced in his new vocation, there was personal happiness. Shortly after his return from Europe, he began his courtship of Mary Potter, daughter of Judge Barrett Potter; she was a Portland neighbor who was a friend of his sister Anne. Longfellow and Mary Potter were married 14 September 1831. After a period in a boardinghouse near Bowdoin, they set up housekeeping in Brunswick even as the young husband explored every possible avenue of escape from that all-too-familiar environment. Longfellow sought diplomatic posts, considered opening a girls' school in New York or taking over the Round Hill School in Northampton, and applied for professorships in Virginia and New York before release came in the form of an invitation to succeed Ticknor as Smith Professor of Modern Languages at Harvard. To prepare himself for the new opportunity, Longfellow undertook another period of European travel–this time accompanied by his wife and two of her friends.

Longfellow's goal in this second European journey was to acquaint himself with Scandinavian languages while strengthening his command of German language and literature. The trip began happily with a London visit and Longfellow's introduction to Thomas Carlyle, whose excitement over Johann Wolfgang von

Goethe and Friedrich Schiller heightened Longfellow's interest in German Romanticism. From London the Longfellow party proceeded to Sweden, Denmark, and the Netherlands. Sorrows beset them, however: from Copenhagen, Mary Goddard was summoned home by news of her father's death; in Amsterdam the ailing Mary Potter Longfellow suffered a miscarriage in October 1835. Although she rallied sufficiently to advance with her husband and Clara Crowninshield to Rotterdam, Mary's health declined over the next weeks and she died on 29 November, leaving her widower stricken and disbelieving. In his grief Longfellow moved on to Heidelberg and immersion in German literature–readings in Goethe, Schiller, Ludwig Uhland, Jean Paul Richter, E. T. A. Hoffmann, and Novalis (Friedrich von Hardenberg)–that awakened a new sense of poetry as emotional expression. In that university town he met William Cullen Bryant, who had been a major influence on his early poetry and an inspiring model of American authorship. Restless and sorrowful, Longfellow then set out alone to travel through the Tyrol and Switzerland. Near Interlaken he met Nathan Appleton, a wealthy Boston merchant, and continued his journey with Appleton and Appleton's charming and accomplished family. After falling in love with seventeen-year-old Frances Appleton, Longfellow returned to Heidelberg to escort Mary's friend Clara Crowninshield home to the United States. There he settled down to his professorial duties at Harvard, freed from some of the Bowdoin drudgery but still feeling oppressed by responsibilities to supervise native-language instructors and provide some basic instruction himself in each of the languages in the curriculum of the university while preparing lectures on European literatures.

After a brief period of boarding on Professors' Row in Cambridge, Longfellow found lodging in the Craigie mansion on Brattle Street, occupying the room that had once been George Washington's headquarters. Resuming friendship with Fanny and Mary Appleton and their brother Tom, Longfellow was crushed by Fanny's rejection of his 1837 marriage proposal. Again, he sought solace by flinging himself into his work. He was still writing learned essays for the *North American Review*–this time concentrating attention on Teutonic languages, including Swedish and early English. Still committed to the native writers of the United States, he wrote a July 1837 review in praise of Hawthorne's *Twice-Told Tales* (1837) even as he turned his own ambitions back toward the writing of poetry. "A Psalm of Life" (1838) expresses both the confusion of his feelings in that time of discouragement and his resolve not to succumb to mournful passivity. Its counsel to "Act,–act in the living Present!" and its injunction to "be up and doing, / With a heart for any fate" gave poetic expression to the motto he had discovered in a German graveyard and translated in the epigraph to *Hyperion, A Romance* (1839) as "Look not mournfully into the Past. It comes not back again. Wisely improve the Present. It is thine. Go forth to meet the shadowy Future, without fear, and with a manly heart."

Mary Potter Longfellow, the poet's first wife (Longfellow House, Cambridge, Massachusetts)

Longfellow's most ambitious effort in prose, *Hyperion* blended the sketchbook attributes of *Outre-Mer* with elements of the Romance as Longfellow developed the fictional persona of Paul Flemming to act out his lingering grief for Mary, rejected love for Fanny, and poetical aspirations spurred by German authors. The book met with only modest success while deepening Fanny's estrangement, sparking considerable Boston gossip, and drawing mixed but often hostile responses from reviewers. The failure of its first publisher kept half the first edition of 1,200 copies from distribution, and the eventual readership of the book, American travelers in Europe, probably discovered *Hyperion* based on its author's later reputation rather than its inherent merits as prose fiction.

More important, Longfellow turned back to poetry after that second European journey and found encouragement in the warm reception of a group of poems he classified loosely as "psalms." Although he never received any money from *Knickerbocker's,* where several of these poems first appeared, Longfellow discovered an appreciative public response to the sad wisdom he had distilled from the disappointments of life; sadness empowered him to speak comforting, encouraging words to the many readers who responded gratefully to "A Psalm of Life," "The Reaper and the Flowers," "The Light of Stars," "Footsteps of Angels," and "Midnight Mass for the Dying Year." He collected these and other early poems in *Voices of the Night,* like *Hyperion* published in 1839, and followed up on that success with *Ballads and Other Poems* (1842), which featured short narrative poems such as "The Skeleton in Armor" and "The Wreck of the Hesperus," a character sketch that he thought of as another psalm titled "The Village Blacksmith," and a poem of Romantic inspiration, "Excelsior." He was exploring American subject matter in many of these poems–even in "The Skeleton in Armor," which drew an unexpected link between medieval Scandinavian war songs and New England antiquities. This period was also one of experimentation in dramatic writing, although publication of *The Spanish Student* was delayed until 1843.

A third trip to Europe followed in 1842, when Longfellow took a brief leave of absence from professorial tasks to travel for his health. Although the sonnet "Mezzo Cammin," written toward the end of that stay in Germany, laments how "Half of my life is gone, and I have let / The years slip from me and have not fulfilled / The aspiration of my youth, to build / Some tower of song," he was entering into a vigorously productive period of his career. In Germany, Longfellow formed a close friendship with the poet Ferdinand Freiligrath, and in England he deepened an earlier acquaintance with Charles Dickens. Inspired by social concerns raised by both writers, Longfellow devoted the voyage home to writing seven of the eight poems published on his return as *Poems on Slavery* (1842). "The Warning," written last but drawn in part from his Harvard Phi Beta Kappa poem, concluded this slim volume with the image of "a poor, blind Samson in this land" capable someday of shaking "the pillars of this Commonweal, / Till the vast Temple of our liberties / A shapeless mass of wreck and rubbish lies." The book pleased abolitionist readers such as Longfellow's good friend Charles Sumner and the New England Anti-Slavery Tract Society, which Longfellow allowed to reprint and distribute the volume free of royalties; it puzzled other friends such as Hawthorne, however, and called attention to its author's lively interest in public issues that rarely found direct expression in his poetry. Now that he had discovered his voice and his audience as a poet, Longfellow achieved personal happiness as well. On 13 July 1843 he married Frances Appleton; her father presented the couple with Craigie House as his wedding gift.

The marriage was an exceptionally happy one for both partners and brought Longfellow the domestic stability he had missed. Six children were born to the couple–Charles, Ernest, Fanny, Alice, Edith, and Anne Allegra. Both Craigie House in Cambridge and the beach home in Nahant, Massachusetts, where the Longfellows summered from the 1850s became centers of warm hospitality extended to American and European guests–many of them literary figures–and Longfellow's many admirers. Fanny Longfellow took pride in her husband's growing reputation and actively assisted him. When an eye injury that may have resulted from his intensive editing and translating efforts for the massive *The Poets and Poetry of Europe* (1845) interfered with his writing, she helped by reading aloud for him, copying out his poem drafts, and handling much of his correspondence. Fanny is also credited with directly inspiring two poems that emerged from their wedding trip–"The Arsenal at Springfield," the peace poem she requested, and "The Old Clock on the Stairs"; both poems appeared in *The Belfry of Bruges and Other Poems* (1845; copyright 1846). Most poems in the book had appeared earlier in *Graham's Magazine,* which had paid both Longfellow and Bryant the unprecedented sum of $50 a poem, and had reappeared in an illustrated edition of Longfellow's poems published earlier that year by Carey and Hart in Philadelphia. As the title suggests, the collection included many poems influenced by his 1842 travels in northern Europe; among them were the title poem, "Nuremberg," "The Norman Baron," "Walter Von Der Vogelweid," and several translations. Other poems had local settings–for example, "The Bridge," which contrasted Longfellow's newfound personal peace with the melancholy of his earlier years in a reflection on the bridge over the Charles River near his home. "To a Child," one of the most popular poems of the book, expressed paternal tenderness toward his first son, while the sonnet "Dante" looked toward a later stage of literary productivity. Longfellow published two collections of verse by other poets, *The Waif* (1845) and *The Estray* (1846), each preceded by an original poem relating to the poet and his audience. "The Day Is Done" (1844) speaks to the comforting quiet offered the weary reader by "some humbler poet" than the Miltonic and Dantean masters–a poet such as Longfellow found himself becoming by virtue of the kindly, sympathetic tone that characterized his popular poems. "Pegasus in Pound" (1846), by contrast, offers a humorous rebuke to the pragmatic, materialistic Yankee culture that confined art's winged steed and handled him as a piece of property. Longfellow returned to this theme three years later in his last major prose composition, *Kavanagh, A Tale* (1849). Although the title character, the liberal-minded young minister of

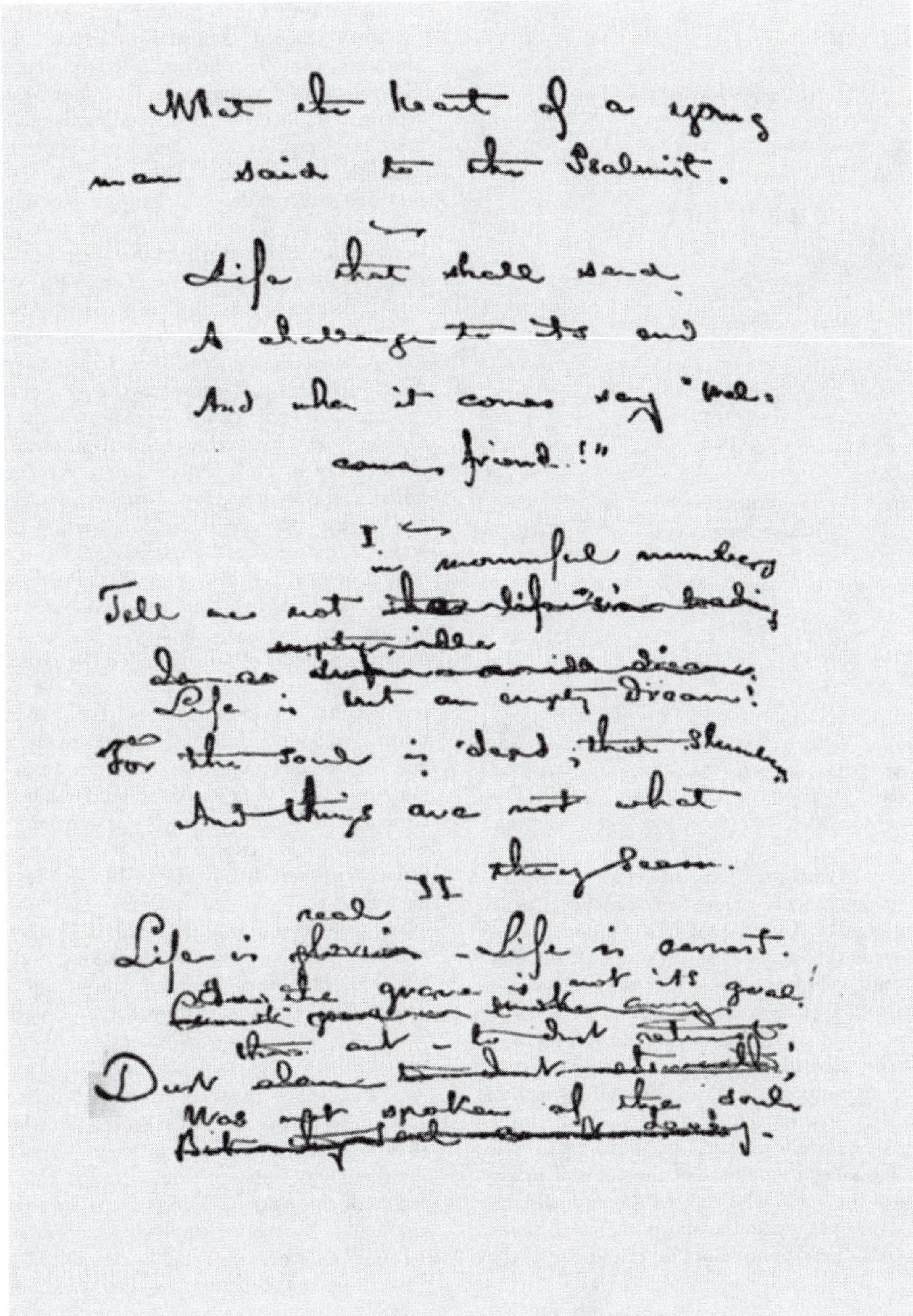
What the heart of a young
man said to the Psalmist.

Life that shall send
A challenge to its end
And when it comes say "Wel-
come, friend!"

I.
Tell me not in mournful numbers
Life is but an empty dream!
For the soul is dead that slumbers
And things are not what
they seem.

II.
Life is real—Life is earnest.
And the grave is not its goal;
Dust thou art—to dust returnest,
Was not spoken of the soul.

Page from the first draft for Longfellow's 1838 poem "A Psalm of Life" (from Samuel Longfellow, ed., Life of Henry Wadsworth Longfellow, *1886)*

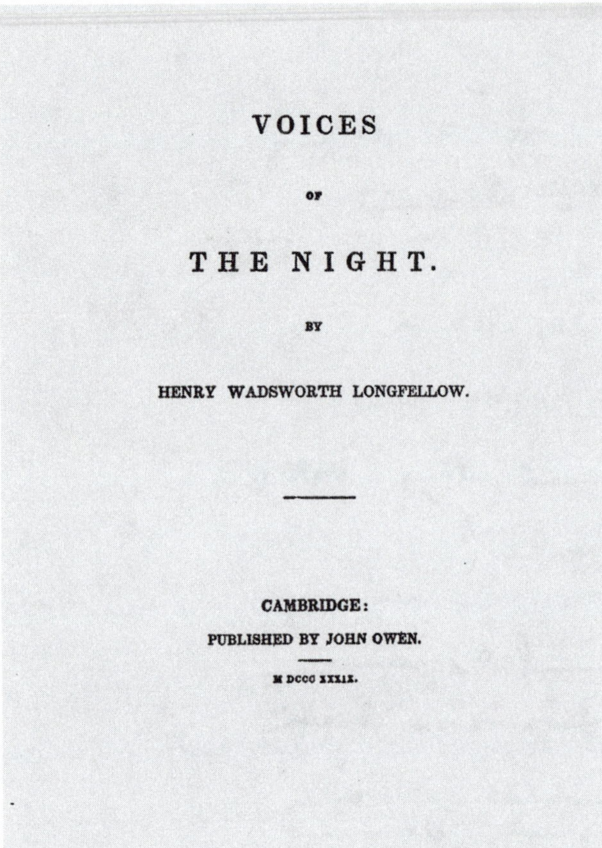
VOICES

OF

THE NIGHT.

BY

HENRY WADSWORTH LONGFELLOW.

CAMBRIDGE:

PUBLISHED BY JOHN OWEN.

M DCCC XXXIX.

Title page for the volume in which Longfellow collected "A Psalm of Life," "The Reaper and the Flowers," "The Light of Stars," "Footsteps of Angels," "Midnight Mass for the Dying Year," and other early poems

a rural New England church, is the central figure of a love triangle involving two close female friends, Cecilia Vaughan and Alice Archer, Longfellow probably took more interest in the schoolmaster, whose literary ambitions are continually frustrated by the press of teaching, fatherhood, and demands made on his time by an aspiring poetess. Although Churchill's failure results most of all from his own limitations–his inattentiveness to sources of inspiration nearest at hand and his lack of driving literary commitment–it also reflects the indifference of Americans to artistic aspirations not in tune with the chauvinistic bombast of the comical magazine editor of the book, who calls for "a national literature altogether shaggy and unshorn, that shall shake the earth, like a herd of buffaloes thundering over the prairies."

Yet, Longfellow achieved perhaps his greatest popular success with *Evangeline, A Tale of Acadie,* a verse romance the geographic sweep of which across French and English America in the eighteenth century makes it a virtual epic, although in the sentimental mode and featuring a heroine notable for her humble, loving endurance rather than military prowess. The germ of the story reached Longfellow through the Reverend Horace L. Conolly, who had failed to interest his friend Hawthorne in developing the legend of Acadian lovers separated on their intended wedding day by an English edict displacing French Canadian settlers in order to establish Nova Scotia. Although the original story involved the maiden's lifelong search only through New England, Longfellow extended its geographic range. Much of the charm of the poem lies in its evocation of place, from the pastoral Grand-Pré, where Benedict Bellefontaine, Evangeline's father, "dwelt on his goodly acres," through the bayous of Louisiana, where the Acadian blacksmith Basil Lajeunesse, Gabriel's father, achieves new prosperity as a rancher, through the forests of French mission territory at the base of the Ozarks, where Evangeline ventures in seeking Gabriel, all the way to Philadelphia, where the aged heroine finds her lover dying in a hospital for plague victims and where they are buried together. There is little action in the story as Longfellow tells it: the Acadians submit quietly to British tyranny; Gabriel's adventures take place out of sight; and Evangeline's quest involves a good deal of travel, admittedly, but no conflict. She serves as a model of "affection that hopes, and endures, and is patient." The crucial event of the story is the reunion that almost happens but fails, when Gabriel's northward-bound boat passes at night by the one in which Evangeline and their priest are resting on their journey to his father's new home. Despite some criticism of the Virgilian dactylic hexameter meter with which Longfellow experimented in *Evangeline,* the poem proved enormously successful. Longfellow completed his writing on his fortieth birthday. The book appeared in late October and was in its sixth edition by mid January. Hundreds of editions, translations, and imitations followed, and *Evangeline* won admiration in Europe (from which Longfellow drew some of his sources) as well as the United States. It was probably the most celebrated American poem of the century.

Longfellow thanked his readers in the "Dedication" to *The Seaside and the Fireside* (1849), which assured all those distant friends responsive to his poetry that "If any thought of mine, or sung or told, / Has ever given delight or consolation, / Ye have repaid me back a thousand-fold, / By every friendly sign and salutation." As the title indicates, this book maintained a balance between poems of nature invoking in various ways the poet's Portland boyhood and oceanic travels and poems of home life–notably "Resignation," an elegy for his year-old daughter Fanny. Both seaside and fireside come together in "The Fire of Drift-Wood," a mood piece employing imagery of light and warmth drawn from shipwreck as a metaphor for intuited estrangement among friends. There were still poems drawn from Longfellow's travels and his readings in European literatures, but the most celebrated poem of the book was among his most patriotic pieces. "The Building of the Ship" combines a tribute to the master builder who designed the ship with a love story linking the master's daughter to the "fiery youth" employed in its construction while making clear that the *Union* stood allegorically for the United States on the eve of secession. Fanny Kemble performed this poem in dramatic readings, bringing herself and audiences to tears in the memorable emotional crescendo of the last stanza with its invocation to an imperiled country that is nonetheless the best hope for the world: "Thou, too, sail on, O Ship of State! / Sail on, O UNION, strong and great!" President Abraham Lincoln, hearing these lines recited in the midst of the Civil War, is reported to have wept before remarking, "It is a wonderful gift to be able to stir men like that."

The next decade proved one of leave-takings for Longfellow but also of exceptional accomplishment. His father died in 1849, his brother Stephen in 1850, and his mother in 1851. In 1854 he resigned his Harvard professorship–partly because of his eyesight, partly for relief from academic pressures and contention with the university corporation on behalf of his department, but probably most of all because he found he could support his household on the strength of his poetry and desired more opportunity for writing. Each new book extended his fame, and he was bombarded with invitations for literary contributions and for autographs. A sociable man known for his graciously winning manners, Longfellow took pleasure in associations with other literary figures through the Saturday Club, founded about 1855 for monthly dinner meetings, and the Atlantic Club, which brought together contributors to the *Atlantic Monthly* after its launching in 1857.

He was engaged in ambitious projects. *The Golden Legend* (1851), set in thirteenth-century Italy, was destined to become the middle section of the work he conceived as his masterpiece, *Christus: A Mystery* (1872). It represented the medieval phase of Christianity and the virtue of faith (mixed, inevitably, with superstition) by dramatizing the story of a peasant girl's willingness to die so that a prince might be healed of his illness. For this work Longfellow drew on European sources, chiefly Hartmann von Aue's *Der Arme Heinrich* (circa 1191). Soon afterward, however, he returned to the most American of topics in *The Song of Hiawatha* (1855) and to the interest in American Indians he had earlier shown at Bowdoin and in "To the Driving Cloud" (1845). Based on Chippewa (Ojibway) culture and traditions as represented by Henry Rowe Schoolcraft and John Tanner, on John G. E. Heckewelder's defense of Delaware culture, and on Longfellow's acquaintance with an Ojibway chief who stayed at his house, the poem also drew on widespread literary and visual representations of the West to construct what Longfellow called his "Indian Edda." "Edda" reflects the Scandinavian influences also evident in this poem, most remarkably in the unrhymed trochaic meter he borrowed from the *Kalevala,* a Finnish folk epic composed by Elias Lönrott. Longfellow's metric choice, which captures the beat of a tom-tom, exposed the poem to parody, as did its insistent repetitions and use of Indian words. But parody did nothing to undermine the success of the book; even more marketable than *Evangeline, Hiawatha* sold fifty thousand copies by 1860 and earned $7,000 in royalties in its first decade. The poem was extensively reviewed, translated into German by Ferdinand Freiligrath in 1856, and set to music as well as featured in dramatic performances. Although Longfellow introduced a love story in his account of Hiawatha's wooing of Minnehaha, their marriage, and her death, for the most part he assembled legends he found in Schoolcraft's many books to exalt his Ojibway hero as a leader of supernatural birth (son of the West Wind, Mudjekeewis, and of Wenonah, whose mother, Nokomis, had fallen from the heavens) who leads his people in ways of peace. Hiawatha introduces his tribe to agriculture through his encounter with the corn god Mondamin, to transportation by inventing the birch canoe, and to picture-writing. Through his friendship with Chibiabos the musician, he encourages the arts; by marrying a Dacotah maiden, he fosters intertribal peace. At the end of the poem, Hiawatha journeys westward alone after enjoining his people to welcome European missionaries with their new culture and Christian faith:

Many moons and many winters
Will have come, and will have vanished,
Ere I come again to see you.
But my guests I leave behind me;
Listen to their words of wisdom,
Listen to the truth they tell you,
For the Master of Life has sent them
From the land of light and morning!

The poem both exalts the Indian and assumes the obliteration of indigenous ways of life.

New England storytelling traditions also engaged Longfellow's attention in these years. He began working on a dramatic poem about Puritan persecution of the Quakers, which was eventually included in one of the three "New England Tragedies" within *Christus.* For immediate publication, in three months beginning late in 1857 he composed the title poem for *The Courtship of Miles Standish and Other Poems* (1858). The most humorous and charming of his longer narrative poems, "The

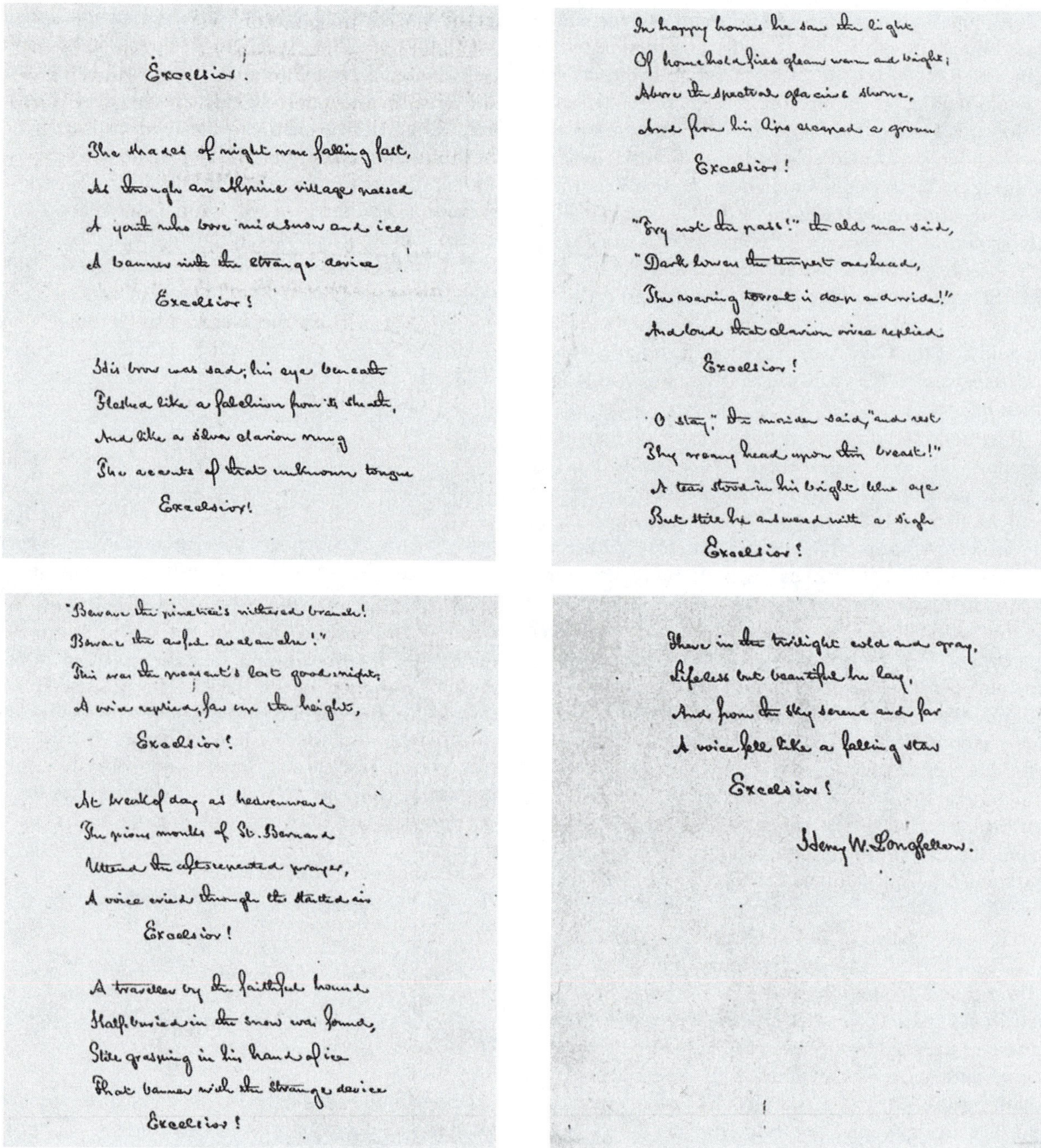

Excelsior.

The shades of night were falling fast,
As through an Alpine village passed
A youth who bore mid snow and ice
A banner with the strange device
Excelsior!

His brow was sad; his eye beneath
Flashed like a falchion from its sheath,
And like a silver clarion rung
The accents of that unknown tongue
Excelsior!

In happy homes he saw the light
Of household fires gleam warm and bright;
Above the spectral glaciers shone,
And from his lips escaped a groan
Excelsior!

"Try not the pass!" the old man said,
"Dark lowers the tempest overhead,
The roaring torrent is deep and wide!"
And loud that clarion voice replied
Excelsior!

"O stay," the maiden said, "and rest
Thy weary head upon this breast!"
A tear stood in his bright blue eye
But still he answered with a sigh
Excelsior!

"Beware the pine-tree's withered branch!
Beware the awful avalanche!"
This was the peasant's last good-night;
A voice replied, far up the height,
Excelsior!

At break of day as heavenward
The pious monks of St. Bernard
Uttered the oft-repeated prayer,
A voice cried through the startled air
Excelsior!

A traveller by the faithful hound
Half-buried in the snow was found,
Still grasping in his hand of ice
That banner with the strange device
Excelsior!

There in the twilight cold and gray,
Lifeless but beautiful he lay,
And from the sky serene and far
A voice fell like a falling star
Excelsior!

Henry W. Longfellow.

Fair copy of a poem Longfellow collected in his 1842 book Ballads and Other Poems *(from* Autograph Leaves of Our Country's Authors, *edited by Alexander Bliss and John Pendleton Kennedy, 1864)*

Craigie House (now Longfellow House) at 105 Brattle Street in Cambridge, which the father of Longfellow's second wife, Frances (Fanny) Appleton, gave the couple as a wedding gift in 1843

Courtship of Miles Standish" relates a story already familiar (especially in Longfellow's family) about John Alden's fortunate failure in his dutiful attempt to woo the maiden he loves on behalf of the widowed captain of Plymouth, his friend Miles Standish. Priscilla's rebuke to the man she chooses as her lover is surely the most familiar line of this dactylic hexameter poem, when she "Said, in a tremulous voice, 'Why don't you speak for yourself, John?'" The book that supplemented this poem with a group of shorter works sold well (twenty-five thousand copies printed in the first two months following its publication) but elicited fewer reviews than *Evangeline* or *Hiawatha.* Of the lyrics Longfellow composed during that period, "My Lost Youth" is a memorable example of the poet's reflection on his personal past. That poem appeared in one of those assemblages of short poems, identified as "Birds of Passage," that Longfellow introduced in *The Courtship of Miles Standish and Other Poems* and returned to frequently in subsequent volumes. The most warmly received of such poems composed in the 1850s, however, was "The Children's Hour," which reflected the poet's delight in his small daughters.

The family's domestic bliss, however, was about to be shattered. On 9 July 1861, Fanny Longfellow suffered fatal burns when the candle she was using to seal packets of her daughters' curls ignited her dress; she died the next day. Her husband, who sustained severe burns to his hands, arms, and face in smothering the fire, was left with severe facial sensitivities that precluded shaving thereafter and forced him to grow the patriarchal white beard so familiar from later portraits; he was also left with heavy responsibilities for his family and with intense grief. While coping with private tragedy at home, he suffered the additional trauma of the Civil War. That ordeal touched his family directly in late 1862, when Charles Longfellow was wounded while fighting for the Union army; his father and brother made an anxious trip to Washington to escort the invalid home.

Again, Longfellow coped with sorrow by plunging himself into literary work–this time of an intensely challenging sort. A project already well in hand that he was able to bring to completion was *Tales of a Wayside Inn,* the first part of which appeared in 1863. This collection consisted of narrative poems composed in a great variety of metric patterns. Although many of the poems had been written and even published separately beforehand, they were loosely held together in this book by the fiction of an assemblage of friends enter-

Five of Longfellow's six children: Charles Appleton and Ernest Wadsworth (left) and Edith, Anne Allegra, and Alice (left: pastel by Eastman Johnson; right: painting by Thomas Buchanan Read; both at Longfellow House, Cambridge)

taining each other by storytelling at a Sudbury, Massachusetts, inn. This collection was Longfellow's version of Geoffrey Chaucer's *Canterbury Tales* or Giovanni Boccaccio's *Decameron.* Although "Paul Revere's Ride" and "The Birds of Killingworth," the most familiar of these poems today, give an impression of New England focus, the great majority had European settings and sources. (Even "The Birds of Killingworth" was adapted from an English story.) Many, especially "Torquemada" and "The Saga of King Olaf," were surprisingly violent for such a gentle poet. The framework Longfellow provided, however, allowed his six storytellers (the Landlord, the Student, the Spanish Jew, the Italian, the Musician, and the Theologian) to criticize each other's presentations and draw out lessons of tolerance, forgiveness, and faith.

The most sustained and most challenging project Longfellow undertook in this period of bereavement was his blank-verse translation of *The Divine Comedy.* A translation of this work had been among his goals when teaching Dante at Harvard, and he had translated small parts of the poem in the early 1840s. Now he plunged into work, translating at the rate of a canto a day. For advice, he gathered weekly evening sessions of his "Dante Club" of writer-scholars–among them James Russell Lowell, who had succeeded Longfellow as Smith Professor; Charles Eliot Norton, who eventually published his own prose translation of Dante's masterpiece; and William Dean Howells. Longfellow's translation, still respected for its linguistic appreciation and literary merit, appeared in an 1865–1867 three-volume edition, although he completed the translation in spring 1864. Among the shorter poems of his late career, Longfellow's sonnets are especially prized. The "Divina Commedia" group of six sonnets written between 1864 and 1866 honor the Tuscan poet Dante–most memorably the first, with its image of the bereaved American poet leaving "my burden at this minster gate, / Kneeling in prayer, and not ashamed to pray" in a quest for spiritual peace.

Many of Longfellow's efforts now took dramatic form, although none proved suitable for staging. After refreshing his soul with Dante, he returned to the task he had long intended as the capstone of his work–the three-part chronicle of Christianity and its virtues initiated with "The Golden Legend." *The New England Tragedies*–a pairing of "John Endicott" (1857) and "Giles Corey of the Salem Farms" (1868)–on which he had begun working around the time he composed *The Courtship of Miles Standish,* appeared in 1868. In these verse dramas set in Puritan Massachusetts, Longfellow attempted to bring forward his story into relatively modern times (post-Reformation) and into the new world, though Quaker persecutions and the Salem witchcraft frenzy may seem unlikely illustrations of Christian charity. Despite relatively tepid public response to this effort, Longfellow persevered with *The Divine Tragedy* (1871), in which he represented Christian hope through dramatization of Christ's Passion and its effects on many characters drawn from the Bible. Sales of this book improved upon those for its predecessor; yet, Longfellow was disappointed by reader indifference to the work he had identified in an 1849 letter as "the sublimer Song whose broken melodies have for so many years breathed through my soul." When all three parts finally came together in *Christus: A Mystery,* book sales were slight (only six thousand copies printed) and critical response even less heartening. Longfellow himself may have recognized that the sections did not cohere and that the historical sequence ended in anticlimax; he thought of adding another drama on the Moravians of Bethlehem to show the positive influence of the Gospel, but he never carried out his intention. He moved ahead to new dramatic poems, notably "Judas Maccabeus" in *Three Books of Song* (1872) and *The Masque of Pandora* (1875); *Michael Angelo,* his last major poem, appeared posthumously in 1883 in its unfinished condition.

Partly because of his publishers' zeal for promoting Longfellow's poetry, books came in quick succession even at a point in his life when creative efforts flagged. Volumes of selected poems emerged along with reprintings of earlier books and individual poems in varied formats and price ranges. *Flower-de-Luce,* a small book of twelve short poems, came out in 1867 with its elegy for Hawthorne and sonnets on Dante. A revised edition of *Hyperion* followed in 1869. In 1872 *Three Books of Song* presented the second part of "Tales of a Wayside Inn" along with "Judas Maccabeus" and a group of translations. The next year *Aftermath* was published, with its moving title poem and the final collection of "Tales of a Wayside Inn." *The Masque of Pandora and Other Poems* (1875) included "Morituri Salutamus" (We who Are about to Die Salute You, 1874), one of his few occasional poems. Written for the fiftieth reunion of his Bowdoin College class, it is a memorable reflection on aging and is Longfellow's most admired ode. That book also featured "The Hanging of the Crane" (1874), which had been Longfellow's most remunerative poem when *The New York Ledger* paid him $3,000 for its serial publication earlier that same year. Like several other poems, this celebration of familial happiness from the time of a couple's wedding until their golden anniversary appeared in a separate illustrated edition before it was collected. *Kéramos and Other Poems* appeared in 1878 with a title poem that linked Longfellow's boyhood interest in Portland pottery with his later travels and readings to present a particularly effective statement of his poetics. *Ultima Thule* (1880), the title of which signaled his expectation that it would be his last collection, featured such lyrics as "The Tide Rises, The Tide Falls" (1879) and "L'Envoi. The Poet and His Song" (1880). *In the Harbor, Ultima Thule–Partz 2* came out just after his death in 1882 and included his final composition, "The Bells of San Blas" (1882). At least as wearing as his original authorship in late years was a massive editorial and translation project he undertook for his publisher, James T. Fields; *Poems of Places* emerged in thirty-one volumes between 1876 and 1879.

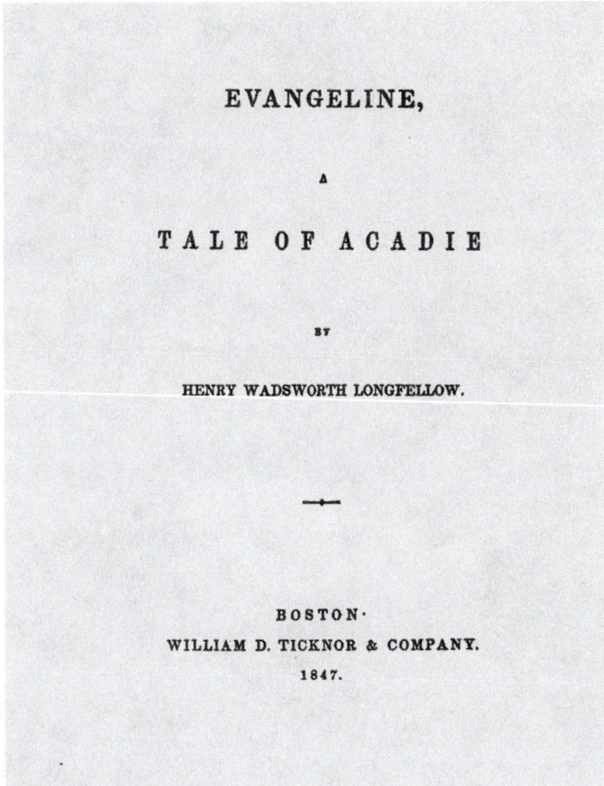
EVANGELINE,

A

TALE OF ACADIE

BY

HENRY WADSWORTH LONGFELLOW.

BOSTON·

WILLIAM D. TICKNOR & COMPANY.

1847.

Title page for one of Longfellow's most popular narrative poems, inspired by the British expulsion of the Acadians from Nova Scotia in 1755

Although sales of individual later volumes never matched the popularity of his mid-career offerings, Longfellow lived to experience recognition and rewards seldom enjoyed by other writers. Tributes of many kinds testified to public affection–visits to Craigie House by prominent literary and political figures and even the emperor of Brazil, public tributes, and escalating requests for autographs. His 1868–1869 final visit to Europe, on which he was attended by a large family party, turned into a triumphal progression framed by honorary degrees awarded by Cambridge and Oxford Universities. Queen Victoria received Longfellow at Windsor Castle; the Prince of Wales invited him as a guest; and he visited with William Gladstone and John

Fanny Appleton Longfellow in middle age (Longfellow House, Cambridge)

Russell as well as Alfred Tennyson. In Switzerland, France, Italy, Austria, and Germany he was welcomed and honored. At home the schoolchildren of Cambridge presented him in 1879 with a chair carved from the wood of the "spreading chestnut-tree" immortalized in "The Village Blacksmith." His picture appeared among "Our American Poets" in classrooms across the United States, thanks to Fields's success in placing Longfellow, Ralph Waldo Emerson, John Greenleaf Whittier, James Russell Lowell, and Oliver Wendell Holmes in textbooks that established canonical readings for many decades. Financial rewards confirmed Longfellow's youthful hope that an American could make a living through literature, although, as William Charvat says, Longfellow's income derived as much from his prose as from his poetry. When he died of phlebitis less than a month after his seventy-fifth birthday and only a few days after completing "The Bells of San Blas," Longfellow left an estate worth $356,320 to his children and grandchildren, with weekly book sales amounting to a thousand copies. He also left a loving family and grateful readers who have continued to honor him by erecting statues and naming parks and schools for him, Evangeline, and Hiawatha.

Longfellow's celebrity as the preeminent poet of America assured him critical respect in the closing decades of the nineteenth century and the beginning of the twentieth; yet, commentators even then recognized his limitations. While readily dismissing Edgar Allan Poe's charges of plagiarism, they acknowledged that Longfellow lacked the originality evident in Whitman, Emerson, and even Poe. Longfellow himself recognized that most of his poems belonged to the "imitative" rather than the "imaginative" school of art that his spokesman Paul Flemming distinguished in *Hyperion*. Longfellow's imitativeness differed significantly from that of many contemporaries, however, in that he early outgrew his tendency to echo Bryant's style or that of English Romantic poets and turned instead to German Romanticism, which he virtually introduced into American poetry, and to traditions of European verse from many countries and eras. Richard Henry Stoddard summed up Longfellow's contribution in an 1881 essay, pointing out how Longfellow remained "true to himself" and to his scholarly impulses by creating and satisfying "a taste for a literature which did not exist in this country until he began to write." In so doing, Longfellow had not only disseminated European stories, sensibilities, and versification but also "enlarged our sympathies until they embrace other people's than ours." Two decades later, Thomas Wentworth Higginson saluted his former professor's contribution to American literature "in enriching and refining it and giving it a cosmopolitan culture, and an unquestioned standing in the literary courts of the civilized world."

Longfellow gave poetry higher standing within American society than it had enjoyed ever before, not only by exemplifying the appeal of graceful, informed writing to an exceptionally wide reading audience but also by making art itself one of his centering themes. In poems throughout his career, he represented persons of all times, cultures, and states of life as turning to creative expression (music, song, poetry, storytelling, and pottery) for entertainment and reassurance. In turn, he received homage from practitioners of other arts: composers set many of his poems to music, and artists illustrated many of his scenes. As he had honored European poets by translating their work into English, he lived to see his own poems translated into twenty-four languages. Longfellow laid the groundwork for other authorial careers by persuading readers of the importance of art as well as by demonstrating how literature could be turned into a paying proposition in a country known for material ambition. According to Charvat, "by shrewd, aggressive, and intelligent management of the business of writing, he raised the commercial value of verse and thereby helped other American poets to get out of the garret."

In an age that judged literature largely in moral terms as expressive of an author's personal virtues, Longfellow became everyman's kindly, sympathizing, gently encouraging friend. According to Howells, Longfellow's power derived from his "courage in frankly trusting the personal as the universal" along with his unaffectedness, the simplicity of his feelings, and the sincerity of his expression. These virtues made him "sovereign of more hearts than any other poet of his generation" while seeming to ensure posterity's regard. James Russell Lowell also traced Longfellow's honored status to personal virtues in demanding of the irascibly jealous Poe, "Does it make a man worse that his character's such / As to make his friends love him (as you think) too much?"

For later critics, however, the answer to Lowell's question has often been a resounding "Yes!" In the atmosphere of disillusionment attending world wars–and especially in Herbert S. Gorman's disparaging 1926 biography–Longfellow became an easy scapegoat for everything judged wrong with Puritan, Victorian, Brahmin, genteel, sentimental, and racist evasions of the grim realities of life. The moralism of his poetry came to seem offensive and even ridiculous as critics attacked his mixed metaphors as evidence of muddled thinking. The dominance of free verse fostered contempt for Longfellow's songlike versification and an indifference to its experimental qualities. New Critics looked for ironies, ambiguities, and complexities not discoverable in Longfellow's work and rejected the didactic conclusions he typically tacked onto his poems. Hyatt Waggoner observed the irony of Longfellow's having been most appreciated in his own time for "A Psalm of Life," noting that "though it intends to mean that life is worth living after all, what it effectively *does* mean is that life *must* be worth living but the poet can't think why."

From a New Historicist standpoint Longfellow is classified with others in Fields's Houghton-Mifflin stable as one of those authors used to impose a presumed "high culture" of English Puritan origins on subsequent generations and immigrant populations, even though Longfellow might also be recognized as one whose broadly inclusive responsiveness to European traditions could have smoothed assimilation for the children of newcomers from central and southern Europe. In many ways Longfellow may be read as a friend of American multiculturalism even if *Hiawatha* fails current tests of anthropological accuracy. His reputation could also

Longfellow in 1859 (photograph by Mathew Brady; Longfellow House, Cambridge)

benefit from renewed critical respect for sentimentalism, especially as that respect gets extended to male authors.

At present, however, Longfellow has been relegated to the status of an historically interesting minor poet whose poems occupy only a few pages in recent anthologies and do so in ways that obscure the reasons for his original popularity. Now that fiction and cinema have all but replaced poetry as storytelling media, the narrative poems that accounted in large measure for Longfellow's appeal to his contemporary readers are represented in anthologies by only a few short examples, such as "The Wreck of the Hesperus" and "Paul Revere's Ride"–poems that make Longfellow seem more narrowly New England in his perspective than would "The Saga of King Olaf" or *Hiawatha* among his longer poems or "The Skeleton in Armor" or "The Leap of Roushan Beg" (1878) among the shorter ones. Whereas nineteenth-century readers had savored the sentimental charms of "The Children's Hour," readers of today look for confessional poetry of a sort Longfel-

The inn in Sudbury, Massachusetts, that Longfellow used as the gathering place for the narrators of the poems he collected as Tales of a Wayside Inn *(1863, 1872)*

low held in reserve; two sonnets particularly admired today for their courageous yet artistically controlled revelations of personal pain, "Mezzo Cammin" and "The Cross of Snow" (composed 1879), both appeared posthumously. In his own time one of Longfellow's chief contributions to American literature was the encouragement he offered to aspiring writers–whether those Boston-Cambridge-Concord literati with whom he interacted through his various clubs or those such as Emily Dickinson, who responded gratefully to him from a distance as the champion of poetry in an otherwise prosaic American society, the Pegasus in the pound of Yankee bookstores. Twentieth-century poets such as Robert Frost, Robert Lowell, and Howard Nemerov have been kinder to Longfellow than literary critics and historians. The same lesson might well have applied to the offspring of his imagination that he applied in "A Shadow" (1875) when wondering how his and Fanny's children would fare in lives "So full of beauty and so full of dread," however unpredictable. "The world," he concluded with characteristic serenity, "belongs to those who come the last, / They will find hope and strength as we have done."

Letters:

The Letters of Henry Wadsworth Longfellow, 6 volumes, edited by Andrew Hilen (Cambridge, Mass.: Belknap Press of Harvard University Press, 1966–1983).

Bibliographies:

Luther S. Livingston, *A Bibliography of the First Editions in Book Form of the Writings of Henry Wadsworth Longfellow* (New York: De Vinne Press, 1908);

H. W. L. Dana, "Henry Wadsworth Longfellow," in *Cambridge History of American Literature,* 4 volumes, edited by William Peterfield Trent and others (Cambridge: Cambridge University Press, 1917), II: 425–436;

Jacob Blanck, *Bibliography of American Literature,* volume 5 (New Haven: Yale University Press, 1969), pp. 468–640;

Richard Dilworth Rust, "Henry Wadsworth Longfellow," in *Fifteen American Authors before 1900: Bibliographic Essays on Research and Criticism,* edited by Robert A. Rees and Earl N. Harbert (Madison: University of Wisconsin Press, 1971), pp. 263–283.

Biographies:

William Sloane Kennedy, *Henry W. Longfellow: Biography, Anecdote, Letters, Criticism* (Cambridge, Mass.: Moses King, 1882);

George Lowell Austin, *Henry Wadsworth Longfellow: His Life, His Works, His Friendships* (Boston: Lee & Shepard, 1883);

Samuel Longfellow, *Life of Henry Wadsworth Longfellow, with Extracts from His Journals and Correspondence,* 2 volumes (Boston: Ticknor, 1886); *Final Memorials of Henry Wadsworth Longfellow* (Boston: Ticknor, 1887); combined as *Life of Henry Wadsworth Longfellow,* 3 volumes (Boston: Houghton, Mifflin, 1903);

Thomas Wentworth Higginson, *Henry Wadsworth Longfellow* (Boston: Houghton, Mifflin, 1902);

Charles Eliot Norton, *Henry Wadsworth Longfellow: A Sketch of His Life* (Boston: Houghton, Mifflin, 1906);

Ernest Wadsworth Longfellow, *Random Memories* (Boston: Houghton Mifflin, 1922);

Herbert S. Gorman, *A Victorian American: Henry Wadsworth Longfellow* (New York: Doran, 1926);

Lawrance Thompson, *Young Longfellow (1807–1843)* (New York: Macmillan, 1938);

Carl L. Johnson, *Professor Longfellow of Harvard* (Eugene: University of Oregon Press, 1944);

Edward Wagenknecht, *Longfellow: A Full-Length Portrait* (New York: Longmans, Green, 1955);

Newton Arvin, *Longfellow: His Life and Work* (Boston: Little, Brown, 1963);

Wagenknecht, *Henry Wadsworth Longfellow: Portrait of an American Humanist* (New York: Oxford University Press, 1966).

References:

Gay Wilson Allen, "Henry Wadsworth Longfellow," in his *American Prosody* (New York: American Book Company, 1935), pp. 154–192;

George Arms, *The Fields Were Green: A New View of Bryant, Whittier, Holmes, Lowell, and Longfellow* (Stanford, Cal.: Stanford University Press, 1953);

Van Wyck Brooks, *The Flowering of New England, 1815–1865* (New York: Dutton, 1936);

Lawrence Buell, "Introduction," in *Selected Poems by Henry Wadsworth Longfellow* (New York: Penguin, 1988);

Kenneth Walter Cameron, *Longfellow's Reading in Libraries: The Charging Records of a Learned Poet Reconsidered* (Hartford, Conn.: Transcendental Books, 1973);

Cameron, ed., *Longfellow among His Contemporaries: A Harvest of Estimates, Insights, and Anecdotes from the Victorian Literary World* (Hartford, Conn.: Transcendental Books, 1978);

Helen Carr, "The Myth of Hiawatha," *Literature and History,* 12 (Spring 1986): 58–78;

William Charvat, "Longfellow" and "Longfellow's Income from His Writings, 1840-1852," in his *The Profession of Authorship in America, 1800–1870,* edited by Matthew J. Bruccoli (Columbus: Ohio State University Press, 1968), pp. 106-167;

Robert A. Ferguson, "Longfellow's Political Fears: Civic Authority and the Role of the Artist in *Hiawatha* and *Miles Standish,*" *American Literature,* 50 (March 1978): 187–215;

Angus Fletcher, "Whitman and Longfellow: Two Types of the American Poet," *Raritan,* 10 (Spring 1991): 131–145;

Dana Gioia, "Longfellow in the Aftermath of Modernism," in *The Columbia History of American Poetry,* edited by Jay Parini and Brett C. Millier (New York: Columbia University Press, 1993), pp. 64–96;

Clarence Gohdes, "Longfellow and His Authorized British Publishers," *PMLA,* 55 (December 1940): 1165–1179;

Eric L. Haralson, "Mars in Petticoats: Longfellow and Sentimental Masculinity," *Nineteenth-Century Literature,* 51 (December 1996): 327–355;

Janet Harris, "Longfellow's *Poems on Slavery,*" *Colby Library Quarterly,* 14 (June 1978): 84–92;

James Taft Hatfield, *New Light on Longfellow, with Special Reference to His Relations with Germany* (Boston: Houghton Mifflin, 1933);

Edward L. Hirsh, *Henry Wadsworth Longfellow* (Minneapolis: University of Minnesota Press, 1964);

Kenneth Hovey, "'A Psalm of Life' Reconsidered: The Dialogue of Western Literature and Monologue of Young America," *American Transcendental Quarterly,* new series 1 (March 1987): 3–19;

William Dean Howells, "The Art of Longfellow," *North American Review,* 184 (1 March 1907): 472–485;

Kent P. Ljungquist, "The 'Little War' and Longfellow's Dilemma: New Documents in the Plagiarism Controversy of 1845," *Resources for American Literary Study,* 23, no. 1 (1997): 28–57;

Joseph Masheck, "Professor Longfellow and the Blacksmith," *Annals of Scholarship,* 10 (Summer–Fall 1993): 345–361;

Joseph Chesley Mathews, ed., *Henry W. Longfellow Reconsidered: A Symposium* (Hartford, Conn.: Transcendental Books, 1970);

Celia Millward and Cecelia Tichi, "Whatever Happened to *Hiawatha?*" *Genre,* 6 (September 1973): 313–332;

George Monteiro, "Introduction," in *The Poetical Works of Longfellow* (Boston: Houghton Mifflin, 1975), pp. xvii–xxvii;

Paul Morin, *Les Sources de l'Oeuvre de Henry Wadsworth Longfellow* (Paris: E. Larose, 1913);

Howard Nemerov, "Introduction," in *Longfellow: Selected Poetry* (New York: Dell, 1959), pp. 7–26;

Chase S. and Stellanova Osborn, *Schoolcraft, Longfellow, Hiawatha* (Lancaster, Pa.: Jaques Cattell Press, 1942); abridged as *"Hiawatha" with Its Original Indian Legends* (Lancaster, Pa.: Jaques Cattell Press, 1944);

Papers Presented at the Longfellow Commemorative Conference, April 1–3, 1982, coordinated by the National Park Service (Washington, D.C.: U.S. Government Printing Office, 1982);

Thomas H. Pauly, "*Outre-Mer* and Longfellow's Quest for a Career," *New England Quarterly,* 50 (March 1977): 30–52;

Norman Holmes Pearson, "Both Longfellows," *University of Kansas City Review,* 16 (Summer 1950): 245–253;

John Seelye, "Attic Shape: Dusting Off *Evangeline,*" *Virginia Quarterly Review,* 60 (Winter 1984): 21–44;

Edmund Clarence Stedman, *Poets of America* (Boston: Houghton, Mifflin, 1885);

Richard Henry Stoddard, "Henry Wadsworth Longfellow," in *The Homes and Haunts of Our Elder Poets* (New York: Appleton, 1881), pp. 67–104;

M. Brook Taylor, "The Poetry and Prose of History: *Evangeline* and the Historians of Nova Scotia," *Journal of Canadian Studies,* 23 (Spring–Summer 1988): 46–67;

W. S. Tryon, "Nationalism and International Copyright: Tennyson and Longfellow in America," *American Literature,* 24 (March 1952): 301–309;

Edward L. Tucker, "References in Longfellow's *Journals* (1856–1882) to His Important Literary Works," in *Studies in the American Renaissance,* edited by Joel Myerson (Charlottesville: University Press of Virginia, 1994), pp. 289–345;

Tucker, *The Shaping of Longfellow's* John Endicott: *A Textual History Including Two Early Versions* (Charlottesville: University Press of Virginia, 1985);

S. Ullmann, "Composite Metaphors in Longfellow's Poetry," *Review of English Studies,* 18 (April 1942): 219–228;

John Van Schaick Jr., *The Characters in "Tales of a Wayside Inn"* (Boston: Universalist Publishing House, 1939);

Edward Wagenknecht, *Henry Wadsworth Longfellow: His Poetry and Prose* (New York: Ungar, 1986);

Hyatt H. Waggoner, "Five New England Poets: The Shape of Things to Come," in his *American Poets from the Puritans to the Present* (Boston: Houghton Mifflin, 1968), pp. 33–85;

Cecil B. Williams, *Henry Wadsworth Longfellow* (New York: Twayne, 1964);

Thomas Wortham, "William Cullen Bryant and the Fireside Poets," in *Columbia Literary History of the United States,* edited by Emory Elliott (New York: Columbia University Press, 1988), pp. 278–288.

Papers:

The chief repository of Henry Wadsworth Longfellow's papers and manuscripts is the Houghton Library, Harvard University. Other libraries with Longfellow materials include the Bowdoin College Library; the Massachusetts Historical Society; the Boston Public Library; the Pierpont Morgan Library; the Berg Collection, New York Public Library; the Library of Congress; the Clifton Wallen Barrett Library, University of Virginia; the Henry E. Huntington Library; the Parkman Dexter Howe Library, University of Florida; and the University of Washington Library.

James Russell Lowell

(22 February 1819 – 12 August 1891)

Thomas Wortham
University of California, Los Angeles

See also the Lowell entries in *DLB 11: American Humorists, 1800–1950; DLB 64: American Literary Critics and Scholars, 1850–1880; DLB 79: American Magazine Journalists, 1850–1900;* and *DLB 189: American Travel Writers, 1850–1915.*

James Russell Lowell (Harvard University Archives)

BOOKS: *Class Poem* (Cambridge, Mass.: Metcalf, Torry & Ballou, 1838);

A Year's Life (Boston: Little, Brown, 1841);

Poems (Cambridge, Mass.: John Owen, 1844);

Conversations on Some of the Old Poets (Cambridge, Mass.: John Owen, 1845; London: Clarke, 1845);

Poems. Second Series (Cambridge, Mass.: Nichols / Boston: Mussey, 1848);

A Fable for Critics (New York: Putnam, 1848; London: Chapman, 1848);

The Biglow Papers (Cambridge, Mass.: Nichols, 1848; London: Trübner, 1859);

The Vision of Sir Launfal (Cambridge, Mass.: Nichols, 1848);

Poems, 2 volumes (Boston: Ticknor, Reed & Fields, 1849);

The Biglow Papers. Second Series, in 3 parts (London: Trübner, 1862); 3 parts collected in 1 volume (London: Trübner, 1864; Boston: Ticknor & Fields, 1867);

Fireside Travels (Boston: Ticknor & Fields, 1864; London: Macmillan, 1864);

Ode Recited at the Commemoration of the Living and Dead Soldiers of Harvard University, July 21, 1865 (Cambridge, Mass.: Privately printed, 1865);

Under The Willows and Other Poems (Boston: Fields, Osgood, 1869);

The Cathedral (Boston: Fields, Osgood, 1870);

Among My Books (Boston: Fields, Osgood, 1870; London: Macmillan, 1870);

My Study Windows (Boston: J. R. Osgood, 1871);

Among My Books. Second Series (Boston: J. R. Osgood, 1876; London: Low, 1876);

Three Memorial Poems (Boston: J. R. Osgood, 1877);

On Democracy: An Address Delivered in the Town Hall, Birmingham, on the 6th of October, 1884 (Birmingham, U.K.: Cond, 1884);

Democracy and Other Addresses (Boston & New York: Houghton, Mifflin, 1887);

Early Poems (New York: Alden, 1887);

Heartsease and Rue (Boston & New York: Houghton, Mifflin, 1888; London: Macmillan, 1888);

Political Essays (Boston & New York: Houghton, Mifflin, 1888);

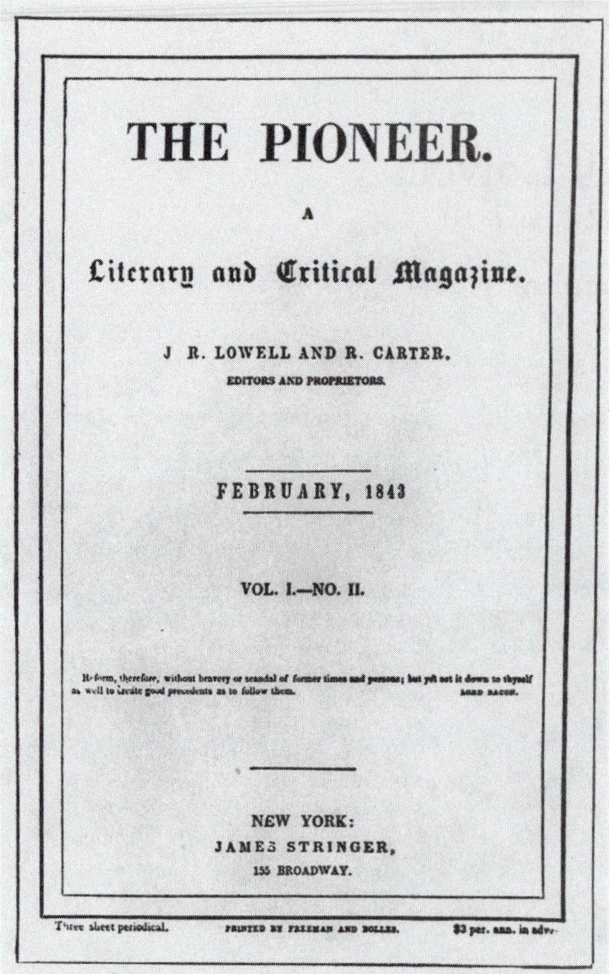

THE PIONEER.

A

Literary and Critical Magazine.

J R. LOWELL AND R. CARTER.
EDITORS AND PROPRIETORS.

FEBRUARY, 1843

VOL. I.—NO. II.

Reform, therefore, without bravery or scandal of former times and persons; but yet set it down to thyself as well to create good precedents as to follow them. LORD BACON.

NEW YORK:
JAMES STRINGER,
155 BROADWAY.

Three sheet periodical. PRINTED BY FREEMAN AND BOLLES. $3 per. ann. in adv.

The first issue of the journal Lowell edited for three months in 1843

The Independent in Politics (New York & London: Putnam, 1888);

The Writings of James Russell Lowell, Riverside Edition, 10 volumes (Boston & New York: Houghton, Mifflin, 1890);

Latest Literary Essays and Addresses, edited by Charles Eliot Norton (Boston & New York: Houghton, Mifflin, 1892; London: Macmillan, 1892);

American Ideas for English Readers, with introduction by Henry Stone (Boston: Cupples, 1892);

The Old English Dramatists, edited by Norton (Boston & New York: Houghton, Mifflin, 1892; London: Macmillan, 1892);

Last Poems, edited by Norton (Boston & New York: Houghton, Mifflin, 1895);

The Power of Sound: A Rhymed Lecture (New York: Gilliss, 1896);

Lectures on English Poets, edited by S. A. Jones (Cleveland: Rowfant Club, 1897);

Impressions of Spain, compiled by Joseph B. Gilder (Boston & New York: Houghton, Mifflin, 1899);

Early Prose Writings (London & New York: John Lane, 1902);

The Anti-Slavery Papers of James Russell Lowell, 2 volumes (Boston & New York: Houghton, Mifflin, 1902);

The Round Table (Boston: Badger, 1913);

The Function of the Poet and Other Essays, edited by Albert Mordell (Boston & New York: Houghton Mifflin, 1920);

Uncollected Poems, edited by Thelma M. Smith (Philadelphia: University of Pennsylvania Press, 1950).

Collection: *The Complete Writings of James Russell Lowell,* Elmwood Edition, edited by Norton, 16 volumes (Boston & New York: Houghton, Mifflin, 1904).

OTHER: *The Works of the Late Edgar Allan Poe: With Notices of His Life and Genius,* 2 volumes, edited by Lowell, N. P. Willis, and R. W. Griswold (New York: Redfield, Clinton Hall, 1850);

The Poetical Works of John Keats, edited by Lowell (Boston: Little, Brown; New York: Evans & Dickerson; Philadelphia: Lippincott, Grambo, 1854);

The Poems of Maria Lowell, edited by Lowell (Cambridge: Privately printed, 1855);

The Poetical Works of Percy Bysshe Shelley, 3 volumes, edited by Lowell (Boston: Little, Brown; New York: Dickerson; Philadelphia: Lippincott, Grambo, 1855);

The Poetical Works of Dr. John Donne, edited by Lowell (Boston: Little, Brown; New York: Dickerson; Philadelphia: Lippincott, 1855);

The Poetical Works of Andrew Marvell, edited by Lowell (Boston: Little, Brown; Cincinnati: Moore, Wilstach, Keys, 1857);

The Complete Angler, or the Contemplative Man's Recreation, of Izaak Walton and Charles Cotton, 2 volumes, edited by Lowell (Boston: Little, Brown, 1889).

The most versatile of the New Englanders during the middle of the nineteenth century, James Russell Lowell was a vital force in the history of American literature and thought during his lifetime. His range and perspicacity in literary criticism are unequalled in nineteenth-century America. He did more than anyone before Mark Twain in elevating the vernacular to a medium of serious artistic expression, and *The Biglow Papers* (1848) ranks among the finest political satires in American literature. His public odes expressed a mind and an outlook that drew the praise of Henry Brooks Adams, William James, and William Dean Howells. His personal charm made him both an effective diplomat during the period of the emergence of

Maria White, whom Lowell married in 1844 (portrait by Samuel W. Rowse; Harvard University)

the United States as a world power and one of its finest letter writers.

Although familiar with the life and literature of the great world, Lowell remained, from first to last, a native of Cambridge, Massachusetts. The New England legacy he inherited was rich by American standards: ministers, judges, and business and political leaders were his ancestry, and being a Lowell was both a privilege and a responsibility. As a result, Lowell's task in his creative life was to work out solutions to the problem not only of self, but also of place and name.

Lowell was a son of the Reverend Charles Lowell and Harriet Traill (Spence) Lowell and the youngest of a clever brood who played hard at games and life during the early years of Andrew Jackson's presidency. In the New England of that time many people had a distinguished ancestry. What mattered more was whether one's grandfather and father had been in the main prudent, and in circumspection the Lowells had for generations been masters. By the twentieth century the name of Lowell, like that of Appleton and Lawrence, had become synonymous with manufacturing wealth and State Street trusts, but this tradition in the social history of New England was not yet firmly established in James Russell Lowell's youth, and, regardless, family wealth, with all its comforts and opportunities, never became his. Still, Lowell did not want for things either of the world or of the spirit. Educated according to the best standards of the day, in due time he entered Harvard College, where his interests proved more literary than academic, a penchant not at all to his preceptors' liking.

Undergraduate glory came with his being elected poet of his senior class in 1838; but the boisterous youth was shamed with suspension by the Harvard faculty six weeks before the all-important Class Day ceremonies at which he would have read, had he only been obedient to college rules, the long, boring verses commemorating his and his classmates' entry into the world. Instead, his *Class Poem* (1838) appeared in print–immortalizing, to Lowell's later regret, his reactionary tendencies and sophomoric opposition to the new thought and reforms then coming into fashion. Transcendentalism, abolition, woman's rights, and temperance came under his satire, but the absence

Elmwood, the Lowell family home in Cambridge

of any genuine humor (or profound sense) left the satire dull, and the performance was a decided failure.

Uncertain as to what he wished to do with his life (other than the impractical desire to write poetry), Lowell took a law degree at Harvard in 1840 and afterward set up practice in Boston. In six months, however, he was convinced that law was for him just as impractical and probably more unprofitable than a literary life, so he gambled all and turned to literature for support.

Though the "golden age of magazines" was still a generation away, periodical publication in America made significant gains during the 1840s and began wielding a far-reaching influence on the development of American literature, particularly the short tale and the sketch, though there was also room for poetry. Lowell even began his own magazine in 1843 and solicited contributions from an impressive group of writers, including Nathaniel Hawthorne and Edgar Allan Poe, but an eye problem that required Lowell's being treated in New York City and a dishonest publisher in Boston were too much for the venture to endure, and *The Pioneer* failed after three months. Other journals were eager for Lowell's offerings, however, and his reputation as a lyric poet was soon established.

This early public recognition of Lowell's poetic abilities was largely undiscriminating and more patriotic than critical, and a few people were not impressed. Margaret Fuller was especially harsh in her assessment; in *Papers on Literature and Art* (1846), she dismissed Lowell as "absolutely wanting in the true spirit and tone of poesy": "His interest in the moral questions of the day has supplied the want of vitality in himself; his great facility at versification has enabled him to fill the ear with a copious stream of pleasant sound. But his verse is stereotyped; his thought sounds no depth, and posterity will not remember him." Throughout his life Lowell attempted to master a lyrical voice, but his efforts were largely unsuccessful. The deficiencies that characterize his work in his first volume of poems, *A Year's Life* (1841), are never entirely absent from his more mature performances–technical infelicities and irregularities, didacticism, obscurity, and excessive literariness. Ralph Waldo Emerson's complaint that Lowell in one of his poems had had to pump too hard describes unfortunately well the forced quality in many of his poems. Lowell seems to have been as much aware of his limitations as were his critics, and he frequently expressed to friends his misgivings. His reference to the book of poems *Under the Willows* (1869) as "Under the Billows or dredgings from the Atlantic" is not only a masterful pun (many of the poems had first appeared in *The Atlantic Monthly*) but close to the truth. As a public poet, however, both in his Pindaric odes and in his satiric verse, Lowell has few equals in American literature.

Toward the end of 1844 Lowell married Maria White. They had four children–three daughters and a son. Drawn into the antislavery movement in the early 1840s, Lowell wrote during that decade scores of articles and poems in defense of abolition and other reform causes. He became a chief editorial writer during the mid 1840s for the *Pennsylvania Freeman* and the *National Anti-Slavery Standard,* and between 1846 and 1848 in the *Standard* and the abolitionist *Boston Courier* first appeared his most important work of the period, the verses of his persona Hosea Biglow.

The use of the rustic Yankee as a voice of political reason was not original with Lowell. John Adams had created Humphrey Ploughjogger eighty years before and through this down-country farmer had made his debut into the political world of controversy in the 1760s. Later, Royall Tyler found the Yankee mask an effective moral point of view in his play *The Contrast* (1787), and Seba Smith used the resources of dialect and region to their full comic possibilities in his *Life and Writings of Major Jack Downing* (1833). By the mid 1840s the Yankee oracle was an established figure in the American mythic imagination. "Plain and pawky," Constance Rourke has described him in her classic *American Humor* (1931):

> he was an ideal image, a self-image, one of those symbols which people spontaneously adopt and by which in some measures they live. Overassertive yet quiet, self-conscious, full of odd new biases, he talked. . . . He was a symbol of triumph, of adaptability, of irrepressible life–of many qualities needed to induce confidence and self-possession among a new and unamalgamated people. No character precisely like him had appeared before in the realm of the imagination.

Lowell's contribution was in turning the Yankee figure into an effective and memorable poet.

The verses of Hosea Biglow were an immediate success; in the opinion of Lowell's fellow abolitionist, John Greenleaf Whittier, "the world-wide laugh" caused by the rustic Yankee poet was enough to "have shaken half the walls of Slavery down." Lowell himself was alarmed at the way Hosea caught on, and in the introduction to the second series of *The Biglow Papers* (1862) he tells of his feelings at that earlier time: "The success of my experiment soon began not only to astonish me, but to make me feel the responsibility of knowing that I held in my hand a weapon instead of the mere fencing-stick I had supposed. . . . I found the verses of my pseudonym copied everywhere; I saw them pinned up in workshops; I heard them quoted and their authorship debated." As the success of his creation

Lowell in 1844

became certain in Lowell's mind, he began imagining a book made out of the Biglow material. Already he had presented, through Hosea's aegis, the unhappy lot of Birdofredum Sawin, a native of Jaalam, who, unlike his townsman Hosea, had hurried off to enlist in the invading army, assured by the promise of wealth and adventure to be had in Mexico. A true picaro, his character provided richer possibilities both for humor and irony than did Hosea's, and the accounts of his adventures in Mexico and the American South, black in their humor, anticipate the absurd quests of twentieth-century antiheroes. Finally, there is Parson Wilbur, or as he is described on the title page, "Homer Wilbur, A.M., Pastor of the First Church in Jaalam, and (Prospective) Member of Many Literary, Learned and Scientific Societies." Lowell's account of the genesis of *The Biglow Papers* describes well the relationship between these three characters:

> When I began to carry out my conception and to write in my assumed character [Hosea Biglow], I found myself in a strait between two perils. On the one hand, I was in danger of being carried beyond the limit of my

> own opinions, or at least of that temper with which every man should speak his mind in print, and on the other I feared the risk of seeming to vulgarize a deep and sacred conviction. I needed on occasion to rise above the level of mere *patois,* and for this purpose conceived the Rev. Mr. Wilbur, who should express the more cautious element of the New England character and its pedantry, as Mr. Biglow should serve for its homely common-sense vivified and heated by conscience. . . . Finding soon after that I needed some one as a mouthpiece of mere drollery, for I conceive that true humor is never divorced from moral conviction, I invented Mr. Sawin for the clown of my little puppet-show. I meant to embody in him that half-conscious *un*morality which I had noticed as the recoil in gross natures from a puritanism that still strove to keep in its creed the intense savor which had long gone out of its faith and life.

The book is a medley of voices and moods, prose and verse, and classic English, Yankee speech, and tortured Latin. Some of it is dated, as one would expect of occasional satire, but much is timeless, classic, though in recent years unrecognized as such. Wilbur and Hosea were meant to be complementary, reflecting two sides of the responsible Yankee character; Birdofredum, the fool, serves as a foil to both. Among the three, Lowell thought he should "find room enough to express . . . the popular feeling and opinion of the time." But in the view of the generally unsympathetic John Jay Chapman, Lowell did something far more important in *The Biglow Papers:*

> At a crisis of pressure, Lowell assumed his real self under the guise of a pseudonym; and with his own hand he rescued a language, a type, a whole era of civilization from oblivion. Here gleams the dagger and here is Lowell revealed. His limitations as a poet, his too much wit, his too much morality, his mixture of shrewdness and religion, are seen to be the very elements of power. The novelty of the Biglow Papers is as wonderful as their world-old naturalness. They take rank with greatness, and they were the strongest political tracts of their time. They imitate nothing; they are real.

Whether Lowell's satire was of consequence to the political events in which it had its origin is a historical problem of no easy solution. Whittier thought its force in the cause of right was immense, but Samuel May, a leading abolitionist, dismissed Lowell and his work when after the Civil War he looked back over the years of controversy and conflict. In a holy war–and for the radical abolitionist the war against slavery was a heavenly battle between the forces of good and evil–there is no place for the humorist, because his point of view is necessarily adjustive, working to establish equilibrium in a world out of balance. Humor is always compromising, but to Lowell and Abraham Lincoln, who relished the humor of *The Biglow Papers,* compromise is essential to man's fleeting and darkling existence.

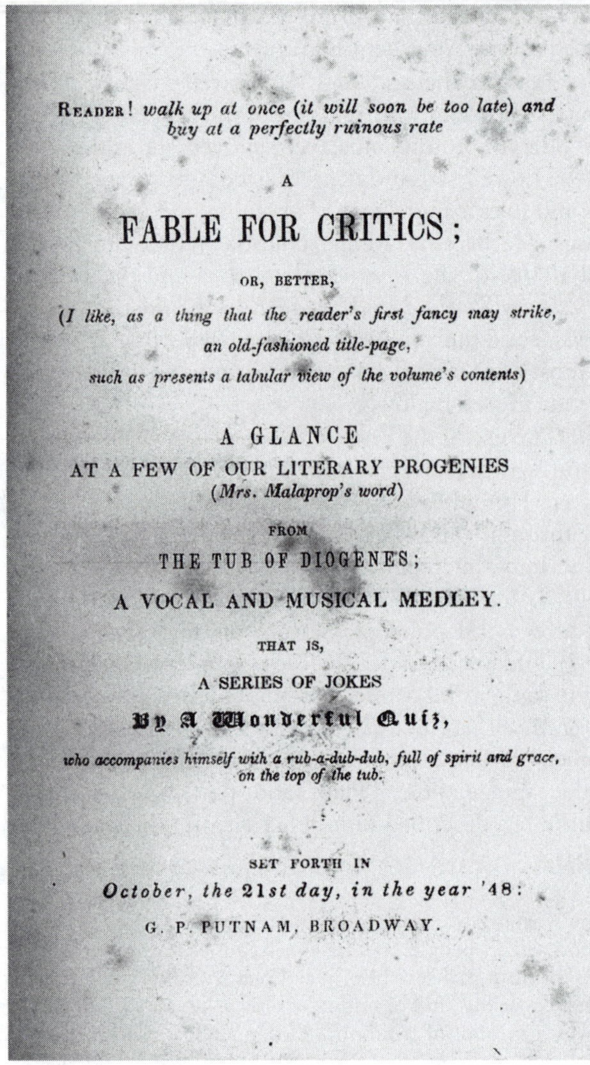
READER! *walk up at once (it will soon be too late) and buy at a perfectly ruinous rate*

A

FABLE FOR CRITICS;

OR, BETTER,

(I like, as a thing that the reader's first fancy may strike, an old-fashioned title-page, such as presents a tabular view of the volume's contents)

A GLANCE
AT A FEW OF OUR LITERARY PROGENIES
(Mrs. Malaprop's word)

FROM
THE TUB OF DIOGENES;
A VOCAL AND MUSICAL MEDLEY.

THAT IS,

A SERIES OF JOKES

By A Wonderful Quiz,

who accompanies himself with a rub-a-dub-dub, full of spirit and grace, on the top of the tub.

SET FORTH IN
October, the 21st day, in the year '48:
G. P. PUTNAM, BROADWAY.

Title page for the long poem in which Lowell satirizes his literary contemporaries (Collection of Joel Myerson)

Better known today than *The Biglow Papers,* at least through quotation and anthology selections, is another of the four books Lowell had published in 1848 (rightly called by his biographers an annus mirabilis)–*A Fable for Critics.* Lowell wrote this book for the sheer fun of writing it and even gave the copyright to a friend he loved and thought needier than himself. But there is nothing easy about *A Fable for Critics,* a fact Amy Lowell discovered when she later tried to imitate her kinsman's work. Nothing in American literary criticism in the nineteenth century compares with Lowell's jeu d'esprit in either its originality or, more importantly, its moral stance. The literary portraits are exact; Ralph Waldo Emerson ("A Plotinus-Montaigne, where the Egyptian's gold mist /

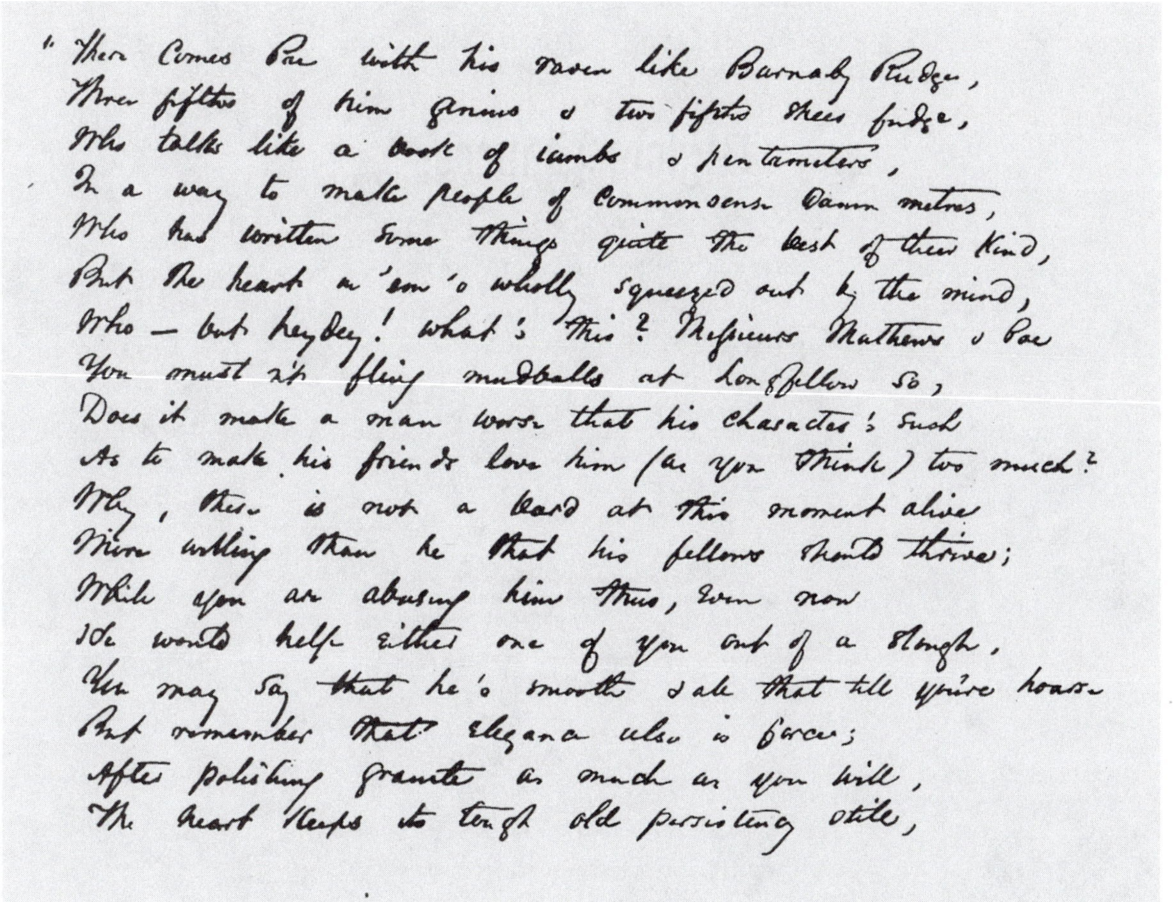
"There comes Poe with his raven like Barnaby Rudge,
Three fifths of him genius & two fifths sheer fudge,
Who talks like a book of iambs & pentameters,
In a way to make people of common sense damn metres,
Who has written some things quite the best of their kind,
But the heart a' 'em 's wholly squeezed out by the mind,
Who—but heyday! what's this? Messieurs Mathews & Poe
You must n't fling mudballs at Longfellow so,
Does it make a man worse that his character's such
As to make his friends love him (as you think) too much?
Why, there is not a bard at this moment alive
More willing than he that his fellows should thrive;
While you are abusing him thus, even now
He would help either one of you out of a slough.
You may say that he's smooth & all that till you're hoarse
But remember that elegance also is force;
After polishing granite as much as you will,
The heart keeps its tough old persistency still,

Lowell's description of Edgar Allan Poe in the manuscript for A Fable for Critics *(from* Autograph Leaves of Our Country's Authors, *edited by Alexander Bliss and John Pendleton Kennedy, 1864)*

And the Gascon's shrewd wit cheek-by-jowl coexist"), Bronson Alcott ("While he talks he is great, but goes out like a taper, / If you shut him up closely with pen, ink, and paper"), Hawthorne ("He's a John Bunyan Fouqué, a Puritan Tieck"), James Fenimore Cooper ("He has drawn you one character [Natty Bumppo], though, that is new, / One wildflower he's plucked that is wet with the dew / of this fresh Western world"), Edgar Allan Poe ("There comes Poe, with his raven, like Barnaby Rudge, / Three fifths of him genius and two fifths sheer fudge"), Henry Wadsworth Longfellow, Washington Irving, Henry David Thoreau, Whittier, Fuller, and even himself ("There is Lowell, who's striving Parnassus to climb, / With a whole bale of *isms* tied together with rhyme")–they are all there, along with a dozen lesser figures now forgotten, and Lowell hits the mark every time.

During the five years preceding his appointment in 1855 as Longfellow's successor as professor of belles lettres at Harvard, Lowell underwent enormous change and loss in his personal life; three of the four children born to him and his first wife, the poet Maria Lowell, died in infancy or early youth, and in October 1853 Maria herself died, leaving Lowell distraught in his grief. But the joy he found in the promise of his sole surviving child, Mabel, sustained him, and he made his study a place of refuge and recreation. Lowell published little during these years; instead, he read what others had done and said. Always an avid reader, he now commonly spent twelve to fifteen hours a day in his library. The range of his literary interests was enormous–including the major modern languages as well as the classics–and his mastery of what he read was thorough. He shared the first fruits of this solitary education with his audiences at the Boston Lowell Institute in January 1855. His success there was what persuaded the Harvard Board of Overseers to name Lowell as Longfellow's replacement. Their choice could not have been happier for the fortunes of Harvard, then just beginning its transformation from a provincial academy to a world-important university, and Lowell prepared himself for the post with a year of diligent study in Germany and Italy. Resettled at Elmwood, the Lowell family house in Cambridge, and remarried in 1857 to a kindly, sympathetic woman named Frances Dunlap–his daughter's govern-

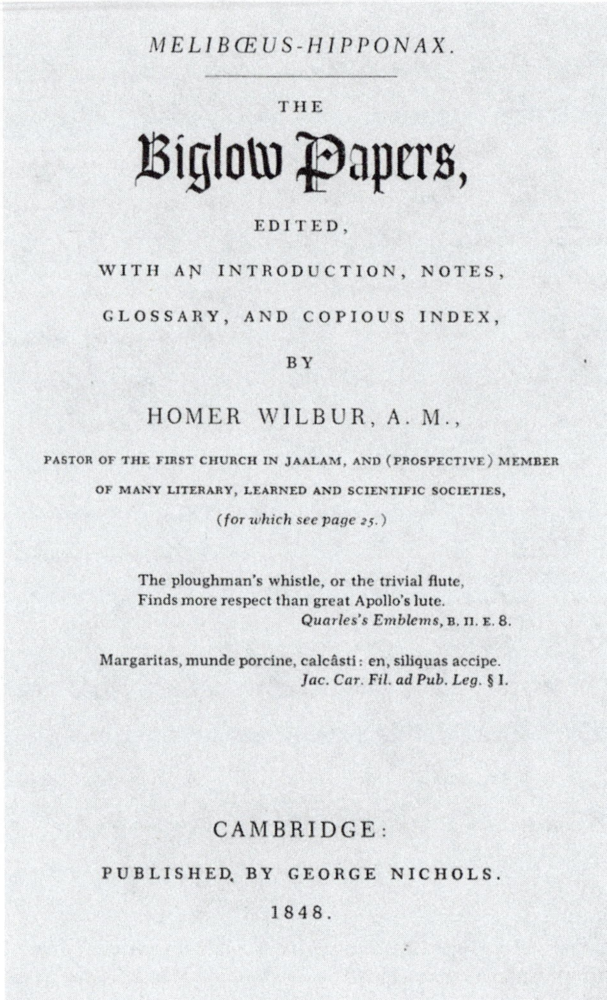

MELIBŒUS-HIPPONAX.

THE

Biglow Papers,

EDITED,

WITH AN INTRODUCTION, NOTES,

GLOSSARY, AND COPIOUS INDEX,

BY

HOMER WILBUR, A. M.,

PASTOR OF THE FIRST CHURCH IN JAALAM, AND (PROSPECTIVE) MEMBER OF MANY LITERARY, LEARNED AND SCIENTIFIC SOCIETIES,

(*for which see page 25.*)

The ploughman's whistle, or the trivial flute,
Finds more respect than great Apollo's lute.
Quarles's Emblems, B. II. E. 8.

Margaritas, munde porcine, calcâsti: en, siliquas accipe.
Jac. Car. Fil. ad Pub. Leg. § I.

CAMBRIDGE:

PUBLISHED BY GEORGE NICHOLS.

1848.

Title page for the first series of the satires in which Lowell's persona, Yankee rustic Hosea Biglow, gives commonsense expression to Lowell's political views

ess during his absence in Europe–Lowell commenced his duties at Harvard in the fall of that year. The terms of his appointment did not burden him with the long hours of recitation that had been Longfellow's bane; instead, Lowell offered each year two courses of formal lectures and in the comfort of his study met with smaller groups of advanced students. Typically he did not overly concern himself with such pedestrian matters as term grades, but he did excite several generations of students who came within his sphere between 1857 and 1876. One of these men was Henry Brooks Adams, Harvard class of 1858, who afterward wrote in his 1907 book *The Education of Henry Adams:*

> Lowell had brought back from Germany the only new and valuable part of its universities, the habit of allowing students to read with him privately in his study. Adams asked the privilege, and used it to read a little, and to talk a great deal, for the personal contact pleased and flattered him, as that of older men ought to flatter and please the young even when they altogether exaggerate its value. Lowell was a new element in the boy's life.

Much more important to the course of American letters was Lowell's instrumental part in the founding of *The Atlantic Monthly* in November 1857 and his editorship of the journal during its first years of publication. That the magazine survived in spite of Lowell's cavalier disregard of editorial routine was owing in large part to the able assistance of F. H. Underwood. But if Lowell was wanting in matters of business efficiency, he more than compensated in literary taste and editorial judgment. Rarely in American journalism has the balance between commercial and aesthetic demands been more satisfactorily achieved than in the early years of *The*

Lowell's daughter Mabel at age ten

Atlantic Monthly. Lowell was also among the principal contributors to the journal, and his pieces, primarily in prose, helped to set the high level of literacy and political responsibility that was long the distinction of the magazine. In the history of American journalism only Edmund Wilson rivals Lowell in the peculiar role each made his own. Unburdened by a philosophical system or program, Lowell possessed a scholar's care for detail and a stylist's delight in expression, and his major essays, particularly "Chaucer" (1870), "Spenser" (1875), and "Dryden" (1868), remain valuable pieces of critical exposition, informed by an appreciation of the literary text in both its historical and linguistic complexities.

During the seemingly interminable, desolate months of the Civil War, long after a speedy resolution of the conflict was thought to be at hand, Lowell resurrected his Jaalam characters, but like their creator, they had been changed by time. The ardor and moral earnestness are still present, but generally the humor is more reflective. Instead of sarcasm and derision, one is more likely to encounter ironic detachment and lyrical simplicity. In such verses as "Sunthin' in the Pastoral Line" in the second *Biglow* volume–written at the suggestion of the British poet Arthur Hugh Clough "that I should try my hand at some Yankee Pastorals, which would admit of more sentiment and a higher tone without foregoing the advantage offered by the dialect"–Lowell most fully succeeds in his mastery of vernacular art. *The Biglow Papers. Second Series* (1862) lacks, however, the unity and harmonious design of the first series, and its success is only to be found in parts.

Following the Civil War, Lowell lived increasingly in the public eye. In *The Cathedral* (1870), "Agassiz" (1874), and the famed *Commemoration Ode* (1865), he spoke nobly and effectively in a manner that can be compared to Walt Whitman's in *Democratic Vistas* (1871) and "Respondez!" and, a little later, Adams's in *Mont-Saint-Michel and Chartres* (1904) and *The Education of Henry Adams.* According to a natural pattern of nineteenth-century American life, Lowell spent his last years as a representative of his government and culture abroad, first as United States minister to the Spanish court (1877–1880) and afterward to the Court of St. James's in England (1880–1885). During these "diplomatic" years Lowell wrote his two finest utterances on the role of the individual in the life of the community, a role he had learned by experience and success: "Democracy"

Lowell in 1857 (Library of Congress)

(1884) and "The Place of the Independent in Politics" (1888). Henry James knew and recalled Lowell in his memorial: "He was strong without narrowness; he was wise without bitterness and bright without folly. That appears for the most part the clearest ideal of those who handle the English form, and he was altogether in the straight tradition. This tradition will surely not forfeit its great part in the world so long as we continue occasionally to know it by what is so solid in performance and so stainless in character."

During the few years remaining of his life, Lowell divided his residence between England and America–great in the public view, a triumph of style and character. Shortly after Lowell's death in 1891, William Dean Howells attempted to express what Lowell had meant, to describe the impression he had made on Howells and his world:

> What I have cloudily before me is the vision of a very loft and simple soul, perplexed, and as it were surprised and even dismayed, at the complexity of the effects from motives so single in it, but escaping always to a clear expression of what was noblest and loveliest in itself at the supreme moments, in the divine exigencies. I believe neither in heroes nor in saints; but I believe in great and good men, for I have known them; and among such men Lowell was of the richest nature I have known. . . . His genius was an instrument that responded in affluent harmony to the power that made him a humorist and that made him a poet, and appointed him rarely to be quite either alone.

In his best poetry, his essays, his letters, and the stories remembered and told afterward about him, humor is never absent, and its range is as varied as the occasions that elicited it–witty and learned at some times, boisterous and close to bawdy at others. There was a place for the lowly pun, even in its flippant disregard of language, but deeper was an ironic bent that became in Lowell second nature. Whether in the Latin of Harvard Wits, the Yankee speech of Hosea Biglow, or the conventional English of William Shakespeare and Henry Fielding, Lowell found cause to poke fun at life; that is not to say he made fun *of* life, for Lowell

"Hosea Biglow Goes to Court," a British editorial cartoonist's impression of Lowell on his way to present his diplomatic credentials to Queen Victoria, 1880

was no cynic. But thoroughgoing skeptic he was, and skepticism combined with humor describes his particular angle of vision. He once defined a sense of humor as "that modulating and restraining balance-wheel," and his assessment of Miguel de Cervantes can, with due adjustment for their unequal worth, be applied to Lowell: "His sense of humor kept his nature sweet and fresh, and made him capable of seeing that there are two sides to every question, even to a question in which his own personal interest was directly involved."

Lowell's reputation at the time of his death in 1891 was, to use William C. Brownell's term, "a superstition." His fame as a man of letters was international, but he was not in any respect a popular writer. Except for a few schoolroom pieces such as "The Vision of Sir Launfal," Lowell's poetry was considered too difficult by most readers; his literary essays, though they enjoyed a larger audience than such do today, nevertheless appealed to a relatively small class of readers; and his early reform writings meant little to a people notorious for their lack of an historical consciousness. His political addresses were widely reported in the press, often quoted at great length in leading newspapers, but compared to such figures as Carl Schurz or even E. L. Godkin, Lowell can hardly be said to have been regarded as an influential political writer in a world increasingly defined by party loyalties. During the last decade of the nineteenth century, in fact, readers read more about Lowell than by him.

Increasingly since then, readers have read little in either category. Lowell's reputation was so much a matter of received opinion that the attack on it made during the early decades of the twentieth century met with little resistance. Unlike Longfellow and Whittier, Lowell has had few advocates, and since World War II only a few significant items have been published about him and his work.

Lowell's decline in the literary marketplace is both an index to changing literary tastes and values, and the result of critical conflicts and misfortunes. His merits as a writer were not those valued by the New Critics, though, ironically, American academic criticism had its first significant manifestation in Lowell. His biography has been another battleground for the continuing war between the North and the South, with writers such as Horace E. Scudder and Ferris Greenslet praising him largely in terms of New England culture, and Richmond Croom Beatty and Leon Howard damning him on the same ground. More recently, Martin Duberman, first attracted to Lowell because of Lowell's abolitionist activities, afterward was disenchanted by Lowell's moderation and

Frances Dunlap Lowell, the author's second wife, in London, circa 1882

eventual suspicion of organized reform movements. While those associated with New Humanism, such as Norman Foerster and Harry Hayden Clark, rightly viewed Lowell as a precursor to their intellectual outlook, their opponents attacked Lowell, labeling him "Victorian," "genteel," "conservative," and "academic"–the same terms they applied to the New Humanists. Finally, the cosmopolitan point of view that characterized Lowell's later life and much of his best work found few admirers during the "national period" of American literary criticism of the 1930s and the 1940s, though Walter Blair, Jennette Tandy, and H. L. Mencken pointed out that Lowell in *The Biglow Papers* contributed greatly to "native" American literature.

The critical silence of the present time, however, should not be taken as an indication that Lowell will be utterly forgotten. Every generation has to reinvent its literary and cultural past, and until Lowell's piece is put back into its rightful place in the puzzle, the picture of American intellectual life of the nineteenth century will remain incomplete. As Robert A. Rees observed in his useful survey of writings about Lowell: "No one as richly versatile and influential as Lowell will forever remain unattractive or unrewarding to scholars."

Letters:

Letters of James Russell Lowell, edited by Charles Eliot Norton, 2 volumes (London: Osgood, McIlvaine, 1894; New York: Harper, 1894); expanded edition, 3 volumes (Boston & New York: Houghton, Mifflin, 1904);

New Letters of James Russell Lowell, edited by M. A. DeWolfe Howe (New York & London: Harper, 1932);

The Scholar-Friends: Letters of Francis James Child and James Russell Lowell, edited by Howe and G. W. Cottrell Jr. (Cambridge: Harvard University Press, 1952);

James C. Austin, *Fields of the Atlantic Monthly: Letters to an Editor, 1861–1870* (San Marino, Cal.: Huntington Library, 1953);

James L. Woodress Jr., "The Lowell-Howells Friendship: Some Unpublished Letters," *New England Quarterly,* 26 (December 1953): 523–528;

Philip Graham, "Some Lowell Letters," *Texas Studies in Literature and Language,* 3 (Winter 1962): 557–582;

Browning to His American Friends: Letters between the Brownings, the Storys and James Russell Lowell, 1841–1890, edited by Gertrude Reese Hudson (New York: Barnes & Noble, 1965);

Transatlantic Dialogue, edited by Paul F. Mattheisen and Michael Millgate (Austin: University of Texas Press, 1965);

"James Russell Lowell and Robert Carter: *The Pioneer* and Fifty Letters from Lowell to Carter," edited by Edward L. Tucker, in *Studies in the American Renaissance 1987,* edited by Joel Myerson (Charlottesville: University Press of Virginia, 1987), pp. 187–246;

Portrait of a Friendship Drawn from New Letters of James Russell Lowell to Sybella Lady Lyttelton, 1881–1891, edited by Alethea Hayter (Wilton, U.K.: Michael Russell, 1990).

Bibliographies:

George Willis Cooke, *A Bibliography of James Russell Lowell* (Boston & New York: Houghton, Mifflin, 1906);

Robert A. Rees, "James Russell Lowell," in *Fifteen American Authors before 1900: Bibliographic Essays on Research and Criticism,* edited by Rees and Earl N. Harbert (Madison: University of Wisconsin Press, 1971).

Biographies:

Horace Elisha Scudder, *James Russell Lowell: A Biography,* 2 volumes (Boston & New York: Houghton, Mifflin, 1901);

Ferris Greenslet, *James Russell Lowell: His Life and Work* (Boston: Houghton, Mifflin, 1905);

Richmond Croom Beatty, *James Russell Lowell* (Nashville, Tenn.: Vanderbilt University Press, 1952);

Martin Duberman, *James Russell Lowell* (Boston: Houghton Mifflin, 1966).

References:

Henry Adams, *The Education of Henry Adams: An Autobiography* (Boston & New York: Houghton Mifflin, 1918);

George Arms, *The Fields Were Green* (Stanford, Cal.: Stanford University Press, 1953);

Walter Blair, "A Brahmin Dons Homespun," in *Horse Sense in American Humor* (Chicago: University of Chicago Press, 1942);

William Crary Brownell, *American Prose Masters* (New York: Scribners, 1909);

John Jay Chapman, *Emerson and Other Essays* (New York: Scribners, 1898);

Harry Hayden Clark, "Lowell–Humanitarian, Nationalist, or Humanist?" *Studies in Philology,* 27 (July 1930): 411–441;

Angus Fletcher, "James Russell Lowell," *Encyclopedia of American Poetry: The Nineteenth Century,* edited by Eric L. Haralson (Chicago & London: Dearborn, 1998), pp. 271–277;

Norman Foerster, *American Criticism: A Study in Literary Theory from Poe to the Present* (Boston: Houghton Mifflin, 1928);

Leon Howard, *Victorian Knight-Errant: A Study of the Early Literary Career of James Russell Lowell* (Berkeley & Los Angeles: University of California Press, 1952);

William Dean Howells, *Literary Friends and Acquaintance* (New York: Harper, 1900);

Henry James, *Essays in London and Elsewhere* (New York: Harper 1893);

H. L. Mencken, *The American Language: An Inquiry into the Development of English in the United States,* fourth edition (New York: Knopf, 1936);

Constance Rourke, *American Humor: A Study in National Character* (New York: Harcourt, Brace, 1931);

Jennette Tandy, *Crackerbox Philosophers in American Humor and Satire* (New York: Columbia University Press, 1925);

Thomas Wortham, ed., *The Biglow Papers [First Series]: A Critical Edition* (DeKalb: Northern Illinois University Press, 1977).

Papers:

The papers of James Russell Lowell are at the Houghton Library, Harvard University. The Berg Collection at the New York Public Library and the Henry E. Huntington Library in San Marino, California, also have major collections.

Horace Mann

(4 May 1796 – 2 August 1859)

D'Ann Pletcher George
Bridgewater State College

Horace Mann, 1859 (The Metropolitan Museum of Art, Gift of I. N. Phelps Stokes, Edward S. Hawes, Alice Mary Hawes, Marion Augusta Hawes, 1937)

BOOKS: *An Oration, Sept. 6, 1825, before the United Brothers' Society of Brown University* (Providence, R.I.: Privately printed, 1825);

Remarks upon the Comparative Profits of Grocers and Retailers, as Derived from Temperate and Intemperate Customers (Boston: Ford & Damrell for the Massachusetts Temperance Society Tracts, 1834);

Annual Report of the Board of Education together with the Annual Report of the Secretary of the Board, 12 volumes (Boston: Dutton & Wentworth, 1838–1849);

Lecture on the Best Mode of Preparing and Using Spelling Books, Delivered Before the American Institute of Instruction, August 1841 (Boston: Privately printed, 1841);

An Oration before the Authorities of the City of Boston, July 4, 1842 (Boston: Privately printed, 1842);

The Common School Controversy; Consisting of Three Letters of the Secretary of the Board of Education, in Reply to Charges Preferred Against the Board by the Editor of the Christian Witness and Edward A. Newton (Boston: Privately printed, 1844);

Reply to the Remarks of Twenty-Nine Boston Schoolmasters, Part of the "Thirty-One" Who Published Remarks on the Seventh Annual Report of the Secretary of the Massachusetts Board of Education (Boston: Privately printed, 1845);

Letter to the Rev. Matthew Hale Smith, In Answer to His "Reply" or Supplement (Boston: Privately printed, 1847);

Letter to His Constituents (Boston: Privately printed, 1850);

Slavery: Letters and Speeches (Boston: Privately printed, 1851);

A Few Thoughts on the Powers and Duties of Women: Two Lectures (Syracuse: Hall, Mills, 1853);

Antioch College Dedication (Yellow Springs, Ohio: Privately printed, 1854);

Report and Resolution on the "Code of Honor," Falsely So-called: Also Report and Resolution on Intemperance, Profanity and the Use of Tobacco in Schools and Colleges (Columbus, Ohio: Privately printed, 1857);

Lectures on Various Subjects (New York: Privately printed, 1859);

Twelve Sermons: Delivered at Antioch College (Boston: Ticknor & Fields, 1861);

Lectures and Annual Reports on Education (Cambridge, Mass.: Privately printed, 1867);

Thoughts Selected from His Writing (Boston: H. B. Fuller, 1867);

The Study of Physiology in Schools (New York: J. W. Schermerhorn, 1869).

Collection: *Life and Works of Horace Mann,* 5 volumes (Boston: Lee & Shepard; New York: C. T. Dillingham, 1891).

Though not the first to propose a common education for all, Horace Mann transformed the idea into action. As the first secretary of the Board of Higher Education in Massachusetts, president of the state senate, U.S. congressman on the eve of the Civil War, and, finally, president of Antioch College, Mann crusaded most notably for a systematic, public education but also for legal restrictions on the sale of alcohol and tobacco, state-supported medical care for the insane, a school for the blind, and the abolition of both slavery and imprisonment of debtors. Among his friends he counted Elizabeth Peabody, William Ellery Channing, Theodore Parker, and George Combe. His adversaries included Orestes Brownson and Daniel Webster.

One of the oldest families in the Bay Colony, the Manns settled in Cambridge, Massachusetts, in 1633. Thomas Mann Jr. belonged to the third generation of his family to farm a substantial plot in Franklin. Horace, born 4 May 1796 to Thomas and Rebecca (Stanley) Mann, worked hard. As an adult Horace Mann regretted the loss of his childhood to ceaseless labor, but he learned from it the Yankee industry and piety that shaped his life as a social reformer and moralist.

The meetinghouse in Franklin provided a place to worship God, hold town meetings after the Sunday services, and reinforce shared social and religious values. The Reverend Nathaniel Emmons, who ministered to the town for fifty-four years beginning in 1773, belonged to the "New Light" school of Congregationalism, begun in response to the preaching of Jonathan Edwards during the Great Awakening. Emmons characterized God as austere, exacting, and unforgiving. He saw human creatures, on the other hand, as morally depraved, unworthy of mercy, and likely to backslide if not constantly prodded by a vigilant minister. Whereas traditional Congregationalists taught that people could increase their chance to obtain grace through such pious acts as prayer, Bible reading, and church attendance, New Lights believed that men are so thoroughly steeped in evil that even their quest for salvation stems from pride and sinful self-preservation.

New Lights thought their theology more consistently Calvinist than that of other Congregationalists. John Calvin emphasized that God's will, rather than man's works, provided the keys to heaven's gates. The proper stance for aspiring Christians, therefore, was "disinterested benevolence," or a willingness to accept God's plan for their life, even if that plan meant eternal damnation. In fact, willingness to "be damned for the glory of God" provided convincing evidence of membership in the fold. Though the young Horace rejected the cold and uncompromising logic of Emmons's theology, his message urged the precocious boy to consider the nature of man and his purpose on earth. For many years to come he struggled to forget the angry, judgmental God of his childhood and to replace this memory with a more compassionate Supreme Being who encouraged man to improve himself and his society.

The Congregational church gradually became less of an authoritative influence over the Mann family. Reasons for the church's waning importance were complex. Like many Franklin families the Manns made a gradual transition from self-sufficient farming to making straw hats for distant markets. Since the father's work produced no more income than the nimble hands of a child, patterns of authority in and out of the household had to adjust. The wedge between the Manns and the meetinghouse deepened after Emmons's insensitive response to the death in 1810 of Horace's older brother Stephen, who drowned while skipping church to go swimming. Emmons used Stephen's backsliding to emphasize the dangers of living outside the fold. For the unconverted, death and damnation lay just around the corner.

Mann's early education was rudimentary and grounded in religious doctrine. His sister Rebecca taught him to read, giving him lessons from Noah Webster's grammar while she went about her chores. Mann's formal instruction began at one of Franklin's six one-room schoolhouses, in session during the winter for six weeks for older children and during the summer for young children. Here he memorized parts of the Westminster Assembly Short Catechism, which taught the doctrine of original sin. Emmons visited classes regularly, questioning children on their knowledge of basic theology. A solid collection of books in the town library, donated by Benjamin Franklin himself, rounded out Mann's early education.

With some tutoring from an itinerant schoolmaster, Mann at the age of twenty was admitted to Brown University as a sophomore. At Brown he found an intellectual community that supported his growing religious faith in the potential for improving the human lot. Membership in a literary society provided opportunities to develop his oratorical skills and test his ideas for reforming government and society. He gave the valedictory address at his graduation in 1819. After a brief stint as a teacher at Brown, Mann studied law with a judge and then at Litchfield Law School. Admitted to the bar in 1823, he practiced law in Dedham, Massachusetts, where his reputation for integrity and superior oratorical skills won him a seat in the state legislature.

As a National Republican who followed John Quincy Adams rather than Andrew Jackson, Mann championed federal support of humanitarian projects for the good of the masses, but not necessarily because he wanted to garner their favor. A conservative moralist, he was concerned not with empowering the common man but with righting moral injustices, particularly those that violated the principles of the U.S. Constitution or natural religion. In 1829 he drew lawmakers' attention to the terrible treatment of the insane in Massachusetts prisons and won funding for the first publicly financed mental hospital in the United States. After gaining a seat in the state senate in 1833, he turned his attention to regulating trade in alcohol, which he believed caused abusers to commit crimes.

Meanwhile, Mann met his first wife, Charlotte Messer, who died in 1832 after only two years of marriage. Descending into a dark gloom, Mann seemed unable to move on with his life until Elizabeth Peabody and Channing intervened. The two spent many evenings by the Peabody fireside helping Mann to resurrect his shattered faith in a benevolent God. Battling the old orthodox doctrine of sin and retribution, Channing characterized God as merciful and man as deserving mercy; indeed, Channing believed that God's design was for man to grow spiritually, intellectually, and morally until he fully realized his natural connection to God. Peabody at one point hoped to revive Mann's spirits with more than fraternal affection, but his romantic intentions focused on her sister Mary, whom he married in 1843.

While talks with Channing nourished Mann's faith in God and his own social reform efforts, he could not separate his passion for doing good from its Puritan origins. In a phrenological reading of himself, documented by his wife in her biography of him, he found "the faculty of mind by which we see effects in causes, and causes in effects, and invest the future with a present reality" to be particularly active in his mind. For Mann, the judgment day was always imminent. Tireless pursuit of humanitarian projects was his way of preparing for it. In 1837 Mann received what he often called the most important appointment of his career, the position of secretary of the newly created Board of Education in Massachusetts.

Mann's second wife, Mary Peabody Mann (Antiochiana Collection, Olive Kettering Library, Antioch College)

At the time Mann decided to accept the offer of this new position, he was finding through the work of George Combe philosophical and scientific justification for his belief in the uplifting power of education. Combe's *The Constitution of Man Considered in Relation to External Objects* (1829), a book of phrenological teachings, proposed that the mind consisted of distinct "propensities," such as benevolence and combativeness, located in specific areas of the brain. In some instances, these localized faculties could be observed as measurable protuberances on the human skull. A skilled phrenologist could predict moral weaknesses and strengths by assessing people's skulls.

Mann, however, was most interested in the implications of faculty psychology for education. After he heard Combe lecture in 1840, the two vacationed together on Cape Cod, where they dreamed about a system of education that would lead men to a new era of moral and intellectual progress. By developing crucial centers in the brain and letting others lie dormant, educators could accentuate students'

Mann's sons: Benjamin, Horace Jr., and George

capacity for goodness and minimize their potential for evil. Furthermore, phrenology claimed the existence of a special class of men and women who possess a propensity for moral greatness and can be identified and trained to become educational leaders. Both men thought that Mann obviously belonged to this special class.

During his twelve-year tenure as secretary, Mann wrote twelve annual reports, in which he noted conditions and practices in the public schools at home and abroad and in which he laid out his rationale for forming a strong public school system. Many of his reports have relevance to educational issues of today, treating subjects such as teacher training, the nature of literacy acquisition, and the need for students to participate actively in their learning.

Mann's ideas concerning student learning and student-teacher relationships were among his most progressive and provocative. Influenced by Combe, Swiss educator Johann Heinrich Pestalozzi, and a visit to Prussian schools, Mann lamented that so many American schoolmasters forced students to learn their lessons out of fear of corporal punishment for failure. Instead, he urged, teachers should attempt to engage students' interest and inspire their learning through a "sweet and humanizing influence." Likening teachers to parents, Mann imagined a kinder classroom based on "tenderness and vigilance." When young people learn to perform their duty voluntarily, in compliance with their inner conscience, the republic will be stronger, he maintained.

In addition to a humanizing influence, Mann argued that teachers need other essential skills that require formal training in a professional school. In the publicly financed normal schools that Mann convinced the state to build, teachers studied subject areas as well as classroom management strategies. At the end of a rigorous course of study, they had to pass difficult qualifying exams. Qualifications of teachers also included marks of gentility, such as good manners, correct pronunciation, and the ability to spread a "nameless charm over whatever circle may be entered." Following the lead of Catharine Beecher, Mann argued that women were best suited to teach young children.

Mann's suggestions for curricular reform focused on active learning and a broad, liberal course

Antioch College, where Mann served as president from its founding in 1852 until his death in 1859

of study. Children acquire the written language more easily when presented initially with familiar words and interesting reading, he believed, than with the rudiments of the alphabet or of proper English grammar. Unlike the strict whole-language approach used in some classrooms today, however, Mann approved of phonics as a method for teaching the mechanics of reading.

To traditional subjects of arithmetic, writing, spelling, and geography, Mann wanted to add the study of human health and vocal music. He also advocated the teaching of oral and written composition, the use of laboratory equipment in sciences, and instruction in the workings of government. To keep politics out of the teaching of government, Mann proposed that controversial ideas be excluded and that the curriculum focus instead on those principles accepted by all factions. In a time when most people thought of popular education only in terms of vocational training, Mann was devoted to a broad liberal education for the masses.

Mann's student-centered ideas angered Boston's schoolmasters, who suspected that their practices were being ridiculed. In a lengthy document thirty-one of them defended their pedagogy and approach to classroom management. The interactive methods of teaching that Mann advocated would prevent "habit of independent and individual effort," they warned, while abolishment of corporal punishment would lead to chaos in the classroom. Furthermore, more gentle forms of persuading students to do what is right amounted to sin against God, since "All authority is of God and must be obeyed."

While Mann refuted the schoolmasters in writing, his best revenge came when several of his political allies ran and were elected to the Boston School Committee. They made the inspection of grammar schools that year more than pro forma, administering to students a standardized written exam instead of the usual oral exams. The results betrayed that lessons focused most often on rote memorization, with the result that students did not know how to think outside the structure of a textbook and had not developed higher cognitive skills. For example, instead of learning to write, students had merely memorized grammar rules. When asked to compose an original piece, they faltered. The report recommended new pedagogy and the immediate suspension of flogging. In addition, four schoolmasters were removed and several others transferred.

In addition to specific proposals for improving instruction and teacher training, the annual reports articulated a larger philosophy of public education. People have an important role to play in creating a good republic, he argued. First, however, they must develop their intellectual, spiritual, and moral dimensions through education and self-culture. Systematically and uniformly educating people will unify them with a set of common moral and religious values that assure a sense of duty to one's God, republic, and fellow men.

Mann felt that there were certain essential Christian truths that virtually everyone believed and that could therefore undergird the moral and civic training provided by the common school system. He was, however, sensitive to the political dangers of allowing schools to proselytize for particular religious denominations. Besides, an 1827 state law made the teaching of sectarian doctrine in public schools illegal. Over and over he sanctioned only the teaching of "nonsectarian" moral and religious principles, believing firmly that the Bible included certain plain and indisputable truths evident to everyone.

Behind Mann's search for a common ground of religious beliefs lay several prejudices and incorrect assumptions. He ignored the possibilities that people might not base concepts of truth on the Holy Scripture and that some religious groups, such as Jews and Catholics, read Bibles different from his own. Furthermore, he mistakenly assumed a set of biblical truths to which all Protestant Christians subscribed. The fallacy of this last assumption threatened to manifest itself every time Mann was forced to spell out, with any detail, which biblical truths were plain and indisputable.

Though members of evangelical denominations as well as Unitarians sat on the Board of Higher Education, antagonists accused them all of advocating Unitarian beliefs. After Mann refused to endorse schoolbooks selected by the American Sunday School Union because he thought they favored evangelical doctrine, Samuel Packard, the editor of the books in question, attacked the board. According to Packard, the board was trying to remove God (by which he meant the Trinitarian conception of God) and Christianity from the public schools.

Brownson, leader of a workingmen's organization in Boston, editor of the *Quarterly Review,* and an agnostic at the time, called for abolishing the board on grounds that it was Godless and, even worse, Whig. Furthermore, he grumbled, schoolhouses never did anything to improve society. In a more judicious criticism of Mann, Brownson charged that the attempt to teach religion impartially was naive: "If they exclude whatever is sectarian, they must exclude all that relates to religion."

If Mann had enemies, he also had friends–Peabody and Parker frequently came to his defense during controversies. Ralph Waldo Emerson considered Mann important enough to hear him speak at a convention, though Emerson wrote afterward in his journal that "Law has touched the business of education with the point of its pen and instantly it has frozen stiff." Nathaniel Hawthorne perceived a similar chill in Mann's character, which he represented as the implacable Hollingsworth in *The Blithedale Romance* (1852). Whatever Mann's personal shortcomings, the Packard and Brownson controversies demonstrate the larger social tension that boiled just below the surface of agreements about the purpose and even the desirability of a common public education.

Given the limited power of the board, Mann's ability with rhetoric and oratory proved crucial to his success in furthering school reform. The state legislature had granted the board power to persuade and recommend but not to pass laws. Still, local districts resented the implied power of the board and suspected its purpose–to counteract poor performance of certain districts, many of which saw their job as one of cutting spending to the barest minimum. Mann in fact did not want to replace power of local citizenry with a centralized approach to education. Instead, the rhetorician hoped to stir up concern and to guide that concern in an appropriate direction.

While Mann usually grounded his arguments for public education in appeals to republican virtue and Christian morality, he varied his message according to audience. Speaking to businessmen, he argued that improved education would reduce crime and boost the economy by providing more diligent, literate workers. To working-class audiences he stressed the natural right of every citizen to a good education and the potential for instruction to prevent class distinctions. To the socially conscious, he claimed reduced poverty and distress. Mann came up with a clever way to garner support from teachers for his progressive views, many of whom subscribed to the doctrine of original sin. How many of their charges, he asked, "could be turned out the blessing, and not the bane, the honor, and not the scandal, of society?"

In addition to philosophical and pedagogical advances, schools made concrete material gains during Mann's tenure. Teachers' salaries rose 62 percent for men and 54 percent for women. Two million dollars were appropriated for better schoolhouses and equipment. Expenditure on private schools dropped from 75 percent of total public monies to 36 percent. Perhaps most impressively, the school year was extended from an average of two months to six months.

When John Quincy Adams died, Mann took his place in the House of Representatives, where he used his rhetorical skills to speak out against slavery. In his first address to his colleagues, he capitalized on his ethos as an education expert, claiming that slavery made edification of common people impossible (by this he meant white people), citing for evidence the low level of literacy in Virginia compared to that found in Northern states. Later, Mann defended a sea captain who tried to free a ship of slaves docked in the District of Columbia, receiving no fee for the case.

Mann's riskiest foray into abolitionist politics came in response to Daniel Webster's eloquent speech in favor of Henry Clay's Fugitive Slave Law. In a forty-page letter to Massachusetts voters, Mann accused Webster of hypocrisy and lack of integrity. His opposition nearly cost him a third term in office when Whig newspapers friendly to Webster lashed out at Mann. Mann's last speech to the House of Representatives, in 1851, challenged the constitutionality and morality of the Fugitive Slave Law. Foreshadowing an even more powerful argument against slavery that later appeared in the form of Harriet Beecher Stowe's *Uncle Tom's Cabin* (1852), Mann claimed that the law "renders the precepts of the gospel and the teachings of Jesus Christ seditious."

After losing a race for governor, Mann ignored the advice of friends and agreed to serve as president of Antioch College, a new venture in Ohio. In a speech at the opening of the college Mann articulated the millennial purpose of the college. Though classrooms were unfinished and buildings unheated, the college played a central role in educating the young people of the United States, particularly those in the West.

The project attracted Mann for several reasons. In many ways Antioch more closely reflected his ideals than any other social reform project. The religious group that founded the institution claimed to be nonsectarian and to base their doctrine on an unbiased reading of the Scripture. Faculty at first seemed at one mind with Mann, disapproving of slavery, tobacco, and alcohol while enthusiastic about phrenology and religious services. Pedagogically progressive, teachers delivered lessons via individual conferences and oral instruction rather than textbooks.

At Mann's urging, the college initially decided not to exclude applicants on the basis of race or gender, a radical principle in 1852. Though coeducational, the institution strictly enforced rules regulating interaction between the sexes. Mann also eliminated honors and prizes at the college, which he felt undermined what should be a natural love of learning for students. While most students and faculty supported Mann's social and educational views, some disapproved of his Unitarianism. Mann died 2

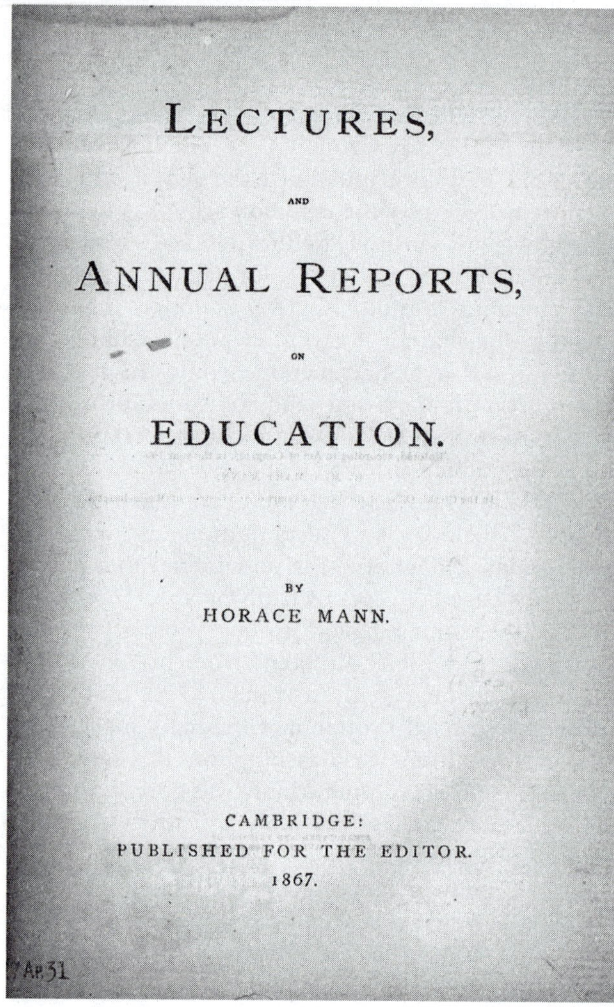
LECTURES,

AND

ANNUAL REPORTS,

ON

EDUCATION.

BY

HORACE MANN.

CAMBRIDGE:
PUBLISHED FOR THE EDITOR.
1867.

Title page for a posthumously published collection of Mann's writings

August 1859 in Yellow Springs, Ohio. Religious conflict and financial problems plagued Antioch until it was reestablished in 1859 with a different board of trustees.

Through his reports, his many public addresses to audiences of teachers and legislators, and his contributions to the *Common School Journal,* Mann influenced educational leaders in other states and beyond the United States. Requests for advice concerned issues such as education for women, lack of adequate funding for schools, public apathy, and teacher preparation. Abroad, Mann's ideas resonated most profoundly with Latin American countries. So impressed was Domingo Faustino Sarmiento with Mann's work that he traveled to the United States, where he spent two days talking to Mann, in whom he found a kindred spirit. Later, as president of his native Argentina, Sarmiento devoted himself to the creation of a public school system. In Chile he founded an elementary school system, established normal schools, and erected statues of Abraham Lincoln and Horace Mann.

Bibliography:

Clyde S. King, *Horace Mann, 1796–1859, A Bibliography* (Dobbs Ferry, N.Y.: Oceana Publications, 1966).

Biographies:

Henry Barnard, "Biographical Sketch of Horace Mann," *American Journal of Education,* 5 (December 1858): 611–656;

Mary Tyler (Peabody) Mann, *Life of Horace Mann* (Boston: Walker, Fuller, 1865);

Joy Elmer Morgan, *Horace Mann: His Ideas and Ideals* (Washington, D.C.: National Home Library Foundation, 1936);

Louise Hall Tharp, *Until Victory: Horace Mann and Mary Peabody* (Boston: Little, Brown, 1953);

Jonathan Messerli, *Horace Mann: A Biography* (New York: Knopf, 1972);

Robert B. Downs, *Horace Mann: Champion of Public Schools* (New York: Twayne, 1974).

References:

Lawrence A. Cremin, "Horace Mann's Legacy," in *The Republic and the School: Horace Mann on The Education of Free Men,* edited by Lawrence A. Cremin (New York: Columbia University Press, 1957);

Raymond B. Culver, *Horace Mann and Religion in the Massachusetts Public Schools* (New York: Arno Press & New York Times, 1969);

Neil Gerard McCluskey, *Public Schools and Moral Education: The Influence of Horace Mann, William Torrey Harris and John Dewey* (New York: Columbia University Press, 1958).

Papers:

Many of Horace Mann's letters, private papers, and manuscripts can be found in the Massachusetts Historical Society; the Brown University Archives; the Dedham Historical Society; and the Houghton Library, Harvard University.

John Lothrop Motley

(15 April 1814 – 29 May 1877)

Deshae E. Lott
University of Illinois at Springfield

See also the Motley entries in *DLB 30: American Historians, 1607–1865* and *DLB 59: American Literary Critics and Scholars, 1800–1850.*

BOOKS: *Morton of Morton's Hope; An Autobiography,* anonymous, 3 volumes (London: Colburn, 1839); republished as *Morton's Hope: or, The Memoirs of a Provincial,* 2 volumes (New York: Harper, 1839);

Merry-Mount; A Romance of the Massachusetts Colony, anonymous (Boston & Cambridge, Mass.: Munroe, 1849);

The Rise of the Dutch Republic: A History, 3 volumes (London: John Chapman/Chapman & Hall, 1856; New York: Harper, 1856);

History of the United Netherlands, 4 volumes (London: Murray, 1860, 1867; New York: Harper, 1861, 1868)–comprises volumes 1 and 2, *History of the United Netherlands: From the Death of William the Silent to the Synod of Dort. With a Full View of the English-Dutch Struggle against Spain, and of the Origin and Destruction of the Spanish Armada* (London: Murray, 1860; New York: Harper, 1861); volumes 3 and 4, *History of the United Netherlands: From the Death of William the Silent to the Twelve Years' Truce–1609* (London: Murray, 1867; New York: Harper, 1868);

Causes of the Civil War in America . . . Reprinted, by Permission, from "The Times" (London: George Manwaring, 1861); republished as *The Causes of the American Civil War* (New York: D. Appleton, 1861) and as *Letters of John Lothrop Motley and Joseph Holt. For Gratuitous Distribution* (New York: Printed by Henry E. Tudor, 1861);

Four Questions for the People, at the Presidential Election. Address of John Lothrop Motley, before the Parker Fraternity, at the Music Hall, October 20, 1868 (Boston: Ticknor & Fields, 1868);

Historic Progress and American Democracy: An Address Delivered before the New-York Historical Society, at Their Sixty-fourth Anniversary, December 16, 1868 (New York: Scribner, 1869);

The Life and Death of John of Barneveld, Advocate of Holland; With a View of the Primary Causes and Movements of the

Thirty Years' War, 2 volumes (London: Murray, 1874; New York: Harper, 1874);

Peter the Great (New York: Harper, 1877; London & Edinburgh: Thomas Nelson, 1887).

Collections: *The Writings of John Lothrop Motley,* 17 volumes, edited by George William Curtis (New York & London: Harper, 1900);

John Lothrop Motley: Representative Selections, with Introduction, Bibliography, and Notes, edited by Chester Penn Higby and B. T. Schantz (New York: American Book Company, 1939).

SELECTED PERIODICAL PUBLICATIONS–UNCOLLECTED: "Goethe," *New York Review,* 3 (October 1838): 397–442;

Friedrich Schiller, "The Diver," translated by Motley, *New Yorker* (19 January 1839);

Novalis, "Wine Song," translated by Motley, *New Yorker* (26 January 1839);

"Goethe's Works," *New York Review,* 5 (July 1839): 1–48;

Ludwig Tieck, *Ritter Blaubart, or Bluebeard: A Story in Five Acts,* translated by Motley, *New World,* 1 (19 December 1840): 449–452, 478–483;

"The Novels of Balzac," *North American Review,* 65 (July 1847): 85–108;

"Polity of the Puritans," *North American Review,* 69 (October 1849): 470–498;

"Florentine Mosaics," *Atlantic Monthly,* 1 (November 1857): 12–22; (December 1857): 129–138;

"Tribute to Dean Milman," *Proceedings of the Massachusetts Historical Society,* 10 (1869): 344–346;

"Cupid Hath Been a God," *Harper's Magazine,* 55 (August 1877): 465;

"Lines Written at Syracuse," *Harper's Magazine,* 55 (September 1877): 610–614.

OTHER: "The Genius and Character of Goethe," in *Literary Pioneers: Early American Explorers of European Culture,* edited by Orie William Long (Cambridge, Mass.: Harvard University Press, 1935), pp. 200–203.

In a memorial poem written in the year John Lothrop Motley died, William Cullen Bryant said of the New England Brahmin, diplomat, and historian: "thy glorious writings speak for thee / And in the answering heart of millions raise / The generous zeal for Right and Liberty." For forty years Motley had upheld in his writings the artist's responsibility to advance democracy. In the historical narratives that earned him fame in America and Europe, Motley found in the past a pattern of Protestants repeatedly liberating themselves from repression and facilitating global social progress.

The second of Thomas and Anna Lothrop Motley's eight children, John Lothrop Motley was born on 15 April 1814 in the Boston suburb of Dorchester, where his father and his uncle Edward Motley had begun their prosperous commercial partnership in 1802. He began his education at Charles W. Green's school in Jamaica Plain the summer after his tenth birthday. In the fall he enrolled in the Round Hill School in Northampton, a new private school for boys organized by its two teachers, Joseph Green Cogswell and George Bancroft. Bancroft introduced Motley to the German language and literature.

Motley entered Harvard College in 1827. There he was particularly influenced by the works of the German authors Friedrich Schiller and Johann Wolfgang von Goethe. His first publication, a translation of Schiller's unfinished novel *Der Geisterseher* (1788) as "The Ghost-Seer," appeared in the Harvard *Collegian* in 1830. At the 1831 senior exhibition Motley, who was third in his class, read his essay "The Genius and Character of Goethe." In 1832–1833 Motley attended the University of Göttingen, where one of his fellow students was Otto von Bismarck, the future prime minister of Prussia and first chancellor of the German Empire. In 1833–1834 Motley and Bismarck studied international law and classical history at the University of Berlin, lodging together at 161 Friedrichstrasse.

Motley traveled in Europe and England before returning to Boston in 1835 to study law. On 2 March 1837 he married Mary Benjamin, the sister of the writer, editor, and critic Park Benjamin. Motley's biographical sketch of Goethe, published in *The New York Review* (October 1838), expresses the principle that "a work of art . . . *must,* if it is true to the principles of aesthetics, exert an ennobling and refining influence" on those who partake of it. In "Goethe's Works" (July 1839), which also appeared in *The New York Review,* Motley reviewed *Wilhelm Meister, Die Wahlverwandschaften* (Elective Affinities, 1809), and *Faust* (1808, 1832), all of which he had translated while he was abroad. The anonymously published novel *Morton of Morton's Hope; An Autobiography* (1839) provides in the character Uncas Morton a sketch of some of Motley's own inclinations: certainty that the American landscape facilitates the emergence of democracy, fondness for the gothic, and skepticism toward transcendentalism. Another character, Otto ("Fox") von Rabenmark, is a sketch of the young Bismarck. The novel, which includes many geographical and chronological discrepancies, received no positive criticism in its own time or since. In 1840 Motley translated Ludwig Tieck's play *Ritter Blaubart* (1797) as *Bluebeard* for the magazine *The New World.*

Motley's parents, Thomas and Anna Lothrop Motley (from Susan Margaret Stackpole St. John Mildmay and Herbert St. John Mildmay, eds., John Lothrop Motley and His Family: Further Letters and Records, *1910)*

In 1841 Motley was appointed secretary of legation to the Russian Mission at St. Petersburg by President William Henry Harrison. His next publications were three essays for the *North American Review* and a second novel. "Peter the Great" (October 1845), which appeared in book form in 1877, reveals for the first time Motley's skill in dramatizing history through figures who represent concepts–a technique also practiced by Thomas Carlyle in *On Heroes, Hero-Worship, and the Heroic in History* (1841) and *The French Revolution* (1859), Thomas Babington Macaulay in his essay "Frederic the Great" in the *Edinburgh Review* (April 1842), and Ralph Waldo Emerson in *Representative Men* (1850). In "The Novels of Balzac" (July 1847) Motley praises Honoré de Balzac's amusing literary style and his lack of didacticism and moralizing; Motley believed that all true art is inherently moral and exerts an ennobling and refining influence without the need for sentimental prefaces or sentimental content. "Polity of the Puritans" (October 1849) provides Motley an opportunity to commend his former teacher, Bancroft, who connects the Puritans with the emergence of self-government. Motley had, however, begun a few years earlier to collect materials for a history of Holland and had found democratic impulses in that country similar to those in North America. He therefore argues that the drive for self-government reaches beyond the Puritans to Protestants in general.

Motley's *North American Review* articles received critical commendation; his novel *Merry-Mount; A Romance of the Massachusetts Colony* (1849) did not. *Merry-Mount* addresses the conflict between the Puritans and their archenemy, Thomas Morton, in the seventeenth century. As compared to *Morton of Morton's Hope,* Motley's depiction of characters and scenes has improved significantly, and the plot is less disjointed. Whereas his contemporaries had chosen not to comment on the earlier novel, the *North American Review* published a twenty-page review of *Merry-Mount* that called for more–and better–works from Motley.

In 1849 Motley served a single term in the Massachusetts legislature. As chairman of the education committee, he proposed an unpopular measure to appropriate revenues to endow state colleges rather than the common schools.

During the next decade Motley researched, wrote, and published the historical works on which his fame is based. Learning that William Hickling Prescott was writing a biography of the Spanish king Philip II, a figure Motley would have to treat in his history of Holland, Motley offered to abandon his project; but Prescott volunteered to share source materials with Motley, and Motley continued his investigations. In 1851 he and his family commenced a five-year stay abroad, during which Motley worked with archival materials in Berlin, Dresden, The Hague, Brussels, and Paris. In 1856 he published at his own expense the three-volume *The Rise of the Dutch Republic: A History*. The work deals with the history of the Netherlands from the abdication of the Holy Roman Emperor Charles V in 1556 to the assassination of William I "the Silent" of Orange in 1584. Motley tells the story as a battle between the Protestant Netherlands, led by his hero, William the Silent, and Catholic Spain, led by his villain, Philip II. Disregarding the large Catholic minority in the northern Netherlands during the sixteenth century, Motley claims that the seven northern provinces were peopled by freedom-loving Protestants, while the ten southern provinces, which ultimately sided with Spain, were inhabited by servile-minded Catholics. Response to the book was overwhelmingly favorable: James Anthony Froude declared in the *Westminster Review* (April 1856) that *The Rise of the Dutch Republic* "will take its place among the finest histories in this or in any language," and Bancroft, Edward Everett, G. S. Hillard, Washington Irving, Francis Lieber, and Charles Sumner praised the work in the *North American Review*. The leading Dutch historian Bakhuizen van den Brink translated the volumes into Dutch, and the French historian François Guizot edited and introduced one of the two French translations. German and Russian translations also appeared. Though Dutch historians welcomed the attention Motley's history directed to their field, one of them, Robert Jacobus Fruin, noted inaccuracies in just the passages that other audiences found particularly compelling. By 1857 more than 15,000 copies of *The Rise of the Dutch Republic* had been sold in London; American and British editions continued to appear until 1908.

Spending the winter of 1856–1857 in Boston, Motley participated in founding *The Atlantic Monthly*, a journal aimed at encouraging the development of American literature. He contributed to the periodical's first two numbers, for November and December 1857, the article "Florentine Mosaics," which drew on his experiences in Florence the previous winter.

In 1858 Motley returned to his archival research in Europe, and by the next year he had outlined his *History of the United Netherlands*. The work, the first two volumes of which were published in 1860 and the final two in 1867, begins in 1584 with the seven northern provinces fighting Spain without their fallen leader, William the Silent, and continues through the recognition of Dutch independence in the Twelve Years' Truce of 1609. The narrative has less dramatic unity than *The Rise of the Dutch Republic*, as Motley widens his scope to describe such matters as how Spain divided its attentions between wars with the Dutch provinces and with Henry IV of France and the English defeat of the Spanish Armada. Motley explained his conception of the volumes in a 4 March 1859 letter to F. H. Underwood: "the history of the United Provinces is not at all a provincial history. It is the history of European liberty. Without the struggle of Holland and England against Spain, all Europe might have been Catholic and Spanish." For Motley, Holland was the model for the rise of religious and political liberty throughout the Western world. For a year following the publication of the first two volumes, articles in the *London Quarterly Review*, the *Edinburgh Review*, and *Blackwood's Magazine* praised Motley's historical research and vivid descriptions; Dutch scholars

Motley's wife, Mary Benjamin Motley (from Susan Margaret Stackpole St. John Mildmay and Herbert St. John Mildmay, eds., John Lothrop Motley and His Family: Further Letters and Records, *1910)*

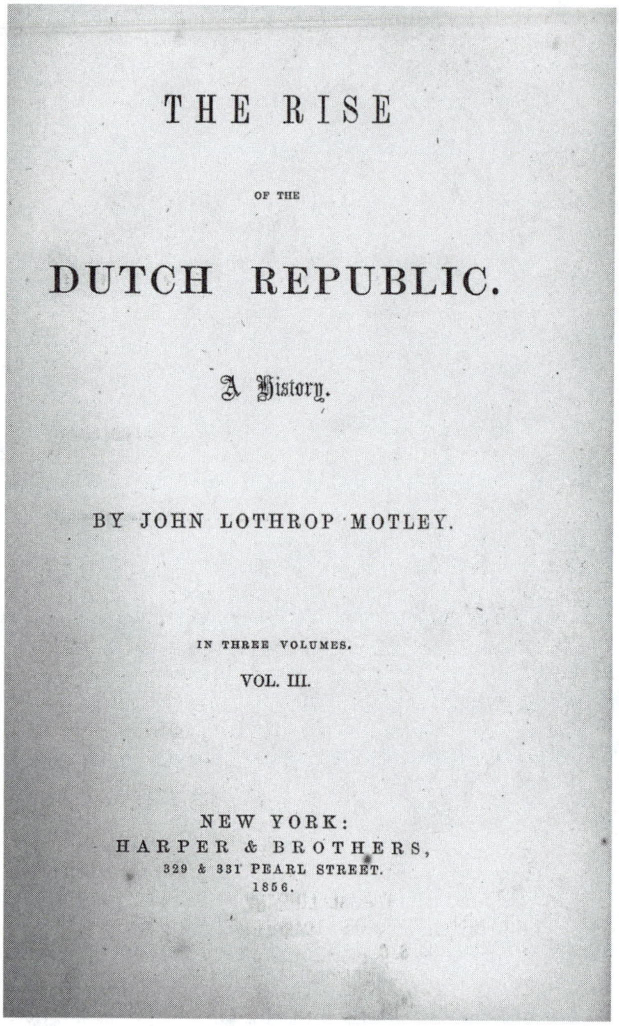
THE RISE

OF THE

DUTCH REPUBLIC.

A History.

BY JOHN LOTHROP MOTLEY.

IN THREE VOLUMES.

VOL. III.

NEW YORK:
HARPER & BROTHERS,
329 & 331 PEARL STREET.
1856.

Title page for the final volume of Motley's history of the Netherlands from 1556 to 1584

lauded the work, as well. American and British editions continued to appear until 1904.

Publication of the third and fourth volumes of the *History of the United Netherlands* was delayed for seven years because Motley was preoccupied with his next diplomatic post, which resulted from the outbreak of the American Civil War. The war began on 12 April 1861 with the Confederate shelling of Fort Sumter in Charleston Harbor, South Carolina; the Union surrendered the fort to the Confederates after thirty-four hours of bombardment. Motley responded with two letters that were published on 23 and 24 May in *The Times* (London) and republished later that year in pamphlet form as *Causes of the Civil War in America.* Motley had heard Europeans express sympathy for the Confederacy, and he wanted to garner their support for the Northern cause. The letters emphasize the importance of preserving the Union and eliminating slavery. They led President Abraham Lincoln to appoint Motley minister to Austria in August 1861; he resigned in 1867 when the U.S. government questioned his integrity because George W. McCrackin, whom Motley did not know, falsely accused him of making derogatory public comments about President Andrew Johnson. Motley then saw the final two volumes of the *History of the United Netherlands* to print.

In the fall of 1868 Motley gave two speeches. "Four Questions for the People, at the Presidential Election," delivered to the Parker Fraternity in Boston's Music Hall on 20 October, was a campaign speech on behalf of Ulysses S. Grant. Motley asserted that the United States had endured the Civil War because "it was founded on the rock of equal rights," an ideal to which, as a sort of missionary country, it would guide other nations. He acknowledged and even glorified the internal tumult that arises with equal rights: "Party spirit is always rife, and in such vivid, excitable, disputatious communities as ours are, and I trust always will be, it is the very soul of freedom. To those who reflect upon the means and end of popular government, nothing seems more stupid than in grand generalities to deprecate party spirit." In "Historic Progress and American Democracy," delivered to the New York Historical Society on 16 December, Motley credited Germany as the primary generator of European and American culture, argued that history reveals a law of progress toward freedom and democracy, and claimed that the American democracy was the culmination of that progress to date.

On the advice of Motley's friend Sumner, who was chairman of the Senate Foreign Affairs Committee, President Grant appointed Motley minister to Great Britain in the spring of 1869. Asked to resign in July 1870 after Sumner and Grant disagreed over the annexation of Santo Domingo, Motley refused to relinquish his post until he was recalled in November. He did research at The Hague in 1871 and part of 1872, returning to England in ill health. His final two volumes of Dutch history, *The Life and Death of John of Barneveld,* covering the period from 1609 to 1623, appeared in 1874. Motley portrays Johan van Oldenbarnevelt as the advocate of religious tolerance and Prince Maurice of Nassau, the son of William the Silent, as the intolerant villain who executed Oldenbarnevelt, his former chief adviser, in 1619. Modern critics contend that the bitter tone in the text reflects Motley's frustrations over his own treatment by the U.S. government in his diplomatic posts. The work received laudatory reviews in the *London Quarterly* and the *Edinburgh*

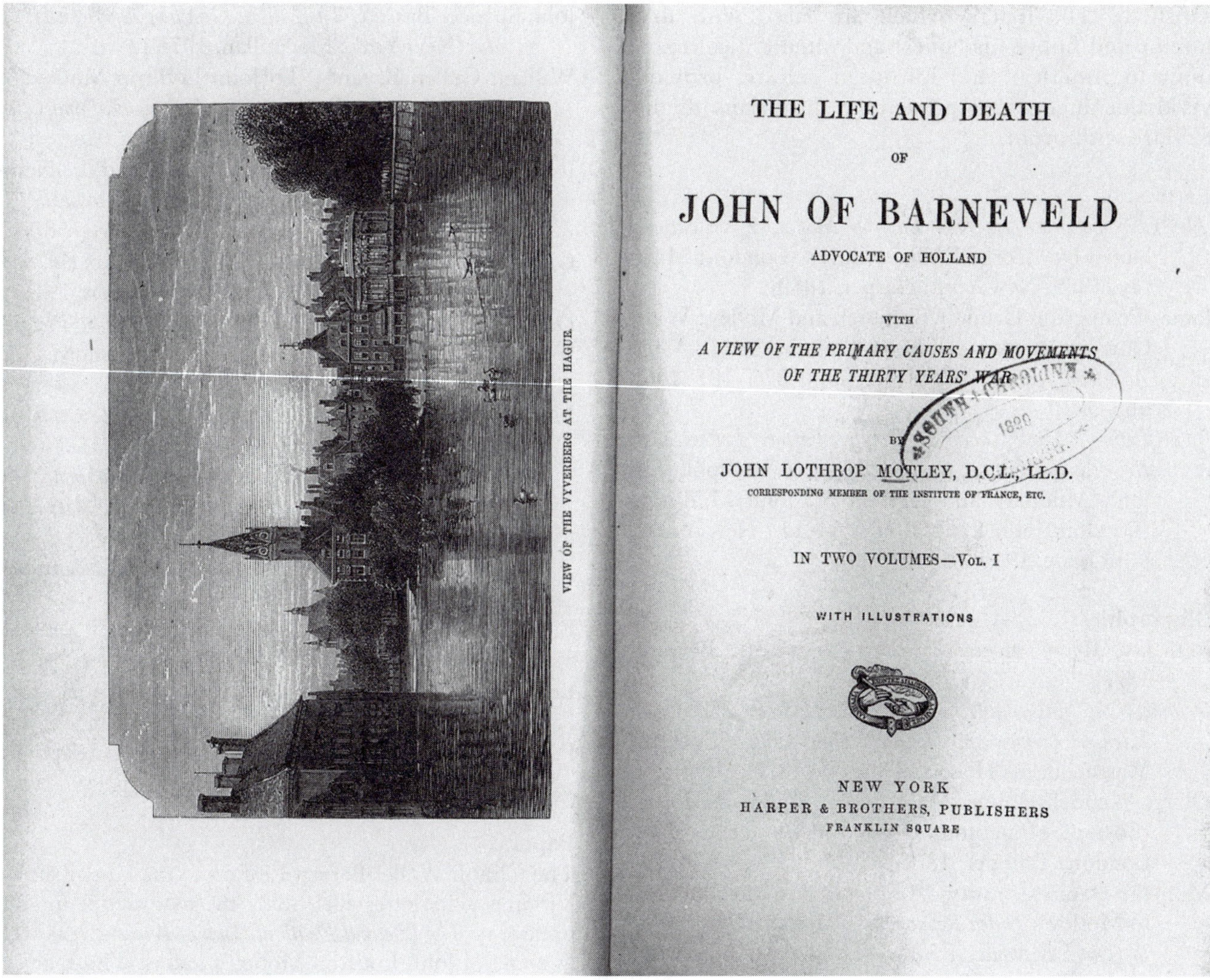

Frontispiece and title page for the last part of Motley's history of the Netherlands, covering the period from 1609 to 1623

Review, and these volumes, like the previous seven, continued to be republished until 1904.

Motley was shattered by his wife's death on 31 December 1874. He made one more trip to the United States in the summer and fall of 1875; then he returned to England, where his daughters lived. He planned to continue his history of the Netherlands by treating the Thirty Years' War, but ill health prevented him from doing so.

Motley received many honorary degrees: doctorates of laws from New York University, Harvard University, and the Universities of Oxford, Cambridge, and Leiden; a doctorate of literature from New York University; and a Ph.D. from the University of Groningen. He was a member of the historical societies of Massachusetts, Minnesota, New York, Rhode Island, Maryland, Tennessee, New Jersey, Utrecht, and Leiden; the American Academy of Arts and Sciences; the American Philosophical Society; the Royal Society of Antiquaries; the Athenaeum Club of London; the Royal Academy of Arts and Sciences of Amsterdam; the French Institute Academy of Moral and Political Sciences; and the Academy of Arts and Sciences of St. Petersburg. He died of a stroke on 29 May 1877 and was buried next to his wife in Kensal Green Cemetery outside London.

Both as a diplomat and as an historian, John Lothrop Motley was sustained by his vision of the inevitability of the progress of political and religious freedom. On 4 January 1854 he had expressed in a letter to Christina Forbes a sentiment that made its way into the preface of *The Rise of the Dutch Republic:* "If ten people in the world hate despotism a little more and love civil and religious liberty a little better in consequence of what I have written, I shall be satisfied." His letters, which are laced with dry humor and full of his honest and often critical reactions to American and European culture, provide vivid documents that present-day historians might explore with profit.

Letters:

The Correspondence of John Lothrop Motley, 2 volumes, edited by George William Curtis (London: Murray, 1889; New York: Harper, 1889);

James Pemberton Grund, "Bismarck and Motley: With Correspondence till Now Unpublished," *North American Review,* 167 (1898): 360–376, 481–496, 569–572;

John Lothrop Motley and his Family: Further Letters and Records, edited by Susan Margaret Stackpole St. John Mildmay and Herbert St. John Mildmay (London: John Lane, Bodley Head / New York: John Lane, 1910).

Biographies:

John Jay, *Motley's Appeal to History* (New York: Barnes, 1877);

Tribute of the Massachusetts Historical Society to the Memory of Edmund Quincy and John Lothrop Motley (Boston: Massachusetts Historical Society, 1877);

Oliver Wendell Holmes, *John Lothrop Motley: A Memoir* (Boston: Houghton, Osgood, 1879 [i.e., 1878]; London: Trübner, 1878);

Moncure Daniel Conway, "A Biographical Introduction to Motley's *Dutch Republic,*" in Motley's *The Rise of the Dutch Republic: A History* (London & New York: George Bell, 1904);

Henry Cabot Lodge, "Some Early Memories," *Scribner's Magazine,* 53 (June 1913): 714–729;

Sister M. Claire Lynch, *The Diplomatic Mission of John Lothrop Motley to Austria, 1861–1867* (Washington, D.C.: Catholic University of America Press, 1944);

Joseph Guberman, *The Life of John Lothrop Motley* (The Hague: Martinus Nijhoff, 1973).

References:

Peter Anton, *Masters in History: Gibbon, Grote, Macaulay, Motley* (Edinburgh: Macniven & Wallace, 1880);

John Spencer Bassett, *The Middle Group of American Historians* (New York: Macmillan, 1917);

William Cullen Bryant, "To John Lothrop Motley: A Poem," in *Atlas Essays, No. 2: Biographical and Critical* (New York: Barnes, 1877);

John L. Edwards, "John Lothrop Motley and the Netherlands," *Bijdragen en Mededelingen Betreffende de Geschiedenis der Nederlanden,* 97 (1982): 561–588;

George Peabody Gooch, *History and Historians in the Nineteenth Century* (London: Longmans, Green, 1913);

David Levin, *History as Romantic Art: Bancroft, Prescott, Motley and Parkman* (Stanford, Cal.: Stanford University Press, 1959);

Meyers and Company, Booksellers, London, *Catalogue of Books from the Library of John Lothrop Motley . . . Mostly with His Autograph Signature or Bookplate, and Including Many Inscribed Presentation Copies, Americana, etc., Just Purchased from the Family, together with Some Rare Early Maps of America and Holland* (London: Meyers, 1932);

E. M. Tilton, "Holmes and His Critic Motley," *American Literature,* 36 (January 1965): 463–474;

Leon Henry Vincent, *American Literary Masters* (Boston: Houghton, Mifflin, 1906), pp. 359–376;

P. J. Wexler, "Motley Datings," *American Speech,* 64 (Spring 1989): 89–94.

Papers:

The Clifton Waller Barrett Library at the University of Virginia, Charlottesville, holds the manuscript for the preface to *The Life and Death of John of Barneveld,* as well as some of John Lothrop Motley's letters. The University of California, Berkeley, has a portfolio of letters. The Houghton Library at Harvard University has the manuscript for Motley's essay on Goethe. Letters from Motley to George Henry Gordon and Henry Cabot Lodge are among the papers of those individuals held by the Massachusetts Historical Society, Boston. Lincoln Memorial University Library, Harrogate, Tennessee, has some of Motley's correspondence with Cassius Marcellus Clay, whose papers it houses. The Concord Free Public Library Special Collections department has the publisher's manuscript of Motley's address on the 1868 presidential election, with Motley's emendations and deletions.

Andrews Norton

(31 December 1786 – 18 September 1853)

Robert D. Habich
Ball State University

BOOKS: *At the Ordination of Rev. Samuel Cary, King's Chapel, Boston, Jan. 1st, 1809* (N.p., 1809);

A Defence of Liberal Christianity (Cambridge, Mass.: William Hilliard, 1812);

A Discourse on Religious Education (Boston: Wells & Lilly, 1818);

Inaugural Discourse, Delivered Before the University in Cambridge, August 10, 1819 (Cambridge, Mass.: Hilliard & Metcalf, 1819);

Review of "Letters to the Rev. Wm. E. Channing, Containing Remarks on His Sermon, Recently Preached and Published at Baltimore. By Moses Stuart, Associate Professor of Sac. Literature in the Theological Sem. Andover" (Boston: Wells & Lilly, 1819);

A Statement of Reasons for Not Believing the Doctrines of the Trinitarians Respecting the Nature of God, and the Person of Christ, Occasioned by Professor Stuart's Letters to Mr. Channing (Boston: Wells & Lilly, 1819);

Thoughts on True and False Religion (Boston: Wells & Lilly, 1820);

Address Delivered Before the University in Cambridge, at the Interment of Professor Frisbie, July XII, MDCCCXXII (Cambridge, Mass.: Hilliard & Metcalf, 1822);

A Review of Professor Frisbie's Inaugural Address (Cambridge, Mass.: Hilliard & Metcalf, 1823);

Remarks on a Report of a Committee of the Overseers of Harvard College, Proposing Certain Changes, Relating to the Instruction and Discipline of the College (Cambridge, Mass.: Hilliard & Metcalf, 1824);

Speech Delivered before the Overseers of Harvard College, February 3, 1825, in Behalf of the Resident Instructers of the College (Boston: Cummings, Hilliard, 1825);

Review of a Sermon Delivered at New York, Dec. 7, 1826 by William Ellery Channing (Boston: Isaac R. Butts, 1826);

A Review of Men and Manners in America (London: J. Miller, 1834);

The Evidences of the Genuineness of the Gospels, volume 1 (Boston: J. B. Russell, 1837); volumes 2–3 (Cambridge, Mass.: John Owen, 1844);

Andrews Norton (bust by Shobal Vail Clevenger, circa 1839; Society for the Preservation of Antiquities, Boston)

A Discourse on the Latest Form of Infidelity; Delivered at the Request of the "Association of the Alumni of the Cambridge Theological School," on the 19th of July, 1839 (Cambridge, Mass.: John Owen, 1839);

Remarks on a Pamphlet Entitled "'The Latest Form of Infidelity' Examined" (Cambridge, Mass.: John Owen, 1839);

Additions Made in the Second Edition of the First Volume of Norton's Evidences of the Genuineness of the Gospels (Cambridge, Mass.: John Owen, 1846);

Additions Made in the Second and Third Volumes of Norton's Evidences of the Genuineness of the Gospels (Cambridge, Mass.: G. Nichols / Boston: W. Crosby, 1848);

Tracts Concerning Christianity (Cambridge, Mass.: J. Bartlett, 1852);
Verses (Boston, 1853);
Internal Evidences of the Genuineness of the Gospels (Boston: Little, Brown, 1855);
The Pentateuch and its Relation to the Jewish and Christian Dispensations, edited by John James Tayler (London: Longman, Green, Longman, Roberts & Green, 1863).

OTHER: *General Repository and Review,* periodical edited by Norton (Cambridge, Mass.: W. Hilliard, January 1812 - April 1813);
Levi Frisbie, *A Collection of the Miscellaneous Writings of Professor Frisbie, with Some Notice of His Life and Character,* selected, with a biographical introduction, by Norton (Boston: Cummings, Hilliard, 1823);
Felicia Dorothea Hemans, *The League of the Alps, The Siege of Valencia, The Vespers of Palermo, and Other Poems,* publication arranged and advertisement written by Norton (Boston: Hilliard, Gray, Little & Wilkins, 1826);
Hemans, *The Forest Sanctuary; and Other Poems,* publication arranged and advertisement written by Norton (Boston: Hilliard, Gray, Little & Wilkins, 1827);
Hemans, *Records of Woman; with Other Poems,* publication arranged and advertisement written by Norton (Boston: Hilliard, Gray, Little & Wilkins, 1828);
Select Journal of Foreign Periodical Literature, periodical edited by Norton and Charles Folsom (Boston: C. Bowen, January 1833 - October 1834);
Silvio Pellico, *My Prisons: Memoirs of Silvio Pellico,* 2 volumes, editor's note by Norton in volume 1 (Cambridge, Mass.: C. Folsom, 1836);
James W. Alexander, Albert B. Dod, and Charles Hodges, *Two Articles from the Princeton Review, Concerning the Transcendental Philosophy of the Germans and of Cousin, and its Influence on Opinion in this Country,* introduction by Norton (Cambridge, Mass.: John Owen, 1840);
A Translation of the Gospels; with Notes, 2 volumes, translated by Norton (Boston: Little, Brown, 1856).

SELECTED PERIODICAL PUBLICATIONS–UNCOLLECTED: "Lord Byron's Character and Writings," *North American Review,* 21 (October 1825): 300–309;
"Recent Publications Concerning Goethe," *Select Journal of Foreign Periodical Literature,* 1 (April 1833): 250–293;
Letter, *Boston Daily Advertiser,* 5 November 1836, p. 1;
"The New School in Literature and Religion," *Boston Daily Advertiser,* 27 August 1838, p. 2.

Few figures in American literary history have been so thoroughly vilified as Andrews Norton. A liberal Unitarian polemicist, teacher of a generation of Harvard-trained ministers (including Ralph Waldo Emerson), editor of an important literary magazine, and author of a massive work of biblical scholarship, Norton has long been known by the dismissive epithet Theodore Parker used in his journals–"Pope Andrews"–for his prominent role in the so-called miracles controversy of the late 1830s. For more than a century Norton's infamy remained securely posited against the Transcendentalist writers whom he opposed; as Perry Miller wryly wrote in 1961, the controversy depicted Emerson as "the purest of white" and Norton "as black as the pit." Modern reappraisals, however, reveal Norton to be at once more consistently principled and more humanly complex than his reputation might suggest.

Andrews Norton was born in Hingham, Massachusetts, on 31 December 1786, the youngest child of Samuel and Jane Andrews Norton. A merchant and town leader, Samuel Norton was by all reports an easygoing man whose strict Calvinism had moderated; Andrews grew up in a household where Christianity was assumed but not vigorously debated. He completed his preparatory studies at the Derby Academy in Hingham and entered Harvard College as a sophomore, graduating in 1804 as the youngest in his class.

Though he published several brief reviews and translations in the *Literary Miscellany* (Cambridge) soon after he graduated, Norton's vocation remained uncertain for nearly a decade. After four years of private study at Cambridge and in his father's house, he accepted a pastorate in Augusta, Massachusetts (now Augusta, Maine), in 1809, only to resign from the pulpit in less than a month; this appointment was his first and last as a minister. Norton took a position as a tutor at Bowdoin College but left within a year; he then became tutor of mathematics at Harvard, but a year later he resigned from that position as well.

In 1812 Norton began his first serious venture as a writer, establishing the *General Repository and Review* in Cambridge. More important in denominational than in literary history, the magazine was, in Lilian Handlin's words, "an expression of liberalism's stormy adolescence," and it provided a platform for the sustained defenses of rational Unitarianism that characterized Norton's career. The *General Repository* lasted only two years, but it apparently gave Norton sufficient visibility to be offered a permanent appointment at Harvard. Beginning in 1813 he served concurrently as librarian (through

1821) and Dexter Lecturer on Biblical Criticism. In 1819 Norton was appointed Dexter Professor of Sacred Literature at the newly founded Divinity School at Harvard, where he taught that generation of ministers soon to be known as the New England Transcendentalists: Emerson, Parker, George Ripley, James Freeman Clarke, and William Henry Channing, among others. By all accounts an austere, reserved man, Norton was an intimidating presence in the classroom who quickly passed into student legend. When he entered heaven, so one joke had it, he would sniff, "It is a *very* miscellaneous crowd."

In the 1820s Norton at last achieved stability in his career and personal life. In 1821 he married Catharine Eliot (born on 7 September 1793), the daughter of the prominent Boston merchant Samuel Eliot, and moved to Shady Hill, a fifty-acre estate in Cambridge. Four of the Nortons' six children survived infancy: three daughters, Louisa (born in 1823), Jane (born in 1824), and Grace (born in 1834); and a son, Charles Eliot (1827–1908), who went on to become Emerson's friend, Thomas Carlyle's editor, and a president of Harvard. But Norton, whose appointment to the Dexter Professorship was nearly derailed because of his combative defenses of liberal religion, gravitated again toward controversy. In the 1820s debate raged over the conduct of Harvard students, especially after riots in 1823, in which fully half of the senior class was expelled. For Norton the issue boiled down to responsible moral governance. When a vacancy opened up on the Harvard governing body in 1824, he and Edward Everett brought forth a bold plan to place control of the college with the faculty. At the same time, the superintendence of the Divinity School–always an awkward arrangement between the college and the private Society for the Promotion of Theological Education–was raised as an issue, and Norton again proposed greater control by the faculty. His proposals failed in both instances. But his commitment to the responsible stewardship of education was established. It surfaced again during the miracles controversy of the 1830s.

Norton divided his energies between institutional politics and literary work. Beginning in the mid 1820s, he reviewed occasionally for periodicals, edited the essays and poetry of his Harvard colleague Levi Frisbie, and supervised the American edition of the works of the British poet Felicia Hemans. Similarly, in 1836 Norton arranged the American publication of the Italian patriot Silvio Pellico's memoir of his incarceration in a Milanese prison. Norton's journeyman work on these projects, disparate though they are, indicates a common purpose. By bringing

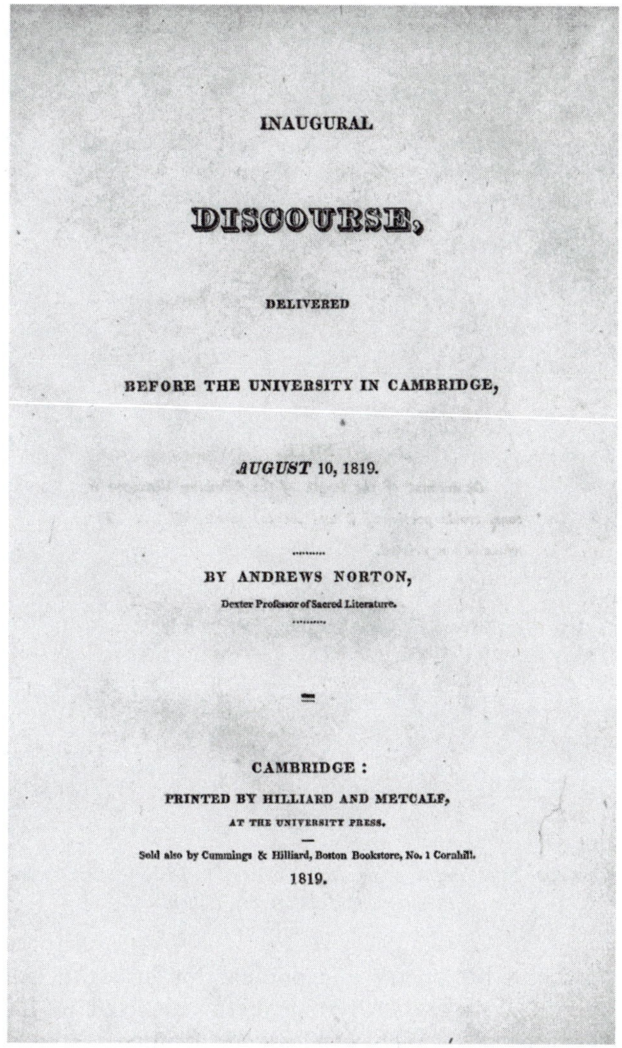

INAUGURAL

DISCOURSE,

DELIVERED

BEFORE THE UNIVERSITY IN CAMBRIDGE,

AUGUST 10, 1819.

BY ANDREWS NORTON,

Dexter Professor of Sacred Literature.

CAMBRIDGE:

PRINTED BY HILLIARD AND METCALF,

AT THE UNIVERSITY PRESS.

Sold also by Cummings & Hilliard, Boston Bookstore, No. 1 Cornhill.

1819.

Title page for the address Norton delivered when he became one of the first professors at the new Harvard Divinity School (Collection of Joel Myerson)

to print Frisbie's essays on the "Moral Constitution of Man," Hemans's polite and sentimental verse, and Pellico's popular story of patient suffering and Christian forgiveness, Norton demonstrated his growing conviction that literary figures, like others of public influence, had a moral responsibility to their readers–and that responsible critics were bound to point readers toward "improving" literature as well as to expose authors whose work was subversive of good character. His essay on George Gordon, Lord Byron, published in the *North American Review* of October 1825, is a case in point.

None of the British Romantic poets was more vexing to the reading public than Byron, whose death in 1824 brought out many reminiscences and reappraisals. Almost universally recognized for the

Catharine Eliot Norton, whom Norton married in 1821 (Society for the Preservation of Antiquities, Boston)

power of his poetry and popular for his exoticism and the rebellious "Byronic hero" depicted in his verse, he was widely condemned for immorality. In some ways Norton's review is conventional, praising Byron's power to create "deep tones of feeling, which dwelt upon the mind, and called forth strong sympathy" while pointing out the poet's "lamentable defects of character." What distinguishes Norton's criticism from the general run of periodical reviews at this time, which tended to be summative with extensive excerpts, is his detailed criticism of Byron's prosody: his imprecise diction, use of archaic terms, defective similes, questionable delineation of characters, and lack of cohesion. The early cantos of *Childe Harold's Pilgrimage* (1812–1818) may capture the "moral purity and elevation of sentiment" of a "mind desolate and unbroken," Norton writes, but Byron's libertinism shackled him, as a man and as a poet. Thus, Norton dismisses *Don Juan* (1819–1824) as "mere drollery" and Byron's poetry generally as "private confessions" of the author's own "vulgar misery." Finally, for Norton the critic, bad art, like bad thinking, is the worse for its public consequences. A "blind Cyclops, aimless and without purpose," the faithless Byron represented more than an aesthetic failure: his seductive poetry "confused and weakened the moral sentiments of his admirers."

Norton's disenchantment with Harvard governance, combined perhaps with a newfound attention to literary work, hastened his decision to leave the Divinity School faculty. In 1828 he took a leave for reasons of health and spent six months in England, where he met Hemans, Robert Southey, William Wordsworth, and Sir Walter Scott. Upon his return Norton resigned the Dexter Professorship and severed his formal connection with Harvard.

If Norton expected to retire quietly at Shady Hill and pursue the life of the independent scholar, he was shortly to be disappointed, for the explosion of interest in foreign–particularly German–writers signaled a disturbing trend that pulled him once again into the public arena. As his review of Byron reveals, he worried about the corrosive effects of indiscriminate reading on a public too naive to understand or too willing to be led astray. In an effort to direct public taste, Norton founded in 1833 *The Select Journal of Foreign Periodical Literature,* which he conducted for two years with his co-editor, Charles Folsom. Filled with reprints from British and French magazines, *The Select Journal of Foreign Periodical Literature* included generous selections of poetry (Hemans's work appeared, not surprisingly, more than any other poet), excerpts of fiction (notably by Victor Hugo and George Sand), and works of history. In their selections and their editorial commentary, as Frank Luther Mott notes in his *History of American Magazines 1741–1850* (1966), Norton and Folsom were "notably conservative."

While Norton's editorial voice in *The Select Journal of Foreign Periodical Literature* is generally confined to prefatory comments, his omnibus review of "Recent Publications Concerning Goethe" in the April 1833 issue is significant, not only for its vitriol but also for the way it foreshadows his later comments on the Transcendentalists. Norton records his amazement at the "despotic" influence of Johann Wolfgang von Goethe in Germany, given the negligible literary quality of his work. (He finds *The Sorrows of Young Werther* [1774] "a book too silly to cry over," for instance.) Largely, though, Norton looks sarcastically at Goethe's admirers, who are convinced of "the blessed era to be brought about by this most extraordinary man." Chief among these admirers is the unnamed author of two recent appreciations, Carlyle, who in Norton's hands receives one of his earliest treatments in America as an exemplar of the "Germanized" school of writing in Europe:

Shady Hill, the Nortons' Cambridge estate

> It is distinguished by its tone of unbounded assumption. Its writers speak forth only mysteries and oracles, and this, often in language as obscure and barbarous, as that in which the ancient mysteries and oracles were involved. They are priests of some one or other new revelation from nature to mankind, which, though it cannot yet be fully understood, is to effect wonderful things; and especially to sweep away all old notions of philosophy, morals, and religion.

Just as Norton's critique of Goethe and Carlyle recalls his earlier review of Byron, so it looks forward–almost verbatim–to his strident condemnation of the American Transcendental writers.

Norton was convinced, at least in 1833, that widespread admiration for things German in the United States was "as improbable as it would be disastrous." But several years later he was far less sure, when faced with the enthusiasm among younger Unitarian ministers for the Germanic school of biblical "higher criticism." Higher criticism placed the scriptures in cultural and historical contexts; ironically, it was the tool Norton himself and other liberal Unitarians had employed earlier to open up the Bible to non-Calvinist interpretations. By the middle 1830s, however, higher criticism threatened scriptural authority in ways Norton found dangerous, particularly the key precept of the historicity of miracles–the belief that biblical miracles validated belief in Christianity. Suddenly, all doctrine seemed interpretable and relative. Norton the rigorous scholar decried the tendency toward slack thinking, and Norton the educational steward brooded over the irresponsibility and bad taste of ministers who speculated about religious fundamentals in potentially destructive ways.

Even worse, for Norton, these speculations were appearing in Unitarian magazines. When his former student Ripley reviewed James Martineau's *Rationale of Religious Enquiry* (1836) in the November 1836 issue of *The Christian Examiner,* Norton was no longer able to remain silent. The *Boston Daily Advertiser* for 5 November carried an angry letter from Norton directed at Ripley's audacity (and that of *The Christian Examiner*) in presenting dangerous speculations about miracles without regard to "the interests of truth and goodness." Ripley replied in the *Boston Daily Advertiser* four days later, on 9 November, with as succinct a summary of the miracles debate as was ever published: "The evidence of miracles depends upon a previous belief in Christianity, rather than the evidence of Christianity on a previous belief in miracles." But, Ripley went on, the real issue was the limits of Unitarian tolerance, revealed by Norton's desire to "place shackles upon the press and to drown the voice of discussion by the cry of alarm."

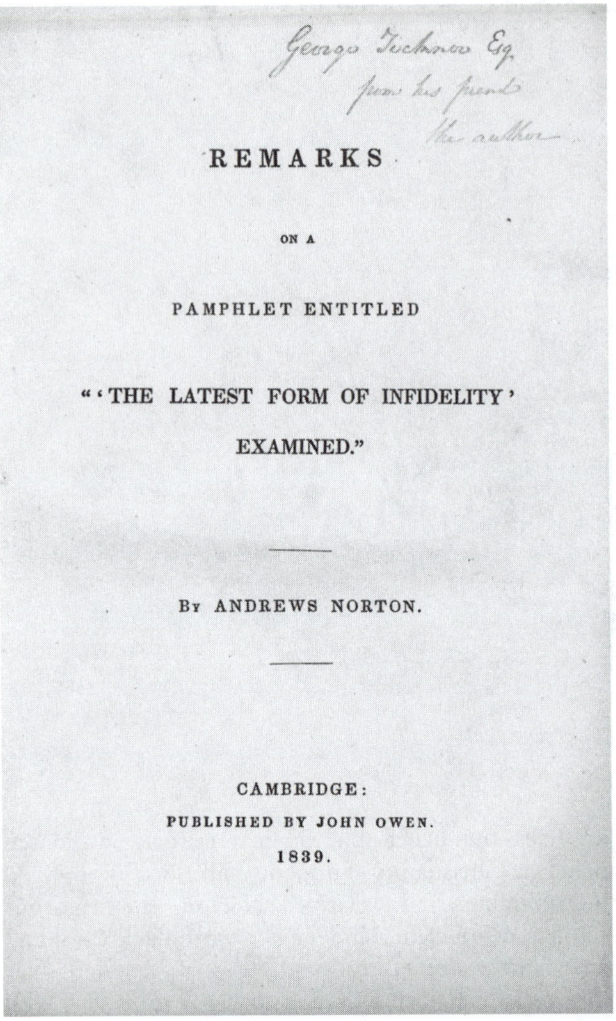
George Ticknor Esq.
from his friend
the author

REMARKS

ON A

PAMPHLET ENTITLED

"'THE LATEST FORM OF INFIDELITY'

EXAMINED."

By ANDREWS NORTON.

CAMBRIDGE:

PUBLISHED BY JOHN OWEN.

1839.

Title page for one of Norton's anti-Transcendentalist salvos in his "pamphlet war" with his former student George Ripley (Collection of Joel Myerson)

Thus, Norton found himself in the middle of the controversy that solidified his reputation as the antagonist of Transcendentalism. With the publication in 1836 of Emerson's *Nature,* Orestes Brownson's *New Views of Christianity, Society, and the Church,* and Ripley's *Discourses on the Philosophy of Religion,* Norton had ample reason for concern. His answer to the "heretical" speculations of these writers was the first volume of his magnum opus, *The Evidences of the Genuineness of the Gospels* (1837). A landmark in American biblical scholarship, the volume develops an empirical defense of Christian miracles and a spirited rebuttal to Transcendental speculations about the inward validation of religious faith. Although massive, scholarly, and carefully modulated in its tone, *The Evidences of the Genuineness of the Gospels* was utterly irrelevant to the Transcendental group, for Ripley and the others never denied the historicity of miracles, only the need for them. If anything, Norton's book merely cemented his connection with reactionary Unitarianism, a position the Transcendentalist editor Clarke began calling "Nortonism."

Events in New England were moving quickly beyond issues of biblical criticism. In the summer of 1838 the Boston "freethinker" Abner Kneeland was tried in the civil courts and jailed for blasphemy. The Harvard Philanthropic Society, a student organization originally intended to support Unitarian missionaries, threatened to bring an abolitionist speaker to campus against the wishes of the faculty. In his *Western Messenger* Clarke was openly criticizing Unitarians such as Norton for intolerance. The young Jones Very, a Harvard tutor and protégé of Emerson, embarrassed the Divinity School faculty publicly by his mercurial behavior and his insistence that he spoke the revealed word of Christ. When Emerson delivered his incendiary address to the Harvard divinity students on 15 July 1838 proclaiming historical Christianity dead and advocating a passionate relationship to God rather than scholarly attention to the "person of Jesus," it must have seemed to Norton the culmination of a decades-long erosion of intellectual responsibility in New England.

Norton's famous response to Emerson's Divinity School address, "The New School in Literature and Religion," was published in the 27 August 1838 *Boston Daily Advertiser.* (He had long ago abandoned hope of publishing in the more traditional Unitarian periodicals.) The "New School" essay charts an "insurrection of folly" overtaking New England with ignorance, arrogance, irrationality, bad taste, "Germanism," and obscure language. While Norton castigates Emerson for his "incoherent rhapsody," he dismisses Emerson's views as "a matter of minor concern." For Norton the central issue was "how it happened, that religion has been insulted by the delivery of those opinions in the Chapel of the Divinity College."

Norton's second response came the following July, in an address before the alumni of the Divinity School (at the First Church, Cambridge, not in Divinity Hall). In *A Discourse on the Latest Form of Infidelity* (1839) Norton concentrates the full force of his rhetoric on the "depraving literature and noxious speculations which flow in among us from Europe" and carefully develops the conventional Unitarian case for the necessity of historical miracles: "Nothing is left that can be called Christianity, if its miraculous character be denied." Norton rallies his old arguments against the fallacy of intuition and in favor of the need to confirm faith empirically, once again claiming that "there is no controlling power of intellect among us." Thus, "men throw out their opinions rashly, reserving to themselves the liberty of correcting them, if they are wrong."

Published reaction to Norton's discourse was lukewarm, even in the Unitarian press; privately, the Transcendentalist Parker called it "a complete failure." Ironically, *A Discourse on the Latest Form of Infidelity* exacerbated the controversy it was designed to put to rest. By so scrupulously raising the arguments in favor of historical Christianity, Norton invited more debate about miracles and the methods of biblical higher criticism. In October 1839 Ripley's *"The Latest Form of Infidelity" Examined* was published; Norton answered him a month later with *Remarks on a Pamphlet Entitled "'The Latest Form of Infidelity' Examined"* (1839). Ripley countered with two more pamphlets, and Parker–writing as "Levi Blodgett"–weighed in with *The Previous Question between Mr. Andrews Norton and His Alumni* (1840).

Norton gave up the "pamphlet war" in 1840, exhausted by a controversy that had become vicious and personal. (Brownson caricatured Norton in *The Boston Quarterly Review* of July 1840: "It is said that he usually sits in a room with the shutters closed, which has the double effect of keeping the light out and the darkness in.") Moreover, Norton had been privately negotiating a return to the Divinity School faculty to replace the retiring dean, John Gorham Palfrey. When the arrangement fell through, Norton washed his hands of the school and returned once again to a life of scholarship at Shady Hill. The publication of volumes 2 and 3 of *The Evidences of the Genuineness of the Gospels* (1844) signaled a belated close to Norton's career as a polemicist. *Tracts Concerning Christianity,* a gathering of his religious writings, was published in 1852, and a slight collection of poetry, *Verses,* was printed in 1853. On 18 September 1853 Norton died at his summer retreat in Newport, Rhode Island.

Had Norton never engaged the Transcendentalists in debate, his editing of *The Select Journal of Foreign Periodical Literature* would likely have earned him a footnote in American letters. His reviews of literary works, though few in number, were powerfully written and closely attentive to texts and authors. At their best, they revealed a perceptive aesthetic sense that set them apart from the polite but vacant excerpting that passed for literary analysis in the magazines of his time. Like Margaret Fuller a generation later, Norton in his periodical criticism tried to educate a readership–in Norton's case, to the dangers of aesthetic nonsense and moral license. The distinction between creative and religious writing would have made little sense to him. With many of his contemporaries, he accepted the broad definition of literature as outlined by Dr. William Ellery Channing in his "Remarks on National Literature" (1830): "all the writings of superior minds, be the subjects what they may."

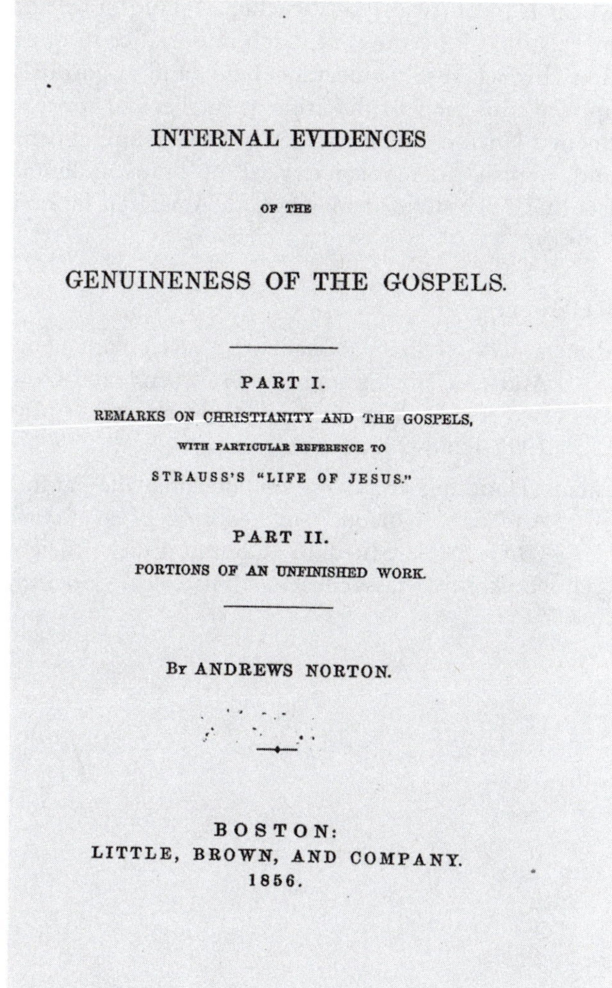
INTERNAL EVIDENCES

OF THE

GENUINENESS OF THE GOSPELS.

PART I.

REMARKS ON CHRISTIANITY AND THE GOSPELS,

WITH PARTICULAR REFERENCE TO

STRAUSS'S "LIFE OF JESUS."

PART II.

PORTIONS OF AN UNFINISHED WORK.

BY ANDREWS NORTON.

BOSTON:
LITTLE, BROWN, AND COMPANY.
1856.

Title page for one of several works in which Norton asserted the historical truth of the miracles described in the New Testament

Norton's notorious role in the Transcendental controversy, while it called forth his most impassioned rhetoric, is important chiefly for showing how consistently he applied two principles to Channing's expanded definition of literature: first, that writers have a moral responsibility not only to live with rectitude but also to write with an eye toward the public good; and second, that critics and scholars must adjudicate on moral, not merely aesthetic grounds, mediating between potentially subversive authors and their vulnerable reading public. What Norton says in his review of Goethe applies equally well to his position on fiction, poetry, social commentary, and history: "It is only when the writer of such works is put forward as a teacher of philosophy and morals, that it becomes of much importance to question his claims." Sincerely held and rigorously applied, this view of the critic as intellectual steward opened Norton to the charges of censorship, elitism, and "popish" antagonism toward the Transcendentalists that have defined his place in American literary history.

References:

Robert D. Habich, "Emerson's Reluctant Foe: Andrews Norton and the Transcendental Controversy," *New England Quarterly,* 65 (June 1992): 208–237;

Lilian Handlin, "Babylon est delenda–the Young Andrews Norton," in *American Unitarianism, 1805–1865,* edited by Conrad Edick Wright (Boston: Massachusetts Historical Society/ Northeastern University Press, 1989), pp. 53–85;

William R. Hutchison, *The Transcendentalist Ministers* (New Haven: Yale University Press, 1959);

William Newell, "Andrews Norton," *Christian Examiner,* 55 (November 1853): 425–452;

Charles Eliot Norton, *Letters of Charles Eliot Norton,* 2 volumes, edited by Sara Norton and M. A. DeWolfe Howe (Boston & New York: Houghton Mifflin, 1913);

David Robinson, *The Unitarians and the Universalists* (Westport, Conn.: Greenwood Press, 1985).

Papers:

The largest collection of Andrews Norton's papers, including correspondence, notebooks, and reading lists, is at the Houghton Library, Harvard University. Other important papers are in the Andover-Harvard Theological Library.

Charles Eliot Norton

(16 November 1827 – 21 October 1908)

M. David Samson
Worcester Polytechnic Institute

See also the Norton entry in *DLB 64: American Literary Critics and Scholars, 1850–1880.*

BOOKS: *Considerations on Some Recent Social Theories,* anonymous (Boston: Little, Brown, 1853);

Notes of Travel and Study in Italy (Boston: Ticknor & Fields, 1860);

A Review of a Translation into Italian of the Commentary by Benvenuto da Imola on the Divina Commedia (Cambridge, Mass.: Printed by H. O. Houghton, 1861);

The Soldier of the Good Cause, Army Series, no. 2 (Boston: American Unitarian Association, 1861);

On the Original Portraits of Dante (Cambridge, Mass.: Privately printed at the Harvard University Press, 1865);

The Holbein Madonna (N.p.: Privately printed, 1872);

List of the Principal Books Relating to the Life and Works of Michelangelo; with Notes, edited by Justin Winsor, Bibliographical Contributions of the Library of Harvard University, no. 3 (Cambridge, Mass.: Wilson, 1878);

Historical Studies of Church-Building in the Middle Ages: Venice, Siena, Florence (New York: Harper, 1880; London: Low, Marston, Searle & Rivington, 1881);

Address at the Celebration of the Two Hundredth Anniversary of the Building of the Old Meeting-house at Hingham, on the Eighth of August, 1881 (Cambridge, Mass.: Wilson, 1882);

History of Ancient Art: Prepared by H. F. Brown and Wm. H. Wiggin, jr. from Lectures Delivered by Professor Charles Eliot Norton, at Harvard College, Cambridge, Mass., edited by Harry Fletcher Brown and William Harrison Wiggin Jr. (Boston: A. Mudge, 1891);

Rudyard Kipling: A Bibliographical Sketch (New York: Doubleday & McClure, 1899);

The Poet Gray as a Naturalist with Selections from his Notes on the Systema naturæ of Linnæus and Facsimiles of some of his Drawings (Boston: Goodspeed, 1903);

Ashfield Children's Exhibit and Prize Day, Massachusetts Civic League Leaflets, no. 2 (Boston, 1905);

A Leaf of Grass from Shady Hill: With A Review of Walt Whitman's Leaves of Grass; Written by Charles Eliot Norton in 1855 (Cambridge, Mass.: Printed at the Harvard University Press, 1928).

OTHER: *A Book of Hymns for Young Persons,* edited by Norton (Cambridge, Mass.: Bartlett, 1854);

Andrews Norton, *A Translation of the Gospels: With Notes,* edited by Norton (Boston: Little, Brown, 1854);

Dante Alighieri, *The New Life of Dante: An Essay, with Translations,* translated, with an essay, by Norton (Cambridge, Mass.: Privately printed at the Riverside Press, 1859); revised as *The New Life of*

Dante Alighieri (Boston: Ticknor & Fields, 1867; revised edition, Boston & New York: Houghton, Mifflin, 1892; revised edition, Cambridge, Mass.: Privately printed, 1906);

Andrews Norton, *The Evidences of the Genuineness of the Gospels,* edited and abridged by Norton (Boston: American Unitarian Association, 1867);

William Blake, *William Blake's Illustrations of the Book of Job: With Descriptive Letterpress, and a Sketch of the Artist's Life and Works,* edited by Norton (Boston: Osgood, 1875);

Chauncey Wright, *Philosophical Discussions,* edited, with an introduction, by Norton (New York: Holt, 1877);

Thomas Carlyle and Ralph Waldo Emerson, *The Correspondence of Thomas Carlyle and Ralph Waldo Emerson, 1834–74,* 2 volumes, edited by Norton (Boston: Osgood, 1883);

Carlyle and Emerson, *The Correspondence of Thomas Carlyle and Ralph Waldo Emerson, 1834–74: Supplementary Letters,* edited by Norton (Boston: Ticknor, 1886);

Carlyle, *Early Letters of Thomas Carlyle, 1814–1836,* 2 volumes, edited by Norton (London & New York: Macmillan, 1886);

Johann Wolfgang von Goethe and Carlyle, *Correspondence Between Goethe and Carlyle,* 2 volumes, edited by Norton (London & New York: Macmillan, 1887);

Carlyle, *Reminiscences,* 2 volumes, edited by Norton (London & New York: Macmillan, 1887);

Carlyle, *Letters of Thomas Carlyle, 1826–1836,* 2 volumes, edited by Norton (London & New York: Macmillan, 1888);

John Ruskin, *The Brantwood Edition of the Works of John Ruskin,* 20 volumes, introductions by Norton (New York: Merrill / London: George Allen, 1890–1893);

James Russell Lowell, *Latest Literary Essays and Addresses of James Russell Lowell,* edited by Norton (Cambridge, Mass.: Riverside Press, 1891);

Dante, *The Divine Comedy of Dante Alighieri,* 3 volumes, translated by Norton (Boston: Houghton, Mifflin, 1891–1892; revised, 1902);

Lowell, *The Old English Dramatists,* preface by Norton (Boston & New York: Houghton, Mifflin, 1892);

Lowell, *Letters of James Russell Lowell,* 2 volumes, edited by Norton, (New York: Harper, 1893);

George William Curtis, *Orations and Addresses of George William Curtis,* 3 volumes, edited by Norton (New York: Harper, 1894);

"Harvard," in *Four American Universities: Harvard, Princeton, Yale, Columbia* (New York: Harper, 1895), pp. 1–43;

Lowell, *Last Poems of James Russell Lowell,* edited by Norton (Boston & New York: Houghton, Mifflin, 1895);

John Donne, *The Poems of John Donne, from the Text of the Edition of 1633 revised by James Russell Lowell,* 2 volumes, preface, introduction, and notes by Norton (New York: Grolier, 1895);

Anne Bradstreet, *The Poems of Mrs. Anne Bradstreet (1612–1672); Together with Her Prose Remains,* introduction by Norton (New York: Duodecimos, 1897);

Carlyle, *Two Note-Books of Thomas Carlyle, from 23d March 1822 to 16th May 1832,* edited by Norton (New York: Grolier, 1898);

Emerson, *Letters from Ralph Waldo Emerson to a Friend, 1838–1853,* edited by Norton (Boston & New York: Houghton, Mifflin, 1899);

Ruskin, *Comments of John Ruskin on the Divina Commedia,* compiled by George P. Huntington, introduction by Norton (Boston & New York: Houghton, Mifflin, 1903);

"Address of Charles Eliot Norton," in *The Centenary of the Birth of Ralph Waldo Emerson as Observed in Concord May 25, 1903 under the Direction of the Social Circle of Concord* (Concord, Mass.: Printed at the Riverside Press for the Social Circle in Concord, 1903), pp. 45–58;

"The Intellectual and Moral Awakening of Italy," in *Aids to the Study of Dante,* compiled by Charles Allen Dinsmore (Boston & New York: Houghton, Mifflin, 1903);

Ruskin, *Letters of John Ruskin to Charles Eliot Norton,* 2 volumes, edited by Norton (Boston & New York: Houghton, Mifflin, 1904);

Donne, *The Love Poems of John Donne,* selected and edited by Norton (Boston: Houghton, Mifflin, 1905);

Henry Wadsworth Longfellow, *Henry Wadsworth Longfellow: A Sketch of His Life by Charles Eliot Norton, Together with Longfellow's Chief Biographical Poems,* edited, with an introduction, by Norton, Riverside Literature Series, no. 167 (Boston & New York: Houghton, Mifflin, 1906).

SELECTED PERIODICAL PUBLICATIONS–UNCOLLECTED: "Whitman's Leaves of Grass," anonymous, *Putnam's Magazine,* 6 (September 1855): 321–323;

"Abraham Lincoln," anonymous, *North American Review,* 100 (January 1865): 1–21;

"Mr. Emerson's Poems," anonymous, *Nation,* 4 (30 May 1867): 430–431;

"Female Suffrage and Education," anonymous, *Nation,* 4 (19 September 1867): 152;

"The Intellectual Life of America," *New Princeton Review,* 6 (November 1888): 312–324;

"James Russell Lowell," *Harper's Magazine,* 56 (May 1893): 846–857.

Charles Eliot Norton's aim throughout his career was to demonstrate how literature and art could serve as moral exemplars for the United States. Intimately connected by birth and associations to Ralph Waldo Emerson's generation, Norton worked to continue the shift in New England culture from mercantile and theological concerns to literary, intellectual, and reformist ones. His primary legacy to this earlier generation of New England writers was to preserve and publish the documents of its intellectual development, especially those of Emerson and James Russell Lowell.

Norton's friendships with Emerson and with John Ruskin, and his actions as a go-between for Emerson and Thomas Carlyle, made him an especially important witness to the contacts between American and European Romanticism. At the same time, Norton was far more pessimistic about the possibilities for human progress than the American Renaissance generation had been. Insisting that faith in self-reliance must be tempered by knowledge of European traditions of high culture, he made essential contributions to art history, classical and medieval studies, and literary scholarship in the United States. As an editor, teacher, and adviser to writers and thinkers–roles that far outweigh his own accomplishments as a writer–Norton worked to turn Emerson's legacy into a mature program of humanistic knowledge and institution-building. Despite his pessimism, Norton did a great deal to suggest how Transcendentalist goals of intellectual freedom and active idealism could be preserved into a more complex world.

Norton's family had been important in Massachusetts intellectual and religious affairs since the seventeenth century. His father, Andrews Norton, was the most eminent Unitarian man of letters in New England and the leading opponent of Transcendentalism on religious grounds, and his mother, Catherine (Eliot) Norton, came from a wealthy Boston family. Born 16 November 1827, Charles Eliot Norton grew up at the family estate in Cambridge, Shady Hill, steeped in literary and theological matters and surrounded by the intellectual celebrities of Boston. The persona Norton wore throughout his adult life–sickly, dutiful, reverent of cultural authority, and eager to please but prone to didacticism–seems to have been acquired in childhood. A famous family legend has the ten-year-old Charles on his sickbed stating that he hoped to get better so he could "live to edit Father's works." Norton began to live up to this vocation after graduating from Harvard College in 1846, helping the twenty-six-year-old Francis Parkman prepare for press his *The California and Oregon Trail: Being Sketches of Prairie and Rocky Mountain Life* (1849).

Norton as a young man (Charles Eliot Norton Papers, Houghton Library, Harvard University)

Norton's first attempt at a career was mercantile, as an employee in the counting house of the trading firm Bullard and Lee. Assisting Parkman, writing occasional reviews and essays, and operating an evening school for working boys and men made up Norton's intellectual life until he was sent to India by Bullard and Lee in 1849. Norton's travels lasted until 1851 and took him to Italy and England as well as India. What he saw on his trip, particularly the workings of the British colonial administration in India, made him acutely conscious of social inequalities and injustices. The experience also gave him an enduring love of Italy and introduced him to the literary and intellectual circles of London. His English friendships came to take in such diverse figures as Charles Dickens, William Makepeace Thackeray, Elizabeth Gaskell, Dante Gabriel Rossetti, William Morris, Matthew Arnold, A. C. Swinburne, and Charles Darwin.

Although Norton remained a businessman until 1855, his preoccupations after returning to the United States became increasingly reformist and literary. In 1853 he built two "model lodging-houses" for the poor of Boston. Nonetheless, his social and cultural outlook remained at first conservative. Norton's anonymous 1853 book *Considerations on Some Recent Social Theories*

Norton in November 1861 (Society for the Preservation of Antiquities, Boston)

condemned mass democracy as well as the socialism of Charles Fourier and Robert Owen and urged instead a program of education and charity by the enlightened elite of the United States. In that year Andrews Norton died, and his son began to "edit Father's works." The process, ultimately left unfinished, seems to have led to disillusionment with the senior Norton's theological outlook. A visit to the South Carolina plantation of the eminent Middleton family focused Norton's social ideas on the evils of slavery (although Norton feared for the moral health of slave owners far more than he regretted the enslavement of blacks). Renewed acquaintance with Emerson opened Norton to the influence of those idealist and Romantic currents his father had resisted. Norton was invited to review the first edition of Walt Whitman's *Leaves of Grass* (1855) for the September 1855 issue of *Putnam's Magazine*. Norton's anonymous review calls the book "preposterous yet somehow fascinating" and describes Whitman as equal parts "Concord philosopher" and "New York fireman"; the reviewer finds a "most perfect harmony" in the fusion of incongruities in the book and praises Whitman's "original perception of nature," "epic directness," and "manly brawn." The poem even moved Norton to attempt his own free-verse pastiche, never published in his lifetime, appearing in 1928–along with the review for *Putnam's Magazine*–as *A Leaf of Grass from Shady Hill: With A Review of Walt Whitman's Leaves of Grass; Written by Charles Eliot Norton in 1855.*

Throughout the next decade Norton was a close associate of Emerson, Lowell, and Oliver Wendell Holmes Sr., working with them to establish the *Atlantic Monthly* and joining their Saturday Club. He became especially close to Lowell and tried to make him share his enthusiasm for Whitman, an attempt that Lowell rebuffed. Nonetheless, Norton came to share much of the Transcendentalist outlook. Drawn to the antislavery cause, Norton shared the Boston writers' regard for John Brown as a tragic hero; perhaps more importantly, his sense of the rapid progress of abolitionism brought him as close as he ever came to the Transcendentalist mood of human perfectionism.

In 1855, in the midst of these literary and reformist activities, Norton left with his mother and sisters for a two-year stay in Europe, pleading ill health. This illness was the first of many near-collapses that interrupted his career and that seem to have been largely psychosomatic or depressive. On this journey, however, Norton discovered his true vocations: as an interpreter of medieval art and culture to Americans and as a spokesman for the higher social and moral values he saw in them. The catalyst was Norton's reading of the works of Ruskin, accelerated by his friendship with the English art critic and historian. A chance encounter between the two men in Switzerland led to travels together and frequent visits by Norton to Ruskin's London home. Norton became a sympathetic listener for Ruskin and encouraged the older man to continue working despite the doubt and depression from which he suffered, as did Norton himself. Portions of Norton's 1860 book, *Notes of Travel and Study in Italy,* first appeared in 1856 as essays in the American art journal *The Crayon,* begun by Norton's acquaintance William J. Stillman to spread Ruskin's ideas in the United States. The book mixes loving descriptions of the Italian landscape with the thesis, taken from Ruskin, that Italian Gothic cathedrals were essentially democratic products, the common expression of a people's "temper." Ruskin's quasi-evangelistic vision of medieval Italian art made artistic form a register of the social health of a culture and of its apprehension of God in nature. This interpretation gave Norton's love of medieval Italy a sense of moral mission that lent purpose to his enjoyment of it. For Norton, as a follower of Ruskin, art is

Villa Spannocchi, Siena, where Norton stayed in 1870 while researching his Historical Studies of Church-Building in the Middle Ages: Venice, Siena, Florence *(1880)*

not an indulgence but a call to mankind to better and unify itself. The implication that Americans should emulate the aesthetic, moral, and social aims of medieval Orvieto or Florence, muted in *Notes of Travel and Study in Italy,* soon became a strident demand.

At the same time that he prepared *Notes of Travel and Study in Italy,* Norton prepared and privately published *The New Life of Dante: An Essay, with Translations* (1859), his translation of Dante Alighieri's *La Vita nuova* (circa 1293). His reverence for Dante remained strong for the rest of his life; in "The Intellectual and Moral Awakening of Italy" (1903) he explained Dante as "the chief poet of man as a moral being," calling on his readers to better themselves. Homer and William Shakespeare, Norton stated, each "simply holds the mirror up to nature, and lets us see the reflection . . . They are primarily poets. [Dante] is primarily a moralist who is also a poet." Emerson came to seem to Norton the same kind of figure for the United States that Dante had been for Florence: a teacher of right values to a nation at the threshold of momentous change. In a 17 December 1860 letter to George William Curtis, he described Emerson's *The Conduct of Life* (1860) as "full of councils to rebuke cowardice, to confirm the moral principles of man, and to base them firmly on the unshaken foundations of eternal laws."

In May 1862 Norton married Susan Ridgely Sedgwick; their first child, Eliot, was born in July 1863, and a daughter, Sara, was born in September 1864. During the Civil War, Norton solicited Emerson's contributions to *The North American Review,* which he edited (at first in tandem with Lowell) from 1863 to 1868. Norton also edited the Loyal Publication Society, a bureau service supplying pro-Union writings to newspapers, from 1863 until the end of the war in 1865. In both capacities he fostered a mood of crusading idealism, hopeful that the United States was finally overcoming its moral and cultural shortcomings. In 1865 Norton joined with E. L. Godkin and Frederick Law Olmsted to found the weekly journal *The Nation,* in which the pro-Union intellectuals added more caustic criticism to their earlier calls for reform. In both journals Norton helped set the intellectual course of the postwar years, giving an outlet to younger writers such as William Dean Howells and Henry Adams.

The decade following the war brought Norton both public and private disappointment. In July 1868 he once again gave up his responsibilities and took his family–which by now included Elizabeth, born in June 1866, and Rupert, born in July 1867–on a five-year stay in Europe, where their third daughter, Margaret, was born in January 1870. Susan Norton died in Dresden in February 1872, shortly after giving birth to the Nortons' sixth child, Richard. By the time of his wife's death, Norton was already assuming the stoic pessimism that became his public posture, and he never remarried. His wartime optimism was soured by the corruption and (as Norton saw it) coarsening public taste that characterized the United States under the administration of Ulysses S. Grant (1869–1877). In Europe, Norton's literary friends seemed oblivious to the social and cultural disintegration he saw around them, a disillusionment sharpened by Carlyle when Norton met him in 1869.

In this mood Norton became preoccupied with the inadequacies of Carlyle's friend Emerson as a guide for the United States. He praised Emerson's poetry in *The Nation* in 1867, less for its literary merits than for its reflection of the poet's personal fineness of soul. Writing from the Villa Spannocchi in Siena, Italy, he could still remark in a 13 September 1870 letter to the philosopher Chauncey Wright that Emerson's qualities as a spiritual leader made him indispensable: "we have nobody to take his place in supplying us with the thought itself on which the spiritual growth in good of the nation mainly depends." Yet, Emerson also struck Norton as a figure who "belongs to the pure and innocent age of the Presidency of Monroe or John Quincy Adams . . . he is as remote almost from us as is Plato himself." Emerson was an intuitive thinker, and postwar America needed "the wisdom of the reflective and rational understanding, not that of the intuitions." Carlyle, not Emerson, now seemed to Norton the modern Dante. In 1873 Norton and Emerson shared the same steamship from England to Boston, and during the voyage the two men talked at length about Emerson's beliefs and intellectual development. The intimate encounter, recorded at length by Norton in his journal entry for 15 May 1873, published in *Letters of Charles Eliot Norton, with Biographical Comment* (1913), left Norton both impressed by "the pure whiteness of his [Emerson's] soul" and in despair over Emerson's naive faith in the goodness of the universe: "He is the most innocent, the most inexperienced of men who have lived in and reflected on the world."

Upon his return from Europe in 1873, Norton was asked by his cousin Charles Eliot, president of Harvard University, to teach art history at the school. He began as a lecturer in 1874 and was appointed professor of art history in 1875, a position he held until 1897. (A believer in coeducation, Norton taught at Radcliffe College as well.) In his popular, even famous, courses, Norton limited his subjects to Classical Greece and medieval Italy–epochs in which (according to Norton) public spiritual ideals and artistic accomplishment were most harmoniously in unity. Norton's course material on Italian Gothic cathedrals, based in large part on his own archival research, appeared in 1880 as *Historical Studies of Church-Building in the Middle Ages*. Like Ruskin's works, Norton's book describes cathedral building (Siena and Florence Cathedrals, and St. Mark's Basilica in Venice) as the idealism of free men channeled into a unified civic expression. Norton did not believe that the Catholicism of medieval Italy accounted for its cultural and spiritual excellence; Emerson's *An Address Delivered Before the Senior Class in Divinity College, Cambridge* (1838) had converted Norton to free thought, and his acquaintance with Wright left him an agnostic. Rather, the Church had offered a narrow but all-encompassing basis on which the citizens of the medieval city-states built an active civic idealism. Norton concluded that Italian culture had failed morally in the Renaissance, when luxury and greed replaced expressions of ideals in the arts and society. Norton also applied this lesson to Classical Athens in his Harvard lectures and also to his own time and place in sharply worded asides during his lectures.

Norton's wife, Susan Ridgely Sedgwick Norton, in 1871
(Society for the Preservation of Antiquities, Boston)

Norton's children in 1872: (rear) Eliot, Elizabeth, and Sara; (front) Margaret, infant Richard, and Rupert (Society for the Preservation of Antiquities, Boston)

Norton brought the outlook and message of his courses into his writings on art and culture in *The North American Review* and *The Nation,* often turning ostensible reviews of others' scholarship into long displays of his own learning and opinions. These reviews and articles made up the bulk of his art-historical scholarship. Although Norton was the most eminent art historian in post–Civil War United States, he published comparatively few scholarly essays or books. This falling-off in productivity can be attributed to Norton's frequent periods of depression, but also to his distaste for the German methods of scholarship and postgraduate education that were being introduced in American universities–Norton never gave a seminar, nor did he even use slides of the art works he discussed until his last decade as a professor. Another factor was undoubtedly the sheer number of fronts on which Norton worked to raise aesthetic and intellectual standards. In addition to many private acts of encouragement, he helped to found the Archeological Institute of America in 1879, the Dante Society of America (with the poet Henry Wadsworth Longfellow) in 1881, and the American Academy of Arts and Letters in 1898. His profile as a spokesman for public causes as well as a scholar was maintained through work on *The Nation,* frequently behind the scenes, and through the well-publicized "Ashfield Dinners" he and Curtis held for public figures between 1879 and 1903 at Norton's rural Massachusetts summer home. Norton held a firm place among the leadership of the "Mugwumps," the dissident Republicans who spoke out for tariff reform, black education, and anti-imperialism during the Gilded Age. He quietly worked from 1880 to 1883 to save Niagara Falls from industrial development. His stance against overseas imperialism earned him wide public criticism in 1898, when he condemned the Spanish-American War and implied that any Harvard man who fought in it was behaving immorally.

Norton's most important legacy to New England literary culture–and to literature in general–was as custodian and editor of the papers of the Romantic writers of Emerson's period. Personal friendships brought Norton into this role. In 1873 Norton began to help Emerson obtain for Harvard a large number of Carlyle's books and papers. Emerson also gave Norton his own correspondence with Carlyle. Shortly after Car-

George William Curtis and Norton in the early 1880s (Society for the Preservation of Antiquities, Boston)

lyle's death in 1881, his friend and literary executor James Anthony Froude published Carlyle's *Reminiscences* and included excerpts from private family papers. Norton, who disliked Froude, publicly declared Froude's volume a libel upon Carlyle and a grossly misleading work of editing. To offer a corrected picture, Norton published a two-volume edition of the Emerson-Carlyle correspondence in 1883 and his own edition of Carlyle's *Reminiscences* in 1887.

Norton's introduction to the first volume of *The Correspondence of Thomas Carlyle and Ralph Waldo Emerson* describes the two men at the time of their first meeting as prophets "in the desert," shortly to become leaders of "the hitherto unexpressed tendencies and aspirations of their age." Beneath Emerson's optimism and Carlyle's pessimism, the two were "united in their faith in spiritual truth, and in their reverence for it." In the text that follows, Norton's editorial hand and voice are undetectable. This silence is characteristic of Norton's editorial method; however, it also gives no clue as to the personal material Norton cut out of the letters, so that the correspondence remains a record purely of intellectual and spiritual matters. Norton went on to publish several more volumes of Carlyle's letters and memoirs, consciously using them to undo the picture Froude had created in his own editing of Carlyle's papers.

For the last two and a half decades of his life, Norton's literary projects were largely ones of translation and editing. His prose translation of Dante's *Divine Comedy* (circa 1310–1314) appeared in three volumes in 1891 and 1892. In the 1880s and 1890s he edited volumes of the work and letters of Lowell and Curtis, and in 1906 he edited a selection of Longfellow's more autobiographical poetry. Norton became Ruskin's literary executor after his English friend became mentally incapacitated, and he prepared the Brantwood Edition of Ruskin's works for publication in 1890–1893. Norton moved into seventeenth-century literary scholarship when he completed Lowell's editorial work on the poetry of John Donne in 1895. In 1897 he published an edition of the works of Anne Bradstreet. In all these endeavors, Norton furthered the ideals of his authors, as he saw them, by expurgating material he saw as immoral, discreditable, or simply too personal. In 1904 Norton published two volumes of Ruskin's letters to him; although Norton's comments in the edition sympathetically describe Ruskin's loss of his evangelical faith, he includes no mention of his failed marriage, and the publication of the volumes forestalled English attempts to publish a wider selection of Ruskin's private papers. Norton often declared that his omissions were countermeasures against what he called the modern taste for intrusive publicity. By Norton's last years, this insistence on the author's privacy became itself intrusive. In his edition of Longfellow's autobiographical poems, published the year before Norton's own death, he paradoxically praises the poet for not revealing himself in his first-person poems.

To critics in Norton's later years and afterward, his shrinking-back from the personal or emotional was not so much idealistic as (in John Jay Chapman's words) "old-maidish." Norton's immersion in art and literature, and his insistence that they should deal with the higher aspirations of humanity, did frequently lead him into simplistic calls for "refinement." Writing in Platonic terms about "the ideal," without the spiritual and philosophical convictions of the Transcendentalists, Norton often fell back on nebulous formulations about higher, or at least more gracious, things. On occasion, his distaste for the "vulgar" was aimed at the ethnic and social groups who remade post–Civil War America. This distaste also encompassed writers who did not share Norton's standards of refinement, such as Mark Twain, or who, in Norton's opinion, lapsed from them, such as Howells. It is easy for the reader to see in Norton, as did Van Wyck Brooks, a stereotype of New England Victorian culture: scholarly, finely tuned in taste, mouthing hopes for human betterment, but squeamish and xenophobic.

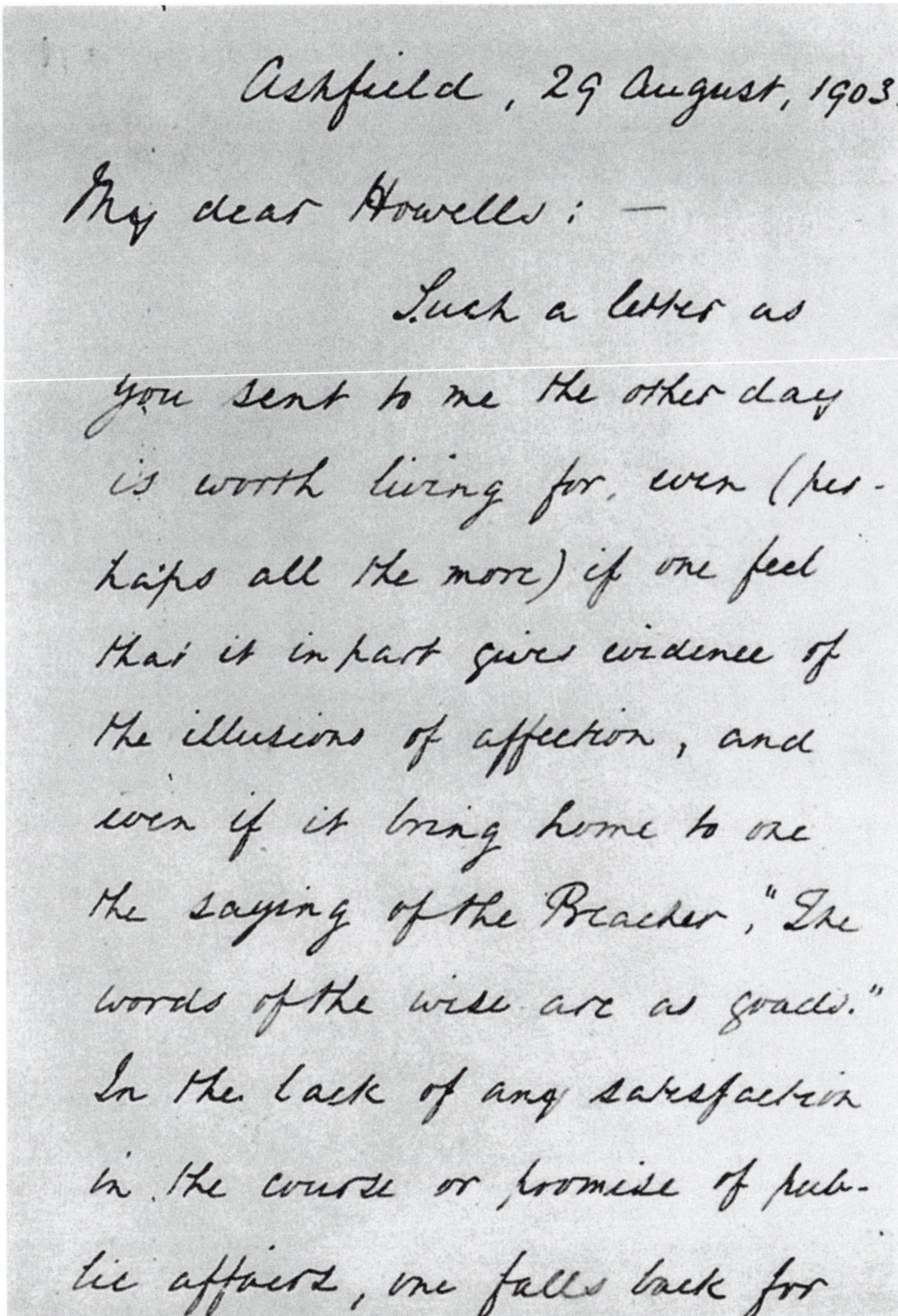

Ashfield, 29 August, 1903.

My dear Howells: —

Such a letter as you sent to me the other day is worth living for, even (perhaps all the more) if one feel that it in part gives evidence of the illusions of affection, and even if it bring home to one the saying of the Preacher, "The words of the wise are as goads." In the lack of any satisfaction in the course or promise of public affairs, one falls back for

First page of a letter from Norton to the novelist William Dean Howells (Charles Eliot Norton Papers, Houghton Library, Harvard University)

Norton in his study at Shady Hill, the family estate in Cambridge, Massachusetts (Society for the Preservation of Antiquities, Boston)

Arguably, this image of post–Civil War New England originated in large degree with Norton. For a writer whose output was mostly editorial or ephemeral, and whose scholarship was soon surpassed, his influence was remarkably widespread. Much of it stemmed from the personal charm and talent for sympathetic companionship that both Norton's London and Boston friends recalled, a charm that brought him intimacy with both the sunny Emerson and the erratic Ruskin. Norton's character as well as his interests left a deep mark on Harvard University, where his almost unearthly immersion in the arts became, in the hands of student and faculty admirers, a pose of extreme aestheticism that stereotyped the college until World War I. It should be noted that Norton, who saw the humanities as a call to moral duty, disliked the amoral, "art-for-art's sake" stance of Walter Pater and Oscar Wilde even more than he disliked literary realism. Both in the college and in greater New England, Norton's demonstration that a life spent in the fine arts could be fulfilling shaped the destinies of Bernard Berenson and Isabella Stewart Gardner, among others. In the fine arts in general, Norton's influence discouraged interest in contemporary American art and encouraged Americans to overvalue European masterworks; however, Norton's insistence on scholarship using primary sources, and his demonstration that the history of fine art had to be taught as the history of an entire civilization, shaped the methods of a generation of U.S. medievalists.

Finally, Norton made a conscious effort throughout his career to appeal to those moneyed men and women who could fund the means–art departments, fellowships, archeological institutes, intellectual journals, well-illustrated books, first-rate architecture, and conservation efforts–by which the United States could be bettered. His appeals to elites did not make him subservient to their interests and beliefs. As Alan Trachtenberg has pointed out, Norton and his intellectual comrades in arms of the Gilded Age were almost always in opposition to the status quo, setting, perhaps, the pattern for the American intellectual as an alienated figure. Norton led his campaigns in the face of his own belief that there was no knowable God, that human progress was probably a myth, and that Emerson's optimism was best met with, as he wrote in a letter, "a modified stoical attitude of mind." The "modification" comes from Norton's hope that poets or artists could lift man "from the petty, transient or physical interests . . . to the large, permanent, and spiritual interests that ennoble his nature, and transform him from a solitary individual into a member of a brotherhood of the human race," as he wrote in his 1903 essay, "The Intellectual and Moral Awakening of Italy."

Norton retired from his Harvard professorship in 1898, although as emeritus professor he offered a course on Dante for several more years. His anti-imperialist stand in 1898 was his last major involvement in a public cause, though he continued to invite scholars and students to Shady Hill to share his artistic and literary treasures. Norton came more and more to see himself as a survivor from Emerson's more innocent New England, and in an address delivered on the centennial of Emerson's birth in 1903 he found a lasting legacy in Emerson's "habitual loftiness of view." Charles Eliot Norton died at Shady Hill on 21 October 1908.

Letters:

Sara Norton and Mark A. DeWolfe Howe, eds., *Letters of Charles Eliot Norton, with Biographical Comment,* 2 volumes (Boston: Houghton Mifflin, 1913);

Jane Whitehill, ed., *Letters of Mrs. Gaskell and Charles Eliot Norton, 1855–1865* (London: Oxford University Press, 1932; Folcroft, Pa.: Folcroft Library Editions, 1973);

John Lewis Bradley and Ian Ousby, eds., *The Correspondence of John Ruskin and Charles Eliot Norton* (Cambridge & New York: Cambridge University Press, 1987).

Bibliography:

James Turner, "The Published Writings of Charles Eliot Norton," in his *The Liberal Education of Charles Eliot Norton* (Baltimore & London: Johns Hopkins University Press, 1999), pp. 481–494.

Biographies:

Kermit Vanderbilt, *Charles Eliot Norton: Apostle of Culture in a Democracy* (Cambridge, Mass.: Belknap Press, 1959);

James Turner, *The Liberal Education of Charles Eliot Norton* (Baltimore & London: Johns Hopkins University Press, 1999).

References:

Van Wyck Brooks, *New England: Indian Summer, 1865–1915* (New York: E. P. Dutton, 1940);

Jackson Lears, *No Place of Grace: Antimodernism and the Transformation of American Culture, 1880–1920* (New York: Pantheon, 1981);

Alan Trachtenberg, *The Incorporation of America: Society and Culture in the Gilded Age* (New York: Hill & Wang, 1982).

Papers:

The major collection of Charles Eliot Norton's papers is held by the Houghton Library, Harvard University.

John Gorham Palfrey

(2 May 1796 – 26 April 1881)

Alfred G. Litton
Texas Woman's University

See also the Palfrey entry in *DLB 30: American Historians, 1607–1865.*

John Gorham Palfrey, 1826 (portrait attributed to Rembrandt Peale; from Frank Otto Gatell, John Gorham Palfrey, *1963)*

BOOKS: *A Sermon Preached to the Society in Brattle Square, June 8th, 1823; the Lord's Day after the Interment of the Late Hon. John Phillips* (Boston: Printed by Munroe & Francis, 1823);

A Sermon Preached in the Church in Brattle Square, in Two Parts, July 18, 1824 (Boston: Printed for O. C. Greenleaf, by Phelps & Farnham, 1825);

The Prospects and Claims of Pure Christianity; a Sermon Preached at the Dedication of the 12th Congregational Church in Boston, October 13, 1824 (Boston: W. W. Clapp, 1825);

Discourses on Intemperance, Preached in the Church in Brattle Square, Boston, April 5, 1827, the Day of Annual Fast, and April 8, the Lord's Day Following (Boston: Nathan Hale, 1827);

A Sermon Occasioned by the Death of John Gorham, M.D. and Preached at the Church in Brattle Square, Boston, April 9th 1829 (Boston: S. G. Goodrich, 1829);

A Sermon Preached in the Church in Brattle Square, Boston, August 1, 1830, the Lord's Day after the Decease of the Honourable Isaac Parker (Boston: Nathan Hale/Gray & Bowen, 1830);

An Address Delivered Before the Society for Promoting Theological Education, June 5, 1831 (Boston: Gray & Bowen, 1831);

An Oration Pronounced Before the Citizens of Boston, on the Anniversary of the Declaration of Independence, July 4th, 1831 (Boston: J. H. Eastburn, 1831);

A Discourse Delivered in the Church in Brattle Square, Boston, Aug. 9, 1832–The Day Appointed for Fasting and Prayer in Massachusetts on Account of the Cholera (Boston: Gray & Bowen, 1832);

A Sermon Preached in the Church in Brattle Square, December 1, 1833, the Lord's Day after the Decease of Miss Elizabeth Bond (Boston: Nathan Hale, 1833);

The Worthy Student of Harvard College. A Sermon Preached in the Chapel of that Institution on Lord's Day Afternoon, March 23, 1834 (Cambridge, Mass.: J. Munroe, 1834);

Sermons on Duties Belonging to Some of the Conditions and Relations of Private Life (Boston: C. Bowen, 1834);

A Sermon Preached at the Installation of Rev. Samuel Kirkland Lothrop, as Pastor of the Church in Brattle Square, Boston, June 18, 1834 (Boston: Nathan Hale, 1834);

The Claims of Harvard College Upon its Sons; a Sermon Preached in the Chapel of that Institution, on Lord's Day Afternoon, July 13, 1834 (Cambridge, Mass.: J. Munroe, 1834);

Elements of Chaldee, Syriac, Samaritan, and Rabbinical Grammar (Boston: Crocker & Brewster, 1835);

A Plea for the Militia System, in a Discourse Delivered Before the Ancient and Honorable Artillery Company, on Its

CXCVIIth Anniversary (Boston: Dutton & Wentworth, 1835);

Academical Lectures on the Jewish Scriptures and Antiquities, 4 volumes (1838–1852); volumes 1 and 2 (Boston: J. Munroe, 1838, 1840); volumes 3 and 4 (Boston: Crosby & Nichols, 1852);

The Theory and Uses of Natural Religion; Being the Dudleian Lecture Read Before the University of Cambridge, May 8, 1839 (Boston: F. Andrews, 1839);

Remarks Concerning the Late Dr. Bowditch, with the Replies of Dr. Bowditch's Children (Boston: C. C. Little, 1840);

A Discourse on the Life and Character of the Reverend John Thornton Kirkland, D.D., LL.D., Late President of Harvard College; Pronounced on Thursday, June 5 1840, in the New South Church in Boston (Cambridge, Mass.: J. Owen, 1840);

A Discourse Pronounced at Barnstable on the Third of September 1839, at the Celebration of the Second Anniversary of the Settlement of Cape Cod (Boston: F. Andrews, 1840);

A Discourse on the Life and Character of the Reverend Henry Ware, D.D., A.A.S. . . . Pronounced in the First Church in Cambridge, September 28, 1845 (Cambridge, Mass.: J. Owen, 1845);

Abstract from the Returns of Agricultural Societies in Massachusetts, for the Year 1845 (Boston: Dutton & Wentworth, 1846);

An Address to the Society of Middlesex Husbandmen and Manufacturers, Delivered at Concord, October 7, 1846 (Cambridge, Mass.: Metcalf, 1846);

Papers on the Slave Power, First Published in the "Boston Whig," in July, August, and September, 1846 (Boston: Merrill, Cobb, 1846);

Speech of Mr. Palfrey of Massachusetts, on the Political Aspects of the Slave Question. Delivered in the House of Representatives, January 26, 1848 (Washington, D.C.: J. & G. S. Gideon, 1848);

A Chapter of American History. Five Years' Progress of the Slave Power; a Series of Papers First Published in the Boston "Commonwealth" in July, August, & September, 1851 (Boston: B. B. Mussey, 1852);

Remarks on the Proposed State Constitution. By a Free Soiler from the Start (Boston: Crosby & Nichols, 1853);

The Relation between Judaism and Christianity, illustrated in Notes on Passages in the New Testament Containing Quotations from, or References to, the Old (Boston: Crosby & Nichols, 1854);

Letter to a Whig Neighbor, on the Approaching State Election, by an Old Conservative (Boston: Crosby & Nichols, 1855);

The Inter-State Slave Trade (New York: American Anti-Slavery Society, 1855);

History of New England, 5 volumes (Boston: Little, Brown, 1858–1890).

SELECTED PERIODICAL PUBLICATION–UNCOLLECTED: "Thoughts on Controversy," *Christian Disciple,* 11 (July/August 1823): 261–262.

Though John Gorham Palfrey was not the most influential person of his age, his life and works intersected frequently with many of those who were. As a minister, scholar, editor, abolitionist, and congressman, Palfrey developed friendships with Ralph Waldo Emerson, Charles Sumner, William Lloyd Garrison, and many other important writers, theologians, politicians, and reformers. In his nearly eighty-five years Palfrey became well known among his contemporaries in Boston.

Born on 2 May 1796 into a struggling Boston merchant family, John Gorham Palfrey did not have bright prospects, and were it not for the beneficence of family friends and his own determination, the young man might never have received an education at Harvard. Palfrey's mother, Mary Sturgis (Gorham) Palfrey, died when the boy was only six. His father, John Palfrey, was the son of William Palfrey, a merchant and secretary of the Sons of Liberty. John Palfrey remained a distant figure who contributed little emotionally or financially to Gorham's life, moving to Louisiana to pursue farming only two years after the death of his wife. After studying Greek and Latin at the Berry Street Academy and at Phillips Exeter Academy in Exeter, New Hampshire, Palfrey received support from an Exeter fund to assist indigent scholars and went on to study at Harvard in 1812, graduating in 1815 and completing his theological studies in 1817.

Palfrey was ordained as minister of Brattle Street Church on 17 June 1818. The church was one of the most prominent Unitarian congregations in Boston, but it had not had stable leadership since the death of Joseph Buckminster in 1812. The congregation was pleased with the young minister, though his growing reputation made some wonder if he might not choose to seek opportunities elsewhere. They were relieved somewhat when Palfrey married one of his parishioners, Mary Ann Hammond, on 11 March 1823. The couple had six children, the oldest of whom, Sarah Hammond Palfrey, became a writer of poetry and fiction. The young minister's achievements at Harvard had established him as one of the brightest scholars of his class, and his sermons at Brattle Street (though hastily composed) distinguished Palfrey as a thoughtful and capable young Unitarian. He soon sought to distinguish himself as an editor and scholar.

Palfrey in 1848

Having already worked closely with Henry Ware Jr. and Andrews Norton, two Unitarians who were among those most interested in publishing denominational periodicals, Palfrey was soon invited by them and other prominent Unitarians to edit the *Christian Disciple,* a magazine that had been established ten years earlier by William Ellery Channing and others as a voice for "liberal Christians." In recent years it had suffered from inattention and poor management. Palfrey's strong organizational skills and commitment to matters of principle were precisely what the periodical needed. Though his editorship was brief, from 1824 through most of 1825, Palfrey made important changes that positioned the magazine as the most important vehicle for liberal religious thought in New England. During Palfrey's tenure its name was changed to the *Christian Examiner,* signaling a significant shift in posture for the leading organ of nineteenth-century Unitarianism. Before he became editor of the *Christian Disciple,* serving somewhat as a prelude to his new editorial philosophy with the *Christian Examiner,* Palfrey wrote "Thoughts on Controversy" (1823) in which he boldly proclaimed: "I look upon controversy, as one of the great dispensations of God. It results from the very constitution of our minds. . . . Let us not make *too much* of being in a state of controversy . . . first, because it is what falls out in the natural course of things, and secondly, because it may be, and *is* productive of many advantages." Under Palfrey's leadership, the magazine did truly "examine" the presumed errors of orthodoxy in a much more aggressive manner than in the past. This approach was consistent with his close friend Andrews Norton's views concerning the existing conflicts between Congregationalists and Unitarians. Norton had written Palfrey in 1820 that "to relax our efforts now would be like drawing off to encamp in the midst of an engagement just as the enemy is beginning to break." In *The Prospects and Claims of Pure Christianity,* a sermon delivered during his editorship of the *Christian Examiner* and published as a pamphlet in 1825, Palfrey echoes this view in observing that "the system of orthodoxy had its birth in a very ignorant period of the world. Such a period is its natural element; and, tenacious as it is of life, it does not seem properly constituted to thrive in any other." His thoughts on the subject came at a time when Unitarianism was struggling to define itself as a coherent religious movement. Palfrey's assumption of the editorship of the leading Unitarian magazine came on the eve of the founding of the American Unitarian Association, and his voice was an important one in the defense of "liberal Christianity" against Congregationalist attacks.

Palfrey carried these sentiments into the classroom in 1830, when he gave up his position with the Brattle Street congregation and assumed the post of professor of sacred literature at the Harvard Divinity School. Palfrey had already been contributing to the work of his alma mater. In 1827 he had become the secretary for the Society for Promoting Theological Education at Harvard and had become a Harvard Overseer one year later, teaching at the school part-time. Palfrey's students became some of the most important religious, literary, and artistic figures of their time and included individuals such as William Henry Channing, Frederic Henry Hedge, James Freeman Clarke, Theodore Parker, Christopher Pearse Cranch, and John Sullivan Dwight. In the early 1830s the school was thoroughly Unitarian and just as thoroughly mismanaged. Shortly after joining the faculty, Palfrey was chosen dean of the Divinity School. His early experiences with the *Christian Examiner* helped to shape his tenure there. Palfrey had maintained in his days as editor that controversy was productive of good, and he certainly experienced ample amounts of it while presiding over the Divinity School. In a bold move signaled in *An Address Delivered Before the Society for Promoting Theological Education* (1831), Palfrey outlined his vision for the school, including a stronger curriculum and higher standards. The vision, as society members soon learned, was not one that included a continued management role for the society. Placing the management and budget of the school on a more sound footing, Palfrey also reformed the curriculum, making it more demanding and more comprehensive. He was also known for reforming the students themselves, many of whom initially balked at but later resigned themselves to accepting "Palfrey's Code." Palfrey's ability to inspire the students through reasoned eloquence can be seen in his sermon *The Claims of Harvard College Upon its Sons* (1834). This work, along with his *Sermons on Duties Belonging to Some of the Conditions and Relations of Private Life* (1834), soon won him many admirers among the divinity students. One student, Andrew Preston Peabody, recalled these works many years later for the strong impression that they made on a young would-be clergyman: "methodical in arrangement, exhaustive in division, philosophically sound, and religiously impressive, based on the intrinsic and eternal Right." Though he demanded much from students, Palfrey encouraged debate and dialogue concerning theological questions.

No doubt, these reforms and Palfrey's openness contributed to the senior students' decision in 1838 to invite Ralph Waldo Emerson to lecture in the chapel of Divinity Hall. Palfrey's reaction to the address was as one might expect. "Emerson preached odiously," he wrote in his journal. Palfrey could tolerate the "matters of poetry" in the earlier moments of the address, but not what he saw as the direct criticism of the Unitarian beliefs of the school and its new curriculum. Having invested a considerable portion of his first years at the Divinity School reforming the curriculum, he could not have been pleased by Emerson's view that the professors and program at Harvard were archaic. Though Palfrey chose not to reply publicly to Emerson's address, he asserted privately, in a 16 October 1843 letter to George Edward Ellis, that "the prospect that even the small number of pupils were to be reared up to be useful servants of the church, was lessened by the introduction among them, to some extent, of infidel opinions. Mr. Emerson's Address . . . with the indications accompanying it, has been a bad blow to our hopes." Perhaps his decision not to respond publicly and not even to aid Andrews Norton in his attempts at a public response were owing to Palfrey's confidence in the fact that the position of the Divinity School had risen considerably during his tenure as dean. That Emerson had been allowed to deliver his address at the school demonstrated its commitment to liberal principles even if its principals had not proved themselves quite so liberal. The following summer, after eight years of leadership at the Divinity School, Palfrey left to pursue another vocation.

Palfrey had been interested in an editing position with *The North American Review* as far back as 1817, when his friend Jared Sparks had become editor. Though Palfrey was not offered a shared editorship at the time, he began a long connection with the magazine, contributing pieces and helping to improve its circulation. When the publication came into the hands of Edward and Alexander Everett, the financial prospects of the magazine were not bright despite its growing reputation. In 1835 Edward Everett had offered Palfrey the opportunity to purchase *The North American Review,* and despite its financial difficulties, he decided to purchase it, hoping to supplement his income from Harvard. His hopes of deriving an adequate income from the work led him to leave Harvard in 1839 to devote his complete attention to the magazine. Palfrey's financial state grew increasingly dire as he saw subscriptions plummet and costs rise after he left the secure income of his position at Harvard. Despite his success in recruiting several important writers–including Henry Wadsworth Longfellow, William Hickling Prescott, and Francis Bowen–for the magazine, Palfrey was required to contribute a considerable amount of the material for each issue himself. The result was that *The North American Review* bore the indelible imprint of Palfrey's personality, something critics such as Edgar Allan Poe did not hesitate to assail. Writing in *Graham's Magazine* (November 1841), Poe opined that the magazine suffered because the editor "seems to dwell altogether within the narrow world of his *own* conceptions." Palfrey's writings, said Poe, showed "a total deficiency in the sense of the beautiful," and "however much we may admire the mere knowledge of the man who writes thus, it will not do to place any dependence upon his wisdom or upon his taste." Poe treated many writers of the era with this sort of brutal frankness, but there is little doubt that Palfrey's writing lacked an appreciation for the finer points of style. Nor was the enhanced reputation of *The North American Review* based on any creative new approach. Instead, the chief criticism that the periodical was "dull and hoary" seems a deserved one. Its Whig political affiliation, its lack of interest in reform issues, and its exclusion of Transcendentalist writers such as Orestes Brownson, Emerson, and Henry David Thoreau all went far in solidifying its position as a "New England establishment" magazine. But Palfrey's interest in the journal was not merely literary. It provided him with a platform for his political views and served as a springboard for another major period in his career.

One year prior to his selling *The North American Review* in 1842, Palfrey was elected to the Massachusetts state legislature as a Whig representative from

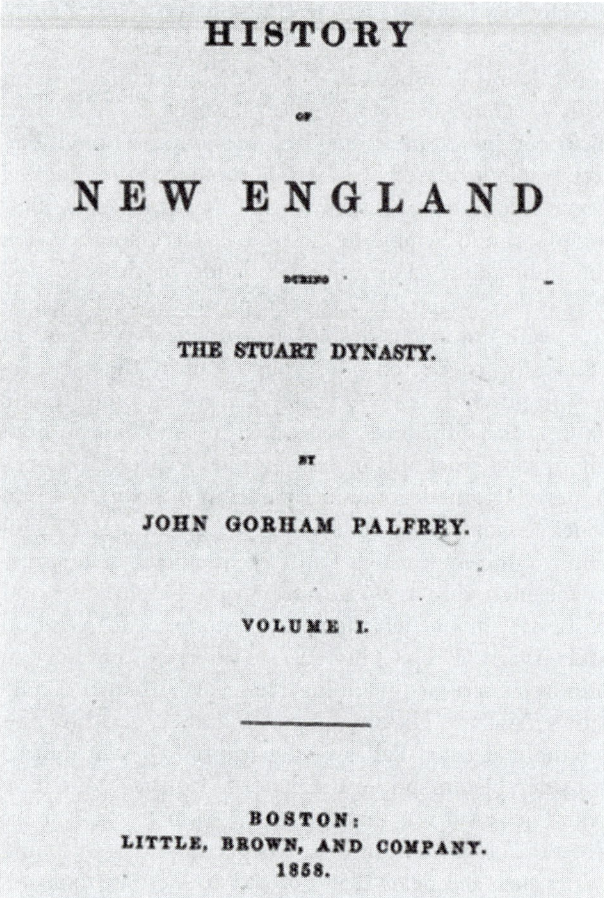
HISTORY

OF

NEW ENGLAND

DURING

THE STUART DYNASTY.

BY

JOHN GORHAM PALFREY.

VOLUME I.

BOSTON:
LITTLE, BROWN, AND COMPANY.
1858.

Title page for the first volume of Palfrey's account of the colonial period in his native region (courtesy of the John Carter Brown Library at Brown University)

Boston. As chair of the House Standing Committee on Education, he worked with Horace Mann to introduce many educational reforms, including the establishment of normal schools and school libraries. His entry into politics is most notable, however, for the impact that Palfrey eventually had among fellow Bostonians on the issue of slavery. In his brief but tumultuous political career, Palfrey gradually moved toward a more radical stance on the slavery issue, and his increasing outspokenness on the subject was responsible for his election and eventual ouster from public office. The issue confronted Palfrey in a personal way shortly after he was elected to office. Palfrey's father, who had managed to establish a profitable plantation in Louisiana after many failed business ventures, died and left the fledgling politician one-third of his "property." Despite the objections of his brothers, and at considerable personal expense, Palfrey arranged to inherit as many of the slaves as possible so that he might immediately emancipate them. The expenses related to the legal maneuvers and the transportation to the North were offset somewhat by friends such as Lydia Maria Child, but they were still burdensome for Palfrey. Nevertheless, he carried out what he felt was his moral duty and chose not to disclose his actions for political gain.

In 1846, after briefly serving as Secretary of State for Massachusetts, Palfrey was elected to the U.S. House of Representatives. His party loyalty was continually a matter of debate between the two factions of the Whig party. "Conscience Whigs" urged him to take a more abolitionist stance and conservatives threatened to withdraw their support should he appear to harbor any sympathies with abolitionists such as William Lloyd Garrison or Wendell Phillips. Throughout his brief tenure, Palfrey seems not to have allowed the ongoing debate about his sentiments to influence his position on the issue. As his published *Speech of Mr. Palfrey of Massachusetts, on the Political Aspects of the Slave Question* (1848) illustrates, he gradually drew nearer to those "Conscience Whigs" and even the Free Soilers, who advocated outright abolition. The evolution of his thoughts on slavery eventually led to one of the most notable political stalemates of the era. When Palfrey failed to receive a clear majority of the electorate in his 1848 bid for reelection, there ensued an unprecedented fourteen "trials," or runoff elections. Despite even the endorsement of Ralph Waldo Emerson, however, Palfrey was unable to maintain his seat in Congress. The yearlong struggle, which produced a noticeable vacancy for the Fourth District of Massachusetts in the U.S. House of Representatives, underscores the divisiveness of the slavery question even among Bostonians. Palfrey, always a man guided by his conscience, brought the issue directly to the electorate in dramatic fashion.

Palfrey's life after politics was not nearly so eventful. After leaving Washington, he continued to write on the issue of slavery, first publishing a collection of his impassioned essays for the *Boston Commonwealth* as *A Chapter of American History. Five Years' Progress of the Slave Power* (1852) and then publishing the more analytical treatise *The Inter-State Slave Trade* (1855), a work in which he detailed the political and economic quagmire that slavery had become. With the onset of the Civil War, Palfrey's position on slavery was no longer so controversial as it had been. His political views of a decade earlier undoubtedly led to his appointment as postmaster of Boston in 1861. The appointment also owed much to Palfrey's long friendship with Charles Sumner. Though some might have viewed the position as a sinecure, Palfrey approached the duties of the post with characteristic zeal. During the period, he applied the same sort of energy to his multivolume *History of New England* (1858–

1890). Work on the history spanned more than three decades, and though it was a considerable achievement for the time, it brought him little money and no lasting fame as a writer. When the first volumes were published just before and during the war, their vigorous denunciation of England and favorable portrayal of Puritan New Englanders won a politically sympathetic audience that had grown increasingly uneasy with the prospects of a British-Confederate alliance. With modern readers, however, the value of the work seems to lie in what it demonstrates regarding nineteenth-century historiography.

After five volumes, poor health prevented Palfrey from continuing the work. Despite mediocre sales of his *History of New England,* Palfrey was able to achieve financial security in his later years and enjoyed a considerable reputation as one of the most public-spirited citizens of Boston. His contributions to the Harvard Divinity School, his ministerial career, his conscientious stand on the slavery issue, and his contributions in the area of letters all marked him as one of the most esteemed men of the city. In 1873 he suffered a stroke but continued to meet his public engagements, but by 1877 his health was so poor that he was no longer able to keep a journal. On 26 April 1881, John Gorham Palfrey died quietly in his sleep. "The Good Old Dr. Palfrey," as many called him, was remembered by his friends as a man whose convictions were his greatest legacy.

Letters:

Hannah Palfrey Ayer, ed., *A Legacy of New England: Letters of the Palfrey Family* (Milton, Mass.: Privately printed, 1950).

Biography:

Frank Otto Gatell, *John Gorham Palfrey and the New England Conscience* (Cambridge, Mass.: Harvard University Press, 1963).

References:

Gary Collison, "'A True Toleration': Harvard Divinity School Students and Unitarianism, 1830–1859," in *American Unitarianism, 1805–1865,* edited by Conrad Edick Wright (Boston: Massachusetts Historical Society / Northeastern University Press, 1989), pp. 209–237;

Guy Litton, "From *Disciple* to *Examiner:* The Early Years of Unitarianism's Leading Nineteenth-Century Periodical," *Journal of Unitarian Universalist History,* 26 (1999): 47–71;

Andrew Preston Peabody, "John Gorham Palfrey," in *Harvard Reminiscences* (Boston: Ticknor, 1888), pp. 107–115.

Papers:

The largest collection of John Gorham Palfrey's manuscripts, including his correspondence and extensive diary, is the Palfrey Papers in the Houghton Library at Harvard University. Other important collections include the Andrews Norton Papers, the Charles Sumner Papers, and the Jared Sparks Papers, also at the Houghton Library; the Unitarian Universalist Ministers File at the Andover Harvard Theological Library; and the George Bancroft Papers and the Charles Deane Papers at the Massachusetts Historical Society.

Theodore Parker

(24 August 1810 – 10 May 1860)

Dean Grodzins
Meadville/Lombard Theological School

BOOKS: *The Previous Question between Mr. Andrews Norton and His Alumni, Moved and Handled in a Letter to Those Gentlemen,* as Levi Blodgett (Boston: Weeks, Jordan, 1840);

A Discourse on the Transient and Permanent in Christianity (Boston: Privately printed, 1841);

Lecture on the Education of the Laboring Classes (Boston: William D. Ticknor, 1842);

A Discourse of Matters Pertaining to Religion (Boston: Little, Brown, 1842; London: Chapman, 1846; revised edition, Boston, 1855);

An Humble Tribute to the Memory of William Ellery Channing, D.D. (Boston: Little, Brown, 1842; London: John Green, 1842);

The Critical and Miscellaneous Writings of Theodore Parker (Boston: J. Munroe, 1843; London: John Green, 1843);

A Sermon of Slavery (Boston: Thurston & Torrey, 1843);

A Letter to the Boston Association of Congregational Ministers, Touching Certain Matters of Their Theology (Boston: Little, Brown, 1845);

The Relation of Jesus to His Age and the Ages (Boston: Little, Brown, 1845);

The Excellence of Goodness (Boston: B. H. Greene, 1845);

The True Idea of a Christian Church (Boston: B. H. Greene, 1846);

A Sermon of War (Boston: Little, Brown, 1846);

A Sermon of the Perishing Classes in Boston (Boston: George Coolidge, 1846);

A Sermon of Immortal Life (Boston: George Coolidge, 1846);

A Sermon of Merchants (Boston: Published by request, 1847);

A Sermon of the Dangerous Classes in Society (Boston: C. & J. M. Spear, 1847);

A Letter to the People of the United States Touching the Matter of Slavery (Boston: J. Munroe, 1848);

Some Thoughts on the Most Christian Use of the Sunday (Boston: B. H. Greene, 1848);

A Discourse Occasioned by the Death of John Quincy Adams (Boston: Bela Marsh, 1848);

Theodore Parker

A Sermon of the Mexican War (Boston: Coolidge & Wiley, 1848);

A Sermon of the Moral Condition of Boston and a Sermon of the Spiritual Condition of Boston (Boston: Crosby & Nichols, 1849);

The Public Education of the People (Boston: Crosby & Nichols, 1850);

Theodore Parker's Review of Webster (Boston: R. F. Wallcut, 1850);

The Function and Place of Conscience, in Relation to the Laws of Men (Boston: Crosby & Nichols, 1850);
The State of the Nation (Boston: Crosby & Nichols, 1851);
The Chief Sins of the People (Boston: B. H. Greene, 1851);
The Three Chief Safeguards of Society (Boston: Crosby & Nichols, 1851);
Speeches, Addresses and Occasional Sermons, 2 volumes (Boston: Crosby & Nichols, 1851);
The Boston Kidnapping: A Discourse to Commemorate the Rendition of Thomas Sims (Boston: Crosby & Nichols, 1851);
A Discourse Occasioned by the Death of Daniel Webster (Boston: Benjamin B. Mussey, 1853; London: William Tweedie, 1853);
Two Sermons Preached before the Twenty Eighth Congregational Society in Boston . . . on Leaving Their Old and Entering a New Place of Worship (Boston: Crosby & Nichols, 1853);
Ten Sermons of Religion (Boston: Crosby & Nichols, 1853; London: Chapman, 1853);
A Sermon of the Public Function of Woman (Boston: R. F. Wallcut, 1853; London: Chapman, 1853);
A Friendly Letter to the Executive Committee of the American Unitarian Association Touching Their New Creed or General Proclamation of Unitarian Views (Boston: Benjamin Mussey, 1853);
Sermons of Theism, Atheism, and the Popular Theology (Boston: Little, Brown, 1853; London: Chapman, 1853);
A Sermon of Old Age (Boston: Benjamin Mussey, 1854);
The Nebraska Question: Some Thoughts on the New Assault upon Freedom in America, and the General State of the Country in Relation Thereto (Boston: Benjamin Mussey, 1854);
An Address Delivered before the New York City Anti-Slavery Society (New York: American Anti-Slavery Society, 1854);
The New Crime Against Humanity . . . with the Lesson for the Day of the Previous Sunday (Boston: Benjamin Mussey, 1854);
The Law of God and the Statutes of Men (Boston: Benjamin Mussey, 1854);
A Sermon of the Dangers which Threaten the Rights of Man in America (Boston: Benjamin Mussey, 1854);
A Sermon of the Moral Dangers Incident to Prosperity (Boston: B. H. Greene, 1855);
A Sermon of the Consequences of an Immoral Principle and False Idea of Life (Boston: B. H. Greene, 1855);
Additional Speeches, Addresses and Occasional Sermons, 2 volumes (Boston: Little, Brown, 1855);
A Discourse of the Function of a Teacher of Religion in these Times (Boston: B. H. Greene, 1855);
The Trial of Theodore Parker (Boston: Privately published, 1855);
The Great Battle Between Slavery and Freedom, Considered in Two Speeches Delivered Before the American Anti-Slavery Society (Boston: B. H. Greene, 1856);
A New Lesson for the Day (Boston: B. H. Greene, 1856);
The Present Aspect of Slavery in America and the Immediate Duty of the North (Boston: Bela Marsh, 1858);
A Sermon of False and True Theology (Boston: William L. Kent, 1858);
A False and True Revival of Religion (Boston: William L. Kent, 1858);
The Revival of Religion which We Need (Boston: William L. Kent, 1858);
The Relation of Slavery to a Republican Form of Government (Boston: William L. Kent, 1858);
The Biblical, the Ecclesiastical and the Philosophical Notion of God, and Soul's Normal Delight in Him (New York: John F. Trow, 1858);
The Effect of Slavery on the American People (Boston: William L. Kent, 1858);
A Sermon for the New Year: What Religion May Do for a Man (Boston: Fraternity, 1859);
Theodore Parker's Experience as a Minister (Boston: Rufus Leighton, 1859; London: Chapman, 1859);
A Sermon for Midsummer Day: Beauty in the World of Matter Considered as Revelation from God (Boston: Fraternity, 1859);
The Two Christmas Celebrations: A.D. I and MDCCCLV: A Christmas Story for MDCCLVI (Boston: Rufus Leighton, 1859);
John Brown's Expedition Reviewed (Boston: Fraternity, 1860);
The Material Condition of the People of Massachusetts (Boston: Fraternity, 1860);
Prayers (Boston: Walker, Wise, 1862; London: Whitfield, 1862);
Lessons from the World of Matter and the World of Man (Boston: Charles Slack, 1865; London: Trübner, 1865);
Historic Americans (Boston: Horace Fuller, 1870; London: Trübner, 1871);
Transcendentalism (Boston: Free Religious Association, 1876);
Theodore Parker to a Young Man (Boston: Christian Register Association, 1885);
West Roxbury Sermons, edited by Samuel J. Barrows (Boston: Roberts, 1892).

Collections: *The Collected Works of Theodore Parker,* 14 volumes (London: Trübner, 1863–1865; 1871–1872);
Centennial Edition: The Works of Theodore Parker, 15 volumes (Boston: American Unitarian Association, 1907–1913).

OTHER: *A Critical and Historical Introduction to the Canonical Scriptures of the Old Testament, from the German of Wilhelm Martin Leberecht De Wette,* translated and enlarged by Parker, 2 volumes (Boston: Little, Brown, 1843);

Massachusetts Quarterly Review, edited by Parker (1848–1851).

SELECTED PERIODICAL PUBLICATIONS–UNCOLLECTED: "A Translation and Exposition of Isaiah LII.13–LIII.12," *Scriptural Interpreter,* 6 (April 1836): 174–190;

"Palfrey's Lectures on Jewish Scriptures and Antiquities," *Boston Quarterly Review,* 1 (July 1838): 261–310;

"The Divine Presence in Nature and in the Soul," *Dial,* 1 (July 1840): 58–70;

"Hollis Street Council," *Dial,* 3 (October 1842): 201–221.

If Ralph Waldo Emerson represents what literary historians call the New England "Renaissance," Emerson's fellow Transcendentalist Theodore Parker represents what might be called the New England "Reformation." Both men started their careers as Unitarian clergymen, but Emerson left the ministry to become a lecturer, essayist, and poet, while theological themes, often overt in his early writings, over time became implicit. Parker also became a popular lecturer and important essayist but never changed his profession; in the 1850s he was one of the most prominent preachers and theologians in the United States. Again, although Emerson sympathized with reform, was respected by reformers, and even inspired others to become reformers, he confined himself to a minor role in the many reform movements of his day. Parker helped lead the crusades for church reform, alleviation of urban poverty, woman's rights, and abolition of slavery. He also emerged as an important theorist of American democracy. Emerson aptly called him "our Savonarola," and, like the Florentine monk, Parker was an extremely controversial figure. Many loved him as a prophet, while others hated him as an infidel and a demagogue.

Parker descended from generations of farm families who lived in the little villages northwest of Boston. His father's father, Captain John Parker, had earned patriotic immortality by commanding the Lexington militia in the first skirmish of the Revolutionary War. Theodore's own parents were intelligent and respectable, but not prosperous. John and Hannah Stearns Parker strained the resources of their modest Lexington farm to support their eleven children, of whom ten survived infancy. Theodore, "the gift of God," was the youngest born on 24 August 1810.

The boy showed intellectual precocity and an indomitable determination to rise in the world, even as tragedy repeatedly struck his family. His mother died of tuberculosis when he was eleven, after which his sisters Mary and Emily took over the maternal role, but they both died, also of tuberculosis, before he was twenty-one. By the time he turned twenty-eight Theodore had only two living brothers to whom he never felt especially close (one was a stolid farmer, the other an alcoholic carpenter). Parker rarely wrote or spoke about this private holocaust; yet, it affected his religious outlook deeply, moving him toward an emotional faith in immortality and in God as a just and loving parent who would never allow any ultimate harm to come to him or any other creature. This piety directed his ambition toward a clerical career.

From boyhood, he never intended to be a farmer. His desire to rise in the world is indicated by his choice of a bride–Lydia Dodge Cabot, of the distinguished and wealthy Boston Cabots, whom he married in April 1837–and possibly by his decision to become a Unitarian. Although the Lexington church had become more liberal when he was a child, he had been exposed to diverse religious influences growing up and was attracted enough to evangelicalism that when he was twenty he attended the preaching of Lyman Beecher for a year and even sat through one of Beecher's five-day revival meetings. Parker did not convert, however, perhaps because evangelicalism was the faith of the rural and lower classes he wanted to leave, while liberalism was the religion of the urban, middle, and upper classes he wanted to join.

His ambition may be seen most clearly in the extraordinary efforts he devoted to his education. As a child he excelled in his studies, becoming one of the few local boys to study Latin and Greek. At age seventeen he began teaching in the common schools. At age twenty he took and passed the entrance examinations for Harvard College, but lacking the money to enroll, he read the entire Harvard curriculum on his own and much else besides. He taught at an academy in Boston for a year and then, starting in 1831, ran a small academy in Watertown, Massachusetts. By 1834 he had enough money saved (despite spending a large proportion of his income on books) that with the help of a patron he entered Harvard Divinity School. Although he lacked an undergraduate degree, his private studies allowed him to enroll with advanced standing. He finished the course at Harvard in two years instead of the usual three, while earning an outstanding reputation for scholarly ability and diligence. When he left Cambridge in 1836 he had a reading knowledge of twenty languages.

On 21 June 1837 Parker was ordained pastor of the suburban Unitarian parish at West Roxbury, Massachusetts. His congregation had only sixty adult

Lydia Dodge Cabot Parker, whom Parker married in 1837 (American Unitarian Association)

members, and the salary was meager. He felt dissatisfied with the position but took it to please his wife's family, who lived nearby and owned land in the area. His wife's rich, invalid maiden aunt, Lucy Cabot, bought a house for him and Lydia, moved in with them, and supported them financially. Parker came to resent this position of dependence, especially as he and Cabot got along poorly. He thought her insufferably selfish and peevish and believed she turned the affections of his wife against him. She seems to have thought him an "infidel" because his theological views grew rapidly heterodox.

Parker had come to adulthood firmly convinced of the miraculous authority of the Scriptures but had found this conviction shaken by modern biblical criticism. He had been introduced to biblical studies by the scholarly Unitarian minister in Watertown, Convers Francis, who became his intellectual mentor. Later, at Harvard, Parker discovered radical ideas, originating in the universities of Germany, that the Bible was full of errors and legends. In 1836 he published his first dissent from received tradition in an article for *The Scriptural Interpreter,* a student magazine, in which he denied that the prophet Isaiah had predicted the coming of Christ. In the fall of 1836 Parker embarked on what turned out to be a seven-year project, translating and expanding one of the most revisionist accounts of the Hebrew Scriptures, the dryly titled *Lehrbuch der historisch-kritisch Einleitungen die kanonischen und apokryphischen Bücher des Alten Testaments* (An Historico-Critical Introduction to the Canonical and Apocryphal Books of the Old Testament, 1817) by Wilhelm Martin Leberecht de Wette, Professor at Basel. De Wette denied the authenticity of most Old Testament books and believed they were all, to a greater or lesser degree, historically inaccurate or mythical. By 1839 Parker had come to accept as valid many of the arguments of the German critic David Friedrich Strauss, who argued in his famous *Das Leben Jesu, kritisch bearbeitet* (The Life of Jesus, Critically Examined, 1835, 1836) that the New Testament was largely mythological as well.

Parker found Transcendentalism attractive because it offered what seemed to him an alternative to the Bible as a basis for faith and practice–the intuitive knowledge of religious truth. His connection to Francis won him entree into the so-called Transcendental Club, and he joined in most of its discussions from 1837 to 1840. He came greatly to admire Emer-

Spring Street Church in West Roxbury, Massachusetts, where Parker became pastor in 1837

son, whose lectures he attended regularly in Boston. In 1838 Parker sat in the audience that heard Emerson's Divinity School Address, which thrilled him more than anything else Emerson ever wrote and inspired him to begin writing his own sermons in a more prophetic vein. When the Transcendentalist Unitarians began meeting resistance from denominational conservatives, who favored the idea of Christianity as a unique, miraculous revelation, Parker sided with the "New School." While his Transcendentalist connections were pulling him in a radical direction, he was being pushed away from conservatism by his increasingly difficult relations with his wife's family and even with his wife herself. Gradually he discovered that the Cabots and their class were not his kind of people.

In this period Parker began to find his literary voice, developing it in the scores of anonymous and pseudonymous pieces he wrote for *The Christian Register, Christian Examiner,* and other publications, and especially in his sermons, hundreds of which survive in manuscript. Sermons served for Parker the role that journals served for Emerson–the principal site where he worked out his ideas and rhetoric.

In 1840 Parker emerged as a significant Transcendentalist spokesman. He had followed closely the pamphlet exchange, which had been running since 1839, between Andrews Norton, the former Harvard professor who despised Transcendentalism, and George Ripley, the New School champion. Believing that the two disputants were getting sidetracked into scholarly matters and therefore were neglecting the central issue of whether or not religious truths required miraculous authority, he produced in the spring of 1840 *The Previous Question between Mr. Andrews Norton and His Alumni, Moved and Handled in a Letter to Those Gentlemen,* under the pseudonym "Levi Blodgett." Supposedly a plain Yankee farmer, Blodgett took the "common sense" position that religious truth required no miracle to be recognized by the soul.

This pamphlet, Parker's first, received little attention, but his other activities that year began to win him a reputation as a radical. Most controversial was his decision to sign the call for, and to speak at, the religious reform convention at Chardon Street in Boston, which debated the significance of the Sabbath. Parker had become committed to reconstructing religious institutions on a new basis so that they no longer claimed divine authority over the reason and conscience of individuals. As Parker saw the matter, freeing the people from this ancient and universal spiritual tyranny was the first step toward ending all forms of social repression. Parker remained sympathetic to the other Transcendentalist social reform projects of the period, in particular the Brook Farm community, which Ripley started in West Roxbury in 1841. Parker regularly visited Brook Farm, and many of the residents of Brook Farm attended his church.

Parker moved to the center of the Transcendentalist controversy in May 1841 when he delivered his first ordination sermon–for Charles C. Shackford of the Unitarian Church at South Boston. Parker did not intend *A Discourse on the Transient and Permanent in Christianity* to be a Transcendentalist manifesto. The main point of the discourse, as Parker saw it, was that Christianity would never be superseded, because Jesus had preached the Absolute Religion, so his words were permanently true. Yet, Parker's audience heard only the negative part of his argument, in which he attacked as a "transient" notion that Jesus and the Bible had miraculous authority. Three evangelical ministers who were attending Shackford's ordination raised an outcry. They published an inflammatory account of the discourse in the newspapers and demanded to know if the Unitarians considered Parker a Christian minister. Most of the Unitarian clergy denied that he was.

Although the Unitarian denomination lacked both the procedural mechanisms and the collective will to excommunicate him formally, individual Unitarian ministers, each acting separately, decided to deny Parker pulpit exchanges. Swapping pulpits for a Sunday was a popular practice among the congregational clergy around Boston; Parker himself, before the controversy started, exchanged often. Congregations enjoyed a greater variety of preaching, while ministers enjoyed wider audiences and the break from having to write (as New England ministers of that era were expected to do) two new sermons every week. Among Unitarians, pulpit exchanging had theological significance. Many liberals saw it as a right of ministerial fellowship and believed that no Christian minister should exclude another from his pulpit on doctrinal grounds. Parker was excluded from Unitarian pulpits, nonetheless. Most ministers refused to invite him because they thought he was not a Christian; others refused because they feared that an invitation would offend a significant portion of their congregations–generally made up of the older, wealthier, more powerful members.

Parker's becoming a pariah within Unitarianism changed the course of his career. His early ambition to rise to eminence and respectability was forever thwarted, and he afterward resented the Boston elite. Although his West Roxbury congregation remained loyal to him, he feared that he would be shut up in his tiny parish and effectively silenced. He found a new outlet, however, in lecturing. In the fall of 1841 Parker delivered a course of five lectures on "Religion" to large, attentive audiences in Boston and surrounding towns. In the spring of 1842 he published the lectures in expanded form as *A Discourse of Matters Pertaining to Religion.*

In this work Parker offered a systematic presentation of Transcendentalist views, written in a vivid, popular style but buttressed by hundreds of erudite footnotes. The book shows the influence on him of Friedrich Schleiermacher, Benjamin Constant, August Comte (*A Discourse of Matters Pertaining to Religion* was the first book in English to make use of Comte's ideas), the German biblical critics, and the English neoplatonists. Parker held that the "religious sentiment" was innate, and he described it, using Schleiermacher's language, as a "sense of dependence" on God. All religions throughout history sprang from this sentiment, Parker argued, each successive manifestation a progressively better approximation of the Absolute Religion. The Bible was a collection of such approximations from the period of early Jewish history to the time of Jesus; it had no miraculous authority. Neither had Jesus, whom Parker acknowledged to be fallible. Nonetheless, Parker insisted, as he had in *A Discourse on the Transient and Permanent in Christianity,* that the historical Jesus actually had preached the Absolute

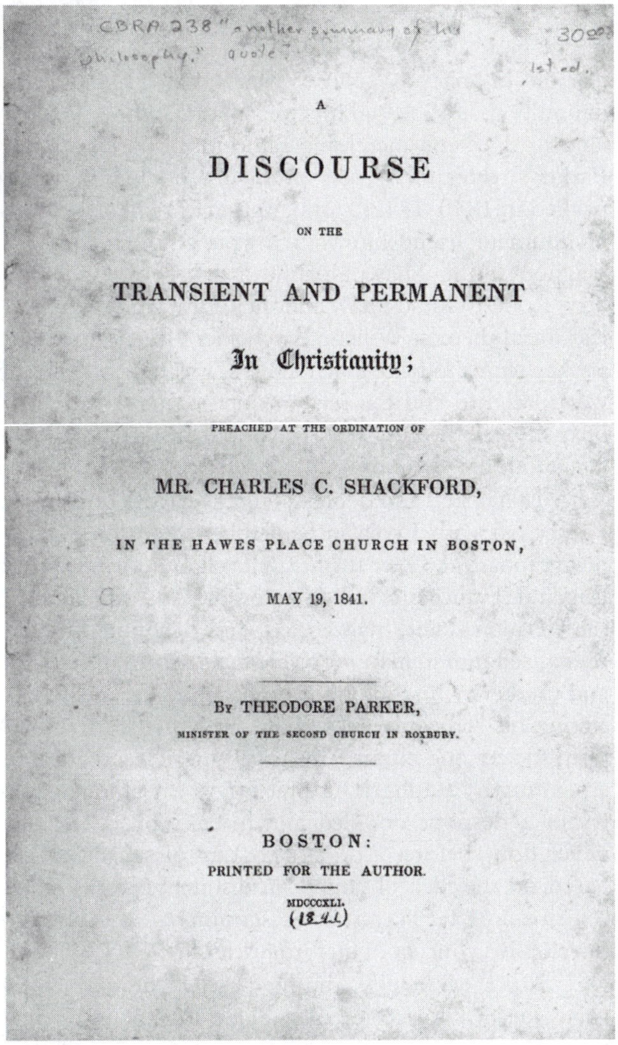
A

DISCOURSE

ON THE

TRANSIENT AND PERMANENT

In Christianity;

PREACHED AT THE ORDINATION OF

MR. CHARLES C. SHACKFORD,

IN THE HAWES PLACE CHURCH IN BOSTON,

MAY 19, 1841.

By THEODORE PARKER,

MINISTER OF THE SECOND CHURCH IN ROXBURY.

BOSTON:

PRINTED FOR THE AUTHOR.

MDCCCXLI.

Title page for the sermon that provoked some clergymen to question if Parker could be considered a Christian (Collection of Joel Myerson)

Religion. Parker criticized every existing "party" within Christianity, including Unitarianism, and argued that the Soul was greater than the Church.

Parker had written *A Discourse of Matters Pertaining to Religion,* a five-hundred-page book of theology, in only nine months. The effort exhausted him, but he did not stop working. He published more articles, more pamphlets, two more books, a collection of his *Critical and Miscellaneous Writings* (1843), and (after seven years of scholarly labor and many delays) his massive two-volume translation and expansion of de Wette's *Introduction to the Canonical Scriptures of the Old Testament* (1843). Altogether, between the spring of 1841 and the fall of 1843, he published more than three thousand pages of material. Besides, Parker continued his regular preaching and delivered another series of lectures around Boston in 1842–1843, "Six Plain Sermons of the Times" (never published).

These years of controversy were marked for Parker not only by toil but also by emotional trial. He lost the intimacy of several friends, most notably and painfully that of his old mentor, Francis, who was alienated by Parker's increasing radicalism. To compound Parker's difficulties, the problems of his marriage peaked in 1840–1842. During these years he developed an intimate friendship with a young West Roxbury neighbor, Anna Shaw, an aunt of the future Civil War hero Robert Gould Shaw and the future wife of the radical social theorist William Batchelder Greene. Secretly, Parker seems to have fallen in love with her. In 1842 he was forced to end the relationship because of the jealousy of his wife and because gossip had started to circulate about the situation.

Exhausted and depressed by overwork and stress, Parker left with Lydia in September 1843 for a European sabbatical. Over the next eleven months he visited England, France, the Italian states, the Austrian Empire, the German states, Switzerland, and Belgium. The trip revitalized him in many ways. He met scores of scholars and thinkers who took him and his work seriously, bolstering his self-confidence. Too, his exposure to European society and culture–his first sight of a cathedral or a painting by Raphael, his first trip to a Catholic country or a despotic one–led him to envision, as he had never done before, a broad program of social reform, based on the idea of American distinctiveness. On his return home he began in his sermons and lectures to develop his concept of an "American Idea."

More personally, during this trip he and Lydia spent large amounts of time alone together, the first time they had done so since their wedding, and they reconciled. There was still pain in their marriage (in particular, they were both saddened by their childlessness), but they would never again be so alienated from one another. By the time Parker returned home, his mood had improved dramatically. Although in the future he faced far more dangerous controversies than he had in 1841–1843, none affected him so deeply.

In the fall of 1844 Parker once again became the center of a polemical storm. In November he conducted an exchange with John Sargent, minister of a Unitarian chapel for the poor in Boston, which caused a protest from Sargent's congregation and from the directors of the chapel, who demanded he not exchange with Parker again. Sargent resigned, arguing that freedom of the pulpit was at stake. His case prompted James Freeman Clarke, minister of the new Church of the Disciples in Boston, to offer Parker an exchange. Although Clarke was a Unitarian allied with the Transcendentalists, he strongly disagreed with Parker's naturalistic interpretation of Jesus. He believed, however, that his own liberal principles required him to open his pulpit to Parker. Clarke's action prompted a significant section of his congregation to secede in protest.

The troubles of Sargent and Clarke provoked enormous discussion within the denomination, and in January 1845 a group of Unitarians, designating themselves the "Friends of Theodore Parker," met and resolved to offer him "a chance to be heard in Boston." They rented the Melodeon Theater and invited him to preach there Sunday mornings. Parker accepted, while continuing to preach in West Roxbury Sunday afternoons. Large audiences came to the Melodeon to hear what he had to say, and in the fall of 1845 his supporters decided formally to organize themselves into a church called the 28th Congregational Society (because it was the 28th Congregational church in the city). Parker officially became minister there in January 1846, preaching his own installation sermon (*The True Idea of a Christian Church*). He resigned his West Roxbury pulpit a month later.

Parker now had a large salary, which he supplemented by lecture fees. He could afford to move out of Lucy Cabot's house, and in January 1847 he and Lydia took up residence at Exeter Place in Boston, a few blocks southeast of the Public Garden. His career had entered a new phase. His controversy with Unitarianism had passed from a "hot" phase to a "cold" one, flaring up only occasionally (as in 1853, when the denomination approved a creedlike statement, prompting Parker to question it in his *Friendly Letter to the Executive Committee of the American Unitarian Association Touching Their New Creed or General Proclamation of Unitarian Views*). Meanwhile, his interests grew more diverse and his influence, wider.

Despite continued ostracism by the Unitarian social elite of the city, or perhaps because of it, Parker drew more and more people to his regular Sunday services as the years passed. Regular attendance rose from close to one thousand at the time of his installation to twice that number a decade later (altogether, nearly two percent of the non-Catholic population of Boston). Even more people came whenever some significant public event occurred, because everyone was curious to hear what Parker would say about it. His popularity led the 28th Congregational Society to move in 1852 from the Melodeon to the new, larger Boston Music Hall (today the Orpheum Theater).

His sermons–especially the topical, political ones–received extensive coverage in newspapers around the country and often were published as pamphlets. Parker came to be regarded as an innovator of the sermon form. He had been trained in the Unitarian tradition of preaching, which held that sermons should be carefully composed, elegant literary productions. From this starting point he moved on to test the bound-

The Melodeon Theatre in Boston, where Parker began preaching in 1845

aries of what a preacher could do. He abandoned the tradition that sermons should be expositions of Scriptural passages. Although he prefaced most of his sermons with biblical texts, they were merely mottoes; sometimes Parker used non-Scriptural "texts," such as popular sayings or even topical events. He made a point to raise issues in his preaching that most other ministers regarded as too political or controversial to be proper subjects for sermons and removed from his discourses much traditional theological language, sometimes replacing it with the rhetorical effects and polemical style of political oratory. Parker believed the traditional pulpit oratory had grown moribund and dull, and he was reviving it. The popularity of his preaching indicates the success of his strategy.

Again, Parker became a successful lecturer. At his peak, in the mid 1850s, he delivered about seventy lectures a year and often made more money from lecture fees than from his ministerial salary. Only once more did he work up a lecture series, as he had in 1841 or 1842; that was in 1858, when he prepared four talks on "Historic Americans." Otherwise, he would deliver one, or at most two, lectures to a given lyceum during a year. Through the mid 1840s he spoke only in New England, but starting in 1848 he made an annual excursion to the West, traveling by rail and stagecoach as far as Illinois and Wisconsin. By his own estimate he spoke altogether to between sixty and a hundred thousand people a year on the lyceum circuit. Many of his lectures he published as essays, while a few were published after his death–for example, *Transcendentalism,* published in 1876.

Besides these activities Parker cultivated extensive connections among the learned. He was elected an officer of the American Oriental Society and a member of the Boston Society of Natural History and became recognized as a significant scholarly resource, not only because of his personal erudition but also because of his extraordinary private research library, painstakingly accumulated, of nearly fourteen thousand volumes, one of the largest libraries of any kind in the United States, items of which he lent freely and every book of which he was believed to have read. In 1848 he founded *The Massachusetts Quarterly Review* and served as its editor until financial problems of the publisher forced publication to cease three years later. Parker used *The Massachu-*

setts Quarterly Review, the most significant Transcendentalist periodical after the *The Dial,* as a forum for his intellectual circle, publishing their essays, as well as his own, on politics (both national and international), science, religion, and literature. Despite all his scholarly activity, he never had time to complete what he intended to be his major scholarly project–a study of the development of religion across the course of human history.

In Parker's mature theology his attachment to historical Christianity grew more attenuated. Around 1850 he concluded, contrary to his earlier view, that Jesus had not in fact preached the Absolute Religion but had made what Parker considered significant errors (he thought Jesus mistakenly believed in Hell, for example, and in the miraculously ordained nature of his own Messiahship). Parker laid out his new position in the fourth, revised edition of the *Discourse of Matters Pertaining to Religion* (1855).

Meanwhile, he moved from the anthropological concerns of his early years (when he stressed that people were naturally religious and naturally received divine inspiration) toward an emphasis on the absolute perfection of God. Parker may have made this shift in part as a reaction against the anthropological interpretation of God advanced by the German atheist Ludwig Feuerbach. Feuerbach argued that humans created God as a projection of their own qualities. After learning (in 1852) that Feuerbach's ideas were widespread among young German intellectuals, Parker predicted in his journal that "I shall appear in the ranks of conservatives in theology long before I looked for that result." He therefore insisted that humans had divine qualities (not the other way around) and that God had a real, independent existence. Parker's new concerns are evident in his major theological books of this period, especially *Sermons of Theism, Atheism, and the Popular Theology* (1853).

Alongside these developments Parker began analyzing society and social problems in new ways. His analysis turned sociological in the mid 1840s, as he started lavishly illustrating his arguments with statistics. He sought to show with census data, for example, that slavery was uneconomical and socially destructive. Parker's fascination with statistics has been held by some scholars to sit poorly with his intuitionist philosophy. They argue, for example, that if Parker really believed human bondage was intuitively and absolutely wrong, he should have found irrelevant the question of whether or not slavery hindered economic development. Parker, however, saw no contradiction. He believed that God infused both matter and mind with the same moral structure. Moral truth, therefore, would be the same whether perceived by an insight of "Conscience" or deduced from the accumulation and analysis of "Facts." Parker believed, moreover, that the two approaches to truth complemented one another psychologically, because the study of external facts by itself could not yield certainty, while intuition, unconstrained by facts, might leap to arbitrary and false conclusions.

In addition to statistics Parker began using race as a category of social analysis. In particular he became fascinated by the study of ethnology and racial classification. His later writings, especially on history and politics, often include lengthy discussions of the distinct strengths and characteristics of different human "races," "families," and "tribes"–for example, "The Political Destination of America" (1848), in *Speeches, Addresses and Occasional Sermons,* volume 2 (1851); "Some Thoughts on the Progress of America" (1854), in *Additional Speeches, Addresses and Occasional Sermons,* volume 2 (1855); and *The Present Aspect of Slavery in America and the Immediate Duty of the North* (1858).

Parker's interest in ethnology grew in significant ways from his Transcendentalism. German Romantic theorists had strongly influenced his conception of race–notable among them Johann Gottfried von Herder, who held that each people had a characteristic spiritual "genius," which expressed itself in culture and language, and a characteristic "idea" that God intended them to develop in world history. Race, for Parker, therefore had a spiritual dimension, and ethnology allowed him to talk, in what he felt was a "scientific" way, about the progress of spirit in history. Also, race seemed to him a way to repudiate certain materialistic conceptions of history, which held that everything about a people could be determined by the physical environment in which it lived (climate and terrain, for example) and by its political and economic institutions. Parker never doubted the importance of these factors, but when he insisted on the significance of "blood" and "racial stock," his purpose was to assert the significance of spirit, culture, and ideas.

In adopting the theories and language of ethnology, however, he also accepted the idea of a hierarchy of races, based on the "progressive" power of each. He came to believe that the "Caucasian" race was more progressive than all the others; that within that race the "Germanic family" was the most progressive; and that within that family the "Anglo-Saxon tribe" was the most progressive. Parker's proclivity to rank races, however, caused him difficulties as an abolitionist.

While his interest rose in statistics and race, he reconceived his social reform program. In particular he moved from his earlier idea that changing the Church would by itself transform society. He remained interested in the reform of ecclesiastical institutions. He encouraged the 28th Congregational Society to adopt innovative practices (they had only one sermon on Sunday, for example, instead of the usual two, because Parker thought that there were better

Parker's study in the house on Exeter Place in Boston where he and his wife took up residence in 1847

places for people to spend the day than at a religious service). He also participated in a major Sabbath reform convention in 1848. But he no longer saw the Church as the cornerstone of social organization. By the mid 1840s the key social building blocks appeared to him to be economic and political. Religion remained an essential element of his reform vision, but his priority was no longer to create a new church. Instead, he wanted the United States to become what he came to call an "Industrial Democracy."

Industrial Democracy grew, according to Parker, out of an inexorable, divinely sanctioned historical trend. Earlier ages were characterized by "military despotism," when a few aristocratic warriors dominated society for their own benefit. Now this system was giving way around the world, but most rapidly and obviously in the United States. Instead of aristocrats and warriors, merchants held sway, which meant greater general prosperity and more rapid social advancement for all, although merchants tended to view labor, especially manual labor, with contempt. They therefore sought to accumulate enough wealth that they or their children could live idly. Parker believed that in the ideal society toward which America was heading work no longer would be seen as a curse, but be valued as a school to train the mind and body; all laborers, including manual laborers, would be honored for their efforts; and everyone would work, with work being distributed fairly throughout society, so that none would be ruined by luxurious idleness or oppressive toil.

As America became "industrial," Parker believed, it also became a "democracy," which he defined as "government by all the people, for all the people, and of all the people." He first put in print a version of this definition in his *A Sermon of Merchants* (1846; published 1847); Abraham Lincoln later adapted it for the "Gettysburg Address" (1863). Lincoln, however, changed Parker's meaning. The president referred to a particular form of political polity. Parker envisioned an ideal kind of just society. "Government of all the people" suggests that the action of the whole people should result from the will of the whole people, not of an individual or social group, while "by all the people" indicates that social power should be distributed widely, so that no social group could be despotic. But Parker held the most morally important part of the phrase to be "for all the people" (or "for the sake of all the people"), by which he meant that no social group would behave selfishly, and that government, like God, would watch out for the welfare of each individual.

Parker saw Industrial Democracy as the ultimate manifestation of what he called the "American Idea,"

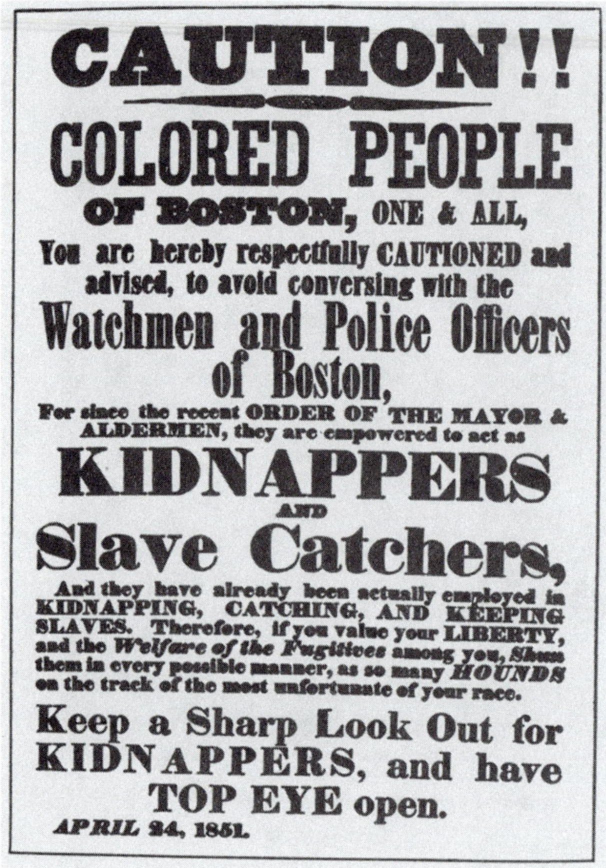

Warning to fugitive slaves, written by Parker and published by the Boston Vigilance Committee

which he believed was expressed in the Declaration of Independence, that everyone was created equal and endowed by God with inalienable rights. At the same time an Industrial Democracy would be the most *religious* kind of society, because it would provide the greatest opportunity for individual spiritual development. Every person, according to Parker, should strive to become perfect in mind, conscience, heart, and soul, and to become in this sense like God. Industrial Democracy would encourage all people to strive for such perfection.

Parker attacked what he perceived as the obstacles to the realization of this vision, and in the process he developed a comprehensive critique of American culture and society. He found that most American literature reflected "aristocratic" values, as did much of American higher education. He argued that both must become more democratic. He supported the temperance movement, in part because he believed that alcohol abuse produced widespread spiritual destruction, especially among the poor, and in part because he saw the liquor trade as a case of the strong exploiting the weak in order to become rich. Parker never endorsed prohibition legislation, however, believing it both destructive of personal liberties and ineffective; instead, he favored a regulatory approach. Again, he was active in the effort to improve the condition of the urban poor and the treatment of criminals. His major sermons on these subjects were pioneering examples of sociological analysis as well as moral exhortations–for example, *A Sermon of the Perishing Classes in Boston* (1846); *A Sermon of the Dangerous Classes in Society* (1847); and "A Sermon of Poverty," in volume 1 of *Speeches, Addresses and Occasional Sermons.* He supported, too, the efforts of his friend Horace Mann to better Massachusetts public education by providing teachers with professional training, establishing public high schools, and opening up schools for girls as well as boys.

Parker's support for women's education, which he showed from his earliest days as a schoolteacher, became part of a larger campaign for woman's rights. He came to see the "degradation of woman" as one of the greatest obstacles to Industrial Democracy. He joined the attempt to persuade the Massachusetts Constitutional Convention of 1853 to grant the vote to women of the state. Parker gave notable testimony before the convention, in which he called the woman's rights movement the "deepest of all reforms," and he endorsed woman's suffrage in one of his most important and often-reprinted sermons, *A Sermon of the Public Function of Woman* (1853). Although the convention rejected the suffrage measure, Parker demonstrated his ongoing commitment to woman's rights with significant symbolic gestures. He began to address God in his sermons and public prayers not only as "Father" but as "Mother"; he arranged for women preachers and lecturers to address his congregation; he encouraged his church to choose women officers (in 1855 his congregation became among the first ever to elect women to its Standing Committee).

Parker preferred to say that men and women were "equivalent" rather than "equal." He thought that women had less power of Body and Reason than men, but more of the "higher" spiritual powers of Conscience, Affection, and Religion. Again, although he happily served as mentor to many prominent intellectual women, among them Julia Ward Howe and Caroline Healey Dall, he had difficulty accepting women as intellectual peers–and therefore could never feel comfortable with Margaret Fuller. Yet, Parker's softer, sentimental version of woman's rights had considerable appeal among the middle-class women of Boston, who were educated, accomplished, and interested in reform but who still prided themselves on their domestic skills and supposedly "feminine" traits.

More even than woman's rights, however, Parker became associated with abolitionism. He considered slavery to be the greatest threat to Industrial Democracy, and through the antislavery movement he had his greatest immediate impact on American life. He had denounced slavery from the pulpit as early as 1837 and had published his first antislavery sermon in 1843, but for years he avoided speaking at abolitionist gatherings and did not vote for antislavery political parties, preferring instead to support the Whigs.

Then came the annexation of Texas (1845) and the Mexican War (1846–1848), which together vastly increased the territory into which slavery could expand. Parker strongly opposed both and believed the Whigs had done little to prevent either. He began associating more openly with abolitionists, becoming good friends with many of them, especially Wendell Phillips, who was his neighbor in Boston, and William Lloyd Garrison, who with his wife began attending Parker's church. Parker started making speeches at abolitionist conventions and in 1847 wrote his long *Letter to the People of the United States Touching the Matter of Slavery* (published in 1848), an attempt to demonstrate the wrong of slavery on many grounds, both moral and practical. Here Parker helped popularize the argument that slavery was economically destructive for the South. When the Free Soil Party was organized in 1848, he became an active supporter and a close adviser to state Free Soil leaders.

Parker was welcomed into the antislavery movement, in part because he brought with him both a large following and an impressive scholarly reputation. People would go to hear him who would never listen to Garrison or Phillips, and newspapers that would never report their speeches would report his. Parker also proved himself adept at avoiding the pitfalls of abolitionist factionalism. He worked to bridge the most conspicuous division in antislavery ranks, between those, such as Garrison and Phillips, who thought that the federal Constitution was a proslavery document and that no true abolitionist could be involved in constitutional political action, and those who held the Constitution to be neutral or even hostile toward slavery, and who therefore thought they could vote and hold office. Parker could be truly neutral on this issue, because he interpreted the Constitution in a way similar to the way he interpreted the Bible. Just as the Bible was a provisional statement of Absolute Religion, to be respected and honored insofar as it was true but set aside when it has been found false, so the Constitution was a provisional statement of the American Idea, to be respected and honored insofar as it was useful and just but set aside when it was not. With this view Parker believed he could support antislavery action whether it was constitutional or unconstitutional, legal or illegal.

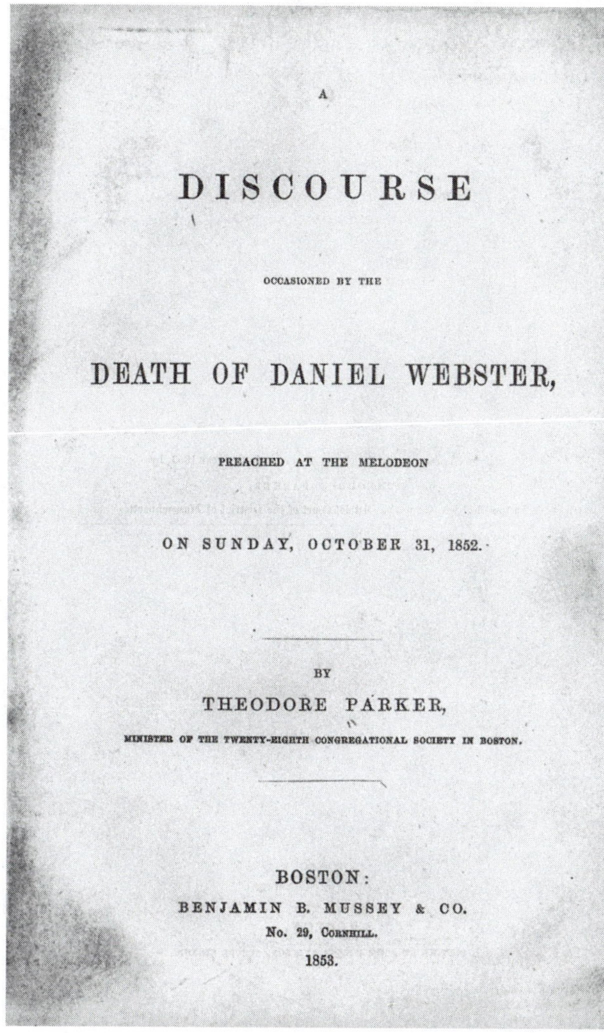
A

DISCOURSE

OCCASIONED BY THE

DEATH OF DANIEL WEBSTER,

PREACHED AT THE MELODEON

ON SUNDAY, OCTOBER 31, 1852.

BY

THEODORE PARKER,

MINISTER OF THE TWENTY-EIGHTH CONGREGATIONAL SOCIETY IN BOSTON.

BOSTON:
BENJAMIN B. MUSSEY & CO.
No. 29, CORNHILL.
1853.

Title page for the sermon in which Parker called a much-admired New England statesman a tragic failure for his willingness to compromise on the issue of slavery, "the most hideous snake which Southern regions breed" (Collection of Joel Myerson)

Parker's role in the antislavery movement grew even more important in 1850, when Congress, as part of the famous Compromise Measures of that year, passed a new fugitive slave law. This measure, which its supporters pronounced a necessary concession to the South that would prevent disunion and civil war, in effect established a federal slave-catching bureaucracy made up of federal court commissioners. Until the 1850 law took effect, fugitive slaves merely had to escape to the free states to be safe, and in Massachusetts many people were proud that their state had never returned a fugitive. Now there were "Fugitive Slave Commissioners" at work in Boston, and fugitives there had to flee to Canada.

Parker openly called for people to disobey the law, as in his sermon on *The Function and Place of Con-*

Theodore Parker

science, in Relation to the Laws of Men (1850). His kind of civil disobedience differed from the more famous version put forward by his fellow Transcendentalist Henry David Thoreau. Thoreau wanted to retain his personal and spiritual integrity by refusing to participate in evil; Parker wanted to stop legislation he saw as evil from taking effect. Parker's version of civil disobedience, in other words, was far more explicitly political. He justified resistance to the government, for example, partly by drawing on the political precedents of the English and American revolutions, and he began to extol the example of his heroic paternal grandfather. Again, Parker conceived of disobedience within a framework of political institutions. He became an advocate of what is today called "jury nullification," arguing that a conscientious juror should never vote to punish someone who had rescued a fugitive slave, whatever the law mandated. Most obviously, civil disobedience was not for Parker a solitary, private act, as it was for Thoreau. Parker organized groups of people publicly to flout the law.

He was chosen, by a public protest meeting, to be Minister at Large for all fugitive slaves in Boston. He helped set up the Boston Vigilance Committee and became chairman of its executive committee; the Vigilance Committee, made up of hundreds of men (women played an informal role), provided fugitives with financial assistance, legal aid, and above all, help in avoiding capture. As part of this effort Parker once hid a famous fugitive, Ellen Craft, for a week in his home. While she was there, he wrote his sermons with a loaded pistol on his desk and a sword beside him.

Parker's opposition to the Fugitive Slave Law had several sources. There were fugitive slaves in his congregation, Craft among them, and Parker insisted that he had an obvious pastoral duty to protect his parishioners from "kidnappers." Yet, he had a complex relationship with the African Americans of Boston, both fugitive and free. They resented his ethnological ideas. He insisted that the "African" race was docile and incapable of spontaneous progress. More than one black abolitionist (Williams Wells Brown, for example, and Charles Rock) and a few white ones (Phillips) criticized his views publicly and to his face. Most African Americans respected him, however, as a powerful ally on practical matters, with a strong commitment to abolition and even to equal rights. The 28th Congregational Society was one of the few integrated churches in Boston, and Parker supported the effort to repeal legal segregation of the Boston schools. The leader of the desegregation movement, the African American historian William C. Nell, admired Parker and worked as sexton of his church. Still, Parker felt a certain personal discomfort around blacks and expressed the hope, in some unpublished sermons from the late 1850s, that through race mixing the African race in the United States would be "absorbed" by the Caucasian race and would disappear from sight.

Parker had other motives to oppose the Fugitive Slave Law than empathy with its victims. Above all, his ideological commitment to democracy became combined with his powerful resentment of the Boston elite, who in 1850 united to support the capture of fugitives. The driving force behind the elite's stand was Senator Daniel Webster, for decades the monarch of Massachusetts Whiggery, who threw his huge reputation behind the Fugitive Slave Law, endorsing the legislation in a spectacular Senate speech and then, when President Millard Fillmore appointed him Secretary of State, working hard to see that the enactment was enforced. Webster, with the help of his supporters and allies, convinced a large body of "establishment" Massachusetts opinion that the Fugitive Slave Law would settle the sectional controversy forever.

Parker's hostility to the elite had been high since the late 1830s and early 1840s, when he was scorned by the Cabots and then by the "respectable" Boston churches. His feelings had grown even more bitter in 1848, when Lucy Cabot died and Lydia Parker received only a fraction of her money. Parker himself believed his wife's Brahmin relations, because of their contempt for him, had used legal chicanery to cheat her out of $30,000. Now he believed that the elite was opposing the American Idea.

He began to argue that there was not just one great idea in America, but two, fighting a struggle to the death: Freedom versus Despotism. On the side of Freedom, he believed, massed the ordinary people of the North; on the side of Despotism stood the slaveholders of the South and, in the North, most of the wealthy, educated, and powerful classes. Daniel Webster became for Parker the symbol of this morally bankrupt Northern aristocracy. When Webster died in October 1852, preachers around the country eulogized him as a statesman and hero, but Parker took a different approach. In his *Discourse Occasioned by the Death of Daniel Webster* (1852; published 1853), he portrayed his subject as a tragic failure, gifted with immense powers of mind but lacking a moral core and therefore willing to see fugitive slaves arrested in order to win Southern support in a bid for the presidency. Parker's sermon, which some contemporaries regarded as the greatest he ever wrote, caused a sensation and earned him the enduring enmity of Webster's supporters.

Contrary to their claims, Parker always had argued that the Fugitive Slave Act would not settle the slavery issue but that Northern appeasement of the "Slave Power" would lead to renewed "assaults upon Freedom in America." His view seemed to receive powerful confirmation from the events of 1854. That spring, Congress passed the Kansas-Nebraska Act, which potentially opened the entire West to slavery. Parker attacked it in speeches and sermons. In June, Anthony Burns, a fugitive slave and Baptist preacher from Virginia, was arrested in Boston and brought before Fugitive Slave Commissioner Edward G. Loring, a conservative Whig, who after a weeklong hearing ordered Burns returned to his master.

The Burns case, coming on the heels of the Kansas-Nebraska Act, roused outrage in Boston, for which Parker became the spokesman. While he was addressing a Faneuil Hall rally called to protest Burns's arrest, a riot broke out. Rioters tried to break into the jail where Burns was being held and free him. The rescue attempt failed, but an Irish policeman guarding Burns was killed. These events became the subject of bitter contention. Parker publicly blamed the policeman's death on Commissioner Loring and helped launch a

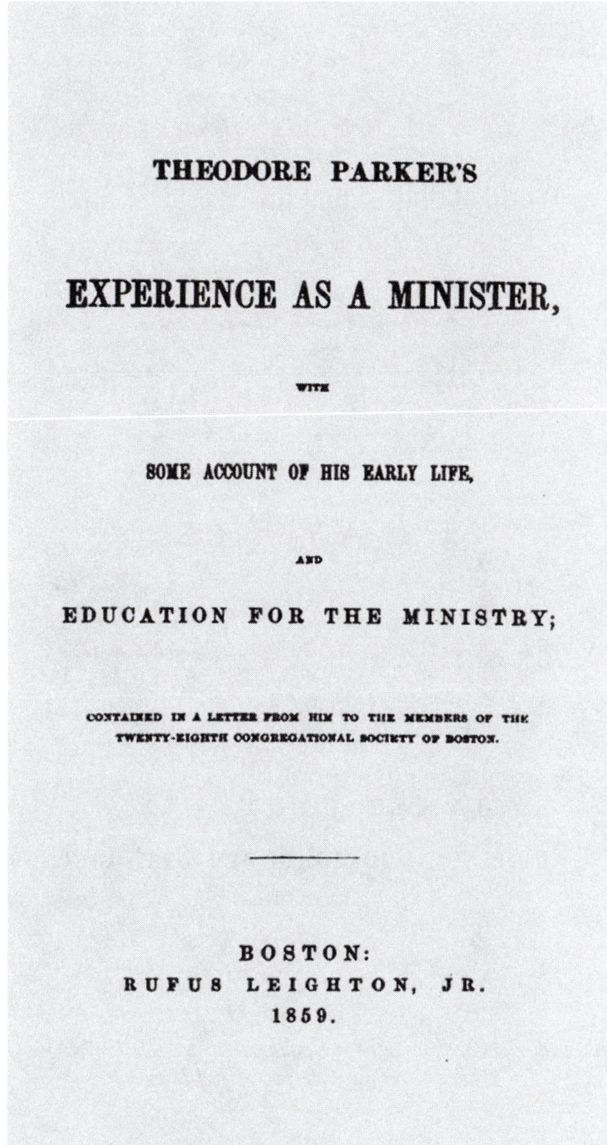
THEODORE PARKER'S

EXPERIENCE AS A MINISTER,

WITH

SOME ACCOUNT OF HIS EARLY LIFE,

AND

EDUCATION FOR THE MINISTRY;

CONTAINED IN A LETTER FROM HIM TO THE MEMBERS OF THE TWENTY-EIGHTH CONGREGATIONAL SOCIETY OF BOSTON.

BOSTON:
RUFUS LEIGHTON, JR.
1859.

Title page for the letter to his congregation in which Parker summarized his career

campaign, which quickly became a cause célèbre, to have Loring removed from one of his other jobs, that of state probate judge. Meanwhile, the Whig elite and the Boston Irish together denounced Parker as a demagogue. Some Irish threatened to burn his house, while an Irish politician on the Boston City Council sought to revoke his right to speak at Faneuil Hall. Meanwhile, some former Webster Whigs tried to evict Parker's church from the Boston Music Hall, while others had Parker indicted before a federal grand jury for obstructing execution of federal law. He was arrested the day before Thanksgiving, 1854, but released on bail.

Meanwhile, a political sea change had occurred in Massachusetts, one that considerably strengthened

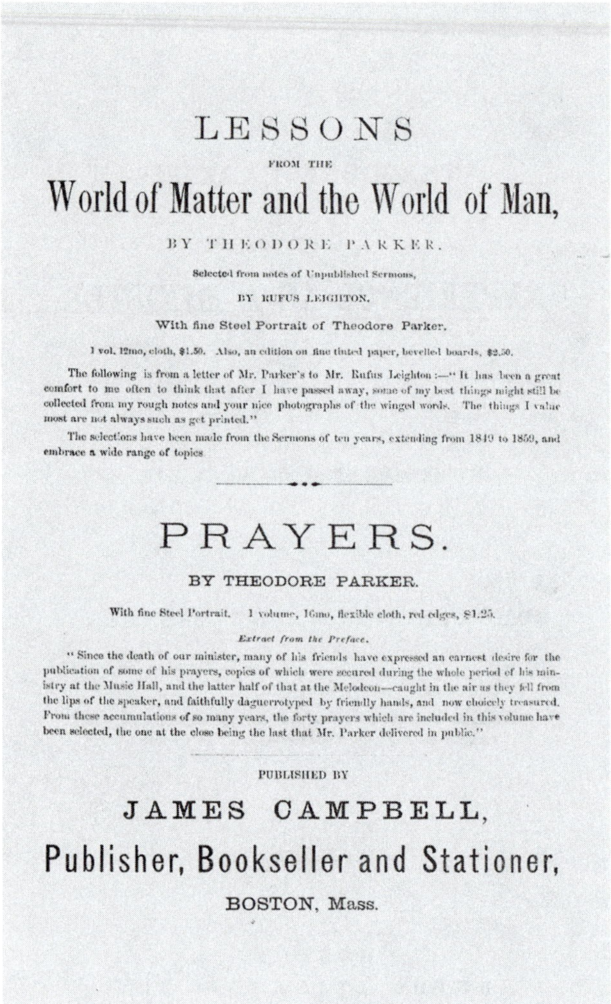

LESSONS

FROM THE

World of Matter and the World of Man,

BY THEODORE PARKER.

Selected from notes of Unpublished Sermons,

BY RUFUS LEIGHTON.

With fine Steel Portrait of Theodore Parker.

1 vol. 12mo, cloth, $1.50. Also, an edition on fine tinted paper, bevelled boards, $2.50.

The following is from a letter of Mr. Parker's to Mr. Rufus Leighton :—" It has been a great comfort to me often to think that after I have passed away, some of my best things might still be collected from my rough notes and your nice photographs of the winged words. The things I value most are not always such as get printed."

The selections have been made from the Sermons of ten years, extending from 1849 to 1859, and embrace a wide range of topics

PRAYERS.

BY THEODORE PARKER.

With fine Steel Portrait. 1 volume, 16mo, flexible cloth, red edges, $1.25.

Extract from the Preface.

" Since the death of our minister, many of his friends have expressed an earnest desire for the publication of some of his prayers, copies of which were secured during the whole period of his ministry at the Music Hall, and the latter half of that at the Melodeon—caught in the air as they fell from the lips of the speaker, and faithfully daguerrotyped by friendly hands, and now choicely treasured. From these accumulations of so many years, the forty prayers which are included in this volume have been selected, the one at the close being the last that Mr. Parker delivered in public."

PUBLISHED BY

JAMES CAMPBELL,

Publisher, Bookseller and Stationer,

BOSTON, Mass.

Bookseller's advertisement for two posthumously published collections of Parker's writings (Collection of Joel Myerson)

Parker's position. In the 1854 elections state voters had repudiated both the Whigs and the Irish by sweeping into power an upstart organization, called the American or "Know Nothing" Party. The rise of the Know Nothings destroyed the Whigs' political base, while the principal plank of the Know Nothing platform was to restrict the political rights of Irish Catholic immigrants, who had been flooding into the state by the tens of thousands since the mid 1840s, fleeing the terrible famine in their homeland. Parker himself initially had felt some sympathy for the impoverished new arrivals, but over time he turned against them. Partly, he felt repulsed by their "Celtic" mores, but more importantly, he came to regard their Catholicism and their politics as threats to his religious and social vision. The Irish bishops and politicians rejected the reforms he held dear, in particular abolitionism. He believed that the Irish were allied with the Boston elite against the idea of Freedom. Starting with his sermon on 4 July 1854, he began listing Catholicism as one of the political detriments in *A Sermon of the Dangers which Threaten the Rights of Man in America.* Parker's own long struggle for religious liberty led him to reject legal discrimination against Catholics as Catholics, but he did come to favor the Know Nothing idea of requiring immigrants to wait up to twenty-one years before they could vote or hold political office. Parker never seems to have joined the Know Nothing Party (he voted Free Soil and later Republican); yet, he had an affinity with the nativists, as many Know Nothings themselves recognized. In January 1854 the Know Nothing-dominated state House of Representatives nearly elected Parker its chaplain.

Parker's local political influence reached its peak in 1855 with the Know Nothing legislature. It was full of his admirers and supporters, who, with his encouragement, passed a raft of reform and antislavery legislation, including strong protection for fugitive slaves, the end of legal segregation of the Boston schools, the end of imprisonment for debt, and the expansion of the property rights of married women. Parker's political standing was so high that jailing him became an impossibility. In April 1855 the indictment against him was quashed. He took the speech to the jury he had written but never had the chance to deliver, expanded it, and published it as *The Trial of Theodore Parker* (1855).

Parker grew convinced, in the mid 1850s, that civil war in the United States was unavoidable. He did not foresee a conflict between the sections, however, but between Freedom and Despotism. The battle, he believed, would take place within the North as well as between North and South. When free-state and slave-state settlers in Kansas began fighting for control of that territory, Parker noted that the slave-state cause had the support of prominent Northern politicians, including President Franklin Pierce. Parker strongly backed the free-state side and in 1855 and 1856 raised money to buy weapons for emigrants from Massachusetts. Again, in 1856, when Parker's friend Charles Sumner, the antislavery Senator from Massachusetts, was beaten nearly to death on the Senate floor by a South Carolina congressman, Parker argued (in *A New Lesson for the Day,* 1856) that the deed was done with the tacit encouragement of proslavery Bostonians. After the presidential election of 1856, won by the proslavery Northerner James Buchanan, Parker was so sure that war was at hand and that his local enemies would soon try again to jail him or even attempt to assassinate him, as they had Sumner, he drastically cut his expenses and transferred much of his property to his wife for safekeeping. Such was his apocalyptic mood when, in January 1857, he met the apocalyptic apostle of abolitionist violence, John Brown.

Christopher Cranch's cartoon poking fun at his friend Parker's enthusiasm for German scholarship (from Frederick De Wolf Miller, Christopher Pearse Cranch and His Caricatures of New England Transcendentalism, *1951)*

Parker became an immediate admirer of "Old Brown," whose sense of urgency about the slavery issue matched his own. The two men agreed that only violent resistance now could stop the Slave Power from taking over the country. In February 1858 Brown informed Parker of his secret, long-contemplated plan to start a guerrilla insurrection among the slaves of Virginia. Parker supported the plan as he understood it–he in fact had argued for years that a slave insurrection would be the most direct way to destroy slavery–and helped organize a clandestine committee to provide Brown with weapons and money. In May 1858, however, Parker learned that a member of Brown's secret army, Hugh Forbes, had threatened to reveal details of the conspiracy to the government. Parker persuaded the majority of his fellow committee members, over Brown's objections, to postpone the Virginia war until 1859. Although Parker had little direct involvement with Brown's activities after this time, he continued to predict that slavery soon would fall in "violence and blood."

During the months Parker secretly conspired with Brown, he publicly battled evangelical Christians. Religious revivals swept the country in 1858, but for Parker they were merely "theological," not "religious." He thought they did not advance real goodness and piety but merely popularized what he considered spurious notions, such as salvation by Christ and eternal damnation. He attacked the revivals in two sermons, *A False and True Revival of Religion* and *The Revival of Religion which We Need,* which when published in 1858 became instant national best-sellers. Until this point many evangelicals had tolerated Parker, seeing him as a thorn in the side of their enemies, the Unitarians. Now Parker himself became their principal opponent, and their attacks on him became unrelenting.

Meanwhile, Parker's health was failing. Stress and overwork seem to have revived the tuberculosis he had been exposed to as a child. He suffered a collapse in February 1857 and took months to recover. Afterward, he lectured much less, but he continued to preach and write. In the winter of 1858 he had an operation on a fistula that weakened him further, and in January 1859 he suffered a severe attack of bleeding in the lungs that obliged him to give up preaching. Hoping at least for a partial recovery, in February he left Boston, sailing with Lydia and some friends for the more salubrious climate of the Caribbean. While staying on the island of Santa Cruz in March and April, Parker rallied enough strength to write a long letter to his congregation, soon published as *Theodore Parker's Experience as a Minister* (1859). In the letter Parker summarized his career, which he now assumed to be over, and provided one of the finest Transcendentalist confessions of faith.

From the Caribbean, Parker traveled to Europe–staying in England, France, Switzerland, and finally, in the winter of 1858–1859, Rome. There he learned that John Brown had made the attempt to start his Virginia war but that the insurrection had failed and Brown had been arrested and was to be hanged. In November 1859 Parker wrote a letter to a parishioner defending Brown and the right of slaves to kill their masters. The letter appeared in print in 1860 as a pamphlet–*John Brown's Expedition Reviewed*–Parker's last publication to appear during his lifetime. In early 1860 he also attempted to write an autobiography but soon had to abandon the project as his health worsened. In late April, he took his final trip, from Rome to Florence. He died in the city of Savonarola a few weeks later on 10 May, where he was buried in the English Cemetery.

No eulogy was delivered at his graveside. As he requested, only the first eleven verses of the Sermon on the Mount were read. When news of his passing reached Boston, however, his friends said many words in his honor. Among them was the astute judgment of Emerson, who predicted that when "coming generations" wanted to study what "really befell," they would find "in the plain lessons of Theodore Parker . . . the true temper and authentic record of these days."

Biographies:

John Weiss, *The Life and Correspondence of Theodore Parker, Minister of the Twenty-Eighth Congregational Society, Boston,* 2 volumes (Boston: D. Appleton, 1864);

Octavius Brooks Frothingham, *Theodore Parker: A Biography* (Boston: James R. Osgood, 1874);

John White Chadwick, *Theodore Parker: Preacher and Reformer* (Boston: Houghton, Mifflin, 1900);

Henry Steele Commager, *Theodore Parker: Yankee Crusader* (Boston: Little, Brown, 1936);

Dean Grodzins, "Theodore Parker and Transcendentalism," dissertation, Harvard University, 1993.

References:

Gary L. Collison, "A Calendar of the Letters of Theodore Parker," *Studies in the American Renaissance,* edited by Joel Myerson (Charlottesville: University Press of Virginia, 1979), pp. 159–229; (1980), pp. 317–408;

Henry Steele Commager, "The Dilemma of Theodore Parker," *New England Quarterly,* 6 (June 1933): 257–277;

Michael Fellman, "Theodore Parker and the Abolitionist Role in the 1850s," *Journal of American History,* 61 (December 1974): 666–684;

Dean Grodzins, "Theodore Parker and the 28th Congregational Society: The Reform Church and the Spirituality of Reformers in Boston, 1845–1859," in *The Transient and Permanent: The Transcendentalist Movement and its Contexts,* edited by Charles Capper and Conrad E. Wright (Boston: Massachusetts Historical Society, 1999), pp. 73–117;

Grodzins, and Joel Myerson, "Theodore Parker's Preaching Record, 1836–1859," *Studies in the American Renaissance 1994* (Charlottesville: University Press of Virginia, 1994), pp. 57–123;

Elisabeth Hurth, "From Idealism to Atheism: Theodore Parker and Ludwig Feuerbach," *Journal of Unitarian Universalist History,* 26 (1999): 18–46;

Paul Teed, "Racial Nationalism and Its Challengers: Theodore Parker, John Rock, and the Antislavery Movement," *Civil War History,* 41 (June 1995): 142–160.

Papers:

The Andover-Harvard Theological Library at Harvard University holds the largest collection of Theodore Parker's papers, including more than seven hundred manuscript sermons and lectures, four volumes of his journal and many notebooks, manuscripts for several of his books, and many letters. The Massachusetts Historical Society holds the largest collection of letters from and to Parker, two more volumes of his journal, and notebooks. The Boston Public Library holds many letters, some important manuscripts, as well as many notebooks and scrapbooks; the Boston Public Library also inherited Parker's library, and a few of the books include his marginal notes. Other important collections include those at the Houghton Library, Harvard University; the Library of Congress; and the Huntington Library.

Francis Parkman

(16 September 1823 – 8 November 1893)

Sally A. Hawthorne

See also the Parkman entries in *DLB 30: American Historians, 1607–1865; DLB 183: American Travel Writers, 1776–1864;* and *DLB 186: Nineteenth-Century American Western Writers.*

Francis Parkman

BOOKS: *The California and Oregon Trail: Being Sketches of Prairie and Rocky Mountain Life* (New York & London: Putnam, 1849); revised as *Prairie and Rocky Mountain Life; or the California and Oregon Trail* (New York: Putnam, 1852); revised as *The Oregon Trail: Sketches of Prairie and Rocky-Mountain Life* (Boston: Little, Brown, 1872; revised edition, Boston: Little, Brown, 1892; London: Macmillan, 1892);

History of the Conspiracy of Pontiac, and the War of the North American Tribes against the English Colonies after the Conquest of Canada (2 volumes, London: Bentley, 1851; 1 volume, Boston: Little, Brown / London: Bentley, 1851; revised edition, Boston: Little, Brown, 1868); revised and enlarged as *The Conspiracy of Pontiac and the Indian War after the Conquest of Canada,* 2 volumes (Boston: Little, Brown, 1870);

Vassall Morton: A Novel (Boston: Phillips, Sampson, 1856);

Pioneers of France in the New World, part 1 of *France and England in North America: A Series of Historical Narratives* (Boston: Little, Brown, 1865; London: Routledge, 1868; revised edition, Boston: Little, Brown, 1886);

The Book of Roses (Boston: Tilton, 1866);

The Jesuits in North America in the Seventeenth Century, part 2 of *France and England in North America: A Series of Historical Narratives* (Boston: Little, Brown, 1867; London: Routledge, 1868);

The Discovery of the Great West, part 3 of *France and England in North America: A Series of Historical Narratives* (Boston: Little, Brown, 1869; London: Murray, 1869); revised and enlarged as *La Salle and the Discovery of the Great West* (Boston: Little, Brown, 1879);

The Old Régime in Canada, part 4 of *France and England in North America: A Series of Historical Narratives* (Boston: Little, Brown, 1874; London: Sampson Low, 1875; revised and enlarged edition, Boston: Little, Brown, 1894);

Count Frontenac and New France under Louis XIV, part 5 of *France and England in North America: A Series of Historical Narratives* (Boston: Little, Brown, 1877);

Some of the Reasons against Woman Suffrage (N.p., 1883);

Montcalm and Wolfe, part 7 of *France and England in North America: A Series of Historical Narratives,* 2 volumes

(Boston: Little, Brown, 1884; London: Macmillan, 1884);

Our Common Schools (Boston: Citizens' Public School Union, 1890);

A Half-Century of Conflict, part 6 of *France and England in North America: A Series of Historical Narratives,* 2 volumes (Boston: Little, Brown, 1892; London: Macmillan, 1892);

The Journals of Francis Parkman, 2 volumes, edited by Mason Wade (New York & London: Harper, 1947).

Editions and Collections: *The Works of Francis Parkman,* 20 volumes (Boston: Little, Brown, 1897–1898);

France and England in North America, 2 volumes, The Library of America (New York: Literary Classics of the United States, 1983);

The Oregon Trail; The Conspiracy of Pontiac, The Library of America, no. 53 (New York: Literary Classics of the United States, 1991).

OTHER: William Smith, *Historical Account of Bouquet's Expedition against the Ohio Indians, in 1764,* preface by Parkman (Cincinnati: Clarke, 1868);

"Louis, Count Frontenac," in *Appleton's Cyclopaedia of American Biography,* volume 2, edited by James Grant Wilson and John Fiske (New York: Appleton, 1887), pp. 553–555;

"Marquis de Montcalm," in *Appleton's Cyclopaedia of American Biography,* volume 4, edited by Wilson and Fiske (New York: Appleton, 1889), pp. 363–365;

Mary Hartwell Catherwood, *The Romance of Dollard,* preface by Parkman (New York: Century, 1889);

"Robert Cavalier de la Salle," in *Appleton's Cyclopaedia of American Biography,* volume 3, edited by Wilson and Fiske (New York: Appleton, 1900), pp. 621–622.

SELECTED PERIODICAL PUBLICATIONS–UNCOLLECTED: "The Scalp-Hunter," anonymous, *Knickerbocker Magazine,* 25 (1845): 297–303;

"The History of the Conspiracy of Pontiac," *North American Review,* 73 (1851): 495–529;

"The Works of James Fenimore Cooper," *North American Review,* 74 (December 1852): 147–161;

"Exploring the Magalloway," *Harper's Magazine,* 29 (1864): 735–741;

"The Tale of the Ripe Scholar," *Nation,* 234 (1869): 558–560.

Francis Parkman is best remembered for *The California and Oregon Trail: Being Sketches of Prairie and Rocky Mountain Life* (1849), a lively account of his adventures with Indians, pioneers, and buffalo in the Wild West of the 1840s. But he was no rugged frontiersman. He lived almost all of his life in Boston, the hub of New England culture, and his literary work reflects this intellectual milieu. He was imbued early with the attitude that colors all his writings: that white men (not women; he was opposed to woman suffrage) of good birth and good breeding have the only qualities that matter. While this outlook appears embarrassingly bigoted from a present-day standpoint, his wealth and social position made it possible for him to travel in the United States and abroad, to acquire the education that gave polish to his literary style, to procure copies of documents necessary to his historical research, and to have the leisure to read and write. Furthermore, he suffered from chronic ill health. His illness, however, may have been a key contributor to the lyrical flow of his prose, for it forced him to dictate much of his work: alert to the cadence of his lines, he was able to match the beat of his language to the tempo of the action. He had an inimitable knack for creating suspense and for arranging the threads of his narratives so that shadowy figures known only through archival records spring to life. He was also adept at depicting setting, having traveled to many of the places he describes. His great achievement was to combine sensory, dramatic, and documentary elements into compelling and enduring narratives such as *The California and Oregon Trail* and his seven-part history of the conflicts among the French, English, and Indian inhabitants of North America up to the Battle of Quebec, *France and England in North America: A Series of Historical Narratives* (1865–1892).

Parkman was born in Boston on 16 September 1823. His grandfather Samuel Parkman, a merchant, had built the family fortune; his father, the Reverend Francis Parkman, was the minister of the Unitarian New North Church; and his mother, Caroline Hall Parkman, was a descendant of the Puritan clergyman John Cotton. Although they were well-respected members of New England's patrician class, Parkman's family did have a few skeletons in its closet: one of Parkman's uncles, a moneylender, was murdered in a debt-repayment scandal, and another got a divorce and ran off to Europe under the shadow of forgery charges.

Because of poor health, Parkman spent the years from 1831 to 1836 at the farm of his maternal grandparents in Medford, Massachusetts. He attended the day school run by John Angier but devoted the greater part of his energy to romping in the woods of Middlesex Fells. During these years he acquired his love of woodcraft and developed the keen sensibilities for the sights, sounds, and smells of the forest that he later incorporated into his histories. From 1836 to 1840 he attended the Chauncy Hall School in Boston, where he studied Greek, Latin, and English literature. He devoured the adventure novels of Sir Walter Scott and James Fenimore Cooper and admired the poetry of George Gordon, Lord Byron, praising these writers for what he deemed the manly spirit of their art. In his spare time he conducted chemical experiments, which he later claimed were deleterious to his health, and participated in amateur plays with his friends.

In 1840 Parkman entered Harvard College. There he conceived his life's ambition: to write the history of France and England in the New World. At Harvard he immersed himself in ethnology and frontier history, sometimes to the detriment of his other studies. Jared Sparks, Harvard's first professor of modern history and a family friend, sent him a bibliography to help him get started and in later years put him in touch with people who could direct him to useful libraries and archives in the United States and other countries.

While at college Parkman developed his athletic skills, often pushing himself well beyond the limits of ordinary and sensible endurance. He spent hours boxing in the gymnasium, riding horses, and shooting. He was such a vigorous hiker that friends who accompanied him complained that their enjoyment was spoiled in trying to keep up with him. He made a series of wilderness trips to the northern states and Canada, visiting Lake Magalloway, Lake George, Lake Champlain, and the White Mountains, touring the sites of many of the incidents he intended to recount in his histories. He had difficulty inducing his companions to press on once the last outposts of civilization had been reached, and his journals from the summers of 1841 and 1842 record his frustration with Daniel Slade on an excursion to the White Mountains and with Henry Orne White on a trip to Lake George when they failed to share his avidity for outdoor challenges.

Parkman's strenuous regimen, coupled with his weak constitution, resulted in 1843 in the first of a series of physical breakdowns. He traveled to Europe for what was supposed to be a restful holiday but spent the winter and spring roaming energetically through Italy, Switzerland, France, and England. He traveled with Theodore Parker from Naples to Rome, where he learned more than his Protestant family thought was beneficial about Catholicism and even stayed for a few days at the convent of the Passionist Fathers. In his journals he ruminates on the lure of the faith that had played such a key role in the French conquest of Canada. After touring the Apennines with his friend William Morris Hunt, he visited his uncle in Paris and then went on to England before returning home.

In 1844, under pressure from his father, Parkman entered Harvard Law School; but his real interest continued to be the settlers' struggles for control over the New World. Drawing on his wilderness experiences, he wrote several stories and had them published in the *Knickerbocker Magazine,* either anonymously or under the pseudonym Captain Jonathan Carver Jr. In the summer of 1845, while researching material for a book on the Indian uprising led by Pontiac, he toured the Great Lakes region and the Mohawk Valley. In Palmer, Michigan, he sifted through six trunks of papers belonging to Lieutenant M'Dougal, who had been captured by the Indians during the uprising. He also interviewed Robert Stuart, the superintendent of Indian affairs for Michigan and a former fur trader, and Lyman C. Draper, the founder of the Wisconsin State Historical Society and collector of early Western documents.

Parkman during his student years at Harvard College

In 1846 Parkman and his cousin, Quincy Adams Shaw, who also had health problems, embarked on a curative trip to the West. Parkman had a second motive for undertaking the journey: he wanted to acquire firsthand knowledge of Indians for his histories. At Fort Laramie, Wyoming, he learned that a large Sioux war party was to rendezvous at La Bonte's Camp on the Platte River, and he went to meet it. When the assemblage of warriors did not occur, he decided to follow a band of Oglalas, who

Parkman's wife, Catherine Bigelow Parkman, and their daughter Grace

had a five-day head start, on their annual trek to the Medicine Bow range to cut lodge poles. Shaw declined to join the expedition, so Parkman, weakened by illness and poor diet to such a degree that he could barely sit upright on his horse, pursued the Indians accompanied only by his hired hand, Raymond. Parkman lived with the Sioux for nineteen days.

Dysentery, exposure, poor nutrition, and the physical demands of travel contributed to the complete breakdown of Parkman's health on his return from the West. He suffered from a nervous condition that caused a tumult in his brain if he attempted to concentrate on a single subject for more than a few moments. Furthermore, he could not bear bright sunlight and experienced great difficulty in reading and writing. For the next two years he lived primarily in Manhattan and Staten Island, New York, receiving treatment for his failing eyesight and taking occasional trips to spas in the Catskills and in Brattleboro, Vermont. Working by dictation and using the journals of his expedition, he began publishing his adventures in the *Knickerbocker Magazine* in 1847. Initially he signed the installments "A Bostonian," but by February 1849, when the final installment was published, he was using his real name. The appearance of that installment was delayed by several months because Parkman wanted to get the work published in book form before its serial completion to prevent piracy.

The California and Oregon Trail was published in 1849. Parkman made a few stylistic revisions to the serialized version and added two new chapters. In addition to his ethnographic study of the Oglalas, Parkman records his observations of the pioneers. The work is marked by a wry, aristocratic tone and a confidence that his readers share his class consciousness. He takes a cynical view of the settlers' motives for leaving their homes, speculating that they hoped to escape the restraints of the law and civilized society or that they foolishly dreamed of bettering their condition and that, hating the journey and dissatisfied with the final destination, they would be happy to return whence they came. Parkman does, however, respect manliness above any other quality, and he found it in abundance on the plains. He admires the illiterate guide Henry Chatillon's skill with the rifle and steadiness in surmounting wilderness hardships, and he speaks well of a group of mountaineers from Virginia who, though lacking Yankee polish, combine muscular hardiness with pleasing manners. Nevertheless, the overall effect of the book is to affirm the superiority of Parkman's own class.

Parkman married Catherine Scollay Bigelow, the daughter of the eminent Boston physician Jacob Bigelow, on 13 May 1850. With her help and that of other amanuenses he worked on his book about the Pontiac uprising. He eventually adopted the writing method used by the historian William Hickling Prescott, who also suffered from seriously impaired eyesight, in which wire grids were fitted to a frame as a guide for the hand. In 1851 he began suffering from arthritis in the knees, a condition that later required him to resort to the occasional use of a wheelchair.

Parkman's *History of the Conspiracy of Pontiac, and the War of the North American Tribes against the English Colonies after the Conquest of Canada* was published in September 1851. The book tells the story of the uprising (1763–1765) in which the Indians suffered their most crushing defeat at the hands of the English settlers. Parkman's greatest challenge was how to present Pontiac, whose leadership, cunning, and determination gave the Indians their final chance to beat back the settlers. The warrior chief's bravery and single-mindedness of purpose receive much emphasis; but, believing Indians in the last analysis to be irredeemable savages, Parkman could not depict Pontiac as entirely heroic. Ultimately siding with the white man's virtue and downplaying the white man's vice, Parkman was criticized by Parker for undue harshness toward the Indians and for undeserved leniency toward the settlers.

In 1852 Putnam republished *The California and Oregon Trail,* changing the title to *Prairie and Rocky Mountain Life; or the California and Oregon Trail* and including the author's "Preface to the Third [*sic*] Edition." In 1853–1854 poor health prevented Parker from pursuing historical research. During this period he wrote the semi-autobiographical, melodramatic novel *Vassall Morton* (1856), which includes details from his 1843 European holiday. The novel was poorly received, and Parkman later omitted it from a list of his published works.

Parkman employed copyists to reproduce primary documents. In 1856 he discovered that the journalist, author, and editor Benjamin Perley Poore, to whom he had advanced a fair sum of money for the copying of documents, had not performed in accordance with their agreement. The dispute was turned over to arbitration.

Parkman's three-year-old son, Francis, died in 1857, and his wife died in 1858 after the birth of their second daughter. Also in 1858 he traveled to Paris to consult with the brain specialist Charles Edouard Brown-Séquard. Too distraught from these calamities to concentrate on his historical projects, he took up gardening, creating the hybrid *Lilium Parkmanii.* During the Civil War years he wrote letters to the *Boston Daily Advertiser* on the political situation and resumed work on his histories with the help of his sisters, Mary and Eliza.

In the early 1860s Parkman began publishing chapters of his *Pioneers of France in the New World* in the *Atlantic Monthly.* The work was published in book form in 1865 and won him acclaim as an historian. It was the first volume of the projected series *France and England in North America* that he had envisioned twenty years previously as a Harvard undergraduate. As he notes in the introduction, completion of the book was delayed by his illness and impaired vision. The introduction lays out key themes of his histories, including the triumph of British liberty over French absolutism, which he likens to the victory of the Union over the Confederacy, and he makes the comparison more pointed by dedicating the book to relatives who had fallen in the late conflict. In his Civil War letters he had used the analogy of the democratic North resembling a body with no head while the authoritarian South appeared to be all head with no body. In his histories he returned to this image, arguing repeatedly that the French ultimately failed to gain control of North America because the absolutist head gave the pioneering body no freedom to develop and filled Canada with courtiers and priests; British settlers, on the other hand, lacked unified guidance but were able to respond to their new environment in more enterprising and productive ways. *Pioneers of France in the New World* describes Spanish and French explorations of Florida, clashes between those rival nations, and Samuel de Champlain's explorations of Canada. In prefatory passages to each of the main sections of the book Parkman points out his meticulous use of primary sources, and footnotes throughout the text serve as constant reminders of the author's immersion in firsthand sources. By this means, he asserted himself as a painstakingly careful scholar–so careful, in fact, that not until 1885, after twenty-three reprintings, was a new edition of *Pioneers of France in the New World* published. In his revisions Parkman corrected several geographical errors and added fuller descriptions of Florida, which he had not been able to visit before the book's original publication because of the Civil War.

In 1866 Parkman published *The Book of Roses,* a horticultural treatise. That same year he began a lifelong correspondence with Abbé Henri-Raymond Casgrain of Quebec; the two men had in common poor eyesight and a love of history.

In 1867, after traveling in Canada, Parkman published *The Jesuits in North America in the Seventeenth Century,* the second volume of *France and England in North America.* He prefaces the narrative with an overview of the Indians' culture and character in which he suggests that the destruction of tribal life resulted from their refusal or inability to move beyond savagery and adapt to white civilization. In the text of *The Jesuits in North America in the Seventeenth Century* he plays up Indian savagery more than he does in any of his other histories. He tells, for example, of Father Isaac Jogues, who, after enduring torture and mutilation at the hands of the Iroquois, escaped–only to return with hopes of furthering the work of conversion but also with the certainty of greater agony and death. Claiming to be sparing the reader the full details, Parkman relates that the Indians chopped off one of Jogues's thumbs, gnawed the flesh from his hands, tore out his hair, burned him with red-hot coals, peeled away strips of his skin, and cut off his head. He also cites Father Jean de Brebeuf's *Relation de Hurons* (1636), which states that some Indians practiced cannibalism. Critics have pointed out that the priests may have exaggerated the stories of torture in hopes of gaining sympathy and monetary contributions from supporters in France, and that Parkman may have selected the grisliest episodes in order to rivet his readers' attentions with suspense and horror.

In January 1869 Parkman was in Paris, having learned of the archivist Pierre Margry's vast collec-

The "gridiron," consisting of wires stretched across a frame, that Parkman used to guide his hand when writing after his eyesight failed (photograph by W. R. Jacobs)

tion of old Northwest and colonial New York documents, including much material on the explorer René-Robert Cavelier, Sieur de La Salle. Margry, however, denied Parkman and all other researchers access to the material until it could be published. Using the sources available to him, in 1869 Parkman published *The Discovery of the Great West,* the third part of *France and England in North America.* The work is an account of La Salle's explorations and a consideration of how the lure of the far West influenced colonization and fortification efforts east of the Mississippi River. Much of the drama of the book derives from La Salle's character and conduct: his wrangling with financial backers, his harsh treatment of subordinates, and his refusal to admit defeat in the face of the most daunting obstacles. The explorer may have suffered from insanity, but Parkman treats La Salle as a classical hero whose tragic flaw was arrogance rather than as a madman beset by paranoia and delusions.

Parkman revised *History of the Conspiracy of Pontiac* for the fourth edition in 1868. His final revisions appear in the two-volume 1870 edition, for which he was able to use the papers of Colonel Henry Bouquet and General Frederick Haldimand, which included the story of the colonists' plans to weaken the Indians by giving them rum and smallpox-contaminated blankets. For this edition Parkman changed the title to *The Conspiracy of Pontiac and the Indian War after the Conquest of Canada* and added a new preface in which he explains the place of the work in relation to his still-incomplete *France and England in North America.* Falling chronologically after the last book in that series, *The Conspiracy of Pontiac* serves as a sequel to it, and the opening chapters recapitulate earlier events in the French-English conflict.

Parkman and Casgrain finally met in person in 1871. The next year Casgrain published a biographical sketch in which he praised his friend's rationalism, loyalty, and honor but chided Parkman for rejecting both Catholicism and Protestantism.

A "fourth"–actually third–edition of *The California and Oregon Trail* was published in 1872; it carried the title by which the work has become best known: *The Oregon Trail,* with the subtitle *Sketches of Prairie and Rocky-Mountain Life*. This edition included a dedication to Parkman's cousin Shaw and a new preface. Parkman also made many stylistic revisions, removing the epigraphs from Scott and Byron at the beginning of each chapter, formalizing colloquialisms, and abbreviating or omitting much of the biographical and autobiographical detail.

The fourth part of *France and England in North America, The Old Régime in Canada* (1874), is the only one to employ a topical rather than a narrative organization. Instead of focusing on heroic action, it holds a significant if relatively undramatic place in the series by filling in certain gaps in Parkman's discussion of New France. *The Old Régime in Canada* covers developments in Acadia, intrigues of the missionaries, and the exploitation of Canada by the French government. It examines clashes between fur traders, who wanted Canada left wild, and farmers, who wanted to clear the forests for agriculture; disparities between colonists' needs in New France and administrative policies in the mother country; and conflicts among religious, civil, and military aims. Favorable remarks by William Dean Howells in an 1874 review in the *Atlantic Monthly* brought Parkman wider marketplace appeal both in America and in England. Casgrain, on the other hand, reviewed it scathingly in the *Revue Canadienne* (April 1875), claiming that Parkman exaggerated Canadian defects while brushing aside the country's merits. Parkman responded that he had suppressed objectionable material when he could make his point without it; nevertheless, he made his biases clear when he concluded that the British conquest of Canada had proved to be a happy calamity. He believed that French absolutism encouraged unmanly dependence, whereas British policies engendered liberty and industry. He elaborated on the problems of absolutist rule in *Count Frontenac and New France under Louis XIV* (1877), part five of *France and England in North America,* which discusses the rivalry between France and England for control of trade and administrative authority. The crusty but capable general and colonial administrator Louis de Baude, Comte de Frontenac et Palluau, is the central figure.

In 1878 Casgrain recommended Parkman for an honorary doctorate from Laval University in Quebec, which was denied because of the committee's distaste for what it perceived as the candidate's abuse of Catholics in his histories. Parkman did receive an honorary doctorate of laws from McGill University, which was dominated by Protestants, the following year. The affair of the honorary doctorates drew attention to real or imagined religious biases in Parkman's histories, although he prided himself on keeping to the facts regardless of his personal views.

Abbé Henri-Raymond Casgrain of Quebec, who objected to some of Parkman's interpretations of Canadian history but continued to correspond with Parkman until the latter's death

In 1873 Parkman had persuaded the United States Congress to appropriate $10,000 for the publication in Paris of a six-volume set of Margry's papers. The volumes appeared between 1876 and 1888, and Parkman revised *The Discovery of the Great West* to incorporate the new material. He did not change his interpretation of La Salle, however, and he gave the explorer even more weight as the central figure of the book by titling the revised edition *La Salle and the Discovery of the Great West* (1879).

Montcalm and Wolfe, the seventh and final part of the *France and England in North America* series,

Pierre Margry, the Paris archivist who refused to allow Parkman to consult his documents relating to French colonization of North America until Parkman obtained a grant from the U.S. Congress to publish the collection

appeared in two volumes in 1884. Parkman published the work out of chronological sequence because he feared that if he waited, he might not live to complete it. The volumes cover the French and Indian War through the climactic battle on the Plains of Abraham. Parkman analyzes the policies of the European powers as a key driving force in the conflict. But even more significant are the characters of the opposing military leaders, France's Louis-Joseph de Montcalm-Grozon, Marquis de Montcalm, and Britain's James Wolfe. Parkman had met Montcalm's great-grandson in Paris and had obtained permission to copy the family papers. His research helped him to humanize the antagonists by noting their unwarriorlike soft spots–for Montcalm, an affectionate domestic side; for Wolfe, moments of poetic sentiment. In describing the ailing Wolfe faced with the challenge of climbing the steep banks during the attack on Fort William Henry, Parkman echoes an incident from his own youth, recorded in his journal, in which he became stuck while climbing the side of a ravine in the White Mountains. His description of Wolfe's death has such realism and immediacy that his sister Eliza wept while reading it.

In the second volume (1885) of his complete works (1884–1896) Casgrain criticized *Montcalm and Wolfe* for claiming that the Catholic Church in Canada had done nothing to check corruption in the colony. In a letter of 28 November 1885 Parkman defended his claim and retorted that no Canadian had equaled the thoroughness of his own research. When Casgrain published *Un pèlerinage au pays d'Evangéline* (A Pilgrimage to the Country of Evangeline, 1887) to refute the two chapters on Acadia in Parkman's book, Parkman lambasted the work in a letter of 23 October 1887 as having been built on animosity, not historical data. Despite their differences, Parkman and Casgrain never broke off their correspondence; it was ended only by Parkman's death.

Parkman heightened the dramatic impact of *Montcalm and Wolfe* by relegating mundane elements to the sixth installment of the *France and England in North America* series, *A Half-Century of Conflict* (1892), which covers the period 1700 to 1748 and provides the background of the Battle of Quebec. Long and somewhat disorganized, it provides many details necessary to clarify the causes of the French and Indian War and closes the last gap in Parkman's monumental study. Taken as a whole, the *France and England in North America* volumes form the most complete account of the struggle for dominance over the wilderness that had yet been written and, perhaps, the most readable and lively that ever will be written.

Another edition of *The Oregon Trail* appeared in 1892. Parkman made only a few revisions to it, but it is significant for featuring illustrations drawn by the great Western artist Frederic Remington from photographs and descriptions provided by the author nearly fifty years after his journey. Scholars remain divided over which version of *The Oregon Trail* best represents the American West as Parkman experienced it; some insist that the journals give a more intimate, immediate, and accurate picture than any edition of the work.

Parkman died on 8 November 1893 at his home on Jamaica Pond in Boston. Although his reputation has waned from the days when he was considered a leading historian and *The Oregon Trail* was required reading in many public schools, his popularity may again be on the rise. In 1983 the Library of America published a two-volume edition of *France and England in North America,* with a combined edition of *The Oregon Trail* and *Conspiracy of Pontiac* following in 1991. Although multiculturalists today frown on Parkman's none-too-discreet bigotry against Indians, emigrants, women, Catholics, and generally anyone not of the same class and upbringing as himself, his very openness about his biases encourages the reader to confront them. Some critics fault him for overuse of secondary sources–often without attribution–but the presence of these sources in Parkman's work may have been his way of bowing to his contemporaries and exhibiting his familiarity with their work, and the lack of attribution may be explained by his assumption that any educated reader would recognize the parallels. Whatever the shortcomings of his books may be from a technical standpoint, the liveliness of his prose and his use of his own experiences to re-create the scenes and incidents of the past still make for compelling reading.

Letters:

Letters of Francis Parkman, 2 volumes, edited by Wilbur R. Jacobs (Norman: University of Oklahoma Press, 1960).

Biographies:

Henri-Raymond Casgrain, *Francis Parkman* (Quebec: Darveau, 1872);

Charles Haight Farnham, *A Life of Francis Parkman* (Boston: Little, Brown, 1900);

Henry Dwight Sedgwick, *Francis Parkman* (Boston: Houghton, Mifflin, 1904);

Mason Wade, *Francis Parkman: Heroic Historian* (New York: Viking, 1942);

Wilbur R. Jacobs, *Francis Parkman, Historian as Hero: The Formative Years* (Austin: University of Texas Press, 1991).

References:

Howard Doughty, *Francis Parkman* (New York: Macmillan, 1962);

Robert L. Gale, *Francis Parkman* (New York: Twayne, 1973);

David Levin, *History as Romantic Art: Bancroft, Motley, Prescott, and Parkman* (Stanford, Cal.: Stanford University Press, 1959);

Otis Pease, *Parkman's History: The Historian as Literary Artist* (New Haven: Yale University Press, 1953);

Richard C. Vitzthum, *The American Compromise: Theme and Method in the Histories of Bancroft, Parkman, and Adams* (Norman: University of Oklahoma Press, 1974).

Papers:

Most of Francis Parkman's papers are at the Massachusetts Historical Society, Boston. His library and maps are held by Harvard University.

Wendell Phillips

(29 November 1811 – 2 February 1884)

Len Gougeon
University of Scranton

BOOKS: *The Constitution a Pro-Slavery Compact; or, Extracts from the Madison Papers, etc.* (Boston, 1844);

Daniel O'Connell, the Irish Patriot (Boston: Lee & Shepard / New York: C. T. Dillingham, 1844);

Review of Lysander Spooner's Essay on the Unconstitutionality of Slavery: Reprinted from the "Anti-Slavery Standard," with Additions (Boston: Printed by Andrews & Prentiss, 1847);

Review of Webster's Speech on Slavery (Boston: American Anti-Slavery Society, 1850);

Sketch of the Life of Mrs. Eliza Garnaut (Boston?, 1850);

Freedom for Women: Speech at the Convention Held at Worcester, Oct. 15 and 16, 1851 (New York: American Equal Rights Association, 1851);

Speeches Before the Massachusetts Anti-Slavery Society: January, 1852 (Boston: R. F. Wallcut, 1852);

Speech of Wendell Phillips: at the Melodeon, Thursday Evening, Jan. 27, 1853 (Boston, 1853);

Argument of Wendell Phillips, Esq., Before the Committee on Federal Relations (Of the Massachusetts Legislature) in Support of the Petitions for the Removal of Edward Greely Loring from the Office of Judge of Probate, February 20, 1855 (Boston: J. B. Yerrinton, 1855);

Speech of Wendell Phillips, Esq. at the Worcester Disunion Convention, January 15, 1857 (Boston: American Anti-Slavery Society, 1857);

Fraternity Lecture of Wendell Phillips, Esq.: Boston, Oct. 4, 1859 (Boston: R. F. Wallcut, 1859);

The Lesson of the Hour: Lecture of Wendell Phillips, Delivered at Brooklyn, N.Y., Tuesday Evening, November 1, 1859 (N.p., 1859);

No Slave-hunting in the Old Bay State: Speech of Wendell Phillips, Esq., Before the Committee on Federal Relations, in Support of the Petitions Asking for a Law to Prevent the Recapture of Fugitive Slaves in the Hall of the House of Representatives, Thursday, February 17, 1859 (Boston: R. F. Wallcut, 1859);

The Philosophy of the Abolition Movement (New York: American Anti-Slavery Society, 1860);

The Pulpit, a Discourse (Boston: Published by the Fraternity, printed by Ripley, 1860);

The St. Domingo Insurrection: Toussaint L'Ouverture, the John Brown of St. Domingo (New York, 1860);

Argument of Wendell Phillips, Esq. Against the Repeal of the Personal Liberty Law: Before the Committee of the Legislature, Tuesday, January 29, 1861 (Boston: R. F. Wallcut, 1861);

Disunion: Two Discourses at Music Hall, on January 20th, and February 17th, 1861 (Boston: R. F. Wallcut, 1861);

The War for the Union: A Lecture (New York: E. D. Barker, 1862);

Speeches, Lectures, and Letters (Boston: James Redpath, 1863);

Wendell Phillips Esq., on a Metropolitan Police (Boston, 1863);

An Address, Delivered in Tremont Temple, Boston, April 19th, 1865 (Worcester, Mass.: Printed by Chas. Hamilton, 1865);

The Laws of the Commonwealth, Shall They Be Enforced?: Speech of Wendell Phillips, Esq., Before the Legislative Committee, February 28, 1865 (Boston: Wright & Potter, 1865);

The Maine Liquor Law in Massachusetts; Speech Before the Massachusetts Legislative Committee, February, 28th, 1865 (Manchester, U.K.: United Kingdom Alliance, 1865);

Remarks of Wendell Phillips at the Mass Meeting of Workingmen in Faneuil Hall, Nov. 2, 1865 (Boston: Voice Printing and Publishing Company, 1865);

Women's Suffrage (London, 187?);

The People Coming to Power! Speech of Wendell Phillips, Esq., at the Salisbury Beach Gathering, September 13, 1871 (Boston: Lee & Shepard, 1871);

"Stand and Be Counted": Speech at the Convention Held at Boston, Oct. 6, 1875 (Boston, 1875);

Wendell Phillips in Faneuil Hall: on Louisiana Difficulties (Boston: Wright & Potter, 1875);

Oration Delivered in the Old South Church (Boston: R. Hildreth, 1876);

Speech of Hon. Wendell Phillips for Aid in the Preservation of the Old South Meeting-House (Boston: A. Mudge, 1878);

Who Shall Rule Us? Money, or the People? (Boston: Franklin Press/Rand & Avery, 1878);

The Scholar in a Republic: Address at the Centennial Anniversary of the Phi Beta Kappa of Harvard College, June 30, 1881 (Boston: Lee & Shepard / New York: C. T. Dillingham, 1881);

Eulogy of Garrison: Remarks of Wendell Phillips at the Funeral of William Lloyd Garrison (Boston: Lee & Shepard / New York: C. T. Dillingham, 1884);

The Labor Question (Boston: Lee & Shepard / New York: C. T. Dillingham, 1884);

The Lost Arts (Boston: Lee & Shepard / New York: C. T. Dillingham, 1884);

Oration Delivered in the Old South Meeting-House (Boston: Sold at the Old South, 1884);

The Freedom Speech of Wendell Phillips: Faneuil Hall, December 8, 1837, with Descriptive Letters from Eye Witnesses (Boston: Wendell Phillips Hall Association, 1890);

Speeches, Lectures, and Letters, second series (Boston: Lee & Shepard / New York: C. T. Dillingham, 1891);

Touissant L'Ouverture: An Address by Wendell Phillips, Delivered at New York, March 11, 1863 (Cleveland: Rewell, 1891);

Wendell Phillips to the School Children (Boston: Wendell Phillips Hall Association, 1892);

Speeches on Rights of Women (Philadelphia: A. J. Ferris, 1898).

Collection: *Wendell Phillips on Civil Rights and Freedom,* edited by Louis Filler (New York: Hill & Wang, 1965)–comprises eighteen selections from *Speeches, Lectures, and Letters* and *Speeches, Lectures, and Letters,* second series.

OTHER: "The Immediate Issue," in *The Equality of All Men Before the Law: Claimed and Defended in Speeches by Hon. William D. Kelley, Wendell Phillips, and Frederick Douglass, and Letters from Elizur Wright and William Heighton* (Boston: Rand & Avery, 1865).

Wendell Phillips was one of the most influential and eloquent advocates for social reform in the nineteenth century. He is most prominently associated with the American antislavery movement, in which he worked closely for many years with William Lloyd Garrison, the most famous of all the New England abolitionists. Phillips was exceptional in many ways. Well-educated, handsome, and wealthy, he socialized with a small group of affluent and like-minded reformers known as the "Boston Clique." This group included Maria Weston Chapman and her sisters, Anne and Caroline, and Edmund Quincy. In addition to antislavery, Phillips spent his life supporting a variety of reform causes, including temperance, penal reform, the abolition of capital punishment, the rights of women, emancipated Negroes and Native Americans, and labor reform. He became notorious during his lifetime for his absolute dedication to these causes and his unsparing criticisms of those deemed opponents of social justice. Phillips's speeches, however, were never bombastic but always poised, controlled, and rhetorically sophisticated. Thus, a writer for the *Boston Courier* once noted that "Mr. Phillips thinks like a Billingsgate fishwoman, or a low pothouse bully, but he speaks like Cicero." Another critic claimed that Phillips practiced "the eloquence of abuse." Because of his remarkable speaking ability, however, Phillips was in great demand as a lecturer throughout his life. Some of his most popular speeches were "The Lost Arts," a topic on which he spoke some two thousand times, "Street Life in Europe," "The Scholar in a Republic," and "Touissant L'Ouverture."

Wendell Phillips, born on 29 November 1811, was the eighth child and fifth son of John and Sarah Walley Phillips. His father's family, one of the most distinguished in Boston, had arrived in Massachusetts with John Winthrop in 1630. Phillips's paternal grandfather was a wealthy businessman; his father, after

Phillips's boyhood home, the family mansion on Beacon Hill in Boston

graduating from Harvard at the top of his class, established a successful law practice and eventually served in the Massachusetts State Senate for eighteen years, ten as its presiding officer. Phillips attended Boston Public Latin School and, later, Harvard College, from which he graduated sixth in his class in 1831. Following graduation he entered Harvard Law School, where he became a close friend of Charles Sumner. Sumner later distinguished himself as the most eloquent opponent of slavery in the United States Senate, a distinction for which he nearly paid with his life when he was attacked on the Senate floor and beaten senseless by an enraged Southern congressman in 1856.

After completing law school, Phillips established himself in a modest practice in Boston, but the practice of law was never his primary interest. On 12 October 1837 he married Ann Terry Greene, the daughter of a wealthy Boston businessman. She was a staunch abolitionist and encouraged her husband to take an interest in the cause. Because of her frail health, a condition which persisted throughout the couple's life together, her own activities were limited. They had no children, but apparently their like-mindedness on most important issues resulted in a happy marriage.

Phillips's first exposure to the challenges of the abolition movement came in 1835, when he witnessed an attack on the abolitionist William Lloyd Garrison by a street mob, which took place a short distance from Phillips's Boston law office. He later met the heroic Garrison at Chapman's house, a meeting that he considered a turning point in his life. Soon afterward, Phillips began reading Garrison's *Liberator* (1831–1865) and attending antislavery meetings. In March 1837 he gave his first antislavery address, in which he defended the right of free speech, which had been threatened by a gag rule imposed in the House of Representatives to prevent antislavery petitions from coming to the floor. Phillips's concern for the protection of free speech was increased by the shocking murder of Elijah P. Lovejoy, an abolitionist publisher, in Alton, Illinois, in November 1837. Lovejoy died defending his press against an antiabolitionist mob. When a meeting to protest the murder was called in Boston at Faneuil Hall, Phillips rose to the occasion and delivered an eloquent address condemning the assassins and their defenders.

Eventually, Phillips was elected president of the Boston Anti-Slavery Society, and in 1838 he became an agent for the Massachusetts Anti-Slavery Society, Garrison's organization. The Boston patrician's commitment to the outré cause of abolition scandalized his family and many friends, but he was unequivocal in his commitment. Like other abolitionists, Phillips felt the cause was an expression of his religious faith and the need to address the serious moral ills of American society. He lived in an era of reform and was religiously determined to play his role in it, no matter what the social costs.

In the summer of 1839 Phillips and Ann traveled to Europe in an effort to improve her health. After a year of touring the two attended the first world antislavery convention in London as American delegates. On this occasion Phillips made history by arguing for the seating of all persons bearing credentials from any antislavery body, regardless of gender. The British, shocked at this attempted breach of tradition and social decorum, could not be persuaded, and the ladies were relegated to the balcony, where Garrison later joined them in protest.

After returning to the United States in July of 1841, Phillips continued the struggle against racial discrimination. Unlike many others, including some abolitionists, he believed that Negroes were as competent as whites in all areas. He especially admired Frederick Douglass, the former slave whose *Narrative of the Life of Frederick Douglass, an American Slave* (1845) was destined to become an American classic. Douglass, like Phillips, was an agent for the Massachusetts Anti-Slavery Society and a dynamic orator. The two often shared the platform, and Phillips admired Douglass's language, taste, eloquence, and the vigor of his thoughts, as well as his manliness. In view of these qualities, as far as Phillips was concerned, race meant nothing, and neither man considered it an issue. Because of his beliefs Phillips fought against discrimination wherever it raised its ugly head, including on trains, where Negroes were forced to occupy segregated cars and where he often rode with them as a protest. He also led the fight against discrimination in the public school system of Boston.

In the early 1840s Phillips, like Garrison, reached the conclusion that the federal government was so utterly corrupted by the influence of slavery that the only way to reform it was to dissolve it. Accordingly, in February 1842 Phillips proposed circulating petitions asking Congress to take measures for the immediate dissolution of the Union. The "no Union with slaveholders" movement grew quickly among abolitionists. By April, Garrison was describing the United States Constitution in the *Liberator* as a "covenant with death and an agreement with hell" that he refused to recognize. In 1844 Phillips published a 123-page pamphlet on the topic, titled *The Constitution a Pro-Slavery Compact.* Both he and Garrison maintained this antigovernment position until the advent of the Civil War, which presented itself as an expedient way of annihilating the institution of slavery.

Because of his views on abolition and government, as well as his personal attacks on people whom he saw as the enemies of reform, Phillips was an extremely controversial figure throughout his life. Ralph Waldo Emerson, a major proponent of reform throughout the period, once noted, "The first discovery I made of Phillips was, that while I admired his eloquence, I had not the faintest wish to meet the man." Despite such reservations, however, throughout the 1840s Emerson found himself irresistibly drawn to Phillips and the cause of abolition. When the controversial speaker was suggested for a lecture at the Concord Lyceum in the spring of 1845, several officers objected. Emerson and Henry David Thoreau, however, were adamant that Phillips be allowed to speak in Concord on the topic of slavery. When two curators resigned in protest, Emerson and Thoreau took their places, and the invitation was extended to Phillips. Emerson, who had made his own debut in the antislavery debate with a major address in the previous summer, was most impressed by what he heard. The next day he wrote to a friend that "I have not learned a better lesson in many weeks than last night in a couple of hours." Thoreau was similarly affected and responded to the presentation by sending his first and only letter to an editor, which recounted the speech. Garrison published Thoreau's letter in the *Liberator* on 28 March 1845. Like Emerson, deeply impressed by Phillips's personal courage, virtue, and commitment, Thoreau notes in his letter that

> in this man the audience might detect a sort of moral principle and integrity, which was more stable than their firmness, more discriminating than his own intellect, and more graceful than his rhetoric, which was not working for temporary or trivial ends. It is so rare and encouraging to listen to an orator who is content with another alliance than with the popular party, or even with the sympathizing school of the martyrs, who can afford sometimes to be his own auditor if the mob stay away, and hears himself without reproof, that we feel ourselves in danger of slandering all mankind by affirming that here is one who is at the same time an eloquent speaker and a righteous man.

Although Phillips was always somewhat skeptical of the Transcendentalists because of what he saw as their tendency toward philosophical abstraction, he eventually formed an alliance of sorts with them, especially with Emerson. From the mid 1840s on, Garrison and Phillips frequently visited Concord to speak on slavery, and they found ready listeners in Emerson, Thoreau, and the women of Concord, who had established their own antislavery society in the late 1830s. Emerson's wife, Lidian, as well as the women in the Thoreau family, were members. Emerson came to develop an enduring respect for Phillips and joined him on the antislavery lecture platform when the times demanded another assured voice. After the Civil War, Emerson lent his prestige, as well as his eloquence, to the promotion of woman's suffrage, another of Phillips's special causes and one for which he had long sought Emerson's support.

The passage of the Fugitive Slave Law in September of 1850 brought with it a special challenge for Phillips and other militant abolitionists. The law, which was one element of a five-part legislative initiative known as "The Compromise of 1850," provided for the return of fugitive slaves who were living in the free states. Under the law, a Negro who was accused of being a fugitive was brought before a special commissioner who adjudicated the case. The accused was not allowed to speak in his own defense, nor was he granted the protection of habeas corpus. If the commissioner found that the accused was, indeed, a fugitive, he was remanded to his captors, and the commissioner was paid $10. If the accused was released, the commissioner was paid $5. The law caused an outcry in the free states, and nowhere was opposition more pronounced than in Boston. A "Vigilance Committee" was quickly formed, and Phillips was a member. The group was able successfully to defend Ellen and William Craft, who had escaped from slavery in Georgia in 1848, from would-be captors in October 1850. A fugitive slave known as Shadrach was released by violence and hurried off to Canada in February 1851. Federal officers, however, were determined that this kind of escape would not happen again. When Thomas Sims was arrested in April 1851, a large military presence assured that there would be no rescue. Thus, despite the protests of Phillips, Garrison, and others, Sims was returned to Savannah, Georgia, where he was publicly whipped on 19 April.

Boston was shocked, and the social status of the abolitionists was strengthened by virtue of their strong opposition to the increasingly intrusive influence of the slave power in New England. Phillips now emerged as one of the most prominent leaders of the abolitionist movement. In a subsequent oration on the Sims affair he was uncompromising in his attack on the moral enervation of Boston's merchant class, whom he saw as largely responsible for the city's willingness to accommodate any outrage to placate the slave owners of the South. "Do you ask why the Abolitionists denounce the traders of Boston?" he asked. "It is because the merchants chose to send back Thomas Sims,–pledged their individual aid to Marshal Tukey, in case there should be any resistance; it is because the merchants did it to make money. Thank God they have not made any! . . . If only slave-hunting can save them, may bankruptcy sit on the ledger of every one of those fifteen hundred scoundrels who offered Marshal Tukey their aid!"

When Anthony Burns, another fugitive slave, was arrested in May 1854, Phillips came to his defense, convincing Richard Henry Dana Jr. to take the case. Despite extensive legal maneuvering and a failed attempt at a physical rescue which resulted in the death of a deputy, Burns, like Sims, was returned to his master. This time, Phillips, Theodore Parker, and others who were suspected of being behind the violent effort to free Burns were arrested. Phillips and Parker were delighted with their arrest, which they considered an honor, and looked forward to a public trial that would allow them to showcase the grotesque immorality of the law. Both were disappointed when the case was dismissed on a technicality.

Events in the 1850s continued to deepen the discord between North and South. The Burns affair ignited the fires of protest in many hearts, and Phillips was there to fan the flames. Thus, on 4 July 1854 he attended an antislavery gathering in Framingham, Massachusetts, and sat on the platform as Thoreau delivered his fiery "Slavery in Massachusetts" address, in which he castigated the immorality of the government and announced that "My thoughts are murder to the state." At the same meeting Garrison burned a copy of the Constitution while crying out, "So perish all compromises with tyranny!" This inflammatory ire reached its climax at the end of the decade with John Brown's famous raid on the federal arsenal at Harpers Ferry, Virginia, on 16 October 1859. While most of the nation expressed shock at this extraordinary event, Phillips, along with Emerson, Thoreau, and others, applauded Brown. Emerson considered Brown a martyr to the abolitionist cause, a Puritan moralist who put his creed into his deed. Phillips saw Brown in the same light and praised him without reservation. Brown was found guilty of treason and conspiracy to incite a slave insurrection and sentenced to death. After his execution, on 2 December 1859, Phillips was one of his pallbearers and gave the funeral oration at his burial in North Elba, New York. To the small group gathered there Phillips remarked that "Your neighbor farmer went, surrounded by his household, to tell the slaves there were still hearts and right arms ready and nerved for their service. From this roof four, from a neighboring roof, two, to make up that score of heroes. How resolute each looked into the face of Virginia, how loyally each stood at his forlorn post, meeting death cheerfully, till that master-voice said, 'It is enough.'"

The advent of the Civil War was welcomed by Phillips and many other abolitionists. He never shared Garrison's nonresistant philosophy (Phillips began carrying a pistol for personal protection in the late 1850s), and he came to feel that the power of the sword would provide the final solution to the problem of slavery, a problem that had proved impervious to the influence of moral suasion alone. Similarly, Phillips quickly abandoned his no-government position following the firing on Fort Sumter in April 1861. The Union that he once defined as "an agreement with hell" was now worth preserving, as long as the stain of slavery was washed away.

Initially, Phillips was unimpressed with President Abraham Lincoln, a relatively unknown and untested politician from Illinois. Lincoln's refusal to make emancipation an objective of the war early on rankled Phillips who, like other abolitionists, saw slavery as the fundamental cause of the conflict. When Lincoln announced his Preliminary Emancipation Proclamation following the Union victory at the Battle of Antietam in September 1862, Phillips was at least partially mollified. During the war he met with Lincoln twice to urge a more vigorous emancipation policy. Because of his singular dedication to this goal, it is perhaps not surprising that in 1864 Phillips did not support Lincoln's reelection bid, finding in John C. Fremont a more vigorous proponent of the abolitionist cause. When Atlanta fell to General William T. Sherman on 2 September 1864, Lincoln's reelection was virtually guaranteed. Ultimately, Phillips's attacks on Lincoln caused a rift between himself and Garrison, who was a Lincoln supporter. This rift grew into a gulf when Garrison attempted

Phillips and other prominent abolitionists as depicted in an 1864 engraving by John Chester Buttre

to disband the American Anti-Slavery Society following the passage of the Thirteenth Amendment (1865), which outlawed slavery forever. Garrison felt that the work of the society and the labor of his life had been fulfilled by the passage of this amendment. Phillips disagreed, arguing that the fight for Negro rights following emancipation was imperative. As a result of the disagreement Garrison left the organization, which he had led for thirty years, and Phillips succeeded him as president.

During the years following the war Phillips became a national institution. A volume of his work titled *Speeches, Lectures, and Letters,* published in Boston in 1863, sold out in four days. He came to be seen as the spokesperson for a considerable constituency of reform-minded citizens and aligned himself with the Radical Republicans in pressing for a more extensive reconstruction of the South than that envisioned by President Andrew Johnson. When the president resisted, Phillips supported his impeachment. He also threw himself vigorously behind the legislative proposal that became the Fifteenth Amendment to the Constitution in March 1870. This amendment provided for black male suffrage, which Phillips felt was a key element in assuring black Americans their civil rights.

Throughout the post–Civil War period, Phillips served as the champion of many causes. In an age that witnessed the excesses of the "Captains of Industry," Phillips was among the first to support labor reformers. Not surprisingly, he suggested that they pattern their efforts on those of the abolitionists in order to raise the consciousness of society regarding such issues as the eight-hour workday. When the coal miners known as the Molly Maguires were prosecuted for bringing violence to the Pennsylvania coal fields, Phillips defended them as he had Brown, and he accused the mine owners of degrading the lives of their employees and brutally exploiting them.

At this same time Phillips also continued to support the goals of the woman's movement, as he had since its inception in the 1840s. In this effort he worked with and supported such notables as Lucretia Mott, Susan B. Anthony, and Elizabeth Cady Stanton. When the movement took a radical turn, supporting more liberal divorce laws, for example, Phillips became somewhat uncomfortable. When the woman's movement finally split, with the radicals aligning themselves with Stanton and Anthony and the conservatives aligning themselves with Lucy Stone and Julia Ward Howe, Phillips gravitated toward the conservatives. He remained, however, a staunch supporter of woman's suffrage and other key issues in the movement.

Indefatigable in the cause of social reform, Phillips also spoke out against capital punishment and supported the movement to protect the interests of Native Americans, as well as those of Irish immigrants. At the time of his death on 2 February 1884, Phillips was revered by those at the bottom of the social ladder whose causes were always his. This son of wealth and privilege had spent his life in defense of the lowly, the poor, the downtrodden, the ignorant, and the oppressed.

Biographies:

George Austin, *The Life and Times of Wendell Phillips* (Boston: Lee & Shepard, 1884);

Lorenzo Sears, *Wendell Phillips: Orator and Agitator* (New York: Doubleday, Page, 1909);

Charles E. Russell, *The Story of Wendell Phillips: Soldier of the Common Good* (Chicago: C. H. Kerr, 1914);

Irving H. Bartlett, *Wendell Phillips: Brahmin Radical* (Boston: Beacon Press, 1961);

James Brewer Stewart, *Wendell Phillips: Liberty's Hero* (Baton Rouge: Louisiana State University Press, 1986).

References:

Irving Bartlett, "New Light on Wendell Phillips and the Community of Reform, 1848–1880," *Perspectives in American History,* 12 (1979): 3–251;

Bartlett, "The Persistence of Wendell Phillips," in *The Antislavery Vanguard: New Essays on the Abolitionists,* edited by Martin Duberman (Princeton: Princeton University Press, 1965);

Austin Bearse, *Reminiscences of Fugitive Slave Days in Boston* (Boston: Printed by W. Richardson, 1880);

Thomas Wentworth Higginson, *Contemporaries* (Boston: Houghton, Mifflin, 1899);

Richard Hofstadter, "Wendell Phillips: The Patrician as Agitator," in his *The American Political Tradition and the Men Who Made It* (New York: Knopf, 1948);

Robert D. Marcus, "Wendell Phillips and American Institutions," *Journal of American History,* 56 (June 1969): 39–56;

Oswald Garrison Villard, "Wendell Phillips After Fifty Years," *American Mercury,* 34 (January 1935): 89–99;

George Woodberry, "Wendell Phillips: The Faith of an American," in his *Heart of Man, and Other Papers* (New York: Harcourt, Brace & Howe, 1920).

Papers:

There are substantial collections of Wendell Phillips's papers in the Houghton Library, Harvard University; the Boston Public Library; the Massachusetts Historical Society; and the Library of Congress.

William Hickling Prescott

(4 May 1796 – 28 January 1859)

Scott E. Casper
University of Nevada, Reno

See also the Prescott entries in *DLB 30: American Historians, 1607–1865* and *DLB 59: American Literary Critics and Scholars.*

BOOKS: *History of the Reign of Ferdinand and Isabella, the Catholic,* 3 volumes (Boston: American Stationers' Company, 1838; London: Bentley, 1838);

History of the Conquest of Mexico, with a Preliminary View of the Ancient Mexican Civilization, and the Life of the Conqueror, Hernando Cortés, 3 volumes (London: Bentley, 1843; New York: Harper, 1843);

Biographical and Critical Miscellanies . . . (London: Bentley, 1845; New York: Harper, 1845); revised and enlarged as *Critical and Historical Essays* . . . (London: Bentley, 1850);

History of the Conquest of Peru, with a Preliminary View of the Civilization of the Incas, 2 volumes (London: Bentley, 1847; New York: Harper, 1847);

Memoir of Hon. John Pickering, LL.D. (Cambridge, Mass.: Metcalf, 1848);

History of the Reign of Philip the Second, King of Spain, 3 volumes: volumes 1 and 2 (London: Bentley, 1855; Boston: Phillips, Sampson, 1855); volume 3 (Boston: Phillips, Sampson, 1858; London: Routledge, 1858);

Memoir of the Honorable Abbott Lawrence, Prepared for the National Portrait Gallery . . . (N.p.: Privately printed, 1856);

William Hickling Prescott: Representative Selections, edited by William Charvat and Michael Kraus (New York & Cincinnati: American Book Company, 1943);

The Literary Memoranda of William Hickling Prescott, 2 volumes, edited by C. Harvey Gardiner (Norman: University of Oklahoma Press, 1961);

The Papers of William Hickling Prescott, edited by Gardiner (Urbana: University of Illinois Press, 1964).

Collections: *Prescott's Works,* 15 volumes, edited by John Foster Kirk (Philadelphia: Lippincott, 1873–1875);

William Hickling Prescott

The Works of William Hickling Prescott, 22 volumes, Montezuma Edition, edited by Wilfred Harold Munro (Philadelphia & London: Lippincott, 1904).

OTHER: "Life of Charles Brockden Brown," in *Library of American Biography,* first series, volume 1, edited by Jared Sparks (Boston: Hilliard, Gray, 1839; London: Richard James Kennett, 1839), pp. 117–180;

William Robertson, *History of the Reign of the Emperor Charles the Fifth,* 2 volumes, edited by Prescott, with "The Life of Charles the Fifth after his Abdication" by Prescott (London: Routledge, 1857); 3 volumes (Boston: Phillips, Sampson, 1857).

SELECTED PERIODICAL PUBLICATIONS–UNCOLLECTED: "Club-Room," *Club Room,* no. 2 (March 1820): 43–50;

"Calais," *Club Room,* no. 2 (March 1820): 78–84;

"The Vale of Alleriot," *Club Room,* no. 3 (April 1820): 130–137;

"Letter to . . . on the Rev. W. L. Bowles' Stricture on the Life and Writings of Pope. By R. H. Lord Byron," *North American Review,* 13 (October 1821): 450–473;

"Essay Writing," *North American Review,* 14 (April 1822): 319–350;

"French and English Tragedy," *North American Review,* 16 (January 1823): 124–156;

Review of *Boston Prize Poems and Other Specimens of Dramatic Poetry,* by Charles Sprague, *North American Review,* 19 (July 1824): 253–256;

Review of *The Orlando Innamorato,* by Francesco Berni, and *The Orlando Furioso,* by Ludovico Ariosto, translated by W. S. Rose, *North American Review,* 19 (October 1824): 337–389;

"Da Ponte's Observations," *North American Review,* 21 (July 1825): 189–217;

Review of *Leisure Hours at Sea; Being a Few Miscellaneous Poems by an Anonymous Midshipman, North American Review,* 22 (April 1826): 453–455;

Review of *The Songs of Scotland, Ancient and Modern,* by Allan Cunningham, *North American Review,* 23 (July 1826): 124–142;

Review of *Almack's,* attributed to Marianne Spencer Stanhope Hudson, and *Vivian Grey,* by Benjamin Disraeli, *North American Review,* 25 (July 1827): 183–203;

Review of *Histoire de la Vie et des Ouvrages de Molière,* by Jules-Antoine Taschereau, *North American Review,* 27 (October 1828): 372–402;

Review of *A Chronical [sic] of the Conquest of Granada, by Fray Antonio Agapida,* by Washington Irving, *North American Review,* 29 (October 1829): 293–314;

"Essay on An Act to Incorporate the New-England Asylum for the Blind. Approved, March 2d, 1829," *North American Review,* 31 (July 1830): 66–85;

"Obituary Notice of the Rev. Dr. Gardiner," *Columbian Centinel,* no. 4844 (11 September 1830): 1;

"Poetry and Romance of the Italians," *North American Review,* 33 (July 1831): 29–81;

"Edinburgh Review," *New-England Galaxy,* 14 (31 December 1831): 2;

"North American Review," *New-England Galaxy,* 15 (7 April 1832): 3;

Review of *English Literature of the Nineteenth Century: American Library of Useful Knowledge,* volumes 2, 3, 4, *North American Review,* 35 (July 1832): 165–195;

"For the New-England Galaxy," *New-England Galaxy,* 16 (12 January 1833): 2;

Review of *El ingenioso hidalgo Don Quijote de la Mancha,* by Miguel de Cervantes, edited by Francisco Sales, *North American Review,* 45 (July 1837): 1–34;

Review of *Memoirs of the Life of Sir Walter Scott,* by J. G. Lockhart, and *Recollections of Sir Walter Scott, North American Review,* 46 (April 1838): 431–474;

Review of *Poems and Rhymed Plea for Tolerance,* by John Kenyon, *North American Review,* 48 (April 1839): 401–415;

Review of *Sketches of English Literature,* by Chateaubriand, *North American Review,* 49 (October 1839): 317–348;

Review of *History of the United States from the Discovery of the American Continent,* volume 3, by George Bancroft, *North American Review,* 52 (January 1841): 75–103;

Review of *Italy, General Views of its History and Literature in Reference to its Present State,* by Luigi Mariotti (Antonio Gallenga), *North American Review,* 54 (April 1842): 339–356;

Review of *Life in Mexico During a Residence of Two Years in that Country,* by Frances Calderon, *North American Review,* 56 (January 1843): 137–170;

Review of *History of Spanish Literature,* by George Ticknor, *North American Review,* 70 (January 1850): 1–56.

William Hickling Prescott won critical acclaim, popular success, and enduring influence as the first scholarly United States historian of Spain and Spanish America. A Boston Brahmin who made letters his career, he belonged to the community of Harvard-educated, Unitarian historians that also included Jared Sparks, George Bancroft, and George Ticknor. Prescott combined intensive research with compelling literary narrative in the Romantic vein. His best-selling, much-reprinted histories of the fifteenth- and sixteenth-century Spanish monarchies and conquests in Latin America added color to a history that had previously been told more dryly; he also gave scholarly depth to episodes that had been the province of romantic fiction. Prescott's historical interpretations sprang from his own milieu and have exerted continuing influence on the popular imagination and on historical

Members of "Club": (seated) Henry Warren, John Chipman Gray, William Powell Mason, Charles Folsom, William Howard Gardiner, Jare d Sparks, Prescott, and Octavius Pickering; (standing) John Gorham Palfrey, Samuel Atkins Eliot, Theophilus Parsons, Franklin Dexter, and Charles Greeley Loring.

scholarship. In particular, his *History of the Conquest of Mexico, with a Preliminary View of the Ancient Mexican Civilization, and the Life of the Conqueror, Hernando Cortés* (1843) is among the most enduring nineteenth-century works of history.

William Hickling Prescott was born on 4 May 1796 in Salem, Massachusetts, into a distinguished family; his patrician status enabled him to pursue a life of letters. His paternal grandfather, William Prescott, had commanded the American troops at Bunker Hill. His father, William, practiced law in Salem until 1808, then moved the family into Boston, where he amassed a substantial fortune through his legal practice and investments. His politics were Federalist in one of that party's last strongholds: he became a judge and joined the Hartford Convention that opposed the War of 1812. Prescott's mother, Catherine Greene Hickling Prescott, was the daughter of a wealthy merchant with business interests in the Azores. Thomas Hickling resided largely on St. Martin's Island, Azores, where Catherine spent two years during the American Revolution and learned Portuguese. Prescott was educated as other young men of patrician families were: classical instruction in Latin, Greek, and English under the Reverend John S. Gardiner (whose obituary Prescott wrote two decades later) from 1808 to 1811, then into Harvard as a sophomore. Membership in the Porcellian Club at Harvard, attendance at the Unitarian Church, and Federalist political leanings all marked young Prescott as a man of his station. In his first two years at Harvard he approached his studies without rigor.

In 1813 a dining-hall accident changed his life. In a student protest typical of the day, food flew across the hall. One hard crust of bread hit Prescott and blinded him in the left eye. This occurrence apparently sobered him; he applied himself to study until his graduation in August of the following year. The accident also began a pattern of lifelong afflictions, as he developed chronic rheumatism (a family illness) about the same time. Legal study in his father's office proved brief: Prescott had little interest in law, and in 1815 the rheumatism inflamed his right eye, rendering him temporarily sightless. Although he recovered, for the rest of his life Prescott's sight varied in strength, and he lived primarily in darkened rooms to prevent further damage. A series of secretaries enabled him to pursue his scholarship and writing–but he always knew that his eyesight impeded his literary production.

To regain his health, Prescott traveled in 1815 to his grandfather's plantation in the Azores–the only time in his life that he visited an Iberian culture. No doubt influenced by his upbringing in commercial, capitalist New England, Prescott found the Portuguese Azores culture economically backward yet fascinating, debased because "crampt by an arbitrary government and Papal superstition," as he wrote to his parents on 15 March 1816. Next he sailed for Europe, primarily to visit specialists in London who offered no hope for his optical recovery. He also saw France and Italy, sometimes in the company of his friend Ticknor, whom Prescott had known since their student days with Gardiner. After his return to the United States he married Susan Amory on 4 May 1820. The couple had four children. Like his mother, Prescott's new wife was the daughter of a prosperous merchant, and she helped her husband maintain the regimen he followed for the rest of his life for the sake of his health and sight: careful diet, limited social activity, seven-and-a-half-hour days of study.

Prescott approached literature first as a dilettante. With several friends from Harvard–including Ticknor and Sparks–he founded a literary group, called simply "Club," in 1818. With nine members at first, eventually twenty-four, "Club" produced four issues of a periodical, *The Club-Room,* in the spring and summer of 1820, but the journal soon expired. In 1821 the *North American Review* published its first Prescott piece, a review of George Gordon, Lord Byron's letter on Alexander Pope. With Edward Everett and then Sparks as editors, the *North American Review* became the leading American quarterly review. Its criticism embraced foreign literature, and its articles treated contemporary political subjects. Also in the early 1820s Prescott studied Italian and French and applied himself to English and classical literature and composition. These studies led to a series of long articles for the *North American Review,* edited by his friend Sparks from 1823 to 1829.

Prescott's fascination with Italian literature, especially epic poetry, influenced him in several ways in 1823 and 1824. It directed his attention toward the sixteenth century, which soon became central to his own studies of Spain. It pointed the way toward his sweeping narratives and his emphasis on heroic figures. Finally, it occasioned a reflection in his literary memoranda for 14 September 1823, in the American Romantic style, on the effects of national identity: "There has never been among modern Italians that nationality, wh[ich] existed when they constituted but one indivisible people. – There is not now in any of their separate states that proud spirit of liberty conspicuous in their earlier modern history. This ceased, when they ceased to be their own masters." By the mid 1820s Prescott was determined to devote his life to literature, but he hesitated about exactly what to pursue: Roman history, European literature, or Spanish history.

Prescott's interest in Spain began during one of his bouts with weakened eyesight in 1824. His friend Ticknor, now the first professor of modern languages at Harvard, read Prescott his lectures on Spanish literature. On 1 December of that year, Prescott started studying Spanish. Within months he had learned the language and read extensively in it. Also, in this era of the Monroe Doctrine, Sparks was publishing articles on Latin American revolutions in the *North American Review;* doubtless these contributed as well to Prescott's burgeoning interest. Like other Unitarian, New England historians of his coterie, Prescott read Spanish literature with his own biases–toward the Massachusetts past as well as toward Catholicism: Alonso de Ercilla y Zúñiga's epic poem, *La Araucana* (1569–1589), and Antonio de Solís's *Historia de la conqvista de Mexico* (1684), both "perpetually disgust the temperate reader," Prescott wrote on 27 February 1825, "by the little value they set upon the sufferings of the Heathen. The opinions of the most enlightened *Spanish* writers of the most enlightened ages, are not one jot in advance of the persecuting uncharitable bigotry of our puritan ancestors."

By January 1826 Prescott had decided to pursue Spanish history through the biography of Ferdinand and Isabella. He envisioned correctly that this topic would allow him to treat subjects of epic proportion: the Inquisition, the conquest of Granada, the discoveries of Columbus, and the development of monarchical state authority in Europe. Prescott resolved (for the most part, successfully) to limit his other writing to one *North American Review* article a year. He hoped to complete his *History of the Reign of Ferdinand and Isabella, the Catholic* (1838) by 1833, particularly because he imagined other writers on the same track. Washington Irving's *History of the Life and Voyages of Christopher Columbus* appeared in 1828, his *Chronicle of the Conquest of Granada* the following year; Prescott reviewed the latter for the *North American Review*. Robert Southey, Prescott feared, was also working on Spanish history.

The project took longer than anticipated: Prescott did not complete *History of the Reign of Ferdinand and Isabella, the Catholic* until June 1836. In the meantime he wrote a life of Charles Brockden Brown for Sparks's *Library of American Biography* series, which appeared in 1839. Sparks asked Prescott to undertake the biography, perhaps because author and subject both had chosen lives of letters after initial plans to enter the law. Prescott found the task unpleasant, however, for he did not admire the writer whom modern critics describe as a pioneer in American literature. Instead, the romantic

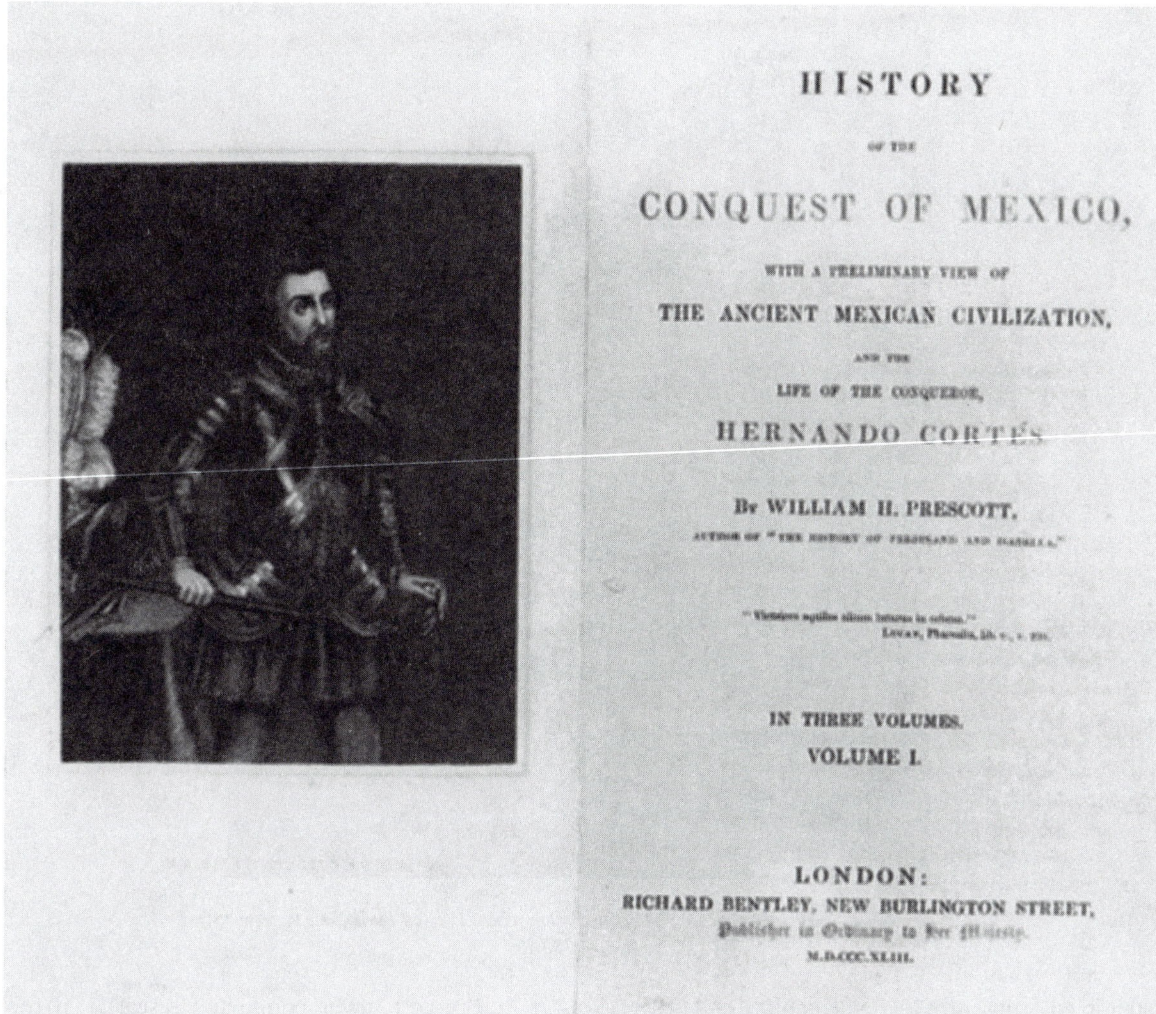
HISTORY

OF THE

CONQUEST OF MEXICO,

WITH A PRELIMINARY VIEW OF

THE ANCIENT MEXICAN CIVILIZATION,

AND THE

LIFE OF THE CONQUEROR,

HERNANDO CORTÉS.

BY WILLIAM H. PRESCOTT,

AUTHOR OF "THE HISTORY OF FERDINAND AND ISABELLA."

IN THREE VOLUMES.

VOLUME I.

LONDON:

RICHARD BENTLEY, NEW BURLINGTON STREET,

Publisher in Ordinary to Her Majesty.

M.DCCC.XLIII.

Frontispiece and title page for the first British edition of the book Prescott called his Iliad, *notable for the striking contrasts he drew between the Spanish conquistador Hernando Cortés and the Aztec chief Montezuma*

Prescott chafed at reading Brown's gothic novels. (Rather than read them fully, Prescott in fact relied heavily on William Dunlap's often pejorative survey of Brown's work.) Prescott particularly complained of Brown's Enlightenment attempts to "explain the *supernaturalities*" in novels such as *Wieland* (1798): perhaps earlier English authors had written for superstitious audiences, but now "all this is changed." Only when writing of earlier times–and Prescott tellingly used the example of Sir Walter Scott, his own favorite–was the use of superstition effective. Prescott admitted that Brown's novels "first opened the way to the successful cultivation of romantic fiction in this country," but noted that unlike Irving or James Fenimore Cooper, Brown focused on the psychological rather than the social. Before concluding the memoir with the customary praise, Prescott criticized Brown's infelicities of language and inability to say things simply.

The biography of Brown, which Prescott saw as a chore, revealed his own literary preferences. Throughout his memoranda Prescott prescribed "rules of composition" for himself, dealing with both literary style and historical practice. As early as May 1824 he listed nearly two dozen such rules, such as writing "freely & boldly," discarding "little qualifying particles, limping participles," and so on, avoiding excessive quotation (the favored style in contemporary reviews), and modeling his work on nobody else's. As his literary memoranda for 1828 and 1829 reveal, another set of concerns emerged once he had chosen historical composition. On the one hand, he could "Never sacrifice truth or correct view, to effect in composition. Facts, facts, whether in the shape of incidents, or opinion, are what I must rely upon, by which I must stand or fall." On the other he "must make the mere narrative very interesting." Thus "great latitude may be reasonably allowed

The house on Beacon Street in Boston where Prescott lived from 1845 to 1859

for dramatic coloring, provided such coloring be true." Dialogue and anecdotes became essential vehicles for drama. Prescott was devising the style that popularized his works.

Creating those works proved time-consuming. Prescott's good right eye functioned well only a few hours a day, and he suffered intermittent rheumatic relapses. From the 1820s on, he employed a series of secretaries versed in foreign languages, who could read to him and mark passages for notes. While in London in 1816 he had purchased a noctograph, a writing machine he described in 1857 as "the size of a sheet of paper, traversed by brass wires . . . with a sheet of carbonated paper . . . pasted on the reverse side." The writer placed a white sheet below the carbon paper, and used an ivory stylus to create lines of print between the wires. Prescott's noctograph enabled him to make notes as his secretary read and to draft some of his work himself. He also composed whole chapters of his book, running to fifty pages or more, in memory, then wrote them out in flowing prose on the noctograph. His secretary made a fair copy of these pages and read them back to Prescott for revision.

Prescott never conducted research in the European archives where American scholars such as Sparks were increasingly delving for their histories. He borrowed books from libraries around Boston, but more often from his friend Ticknor's library. More important, a network of friends in Europe–American consuls, booksellers, fellow American researchers, and European scholars of Spain–assisted him. Alexander H. Everett, the American minister to Spain, and a Massachusetts-born London-based bookseller named Obadiah Rich purchased books for Prescott as he prepared *History of the Reign of Ferdinand and Isabella, the Catholic.* Edward Everett, Sparks, and other friends examined archival materials from Italy to London on Prescott's behalf and arranged for copyists as necessary. Most important, Prescott enjoyed a twenty-year relationship with Pascual de Gayangos, a Spanish scholar of Spanish history. Gayangos, who praised *History of the Reign of Ferdinand and Isabella, the Catholic* in the *Edinburgh Review,* indexed and searched manuscripts for Prescott thereafter, as well as supervising still more copying. By 1845 Prescott owned four or five thousand books and thousands of pages of manuscripts.

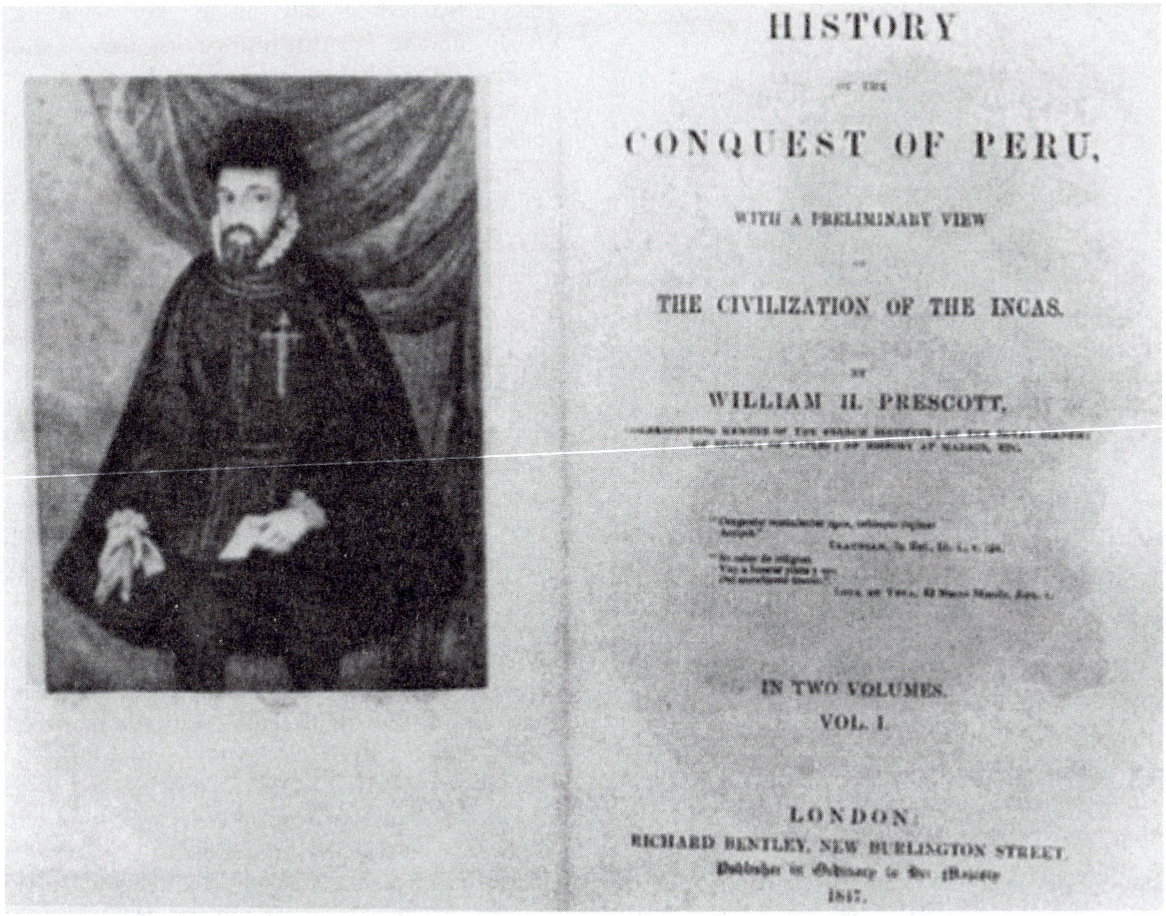

Frontispiece and title page for the first British edition of the book Prescott called his Odyssey, *a lesser achievement than his history of Mexico because he found Francisco Pizarro an unappealing central figure*

By 1836 Prescott was ready to submit *History of the Reign of Ferdinand and Isabella, the Catholic* for publication. His father dispelled Prescott's reluctance to publish the work, telling him (as recounted in his friend Ticknor's biography) that "the man who writes a book which he is afraid to publish is a coward." The manuscript ran to three volumes rather than the two Prescott had originally projected. With this work the author began a publishing practice he followed for all but one of his subsequent works: he had his manuscript stereotyped before submitting it to publishers. Still a relatively new technology, stereotyping involved casting type into molten metal plates from which pages were printed. Stereotype plates were thus a form of capital: their owner controlled the work and could transfer them from one publisher to another. Usually publishers had their works stereotyped and retained ownership of the plates. By making his own stereotyping contracts with Folsom, Wells, and Thurston of Boston, Prescott averted this publishing relationship and arranged for his pages to look exactly as he wanted them. By remaining with this printing firm throughout his career and through several different publishers, Prescott maintained a uniform style (type size, leading between lines, and style of notes) through all his works. He also arranged for English publication of his book with Richard Bentley of London. In this era before international copyright legislation, all of Prescott's works were published separately in England, usually prior to the American edition, to guarantee protection to Bentley as well as to the American publishers.

The *History of the Reign of Ferdinand and Isabella, the Catholic* introduces many of the themes and characteristics of all Prescott's histories. It narrates a sweep of scenes and events: the exotic nature of medieval Spain, with its population of Moors and its internecine conflicts among proud nobles; the condition of Aragon and Castile before the accession of Ferdinand and Isabella; the unification of the kingdoms under these young monarchs; the conquest of Granada, the last Moorish stronghold; the support of Columbus; the Spanish involvement in the Italian Wars; the Inquisition; the

Prescott using the noctograph, a device that enabled him to write despite his failing eyesight (photograph by Whipple and Black; Massachusetts Historical Society)

expulsion of Jews and Moors from Spain; and the oppression of native peoples in America. It featured a central character, a "representative" figure in Romantic terms: Isabella, the humble, pious, naturally kind, energetic young queen. At the center of all his works Prescott employed individual characters, usually of the noble classes, to reveal national or tribal traits. The Spanish people's attachment to beautiful, young Isabella exhibited their chivalrous, romantic character. Ferdinand was the monarch of his age, a Machiavellian prince who stood alongside Henry VII of England and Louis XI of France, the man who unified the Spanish nation and created a system of central authority to supplant the warring nobles. But Prescott's Isabella rose above her own time. He excused the Catholic queen from the excesses of Catholicism during her reign and depicted the fair-featured monarch in terms similar to the heroines of Scott's and Cooper's contemporary romantic fiction.

Above all, in *History of the Reign of Ferdinand and Isabella, the Catholic* Prescott introduced ideas that ran through his subsequent works on Spain and Spanish America. Each of these ideas was rooted in his own beliefs as a New England Unitarian Whig in Jacksonian America. With his fellow Romantic historians Bancroft, John Lothrop Motley, and Francis Parkman, Prescott believed in historical progress, the idea that civilization had advanced steadily in an ever-ascending spiral. Early modern Spanish history was part of this spiral: Ferdinand and Isabella had unified Iberia into a modern nation-state; they had conquered Moorish backwardness for Christendom; and they had helped civilize and Christianize America. Their victories in the Italian Wars proved the superiority of unified nations over fragmented provinces, a lesson for Americans in the decade when South Carolina had attempted to "nullify" the federal tariff law in the name of state sovereignty.

Sixteenth-century Spain, however, became the victim, not the master, of progress. Spanish decline stemmed in part from national character: the same chivalry that adored Isabella became, in Prescott's hands, a vestige of romantic, pre-modern times. Authoritarianism and clericalism, embodied by the power of the Catholic Church, were more significant institutional barriers to progress. Monkish influence over even the heroic Isabella led to the Inquisition. Under the Habsburg Philip II, the Protestant, capitalist Dutch republic superseded Spain in world power (which is where Motley's story began). For Prescott, Spanish decline also had lessons for nineteenth-century Americans. Like other Unitarians–fiction writers such as Nathaniel Hawthorne as well as historians–Prescott saw in the Puritan past of New England the same kind of bigoted theocracy he criticized in the Spanish Inquisition. Unitarianism represented enlightened religion, and the capitalism of the Dutch found its 1830s analogue in prosperous, proto-industrial Massachusetts.

The spiral of progress also includes the dispossession of "savage" or "semi-civilized" peoples, such as the Moors and the Aztecs, by "civilized" ones. Spain battled Moors and persecuted Jews at home, and conquered native peoples in the American colonies. The United States warred with Native Americans and Mexicans in the 1830s and 1840s. In each case, "semi-civilization" included an unhealthy attachment to worldly riches and luxuries rather than trade and industry–a fixation that ultimately helped bring Spain down as the spoils of empire increased. To Whigs such as Prescott, American empire foreshadowed similar dangers: Prescott vigorously opposed the annexation of Texas and the Mexican War. At the very moment of their doom Prescott's "semi-civilized" people became legitimately poetic subjects for sentimental treatment. Like the contemporary depiction of Native Americans as romantic figures, Prescott's Moors and Aztecs could be at once pitied and exoticized. Prescott also distinguished between the historical inevitability of progress and the "right of conquest" in which early-modern Europeans–and many of his American contemporaries–believed. When fueled by base motives (usually, for Prescott, religious fanaticism), conquest turned to oppression, as with Torque-

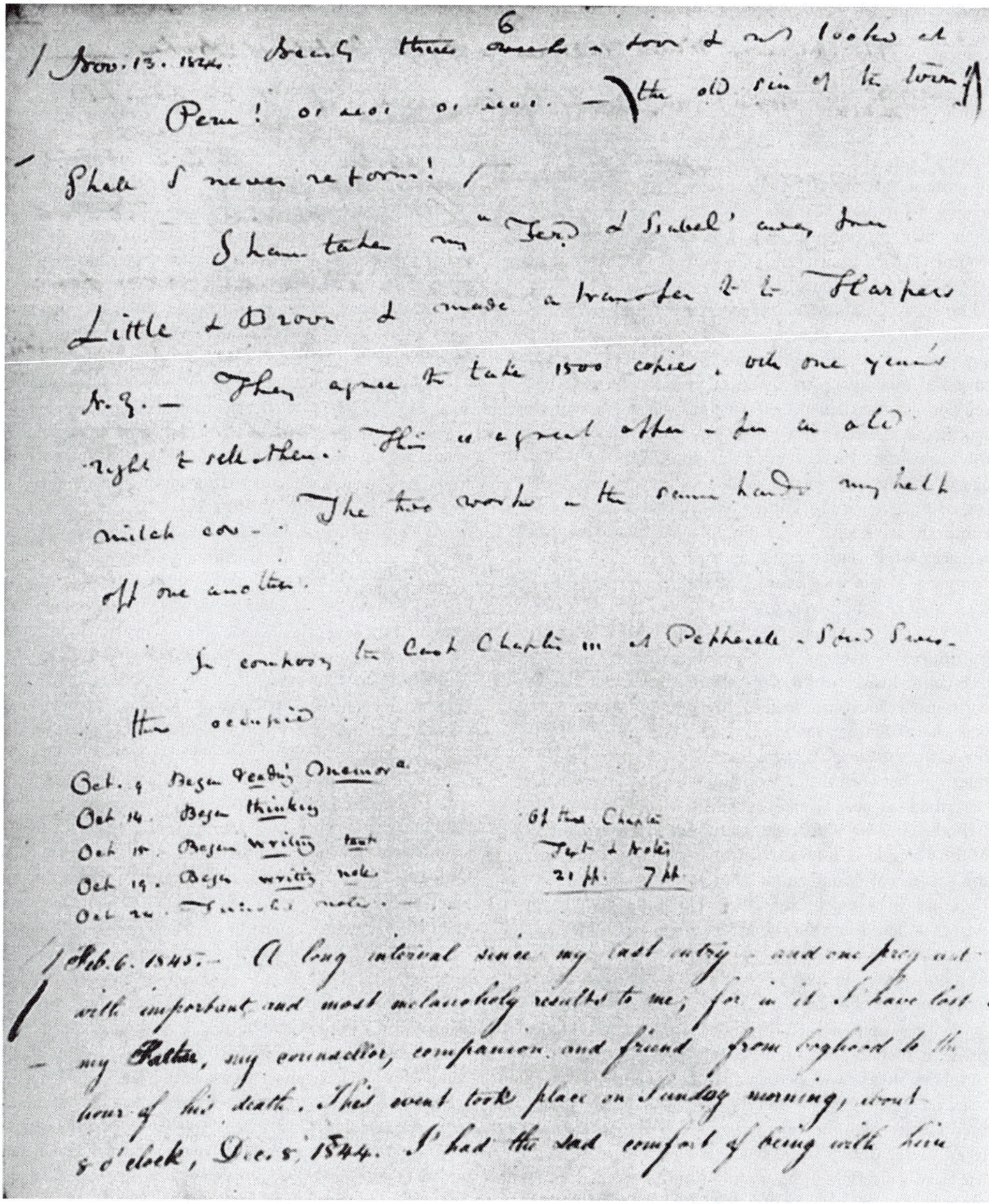

6

Nov. 13. 1844. Nearly three weeks in town & not looked at Peru! or next or next. — the old sin of the town!!

Shall I never reform!

I have taken my "Ferd. & Isabel" away from Little & Brown & made a transfer of it to Harpers N.Y. — They agree to take 1500 copies, with one year's right to sell them. This is a great affair — for an old [illegible]. The two works — the same hands — my best milch cow — [illegible] off one another.

In continuing the Conq. Chapter in A Pepperell — [illegible] then occupied

Oct. 9 Began reading memor^a
Oct 14. Began thinking — Of this Chapter
Oct 18. Began writing text — Text & Notes
Oct 19. Began writing notes — 21 pp. 7 pp.
Oct 22. Finished notes. —

Feb. 6. 1845. — A long interval since my last entry — and one pregnant with important and most melancholy results to me; for in it I have lost my Father, my counsellor, companion and friend from boyhood to the hour of his death. This event took place on Sunday morning, about 8 o'clock, Dec. 8, 1844. I had the sad comfort of being with him

Page from one of Prescott's notebooks; all but the last five lines are in Prescott's handwriting (Massachusetts Historical Society)

mada's Inquisition of the Jews or Philip II's quashing of the Morisco rebellion.

Prescott's subsequent histories continued the epic of Spain across the Atlantic and through the sixteenth century. The *History of the Conquest of Mexico,* his most popular and enduring work, traced the conquistador Cortés from triumph to near-defeat and back ultimately to conquest. Cortés as representative man faced challenges from two quarters: the Aztecs and especially their chief, Montezuma, the conquistador's heroic but doomed counterpart; and the Spanish enemies who sought to replace him. In the first book of the volume, "The Aztec Civilization," Prescott creates his romantic setting. The Aztecs had developed state institutions, a sophisticated chronology and hieroglyphics, agriculture and metalwork, and cultural refinement. But their religion limited their progress: cannibalism and human sacrifice evidenced even greater priestly tyranny than in the Inquisition. Prescott ends this book with the golden age of the Aztecs' neighbors the Tezcucans, who possessed an even more impressive culture, established a comprehensive legal code, and encouraged the arts and sciences while outlawing human sacrifice. The Aztecs' conquest of the Tezcucans laid the moral ground for their own conquest by Cortés.

At the beginning of the second book Prescott introduces Cortés as the Spanish knight-errant who overcame his youthful irresponsibility to emerge the constant, resourceful leader. In contrast, Montezuma was a vacillating, fatalistic chief. Through the fifth book, the *History of the Conquest of Mexico* foregrounds the interplay between these two leaders in a series of richly described events: Cortés's defeat of the Tlascalans (who became his allies against the Aztecs); his massacre of the Cholulans after discovering a plot to kill his men; the seizure of Montezuma; the storming of the Great Pyramid in Mexico; the "Noche Triste" (when the Aztecs killed four hundred retreating Spaniards and four thousand of their Indian allies); Cortés's discovery of a conspiracy in his own ranks; and finally the siege and conquest of Mexico.

This epic, which Prescott narrates in detailed prose, is suspenseful and picturesque. On the one hand, numbers always weighed against the Spanish invaders: Prescott consistently reminds the readers how many men Cortés had and how many more the Aztecs mustered. Aztec priests stood ready with knives to sacrifice the Spanish leaders if they could. On the other, the conquerors possessed superior leadership, tactics, armaments, and horses, and the Aztecs' superstitions worked against them. Prescott describes every battle distinctly, offering glimpses of Mexican scenery. For this element he relied on his correspondence with Frances Erskine Calderon de la Barca, a former Bostonian who married the Spanish ambassador to the United States and Mexico. Thanks to her descriptions of Mexican topography, scenery, and people, Prescott convinced contemporaries that he had traveled in Mexico–including Alexander von Humboldt, the expert on Mexican geography. (His descriptions are less persuasive to twentieth-century scholars who have been there.) Appearing in print just three years before the Mexican War, *History of the Conquest of Mexico* undoubtedly gained popularity when Americans wanted to learn more about the people and sights of their contemporary adversary. Newspapers, pamphlets, and prints all depicted the Mexicans of the 1840s much as Prescott portrayed those of 1519: as exotic, backward, bloodthirsty, and ultimately doomed to defeat.

Reviewers of *History of the Reign of Ferdinand and Isabella, the Catholic* and *History of the Conquest of Mexico* praised Prescott's historical research and literary skill. The *North American Review* lauded the works most fulsomely, which is not surprising given Prescott's long connection with the Boston quarterly. As Prescott wrote to Ticknor in January 1838, one of his friends joked that William H. Gardiner's ninety-page article in the *North American Review* "should be called the fourth volume" of *History of the Reign of Ferdinand and Isabella, the Catholic.* Prescott also won acclaim from most British periodicals, although Richard Ford in the London *Quarterly Review* (1839) observed a quality that later reviewers also noticed. Prescott's strength was "synthetical, not analytical. . . . He is less successful in his attempts to unravel the web, to separate causes from effects, to distinguish motives from pretexts–in a word, to catch a fixed definite insight into the spirit of the fifteenth century." Complaining of Prescott's "republican sneer" at monarchies, Ford blamed this fault on Prescott's context: "He cannot abstract himself from America and 1838."

The critical success of Prescott's first work smoothed his writing of the subsequent histories. The Spanish Royal Academy of History elected him to membership in 1839, giving him access to private archives in Spain; Gayangos's review of *History of the Reign of Ferdinand and Isabella, the Catholic* began Prescott's long association with this leading Spanish scholar; and Prescott and his friends distributed copies to other scholars and archivists. Critics and readers also greeted *History of the Conquest of Mexico* warmly. Fanny Appleton Longfellow revealed its appeal when she wrote in her diary, "It has the fascination of a romance and cannot be left . . . Mr. Prescott seems to have seen it all with his own eyes as he makes his reader." American soldiers took it with them to Mexico. Across the political divide from the Whig historian, the *United States Magazine and Democratic Review* relied on the sixteenth-century chronicler Bernal Diaz to argue that Prescott had romanticized Cortés, who merited condemnation instead. Still, most reviewers agreed that Prescott had added depth of research, picturesque detail, and human richness to the Spanish saga, which the eighteenth-century British historian William Robertson had told more sparely and which Irving had dressed in the garb of Romantic fiction.

Prescott's later works–the *History of the Conquest of Peru, with a Preliminary View of the Civilization of the Incas* (1847), the unfinished *History of the Reign of Philip the Second, King of Spain* (1855–1858), and his edition and extension of Robertson's *History of the Reign of the Emperor Charles the Fifth* (1857)–were no less deeply researched, but none appealed to him as had his first two masterpieces. The conquistador Francisco Pizarro was no Cortés: an illegitimate, illiterate, cruel, greedy former swineherd, sixty years old by the time he reached Peru. The Incas did not practice human sacrifice and other bloody religious rites, and they never met their Spanish foes with the military might of the Aztecs; thus this story had neither the moral grounds nor the suspense of conquest. In Prescott's view *History of the Conquest of Peru* was his *Odyssey* to the Mexican *Iliad:* more rambling, less coherent as narrative. Donald G. Darnell, in *William Hickling Prescott* (1975), called *History of the Conquest of Peru* a triumph of the historian over his materials.

Prescott next turned to a project he had contemplated since 1833 and planned since at least 1841: a history of Philip II, Ferdinand and Isabella's great-grandson and a nemesis of Queen Elizabeth. Here the problems were threefold: a surfeit of materials, an unheroic central character, and the historian's renewed infirmities. By now Prescott had amassed more than eight thousand folio pages of manuscripts copied from Spanish archives, plus more from sources in England, France, and Italy. This work possessed more scholarly authority than anything he had previously written, but he debated how to arrange the materials. He chose the memoir form, which would enable him to emphasize "the great transactions of the reign" and discard the "constitutional, financial, ecclesiastical details." Philip II posed a larger problem. If he was a representative man, he represented sixteenth-century Spanish decline. Philip had none of his great-grandparents' heroic traits: a religious fanatic but never a soldier, he vacillated in statecraft while having opponents of the Inquisition executed. Only the Spanish wars provided Prescott the battle scenes in which his descriptive talents always shone. Throughout the decade of work on *History of the Reign of Philip the Second,* recurrent eye troubles and rheumatism plagued Prescott. He traveled to London in 1850 for relief and found himself lionized by British literati and aristocrats. He returned to America with renewed spirits and wrote two volumes within the next four years. As he was completing the third volume in February 1858, he suffered a slight stroke. He managed to conclude that volume but not to begin writing the fourth; a second stroke killed him on 28 January 1859.

Prescott's works have retained their popularity and scholarly importance since his lifetime. By 1860 more than ninety-one thousand copies of his works had been sold. *History of the Reign of Ferdinand and Isabella, the Catholic* has gone through more than one hundred and forty editions and printings; the *History of the Conquest of Mexico* has gone through more than two hundred editions and has been translated into ten languages. Twentieth-century scholars of Spanish America have challenged Prescott's characterization of its indigenous people. To reveal those people's vantage points, they employ archaeological and ethnographic methods that were unavailable or in their infancy in the mid nineteenth century. These scholars also read the Spanish sources more critically than did Prescott. Modern scholars further contest Prescott's romantic depictions of the Moors and Native Americans: in emphasizing their resemblance to "oriental" peoples, he failed to see their cultures on their own terms. The *History of the Conquest of Mexico,* then, has met considerable scholarly challenge even as it has remained Prescott's most popular work.

More enduring among scholars has been Prescott's depiction of Spain. Prescott's New England contemporaries shared his view: Motley in his *Rise of the Dutch Republic,* Ticknor and Lowell in describing their travels in Spain. In the era of the Spanish-American War, the next generation of gentleman-historians agreed: Henry Charles Lea argued in 1898 that "clericalism," absolutism, and the anti-intellectual Inquisition corroded Spain. Even early American historians of Spanish art favored works of the medieval period, before the Habsburg decline of Spanish liberty. The professionalization of history from the 1890s forward echoed Prescott, even as it changed his emphasis: Spanish decline resulted not from Catholicism or intrinsic national character but from pre-commercial economic stagnation. Prescott's influence began a century of interpretation that marked Spain as exceptional, distinct from the rest of Europe or "Western culture." Examining Spain more minutely–regional economic variations and the everyday lives of individuals and groups beyond Prescott's nobles and clerics–twentieth-century historians have begun to complicate Prescott's picture and place Spanish history back into the larger history of Europe. But for the broad public whose knowledge of Spain comes primarily in elementary and secondary school, Prescott's grand saga persists: a story of Spanish unification under the heroic Isabella and Ferdinand, Latin American conquest, and Habsburg decline in the wake of capitalism, Protestantism, and republican liberty.

Letters:

The Correspondence of William Hickling Prescott, 1833–1847, transcribed and edited by Roger Wolcott (Boston & New York: Houghton Mifflin, 1925);

Prescott, Unpublished Letters to Gayanos in the Library of the Hispanic Society of America, edited by Clara Louisa Penney (New York: Hispanic Society of America, 1927).

Bibliography:

C. Harvey Gardiner, *William Hickling Prescott: An Annotated Bibliography of Published Works,* Hispanic Foundation Bibliographical Series, no. 4 (Washington, D.C.: Library of Congress, 1958).

Biographies:

George Ticknor, *The Life of William Hickling Prescott* (Boston: Ticknor & Fields, 1864);

Rollo Ogden, *William Hickling Prescott* (Boston & New York: Houghton, Mifflin, 1904);

Harry T. Peck, *William Hickling Prescott* (New York & London: Macmillan, 1905);

C. Harvey Gardiner, *William Hickling Prescott, A Biography* (Austin: University of Texas Press, 1969).

References:

Howard F. Cline, C. Harvey Gardiner, and Charles Gibson, eds., *William Hickling Prescott: A Memorial* (Durham, N.C.: Duke University Press, 1959);

Donald G. Darnell, "Rationalism and Romantic History: William Hickling Prescott and the Church of Rome," *Mid-Hudson Language Studies,* 10 (1987): 15–23;

Darnell, *William Hickling Prescott* (Boston: Twayne, 1975);

John Ernest, "Reading the Romantic Past: William H. Prescott's *History of the Conquest of Mexico,*" *American Literary History,* 5 (Summer 1993): 231–249;

C. Harvey Gardiner, *Prescott and his Publishers* (Carbondale: Southern Illinois University Press, 1959);

Frank Goodwyn, "The Literary Style of William Hickling Prescott," *Inter-American Review of Bibliography,* 9 (March 1959): 16–39;

Richard L. Kagan, "Prescott's Paradigm: American Historical Scholarship and the Decline of Spain," *American Historical Review,* 101 (April 1996): 423–446;

David Levin, *History as Romantic Art: Bancroft, Prescott, Motley, and Parkman* (Stanford, Cal.: Stanford University Press, 1959);

Eric Wertheimer, "Noctography: Representing Race in William Prescott's *History of the Conquest of Mexico,*" *American Literature,* 62 (June 1995): 303–327.

Papers:

William Hickling Prescott's papers are at the Massachusetts Historical Society; Houghton Library, Harvard University; Boston Public Library; Historical Society of Pennsylvania; Henry E. Huntington Library; British Museum; Library of Congress; and New York Public Library.

Sampson Reed

(10 June 1800 – 8 July 1880)

Arthur Wrobel
University of Kentucky

BOOKS: *Observations on the Growth of the Mind* (Boston: Cummings, Hilliard, 1826);

Correspondences for Children of the New Church (Boston: Otis Clapp, 1839);

An Address Delivered Before the Boston Society of the New Jerusalem (Boston: Otis Clapp, 1842);

Swedenborg and his Mission: A Lecture Delivered Before the Massachusetts Association of the New-Jerusalem Church, at its Session in Boston, April 7, 1859 (Boston: Phinney, 1859);

The Correspondence of the Sun, Heat, and Light, second edition (Boston: William Carter, 1862);

The Future of the New Church (Boston: New-Church Union, 1875);

A Biographical Sketch of Thomas Worcester, D.D. (Boston: New-Church Union, 1880).

OTHER: "Oration on Genius," M.A. oration, 1821, in *Aesthetic Papers,* edited by Elizabeth P. Peabody (Boston: Privately printed, 1849), pp. 58–64; republished in Kenneth Walter Cameron, *Emerson the Essayist,* volume 2 (Hartford, Conn.: Transcendental Books, 1972), pp. 9–11.

Sampson Reed

Aside from two modest-sized works from a literary output that numbered more than one hundred items–including reviews, essays, books, and prefaces–Sampson Reed is largely remembered for tirelessly working to promote the doctrines of Emanuel Swedenborg (1688–1772) within New England Transcendental circles and to establish the New Jerusalem Church in America. What slight literary reputation Reed currently enjoys rests on two short works, "Oration on Genius" (1821) and *Observations on the Growth of the Mind* (1826); these works, however, are themselves largely remembered less for their own merit than for the impetus they gave Ralph Waldo Emerson to pursue a literary career and, more especially, for providing him with the vocabulary and concepts that significantly inform his writings from *Nature* (1836) to the end of his career. Through his readings in Reed, Emerson absorbed some specifically Swedenborgian doctrines, most notably the existence of a universal "correspondence" between the natural and spiritual realms and the idea that the source of wisdom lies in one's receptivity to the "divine influx"; these beliefs, however, he transformed into more secularized forms. Never a member of the inner circle of Transcendentalism, Reed nevertheless shared with his generation various Romantic assumptions and attitudes–a philosophical optimism that viewed nature as existing for the soul's use, a faith in the inherent godlikeness of man, a belief in the unique genius of each individual, and a confidence that all the elements of the creation are linked together according to a benevolent divine order. With his generation, he expressed an impatience with familiar usage and a hostility toward John Locke's empiricism and Unitarianism. Most of Reed's other writings appear in New Church publications. If for no other reason, Reed warrants study for being, in Emerson's own words, his "early oracle"; beyond that, however scant the critical attention they have received and however limited their accessibility, Reed's writings reflect most of the optimistic tenets of a newly surging Romanticism that were eventually to comprise the core beliefs of thinking men and women of this age.

Sampson Reed was born on 10 June 1800 in what is now known as West Bridgewater, Massachusetts, the youngest of the three sons of John Reed, D.D., pastor of the First Church, a Unitarian congregation. Reed grew up on his father's farm and was educated at home; in 1814 he took the entrance examination for admission to Harvard College and to prepare for the Unitarian ministry. An outstanding scholar, Reed graduated with high honors in 1818 and subsequently entered the Divinity School at Cambridge. However, his chance rooming with Thomas Worcester proved fateful. Assailed by growing doubts about Unitarianism, Worcester started reading the works of Emanuel Swedenborg. "The Writings" (as they were collectively known) offered vivid descriptions of the afterlife, gave a startlingly new interpretation of the Bible, and taught that the Second Coming of Christ had already occurred, not in a physical but in a symbolic sense, the prophesied new church of Revelation evident in the new understanding of the Word of God given to mankind as revealed through his prophet Emanuel Swedenborg. Worcester's enthusiasm attracted others in his class; in 1818 twelve believers founded the Boston Society of the New Jerusalem for the purposes of study and prayer. When Reed joined the society two years later, he signaled his abandonment of plans to become a Unitarian minister.

Also in 1820 Reed wrote as his dissertation "On the Evidence from the Light of Nature of a Future Retribution" (unpublished), a document that has nothing to do with either nature or retribution and everything to do with the distinction between natural and revealed truth, between truth that men hold as reasonable and that has its foundation in the nature of things and truth that has its origins in the Word of God. Though in some measure a doctrinal elucidation of Swedenborgian concepts and imagery, the work never explicitly mentions the source of Reed's ideas. It systematically presents, however, the premises that were to undergird all of his subsequent writings; in addition, it proposes an aesthetic theory that was to shape Emerson's thinking, particularly in "The Poet" (1844), and to flower in Walt Whitman's practice.

In this work, Reed distinguishes between natural and revealed truth in order to account for differing ideas about the Creator and conflicting and erroneous interpretations of God's Word. Reed conceptualizes God as Love, who, acting out of his "love of being useful," created the world; God's truth, the other component of God's Being, suffuses the world. Emerson later gives this idea of nature as an image of truth accessible to man's senses a more secularized expression.

Reed also examines the consequences that arise from the separation of mankind's nature from God's. Because Man conceptualizes God according to his own nature, or what Reed dismissively calls "the light of nature," Man's corrupt understanding gives rise to such monstrous notions as a wrathful God, divine election, the tortures of hellfire, Christ's atonement through suffering and death, and God's arbitrary rewarding and punishment of his children. These ideas, Reed contends, reflect rather man's own defective nature, the consequence of man reducing the spiritual to his own level: "Human theology has indeed, in all ages, and all places, . . . cast its own vileness on our maker. . . . Human systems have brought down God to the image of man." Instead, Reed insists that God's Word is the ultimate measure against which truths that man derives from nature must be judged; this belief was to become the flashpoint for his later estrangement from Emerson. Even this early in his career, Reed declares that man's attribution of godlike powers to himself without recourse to the Word of God is merely the mind of man throwing "its own filthiness over the pure light of revealed thought."

The following year, Reed delivered the baccalaureate during the Harvard Master of Arts commencement ceremonies. The address, "Oration on Genius," was so powerfully inspiring to the eighteen-year-old Emerson, who was in attendance, that, fifteen years after the occasion, he identified Reed in a 22 June 1836 journal entry as his "early oracle"; on 29 October of that same year, Emerson declared the "Oration on Genius," together with William Collins's "Ode on the Passions" and William Shakespeare's plays, as works of genius.

The "Oration on Genius" was so startlingly fresh or, in the words of William Ellery Channing, "so utterly original and full of life" because it captured the first stirrings of a nascent Romanticism in this country in tones that were at once oracular and authoritative; in style it often approaches the epigrammatic. It aroused expectations of mankind's spiritual rejuvenation, elevated intuition over Lockean empiricism, asserted that the genius of the individual's mind links him to the infi-

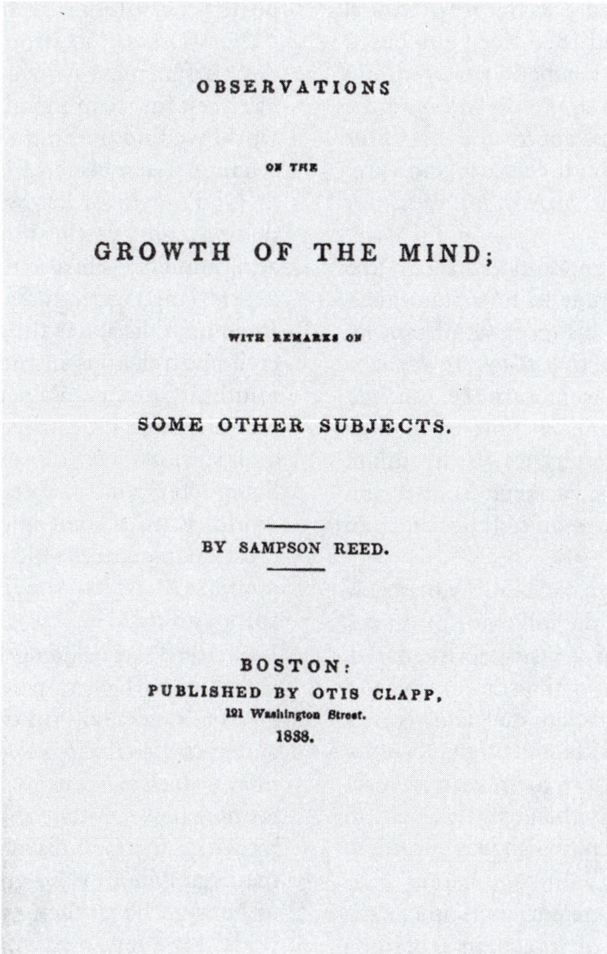

OBSERVATIONS

ON THE

GROWTH OF THE MIND;

WITH REMARKS ON

SOME OTHER SUBJECTS.

BY SAMPSON REED.

BOSTON:
PUBLISHED BY OTIS CLAPP,
121 Washington Street.
1838.

Title page for the third edition of Reed's popular pamphlet, which Ralph Waldo Emerson called "the best thing since Plato of Plato's kind, for novelty & wealth of truth"

nite, exalted the uniqueness of each individual and his potential for greatness, and proposed that lasting art has its foundation in nature; poetry, he asserts, achieves lasting perfection when "words make one with things, and language is lost in nature."

Despite such exuberant Romantic notions, Reed nevertheless tempers them with Swedenborgian thought. Mankind's spiritual rejuvenation will occur when science recognizes the moral order of nature and is reconciled with religion; wisdom flows from a heart charged with a divine influx; genius acknowledges that all powers are from God ("Here is the link of the finite with the infinite, of the divine with the human: this is the humility which exalts."); the individual cultivates his inner moral and spiritual being and vitally serves the commonweal; and the arts reflect the work of an artist whose purified heart is receptive to the love and wisdom that flow from God. Toward the end of his oration, he makes a statement, the echoes of which are to be heard throughout Emerson's canon: "There is a union of spirit and nature. The genius of the mind will descend, and unite with the genius of the rivers, the lakes, and the woods. Thoughts fall to the earth with power, and make a language out of nature."

Its Swedenborgian elements aside, six of Emerson's journal entries–either allusions or direct quotations–testify to the pleasure he took in this work. When Elizabeth P. Peabody in 1849 assembled the essays that appeared in the *Aesthetic Papers,* Emerson was likely the person who lent her his manuscript copy of the "Oration on Genius."

However triumphant the reception of his commencement address, Reed now found himself trained to preach in a faith from whose doctrines he had distanced himself and without a congregation to lead in his newly chosen faith. He briefly taught school in Boston, then resolved on studying medicine; but lacking means, Reed bound himself for three years to an apothecary, or druggist. During these years, he was troubled by his seeming failure to determine his "peculium" or "use" (a

Swedenborgian concept that embraces one's vocational and spiritual fulfillment). Around 1825 Reed purchased an apothecary shop, which he eventually parlayed into a wholesale drug firm; with this stroke, Reed found the peculium that was to remain constant for the rest of his life–that of committing his financial, literary, and spiritual resources to nurturing the growth of the New Jerusalem Church in America.

Evidently, during his apprenticeship in the apothecary shop, Reed found time to formulate ideas and write what was to become his most significant literary work, *Observations on the Growth of the Mind,* a forty-four-page pamphlet that went through ten editions from 1826 to 1886. A grand synthesis, it fuses everything from God and metaphysics to the mind, the laws of the natural sciences, aesthetics, civil and religious institutions, and even man's duties into an all-encompassing scheme.

Reed begins his essay on a millennial note; new inventions and discoveries and the influence of revelation operating on the human mind testify to the dawning of a new age. Unconditional optimism, however, is unwarranted; he reminds his readers that man is in a fallen state and that meaningful change originates only in the mind that lives in the spirit of the revealed word. His purpose in the ensuing essay, he announces, is "to trace summarily that development which is required, in order to render [the mind] truly useful and happy."

The first section treats of memory and time, each discussed against the backdrop of revelation according to Swedenborgian doctrine. Relating memory to the affections, he argues that the mind best retains that which it likes. To that end, he urges man to make learning a living principle directed toward use. The highest use to which learning can be applied is in approaching and identifying with the eternal. At this point, Reed repudiates Locke's theory of tabula rasa, as he did in the "Oration on Genius"; rather, he conceptualizes the mind as growing from an internal principle unique to each individual and nourished by both the material and the spiritual creations.

The second part identifies the shaping influences on the development of the mind–the natural sciences, society, and the Word of God, each acting, in the Swedenborgian scheme, much as the earth, atmosphere, and sun act on the seed in nature. The facts of the natural world impart useful knowledge and, more importantly, provide the objects that invigorate man's moral and intellectual sensibilities. In this latter sense, the arts, particularly poetry, are integrally related to nature–immortal poetry capturing the creative spirit of God in nature. For this reason, the true measure of the state of science and poetry at any given time is reflected in the state of its poetry. Reed also dismisses poetic conventions as having no sanction in nature: "They possess too strongly the marks of art, and produce a sameness which tires, and sometimes disgusts. We seek for them in vain in nature. . . . In the natural world we find nothing which answers to them, . . . but a happy assemblage of living objects springing up . . . in God's own order, which by its apparent want of design, conveys the impression of perfect innocence and humility." He also explores the ideal of employing a pure language founded not on words but on things. Reed next discusses the limited spiritual influence that civil and religious institutions exert in developing the mind. Because man's nature is fallen, he cannot recognize anymore the correspondence between the natural and spiritual worlds; even worse, man's disordered being alters and distorts his perception of the natural world. Reed's point is clear: having lost his place in creation, man needs the power of God's Word to effect a union between the Divine and himself, between spirit and nature.

Reed's concluding remarks center on the need to realize one's highest potential, but they are once again given a Swedenborgian cast: "It becomes us then to seek and to cherish this *peculium* of our own minds, as the patrimony which is left us by our Father in heaven . . . as the forming power within us, which gives to our persons that by which they are distinguished from others. . . . Let a man's ambition to be great, disappear in a willingness to be what he is; then may he fill a high place without pride, or a low one without dejection." Governed by such sentiments, man meets his moral responsibilities toward regenerating the world and gains his fullest spiritual potential.

While some reviews were unfavorable–the October 1826 issue of *The Christian Examiner* calling *Observations on the Growth of the Mind* "unintelligible and useless"–and others mixed–*The United States Review* for November 1826 complaining about Reed's failure to define various terms–no such misgivings clouded Emerson's enthusiasm. Within twelve days of its publication, Emerson described it in a 10 September journal entry as "having to my mind the aspect of a revelation such is the wealth and such is the novelty of the truth unfolded in it"; and in a 29 September letter to his brother William he declared it "the best thing since Plato of Plato's kind, for novelty & wealth of truth." A skeptical letter from his aunt Mary Moody Emerson in October elicited a fervent defense of *Observations on the Growth of the Mind* in the form of questions: "Can anything be more greatly, more wisely writ? Has any modern hand touched the harp of great nature so rarely? Has any looked so shrewdly into the subtle and concealed connexion of man and nature; of earth and heaven?" In May 1834 Emerson sent Thomas Carlyle a copy of

Observations on the Growth of the Mind and in November of that same year alerted James Freeman Clarke to the volume, observing, "I rejoice to be contemporary with that man, and cannot wholly despair of the society in which he lives; there must be some oxygen yet. . . ." Even as late as 1844, *Observations on the Growth of the Mind* continued to exert its hold on Emerson: he gave Dr. Samuel Brown, a Scottish acquaintance, a copy of the second edition (1829) with marked passages that he found especially compelling. A measure of how much Emerson esteemed *Observations on the Growth of the Mind* is suggested by his mentioning it by title seven times from the date of its publication to 1871.

Clarence Hotson's conclusion that "This book gave Emerson his first definite literary impulse" is convincing. Judging from Emerson's reaction, it seems to have been epiphanic in its hopeful, oracular power. As in Reed's other discourses, Romantic doctrines that were to constitute some of Emerson's core beliefs, if not those of Transcendentalism, are present–physical nature as an externalization of the soul; the correspondence of every natural fact to a spiritual truth; imagination's power to unfold spiritual truth through a perfect reconciliation of mind and matter; the genius of every individual; Locke's debasing sensualism; and an aesthetics that viewed poetry as a moral endeavor and repudiated poetic artifice in favor of giving spontaneous expression to the forms of nature. All of these ideas are, in varying degrees, explicit in Emerson's *Nature* essay in 1836 and in Emerson's conception of the poet in his 1844 essay by that same name. Kenneth Walter Cameron even suggests that many of Emerson's manuscript poems that have the appearance of being "incomplete or unpolished experiments" reflect his efforts to put into practice, however unsuccessfully, Reed's curious aesthetics. It took Whitman's daring and his lack of exposure to poetic culture other than that which he absorbed from Emerson to realize more fully Reed's aesthetic. At his best, Whitman eschews formal poetic conventions and constructs poems whose rhythm is derived from their thought and their inspiration from observable phenomena; growing organically like melons and pears, Whitman asserts, the form of his poems are "transcendent and new."

In the decade following the publication of *Observations on the Growth of the Mind,* Reed attended to his growing drug business and continued his church and literary activities. He contributed several essays to the *New Jerusalem Magazine,* the Boston Society's literary and religious publication, which he cofounded in September 1827 and edited after 1854 and to which he heavily contributed throughout his lifetime. From its pages Emerson drew almost all of his understanding of Swedenborgianism, and, as his journals and notebooks show, he homed in especially on Reed's articles. In December 1832 Reed married Catharine Clark, the sister of the Reverend Thomas Worcester's wife; the couple had three sons and a daughter.

Despite the many compelling intellectual affinities between Reed and Emerson and Boston's intellectual elite, they were not enough to prevent an estrangement when, in his 1838 preface to the third edition of *Observations on the Growth of the Mind,* Reed emphatically repudiated Transcendentalism and avowed Swedenborg as the prophet of the Second Coming. The modest literary success that both men had achieved to this time resulted in part from their use of Swedenborgianism, which in most quarters was viewed skeptically if not hostilely. Initially, Boston was friendly to Swedenborgianism, its neo-Platonism, and, in Emerson's case, Samuel Taylor Coleridge's philosophy, since it was reasonably compatible with religious liberalism. But the Transcendentalists emphatically drew the line over doctrinal matters, including the divinity of Swedenborg's revelations as being the Word of God, the literal reality of the afterlife, the Bible as the basis for eternal truth, and the mode by which this truth is perceived. While the Transcendentalists were inclined to place their trust in personal revelation vouchsafed by mankind's godlike powers, the Swedenborgians adhered to scriptural orthodoxy, turning to the Bible for revelation first before linking its truths through correspondence to natural and spiritual phenomena.

Despite his awareness of public prejudice against his faith, Reed's conscience required that he speak truth even at the risk of jeopardizing his literary career. Asserting that "the sacred Scripture is the only door through which we can enter into life, or conceive living things," he accuses Transcendentalism of being "the product of man's own brain," and says that its adherents, "imagining themselves spiritual . . . [,] only give to their sensuality wings, by which it may gain an apparent elevation without any real change in its nature."

Stung by these remarks, Emerson gave vent in a June journal entry, deploring "the malign influences of this immense arrogancy and subtle bigotry of his [Reed's] church." The following month Emerson confirmed Reed's worst suspicions in the Divinity School Address: he repudiated Christ's divinity and the Bible as Divine Revelation.

The rift between Reed and Emerson was underscored during an 1842 conversation in which Emerson iterated his view of Swedenborg as primarily a poet and denied the literalness of Swedenborg's description of the afterlife. For a period of twenty years, references to Reed in Emerson's journals disappear, though by mid 1865 conversations and nostalgic recollections of Reed's works begin to appear once again. All told,

Emerson alluded to Reed and his works fifty times in his journals and correspondence.

After the 1838 preface, the details of Reed's personal life and literary career become as sketchy and unrevealing as those he provided in an 8 July 1864 autobiographical letter. He served on the Board of Aldermen in 1852 and 1853; attended the Constitutional Convention in 1853; chaired the Committee of Finance in the Massachusetts House of Representatives in 1854; and transferred his interests in the drug business to his son in January 1861. His public literary career was thenceforth largely confined to New Church venues: in 1843 he founded, edited, and contributed to the *New Church Magazine for Children* (later titled *Children's New Church Magazine*); he contributed extensively to *New Jerusalem Magazine,* and wrote several pamphlets describing his interpretation of Swedenborgianism. Most notable among these is *The Correspondence of the Sun, Heat, and Light* (1862), an elucidation of the Swedenborgian doctrine of correspondences.

Contemporary with the heyday of Boston Transcendentalism, Reed shared its optimistic anticipation of an imminent unfolding of a more humane social order and mankind's spiritual regeneration; however, in parting philosophically from his contemporaries over the source for this change, "the gifted Sampson Reed became," in the words of Sylvia Binney Shaw, "one of America's forgotten writers." He died in Boston on 8 July 1880, barely remembered except in Swedenborgian circles.

References:

Kenneth Walter Cameron, *Emerson the Essayist,* 2 volumes (Hartford, Conn.: Transcendental Books, 1972);

Clarence Paul Hotson, "Emerson and Swedenborg," dissertation, Harvard University, 1929;

Hotson, "Sampson Reed, A Teacher of Emerson," *New England Quarterly,* 2 (April 1929): 249–277;

Elizabeth A. Meese, "Sampson Reed," in *The Transcendentalists: A Review of Research and Criticism,* edited by Joel Myerson (New York: Modern Language Association, 1984), pp. 372–374;

Meese, "Transcendental Vision: A History of the Doctrine of Correspondence and its Role in American Transcendentalism," dissertation, Wayne State University, 1972;

Meese, "Transcendentalism: The Metaphysics of the Theme," *American Literature,* 47 (March 1975): 1–20;

Sylvia Binney Shaw, "Preface," in *Sampson Reed: Primary Source Material for Emerson Studies,* compiled by George F. Dole (New York: Swedenborg Foundation, 1992), pp. ii–xii;

Shaw, "Sampson Reed: Swedenborgian Pioneer in American Literature," M.A. thesis, Clark University, 1986;

Carl F. Strauch, "Introduction," in *Observations on the Growth of the Mind with Remarks on Some Other Subjects (1838)* (Gainesville, Fla.: Scholars' Facsimiles & Reprints, 1970), pp. v–xvi.

Papers:

The Swedenborg Library at Bryn Athyn College, Pennsylvania, has an incomplete run of letters dating between 1827–1860. It also has a large selection of Reed's published writings including printed flyers, pamphlets, and full-length books. The Swedenborg School of Religion (Newton Center, Massachusetts) has some scattered correspondence of Reed's and two manuscript articles.

George Ripley

(3 October 1802 – 4 July 1880)

Susan M. Stone
University of South Carolina

See also the Ripley entries in *DLB 64: American Literary Critics and Scholars, 1850–1880* and *DLB 73: American Magazine Journalists, 1741–1850.*

BOOKS: *The Divinity of Jesus Christ* (Boston: Gray & Bowen, 1831);

The Doctrines of the Trinity and Transubstantiation Compared (Boston: Charles Bowen, 1833);

Discourses on the Philosophy of Religion. Addressed to Doubters Who Wish to Believe (Boston: J. Munroe, 1836);

The Temptations of the Times (Boston: Hilliard, Gray, 1837);

"The Latest Form of Infidelity" Examined. A Letter to Mr. Andrews Norton, Occasioned by His "Discourse Before the Association of the Alumni of the Cambridge Theological School" on the 19th of July, 1839 (Boston: J. Munroe, 1839);

Defence of "The Latest Form of Infidelity" Examined. A Second Letter to Mr. Andrews Norton, Occasioned by His Defence of a Discourse on "The Latest Form of Infidelity" (Boston: J. Munroe, 1840);

Defence of "The Latest Form of Infidelity" Examined. A Third Letter to Mr. Andrews Norton, Occasioned by His Defence of a Discourse on "The Latest Form of Infidelity" (Boston: J. Munroe, 1840);

A Letter Addressed to the Congregational Church in Purchase Street (Boston: Freeman & Bolles, 1840);

The Claims of the Age on the Work of the Evangelist (Boston: Weeks, Jordan, 1840);

A Farewell Discourse, Delivered to the Congregational Church in Purchase Street, March 28, 1841 (Boston: Freeman & Bolles, 1841);

Constitution of the Brook Farm Association for Industry and Education (Boston: I. R. Butts, 1844);

Constitution of the Brook Farm Phalanx, Adopted May 1, 1845 (West Roxbury, Mass.: The Phalanx, 1845);

To the Patrons of the American Cyclopaedia (New York, 1874).

Collection: *Letters on the Latest Form of Infidelity, Including a View of the Opinions of Spinoza, Schleiermacher, and de Wette* (Boston: J. Munroe, 1840).

OTHER: *Specimens of Foreign Standard Literature,* 15 volumes, edited by Ripley (volumes 1–11, Boston: Hilliard, Gray, 1838–1842; volumes 12–14, Boston: J. Munroe, 1842; volume 15, New York: Wiley, 1845);

Hand-book of Literature and the Fine Arts, compiled by Ripley and Bayard Taylor (New York: Putnam, 1852); republished as *Cyclopedia of Literature and the Fine Arts* (New York: Barnes, 1854);

The New American Cyclopaedia: A Popular Dictionary of General Knowledge, 16 volumes, edited by Ripley and Charles Anderson Dana (New York & London:

Appleton, 1858–1863); revised as *The American Cyclopaedia* (New York: Appleton, 1873–1876);

"Philosophic Thought in Boston," by Ripley and George P. Bradford, in *The Memorial History of Boston,* edited by Justin Winsor, volume 4 (Boston: J. R. Osgood, 1881), pp. 295–330;

"Articles of the Association of the Subscribers to the Brook Farm Institute of Agriculture and Education," in *George Ripley,* by Octavius Brooks Frothingham (Boston: Houghton, Mifflin, 1882), pp. 112–117.

SELECTED PERIODICAL PUBLICATIONS–UNCOLLECTED: "De Gerando on Self-Education," *Christian Examiner,* 9 (September 1830): 70–107;

"Religion in France," *Christian Examiner,* 10 (July 1831): 273–293;

"Pestalozzi," *Christian Examiner,* 11 (January 1832): 347–373;

"Herder's Theological Opinions," *Christian Examiner,* 14 (November 1835): 172–204;

"Schleiermacher as a Theologian," *Christian Examiner,* 20 (March 1836): 1–46;

"Cousin's Philosophy," *Christian Examiner,* 21 (September 1836): 33–64;

"Martineau's *Rationale,*" *Christian Examiner,* 21 (November 1836): 225–254;

"To Mr. Andrews Norton," *Boston Daily Advertiser,* 9 November 1836;

"Theological Aphorisms," *Christian Examiner,* 21 (January 1837): 385–398;

"Brownson's Writings," *Dial,* 1 (July 1840): 22–46;

"Letter to a Theological Student," *Dial,* 1 (October 1840): 183–187;

"Channing's Works," *Dial,* 1 (October 1840): 246–247;

"Harwood's Materialism in Religion," *Dial,* 1 (October 1840): 267–271;

"Introductory Notice," *Harbinger,* 1 (14 June 1845): 8–10;

"Influence of Machinery," *Harbinger,* 1 (14 June 1845): 14;

"Tendencies of Modern Civilization," *Harbinger,* 1 (28 June 1845): 33–35;

"Association in this Country," *Harbinger,* 1 (1846): 189–190;

"Influence of Social Circumstances," *Harbinger,* 5 (26 June 1847): 46.

Although George Ripley was instrumental in the development of the New England philosophical, social, religious, and literary reform movement known as American Transcendentalism, he has been largely overlooked by literary scholars and historians, perhaps because he espoused multiple, seemingly unrelated causes rather than a single endeavor to which his name might be indisputably linked. Ripley was a true "American Renaissance man" whose forward-looking literary and social endeavors influenced not only the handful of nineteenth-century New England intellectuals associated with Transcendentalism but also the great masses of literate, knowledge-hungry, working-class American citizens. Like Ralph Waldo Emerson, Ripley believed in the need to de-emphasize required forms and eliminate hierarchized religious intermediation from Unitarian doctrine; and like Henry David Thoreau, Ripley sought to change society for the better by reforming the individual. Similarly, like Margaret Fuller, Elizabeth Palmer Peabody, and Bronson Alcott, Ripley believed that education ought to be participatory, imaginative, and available to all, regardless of race, class, or gender. But Ripley, arguably to a greater extent than his fellow Transcendentalists, believed that the human race could only be bettered by improving every aspect of life–mental, physical, spiritual, and emotional–on both the individual and societal levels.

Ripley saw beyond Transcendentalism, helping to make its precepts and those of socialism and associationism accessible to and applicable by the American masses in unconventional and often overlooked ways. Without understanding Ripley's egalitarian ideals and breadth of purpose, many modern historians and literary critics have labeled Ripley as less focused than his contemporaries. Critics, dazzled by the intensity of his Transcendentalist peers' singular efforts, have failed to recognize that Ripley's multivalent approach to social reform and Transcendentalism more closely mirrored the way the average mid-nineteenth-century American actually lived and invested his or her time in various efforts; Ripley's eclecticism was and still is, in some respects, more thorough, positive, and realistic to the "normal" citizen than the often abstract and ephemeral behavior of his colorful contemporaries. His vision was to create a better world not only by improving himself, but also by enabling others to uplift themselves and fix ailing community relationships. Ripley embraced both the individual and the world, validating difference yet working toward the common good.

George Ripley was born in Greenfield, Massachusetts, on 3 October 1802, shortly after the rural village had been ravaged by smallpox and dysentery. Ripley's mother, Sarah Franklin Ripley, was mourning the death of a two-year-old son just a few weeks before she delivered Ripley, her ninth child. She convinced her merchant husband, Jerome Ripley, to allow their newborn to be christened with the deceased toddler's name: George. The second George Ripley survived a somewhat sickly childhood.

Ripley, who was spoon-fed Calvinist doctrine by his conservative mother and raised a devout, orthodox Congregationalist, graduated from Harvard in 1823 at the top of his class and immediately entered the Divinity School, where he continued to excel academically. His views began to shift away from the gloomy rigidity of Calvinism. When Ripley left Harvard in 1826, trained as a Unitarian minister and becoming more of a liberal thinker, his reputation was impeccable; he quickly earned a position as an officer in the American Unitarian Association, accepted the duties of both editor and author for the *Christian Register,* and took possession of the Purchase Street Church pulpit in Boston. He married Sophia Willard Dana in 1827, and his future looked bright and predictable. Although Ripley earned a great deal of respect for his early sermons and pamphlets, his writings during the 1830s, particularly surrounding the "Norton Debates," made some of the religious elders nervous.

Already positively influenced by Friedrich Schiller and unsatisfied with John Locke's idea of the mind as a tabula rasa upon which all experience perceived solely by the five senses is engraved, Ripley began to explore more radical European ideas of philosophy and theology. In consideration of these topics, he wrote ten essays for the *Christian Examiner* over a seven-year period, including two in praise of French and Swiss educational philosophies and practices: "De Gerando on Self-Education" (September 1830) and "Pestalozzi" (January 1832). Other essays published in the *Christian Examiner* between 1830 and 1837 began to express Ripley's growing investment in a more democratic, optimistic, and nonauthoritarian form of theology that ultimately became linked to Transcendentalism, including "Religion in France" (July 1831), "Herder's Theological Opinions" (November 1835), "Schleiermacher as a Theologian" (March 1836), and "Cousin's Philosophy" (September 1836). Ripley's writing reflected his zeal for liberal European thought; ultimately these beliefs earned him friendships with the great thinkers, theologians, and teachers who became leaders in the Transcendental movement: Fuller, Alcott, Theodore Parker, John Sullivan Dwight, Orestes A. Brownson, and Emerson, Ripley's cousin.

Although perhaps most often identified as the reform-oriented literary movement prompted by Emerson's famous trio of works–*Nature* (1836), "The American Scholar" (1837), and the Divinity School address (1838)–or as the reason for Thoreau's "Civil Disobedience" (1849) and his famous sojourn at Walden Pond, the American Transcendental movement can also be traced back to earlier transitional figures such as Sampson Reed, the author of *Oration on Genius* (1821) and *Observations on the Growth of the Mind* (1826), and William

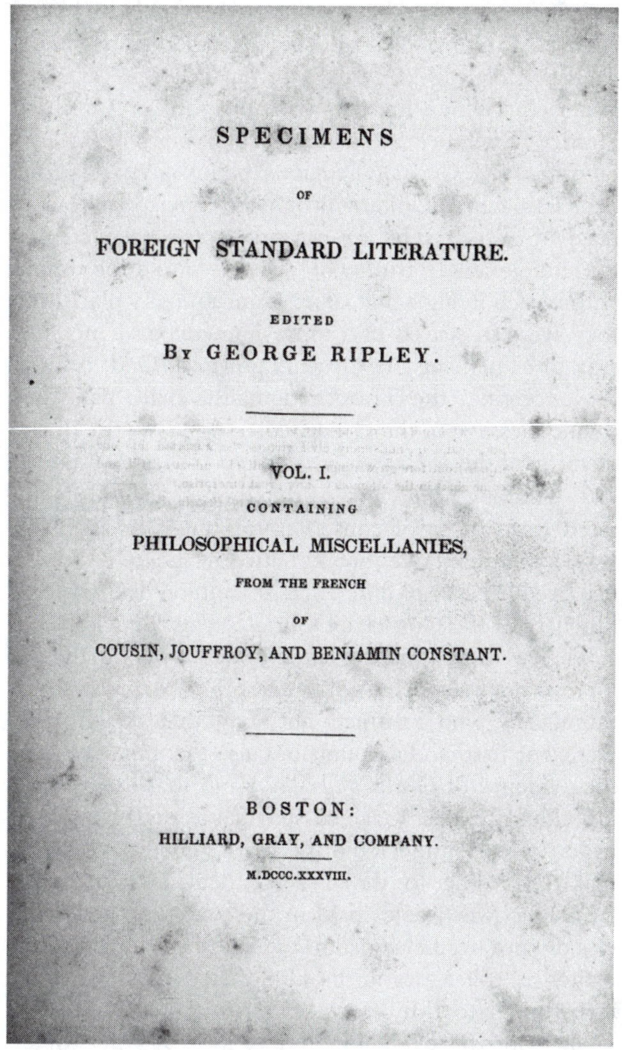
SPECIMENS

OF

FOREIGN STANDARD LITERATURE.

EDITED

BY GEORGE RIPLEY.

VOL. I.

CONTAINING

PHILOSOPHICAL MISCELLANIES,

FROM THE FRENCH

OF

COUSIN, JOUFFROY, AND BENJAMIN CONSTANT.

BOSTON:

HILLIARD, GRAY, AND COMPANY.

M.DCCC.XXXVIII.

Title page for the first volume of the series in which Ripley sought to make the best European ideas accessible to general readers (Collection of Joel Myerson)

Ellery Channing, a liberal theologian who, by asserting not only that intuition was superior to inductive reasoning but also that God was everywhere in nature, to some extent established a middle ground between Unitarianism and what became Transcendentalism. Both of these men, and dozens of foreign-born writers, made Ripley and a handful of his peers question and seek to move beyond the theological status quo. Specifically, full-blown Transcendentalism, although ultimately also a social, political, educational, literary, and philosophical movement, emerged in the early to mid 1830s because of religious dissatisfaction on the part of Ripley, Emerson, Parker, William Henry Furness, Convers Francis, and other rebellious young New Englanders, most of whom had first attended the Divinity School at Harvard and been trained by its conservative ministers. In the opinions of Ripley and his colleagues, who had been influenced not only by liberal American thinkers but also by the writings of Samuel Taylor Coleridge, Victor Cousin, Thomas Carlyle, Heinrich Heine, Immanuel Kant, Johann Gottfried Herder, Emanuel Swedenborg, and one of Ripley's favorites, the German religious philosopher Friedrich Schleiermacher, Unitarianism was impersonal and in need of reform. The Transcendentalists believed that the fundamental truths of religion could be found within each living being, at any time and any place, and they were in search of a more immediate, democratic way of evidencing the supreme power of God. As Ripley once said, the Transcendentalists held that "The divine message of the Gospel corresponds to the divine instincts of the soul."

Although the views of the Transcendentalists differed from those of conservative Unitarians in many ways, the definitive break between the two groups occurred because of differences in opinion over the genuineness of the Gospels of Christ. "The Miracles Controversy," as this dispute came to be known, made the Transcendentalists seem like heretics in the eyes of traditionalists who assumed not only that the Gospels were true firsthand accounts but also that miracles were the evidence of Christ's divinity, and that the average individual needed a trained spiritual leader or guide in order to truly understand the word and receive God's will. According to the Transcendentalists, however, Christ's power was evident in the everyday, and miracles did not need elucidation by Andrews Norton or his orthodox colleagues in the Unitarian Church in order to be understood by the masses. On the contrary, religious truth was evident in and verified by what Ripley called its "correspondence with the divine spirit in man." In other words, Ripley believed that Reason, or the ability to ascertain higher truths by looking inward, enabled each individual to interpret God's message and made historical Christianity problematic.

Predictably, Ripley rose to a prominent role in the Transcendentalist movement. He volunteered to be the first host of–and willingly served as a regular participant in–the famous Transcendental Club, which began on 19 September 1836, a weekly gathering of articulate New Englanders such as Ripley, Emerson, Alcott, Francis, Fuller, Peabody, Parker, William Henry Channing, and James Freeman Clarke. Yet, the more popular Ripley became with the Transcendentalists, the more frequently he found himself at odds with his Harvard past and his early religious training.

Norton, the conservative minister who served as Dexter Professor of Sacred Literature at Harvard until 1830 and was sarcastically dubbed the "Unitarian Pope" of Boston, is perhaps best remembered for his vehement response to Emerson's Divinity School address in 1838. Yet, he and his former pupil, Ripley, had an even longer and more heated history of disagreeing. Two years prior to the Norton/Emerson conflict, in response to Ripley's *Christian Examiner* critique of British minister James Martineau's *Rationale of Religious Inquiry* (1836), Norton publicly chastised Ripley in the *Boston Daily Advertiser* for what he and other orthodox Unitarian ministers felt to be sensationalistic liberal beliefs bordering on religious infidelity and atheism. In his review of Martineau, Ripley had declared that "The power of the soul, by which it gains the intuitive perception of spiritual truth, is the original inspiration that forms the common endowment of human nature." He then suggested that Reason, or intuition, allows each human, regardless of education, gender, class, or religious training, to perceive "Divine Truths." That thought was a step too radical for Norton and his colleague Henry Ware, the Unitarian minister who had proudly ordained Ripley a decade earlier. Ripley quickly slipped from misguided nuisance to conscious threat, becoming the object of Norton's scathing reprimand. Thus began one of the most heated theological debates in American history, a public holy war that ultimately, in part, backfired on Norton and earned new followers for both Transcendentalism and Ripley. In his carefully crafted yet controversial initial response, which appeared four days later in the same newspaper as his adversary's attack, Ripley calmly and clearly thanked Norton for drawing attention and support to his cause; described the latter's claims as vague, unfounded, and elitist; dismissed Norton's Lockean school of philosophy; endorsed the respect of Transcendentalists for individualism and original thinking; and declared that the "evidence of miracles depends on a previous belief in Christianity," not vice versa.

A few weeks later Ripley took the issue a step further and, with James Munroe's backing, published a forty-page rebuttal of Norton's brief yet vicious *Advertiser* article. Ripley used more than two years' worth of his own sermons–and the argument that miracles do not require intermediation–to craft *Discourses on the Philosophy of Religion. Addressed to Doubters Who Wish to Believe* (1836). In this significant piece, he suggests that those, like Norton, who only believe what can be verified by their senses or their understanding, were "Doubters." Although they might want to be truly enlightened, "Doubters" are not "true Believers" because they ignore or disregard the invisible and intangible signs of divinity that might be ascertained without mediation through Reason, or intuition, by each individual. Norton, outraged at the insinuation that he was a "Doubter," responded with *Genuineness of the Gospels* (1837), in which he disagreed vehemently with Ripley's stance, and tensions between the two remained elevated.

Although Norton's attack *The Latest Form of Infidelity* (1839) was largely a response to Emerson's writings, particularly the Divinity School address, which Norton thought a dangerous call for both the reformation of theology and the rejection of formal ritual required by institutionalized religion, the work also excited an immediate response from Ripley, himself a leader of what Norton sarcastically referred to as the misdirected "New School." In the first and most intricate of three lengthy pamphlets addressing Norton's critique, *"The Latest Form of Infidelity" Examined. A Letter to Mr. Andrews Norton, Occasioned by His "Discourse Before the Association of the Alumni of the Cambridge Theological School" on the 19th of July, 1839* (1839), Ripley convincingly asserts that Norton and his colleagues were guilty of the same philosophical narrowness and stagnant theology against which they once fought in order to establish Unitarianism. In this work Ripley argues for diversity of thought, trust in nature, and self-dependence. In the second and third letters of the same series, which appeared the following year from the same publisher, Ripley reinforces his earlier assertions and defends Benedict de Spinoza, Wilhelm Martin Leberecht de Wette, and Schleiermacher against Norton's charge of atheism. Moreover, as he had in *The Temptations of the Times* (1837), Ripley calls for social awareness and a shift away from the traditional Unitarian doctrine of miracles on the grounds that they were un-American and elitist.

As he continued to embrace German Romantic idealism and the power of intuition in pamphlets and articles such as "Theological Aphorisms" (January 1837) in the *Christian Examiner,* Ripley realized that his Transcendental affinities would ultimately make working for the *Christian Register* and preaching from the Purchase Street pulpit problematic. In 1837 Ripley left the Unitarian journal and undertook the first of several editorial projects, some of which seemed to appeal to a broad, nonspecific audience and some of which were decidedly reform-oriented and Transcendental in scope. The earliest of these general editorial endeavors, the first volumes of Ripley's *Specimens of Foreign Standard Literature,* appeared in 1838. With the assistance of many Transcendentalists, including later volume editors William Henry Channing, Fuller, Clarke, and Dwight, Ripley compiled and edited a total of fifteen volumes of European translations for this series. The project, which took seven years, was designed to be "palatable to general readers"; it was written and compiled so that others might become exposed to and influenced by works he and the other Transcendentalists considered necessary albeit rebellious literary "standards": those by German idealists, French philosophers, and other like-minded radical poets, essayists, historians, and theologians. *Specimens of Foreign Standard Literature* acquainted many Americans with Herder, Johann Wolfgang von Goethe, Gotthold Ephraim Lessing, and Schleiermacher, the man whom Ripley described in an 1852 letter to Parker as "the greatest thinker who ever undertook to fathom the philosophy of religion."

Ripley's praise was not limited to the German thinkers; on the contrary, in the introductory notice for the first two volumes in the series, *Philosophical Miscellanies from the French of Cousin, Jouffroy, and Benjamin Constant* (1838), Ripley declared the French thinkers just as enlightening, specifically admiring Cousin's ability to "put the general reader in possession of the most valuable results of a profound philosophy." Although he had to some extent done so previously, Ripley, ever conscious of Cousin's ripple effect, took even greater pains to make his own writing accessible to what he called "the great mass of an intelligent population." Much in the same vein as Emerson's "American Scholar" address, which had been delivered before the Phi Beta Kappa Society at Harvard less than a year earlier, Ripley's introduction to *Philosophical Miscellanies from the French of Cousin, Jouffroy, and Benjamin Constant* attempts to define "the office of the true scholar." The remainder of the work, which endeavors to make the reader feel like the author's partner in learning, is an anthology of the writings of French philosophers and German idealists, a sort of guide to metaphysics and survey of the philosophical principles of democracy.

In 1840, buoyed by the reception of *Specimens of Foreign Standard Literature,* Ripley did what Emerson called "a brave thing." After offering unsuccessfully to resign from his religious post on 21 May 1840, he wrote *A Letter Addressed to the Congregational Church in Purchase Street* (1840), a moving explanation of his need to step down from his ministerial position because of personal differences in perceptions of spirituality. Although Ripley had a devoted following, and although he and his family were guaranteed financial security by the position, he could no longer meet the needs of his congregation or serve as their like-minded spiritual leader with a clear conscience or in good faith. Even so, the Purchase Street committee was so fond of Ripley that they would not let him go for another six months; moreover, when Ripley preached his final sermon, *A Farewell Discourse,* on 28 March 1841, the church members had it printed.

Although his alliance with traditional Unitarianism drew to a close, Ripley's concern with spiritual matters increased in the late 1830s and early 1840s, especially as religion pertained to social thought. Without a regular journal in which to publish their views–

other than Brownson's somewhat "dogmatic" and politically "rigid" *Boston Quarterly Review*–Ripley and several other Transcendentalists were becoming frustrated. Along with Fuller and Emerson, Ripley played a crucial role in the establishment and production of *The Dial,* a Transcendentalist forum for the discussion of religion, philosophy, poetry, literature, art, and social reform. Encouraged by the popular success of the introductory volumes of his *Specimens of Foreign Standard Literature,* Ripley approached Fuller in 1839 about publishing a new Transcendentalist periodical. A brief discussion at the September meeting of the Transcendental Club led to the first issue in July 1840 of the publication that Fuller and Emerson in their introductory notice called "one cheerful rational voice amidst the din of mourners and polemics." Before leaving Boston, Ripley held an editorship, acted as the business manager of the journal, and contributed eight essays for the first volume. Many of Ripley's articles for *The Dial,* such as "Brownson's Writings" (July 1840) and "Channing's Works" (October 1840), were religious endorsements. In "Brownson's Writings" Ripley embraced his friend's enthusiasm for social progress and "spiritual philosophy," and in "Letter to a Theological Student" (October 1840), a heartfelt response to a prospective young minister, Ripley praises Herder and recommends the philosophy of looking both inward and upward for spiritual guidance.

In April 1841, mere days after his resignation of the Purchase Street pulpit, Ripley began a radical experiment in communal living on a 170-acre dairy farm in West Roxbury, Massachusetts. Brook Farm was a controversial group effort to actualize the social idealism of the Transcendental movement; Emerson, Fuller, and Alcott were simultaneously sympathetic and skeptical. Since Ripley, as president of Brook Farm, believed that the chief aim of Christianity was "to redeem society as well as the individual from all sin," no member was to be excluded from the responsibilities, events, and opportunities of the association, regardless of gender, religious beliefs, or previous social station. The Charles River community, the goal of which Ripley claimed in a 9 November 1840 letter to Emerson was to "combine the thinker and the worker as far as possible in the same individual," was designed to be a true democracy, a utopian haven where philosophers milked cows and laundresses might teach poetry. Ripley and his wife, Sophia, invested everything they had in the Brook Farm cause, committing their time, labor, money, and enthusiasm.

For a while, other forward-looking hopefuls shared the Ripleys' zeal, and the joint-stock-based community succeeded. The school, which admitted boys and girls, boarders and day students, was particularly well-received, both in New England and the South. Depicted favorably in the *Monthly Miscellany of Religion and Letters, The Dial,* the *United States Magazine and Democratic Review,* and the *New-York Daily Tribune,* the school attracted many ambitious, hardworking youths from a multitude of dissimilar backgrounds. Word spread of the nurturing environment and democratic ideals at Brook Farm, and membership increased to almost 150 people. In addition to the many students, new recruits enlisted, taking on the responsibilities of the other divisions–Agriculture, Finance, and General Direction. Intrigued by the egalitarian principles for which Brook Farm stood, these later disciples welcomed the opportunity to participate in the caste-free cooperative promised by Ripley in the "Articles of the Association of the Subscribers to the Brook Farm Institute of Agriculture and Education" (1841; published, 1882). Brook Farm was, the "Articles" declared, an attempt to put theory and philosophy into practice both for the individual and the community as a whole.

Logical on paper, "Articles" fell short in practice. Although Article 15 proclaimed that each of the four Brook Farm departments would be considered equal in importance, the agriculture group was disadvantaged from the outset because the majority of the participants lacked previous farming experience. Initially, soaring profits from the educational branch of the community compensated for gradual losses in the farming department. Toward the close of 1843, however, circumstances looked dismal. In an effort to revitalize and reorganize the association, Ripley and his peers turned to Fourierism, a highly structured form of socialistic collectivism based upon the ideals of Charles Fourier, a French radical theorist who proposed arranging people into small, efficient, family-like groups called phalanxes. After this change and the public appearance of Ripley's *Constitution of the Brook Farm Association for Industry and Education* (1844) and *Constitution of the Brook Farm Phalanx, Adopted May 1, 1845* (1845), the community erased some of its debt; however, although hopeful and inspired, part 2 of Ripley's lofty social experiment was short-lived. On 3 March 1846 an extensive fire involving a half-built, uninsured, central dormitory structure called the Phalanstery destroyed any hopes that the debt-plagued community had of survival.

Although the Brook Farm Association went bankrupt and disbanded in 1847, another of Ripley's socialist endeavors flourished, albeit with unexpected changes. When *The Dial* fell out of circulation in 1844, Ripley, then at Brook Farm, began a new Fourierist journal called *The Harbinger.* In the 14 June 1845 "Introductory Notice" Ripley claimed that the publication would strive to be democratic, comprehensive, sincere, and devoted to the improvement of humankind. Its contents would be uplifting and reform-oriented; its writers would challenge racial discrimination, poor working environments, educational elitism, prison conditions, unfair compensation for labor, unnecessary involvement in the Mexican-American War, and gender bias. Purportedly, global problems could be solved if everyone would reject capitalism and embrace socialism and the Association Movement.

For two years Ripley served as both the main editor and a frequent contributor to the weekly publication. He wrote more than three hundred pieces for the journal during its four-year run, including social commentaries such as "Influence of Machinery" (14 June 1845), "Tendencies of Modern Civilization" (28 June 1845), and "Influence of Social Circumstances" (26 June 1847). Often Ripley's writing combined the personal with the political, as in his 1846 *Harbinger* article "Association in this Country." In this poignant piece Ripley reflected upon Brook Farm, noting that the Transcendentalist pilgrims there set out to replace vice-riddled anti-intellectuals with "a race of free, noble, and holy men and women." Ripley was not the sole voice of *The Harbinger;* many other esteemed authors and critics–including Dwight, William Henry Channing, George Curtis, Thomas Wentworth Higginson, James Russell Lowell, John Greenleaf Whittier, Christopher Pearse Cranch, and Charles Anderson Dana–also contributed their views on literature, poetry, art, politics, business, and social reform.

In 1847, however, when Brook Farm closed and the American Union of Associationist leaders voted to move *The Harbinger* to New York, Ripley was forced to turn the position of editor in chief over to Parke Godwin and to accept the less prestigious but more demanding role of assistant editor. Godwin, however, was largely a leader in title only, and Ripley was determined not to let his brainchild die. At this time, perhaps because of its radical content and the increasing social unrest in the lower-income areas of the city, writers for several New York papers began to lambaste *The Harbinger* and Ripley. Agents of local tabloids such as the Rochester *Evening Post,* statewide publications such as *The Observer* and *The Express,* and even the more supposedly open-minded regional magazines such as *The Democratic Review* accused Ripley and the American Union of Associationists of endorsing immorality, condemning capitalism, and agitating the masses. Convinced that *The Harbinger* was truly the voice of and for the people, Ripley tried desperately to keep the socialist journal in print, regardless of the negative press, but lack of funding and Godwin's frequent absences made the demise of *The Harbinger* inevitable. On 10 February 1849 the journal folded, and

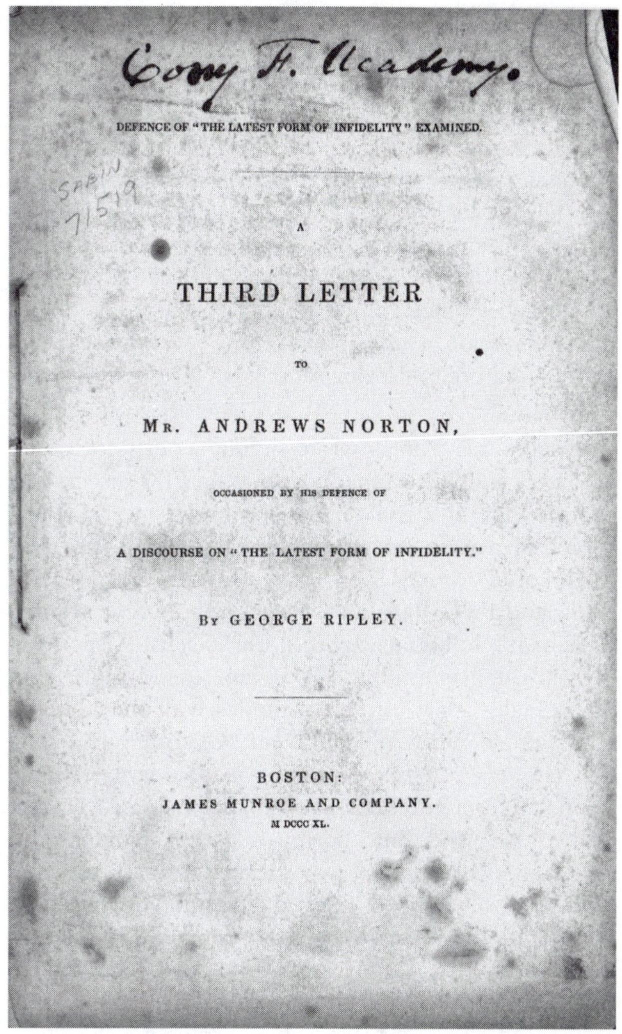
DEFENCE OF "THE LATEST FORM OF INFIDELITY" EXAMINED.

A

THIRD LETTER

TO

MR. ANDREWS NORTON,

OCCASIONED BY HIS DEFENCE OF

A DISCOURSE ON "THE LATEST FORM OF INFIDELITY."

BY GEORGE RIPLEY.

BOSTON:
JAMES MUNROE AND COMPANY.
M DCCC XL.

Title page for the last in Ripley's responses to his former teacher's attacks on Transcendentalism (Collection of Joel Myerson)

after a brief period of recovery, Ripley shifted his editorial and authorial interests elsewhere.

Beginning in 1849, still dealing with Brook Farm debts, Ripley became a regular and highly sought-after "penny-a-line" reviewer and essay writer for more than a dozen publications, including *Putnam's Magazine,* the *Atlantic Monthly Magazine,* the New York *Quarterly,* the *Charleston Literary Gazette,* the Boston *Globe,* the New Orleans *Picayune,* the *National Era, Hearth and Home,* the *Southern Literary Messenger,* the *Washingtonian,* the *Independent,* and Horace Greeley's *New-York Daily Tribune.* Working for this last paper, Ripley established himself as one of the most competent, versatile, and respected journalists in the profession. Initially hired by Greeley to assume Fuller's role as head literary critic for the paper, Ripley also worked part-time in the capacities of literary assistant, assistant editor, and obituary writer. With his Transcendental ability to judge works according to the ideals that they propose to the reader, Ripley acted as a full-time book reviewer for the *New-York Daily Tribune,* writing thousands of commentaries on the literature, philosophy, and poetry of the day. He remarked on writers such as Edgar Allan Poe, Herman Melville, Nathaniel Hawthorne, Mark Twain, William Dean Howells, Louis Kossuth, Heinrich Heine, Charles Sumner, and George Eliot. For *Harper's New Monthly Magazine,* which he helped to establish in 1850, Ripley initially wrote literary notices and later acted as one of the submission readers, evaluating everything from travel literature to theological pieces.

Hoping to earn enough money to settle his Brook Farm accounts, Ripley wrote simultaneously for multiple publications, earning meager wages for discussions of the temperance movement, antislavery meetings and speeches, artistic debuts, the latest operas, the New York social scene, United States history, the ideas of Kant, and P. T. Barnum's circus. Although he wanted to remain a full-time activist in the socialist Association Movement, Ripley found little time to do more than occasionally assist former comrades with their efforts. For example, when William Henry Channing's journal, the *Spirit of the Age,* was waning in popularity, Ripley stepped in as a guest editor; this task proved somewhat discouraging and futile, however, as the tabloid was on the brink of bankruptcy when Ripley resigned the temporary post. Ripley enjoyed constant favor as a reviewer and critic; as a 14 November 1850 editorial in the Boston *Daily Bee* proclaimed, his evaluations were "characterized by eminent sagacity, knowledge, judgment, and light." Moreover, according to the same piece, Ripley's critiques were thought to "frequently exhibit more sound sense and true philosophy and twice the genius of the book criticized; and are often read in preference to the work itself."

Ripley continued to contribute his reviews, articles, essays, and gossip columns to various venues for more than thirty years, but he began in the 1850s to turn his attentions to works that might reach, educate, and motivate the "average American." Determined to make knowledge available to all who desired it, even about traditionally class-exclusive topics such as aesthetics, Ripley and Bayard Taylor, with Putnam's backing, published the *Hand-book of Literature and the Fine Arts* (1852). A popular guide for those seeking an introduction to art, this compilation explained the arts clearly and succinctly, defining terminology, demystifying standards of excellence, and elucidating subtleties. This respected resource was republished by Barnes in 1854 as *Cyclopedia of Literature and the Fine Arts,* but it was superseded by Ripley's all-encompassing encyclopedia, which was geared toward any curious reader.

The New American Cyclopaedia: A Popular Dictionary of General Knowledge, published by Appleton between 1858 and 1863, was a sixteen-volume resource written and edited by Ripley and Charles Anderson Dana. Immediately well-received by the general public as an accessible reference tool–and greeted by critics for such periodicals as the *Massachusetts Quarterly,* the *Chicago Tribune,* and *The Daily Graphic* as one of the best American encyclopedias ever written–this financially lucrative endeavor finally gave Ripley, who was still mourning the death of his wife in 1861, a long-awaited but bittersweet sense of economic security. Even more popular a decade after its initial appearance, the series, which was designed both to spark and satisfy curiosity in the average reader rather than the Harvard-educated theologian or Transcendental philosopher, had earned its editors approximately $180,000. By 1880, after having been revised as *The American Cyclopaedia* (1873–1876), it had sold more than 1.4 million copies; it was reprinted again in 1883.

After his wife's death Ripley, convinced that no one could ever equal Sophia's understanding, warmth, and patience, resolved to remain unmarried. After a three-year period of mourning and intense work, however, he reconsidered. In 1865 Ripley wed a much younger woman he had initially considered adopting, a lively German widow named Louisa Augusta Schlossberger.

Ripley remained a comprehensive reviewer, literary critic, and newswriter throughout his later years, serving during a summer visit in 1866 to Germany, Austria, France, and Switzerland as war correspondent for the *New-York Daily Tribune* and contributing pieces on subjects such as Nathaniel Parker Willis, Cousin, Carlyle, Voltaire, Jean-Jacques Rousseau, Albion W. Tourgée, Daniel Webster, and Charles Darwin not only to the *New-York Daily Tribune* but also to other publications such as the *Independent.* Ripley's postbellum activities were as diverse as those from his early Transcendentalist days. He kept a detailed journal of his daily activities and conversations; involved himself in the ultimately unsuccessful efforts to organize a national institute of letters, arts, and sciences; received an honorary LL.D. degree from the University of Michigan; and agreed to write a chapter for the fourth volume of Justin Winsor's *The Memorial History of Boston* (1880–1881). The chapter, "Philosophic Thought in Boston," was completed by George P. Bradford after Ripley's death. Although he never achieved the contemporaneous celebrity of his cousin Emerson or the posthumous fame of Thoreau, Ripley was a man of many successes and far-reaching influence. In all of his roles–minister, essayist, community leader, educator, journal founder, magazine editor, literary critic, translator, foreign correspondent, and encyclopedia coordinator–Ripley acted as an intermediary between the few and the masses, the privileged and the less fortunate, the theoretical and the actual.

On 4 July 1880, following a prolonged illness, Ripley was found slumped over in his writing chair in the study of his New York home, his final notes for another barely begun article in his hands. Up until his death–and perhaps, considering his textual legacy, even past it–Ripley sought to actualize his Brook Farm dream. For half a century he worked on many fronts, hoping ultimately to make the world a more egalitarian and truly divine place.

Letters:

Mathew David Fisher, "A Selected, Annotated Edition of the Letters of George Ripley, 1828–1841," dissertation, Ball State University, 1992.

Bibliographies:

Joel Myerson, *Brook Farm: An Annotated Bibliography and Resources Guide* (New York: Garland, 1978);

Charles Crowe, "George Ripley," in *The Transcendentalists: A Review of Research and Criticism,* edited by Myerson (New York: The Modern Language Association, 1984), pp. 242–249.

Biographies:

Octavius Brooks Frothingham, *George Ripley* (Boston: Houghton, Mifflin, 1882);

Charles Crowe, *George Ripley: Transcendentalist and Utopian Socialist* (Athens: University of Georgia Press, 1967).

References:

Brian M. Barbour, ed., *American Transcendentalism* (Notre Dame, Ind.: University of Notre Dame Press, 1973);

Lawrence Buell, *Literary Transcendentalism: Style and Vision in the American Renaissance* (Ithaca, N.Y.: Cornell University Press, 1973);

Henry L. Golemba, *George Ripley* (Boston: Twayne, 1977);

Philip F. Gura and Joel Myerson, *Critical Essays on American Transcendentalism* (Boston: G. K. Hall, 1982);

Perry Miller, *The Transcendentalists: An Anthology* (Cambridge, Mass., & London: Harvard University Press, 1950).

Papers:

The Boston Public Library has some of George Ripley's letters (1836–1870) in four collections: thirty-seven are in the John Sullivan Dwight collection; thirty-five are in the Brook Farm collection; eighteen are in the Anti-Slavery collection; and seventeen are in the Weston Papers. The Houghton Library at Harvard University has many additional documents and items of memorabilia, including clippings, Brook Farm account books, manuscripts, and fifteen letters collected in four Ripley folders. The Massachusetts Historical Society holds multiple sermons and manuscripts as well as Ripley's memorandum book, the Brook Farm Constitution drafts, thirty-eight letters in the George Bancroft collection, thirty-four letters in the Octavius Brooks Frothingham collection, eighteen correspondences in the Theodore Parker Papers, and seventeen in the Charles Anderson Dana collection (1830–1880). The *New York Herald Tribune* files, now a part of the Queens Borough Public Library collection, include 106 letters, notes, and memoranda written by Ripley between 1849 and 1880. The State Historical Society of Wisconsin also holds twenty-five letters, both originals and facsimiles, to and from Ripley. The Fruitlands Museums at Harvard, Massachusetts, holds ten letters written between 1841 and 1847. Cornell University Library, Yale University Library, Notre Dame University, the American Unitarian Association, and the New York Public Library each hold three or fewer additional Ripley correspondences.

Benjamin Penhallow Shillaber

(12 July 1814 - 25 November 1890)

Daniel Royot
La Sorbonne Nouvelle, Paris

Benjamin Penhallow Shillaber

BOOKS: *Rhymes, with Reason and Without* (Boston: Abel Tompkins & B. B. Mussey, 1853);

Life and Sayings of Mrs. Partington and Others of the Family (New York: J. C. Derby / Boston: Phillips, Sampson / Cincinnati: H. W. Derby, 1854); republished as *The Sayings and Doings of the Celebrated Mrs. Partington, "Relic" of Corporal P. P., and Others of the Family* (London: James Blackwood, 1854);

Knitting-Work: A Web of Many Textures, Wrought by Ruth Partington (Boston: Brown, Taggard & Chase / New York: Sheldon, 1859);

Mrs. Partington's Ridicule: A Collection of Wit and Humor, Which the Old Lady Offers to Her Friends (Boston: Thomes & Talbot, 1870?);

Partingtonian Patchwork (Boston: Lee & Shepard / New York: Lee, Shepard & Dillingham, 1873);

Lines in Pleasant Places; Rhythmics of Many Moods and Quantities, Wise and Otherwise (Chelsea, Mass.: Privately printed, 1874);

"Lively Boys! Lively Boys!" Ike Partington; or, The Adventures of a Human Boy and His Friends (Boston: Lee & Shepard / New York: C. T. Dillingham, 1879);

Ike Partington and His Friends: Cruises With Captain Bob on Sea and Land (Boston: Lee & Shepard / New York: C. T. Dillingham, 1880);

The Double-Runner Club; or, the Lively Boys of Rivertown (Boston: Lee & Shepard / New York: C. T. Dillingham, 1882);

A Midnight Race (Boston: Ticknor, 1888);

Mrs. Partington's New Grip-Sack, Filled with Fresh Things (New York: J. S. Ogilvie, 1890).

OTHER: *The Carpet-Bag, a Literary Journal,* edited by Shillaber (1851-1853).

SELECTED PERIODICAL PUBLICATIONS–UNCOLLECTED: "Experiences During Many Years," *New England Magazine,* 8 (1893): 511-525, 618-627, 719-724; 9 (1893): 88-95, 153-160, 529-553, 625-631; 10 (1894): 29-36, 247-256, 286-294.

As a Boston writer and editor, Benjamin Shillaber adapted the popular Yankee traditions of the country bumpkin and crackerbox philosopher to a new urban environment. In the mid nineteenth century, his short-lived journal *The Carpet-Bag* was a landmark in the transition from regional vernacular humor to a national comedy of manners and characters, owing to contributors such as Charles Farrar Browne and Samuel Langhorne Clemens (Mark Twain). A shrewd ignoramus but a benevolent successor to Benjamin Franklin's Silence Dogood, Shillaber's Mrs. Partington represented the central figure of his little world of hilarious though resilient misfits at odds with the many "Apostles of the Newness," so named by Ralph Waldo Emerson, who dominated New England culture at midcentury.

Born in Portsmouth, New Hampshire, Benjamin Penhallow Shillaber was one of six children of William and Sarah Leonard Sawyer Shillaber. Both of his grandfathers had served in the Revolutionary War. He never lost his affection for his native town and incorporated many youthful memories in his books for boys. Shillaber attended Portsmouth district schools until he was sixteen and then continued his education as an apprentice with the *New Hampshire Palladium and Strafford Advertiser* in Dover. When this newspaper failed in 1833, he went to Boston at the age of eighteen. He found lodging in a boardinghouse on Union Street and worked first as a printer's devil and then as a compositor for the book-printing firm of Tuttle and Weeks. A gregarious young man, Shillaber soon became acquainted with several writers and editors, including James T. Fields, who was then employed by the publishing house of John Allen and William D. Ticknor and later became the partner of Ticknor. When President Andrew Jackson received a controversial honorary doctorate from Harvard on a visit to New England in 1833, Shillaber was one of his unfailing supporters, and throughout his life he remained a staunch Democrat. In the 1830s he attended the Reverend Hosea Ballou's Unitarian Universalist Church and came to share the optimistic views of life and death espoused by this denomination. Sometimes deemed superficial and excessive in later years, Shillaber's joy of life always appeared to reflect an unshakable faith in man and nature.

After moving to the south of Boston in 1835, Shillaber lived with the Tappan de Rochemont family. That same year he suffered a severe nasal hemorrhage and was advised by his physician to seek a warmer climate to recover. He accompanied a son of his host family to British Guiana, where he worked for two years as a compositor on the *Royal Gazette of British Guiana* in Demerara. When his health was restored, he returned in 1837 to Boston, where Tuttle and Weeks employed him again as a printer. Shillaber married young Ann Tappan de Rochemont on 15 August 1838. The couple had eight children, four of whom died at a young age.

In 1840 Shillaber joined the *Boston Post* as a printer; after a few years the editor, Charles Gordon Greene, made him a journalist. In charge of a column titled "All Sorts of Paragraphs," Shillaber wrote anecdotes, aphorisms, and national news items. He created the character of Mrs. Partington in the 26 February 1847 issue. Within a few weeks the doings and sayings of the old Yankee lady were being reprinted by newspapers all over the country. In a city noted for its genteel culture, Mrs. Partington was an unlettered provincial among the Brahmins. Although the *Boston Post* supported the Mexican War, opposed the abolitionists, and disliked James Russell Lowell's *The Biglow Papers* (1848), the persona of Mrs. Partington was too whimsical and unsophisticated to voice Shillaber's political opinions clearly. He had borrowed her name from a speech of 1831 by Sydney Smith, the English clergyman and essayist, in which Smith castigated the opposition of the aristocracy to the reform movement through an anecdote about a Mrs. Partington of Sidmouth who, during a great storm, had attempted to sweep back the Atlantic Ocean with her broom.

Shillaber left the *Boston Post* in 1850 to join the *Pathfinder and Railway Guide,* distributed by "news-butchers" on railroads and steamboats. A year later he became coeditor of *The Carpet-Bag,* the first exclusively comic magazine in the United States. The first issue came out on 29 March 1851. Despite the quality of the contributions, it never had a wide circulation and was discontinued in March 1853. The failure of the magazine may be explained by a rising tide of sectional chauvinism averse to mere joking about burning issues. A beautifully printed eight-page weekly, *The Carpet-Bag* first sought to win readers as a solicitous companion, pledging "harmless witticisms," good jokes, and "anything cheerful," appealing to "good-natured taste." Nearly all the contributors wrote under one or more pseudonyms. Though the journal was nonpartisan, associate editor Charles G. Halpine burlesqued political propaganda through the candid comments of "Private Miles O'Reilly." Correspondents from New England, the South, and the West derided amateur dramatic companies staging the plays of William Shakespeare; made fun of Neal Dow's state prohibition law, passed in Maine in 1851; and supplied tall tales cultivated either on Puritan granite or in Tennessee canebrakes. In 1852 Benjamin Drew, writing under the pseudonym Trismegistus, originated the campaign hoax of Ensign Jehiel Stebbings, an imaginary native of Spunkville and veteran of the Aroostook "War," running for president against Winfield Scott and Franklin Pierce. But this lightedhearted spoof of national politics harmed *The Carpet-Bag* by antagonizing readers on both sides.

Besides established writers such as John Townsend Trowbridge, Shillaber encouraged a new generation of native humorists such as Matthew Whittier, who used the psuedonym Ethan Spike, and George Horatio Derby, who used the pseudonym John Phoenix. In the 19 June 1852 issue of *The Carpet-Bag* Browne, writing as Artemus Ward, imagined in "Oil vs. Vinegar; or, the Rantankarous Lecturer" a traveling temperance speaker faced with Old Uncle Thad, "a wealthy, jolly, toddy-drinking farmer" whose dialect

Flag for the first American humor magazine, edited by Shillaber from 1851 until it ceased publication in 1853

speech uproariously subverted established values. Clemens's first published yarn, "The Dandy Frightening the Squatter," appeared in the 1 May 1852 issue. The story begins with the docking of a Mississippi steamboat at Hannibal, Missouri. A spruce city slicker wants to impress young ladies on board with "a formidable-looking bowie knife" in his belt and "a large horse-pistol in each hand." He challenges "a tall, brawny woodsman," advising him to say his prayers before stating: "you'll make a capital barn door and I shall drive the key-hole myself." The squatter looks at him calmly and then plants "a huge fist directly between the eyes of the antagonist," who falls in the "turbid waters" of the Big Muddy. In an effort to transcend antebellum conflicts, *The Carpet-Bag* maintained a tone of cheerfulness, painstakingly combining truculence with good taste. Well known far beyond the reaches of Boston, it provided a forum for new talents, achieving distinction among dozens of humor magazines.

In 1853 Shillaber returned to the *Boston Post* as a local editor and reintroduced Mrs. Partington on a regular basis. That same year a compilation of his earlier humorous verses from the *Boston Post* and *The Carpet-Bag* was gathered in a handsome volume under the title *Rhymes, with Reason and Without. Life and Sayings of Mrs. Partington and Others of the Family,* published the following year, sold fifty thousand copies. Being possessed, as he said, of "a fatal facility for rhyming," Shillaber then entered the field of public speaking as a reader of his own poems in order to capitalize on his nationwide success. Though he never achieved the reputation of Browne or Clemens on stage, his performances became increasingly popular over the years. In a biographical sketch George Bungay saw Shillaber in 1854 as "a stout hale, hearty man, considerable above the common stature, with a plain, frank face, a full breast, an honest heart and a head clear as crystal," and concluded: "He has dark hair, is of the bilious-nervous temperament, dresses in a careless manner. Since he has become an author, the hole in his coat has disappeared."

In 1856 Shillaber left his position with the *Boston Post* to become associate editor of the *Saturday Evening Gazette,* published by his close friend William W. Clapp. The only Sunday paper in Boston, it offered verse, tales, and anecdotes. Shillaber wrote two regular columns, "Melange" and "Saturday Notes," which were devoted to the week's news, travel sketches, and aphorisms. In addition to Mrs. Partington he created a gallery of burlesque figures such as Dr. Spooner, Old Roger, Wideswarth, Blifkins, and Ike Partington, who also came to be prominently featured in the *Saturday Evening Gazette. Knitting-Work: A Web of Many Textures, Wrought by Ruth Partington* (1859), a collection of miscellaneous sketches pieced together with no coherent plan in mind, was culled from columns in the *Boston Post* and the *Saturday Evening Gazette.* Failing health, especially attacks of gout, compelled Shillaber to resign his editorial tasks in 1867.

Until 1871 Shillaber was loosely connected with *The Flag and Banner,* a Boston newspaper. *Partingtonian Patchwork* was published in 1873 and *"Lively Boys! Lively*

Boys!" Ike Partington; or, The Adventures of a Human Boy and His Friends in 1879. Sometime in the 1880s Shillaber wrote a weekly column for the *Hartford Post* titled "Old Man With a Cane." He could not complete his autobiography, which was published posthumously in serial form as "Experiences During Many Years" by *New England Magazine* in 1893–1894. The last decade of Shillaber's life was marked by sickness and poverty. He had little property except for a house in Chelsea, Massachusetts, bought with the royalties from his popular books. His wit and geniality were acknowledged in reminiscences written by lifelong acquaintances, who also stressed his humility and kindness. For John Townsend Trowbridge, who knew him well, Shillaber "had never made an enemy."

The comic character Mrs. Partington brought fame to Shillaber. The first forty-six pages of *Life and Sayings of Mrs. Partington and Others of the Family* serve as a biographical introduction to the character, mingling a nostalgic tone with folk humor about "huskings full of incidents and red ears"; "jolly quilting, great with tattle and tea"; and mock-epic rivalry "for the possession of the belle of Dog's Bondage." Descended from the Puritans, Mrs. Partington was born Ruth Trotter and first lived in the village of Beanville, Massachusetts. After her husband, Paul, died, she took charge of her orphaned nephew, Ike, and they moved to Boston when their house was pulled down to make way for a railroad. A steady churchgoer, Mrs. Partington is addicted to souchong tea and snuff and loves knitting, gardening, and patent medicines. Confronted with the intricacies of city life, this outspoken, archaic observer of manners takes after Richard Brinsley Sheridan's Mrs. Malaprop, but her idiosyncrasies are expressed through colorful imagery and New England dialect. In the tradition of the Yankee wise fool, homespun truths paradoxically emerge from Mrs. Partington's strings of incongruous analogies and suspension of evidence.

Mrs. Partington's statements are made nonsensical by the sense of discordance between the language of her everyday experience and her use of highbrow phraseology. Her speech is full of malapropisms, jumbling together misconstrued notions through catachresis, tautology, and misspelling. In "Fancy Diseases" she says, "The Doctor tells me that poor old Mrs. Haze has got two buckles on her lungs! It is dreadful to think of, I declare. . . . One way we hear of people's dying of hermitage of the lungs; another way of the brown creatures; here they tell us of the elementary canal, being out of order . . . we hear of men being killed by getting a pound of tough beef in the sarcofagus, and there another kills himself by discovering his jocular vein."

Mrs. Partington's muddled mind likewise transcends incoherence through reverse logic. In "The Cat and Kittens" she reconciles sheer necessity with an absurd act of benevolence. Finding a litter of kittens in her workbasket, she decides that she has to get rid of them and instructs Ike to do so: "'Isaac,' said the dame, 'take the big tub, and drown them.' There was a determination in her eyes, and authority in her tone, and Ike clapped his hands as he hastened to obey her. 'Stop, Isaac a minute,' she cried, 'and I'll take the chill off the water; it would be cruel to put 'em into it stone-cold.'" Jesse Bier sees the anecdote as a paradigm of the American humorist's unromantic confrontation with a cruel world. At least Mrs. Partington is no pharisee sententiously moralizing about good and evil. Between the ideal and the real, she readily acknowledges her inhumanity, being no exception in an imperfect universe, and never lies to herself.

Mrs. Partington always creates verbal anarchy while interpreting reality in terms of her narrow, though safe, Down East perspectives, but literalness can also be interpreted as a welcome recess from snobbery and the vagaries of the intellect. In "Mrs. Partington's Phrenology," written for *The Carpet-Bag,* Shillaber even playfully parodies contemporary fashions by ascribing her peculiar turn of mind to a "very uneven head." Her aberrant, regressive attitudes recapture the oracular wisdom and innocent pose of Seba Smith's Jack Downing, the Down East peddler who commented on the plight of the common man in the Jacksonian era. Each anecdote takes on a ritualistic value through a recurrent pattern. Mrs. Partington first makes a casual remark, followed by the narrator's perplexed comments on her bizarre syllogisms. She then develops her point of view by accumulating absurdities. Averse to abstraction, Mrs. Partington also appears to be a Down East version of Frances Whitcher's Widow Bedott, whose comments on philistine New Yorkers were widely read in the early 1850s. Both are parochial and semiliterate, yet instinctively apt at unmasking humbug. Mrs. Partington's characterization induces sympathetic smiles whenever Shillaber shows her as the precious relic of a lost New England pastoral; her harmless eccentricity constitutes a haven of mirth amid modern complexities.

A discernible thread of satire runs through the Mrs. Partington sketches. Despite her instinctive charity, she finds fault with a dog who "could not have been more ungrateful if he had been a human critter." As for her cultural environment, after listening to Emerson she admits: "he is such a queer man that you have to watch every word or you can't understand him. If you lose one word, it's jest like a stitch broke in a seam, made by some of the sowing-machines–the work is good for nothing." When asked her opinion about the humor of Hawthorne, Mrs. Partington replies: "syrup of buckthorne is good for all sorts of

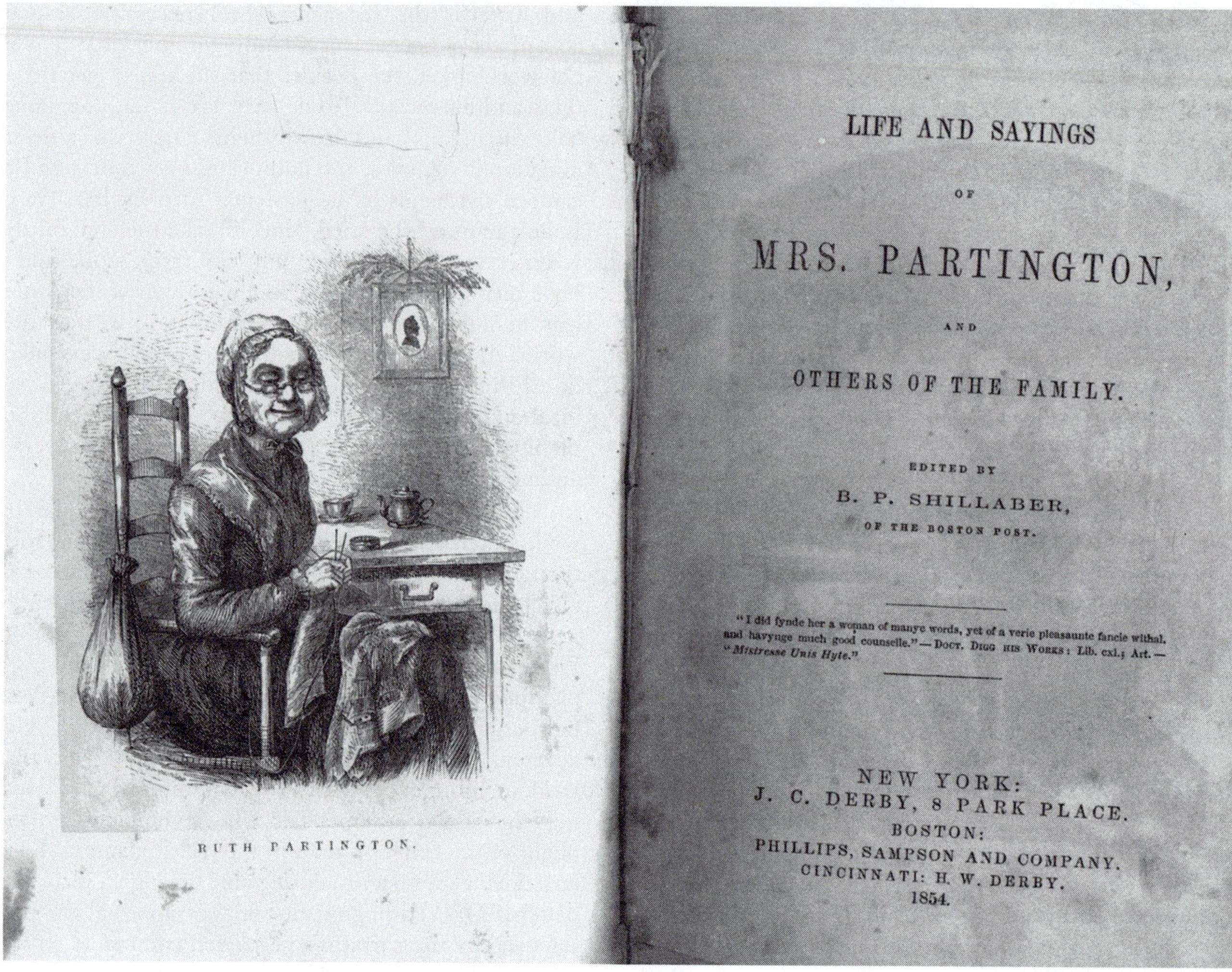

RUTH PARTINGTON.
LIFE AND SAYINGS
OF
MRS. PARTINGTON,
AND
OTHERS OF THE FAMILY.
EDITED BY
B. P. SHILLABER,
OF THE BOSTON POST.
"I did fynde her a woman of manye words, yet of a verie pleasaunte fancie withal, and havynge much good counselle." — Doct. Digg his Works: Lib. cxl.; Art.— "Mistresse Unis Hyte."
NEW YORK:
J. C. DERBY, 8 PARK PLACE.
BOSTON:
PHILLIPS, SAMPSON AND COMPANY.
CINCINNATI: H. W. DERBY.
1854.

Frontispiece and title page for the volume in which Shillaber collected some of his humorous sketches featuring his popular comic persona Ruth Partington

diseases of that kind." In addition to offering critical judgments on reform movements ("men's rights of sufferings") or spiritualism ("spirituous knockings"), Mrs. Partington upbraids individuals who are "no better than scribes, pharisees and hippocriffs, that say one thing and do another." In "A Home Truth," she sadly mentions "a poor old colored man here in Boston that they treat jest like a nigger."

The interplay of mild emotion with sly humor generally lends an antiquarian quality to Shillaber's evocations of Down Easters turned urban dwellers. First used as foils, other characters gradually assume an independent existence. A dedicated Brahmin, Old Roger shares the utopian concerns of his fellow Transcendentalists, Philanthropos and Poo-Poo. He compensates for his painful dyspepsia with an overindulgence in spoonerisms but also often accuses his contemporaries of being unequal to his expectations. An Emersonian idealist, Doctor Spooner displays generosity in the abstract, warning workers against slavish devotion to industry at the expense of spiritual gratification. But when his carpenter takes his advice, he exclaims, "if the work is not done by tomorrow night, you will receive no dimes therefor. In this particular case a little industry is a great virtue." As his name indicates, Wideswarth is a caricature of the Romantic poets. He cannot escape from poetic diction in his high-flown lyrical verse and imagines that he has a heroic stature while his lofty aims prove grotesque. A storekeeper and henpecked husband, Benjamin Blifkins's resignation results from his losing battle against his wife's unrelenting domination. Vainly coping with domestic problems, he is a born loser who finds refuge in daydreaming, only to be brutally awakened to reality by Mrs. Blifkins. Foreshadowing James Thurber's Walter Mitty, Blifkins sheepishly accepts humiliation to live in peace.

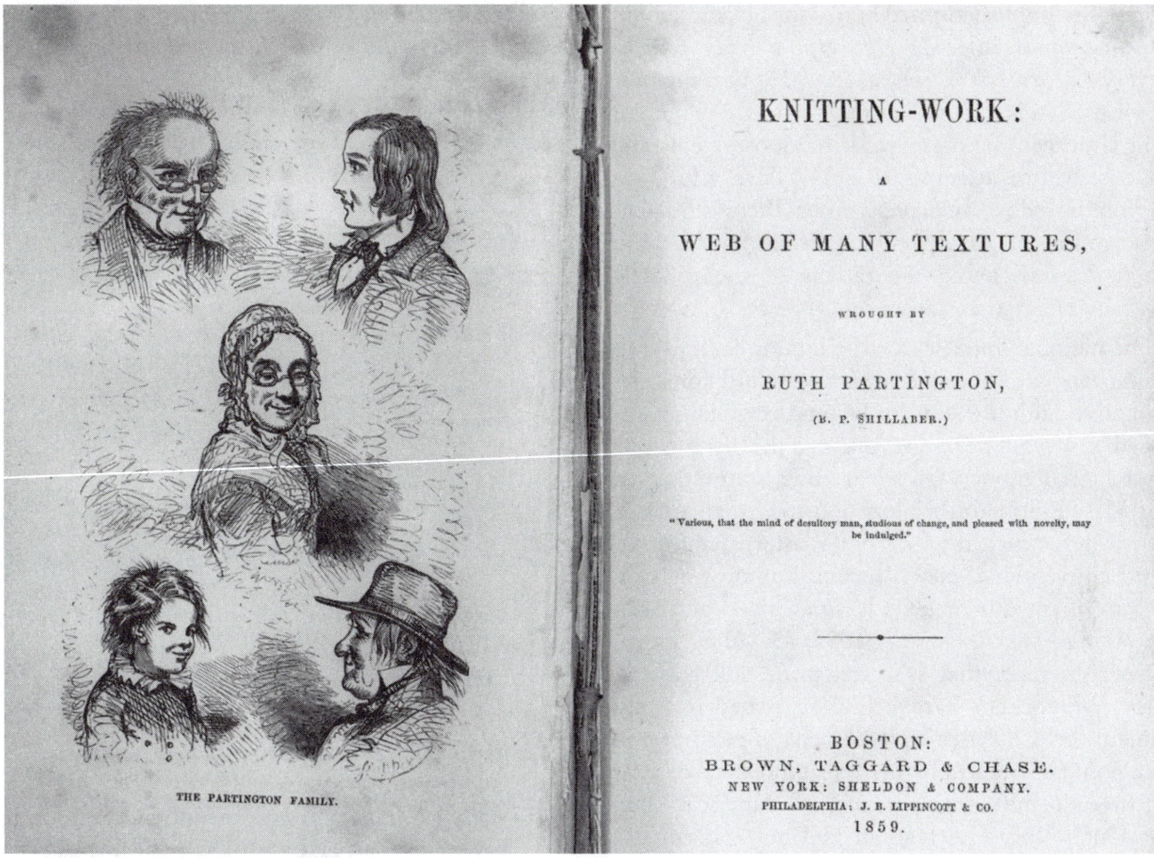

Frontispiece and title page for Shillaber's second collection of humorous sketches, previously published in the Boston Post *and the* Saturday Evening Gazette

Shillaber created Ike Partington in 1848 in the *Boston Post* as a satire of heroic boyhood as exemplified in the Dickensian bildungsroman. Genuinely mischievous, the eleven-year-old boy plagues everyone with his practical jokes without ever incurring the reprobation of his indulgent aunt. Shillaber defines Ike: "His tricks do not flow from any premeditation of fun even; they spring spontaneously and naturally as the lambs skip or the birds sing." Inspired by adventure stories and always acting from impulses, the romantic Ike wants to become a pirate wreaking havoc in his aunt's house. In "Paul's Ghost" he dresses in the uniform of his deceased uncle to frighten his aunt. Cruel though they may be, especially to animals, Ike's pranks are evoked with the distance of slapstick comedy. In "Ike in the Country" the boy ties clamshells to a cat's paws and puts her on a frozen river so that the flurries will soon carry her into cold waters. In "How Ike Dropped the Cat," after Mrs. Partington becomes weary of the antics of her cat and asks Ike to drop her somewhere, he dutifully complies with her request. When she sees the cat dangling from an apple tree, Ike assures her that, despondent for being rejected, she committed suicide by hanging herself. Despite such practices, Shillaber sees Ike not as a sadistic rebel but as "an imitation of the universal human boy," demonstrating his inventiveness through elaborate devices and revealing inborn vitality and resourcefulness by sowing his wild oats in a nascent business culture.

Clemens's portrayal of Aunt Polly in *The Adventures of Tom Sawyer* (1876) is clearly reminiscent of Shillaber's Mrs. Partington, whose image on the frontispiece for *Life and Sayings of Mrs. Partington and Others of the Family* was later used as an illustration in *The Adventures of Tom Sawyer* representing Aunt Polly, captioned "Contentment." The resemblance is more than physical. Both ladies have trouble because doctors change their treatments too often. Ike and Tom are keen on torturing cats, but their aunts are too tender-hearted to enforce the Calvinistic principles they profess for educating youngsters. So marked was Shillaber's influence that in Albert Bigelow Paine's *Mark Twain, a Biography: The Personal and Literary Life of Samuel Langhorne Clemens* (1912), the drowning of kittens in warm water is strangely attributed by Clemens to his mother, also allegedly his model for the character of Aunt Polly.

Shillaber published three books for boys in which Ike plays a minor role. *Ike Partington and His Friends: Cruises With Captain Bob on Sea and Land* (1880) is the best of the series. Unlike Tom Sawyer's world, Ike's environment is peaceful and secure. If the loosely episodic narrative structure attempts to show Ike's efforts to escape from boredom by playing pirate, there is no genuine re-creation of an authentic juvenile world. Shillaber thus cannot avoid the pitfalls of the didactic moralism he satirized in his periodical pieces.

The national impulse to write humor coalesced in *The Carpet-Bag,* which established a standard for antebellum native humor that went beyond regionalism, as interfused grotesqueries were making the distinctions among regional modes less clear. Bier states that in reading Mrs. Partington's injunction to drown cats in warmed water, which moves from Western folklore to prim and conventional New England humor, one cannot be sure if regions or texts have changed at all. In *Beneath the American Renaissance* (1989) David S. Reynolds also recognizes that sectional pride still allowed space for self-mockery. Urban humor treated with sly detachment the problematic phenomena of culture, politics, religion, and reform by making a mockery of vital issues through the carnivalization of American language. Walter Blair and Hamlin Hill make it equally clear that Shillaber's humor was instrumental in distancing subversive themes and establishing comic characters as reputable funny fellows, putting pretentious contemporary culture on display as a public joke.

While through Mrs. Partington's discourse threatening social realities and the acute awareness of changing times were joyfully converted into mere entertainment, in *The Carpet-Bag* Clemens and Browne strikingly fused the topicality of Northeastern urban comedy with the voice of frontier humor. In retrospect, Shillaber's verbal performances may be overdrawn, belabored, and vapid. But the sanity and decorum of his humorous productions, outdated though they may seem, still echo a stubborn willingness to avoid aggressive, biting irony among Americans hopefully sharing a sense of relativity and intent on reaching a consensus by observing the smiling facts of life in a restless age.

Biography:

Cyril Clemens, *Shillaber* (Webster Groves, Mo.: International Mark Twain Society, 1946).

References:

James C. Austin, *Artemus Ward* (New York: Twayne, 1964);

Jesse Bier, *The Rise and Fall of American Humor* (New York: Holt, Rinehart & Winston, 1968);

Walter Blair, *Native American Humor* (New York: American Book Company, 1937);

Blair and Hamlin Hill, *America's Humor: From Poor Richard to Doonesbury* (New York: Oxford University Press, 1978);

George W. Bungay, *Off-Hand Takings; or, Crayon Sketches of the Noticeable Men of Our Age,* third edition (New York: Robert M. DeWitt, 1869), pp. 372–376;

Cyril Clemens, "Benjamin Shillaber and His '*Carpet Bag*,'" *New England Quarterly,* 14 (September 1941): 519–537;

Bernard DeVoto, *Mark Twain's America* (Boston: Houghton Mifflin, 1932);

Franklin J. Meine, "American Comic Periodicals, No. 1–The Carpet Bag," *Collector's Journal,* 4 (October/November/December 1933): 411–413;

Cameron Nickels, *New England Humor: From the Revolutionary War to the Civil War* (Knoxville: University of Tennessee Press, 1993);

John Q. Reed, *Benjamin Penhallow Shillaber* (New York: Twayne, 1972);

David S. Reynolds, *Beneath the American Renaissance* (Cambridge, Mass.: Harvard University Press, 1989), pp. 441–483;

David E. E. Sloane, *American Humor Magazines and Comic Periodicals* (Westport, Conn.: Greenwood Press, 1987), pp. 44–51;

Sloane, ed., *The Literary Humor of the Urban Northeast, 1830–1890* (Baton Rouge: Louisiana State University Press, 1983).

Jared Sparks

(10 May 1789 – 14 March 1866)

William Baller
Worcester Polytechnic Institute

See also the Sparks entry in *DLB 30: American Historians, 1607–1865.*

Jared Sparks, 1828 (unfinished portrait by Gilbert Stuart; from Herbert B. Adams, The Life and Writings of Jared Sparks, *1893)*

BOOKS: *Letters on the Ministry, Ritual, and Doctrines of the Protestant Episcopal Church, Addressed to the Rev. Wm. E. Wyatt, D.D., . . .* (Baltimore: N. G. Maxwell, 1820);

A Sermon, Preached in the Hall of the House of Representatives in Congress, Washington City, March 3, 1822; Occasioned by the Death of the Hon. Wm. Pinkney, Late a Member of the Senate of the United States (Washington, D.C.: Davis & Force, 1822);

An Inquiry into the Comparative Moral Tendency of the Trinitarian and Unitarian Doctrines. In a Series of Letters to the Rev. Dr. Miller, of Princeton (Boston: Wells & Lilly, 1823);

A Historical Outline of the American Colonization Society, and Remarks on the Advantages and Practicability of Colonizing in Africa the Free People of Color from the United States (Boston: Oliver Everett, 1824);

An Account of the Manuscript Papers of George Washington, Which Were Left by Him at Mount Vernon; With a Plan for Their Publication (Boston, 1827);

The Life of John Ledyard, the American Traveller; Comprising Selections from His Journals and Correspondence (Cambridge, Mass.: Hilliard & Brown, 1828); republished as *Memoirs of the Life and Travels of John Ledyard, from His Journals and Correspondence* (London: H. Colburn, 1828);

The American Almanac and Repository of Useful Knowledge, volume 1 (Boston: Gray & Bowen, 1829);

The Life of Gouverneur Morris, volume 1 of *The Life of Gouverneur Morris, with Selections from his Correspondence and Miscellaneous Papers; Detailing Events in the American Revolution, the French Revolution, and in the Political History of the United States,* 3 volumes, edited by Sparks (Boston: Gray & Bowen, 1832);

The Life of George Washington, volume 1 of *The Writings of George Washington; Being His Correspondence, Addresses, Messages, and Other Papers, Official and Private, Selected and Published from the Original Manuscripts; With a Life of the Author, Notes and Illustrations,* 12 volumes, edited by Sparks, volumes 1, 12 (Boston: American Stationers' Company/J. B. Russell, 1837); volumes 2–9 (Boston: Russell, Odiorne & Metcalf/Hilliard, Gray, 1834–1835); volumes 10, 11 (Boston: Russell, Shattuck & Williams/Hilliard, Gray, 1836);

The Life of Benjamin Franklin, volume 1 of *The Works of Benjamin Franklin; Containing Several Political and His-*

torical Tracts Not Included in Any Former Edition, and Many Letters Official and Private, Not Hitherto Published; with Notes and a Life of the Author, 10 volumes, edited by Sparks (Boston: Hilliard, Gray, 1836–1840);

A Reply to the Strictures of Lord Mahon and Others, on the Mode of Editing the Writings of Washington (Cambridge, Mass.: John Bartlett, 1852);

Letter to Lord Mahon, Being an Answer to His Letter Addressed to the Editor of Washington's Writings (Boston: Little, Brown, 1852);

Remarks on a "Reprint of the Original Letters from Washington to Joseph Reed, During the American Revolution, Referred to in the Pamphlets of Lord Mahon and Mr. Sparks" (Boston: Little, Brown, 1853).

OTHER: *A Collection of Essays and Tracts in Theology, from Various Authors, with Biographical and Critical Notices,* 6 volumes, edited by Sparks (Boston: Oliver Everett, 1823–1826);

The Diplomatic Correspondence of the American Revolution; Being the Letters of Benjamin Franklin, Silas Deane, John Adams, John Jay, Arthur Lee, William Lee, Ralph Izard, Francis Dana, William Carmichael, Henry Laurens, John Laurens, M. de Lafayette, M. Dumas, and Others, Concerning the Foreign Relations of the United States During the Whole Revolution . . . , 12 volumes, edited by Sparks (Boston: N. Hale/Gray & Bowen, 1829–1830);

A Collection of the Familiar Letters and Miscellaneous Papers of Benjamin Franklin; Now for the First Time Published, edited by Sparks (Boston: Charles Bowen, 1833; London: Jackson & Walford, 1833);

The Library of American Biography, edited with contributions by Sparks, first series, 10 volumes (Boston: Hilliard, Gray, 1834–1838); second series, 15 volumes (Boston: Little, Brown, 1844–1848); first and second series, 25 volumes (London: Richard James Kennett, 1834–1848);

Correspondence of the American Revolution; Being Letters of Eminent Men to George Washington, from the Time of His Taking Command of the Army to the End of His Presidency, 4 volumes, edited by Sparks (Boston: Little, Brown, 1853).

Many scholars consider Jared Sparks the first great editor of American history and compiler of national records. His ambitious travels and persistence opened up many resources for historians. His reliance on primary sources and work at Harvard University furthered the writing and study of professional history. Although questions remain about some of his editorial methods, Sparks helped make the facts of history public property. No less important for American letters and culture, he made writing a more viable profession in America: simply put, Sparks made writing pay. He managed to publish more than sixty volumes, many of which sold well, without much patronage or institutional support.

Jared Sparks was born on 10 May 1789 in Willington, Connecticut, to Eleanor Orcutt. Joseph Sparks, generally presumed to be Jared's father, married Eleanor on 24 December of that year. The family struggled economically, and at six years of age Jared was sent to live with Eleanor's childless sister and her none-too-successful husband, Ebenezer Eldridge. Although both households barely eked out a living as marginal farmers and tradesmen, Eleanor and her sister did provide Jared with a fondness for literature that nurtured his aspirations. In search of a better living, the Eldridges moved to eastern New York when Sparks was eleven. In 1805, however, Sparks was returned to Willington as concerns arose about the quality of his education in New York. Back in Connecticut, he was sent to school in nearby Tolland, and he also apprenticed as a carpenter. A brilliant student and a prodigy in music, he learned the principles of navigation and astronomy on his own.

Sparks's intelligence and academic achievements attracted a good deal of attention. In 1807 he became a schoolmaster in Tolland, where he taught for four months and earned eight dollars a month. Limited finances meant that he still had to work part-time as a carpenter rather than devote all of his efforts to the life of the mind. The assistance of friends helped Sparks win a scholarship to the prestigious Phillips Academy at Exeter, New Hampshire. While studying at Exeter he wrote articles on astronomy for a New Hampshire newspaper. In 1811, at the age of twenty-two, he was admitted to Harvard University. During breaks in his studies at Harvard, Sparks tutored in Maryland.

Graduating from Harvard in 1815 gave Sparks the opportunity to devote all his energies to academic pursuits. After teaching in Lancaster, Connecticut, for a short time, he returned to Harvard to tutor in mathematics and natural history. Although Sparks enjoyed his time as a schoolmaster and made important contributions to college teaching, his real love was research and editing. In 1817 the then two-year-old *North American Review* named Sparks its new managing editor. His tasks included proofreading, getting articles ready for press, and supervising distribution.

A higher calling, however, led Sparks to place his editing and literary career on hold during the second religious awakening in America. He left *The North American Review* and Boston to pursue a religious vocation. Ordained in 1819, he spent several years in Baltimore and Washington, D.C., working as a Unitarian minister. He also began publishing the *Unitarian Miscellany* as

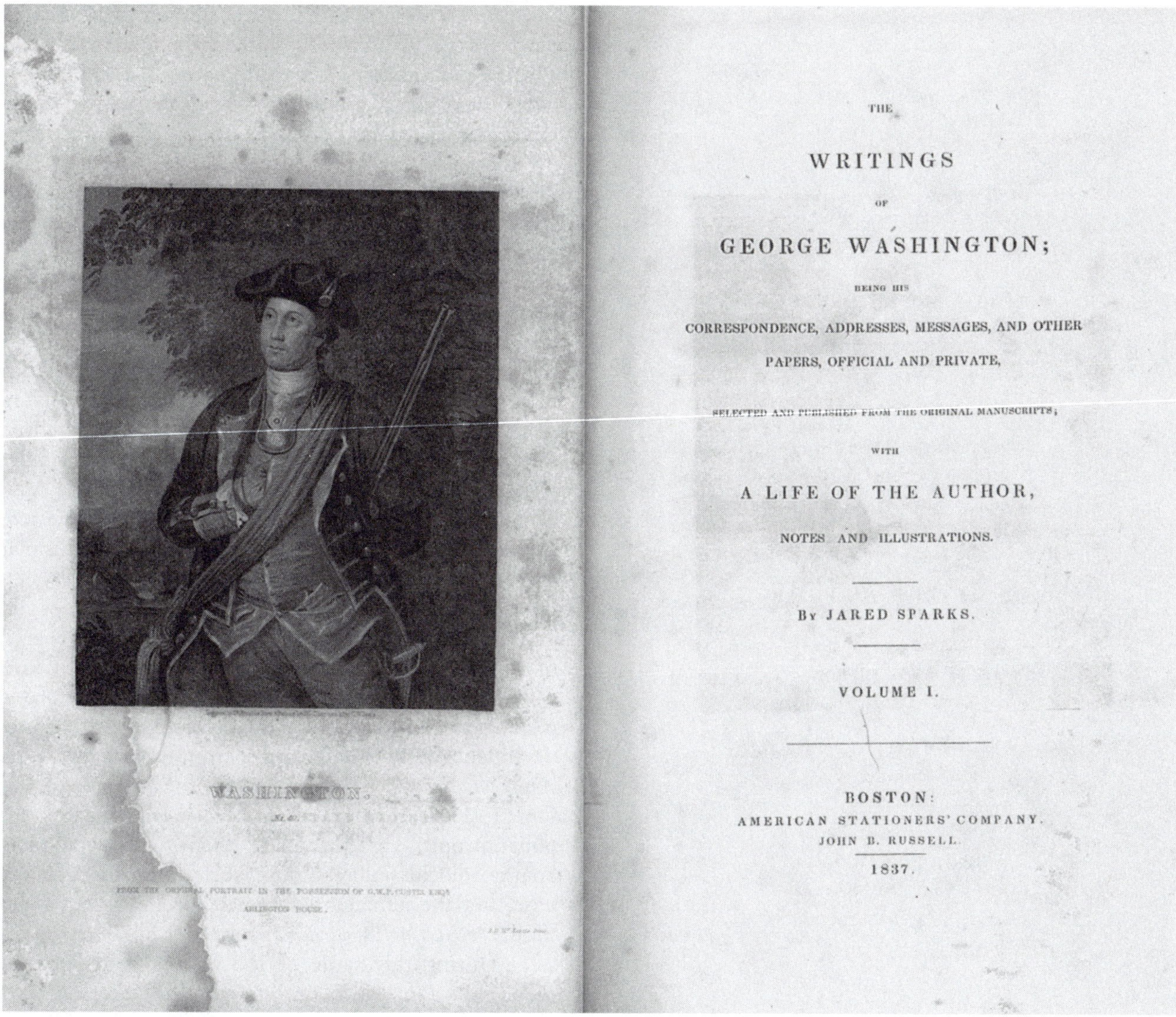

Frontispiece and title page for one of the books that drew praise for Sparks's research and criticism for his editorial practices

a vehicle for spreading and defending religious ideas. Doing much of the writing himself and demonstrating the editorial skills and business acumen he manifested throughout his literary career, he made the *Unitarian Miscellany* a success. This endeavor helped him garner a highly sought position as chaplain of the House of Representatives, which he held from 1821 to 1822.

During this time Sparks also worked on the publication of *A Collection of Essays and Tracts in Theology, from Various Authors, with Biographical and Critical Notices* (1823–1826). Compiling papers on religious subjects by writers such as John Locke, Isaac Newton, and William Penn, Sparks hoped to stress the rationality of religion and the essential agreement that existed among Christian sects. The publication of the series ended in 1826 and signaled Sparks's interest in a more philosophical and historical literature. While his subjects changed, his goals in writing remained consistent. "Among the use of biography," Sparks noted in his preface to the third volume of the series, "none is more valuable, than that which inspires good purposes, awakens energy, and incites to exertion. The events of a person's life, who has risen to eminence, are always interesting, because they are rare; they are always instructive, because they serve as a light and a guide to others, whose early fortunes may be equally unpropitious."

Despite his success as a Unitarian minister, Sparks resigned in 1823 and resumed a full-time literary career in Boston. With borrowed money and enhanced literary and forensic skills honed in defending the Unitarian church, Sparks purchased the *North American Review* and made it into the leading American literary

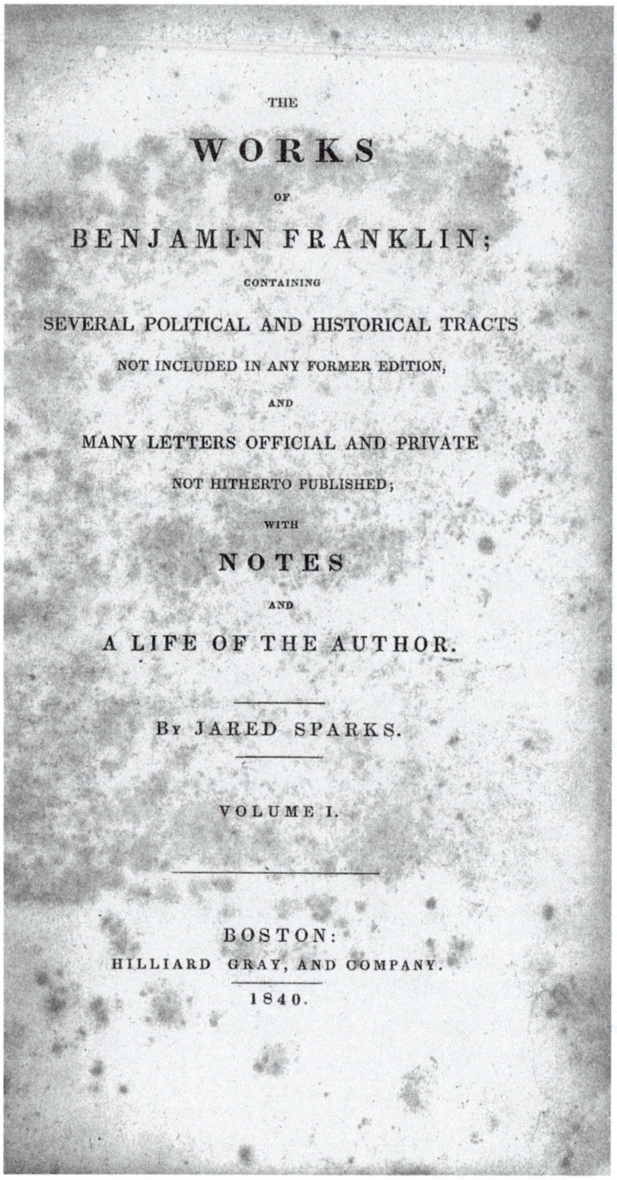
THE
WORKS
OF
BENJAMIN FRANKLIN;
CONTAINING
SEVERAL POLITICAL AND HISTORICAL TRACTS
NOT INCLUDED IN ANY FORMER EDITION,
AND
MANY LETTERS OFFICIAL AND PRIVATE
NOT HITHERTO PUBLISHED;
WITH
NOTES
AND
A LIFE OF THE AUTHOR.
BY JARED SPARKS.
VOLUME I.
BOSTON:
HILLIARD GRAY, AND COMPANY.
1840.

Title page for one of Sparks's most important editorial projects, in which he included many newly discovered documents

journal. His long-standing interest in Africa and in improved relations between the United States and Latin America helped make the journal more international in scope and appeal. Sparks studied Spanish so as to better understand Latin American events and revolutionary fervor and to include news of other nations of the Americas in the *North American Review*. He also began paying writers one dollar per page for their articles, much more than other venues were paying then.

Sparks's time-consuming work on the *North American Review* did not preclude work on his biography of the American explorer John Ledyard. *The Life of John Ledyard, the American Traveller; Comprising Selections from His Journals and Correspondence* was published in 1828. Ledyard proved a fascinating subject for Sparks: born in 1751 in Connecticut, Ledyard shared Sparks's love of adventure, travel, and distant locales. After living among the six nations of the Iroquois Indians and learning their language, Ledyard journeyed to Russia and Alaska as well as England, where he met Captain James Cook and sailed with him during Cook's last voyage around the world. Ledyard died in Cairo in 1788.

Sparks spent almost a decade collecting research material for this biography. His trips to archives in Canada, Europe, and across America set a standard for later scholars, and his book was well received. Sparks utilized the same format in his Ledyard biography that he employed in subsequent monographs: fairly extensive selections from the subject's writings were included with Sparks's biographical analysis.

After the publication of *The Life of John Ledyard, the American Traveller,* Sparks turned his attention to his plan for an American statistical annual. Inspired by the growth of America as well as its burgeoning democracy and nationalism, Sparks set out to record the progress of the United States. In addition to providing the names of public officials and information on internal improvements, banks, and canals, Sparks sought government documents and printed reports from friends. With *The American Almanac and Repository of Useful Knowledge,* volume 1 (1829), Sparks hoped to assist lawmakers and philanthropists by providing them with vital facts. Sparks sold his interest after working on the first volume, but the almanac continued for thirty-four years until *The National Almanac* supplanted it in 1863.

During this same period Sparks completed his more important works dealing with the American Revolutionary era. Through an 1818 congressional resolution, Sparks won the right to oversee the publication of diplomatic correspondence associated with the American Revolution. After examining the letters of Benjamin Franklin, John Adams, John Jay, and other patriots as well as the French foreign ministers, Sparks published his twelve-volume edited collection *The Diplomatic Correspondence of the American Revolution* between 1829 and 1830. While that collection attracted a good deal of attention, a parallel publication, the twelve-volume *Writings of George Washington,* generated more interest among the public and critics when it appeared between 1834 and 1837.

Like most of his works, *The Writings of George Washington* was meticulously researched. To locate letters sent and received by Washington, Sparks visited the homes of James Madison and John Quincy Adams as well as less obvious repositories of important research materials. After traveling to the Pittsburgh area to examine records of Washington's military service with General Edward Braddock during the French and Indian War, Sparks journeyed to England, where he examined British correspondence with British officers in America. His research in the British foreign office opened the door for other historians, and his use of county histories respecting Washington's family also demonstrated insight.

Some of Sparks's methods drew the ire of his peers, however. Several prominent reviewers accused him of tampering with American history by changing the words of texts and not including key facts relating to his subjects. In the sixth volume of his *History of England from the Peace of Utrecht to the Peace of Versailles* (1836–1854), Lord Mahon (Philip Henry Stanhope) chastised Sparks for omitting strong words that Washington had used to characterize British actions during the Revolution. Sparks also omitted Washington's reference to the Scotch as "those universal instruments of tyranny." His tampering with language caused greater concern. He frequently altered language and corrected grammar to make his subject appear more articulate and knowledgeable. When Washington referred to "Old Put," as his contemporaries commonly did, Sparks changed it to "General Putnam" for his book. Finding Washington's reference to a small sum of money as "but a flea-bite at present" too colloquial, Sparks changed it to "totally inadequate to our demands at this time."

Like other historians working well into the twentieth century, Sparks did overlook key incidents in Washington's life in order to place the first president in the most positive light. Sparks did not mention Washington's harsh dealings with Native Americans and his failures on Revolutionary battlefields. Although most scholarly commentators faulted Sparks, Colonel Thomas Wentworth Higginson defended Sparks's alterations of his subject's words. "It is only very lately," observed Higginson in a letter to Sparks's biographer Herbert B. Adams, "that there has come to be any strict sense of the value of a quotation mark. Bancroft, Hildreth, Frothingham (R.), all revised their quotations without saying so."

While completing his work on Washington, Sparks was also working on biographies of Gouverneur Morris and Ben Franklin. *The Life of Gouverneur Morris,* appearing in three volumes in 1832, neither sold particularly well nor created much of a stir among critics or the public. *The Works of Benjamin Franklin* made more of an impression when it came out in ten volumes between 1836 and 1840. Planned as early as 1830, *The Works of Benjamin Franklin* benefited from two trunks of Franklin papers that Sparks had found locked away in a Philadelphia garret and the presence of 450 items from Franklin's collection that had never appeared in print up to that time.

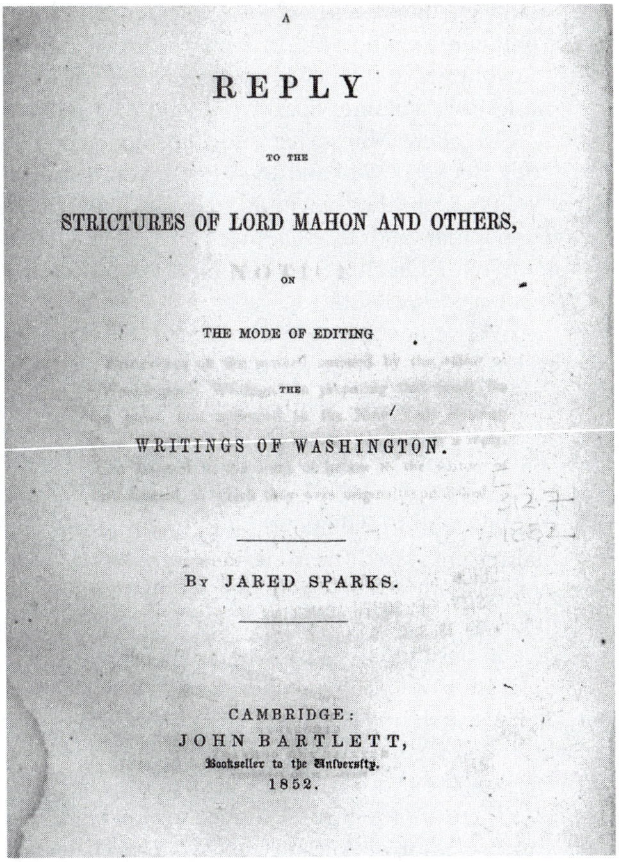
A

REPLY

TO THE

STRICTURES OF LORD MAHON AND OTHERS,

ON

THE MODE OF EDITING

THE

WRITINGS OF WASHINGTON.

By JARED SPARKS.

CAMBRIDGE:
JOHN BARTLETT,
Bookseller to the University.
1852.

Title page for a pamphlet in which Sparks responded to criticisms that he altered quotations and omitted unflattering incidents in his portrayal of George Washington

Years of work on the *North American Review,* publishing success, wide travels, and an active social life brought Sparks into contact with many influential people, including Daniel Webster, Henry Clay, Caleb Cushing, Edward Everett, Henry Wadsworth Longfellow, William Wordsworth, Samuel Taylor Coleridge, Thomas Macaulay, and the Marquis de Lafayette. In 1832 Sparks married Frances Anne Allen of Hyde Park, New York. They settled in Cambridge, Massachusetts, where she helped prepare illustrations for Sparks's editions. After Frances's death from tuberculosis in 1835, Sparks married Mary Crowninshield Silsbee of Salem, Massachusetts, in 1839. His two marriages produced five daughters and a son.

Married life and financial success did not make Sparks complacent. His popular biographical endeavors and close contacts with many of the most highly regarded American authors led him to produce his *Library of American Biography* between 1834 and 1838. Aiming to entertain and instruct general readers, Sparks recruited well-known authors to write extended biographies of the most important American historical figures. The ten volumes in the first series sold well. In addition to editing each volume, Sparks contributed studies of Ethan Allen, Pere Marquette, and Benedict Arnold to the series. Between 1844 and 1848 he edited another fifteen volumes in the biographical series; these also proved popular and foreshadowed monumental biographical works such as Francis Drake's *Dictionary of American Biography* (1872).

Sparks's popularity was not limited to the literary world. His lectures on the Revolutionary War attracted large audiences. In the autumn of 1841 two thousand people heard his lecture in New York City on "The Treason of Benedict Arnold and the Fate of Major Andre," and he was also asked to lecture in Newark, Philadelphia, and Baltimore. His intelligence and nationalism impressed the Whigs enough for the party to ask him to run as its candidate for the Cambridge seat in Congress. He turned down the offer, however, to pursue another career.

His love of learning, experience as a schoolmaster, and research and lecturing skills ultimately drove Sparks toward college teaching. While serving as a member of the Massachusetts Board of Education from 1837 to 1840, Sparks agreed to serve as the McLean Professor of Ancient and Modern History at Harvard University. This position was particularly noteworthy as it was the first time that an American college recognized the study of history as significant enough to establish a professorial chair. Although only a mediocre instructor, Sparks did work to improve pedagogical techniques and based his lectures on his original research.

After a lengthy research trip to Europe to gather research materials for a history of the American Revolution, Sparks became president of Harvard in 1849. Although he never really warmed to the position, he oversaw the completion of the plant that housed the Harvard Observatory and the rearrangement and reclassification of the archives of the college. Sparks never completed his proposed study of the Revolution, but he did finish his *Correspondence of the American Revolution,* in four volumes, in 1853, the year he resigned as president of Harvard. Other than touring Europe with his family in 1857 and 1858, Sparks spent the rest of his life in Cambridge collecting research materials and answering correspondence. He died of pneumonia on 14 March 1866, in Cambridge. His efforts in editing, collecting, and publishing historical documents and helping provide writers and historians with a more substantial income make Sparks a pivotal figure of the nineteenth-century literary world.

Letters:

"The Correspondence of George Bancroft and Jared Sparks," edited by John Spencer Bassett, *Smith College Studies in History,* 2 (January 1917): 67–143.

Biography:

Herbert B. Adams, *The Life and Writings of Jared Sparks Comprising Selections from His Journals and Correspondence,* 2 volumes (Boston & New York: Houghton, Mifflin, 1893).

References:

John Spencer Bassett, *The Middle Group of American Historians* (New York: Macmillan, 1917);

Galen Broeker, "Jared Sparks, Robert Peel and the State Papers Office," *American Quarterly,* 13 (Summer 1961): 140–152;

George E. Ellis, "Memoir of Jared Spark, LL.D.," *Massachusetts Historical Society Proceedings,* 10 (1869): 211–310.

Papers:

One major collection of Jared Sparks's papers is located at the Houghton Library, Harvard University; another collection of correspondence is at the Massachusetts Historical Society.

William Wetmore Story

(12 February 1819 – 7 October 1895)

Ronald A. Bosco

State University of New York at Albany

BOOKS: *Address Delivered Before the Harvard Musical Association in the Chapel of the University at Cambridge, August 24, 1842* (Boston: S. N. Dickinson, 1842);

Nature and Art: A Poem Delivered before the Phi Beta Kappa Society of Harvard University; August 29, 1844 (Boston: Little, Brown, 1844);

A Treatise on the Law of Contracts Not under Seal (Boston: Little and Brown, 1844); revised and enlarged as *A Treatise on the Law of Contracts Not under Seal* (Boston: Little, Brown, 1847);

A Treatise on the Law of Sales of Personal Property, with Illustrations from Foreign Law (Boston: Little, Brown, 1847);

Poems (Boston: Little, Brown, 1847);

Life and Letters of Joseph Story, Associate Justice of the Supreme Court of the United States, and Dane Professor of Law at Harvard University, edited by his son, 2 volumes (Boston: Little, Brown, 1851);

Poems (Boston: Little, Brown, 1856);

Poems (Boston: Little, Brown, 1861; London: Chapman & Hall, 1863);

The American Question (London: Manwaring, 1862);

Roba di Roma, 2 volumes (London: Chapman & Hall, 1863); enlarged as *Roba di Roma,* 2 volumes (London: Chapman & Hall, 1871);

The Proportions of the Human Figure, According to a New Canon, for Practical Use; With a Critical Notice of the Canon of Polycletus, and of the Principal Ancient and Modern Systems (London: Chapman & Hall, 1864);

Graffiti d'Italia (Edinburgh and London: Blackwood, 1868; New York: Scribner, 1868);

Nero, An Historical Play (Edinburgh & London: Blackwood, 1875; New York: Scribner, Welford & Armstrong, 1875);

Stephania, A Tragedy in Five Acts, with a Prologue (Edinburgh: Blackwood, 1875);

Castle St. Angelo, and the Evil Eye. Being Additional Chapters to "Roba di Roma" (Philadelphia: Lippincott, 1877; London: Chapman & Hall, 1877);

Second Thoughts. A Comedy, in Three Acts (Bagni de Lucca, 1878; New York, 1878);

Stale Mate (New York, 1878);

Ode on the Anniversary of the Fifth Half Century of the Landing of Gov. John Endicott . . . Delivered Before the Essex Institute, at Salem, Sept. 18, 1878 (Salem, Mass.: Salem Press, 1879);

Vallombrosa (Edinburgh & London: Blackwood, 1881);

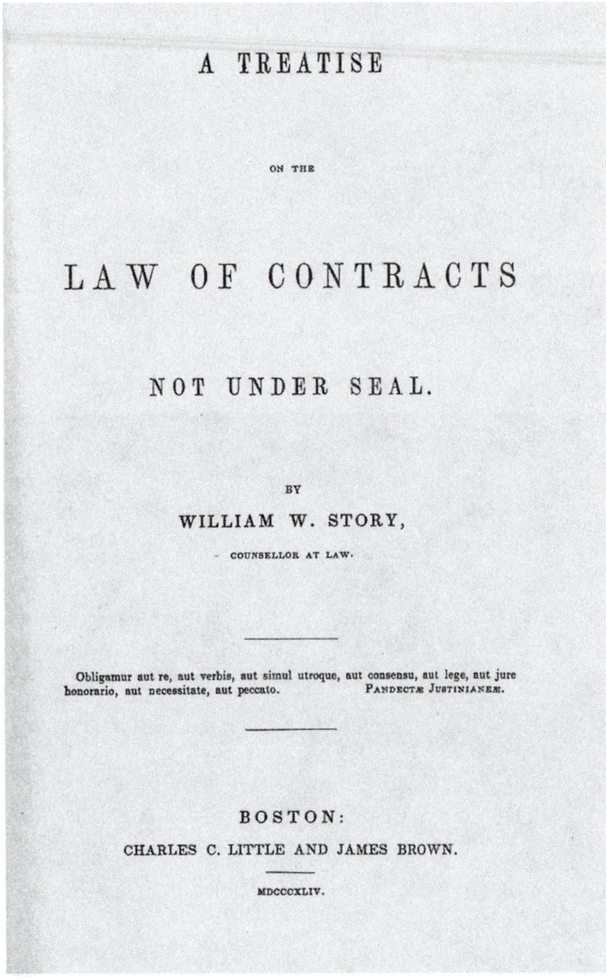
A TREATISE

ON THE

LAW OF CONTRACTS

NOT UNDER SEAL.

BY

WILLIAM W. STORY,

COUNSELLOR AT LAW.

Obligamur aut re, aut verbis, aut simul utroque, aut consensu, aut lege, aut jure honorario, aut necessitate, aut peccato. PANDECTÆ JUSTINIANEÆ.

BOSTON:

CHARLES C. LITTLE AND JAMES BROWN.

MDCCCXLIV.

Title page for one of the books Story wrote while he was practicing law in Boston

He and She; or, A Poet's Portfolio (Boston: Houghton, Mifflin, 1883); revised and enlarged as *A Poet's Portfolio; Later Readings* (Boston & New York, Houghton, Mifflin, 1894);

Poems, 2 volumes (Edinburgh & London: Blackwood, 1885; Boston & New York: Houghton, Mifflin, 1886);

Fiammetta: A Summer Idyl (Boston & New York: Houghton, Mifflin, 1886);

Conversations in a Studio, 2 volumes (Boston & New York: Houghton, Mifflin, 1890);

Excursions in Art and Letters, 2 volumes (Boston & New York: Houghton, Mifflin, 1891).

OTHER: Joseph Story, *Commentaries on the Conflict of Laws, Foreign and Domestic, in Regard to Contracts, Rights and Remedies, and Especially in Regard to Marriages, Divorces, Wills, Successions, and Judgments,* first published in 1835, revised, corrected, and enlarged by William Wetmore Story (Boston: Little, Brown, 1846; London: Maxwell, 1846);

Joseph Story, *Commentaries on the Bills of Exchange, Foreign and Domestic, as Administered in England and America,* first published in 1843, revised and edited by William Wetmore Story (Boston: Little, Brown, 1847).

William Wetmore Story was an expatriate American attorney and legal scholar, poet, art theorist, essayist, and sculptor whose successes in multiple endeavors encouraged the belief among many of his contemporaries and all of his intimates that he was an original "Renaissance man." Although he was committed to Romantic aesthetic theory and practice, Story rarely endorsed any of the intellectual, social, or political movements associated with the nineteenth-century American Renaissance. During brief sojourns in Italy during the 1840s and early 1850s, and then as a permanent resident from 1856 until his death in 1895, he served aesthetic, social, and political ideas primarily as a facilitator of them in conversations among his many American and English friends who gathered at his studio on Via Sistina in Rome or at the apartment he and his wife maintained in the Palazzo Barberini. For nearly fifty years, the Storys were at the center of the expanding Anglo American communities in Rome and Florence. Over time these communities included Margaret Fuller, James Russell Lowell, Nathaniel and Sophia Hawthorne, and Robert and Elizabeth Barrett Browning–with whom the Storys were especially close–as well as William Cullen Bryant, Horatio Greenough, Leigh Hunt, Harriet Hosmer, Walter Savage Landor, Charles Eliot Norton, Hiram Powers, and William Makepeace Thackeray.

The second son and sixth child of the eminent American jurist Joseph Story and Sarah Waldo (Wetmore) Story, William Wetmore Story was born in Salem, Massachusetts, on 12 February 1819. When William was ten years old, Judge Story moved his family to Cambridge, where he taught at the Harvard Law School (1829–1845), while he also continued to serve as an associate justice of the United States Supreme Court (1811–1845). Reared in the elite social circles of Cambridge and Boston, William was prepared for college by William Wells, lived in a household visited routinely by such leading political figures of the day as Daniel Webster, and enjoyed the companionship and support of Lowell, Charles Sumner, and Thomas Wentworth Higginson, who were roughly his contemporaries. William Story received his A.B. degree in 1838 and his LL.B. in 1840 from Harvard University. After graduation he began to practice law in the Boston firm of Hillard and Sumner, but by 1842 he had comfortably settled into a practice with George Ticknor Curtis. On 31 October 1843 Story married Emelyn Bartlett Eldridge of Boston. By all accounts, theirs was an exceedingly congenial marriage; of their four children–Edith Marion, Joseph, Thomas Waldo, and Julian Russell–Thomas eventually became a sculptor and Julian, a painter.

Story's inclination to pursue multiple interests appeared early in his career. During much of the 1840s, when he was starting a family and what later proved to be a successful law practice, he also served as a commissioner in bankruptcy court and in the Massachusetts, Maine, and Pennsylvania federal courts, delivered the Phi Beta Kappa poem at Harvard, placed a few essays and poems in the *Boston Miscellany* and Lowell's *Pioneer,* published two textbooks on the law, revised and enlarged two of his father's commentaries on the law, and published a volume of his own poems–all between 1843 and 1847. Except as exhibitions of youthful enthusiasm and sentiment, neither *Nature and Art* (1844), the Phi Beta Kappa poem, nor *Poems* (1847), in which Story collected his earlier published pieces, is remarkable. By contrast, *A Treatise on the Law of Contracts Not under Seal* (1844) and *A Treatise on the Law of Sales of Personal Property* (1847), together with Story's revised and enlarged editions of his father's *Commentaries on the Conflict of Laws, Foreign and Domestic* (1846) and *Commentaries on the Bills of Exchange, Foreign and Domestic* (1847), are major achievements in the annals of legal studies. Revised and enlarged by other hands in later editions, Story's volumes on contracts and on the sales of personal property became the standard treatments of these subjects in the profession of law and remained in print until the 1870s. Throughout much of the 1840s Story also tested his abilities in music, modeling in clay, and painting, often getting up early in the morning and pursuing one or another of these activities before going to his law office.

The year 1845 proved to be pivotal in Story's life. At the beginning of the year Story suffered a physical and mental breakdown undoubtedly brought on by the pressures associated with dividing his life among so many pursuits; as Story recovered, his father's death later in the year cast him back into the hectic lifestyle that he had lived since taking his law degree. His publication record shows that literature and the law vied for his principal attentions between 1845 and 1847, when he accepted a commission from the trustees of Mount Auburn Cemetery to undertake a statue of his father. Between 1847 and 1851 he made two trips to Europe with his young family, studying the latest techniques in sculpture and working at sketches when in Italy, and practicing law when in America. When the Mount Auburn trustees accepted his sketch of the statue of his father, Story returned to Italy, where he executed the statue in marble.

Story's bust of Elizabeth Barrett Browning (1866), one of the British expatriates with whom he associated after settling in Rome (Boston Athenaeum)

Back in the United States, he spent most of the early 1850s balancing between a career in sculpture and literature and a new life in Italy, and a full-time career in law in the comfortable surroundings of Boston. Although he eventually chose the former, the choice was not easily made. In a late-in-life brief autobiography, which he circulated among friends and which was quoted at length by Henry James in *William Wetmore Story and His Friends* (1903), Story described the emotional turbulence surrounding his decision. Finishing the statue of his father–which was originally placed in the Bigelow Chapel at Mount Auburn Cemetery in Cambridge, Massachusetts, and is today at the Harvard University School of Law–Story then completed writing his monumental tribute to his father and his father's primary devotion to the law and politics and his secondary pursuit of poetry and the arts. Story's *Life and Letters of Joseph Story* appeared in 1851, and in the best tradition of nineteenth-century American life-and-letters

Story's second version (1868) of his 1860–1861 Libyan Sibyl *(National Collection of Fine Arts, Smithsonian Institution)*

biography, the two volumes of this work reveal almost as much about the author as they do about his subject. Tracing his father's life through correspondence, unpublished journals, and reminiscences by family and friends, Story recognized that his father's life cast into large relief the crucial decision he had to make about his own life. His father had chosen law, and for a time it appeared that the son would do the same. But in his autobiography, Story reveals that even as he was writing the biography of his father and occasionally practicing law, he "was haunted . . . by dreams of art and Italy, and every night fancied [he] was again in Rome and at work in [his] studio." His mother, he reports, "thought me mad and urged me to pursue my legal career, in which everything was open to me, rather than take such a leap in the dark." In spite of his mother's foreboding and his own sense of urgency about providing for his growing family, Story's "dreams of art and Italy" prevailed, and he settled in Rome in 1856 to devote his life to art.

In an untitled and undated couplet that he included in *Poems* (1885), his last collection of verse, Story wrote, "All Arts are one, howe'er distributed they stand; / Verse, tone, shape, color, form, are fingers on one hand." After 1856 Story concentrated on three artistic pursuits: poetry, nonfiction prose, and sculpture. All of them disclose not only his early acceptance of the dominant Romantic aesthetic impulses of the day, such as description, sentiment, and idealization of subject through form, but also his continuance in these impulses long after Romanticism and the "Renaissance" in America associated with it declined during and after the 1860s.

Although his early poetry is easily dismissed, the volumes of verse Story composed and collected between 1856 and the 1880s show both an increasingly competent and varied hand and the influence of those English and American poets with whom he came into close contact in Italy: Landor, Hunt, the Brownings, Bryant, and Lowell, his lifelong friend. First in *Poems,* which he dedicated to Lowell in 1856, then in another volume, also called *Poems,* in 1861, *Graffiti d'Italia* (1868), *He and She; or, A Poet's Portfolio* (1883), and the two volumes of *Poems* in which in 1885 he collected all his major verse, Story experimented with and succeeded in many poetic forms. For instance, in "A Roman Lawyer in Jerusalem," in which legal arguments are made in defense of Judas, as well as in "Marcus Aurelius to Lucius Verus," "Padre Bandelli Proses to the Duke Ludovico Sforza about Leonardo da Vinci," "Leonardo da Vinci Poeticizes to the Duke in His Own Defense," and "Ginevra da Siena," Story merged techniques of historical narration and character development that he had learned from Landor and Lowell with Robert Browning's brand of dramatic monologue to produce what might well strike readers of today as a multiple-part mini-series in verse. In many poems–such as "Pan in Love," "Cassandra," "Cleopatra," "Zia Nica," and "Guilietta"–Story employed the lyric form to develop and romanticize classical and historical figures as well as characters such as Zia Nica, whom he drew from everyday Italian life. Finally, he experimented with both the sonnet and what he called "scherzi," or improvised ballads, to produce poems in which he could develop traditional romantic treatments of love, immortality, imagination, and memory. In content and style, "A Glance" is typical of Story's writing in both of these forms:

Little we know what secret influence
A word, a glance, a casual tone may bring,
That, like the wind's breath on a chorded string,
May thrill the memory, touch the inner sense,
And waken dreams that come we know not whence;

Story (fourth from left, middle row) and his assistants outside his studio in Rome (from Gertrude Reese Hudson, ed., Browning to His American Friends: Letters between the Brownings, the Storys, and James Russell Lowell, 1841–1890, *1965)*

Or like the light touch of a bird's swift wing,
The lake's still face a moment visiting,
Leave pulsing rings, when he has vanished thence.
You looked into my eyes an instant's space,
And all the boundaries of time and place
Broke down, and far into a world beyond
Of buried hopes and dreams my soul had sight,
Where dim desires long lost, and memories fond,
Rose in a soft mirage of tender light.

Poetry represents Story's most sustained effort in imaginative literature during his career. However, in the 1870s and 1880s, he also tried his hand at drama and fiction. Attempting to capitalize on his success with historical narrative and lyric treatment of love and loss in poetry, he wrote *Nero, An Historical Play* (1875), *Stephania, A Tragedy in Five Acts, with a Prologue* (1875), *Second Thoughts. A Comedy, in Three Acts* (1878), and *Stale Mate* (1878), a play in two acts; he published *Fiammetta: A Summer Idyl,* his only novel, in 1886. Although Story composed the plays for private production, Henry James critiqued them, as well as *Fiammetta,* as tedious in their exposition of historical detail and overbearingly sentimental. In *Nero,* for example, Story loses control of both dialogue and action in order to incorporate virtually all known facts about this Roman emperor's life and death into his plot. Similarly, from the outset, the plot of *Stephania,* which treats of the historical character Stephania's avenging of the execution of Crescentius, her husband and the Consul of Rome, by the Holy Roman Emperor Otho III in 1002, becomes bogged down in a host of obscure details that neither justify the action taking place across five acts nor serve Story's interest in heroically portraying Stephania. In the novel *Fiammetta,* however, Story exhibits a reasonable degree of mastery over both his subject and his form. A romantic tale of love offered and love rejected, which Story composed for the entertainment of his wife, Emelyn, and daughter, Edith, during a summer visit to Edith's home in Vallombrosa, the book tells the story of Fiammetta, an innocent who is herself the result of one of her mother's illicit affairs, falling in love with a young painter for whom she has posed as a woodland and water sprite. Knowing of her unfortunate origin, the artist, who has no desire to compound one sorry history with another, rejects Fiammetta's overtures. Although he acts out of the purest of motives, the artist's rejection causes Fiammetta to die of a broken heart.

Although his drama and fiction provided him with no real following, Story's poetry did provide him with a considerable enough following to justify the reprinting of his *Poems* (1885) in 1886, 1887, 1888, 1890, 1891, and 1893; two additional printings occurred after his death, the first in 1897 and the second in 1900. Just as popular with the American and English reading public were his essays on Italian history and nineteenth-century Italian life, which he collected as *Roba di Roma*–first in 1863 and then enlarged with new essays under the same title in 1871; Story supplemented *Roba di Roma* with *Castle St. Angelo, and the Evil Eye,* which he published in 1877 and reprinted in 1878, and with *Vallombrosa,* a series of light descriptive essays on Tuscan landscape and history, in 1881. Between its first printing in 1863 and its last printing in 1894, the year before Story's death, *Roba di Roma* went through a total of twelve printings, or eight "editions"; except for his enlarged edition of the collection in 1871, however, editions of *Roba di Roma* are distinguishable only by the prefaces Story wrote for each of them, the last of which, "Preface to the Eighth Edition," first appeared in 1887.

Roba di Roma represents Story's most sustained and popular writing in any form, although it is virtually ignored by readers and literary historians of today. Consisting of twenty-one essays in the enlarged edition published during and after 1871, *Roba di Roma* re-creates the ancient and modern charm of Italy for nineteenth-century readers by moving them back and forth between mid-nineteenth century Rome and the much larger background of Italian history against which the Eternal City has evolved and which it reflects. Story's writing in this work–just as the customs, landscape, and people he describes–is poetic, and even today it appears capable of seducing even the strictest formalist imagination; these popular essays may have done much to wear away the provincialism of many of Story's American contemporaries. Among other subjects, his essays treat Roman holiday celebrations, café and theater life, street music, archaeological excavations, fountains, and the impressive architecture of the Colosseum and the Vatican. While reading them, readers unconsciously become tourists, imagining grand but silent histories that lie hidden behind the ancient walls and beneath the worn walks that Story describes, and vicariously experiencing the inspiration that the splendor of Italian churches, the art of great Italian masters, and the simplicity of peasant and monastic life has provided their narrator. The Italy that Story most prizes is pre-revolutionary Italy, the last stages of which he witnessed firsthand in the 1840s and for which he left America in 1856. Story's Italy in *Roba di Roma* ultimately looks back to the time when culture grew as a function of faith, not of nationalistic politics–a time that he captures in these essays as existing now only as a dream, for which he "sighs," as he states in his "Preface to the Eighth Edition," as he recollects "how pleasant and soothing that dream of life was."

In addition to *Roba di Roma, Castle St. Angelo, and the Evil Eye,* and *Vallombrosa,* Story prepared four other nonfiction prose works. Of these works, *The American Question* (1862)–which reprinted a series of letters he published in the London *Daily News* on 25, 26, and 27 December 1861–is the most significant. Written in response to the lukewarm support of the British press for the Union position at the outset of the Civil War, Story's *Daily News* letters explain the Northern cause and justify the merits of abolition to English readers. *The Proportions of the Human Figure, According to a New Canon, for Practical Use* (1864) is important for what it reveals about Story's evolution as a sculptor of literary and classical subjects who neither had nor sought formal training. In its rejection of verisimilitude in the execution of human subjects, Story's treatise shows his adherence to the Romantic disposition to believe that the purpose of the artist and the function of art are to improve upon nature and life. Finally, in his rambling, unsystematic *Conversations in a Studio* (1890) and *Excursions in Art and Letters* (1891), the last major publications of his career, Story collected his thoughts on art, history, literature, politics, and religion. Neither work conveys the strength of vision or intellectual purpose that Story revealed in his early legal writings or in *Roba di Roma;* instead, and much to the misfortune of Story's literary reputation, both works disclose an extreme late-in-life eclecticism that leaves the reader unsure of just where Story stands on any of the subjects about which he writes.

Although Story's career as a writer ended on an uneven note, none of his admirers took notice of the fact. Instead, Story's contemporaries invariably thought of him as an accomplished sculptor and placed him squarely in the company of such sculptors as Horatio Greenough, Harriet Hosmer, and Hiram Powers, all of whom were American expatriates living in Italy. Indeed, as far back as the 1840s and early 1850s, when he dreamed of leaving Boston and the law for Italy and his studio in Rome, Story thought of himself in precisely this way. When he moved his family to Rome in 1856, he threw himself into sculpture with the same single-minded determination with which he had earlier written on the law. He spent most of the late 1850s discouraged by the public's lack of interest in his work; however, after 1862, when his earliest marbles, *Cleopatra* and *Libyan Sibyl,* were acclaimed by critics at the International Exhibition in London, Story was never without patrons.

Story's sculptures are distributed over two general categories–ideal figures representing mythological, literary, and religious subjects executed in marble in the classic Romantic style; and marble or bronze busts, portraits, and statues of prominent figures. Of these two categories, the first contributed most to Story's reputation in his time, and today art historians generally agree that this category includes his most enduring works. In addition to *Cleopatra*–which exists in two versions, an original executed in 1858 and now in the Goldsmiths' Company Hall in London and a second version carved in 1869 and now in the Metropolitan Museum of Art in New York City–and *Libyan Sibyl,* executed in 1860–1861 and now at the Smithsonian Institution in Washington, D.C., Story's most famous classical, literary, and religious figures include *Medea,* executed in two versions, the first in 1864 and now at the Essex Institute in Massachusetts and the second in 1868 and now at the Metropolitan Museum of Art; *Venus* (ca. 1865) now in the Museum of Fine Arts in Boston; *Delilah* (1866–1867) now in the M. H. de Young Museum in San Francisco; *Salome* (1870) now in the Metropolitan Museum of Art; and *Jerusalem in her Desolation* (1873) now in the Pennsylvania Academy of the Fine Arts in Philadelphia. In contrast to the critical attention shown to these works, the busts, portraits, and statues included in Story's second category have not generally attracted great public interest or scholarly comment. Notable exceptions to this rule include his marble bust of Theodore Parker (ca. 1860) now in the Boston Public Library; his marble statue of Josiah Quincy (ca. 1860) now at Harvard University; his marble bust of Elizabeth Barrett Browning, first executed for Robert Browning after his wife's death in 1861, then executed in another version in 1866, now in the Boston Athenaeum; his bronze statue of Edward Everett (1867) now in the Boston Public Garden; and his bronze statues of Chief Justice John Marshall and the American physicist Joseph Henry, both in the early 1880s and now in Washington, D.C.

Story maintained his studio in Rome into the 1890s. Among his last carvings was a gravestone for his wife, Emelyn, who died in 1894. After his wife's death, Story's own health declined rapidly. He died at his daughter's home in Vallombrosa on 7 October 1895, and two days later he was buried beside his wife in the Protestant Cemetery at Rome.

Favored among his contemporaries as a conversationalist and facilitator of Anglo American literary and intellectual relations, Story was respected in the nineteenth century as one of the premier American expatriate sculptors. He is a prominent figure in the correspondence and journals of virtually all major and many minor authors, artists, and travelers who frequented the Anglo American communities of Italy from the 1840s to the 1890s; the writings of Fuller, Hawthorne, and the Brownings provide the most sustained commentary on Story's life and work, and in their assessments all are uniformly positive. However, the passage of time, the

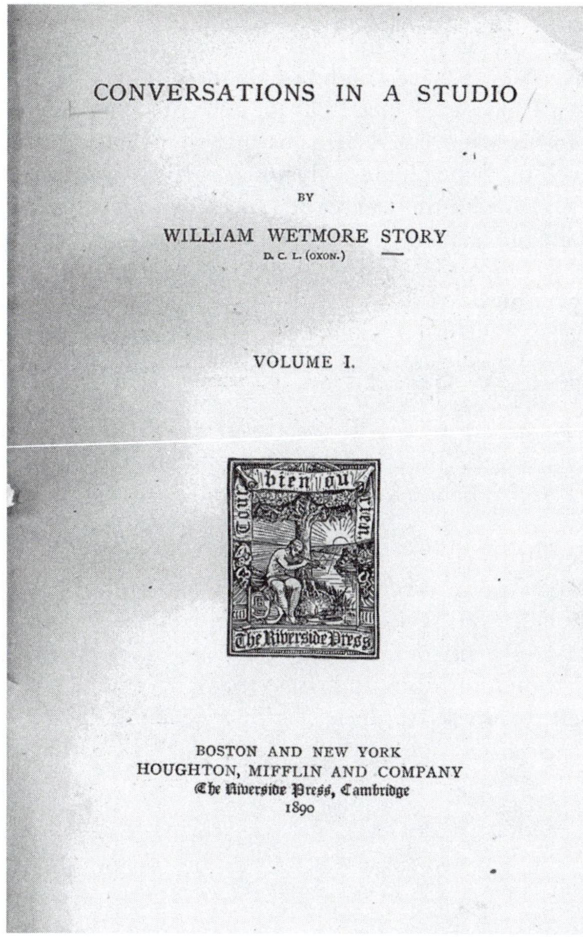
CONVERSATIONS IN A STUDIO

BY

WILLIAM WETMORE STORY

D. C. L. (OXON.)

VOLUME I.

BOSTON AND NEW YORK
HOUGHTON, MIFFLIN AND COMPANY
The Riverside Press, Cambridge
1890

Title page for a collection of Story's miscellaneous observations on art, history, literature, politics, and religion

lack of sustained interest in his biography and the decline of scholarly interest in either his writing or his sculpture, and the increased visibility of contemporaries such as Hosmer and Powers have severely diminished Story's appeal. In fact, Story himself, for whom discouragement in any of his endeavors was reason enough to consider a return to the law, anticipated this reversal of his reputation. So, too, did Hawthorne, one of his closest American friends, and James, his sympathetic and, to date, only major biographer. Both expressed the fear that Story's mastery of so many talents threatened him with the multiple risk of being remembered for none. Nevertheless, in their respective accounts of him, Hawthorne and James preserve their subject's luster. Hawthorne immortalized Story and his *Cleopatra* in his "Preface" to *The Marble Faun* (1860), arguing the artist's claim on the attention of his own and later American generations for having conceived of and executed this "magnificent" statue. That public testimony certainly accords with Hawthorne's remarks in private, as when he wrote in his *French and Italian Notebooks* on 4 October 1858: "Mr. Story is the most variously accomplished and brilliant person–the fullest of social life and fire–whom I have ever met." But the ultimate compliment to Story's achievement remains that from James, who opened the two volumes of his *William Wetmore Story and His Friends* with this praise: he "succeeded in living the real life of his mind."

Biographies:

Mary E. Phillips, *Reminiscences of William Wetmore Story, the American Sculptor and Author* (Chicago: Rand, McNally, 1897);

Henry James, *William Wetmore Story and His Friends,* 2 volumes (Boston: Houghton, Mifflin, 1903; London: Thames & Hudson, 1903).

References:

Wayne Craven, *Sculpture in America* (New York: Crowell, 1968; revised and enlarged edition, Newark: University of Delaware Press, 1984; New York & London: Cornwall Books, 1984);

Albert TenEyck Gardner, *Yankee Stonecutters: The First American School of Sculpture, 1800–1850* (New York: Columbia University Press for the Metropolitan Museum of Art, 1945);

William H. Gerdts Jr., "William Wetmore Story," *American Art Journal,* 4 (November 1972): 16–33;

Gertrude Reese Hudson, ed., *Browning to His American Friends: Letters between the Brownings, the Storys, and James Russell Lowell, 1841–1890* (London: Bowes and Bowes for the Keats-Shelley Memorial Association, 1965; New York: Barnes & Noble, 1965);

Robert N. Hudspeth, ed., *The Letters of Margaret Fuller,* 6 volumes (Ithaca, N.Y.: Cornell University Press, 1983–1994);

Lorado Taft, *The History of American Sculpture* (New York: Macmillan, 1903);

Margaret Farrand Thorp, *The Literary Sculptors* (Durham, N.C.: Duke University Press, 1965).

Papers:

Many of William Wetmore Story's letters and private papers can be found in the Houghton Library and the University Archives, Harvard University; the Massachusetts Historical Society, Boston; and the Beinecke Library, Yale University.

Charles Sumner

(6 January 1811 – 11 March 1874)

Jo Ann Manfra
Worcester Polytechnic Institute

BOOKS*: *The True Grandeur of Nations* (Boston: Ticknor, 1845; London: Smith, 1846);

White Slavery in the Barbary States (Boston: Ticknor, 1847; London: Low, 1853);

The Law of Human Progress (Boston: Ticknor, 1849);

The War System of the Commonwealth of Nations (Boston: Ticknor, Reed & Fields, 1849);

Argument of Charles Sumner, Esq., Against the Constitutionality of Separate Colored Schools (Boston: Roberts, 1849); republished as *Equality Before the Law: Unconstitutionality of Separate Colored Schools in Massachusetts* (Washington, D.C.: Rives & Bailey, 1870);

Orations and Speeches, 2 volumes (Boston: Ticknor, Reed & Fields, 1850);

Justice to the Land States (Washington, D.C.: Buell & Blanchard, 1852);

Freedom National; Slavery Sectional (Washington, D.C.: Buell & Blanchard, 1852; Edinburgh: Johnstone & Hunter, 1853);

The Landmark of Freedom (Washington, D.C.: Buell & Blanchard, 1854);

The Anti-Slavery Enterprise: Its Necessity, Practicability, and Dignity (Boston: Ticknor & Fields, 1855; London: Watts, 1855);

The Crime Against Kansas (Washington, D.C.: Buell & Blanchard, 1856);

Recent Speeches and Addresses (Boston: Higgins & Bradley, 1856);

The Barbarism of Slavery (Washington, D.C.: Buell & Blanchard, 1860);

Our Foreign Relations; Showing Present Perils from England and France (New York: Young Men's Republican Union, 1863);

Our Domestic Relations; or, How to Treat the Rebel States (Boston: Ticknor & Fields, 1863);

Security and Reconciliation for the Future (Boston: Rand & Avery, 1865);

*Sumner's addresses were frequently revised and republished, often with variant titles. There is no comprehensive checklist of these works. This list relies heavily on evidence in David Herbert Donald's biography.

Charles Sumner, 1846 (woodcut after a portrait by Eastman Johnson; Library of Congress)

The Equal Rights of All (Washington, D.C.: Congressional Globe Office, 1866);

Are We a Nation? (Boston: Wright & Potter, 1867);

Claims on England–Individual and National (Washington, D.C., 1869); republished as *The Alabama Claims* (London: Stevens, 1869);

The Question of Caste (Boston: Wright & Potter, 1869);

Naboth's Vineyard (Washington, D.C.: Rives & Bailey, 1870);

Republicanism vs. Grantism (Washington, D.C.: Rives & Bailey, 1872);

Prophetic Voices Concerning America (Boston: Lee & Shepard / New York: Lee, Shepard & Dillingham, 1874);

Sumner during his first term in the U.S. Senate (National Archives)

The Works of Charles Sumner, 15 volumes (Boston: Lee & Shepard, 1870–1883); republished with new introductory material as *Charles Sumner: His Complete Works,* 20 volumes (Boston: Lee & Shepard, 1900).

OTHER: *Reports of Cases Argued and Determined in the Circuit Court of the United States for the First Circuit,* edited by Sumner, 3 volumes (Boston: Hilliard & Gray, 1836, 1841);

Francis Vesey, *Reports of Cases Argued and Determined in the High Court of Chancery,* 20 volumes, edited by Sumner, J. C. Perkins, and C. B. Goodrich (Boston: Little, Brown, 1844–1845);

Andrew Dunlap, *A Treatise on the Practice of Courts of Admiralty,* second edition, completed and edited by Sumner (New York: Halsted, 1850);

Joseph Story, *Commentaries on the Law of Agency as a Branch of Commercial and Maritime Jurisprudence,* fourth edition, revised and enlarged, edited by Sumner (Boston: Little, Brown, 1851).

Charles Sumner, a distinguished legal scholar and ardent reformer who served in the U.S. Senate from 1851 until his death in 1874, was one of the most prominent political figures of the mid nineteenth century. His major contributions to decision making at the national level were his involvement in wartime foreign-policy decisions during an era when U.S. interests were endangered abroad and his relentless espousal of antislavery initiatives and full civil equality for African Americans.

Sumner's racial progressivism continues to earn the admiration of scholars. He was the highest-ranking political leader of the Civil War era to make black equality the primary goal of his adult life. In the long course of his highly personalized reform program, Sumner's policy responses to the biracial character of American society proved far in advance of political opinion in Congress and the nation at large. Although not a prewar supporter of the Garrisonian doctrine of immediate abolition, Sumner vigorously advocated the abolitionist position on black rights as early as 1849, and in 1852, with little support, he urged congressional repeal of the Fugitive Slave Law. Like many of his Republican colleagues, Sumner revised his views and called for immediate emancipation during the Civil War. Unlike most of them, he steadfastly promoted far- reaching postwar Reconstruction policies. Throughout his many years in the Senate his goal, said Sumner, was "absolute human equality, secured, assured, and invulnerable."

Charles Sumner was born in Boston to a couple whose seventeenth-century New England lineages were impeccable, but who were far from prosperous "Boston Brahmins." His mother, Relief Jacob Sumner, supported herself as a seamstress until she married Charles Pinckney Sumner, a Harvard-educated attorney whose interests lay more with history and literature than with the law. He did not become financially secure until he was appointed Suffolk County sheriff in 1826–just in time to afford a university education for his precocious son. Young Sumner graduated from Harvard in 1830. A year later, after considerable indecision, he entered Harvard Law School and completed its two-year professional-training program in 1833.

Sumner's brilliance at Harvard Law School earned him the patronage of its most distinguished teacher, Supreme Court Justice Joseph Story, and Sumner was groomed as Story's eventual replacement on the faculty. To further his suitability for the appointment Sumner spent early 1834 in Washington, attending sessions of the Supreme Court and enjoying a friendly association with the renowned Chief Justice John Marshall and his colleagues.

SOUTHERN CHIVALRY _ ARGUMENT VERSUS CLUB'S.

An editorial cartoonist's depiction of Congressman Preston Brooks assaulting Sumner on the Senate floor after Sumner delivered his speech The Crime Against Kansas, *May 1856* *(New York Public Library, Astor, Lenox, and Tilden Foundations)*

On his return to Cambridge, Sumner's passion for legal scholarship left him little time or energy for building a successful law practice. He became an editor of, and a major contributor to, *The American Jurist.* In 1835 Story appointed him reporter for the federal circuit court in Boston, which resulted in *Reports of Cases Argued and Determined in the Circuit Court of the United States for the First Circuit* (1836, 1841)–generally known as *Sumner's Reports.* In the fall of 1835 Story was delayed in Washington, and Sumner was hired to teach the justice's courses at Harvard. He substituted for the justice again in 1836 and 1837.

Against Story's advice, Sumner borrowed money and late in 1837 left for an indefinite sojourn abroad, intent on a study tour of European legal and political institutions rather than general intellectual cultivation. While in Europe he mastered the French, German, and Italian languages and established close acquaintanceships with leading political and literary figures.

During the first few months after Sumner's reluctant homecoming in the spring of 1840, the Boston elite warmly received him, and he returned to the practice of law. But it soon became clear that he could neither settle comfortably into Boston society nor maintain sufficient interest in routine common-law matters.

Meanwhile, the Reverend William Ellery Channing had introduced Sumner to the challenge of social reform. Initially the young lawyer adopted the Unitarian minister's arguments but refused to assume public leadership of any cause. By 1844, however, Sumner's disinclination had disappeared, and he embarked on his historic calling as a reformer.

Throughout his adult life Sumner wrote tirelessly, creating and revising speeches and essays that in final form sometimes exceeded one hundred pages in length. His most important addresses and essays were polemics, often cast in uncompromising language. His inability to give any leeway to policy opponents was notorious. "Yes, but you forget the other side," a friendly critic, George W. Curtis, once protested. To which Sumner, his resonant voice seeming to shake the room, replied: "There *is* no other side." In Senate debate he displayed little patience for the objection that his antislavery initiatives were unconstitutional. "*Nothing against Slavery can be unconstitutional,*" thundered Sumner. To fellow reformer Carl Schurz, Sumner was best characterized as a "moral terrorist."

In 1845, because of Sumner's increasing visibility in civic affairs, he was honored with an invitation to deliver the official Boston July Fourth oration. Those

An editorial cartoon depicting the Republican reaction to Sumner's June 1860 Senate speech The Barbarism of Slavery *(Library of Congress)*

listeners who expected the usual remarks extolling American virtue were unpleasantly surprised by *The True Grandeur of Nations* (1845), which not only strongly criticized U.S. expansionist aims in Texas and Oregon, but also eloquently denounced the military actions of all nations as dishonorable. Modern war, Sumner said, was prompted by ignorance of human progress, by institutional Christianity, by aggressive patriotism, and by what became known in the twentieth century as the military-industrial complex.

Although the speech outraged the Boston political and social establishment and ended Sumner's hopes for a permanent faculty appointment at Harvard Law School, it abruptly elevated him to importance within the flourishing New England peace movement. In *The War System of the Commonwealth of Nations* (1849), delivered to the American Peace Society, he urged creation of institutions similar to the twentieth-century United Nations Organization and World Court. Yet, Sumner's acceptance of the legitimacy of defensive war and of violent revolution alienated him from the core of "non-resisting" pacifists in the movement. Indeed, when the Civil War broke out in 1861, Sumner demanded that it be waged aggressively.

As the antislavery crusade and its concomitant Civil Rights movement absorbed most of his time and energy, Sumner also gradually moved away from two other early interests, the reform of prisons and schools. His *White Slavery in the Barbary States* (1847), another Boston talk, compared conservative northern Whigs to the mercantile interests that had prevented the British from exterminating slavery in Tripoli, and it likened American slaveholders to the Algerian pirates. In 1848 Sumner joined Charles Francis Adams in calling for a convention of Bay Staters opposed to the further spread of slavery into the West, a meeting that led to the formation of the Free Soil Party of Massachusetts. *The Law of Human Progress* (1849), a college lecture, explained the basis of Sumner's political activism. Although human progress was certainly inevitable, said Sumner, it remained the duty of reformers to induce progress by stirring up public opinion. According to historian Arthur Ekirch, Sumner–of all his antebellum contemporaries–had probably "the most adequate and significant" understanding of the idea of progress.

In the successful *Roberts* v. *Boston* school desegregation case, the *Argument of Charles Sumner, Esq., Against the Constitutionality of Separate Colored Schools* (1849) proved decisive. Years later, during debates over Reconstruction policy in the U.S. Senate, the brief was republished as *Equality Before the Law* (1870) in aid of Sumner's campaign for racially integrated schools in the South. His argument asserted the harmful sociological and psychological effects of segregated education on both black and white children, a view ultimately accepted by the U.S. Supreme Court in its landmark *Brown* v. *Board of Education* decision (1954).

In 1851 the Free Soil/Democratic coalition that dominated the Massachusetts legislature elected Sumner to represent the Bay State in the U.S. Senate. It was the first public office of any kind he had ever held. The legislature reelected him in 1857, 1863, and 1869.

In the Senate, Sumner immediately called attention to himself as a speaker of rare skill and colossal erudition. He offered a disputatious early oration on the public lands question, *Justice to the Land States* (1852), simply to prove his versatility on issues other than slavery. Yet, *Freedom National; Slavery Sectional* (1852), delivered to a packed Senate gallery in support of his motion for repeal of the Fugitive Slave Law, marked him as the most eloquent congressional opponent of the "peculiar institution." In *The Landmark of Freedom* (1854), another widely publicized Senate address, he condemned the Kansas-Nebraska Bill for opening the trans-Missouri West to slavery. *The Anti-slavery Enterprise: Its Necessity, Practicability, and Dignity* (1855), presented before audiences in New York and Massachusetts, solidified his identification with the new Republican Party and its commitment to opposing the westward spread of slavery.

Sumner's Senate oration *The Crime Against Kansas* (1856) is his best-known speech–less because of its content than its results. Reflecting the Republicans' dismay over the invasion of Kansas Territory by proslavery settlers, Sumner's lengthy and rhetorically elaborate address included a particularly venomous attack on an absent senator from South Carolina. Congressman Preston Brooks, another South Carolinian, consequently assaulted Sumner on the Senate floor with a heavy cane, causing potentially fatal wounds. The coincidence of the Brooks assault and the Kansas escalation energized politicians and newspaper editors all across the North. Historians now regard the speech and the attack it provoked as responsible for abruptly returning the slavery issue to center stage.

A fully recovered Sumner returned to the Senate just in time for the critical 1860 presidential campaign and the impending breakup of the Union. *The Barbarism of Slavery* (1860), a scathing indictment of southern society, proved that he was back in form. The subsequent national election and southern secession gave Republicans their first working majority in Washington. Sumner's widely acknowledged expertise in foreign affairs–the result of his early legal scholarship, his fluency in languages, and his personal acquaintances with European notables, renewed during his recent medical convalescence abroad–prompted his selection as chairman of the Senate Foreign Relations Committee. From this powerful post Sumner commanded wary respect from the administrations of Abraham Lincoln, Andrew Johnson, and Ulysses S. Grant. Although Mary Todd Lincoln's social intimacy with Sumner eased his strained relationship with her husband, no such buffer mediated his stormy association with either Johnson or Grant.

For the United States its most important foreign dispute of the 1860s was with Great Britain, whose wartime policies–particularly in permitting the building in British shipyards of powerful Confederate warships such as the *Alabama*–flagrantly favored the Confederacy. *Our Foreign Relations; Showing Present Perils from England and France* (1863), written first as an *Atlantic Monthly* article and then delivered as a speech in New York City, was a harsh indictment of British, and derivative French, policy. Sumner's passionate postwar address, *Claims on England–Individual and National* (1869), republished in London as *The Alabama Claims,* proved influential in defining the initial bargaining terms in negotiating reparations for wartime damages caused by British-built Confederate commerce-raiders. Sumner maintained that the British government was accountable not only for private citizens' losses but also for all the costs of the war after mid 1863, since by then, in his opinion, the Confederates had been defeated except for their maritime operations. He proposed a compensation of $2 billion and advocated the cession of Canada as well. These harsh recommendations shocked the British into being amenable to more moderate terms, leading to resolution of the dispute in the Treaty of Washington (1871).

Sumner's outspoken proposals with respect to the Civil War and its relationship to the postwar fate of African Americans held less sway. From the war's outbreak he urged that it be waged to abolish slavery, not just to preserve the Union. He regularly pressed President Lincoln to free the slaves, to grant them civil equality, and to enlist black males in the army at equal pay with whites. Convinced that there would be no genuine peace without a complete overhaul of Southern society, Sumner proposed his own plan for the postwar years in a second *Atlantic Monthly* article, *Our Domestic Relations; or, How to Treat the Rebel States* (1863), which was reprinted as a pamphlet. His *Security and Reconciliation for the Future* (1865), another pamphlet, includes several of his most important wartime speeches, resolutions, and articles on race and Reconstruction. Sumner's Senate oration *The Equal Rights of All* (1866) concluded with what David Herbert Donald terms "one of his finest perorations in behalf of human equality." And Sumner's public lecture *The Question of Caste* (1869), given

Sumner at the outbreak of the Civil War (Harvard University Archives)

in a dozen northern cities, articulated a full-fledged case against racial segregation in all aspects of the nation's civic life.

As fully developed, Sumner's proposal for racial justice in the South included four measures that went far beyond emancipation. Congress, he insisted, must mandate that to reenter the Union all former Confederate states had to guarantee full civil rights for all African Americans, the right to vote and hold office for black adult males, and free public schooling for black children. In addition, Congress must transfer ownership of the lands of rebellious former slaveholders to emancipated slaves as family homesteads. Absent such measures, Sumner thought, black freedom would prove a delusion.

Only modified versions of two of Sumner's four proposals had anything like majority support in Congress. The most its progressive members seemed willing or able to do was to bring their colleagues to an agreement on voting rights and on those basic civil rights that plausibly could be defended as incidences of the freedom required by the abolition of slavery. Few accepted Sumner's position on the unambiguous guarantee of full civil rights, on education, and on southern homesteads. A stranger to compromise, Sumner maintained that the Thirteenth, Fourteenth, and Fifteenth Amendments to the Constitution failed to go far enough.

A significant postwar event in Sumner's personal life was marriage. As a young man Sumner had been strikingly handsome, over six feet tall and exceedingly charming and personable in private intercourse. Yet, as the twenty-one-year-old Sumner once admitted, courtship baffled him, and he did not marry until 17 October 1866, when he was wed to Alice Mason Hooper, a war widow almost thirty years his junior. The union proved disastrous. As Alice complained, "I am always left alone. Mr. Sumner is always reading, writing and snoring." Separated in June 1867, the couple divorced on 10 May 1873.

During this same period, prompted by the pending American purchase of Alaska from Russia, Sumner produced two major pieces on the future territorial expansion of the United States: *Prophetic Voices Concerning America* (1874), originally an 1867 *Atlantic Monthly* article, and *Are We a Nation?* (1867), a public address

Sumner in the study of his Washington home (Frank Leslie's Illustrated Weekly Magazine)

delivered some two dozen times. Sumner's expansionist vision stopped at the water's edge. When a pet project of President Grant's, a treaty annexing Santo Domingo, came up for ratification, Sumner opposed it on grounds that the underlying negotiations were corrupt. Delivered after the Senate had already rejected the treaty, Sumner's scathing speech was titled *Naboth's Vineyard* (1870), a reference to a biblical king's desire to possess the garden of an humble neighbor. For those colleagues who had long been annoyed by Sumner's obstreperous style, this needlessly antagonizing performance was an excuse to remove him from the chairmanship of the Foreign Relations Committee. Sumner nevertheless continued to be a voice to be reckoned with and was regularly consulted on the *Alabama* Claims negotiations with the British.

In 1872, as the so-called Liberal Republicans began deserting the regular party over President Grant's renomination, Sumner weighed in with a lengthy oration. *Republicanism vs. Grantism* (1872) sought to prove that Grant was no longer a legitimate GOP leader. When the regulars renominated Grant, Sumner hesitantly supported Horace Greeley (the joint nominee of the Liberals and the Democrats), thereby alienating himself from the most powerful Republican figures in Massachusetts.

Only sympathy for the illness in his last years and disillusionment over the increasingly obvious corruption of the Grant Administration prolonged Sumner's dwindling political support within the Bay State. He died in 1874, ten months before the Massachusetts legislature might well have voted to deny him another term.

In the pre–Civil War decade publishers collected Sumner's writings as *Orations and Speeches* (1850) and *Recent Speeches and Addresses* (1856). What Sumner in later life termed his "book" was the aggregation of lectures, newspaper articles and notices, journal essays, public lectures, and other short pieces, often thoroughly revised and with slightly altered titles, that he began publishing after the war. The posthumous collection of this voluminous prose continued into the 1880s, eventually reaching fifteen volumes. *The Works of Charles Sumner* (1870–1883), however, includes only about half of Sumner's public utterances. In 1900 the series was republished, with new introductory material, as a twenty-volume set misleadingly titled *Charles Sumner: His Complete Works.*

Letters:

E. L. Pierce, *Memoir and Letters of Charles Sumner,* 4 volumes (Boston: Roberts, 1877–1893);

The Selected Letters of Charles Sumner, 2 volumes, edited by Beverly Wilson Palmer (Boston: Northeastern University Press, 1990).

Biographies:

D. A. Harsha, *The Life of Charles Sumner* (New York: Dayton & Burdick, 1856);

Jeremiah Chaplin and J. D. Chaplin, *Life of Charles Sumner* (Boston: Lothrop, 1874);

C. Edwards Lester, *Life and Public Services of Charles Sumner* (New York: U.S. Publishing Company, 1874);

Elias Nason, *The Life and Times of Charles Sumner* (Boston: Russell, 1874);

Anna Laurens Dawes, *Charles Sumner* (New York: Dodd, Mead, 1892);

Archibald H. Grimke, *The Life of Charles Sumner: The Scholar in Politics* (New York: Funk & Wagnalls, 1892);

Moorfield Storey, *Charles Sumner* (Boston: Houghton Mifflin, 1900);

George H. Haynes, *Charles Sumner* (Philadelphia: Jacobs, 1909);

Walter G. Shotwell, *Life of Charles Sumner* (New York: Crowell, 1910);

Carl Schurz, *Charles Sumner,* edited by Arthur Reed Hogue (Urbana: University of Illinois Press, 1951);

David Herbert Donald, *Charles Sumner and the Coming of the Civil War* (New York: Knopf, 1960); *Charles Sumner and the Rights of Man* (New York: Knopf, 1970); republished in one volume as *Charles Sumner* (New York: Da Capo, 1996);

Frederick J. Blue, *Charles Sumner and the Conscience of the North* (Arlington Heights, Ill.: Harlan Davidson, 1994).

References:

D. H. Chamberlain, *Charles Sumner and the Treaty of Washington* (Boston: Clarke, 1902);

J. C. B. Davis, *Mr. Sumner, the Alabama Claims, and Their Settlement* (New York: Douglas Taylor, 1878);

Arthur Alphonse Ekirch Jr., *The Idea of Progress in America, 1815–1860* (New York: Columbia University Press, 1944), pp. 258–259;

William E. Gienapp, "The Crime Against Sumner: The Caning of Charles Sumner and the Rise of the Republican Party," *Civil War History,* 25 (September 1979): 218–245;

Bill Ledbetter, "Charles Sumner: Political Activist for the New England Transcendentalists," *Historian,* 44 (May 1982): 347–363;

Elaine Pagel and Carl Dallinger, "Charles Sumner," in *A History and Criticism of American Public Address,* edited by William Norwood Brigance (New York: McGraw-Hill, 1943), pp. 751–776;

Louis Ruchames, "Charles Sumner and American Historiography," *Journal of Negro History,* 38 (April 1953): 139–160;

Laura A. White, "Was Charles Sumner Shamming, 1856–1859?" *New England Quarterly,* 33 (September 1960): 291–324.

Papers:

The main collection of Charles Sumner's papers is at Harvard University. Sumner's letters can be found in many collections in the United States, Canada, and Great Britain. These materials are available on eighty-five reels of microfilm, *The Papers of Charles Sumner,* edited by Beverly Wilson Palmer (Alexandria, Va.: Chadwyck-Healy, 1988); see also Palmer's *Guide and Index to the Papers of Charles Sumner* (Alexandria, Va.: Chadwyck-Healy, 1988).

George Ticknor

(1 August 1791 - 26 January 1871)

Sally C. Hoople

See also the Ticknor entries in *DLB 59: American Literary Critics and Scholars, 1800–1850* and *DLB 140: American Book-Collectors and Bibliographers, First Series.*

BOOKS: *Syllabus of a Course of Lectures on the History and Criticism of Spanish Literature* (Cambridge, Mass.: Hilliard & Metcalf, 1823);

Remarks on Changes Lately Proposed or Adopted in Harvard University (Boston: Cummings, Hilliard, 1825);

Outlines of the Principal Events in the Life of General Lafayette (Boston: Cummings, Hilliard, 1825);

Remarks on the Life and Writings of Daniel Webster of Massachusetts (Philadelphia: Carey & Lea, 1831);

Lecture on the Best Methods of Teaching the Living Languages. Delivered Before the American Institute, August 24, 1832 (Boston: Carter, Hendee, 1833);

History of Spanish Literature, 3 volumes (New York: Harper; London: John Murray, 1849); corrected and enlarged (Boston: Houghton, Mifflin; Riverside Press Cambridge, 1891);

Union of the Boston Athenaeum and the Public Library (Boston: Dutton & Wentworth, 1853);

Life of William Hickling Prescott (Boston: Ticknor & Fields, 1864).

OTHER: Johann Wolfgang von Goethe, *The Sorrows of Young Werter,* translated by Ticknor (1814) in *George Ticknor's The Sorrows of Young Werter,* edited by Frank G. Ryder (Chapel Hill: University of North Carolina Studies in Comparative Literature, 1952).

SELECTED PERIODICAL PUBLICATIONS–UNCOLLECTED: "Biography of Michael Stiefel," *North American Review,* 4 (January 1817): 166–176;

"Griscom's Tour in Europe," *North American Review,* 18 (January 1824): 178–192;

"Essays on Scenes in Italy," *North American Review,* 18 (January 1824): 192–204;

"Free Schools of New England," *North American Review,* 19 (October 1824): 448–457;

George Ticknor, 1828 (portrait by Thomas Sully; Trustees of Dartmouth College)

"Lafayette," *North American Review,* 20 (January 1825): 147–180;

"Mr. Sullivan's Address," *North American Review,* 21 (July 1825): 225–230.

George Ticknor, a groundbreaking New England intellectual, is known primarily for his monumental three-volume *History of Spanish Literature* (1849). Appearing at a time when Americans were struggling to prove to skeptical Europeans that the New World could produce significant literature, Ticknor's work stands out as an important achievement. A champion of education for everyone, he deliberately wrote his book not only for scholars but also for general readers. As a professor at Harvard College for many years, Ticknor worked tirelessly for educational reform in spite of discouragement and opposition. Ever gregarious, he cultivated friendships with both ordinary people and distinguished scholars, artists, and statesmen. Several extended visits to Europe enhanced his international outlook and cultural sophistication. Besides his notable history, he wrote biographies of Daniel Webster and William Hickling Prescott, contributed many articles to journals, engaged in extensive correspondence, and wrote copious journal entries that give readers a vivid picture of an exceptional personality.

George Ticknor was born in Boston on 1 August 1791. His father, Elisha Ticknor, graduated from Dartmouth College in 1783 and was a teacher and school administrator for a few years; from 1795 until his retirement in 1812, he was a grocer in Boston. Until his death in 1821, he participated in many worthy public projects. George's mother, Elizabeth (Billings) Ticknor, a teacher, married Benjamin Curtis, who died in 1784. The couple had four children: Eliza, Benjamin, Harriet, and Augustus. In 1790 Elizabeth married Elisha Ticknor. George Ticknor was the only child of that marriage. The family was comfortable financially. Ticknor had little institutional education as a child, but his father prepared him for college and introduced him to many influential people. When George was fourteen years old, he was admitted to Dartmouth College as a junior and remained there from 1805 to 1807. Later he reported that he was fairly idle but happy at Dartmouth. After graduation he studied the classics avidly with John Sylvester John Gardiner, rector of Trinity Church. In 1810 he entered the law office of William Sullivan, Esq., read law conscientiously, and was admitted to the bar in 1813. He opened an office and practiced law successfully for a year; he wearied of the profession, however, and gave it up to study German in preparation for study in Europe. After a trip to Virginia in late 1814 and early 1815, during which he met many influential dignitaries–including former president John Adams, President James Madison at the White House in Washington, and Thomas Jefferson at Monticello–he reluctantly left his comfortable home and sailed for Europe with Edward Everett on 16 April 1815.

Ticknor's copious journals and correspondence document his European itinerary. He landed in Liverpool, which he likened to Boston, and was dismayed to learn that Napoleon Bonaparte had returned to Paris to reopen hostilities. From Liverpool he journeyed to London and visited galleries, theaters, and intellectual circles where, often facilitated by letters of introduction from Adams and Jefferson, he met many celebrities, such as Sir Humphry Davy and George Gordon, Lord Byron and Lady Byron. A month later, he traveled through Holland and in early August arrived in Göttingen, where he studied for nearly two years. While there he translated Johann Wincklemann's *Gedanken über die Nachahmungen der griechishen Werke in der Malerei und Bildhauerkunst* (1755; Thoughts upon the Imitation of the Works of Greeks in Painting and Statuary). He responded positively to German instruction and scholarship but was appalled by what he considered excessive academic freedom and lax moral behavior. In November 1816 Ticknor received a letter from Harvard President John Kirkland, offering him two professorships–belles lettres and the Smith Professorship of Modern Languages. Passing up an anticipated trip to Greece, for which he had consulted Byron, he journeyed to Paris, where he studied French and Italian, and associated with brilliant intellectuals such as Madame Anne-Louise-Germaine de Staël, August Wilhelm von Schlegel, Robert Southey, and François de Chateaubriand. Overall, however, he was disturbed by the superficiality of French society and political extremism. He found Geneva much more to his taste than Paris, and he considered Rome "worth all the other cities in the world." Especially significant was his visit to Spain, where his stagecoach journey, especially between Barcelona and Madrid, was difficult and accommodations miserable. To combat tedium, Ticknor read aloud from Miguel de Cervantes's *Don Quixote de la Mancha* (1605) to entertain his companions. Once in Madrid, he read Spanish poetry with scholar Joseph Antonio Conde for several hours a day. He found romance in the common life of the Spanish people but fainted at the sight of bullfight slaughter. He was enchanted by the Alhambra in Granada and for protection traveled cheerfully from Seville, Spain to Lisbon, Portugal in the company of contrabandists. Back in Great Britain, he visited William Hazlitt in London, met Walter Scott in Edinburgh, called on William Wordsworth in the Lake Country, and took a brief side trip to Paris to purchase books, including some for Thomas Jefferson. In the spring of 1819 Ticknor returned home.

Zealous to improve the quality of education, scholarship, and culture in the United States, on 10 August 1819 Ticknor formally became an Abiel Smith Professor of the French and Spanish Languages and Literatures and Professor of Belles Lettres at Harvard. He had a light teaching load, for which he prepared conscientiously, and arranged to live at home in Boston instead of on campus as a parietal officer. Thus, he could pursue his own scholarly interests. His earnestness appealed to many scholarly people, and he counted among his friends Daniel Webster, Joseph Story, William Ellery Channing, George Bancroft, Nathaniel Bowditch, Joseph Cogswell, Andrews Norton,

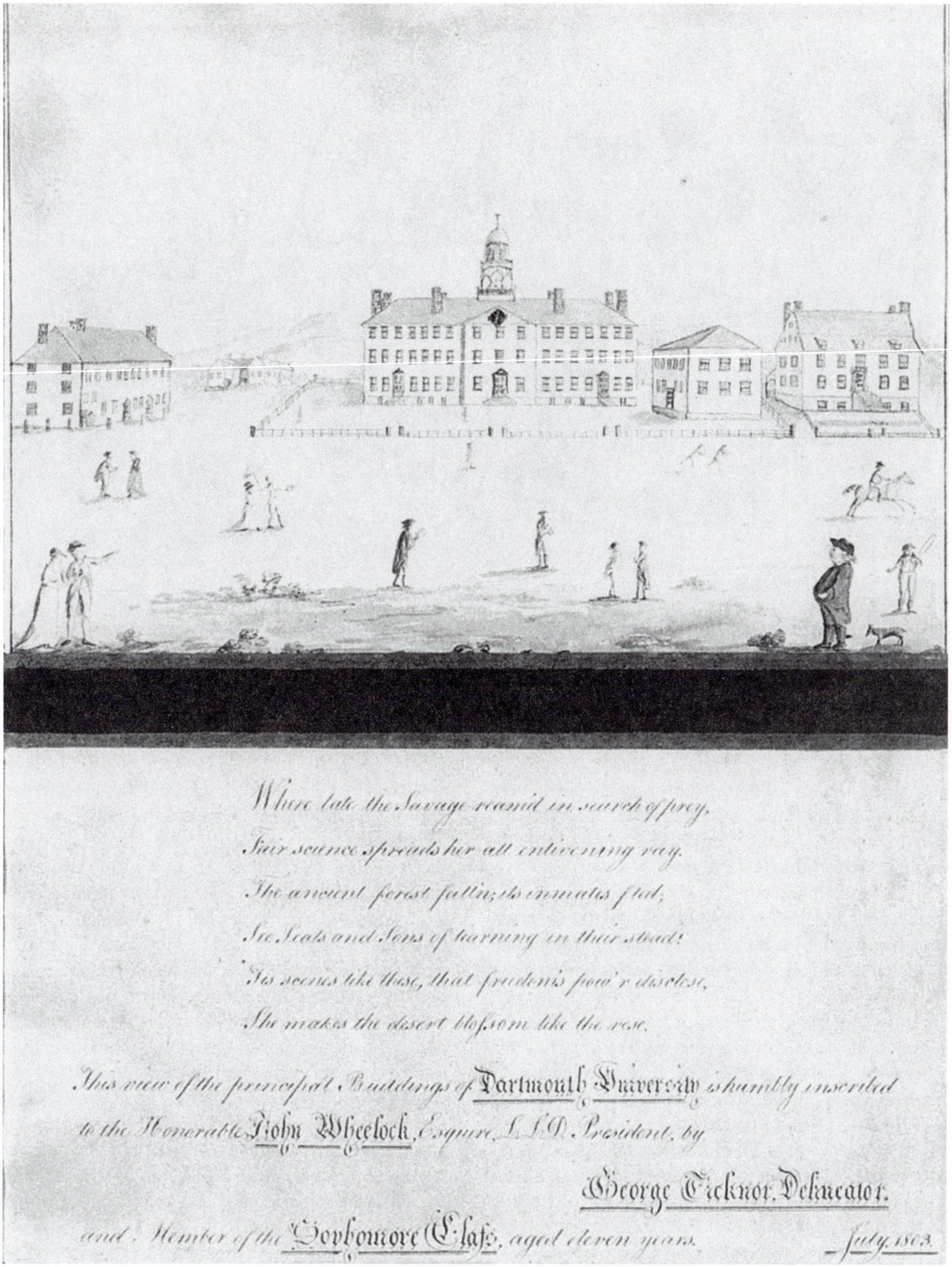

Eleven-year-old George Ticknor's watercolor of Dartmouth College (Trustees of Dartmouth College)

Ticknor's house (at left) in an 1858 photograph of Park Street in Boston

Jared Sparks, and Washington Allston. He also met Samuel Eliot's sister Anna, and they were married on 18 September 1821. Both George and Anna had inheritances that enabled them to live well.

An ardent supporter of his friend Webster, Ticknor published the article "Webster's Speeches and Forensic Arguments" in the *American Quarterly Review* in 1831. Late that year it was reprinted with additions as *Remarks on the Life and Writings of Daniel Webster of Massachusetts.* Idealizing his hero, Ticknor portrayed Webster as a paragon of statesmanship who represented the finest aspirations of his country. Ticknor linked Webster with the American people and saw in Webster's political views a loftiness that precluded partisanship. After hearing Webster orate at Plymouth Rock, Ticknor was so excited that he thought his "temples would burst with the gush of blood" and was afraid to go near him: "It seemed to me as if he was like the mount that might not be touched and that burned with fire."

Ticknor was considered a scholarly, vibrant professor, and he exhibited great interest in techniques of foreign language teaching, as seen in his *Lecture on the Best Methods of Teaching the Living Languages* (1833). He also developed texts and readings for class instruction and demanded that Harvard secure native speakers for foreign-language instruction. He strove to counteract the tendency to teach by memorization by expanding the range of the subject, stimulating thinking, and revising classroom methods. His attempts to reform the institutional structure of Harvard met with resistance from both administration and faculty members. He further angered his antagonists by praising the new University of Virginia, where he was offered a professorship, which he declined. He also tried to tighten discipline, improve moral behavior, and increase the rigor of entrance and final examinations. He adapted to American circumstances elements of German education, which he admired. In a pamphlet, *Remarks on Changes Lately Proposed or Adopted in Harvard University* (1825), Ticknor discussed the problems of the college and defended new laws that had been enacted. When *North American Review* editor Sparks rejected his article, Ticknor refused to contribute any more articles to that journal. Although his language program flourished, Ticknor resigned from Harvard in 1835 and was succeeded by Henry Wadsworth Longfellow. In spite of his disappointments,

Ticknor, a reformer years ahead of his time, profoundly influenced the development of education at Harvard and in the United States.

Ticknor was devoted to his wife and four children. Anna Eliot, the oldest, never married, but she developed the Society to Encourage Studies at home, a correspondence program for adults. She also published anonymously a children's book, *An American Family in Paris* (1869). Daughter Susan Perkins died in infancy in 1825. Daughter Eliza Sullivan married William Dexter. Ticknor's only son, George Haven, who was born in 1829, died at the age of five on 4 August 1834. As a consolation for his overwhelming sorrow and to find a change of scene for his ill wife, Ticknor took his family to Europe in June 1835.

After a voyage that nearly ended in shipwreck, they landed in England and traveled to Oxford in elegant style and then to London. Ticknor's journal includes a dazzling account of his meetings with royalty, aristocrats, and literary intellectuals. The Ticknor family toured England, Wales, and Ireland that summer and then journeyed to Dresden, Germany, to spend the winter. There Ticknor developed a close friendship with Prince John, who in 1845 became king of Saxony. In June 1836 the Ticknors visited Vienna, where Ticknor frequently conversed with Prince Metternich. The Ticknor family spent the winter in Rome; the winter of 1837–1838 they spent in Paris, although Ticknor disapproved of what he considered artificial, immoral French drama and of such writers as Victor Hugo, Honoré de Balzac, and George Sand.

During Ticknor's second trip to Europe, he met (in London) Don Pascual de Gayangos, a young Spanish scholar, who reviewed Prescott's *History of the Reign of Ferdinand and Isabella* (1838). After the Ticknors returned to Boston in June 1838, George Ticknor corresponded copiously with Gayangos. Those letters were published by the Hispanic Society of America in 1927. Gayangos translated Ticknor's *History of Spanish Literature* into Spanish (Madrid, 1851) and contributed invaluable notes and additions to the work.

Until September 1839, when the Ticknors again occupied their house in Boston, they led itinerant lives–visiting friends and relatives and living in hotels. After 1839, however, they spent their winters in Boston and went to the seashore in the summers of 1840, 1841, and 1842. They spent the summer of 1844 traveling in Pennsylvania and southern New York State. Ticknor closely associated with the Boston Brahmins, and although he shared with many of them ambivalence about participating in politics, nevertheless he demonstrated keen interest in the compelling political issues of his time. The Ticknors belonged to the most influential circles and also lavished hospitality on visiting foreign

Ticknor in 1848 (portrait by G. P. A. Healy; Trustees of Dartmouth College)

dignitaries as well as poor scholars and artists. Ticknor's influence was so great that he and his associates ostracized those men whose ideas differed drastically from theirs. Ticknor justified his actions as a defense of Boston's moral standards and politics.

In spite of having published many reviews and essays, translated many works from the classics and German authors, and produced copious lectures, Ticknor, influenced by the Boston work ethic, deplored his dearth of written output after 1835. He found his love for society a time-consuming distraction that he was unwilling to forgo. However, during his second European trip he amassed a personal library of Spanish books that was considered one of the finest in the world. Determined to devote his intellectual explorations to Spain, he expanded the ideas and information that he had developed for his lectures at Harvard. Although he was intensely patriotic and championed the cause of American authorship, he did not believe that an American author must necessarily limit his or her writing to American themes. Thus, he justified his many years of attention to Spanish literature.

Because of his devotion to his subject, Ticknor worked at a leisurely pace on his *History of Spanish Literature*. In 1842 he wrote a letter to Washington Irving,

The library in Ticknor's Boston home

then the new minister to Spain from the United States, telling him about his project and asking him to facilitate Ticknor's attempt to secure manuscripts in Madrid. In late 1849 the first edition of Ticknor's *History of Spanish Literature* was published in three volumes by Harper in New York, while simultaneously in London, John Murray published a small edition. Gayangos's Spanish translation appeared in 1851. The work was extremely successful, and by 1863 an expanded third edition with revisions appeared. For the rest of his life Ticknor labored to enlarge and improve his major work.

Tickor's *History of Spanish Literature* reveals his belief in the distinctive character of the literature of Spain and its reflection of the political, social, and religious distinctions of its culture. While he is didactic in his approach to national literature, he also seeks to present its characteristic romantic lore. Exploring Spain's earliest writings, Ticknor discusses "The Poem of the Cid" as the oldest monument of Spanish poetry and illuminates the early ballads, which he considers the true basis of Spanish literature. He points to two outstanding traits in the earliest Spanish literature: "religious faith and knightly loyalty" expressed in the poetry as "an outpouring of the popular feeling and character." He discusses in great detail the chronicles of royalty and other national leaders. During the sixteenth century, according to Ticknor, historical chronicles were becoming passé, and for many years drama was forbidden. The Spaniards, however, had an extreme passion for romances of chivalry. Citing the alarming fanaticism for romances during the sixteenth century, Ticknor notes that Cervantes successfully wrote *Don Quixote* to counteract the negative effects of those romances. Although Ticknor criticizes some of the inconsistencies in *Don Quixote,* overall he regards it as a monumental work of genius. Toward the end of Ferdinand and Isabella's reign he perceives a disintegration in the courtly literature, a growth of intolerance among Spanish Christians, and the rise of the Inquisition. Ticknor's *Spanish Literature* is a detailed, impressive history that starts with the earliest Spanish literature and extends to the middle of the nineteenth century.

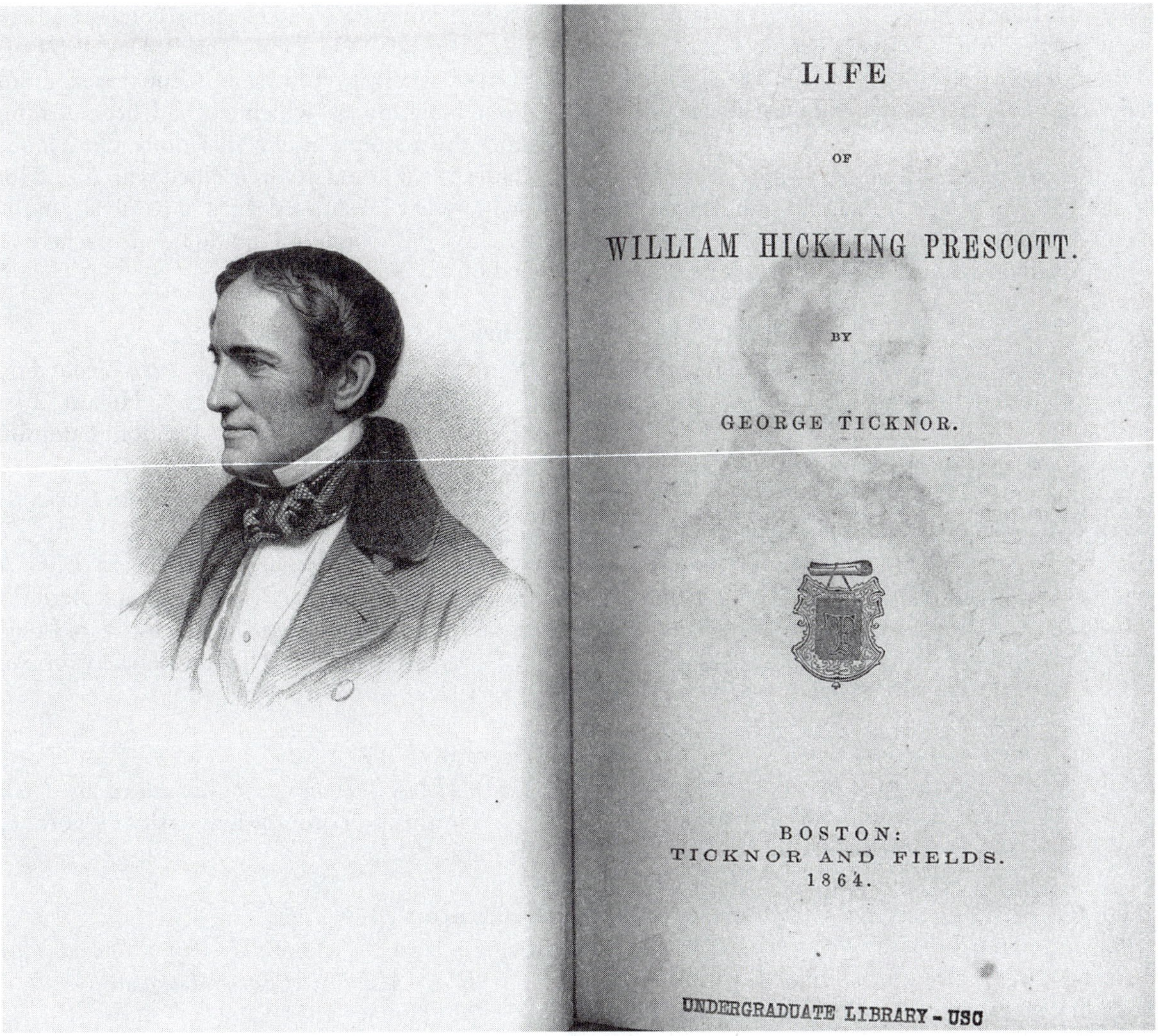

Frontispiece and title page for Ticknor's biography of a friend and fellow Harvard professor

Like his father, Ticknor was dedicated to public works and education. He was a member of the Boston Primary School Board and the treasurer for the Farm School for Boys. Most notably, he and Edward Everett were the prime movers for the establishment of the Boston Public Library, which the General Court of Massachusetts had authorized in 1848. Convinced especially by his trips to Europe of the importance of easy accessibility to great libraries, he wrote most of the 1852 planning report of the Trustees of the Boston Public Library. Countering Everett's fear that books would be damaged and lost, he proposed a free library and the purchase of multiple copies of popular books to encourage simultaneous readings of the same texts. With his own funds he purchased multiple copies of several inspirational works. Ticknor and Everett were both named to the Board of Trustees, and finally Everett agreed to give Ticknor's ideas a fair trial. Ticknor also proposed that library privileges be granted to well-behaved public school students and that library patrons be permitted to submit requests for book purchases. In the summer of 1856 Ticknor reluctantly agreed to journey to Europe to consult with library benefactor Joshua Bates. Traveling entirely at his own expense and refusing commissions for his book purchases, he and his family remained in Europe for fifteen months. After consulting with Bates for three months in London, Ticknor went to the Continent to purchase books. Finding Rome and Florence the most fertile markets for buying books, Ticknor and his family wintered in Rome. After his return home, he was appointed chairman of the committee to move books to the new library building. In April 1860 he donated 2,400 volumes to the library, and in October he donated a 143-volume collection on Molière. In October 1864 he gave the library 160 volumes of Provençal literature. Upon his death, he willed to the library his entire vast collection of Spanish books. After Everett's death, Ticknor was elected president of the Board of Trustees, but he resigned after one year, leaving the post to his friend Horatio Greenough.

Like Greenough, Ticknor was ambivalent about slavery. In 1852 in a letter to Sir Edmund Head, he described "the slavery question" as "the rock on which not only our Union may split, but our well-being and civilization may be endangered." Critical of Harriet Beecher Stowe's *Uncle Tom's Cabin* (1852), he believed that it would offend not only the slaveholders but also those who considered slavery evil, "the very class whom Mrs. Stowe should, both as a Christian woman and politician, have sustained and conciliated." He concluded that the book would "neither benefit the slaves nor advance the slave question one iota towards its solution." He wrote articles defending his friend Webster's defense of the Fugitive Slave Law and assailed abolitionists because he believed that abolition (in his opinion a heresy) would destroy the country and injure the blacks. He believed that the freed slaves, who, in his opinion, could never realize true equality because of "inherent and ineffaceable differences of character between the Anglo-Saxon and the black race," would be outcasts in the country, doomed people with no choice but "emigration or extermination." In his opinion, emancipation was unconstitutional.

Thus, the events of the Civil War dismayed Ticknor and his like-minded friends. They struggled against secession and met in December 1860 to discuss measures that they might take, including repeal of the Massachusetts law that prevented the return of fugitive slaves. Ticknor often entertained Southerners in his home, though he never doubted that the North would win the war and that the South, upon which "the blackness of thick darkness" rested, deserved "all they will suffer." The disasters of the Civil War and the assassination of President Abraham Lincoln horrified him.

In spite of Ticknor's despairing vision of the disintegration of America, his biographers report that generally his later years were serene and his intellect undiminished. During the war he wrote a biography of his friend Prescott. It was published in Boston in 1864 and received an enthusiastic reception. He gave away many copies of it because he did not intend to profit from its sales. He continued to devote his efforts to the work of the Boston Public Library, as well as the Zoological Museum of Cambridge. He spent his last five summers in a charming cottage in Brookline, Massachusetts. On New Year's Day 1871 Ticknor received several visitors and conversed animatedly about biographies, which he had been reading, and about the dissolution of civilizations. On 2 January his children and grandchildren dined with him. However, on 3 January he showed signs of paralysis; in the ensuing days his condition gradually worsened, and he died on 26 January.

Letters:

Life, Letters, and Journals of George Ticknor, edited by Anna Eliot Ticknor and George S. Hillard, 2 volumes (Boston: Osgood, 1876; London: Sampson Low, Marston, Searle & Rivington, 1876);

West Point in 1826, edited by H. Pelham Curtis (Boston, 1886);

Briefwechsel König Johann von Sachsen mit Georg Ticknor, edited by Johann Georg (Leipzig & Berlin, 1920);

Letters to Pascual de Gayangos, edited by Clara Louisa Penney (New York: Hispanic Society of America, 1927).

Biography:

George Ticknor's Travels in Spain, edited by George T. Northrup (Toronto: University of Toronto Studies, 1913).

References:

Richard Ford, "Ticknor's *History of Spanish Literature,*" *Eclectic Magazine of Foreign Literature, Science, and Art,* 22 (January 1851): 1–24;

Thomas R. Hart Jr., "George Ticknor's *History of Spanish Literature:* The New England Background," *PMLA,* 69 (March 1954): 76–88;

Thomas S. Perry, "Life, Letters, and Journals of George Ticknor," *Lippincott's Magazine,* 17 (May 1876): 629–634;

David B. Tyack, *George Ticknor and the Boston Brahmins* (Cambridge, Mass.: Harvard University Press, 1967).

Papers:

The most significant collection of George Ticknor manuscripts is on deposit in the Dartmouth College Library Archives. Other important sources are the Massachusetts Historical Library, the Rare Books Room of the Boston Public Library, Houghton Library at Harvard, and the Harvard University Archives.

Henry Ware Jr.

(21 April 1794 – 22 September 1843)

Susan L. Roberson
Alabama State University

BOOKS: *A Poem Pronounced at Cambridge, February 23, 1815, at the Celebration of Peace Between the United States and Great Britain* (Cambridge, Mass.: Printed by Hilliard & Metcalf, 1815);

A Sermon, Preached at the Interment of the Rev. Thomas Prentiss, Minister of the Second Congregational Church and Society in Charlestown; Who Died Oct. 5, 1817, in the 25th Year of His Age (Charlestown, Mass.: Printed by Samuel Etheridge, 1817);

A Sermon Delivered at Dorchester, Before the Evangelical Missionary Society in Massachusetts, at Their Semi Annual Meeting, June 7, 1820 (Boston: J. W. Burditt, 1820);

Two Letters on the Genuineness of the Verse, 1 John, v. 7, and on the Scriptural Argument for Unitarianism; Addressed to Rev. Alexander M'Leod (Boston: J. W. Burditt, 1820);

Two Letters to the Rev. Alexander McLeod, D.D., Pastor of the Reformed Presbyterian Church, Containing Remarks upon the Texts from Which He Preached on the Evenings of April 30 and May 7 (New York: Printed by C. S. Van Winkle, 1820);

Two Discourses Containing the History of the Old North and New Brick Churches, United as the Second Church in Boston: Delivered May 20, 1821, at the Completion of a Century from the Dedication of the Present Meeting-House in Middle-Street (Boston: J. W. Burditt, 1821);

Three Important Questions Answered, Relating to the Christian Name, Character, and Hopes (New York: New York Unitarian Book Society, 1822; Bristol: W. Brown, 1825); also published as *A Sermon, Preached at Amherst, N.H. on Lord's Day, August 4, 1822* (Amherst, N.H.: Luther Roby, 1822);

The Criminality of Intemperance: An Address Delivered at the Eleventh Anniversary of the Massachusetts Society for the Suppression of Intemperance (Boston: Printed by Phelps & Farnham, 1823);

Hints on Extemporaneous Preaching (Boston: Cummings, Hilliard, 1824; London: E. Rainford, 1830);

The Recollections of Jotham Anderson, Minister of the Gospel (Boston: Christian Register Office, 1824);

The Vision of Liberty: Recited Before the Phi Beta Kappa Society of Harvard University (Boston: Oliver Everett, 1824);

Discourses on the Offices and Character of Jesus Christ (Boston: Office of the Christian Register, 1825);

The Faith Once Delivered to the Saints (Boston: American Unitarian Association Tracts, 1825);

A Sermon Delivered at the Ordination of the Rev. William Henry Furness, as Pastor of the First Congregational Unitarian Church in Philadelphia, January 12, 1825 (Philadelphia: Abraham Small, 1825; Liverpool: F. B. Wright / London: C. Fox, 1825);

A Sermon, Preached at the Dedication of the Second Congregational Church in Northampton, Dec. 7, 1825 (Northampton, Mass.: Printed by T. Watson Shepard, 1825; Liverpool: F. B. Wright, 1825);

To the Ursa Major (N.p., 1825?);

A Sermon on Small Sins (Boston: Nathaniel S. Simpkins, 1827);

An Address, Delivered at Kennebunk Before the York County Unitarian Association, October 24, 1827 (Kennebunk, Me.: Printed by James K. Remich, 1828);

A Farewell Address, to the Second Church and Society in Boston, Delivered October 4, 1830 (Boston: Printed by Isaac R. Butts, 1830);

The Connexion between the Duties of the Pulpit and the Pastoral Office: An Introductory Address Delivered to the Members of the Theological School in Cambridge, October 18 and 25, 1830 (Cambridge, Mass.: Hilliard & Brown, 1830);

The Duty of Improvement: A New Year's Sermon (Boston, 1831; London: John Mardon, 1831);

On the Formation of the Christian Character, Addressed to Those Who Are Seeking to Lead a Religious Life (Boston: Gray & Bowen / Cambridge, Mass.: Hilliard & Brown, 1831);

The Combination against Intemperance Explained and Justified: An Address Delivered before the Cambridge Temperance Society, March 27, 1832 (Cambridge, Mass.: Hilliard & Brown, 1832);

Outline of the Testimony of Scripture Against the Trinity (Boston: Gray & Bowen, 1832);

The Life of the Saviour (Cambridge, Mass.: Brown, Shattuck / Boston: Hilliard, Gray, 1833);

A Sermon Delivered at the Ordination of Rev. Chandler Robbins, over the Second Congregational Church in Boston, December 4, 1833 (Boston: J. W. Burditt, 1833);

The Promise of Universal Peace: A Sermon Preached in the Chapel of Harvard University, Lord's Day, Dec. 15, 1833 (Boston: Russell, Odiorne & Metcalf, 1834);

Memoir of the Rev. Nathan Parker, D. D., Late Pastor of the South Church and Parish in Portsmouth, N. H. (Portsmouth: J. W. Foster and J. F. Shores / Boston: J. Munroe, 1835);

Sober Thoughts on the State of the Times, Addressed to the Unitarian Community (Boston: Isaac R. Butts, 1835);

On the Use and Meaning of the Phrase "Holy Spirit" (Boston: American Unitarian Association, 1836);

The Duties of Young Men in Respect to the Dangers of the Country (Cambridge, Mass.: Metcalf, Torry & Ballou, 1837?);

Education the Business of Life: Two Discourses Preached in the Chapel of Harvard University, on the Last Sabbath of the Academical Year, 16. July, 1837 (Cambridge, Mass.: Metcalf, Torry & Ballou, 1837);

The Feast of Tabernacles: A Poem for Music (Cambridge, Mass.: J. Owen, 1837);

The Nature, Reality and Power of Christian Faith (Boston: American Unitarian Association, 1837);

The Object and Means of the Christian Ministry: a Sermon, Preached at the Ordination of the Rev. Cyrus A. Bartol, as Junior Pastor of the West Church in Boston, Wednesday, March 1, 1837 (Cambridge, Mass.: Folsom, Wells & Thurston, 1837);

The Duty of Promoting Christianity by the Circulation of Books: A Discourse Delivered Before the Unitarian Book and Pamphlet Society, at the Annual Meeting, May 31, 1838 (Boston: Book and Pamphlet Society, 1838);

The Law of Honor: A Discourse, Occasioned by the Recent Duel in Washington, Delivered March 4, 1838, in the Chapel of Harvard University, and in the West Church, Boston (Cambridge, Mass.: Folsom, Wells & Thurston, 1838);

The Personality of the Deity; a Sermon, Preached in the Chapel of Harvard University, September 23, 1838 (Boston: J. Munroe, 1838);

How to Spend a Day (Boston: American Unitarian Association, 1839; London: J. Green, 1840);

A Discourse Preached at the Ordination of Mr. Robert C. Waterston, as a Minister at Large, Nov. 24, 1839 (Boston: Isaac R. Butts, 1840);

Thoughts for the New Year on the Duty of Improvement (Boston: American Unitarian Association, 1840);

Christ the Head of the Church: a Sermon Delivered at the Installation of the Rev. Edmund H. Sears, in Lancaster, Mass., December 23, 1840 (Boston: J. Munroe, 1841);

A Letter to Nehemiah Adams, Occasioned by His Sermon Entitled 'Injuries Done to Christ,' by a Unitarian (Boston: Christian Register Office, 1841);

Sermon. The Moral Principle of the Temperance Movement. A Sermon Preached in the Chapel of Harvard College, October 17, 1841 (N.p., 1841?);

Small Sins (Boston: American Unitarian Association, 1843);

Unitarianism, the Doctrine of Matthew's Gospel (Boston: American Unitarian Association, 1843);

Memoirs of the Rev. Noah Worcester, D. D. (Boston: J. Munroe, 1844);

David Ellington. By Henry Ware, Jr. With Other Extracts from His Writings (Boston: W. Crosby & H. P. Nichols, 1846);

Progress of the Christian Life; being a Sequel to "The Formation of the Christian Character" (Boston: J. Munroe, 1847);

Correspondence Relative to the Prospects of Christianity, and the Means of Promoting its Reception in India (Cambridge, Mass.: Hilliard & Metcalf, 1849).

Collection: *The Works of Henry Ware, Jr., D. D.,* 4 volumes, edited by Chandler Robbins (Boston: J. Munroe / London: Chapman, 1846–1847).

OTHER: *Christian Disciple and Theological Review,* edited by Ware (1819–1823);

John Emery Abbot, *Sermons by the Late Rev. John Emery Abbot, of Salem, Mass.; with a Memoir of His Life, by Henry Ware* (Boston: Wait, Greene, 1829).

SELECTED PERIODICAL PUBLICATIONS–UNCOLLECTED: "Sacred Music," *Christian Examiner,* 3 (November–December 1826): 489–498;

"Church Music," *Christian Examiner,* 4 (January–February 1827): 67–77;

"Present Movements Respecting Intemperance," *Christian Examiner,* 12 (May 1832): 243–257;

"An Address Delivered before the Ministerial Conference in Berry Street, May 27, 1835," *Christian Examiner,* 19 (September 1835): 98–108.

Henry Ware Jr. was one of the most influential leaders of the Unitarian Church at a time of much religious and literary activity in New England. An active proponent of Unitarianism and the model of the ideal parish minister, he was a mentor for young men who were entering the ministry, including Ralph Waldo Emerson. As the first professor of pulpit eloquence and pastoral care at the Harvard Divinity School from 1830 to 1840 and then Parkman Professor until 1842, Ware influenced and guided the next generation of Unitarian ministers. A man of considerable energy despite his chronic ill health, he wrote extensively in a variety of genres, including sermons and devotional pieces, fiction, poetry, and hymns, and he took a leading role in several social reform organizations, all the while maintaining the strength of character that won many people to him and his cause, the religious life. David Robinson remarked in *The Unitarians and the Universalists* (1985) that Ware's work "is the best single refutation of the commonplace historical assumption that Unitarianism was a public, rational, and emotionally cold religion."

Henry Ware Jr. was born on 21 April 1794 to Henry and Mary Clarke Ware (who died in 1805) in Hingham, Massachusetts, where his father was the village minister. Born to a family of much devotion and talent, young Henry was not the only Ware to achieve distinction. His father was named Hollis Professor of Divinity at Harvard College in 1805, marking a shift in the theology school toward liberalism in religion, and his brother William ministered to the Unitarian church in New York City and wrote several popular novels, including *Zenobia* (1837). His brother John was one of the leading American physicians and later became his

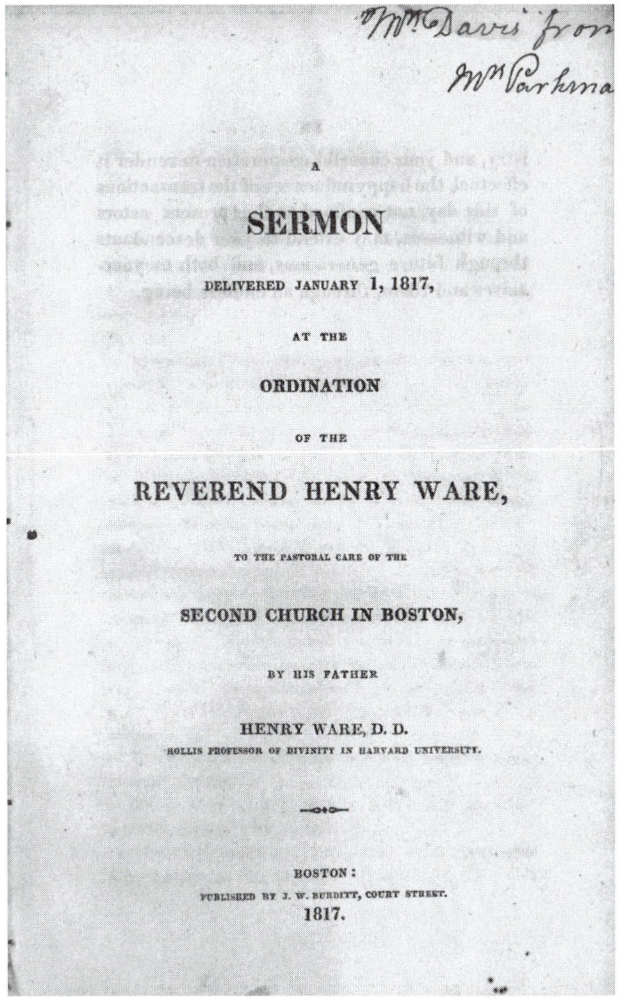
A
SERMON
DELIVERED JANUARY 1, 1817,
AT THE
ORDINATION
OF THE
REVEREND HENRY WARE,
TO THE PASTORAL CARE OF THE
SECOND CHURCH IN BOSTON,
BY HIS FATHER
HENRY WARE, D. D.
HOLLIS PROFESSOR OF DIVINITY IN HARVARD UNIVERSITY.
BOSTON:
PUBLISHED BY J. W. BURDITT, COURT STREET.
1817.

Title page for the sermon Ware's father delivered at his son's installation as minister of the Boston church once served by Increase and Cotton Mather (Collection of Joel Myerson)

biographer. After being schooled partly at home and partly in private and public schools, Ware attended Phillips Academy in Andover, Massachusetts, until he was admitted into the freshman class at Harvard in 1808, during which time he resided with his family in Cambridge. After his graduation in 1812, he was engaged as an assistant at Phillips Academy in Exeter, New Hampshire, for two years and decided to pursue a ministerial career. In *Memoir of the Life of Henry Ware, Jr.* (1846) his brother John remarks of this period, "I doubt if there were any equal portion of his life, in which so distinct a progress and development of character were to be noticed." Ware returned to Harvard in 1814 to finish his theological studies and was approbated to preach on 31 July 1815. After preaching in a variety of places, he was ordained at the Second Church of Boston on 1 January 1817, with his father preaching the ordination sermon.

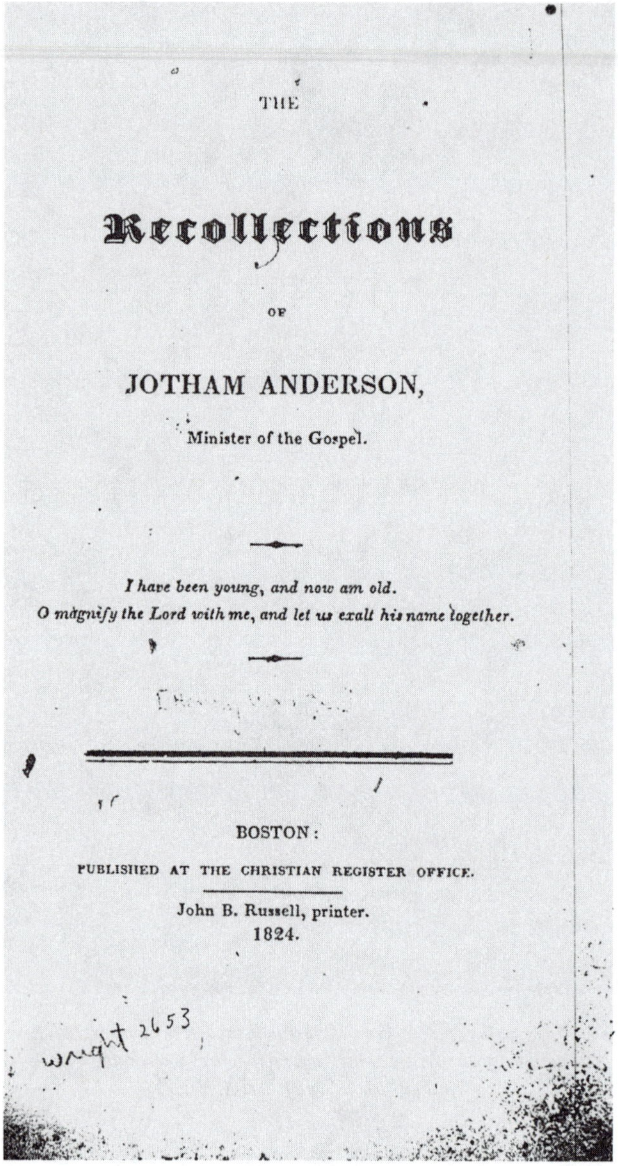
THE

Recollections

OF

JOTHAM ANDERSON,

Minister of the Gospel.

I have been young, and now am old.
O magnify the Lord with me, and let us exalt his name together.

BOSTON:

PUBLISHED AT THE CHRISTIAN REGISTER OFFICE.

John B. Russell, printer.
1824.

wright 2653

Title page for the work of fiction Ware based on his experiences as a young man

Once the church of Increase and Cotton Mather, the Second Church in 1817 had one of the smallest congregations and was the least opulent of the Unitarian churches in Boston. But during the years that Ware ministered to it, the Second Church experienced a religious awakening that ushered in "another golden age," according to Chandler Robbins, a successor of Ware. A popular preacher, Ware emphasized the role of pastoral care and the need for a personal acquaintance with the members of his parish, noting in his farewell address in 1830 "that the private duties of personal and pastoral intercourse are, at least, as important as the public exercises of the pulpit, and in fact necessary to their efficiency and success." He also exerted himself on behalf of the young people of his parish, establishing a Sunday School in the northern section of town and meeting regularly with the young men of his congregation. In addition to his ministerial duties, Ware was involved in the Association for Mutual Religious Improvement, formed to provide religious instruction to the poorer classes in Boston, and from 1819 to 1823 served as the editor of the *Christian Disciple and Theological Review,* which was renamed the *Christian Examiner* in 1824. He was a frequent contributor to the *Christian Examiner.*

All of his exertions, however, wore on his health, and he suffered from a variety of infirmities, including headaches and chest pains. His wife, Elizabeth Watson Waterhouse Ware, whom he had married in October 1817, also suffered a decline in health and died on 9 February 1824 at age thirty, leaving Ware with two young children. In a letter to his sister he wrote, "The event sets me adrift in the world, breaks up my plans, and changes my whole lot." Nonetheless, he continued to work, publishing *Hints on Extemporaneous Preaching* (1824), in which he declares that in extemporaneous preaching "there is more natural warmth in the declamation, more earnestness in the address, greater animation in the manner, more of the lighting up of the soul." He also published a fictional piece, *The Recollections of Jotham Anderson, Minister of the Gospel* (1824), a sentimental, loosely autobiographical story of the religious trials and tribulations of its narrator. In 1825 his *Discourses on the Offices and Character of Jesus Christ* was published; in it he asserts that Jesus is the "prime and only sufficient Teacher" of Christianity and points to Jesus' roles as messiah, mediator, savior, and high priest.

That same year Ware was much involved in the formation of the American Unitarian Association. In 1827 he married Mary Lovell Pickard, with whom he went on to have six children; he was also actively involved with recruiting young men to the ranks of the ministry and raising money to help offset the cost of a Harvard education for them through a series of public lectures on the geography of Palestine. Ware's concern for recruiting and educating men for the ministry also prompted him to propose a school (later established as the Meadville Theological School) for those distanced from Harvard by geography, education, and money. John Ware writes of his brother: "He was probably at no period of his life more busily engaged in every method of exertion, than during this season. He was literally crowded with occupation of every kind."

Ware suffered a relapse in health when he was exposed to the elements on a trip in May 1828 from Boston to Northampton. He suffered severe inflammation of the lungs and was bedridden for more than six weeks. During his convalescence, plans were made to establish a professorship at Harvard for him. Upon his return to Boston, he offered his letter of resignation to the Second Church, but rather than part with him, the congregation decided to appoint a colleague pastor to take up the active duties of ministering to the church. They settled on Emerson, who had for some time supplied the pulpit, and he was ordained on 11 March 1829. On 1 April, Ware and his wife sailed for Europe in an attempt to regain his health; they remained abroad until August 1830, at which time he tendered his resignation, leaving the care of the church in Emerson's hands.

In October 1830 Ware joined his father on the faculty of the new Divinity School that the elder Ware had helped to establish at Harvard. In his introductory remarks to the students on 18 and 25 October, Ware stressed the need for training in both eloquence and pastoral care: "The minister is the better preacher for having his heart warmed by intercourse with his hearers in private; and he goes to them in private with the greater influence and effect, because he carries with him the sacredness and sanction of the pulpit." He defined pulpit eloquence as "the power and habit to select judiciously, arrange clearly, and express forcibly and fervently, the topics suited to the pulpit, and to utter them in that distinct, correct, and pleasant elocution, which shall insure for them the attention of the people." In subsequent lectures to the students on homiletics, he recommended the use of narrative, anecdote, and analogy, but warned against references to the arts and to common life as too profane. Indeed, he had earlier complained that Emerson cited Scripture too little, prompting Emerson to respond on 30 December 1826: "I have affected generally a mode of illustration rather bolder than the usage of our preaching warrants." Pastoral care, Ware told his Harvard students, is "that duty toward individuals and families which consists in personal acquaintance and intercourse for the purpose of knowing the character and condition of the flock, that so the minister may be ready to seize opportunities of usefulness among them."

As Ware's comments indicate, he was concerned with touching people's affections to bring them to the religious life. Adapting his method of ministering and his inclination toward spontaneity to teaching, he preferred conversation with his students to lectures. He explained in a letter of 7 March 1830, "I have turned the exercise of extempore preaching into an extempore discussion, which acts much like a conference meeting. I propose a subject, of a practical character rather than speculative; four speak upon it from the pulpit in order; then all are at liberty to speak from their places. It proves interesting, and I flatter myself it tends to promote personal religion." He also opened his home to students, regularly inviting them to tea or breakfast to

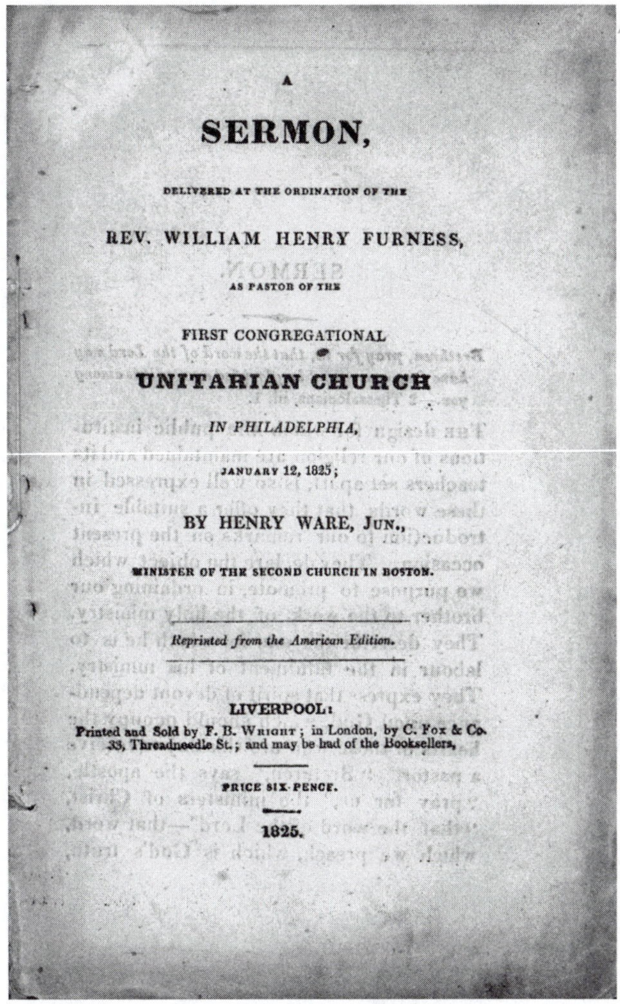
A

SERMON,

DELIVERED AT THE ORDINATION OF THE

REV. WILLIAM HENRY FURNESS,

AS PASTOR OF THE

FIRST CONGREGATIONAL

UNITARIAN CHURCH

IN PHILADELPHIA,

JANUARY 12, 1825;

BY HENRY WARE, JUN.,

MINISTER OF THE SECOND CHURCH IN BOSTON.

Reprinted from the American Edition.

LIVERPOOL:

Printed and Sold by F. B. WRIGHT; in London, by C. Fox & Co. 33, Threadneedle St.; and may be had of the Booksellers.

PRICE SIX-PENCE.

1825.

Title page for Ware's ordination sermon for a fellow clergyman and author (Collection of Joel Myerson)

more intimately discuss their progress. His brother John quotes Robbins, who had been a student of Ware: "As a Teacher, Mr. Ware's principal aim seemed to be, not so much to impart knowledge, as to provoke and elicit thought." Though the professorship was meant to ease Ware's exertions and increase his health, Ware continued to push himself and was plagued for the rest of his life with bouts of illness.

In addition to his assigned duties at Harvard, Ware was a zealous proponent of many religious and social causes such as the students' Philanthropic Society, the Cambridge Temperance Society, religious publications for young people, and the Anti-Slavery Society of Cambridge, which he helped form, serving as its president. As he made clear in an essay on intemperance for the *Christian Examiner* (May 1832), his methods for bringing about reform, while energetic, were fairly conservative and of the type to be expected by a man of religion: "*Our object, Reform; our means, Moral Influence.*"

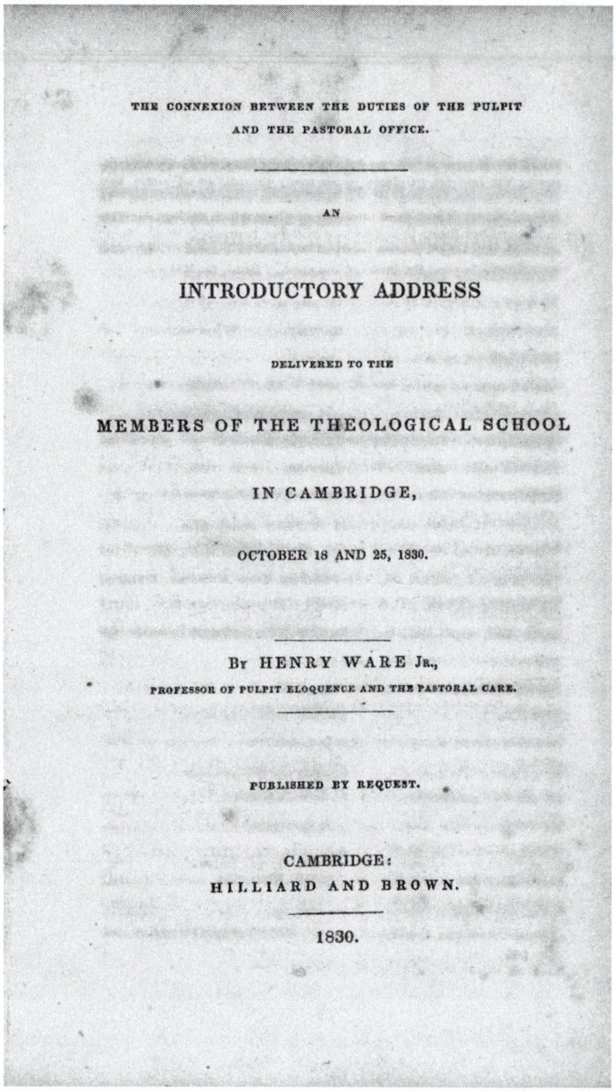

THE CONNEXION BETWEEN THE DUTIES OF THE PULPIT AND THE PASTORAL OFFICE.

AN

INTRODUCTORY ADDRESS

DELIVERED TO THE

MEMBERS OF THE THEOLOGICAL SCHOOL

IN CAMBRIDGE,

OCTOBER 18 AND 25, 1830.

BY HENRY WARE JR.,

PROFESSOR OF PULPIT ELOQUENCE AND THE PASTORAL CARE.

PUBLISHED BY REQUEST.

CAMBRIDGE:
HILLIARD AND BROWN.

1830.

Title page for Ware's remarks on becoming the first professor of pulpit eloquence and pastoral care at Harvard Divinity School (Collection of Joel Myerson)

Even so, his antislavery activities, though by no means those of a radical abolitionist, met with considerable criticism. In his biography John Ware comments, "It was reported, and believed by many, that the Government of the College had expressly made his silence in this matter a condition of his continuance in his office."

During his ten-year tenure as a professor, Ware continued to write. The most important publication was *On the Formation of the Christian Character* (1831), a manual on personal religion that promoted self-culture, one of the keystones of Unitarian practice. The book went through fifteen editions of a thousand copies each in the United States and also sold well in Great Britain. Its effect on readers was tremendous; as Ware noted in a letter to his wife, "They speak to me of it with tears in their eyes." In the book he wrote that "Men need to be made sensible that religion is a personal thing, a matter of personal application and experience," and he outlined means of raising the religious affections through reading, meditation, prayer, preaching, the acquisition of appropriate habits, and self-discipline. He planned to follow with a sequel, *Progress of the Christian Life* (1847), which remained unfinished and was published posthumously. The extant chapters warn Christians against complacency and urge continued religious self-cultivation. Concerned with the state of religion in America, in 1835 he published *Sober Thoughts on the State of the Times,* in which he reviewed the ideas of Unitarianism and urged Unitarians to be true to the principles of the Reformation.

Then in 1838 Emerson gave his Divinity School address and shook the Unitarian community, Ware among them. Following the address Ware and Emerson met to discuss it and carried on a correspondence that remained friendly despite their difference of opinions. Ware wrote on 15 July 1838, "On this account, I look with anxiety and no little sorrow to the course which your mind has been taking." Ware's more formal response came in September in the form of a sermon, *The Personality of the Deity* (1838), one of a three-part series of sermons on the Deity that Ware had already planned. The first two sermons took up the "Existence of the Deity" and "The Divine Perfections," and Ware followed with sermons on miracles, the character and progress of Christianity, and obedience. In *The Personality of the Deity* Ware argued that "to exclude personality from the idea of God, is, in effect, to destroy the object of worship, and thus to annihilate that essential duty of religion." He used the analogy of the orphan to bring home his point that without "the Father of the universe" we are "but a company of children in an orphan asylum." Emerson's Transcendentalist position seemed to Ware to threaten the authority of Christianity and to undermine the entire religious project, and, as William R. Hutchison points out in *The Transcendentalist Ministers* (1959), the sermon makes implicit references to Emerson's address even if Ware did not directly refer to it. Urged by his friends to publish the sermon, Ware first sent a copy of it to Emerson, commenting to his young friend, "I confess, that I esteem it particularly unhappy to be thus brought into a sort of public opposition to you; for I have a thousand feelings which draw me toward you." An anonymous reviewer for the *Christian Examiner* (November 1838) said of *The Personality of the Deity,* "It is good; it is seasonable," and praised Ware's style as "simple, manly, straight forward."

Continuing to be plagued by the weakness of his body that had left him unable to read or write in 1836, Ware resigned from his professorial duties in 1842 and retired to Hingham, Massachusetts, where he died on 22 September 1843, "worn down by . . . exertion, both of body and mind," according to his biographer. He was, as fellow minister and writer James Freeman Clarke put it, "a man of rare religious genius" and, as Robinson posits in *Apostle of Culture: Emerson as Preacher and Lecturer* (1982), "second only to Dr. Channing in popular esteem." After his death, Robbins collected and edited Ware's writings into four volumes. He included not only the major works but much of the poetry, fiction, and miscellaneous writings. The poetry tends toward the sentimental and familiar, with many of the poems addressed to specific people or occasions and leaning toward the patriotic and religious. His major poetic endeavor, "My Dream of Life," a poetical autobiography in the fashion of William Wordsworth, remained unfinished. Reviewing the collection for the *Christian Examiner* (May 1847), A. P. Peabody noted Ware's "versatility of talent,–of *manysidedness*" and commented of his sermons that "His style is unsurpassed in transparency. It is eminently pure and graceful" and that "all who heard him preach will so perpetually miss his eloquent presence and his impressive tone."

Biography:

John Ware, *Memoir of the Life of Henry Ware, Jr.*, 2 volumes, new edition (Boston: J. Munroe, 1846).

References:

Gary Collison, "'A True Toleration': Harvard Divinity School Students and Unitarianism, 1830–1859," in *American Unitarianism, 1805–1865,* edited by Conrad Edick Wright (Boston: Massachusetts Historical Society and Northeastern University Press, 1989), pp. 209–237;

George Willis Cooke, *Unitarianism in America: A History of Its Origins and Development* (Boston: American Unitarian Association, 1902);

Daniel Walker Howe, *The Unitarian Conscience: Harvard Moral Philosophy, 1805–1861* (Middletown, Conn.: Wesleyan University Press, 1970);

William R. Hutchison, *The Transcendentalist Ministers* (New Haven: Yale University Press, 1959);

David Robinson, *Apostle of Culture: Emerson as Preacher and Lecturer* (Philadelphia: University of Pennsylvania Press, 1982);

Robinson, "The Sermons of Ralph Waldo Emerson: An Introductory Historical Essay," in *The Complete Sermons of Ralph Waldo Emerson,* edited by Albert J. von Frank, volume 1 (Columbia: University of Missouri Press, 1989), pp. 1–32;

Robinson, *The Unitarians and the Universalists* (Westport, Conn.: Greenwood Press, 1985).

Papers:

There are five boxes of Henry Ware Jr.'s papers in the Harvard University Archives at Pusey Library, including sermons and personal correspondence, and the Andover-Harvard Theological Library at the Harvard Divinity School has some additional letters and miscellaneous manuscripts. The Massachusetts Historical Society has manuscripts in the records of the Second Church of Boston.

William Ware

(3 August 1797 – 19 February 1852)

Noelle A. Baker
University of Wisconsin Oshkosh

BOOKS: *A Sermon on the Communion: Preached, March 6, 1825, in the First Congregational Church in the City of New-York . . . Published at the Request of the Trustees* (New York: Clayton & Van Norden, 1825);

Address, Delivered at the Laying of the Corner Stone of the Second Congregational Unitarian Church, At the Corner of Prince and Mercer Sts., New-York, November 24, 1825 (New York?: Printed by John Tryon, 1825);

Three Sermons, Illustrative of the Principles of Unitarian Christianity, Preached in Utica, on Sunday, the 12th, of October, 1828 . . . Published by Request (Utica, N.Y.: Northway & Porter, 1828);

The Danger of Delay (Boston: Printed for the American Unitarian Association by Gray & Bowen, 1829);

The Antiquity and Revival of Unitarian Christianity (Boston: Printed for the American Unitarian Association by Gray & Bowen, 1831);

And They Shall Say, Every Man to His Neighbour, Wherefore Hath the Lord Done This unto This Great City? A Sermon, Preached on the Sunday Succeeding the Great Fire, Which Occurred on the Night of December the 16th, 1835 (New York: Charles S. Francis, 1835);

Letters of Lucius M. Piso, from Palmyra, to His Friend Marcus Curtius, at Rome. Now First Translated and Published, 2 volumes (New York: Charles S. Francis / Boston: Joseph H. Francis, 1837); republished as *Zenobia: Or the Fall of Palmyra. An Historical Romance. In Letters of Lucius M. Piso from Palmyra, to His Friend Marcus Curtius at Rome,* 2 volumes (New York: Charles S. Francis / Boston: Joseph H. Francis, 1838); republished as *Zenobia, Queen of the East; or, Letters from Palmyra,* as Lucius Manlius Piso, 2 volumes (London: Bentley, 1838); republished as *Palmyra: Being Letters of Lucius M. Piso, from Palmyra, to His Friend Marcus Curtius at Rome. Now First Translated and Published,* 2 volumes (Edinburgh: Chambers, 1839); republished as *Zenobia: Queen of Palmyra; a Tale of the Roman Empire in the Days of the Emperor Aurelian* (London: Warne, 1868); republished as *The Last Days and Fall of Palmyra, Being Letters of Lucius M. Piso, to His Friend, Marcus Curtius, at Rome. With a Preface by the Rev. Henry Allon, D.D.* (London & New York: Cassell, 1885);

Probus; or, Rome in the Third Century: In Letters of Lucius M. Piso from Rome, to Fausta, the Daughter of Gracchus, at Palmyra, 2 volumes (New York: Charles S. Francis / Boston: Joseph H. Francis, 1838); republished as *The Last Days of Aurelian; or, the Nazarenes of Rome: A Romance by the Author of "Zenobia, Queen of the East,"* 2 volumes (London: Bentley, 1838); republished as *Rome and the Early Christians: Being Letters of Lucius M. Piso, from Rome, to Fausta, the Daughter of Gracchus, at Palmyra* (Edinburgh: Chambers, 1840); republished as *Aurelian: or, Rome in the Third Century. In Letters of Lucius M. Piso from Rome, to Fausta, the Daughter of Gracchus, at Palmyra,* 2 volumes (New York: Charles S. Francis / Boston: Joseph H. Francis, 1848);

Julian: or, Scenes in Judea. By the Author of Letters from Palmyra and Rome, 2 volumes (New York: Charles S. Francis / Boston: Joseph H. Francis, 1841; London: Wiley, 1841);

Unitarianism the Doctrine of Matthew's Gospel (Boston: J. Munroe, 1843);

Righteousness before Doctrine: Two Sermons Preached on Sunday, March 16, 1845 . . . Printed by Request (Boston: Charles C. Little & James Brown, 1845);

Justification by Faith (Boston: Printed for the American Unitarian Association by William Crosby & H. P. Nichols, 1846);

Sketches of European Capitals (Boston: Phillips, Sampson, 1851);

Lectures on the Works and Genius of Washington Allston (Boston: Phillips, Sampson, 1852).

OTHER: "The Right Hand of Fellowship, and Address to the Society," in *A Sermon Delivered at the Ordination of the Rev. William Parsons Lunt: as Pastor of the Second Congregational Unitarian Society in the City of New York, June 19, 1828,* by F. W. P. Greenwood (New York: D. Felt, 1828), pp. 34–47;

"The Charge," in *The Spirit of Jesus: A Sermon Preached at the Installation of Rev. D. H. Barlow, in Brooklyn, New York, September 17, 1834 by W. H. Furness; with The Charge, The Right Hand of Fellowship, and The Address to the People* (Brooklyn, N.Y.: A. Spooner, 1834), pp. 16–22;

"A Memoir of Nathaniel Bacon," in *The Library of American Biography: Lives of John Sullivan, Jacob Leisler, Nathaniel Bacon, and John Mason,* edited by Jared Sparks, volume 3 (Boston: Charles C. Little & James Brown, 1844), pp. 239–306;

American Unitarian Biography: Memoirs of Individuals Who Have Been Distinguished by Their Writings, Character, and Efforts in the Cause of Liberal Christianity, edited by Ware, 2 volumes (Boston & Cambridge, Mass.: J. Munroe / London: E. T. Whitfield, 1850, 1851).

SELECTED PERIODICAL PUBLICATIONS–UNCOLLECTED: "Critical Notices," review of *Two Articles from the Princeton Review, Concerning the Transcendental Philosophy of the Germans, and of Cousin, and Its Influence on Opinion in This Country,* by James W. Alexander, Charles Hodge, and Albert B. Dod, anonymous, *Christian Examiner,* 28 (July 1840): 378–389;

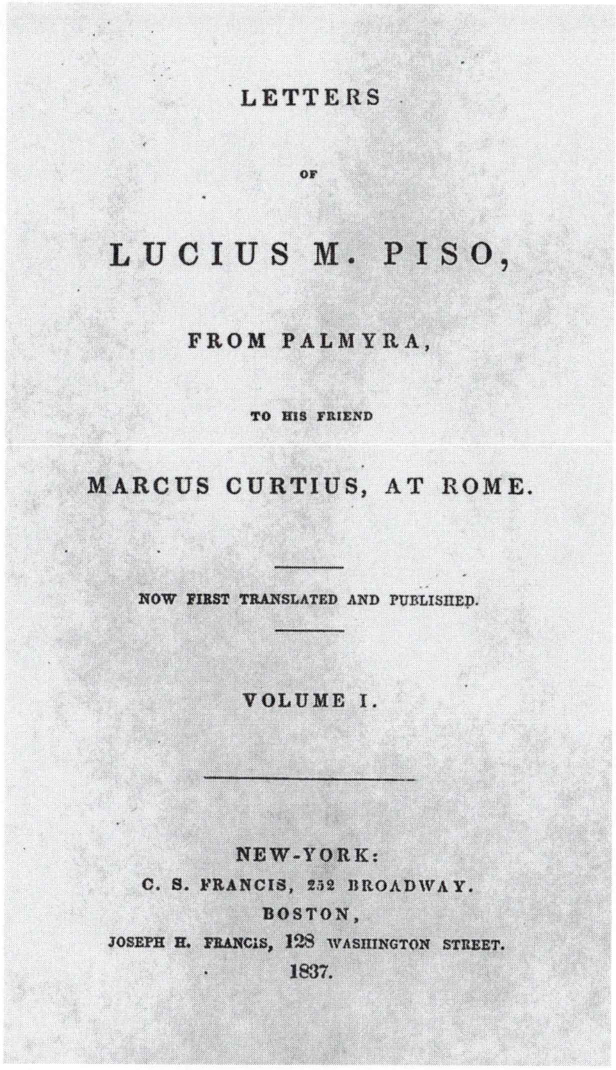

LETTERS

OF

LUCIUS M. PISO,

FROM PALMYRA,

TO HIS FRIEND

MARCUS CURTIUS, AT ROME.

NOW FIRST TRANSLATED AND PUBLISHED.

VOLUME I.

NEW-YORK:
C. S. FRANCIS, 252 BROADWAY.
BOSTON,
JOSEPH H. FRANCIS, 128 WASHINGTON STREET.
1837.

Title page for the first edition of Ware's novel, better known under its later title Zenobia, *about the queen of Palmyra who rebelled against the Roman emperor Aurelian*

"Poems on Slavery" [review of *Poems on Slavery,* by Henry Wadsworth Longfellow], anonymous, *Christian Examiner,* 33 (January 1843): 353–358;

"Jay's Results of Emancipation in the West Indies," anonymous, *Christian Examiner,* 33 (January 1843): 382–388;

"Discourses on Slavery" [review of *Two Discourses Occasioned by the Approaching Anniversary of the Declaration of Independence,* by William H. Furness; *A Sermon of Slavery,* by Theodore Parker; and *Caste and Slavery in the American Church,* by "A Churchman"], anonymous, *Christian Examiner,* 35 (September 1843): 128–130;

"Doctrinal Discourses" [review of *A Discourse, Embracing Several Important Objections to the Doctrine, "That Jesus Christ . . . Possesses Two Natures . . . ,"* by J. B. Pit-

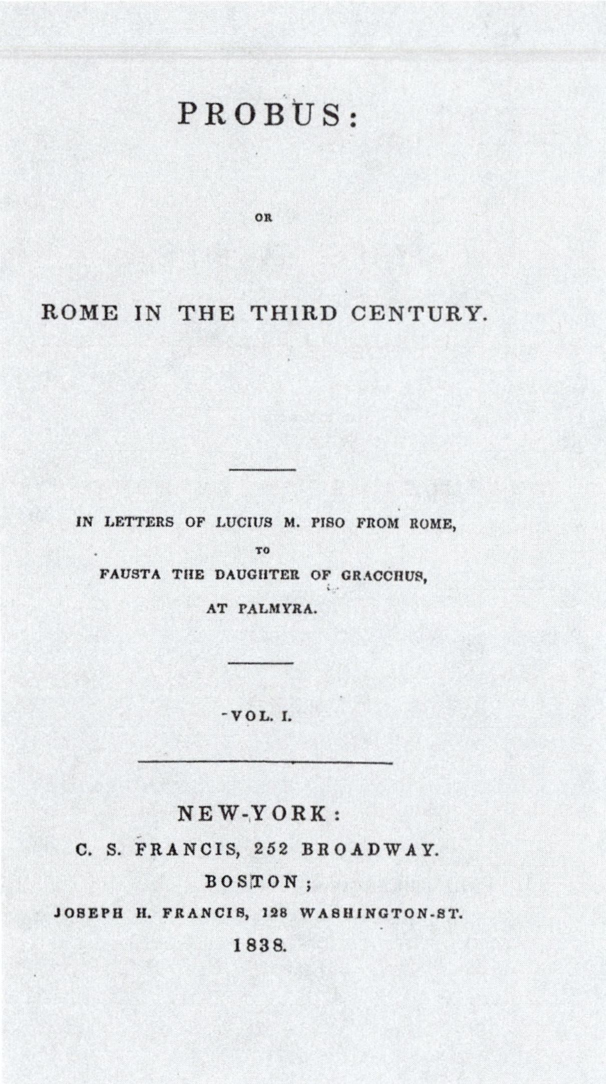

PROBUS:

OR

ROME IN THE THIRD CENTURY.

IN LETTERS OF LUCIUS M. PISO FROM ROME,

TO

FAUSTA THE DAUGHTER OF GRACCHUS,

AT PALMYRA.

VOL. I.

NEW-YORK:

C. S. FRANCIS, 252 BROADWAY.

BOSTON;

JOSEPH H. FRANCIS, 128 WASHINGTON-ST.

1838.

Title page for the sequel to Zenobia, *about the persecution of Christians in third-century Rome (Rice University Library)*

kin; *A Sermon Preached on Fast Day . . . ,* by George G. Ingersoll; *Our Faith. A Sermon . . . ,* by Christopher T. Thayer; and *"What Thinkest Thou?" A Sermon . . . ,* by Samuel Barrett], anonymous, *Christian Examiner,* 35 (January 1844): 385–393.

William Ware is best known as the pioneering New York Unitarian minister who left the pulpit in 1836 to write the three earliest popular American religious novels. While Ware was not a Transcendentalist, he represents the broad spectrum of liberal Unitarian thinking that fostered the Transcendentalism of Ralph Waldo Emerson, Theodore Parker, Frederic Henry Hedge, and George Ripley. In all three of his novels Ware stresses the humanity of Jesus and the intuitive nature of the religious sentiment, notions Parker and Emerson later took to a further extreme.

Born in Hingham, Massachusetts, on 3 August 1797, Ware was one of ten children of Henry Ware, minister of the First Unitarian Church, and Mary Clark Ware. His older brother, Henry Jr., went on to become pastor of the Second Unitarian Church of Boston, editor of the *Christian Disciple,* and a professor at Harvard Divinity School. Mary Ware died in 1805; that year the rest of the family moved to Cambridge, where Henry Ware Sr. became Hollis Professor of Divinity at Harvard. William prepared for college under the guidance of his cousin Ashur Ware, who later became a professor of Greek at Harvard, and the Reverend John Allyne of Duxbury, Massachusetts.

Ware spent four years at Harvard College, graduating in 1816, then returned to Hingham to study under the Reverend Henry Coleman, his father's successor at First Church, and to teach in the local school. In 1817 he entered Harvard Divinity School; during his three years there he taught at the Cambridge town school and assisted Andrews Norton, the Harvard College librarian. Ware began preaching in 1820, principally in Brooklyn, Connecticut; Burlington, Vermont; and, finally, New York City, where he was ordained on 18 December 1821 as pastor of the First Unitarian Church. He was the first Unitarian minister in the city.

On 10 June 1823 Ware married Mary Waterhouse, daughter of the prominent scientist Benjamin Waterhouse. The couple had seven children, four of whom survived their father. Ware's early published sermons include *A Sermon on the Communion: Preached, March 6, 1825, in the First Congregational Church in the City of New-York . . . Published at the Request of the Trustees* (1825); *Three Sermons, Illustrative of the Principles of Unitarian Christianity, Preached in Utica, on Sunday, the 12th, of October, 1828 . . . Published by Request* (1828); and *The Danger of Delay* (1829). In a letter of 18 February 1863 Ware's friend, Orville Dewey, wrote that soon after settling in New York, Ware declared that he had made a fatal "mistake for a life" in choosing the ministry. Henry Ware Jr. persuaded his brother not to retire, but William reiterated this sentiment frequently. He suffered from extreme self-consciousness when speaking before his congregation; both Dewey and Henry Ware Jr. remarked on the contrast between his dull and restrained sermons and his lively letters. He edited the *Unitarian* magazine from November 1827 to February 1828. In 1831 he published the pamphlet *The Antiquity and Revival of Unitarian Christianity,* in which he claims to find the tenets of Unitarianism expressed in the New Testament and in historical records from the third century to the nineteenth century. In this pamphlet Ware decries the "deadly hate and hostility" expressed in the

Trinitarian doctrine, which he associates with "superstition, prejudice and bigotry," and allies Unitarianism with the common people, courage, liberty, truth, and tolerance.

Ware published portions of his first novel as "Letters from Lucius M. Piso" in the *Knickerbocker Magazine* between March and May 1836. He resigned his position at the First Unitarian Church in October 1836 and moved to Brookline, Massachusetts. There he completed the novel, which was published as *Letters of Lucius M. Piso, from Palmyra, to His Friend Marcus Curtius, at Rome* in 1837; it was republished in 1838 as *Zenobia: Or the Fall of Palmyra. An Historical Romance. In Letters of Lucius M. Piso from Palmyra, to His Friend Marcus Curtius at Rome.* Ware's most popular novel, *Zenobia,* was republished under the titles *Zenobia, Queen of the East; or, Letters from Palmyra* (1838); *Palmyra: Being Letters of Lucius M. Piso, from Palmyra, to His Friend Marcus Curtius at Rome* (1839); *Zenobia: Queen of Palmyra; a Tale of the Roman Empire in the Days of the Emperor Aurelian* (1868); and *The Last Days and Fall of Palmyra, Being Letters of Lucius M. Piso, to His Friend, Marcus Curtius, at Rome* (1885). The novel is set in the third century, during the conflict between the Roman emperor Aurelian and the rebellious Queen Zenobia of the province of Palmyra in present-day Syria. Most of the characters are non-Christians, including Aurelian, Zenobia, her daughter Julia, her friends Gracchus and Fausta, the Platonic philosopher Longinus, and the noble Roman narrator, Lucius Manlius Piso. The only Christian figures, Probus and St. Thomas, contribute primarily to chapters devoted to the main characters' philosophical and religious investigations. The least anachronistic of Ware's novels, *Zenobia* nevertheless presents a thinly veiled exposition of nineteenth-century Unitarian thinking. Third-century Christianity is characterized by a Unitarian emphasis on tolerance, the unifying power of love, and a nonsectarian spirituality sustained by reason and historical evidence. Ware characterizes Jesus as human, albeit inspired with a divine mission, and the novel's most thoroughgoing Christian, St. Thomas, asserts that "in goodness, and faithfulness to the sense of duty, lies the chief good." Critics from John Stuart Mill to the present day have recognized a strong feminist strain in Ware's characterization of the queen and her militant friend, Fausta, both of whom fight in war alongside the men.

Ware assumed a ministerial post at the Second Congregational Church in Waltham, Massachusetts, in June 1837 but resigned in April 1838 and bought a small farm in Jamaica Plain. *Probus; or, Rome in the Third Century: In Letters of Lucius M. Piso from Rome, to Fausta, the Daughter of Gracchus, at Palmyra,* the sequel to *Zenobia,* was published in two volumes in June 1838. *Probus* is a Christian martyr tale: the narrator, Piso, has married

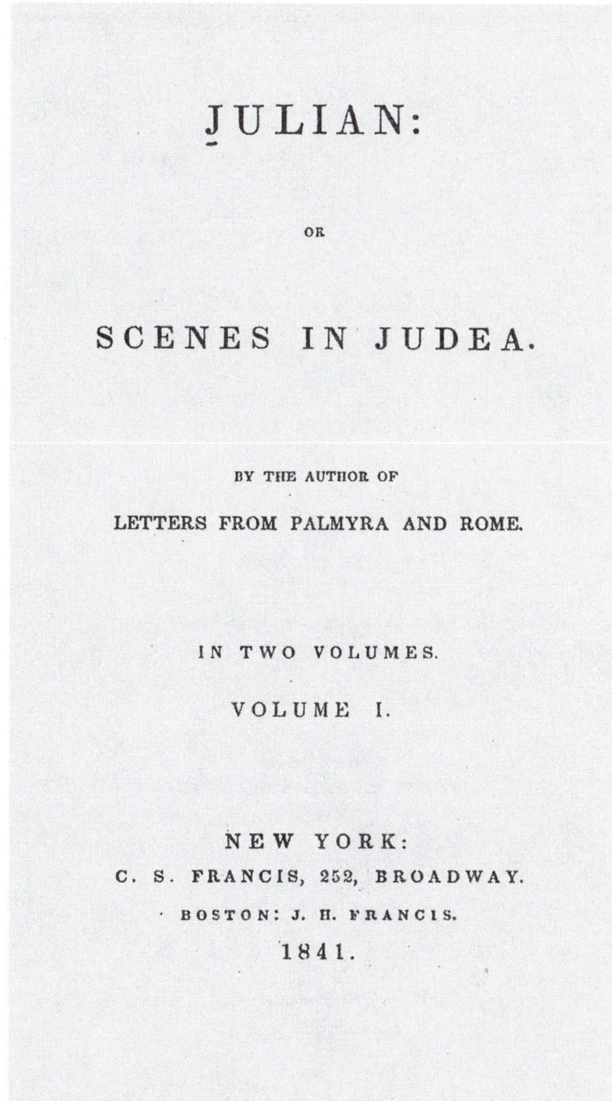
JULIAN:

OR

SCENES IN JUDEA.

BY THE AUTHOR OF

LETTERS FROM PALMYRA AND ROME.

IN TWO VOLUMES.

VOLUME I.

NEW YORK:

C. S. FRANCIS, 252, BROADWAY.

BOSTON: J. H. FRANCIS.

1841.

Title page for Ware's novel about a Roman Jew who investigates the life of Jesus (Rice University Library)

Julia, and both have become Christians; they suffer Aurelian's brutal persecution, along with the novel's other Christian characters, Probus, Macer, and Felix. Macer and Felix represent immoderate and sectarian modes of Christianity that divide the faithful and only accelerate the persecution, torture, and execution of Christians by the pagan Roman populace. Probus, who resembles the Unitarian clergyman William Ellery Channing in his theology, attempts to explain Christianity to Aurelian without success. All the major characters except Piso and Julia die for their faith. *Probus* also includes Ware's strongest fictional statements about the evils of slavery. The ideological similarities between 1830s Boston and third-century Rome are even more apparent in this novel than in its predecessor.

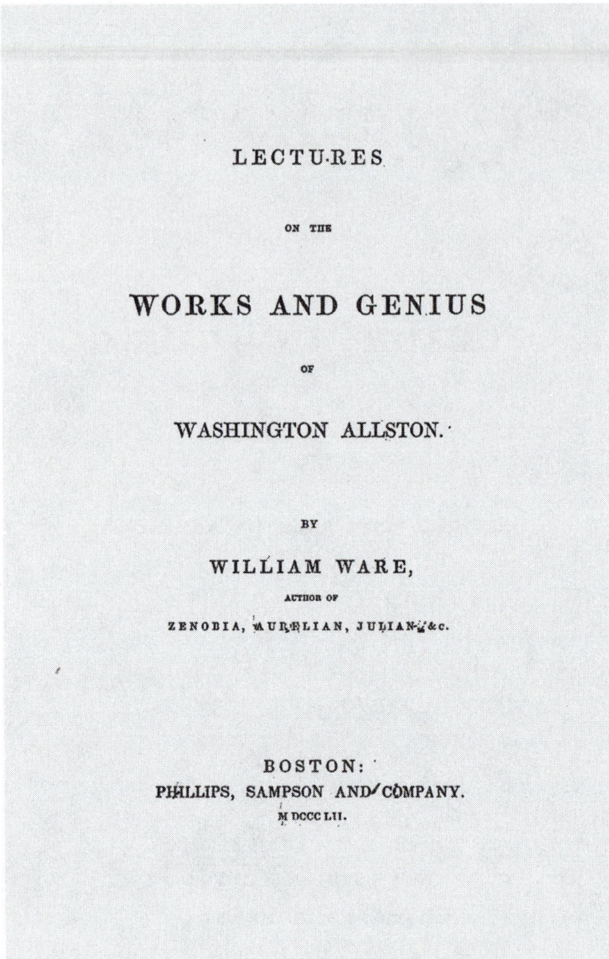
LECTURES

ON THE

WORKS AND GENIUS

OF

WASHINGTON ALLSTON.

BY

WILLIAM WARE,

AUTHOR OF

ZENOBIA, AURELIAN, JULIAN, &c.

BOSTON:

PHILLIPS, SAMPSON AND COMPANY.

M DCCC LII.

Title page for Ware's posthumously published analysis of the Romantic painter

In July 1839 Ware moved back to Cambridge and became the proprietor and editor of *The Christian Examiner.* During his tenure Ware increased the number of book reviews and critical notices of American and foreign periodicals and enlarged the poetry section. He rebuked Emerson for pantheism in his review of James W. Alexander, Charles Hodge, and Albert B. Dod's *Two Articles from the Princeton Review, Concerning the Transcendental Philosophy of the Germans, and of Cousin, and Its Influence on Opinion in This Country* (July 1840). He chastened Parker and William H. Furness for preaching against slavery in their sermons in his September 1843 review of the published versions of the sermons, yet he also celebrated antislavery writings in *Christian Examiner* reviews. In his mind, periodical publication was the appropriate venue for such political discussions. He remained relatively neutral during the "miracles controversy"–the dispute between Transcendentalists, such as Ripley, who claimed that miracles were not necessary to validate faith, and traditionalists, such as Norton, who claimed that they were. While certainly not welcoming Transcendentalist writers, in 1840 Ware rejected Norton's suggestion that he castigate Ripley in *The Christian Examiner.*

Ware published the initial chapters of what is now considered the prototype of the American Christological novel, *Julian: or, Scenes in Judea,* in *The Christian Examiner* from September 1839 to May 1840. The work appeared in book form in two volumes in 1841. The wealthy Roman Jew Julian returns to Judea after experiencing anti-Semitism in Rome and rediscovers his religious heritage in the context of political infighting among the Pharisees and Sadducees–another veiled reference by Ware to Christian sectarianism. Julian joins Herod Antipas's revolt against Rome and becomes interested in Jesus as a possible Messiah. With true Unitarian rationalism Julian explores the question empirically through secondary accounts, his own observations, and the elders' teaching; he even spends time with Jesus' family and learns of their doubts about their relative's divine status. Julian concludes that Jesus was merely "a messenger and prophet of God." Modern scholars recognize the Unitarian impulse in this novel, its condemnation of anti-Semitism, and its seminal role for subsequent fictional lives of Christ. But *Julian* never gained the popular success of *Zenobia* and *Probus.*

After the mediocre reception of *Julian,* Ware gave up fiction writing. In 1843 he began negotiations to terminate what had become an arduous connection to *The Christian Examiner,* and in January 1844 he accepted a ministry in West Cambridge. He had suffered from ill health for some years, and at this time he was diagnosed with epilepsy. In the wake of the controversy over Theodore Parker's 1844 Thursday Lecture, in which Parker said that Jesus was "the greatest person of the ages" but that "God has greater men in store," Ware delivered and published the sermon *Righteousness before Doctrine* (1845), a protest against the majority who were solidifying Unitarian theology into sectarianism in order to exclude Parker. Without mentioning Parker by name, Ware criticized his colleagues' "hostile attitude toward this person, solely because of his opinions . . . instead of drawing towards him on account of the righteousness which he preaches, and the righteousness which he lives." In the same year Ware joined 173 other Unitarian ministers in signing James Freeman Clarke's declaration that slavery was "utterly opposed to the principles and spirit of Christianity." Soon thereafter Ware experienced an epileptic seizure that resulted in paralysis; friends raised $6,280 to support his family.

Ware never fully recovered from his affliction. In 1847 he returned to Cambridge and joined the Ministry at Large in Boston, a mission that he had supported in his 1843 *Christian Examiner* reviews. He traveled in Europe, primarily in Italy, in 1848–1849. On his return he delivered his observations on European architecture, history, culture, and art in a winter 1849–1850 lecture series that he published as *Sketches of European Capitals* (1851). During the summer of 1851 Ware composed a second lecture series on the Romantic painter Washington Allston; he was completing the arrangements for Boston engagements when he died on 19 February 1852. *Lectures on the Works and Genius of Washington Allston* (1852) was published posthumously. Asserting the importance of religious sentiment in the artist, Ware also emphasizes Allston's use of color to suggest light and truth; thus, Allston's technique demonstrates that it is only by "pure intellect, set forth in the strictest forms of logic, that mankind are to be moved or permanently benefited." Despite this Unitarian emphasis on reason, Ware extolls Allston's *Elijah in the Desert* (1818). Unitarian Bostonians generally objected to the painting's ambiguous treatment of religious subjects, but Ware admires the work's "landscape, which, in its sublimity, excited the imagination as powerfully as any gigantic form of the Elijah could have done."

William Ware exemplifies the place occupied by Unitarians in the evolution of antebellum literature. As a novelist, author, and critic he demonstrates the connections between spirituality and the arts in the Unitarian community from which Transcendentalism derived. Nevertheless, his novels, art criticism, and editorship of *The Christian Examiner* have received limited scholarly treatment, and no complete bibliography of his writings exists. Much remains to be learned about this interesting figure.

References:

David Bjelajac, "The Boston Elite's Resistance to Washington Allston's *Elijah in the Desert*," in *American Iconology: New Approaches to Nineteenth-Century Art and Literature,* edited by David C. Miller (New Haven: Yale University Press, 1993), pp. 39–57;

Bjelajac, "Milk of the Word or Milk of Poison," in his *Washington Allston, Secret Societies, and the Alchemy of Anglo-American Painting* (Cambridge, Mass.: Cambridge University Press, 1997), pp. 108–132;

Curtis Dahl, "New England Unitarianism in Fictional Antiquity: The Romances of William Ware," *New England Quarterly,* 48 (March 1975): 104–115;

Ann Douglass, *The Feminization of American Culture* (New York: Knopf, 1977), pp. 115–117;

George Edward Ellis, George Putnam, and Orville Dewey, "The Rev. William Ware," *Christian Examiner,* 52 (May 1852): 406–412;

Louis Harap, *The Image of the Jew in American Literature from Early Republic to Mass Immigration* (Philadelphia: Jewish Publication Society of America, 1974), pp. 157–161;

William R. Hutchison, *The Transcendentalist Ministers: Church Reform in the New England Renaissance* (New Haven: Yale University Press, 1959), pp. 89–92, 126;

Frederick Paul Kroeger, "The Unitarian Novels of William Ware," dissertation, University of Michigan, 1967;

Alfred Guy Litton, "'Speaking the Truth in Love': A History of the *Christian Examiner* and Its Relation to New England Transcendentalism," dissertation, University of South Carolina, 1993, pp. 250–252;

David C. Miller, "Washington Allston and the Sister Arts Tradition in America," *European Romantic Review,* 5, no. 1 (1994): 49–72;

Allene Stuart Phy, "The Representation of Christ in Popular Fiction," dissertation, George Peabody College for Teachers, pp. 39–56;

David Reynolds, *Faith in Fiction: The Emergence of Religious Literature in America* (Cambridge, Mass. & London: Harvard University Press, 1981), pp. 35–37, 139–144;

Malini Johar Schueller, "Missionary Colonialism, Egyptology, Racial Borderlands, and the Satiric Impulse: M. M. Ballou, William Ware, John DeForest, Maria Susanna Cummins, David F. Dorr," in her *U.S. Orientalisms: Race, Nation, and Gender in Literature, 1790–1860* (Ann Arbor: University of Michigan Press, 1998), pp. 75–108;

William B. Sprague, "William Ware," in his *Annals of the American Unitarian Pulpit; Or, Commemorative Notices of Distinguished Clergymen of the Unitarian Denomination in the United States, from Its Commencement to the Close of the Year Eighteen Hundred and Fifty-Five* (New York: Robert Carter, 1865), pp. 511–518;

Gardner B. Taplin, "The Brownings and the Reverend William Ware," *Browning Newsletter,* 7 (Fall 1971): 3–8.

Papers:

The primary collections of correspondence and papers related to William Ware are at the Massachusetts Historical Society, Boston; and the Houghton Library, Harvard University. Other minor collections include the Boston Public Library; the New York Society Library; the Historical Society of Pennsylvania, Philadelphia; the Alderman Library, University of Virginia; the Pierpont Morgan Library, New York; and the Beinecke Library, Yale University.

Joseph Emerson Worcester

(24 August 1784 – 27 October 1865)

Mariane Wurst Schaum

Joseph Emerson Worcester

BOOKS: *A Geographical Dictionary; or, Universal Gazetteer, Ancient and Modern,* 2 volumes (Salem, Mass.: Whipple, 1817); revised and enlarged edition, Boston: Cummings & Hilliard, 1823);

Elements of Geography, Ancient and Modern: With an Atlas (Boston: Swan, 1819; revised edition, Boston: Hilliard, Gray, Little & Wilkins, 1830);

Epitome of Modern Geography, with Maps: For the Use of Common Schools (Boston: Cummings, Hilliard, 1820);

Sketches of the Earth and Its Inhabitants: With One Hundred Engravings, 2 volumes (Boston: Cummings, Hilliard, 1823);

Elements of History, Ancient and Modern: With Historical Charts (Boston: Cummings, Hilliard, 1826; revised and enlarged, Boston: Taggard & Chase, 1849);

An Epitome of History, with Historical and Chronological Charts (Cambridge, Mass.: Hilliard & Brown, 1827);

Outlines of Scripture Geography, With an Atlas (Boston: Bowles & Dearborn / Hilliard, Gray, Little & Wilkins, 1828);

A Comprehensive Pronouncing and Explanatory Dictionary of the English Language, With Pronouncing Vocabularies of Classical, Scripture and Proper Names (Boston: Hilliard, Gray, Little & Wilkins, 1830; revised and enlarged edition, Boston: Jenks & Palmer / Philadelphia: Thomas, Cowperthwait, 1840); revised and enlarged as *A Pronouncing, Explanatory, and Synonymous Dictionary of the English Language* (Boston: Hickling, Swan & Brown, 1855);

Elementary Dictionary of the English Language (Boston: Jenks, Palmer, 1835); revised and enlarged edition, Boston: Brewer & Tileston, 1860);

A Pronouncing, Explanatory, and Synonymous Dictionary of the English Language (Boston: American Stationers / Russell, 1837);

An Elementary Dictionary for Common Schools: With Pronouncing Vocabularies of Classical, Scripture, and Modern Geographical Names (Boston: American Stationers / Russell, 1837; revised and enlarged edition, Boston: Jenks, Hickling & Swan, 1852);

Elements of Ancient Classical and Scripture Geography: With an Atlas (Boston: Phillips, Sampson, 1839);

A Universal and Critical Dictionary of the English Language; to Which Are Added Walker's Key to the Pronunciation of Classical and Scripture Proper Names, Much Enlarged and Improved; and a Pronouncing Vocabulary of Modern Geographical Names (Boston: Wilkins, Carter, 1846); republished as *A Universal, Critical, and Pronouncing Dictionary of the English Language: Including Scientific Terms, Compiled from the Materials of Noah Webster, LL.D. by Joseph E. Worcester. New Edition, to Which Are Added Walker's Key to the Pronunciation of Classical and Scripture Proper Names, Enlarged and*

Improved; a Pronouncing Vocabulary of Modern Geographical Names: And an English Grammar (London: Bohn, 1853);

A Primary Pronouncing Dictionary of the English Language: With Vocabularies of Classical, Scripture and Modern Geographical Names (Boston: Jenks, Palmer, 1850);

A Gross Literary Fraud Exposed: Relating to the Publication of Worcester's Dictionary in London (Boston: Jenks, Hickling & Swan, 1853); enlarged as *A Gross Literary Fraud Exposed: Relating to the Publication of Worcester's Dictionary in London: Together with Three Appendices; Including the Answer of S. Converse to an Attack on Him by Messrs G. & C. Merriam* (Boston: Jenks, Hickling & Swan, 1854);

A Pronouncing Spelling-Book of the English Language (Boston: Brewer & Tileston / Cleveland: Ingham & Bragg, 1857);

A Dictionary of the English Language (Boston: Swan, Brewer & Tileston, 1860);

Elementary Spelling-Book, Designed for Primary and Common Schools and as an Introduction to Worcester's Pronouncing Spelling Book (Boston: Swan, Brewer & Tileston / Cleveland: Ingham & Bragg, 1861);

A Comprehensive Spelling-Book on the Plan of the Pronouncing Spelling-Book (Boston: Ware / Brewer & Tileston, 1864).

OTHER: Samuel Johnson, *English Dictionary, as Improved by Todd and Abridged by Chalmers, with Walker's Pronouncing Dictionary Combined, to which is added Walker's Key to the Classical Pronunciation of Greek, Latin and Scripture Proper Names,* revised and edited by Worcester (Boston: Charles Ewer & T. Harrington Carter, 1828);

Noah Webster, *An American Dictionary of the English Language; Exhibiting the Origin, Orthography, Pronunciation and Definitions of Words: Abridged from the Quarto Edition of the Author; to Which are Added, a Synopsis of Words Differently Pronounced by Different Orthoëpists; and Walker's Key to the Classical Pronunciation of Greek, Latin, and Scripture Proper Names,* edited by Worcester (New York: Converse, 1829);

The American Almanac and Repository of Useful Knowledge, edited by Worcester (Boston: Gray & Brown, 1831–1843);

"Remarks on Longevity and the Expectation of Life in the United States, Relating more Particularly to the State of New Hampshire, with Some Comparative Views in Relation to Foreign Countries," in *Memoirs of the American Academy of Arts and Sciences,* new series, volume 1 (Cambridge, Mass.: American Academy of Arts and Sciences, 1833), pp. 1–44.

Virtually unknown today both to the general public and to most academicians, Joseph Emerson Worcester was one of the two most revered lexicographers in the United States from 1830 until the last decades of the nineteenth century. A quiet, dignified, and unassuming man, Worcester was a linguistic conservative; he used the educated speech of London as his standard for spelling and pronunciation, and he cited British writers to illustrate word usage. His rival, Noah Webster, wanted to Americanize spelling and pronunciation, and when he could not find an American writer to cite, he made up his own illustrations. Webster thought it his duty to set the standard of American English that should be followed by everyone in every part of the country. As much as Worcester admired the British standard, however, he believed that a lexicographer's task was to reflect the language of the people, not to impose a language upon them. Worcester's dictionaries reflected his common sense, judgment, and diligent scholarship, and they became the standard for spelling and pronunciation at Harvard and at the University of Virginia.

Almost from the beginning of his career as a lexicographer, Worcester was hounded by Webster and, particularly after Webster's death, by his publishers, who were threatened not only philosophically but also financially by Worcester's success. The dispute, which came to be called the "War of the Dictionaries," was an ugly imbroglio that eventually turned literary figures, educators, politicians, and even family members against one another. Webster, or at least his name, eventually won the "War." When Worcester died, he had no successor to continue his work, and Webster's publisher had the resources to capture the market; however, the text that established Webster's dictionary as the preeminent U.S. dictionary had been compiled by lexicographers so influenced by Worcester that it bore hardly any resemblance to the work of Webster.

A direct descendant of the Reverend William Worcester, first minister of the Congregational Church in Salisbury, Massachusetts, Joseph Emerson Worcester was born on 24 August 1784 in Bedford, New Hampshire, the second of fifteen children born to Jesse Worcester and Sarah Parker Worcester. His father, who had retired from school teaching to farm in Hollis, New Hampshire, published pieces in several periodicals and wrote an unpublished work, "Chronicles of Nissitissit." Like him, at some point in their lives, fourteen of his children taught in public schools. Joseph and his older brother, Jesse, worked on the farm during the day and studied at home at night, occasionally attending the district school when their farming duties permitted. In a biographical sketch published in *The Granite Monthly* (1880), his younger brother Samuel recalled that Joseph applied himself to his studies with "quiet and unwearied perseverance and resolute energy, which were marked traits of his character through his whole life." When Joseph was twenty-one years old, he and Jesse entered Phillips Academy in Andover, Massachusetts, where they attended classes with children of eight and nine. The two brothers graduated from the Academy in 1809, when Joseph was twenty-five. Two years later he graduated from Yale, where he was elected to Phi Beta Kappa.

The rest of Worcester's long life was spent in the "quiet perseverance" to which his brother referred. Other than the steady publication of his books and a protracted dispute with Webster's publishers, the only notable events of Worcester's life were his receiving honorary degrees from Yale, Brown, and Dartmouth; his election to the Massachusetts Historical Society, the American Academy of Arts and Sciences, and the Royal Geographic Society; and his marriage on 29 June 1841, when he was fifty-seven years old, to Amy Elizabeth McKean, the forty-year-old daughter of the Reverend Joseph McKean, professor of rhetoric and oratory at Harvard. Amy Worcester assisted her husband in his work. They had no children.

Immediately after graduating from Yale, Worcester took his first teaching job in Salem; young Nathaniel Hawthorne was one of his pupils. He taught in Salem from 1811 until 1816 while he prepared his first book, *A Geographical Dictionary; or, Universal Gazetteer, Ancient and Modern,* which was printed in 1817 by the Andover firm of Flagg and Gould and was published and sold by Henry Whipple in Salem. After leaving Salem, Worcester taught in Andover for two years; then in 1819 he moved to Cambridge, where he spent the rest of his life.

The first book Worcester published after moving to Cambridge was his *Elements of Geography, Ancient and Modern: With an Atlas* (1819). The work was widely used in the public schools and academies of New England and became the required geography text for admission to Harvard; Henry David Thoreau used the 1832 edition of this text in his student days at Concord Academy.

Between 1823 and 1828 Worcester brought out several more books of history and geography. Praised for their accuracy and style, these books went through many editions and were used extensively as textbooks. In 1825 Worcester was elected to the American Academy of Arts and Sciences, which published his essay on longevity and life expectancy in the United States.

In 1828 Worcester published his first work in lexicography, an edition of Samuel Johnson's *Dictionary of the English Language* (1755) as it had been revised by Henry John Todd in 1818 and 1825 and by Alexander Chalmers in 1820. Worcester's edition included the key to pronunciation devised by John Walker in his 1791 dictionary. He was far along in work on his own dictionary, *A Comprehensive Pronouncing and Explanatory Dictionary of the English Language, With Pronouncing Vocabularies of Classical, Scripture and Proper Names* (1830), when Worcester reluctantly agreed to prepare an abridgement of Webster's two-volume *An American Dictionary of the English Language* (1828) under the supervision of Webster's son-in-law, Chauncey A. Goodrich, a professor at Yale. Webster expected Goodrich to make sure that the abridgement complied with the principles he had laid down in the 1828 edition, but Goodrich seemingly gave Worcester a free rein in terms of content decisions. Worcester added words taken from Todd's edition of Johnson's dictionary and elsewhere, compressed many definitions and added others omitted by Webster, and deleted most of Webster's illustrative citations and all but the "most important" etymologies. Worcester also introduced more spelling variants than Webster had allowed, changed the pronunciation of some words (for example, he gave *medicine* three syllables instead of Webster's two), and added the "Synopsis of Words Differently Pronounced by Different Orthoepists" and "Walker's Key [to Pronunciation]," which ran at the foot of every page. For his services, Worcester was paid $2,000.

When the dictionary was published in 1829, Webster was furious not only with Worcester but also with Goodrich. Fourteen years after publication of the abridged dictionary and a month before his death, Webster wrote a letter to William Chauncey Fowler, another son-in-law, saying he regretted he had "suffered the American Dictionary to be abridged" and declaring "the work must not be considered as mine."

In 1830 Worcester published the first edition of his own dictionary, *A Comprehensive Pronouncing and Explanatory Dictionary of the English Language,* which comprises 43,000 entries. In the preface Worcester says that he conceived the plan for the dictionary while editing Johnson's dictionary and that he gave a great deal of attention to pronunciation in the work. According to the introduction, he consulted many dictionaries and the work of twenty-seven lexicographers and orthoepists while drafting the work.

The importance of pronunciation to Worcester is evident in the dictionary. It includes "A Synopsis of Words Differently Pronounced by Different Orthoepists," which he says he had prepared for this work but decided to include in his abridgement of Webster's *An American Dictionary of the English Language* when publication of his own dictionary was delayed by preparation of the abridgement. In the "Key to Sounds of the Marked Letters," Worcester distinguishes seven sounds for the letter *a,* five for *e,* six for *u* and *o,* and four for *y,* and he notes the diphthongs *oi, oy, ou, ow,* and *eu.* In this dictionary Worcester made his lasting contribution to the pronunciation of American English: a sound between the *a* of *father* and the *a* of *hat,* to be used in words such as *fast, grass,* and *dance.* For such words, Worcester preferred this sound, which came to be known as the "compromise vowel," to either the vowel sound of *hat,* then considered fashionable, or the vowel sound of *father,* which he considered vulgar.

An innovative feature of *A Comprehensive Pronouncing and Explanatory Dictionary of the English Language* is a system of diacritical marks that allowed Worcester to indicate punctuation without having to respell the word. He also distinguished between the primary and secondary stresses in words.

The standard of pronunciation, Worcester says in the preface, should be that of the so-called best society of London; "yet this is not the only thing to be observed. The usage of the best society in the place or district where one resides, is not to be disregarded." Despite his preference for the pronunciation of London, he believed the orthoepist should record pronunciation as it is, not as the orthoepist thinks it should be. Webster, on the other hand, had decided that the pronunciation of the best educated people in New England was to be the standard of pronunciation because it had not been tainted by what he considered to be corruptions of the mother tongue in England, and he desired to establish his own pronunciations as the national standard. In orthography Worcester is usually respectful of usage, although his conservative bias sometimes surfaces; for example, he drops the *u* in such words as *honor* and *labor* but prefers the *re* spelling to *er* in such words as *centre* and *theatre.*

As he did in later books, in *A Comprehensive Pronouncing and Explanatory Dictionary of the English Language* Worcester introduced features that became standard in American lexicography: foreign words that have not become a part of the English language are printed in italics; obsolete words are included if they appear "in works not obsolete," and irregular noun forms, preterits, and past participles are given. His definitions are usually short, and his explanatory descriptions cite British writers and avoid Webster's loquacious, provincial illustrations.

In his *The English Language in America* (1925), George Phillip Krapp praises Worcester's 1830 dictionary as "a discriminating and scholarly piece of work" and says that Worcester "in general . . . showed greater common sense and better judgement than Webster." In his dictionary, Webster had made many errors in etymology, errors Worcester avoided, says Krapp, "by not giving any etymologies"; however, as Joseph H. Friend notes in his 1967 work, *The Development of American Lexicography, 1798–1864,* "The omission of etymologies saved space and avoided howlers, but so negative a virtue scarcely warrants praise." *A Comprehensive Pronouncing and Explanatory Dictionary of the English Language* quickly became the preferred dictionary for use at Harvard and was embraced by Anglophiles and conservative linguists throughout the country.

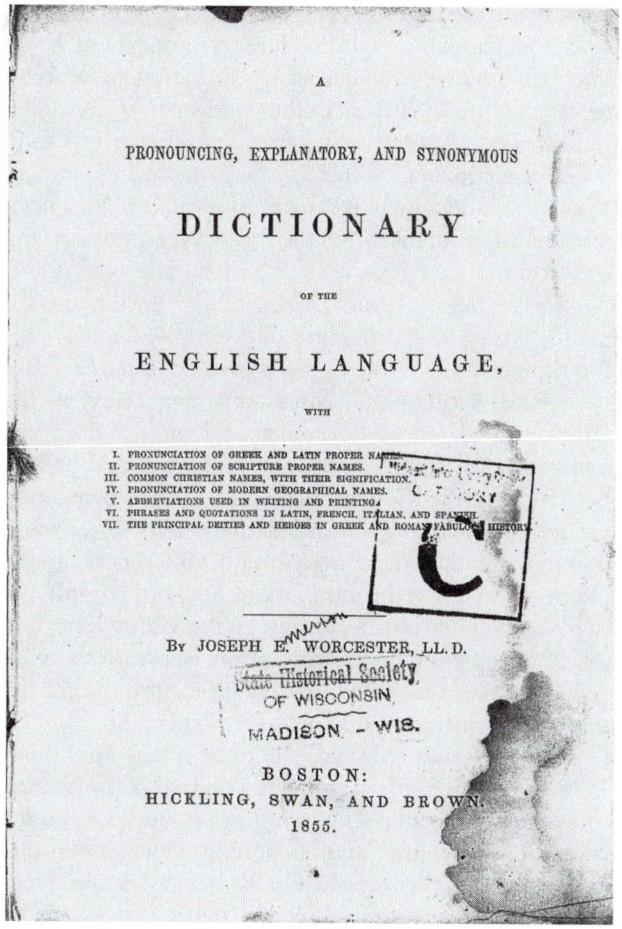
A

PRONOUNCING, EXPLANATORY, AND SYNONYMOUS

DICTIONARY

OF THE

ENGLISH LANGUAGE,

WITH

I. PRONUNCIATION OF GREEK AND LATIN PROPER NAMES.
II. PRONUNCIATION OF SCRIPTURE PROPER NAMES.
III. COMMON CHRISTIAN NAMES, WITH THEIR SIGNIFICATION.
IV. PRONUNCIATION OF MODERN GEOGRAPHICAL NAMES.
V. ABBREVIATIONS USED IN WRITING AND PRINTING.
VI. PHRASES AND QUOTATIONS IN LATIN, FRENCH, ITALIAN, AND SPANISH.
VII. THE PRINCIPAL DEITIES AND HEROES IN GREEK AND ROMAN FABULOUS HISTORY.

BY JOSEPH E. WORCESTER, LL. D.

State Historical Society
OF WISCONSIN
MADISON - WIS.

BOSTON:
HICKLING, SWAN, AND BROWN.
1855.

Title page for Worcester's second revision and expansion of his 1837 dictionary, the main American competitor for the Noah Webster dictionaries published by George and Charles Merriam

In 1831 Worcester went to Europe to do research, collecting books of geography, history, philology, and lexicography in England, Scotland, France, Holland, and Germany. When he returned to the United States, he became editor of the *American Almanac and Repository of Useful Knowledge,* a statistical annual of 300 to 375 pages for which he prepared all the contents except those pertaining to astronomy. He edited the *American Almanac* until 1843.

The first volley in what came to be known as the "War of the Dictionaries" was fired in the *Worcester (Mass.) Palladium* of 26 November 1834. An anonymous article on the editorial page accused Worcester of "gross plagiarism . . . on the literary property of Noah Webster, Esq." The article charged that while Worcester was aiding Webster "in the drudgery" of abridging *An American Dictionary of the English Language,* he "published a dictionary, which is a very close imitation of Webster's; and which, we regret to learn, has since been introduced into many of the primary schools of the country."

Even before Worcester knew the attack had been made, Sidney Willard, editor of the *Boston Christian Register,* immediately wrote to the *Worcester (Mass.) Palladium* to defend Worcester. Worcester's own reply to the attack was dated 3 December and appeared in the newspaper on 10 December 1834. He said that he had begun work on his own dictionary before being persuaded to undertake the abridgement of Webster's and pointed out that there were many differences in the plans, vocabulary, pronunciation, and orthography of the two dictionaries. In contrast to the vituperative language of the anonymous accusation, Worcester's reply was dignified, restrained, reasonable–and futile. In the same issue, just above Worcester's letter, the *Worcester (Mass.) Palladium* printed another attack on both Worcester and Willard, accusing Willard of pretending to defend Worcester only to indulge in his "passion for pedantic exhibitions" and reasserting the charge of plagiarism against Worcester. On 17 December the paper published a letter from Webster himself in which he accused Worcester of plagiarizing his definitions. Another letter from Webster on 28 January 1835 listed 121 words that Webster said had been taken from his dictionary. He challenged Worcester to prove that he had found them anywhere but in Webster's dictionary.

In his reply to Webster on 11 February, Worcester referred to the fifty-six other dictionaries or glossaries, dating back more than a century, in which he had found 90 of the 121 words. He said that 6 or 7 of the words had not been in Webster's quarto edition and that one of them was among the 3,000 words from the Todd-Johnson dictionary he himself had inserted in the abridged version. He further pointed out that he had deliberately avoided including in his dictionary any words coined by Webster, not even mentioning them in the "Vocabulary of Words of Various Orthography."

Another letter from Webster to Worcester appeared in the *Worcester (Mass.) Palladium* on 18 February 1835. Webster repeated his charge that Worcester had used his definitions and accused him of using his rules of orthography also. This time he said that he had spent *"twenty years of labor and 20,000 dollars"* to complete his quarto *An American Dictionary of the English Language* and accused Worcester of robbing him of remuneration that he should have received. Worcester replied on 11 March, Webster answered on 25 March, and there the matter came to rest for a while.

The public controversy seems to have had no effect on the esteem with which Worcester's dictionaries were held. A second edition of *A Comprehensive Pronouncing and Explanatory Dictionary of the English Language* had been published in 1831, and a revised and enlarged edition was published to favorable reviews in 1840. In 1835 Worcester brought out his *Elementary Dictionary of the English Language* for use in the schools. It included more than 44,000 words and sold for 60¢. Webster brought out an unabridged edition of his dictionary in 1841, but it did not sell well because it was insufficiently revised to satisfy its critics and its $15 price was too high. As a result, Worcester's dictionary was all the more in demand. When Webster died in 1843, Worcester was considered by many to be the preeminent lexicographer of the United States.

As soon as he had finished *A Comprehensive Pronouncing and Explanatory Dictionary of the English Language,* Worcester began recording all the English words he came across that were not found in Todd's edition of Johnson's dictionary. He intended to revise his 1830 dictionary to include these words, but the list grew so long that he decided to make a new, larger dictionary that would include a vocabulary as complete as he could compile. In 1846 he published in octavo a dictionary of more than a thousand pages, including front matter. *A Universal and Critical Dictionary of the English Language; to Which Are Added Walker's Key to the Pronunciation of Classical and Scripture Proper Names, Much Enlarged and Improved; and a Pronouncing Vocabulary of Modern Geographical Names* sold for $3.50 and, in the library edition, $5.

Worcester's 1846 dictionary includes more than 83,000 words, without listing the participial forms as separate words as some dictionaries did. Authorities are cited for all the new words. Once again Worcester cited English authorities because he thought "it is satisfactory to many readers to know, in relation to a new, uncommon, or doubtful word, that it is not peculiar to American writers, but that a respectable English authority may be adduced in support of its use." As he always had, he cited all the predecessors whose work he had consulted and used. He called Webster's *American Dictionary of the English Language* "the greatest and most important" dictionary since that of Johnson, but added "the taste and judgement of the author are not generally esteemed equal to his industry and erudition." Worcester was careful to say that he was "not aware of having taken a single word, or the definition of a word" from "Webster's Dictionary."

In addition to the material on pronunciation and orthography taken from his *Comprehensive Pronouncing and Explanatory Dictionary of the English Language,* Worcester includes in the 1846 dictionary an outline of English grammar; a section on the origin and formation of the language with etymologies; a survey of archaisms, provincialisms, and Americanisms with an essay on the differences between American and British English that gives an explanation as to why there are more local dialects in England than in the United States; and a seventeen-page "History of English Lexicography," which has been noted for "its objectivity and scholarly command of the material." In addition to these merits, the dictionary has been cited for its brilliant explanations of idiomatic verbal phrases.

After the publication of his *Universal and Critical Dictionary of the English Language,* Worcester lost the use of his eyes because of cataracts. Between 1847 and 1849 he had five operations that saved his left eye but left him nearly blind in the right. During this time, while he was unable to work, the scene was set for the second round in "The War of the Dictionaries."

After Webster's death in 1843, George and Charles Merriam took over the publication of the Webster dictionaries. In 1847, a year after Worcester's *A Universal and Critical Dictionary of the English Language* was published, Merriam brought out a new edition of *An American Dictionary of the English Language,* revised and enlarged by Goodrich. The old personal quarrel between Webster and Worcester now became a fight between publishers and eventually also between linguists, regions, social classes, and academic institutions. Yale men were proponents of Webster's dictionary and its emphasis on American English; at Harvard and Boston, literary men swore by Worcester's dictionary. The real war, however, was fought between publishers. With the rise in immigration and the extension of public education, the need for dictionaries in secondary schools was growing; the publisher who could secure the market would drive the other out of the dictionary publishing business.

Both Webster's and Worcester's publishers bombarded the public with advertising that included letters of endorsement, testimonials, and claims of superiority. A rumor that Worcester had regained the use of his eyes and was engaged in the making of a new dictionary spurred Webster's publisher into such a frenzy that Worcester's Philadelphia publisher, Thomas, Cowperthwait, and Company, charged Merriam with unscrupulous practices intended to "vilify, traduce, and slander both Dr. Worcester and ourselves." They published a series of letters from Merriam threatening to destroy the market for Cowperthwait's geography textbooks "unless they 'show their flag' in favor of Webster's Dictionary."

To make matters worse, Worcester had no control over the publishing of his 1846 dictionary, and it passed from Wilkins, Carter, and Company to Jenks, Hickling, and Swan in the United States. Before the transfer, however, Wilkins, Carter, and Company had authorized negotiations for the publication of Worcester's dictionary in England. Lack of an international copyright law enabled the English publisher, Henry G. Bohn, to bring out a pirated edition in 1846 with an altered title page and preface that deleted Worcester's statement that he had not made use of any words or definitions of Webster's; significantly, the new subtitle read, in part, *Compiled from the Materials of Noah Webster, LL.D. by Joseph E. Worcester,* seeming to indicate that the dictionary Worcester had published in 1846 was in fact based on Webster's 1828 dictionary.

A flurry of pamphlets and letters on both sides fed the flames of the rivalry between publishers. Merriam accused Worcester of trying to profit by using Webster's name. Worcester remained dignified and restrained in his contributions to the pamphlets put out by his publisher, Jenks, Hickling, and Swan. In a twenty-four-page pamphlet titled *A Gross Literary Fraud Exposed: Relating to the Publication of Worcester's Dictionary in London* (1853), he attempted to establish that he had no responsibility for the British edition of his dictionary and, once again, to clear himself of charges of plagiarism. The pamphlet included a letter to Worcester from the publisher of the abridgment, Sherman Converse, saying that the abridgement of Webster's dictionary had been "performed . . . to my entire satisfaction, and I believe to that of Professor Goodrich." In the pamphlet Worcester also pointed out in meticulous detail examples of the differences between his and Webster's dictionaries.

After the Merriams published a pamphlet in response, Worcester replied in January 1854 with a new edition of his pamphlet that included a four-page appendix, in which he quoted from a letter from Goodrich: "I have always felt and said, that I knew of no ground whatever for any imputation upon you, as though you had made use of Dr. Webster's Dictionary in the production of your own. . . . I have uniformly stated . . . that if any coincidences should be discovered between the two works, I had no belief they were intentional or conscious ones on your part." The battle between publishers continued through the 1850s, with outrageous advertising and many more pamphlets reproducing letters and documents dating back to the 1830s, testimonials for both sides by educators, quotations from anonymous sources, wooing of school boards, and, of course, accusations of falsifications. Reviewers for many magazines and newspapers also joined in the fray, and eventually the reviewers began

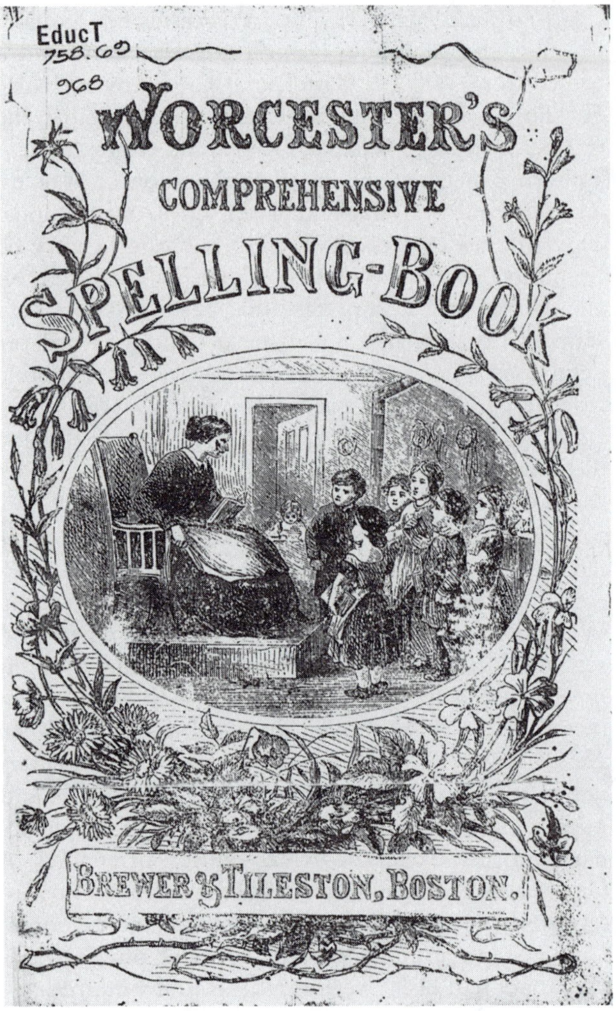

Decorated title page for Worcester's 1864 textbook

reviewing one another's reviews and hurling invectives at one another.

After he recovered his sight, Worcester brought out enlarged revisions of *A Comprehensive Pronouncing and Explanatory Dictionary of the English Language* in 1847 and 1849, and his *A Primary Pronouncing Dictionary of the English Language: With Vocabularies of Classical, Scripture and Modern Geographical Names* for use in schools in 1850. New editions of that dictionary appeared in 1857 and 1861; it continued to sell about ten thousand copies a year until 1877. In 1855 he revised and expanded the *Comprehensive Pronouncing and Explanatory Dictionary of the English Language* still more and brought it out as *A Pronouncing, Explanatory, and Synonymous Dictionary of the English Language*. Its most notable new feature was a discriminative synonymy; it was the first dictionary to use synonyms for a head word and to make distinctions among the synonyms.

Worcester's last dictionary was his most important and elaborate. *A Dictionary of the English Language* was published in 1860, when Worcester was seventy-six years old. He had worked on it for fifteen years, but because of his age, toward the end of the process Worcester was assisted in the preparation of this dictionary by six assistants who insisted that the publisher provide them with a place to work "separately indeed, but in such proximity as will afford the opportunity of brief consultation, each with each, without engaging the attention of the rest." The result of their work was not only to include some obvious derivatives and compounds (for example, "twenty pages of words formed with the prefix *-un,*" a trait also characteristic of later Merriam-Webster dictionaries) but also to exceed previous dictionaries in the scope of the appended matter. Worcester had "hit upon the particular pattern that distinguishes the American dictionary," an encyclopedic pattern he had been working toward for thirty years.

A noticeable improvement over his earlier dictionaries is the writing of definitions, which Ezra Abbott praised for "neatness and precision." In this dictionary Worcester also introduced the discriminatory synonymy with cross references, establishing the form that has been used in American dictionaries ever since. This quarto edition of 1,800 pages was obviously superior to the edition of Webster's dictionary that Merriam brought out in 1859, and the reviews were laudatory. The *Atlantic Monthly* (May 1860) declared, "Dr. Worcester has unquestionably come off victorious" in the war with Webster. Reviewing Worcester's dictionary in *The Christian Examiner* (May 1860), Edward Everett Hale said that if a new civilization ever had to be established, only two books would be needed: "Shakespeare and this dictionary."

The war was not over, however, and, paradoxically, the book that won was written by neither Webster nor Worcester. C. A. F. Mahn, a German philologist, had been commissioned by the Merriams to overhaul Webster's etymologies, which had always been fanciful at best, in the light of new information about the development of the English language. With the etymologies cleaned up by Mahn and other deficiencies rectified by many lexicographers in the employ of Merriam, only a scattering of Webster's original definitions remained in the *American Dictionary of the English Language, Unabridged,* bearing Webster's name, that was published in 1864. Only a few critics refused to acclaim it the best dictionary ever published in this country.

During his last five years, Worcester continued to make annotations for a planned revision of his 1860 dictionary, but he died in Cambridge on 27 October 1865 before he was able to challenge the 1864 Webster-Mahn edition. Although Worcester's dictionaries remained popular until the end of the nineteenth century–as late as the 1890s Harvard specified Worcester's dictionary as the spelling authority to be followed in entrance examinations–Webster's dictionaries eventually won the field. Webster's victory, however, was more that of his name than his lexicography. As Krapp says, the victory of Webster's dictionary was "largely due to judicious editing, manufacturing and selling." Indeed, after Webster's death, Merriam adopted Worcester's philosophy that a dictionary should reflect usage rather than dictate it, and the firm published under Webster's name dictionaries he would have disavowed.

Although today his name is almost unknown to the general public, Worcester had a crucial impact on American lexicography. As Friend writes, he "had qualities of mind that Webster lacked, which enabled him to produce work more balanced and judicious, less extravagant, biased, and partisan. . . . Worcester's neatness, precision, caution, moderation, and elegance, together with his handling of synonymy and of such things as divided usage and idiomatic phrases, clearly influenced the Merriam product."

Biographies:

Ezra Abbott, "Joseph Emerson Worcester," *Proceedings of the American Academy of Arts and Sciences,* 7 (1865–1868), pp. 112–116;

Samuel T. Worcester, "Joseph E. Worcester," *Granite Monthly,* 3 (April 1880): 245–252;

Franklin B. Dexter, *Biographical Sketches of the Graduates of Yale College,* volume 6 (New Haven: Yale University Press, 1912);

Sarah A. Worcester, *The Descendants of Rev. William Worcester* (1914).

References:

Eva Marie Burkett, *American Dictionaries of the English Language Before 1861* (Metuchen, N.J.: Scarecrow Press, 1979);

Joseph H. Friend, *The Development of American Lexicography, 1798–1864* (The Hague: Mouton, 1967), pp. 82–110;

Arthur G. Kennedy, *A Bibliography of Writings on the English Language from the Beginning of Printing to the End of 1922* (Cambridge, Mass.: Harvard University Press / New Haven: Yale University Press, 1927);

George Philip Krapp, *The English Language in America,* 2 volumes (New York: Modern Language Association of America, 1925);

Janice A. Kraus, "Caveat Auctor: The War of the Dictionaries," *Journal of the Rutgers University Libraries,* 48 (December 1986): 75–90.

Papers:

There appear to be no collections of Joseph Emerson Worcester's papers. A letter dated 1820 and an undated engraving are at the University of Virginia Alderman Library. A letter dated 8 March 1824, to George Ticknor, is in the Dartmouth College Library. Two letters from Charles Folsom, one to Worcester and one to William D. Swan regarding arrangements to prepare the manuscript of the 1860 dictionary for publication, are in the Folsom Collection, Boston Public Library.

Appendix

Boston & Cambridge: Eyewitness Account of the New England Literary Renaissance

Near the beginning of the twentieth century, William Dean Howells looked back on the Boston he had found in 1860–just before the outbreak of the Civil War–when as a twenty-three-year-old aspiring writer from Ohio he made his first literary pilgrimage to the East. In awe he declared that "there is no question but our literary centre was then in Boston. . . . At Boston chiefly, if not at Boston alone, was there a vigorous intellectual life" among the leading authors in the United States. Bostonians were only too happy to concur with this judgment. The city that seventeenth-century Puritans conceived as a "Citie upon an hill"–as glorious in God's eyes as the biblical Jerusalem–had become, with post-Revolutionary achievements in education, commerce, and culture, the "Athens of America." The center of the American literary renaissance, Boston would soon be popularly known, with even less modesty, as the "Hub of the Universe." Howells confessed that "it rather surprised me to find that the literary associations of Boston referred so largely to Cambridge." In this town across the Charles River from Boston, Harvard College had educated a generation of ministers and writers who transformed the culture of New England and the nation, and Harvard itself was at various times home to eminent theologians such as Andrews Norton, scholars such as Francis James Child, and major writers such as Henry Wadsworth Longfellow and James Russell Lowell.

The following essay is a retrospective on antebellum Boston and Cambridge by George Ripley and George P. Bradford, both of whom participated in the literary renaissance in those cities. Boston may have basked in the glow of its powerful institutions and reputation, but in his essay "Boston," Ralph Waldo Emerson, the central figure of the age, reminded his readers that "a good principle of rebellion," "some thorn of dissent and innovation and heresy to prick the sides of conservatism," had been a trademark of the city of his birth since colonial times. The "moral" atmosphere that continued to pervade Boston and Cambridge in his own day fostered the influential reform community at Brook Farm, the principal founder of which was George Ripley. Ripley was commissioned to write the essay on "Philosophic Thought in Boston" for Justin Winsor's monumental four-volume The Memorial History of Boston *(1881), but he died before completing the assignment. George P. Bradford (1807–1890), a teacher at Brook Farm and friend of several Transcendentalists, completed this remarkable essay, which discusses the significance of Harvard, Transcendentalism, and Reform to the literary renaissance. Winsor's* History *was published the year before the death of Emerson.*

By the twentieth century, Howells had to admit, "Certainly the city of Boston has distinctly waned in literature, though it has waxed in wealth and population." But the antebellum literary renaissance centered in Boston and Cambridge left an enduring mark on the literature and wider culture of the nation.–Wesley T. Mott

Philosophic Thought In Boston

By George Ripley, LL.D., and George P. Bradford

The brief space allotted to the subject of the present chapter permits only a few rapid notices (mostly from personal recollections) of some of the eminent men who have exerted a marked influence on the tendency and development of thought in Boston during the nineteenth century, without any attempt at the profound discussion of philosophical principles, or the illustration of their character and influence. No powerful school of philosophy, with the qualities of unity and permanence, has sprung up among the people of Boston; but several individual, isolated essays have been made by her studious and thoughtful men to reach a higher sphere of intellectual life, which are perhaps entitled to a place in the modest records of speculative opinion.

In treating the subject of the following pages, I shall regard the University of Cambridge and the city of Boston as so closely identified in all the relations of literature and cultivation, that no account can be given of the intellectual progress of one, without assigning a large and most conspicuous place to the influence of the other. The prominent thinkers of Boston, with few exceptions, have been children of Harvard; most of them have been the pupils of her schools; many of them teachers in her halls, and the ministers of her discipline. With the widest differences of mental habit and achievement, wearing their opinions like the Hebrew garment of many colors, forming no sect for winning proselytes, no clan for urging conquests, they have met only on the common ground of love of learning, interest in the pursuit of truth, and affectionate devotion to the fair and venerable "mother of their minds."

Soon after the beginning of the present century an intellectual movement arose in Massachusetts which has been not unhappily compared to the Renaissance in Italy, that succeeded the dreary monotony of the Middle Ages. Art, letters, poetry, philosophy, social intercourse, domestic culture, public education, alike felt the genial impulse. The cradle and centre of this movement was Harvard College. Without precisely defining the date, the accession of John Thornton Kirkland to the presidency of the college, in 1810, may be said to mark the beginning of the era which has been so prolific in its results and so auspicious in its influence.

President Kirkland, indeed, made no pretensions to the character of a pioneer or a discoverer in the sphere of philosophy. His admirably balanced mind was not speculative, much less controversial. He had little genius, and no taste for the discussion of purely abstract questions; nor was he profoundly versed in the history of opinions: but the transparent clearness of his mental perceptions, the fine and subtile delicacy of his ethical instincts, his sympathy with whatever was rare and beautiful in literature, and the sagacity and firmness of his common-sense created around him an atmosphere in the highest degree favorable to the cultivation of thought, freedom of research, and frankness of expression. His personal aversion to the toil of composition has prevented him from leaving any adequate memorial of his affluent mind; but the magnetic charm of his conversation, the sweet amenity of his manner, and the quaint and fertile suggestions of his original imagination, must always be noted among the influences which led to the revival of a sound literature and an ideal philosophy among the descendants of the Puritans.

Seven years after the entrance of Dr. Kirkland upon the presidency, the chair of Moral Philosophy was filled by the appointment of Professor Levi Frisbie (1817), a graduate of the celebrated class of 1802, who held the office until his death, in 1822. During the brief period of five years he gave an impulse to the study of philosophy, and a direction to its subsequent development, which form an important feature in the history of modern thought in the vicinity of Boston. Professor Frisbie was a man of a peculiar and remarkable nature. His influence was founded on his personal character rather than on his writings. A chronic infirmity of sight prevented his free use of the pen, and his stores of learning and speculation were illustrated by his oral teachings in the class-room, and not by the composition of books. His presence afforded a lucid example of the ideal beauty of human character, or, to use the words of Professor Norton, his friend and biographer, of "the holy charm of moral loveliness," while the sweetness and dignity of his discourse inspired the fancy that the classical bees of Plato had once more settled on modern lips. A devotee of ancient literature, especially of the Latin classics, he was deeply interested in the whole range of elegant letters in the English language. He was a fervent admirer of the terse vigor and ethical severity of Tacitus, while his æsthetic tastes inspired him with a profound sympathy with the graceful ease and masculine sense of the writings of Maria Edgeworth. He was equally addicted to the cultivation of poetry and the study of philosophy. His rare speculative insight was united with singular critical acuteness, a lively and delicate fancy, and an unerring taste in literary composition. The influence of Professor Frisbie was not lost on the plastic minds that waited reverently on his words, and has been reproduced more or less directly in the solution of high problems of philosophy from that day to the present.

Professor Frisbie's examination of Adam Smith's *Theory of Moral Sentiments,* first published in 1819, is a master-piece of philosophical analysis, pointing out the defects and shortcomings of the author with equal insight and discrimination, and incidentally exposing the superficial and untenable conclusions of Paley, who until that time had been an important ethical authority with American students. The point which Professor Frisbie insisted on most urgently in his lectures on moral philosophy was the independent character of the idea of Right. This was an emphatic departure from the empirical theory of the sensuous philosophy,–the philosophy founded on the experience of the senses, as the antithesis of the intuitions of the soul, and which will be designated respectively in this chapter, and without any invidious intent, as the Sensuous and the Intuitive systems,–in which the followers of Locke and Paley had found a placid repose, and which had been made the cardinal principle of ethics in some of the most prominent seats of learning in this country. The spirit of Professor Frisbie's teachings is tersely expressed in a sentence from his inaugural discourse: "There will always be a Hobbes, a Rousseau, and a Godwin; let us then have also our Cudworths, our Butlers, and our Stewarts." The term Right, according to his theory, denotes an action which an intelligent moral agent is morally obliged to perform. Absolute right is a perception of the understanding–or, as we should say, the reason–discerning a real and inherent quality in actions. The idea of right is essentially distinct from that of utility, of the greatest happiness, of obedience to the divine will, or of a course of conduct determined by the assurance of reward or punishment. It is a simple idea; it can be described only by synonymous words; it possesses an identity of its own by its very essence, independent of any tendency or consequence. It is that which impresses the belief that an action should be performed, which we approve in the actions of others, and reflect upon with satisfaction in our own; which is perceived in a manner precisely similar to the perception of other ideas. The general tendency of right actions, Professor Frisbie affirms, is indeed to produce good or happiness; but the perception of right is distinct from the perception of happiness. There is another principle of action by which good is to be distributed besides a regard to the greatest good; and this principle is rectitude, or, in the widest sense, justice. Hence those actions are right which, on the whole, are of a nature to produce good or prevent harm, under the control of the principle of rectitude; but the idea of rectitude or absolute right is simple and intuitive, not the fruit of sensuous experience, of traditional teaching, of external authority, or of a rapacious selfhood. The ethical theory thus enunciated by Professor Frisbie forms the silver thread that runs through the most conspicuous philosophical suggestions–we can scarcely call them systems–which have found powerful representatives among the thinkers of Boston. It was the dawn of the intuitive philosophy, in its application to ethics, which has since cast a healing splendor over modern thought, and illustrated the place of Boston in the development of philosophy.

The name of Professor Levi Hedge, who succeeded to the chair of Moral Philosophy after the death of Professor Frisbie, although he had previously taught for a series of years in a kindred department of the college, recalls the memory of a modest, capable, and faithful worker in the sphere of philosophy, whose example was a lesson in the pursuit of truth, in exactness of expression, in felicity of illustration, and in thoroughness of exposition. He was an adherent of the Scottish philosophy, as represented by Dugald Stewart and Thomas Brown; and, as an expounder of their protest against the principles of Locke and of Paley, may be regarded as the fellow-laborer of Frisbie in anticipating the developments of the intuitive philosophy. His clearness of mind, his native good sense, his sound learning, and his austere integrity, gave him a wide influence among the clerisy of Massachusetts; and he will always hold an eminent place among the pioneers of philosophic thought in the capital of the State.

Contemporary with Professor Frisbie, and united with him by the most intimate ties of friendship and sympathy, was Andrews Norton, who, though trained in a different philosophical school, the principles of which he always cherished with singular tenacity, holds a distinguished place among the intellectual influences which have helped to stamp the society of Boston with an impress of liberal inquiry and original thought in the sphere of letters, philosophy, and art. Mr. Norton may be said to have formed a connecting link between the past and the future in American literary cultivation. He appeared at the moment when the scholastic attainments since the period of the Revolution were about to ripen into a more generous development. In early life he was far in advance of most of his contemporaries in sound and exact learning, and in what was then deemed an excessive freedom of speculation. He was connected with Harvard, first as tutor, then as librarian, and afterward as Professor of Sacred Literature. In each of these offices his influence was marked and salutary. His thorough scholarship served to give form and substance to the literary enthusiasm which at that time prevailed in Cambridge. His refined and exquisite taste cast an air of purity and elegance around the spirit of the place. His habits were as severe as those of a mediæval monk. His love of literature was a passion. The predominant qualities of his mind were clearness of perception, rigidity of judgment, accuracy of expression, and a chaste imagination. His peculiar sphere was that of theology and criticism, but no department of elegant letters was foreign to his tastes. Every scholar in Cambridge received an inspiring impulse from his example. The lucidity of his intellect, the depth of his erudition, and the choice felicities of his language presented a new standard of excellence, and gave a higher tone to the literary character of Boston. But the personal traits of Mr. Norton exerted a still more powerful influence. His hatred of pretension was equalled only by his devotion to truth. He spurned with a beautiful disdain whatever he deemed to be false, or shallow, or insincere. He demanded the stamp of genuineness, reality, harmony of proportion and perspective on everything which challenged his approval. His sympathies were not easily won, nor was he lavish in the expression of even favorable judgments. He was free, perhaps, from what may be called moral suspicion, but he certainly often evinced an excess of intellectual caution. A man of stainless purity of purpose, of high integrity of life, with a profound sense of religion, and severe simplicity of manners, his example was a perpetual rebuke to the conceitedness of learning, the vanity of youthful scholarship, and the habit of "vain and shallow thought." His influence is deeply stamped on the literature of Harvard; the intellectual atmosphere has not yet lost the fragrance of his presence; and if he solved no deep problems of philosophy, if his insight was restricted within a comparatively narrow compass, and he failed to appreciate justly the philosophic tendencies of the age, yet the course of speculative thought in Boston, it is believed, is largely indebted to the influence of his character and example for whatever tincture of sound learning it may exhibit, for its thoroughness of inquiry, its accuracy of research, and its comparative freedom from extreme and erratic conclusions.

The tendency of Mr. Norton's mind in regard to themes of philosophical inquiry was in a sceptical direction. Adopting the cardinal principles of Locke and Hume in regard to the origin of knowledge and the foundations of belief, he pursued them with strict logical sequence to their natural conclusions. In his view there could be but two sources of ideas,–experience and testimony,–which in the final analysis were resolved into one. We have the teachings of experience in regard to the facts of the material universe; and concerning the realm of spiritualities, we are dependent on the authority of divine revelation. The human mind has no inherent faculty of perception in the sphere of facts which transcend the cognizance of the senses. We cannot rely upon the intuitions of reason as the ground of faith in the suggestions of the soul. The veracity of the human spirit as the condition of truth formed no part of his scheme of philosophy. There is no absolute certainty, Mr. Norton affirms, beyond the limit of momentary consciousness,–a certainty that vanishes at once into the region of metaphysical doubt. The doctrine of an intuitive faculty for discovering the truths of religion is utterly untenable; we are not conscious of possessing any such faculty, and there can be no other proof of its existence. Intuition can inform us of nothing but what exists in our own minds, including the relations of our own ideas; it is therefore a mere absurdity to maintain that we have an intuitive knowledge of the truths of religion. I am not aware that Mr. Norton reduced these principles to the form of a connected system, or that he would not have shrunk from the ultimate consequences which they involved. He held them, I think, as incidental to certain theories of dogmatic theology, of which he was the strenuous champion, rather than as a formal, coherent, and uniting body of philosophical truth; but that their spirit pervaded his writings, especially in the latter years of his life, and that they were interwoven with the whole fabric of his mental convictions, will not, I believe, be called in question by those who are the most intimately acquainted with the character of his mind and the tendency of his opinions. The influence of Mr. Norton in philosophy, however, was provocative rather than creative; he led to doubt with regard to the ancient foundations rather than to sympathy with his peculiar ideas; he prepared the way for vigorous combat, and not for docile acceptance; and, like the influence of Hume on the virile mind of Kant, which "aroused him from his dogmatic slumbers," and sent him forth in quest of new achievements in the pursuit of truth, he inspired not a few of the earnest-minded young men of the day with a passionate zeal for the conquest of the holy Graal,–the discovery of the golden chalice which was brimming with pure wine for the life of the soul.

Mr. Ripley was prevented from completing this chapter by his death. In accordance with his plan, of which he left a sketch, we shall continue the subject principally with an account of some of the persons and writers who may be considered as the exponents or organs of the various phases of thought, and whose works had a special influence in developing or directing its tendencies. The period beginning in 1830, or a little earlier, may be noted as one of especial activity and fertility in this respect as well as in many others. Among the salient points and conspicuous influences which marked this period we may signalize the early days of the *Liberator* and of Garrison, like "a voice crying in the wilderness;" the preaching and writings of Dr. Channing; the lectures and writings of Mr. Emerson; Dr. Hedge's articles in the *Christian Examiner* on German Philosophy, Coleridge, and other topics, and his Dudleian Lecture; Theodore Parker at West Roxbury, and later in Boston; Carlyle's various writings; the writings of Dr. O. A. Brownson; the conversations at the house of Dr. Channing, in which Mr. Jonathan Phillips, Dr. Follen, George Ripley, and others took part; the controversy between Professor Norton and Mr. Ripley; and the inception of the Brook Farm enterprise, and the steps taken for its actual realization in 1841.

The period thus indicated was one of great excitement of thought on moral and intellectual questions, especially with the young and the generation just coming upon the stage. Before the impulse given to the revival of thought which Mr. Ripley, in a general way, places about the time of the accession of Dr. Kirkland to the presidency of Harvard College, there had been little taste for abstract speculation, and the Sensuous System of Locke (to adopt, for convenience, the term used by Mr. Ripley) was generally accepted as authority on questions of this kind. A step away from this was taken when the famous *Essay on the Understanding* was disused as a text-book at Harvard, and the rational, but not very profound, metaphysics of the Scotch school adopted in its place. The *Natural Theology, Evidences of Christianity,* and *Moral Philosophy* of Paley were text-books in the college, and were accepted, and perhaps generally acquiesced in, as authority in the fields of morals and theology. In this condition of thought the fervent eloquence of Channing, the inspiring words of Emerson and Carlyle, the stirring appeals of Parker and other reformers to high and abstract principles, came like a fresh and invigorating breeze into a dull and sluggish atmosphere.

Of the influences of which we have spoken, Dr. Channing's preaching and writings are among the earliest in point of time. His connection with our theological and Antislavery history has been treated by other hands.[1] He belonged quite decidedly and avowedly to what we may call, in accordance with the distinctive terms before indicated, the Intuitive School. This philosophy derives our knowledge from the intuitions of the soul, and is in opposition to that recognizing the senses and experience as its only ultimate source. We are informed by an intimate friend of Channing, who was very familiar with his thought, that he repudiated Locke's philosophy while in college, and accepted, on moral and metaphysical questions, the statements of Price in his *Dissertations on Matter and Spirit,* and of Hutcheson's moral philosophy. He recognized also a harmony between his own thought and that of the German systems of philosophy as reported by Madame de Staël. He acknowledged his obligation to the poetry of Wordsworth and Coleridge, and to the philosophy of the latter he considered himself specially and greatly indebted. He also read with pleasure Cousin's *Philosophy* and the writings of Carlyle, particularly his *Sartor Resartus.* These tastes will indicate, to those acquainted with the currents of thought at that period, his position with regard to the two parties, which we may designate as the Old and the New,–or, as the latter was called in the language of the time, the Transcendental School. This attitude of his, especially after his part in the Antislavery movement, and in advocating the broadest toleration and freedom in some unpopular cases,–like that of Abner Kneeland, who was indicted for blasphemy,–grieved some of his friends, and offended and disaffected others among the conservatives, who had been wont to listen with delight to his preaching, and who had reverenced the saintliness of his character. In the controversy between Professor Norton and Mr. Ripley we think his sympathy was with the latter, though the former had long been his personal friend.

Although Dr. Channing did not have occasion to advocate distinctly any special system of philosophy, yet the spirit of the school most in harmony with his own thought and pervading his preaching and writing, whose influence was so widely felt, must have had its effect on the prevailing thought of the day. Notwithstanding his philosophic tendencies were decidedly in the direction we have indicated, he must not be regarded as sympathizing fully with all the forms and phases of the Transcendental[2] movement; but his chief interest in philosophy we may suppose was in its relation to religion and morals; and this philosophy, in his view, formed the only true foundation for these.

The fermentation of thought and feeling developed by the Transcendental movement, especially among the young, has, we think, nothing similar at the present day, and is something very interesting to recall: perhaps devotion to art and practical philanthropy have taken its place. Foremost among the influences that stimulated and sustained this state of feeling were the writings and the public addresses, lectures, etc. of Mr. Emerson. At first he was known to a small but admiring circle as a most interesting preacher, remarkable for independence and originality of thought as well as charm of style and manner; and by many, especially of the congregation of which he was pastor, and by those who knew him more familiarly, he was valued also for higher and more intimate qualities. But he had not much attracted the notice of the general public until his opinion and action in relation to the observance of the communion service caused a good deal of feeling in the body of Christians with which he was associated. As he could not, with his views, continue to administer the rite, his connection with the society of which he was the minister was dissolved. After his return from a visit to Europe he gave a number of lectures; and several of them relating to his tour abroad were of a descriptive character. These were afterward followed by several courses in 1835 and successive years; and, besides, he delivered public addresses on different occasions. The subjects of these discourses were some of a literary, but mostly of a philosophical and ethical, character.[3]

In 1836 appeared a little volume called *Nature,* which, like his other early works, excited the enthusiastic admiration of some, and provoked the adverse criticism or ridicule of others. The earlier courses of the lectures are pleasantly associated, in the recollections of some, with the hall of the Old Masonic Temple in which they were given; and they constituted an era in the social and literary history of Boston, as well as in the life and culture of many individuals. They were looked for from year to year as one of the special pleasures of the winter season. Thus the influence of his writings, but more particularly of his lectures, was deeply and widely felt. To his hearers they seemed to open a new world,–new charms in literature, in Nature, and in thought; new and deeper delights and significance in living,–giving an interpretation of their own minds, souls, and being, so different from the dogmatic formulas and conventional statements common in that sterility of thought in which "the hungry sheep look up, and are not fed." To what were these effects due? What was the secret of this influence? We may say, perhaps, that it was the assertion of the high powers, dignity, and integrity of the soul, its absolute independence and right to interpret for itself the meaning of life, untrammelled by tradition and conventions; the assertion of the soul with its ideas and instincts as the oracle within, the source to us of knowledge and thought in its intimate connection with the source of all life and truth; of the right and duty of all to look at truth and the facts of the universe face to face, thus calling to self-reliance and cheerful hope; teaching and inspiring by his own deep conviction the reality of truth and good; opening glimpses of the eternal beauty, and imparting the joy of high thoughts and lofty purpose. These, with the incidental charm of the beauty, piquancy, and condensed expressiveness of his style; the refined simplicity of his manner; the calm earnestness and sincerity pervading his words,–combined with the remarkable ethical character, the power of touching the springs of highest moral emotion and of lifting his hearers into a loftier sphere, "an ampler ether, a diviner air,"–were some of the attractions which drew year after year, with increasing interest, multitudes of young and old, conservatives and radicals, the highly cultivated and those in whom a quick sensibility to what is high and pure supplied the place of culture. In hearing him, a serene and cheerful faith and hope seemed to them to flow over the world and over human life like a brighter atmosphere. And this it was which the young could feel and understand; so that when, if we may be allowed to repeat once more a jest which has been told over and over again to weariness, a man of distinction for learning and ability declared that he could not understand Mr. Emerson but his daughters could, he spoke more truly than he knew.

The term excitement, applied to the feelings of his hearers, seems hardly the proper one. It was rather sometimes like the enlivening effect of the morning breeze, sometimes like the transporting and at the same time tranquilizing effect of high and solemn music, dissolving the hard rigors of life, and infusing sweetness and hope.

The feelings, however, excited by Mr. Emerson's position and words were not all admiration, but some of a quite opposite character. It is amusing and instructive (when we consider the position he now holds, and how almost universally he is the object of such loving and reverent regard, distinguished and admired in the literature and thought of both hemispheres) to recall the way in which he was once regarded and spoken of by a large number of those considered to be the dispensers of correct opinion and taste, and equally so to read the current criticism of his earlier productions.[4]

Many who disliked the general tone of what he said contented themselves with ridicule, for which some peculiarities of his style seemed to offer opportunity; others laughed at what they deemed his fanciful and unsound notions, and at the craze of the young people concerning him. Among these, some who knew and esteemed him personally smiled good-naturedly at what seemed novelties or oddities, and at the infatuation of their children; but others took it more seriously. Wise and good men who had labored with earnestness and fidelity in the belief of certain opinions and religious doctrines, the foundations of which seemed assailed or threatened by the freedom with which Mr. Emerson spoke, were pained and offended, especially by his address before the students of the Cambridge Theological School, in July, 1838, in which he spoke of beliefs devoutly cherished by many, not irreverently indeed, but with a freedom which was to them a grief and an offence. Some of his hearers of the conservative class, attracted by the charm of his lectures, tolerated as they might the freedom with which he touched on the exciting and controverted questions of the day in consideration of their enjoyment in listening to him, though at times disturbed or offended when he came too near matters connected with fierce debate and controversy.[5]

Although Mr. Emerson cannot be said to belong to any school or system of philosophy as such, yet the character and tendency of his thought place him most decidedly with the Idealist, Intuitive, or Transcendental School,[6] of which in popular estimation he stood for the representative and type.

The connection of Dr. Hedge with the Transcendental movement was close and important. His education in Germany, where he had passed some years in the earlier part of his life, had given him, besides a familiarity with the language of that country, an interest in its literature, and developed the taste which has led to his wide and intimate acquaintance with the German philosophy and sympathy with its spirit and ideas. This tendency showed itself while he was a student in the theological school at Cambridge, and then and afterward inspired many of his friends with something of his own interest and enthusiasm. In an article on Coleridge,[7] he took occasion to give some account of the leading metaphysicians of Germany–Kant, Fichte, Schelling–and of their systems of philosophy; and thus placed before the public a distinct exposition and defence of the Transcendental philosophy, which may be regarded as an important point in the history of that phase of thought in this vicinity. Speaking of the Transcendtal philosophy, he characterizes it as "an attempt to penetrate into the most hidden mysteries of our being." To the opponents of this philosophy this attempt seemed both futile and a fruitful source of obscurities and absurdities. In illustration of this view they liked to instance the seemingly unintelligible, or what they chose to consider ridiculous, utterances of those who had a taste for the speculations of that school, or were ranked among its adherents.

In 1851 Dr. Hedge delivered the Dudleian lecture at Harvard College. His subject was "Natural Religion."[8] In this he takes the ground that all religious truth is properly revealed; that this belongs to a higher power than the unassisted human understanding; and that it has received its original light from revelation. The most striking part of this discourse, and what particularly characterizes it, is his criticism of the common argument for the existence of God from instances of design in the universe. He maintains that design is no adequate proof, and indeed is worthless as a proof by which to establish this truth, since in all such reasoning or proof we carry with us an idea of God already existing in our own minds and in no way dependent on the instances of design. He says:–

> "The argument from design has its origin in a law of the mind which demands intelligence as the co-ordinate of being. Whatever conviction it produces is due to that law. Besides, though we grant the argument from design the uttermost that can be claimed for it, what does it give us after all, but the wonderful mechanician, the unfathomable artist? What religion wants and declares is a Father in Heaven, a moral Governor, Ruler, and Judge of the rational world. Of this God the natural proofs are our own consciousness, our moral instincts, and the universal consent of mankind."

Earlier than this, Dr. Hedge had taken some part in the discussion of phrenology, which excited a lively but rather short-lived interest in this community on the occasion of a visit of Dr. Spurzheim, one of its founders and chief advocates. This system excited a good deal of interest, and had a certain popularity, as it seemed to offer a cheap and easy philosophy of the mental and moral faculties (a subject of so much interest), and to put the matter almost literally, so to speak, into the hands of all. Its claims and pretensions were attacked by Dr. Hedge[9] in a tone more sarcastic and less respectful than was his wont in dealing with what was opposed to his views, as its pretensions seemed to him unfounded, and its methods as well as doctrines unphilosophical. He points out the materialistic character of the system, as well as its insufficiency as an account of the mental and moral phenomena of our constitution.

Already, in November, 1833, there had appeared in the *Examiner* Dr. Hedge's paper on Swedenborg, which is on the whole a favorable view of him and of his place in the philosophy of religion; and it treats his claims with respect and impartiality. A strong interest in the religious doctrines and writings of the Swedish theosopher characterized many other thoughtful persons, and those who consciously or unconsciously were in sympathy with the spiritual philosophy. In Mr. Emerson's *Representative Men* we find Swedenborg taken as the type of the Mystic, and a very high place assigned to him among the seers, teachers, and prophets of the world. The writings of Sampson Reed, too, an able and devoted follower of Swedenborg, were inspired and pervaded by his teachings. The writings of Swedenborg were also read and admired by many serious and thoughtful persons who did not accept him in the same sense with Mr. Reed, as an inspired teacher, but who found the truths of divine and human knowledge illustrated by the remarkable insight and profound thought of the Swedish seer. Thus his teachings have had a much wider influence, and have been much more deeply felt, than is represented by the number of the professed receivers of his doctrine.[10]

Mr. Henry James, too, has devoted much time and subtile thought, in various writings, to illustrate and explain in numerous relations the truths found in the works of Swedenborg, for whose mind and teachings he has shown profound reverence and admiration.

The part and position of George Ripley in the Transcendental movement was an important and prominent one in various ways. His early life was passed at Greenfield, Mass., where he was brought up in the faith and influence of the Orthodox Congregational Church. After the years spent at the University and the Divinity School at Cambridge, he was settled in 1828 as a clergyman over a Unitarian society in Boston, where he continued as minister for several years. He had an ardent love of knowledge and remarkable power of rapid acquisition; and as his taste led him in the direction of theological and metaphysical studies, he became an acute and accomplished scholar in these departments. His ardent spirit was ever active, and his industry untiring. While connected with the religious society he undertook an important literary enterprise,–the publication of a work called *Specimens of Foreign Standard Literature,* which was continued for some time, and embraced several valuable works. In this series the *Philosophical Miscellanies* of Cousin, Constant, and Jouffroy were translated by Mr. Ripley himself; some of the other volumes, by Mr. John S. Dwight, Miss Margaret Fuller, Mr. W. H. Channing, and Dr. S. Osgood. The first volumes appeared in 1838, the last in 1842. Most of these works were imbued with the new and fresh thought of the time, and in their general tendency were opposed to the philosophy of experience, as represented by the Locke school. The wide researches of Mr. Ripley led him to acquaintance with the German philosophy and theology which then occupied so important a place in the intellectual world, and he became warmly interested in many of the writers of Germany,–in Kant and Herder, and more particularly in Schleiermacher, whom he much admired, and whose statement of religion he found very satisfactory.

Mr. Ripley was always a busy writer, and while minister of the society in Boston he contributed a number of articles to the *Christian Examiner,* which for a long time was a leading journal of the Unitarian denomination, and embraced in its pages a wide range of discussion on philosophy, morals, and religion. A paper by him on Sir James Mackintosh's work on the moral sentiment goes into a lucid and able discussion of the relation of virtue to utility, and advocates the Intuitive in opposition to the Utilitarian theory of morals and of the ground and origin of moral obligation. This placed him, on the question of morals, as his other writings do on those of religion and philosophy, decidedly in the ranks of the Spiritual or Transcendental school.

An important occasion in Mr. Ripley's literary life, and one which added a good deal to his reputation in the theological world, was his controversy with Professor Andrews Norton, of the Cambridge Theological School.[11] Its chief interest consists in our having in conflict before us representatives of the two different schools of philosophy,–Professor Norton representing that of experience and the senses, in the last resort, as the only source of our knowledge; Mr. Ripley, that which we have called the Intuitional, which regards the mind itself, with its intuitions and cognitions, as an independent source of knowledge and belief,–which latter, claiming in the past the names of Plato, Descartes, Cudworth, Malebranche, and Berkeley, was destined to exert so wide an influence among us from the works of Coleridge, Carlyle, Emerson, Hedge, Alcott, Marsh, and others. Though the controversy seems mainly theological and personal, the roots of the positions of the antagonists strike down into the two divergent systems of philosophy, and the theological ground rests on the philosophical.[12]

We pass now to speak of Mr. Ripley's connection with the famous socialistic experiment conducted by the Brook Farm Phalanx. This enterprise was the object of much misapprehension, of a good deal of ridicule and even bitter hostility. It was natural enough that an institution so novel in its arrangements and its claims, so opposed to conservative notions and feelings, should encounter prejudice, misapprehension, and ridicule; neither is it strange that many mistakes, and ludicrous ones, should have been made. Embracing in its numbers such heterogeneous materials, and naturally attracting persons of fantastic notions, with various peculiarities and singularities of character, it was to be expected that some would have vagaries, and some affect singular ways. So the public very legitimately had its laugh. But perhaps it was hardly fair, though natural enough, to fix on these oddities and absurdities as the salient and chief characteristics of the enterprise in which many sensible, thoughtful, worthy, and benevolent persons set themselves seriously to work to carry out an experiment which had attractions for themselves, and which they fondly and generously, if not wisely, hoped would lead to important benefit for mankind. To overlook their humane and generous aims and objects, and what were in many respects their wise, skilful, and efficient arrangements,–to ignore, too, what was really accomplished, and to fix attention only on the mistakes and ludicrous aspects of the enterprise,–was not quite just, nor was it a true view of the matter. The mistakes were necessarily the more obvious features to those outside; often made known, too, from the unfriendly gossip of some who became dissatisfied. The better accomplishments could not be so well known without interior acquaintance, or at least sympathy, with the movement. It is, of course, not possible to form any proper estimate of the influence of this experiment, or of what was really accomplished by it. It certainly taught some lessons about associated life, though it may not have demonstrated either its feasibility or the contrary; but that it had various and important influences in the spirit and direction of the ideas with which it was started, we think many who were there will testify. Some of these look back on it as a very profitable as well as delightful part of their lives, and no doubt owe to it–beside valuable practical experience–higher and more generous aims, a free and varied culture, wider sympathies, and more humane views of the relations of society.

The influence on the young, we may perhaps say, was especially valuable; affording them as it did a wide opportunity for out-of-door life, with its broadening and emancipating effects, combined with instruction from many different teachers of diversified character, and bringing them into daily intimacy with persons of various culture and experience, and with principles of humanity and brotherhood as the basis of daily life. And may we not believe that with all the shortcomings and unfaithfulness to its ideal, with the collisions and heartburnings almost inseparable from associations of human beings in any enterprise, a large spirit of humanity was developed and prevailed, and that this brief and imperfect experiment had an important influence in enlarging, emphasizing, defining, and deepening the spirit of true democracy?

It would seem that Mr. Ripley was not satisfied with the efficacy of the church modes of administering Christianity, in promoting its objects and combating the evils of the present social arrangements, and was led to hope for more effective benefit to the cause of humanity and for the protection of human brotherhood, from some organization of labor on the principle of co-operation instead of competition, and with agricultural labor as the basis. Questions relating to this matter were discussed between him and some of the leading philanthropists of the day; and these, Dr. Channing among them, took an interest in his ideas, though probably none of them had the same sanguine hopes. Thus the plan of doing something toward a reform of social organization, by some form of association, gradually took shape in his mind. The subject of Life in Community, or Association, as a remedy for the evils of the present form of social life, seems to have been in the air at the time. The Mendon Association of Adin Ballou and his associates, and perhaps other similar experiments, were in agitation or actually begun. But whatever aid and incitement Mr. Ripley may have owed to the sympathy and thought of others, we may assert that this enterprise derived its origin from his philanthropic idealism, and that to him belongs the credit of having given form to the scheme as actually carried out, and of having devised and fixed upon the ways and means of its inception and realization.[13]

This movement, in the mind of Mr. Ripley and others, was one form of the strong and rising feeling of humanity and of the brotherhood of man, then so widely pervading the community. With it, too, came the desire and hope for better conditions of life, in which the less fortunate classes might come to share in the privileges, comforts, and various advantages belonging to civilized society.

The feeling which at this time manifested itself in an excited form in the Antislavery agitation may indirectly have had some effect in suggesting or stimulating this movement. Mr. Ripley, and others with him, while sympathizing with the object of the Abolitionists, thought that as the evils of which slavery is so signal and conspicuous a form lay deep in the present constitution and arrangement of society, so their remedy could only be found in a modification or radical change of ordinary life. The feeling, then, which lay at the bottom of the Brook Farm enterprise, and from which it mainly sprang, we may say, from acquaintance with many of its chief actors and friends, was dissatisfaction with the existing conditions of society,–that, under these, some classes enjoy the advantages of high culture and the gratification of the intellect and taste, and if obliged to work in some way for subsistence they yet have leisure and opportunity for refined recreation and for the enjoyment of comfortable or elegant modes of living, and are in some respects subject to more favorable moral influences; while under these, also, other classes are doomed to wearisome or painful drudgery and incessant toil, without opportunity for the enjoyments of intellect and taste, confined to dreary and squalid conditions of existence, and more exposed to temptations at least to the more flagrant crimes. Then, again, there was the feeling that there is something wrong in the mode of industry as now constituted,–namely, competitive industry; a point so much insisted on by Fourier and other advocates of association, in which one man's gain is another man's loss, and the necessities of which make it the interest of each to get away from others, and to appropriate to himself as large a share as possible of this world's goods,–a condition of things seemingly so contrary to the spirit of Christian brotherhood. Consequently a mode of life was desired, and even anticipated with more or less confidence by different persons, according to character or mental bias, in which this evil condition of the relations of society might be corrected.

The views and feelings we have thus attempted to indicate, and which so readily suggest themselves to the thoughtful and humane, seem to have lain at the bottom of the movement, and most of those attracted to it shared more or less in them; but, besides these, there were various other considerations inciting to an interest in the enterprise and a wish to take part in it. The idea of a pleasant social life, with congenial society, somewhat free from burdensome conventions, moved some. Then there was the idea of a life of mingled physical and intellectual labor, as more proper and healthful, combined with the notion that exclusive occupation in one or the other is unfavorable to mental and bodily health, and that the alternation of the two, as it is the duty and benefit of all, is also the right and privilege of all. Other considerations were those of the economies of a united household of several families,–economies of fuel and labor, and of the apparatus for cooking, washing, agricultural uses, etc. Among those drawn to it there were some, who, willing to work, were yet indisposed to the struggle for existence in civilized society, or who in the struggle had been unsuccessful. Young women, too, who had found no sphere suited to their taste, culture, or capabilities, hailed the opportunity of a home and a support, in return for work they were willing and glad to give, in conditions of society agreeable to their tastes and character. Some were mainly attracted by the agricultural feature, to whom the cultivation of the soil, as the most primitive and natural, seemed also the most innocent and agreeable, form of industry, and Mr. Ripley himself took much interest in this aspect.

These various considerations and feelings were mingled in different proportions in the different individuals, and had their influence; and they were perhaps more or less shared as motives by all who came with thought and reflection to the enterprise. If it may seem that most of the thoughts and feelings adopted and proclaimed with so much enthusiasm and emphasis are quite commonplace, indeed mere platitudes, it should be considered that since then the mind of society has made progress in democratic ideas; and may we not believe that this, too, is due in some degree to the zeal with which they were adopted and proclaimed at that time? It should be considered, too, that this was an attempt to give substantial form and embodiment to these thoughts and feelings. Mr. Ripley, who was of a sanguine temperament, with remarkable power of quick perception and rapid apprehension, when this matter of associative industry as a remedy for the ills of society was brought to his mind, was seized with the idea of some form of community, some mode of life in association and of co-operative industry, which might secure better conditions for humanity. Finding a number of persons disposed to sympathize, either practically or theoretically, with his views and hopes, he went forward with an ardor very inspiring to those who came in contact with him. He threw himself with enthusiastic and disinterested zeal into his plans and schemes, worked long and generously, amid many discouragements, with unselfish and never-failing devotion for their accomplishment and success. While under these influences the opportunity of securing a farm which seemed to offer various advantages for trying his experiment induced him to take it. This property was situated in West Roxbury, now a part of Boston, and touched on the towns of Dedham and Newton. It consisted of about two hundred acres, part of it rocky and not very fertile land; part an extensive meadow, reaching to and bordering on Charles River, which was mainly its Dedham boundary. There was on the farm a pleasant old family mansion, on rising ground or sort of knoll, along which, and winding through the meadow till it reached the river, was a lively brook, whence the farm had its name, and which to the younger people was a source of amusement and pleasure, as they wandered along its banks or trapped the wild game of its neighborhood. The nearness of the farm to the city was an advantage in several ways, as for instance affording a market for its products. It was, too, an attraction to some not yet entirely emancipated from the benefits and charms of that civilization which, theoretically, seemed so full of evils; for it should be considered that of those who were early members of the family there were quite a number who had enjoyed many of the advantages and luxuries of civilization and high culture. There was the hope, however, that in time it would not be necessary to go so far to seek those delights of music, art, etc., which on the true theory of life in association were to find place and cultivation among themselves.

A small company,–the pioneers in the work,–first planted themselves on the ground early in April, 1841. Among those who thus began the work were Mr. and Mrs. Ripley, and Miss Marianne Ripley, his sister, who had had a school for young children in Boston, some of whom she brought with her. She made a separate family with them in a small house near the farm; and, in the rather fanciful nomenclature adopted, this was called the Nest, as the principal house was named the Hive.[14]

Mrs. Ripley, who was of an energetic and enthusiastic temperament, entered very heartily into the views and plans of her husband, and was always a prominent person in the conduct of affairs. She threw herself with zeal and efficiency into the various departments in which she could take part; especially that of teaching, for which she was so well qualified by her knowledge and previous experience.[15] Besides the principal persons and workers, there were a number of young persons who were here mainly for education, but who sometimes took part in the farm and other work, not always in the most efficient way. There were in the community first and last a large number of such young persons, as many of the principal members were well qualified to give instruction by previous experience, or by their knowledge in different departments. There were also, much of the time, a number of boarders, attracted by the agreeable society, by the pleasant situation, or by sympathy with the idea and mode of life. This appendage of the school and boarders, though not strictly in accordance with the idea of the community life, was taken advantage of to furnish the necessary means for the first starting of the experiment and carrying it on in its early stages, toward which the proceeds of the farm would not have gone far.

And we may here say something of the ways and means of meeting the expenses, and providing for the wants of the company. The food was furnished either from the products of the farm, or was purchased. The necessary funds came from the sale of the farm products, or from other sources indicated above. The clothing of those properly to be reckoned members was also provided for in a similar way, and set off against services of one kind or another. This for the most part could be afforded at a somewhat reduced rate, the material being purchased in quantity, and made up among themselves by those who brought the requisite skill and practice with them,–for in this microcosm a considerable variety of occupations and industries was represented. The school was an important source of income; and this was continued till the end, or nearly so, of the existence of the association. Some of the pupils took part in the work, and thus defrayed a portion of the expense of board, etc. There were always a large number of young persons, scholars, boarders, etc., and this led to a considerable mingling of amusement of various kinds. Moreover, some of the company had a special skill in arranging and directing this element. We may in this connection remark that a prominent feature of the life was the opportunity given for the exercise of divers gifts and faculties; and the way in which they may be easily and naturally brought into play is one of the claims of the theory of association. There were amusements suited to the different seasons,–tableaux, charades, dances; in the winter, skating and coasting, for which the knolls, wide meadows, and river afforded favorable opportunities; in summer, rural fêtes, masquerades, etc., in the charming localities, rocks, and woods around the place.

A great charm of the life was the free and natural intercourse for which it gave opportunity, and the working of the elective affinities, which here had more full play; so that while a kindly feeling was the general spirit of the family, little groups of friends, drawn together in closer relations by taste and sympathy, soon declared themselves. By most who were there the life was felt to be very charming. The relief from the fetters and burdensome conventions of society, from the

> "greetings where no kindness is, and all
> The dreary intercourse of daily life,"

was a constant delight to those who had suffered from them in the artificial arrangements and forms of society. At the same time the relief and pleasures of solitude were not wanting, as the taste that might lead any to withdraw to the solitude of the woods or of their own rooms was respected. There was for a long time a large infusion of romantic feeling and enthusiasm, especially among the younger and more inexperienced, who knew nothing of the embarrassment of providing ways and means. Nor was this enthusiasm confined to these. There was something of the "tête montée" pervading to a great extent the company, and of the feeling expressed in the verse of Virgil,–

> "Magnus ab integro sæclorum nascitur ordo."

And if in some instances there was a slight falsetto tone, at the same time there was a great deal of genuine faith in the idea; and a conviction obtained that such a life was in many respects a truer and better as well as a happier one than that of the unfortunates who, according to the current phraseology, were still in *civilization,*– which was a word of somewhat sinister import in the Brook Farm community. Among the less wise and thoughtful there was indeed carried to a silly exaggeration a pity for the *civilisées.* Notwithstanding all this, justice should be done to the feeling of the more wise and thoughtful in entering upon and going through the enterprise. This, we think, those well acquainted with them would bear witness was for the most part simple; and, though colored with an enthusiasm which seemed exaggerated to many, was without that special consciousness and pretension with which they were charged.

The agricultural feature was always a very important one, and of great interest to many of the company, to whom its various aspects and phases were a novelty. Hawthorne, who was there during most of the first summer, and also part of the following winter, was an efficient and stalwart worker in this department, and found amusement in his apprenticeship to some parts of the farm work,–as milking, etc., and especially, for a long time, in the pleasant operations of hay-making, which was an important part in consequence of the extensive meadows. He was attracted thither, as we understood, by the hope of an opportunity of leading a life more in conformity with his tastes and feelings than was possible in the common arrangements of society, and also of uniting successfully manual with intellectual work. But we think he was disappointed in this, and found it not easy to combine writing with severe bodily toil; and as the former was so manifestly his vocation, he gave up the farm work in the course of the first summer, and though he remained there for some time longer, it was as a boarder, not a worker. The younger people had, as usual, their admirations and worships; and Hawthorne was eminently fitted to be one of these, partly by the prestige of his reputation, but more in consequence of a real appreciation of his genius as a writer, as well as from the impression made by his remarkable and fine personal appearance and by his whole bearing. He was shy in his ways; and though he mingled with the rest of the company in the evening gatherings in the hall or parlor of the Hive, he was silent and apparently self-absorbed, but no doubt carefully observing as was his wont, and finding material for his writing.[16] There was something about him, however, that attracted, notwithstanding this reserve.

In process of time new arrangements were found necessary to accommodate the increasing numbers. The original mansion-house, the Hive, was enlarged by successive additions; and then, with the further increase of numbers, the Eyrie, and afterward the Cottage and the Pilgrim House, were added. Later, some workshops for the exercise of several new branches of industry were erected,–among these, shoemaking, though never on a large scale; the manufacture of Britannia ware, lamps, teapots, etc.; carpenters' rules; carpentry; sash and blind making. The most profitable work, we are informed, was that of the farm, and branches connected with it,–like the nursery, and the business of the trees and greenhouse.

As to compensation, the principle was to apportion it in general to the number of hours, and also to the difficulty and disagreeableness of the kind of work. This was received in the form of board, clothing, and dividends on labor. Compensation was also allowed for extra work.

At the beginning the arrangements were quite simple, and the organization slight; but the tendency was constantly to a more scientific form, according to the principles of Fourier, especially after the scheme had attracted some of his professed disciples and students. It was the aim and hope to have it eventually organized and conducted wholly on that system; though (perhaps from want of sufficient numbers) this was never thoroughly carried out.[17] The last building, the Phalanstery, was arranged in some measure in conformity with these principles. It was on a large scale, and had many suites of apartments for different families, but was destroyed by fire before completion. The institution thus suffered a loss from which it never recovered, and finally came to an end in the fall of 1847, about six years after it began. Pecuniary difficulties in conducting it, we presume, may be stated as the main cause of its failure and of the necessity for its abandonment.

Most of the time there were no religious observances by the association as such,[18] as many of the inmates attended Theodore Parker's church, or others in the neighborhood, while some went to Boston. At one time, however, there were religious services conducted by William H. Channing, or other clergymen who may have been present. Also for a considerable period meetings were held in Boston on Sunday; and these, too, were generally conducted by Mr. Channing, and often had reference to the doctrines of association, in which he was much interested.

An important point to be noted in the history of this movement was the publication of a journal called the *Harbinger,* to advocate the principles of association. The first number is dated June 14, 1845. It was continued for several years, and was first printed at Brook Farm, afterward at New York. In the manifesto of the first number we find its object thus stated: "It is proposed to publish a weekly newspaper for the examination and discussion of the great questions in social science, politics, and the arts which command the attention of all believers in the progress and elevation of humanity, . . . and to be devoted to the cause of a radical, organic social reform, as essential to the highest development of man's nature. . . . The principles of universal unity, as taught by Charles Fourier, in their application to society, we believe are at the foundation of all genuine social progress; and it will be our aim to discuss and defend these principles. . . . The social reform, of which the signs are everywhere visible, comprehends all others." This journal, which was conducted with zeal and ability, is important as showing the faith, earnestness, and seriousness of purpose, as well as hopeful confidence, which the advocates of association had in the truth and ultimate success of their principles. Besides the special subject of association, the *Harbinger* embraced a variety of other topics, particularly in relation to matters of art. The musical articles occupy much space, and were mainly written by John S. Dwight; and these were in the sense and spirit of his other writings on the subject, characterized by warm and discriminating zeal in advocating and expounding the highest forms of musical art, and instructing and elevating the public taste. Mr. Dwight was himself, with other members of his family, a long time at Brook Farm, and had direction of the musical department.[19]

From this episode of associated endeavor we turn to trace the influence of the new philosophical thought and tendency in other fields. It was naturally felt in an especial manner in the Divinity School at Cambridge, although among its professors Mr. Norton was decidedly opposed, and others were by no means favorable, to it; but the students, as belonging to a younger generation, and moreover by their studies particularly occupied with questions of philosophy, were more open to its influence. Various circumstances, which brought the philosophy and literature of Germany to their acquaintance, served further to awaken interest. The coming of Dr. Follen as teacher of German, about 1826–27, had already given an impulse to the study of that language, and Dr. Hedge, then a student of the school, helped to spread it among his personal friends. The writings of Carlyle, in so far as they illustrated German literature and its distinguished representatives, also contributed much to stimulate taste and diffuse knowledge in this direction. Dr. Hedge's book of translations, *Prose Writers of Germany,* was another indication of this tendency. It is proper to connect the interest in the language, literature, and philosophy of Germany with the Transcendental tendency, as they were associated together in the popular mind, and looked upon alike with a vague dislike, suspicion, or dread, as closely connected with infidelity, or at best with mysticism, obscurity, absurdity, and nonsense, and tending to pernicious radicalism; so that the word *German* came to carry with it all sorts of ridiculous and extravagant associations,[20]–and to this some color was lent by the specimens from which the popular, but very slight and imperfect, notion had been derived. Such were the translations of Schiller's *Robbers,* a work belonging to a very crude period of his life, and Goethe's *Sorrows of Werther,* which in itself, in some respects rather remote from the New England style of thought and sentiment, had the further disadvantage of being known from a poor and sickly French version, probably still further disfigured by its translation into English.

The books most in vogue at any period, and especially those which are favorites with the active and influential minds whose mission is to give character and direction to the prevalent thought, may be taken as indications of the tendencies of the time; and so we may fitly notice here some of those which were so regarded at that time.

Besides the taste for German literature and philosophy, the writings of Coleridge excited much interest and awakened a taste for profound and abstract thought on literary and philosophical subjects. First, his *Biographia Literaria,* and then, more exclusively philosophical, his *Aids to Reflection,* with the valuable introductory essay by President J. Marsh.[21] This is more particularly addressed to those interested in questions of theology; but as it is written from the ground of the Transcendental philosophy, and pervaded by its spirit, it was not a small element in the influence in that direction. In this work the very important distinction of the *Understanding* and the *Reason* is much emphasized and insisted on; and this is of the very essence of that philosophy, and the whole spirit of the work is very strong and decided in opposition to the sensuous system.

The works of Cousin also were favorite books,– the *Introduction to Philosophy,* translated by Professor C. Henry, and the *Comparative View of the Different Philosophical Systems.* His able and lucid criticism of Locke and his system, and of the philosophy of sensation and experience, was read and valued as pointing out the defects and tendencies of that system.

Besides the writings of Carlyle relating to German literature, other works of his awakened still greater interest, and had a still more inspiring influence; among these, several articles in the *Edinburgh Review,*[22] and the *Sartor Resartus.*[23] It is hardly possible for those not contemporary with the first appearance in this country of Carlyle's earlier works to understand or appreciate the extent and vividness of this excitement. It was an era in the thought, experience, and culture of many, provoking in the same person the most opposite feelings,– delight, admiration, sympathy, at the same time dissent, questioning, and opposition; and stimulating thought by the opposition thus aroused. There was also the charm of his style, then a novelty, so rich and strong, so picturesque and poetical, and at times marked by touching strains of tender humanity. We connect the taste for the writings of Carlyle with the history of thought in Boston, since they nowhere else found so early and cordial recognition;[24] and this, we may presume, because their tone was so much in harmony, in some respects, with the growing tendency among us. At the same time, like those of Mr. Emerson, his writings aroused dislike and ridicule, so that with some of his younger admirers the reading of them was a sort of stolen pleasure. It was one of the jests of the day, ridiculing the tastes and enthusiasm of the young people, that in a group of school-girls the talk would be not of balls and beaux, but of Emerson and Carlyle.

Among the interesting features of this period was the Transcendental Club, of which Dr. Hedge, Mr. Emerson, Mr. Alcott, Mr. George Ripley, Theodore Parker, and some others were the founders. It was instituted with the object of bringing together those who agreed in general tendency of philosophical thought, or rather with the broader object of free and untrammelled discussion of questions of high moment then abroad in the community. The meetings of this club, the character and arrangements of which were quite informal, usually took place at the time of the religious anniversaries, or of the Harvard Commencement. They were held at various residences of persons interested,–as of Mr. Parker in West Roxbury, Caleb Stetson in Medford, Mr. Emerson at Concord, Dr. Francis at Watertown, or at Mr. Ripley's, Mr. Alcott's, and Dr. Bartol's, in Boston.[25] The talk took a wide range, and was at times of a very inspiring character, relating to topics of religion, philosophy, morals, etc.[26]

There were few who occupied a more prominent position, or one of wider influence in the period of which we write, than Theodore Parker. His independence of mind, his devotion to the cause of freedom and humanity in every aspect, and unshrinking courage in advocating and upholding their claims, and his interest in all knowledge and thought, with his warm, genial, and tender affection, made him a very noteworthy and efficient influence in these causes. His strong feeling against what he deemed errors of doctrine, and his own ardent and uncompromising spirit, led him into the ranks of controversy; and his language toward those whom he considered as faithless or hostile to freedom of thought, or to the relief of humanity from its wrongs and burdens, was harsh and unsparing: but this did no justice to his really kind, tender, and loving nature. His biography has been amply given in various forms; to this paper it belongs to say something of his influence on the thought of his period. This was chiefly in the direction of theology and of moral and social reform. He made it his mission to expose and attack the iniquities and falsehood that, in his view, are embodied in the present constitution of society; to assail the evils that oppress humanity and impede its progress, and more especially to expose and combat the errors that are mingled in the religious notions and institutions of the day, especially those which to him seemed to darken and disfigure our conceptions of the Divine Nature, and, though clothed in the garb of reverence and worship, to deface the pure, free, and beneficent character of Christianity and its founder. Settled at first over a small parish in West Roxbury, he drew a number of hearers from abroad, many coming out from Boston to listen to his earnest and eloquent speech. What attracted these hearers was not, we think, any very remarkable original intellectual power, but a strong common-sense, entire freedom in exploring and judging of questions of religion, perfect fearlessness in uttering his thoughts, and above all an earnest spirit of humanity and a high moral purpose, united with a profoundly reverent spirit.

His sermon on the "Transient and Permanent in Christianity," at an ordination in South Boston (May 19, 1841), was the occasion of a strong outbreak of feeling against him. The doctrine which was the subject of this discourse was a favorite topic with him,–namely, the distinction on the one hand between the *permanent* and immortal element in Christianity, which is the true religion, suited to all times and all men, and destined to imperishable life, and which was taught by Jesus himself; and, on the other hand, the *transient,* consisting of the opinions of men, the dogmas and forms, the ecclesiastical arrangements, creeds, etc., which embody the notions of men about the absolute and eternal, and are destined to change from age to age. What most caused the commotion in the community and the churches was the freedom with which he spoke of the inspiration of the Scriptures and of the miracles there recorded. Many were shocked, many offended and irritated; and a sort of dismay, arising from various causes, pervaded the religious denomination with which he was connected, and, with few exceptions, their ministers withdrew from ministerial intercourse with him. A warm and excited controversy followed; his opinions and utterances were denounced and opposed in various forms, and journals and pamphlets carried on the war. A few came out in the pulpit and elsewhere in his defence, and without assenting to his opinions declared themselves in favor of free and independent speech, and opposed his being excluded from the old intercourse merely on the ground of free utterance of opinions discordant with their own.

His views naturally spread in the train of the discussion, as this became more and more widely remarked and followed. A gift of clear and strong statement helped their acceptance, so that they found ready access to many minds. The inspiration of the freedom with which he spoke, and assailed the opinions and dogmas which oppressed and hampered the minds of so many, attracted not a few. His ardent interest in the great questions of humanity then agitating society, especially that of slavery,[27] commended to the ardent partisans in these matters his opinions on more abstract questions. He was naturally connected with the Transcendental party, and generally attended the meetings of the club before mentioned; was connected with the publication of the *Dial,* for which he wrote much, and was associated in social intercourse and intimacy, as he was in the public mind, with many of the prominent members of that party.

About the end of 1845 he was invited to preach to a congregation in Boston, to afford him the opportunity of teaching freely in a wider sphere, and where more could hear him, the views and doctrines now of so wide interest. He entered on this new position early in 1846. This society, which became known as the Twenty-eighth Congregational Society, met first in the Melodeon, afterward in the Music Hall, where for many years he preached to large multitudes with strong and stirring eloquence. Here he gave his views on religion and morals, and on the exciting topics of politics, especially slavery and the fugitive-slave law. On these occasions he attacked unsparingly some of the prominent and distinguished characters of the day, whom he considered treacherous to the cause of humanity.

These practical questions did not, however, draw him away from his theological studies; and in the midst of the warfare he published several editions of his *Discourse of Religion,* the object of which was to present to the community the grounds of belief in the doctrines of what are called Natural and Revealed Religion.[28] This, and other works in the like tone and direction, were widely read and accepted. Many hailed them as a new light to their minds, and found satisfaction in the clear and earnest statement of grounds of belief in what specially concerned their highest nature, and which seemed to afford a more stable and satisfactory foundation than they had before known. Mr. Parker's position in the theological and antislavery controversies engaged him in a very extensive acquaintance and correspondence. Persons from near and far, whom his words had reached, were eager for closer intercourse with one to whom they felt themselves so much indebted. Many came to his house to see and talk with him; and notwithstanding his overwhelming occupations, and the varied and complicated network of his engagements, he rarely denied himself to such, however trifling or unprofitable their demands.

The Sunday services at the Music Hall became a very notable and conspicuous institution of our city. Here he sometimes treated the great problems of religion and life, assailing moral abuses or dogmatic errors; or from week to week, as any great event or occasion bearing on the claims, rights, or duties of humanity came along,–any exciting questions or incidents, legislative injustice, or popular violence,–in that most electric period of fierce excitement he "fulmined" over Boston from his pulpit, or pleaded with gentler appeals in behalf of the elevation and relief of the suffering and distressed in every form. Mr. Parker maintained all this varied existence, in spite of failing health, until he was finally obliged to give up his work and go abroad for his health. He died not long after in Florence. [29]

In 1835 Mr. A. Bronson Alcott opened a school for young children at the Masonic Temple in Boston. This was a remarkable and noteworthy experiment, and claims some notice, since marked philosophical thought and a high ideal were embodied in its conception, and in the novel and peculiar way in which it was conducted. Whatever we may think of the success of the experiment, we may say at least, if he failed, *Magnis tamen excidit ausis.* It was founded on the principle of the Platonic philosophy, that all abstract truth exists in the soul of man; and its aim was not to impart knowledge from without, but to educe both truth and knowledge from the mind of the child, where it lies, unrecognized and unknown perhaps, but still existing in a purer form, or less encumbered by errors, than in later life.[30]

The famous ode of Wordsworth on Immortality may almost be taken as Mr. Alcott's creed in this matter. His thought, as shown in this and in various other manifestations, placed him, in the public estimation, very decidedly among the Transcendentalists, and in the category which we presume he himself would choose, if any, of Platonism. The thought, idea, method, and genius of Plato were the especial objects of his admiration and sympathy; and he may, with as much justice as any modern man, be reckoned among his disciples, and has ever reproduced, expounded, and preached his doctrines. He has always most persistently followed in practice the Platonic or Socratic method of teaching or developing truth,–by conversation; having a profound and unfailing confidence in its value, its power, and its efficacy, and laying the greatest stress on these. For many years he has, when favorable opportunities have offered, embraced them to practise his favorite mode of instruction, and to impart the views he holds so important (of the spiritual nature and destiny of man, and his close relation to the divine), at the same time always manifesting a warm sympathy with whatever in literature and religious history he found cognate with his fervent and unwavering faith in man's divine origin and immortal being. These conversations have at times had very impressive and inspiring effects, and have met with a warm response from large numbers,– of late years particularly at the West, where he has found many to welcome his presentation of high and spiritual truth. He generally attended the meetings of the Transcendental Club, of which he was an early and zealous member, and contributed some papers to the *Dial,* with the title of "Orphic Sayings." What most deserves our interest and respect in his course and position is his unwavering and unfailing loyalty to the principles of thought of which we have spoken, and his persistent devotion to the highest conception of the soul and the spiritual life.

The position of Miss Margaret Fuller, as producing a marked influence on the mind of a large circle both of the young and of her contemporaries in age, demands some notice. Her conversations, held in Boston with an audience of thoughtful and cultivated women, seem to have been her opportunity. They were continued for several successive winters. It is sufficient to mention some of the topics discussed to show something of their character, or at least their aim,–namely, Greek Mythology, Fine Arts, Faith, Creeds, Woman, Culture, Prudence, etc. She was also at one time editor of the *Dial*. Her influence on the circle she drew around her, especially on her intimate friends, was remarkable, being both intellectual and moral; particularly on women, to whose hearts and minds she seems to have had a peculiar and most direct access. In exciting them to thought and aspiration for higher culture, or perhaps more especially in leading them to disregard some conventional trammels, and in assisting their endeavors to a higher, more religious, and self-sustained life, she found her mission.[31]

Of course this new phase of thought called Transcendentalism had many opponents. Persons of conservative opinions in religion, morals, politics, and literature were disturbed, offended, or disgusted at what seemed to them its pernicious influences on the great interests of society. Some were amused at what appeared to be its extravagances or absurdities; and some attacked its arguments and its doctrines, or criticised what they deemed to be its inconsistencies and false pretensions, in elaborate counter statements and arguments, or they deplored with sincere dislike and apprehension what seemed to them its disastrous tendencies. Others used freely the weapons of ridicule and sarcasm, for which the novelty, to say the least, of some of the utterances of its adherents and organs appeared to offer fair opportunity.[32]

Let us in conclusion glance rapidly at some of the salient features of the excitable condition of mind which characterized the period with which we are dealing. In the sphere of morals, the strong assertion by Mr. Garrison and his followers of first and absolute principles opened the minds and roused the feelings of the community; and while it powerfully moved the sympathy of those favorably inclined by nature or education, aroused the fears, disgust, or bitter hostility of the adverse element. Two parties were thus arrayed in fierce antagonism, which showed itself in excited meetings and conventions on the one side and the other, or, with those of more brutal instincts, in mobs and violence. The discussion of abstract principles, provoked primarily by the Abolition doctrines, soon ran off in all directions, and brought up all sorts of abstract questions and their unqualified application. Thus the whole theory of government, of social life, its arrangements and usages,–questions of the right to take life at all, leading logically to the doctrine of absolute non-resistance, and thus striking at the foundation of all governmental control and organization,–were brought under consideration. So the right of taxation to support a government of force was denied; and with some the Constitution of the United States, as not condemning slavery,–"the sum of all villanies,"–was of no binding value. Then followed the denial of the right to take animal life, thus leading to the disuse of animal food and of substances derived to the use of man from the enslavement and slaughter of the brute creation. Then came the question of women having an equal right with men on the platforms of the free societies, which came up most naturally in connection with the broad principles of freedom professed; and this opened the whole question of woman's prerogatives, and of the right to exclude her from equal participation in the duties and offices of society and government. These, and allied questions, led to inconveniences and embarrassments, and sometimes to ludicrous scenes and incidents, of which the hostile critics were not slow to make the most.

Another extreme question, which to some seemed to flow logically from acknowledged principles, as well as from those recognized as the very essence of Christianity, was that of the right to hold and use money, as involving, in substance, consequences inconsistent with human brotherhood. A small journal was published, and continued for a few numbers, called, we think, the *Herald of Holiness*, which maintained the moral evil of the use of money, and by its earnestness and appeals to high moral considerations interested and impressed some minds.

In all this tendency to extremes, and indeed to what may be called extravagances, it is interesting and gratifying to observe that in this region at least there was not that tendency to run into licentious doctrine or practice, or more lax principles of morality, which has sometimes shown itself in times of similar mental and moral excitement. On the contrary, the tendency was to a more strict and even ascetic behavior.

The excitement and interest of this discussion and action of the time reached and pervaded various classes of society,–alike those of high culture and those less educated, but in whom the moral instincts and principles asserted themselves with force, and often in language of rough strength, which was quite current at the time. The Antislavery meetings naturally abounded in specimens of forcible and often rude eloquence, as they had for their staples the exciting and inspiring themes which easily lent themselves to stirring oratory. On their platform might be witnessed a remarkable combination of the higher mixed with the ruder but forcible oratory. Here were, indeed, the refined feeling and feminine dignity of Lucretia Mott and the Misses Grimké; the splendid power, rare brilliancy, glowing words, and trenchant logic of Thompson and Phillips; but also the more rude, but most effective and telling blows of the Goodells and Burleighs and Fosters. That this period has left an abiding influence on the moral and intellectual thought and culture of the country we cannot doubt; and may we not hope, too, that the later, broader, and freer spirit, grafted on the strong and sturdy Puritan stock, will yield rich and wholesome fruits?[33]

Though the phase of thought which gave its name and character to this period is no longer so marked and conspicuous, it doubtless gave a permanent and still existing impulse to the mode of thinking and feeling on matters of philosophy and religion. New questions have since arisen to take the place of the old; or more accurately, perhaps, the old ones have passed into new forms and aspects. The hostility and ridicule which it aroused have died away, and its modifying influence is now silently, perhaps unconsciously, felt in many minds to whom it once seemed portentous in its aspect and pernicious in its consequences, and has undermined or lessened the hold of other opinions and doctrines. If we may venture to draw a lesson from a retrospect of the field which we have passed over, when we look back on the angry controversies and bitter hostilities of the past, it may impress upon us that what when novel and strange often seems sinister and threatening, a meteor "shaking from its horrid hair" all sorts of evils and disasters, "may by and by," to borrow the language of another, "take its place in the clear upper sky, and blend its light with all our day."

NOTES

1. [See Dr. Peabody's and Dr. Clarke's chapters in Vol. III.–ED.]

2. As we shall have frequent occasion to use the terms Transcendental, etc., we wish to say that this will not be in any very exact or strictly accurate sense, but in a rather vague and popular one, as convenient for our purpose to denote certain general tendencies of thought and opinion.

3. Here are some of them: "Philosophy of History," "Conduct of Life," "Representative Men," "Human Life," "Human Culture," etc.

4. The following remarks from an article in the *Christian Examiner,* May 1841, by a scholar of distinguished reputation and position, may be taken as a specimen of the way in which Emerson's writings, both as to style and thought, were regarded at the time: "Mr. Emerson is an extravagant and erratic genius, setting all authority at defiance, sometimes writing with the pen of an angel, and sometimes gravely propounding the most amazing nonsense. . . .He has expressed such sovereign contempt for consistency, that we must not look for that virtue in what he may choose to say; if we do, we shall look in vain. In its place we shall often encounter point blank contradictions. . . . His writings are thickly studded with oddities gathered from the most unfrequented paths of English literature; and when we add to this the supersublimated transcendentalism of the New Platonic style which he now and then affects, we must not wonder if Mr. Emerson's phraseology frequently passes the comprehension of the vulgar. Moreover, he plays certain tricks with words which disfigure his pages not a little." Of his Essays the same writer says: "The Essay under the affected title of the 'Oversoul' is the most objectionable of all of them, both as regards sentiment and style. . . . From the praises which the author's genius would otherwise deserve, large deductions must be made on the score of whim, oddity, and affectation." These things read curiously to us who have lived to know the estimation in which Mr. Emerson and his works are now held.

5. A striking instance of this occurred in the inspiring and profoundly touching lecture on Heroism, so full of deepest eloquence. The audience had been carried on and lifted up by its calm and solemn tone to the passage beginning, "Times of heroism are generally times of terror; but the day never shines in which this element may not work." Going on, he says: "More freedom [*i.e.* at this time] exists for culture. It will not now run against an axe at the first step out of the beaten track of opinion. But whoso is heroic will always find crises to try his edge. Human virtue demands her champions and martyrs, and the trial of persecution always proceeds. It is but the other day that the brave Lovejoy gave his breast to the bullets of a mob, for the right of free speech and opinion, and died when it was better not to live." We remember how some of his friends and sympathizers felt the sort of cold shudder which ran through the audience at this calm braving of the current opinion. "He died as the fool dieth" had been the popular dictum about Lovejoy and his death; and this solemn exalting him as a hero and martyr seemed almost an insult to the admiring crowd, who were wholly unprepared for this unexpected turn and shock to their feelings and notions. We have heard some of those who had for him a special regard and sympathy describe their terror, almost, at what they felt was so obnoxious to his audience. Mr. Emerson also delivered addresses, by invitation, before the literary societies of Dartmouth and Waterville colleges.

6. [See a chapter on "Emerson the Seer" in Frothingham's *Transcendentalism in New England;* and the chapter on "Transcendentalism" in Dr. Bartol's *Radical Problems.*–ED.]

7. *Christian Examiner,* March 1833.

8. The substance of this discourse may be found in an article in the *Christian Examiner,* vol. xvii. 1852, entitled "Natural Religion."

9. *Christian Examiner,* 1834.

10. [See the chapter on the "The New Jerusalem Church in Boston" in Vol. III., by a son of Sampson Reed.–ED.]

11. Mr. Norton, in an address before the alumni of the Theological School on what he called the "Latest Form of Infidelity," took occasion to attack what seemed to him the novel and dangerous views of the evidences of Christianity, which, while they either denied or undervalued the proof from miracles, laid the chief stress on the general character of the teachings of Christ and their adaptation to the moral wants and natural religious instincts of mankind. Professor Norton regarded this rejection or undervaluing of the historical miracles as dangerous to the foundation of Christianity. He, indeed, deemed the denial of the miracles as equivalent to a denial of the divine origin of Christianity, and as nothing more nor less than infidelity, to which he gave the title of "Latest Form," in contradistinction to the Deism of the last century of Collins, Toland, etc. As less open and declared it seemed to him only the more insidious and pernicious. Mr. Ripley girded

himself to reply with a sort of joyous confidence, like the rejoicing of a strong man to run a race. From his knowledge and appreciation of the views attacked, and from his confidence in their truth and strength, as well as from his acquaintance with the recent theology and philosophy of Germany he was extremely well qualified for the occasion. The controversy turned mainly on the value and importance of miracles as ground and proof of the Christian religion.

Mr. Norton maintained their absolute indispensableness, and affirmed that a denial or disbelief of them was equivalent to a rejection of any proper belief in religion as a divine revelation. "Christianity," he says, "claims to reveal facts, a knowledge of which is essential to the moral regeneration of men, and to offer in attestation of these facts the only satisfactory proof,–the authority of God evidenced by miraculous displays of his power." Referring to Mr. Ripley's views he adds: "The latest form of infidelity is distinguished by assuming the Christian name while it strikes at the root of faith in Christianity, and indirectly at all religion, by denying the miracles attesting the divine mission of Christ." In the course of his discourse he attacked German theology and philosophy; and first Spinoza, who, though not a German, he says, "is regarded as a profound teacher and patriarch by some of the most noted among the infidel philosophers and theologians of Germany," and afterward gave an account, in a very unfavorable spirit, of some distinguished recent theologians.

Mr. Ripley in reply controverted Mr. Norton's position that miracles are the *only* proof of Christianity. After quoting his words, "that the divine authority of him whom God commissioned to speak to us in his name was attested in the *only* mode in which it could be, by miraculous displays of his power," and other statements to the same effect, he went on to examine this doctrine, and made many citations to show that Mr. Norton's doctrine, though not absolutely novel, was contrary to the opinion and statements of many of the most distinguished divines and theologians of Europe and America; that it was contrary to the teachings of the Old and New Testaments; and he showed that other proofs, called internal evidence, have ever been admitted to have a force and power that are disparaged by Mr. Norton's claim for miracles as the *essential* and *only* satisfactory proof of divine origin. (It should be said, at the same time, that Mr. Norton did not deny to this internal evidence a high comparative value and use.) To the charges made against some distinguished modern German theologians, and to the severe terms in which Professor Norton had spoken of them as Pantheists and Infidels, Mr. Ripley replied with an elaborate statement of their belief and philosophy, which he substantiated by quotations from their works. He also criticised the translation of passages from them made by Mr. Norton, and charged such versions with incorrectness. To this Mr. Norton replied in a pamphlet criticising and controverting Mr. Ripley's arguments, while he reiterated his own former positions and assertions, and adduced citations in confirmation of them. To this Mr. Ripley replied in a second letter, in which he gives an account of the system and doctrines of Spinoza, to refute the common notion of his Atheism, Pantheism, etc., and defends some of his own former assertions and translations. This was followed by a third letter by Mr. Ripley, which is specially occupied with a defence of Schleiermacher and De Wette; and this concluded the controversy.

12. In this controversy we believe that it was the general opinion among those who took an interest in the subject, that Mr. Ripley acquitted himself with great credit, both as respects the learning and ability displayed, and the good temper and courtesy shown to his adversary, for whom, as appears from the discriminating notice in the early part of this chapter, he ever retained a high respect.

13. The question here naturally occurs, how much Mr. Ripley owed to the theories and writing of Charles Fourier, who had written so largely on the subject of associated life and industry. So far as we learn, it would seem he was acquainted with Fourier's theories through the writings of Albert Brisbane, one of his zealous disciples and expounders in this country, but not with the works of Fourier himself till sometime later, and after being settled at Brook Farm. At any rate he did not at first adopt in their full extent the ideas or system of Fourier, his own notions on the subject being far less systematic and *doctrinaire,* so to speak.
VOL. IV.–40.

14. Mr. Warren Burton, who had been a clergyman, and an author of some small books, accompanied them. He however did not remain long. Hawthorne also came at the beginning, or very early. There were a few who had had some experience in farming, and whose knowledge and skill were highly esteemed in the general lack of this accomplishment. Mr. William Allen, a young farmer from Vermont, had in some way become *interested in the idea.* This was one of the pet phrases. He afterward married, and brought his wife, and continued some time at the farm. Mr. Frank Farley, who is still living, had had also some experience in farming at the West. Several young women were also there, of marked character and intelligence.

15. She has recently been very favorably and justly noticed in some articles on Brook Farm in the *Atlantic Monthly,* by Miss Amelia Russell, since deceased, who was herself a long time a member of the association, and was a zealous, active, and valuable co-worker. There were also some young women who were there partly for education, or drawn there by some other consideration. Later than this, but in the course of the first summer, came Charles A. Dana, now editor of the *New York Sun.* With the ardor of youth, and bringing fresh from Harvard, where he had been a student, the latest improvements in scholarly lore, he embraced the ideas and modes of operation of the enterprise with zeal and systematic energy, and long filled an important place as teacher, worker, counsellor, and director. In the course of the first summer, too, came Minot Pratt, with his family. He had been a printer, but was attracted by sympathy and interest in the mode of life, as well as by a taste for agriculture, which he retained until his death, a few years since. He was a man of singular purity and uprightness of character, simplicity of taste, and great intelligence. He was in many ways a valuable member, and for a long time had the chief direction of the farming operations.

16. In his *Blithedale Romance,* which was the fruit of his experience here, in order to deepen the shadows of his picture he avails himself of a most painful and tragic incident, which did not occur here, but elsewhere. Some of the Brook Farmers were sorry to have anything so ghastly connected with what for them had, for the most part, pleasant and beautiful associations.

17. There had been at earlier stages some statements of the plan, but the final formulating of their intents appears in a constitution dated May 1, 1845, in the introduction to which are these words, which show a more sanguine confidence, after about four years' actual experience, and more hope of realizing their expectations, than is commonly supposed to have existed: "We have laid the foundation, and now stand ready to rear the superstructure, which will approach more nearly the ideal of human society than any that has ever existed,–a society which will establish justice between all interests and all men; which will guarantee education, right to labor, and the rights of property to all; and which, by actual demonstration of a state of things every way better and more advantageous, will put an end to the great evils which at present burden even the most fortunate classes. What we have already been able to accomplish ought to give weight to our words. We speak not from abstract conviction, but from experience; as men of practical common-sense, holding in our hands the means of escape from the present conditions of society, and from that more frightful state to which in all countries it is hurrying."

The preamble reads thus: "In order more effectually to promote the great purposes of human culture, . . . to substitute a system of brotherly love for one of selfish competition, . . . to guarantee to each other forever the means of physical support and spiritual progress, etc., we unite, etc."

Its principles may be thus summarized: "*The Government.*–It shall be vested in a General Council which shall consist of four branches, viz.: first, a Council of Industry; second, a Council of Finance; third, a Council of Science; fourth, a President, who together with a chairman of each of the foregoing councils shall constitute a General Council. *Organization of Labor.*–The labor of the Phalanx shall be arranged in Groups and Series, as far as practicable, according to the system of Charles Fourier. *Groups.*–A group is a little company of from three to twenty persons, engaged in some special division of labor or study. In this sphere it governs and is responsible; it makes its rules, and decides upon the management of its own operations. In it the highest talent of its members for its particular duty is called out. *Series.*–The different groups, engaged in divisions of the same employment, are united into a higher combination called a Series, which, through its proper officers, governs and is responsible in that department.

These again are concentrated in the Councils of Industry and Science, which have a like power and responsibility.* *Division of Profits.*–The striking features of this, and which are especially in contrast with the usual arrangements of civilized society, are, first, that the net profits after all general expenses are paid are to be divided, one third to Capital and two thirds to Labor; second, that the two thirds allotted to Labor shall be distributed so that the labor of the Class of Necessity shall receive the highest dividend, labor of the class of Usefulness a medium dividend, and labor of the Class of Attractiveness the lowest dividend,–*i.e.,* that the necessary and important, which at the same time may be the most disagreeable and repulsive, shall receive the highest dividend. *The General Council.*–This shall classify all labor, according to its necessity, its usefulness, or its attractiveness, and with reference to the promotion of Social Harmony; and this classification may be varied from time to time, so as to prevent an excess of laborers in any branch of industry, and secure the performance of the labor required."

A distinction should not be overlooked between the earlier and later periods of this experiment. The first was one of much generous enthusiasm, with somewhat vague feelings of humanity, and of hope for better and more humane conditions of life; and this was combined with the undefined and unsystematic way in which it was attempted to carry out the ideas that prompted the movement. The later was a more mature period, when the more scientific and systematic forms of organization were gradually approximated and introduced. The first phase was more agreeable to some of the zealous first-comers.

*We would remark, for the information of those unacquainted with the subject, that the groups and series, etc., are important and characteristic features of the system and nomenclature of Fourier. [Octavius B. Frothingham's *Transcendentalism in New England,* Boston, 1876, gives at full length, p. 159, the constitution of the Brook Farm community. The literature of the subject is somewhat scattered. See the paper on their "Home-Life" in the *Atlantic Monthly,* 1878; also the number for May, 1866, p. 565. Other estimates and glimpses can be found in Greeley's *Recollections of a Busy Life;* the various sketches of Hawthorne, including M. D. Conway's introduction to the English edition of Hawthorne's *Note-books,* and in general the reviews of *The Blithedale Romance;* Dixon's *New America;* Noyes's *American Socialisms.*–ED.]

18. In the Phalanstery was a hall intended for meetings of the company, and to be used for religious services by those who might so wish.

19. In the list of writers given in the first number we find the names of Albert Brisbane, W. H. Channing, C. P. Cranch, G. W. Curtis, C. A. Dana, Parke Godwin, Horace Greeley, T. W. Higginson, G. Ripley, J. R. Lowell, F. G. Shaw, William W. Story, and J. G. Whittier. The translations of George Sand's *Consuelo* and *Countess of Rudolstadt,* by F. G. Shaw, were printed first in this journal.

20. The prevailing misapprehension was also aggravated by the unfavorable representations of English Reviews, from which, at that time, many of the popular literary notions were derived.

21. Published in Burlington, Vt., 1840.

22. "Characteristics," "Signs of the Times," "Burns," etc.,–the first-named especially.

23. [This first appeared serially in *Fraser's Magazine,* and was published for the first time in a collected form in Boston, in 1836, at the instance of Dr. Le Baron Russell, and Rev. Wm. Silsbee, with an introduction by R. W. Emerson.–ED.]

24. [Carlyle's will, but recently made public says, in connection with a bequest of books which he makes to Harvard University:–

"Having with good reason, ever since my first appearance in literature, a variety of kind feelings, obligations, and regards toward New England, and indeed long before that a hearty good will, real and steady, which still continues, to America at large, and recognizing with gratitude how much of friendliness, of actually credible human love, I have had from that country," etc.–ED.]

25. Besides those already mentioned, Miss Margaret Fuller, Miss Elizabeth Peabody, Mrs. Ripley of Waltham, the Rev. James Freeman Clarke, John S. Dwight, and others were sometimes present.

26. One of these meetings, held in Boston, was rendered memorable by one of the remarkable and impressive outbursts of Father Taylor's eloquence. The subject of discussion was, we think, something relating to the influence of preaching and of the administration of religion, and how they might be rendered more effective. Father Taylor, who was present by invitation, was requested to give his views and experience. He had been sitting silent while the others talked, knitting his brows, with his green spectacles thrown up on his forehead, leaning forward or shifting about on his chair, in the attitudes so familiar to those who remembered him. When he began to speak he soon rose to his feet, and warming as he went on, in a sort of indignant or sorrowful eloquence, by-and-by took his hearers off their feet, and they were carried away as by a flood. He rebuked the shortcomings of the various religious sects, not sparing his own, the Methodists; characterizing the faults or peculiarities of each with sarcastic wit, and a sort of grim but fervent satire. The points he made were commonplace enough perhaps,–namely, that all that is needed to move men is simple earnestness and living faith, and that this will conquer coldness and indifference in the hearers; so that what he said was not so remarkable as the pervading, fervent power of his utterance. When he got through, the company were so deeply impressed that they were for the most part disposed to entire silence, and though some desultory attempts were made to renew and continue the discussion, all other speech seemed so cold and hard after the glowing words they had heard, and so out of harmony with their mood, that the company soon broke up. [See *Incidents and Anecdotes of the Rev. Edward T. Taylor,* by G. Haven and T. Russell. Boston, 1872.–ED.]

27. [See James Freeman Clarke's chapter on "The Antislavery Movement."–ED.]

28. He thus states the primitive ground of our belief, or rather of our knowledge, of the existence of God. "It may be called," he says, "in the language of philosophy, an intuition of the reason. . . . Our belief in God's existence does not depend on the *à posteriori* argument, on considerations drawn from the order, fitness, or beauty discovered by observations made on the material world. It depends primarily on no argument whatever; on no reasoning, but on Reason. . . . The intuitive perception of God is afterward fundamentally and logically established by the *à priori,* and beautifully confirmed by the *à posteriori,* argument; but we are not left without the idea of God till we become metaphysicians and naturalists, and so till we can discover it by much thinking."

It may also be mentioned, that, in 1847–50, Mr. Parker shared with others the editorship of the *Massachusetts Quarterly.*

29. [See John T. Sargent's *Theodore Parker, the Reform Pulpit, and the Influences that Oppose it.* Boston, 1852; and other references in the note to Parker's portrait in Vol. III.–ED.]

30. A few extracts from the preface to the *Conversations on the Gospels,* which is a sort of record of the course pursued, will show something of the aim and methods of this attempt to educe moral and spiritual thought from the minds of children. "It is," he says, "an attempt to unfold the idea of spirit from the consciousness of childhood, and to trace its intellectual and corporeal relations, its struggles and conquests, while in the flesh. . . . Assuming as a fact the spiritual integrity of the young mind, he [Mr. Alcott] was desirous to place under the inspection of children a character so much in conformity with their own as that of Jesus of Nazareth. . . . It [the record of these conversations] is a revelation of the divinity in the soul of childhood."

31. [See Mrs. Cheney's chapter in this volume.–ED.]

32. Among the more decided and declared antagonists of this philosophy, besides Professor Norton, was Mr. Bowen, professor of moral and metaphysical science in Harvard University. Mr. Emerson's *Nature,* which appeared in 1836, gave occasion for a review of the work in the *Christian Examiner,* January, 1837, by Mr. Bowen. As that little book was looked upon as a sort of con-

densed essence of the spirit of Transcendentalism, and open to all the charges brought against it, Mr. Bowen took the opportunity to oppose the obnoxious system, in an adverse and unfavorable criticism, with charges of novel and unwarrantable language, of new and barbarous words, indicating vagueness and incompleteness of thought in the minds of the writers, and producing obscurity to their readers. Other charges, besides innovation and obscurity, are those of dogmatism and arrogance in the assertion of their opinions. He then goes on to a more direct discussion of the philosophy, to show its shallowness and falsehood, and incidentally eulogizes Locke, whose philosophy was especially assailed and disparaged by the opposite party. We give in his own words one of the objections which he, in concert with the popular voice, makes to this philosophy: "The distinguishing trait of the Transcendental philosophy is the appeal which it makes from the authority of reason to that of passion and feeling,"–a statement to which the advocates and receivers of this system would doubtless most decidedly object. He also brings a charge which they might not be very anxious to repel, of its being a revival of the old Platonic School. In the *Examiner,* in November of the same year, Professor Bowen returns to the charge, and in a long and elaborate article compares and contrasts the claims of the philosophy of Locke, or that of experience, with that of this new school. In this he pursues substantially the same line of argument and criticism, but in a more extended and elaborate way, and repeats the charges and objections against the Transcendental system and its adherents,–of arrogance, and obscure and unwarrantable use of language. He naturally has a good deal to say of the German metaphysicians, of whom he takes a very unfavorable view; and of Coleridge, too, who among the English thinkers was considered as rather the type of this mode of thought and speculation. [There is a portrait and sketch of Mr. Bowen in the *Harvard Register,* May, 1881.–ED.]

33. Our limits have obliged us to omit the mention of several who deserve notice among those whose teaching or writing has had an influence in modifying, directing, or enlightening the thought of our community, like the Rev. O. A. Brownson, Professor C. C. Everett, and others; but we have chosen to dwell at some length upon some prominent names, rather than furnish little more than a bare catalogue of all who might seem to require notice. We cannot, however, allow ourselves to pass by the name of Miss Elizabeth P. Peabody, without some reference at least to her long-continued, disinterested, and unfailing exertions and zeal in promoting everything that promised greater freedom, elevation, and breadth of philosophic, philanthropic, or religious thought or action. We trust that better justice may be done to her character and efficient services than belongs to our subject. Her conversations with Dr. Channing, reported in the volume recently published by her, are in this wise very important, as through various channels they found their way to the minds of a wide circle in the community. This influence was also felt in her teaching, which has ever been characterized by high and ideal aims.

At one time (about 1840) she opened a room for a circulating library and the sale of foreign books and journals. This became a sort of Transcendental Exchange. Persons young and old resorted here, partly to talk with the learned and active-minded proprietor, to get the literary news of the day, the last word of philosophy, of religious literature and thought. Many persons of high culture, or of distinction in the sphere of religious philosophy, philanthropy, or literature, were often here, and likely to meet others, like themselves, interested in the questions then agitating the community, or to talk on the calmer topics of literature and philosophy. Some of Miss Fuller's conversations were held at Miss Peabody's house in West Street.

VOL. IV.–42.

From *The Memorial History of Boston,* edited by Justin Winsor. 4 volumes (Boston: James R. Osgood and Company, 1881), 4: 295–330.

Checklist of Further Readings

The following selective list should be of value to those wishing to read more about the American Renaissance. Additional information may he obtained from Clarence Gohdes, *Bibliographical Guide to the Study of the Literature of the U.S.A.,* fourth edition (Durham, N.C.: Duke University Press, 1976); Lewis Leary, *Articles on American Literature, 1900–1930* (Durham, N.C.: Duke University Press, 1954); Leary, *Articles on American Literature, 1950–1967* (Durham, N.C.: Duke University Press, 1970); Joel Myerson, ed., *The Transcendentalists: A Review of Research and Criticism* (New York: Modern Language Association of America, 1984); the annual MLA bibliography; and *American Literary Scholarship: An Annual* (Durham, N.C.: Duke University Press, 1965–). Specialized bibliographies appear annually in the *Emerson Society Papers* and quarterly in the *Thoreau Society Bulletin.* Journals that regularly publish articles about the American Renaissance include *American Literature; American Transcendental Quarterly; ESQ: A Journal of the American Renaissance;* and *New England Quarterly.* The *Emerson Society Quarterly* was published from 1953 to 1971. See also *Studies in the American Renaissance,* edited by Joel Myerson (Boston: Twayne, 1977–1982 / Charlottesville: University Press of Virginia, 1983–1996).

Aaron, Daniel. *Men of Good Hope: A Story of American Progressives.* New York: Oxford University Press, 1951.

Adams, Grace, and Edward Hutter. *The Mad Forties.* New York: Harper, 1942.

Ahlstrom, Sydney E. "The Middle Period (1840–1880)," in *The Harvard Divinity School: Its Place in Harvard University and in American Culture,* edited by George Huntston Williams. Boston: Beacon, 1954, pp. 78–147.

Ahlstrom. *A Religious History of the American People.* New Haven: Yale University Press, 1972.

Ahlstrom and Jonathan S. Carey, eds. *An American Reformation: A Documentary History of Unitarian Christianity.* Middletown, Conn.: Wesleyan University Press, 1985.

Albanese, Catherine L. *Corresponding Motion: Transcendental Religion and the New America.* Philadelphia: Temple University Press, 1977.

Allen, Joseph Henry. *Our Liberal Movement in Theology.* Boston: Roberts Brothers, 1882.

Allen. *Sequel to "Our Liberal Movement."* Boston: Roberts Brothers, 1897.

Allen and Richard Eddy. *A History of the Unitarians and Universalists in the United States.* New York: Christian Literature Company, 1894.

Anagnos, Julia R. *Philosophiae Quaestor; or, Days in Concord.* Boston: Lothrop, 1885.

Anderson, Quentin. *The Imperial Self: An Essay in American Literary and Cultural History.* New York: Knopf, 1971.

Ando, Shoei. *Zen and American Transcendentalism.* Tokyo: Hokuseido, 1970.

Andrews, William L., ed. *Literary Romanticism in America.* Baton Rouge: Louisiana State University Press, 1981.

Asselineau, Roger. *The Transcendentalist Constant in American Literature.* New York: New York University Press, 1980.

Bacon, Edwin M. *Literary Pilgrimages in New England.* New York: Silver, Burdett, 1902.

Baker, Paul R. *The Fortunate Pilgrims: Americans in Italy 1800-1860.* Cambridge, Mass.: Harvard University Press, 1964.

Barbour, Brian M., ed. *American Transcendentalism: An Anthology of Criticism.* Notre Dame, Ind.: University of Notre Dame Press, 1973.

Barbour, James, and Thomas Quirk, eds. *Romanticism: Critical Essays in American Literature.* New York: Garland, 1986.

Bartlett, George B. *Concord: Historic, Literary and Picturesque,* third edition. Boston: Lothrop, 1885.

Bartlett, Irving H. *The American Mind in the Mid-Nineteenth Century.* New York: Crowell, 1967.

Bauerlein, Mark. *The Pragmatic Mind: Explorations in the Psychology of Belief.* Durham, N.C.: Duke University Press, 1997.

Baym, Max I. *A History of Literary Aesthetics in America.* New York: Ungar, 1973.

Baym, Nina. *American Women Writers and the Work of History, 1790–1860.* New Brunswick, N.J.: Rutgers University Press, 1995.

Baym. *Novels, Readers, and Reviewers: Responses to Fiction in Antebellum America.* Ithaca, N.Y.: Cornell University Press, 1984.

Baym. *Woman's Fiction: A Guide to Novels by and about Women in America, 1820–1870,* second edition. Urbana: University of Illinois Press, 1993.

Bell, Michael. *The Development of American Romance: The Sacrifice of Relation.* Chicago: University of Chicago Press, 1980.

Bercovitch, Sacvan. *The American Jeremiad.* Madison: University of Wisconsin Press, 1978.

Bercovitch. *The Puritan Origins of the American Self.* New Haven: Yale University Press, 1975.

Bercovitch. *The Rites of Assent: Transformations in the Symbolic Construction of America.* New York: Routledge, 1993.

Bercovitch and Myra Jehlen, eds. *Ideology and Classic American Literature.* Cambridge: Cambridge University Press, 1986.

Berlin, James A. *Writing Instruction in Nineteenth-Century American Colleges.* Carbondale: Southern Illinois University Press, 1984.

Bickman, Martin. *The Unsounded Centre: Jungian Studies in American Romanticism.* Chapel Hill: University of North Carolina Press, 1980. Republished as *American Romantic Psychology: Emerson, Poe, Whitman, Dickinson.* Dallas: Spring, 1988.

Blasing, Mutlu Konuk. *American Poetry: The Rhetoric of Its Forms.* New Haven: Yale University Press, 1987.

Blau, Joseph L. *Men and Moments in American Philosophy.* Englewood Cliffs, N.J.: Prentice-Hall,1952.

Bloom, Harold. *Agon: Towards a Theory of Romanticism.* New York: Oxford University Press, 1982.

Bloom. *The Breaking of the Vessels.* Chicago: University of Chicago Press, 1982.

Bloom. *Figures of the Capable Imagination.* New York: Seabury Press, 1976.

Bloom. *Poetry and Repression: Revisionism from Blake to Stevens.* New Haven: Yale University Press, 1976.

Blumenthal, Henry. *American and French Culture, 1800–1900: Interchanges in Art, Science, Literature, and Society.* Baton Rouge: Louisiana State University Press, 1975.

Boas, George, ed. *Romanticism in America.* Baltimore: Johns Hopkins University Press, 1940.

Bode, Carl. *The American Lyceum.* New York: Oxford University Press, 1956.

Boller, Paul F., Jr. *American Transcendentalism, 1830–1860: An Intellectual Inquiry.* New York: Putnam, 1974.

Branch, Douglas E. *The Sentimental Years 1836–1860.* New York: Appleton-Century, 1934.

Brantley, Richard E. *Coordinates of Anglo-American Romanticism: Wesley, Edwards, Carlyle & Emerson.* Gainesville: University Press of Florida, 1993.

Brooks, Paul. *The People of Concord: One Year in the Flowering of New England.* Chester, Conn.: Globe Pequot Press, 1990.

Brooks, Van Wyck. *The Dream of Arcadia: American Writers and Artists in Italy 1760–1915.* New York: Dutton, 1958.

Brooks. *The Flowering of New England 1815–1865.* New York: Dutton, 1936.

Brown, Herbert Ross. *The Sentimental Novel in America 1789–1860.* Chapel Hill: University of North Carolina Press, 1940.

Brown, Jerry Wayne. *The Rise of Biblical Criticism in America, 1800–1870: The New England Scholars.* Middletown, Conn.: Wesleyan University Press, 1969.

Brown, Mary Hosmer. *Memories of Concord.* Boston: Four Seas, 1926.

Buell, Lawrence. *The Environmental Imagination: Thoreau, Nature Writing, and the Formation of American Culture.* Cambridge, Mass.: Harvard University Press, 1995.

Buell. *Literary Transcendentalism: Style and Vision in the American Renaissance.* Ithaca, N.Y.: Cornell University Press, 1973.

Buell. *New England Literary Culture from Revolution through Renaissance.* New York: Cambridge University Press, 1986.

Buell. "The Transcendentalists," in *Columbia Literary History of the United States,* general editor Emory Elliott. New York: Columbia University Press, 1988, pp. 364–378.

Burton, Katherine. *Paradise Planters: The Story of Brook Farm.* London: Longmans, Green, 1939.

Cain, William E. *F. O. Matthiessen and the Politics of Criticism.* Madison: University of Wisconsin Press, 1988.

Calverton, V. F. *The Liberation of American Literature.* New York: Scribners, 1932.

Cameron, Kenneth Walter. *Transcendental Climate,* 3 volumes. Hartford: Transcendental Books, 1963.

Carafiol, Peter. *The American Ideal: Literary History as a Worldly Activity.* New York: Oxford University Press, 1991.

Carpenter, Frederic I. *American Literature and the Dream.* New York: Philosophical Library, 1955.

Carter, Everett. *The American Idea: The Literary Response to American Optimism.* Chapel Hill: University of North Carolina Press, 1977.

Carton, Evan. *The Rhetoric of American Romance: Dialectic and Identity in Emerson, Dickinson, Poe, and Hawthorne.* Baltimore: Johns Hopkins University Press, 1985.

Cavell, Stanley. *Conditions Handsome and Unhandsome: The Constitution of Emersonian Perfectionism.* Chicago: University of Chicago Press, 1990.

Cavell. *In Quest of the Ordinary: Lines of Skepticism and Romanticism.* Chicago: University of Chicago Press, 1988.

Cavell. *This New Yet Unapproachable America: Lectures after Emerson and Wittgenstein.* Albuquerque, N.Mex.: Living Batch Press, 1989.

Chai, Leon. *The Romantic Foundations of the American Renaissance.* Ithaca, N.Y.: Cornell University Press, 1987.

Chapin, Sarah. *Concord, Massachusetts.* Dover, N.H.: Arcadia, 1997.

Charvat, William. *Literary Publishing in America: 1790–1850.* Amherst: University of Massachusetts Press, 1993.

Charvat. *The Origins of American Critical Thought 1810–1835.* Philadelphia: University of Pennsylvania Press, 1936.

Charvat. *The Profession of Authorship in America, 1800–1870,* edited by Matthew J. Bruccoli. Columbus: Ohio State University Press, 1968.

Chase, Richard. *The American Novel and Its Tradition.* Garden City, N.Y.: Doubleday, 1957.

Christy, Arthur. *The Orient in American Transcendentalism.* New York: Columbia University Press, 1932.

Colacurcio, Michael J. *Doctrine and Difference: Essays in the Literature of New England.* New York: Routledge, 1997.

Cole, Phyllis. *Mary Moody Emerson and the Origins of Transcendentalism: A Family History.* New York: Oxford University Press, 1998.

Conrad, Susan P. *Perish the Thought: Intellectual Women in Romantic America 1830–1860.* New York: Oxford University Press, 1976.

Cooke, George Willis. *Unitarianism in America.* Boston: American Unitarian Association, 1902.

Cooke, ed. *The Poets of Transcendentalism: An Anthology.* Boston: Houghton, Mifflin, 1903.

Cowen, Michael H. *City of the West: Emerson, America, and Urban Metaphor.* New Haven: Yale University Press, 1967.

Cowie, Alexander. *The Rise of the American Novel.* New York: American Book Co., 1948.

Crawford, Mary Caroline. *Romantic Days in Old Boston.* Boston: Little, Brown, 1910.

Cunliffe, Marcus. *The Literature of the United States.* London: Penguin, 1954.

Curtis, Edith Roelker. *A Season in Utopia: The Story of Brook Farm.* New York: Nelson, 1961.

Day, Martin S. *History of American Literature from the Beginning to 1900.* Garden City, N.Y.: Doubleday, 1970.

Decker, William Merrill. *Epistolary Practices: Letter Writing in America before Telecommunications.* Chapel Hill: University of North Carolina Press, 1998.

Dekker, George. *The American Historical Romance.* Cambridge: Cambridge University Press, 1987.

Delano, Sterling F. *The Harbinger and New England Transcendentalism: A Portrait of Associationism in America.* Rutherford, N.J.: Fairleigh Dickinson University Press, 1983.

Dickens, Charles. *American Notes for General Circulation.* London: Chapman & Hall, 1842.

Douglas, Ann. *The Feminization of American Culture.* New York: Knopf, 1977.

Duyckinck, Evert A., and George L. Duyckinck, eds. *Cyclopaedia of American Literature,* 2 volumes. New York: Scribner, 1856.

Eakin, Paul John. *The New England Girl: Cultural Ideals in Hawthorne, Stowe, Howells and James.* Athens: University of Georgia Press, 1976.

Ekirch, Arthur A., Jr. *Man and Nature in America.* New York: Columbia University Press, 1963.

Eliot, Samuel A., ed. *Heralds of a Liberal Faith,* 3 volumes. Boston: American Unitarian Association, 1910.

Emerson, Edward Waldo. *The Early Years of the Saturday Club 1855–1870.* Boston: Houghton Mifflin, 1918.

Falk, Robert. *The Victorian Mode in American Fiction.* East Lansing: Michigan State University Press, 1965.

Feidelson, Charles, Jr. *Symbolism and American Literature.* Chicago: University of Chicago Press, 1953.

Fellman, Michael. *The Unbounded Frame: Freedom and Community in Nineteenth Century American Utopianism.* Westport, Conn.: Greenwood Press, 1973.

Fenn, William W. *The Religious History of New England.* Cambridge, Mass.: Harvard University Press, 1917.

Ferguson, Robert A. *Law & Letters in American Culture.* Cambridge, Mass.: Harvard University Press, 1984.

Fiedler, Leslie A. *Love and Death in the American Novel,* revised edition. New York: Stein & Day, 1966.

Fischer, David Hackett, ed. *Concord: The Social History of a New England Town 1750–1850.* Waltham, Mass.: Brandeis University, 1983.

Fish, Carl Russell. *The Rise of the Common Man 1830–1850.* New York: Macmillan, 1927.

Floan, Howard R. *The South in Northern Eyes 1831 to 1861.* Austin: University of Texas Press, 1958.

Flower, Elizabeth, and Murray G. Murphey. "Transcendentalism," in their *A History of Philosophy in America,* 2 volumes. New York: Putnam, 1977, I: 397–435.

Foerster, Norman. *American Criticism.* Boston: Houghton Mifflin, 1928.

Foster, Edward Halsey. *The Civilized Wilderness: Backgrounds to American Romantic Literature, 1817–1860.* New York: Free Press, 1975.

Francis, Richard. *Transcendental Utopias: Individual and Community at Brook Farm, Fruitlands, and Walden.* Ithaca, N.Y.: Cornell University Press, 1997.

Freidel, Frank, ed. *Harvard Guide to American History,* revised edition, 2 volumes. Cambridge, Mass.: Harvard University Press, 1974.

Frothingham, Octavius Brooks. *Transcendentalism in New England: A History.* New York: Putnam, 1876.

Fussell, Edwin. *Frontier: American Literature and the American West.* Princeton: Princeton University Press, 1965.

Gardiner, Harold C., ed. *American Classics Reconsidered: A Christian Appraisal.* New York: Scribners, 1958.

Gelpi, Albert. *The Tenth Muse: The Psyche of the American Poet.* Cambridge, Mass.: Harvard University Press, 1975.

Gilmore, Michael T. *American Romanticism and the Marketplace.* Chicago: University of Chicago Press, 1985.

Gittleman, Edwin, ed. *The Minor and Later Transcendentalists: A Symposium.* Hartford, Conn.: Transcendental Books, 1969.

Goddard, Harold Clarke. *Studies in New England Transcendentalism.* New York: Columbia University Press, 1908.

Gohdes, Clarence. *American Literature in Nineteenth Century England.* New York: Columbia University Press, 1944.

Gohdes. *The Periodicals of American Transcendentalism.* Durham, N.C.: Duke University Press, 1931.

Goodman, Russell B. *American Philosophy and the Romantic Tradition.* New York: Cambridge University Press, 1991.

Gougeon, Len. *Virtue's Hero: Emerson, Antislavery, and Reform.* Athens: University of Georgia Press, 1990.

Green, Martin. *The Problem of Boston: Some Readings in Cultural History.* New York: Norton, 1966.

Green. *Re-appraisals: Some Commonsense Readings in American Literature.* London: Hugh Evelyn, 1963.

Greer, Louise. *Browning and America.* Chapel Hill: University of North Carolina Press, 1952.

Grey, Robin. *The Complicity of Imagination: The American Renaissance, Contests of Authority, and Seventeenth-Century English Culture.* New York: Cambridge University Press, 1995.

Griffin, C. S. *The Ferment of Reform,* 1830–1860. New York: Crowell, 1967.

Gross, Theodore L. *The Heroic Ideal in American Literature.* New York: Free Press, 1971.

Grusin, Richard. *Transcendentalist Hermeneutics: Institutional Authority and the Higher Criticism of the Bible.* Durham, N.C.: Duke University Press, 1991.

Guarneri, Carl J. *The Utopian Alternative: Fourierism in Nineteenth-Century America.* Ithaca, N.Y.: Cornell University Press, 1991.

Gura, Philip F. *The Crossroads of American History and Literature.* University Park: Pennsylvania State University Press, 1996.

Gura. *The Wisdom of Words: Language, Theology, and Literature in the New England Renaissance.* Middletown, Conn.: Wesleyan University Press, 1981.

Gura and Joel Myerson, eds. *Critical Essays on American Transcendentalism.* Boston: G. K. Hall, 1982.

Gustafson, Thomas. *Representative Words: Politics, Literature, and the American Language, 1776–1865.* New York: Cambridge University Press, 1992.

Habich, Robert D. *Transcendentalism and the* Western Messenger: *A History of the Magazine and Its Contributors, 1835–1841.* Rutherford, N.J.: Fairleigh Dickinson University Press, 1985.

Haralson, Eric L., ed. *Encyclopedia of American Poetry: The Nineteenth Century*. Chicago: Fitzroy Dearborn, 1998.

Haraszti, Zoltan. *The Idyll of Brook Farm as Revealed by Unpublished Letters in the Boston Public Library*. Boston: Trustees of the Public Library, 1937.

Harbert, Earl N., and Robert A. Rees. *Fifteen American Authors Before 1900: Bibliographical Essays on Research and Criticism,* revised edition. Madison: University of Wisconsin Press, 1984.

Harris, Susan K. *Nineteenth-Century American Women's Novels*. Cambridge: Cambridge University Press, 1990.

Hart, James D. *The Popular Book: A History of America's Literary Taste*. New York: Oxford University Press, 1950.

Hendrick, George, ed. *The American Renaissance: The History and Literature of an Era*. Berlin: Diesterweg, 1961.

Herreshoff, David. *American Disciples of Marx*. Detroit: Wayne State University Press, 1967.

Hertz, David Michael. *Angels of Reality: Emersonian Unfoldings in Wright, Stevens, and Ives*. Carbondale: Southern Illinois University Press, 1993.

Higginson, Thomas Wentworth, and Henry Walcott Boynton. *A Reader's History of American Literature*. Boston: Houghton, Mifflin, 1903.

Hochfield, George. "New England Transcendentalism," in *American Literature to 1900,* edited by Marcus Cunliffe. New York: Peter Bedrick, 1987, pp. 135–168.

Hochfield, ed. *Selected Writings of the American Transcendentalists*. New York: New American Library, 1966.

Hoffman, Daniel G. *Form and Fable in American Fiction*. New York: Oxford University Press, 1961.

Horton, Rod W., and Herbert W. Edwards. *Backgrounds of American Literary Thought*. New York: Appleton-Century-Crofts, 1952.

Howard, Leon. *Literature and the American Tradition*. Garden City, N.Y.: Doubleday, 1960.

Howe, Daniel Walker. "'At Morning Blessed and Golden Browed,'" in *A Stream of Light: A Sesquicentennial History of American Unitarianism,* edited by Conrad Wright. Boston: Beacon, 1975, pp. 3–61.

Howe. *Making the American Self: Jonathan Edwards to Abraham Lincoln*. Cambridge, Mass.: Harvard University Press, 1997.

Howe. *The Unitarian Conscience: Harvard Moral Philosophy, 1805–1861*. Cambridge, Mass.: Harvard University Press, 1970.

Howe, Irving. *The American Newness: Culture and Politics in the Age of Emerson*. Cambridge, Mass.: Harvard University Press, 1986.

Hutchison, William R. *The Transcendentalist Ministers: Church Reform in the New England Renaissance*. New Haven: Yale University Press, 1959.

Huth, Hans. *Nature and the American: Three Centuries of Changing Attitudes*. Berkeley: University of California Press, 1957.

Irwin, John T. *American Hieroglyphics: The Symbol of the Egyptian Hieroglyphics in the American Renaissance*. New Haven: Yale University Press, 1980.

Jackson, Carl T. *The Oriental Religions and American Thought: Nineteenth-Century Explorations.* Westport, Conn.: Greenwood Press, 1981.

Jarvis, Edward. *Traditions and Reminiscences of Concord, Massachusetts, 1779–1878,* edited by Sarah Chapin. Amherst: University of Massachusetts Press, 1993.

Johnson, James L. *Mark Twain and the Limits of Power: Emerson's God in Ruins.* Knoxville: University of Tennessee Press, 1982.

Jones, Howard Mumford. *American and French Culture 1750–1848.* Chapel Hill: University of North Carolina Press, 1927.

Jones. *Belief and Disbelief in American Literature.* Chicago: University of Chicago Press, 1967.

Jones. *The Theory of American Literature.* Ithaca, N.Y.: Cornell University Press, 1965.

Kaplan, Harold. *Democratic Humanism and American Literature.* Chicago: University of Chicago Press, 1972.

Kaplan, Nathan, and Thomas Katsaros. *The Origins of American Transcendentalism in Philosophy and Mysticism.* New Haven: College and University Press, 1975.

Kateb, George. *The Inner Ocean: Individualism and Democratic Culture.* Ithaca, N.Y.: Cornell University Press, 1992.

Kaufman, Paul. "The Romantic Movement," in *The Reinterpretation of American Literature,* edited by Norman Foerster. New York: Harcourt, Brace, 1928, pp. 114–138.

Kazin, Alfred. *An American Procession: The Major American Writers from 1830 to 1930–The Crucial Century.* New York: Knopf, 1984.

Kazin. *God and the American Writer.* New York: Knopf, 1997.

Kelley, Mary. *Private Woman, Public Stage: Literary Domesticity in Nineteenth-Century America.* New York: Oxford University Press, 1984.

Kern, Alexander. "The Rise of Transcendentalism, 1815–1860," in *Transitions in American Literary History,* edited by Harry Hayden Clark. Durham, N.C.: Duke University Press, 1954, pp. 247–314.

Knight, Denise D., ed. *Nineteenth-Century American Women Writers: A Bio-Bibliographical Critical Sourcebook.* Westport, Conn.: Greenwood Press, 1997.

Knight, Grant C. *American Literature and Culture.* New York: Ray Long & Richard R. Smith, 1932.

Kolb, Harold H., Jr. *A Field Guide to the Study of American Literature.* Charlottesville: University Press of Virginia, 1976.

Kopley, Richard, ed. *Prospects for the Study of American Literature: A Guide for Scholars and Students.* New York: New York University Press, 1997.

Koster, Donald N. *Transcendentalism in America.* Boston: Twayne, 1975.

Kramer, Michael P. *Imagining Language in America: From the Revolution to the Civil War.* Princeton: Princeton University Press, 1992.

Kreymborg, Alfred. *Our Singing Strength: An Outline of American Poetry, 1620–1930.* New York: Coward-McCann, 1929.

Kronick, Joseph G. *American Poetics of History: From Emerson to the Moderns.* Baton Rouge: Louisiana State University Press, 1984.

Kuklick, Bruce. *Churchmen and Philosophers: From Jonathan Edwards to John Dewey.* New Haven: Yale University Press, 1985.

Lader, Lawrence. *The Bold Brahmins: New England's War against Slavery, 1831–1863.* New York: Dutton, 1961.

Layman, Richard, and Joel Myerson, eds. *The Professions of Authorship: Essays in Honor of Matthew J. Bruccoli.* Columbia: University of South Carolina Press, 1996.

Leary, Lewis. *American Literature: A Study and Research Guide.* New York: St. Martin's Press, 1976.

Lease, Benjamin. *Anglo-American Encounters: England and the Rise of American Literature.* Cambridge: Cambridge University Press, 1981.

Lehmann-Haupt, Hellmut, Lawrence C. Wroth, and Rollo G. Silver. *The Book in America: A History of the Making and Selling of Books in the U.S.,* second edition, revised and enlarged. New York: R. R. Bowker, 1952.

Leighton, Walter L. *French Philosophers and New-England Transcendentalism.* Charlottesville: University of Virginia, 1908.

Leisy, Ernest Erwin. *The American Historical Novel.* Norman: University of Oklahoma Press, 1950.

Leisy. *American Literature.* New York: Crowell, 1929.

Leverenz, David. *Manhood and the American Renaissance.* Ithaca, N.Y.: Cornell University Press, 1989.

Lewis, R. W. B. *The American Adam: Innocence, Tragedy and Tradition in the Nineteenth Century.* Chicago: University of Chicago Press, 1955.

Lewisohn, Ludwig. *Expression in America.* New York: Harper, 1932.

Lieber, Todd M. *Endless Experiments: Essays on the Heroic Experience in American Romanticism.* Columbus: Ohio State University Press, 1973.

Loving, Jerome. *Emerson, Whitman, and the American Muse.* Chapel Hill: University of North Carolina Press, 1982.

Loving. *Lost in the Customhouse: Authorship in the American Renaissance.* Iowa City: University of Iowa Press, 1993.

Madden, Edward H. *Civil Disobedience and Moral Law in Nineteenth-Century American Philosophy.* Seattle: University of Washington Press, 1968.

Marchalonis, Shirley, ed. *Patrons and Protegees: Gender, Friendship, and Writing in Nineteenth-Century America.* New Brunswick, N.J.: Rutgers University Press, 1988.

Marr, David. *American Worlds since Emerson.* Amherst: University of Massachusetts Press, 1988.

Martin, Terence. *The Instructed Vision: Scottish Common Sense Philosophy and the Origins of American Fiction.* Bloomington: Indiana University Press, 1961.

Martin. *Parables of Possibility: The American Need for Beginnings.* New York: Columbia University Press, 1995.

Marx, Leo. *The Machine in the Garden: Technology and the Pastoral Ideal in America.* New York: Oxford University Press, 1964.

Matthiessen, F. O. *American Renaissance: Art and Expression in the Age of Emerson and Whitman.* New York: Oxford University Press, 1941.

Maxwell, D. E. S. *American Fiction: The Intellectual Background.* New York: Columbia University Press, 1963.

McDowell, Deborah E., and Arnold Rampersad, eds. *Slavery and the Literary Imagination.* Baltimore: Johns Hopkins University Press, 1989.

McKinsey, Elizabeth R. *The Western Experiment: New England Transcendentalists in the Ohio Valley.* Cambridge, Mass.: Harvard University Press, 1973.

McWilliams, Wilson Carey. *The Idea of Fraternity in America.* Berkeley: University of California Press, 1973.

Mead, David. *Yankee Eloquence in the Middle West: The Ohio Lyceum, 1850–1870.* East Lansing: Michigan State College Press, 1951.

Michaels, Walter Benn, and Donald E. Pease, eds. *The American Renaissance Reconsidered.* Baltimore: Johns Hopkins University Press, 1984.

Miller, Perry. *Nature's Nation.* Cambridge, Mass.: Harvard University Press, 1967.

Miller. *The Raven and the Whale: The War of Words and Wits in the Era of Poe and Melville.* New York: Harcourt, Brace, 1956.

Miller, ed. *The Transcendentalists: An Anthology.* Cambridge, Mass.: Harvard University Press, 1950.

Minnigerode, Meade. *The Fabulous Forties 1840–1850.* New York & London: Putnam, 1924.

Minter, David L. *The Interpreted Design as a Structural Principle in American Prose.* New Haven: Yale University Press, 1969.

Mitchell, Charles E. *Individualism and Its Discontents: Appropriations of Emerson, 1880–1950.* Amherst: University of Massachusetts Press, 1997.

Mitchell, Donald G. *American Lands and Letters: Leather-Stocking to Poe's "Raven."* New York: Scribners, 1899.

More, Paul Elmer. *Paul Elmer More's Shelbourne Essays on American Literature,* edited by Daniel Aaron. New York: Harcourt, Brace & World, 1963.

Mott, Frank Luther. *Golden Multitudes: The Story of Best Sellers in the United States.* New York: Macmillan, 1947.

Mott. *A History of American Magazines,* 5 volumes. Cambridge, Mass.: Harvard University Press, 1938–1968.

Mott, Wesley T., ed. *Biographical Dictionary of Transcendentalism.* Westport, Conn.: Greenwood Press, 1996.

Mott, ed. *Encyclopedia of Transcendentalism.* Westport, Conn.: Greenwood Press, 1996.

Mott and Robert E. Burkholder, eds. *Emersonian Circles: Essays in Honor of Joel Myerson.* Rochester, N.Y.: University of Rochester Press, 1997.

Mumford, Lewis. *The Golden Day: A Study in American Experience and Culture.* New York: Boni & Liveright, 1926.

Myerson, Joel. *Brook Farm: An Annotated Bibliography and Resources Guide.* New York: Garland, 1978.

Myerson. *The Brook Farm Book: A Collection of First-Hand Accounts of the Community.* New York: Garland, 1987.

Myerson. *The New England Transcendentalists and The Dial: A History of the Magazine and Its Contributors.* Rutherford, N.J.: Fairleigh Dickinson University Press, 1980.

Myerson, ed. *The American Transcendentalists.* Detroit: Gale, 1988.

Myerson, ed. *Transcendentalism: A Reader.* New York: Oxford University Press, 2000.

Myerson, ed. *The Transcendentalists: A Review of Research and Criticism.* New York: Modern Language Association, 1984.

Nash, Roderick. *Wilderness and the American Mind.* New Haven: Yale University Press, 1967.

New, Elisa. *The Regenerate Lyric: Theology and Innovation in American Poetry.* New York: Cambridge University Press, 1993.

Newbury, Michael. *Figuring Authorship in Antebellum America.* Stanford, Cal.: Stanford University Press, 1997.

Newfield, Christopher. *The Emerson Effect: Individualism and Submission in America.* Chicago: University of Chicago Press, 1996.

Newton, Annabel. *Wordsworth in Early American Criticism.* Chicago: University of Chicago Press, 1928.

Nilon, Charles H. *Bibliography of Bibliographies in American Literature.* New York: R. R. Bowker, 1970.

Novak, Barbara. *Nature and Culture: American Landscape and Painting, 1825–1875,* revised edition. New York: Oxford University Press, 1995.

Nye, Russel Blaine. *Society and Culture in America 1830–1860.* New York: Harper, 1974.

Nye. *The Unembarrassed Muse: The Popular Arts in America.* New York: Dial, 1970.

O'Connell, Shaun. *Imagining Boston: A Literary Landscape.* Boston: Beacon, 1990.

Oelschlaeger, Max. *The Idea of Wilderness from Prehistory to the Age of Ecology.* New Haven: Yale University Press, 1991.

Orians, G. Harrison. "The Rise of Romanticism, 1805–1855," in *Transitions in American Literary History,* edited by Harry Hayden Clark. Durham, N.C.: Duke University Press, 1954, pp. 161–244.

Packer, Barbara. "The Transcendentalists," in *The Cambridge History of American Literature,* edited by Sacvan Bercovitch, volume 2: *Prose Writing, 1820–1865.* Cambridge: Cambridge University Press, 1995, pp. 329–604.

Papasvily, Helen Waite. *All the Happy Endings.* New York: Harper, 1956.

Parini, Jay, ed. *The Columbia History of American Poetry.* New York: Columbia University Press, 1993.

Parrington, Vernon Lewis. *The Romantic Revolution in America 1800–1860.* New York: Harcourt, Brace, 1927.

Parrington, Vernon Lewis, Jr. *American Dreams: A Study of American Utopias.* Providence: Brown University Press, 1947.

Pattee, Fred Lewis. *The Development of the American Short Story.* New York: Harper, 1923.

Pattee. *The First Century of American Literature 1770–1870.* New York: Appleton-Century, 1935.

Patterson, Anita Haya. *From Emerson to King: Democracy, Race, and the Politics of Protest.* New York: Oxford University Press, 1997.

Patterson, Mark R. *Authority, Autonomy, and Representation in American Literature, 1776–1865.* Princeton: Princeton University Press, 1988.

Payne, Edward F. *Dickens Days in Boston.* Boston & New York: Houghton Mifflin, 1927.

Peach, Linden. *British Influence on the Birth of American Literature.* London: Macmillan, 1982.

Pearce, Roy Harvey. *The Continuity of American Poetry.* Princeton: Princeton University Press, 1961.

Pease, Donald E. *Visionary Compacts: American Renaissance Writings in Cultural Context.* Madison: University of Wisconsin Press, 1987.

Pease, Jane H., and William H. Pease. *Bound Them in Chains: A Biographical History of the Antislavery Movement.* Westport, Conn.: Greenwood Press, 1972.

Perry, Bliss. *The American Spirit in Literature.* New Haven: Yale University Press, 1918.

Perry, Lewis. *Boats against the Current: American Culture between Revolution and Modernity 1820–1860.* New York: Oxford University Press, 1993.

Persons, Stow. *American Minds: A History of Ideas.* New York: Holt, Rinehart & Winston, 1958.

Persons. *Free Religion: An American Faith.* New Haven: Yale University Press, 1947.

Pochmann, Henry A. *German Culture in America: Philosophical and Literary Influences, 1600–1900.* Madison: University of Wisconsin Press, 1956.

Pochmann. *New England Transcendentalism and St. Louis Hegelianism.* Philadelphia: Carl Schurz Foundation, 1948.

Poirier, Richard. *Poetry and Pragmatism.* Cambridge, Mass.: Harvard University Press, 1992.

Poirier. *The Renewal of Literature: Emersonian Reflections.* New York: Random House, 1987.

Poirier. *A World Elsewhere: The Place of Style in American Literature.* New York: Oxford University Press, 1966.

Porte, Joel. *Emerson and Thoreau: Transcendentalists in Conflict.* Middletown, Conn.: Wesleyan University Press, 1966.

Porte. *In Respect to Egotism: Studies in American Romantic Writing.* Cambridge: Cambridge University Press, 1991.

Power, Julia. *Shelley in America in the Nineteenth Century.* Lincoln: University of Nebraska Press, 1940.

Pritchard, John Paul. *Criticism in America.* Norman: University of Oklahoma Press, 1956.

Quinn, Arthur Hobson. *American Fiction: An Historical and Critical Survey.* New York: D. Appleton-Century, 1936.

Quinn, ed. *The Literature of the American People: An Historical and Critical Survey.* New York: Appleton-Century-Crofts, 1951.

Railton, Stephen. *Authorship and Audience: Literary Performance in the American Renaissance.* Princeton: Princeton University Press, 1991.

Rayapati, J. P. Rao. *Early American Interest in Vedanta: Pre-Emersonian Interest in Vedic Literature and Vedantic Philosophy.* London: Asia Publishing House, 1973.

Rees, Robert A., and Earl N. Harbert, eds. *Fifteen American Authors before 1900: Bibliographic Essays on Research and Criticism,* revised edition. Madison: University of Wisconsin Press, 1984.

Reising, Russell J. *The Unusable Past: Theory and the Study of American Literature.* New York: Methuen, 1986.

Reynolds, David S. *Beneath the American Renaissance: The Subversive Imagination in the Age of Emerson and Melville.* New York: Knopf, 1988.

Reynolds. *Faith in Fiction: The Emergence of Religious Literature in America.* Cambridge, Mass.: Harvard University Press, 1981.

Reynolds, Larry J. *European Revolutions and the American Literary Renaissance.* New Haven: Yale University Press, 1988.

Richardson, Robert D., Jr. *Myth and Literature in the American Renaissance.* Bloomington: Indiana University Press, 1978.

Riegel, Robert E. *Young America 1830–1840.* Norman: University of Oklahoma Press, 1949.

Riley, Woodbridge. *American Thought from Puritanism to Pragmatism and Beyond.* New York: Holt, 1915.

Robinson, David. *The Unitarians and the Universalists.* Westport, Conn.: Greenwood Press, 1985.

Rose, Anne C. *Transcendentalism as a Social Movement 1830–1850.* New Haven: Yale University Press, 1981.

Rosenthal, Bernard. *City of Nature: Journeys to Nature in the Age of American Romanticism.* Newark: University of Delaware Press, 1980.

Rourke, Constance. *American Humor: A Study of the National Character.* New York: Harcourt, Brace, 1931.

Rowe, John Carlos. *At Emerson's Tomb: The Politics of Classic American Literature.* New York: Columbia University Press, 1997.

Rowland, William G., Jr. *Literature and the Marketplace: Romantic Writers and Their Audiences in Great Britain and the United States.* Lincoln: University of Nebraska Press, 1996.

Ruland, Richard. *The Rediscovery of American Literature: Premises of Critical Taste, 1900–1940.* Cambridge, Mass.: Harvard University Press, 1967.

Sams, Henry W., ed. *Autobiography of Brook Farm.* Englewood Cliffs, N.J.: Prentice-Hall, 1958.

Saum, Lewis O. *The Popular Mood of Pre-Civil War America.* Westport, Conn.: Greenwood Press, 1980.

Schlesinger, Arthur M., Jr. *The Age of Jackson.* Boston: Little, Brown, 1945.

Schneider, Herbert W. *A History of American Philosophy.* New York: Columbia University Press, 1946.

Scudder, Townsend. *Concord: American Town.* Boston: Little, Brown, 1947.

Sealts, Merton M., Jr. *Beyond the Classroom: Essays on American Authors.* Columbia: University of Missouri Press, 1996.

Seldes, Gilbert. *The Stammering Century*. New York: John Day, 1928.

Sellers, Charles. *The Market Revolution: Jacksonian America 1815–1846*. New York: Oxford University Press, 1991.

Serafin, Steven R., general ed. *Encyclopedia of American Literature*. New York: Continuum, 1999.

Shi, David. *The Simple Life: Plain Living and High Thinking in American Culture*. New York: Oxford University Press, 1985.

Shucard, Alan. *American Poetry: The Puritans through Walt Whitman*. Boston: Twayne, 1988.

Shumway, David R. *Creating American Civilization: A Genealogy of American Literature as an Academic Discipline*. Minneapolis: University of Minnesota Press, 1994.

Simon, Myron, and Thornton H. Parsons, eds. *Transcendentalism and Its Legacy*. Ann Arbor: University of Michigan Press, 1966.

Simpson, David. *The Politics of American English, 1776–1850*. New York: Oxford University Press, 1986.

Slotkin, Richard. *Regeneration through Violence: The Mythology of the American Frontier, 1600–1860*. Middletown, Conn.: Wesleyan University Press, 1973.

Smith, Bernard. *Forces in American Criticism: A Study in the History of American Literary Thought*. New York: Harcourt, Brace, 1939.

Smith, Henry Nash. *Democracy and the Novel: Popular Resistance to Classic American Writers*. New York: Oxford University Press, 1978.

Smithline, Arnold. *Natural Religion and American Literature*. New Haven: College and University Press, 1966.

Spencer, Benjamin. *The Quest for Nationality: An American Literary Campaign*. Syracuse, N.Y.: Syracuse University Press, 1957.

Spengemann, William C. *A Mirror for Americanists: Reflections on the Idea of American Literature*. Hanover, N.H.: University Press of New England, 1989.

Spiller, Robert E. *The American in England during the First Half Century of Independence*. New York: Holt, 1926.

Spiller. *The Cycle of American Literature*. New York: Macmillan, 1956.

Spiller and others. *Literary History of the United States,* 2 volumes, fourth edition, revised. New York: Macmillan, 1974.

Stafford, John. *The Literary Criticism of "Young America": A Study in the Relationship of Politics and Literature 1837–1850*. Berkeley: University of California Press, 1952.

Stange, Douglas C. *Patterns of Antislavery among American Unitarians, 1831–1860*. Rutherford, N.J.: Fairleigh Dickinson University Press, 1977.

Stapleton, Laurence. *The Elected Circle: Studies in the Art of Prose*. Princeton: Princeton University Press, 1973.

Stauffer, Donald Barlow. *A Short History of American Poetry*. New York: Dutton, 1974.

Stearns, Frank Preston. *Sketches from Concord and Appledore*. New York: Putnam, 1895.

Steele, Jeffrey. *The Representation of the Self in the American Renaissance.* Chapel Hill: University of North Carolina Press, 1987.

Stern, Madeleine B. *Imprints on History: Book Publishers and American Frontiers.* Bloomington: Indiana University Press, 1956.

Stewart, Randall. *American Literature and Christian Doctrine.* Baton Rouge: Louisiana State University Press, 1958.

Stoehr, Taylor. *Nay-Saying in Concord: Emerson, Alcott, and Thoreau.* Hamden, Conn.: Archon Books, 1979.

Stovall, Floyd. *American Idealism.* Norman: University of Oklahoma Press, 1943.

Stovall, ed. *The Development of American Literary Criticism.* Chapel Hill: University of North Carolina Press, 1955.

Sundquist, Eric. *Home as Found: Authority and Genealogy in Nineteenth-Century American Literature.* Baltimore: Johns Hopkins University Press, 1979.

Swayne, Josephine Latham. *The Story of Concord Told by Concord Writers,* second edition, revised. Boston: Meador, 1939.

Swift, Lindsay. *Brook Farm: Its Members, Scholars, and Visitors.* New York: Macmillan, 1900.

Tanner, Tony. *The Reign of Wonder: Naivety and Reality in American Literature.* Cambridge: Cambridge University Press, 1965.

Taylor, Walter Fuller. *The Economic Novel in America.* Chapel Hill: University of North Carolina Press, 1942.

Teichgraeber, Richard F., III. *Sublime Thoughts/Penny Wisdom: Situating Emerson and Thoreau in the American Market.* Baltimore: Johns Hopkins University Press, 1995.

Trent, William P. *A History of American Literature 1607–1865.* New York: Appleton, 1903.

Turner, Lorenzo Dow. *Anti-Slavery Sentiment in American Literature Prior to 1865.* Washington, D.C.: Association for the Study of Negro Life and History, 1929.

Unitarianism: Its Origin and History: A Course of Sixteen Lectures Delivered in Channing Hall, Boston, 1888–89. Boston: American Unitarian Association, 1890.

Vanderbilt, Kermit. *American Literature and the Academy: The Roots, Growth, and Maturity of a Profession.* Philadelphia: University of Pennsylvania Press, 1986.

Van Nostrand, A. D. *Everyman His Own Poet: Romantic Gospels in American Literature.* New York: McGraw-Hill, 1968.

Versluis, Arthur. *American Transcendentalism and Asian Religions.* New York: Oxford University Press, 1993.

Vogel, Stanley M. *German Literary Influences on the American Transcendentalists.* New Haven: Yale University Press, 1955.

Von Frank, Albert J. *The Sacred Game: Provincialism and Frontier Consciousness in American Literature.* New York: Cambridge University Press, 1985.

Von Frank. *The Trials of Anthony Burns: Freedom and Slavery in Emerson's Boston.* Cambridge, Mass.: Harvard University Press, 1998.

Wagenknecht, Edward. *A Pictorial History of New England.* New York: Crown, 1976.

Wager, Willis. *American Literature: A World View.* New York: New York University Press, 1968.

Waggoner, Hyatt H. *American Poets from the Puritans to the Present.* Boston: Houghton Mifflin, 1968.

Walls, Laura Dassow. *Seeing New Worlds: Henry David Thoreau and Nineteenth-Century Natural Science.* Madison: University of Wisconsin Press, 1995.

Warren, Joyce W. *The American Narcissus: Individualism and Women in Nineteenth-Century American Fiction.* New Brunswick, N.J.: Rutgers University Press, 1984.

Warren, ed. *The (Other) American Traditions: Nineteenth-Century Women Writers.* New Brunswick, N.J.: Rutgers University Press, 1993.

Webber, Everett. *Escape to Utopia: The Communal Movement in America.* New York: Hastings House, 1959.

Weisbuch, Robert. *Atlantic Double-Cross: American Literature and British Influence in the Age of Emerson.* Chicago: University of Chicago Press, 1986.

Welter, Barbara. *Dimity Convictions: The American Woman in the Nineteenth Century.* Athens: Ohio University Press, 1976.

Welter, Rush. *The Mind of America 1820–1860.* New York: Columbia University Press, 1975.

Wendell, Barrett. *A Literary History of America.* New York: Scribners, 1900.

West, Cornel. *The American Evasion of Philosophy: A Genealogy of Pragmatism.* Madison: University of Wisconsin Press, 1989.

Westbrook, Perry D. *A Literary History of New England.* Bethlehem, Penn.: Lehigh University Press, 1988.

Westbrook. *The New England Town in Fact and Fiction.* Rutherford, N.J.: Fairleigh Dickinson University Press, 1982.

Wheeler, Ruth R. *Concord: Climate for Freedom.* Concord, Mass.: Concord Antiquarian Society, 1967.

Whicher, George F., ed. *The Transcendentalist Revolt against Materialism.* Boston: Heath, 1949; revised as *The Transcendentalist Revolt,* edited by Gail Kennedy. Boston: Heath, 1968.

White, Barbara A. *American Women's Fiction: 1790–1870: A Reference Guide.* New York: Garland, 1990.

White, Morton. *Science and Sentiment in America.* New York: Oxford University Press, 1972.

Whiting, Lilian. *Boston Days.* Boston: Little, Brown, 1911.

Wider, Sarah Ann. *Anna Tilden, Unitarian Culture, and the Problem of Self-Representation.* Athens: University of Georgia Press, 1997.

Williams, Stanley T. *The Beginnings of American Poetry (1620–1855).* Uppsala, Sweden: Almquist & Wiksells, 1951.

Wilmerding, John, ed. *American Light: The Luminist Movement, 1850–1875. Paintings, Drawings, Photographs.* New York: Harper & Row, 1980.

Wilson, R. Jackson. *Figures of Speech: American Writers and the Literary Marketplace, from Benjamin Franklin to Emily Dickinson.* New York: Knopf, 1989.

Wilson, Rufus Rockwell. *New England in Letters.* New York: A. Wessels, 1904.

Wolf, Brian Jay. *Romantic Re-Vision: Culture and Consciousness in Nineteenth-Century American Painting and Literature.* Chicago: University of Chicago Press, 1982.

Wright, Conrad. *The Beginnings of Unitarianism in America.* Boston: Starr King Press, 1955.

Wright. "The Early Period (1811–1840)," in *The Harvard Divinity School: Its Place in Harvard University and in American Culture,* edited by George Huntston Williams. Boston: Beacon, 1954, pp. 21–77.

Wright. *The Liberal Christians: Essays on American Unitarian History.* Boston: Beacon, 1970.

Wright. *The Unitarian Controversy: Essays on American Unitarian History.* Boston: Skinner House, 1994.

Wright, ed. *A Stream of Light: A Sesquicentennial History of American Unitarianism.* Boston: Unitarian Universalist Association, 1975.

Wright, Conrad Edick, ed. *American Unitarianism, 1805–1865.* Boston: Northeastern University Press, 1989.

Ziff, Larzer. *Literary Democracy: The Declaration of Cultural Independence in America.* New York: Viking, 1981.

Contributors

Noelle A. Baker	*University of Wisconsin Oshkosh*
William Baller	*Worcester Polytechnic Institute*
Ronald A. Bosco	*State University of New York at Albany*
Scott E. Casper	*University of Nevada, Reno*
Helen R. Deese	*Tennessee Technological University*
Jane Donahue Eberwein	*Oakland University*
Janice L. Edens	*Macon State College*
D'Ann Pletcher George	*Bridgewater State College*
Len Gougeon	*University of Scranton*
Suzanne Disheroon Green	*Northwestern State University*
Dean Grodzins	*Meadville/Lombard Theological School*
Robert D. Habich	*Ball State University*
Thomas S. Hansen	*Wellesley College*
Sally A. Hawthorne	*Columbia, South Carolina*
Kathleen Healey	*Colby-Sawyer College*
William G. Heath	*Lakehead University*
Alan D. Hodder	*Hampshire College*
Sally C. Hoople	*Castine, Maine*
Camille A. Langston	*Texas Woman's University*
Alfred G. Litton	*Texas Woman's University*
Esther Lopez	*University of Rochester*
Deshae E. Lott	*University of Illinois at Springfield*
Christine Brooks Macdonald	*University of Colorado, Boulder*
Jo Ann Manfra	*Worcester Polytechnic Institute*
James W. Mathews	*State University of West Georgia*
Michael McLoughlin	*University of South Carolina*
Stephen N. Orton	*University of North Carolina at Chapel Hill*
Susan L. Roberson	*Alabama State University*
David M. Robinson	*Oregon State University*
William Rossi	*University of Oregon*
Daniel Royot	*La Sorbonne Nouvelle, Paris*
Ora Frishberg Saloman	*Baruch College and The Graduate School, City University of New York*
M. David Samson	*Worcester Polytechnic Institute*
Mariane Wurst Schaum	*Atlanta, Georgia*
Ellery Sedgwick	*Longwood College*

Scott Slawinski . . . . *University of South Carolina*
E. Kate Stewart . . . . *University of Arkansas at Monticello*
Susan M. Stone . . . . *University of South Carolina*
Peter Valenti . . . . *Fayetteville State University*
Laura Dassow Walls . . . . *Lafayette College*
C. P. Seabrook Wilkinson . . . . *College of Charleston*
Mary Ann Wilson . . . . *University of Louisiana at Lafayette*
Guy R. Woodall . . . . *Tennessee Technological University*
Thomas Wortham . . . . *University of California, Los Angeles*
Arthur Wrobel . . . . *University of Kentucky*

Cumulative Index

Dictionary of Literary Biography, Volumes 1-235
Dictionary of Literary Biography Yearbook, 1980-1999
Dictionary of Literary Biography Documentary Series, Volumes 1-19

Cumulative Index

DLB before number: *Dictionary of Literary Biography,* Volumes 1-235
Y before number: *Dictionary of Literary Biography Yearbook,* 1980-1999
DS before number: *Dictionary of Literary Biography Documentary Series,* Volumes 1-19

A

B

C

E

F

H

I

J

K

L

M

N

O

P

Q

R

S

T

U

V

W

X

Y

Z